Reinforced Concrete Designer's Handbook

Reinforced Concrete Designer's Handbook

TENTH EDITION

Charles E. Reynolds
BSc (Eng), CEng, FICE

and

James C. Steedman
BA, CEng, MICE, MIStructE

London New York
E. & F.N. SPON

First published in 1932, second edition 1939, third edition 1946, fourth edition 1948, revised 1951, further revised 1954, fifth edition 1957, sixth edition 1961, revised 1964, seventh edition 1971, revised 1972, eighth edition 1974, reprinted 1976, ninth edition 1981

This edition first published in 1988 by
E. & F.N. Spon Ltd
11 New Fetter Lane, London EC4P 4EE
Published in the USA by
E. & F.N. Spon
29 West 35th Street, New York NY 10001

Printed in Great Britain at the
University Press, Cambridge

ISBN 0 419 14530 3 (hardback)
ISBN 0 419 14540 0 (paperback)

British Library Cataloguing in Publication Data

Reynolds, Charles E. (Charles Edward)
Reinforced concrete designer's handbook.
—10th ed.
1. Reinforced concrete structures. Design
I. Title II. Steedman, James C.
(James Cyril), 1933–
624.1′8341

ISBN 0–419–14530–3
ISBN 0–419–14540–0 Pbk

Library of Congress Cataloging in Publication Data

Reynolds, Charles E. (Charles Edward)
Reinforced concrete designer's handbook/Charles E. Reynolds and James C. Steedman.—10th ed.
p. cm.
Bibliography: p.
Includes index.
ISBN 0–419–14530–3. ISBN 0–419–14540–0 (pbk.)
1. Reinforced concrete construction—Handbooks, manuals, etc.
I. Steedman, James C. (James Cyril) II. Title.
TA683.2.R48 1988 88–9696
624.1′8341—dc19 CIP

Contents

Preface

Since the last edition appeared under the Viewpoint imprint of the Cement and Concrete Association, this *Handbook* has been in the ownership of two new publishers. I am delighted that it has now joined the catalogue of engineering books published by Spon, one of the most respected names in technical publishing in the world, and that its success is thus clearly assured for the foreseeable future.

As always, it must be remembered that many people contribute to the production of a reference book such as this, and my sincere thanks goes to all those unsung heroes and heroines, especially the editorial and production staff at E. & F.N. Spon Ltd, who have been involved in the process.

Thanks are also due to the many readers who provide feedback by pointing out errors or making suggestions for future improvements. Finally, my thanks to Charles Reynolds' widow and family for their continued encouragement and support. I know that they feel, as I do, that C.E.R. would have been delighted to know that his *Handbook* is still serving reinforced concrete designers 56 years after its original inception.

J.C.S.
Upper Beeding, May 1988

The authors

Charles Edward Reynolds was born in 1900 and educated at Tiffin Boys School, Kingston-on-Thames, and Battersea Polytechnic. After some years with Sir William Arroll, BRC and Simon Carves, he joined Leslie Turner and Partners, and later C. W. Glover and Partners. He was for some years Technical Editor of Concrete Publications Ltd and later became its Managing Editor, combining this post with private practice. In addition to the *Reinforced Concrete Designer's Handbook*, of which well over 150 000 copies have been sold since it first appeared in 1932, Charles Reynolds was the author of numerous other books, papers and articles concerning concrete and allied subjects. Among his various appointments, he served on the council of the Junior Institution of Engineers and was the Honorary Editor of its journal at his death on Christmas Day 1971.

The current author of the *Reinforced Concrete Designer's Handbook*, James Cyril Steedman, was educated at Varndean Grammar School and was first employed by British Rail, whom he joined in 1950 at the age of 16. In 1956 he commenced working for GKN Reinforcements Ltd and later moved to Malcolm Glover and Partners. His association with Charles Reynolds commenced when, following the publication of numerous articles in the magazine *Concrete and Constructional Engineering*, he took up an appointment as Technical Editor of Concrete Publications Ltd in 1961, a post he held for seven years. Since that time he has been engaged in private practice, combining work for the Publications Division of the Cement and Concrete Association with his own writing and other activities. In 1981 he established Jacys Computing Services, an organization specializing in the development of microcomputer software for reinforced concrete design, and much of his time since then has been devoted to this project. He is also the joint author, with Charles Reynolds, of *Examples of the Design of Buildings to CP110 and Allied Codes.*

Introduction to the tenth edition

The latest edition of *Reynold's Handbook* has been necessitated by the appearance in September 1985 of BS8110 'Structural use of concrete'. Although it has superseded its immediate predecessor CP110 (the change of designation from a Code of Practice to a British Standard does not indicate any change of status) which had been in current use for 13 years, an earlier document still, CP114 (last revised in 1964), is still valid.

BS8110 does not, in essence, differ greatly from CP110 (except in price!). Perhaps the most obvious change is the overall arrangement of material. Whereas CP110 incorporated the entire text in Part 1, with the reinforced concrete design charts more usually required (i.e. slabs, beams and rectangular columns) forming Part 2 and the others Part 3, the arrangement in BS8110 is that Part 1 embodies the 'code of practice for design and construction', Part 2 covers 'special circumstances' and Part 3 incorporates similar charts to those forming Part 2 of CP110. There are, as yet, no equivalents to the charts forming Part 3 of CP110.

The material included in Part 2 provides information on rigorous serviceability calculations for cracking and deflection (previously dealt with as appendices to Part 1 of CP110), more comprehensive treatment of fire resistance (only touched on relatively briefly in Part 1), and so on. It could be argued that more logical arrangements of this material would be either to keep all that relating to reinforced concrete design and construction together in Part 1 with that relating to prestressed and composite construction forming Part 2, or to separate the material relating to design and detailing from that dealing with specifications and workmanship.

The main changes between CP110 and its successor are described in the foreword to BS8110 and need not be repeated here. Some of the alterations, for example the design of columns subjected to biaxial bending, represent considerable simplifications to previously cumbersome methods. Certain material has also been rearranged and rewritten to achieve a more logical and better structured layout and to meet criticisms from engineers preferring the CP114 format. Unfortunately this makes it more difficult to distinguish between such 'cosmetic' changes and those where a definite change in meaning or emphasis is intended than would otherwise be the case.

In addition to describing the detailed requirements of BS8110 and providing appropriate charts and tables to aid rapid design, this edition of the *Handbook* retains all the material relating to CP110 which appeared in the previous edition. There are two principal reasons for this. Firstly, although strictly speaking CP110 was immediately superseded by the publication of BS8110, a certain amount of design to the previous document will clearly continue for some time to come. This is especially true outside the UK where English-speaking countries often only adopt the UK Code (or a variant customized to their own needs) some time after it has been introduced in Britain. Secondly, as far as possible the new design aids relating to BS8110 have been prepared in as similar a form as possible to those previously provided for CP110: if appropriate, both requirements are combined on the same chart. Designers who are familiar with these tables from a previous edition of the *Handbook* should thus find no difficulty in switching to the new Code, and direct comparisons between the corresponding BS8110 and CP110 charts and tables should be instructive and illuminating.

When BS8110 was published it was announced that CP114 would be withdrawn in the autumn of 1987. However, since the appearance of CP110 in 1972, a sizeable group of engineers had fought for the retention of an alternative officially-approved document based on design to working loads and stresses rather than on conditions at failure. This objective was spear-headed by the *Campaign for Practical Codes of Practice* (CPCP) and as a result, early in 1987, the Institution of Structural Engineers held a referendum in which Institution members were requested to vote on the question of whether 'permissible-stress codes such as CP114...should be updated and made available for design purposes'. By a majority of nearly 4 to 1, those voting approved the retention and updating of such codes. Accordingly, the IStructE has now set up a task group for this purpose and has urged the British Standards Institution to publish a type TI code for the permissible-stress design of reinforced concrete structures. As an interim measure, the BSI has been requested to reinstate CP114, and the Building Regulations Division of the Department of the Environment asked to retain CP114 as an approved document until the new permissible stress code is ready.

In order to make room for the new BS8110 material in this edition of the *Handbook*, much of that relating specifically to CP114 (especially regarding load-factor design) has had to be jettisoned. However, most of the material relating to design using modular-ratio analysis (the other principal design method sanctioned by CP114) has been retained, since this has long proved to be a useful and safe design method in appropriate circumstances.

Although intended to be self-sufficient, this *Handbook* is planned to complement rather than compete with somewhat similar publications. A joint committee formed by the Institutions of Civil and Structural Engineers published in October 1985 the *Manual for the Design of Reinforced Concrete Building Structures*, dealing with those aspects of BS8110 of chief interest to reinforced concrete designers and detailers. The advice provided, which generally but not always corresponds to the Code requirements, is presented concisely in a different form from that in BS8110 and one clearly favoured by many engineers. Elsewhere in the *Handbook* this publication is referred to for brevity as the *Joint Institutions Design Manual.* Those responsible for drafting CP110 produced the *Handbook on the Unified Code for Structural Concrete*, which explained in detail the basis of many CP110 requirements. A similar publication dealing with BS8110 is in preparation but unfortunately had not been published when this edition of the *Handbook* was prepared. References on later pages to the *Code Handbook* thus relate to the CP110 version. A working party from the CPCP has produced an updated version of CP114* and reference is also made to this document when suggesting limiting stresses for modular-ratio design.

* Copies can be obtained from the Campaign for Practical Codes of Practice, PO Box 218, London SW15 2TY.

In early editions of this *Handbook*, examples of concrete design were included. Such examples are now embodied in the sister publication *Examples of the Design of Buildings*, in which the application of the requirements of the relevant Codes to a fairly typical six-storey building is considered. Since the field covered by this book is much narrower than the *Handbook*, it is possible to deal with particular topics, such as the rigorous calculations necessary to satisfy the serviceability limit-state requirements, in far greater detail. The edition of the *Examples* relating to CP110 has been out of print for some little time but it is hoped that a BS8110 version will be available before long.

Chapter 7 of this *Handbook* provides a brief introduction to the use of microcomputers and similar electronic aids in reinforced concrete design. In due course it is intended to supplement this material by producing a complete separate handbook, provisionally entitled the *Concrete Engineer's Computerbook*, dealing in far greater detail with this very important subject and providing program listings for many aspects of concrete design. Work on this long-delayed project is continuing.

Finally, for newcomers to the *Handbook*, a brief comment about the layout may be useful. The descriptive chapters that form Part I contain more general material concerning the tables. The tables themselves, with specific notes and worked examples in the appropriate chapters, form Part II, but much of the relevant text is embodied in Part I and this part of the *Handbook* should always be consulted. The development of the *Handbook* through successive editions has more or less negated the original purposes of this plan and it is hoped that when the next edition appears the arrangement will be drastically modified.

Notation

The basis of the notation adopted in this book is that employed in BS8110 and CP110. This in turn is based on the internationally agreed procedure for preparing notations produced by the European Concrete Committee (CEB) and the American Concrete Institute, which was approved at the 14th biennial meeting of the CEB in 1971 and is outlined in Appendix F of CP110. The additional symbols required to represent other design methods have been selected in accordance with the latter principles. In certain cases the resulting notation is less logical than would be ideal: this is due to the need to avoid using the specific Code terms for other purposes than those specified in these documents. For example, ideally M could represent any applied moment, but since CP110 uses the symbol to represent applied moments due to ultimate loads only, a different symbol (M_d) has had to be employed to represent moments due to service loads. In isolated cases it has been necessary to violate the basic principles given in Appendix F of CP110: the precedent for this is the notation used in that Code itself.

To avoid an even more extensive use of subscripts, for permissible-stress design the same symbol has sometimes been employed for two related purposes. For example, f_{st} represents either the maximum permissible stress in the reinforcement or the actual stress resulting from a given moment, depending on the context. Similarly, M_d indicates either an applied 'service' moment or the resistance moment of a section assessed on permissible-service-stress principles. It is believed that this duality of usage is unlikely to cause confusion.

In accordance with the general principles of the notation, the symbols K, k, α, β, ζ, ξ and ψ have been used repeatedly to represent different factors or coefficients, and only where such a factor is used repeatedly (e.g. α_e for modular ratio), or confusion is thought likely to arise, is a subscript appended. Thus k, say, may be used to represent perhaps twenty or more different coefficients at various places in this book. In such circumstances the particular meaning of the symbol is defined in each particular case and care should be taken to confirm the usage concerned.

The amount and range of material contained in this book makes it inevitable that the same symbols have had to be used more than once for different purposes. However, care has been taken to avoid duplicating the Code symbols, except where this has been absolutely unavoidable. While most suitable for concrete design purposes, the general notational principles presented in Appendix F of CP110 are perhaps less applicable to other branches of engineering. Consequently, in those tables relating to general structural analysis, the only changes made to the notation employed in previous editions of this book have been undertaken to conform to the use of the Code symbols (i.e. corresponding changes to comply with Appendix F principles have not been made).

In the left-hand columns on the following pages, the appropriate symbols are set in the typeface used in the main text and employed on the tables. Terms specifically defined and used in the body of BS8110 and CP110 are indicated in bold type. Only the principal symbols (those relating to concrete design) are listed here: all others are defined in the text and tables concerned.

$\boldsymbol{A_c}$	Area of concrete
A_{c1}	Area of core of helically reinforced column
$\boldsymbol{A_s}$	Area of tension reinforcement
$\boldsymbol{A'_s}$	Area of compression reinforcement
$\boldsymbol{A'_{s1}}$	Area of compression reinforcement near more highly compressed column face
$\boldsymbol{A_{s2}}$	Area of reinforcement near less highly compressed column face
$\boldsymbol{A_{sc}}$	Total area of longitudinal reinforcement (in columns)
$\boldsymbol{A_{sh}}$	Equivalent area of helical binding (volume per unit length)
$\boldsymbol{A_{sl}}$	Area of longitudinal reinforcement provided for torsion
$\boldsymbol{A_{s\,prov}}$	Area of tension reinforcement provided
$\boldsymbol{A_{sreq}}$	Area of tension reinforcement required
$\boldsymbol{A_{sv}}$	Cross-section area of two legs of link reinforcement
δA_s	Area of individual tension bar
$\delta A'_s$	Area of individual compression bar
A_{tr}	Transformed concrete area
a	Dimension (as defined); deflection
$\boldsymbol{a_b}$	Distance between centres of bars
a_c	Distance to centroid of compression re-

inforcement

a_t Distance to centroid of tension reinforcement

b Width of section; dimension (as defined)

b_t Breadth of section at level of tension reinforcement

b_w Breadth of web or rib of member

C Torsional constant

c_{min} Minimum cover to reinforcement

D Density (with appropriate subscripts)

D_c Density (i.e. unit weight) of concrete at time of test

d Effective depth to tension reinforcement

d' Depth to compression reinforcement

d_{min} Minimum effective depth that can be provided

d_1 Diameter of core of helically bound column

d_c Depth of concrete in compression (simplified limit-state formulae)

E_c Static secant modulus of elasticity of concrete

E_s Modulus of elasticity of steel

e Eccentricity; dimension (as defined)

e_a Additional eccentricity due to deflection in wall

e_x Resultant eccentricity of load at right angles to plane of wall

e_{x1} Resultant eccentricity calculated at top of wall

e_{x2} Resultant eccentricity calculated at bottom of wall

F Total load

F_b Tensile force due to ultimate load in bar or group of bars

F_h Horizontal component of load

F_t Tie force

F_v Vertical component of load

f Stress (as defined) (i.e. f_A, f_B etc. are stresses at points A, B etc.).

f_{bs} Local-bond stress due to ultimate load

f_{bsa} Anchorage-bond stress due to ultimate load

f_{bsd} Local-bond stress due to service load

f_{bsda} Anchorage-bond stress due to service load

f_{cc} Permissible stress or actual maximum stress in concrete in direct compression (depending on context)

f_{cr} Permissible stress or actual maximum stress in concrete in compression due to bending (depending on context)

f_{ct} Permissible stress or actual maximum stress in concrete in tension (depending on context)

f_{cu} Characteristic cube strength of concrete

f_s Service stress in reinforcement (deflection requirements)

f_{s2} Stress assumed in reinforcement near less highly compressed column face (simplified limit-state formulae)

f_{sc} Permissible stress in compression reinforcement

f_{st} Permissible stress or actual maximum stress in tension reinforcement (depending on context)

f_u Specified minimum cube strength of concrete

f_y Characteristic strength of reinforcement

f_{yd} Maximum design stress in tension reinforcement ($=f_y/\gamma_m$) (limit-state analysis)

f_{yd1} Actual design stress in compression reinforcement (limit-state analysis)

f_{yd2} Actual design stress in tension reinforcement (limit-state analysis)

f_{yl} Characteristic strength of longitudinal torsional reinforcement

f_{yv} Characteristic strength of shear reinforcement

G Shear modulus

G_k Characteristic dead load

g Distributed dead load

g_k Characteristic dead load per unit area

H Horizontal reaction (with appropriate subscripts)

h Overall depth or diameter of section

h_c Diameter of column head in flat-slab design; distance of centroid of arbitrary strip from compression face

h_f Thickness of flange

h_s Depth of arbitrary strip

I Second moment of area

I_{tr} Transformed second moment of area in concrete units

i Radius of gyration

J Section modulus; number; constant

j Number

K A constant (with appropriate subscripts)

K_{bal} Moment-of-resistance factor when $K_{dc} = K_{ds}$ (design to BS5337)

K_{conc} Moment-of-resistance factor due to concrete alone ($= M_{conc}/bd^2$)

K_d Link-resistance factor for permissible-service-stress design

K_{dc} Service moment-of-resistance factor for uncracked section (design to BS5337)

K_{ds} Service moment-of-resistance factor for cracked section (design to BS5337)

K_u Link-resistance factor for limit-state design

k A constant (with appropriate subscripts)

k_1, k_2, k_3 Factors determining shape of parabolic-rectangular stress-block for limit-state design

k_4, k_5 Factors determining shape of stress–strain diagram for reinforcement for limit-state design

L Span

l Span

l_e Effective span or height of member

l_{ex} Effective height for bending about major axis

l_{ey} Effective height for bending about minor axis

l_m Average of l_1 and l_2

l_0 Clear height of column between end restraints

l_x Length of shorter side of rectangular slab

l_y Length of longer side of rectangular slab

l_1 Length of flat-slab panel in direction of span measured between column centres

l_2 Width of flat-slab panel measured between column centres

M Bending moment due to ultimate loads

M_{add} Additional moment to be provided by compression reinforcement

M_{conc} Moments of resistance provided by concrete alone (permissible-service-stress design)

M_d Moment of resistance of section or bending moment due to service load, depending on context (permissible-service-stress design)

M_{ds} Design bending moments in flat slabs

M_i Maximum initial moment in column due to ultimate load

M_{ix} Initial moment about major axis of slender column due to ultimate load

M_{iy} Initial moment about minor axis of slender column due to ultimate load

M_{sx}, M_{sy} Bending moments at midspan on strips of unit width and of spans l_x and l_y respectively

M_t Total moment in column due to ultimate load

M_{tx} Total moment about major axis of slender column due to ultimate load

M_{ty} Total moment about minor axis of slender column due to ultimate load

M_u Ultimate moment of resistance of section

M_{ux} Maximum moment capacity of short column under action of ultimate load N and bending about major axis only

M_{uy} Maximum moment capacity of short column under action of ultimate load N and bending about minor axis only

M_x, M_y Moments about major and minor axes of short column due to ultimate load

N Ultimate axial load

N_{bal} Ultimate axial load giving rise to balanced condition in column (limit-state design)

N_d Axial load on or axial resistance of member depending on context (permissible-service-stress design)

N_{uz} Ultimate resistance of section to pure axial load

n Total distributed ultimate load per unit area ($=1.4\,g_k + 1.6\,q_k$)

n_s Number of storeys

Q_k Characteristic imposed load

q Distributed imposed load

q_k Characteristic distributed imposed load per unit area

R Vertical reaction (with appropriate subscripts)

r Internal radius of bend of bar; radius

r_1, r_2 Outer and inner radii of annular section, respectively

S Value of summation (with appropriate subscripts)

s_b Spacing of bars

s_h Pitch of helical binding

s_v Spacing of links

T Torsional moment due to ultimate loads

T_d Torsional moment due to service loads

T° Temperature in degrees

u Perimeter

u_{crit} Length of critical perimeter

u_s Effective perimeter of reinforcing bar

V Shearing force due to ultimate loads

V_d Shearing force due to service loads

V_i Total shearing resistance provided by inclined bars

v Shearing stress on section

v_c Ultimate shearing resistance per unit area provided by concrete alone

v_d Shearing resistance per unit area provided by concrete alone (permissible-service-stress design)

v_{max} Limiting ultimate shearing resistance per unit area when shearing reinforcement is provided

v_t Shearing stress due to torsion

$v_{t\,min}$ Ultimate torsional resistance per unit area provided by concrete alone

v_{tu} Limiting ultimate torsional resistance per unit area when torsional reinforcement is provided

W Total wind load

w Total distributed service load per unit area ($=g_k + q_k$)

x Depth to neutral axis

x_1 Lesser dimension of a link

y_1 Greater dimension of a link

z Lever-arm

$\alpha, \beta, \zeta, \xi, \psi$ Factors or coefficients (with or without subscripts as appropriate)

α_e Modular ratio

γ_f Partial safety factor for loads

γ_m Partial safety factor for materials

$\varepsilon_A, \varepsilon_B$, etc. Strain at points A, B etc.

ε_0 Strain at interface between parabolic and linear parts of stress–strain curve for concrete

ε_s Strain in tension reinforcement

ε'_s Strain in compression reinforcement

ρ Proportion of tension reinforcement ($=A_s/bd$)

ρ' Proportion of compression reinforcement ($=A'_s/bd$)

ρ_1 Proportion of total reinforcement in terms of gross section ($=A_s/bh$ or A_{sc}/bh)

ϕ Bar size

θ Angle

μ Frictional coefficient

ν Poisson's ratio

Part I

Chapter 1
Introduction

A structure is an assembly of members each of which is subjected to bending or to direct force (either tensile or compressive) or to a combination of bending and direct force. These primary influences may be accompanied by shearing forces and sometimes by torsion. Effects due to changes in temperature and to shrinkage and creep of the concrete, and the possibility of damage resulting from overloading, local damage, abrasion, vibration, frost, chemical attack and similar causes may also have to be considered. Design includes the calculation of, or other means of assessing and providing resistance against, the moments, forces and other effects on the members. An efficiently designed structure is one in which the members are arranged in such a way that the weight, loads and forces are transmitted to the foundations by the cheapest means consistent with the intended use of the structure and the nature of the site. Efficient design means more than providing suitable sizes for the concrete members and the provision of the calculated amount of reinforcement in an economical manner. It implies that the bars can be easily placed, that reinforcement is provided to resist the secondary forces inherent in monolithic construction, and that resistance is provided against all likely causes of damage to the structure. Experience and good judgement may do as much towards the production of safe and economical structures as calculation. Complex mathematics should not be allowed to confuse the sense of good engineering. Where possible, the same degree of accuracy should be maintained throughout the calculations; it is illogical to consider, say, the effective depth of a member to two decimal places if the load is overestimated by 25%. On the other hand, in estimating loads, costs and other numerical quantities, the more items that are included at their exact value the smaller is the overall percentage of error due to the inclusion of some items the exact magnitude of which is unknown.

Where the assumed load is not likely to be exceeded and the specified quality of concrete is fairly certain to be obtained, high design strengths or service stresses can be employed. The more factors allowed for in the calculations the higher may be the strengths or stresses, and vice versa. If the magnitude of a load, or other factor, is not known precisely it is advisable to study the effects of the probable largest and smallest values of the factor and provide resistance for the most adverse case. It is not always the largest load that produces the most critical conditions in all parts of a structure.

Structural design is largerly controlled by regulations or codes but, even within such bounds, the designer must exercise judgement in his interpretation of the requirements, endeavouring to grasp the spirit of the requirements rather than to design to the minimum allowed by the letter of a clause. In the United Kingdom the design of reinforced concrete is based largely on the British Standards and BS Codes of Practice, principally those for 'Loading' (CP3: Chapter V: Part 2 and BS6399: Part 1), 'Structural use of concrete' (BS8110: Parts 1, 2 and 3), 'The structural use of concrete' (CP110: Parts 1, 2 and 3), 'The structural use of normal reinforced concrete in buildings' (CP114), 'The structural use of concrete for retaining aqueous liquids' (BS5337) and 'Steel, concrete and composite bridges' (BS5400) 'Part 2: Specification for loads' and 'Part 4: Design of concrete bridges'. In addition there are such documents as the national Building Regulations.

The tables given in Part II enable the designer to reduce the amount of arithmetical work. The use of such tables not only increases speed but also eliminates inaccuracies *provided* the tables are thoroughly understood and their bases and limitations realized. In the appropriate chapters of Part I and in the supplementary information given on the pages facing the tables, the basis of the tabulated material is described. Some general information is also provided. For example, Appendix A gives fundamental trigonometrical and other mathematical formula and useful data. Appendix B is a conversion table for metric and imperial lengths. Appendix C gives metric and imperial equivalents for units commonly used in structural calculations.

1.1 ECONOMICAL STRUCTURES

The cost of a reinforced concrete structure is obviously affected by the prices of concrete, steel, formwork and labour. Upon the relation between these prices, the economical proportions of the quantities of concrete, reinforcement and framework depend. There are possibly other factors to be taken into account in any particular case, such as the use of available steel forms of standard sizes. In the United Kingdom economy generally results from the use of simple formwork even if this requires more concrete compared with a design requiring more complex and more expensive formwork.

Some of the factors which may have to be considered are whether less concrete of a rich mix is cheaper than a greater volume of a leaner concrete; whether the cost of higher-priced bars of long lengths will offset the cost of the extra weight used in lapping shorter and cheaper bars; whether, consistent with efficient detailing, a few bars of large diameter can replace a larger number of bars of smaller diameter; whether the extra cost of rapid-hardening cement justifies the saving made by using the forms a greater number of times; or whether uniformity in the sizes of members saves in formwork what it may cost in extra concrete.

There is also a wider aspect of economy, such as whether the anticipated life and use of a proposed structure warrant the use of a higher or lower factor of safety than is usual; whether the extra cost of an expensive type of construction is warranted by the improvement in facilities; or whether the initial cost of a construction of high quality with little or no maintainance cost is more economical than less costly construction combined with the expense of maintenance.

The working of a contract and the experience of the contractor, the position of the site and the nature of the available materials, and even the method of measuring the quantities, together with numerous other points, all have their effect, consciously or not, on the designer's attitude towards a contract. So many and varied are the factors to be considered that only experience and the study of the trend of design can give any reliable guidance. Attempts to determine the most economical proportions for a given member based only on inclusive prices of concrete, reinforcement and formwork are often misleading. It is nevertheless possible to lay down certain principles.

For equal weights, combined material and labour costs for reinforcement bars of small diameter are greater than those for large bars, and within wide limits long bars are cheaper than short bars if there is sufficient weight to justify special transport charges and handling facilities.

The lower the cement content the cheaper the concrete but, other factors being equal, the lower is the strength and durability of the concrete. Taking compressive strength and cost into account, a concrete rich in cement is more economical than a leaner concrete. In beams and slabs, however, where much of the concrete is in tension and therefore neglected in the calculations, it is less costly to use a lean concrete than a rich one. In columns, where all the concrete is in compression, the use of a rich concrete is more economical, since besides the concrete being more efficient, there is a saving in formwork resulting from the reduction in the size of the column.

The use of steel in compression is always uneconomical when the cost of a single member is being considered, but advantages resulting from reducing the depth of beams and the size of columns may offset the extra cost of the individual member. When designing for the ultimate limit-state the most economical doubly-reinforced beam is that in which the total combined weight of tension and compression steel needed is a minimum. This occurs when the depth of the neutral axis is as great as possible without reducing the design strength in the tension steel (see section 5.3.2). With permissible-working-stress design the most economical doubly-reinforced section is that in which the compressive stress in the concrete is the maximum permissible stress and the tensile stress in the steel is that which gives the minimum combined weight of tension and compression reinforcement. T-beams and slabs with compression reinforcement are seldom economical. When the cost of mild steel is high in relation to that of concrete, the most economical slab is that in which the proportion of tension reinforcement is well below the so-called 'economic' proportion. (The economic proportion is that at which the maximum resistance moments due to the steel and concrete, when each is considered separately, are equal.) T-beams are cheaper if the rib is made as deep as practicable, but here again the increase in headroom that results from reducing the depth may offset the small extra cost of a shallower beam. It is rarely economical to design a T-beam to achieve the maximum permissible resistance from the concrete.

Inclined bars are more economical than links for resisting shearing force, and this may be true even if bars have to be inserted specially for this purpose.

Formwork is obviously cheaper if angles are right angles, if surfaces are plane, and if there is some repetition of use. Therefore splays and chamfers are omitted unless structurally necessary or essential to durability. Wherever possible architectural features in work cast *in situ* should be formed in straight lines. When the cost of formwork is considered in conjunction with the cost of concrete and reinforcement, the introduction of complications in the formwork may sometimes lead to more economical construction; for example, large continuous beams may be more economical if they are haunched at the supports. Cylindrical tanks are cheaper than rectangular tanks of the same capacity if many uses are obtained from one set of forms. In some cases domed roofs and tank bottoms are more economical than flat beam-and-slab construction, although the unit cost of the formwork may be doubled for curved work. When formwork can be used several times without alteration, the employment of steel forms should be considered and, because steel is less adaptable than wood, the shape and dimensions of the work may have to be determined to suit. Generally, steel forms for beam-and-slab or column construction are cheaper than timber formwork if twenty or more uses can be assured, but for circular work half this number of uses may warrant the use of steel. Timber formwork for slabs, walls, beams, column sides etc. can generally be used four times before repair, and six to eight times before the cost of repair equals the cost of new formwork. Beam-bottom boards can be used at least twice as often.

Precast concrete construction usually reduces considerably the amount of formwork and temporary supports required, and the moulds can generally be used very many more times than can site formwork. In some cases, however, the loss of structural rigidity due to the absence of monolithic construction may offset the economy otherwise resulting from precast construction. To obtain the economical advantage of precasting and the structural advantage of *in situ* casting, it is often convenient to combine both types of construction in the same structure.

In many cases the most economical design can be determined only by comparing the approximate costs of different designs. This is particularly true in borderline cases and is practically the only way of determining, say, when a simple cantilevered retaining wall ceases to be more economical than one with counterforts; when a solid-slab bridge is more economical than a slab-and-girder bridge; or when a cylindrical container is cheaper than a rectangular container. Although it is usually more economical in floor construction for the main beams to be of shorter span than the secondary beams, it is sometimes worth while investigating different spacings of the secondary beams, to determine whether a thin slab with more beams is cheaper or not than a thicker slab with fewer beams. In the case of flat-slab construction, it may be worth while considering alternative spacings of the columns.

An essential aspect of economical design is an appreciation of the possibilities of materials other than concrete. The judicious incorporation of such materials may lead to substantial economies. Just as there is no structural reason for facing a reinforced concrete bridge with stone, so there is no economic gain in casting *in situ* a reinforced concrete wall panel if a brick wall is cheaper and will serve the same purpose. Other common cases of the consideration of different materials are the installation of timber or steel bunkers when only a short life is required, the erection of light steel framing for the superstructures of industrial buildings, and the provision of pitched steel roof trusses. Included in such economic comparisons should be such factors as fire resistance, deterioration, depreciation, insurance, appearance and speed of construction, and structural considerations such as the weight on the foundations, convenience of construction and the scarcity or otherwise of materials.

1.2 DRAWINGS

The methods of preparing drawings vary considerably, and in most drawing offices a special practice has been developed to suit the particular class of work done. The following observations can be taken as a guide when no precedent or other guidance is available. In this respect, practice in the UK should comply with the report published jointly by the Concrete Society and the Institution of Structural Engineers and dealing with, among other matters, detailing of reinforced concrete structures. The recommendations given in the following do not necessarily conform entirely with the proposals in the report (ref. 33).

A principal factor is to ensure that, on all drawings for any one contract, the same conventions are adopted and uniformity of appearance and size is achieved, thereby making the drawings easier to read. The scale employed should be commensurate with the amount of detail to be shown. Some suggested scales for drawings with metric dimensions and suitable equivalent scales for those in imperial dimensions are as follows.

In the preliminary stages a general drawing of the whole structure is usually prepared to show the principal arrangement and sizes of beams, columns, slabs, walls, foundations and other members. Later this, or a similar drawing, is utilized as a key to the working drawings, and should show precisely such particulars as the setting-out of the structure in relation to adjacent buildings or other permanent works, and the level of, say, the ground floor in relation to a datum. All principal dimensions such as the distance between columns and overall and intermediate heights should be indicated, in addition to any clearances, exceptional loads and other special requirements. A convenient scale for most general arrangement drawings is 1:100 or 1/8 in to 1 ft, although a larger scale may be necessary for complex structures. It is often of great assistance if the general drawing can be used as a key to the detailed working drawings by incorporating reference marks for each column, beam, slab panel or other member.

The working drawings should be large-scale details of the members shown on the general drawing. A suitable scale is 1:25 or 1/2 in to 1 ft, but plans of slabs and elevations of walls are often prepared to a scale of 1:50 or 1/4 in to 1 ft, while sections through beams and columns with complicated reinforcement are preferably drawn to a scale of 1:10 or 1 in to 1 ft. Separate sections, plans and elevations should be shown for the details of the reinforcement in slabs, beams, columns, frames and walls, since it is not advisable to show the reinforcement for more than one such member in a single view. An indication should be given, however, of the reinforcement in slabs and columns in relation to the reinforcement in beams or other intersecting reinforcement. Sections through beams and columns showing the detailed arrangement of the bars should be placed as closely as possible to the position where the section is taken.

In reinforced concrete details, it may be preferable for the outline of the concrete to be indicated by a thin line and to show the reinforcement by a bold line. Wherever clearness is not otherwised sacrificed, the line representing the bar should be placed in the exact position intended for the bar, proper allowance being made for the amount of cover. Thus the reinforcement as shown on the drawing will represent as nearly as possible the appearance of the reinforcement as fixed on the site, all hooks and bends being drawn to scale. The alternative to the foregoing method that is frequently adopted is for the concrete to be indicated by a bold line and the reinforcement by a thin line; this method, which is not recommended in the report previously mentioned, has some advantages but also has some drawbacks.

The dimensions given on the drawing should be arranged so that the primary dimensions connect column and beam centres or other leading setting-out lines, and so that secondary dimensions give the detailed sizes with reference to the main setting-out lines. The dimensions on working drawings should also be given in such a way that the carpenters making the formwork have as little calculation to do as possible. Thus, generally, the distances between breaks in any surface should be dimensioned. Disjointed dimensions should be avoided by combining as much information as possible in a single line of dimensions.

It is of some importance to show on detail drawings the positions of bolts and other fitments that may be required to be embedded in the concrete, and of holes etc. that are to be formed for services and the like. If such are shown on the same drawings as the reinforcement, there is less likelihood of conflicting information being depicted. This proposal may be of limited usefulness in buildings but is of considerable importance in industrial structures.

Marks indicating where cross-sections are taken should be bold and, unless other considerations apply, the sections should be drawn as viewed in the same two directions throughout the drawing; for example, they may be drawn as viewed looking towards the left and as viewed looking from the bottom of the drawing. Consistency in this makes it easier to understand complicated details.

Any notes on general or detailed drawings should be concise and free from superfluity in wording or ambiguity in meaning. Notes which apply to all working drawings can be reasonably given on the general arrangement with a reference to the latter on each of the detail drawings. Although the proportions of the concrete, the cover of concrete over the reinforcement, and similar information are usually given in the specification or bill of quantities, the proportions and covers required in the parts of the work shown on a detail drawings should be described on the latter, as the workmen rarely see the specification. If the bar-bending schedule is not given on a detail drawing, a reference should be made to the page numbers of the bar-bending schedule relating to the details on that drawing.

Notes that apply to one view or detail only should be placed as closely as possible to the view or detail concerned, and only those notes that apply to the drawing as a whole should be collected together. If a group of notes is lengthy there is a danger that individual notes will be read only cursorily and an important requirement be overlooked.

Chapter 2
Safety factors, loads and pressures

2.1 FACTORS OF SAFETY

The calculations required in reinforced concrete design are generally of two principal types. On the one hand, calculations are undertaken to find the strength of a section of a member at which it becomes unserviceable, perhaps due to failure but also possibly because cracking or deflection becomes excessive, or for some similar reason. Calculations are also made to determine the bending and torsional moments and axial and shearing forces set up in a structure due to the action of an arrangement of loads or pressures and acting either permanently (dead loads) or otherwise (imposed loads). The ratio of the resistance of the section to the moment or force causing unserviceability at that section may be termed the factor of safety of the section concerned. However, the determination of the overall (global) factor of safety of a complete structure is usually somewhat more complex, since this represents the ratio of the greatest load that a structure can carry to the actual loading for which it has been designed. Now, although the moment of resistance of a reinforced concrete section can be calculated with reasonable accuracy, the bending moments and forces acting on a structure as failure is approached are far more difficult to determine since under such conditions a great deal of redistribution of forces occurs. For example, in a continuous beam the overstressing at one point, say at a support, may be relieved by a reserve of strength that exists elsewhere, say at midspan. Thus the distribution of bending moment at failure may be quite different from that which occurs under service conditions.

2.1.1 Modular-ratio design

Various methods have been adopted in past Codes and similar documents to ensure an adequate and consistent factor of safety for reinforced concrete design. In elastic-stress (i.e. modular-ratio) theory, the moments and forces acting on a structure are calculated from the actual values of the applied loads, but the limiting permissible stresses in the concrete and the reinforcement are restricted to only a fraction of their true strengths, in order to provide an adequate safety factor. In addition, to ensure that if any failure does occur it is in a 'desirable' form (e.g. by the reinforcement yielding and thus giving advance warning that failure is imminent, rather than the concrete crushing, which may happen unexpectedly and explosively) a greater factor of safety is employed to evaluate the maximum permissible stress in concrete than that used to determine the maximum permissible stress in the reinforcement.

2.1.2 Load-factor design

While normally modelling the behaviour of a section under service loads fairly well, the above method of analysis gives an unsatisfactory indication of conditions as failure approaches, since the assumption of a linear relationship between stress and strain in the concrete (see section 5.4) no longer remains true, and thus the distribution of stress in the concrete differs from that under service load. To obviate this shortcoming, the load-factor method of design was introduced into CP114. Theoretically, this method involves the analysis of sections at failure, the actual strength of a section being related to the actual load causing failure, with the latter being determined by 'factoring' the design load. However, to avoid possible confusion caused by the need to employ both service and ultimate loads and stresses for design in the same document, as would be necessary since modular-ratio theory was to continue to be used, the load-factor method was introduced in CP114 in terms of working stresses and loads, by modifying the method accordingly.

2.1.3 Limit-state design

In BS8110 and similar documents (e.g. CP110, BS5337, BS5400 and the design recommendations of the CEB) the concept of a limit-state method of design has been introduced. With this method, the design of each individual member or section of a member must satisfy two separate criteria: the ultimate limit-state, which ensures that the probability of failure is acceptably low; and the limit-state of serviceability, which ensures satisfactory behaviour under service (i.e. working) loads. The principal criteria relating to serviceability are the prevention of excessive deflection, excessive cracking and excessive vibration, but with certain types of structure and in special circumstances other limit-state criteria may have to be considered (e.g. fatigue, durability, fire resistance etc.)

To ensure acceptable compliance with these limit-states, various partial factors of safety are employed in limit-state design. The particular values selected for these factors depend on the accuracy known for the load or strength to which the factor is being applied, the seriousness of the consequences that might follow if excessive loading or stress occurs, and so on. Some details of the various partial factors of safety specified in BS8110 and CP110 and their application are set out in *Table 1* and discussed in Chapter 8. It will be seen that at each limit-state considered, two partial safety factors are involved. The characteristic loads are *multiplied* by a partial safety factor for loads γ_f to obtain the design loads, thus enabling calculation of the bending moments and shearing forces for which the member is to be designed. Thus if the characteristic loads are multiplied by the value of γ_f corresponding to the ultimate limit-state, the moments and forces subsequently determined will represent those occurring at failure, and the sections must be designed accordingly. Similarly, if the value of γ_f corresponding to the limit-state of serviceability is used, the moments and forces under service loads will be obtained. In a similar manner, characteristic strengths of materials used are *divided* by a partial safety factor for materials γ_m to obtain appropriate design strengths for each material.

Although serviceability limit-state calculations to ensure the avoidance of excessive cracking or deflection may be undertaken, and suitable procedures are outlined to undertake such a full analysis for every section would be too time-consuming and arduous, as well as being unnecessary. Therefore BS8110 and CP110 specify certain limits relating to bar spacing, slenderness etc. and, if these criteria are not exceeded, more-detailed calculations are unnecessary. Should a proposed design fall outside these tabulated limiting values, however, the engineer may still be able to show that his design meets the Code requirements regarding serviceability by producing detailed calculations to validate his claim.

Apart from the partial factor of safety for dead + imposed + wind load, all the partial safety factors relating to the serviceability limit-state are equal to unity. Thus the calculation of bending moments and shearing forces by using unfactored dead and imposed loads, as is undertaken with modular-ratio and load-factor design, may conveniently be thought of as an analysis under service loading, using limiting permissible service stresses that have been determined by applying overall safety factors to the material strengths. Although imprecise, this concept may be useful in appreciating the relationship between limit-state and other design methods, especially as permissible-working-stress design is likely to continue to be used for certain types of structures and structural members (e.g. chimneys) for some time to come, especially where the behaviour under service loading is the determining factor. In view of the continuing usefulness of permissible-working-stress design, which has been shown by the experience of many years to result in the production of safe and economical designs for widely diverse types of structure, most of the design data given elsewhere in this book, particularly in those chapters dealing with structures other than building frames and similar components, are related to the analysis of structures under service loads and their design by methods based on permissible working stresses.

Note When carrying out any calculation, it is most important that the designer is absolutely clear as to the condition he is investigating. This is of especial importance when he is using values obtained from tables or graphs such as those given in Part II of this book. For example, tabulated values for the strength of a section at the ultimate limit-state must *never* be used to satisfy the requirements obtained by carrying out a serviceability analysis, i.e. by calculating bending moments and shearing forces due to unfactored characteristic loads.

2.2 CHARACTERISTIC LOADS

The loads acting on a structure are permanent (or dead) loads and transient (or imposed or live) loads. As explained above, a design load is calculated by multiplying the characteristic load by the appropriate partial factor of safety for loads γ_f. According to the *Code Handbook* a characteristic load is, by definition, 'that value of load which has an accepted probability of its not being exceeded during the life of the structure' and ideally should be evaluated from the mean load with a standard deviation from this value. BS8110 states that for design purposes the loads set out in BS6399: Part 1 and CP3: Chapter V: Part 2 may be considered as characteristic dead, imposed and wind loads. Thus the values given in *Tables 2–8* may be considered to be characteristic loads for the purposes of limit-state calculations.

In the case of wind loading, in CP3: Chapter V: Part 2 a multiplying factor S_3 has been incorporated in the expression used to determine the characteristic wind load W_k to take account of the probability of the basic wind speed being exceeded during the life of the structure.

2.3 DEAD LOADS

Dead loads include the weights of the structure itself and any permanent fixtures, partitions, finishes, superstructures and so on. Data for calculating dead loads are given in *Tables 2, 3* and *4*: reference should also be made to the notes relating to dead loads given in section 9.1.

2.4 IMPOSED LOADS

Imposed (or transient or live) loads include any external loads imposed upon the structure when it is serving its normal purpose, and include the weight of stored materials, furniture and movable equipment, cranes, vehicles, snow, wind and people. The accurate assessment of the actual and probable loads is an important factor in the production of economical and efficient structures. Some imposed loads, such as the pressures and weights due to contained liquids, can be determined exactly; less definite, but capable of being calculated with reasonable accuracy, are the pressures of retained granular materials. Other loads, such as those on floors, roofs and bridges, are generally specified at characteristic values. Wind forces are much less definite, and marine forces are among the least determinable.

2.4.1 Floors

For buildings is most towns the loads imposed on floors, stairs and roofs are specified in codes or local building regulations. The loads given in *Tables 6* and *7* are based on BS6399: Part 1 which has replaced CP3: Chapter V: Part 1. The imposed loads on slabs are uniformly distributed loads expressed in kilonewtons per square metre (kN/m^2) and pounds per square foot (lb/ft^2). A concentrated load, as an alternative to the uniformly distributed load, is in some cases assumed to act on an area of specified size and in such a position that it produces the greatest stresses or greatest deflection. A slab must be designed to carry either of these loads, whichever produces the most adverse conditions. The concentrated load need not be considered in the case of solid slabs or other slabs capable of effectively distributing loads laterally.

Beams are designed for the appropriate uniformly distributed load, but beams spaced at not more than 1 m (or 40 in) centres are designed as slabs. When a beam supports not less than $40\,m^2$ or $430\,ft^2$ of a level floor, it is permissible to reduce the specified imposed load by 5% for every $40\,m^2$ or $430\,ft^2$ of floor supported, the maximum reduction being 25%; this reduction does not apply to floors used for storage, office floors used for filing, and the like.

The loads on floors of warehouses and garages are dealt with in sections 2.4.8, 9.2.1 and 9.2.5. In all cases of floors in buildings it is advisable, and in some localities it is compulsory, to affix a notice indicating the imposed load for which the floor is designed. Floors of industrial buildings where machinery and plant are installed should be designed not only for the load when the plant is in running order, but for the probable load during erection and the testing of the plant, as in some cases this load may be more severe than the working load. The weights of any machines or similar fixtures should be allowed for if they are likely to cause effects more adverse than the specified minimum imposed load. Any reduction in the specified imposed load due to multiple storeys or to floors of large area should not be applied to the gross weight of the machines or fixtures. The approximate weights of some machinery such as conveyors and screening plants are given in *Table 12*. The effects on the supporting structure of passenger and goods lifts are given in *Table 12* and the forces in colliery pit-head frames are given in section 9.2.9. The support of heavy safes requires special consideration, and the floors should be designed not only for the safe in its permanent position but also for the condition when the safe is being moved into position, unless temporary props or other means of relief are provided during installation. Computing and other heavy office equipment should also be considered specially.

2.4.2 Structures subject to vibration

For floors subjected to vibration from such causes as dancing, drilling and gymnastics, the imposed loads specified in *Table 6* are adequate to allow for the dynamic effect. For structural members subjected to continuous vibration due to machinery, crushing plant, centrifugal driers and the like, an allowance for dynamic effect can be made by reducing the service stresses by, say, 25% or more or by increasing the total dead and imposed loads by the same amount; the advantage of the latter method is that if modular-ratio theory is being used the ordinary stresses and standard tables and design charts are still applicable.

2.4.3 Balustrades and parapets

The balustrades of stairs and landings and the parapets of balconies and roofs should be designed for a horizontal force acting at the level of the handrail or coping. The forces specified in BS6399: Part 1 are given in *Table 7* for parapets on various structures in terms of force per unit length. BS5400: Part 2 specifies the horizontal force on the parapet of a bridge supporting a footway or cycle track to be 1.4 kN/m applied at a height of 1 metre: for loading on highway bridge parapets see DTp memorandum BE5 (see ref. 148).

2.4.4 Roofs

The imposed loads on roofs given in *Table 7* are additional to all surfacing materials and include snow and other incidental loads but exclude wind pressure. Freshly fallen snow weighs about $0.8\,kN/m^3$ or $5\,lb/ft^3$, but compacted snow may weigh $3\,kN/m^3$ or $20\,lb/ft^3$, which should be considered in districts subject to heavy snowfalls. For sloping roofs the snow load decreases with an increase in the slope. According to the Code the imposed load is zero on roofs sloping at an angle exceeding 75°, but a sloping roof with a slope of less than 75° must be designed to support the uniformly distributed or concentrated load given in *Table 7* depending on the slope and shape of the roof.

If a flat roof is used for purposes such as a café, playground or roof garden, the appropriate imposed load for such a floor should be allowed. The possibility of converting a flat roof to such purposes or of using it as a floor in the future should also be anticipated.

2.4.5 Columns, walls and foundations

Columns, walls and foundations of buildings should be designed for the same loads as the slabs or beams of the floors they support. In the case of buildings of more than two storeys, and which are not warehouses, garages or stores and are not factories or workshops the floors of which are designed for not less than $5\,kN/m^2$ or about $100\,lb/ft^2$, the imposed loads on the columns or other supports and the foundations may be reduced as shown in *Table 12*. If two floors are supported, the imposed load on both floors may be reduced by 10%; if three floors, reduce the imposed load on the three floors by 20%, and so on in 10% reductions down to five to ten floors, for which the imposed load may be reduced by 40%; for more than ten floors, the reduction is 50%. A roof is considered to be a floor. These requirements are in accordance with the Code. If the load on a beam is reduced because of the large area supported, the columns or other supporting members may be designed either for this reduced load or for the reduction due to the number of storeys.

2.4.6 Bridges

The analysis and design of bridges is now so complex that it cannot be adequately treated in a book of this nature, and reference should be made to specialist publications. However, for the guidance of designers, notes regarding bridge loading etc. are provided below since they may also be applicable to ancillary construction and to structures having features in common with bridges.

Road bridges. The imposed load on public road bridges in the UK is specified by the Department of Transport in BS153 (as subsequently amended) and Part 2 of BS5400. (Certain requirements of BS153 were later superseded by Department of the Environment Technical Memoranda. These altered, for example, the equivalent HA loading for short loaded lengths, the wheel dimensions for HB loading etc. For details reference should be made to the various memoranda. These modifications are embodied in BS5400.) The basic imposed load to be considered (HA loading) comprises a uniformly distributed load, the intensity of which depends on the 'loaded length' (i.e. the length which must be loaded to produce the most adverse effect) combined with a knife-edge load. Details of these loads are given in *Tables 9*, *10* and *11* and corresponding notes in section 9.2.3. HA loading includes a 25% allowance for imapct.

Bridges on public highways and those providing access to certain industrial installations may be subjected to loads exceeding those which result from HA loading. The resulting abnormal load (HB loading) that must be considered is represented by a specified sixteen-wheel vehicle (see *Tables 9*, *10* and *11*). The actual load is related to the number of units of HB loading specified by the authority concerned, each unit representing axle loads of 10 kN. The minimum number of HB units normally considered is 25, corresponding to a total load of 1000 kN (i.e. 102 tonnes) but up to 45 units (184 tonnes) may be specified.

For vehicles having greater gross laden weights, special routes are designated and bridges on such routes may have to be designed to support special abnormal loads (HC loading) of up to 360 tonnes. However, owing to the greater area and larger number of wheels of such vehicles, gross weights about 70% greater than the HB load for which a structure has been designed can often be accommodated, although detailed calculations must, of course, be undertaken in each individual case to verify this.

If the standard load is excessive for the traffic likely to use the bridge (having regard to possible increases in the future), the load from ordinary and special vehicles using the bridge, including the effect of the occasional passage of steam-rollers, heavy lorries and abnormally heavy loads, should be considered. Axle loads (without impact) and other data for various types of road vehicles are given in *Table 8*. The actual weights and dimensions vary with different types and manufacturers; notes on weights and dimensions are given in section 9.2.2, and weights of some aircraft are given in section 9.2.11.

The effect of the impact of moving loads is usually allowed for by increasing the static load by an amount varying from 10% to 75% depending on the type of vehicle, the nature of the road surface, the type of wheel (whether rubber or steel tyred), and the speed and frequency of crossing the bridge. An allowance of 25% on the actual maximum wheel loads is incorporated in the HA and HB loadings specified in BS153 and BS5400. A road bridge that is not designed for the maximum loads common in the district should be indicated by a permanent notice stating the maximum loads permitted to use it, and a limitation in speed and possibly weight should be enforced on traffic passing under or over a concrete bridge during the first few weeks after completion of the concrete work.

Road bridges may be subjected to forces other than dead and imposed loads (including impact); these include wind forces and longitudinal forces due to the friction of bearings, temperature change etc. There is also a longitudinal force due to tractive effort and braking and skidding. The effects of centrifugal force and differential settlement of the structure must also be considered. Temporary loads resulting from erection or as a result of the collision of vehicles must be anticipated. For details of such loads, reference should be made to BS153 or Part 2 of BS5400.

Footpaths on road bridges must be designed to carry pedestrians and accidental loading due to vehicles running on the path. If it is probable that the footpath may later be converted into a road, the structure must be designed to support the same load as the roadway.

Railway bridges. The imposed load for which a main-line railway bridge or similar supporting structure should be designed is generally specified by the appropriate railway authority and may be a standard load such as that in BS5400: Part 2, where two types of loading are specified. RU loading covers all combinations of rail vehicles operating in Europe (including the UK) on tracks not narrower than standard gauge: details of RU loading are included in *Tables 9* and *10*. Details of some typical vehicles covered by RU loading are given in *Table 8*. An alternative reduced loading (type RL) is specified for rapid-transit passenger systems where main-line stock cannot operate. This loading consists of a single 200 kN concentrated load combined with a uniform load of 50 kN/m for loaded lengths of up to 100 m. For greater lengths, the uniform load beyond a length of 100 m may be reduced to 25 kN/m. Alternatively, concentrated loads of 300 kN and 150 kN spaced 2.4 m apart should be considered when designing deck elements if this loading gives rise to more severe conditions. In addition to dead and imposed load, structures supporting railways must be designed to resist the effects of impact, oscillation, lurching, nosing etc. Such factors are considered by multiplying the static loads by an appropriate dynamic factor: for details see BS5400: Part 2. The effects of wind pressures and temperature change must also be investigated.

For light railways, sidings, colliery lines and the like, smaller loads than those considered in BS5400 might be adopted. The standard loading assumes that a number of heavy locomotives may be on the structure at the same time, but for secondary lines the probability of there being only one locomotive and a train of vehicles of the type habitually using the line should be considered in the interests of economy.

2.4.7 Structures supporting cranes

Cranes and oher hoisting equipment are commonly supported on columns in factories or similar buildings, or on gantries. The wheel loads and other particulars for typical overhead travelling cranes are given in *Table 12*. It is important that a dimensioned diagram of the actual crane to be installed is obtained from the makers to ensure that the necessary clearances are provided and the actual loads taken into account. Allowances for the secondary effects on the supporting structure due to the operation of overhead cranes are given in section 9.2.6.

For jib cranes running on rails on supporting gantries, the load to which the structure is subjected depends on the disposition of the weights of the crane. The wheel loads are generally specified by the maker of the crane and should allow for the static and dynamic effects of lifting, discharging, slewing, travelling and braking. The maximum wheel load under practical conditions may occur when the crane is stationary and hoisting the load at the maximum radius with the line of the jib diagonally over one wheel.

2.4.8 Garages

The floors of garages are usually considered in two classes, namely those for cars and other light vehicles and those for heavier vehicles. Floors in the light class are designed for specified uniformly distributed imposed loads, or alternative concentrated loads. In the design of floors for vehicles in the heavier class and for repair workshops, the bending moments and shearing forces should be computed for a minimum uniformly distributed load or for the effect of the most adverse disposition of the heaviest vehicles. The requirements of the Code are given in *Table 11*. A load equal to the maximum actual wheel load is assumed to be distributed over an area 300 mm or 12 in square.

The loading of garage floors is discussed in more detail in *Examples of the Design of Buildings*.

2.5 DISPERSAL OF CONCENTRATED LOADS

A load from a wheel or similar concentrated load bearing on a small but definite area of the supporting surface (called the contact area) may be assumed to be further dispersed over an area that depends on the combined thicknesses of the road or other surfacing material, filling, concrete slab, and any other constructional material. The width of the contact area of the wheel on the slab is equal to the width of the tyre. The length of the contact area depends on the type of tyre and the nature of the road surface, and is nearly zero for steel tyres on steel plate or concrete. The maximum contact length is probably obtained with an iron wheel on loose metalling or a pneumatic tyre on a tarmacadam surface.

Dispersal of a concentrated load through the total thickness of the road formation and concrete slab is often considered as acting at an angle of 45° from the edge of the contact area to the centre of the lower layer of reinforcement, as is shown in the diagrams in *Table 11*. The requirements of BS5400 'Steel, concrete and composite bridges' differ, as shown in *Table 10*. The dispersal through surfacing materials is considered to be at an inclination of 1 unit horizontally to 2 units vertically. Through a structural concrete slab at 45°, dispersal may be assumed to the depth of the neutral axis only.

In the case of a pair of wheels, on one axle, on two rails supported on sleepers it can be considered that the load from the wheels in any position is distributed transversely over the length of the sleeper and that two sleepers are effective in distributing the load longitudinally. The dispersal is often assumed as 45° through the ballast and deck below the sleepers, as indicated in *Table 11*. Again, the requirements of BS5400 differ, as shown in *Table 10*. When a rail bears directly on concrete, the dispersion may be four to six times the depth of the rail. These rules apply to slow-moving trains; fast-moving trains may cause a 'mounting' surge in front of the train such that the rails and sleepers immediately in front of the driving wheels tend to rise and therefore impose less load in front, but more behind, on the supporting structure.

2.6 MARINE STRUCTURES

The forces acting upon wharves, jetties, dolphins, piers, docks, sea-walls and similar marine and riverside structures include those due to the wind and waves, blows and pulls from vessels, the loads from cranes, railways, roads, stored goods and other live loads imposed on the deck, and the pressures of earth retained behind the structure.

In a wharf or jetty of solid construction the energy of impact due to blows from vessels berthing is absorbed by the mass of the structure, usually without damage to the structure or vessel if fendering is provided. With open construction, consisting of braced piles or piers supporting the deck in which the mass of the structure is comparatively small, the forces resulting from impact must be considered, and these forces depend on the weight and speed of approach of the vessel, on the amount of fendering, and on the flexibility of the structure. In general a large vessel has a low speed of approach and a small vessel a higher speed of approach. Some examples are a 500 tonne trawler berthing at a speed of 300 mm/s or 12 in/s; a 4000 tonne vessel at 150 mm/s or 6 in/sec; and a 10 000 tonne vessel at 50 mm/s or 2 in/s (1 tonne = 1 ton approximately). The kinetic energy of a vessel of 1000 tonnes displacement moving at a speed of 300 mm/s or 12 in/s and of a vessel of 25 000 tonnes moving at 60 mm/s or 2.4 in/s is in each case about 50 kNm or 16 ton ft. The kinetic energy of a vessel of displacement F approaching at a velocity of V is $514FV^2$ N m when F is in tonnes and V is in m/s, and $0.016FV^2$ ton ft when F is in tons and V is in ft/s. If the direction of approach is normal to the face of the jetty, the whole of this energy must be absorbed upon impact. More commonly a vessel approaches at an angle of θ^0 with the face of the jetty and touches first at one point about which the vessel swings. The kinetic energy then to be absorbed is $K[(V \sin \theta)^2 - (\rho\omega)^2]$, where K is $514F$ or $0.016F$ depending on whether SI or imperial units are employed, ρ is the radius of gyration of the vessel about the point of impact in metres or feet, and ω is the angular velocity (radians per second) of the vessel about the point of impact. The numerical values of the terms in this expression are difficult to assess accurately and can vary considerably under different conditions of tide and wind with different vessels and methods of berthing.

The kinetic energy of approach is absorbed partly by the resistance of the water, but most of it will be absorbed by the fendering, by elastic deformation of the structure and the vessel, by movement of the ground, and by the energy 'lost' upon impact. The proportion of energy lost upon impact (considered as inelastic impact), if the weight of the structure is F_s, does not exceed $F_s/(F_s + F)$ approximately. It is advantageous to make F_s approximately equal to F. The energy absorbed by the deformation of the vessel is difficult to assess, as is also the energy absorbed by the ground. It is sometimes recommended that only about one-half of the total kinetic energy of the vessel be considered as being absorbed by the structure and fendering.

The force to which the structure is subjected upon impact is calculated by equating the product of the force and half the elastic horizontal displacement of the structure to the kinetic energy to be absorbed. The horizontal displacement of an ordinary reinforced concrete jetty may be about 25 mm or 1 in, but probable variations from this amount combined with the indeterminable value of the kinetic energy absorbed result in the actual value of the force being also indeterminable. Ordinary timber fenders applied to reinforced concrete jetties cushion the blow, but may not substantially reduce the force on the structure. A spring fender or a suspended fender can, however, absorb a large portion of the kinetic energy and thus reduce considerably the blow on the structure. Timber fenders independent of the jetty are sometimes provided to relieve the structure of all impact forces.

The combined action of wind, waves, currents and tides on a vessel moored to a jetty is usually transmitted by the vessel pressing directly against the side of the structure or by pulls on mooring ropes secured to bollards. The pulls on bollards due to the foregoing causes or during berthing vary with the size of the vessel. A pull of 150 kN or 15 tons acting either horizonally outwards or vertically upwards or downwards is sometimes assumed. A guide to the maximum pull is the breaking strength of the mooring rope, or the power of capstans (when provided), which varies from 10 kN or 1 ton up to more than 200 kN or 20 tons at a large dock.

The effects of wind and waves acting on a marine structure are much reduced if an open construction is adopted and if provision is made for the relief of pressures due to water and air trapped below the deck. The force is not, however, directly related to the proportion of solid vertical face presented to the action of the wind and waves. The magnitude of the pressures imposed is impossible to assess with accuracy, except in the case of sea-walls and similar structures where there is such a depth of water at the face of the wall that breaking waves do not occur. In this case the pressure is merely the hydrostatic pressure which can be evaluated when the highest wave level is known or assumed, and an allowance is made for wind surge; in the Thames estuary, for example, the latter may raise the high-tide level 1.5 m or 5 ft above normal.

A wave breaking against a sea-wall induces a shock pressure additional to the hydrostatic pressure, which reaches its maximum value at about mean water level and diminishes rapidly below this level and less rapidly above it. The shock pressure may be ten times the hydrostatic pressure, and pressures up to 650 N/m^2 or 6 tons/ft^2 are possible with waves from 4.5 to 6 m or 15 to 20 ft high. The shape of the face of the wall, the slope of the foreshore, and the depth of the water at the wall affect the maximum pressure and the distribution of pressure. All the possible factors that may affect the stability of a sea-wall cannot be taken into account by calculation, and there is no certainty that the severity of the worst recorded storms may not be exceeded in the future.

2.7 WIND FORCES

2.7.1 Velocity and pressure of wind

The force due to wind on a structure depends on the velocity of the wind and the shape and size of the exposed members. The velocity depends on the district in which the structure is erected, the height of the structure, and the shelter afforded by buildings or hills in the neighbourhood. In the UK the velocity of gusts may exceed 50 m/s or 110 miles per hour but such gusts occur mainly in coastal districts. The basic wind speed V in the design procedure described in Part 2 of CP3: Chapter V is the maximum for a three-second gust that will occur only once during a 50 year period, at a height above ground of 10 m. Its 1958 predecessor considered the basic wind speed as the maximum value of the mean velocity for a one-minute period that would be attained at a height of 40 ft. The velocity of wind increases with the height above the ground.

The pressure due to wind varies as the square of the velocity and on a flat surface the theoretical pressure is as given by the formula at the top of *Table 13*. When calculating the resulting pressure on a structure, however, it is necessary to combine the effect of suction on the leeward side of an exposed surface with the positive pressure on the windward side.

The distribution and intensity of the resulting pressures due to wind depend on the shape of the surface upon which the wind impinges. The ratio of height to width or diameter seriously affects the intensities of the pressures; the greater this ratio, the greater is the pressure. The 'sharpness' of curvature at the corners of a polygonal structure, and the product of the design wind speed V_s and diameter (or width) b both influence the smoothness of the flow of air past the surface and may thus also affect the total pressure. In practice it is usual to allow for such variations in intensity of the pressure by applying a factor to the normal specified or estimated pressure acting on the projected area of the structure. Such factors are given in *Table 15* for some cylindrical, triangular, square, rectangular and octagonal 'solid' structures with various ratios of height to width; corresponding factors for open-frame (unclad) structures and for chimneys and sheeted towers are also given in CP3, from which the factors given at the bottom of *Table 15* have been abstracted.

The wind pressure to be used in the design of any particular structure should be assessed by consideration of relevant conditions, and especially should be based on local records of velocities.

2.7.2 Buildings

The effect of the wind on buildings is very complex. In any particular case it is necessary to determine the requirements of the local authority.

CP3: Chapter V: Part 2: 'Wind loading' deals with wind forces in some detail, and gives comprehensive data and formulae by which wind pressures on buildings and similar structures may be assessed. The intensity of external pressure is calculated from the characteristic wind speed; this relationship in SI units is as given in the table on the right of *Table 13*. The characteristic wind speed in turn is related to the locality, degree of exposure and height of structure, and is found by multiplying the basic wind speed V, which depends on locality only, by three non-dimensional factors S_1, S_2 and S_3. Values of V for the UK may be read from the map on *Table 13*.

The factor S_1 relates to the topography of environment of the site and in most cases is equal to unity; it may increase by some 10% on exposed hills or in narrowing valleys or it may decrease by some 10% in enclosed valleys. The factor S_3 is a statistical concept depending on the probable life of the structure and the probability of major winds occurring during that period; a recommended value for general use is unity. Thus in the general case $V_s = VS_2$, where S_2 is an important factor relating the terrain, i.e. open country or city centres or intermediate conditions, the plan size of the building and the height of the building. Some values of S_2 over a wide range of conditions are given in *Table 13*.

Having determined V_s, the next step is to assess the characteristic wind pressure w_k which is obtained from the formula $w_k = 0.613 V_s^2$, in which w_k is in N/m^2 and V_s is in m/s. The actual pressure on the walls and roof of a fully clad building is then obtained by multiplying w_k by a pressure coefficient C_{pe} to obtain the external pressure and by C_{pi} to obtain the internal pressure. The net pressure on cladding is then the algebraic difference between the two pressures. Values of C_{pe} for general surfaces and for local surfaces are given on *Table 15*.

To calculate the force on a complete building, the structure should be divided into convenient parts (e.g. corresponding to the storey heights). The value of S_2 relating to the height of the top of each part should be determined and used to calculate the correspondng value of V_s and hence w_k. The force acting on each part is then calculated and the results summed vectorially if the total force on the entire structure is required.

An alternative procedure to the use of external pressure coefficients C_{pe} is to employ the force coefficients C_f which are also tabulated in Part 2 of CP3: Chapter V and included on *Table 15*. The value of w_k is found as previously described and then multiplied by the frontal area of the structure and the appropriate force coefficient to obtain the total wind force.

On a pitched roof the pressures and suctions on the windward and leeward areas depend on the degree of slope, and appropriate external pressure coefficients are included on *Table 14*. The overall coefficients apply to the roof as a whole but for the design of the roof covering and purlins, or other supports, greater local pressures and suctions must be considered as indicated on the table. Curved roofs should be divided into segments as illustrated on *Table 7*. The information presented on *Tables 14* and *15* only briefly summarizes the more important items abstracted from the considerable volume of information provided in the Code itself, which should be consulted for further details.

2.7.3 Chimneys and towers

Since a primary factor in the design of chimneys and similarly exposed isolated structures is the force of the wind, careful consideration of each case is necessary to avoid either underestimating this force or making an unduly high assessment. Where records of wind velocities in the locality are available an estimate of the probable wind pressures can be made. Due account should be taken of the susceptibility of narrow shafts to the impact of a gust of wind. Some by-laws in the UK specify the intensities of horizontal wind pressure to be used in the design of circular chimney shafts for factories. The total lateral force is the product of the specified pressure and the maximum vertical projected area, and an overall factor of safety of at least 1.5 is required against overturning. In some instances specified pressures are primarily intended for the design of brick chimneys, and in this respect it should be remembered that the margin of safety is greater in reinforced concrete than in brickwork or masonry owing to the ability of reinforced concrete to resist tension, but a reinforced concrete chimney, like a steel chimney, is subject to oscillation under the effect of wind. Suitable pressures are specified in CP3, Chapter V: 1958. (Note that the 1972 revision does not cover chimneys and similar tall structures, for which a BSI Draft for Development is in preparation.) These recommendations allow for a variable pressure increasing from a minimum at the bottom to a maximum at the top of the chimney (or tower). A factor, such as given in *Table 15*, to allow for the shape of the structure, can be applied to allow for the relieving effect of curved and polygonal surfaces of chimneys, and of the tanks and the supporting structures of water towers. For cylindrical shafts with fluted surfaces a higher factor than that given in *Table 15* should be applied. Local meteorological records should be consulted to determine the probable maximum wind velocity. The chimney, or other structure, can be divided into a number of parts and the average pressure on each can be taken.

2.7.4 Bridges

The requirements of Part 2 of BS5400 for the calculation of wind loads on bridges are basically similar to those in Part 2 of CP3: Chapter V. However, the analysis is based on basic wind speeds which represent the greatest mean hourly speed that may be attained in a 120 year period at a height of 10 m above open level country. For details, reference must be made to BS5400: Part 2 itself.

2.8 RETAINED AND CONTAINED MATERIALS

2.8.1 Active pressures of retained and contained materials

The value of the horizontal pressure exerted by a contained material or by earth or other material retained by a wall is uncertain, except when the contained or retained material is a liquid. The formulae, rules and other data in *Tables 16–20* are given as practical bases for the calculation of such pressures. Reference should also be made to Code no. 2, 'Earth-retaining structures' (see ref. 1).

When designing structures in accordance with BS8110 it should be remembered that all pressures etc. calculated by using the characteristic dead weights of materials represent *service* loads. Consequently, when designing sections according to limit-state considerations, the pressures etc. must be multiplied by the appropriate partial safety factors for loads to obtain ultimate bending moments and shearing forces.

Liquids. At any h below the free surface of a liquid, the intensity of pressure q per unit area normal to a surface subject to pressure from the liquid is equal to the intensity of vertical pressure, which is given by the simple hydrostatic expression $q = Dh$, where D is the weight per unit volume of the liquid.

Granular materials. When the contained material is granular, for example dry sand, grain, small coal, gravel or crushed stone, the pressure normal to a retaining surface can be expressed conveniently as a fraction of the equivalent fluid pressure; thus $q = kDh$, where k is a measure of the 'fluidity' of the contained or retained material and varies from unity for perfect fluids to zero for materials that stand unretained with a vertical face. The value of k also depends on the physical characteristics, water content, angle of repose, angle of internal friction and slope of the surface of the material, on the slope of the wall or other retaining surface, on the material of which the wall is made, and on the surcharge on the contained material. The value of k is determined graphically or by calculation, both methods being usually based on the wedge theory or the developments of Rankine or Cain. The total pressure normal to the back of a sloping or vertical wall can be calculated from the formulae in *Table 16* for various conditions.

Friction between the wall and the material is usually neglected, resulting in a higher calculated normal pressure which is safe. Friction must be neglected if the material in contact with the wall can become saturated and thereby reduce the friction by an uncertain amount or to zero. Only where dry materials of well-known properties are being stored may this friction be included. Values of the coefficient of friction μ can be determined from *Table 17*. When friction is neglected (i.e. $\mu = 0$), the pressure normal to the back of the wall is equal to the total pressure and there is, theoretically, no force acting parallel to the back of the wall.

Generally, in the case of retaining walls and walls of bunkers and other containers, the back face of the wall is vertical (or nearly so) and the substitution of $\beta = 90°$ in the general formulae for k gives the simplified formulae in *Table 16*. Values of k_1 (maximum positive slope or surcharge), k_2 (level fill) and k_3 (maximum negative slope) for various angles of internal friction (in degrees and gradients) are given in *Table 18*; the values of such angles for various granular materials are given in *Tables 17* and *21*. For a wall retaining ordinary earth with level filling k_2 is often assumed to be 0.3 and, with the average weight of earth as $16\,\text{kN/m}^3$ or $100\,\text{lb/ft}^3$, the intensity of horizontal pressure is $4.8\,\text{kN/m}^2$ per metre of height or $30\,\text{lb/ft}^2$ per foot of height. The formulae assume dry materials. If ground-water occurs in the filling behind the wall, the modified formula given in section 10.1.1 applies. The intensity of pressure normal to the slope of an inclined surface is considered in section 10.1.2 and in *Table 18*.

Effect of surcharge (granular materials). The effects of various types of surcharge on the ground behind a retaining wall are evaluated in *Table 20*, and comments are given in section 10.1.3.

Theoretical and actual pressures of granular materials. In general practice, horizontal pressures due to granular materials can be determined by the purely theoretical formulae of Rankine, Cain and Coulomb. Many investigators have made experiments to determine what relation actual pressures bear to the theoretical pressures, and it appears that the Rankine formula for a filling with a level surface and neglecting friction between the filling and the back of the wall gives too great a value for the pressure. Thus retaining walls designed on this theory should be on the side of safety. The theory assumes that the angle of internal friction of the material and the surface angle of repose are identical, whereas some investigations find that the internal angle of friction is less than the angle of repose and depends on the consolidation of the material. The ratio between the internal angle of friction and the angle of repose has been found to be between 0.9 and 1 approximately. For a filling with a level surface the horizontal pressure given by

$$q = Dh\left(\frac{1 - \sin\theta}{1 + \sin\theta}\right)$$

agrees very closely with the actual pressure if θ is the angle of internal friction and not the angle of repose. The maximum pressure seems to occur immediately after the filling has been deposited, and the pressure decreases as settling proceeds. The vertical component of the pressure on the back of the wall appears to conform to the theoretical relationship $F_v = F_h \tan\mu$. A rise in temperature produces an increase in pressure of about 2% per 10°C.

The point of application of the resultant thrust on a wall with a filling with a level surface would appear theoretically to be at one-third of the total height for shallow walls, and rises in the course of time and with increased heights of wall. According to some investigators, where the surface of the fill slopes downward away from the wall, the point of application is at one-third of the height, but this rises as the slope increases upwards.

Loads imposed on the ground behind the wall and within the plane of rupture increase the pressure on the wall, but generally loads outside the wedge ordinarily considered can be neglected. The increase of pressure due to transient imposed loads remains temporarily after the load is removed. If the filling slopes upwards, theory seems to give pressures almost 30% in excess of actual pressures.

Cohesive soils. Cohesive soils include clays, soft clay shales, earth, silts and peat. The active pressures exerted by such soils vary greatly; owing to cohesion, pressures may be less than those due to granular soil, but saturation may cause much greater pressure. The basic formula for the intensity of horizontal pressure at any depth on the back of a vertical wall retaining a cohesive soil is that of A. L. Bell (derived from a formula by Français). Bell's formula is given in two forms in *Table 16*. The cohesion factor is the shearing strength of the unloaded clay at the surface. Some typical values of the angle of internal friction and the cohesion C for common cohesive soils are given in *Table 17*, but actual values should be ascertained by test.

According to Bell's formula there is no pressure against the wall down to a depth of $2C/D\sqrt{k_2}$ below the surface if the nature of the clay is prevented from changing. However, as the condition is unlikely to exist owing to the probability of moisture changes, it is essential that hydrostatic pressure should be assumed to act near the top of the wall. Formulae for the pressure of clays of various types and in various conditions are given in *Table 19*, together with the properties of these and other cohesive soils. In general, friction between the clay and the back of the wall should be neglected.

2.8.2 Passive resistance of granular and cohesive materials

The remarks in the previous paragraphs relate to the active horizontal pressure exerted by contained and retained materials.

If a horizontal pressure in excess of the active pressure is applied to the vertical face of a retained bulk of material, the passive resistance of the material is brought into action. Up to a limit, determined by the characteristics of the particular material, the passive resistance equals the applied pressure; the maximum intensity that the resistance can attain for a granular material with a level surface is given theoretically by the reciprocal of the active pressure factor. The passive resistance of earth is taken into account when considering the resistance to sliding of a retaining wall when dealing with the forces acting on sheet piles, and when designing earth anchorages, but in these cases consideration must be given to those factors, such as wetness, that may reduce the probable passive resistance. Abnormal dryness may cause clay soils to shrink away from the surface of the structure, thus necessitating a small but most undesirable movement of the structure before the passive resistance can act.

For a dry granular material with level fill the passive resistance is given by the formula in *Table 16*; expressions for the passive resistance of waterlogged ground are given in section 10.1.1. It is not easy to assess the passive resistance when the surface of the material is not level, and it is advisable never to assume a resistance exceeding that for a level surface. When the surface slopes downwards the passive resistance should be neglected.

For ordinary saturated clay the passive resistance is given by the formula in *Table 16*, and the corresponding formulae for clay in other conditions are given in *Table 19*.

2.8.3 Horizontal pressures of granular materials in liquid

The effect of saturated soils is considered in preceding paragraphs. The notes given in section 10.2.1 and the numerical values of some of the factors involved for certain materials as given in *Table 17* apply to granular materials immersed in or floating in liquids.

2.8.4 Deep containers (silos)*

In deep containers, termed silos, the linear increase of pressure with depth, found in shallow containers and described above, is modified. When the deep container is filled, slight settlement of the fill activates the frictional resistance between the stored mass and the wall. This induces vertical load in the silo wall but reduces the vertical pressure in the mass and the lateral pressures on the wall. Janssen has developed a theory giving the pressures on the walls of a silo filled with granular material having constant properties. His expression, shown in *Table 21*, indicates that the maximum lateral pressure arising during filling, at which the force due to wall friction balances the weight of each layer of fill, is approached at depths greater than about twice the diameter or width of the silo.

The lateral pressure q_h depends on D the unit weight of contained material, r the hydraulic radius (obtained by dividing the plan area by the plan perimeter), $\tan\theta'$ the coefficient of friction between the contained material and the silo wall, h the depth of material above the plane considered, and k the ratio of horizontal to vertical pressure. The value of k is often taken as $k_2 = (1 - \sin\theta)/(1 + \sin\theta)$, where θ is the angle of internal friction of the stored material. For reinforced concrete silos for storing wheat grain D is often taken as $8400\,\text{N/m}^3$, with values of k of 0.33 to 0.5 and of $\tan\theta'$ of 0.35 to 0.45. The average intensity of vertical pressure q_v on any horizontal plane of material is q_h/k, but pressure is not usually uniform over the plane. The load carried by the walls by means of friction is $[Dh - (q_h/k)]r$ per unit length of wall.

Unloading a silo disturbs the equilibrium of the contained mass. If the silo is unloaded from the top, the frictional load on the wall may reverse as the mass re-expands, but the lateral pressures remain similar to those that occur during filling. With a free-flowing material unloading at the bottom from the centre of a hopper, one of two completely different modes of flow may occur, depending on the nature of the contained material, and the proportions of the silo and the hopper. These modes are termed 'core flow' and 'mass flow' respectively. In the former, a core of flowing material develops from the outlet upwards to the top surface where a conical depression develops. Material then flows from the top surface down the core leaving the mass of fill undisturbed (diagram(a) on *Table 21*). Core flow give rise to some increase in lateral pressure from the stable, filled condition.

*These notes and those in section 10.3 have been contributed by J. G. M. Wood, BSc, PhD, CEng, MICE.

Mass flow occurs in silos fitted with steep-sided hoppers which are proportioned to ensure that the entire mass moves downwards as a whole, converging and accelerating towards the outlet (diagram(b) on *Table 21*). This action produces substantial local increases in lateral pressure, especially at the intersection between the vertical walls and the hopper bottom where a 'dynamic arch' forms at the transition from parallel vertical flow to accelerating convergent flow. However, mass flow can develop within the mass of material contained in *any* tall silo owing to the formation of a 'self-hopper'. The resulting high local pressures arising at the transition may occur at varying levels where the parallel flow starts to diverge from the walls.

For the routine design of silos in which mass flow cannot develop, the method presented in the West German code of practice DIN1055: Part 6 (ref. 2) provides possibly the most satisfactory current approach for calculating pressures for designing concrete silos: this method is summarized on *Table 21* and in section 10.3. Where mass flow is possible (e.g. where the height from the outlet to the surface of the contained material exceeds about four times the hydraulic radius) specialist information should be sought (ref. 3): reference should be made to the work of Walker and Jenike (refs 4, 5).

When calculating the pressures on and the capacity of the silo, great care must be exercised in establishing the maximum and minimum values of density, angle of repose, angle of internal friction and angle of wall friction for the contained fill. In establishing the coefficient of wall friction, allowance must be made for the full range of moisture contents that may occur in the stored material and the 'polishing' effects of continued use on the surface finish of the silo wall. In general, concrete silo design is not sensitive to the values of vertical wall load, so the maximum density and minimum consistent coefficients of internal friction and wall friction should be used when calculating the lateral and floor pressures. Typical values for some common materials are indicated on *Table 21*, together with the values of density and angle of repose appropriate to calculations of capacity.

The pressures in the silo, the effects of vibration and the presence of fine particles and/or moisture in the stored material may all increase densities from the values given in reference books. For certain materials, e.g. wheat and barley, the density when stored in a silo can be 15% greater than the 'bushel weight' density commonly quoted.

Eccentric filling or discharge tends to produce variations in pressure round the bin wall. These variations must be anticipated when preparing the design, although reliable guidance is limited; with large bins central discharge must be insisted upon for normal designs. The 'fluidization' of fine powders such as cement or flour can occur in silos, either owing to rapid filling or through aeration to facilitate discharge. Where full fluidization can occur, designs must be based on the consideration of fluid pressure at a reduced density.

Various devices are marketed to facilitate the discharge of silos based on fluidization, air slides, augers, chain cutters and vibrators. These devices alter the properties of the mass or the pressure distribution within the mass to promote flow, with a corresponding effect on the pressures in the silo. When vibrating devices are used the effects of fatigue should also be considered during design. Considerable wear can occur due to the flow of material in a silo, particularly close to the hopper outlet.

Agricultural silage silos are subjected to distributions of pressure that differ greatly from those due to granular materials: reference should be made to BS5061 'Circular forage tower silos'.

2.9 PRESSURE DUE TO SONIC BOOMS

A sonic boom is a pressure wave, not dissimilar to that produced by a clap of thunder, which sweeps along the ground in the wake of aircraft flying at supersonic speeds, despite the great altitude at which the aircraft is flying. Limiting pressures of about $100\,N/m^2$ or $2\,lb/ft^2$ have been established as the probable maximum sonic-boom pressure at ground level. Pressures of such low intensities are relatively unimportant when compared with the wind pressures which buildings are designed to resist, but the dynamic effect of the sudden application of sonic pressures may produce effectively higher pressures.

Chapter 3
Structural analysis

The bending moments and shearing forces on freely supported beams and simple cantilevers are readily determined from simple statical rules but the solution of continuous beams and statically indeterminate frames is more complex. Until fairly recently the techniques of structural analysis required to solve such problems were presented and employed as independent self-contained methods, the relationships between them being ignored or considered relatively unimportant. The choice of method used depended on its suitability to the type of problem concerned and also to some extent on its appeal to the particular designer involved.

Recently, the underlying interrelationships between various analytical methods have become clearer. It is now realized that there are two basic types of method: *flexibility* methods (otherwise known as action methods, compatibility methods or force methods), where the behaviour of the structure is considered in terms of unknown forces, and *displacement* methods (otherwise known as stiffness methods or equilibrium methods), where the behaviour is considered in terms of unknown displacements. In each case, the complete solution consists of combining a *particular* solution, obtained by modifying the structure to make it statically determinate and then analysing it, with a *complementary* solution, in which the effects of each individual modification are determined. For example, for a continuous-beam system, with flexibility methods, the particular solution involves removing the redundant actions (i.e. the continuity between the individual members) to leave a series of disconnected spans; with displacement methods the particular solution involves violating joint equilibrium by restricting the rotation and/or displacement that would otherwise occur at the joints.

To clarify further the basic differences between the types of method, consider a propped cantilever. With the flexibility approach the procedure is first to remove the prop and to calculate the deflection at the position of the prop due to the action of the load only: this gives the particular solution. Next calculate the concentrated load that must be applied at the prop position to achieve an equal and opposite deflection: this is the complementary solution. The force obtained is the reaction in the prop; when this is known, all the moments and forces in the propped cantilever can be calculated.

If displacement methods are used, the span is considered fixed at both supports and the resulting moment acting at the end at which the prop occurs is found: this is the particular solution. The next step is to release this support and determine the moment that must then be applied at the pinned end of the cantilever to negate the fixing moment. Lastly, by summing both resulting moment diagrams the final moments are obtained and the reactions can be calculated.

In practical problems there are a number of unknowns and, irrespective of the method of solution adopted, the preparation and solution of a series of simultaneous equations is normally necessary. Whichever basic method of analysis is employed the resulting relationship between forces and displacements embodies a series of coefficients which can be set out concisely in matrix form. If flexibility methods are used the resulting flexibility matrix is built up of flexibility coefficients, each of which represents a displacement produced by a unit action. Similarly, stiffness methods lead to the preparation of a stiffness matrix formed of stiffness coefficients, each of which represents an action produced by a unit displacement.

The solution of matrix equations, either by inverting the matrix or by a systematic elimination procedure, is ideally handled by machine. To this end, methods have been devised (so-called matrix stiffness and matrix flexibility methods) for which the computer both sets up and solves the necessary equations (ref. 6).

It may here be worth while to summarize the basic aims of frame analysis. Calculating the bending moments on individual freely supported spans by simple statics ensures that the design loads are in equilibrium. The analytical procedure which is then undertaken involves linearly transforming these free-moment diagrams in such a way that under ultimate-load conditions the inelastic deformations at the critical sections remain within the limits that the sections can withstand, whereas under working loads the deformations are insufficient to cause excessive deflection or cracking or both. Provided that the analysis is sufficient to meet these requirements, it will be entirely satisfactory for its purpose; the attempt to obtain painstakingly precise results by ever more complex methods in unjustified in view of the many uncertainties involved.

The basic relations between the shearing force, bending moment, slope and deflection caused by a load in a structural member are given in *Table 22*, in which are also given typical diagrams of bending moments and shearing forces for cantilevers, propped cantilevers, freely supported beams, and beams fixed or continuous at one or both supports.

3.1 SINGLE-SPAN BEAMS AND CANTILEVERS

Formulae giving shearing forces, bending moments and deflections produced by various general loads are given on *Table 23*. Similar expressions for particular arrangements of load commonly encountered on beams that are freely supported or fixed at both ends, with details of the maximum values, are presented on *Table 24*. The same information but relating to both simple and propped cantilevers is set out on *Tables 25* and *26*, respectively. Combinations of load can be considered by calculating the moments, deflections etc. required at various points across the span due to each individual load and summing the resulting values at each point.

On *Tables 23* to *26*, expressions are also given for the slopes at the beam supports and the free (or propped) end of a cantilever. Information regarding slopes at other points (or due to other loads) is seldom required. If needed, it is usually a simple matter to obtain the slope by differentiating the deflection formula given with respect to x. If the resulting expression is then equated to zero and solved to obtain x, the point of maximum deflection will have been found, which can then be resubstituted into the original formula to obtain the value of maximum deflection.

The charts on *Table 28* give the value and position of maximum deflection for a freely supported span when loaded with a partial uniform or triangular load. (On this and similar charts, concentrated loads may be considered by taking $\beta = 1 - \alpha$, of course.) If deflections due to combinations of load are required they can be estimated simply by summing the deflection obtained for each load individually. Since the values of maximum deflection given by the charts usually occur at different points for each individual load, the resulting summation will slightly exceed the true maximum deflection of the combined loading. A full range of similar charts but giving the *central* deflections on freely supported and fixed spans and propped cantilevers and the deflection at the free end of simple cantilevers are given in *Examples of the Design of Buildings*. The calculation of such deflections forms part of the rigorous procedure for satisfying the serviceability limit-state requirements regarding deflections in BS8110 and CP110. Comparison between the values obtained from the charts shows that the differences between the central and maximum deflection are insignificant, in view of the uncertainties in the constants (e.g. E_c and I) used to compute deflections. For example, with a partial uniform load or a concentrated load on a freely supported span, the greatest difference, of about 2.5%, between the maximum deflection and that at midspan occurs when the load is at one extreme end of the span, when the deflection values are minimal anyway.

Similar charts giving the value and position of the maximum bending moment on a freely supported span, when loaded with a partial uniform or triangular load, are given on *Table 27*. These may be used to sketch the free bending moment diagrams simply and quickly.

The bending-moment factors for beams of one span which is fixed at both supports are the fixed-end-moment factors (or load factors) used in calculations in some methods of analysing statically indeterminate structures. Such load factors (which should not be confused with load factors used in determining the resistances of members by ultimate-load methods) and notes relating to the methods to which they apply are given in *Table 29*. Coefficients for the fixed-end moments due to a partial uniform and a partial triangular load on a span with fixed supports are given in *Tables 31* and *30* respectively, and similar coefficients for a trapezoidal load, such as occurs along the longer spans of a beam system supporting two-way slabs, are given in *Table 31*.

3.2 CONTINUOUS BEAMS

Various methods have been been developed for determining the bending moments and shearing forces on beams that are continuous over two or more spans. As pointed out above, these methods are interrelated to each other to a greater or lesser extent. Most of the well-known individual methods of structural analysis such as the theorem of three moments, slope deflection, fixed and characteristic points, and moment distribution and its variants, are stiffness methods: this approach generally lends itself better to hand computation than do flexibility methods. To avoid the need to solve large sets of simultaneous equations, such as are required with the three-moment theorem or slope deflection, methods involving successive approximations have been devised, such as Hardy Cross moment distribution and Southwell's relaxation method.

Despite the ever-increasing use of machine aids, hand methods still at present have an important place in the concrete designer's 'tool-kit'. For less complex problems, it may be both cheaper and quicker to use such methods if immediate and continued access to a computer is not possible. Hand methods, particularly those involving successive approximations, also give the designer a 'feel' for analysis that it is impossible to obtain when using machine aids entirely. It is for these and similar reasons that brief details of the best-known hand computation methods are given in the tables corresponding to this section.

3.2.1 Calculation of bending moments and shearing forces

The bending moments on a beam continuous over two or more spans can be calculated by the *theorem of three moments*, which in its general form for any two contiguous spans is expressed by the general and special formulae given on *Table 39*. Notes on the use of the formulae and the calculation of the shearing forces are given in section 12.4.1, and an example is also provided. The formulae establish the negative support moments; the positive bending moments in the spans can then be found graphically or, in the case of spans that are loaded uniformly throughout, from the formulae given on *Table 141*.

Another well-known method is that of slope deflection: this is discussed later when considering the analysis of frames. The principles of slope deflection can be used to develop a graphical method for determining both span and support moments, known as the *method of fixed points*. Details of the procedure involved are summarized on *Table 41* and described in section 12.5. A somewhat similar but perhaps even simpler semi-graphical method is that of *characteristic points*, of which brief details are given on *Table 42*.

If beams having two, three or four spans, and with a uniform moment of inertia throughout, support loads that are symmetrical on each individual span, the theorem of three moments can be used to produce formulae and coefficients which enable the support moments to be determined without the need to solve simultaneous equations. Such a method is presented on *Table 43*. The resulting formulae can also be used to prepare graphs for two- and three-span beams, such as those which form *Tables 44* and *45*, from which the internal support moments can be found very quickly. Further details of this method, together with examples, are given in section 12.7.

Perhaps the system best known at present for analysing continuous beams by hand is that of *moment distribution*, devised by Hardy Cross in 1929. The method, which derives from slope-deflection principles and is described briefly on *Table 40*, avoids the need to solve sets of simultaneous equations directly by employing instead a system of successive approximations which may be terminated as soon as the required degree of accuracy has been reached. One particular advantage of this (and similar approximation methods) is that it is often clear, even after only one distribution cycle, whether or not the final values will be acceptable. If not, the analysis need not be continued further, thus saving much unnecessary work. The method is simple to remember and apply and the step-by-step procedure gives the engineer a quite definite 'feel' of the behaviour of the system. It can be extended, less happily, to the analysis of systems containing non-prismatic members and to frames (see *Table 66*). Hardy Cross moment distribution is described in detail in most textbooks dealing with structural analysis: see for example, refs 7, 8 and 9.

In the succeeding fifty years since it was introduced the Hardy Cross method has begot various (including some rather strange) offspring. One of the best known is so-called *precise moment distribution* (sometimes known as the coefficient-of-restraint method or direct moment distribution). The analytical procedure is extremely similar to and only slightly less simple than normal moment distribution, but the distribution and carry-over factors are so adjusted that an exact solution is obtained after only a single distribution in each direction. The method thus has the advantage of eliminating the need to decide when to terminate the successive approximation procedure. The few formulae that are required are easy to memorize and the use of graphs is not essential. Brief details are given on *Table 40* and the method is described in some detail in *Examples of the Design of Buildings*: more extensive information is given in refs 10 and 11.

It should be noted that the loading producing the greatest negative bending moments at the supports is not necessarily that producing the greatest positive bending moments in the span. The incidence of imposed load to give the greatest bending moments according to structural theory and to the less onerous requirements of BS8110 and CP110 is illustrated in *Table 22* and comments are given in section 12.1. Some dispositions of imposed load may produce negative bending moments in adjacent unloaded spans.

According to both Codes, the appropriate partial safety factors for loads to be considered when analysing systems of continuous beams for ultimate limit-state conditions are 1.6 for imposed load and either 1.4 or 1.0 for dead load, the particular arrangement investigated being that causing the most onerous conditions. In view of the alternative dead-load factors it is often convenient in such calculations to consider instead an ultimate dead load of $1.0g_k$ (or $1.0G_k$) and an 'imposed load' of $0.4g_k + 1.6q_k$ (or $0.4G_k + 1.6Q_k$).

The moment of inertia of a reinforced concrete beam of uniform depth may vary throughout its length because of variations in the amount of reinforcement and because it is considered, with the adjoining slab, to act as a flanged section at midspan but as a simple rectangular section over the supports. It is common, however, to neglect these variations for beams of uniform depth and for beams having small haunches at the supports. Where the depth of a beam varies considerably, neglect of the variation of moment of inertia when calculating the bending moments leads to results that differ widely from the probable bending moments. Methods of dealing with beams having non-uniform moments of inertia are given in *Table 39* and in section 12.4.2.

3.2.2 Coefficients for bending moments and shearing forces for equal spans

For beams continuous over a number of equal spans, calculation of the maximum bending moments from basic formulae is unnecessary since the moments and shearing forces can be tabulated. For example, in *Tables 33* and *34* the values of the bending-moment coefficients are given for the middle of each span and at each support for two, three, four and five continuous equal spans carrying identical loads on each span, which is the usual disposition of the dead load on a beam. The coefficients for the maximum bending moments at midspan and support for the most adverse incidence of imposed loads are also given; the alternative coefficients assuming only two spans to be loaded in the case of the bending moments at the supports are given in curved brackets and those relating to imposed load covering all spans are shown in square brackets; these latter correspond to the critical loading conditions specified in CP110 and BS8110 respectively. It should be noted that the maximum bending moments do not occur at all sections simultaneously. The types of load considered are a uniformly distributed load, a single load concentrated at midspan, trapezoidal loads of various proportions and equal loads at the two third-points of the span.

Similar information is presented in *Tables 36* and *37*, where the bending-moment coefficients corresponding to various arrangements of dead and imposed loads are given together with sketches of the resulting moment envelopes for two- and three-span beams and for the end and interior spans of a theoretically infinite system. This information enables the appropriate bending-moment diagrams to be plotted quickly and accurately.

These theoretical bending moments may be adjusted by assuming that some redistribution of moments takes place.

One principal advantage of employing such moment redistribution is that it enables the effects of ultimate loading to be assessed by employing normal elastic analyses of the structure, thus avoiding the need to undertake a separate structural analysis under ultimate-load conditions using plastic-hinge techniques: the theoretical basis for redistribution is explained clearly in the *Code Handbook*. Since the reduction of moment at a section assumes the formation of a plastic hinge at that point as ultimate conditions are approached, it is necessary to limit the total amount of adjustment possible in order to restrict the amount of plastic-hinge rotation that takes place and to control the amount of cracking that occurs under serviceability conditions. For these reasons both Codes also relate the depth-to-neutral-axis factor x/d (see section 5.3.1) and the maximum permitted spacing of the tension reinforcement (see *Table 139*) to the amount of redistribution allowed.

Such adjustments are convenient to reduce the inequality between negative and positive moments and to minimize the moment and hence the amount of reinforcement that must be provided at a section, such as the intersection between beam and column, where concreting may otherwise be difficult due to the congestion of reinforcement. Both BS8110 and CP110 permit moment redistribution to be undertaken; the procedure is outlined below and described in more detail in section 12.3, while the resulting adjusted bending-moment coefficients are given in *Tables 36* and *37*.

It should be remembered that while the coefficients given apply to the systems of equal spans considered here, moment redistribution can be employed as described in section 12.3 to adjust the moments on any system that has been analysed by so-called exact methods.

It is generally assumed that an ordinary continuous beam is freely supported on the end supports (unless fixity or another condition of restraint is specifically known), but in most cases the beam is constructed monolithically with the support, thereby producing some restraint.

The shearing forces produced by a uniformly distributed load when all spans are loaded and the greatest shearing forces due to any incidence of imposed load are given in *Table 35* for beams continuous over two to five equal spans.

3.2.3 Approximate bending-moment coefficients

The precise determination of the theoretical bending moments on continuous beams may involve much mathematical labour, except in cases which occur often enough to warrant tabulation. Having regard to the general assumptions of unyielding knife-edge supports and uniform moments of inertia, the probability of the theoretical bending moments being greater or less than those actually realized should be considered. The effect of a variation of the moment of inertia is given in section 12.4.2. The following factors cause a decrease in the negative bending moment at a support: settlement of the support relative to adjacent supports, which may cause an increase in the positive bending moments in the adjacent spans and may even be sufficient to convert the bending moment at that support into a positive bending moment; supports of considerable width; and support and beam constructed monolithically. The settlement of one or both of the supports on either side of a given support causes an increase in the negative bending moment at the given support and consequently affects the positive bending moments in adjacent spans.

The indeterminate nature of the actual bending moments occurring leads in practice to the adoption of approximate bending-moment coefficients for continuous beams and slabs of about equal spans with uniformly distributed loads. Such coefficients, including those recommended by BS8110 and CP110, are given in the middle of *Table 32*; notes on the validity and use of the coefficients are given in section 12.1.4.

When the bending moments are calculated with the spans assumed to be equal to the distance between the centres of the supports, the critical bending moment in monolithic construction can be considered as that occurring at the edge of the support. When the supports are of considerable width the span can be considered as the clear distance between the supports plus the effective depth of the beam, or an additional span can be introduced that is equal to the width of the support minus the effective depth of the beam. The load on this additional span can be considered as the reaction of the support spread uniformly along the part of the beam over the support. When a beam is constructed monolithically with a very wide and massive support the effect of continuity with the span or spans beyond the support may be negligible, in which case the beam should be treated as fixed at the support.

3.2.4 Bending-moment diagrams for equal spans

The basis of the bending-moment diagrams in *Tables 36* and *37* is as follows. The theoretical bending moments are calculated to obtain the coefficients for the bending moments near the middle of each span and at each support for a uniformly distributed load, a central load, and loads concentrated at the third-points of each span. The condition of all spans loaded (for example, dead load) and conditions of incidental (or imposed) load producing the greatest bending moments are considered. As the coefficients are calculated by exact methods, moment redistribution as permitted in BS8110 and CP110 is permissible. The support moments are reduced by 10% or 30% to establish the reduced bending moments at the supports, and the span moments are then reduced by 10% or 30% (where possible) to obtain the reduced positive bending moments in the span. *Tables 36* and *37* also give the coefficients for the positive bending moments at the supports and the negative bending moments in the spans which are produced under some conditions of imposed load; it is not generally necessary to take these small bending moments into account as they are generally insignificant compared with the bending moments due to dead load.

The method of calculating the adjusted coefficients is that the theoretical bending moments are calculated for all spans loaded (dead load), and for each of the four cases of imposed load that produce maximum bending moments, that is at the middle of an end span (positive), at a penultimate support (negative), at the middle of the interior span (positive), and at an inner support (positive). For each case, the theoretical bending-moment diagram is adjusted as follows. For the diagram of maximum negative bending moments, the theoretical negative bending moments at the supports are reduced by either 10% or 30% and the positive bending moments are increased accordingly. For the diagram of maximum positive bending moments in the spans, these theoretical positive bending moments are reduced by 10% or more where possible. (In most cases a full 30% reduction of the positive bending moments is not possible.) This redistribution process is described in detail in section 12.3.

3.3 MOVING LOADS ON CONTINUOUS BEAMS

Bending moments caused by moving loads, such as those due to vehicles traversing a series of continuous spans, are most easily calculated by the aid of influence lines. An influence line is a curve with the span of the beam as a base, the ordinate of the curve at any point being the value of the bending moment produced at a particular section of the beam when a unit load acts at the point. The data given in *Tables 46* to *49* enable the influence lines for the critical sections of beams continuous over two, three, four and five or more spans to be drawn. By plotting the position of the load on the beam (drawn to scale), the bending moments at the section being considered are derived as explained in the example given in chapter 13. The curves in the tables for equal spans are directly applicable to equal spans, but the corresponding curves for unequal spans should be plotted from the data tabulated.

The bending moment due to a load at any point is the ordinate of the influence line at the point multiplied by the product of the load and the span, the length of the shortest span being used when the spans are unequal. The influence lines in the tables are drawn for symmetrical inequality of spans. Coefficients for span ratios not plotted can be interpolated. The symbols on each curve indicate the section of the beam and the ratio of spans to which the curve applies.

3.4 ONE-WAY SLABS

3.4.1 Uniformly distributed load

The bending moments on slabs supported on two opposite sides are calculated in the same way as for beams, account being taken of continuity. For slabs carrying uniformly distributed loads and continuous over nearly equal spans, the coefficients for dead and imposed load as given in *Table 32* for slabs without splays conform to the recommendations of BS8110 and CP110. Other coefficients, allowing for the effect of splays on the bending moments, are also tabulated. Spans are considered to be approximately equal if the difference in length of the spans forming the system does not exceed 15% of the longest span.

If a slab is nominally freely supported at an end support, it is advisable to provide resistance to a probable negative bending moment at a support with which the slab is monolithic. If the slab carries a uniformly distributed load, the value of the negative bending moment should be assumed to be not less than $wl^2/24$ or $nl^2/24$.

Although a slab may be designed as though spanning in one direction, it should also be reinforced in a direction at right angles to the span with at least the minimum proportion of distribution steel, as described in section 20.5.2.

3.4.2 Concentrated load

When a slab supported on two opposite sides only carries a load concentrated on a part only of the slab, such as a wheel load on the deck of a bridge, there are several methods of determining the bending moments. One method is to assume that a certain width of the slab carries the entire load, and in one such method the contact area of the load is first extended by dispersion through the thickness of the slab as shown in *Table 11*, giving the dimension of loaded area as a_y at right angles to the span and a_x parallel to the span l. The width of slab carrying the load may be assumed to be $(2/3)(l + a_x) + a_y$. The total concentrated load is then divided by this width to give the load carried on a unit width of slab for the purpose of calculating the bending moments. The width of slab assumed to carry a concentrated load according to the recommendations of BS8110 and the *Code Handbook* is as illustrated in the lower part of *Table 56*.

Another method is to extend to slabs spanning in one direction the theory of slabs spanning in two directions. For example, the curves given in *Tables 54* and *55* for a slab infinitely long in the direction l_y can be used to evaluate directly the bending moments in the direction of, and at right angles to, the span of a slab spanning in one direction and carrying a concentrated load; this application is shown in example 2 in section 14.5. Yet another possibility is to carry out a full elastic analysis. Finally, the slab may be analysed using yield-line theory or Hillerborg's strip method.

3.5 TWO-WAY SLABS

When a slab is supported other than on two opposite sides only, the precise amount and distribution of the load taken by each support, and consequently the magnitude of the bending moments on the slab, are not easily calculated if assumptions resembling practical conditions are made. Therefore approximate analyses are generally used. The method applicable in any particular case depends on the shape of the panel of slab, the condition of restraint at the supports, and the type of load.

Two basic methods are commonly used to analyse slabs spanning in two directions. These are the theory of plates, which is based on an elastic analysis under service loads, and yield-line theory, in which the behaviour of the slab as collapse approaches is considered. A less well-known alternative to the latter is Hillerborg's strip method. In certain circumstances, however, for example in the case of a freely supported slab with corners that are not held down or reinforced for torsion, the coefficients given in BS8110 and CP110 are derived from an elastic analysis but use loads that are factored to represent ultimate limit-state conditions. If yield-line or similar methods are concerned, the sections should be designed by the limit-state method described in section 20.1. In undertaking elastic analyses, both Codes recommend a value of 0.2 for Poisson's ratio.

Distinction must be made between the conditions of free support, fixity, partial restraint and continuity, and it is essential to establish whether the corners of the panel are free to lift or not. Free support occurs rarely in practice, since in ordinary reinforced concrete beam-and-slab construction, the slab is monolithic with the beams and is thereby partially restrained and is not free to lift at the corners. The condition of being freely supported may occur when the slab is not continuous and the edge bears on a brick wall or on unencased structural steelwork. If the edge of the slab is built into a substantial brick or masonry wall, or is monolithic with concrete encasing steelwork or with a reinforced concrete beam or wall, partial restraint exists. Restraint is allowed for when computing the bending moments on the slab but the supports must be able to resist the torsional and other effects induced therein; the slab must be reinforced to resist the negative bending moment produced by the restraint. Since a panel or slab freely supported along all edges but with the corners held down is uncommon (because corner restraint is generally due to edge-fixing moments), bending moments for this case are of interest mainly for their value in obtaining coefficients for other cases of fixity along or continuity over one or more edges. A slab can be considered as fixed along an edge if there is no change in the slope of the slab at the support irrespective of the incidence of the load. This condition is assured if the polar moment of inertia of the beam or other support is very large. Continuity over a support generally implies a condition of restraint less rigid than fixity; that is, the slope of the slab at the support depends upon the load not only on the panel under consideration but on adjacent panels.

3.5.1 Elastic methods

The so-called exact theory of the elastic bending of plates spanning in two directions derives from the work of Lagrange, who produced the governing differential equation for bending in plates in 1811, and Navier, who described in 1820 the use of double trigonometrical series to analyse freely supported rectangular plates. Pigeaud and others later developed the analysis of panels freely supported along all four edges.

Many standard elastic solutions of slabs have been developed (see, for example, refs 13 and 14, and the bibliography in ref. 15) but almost all are restricted to square, rectangular and circular slabs. The exact analysis of a slab having an arbitrary shape and support conditions due to a general arrangement of loading is extremely complex. To solve such problems, numerical techniques such as finite differences and finite elements have been devised. These methods are particularly suited to computer-based analysis but the methods and procedures are as yet insufficiently developed for routine office use. Some notes on finite-element analysis are given in section 3.10.7. Finite-difference methods are considered in detail in ref. 16: ref. 6 provides a useful introduction.

3.5.2 Collapse methods

Unlike frame design, where the converse is true, it is normally easier to analyse slabs by collapse methods than by elastic methods. The two best-known methods of analysing slabs plastically are the yield-line method developed by K. W. Johansen and the so-called strip method devised by Arne Hillerborg.

It is generally impossible to calculate the precise ultimate resistance of a slab by collapse theory, since such slabs are highly indeterminate. Instead, two separate solutions can be found – one upper-bound and one lower-bound solution. With solutions of the first type, a collapse mechanism is first postulated. Then, if the slab is deformed, the energy absorbed in inducing ultimate moments along the yield lines is equal to the work done on the slab by the applied load in producing this deformation. Thus the load determined is the maximum that the slab will support before failure occurs. However, since such methods do not investigate conditions between the postulated yield lines to ensure that the moments in these areas do not exceed the ultimate resistance of the slab, there is no guarantee that the minimum load which may cause collapse has been found. This is one shortcoming of upper-bound solutions such as those given by Johansen's theory.

Conversely, lower-bound solutions may lead to collapse loads that are less than the maximum that the slab will actually carry. The procedure here is to choose a distribution of ultimate moments that ensures that the resistance of the slab is not exceeded and that equilibrium is satisfied at all points across the slab.

Most material dealing with Johansen's and Hillerborg's methods assumes that any continuous supports at slab edges are rigid and unyielding. This assumption is also made throughout the material given in Part II of this book. However, if the slab is supported on beams of finite strength, it is possible for collapse mechanisms to form in which the yield lines pass through the supporting beams. These beams then form part of the mechanism considered. When employing collapse methods to analyse beam-and-slab construction such a possibility must be taken into account.

Yield-line analysis. Johansen's yield-line method requires the designer to postulate first an appropriate collapse mechanism for the slab being considered according to the rules given in section 14.7.2. Any variable dimensions (such as αl_y in diagram (iv)(a) on *Table 58*) may then be adjusted to obtain the maximum ultimate resistance for a given load (i.e. the maximum ratio of M/F). This maximum value can be found in various ways, for example by tabulating the work equation as described in section 14.7.8 using actual numerical values and employing a trial-and-adjustment process. Alternatively, the work equation may be expressed algebraically and, by substituting various values for α, the maximum ratio of M/F may be read from a graph relating α to M/F. Yet another method, beloved of textbooks, is to use calculus to differentiate the equation, setting this equal to zero in order to determine the critical value of α. This method cannot always be used, however (see ref. 21).

As already explained, although such processes enable the maximum resistance moment for a given mode of failure to be determined, they do not indicate whether the yield-line pattern considered is the critical one. A further disadvantage of such a yield-line method is that, unlike Hillerborg's method, it gives no direct indication of the resulting distribution of load on the supports. Reference 21 discusses the possibility that the yield-line pattern also serves to apportion the loaded areas of slab to their respective supporting beams but somewhat reluctantly concludes that there is no justification for this assumption.

Despite these shortcomings, yield-line theory is extremely useful. A principal advantage is that it can be applied relatively easily to solve problems that are almost intractable by other means.

Yield-line theory is too complex to cover adequately in this *Handbook*; indeed several textbooks are completely or near-completely devoted to this subject (refs 17–21). In section 14.7 and *Tables 58* and *59* notes and examples are given on the rules for choosing yield-line patterns for analysis, on theoretical and empirical methods of analysis, on simplifications that can be made by using so-called affinity theorems, and on the effects of corner levers.

Strip method. Hillerborg devised his strip method in order to obtain a lower-bound solution for the collapse load while achieving a good economical arrangement of reinforcement. As long as the steel provided is sufficient to cater for the calculated moments, the strip method enables such a lower-bound solution to be determined. (Hillerborg and others sometimes refer to it as the equilibrium theory: it should not, however, be confused with the equilibrium method of yield-line analysis, with which it has no connection.) Hillerborg's original theory (ref. 22) (now known as the *simple strip method*) assumes that, at failure, no load is carried by the torsional strength of the slab and thus all the load is supported by flexural bending in either of two principal directions. The theory results in simple solutions giving full information regarding the moments over the whole slab to resist a unique collapse load, the reinforcement being arranged economically in bands. Brief notes on the use of simple strip theory to design rectangular slabs supporting uniform loads are given in section 14.7.10 and *Table 60*.

However, the simple strip theory cannot be used with concentrated loads and/or supports and leads to difficulties with free edges. To overcome such problems, Hillerborg later developed his *advanced strip method* which employs complex moment fields. While extending the scope of the original method, this development somewhat clouds the simplicity and directness of the original concept. A full treatment of both the simplified and advanced strip theories is given in ref. 22.

A further disadvantage of Hillerborg's and, of course, Johansen's methods is that, being based on conditions at failure only, they permit unwary designers to adopt load distributions which may differ widely from those which occur under working loads, and the resulting designs may thus be susceptible to early cracking. A recent development which eliminates this problem as well as overcoming the limitations arising from simple strip theory is the so-called strip deflection method due to Fernando and Kemp (ref. 25). With this method the distribution of load in either principal direction is not selected arbitrarily by the designer (as in the Hillerborg method or, by choosing the proportion of steel provided in each direction, as in the yield-line method) but is calculated to ensure compatibility of deflections in mutually orthogonal strips. The method leads to the solution of sets of simultaneous equations (usually eight), and thus requires access to a small computer or similar device.

3.5.3 Rectangular panel with uniformly distributed load

Empirical formulae and approximate theories have been put forward for calculating the bending moments in the common case of a rectangular panel or slab supported along four edges (and therefore spanning in two directions mutually at right angles) and carrying a uniformly distributed load. The bending moments depend on the support conditions and the ratio of the length of the sides of the panel. Because most theoretical expressions based on elastic analyses are complex, design curves or close arithmetical approximations are generally employed in practice. Westergaard has combined theory with the results of tests and his work formed the basis of the service bending-moment coefficients which were given in CP114.

The ultimate bending-moment coefficients given in BS8110 and CP110 are derived from a yield-line analysis in which the coefficients have been adjusted to allow for the non-uniformity of the reinforcement spacing resulting from the division of the slab into middle strips and edge strips. The various arbitrary parameters (e.g. the ratio of the negative moment over the supports to the positive moment at midspan) have been chosen so as to conform as closely as possible to serviceability requirements. For further details see ref. 130, on which the coefficients in CP110 are based. The coefficients for freely supported panels having torsional restraint and panels with continuity on one or more sides are illustrated graphically on *Tables 51* and *52* for BS8110 and CP110 respectively.

The simplified analysis of Grashof and Rankine can be applied when the corners of a panel are not held down and no torsional restraint is provided; the bending-moment coefficients are given in *Table 50* and the basic formulae are given in section 14.2.1. If corner restraint is provided, coefficients based on more exact analyses should be applied; such coefficients for a panel freely supported along four sides are given in *Table 50*. It has been shown by Marcus (ref. 12) that, for panels whose corners are held down, the midspan bending moments obtained by the Grashof and Rankine method can be converted to approximately those obtained by more exact theory by multiplying by a simple factor. This method is applicable not only for conditions of free support along all four edges but for all combinations of fixity on one to four sides with free support along the other edges; the bending moments at the supports are calculated by an extension of the Grashof and Rankine method but without the adjusting factors. The Marcus factors for a panel fixed along four edges are given in *Table 50*, and these and the Grashof and Rankine coefficients are substituted in the formulae given in the table to obtain the midspan bending moments and the bending moments at the supports.

If the corners of a panel are held down, reinforcement should be provided to resist the tensile stresses due to the torsional strains. The amount and position of the reinforcement required for this purpose, as recommended in BS8110 and CP110, are given in *Table 50*. No reinforcement is required at a corner formed by two intersecting supports if the slab is monolithic with the supports.

At a discontinuous edge of a slab monolithic with its support, resistance to negative bending moment must be provided; the expressions in the centre of *Table 50* give the magnitude, in accordance with BS8110 and CP110, of this moment, which is resisted by reinforcement at right angles to the support. The Codes also recommend that no main reinforcement is required in a narrow strip of slab parallel and adjacent to each support; particulars of this recommendation are also given in *Table 50*, the coefficients for use in which are taken from *Tables 51* and *52*.

The shearing forces on rectangular panels spanning in two directions and carrying uniformly distributed load are considered briefly in section 14.8.

3.5.4 Rectangular panel with triangularly distributed load

In the design of rectangular tanks, storage bunkers and some retaining structures, cases occur of walls spanning in two directions and subject to triangularly distributed pressure. The intensity of pressure is uniform at any level, but vertically the pressure varies from zero at or near the top to a maximum at the bottom. The curves on *Table 53* give the coefficients for the probable span and support moments in each direction, calculated by elastic theory and assuming a value of Poisson's ratio of 0.2, as recommended in BS8110 and CP110. The curves have been prepared from data given in ref. 13, suitably modified to comply with the value of Poisson's ratio adopted. Separate graphs are provided for cases where the top edge of the panel is fully fixed, freely supported and unsupported. The other panel edges are assumed to be fully fixed in all cases. In addition, however, the maximum span moments in panels with pinned edges are shown by broken lines on the same graphs. The true support conditions at the sides and bottom of the panel will almost certainly be somewhere between these two extremes, and the corresponding span moments can thus be estimated by interpolating between the appropriate curves corresponding to the pinned-support and fixed-support conditions.

If Poisson's ratio is less than 0.2 the bending moments will be slightly less, but the introduction of corner splays would increase the negative bending moments. Further comments on the curves, together with an example, are given in section 14.9.1.

An alternative method of designing such panels is to use yield-line theory. If the resulting structure is to be used to store liquids, however, extreme care must be taken to ensure that the proportion of span to support moment and vertical to horizontal moment adopted conform closely to the proportions given by elastic analyses, as otherwise the formation of early cracks may render the structure unsuitable for the purpose for which it was designed. In the case of non-fluid contents, such considerations may be less important. This matter is discussed in section 14.9.2.

Johansen has shown (ref. 18) that if a panel is fixed or freely supported along the top edge, the total ultimate moment acting on the panel is identical to that on a similar panel supporting the same total load distributed uniformly. Furthermore, as in the case of the uniformly loaded slab considered in section 14.9.1, a restrained slab may be analysed as if it were freely supported by employing so-called 'reduced side lengths' to represent the effects of continuity or fixity. Of course (unlike the uniformly loaded slab) along the bottom edge of the panel, where the loading is greatest, a higher ratio of support to span moment should be adopted than at the top edge of the panel.

If the panel is unsupported along the top edge, different collapse mechanisms control the behaviour of the panel. The pertinent expressions developed by Johansen (ref. 18) are shown graphically on *Table 61*.

Triangularly loaded panels can also be designed by means of Hillerborg's strip method: for details see ref. 22 and *Table 61*.

3.6 BEAMS SUPPORTING RECTANGULAR PANELS

When designing the beams supporting a panel freely supported along all four edges or with the same degree of fixity along all four edges, it is generally accepted that each of the beams along the shorter edges of the panel carries the load on an area having the shape of a 45° isosceles triangle with a base equal to the length of the shorter side, i.e. each beam carries a triangularly distributed load; one-half of the remaining load, i.e. the load on a trapezium, is carried on each of the beams along the longer edges. In the case of a square panel, each beam carries one-quarter of the total load on the panel, the load on each beam being distributed triangularly. The diagram and expressions in the top left-hand corner of *Table 63* give the amount of load carried by each beam. Bending-moment coefficients for beams subjected to triangular and trapezoidal loading are given in *Tables 23* and *24*; fixed-end moments due to trapezoidal loading on a span can be read from the curves on the lower chart on *Table 31*. The formulae for equivalent uniformly distributed loads that are given in section 14.10 apply only to the case of the span of the beam being equal to the width or length of the panel.

An alternative method is to divide the load between the beams along the shorter and longer sides in proportion to α_{x2} and α_{y2} (*Table 50*) respectively. Thus the load transferred to each beam along the shorter edges is $\alpha_{y2}wl_xl_y/2$, triangularly distributed, and to each beam along the longer edges is $\alpha_{x2}wl_xl_y/2$, trapezoidally distributed. For square panels the loads on the beams obtained by both methods are identical.

When the panel is fixed or continuous along one, two or three supports and freely supported on the remaining edges, the subdivision of the load to the various supporting beams can be determined from the diagrams and expressions on the left-hand side of *Table 63*. The non-dimensional factors α, β and μ denote the distances (in terms of the spans concerned) defining the pattern of load distribution. Alternatively the loads can be calculated approximately as follows. For the appropriate value of the ratio k of the equivalent spans (see *Table 56*), determine the corresponding values of α_{x2} and α_{y2} from *Table 50*. Then the load transferred to each beam parallel to the longer equivalent span is $\alpha_{x2}wl_xl_y/2$ and to each beam parallel to the shorter equivalent span is $\alpha_{y2}wl_xl_y/2$. Triangular distribution can be assumed in both cases, although this is a little conservative for the load on the beams parallel to the longer actual span. For a span freely supported at one end and fixed at the other, the foregoing loads should be reduced by about 20% for the beam along the freely supported edge and the amount of the reduction added to the load on the beam along the fixed or continuous edge.

If the panel is unsupported along one edge or two adjacent edges, the loads on the beams supporting the remaining edges are as given on the right-hand side of *Table 63*.

The above expressions are given in terms of a service load w but are equally applicable to an ultimate load n.

BS8110 provides coefficients for calculating the reactions from two-way slabs supporting uniform loads and taking torsional restraint at the corners into account. Curves derived from these values form *Table 62* and details of their use are given in section 14.8.

3.7 RECTANGULAR PANELS WITH CONCENTRATED LOADS

3.7.1 Elastic analysis

The curves in *Tables 54* and *55*, based on Pigeaud's theory, give the bending moments on a freely supported panel along all four edges with restrained corners and carrying a load uniformly distributed over a defined area symmetrically disposed upon the panel. Wheel loads and similarly highly concentrated loads are dispersed through the road finish (if any) down to the surface of the slab, or farther down to the reinforcement, as shown in *Table 11*, to give dimensions a_x and a_y, and thus the ratios a_x/l_x and a_y/l_y, for which the bending moments α_{x4} and α_{y4} for unit load are read off the curves for the appropriate value of the ratio of spans k. For a total load of F on the area a_x by a_y, the positive bending moments on unit width of slab are given by the expressions in *Tables 54* and *55*, in which the value of Poisson's ratio is assumed to be 0.2. The positive bending moments calculated from *Tables 54* and *55* for the case of a uniformly distributed load over the whole panel (that is $a_x = a_y = 1$) do not coincide with the bending moments based on the corresponding coefficients α_{x3} and α_{y3} given in *Table 50* unless Poisson's ratio is assumed to be zero, as is sometimes recommended. The curves in *Tables 54* and *55* are drawn for $k = 1.0$, 1.25, $\sqrt{2}(= 1.41$ approximately), 1.67, 2.0, 2.5 and infinity. For intermediate values of k, the values of α_{x4} and α_{y4} can be interpolated from the values above and below the given value of k. The curves for $k = 1.0$ apply to a square panel.

The curves for $k = \infty$ apply to a panel of great length (l_y) compared with the short span (l_x) and can be used for determining the transverse (main reinforcement) and longitudinal (distribution reinforcement) bending moments on a long narrow panel supported on the two long edges only. Alternatively the data at the bottom of *Table 56* can be applied to this case which is really a special extreme case of a rectangular panel spanning in two directions and subjected to a concentrated load.

When there are two concentrated loads symmetrically disposed or an eccentric load, the resulting bending moments can be calculated from the rules given for the various cases in *Table 56*. Other conditions of loading, for example, multiple loads the dispersion areas of which overlap, can generally be treated by combinations of the particular cases considered. Case I is an ordinary symmetrically disposed load. Case VI is the general case for a load in any position, from which the remaining cases are derived by simplification.

The bending moments derived directly from *Tables 54* and *55* are those at midspan of panels freely supported along all four edges but with restraint at the corners. If the panel is fixed or continuous along all four edges, Pigeaud recommends that the midspan bending moments should be reduced by 20%. The estimation of the bending moment at the support and midspan sections of panels with various sequences of continuity and free support along the edges can be dealt with by applying the following rules, which possibly give conservative results when incorporating Poisson's ratio equal to 0.2; they are applicable to the common conditions of continuity with adjacent panels over one or more supports, and monolithic construction with the supports along the remaining edges. Find α_{x4} and α_{y4} from the curves in *Tables 54* and *55* for the appropriate value of $k_e = k_1 l_y/l_x$, where k_1 is obtained from *Table 56*, cases (a)–(j). For similar conditions of support on all four sides, that is cases (a) and (j), or for a symmetrical sequence as in case (f), $k_1 = 1.0$; therefore the actual value of l_y/l_x is used in these cases. If in cases (b), (d), and (h) the value of $k_1 l_y/l_x$ is less than unity, l_y and l_x (and consequently a_x and a_y) should be transposed throughout the calculation of α_{x4} and α_{y4}. Having found the bending moments in each direction with the adjusted values of l_y/l_x, the bending-moment reduction factors for continuity given in *Table 56* are applied to give the bending moments for the purpose of design.

Examples of the use of *Tables 54, 55* and *56* are given in section 14.5.

The maximum shearing forces V per unit length on a panel carrying a concentrated load are given by Pigeaud as follows:

$a_x > a_y$: at the centre of length a_x, $V = F/(2a_x + a_y)$
at the centre of length a_y, $V = F/3a_x$

$a_y > a_x$: at the centre of length a_x, $V = F/3a_y$
at the centre of length a_y, $V = F(2a_y + a_x)$

To determine the load on the supporting beams, the rules given for a uniformly distributed load over the entire panel are sufficiently accurate for a load concentrated at the centre of the panel, but this is not always the critical case for imposed loads, such as a load imposed by a wheel on a bridge deck, since the maximum load on a beam occurs when the wheel is passing over the beam, in which case the beam carries the whole load.

3.7.2 Collapse analysis

Both yield-line theory and Hillerborg's strip method can be used to analyse slabs carrying concentrated loads. Appropriate yield-line formulae are given in ref. 18, or the empirical method described in section 14.7.8 may be used. For details of the analysis involved if the advanced strip method is adopted, see ref. 22.

3.8 NON-RECTANGULAR PANELS

When a panel which is not rectangular is supported along all its edges and is of such proportions that main reinforcement in two directions seems desirable, the bending moments can be determined approximately from the data given in *Table 57*, which are derived from elastic analyses and apply to a trapezoidal panel approximately symmetrical about one axis, to a panel which in plan is an isosceles triangle (or very nearly so), and to panels which are regular polygons or are circular. The case of a triangular panel continuous or partially restrained along three edges occurs in pyramidal hopper bottoms (*Table 186*); the reinforcement calculated by the expressions for this case should extend over the entire area of the panel, and provision must be made for the negative moments and for the direct tensions which act simultaneously with the bending moments.

If the shape of a panel approximates to a square, the bending moments for a square slab of the same area should be determined. A slab having the shape of a regular polygon with five or more sides can be treated as a circular slab the diameter of which is the mean of the diameters of the inscribed and circumscribed circles; the mean diameters for regular hexagons and octagons are given in *Table 57*.

Alternatively, yield-line theory is particularly suitable for obtaining an ultimate limit-state solution for an irregularly shaped slab: the method of obtaining solutions for slabs of various shapes is described in detail in ref. 18.

For a panel which is circular in plan and is freely supported or fully fixed along the circumference and carries a load concentrated symmetrically about the centre on a circular area, the total bending moment which should be provided for across each of two diameters mutually at right angles is given by the appropriate expression in *Table 57*. The expressions given are based on those derived by Timoshenko and Woinowsky–Krieger (ref. 14).

In general the radial and tangential moments vary according to the position being considered.

A circular panel can therefore be designed by one of the following elastic methods:

1. Design for the maximum positive bending moment at the centre of the panel and reduce the amount of reinforcement or the thickness of the slab towards the circumference. If the panel is not truly freely supported, provide for the negative bending moment acting around the circumference.
2. Design for the average positive bending moment across a diameter and retain the same thickness of slab and amount of reinforcement throughout the entire panel. If the panel is not truly freely supported around the circumference, provide for the appropriate negative bending moment.

The reinforcement required for the positive bending moments in both the preceding methods must be provided in two directions mutually at right angles; the reinforcement for the negative bending moment should be provided by radial bars normal to, and equally spaced around, the circumference, or reinforcement equivalent to this should be provided.

Circular slabs may conveniently be designed for ultimate limit-state conditions by using yield-line theory: for details see ref. 18.

3.9 FLAT SLABS

The design of flat slabs, i.e. beamless slabs or mushroom floors, is frequently based on empirical considerations, although BS8110 places much greater emphasis on the analysis of such structures as a series of continuous frames. The principles described below and summarized in *Table 64* and in section 14.12 are in accordance with the empirical method described in BS8110 and CP110. This type of floor can incorporate drop panels at the column heads or the slab can be of uniform thickness throughout. The tops of the columns may be plain or may be provided with a splayed head having the dimensions indicated in *Table 64*.

There should be at least three spans in each direction and the lengths (or widths) of adjacent panels should not differ by more than 15% of the greater length or width according to CP110 or 20% according to the *Joint Institutions Design Manual*: BS8110 merely requires spans to be 'approximately equal'. The ratio of the longer to the shorter dimension of a non-square panel should not exceed 4/3. The length of the drop in any direction should be not less than one-third of the length of the panel in the same direction. For the purposes of determining the bending moments, the panel is divided into 'middle strips' and 'column strips' as shown in the diagram in section 14.12, the width of each strip being half the corresponding length or width of the panel according to CP110, but one-half of the shorter dimension according to BS8110. If drop panels narrower than half the panel length or width are provided, the width of the column strip should be reduced to the width of the drop panel and the middle strip increased accordingly, the moments on each strip being modified as a result.

The thickness of the slab and the drop panels must be sufficient to provide resistance to the shearing forces and bending moments: in addition it must meet the limiting span/effective-depth requirements for slabs summarized in *Table 137*. For further details see section 14.12.2.

3.9.1 Bending moments

For the calculation of bending moments, the effective spans are $l_1 - (2/3)h_c$ and $l_2 - (2/3)h_c$, where l_1 and l_2 are the longer and shorter dimensions respectively of the panel and h_c is the diameter of the column or column head if one is provided. The total bending moments to be provided for at the principal sections of the panel are given in *Table 64* and are functions of these effective spans.

Walls and other concentrated loads must be supported on beams, and beams should be provided around openings other than small holes; both Codes recommend limiting sizes of openings permissible in the column strips and middle strips.

3.9.2 Reinforcement

It is generally most convenient for the reinforcement to be arranged in bands in two directions, one parallel to each of the spans l_1 and l_2. Earlier Codes such as CP114 also permitted bars to be arranged in two parallel and two diagonal bands, but this method produces considerable congestion of reinforcement in relatively thin slabs.

BS8110 places similar restrictions on the curtailment of reinforcement to those for normal slabs (see *Table 140*). The requirements of CP110 are that 40% of the bars forming the positive-moment reinforcement should remain in the bottom of the slab and extend over a length at the middle of the span equal to three-quarters of the span. No reduction in the positive-moment reinforcement should be made within a length of $0.6l$ at the middle of the span and no reduction of the negative-moment steel should be made within a distance of $0.2l$ of the centre of the support. The negative-moment reinforcement should extend into the adjacent panel for an average distance of at least $0.25l$; if the ends of the bars are staggered the shortest must extend for a distance of at least $0.2l$.

3.9.3 Shearing force

The shearing stresses must not exceed the appropriate limiting values set out in *Table 142* and *Table 143* for BS8110 and CP110 respectively. Details of the positions of the critical planes for shearing resistance and calculation procedures are shown in the diagrams in *Table 64* and discussed in section 14.12.5.

3.9.4 Alternative analysis

A less empirical method of analysing flat slabs is described in BS8110 and CP110, which is applicable to cases not covered by the foregoing rules. The bending moments and shearing forces are calculated by assuming the structure to comprise continuous frames, transversely and longitudinally. This method is described in detail (with examples) in *Examples of the Design of Buildings*. However, the empirical method generally requires less reinforcement and should be used when *all* the necessary requirements are met.

3.10 FRAMED STRUCTURES

A structure is statically determinate if the forces and bending moments can be determined by the direct application of the principles of statics. Examples include a cantilever (whether a simple bracket or the roof of a grandstand), a freely supported beam, a truss with pin-joints, and a three-hinged arch or frame. A statically indeterminate structure is one in which there is a redundancy of members or supports or both, and which can only be analysed by considering the elastic deformation under load. Examples of such structures include restrained beams, continuous beams, portal frames and other non-triangulated structures with rigid joints, and two-hinged and fixed-end arches. The general notes relating to the analysis of statically determinate and indeterminate beam systems given in sections 3.1 and 3.2 are equally valid when analysing frames. Provided that a statically indeterminate frame can be represented sufficiently accurately by an idealized two-dimensional line structure, it can be analysed by any of the methods mentioned earlier (and various others, of course).

The analysis of a two-dimensional frame is somewhat more complex than that of a linear beam system. If the configuration of the frame or the applied loading is unsymmetrical (or both), side-sway will almost invariably occur, considerably lengthening the analysis necessary. Many more combinations of load (vertical and horizontal) may require consideration to obtain the critical moments. Different partial safety factors may apply to different load combinations, and it must be remembered that the critical conditions for the design of a particular column may not necessarily be those corresponding to the maximum moment. Loading producing a reduced moment together with a greater axial thrust may be more critical. However, to combat such complexities, it is often possible to simplify the calculations by introducing some degree of approximation. For example, when considering wind loads, the points of contraflexure may be assumed to occur at midspan and at the midheight of columns (see *Table 74*), thus rendering the frame statically determinate. In addition, if a frame subjected to vertical loads is not required to provide lateral stability, BS8110 and CP110 permit each storey to be considered separately, or even to be subdivided into three-bay sub-frames for analysis (see below).

Beeby (ref. 71) has shown that, in view of the many uncertainties involved in frame analysis, there is little to choose as far as accuracy is concerned between analysing a frame as a single complete structure, as a series of continuous beams with attached columns, or as a series of three-bay sub-frames with attached columns. However, wherever possible the effects of the columns above and below the run of beams should be included in the analysis. If this is not done, the calculated moments in the beams are higher than those that are actually likely to occur and may indicate the need for more reinforcement to be provided than is really necessary.

It may not be possible to represent the true frame as an idealized two-dimensional line structure. In such a case, analysis as a three-dimensional space frame may be necessary. If the structure consists of large solid areas such as walls, it may not be possible to represent it adequately by a skeletal frame. The finite-element method is particularly suited to solve such problems and is summarized briefly below.

In the following pages the analysis of primary frames by the methods of slope deflection and various forms of moment distribution is described. Most analyses of complex rigid frames require an amount of calculation often out of proportion to the real accuracy of the results, and some approximate solutions are therefore given for common cases of building frames and similar structures. When a suitable preliminary design has been evolved by using these approximate methods, an exhaustive exact analysis may be undertaken by employing one of the programs available for this purpose at computer centres specializing in structural analysis. Several programs are also available for carrying out such analysis using the more popular microcomputers. Further details are given in Chapter 7 and the associated references.

3.10.1 BS8110 and CP110 requirements

For most framed structures it is unnecessary to carry out a full structural analysis of the entire frame as a single unit – an extremely complex and time-consuming task. For example, both Codes distinguish between frames that provide lateral stability for the structure as a whole and those where such stability is provided by other means (e.g. shear walls or a solid central core). In the latter case each floor may be considered as a separate sub-frame formed from the beams at that floor level together with the columns above and below, these columns being assumed to be fully fixed in position and direction at their further ends. This system should then be analysed when subjected to a total maximum ultimate load of $1.4G_k + 1.6Q_k$ acting with minimum ultimate dead load of $1.0G_k$, these loads being arranged to induce maximum moments. The foregoing loading condition may be considered most conveniently by adopting instead a dead load of $1.0G_k$ and 'imposed load' of $0.4G_k + 1.6Q_k$.

As a further simplification, each individual beam may instead be considered separately by analysing a sub-frame consisting of the beam concerned together with the upper and lower columns and adjacent beams at each end (as shown in the right-hand diagram on *Table 1*). These beams and columns are assumed to be fixed at their further ends and the stiffnesses of the two outer beams are taken to be only one-half of their true values. The sub-frame should then be analysed for the combination of loading previously described. Formulae giving the 'exact' bending moments due to various loading arrangements acting on this sub-frame and obtained by slope-deflection methods (as described in section 15.2.1) are given in *Table 68*. Since the method is an 'exact' one, the moments thus obtained may be redistributed to the limits permitted by the Codes. This method is dealt with in greater detail in *Examples in the Design of Buildings*, where graphical aid is provided.

BS8110 also explicitly sanctions the analysis of the beams forming each floor as a continuous system, neglecting the restraint provided by the columns entirely and assuming that no restraint to rotation is provided at the supports. However, as explained above, this conservative assumption is uneconomic and should be avoided if possible.

If the frame also provides lateral stability the following two-stage method of analysis is recommended by both Codes, unless the columns provided are slender (in which case sway must be taken into account). Firstly, each floor is considered as a separate sub-frame formed from the beams comprising that floor together with the columns above and below, these columns being assumed fixed at their further ends. Each sub-frame is subjected to a single vertical ultimate loading of $1.2(G_k + Q_k)$ acting on all beams simultaneously with no lateral load applied. Next, the complete structural frame should be analysed as a single structure when subjected to a separate ultimate lateral wind load of $1.2W_k$ only, the assumption being made that positions of contraflexure (i.e. zero moment) occur at the midpoints along all beams and columns. This analysis corresponds to that described for building frames in section 3.13.3, and the method set out in diagram (c) of *Table 74* may thus be used. The moments obtained from each of these analyses should then be summed and compared with those resulting from a simplified analysis considering vertical loads only, as previously described, and the frame designed for the more critical values. These procedures are summarized on *Table 1*.

In certain cases, a combination of load of $0.9G_k + 1.4W_k$ should also be considered when lateral loading occurs. The *Code Handbook* suggests that this is only necessary where it is possible that a structure may overturn, e.g. for buildings that are tall and narrow or cantilevered.

3.10.2 Moment-distribution method: no sway occurs

In certain circumstances a framed structure may not be subject to side-sway; for example, if the configuration and loading are both symmetrical. Furthermore, if a vertically loaded frame is being analysed storey by storey as permitted by BS8110 and CP110, the effects of any side-sway may be ignored. In such circumstances, Hardy Cross moment distribution may be used to evaluate the moments in the beam-and-column system. The procedure, which is outlined on *Table 66*, is virtually identical to that used to analyse systems of continuous beams.

Precise moment distribution may also be used to solve such systems. Here the method, which is also summarized on *Table 66*, is slightly more complex than in the equivalent continuous-beam case since, when carrying over moments, the unbalanced moment in a member must be distributed between the remaining members meeting at a joint in proportion to the relative restraint that each provides: the expression giving the continuity factors is also less simple to evaluate. Nevertheless, this method is a valid and time-saving alternative to conventional moment distribution. It is described in greater detail in *Examples of the Design of Buildings*.

3.10.3 Moment-distribution method: sway occurs

If sway can occur, moment-distribution analysis increases in complexity since, in addition to the influence of the original loading with the structure prevented from swaying, it is necessary to consider the effect of each individual degree of sway freedom separately in terms of unknown sway forces. These results are then combined to obtain the unknown sway values and hence the final moments. The procedure is outlined on *Table 67*.

The advantages of precise moment distribution are largely nullified if sway occurs: for details of the procedure in such cases see ref. 10.

To determine the moments in single-bay frames subjected to side sway, Naylor (ref. 27) has devised an ingenious variant of moment distribution: details are given on *Table 67*. The method can also be used to analyse Vierendeel girders.

3.10.4 Slope-deflection method

The principles of the slope-deflection method of analysing a restrained member are given in *Table 65* and in section 15.1, in which also the basic formulae and the formulae for the bending moments in special cases are given. When there is no deflection of one end of the member relative to the other (for example, when supports are not elastic as assumed), when the ends of the member are either hinged or fixed, and when the load is symmetrically disposed, the general expressions are simplified and the resulting formulae for the more common cases of restrained members are also given in *Table 65*.

The bending moments on a framed structure are determined by applying the formulae to each member successively. The algebraic sum of the bending moments at any joint equals zero. When it is assumed that there is no deflection (or settlement) a of one support relative to the other, there are as many formulae for the restraint moments as there are unknowns, and therefore the restraint moments and the slopes at the ends of the members can be evaluated. For symmetrical frames on unyielding foundations and carrying symmetrical vertical loads it is common to neglect the change in the position of the joints due to the small elastic contractions of the members, and the assumption of $a = 0$ is reasonably accurate. If the foundations or other supports settle unequally under the load, this assumption is not justified and a value must be assigned to the term a for the members affected.

If a symmetrical or unsymmetrical frame is subjected to a horizontal force the sway produced involves lateral movement of the joint. It is common in this case to assume that there is no elastic shortening of the member. Sufficient formulae to enable the additional unknowns to be evaluated are obtained by equating the reaction normal to the member, that is the shearing force on the member, to the rate of change of bending moment. Sway cannot be neglected when considering unsymmetrical frames subject to vertical loads, or any frame on which the load is unsymmetrically disposed.

Slope-deflection methods have been used to derive the formulae giving the bending moments on the sub-frame illustrated on *Table 68*. This sub-frame corresponds to the simplified system that BS8110 and CP110 suggest may be considered to determine the bending moments in individual members comprising a structural frame subjected to vertical loads only. The method is described in section 15.2.

An example of the application of the slope-deflection formulae to a simple problem is given in section 15.1.

3.10.5 Shearing forces on members of a frame

The shearing forces on any member forming part of a frame can be determined when the bending moments have been found by considering the rate of change of the bending moment. The uniform shearing force on a member AB due to end restraint only is $(M_{AB} + M_{BA})/l_{AB}$, account being taken of the signs of the bending moments. Thus if both restraint moments are clockwise, the shearing force is the numerical sum of the moments divided by the length of the member. If one restraint moment acts in a direction contrary to the other, the numerical difference is divided by the length to give the shearing force. For a member with end B hinged, the shearing force due to the restraint moment at A is M_{AB}/l_{AB}. The variable shearing forces due to the loads on the member should be algebraically added to the uniform shearing force due to the restraint moments, in a manner similar to that shown for continuous beams in *Table 32.*

3.10.6 Portal frames

A common type of simple frame used in buildings is the portal frame with either a horizontal top member or two inclined top members meeting at the ridge. In *Tables 70* and *71*, general formulae for the moments at both ends of the columns, and at the ridge in the case of frames of that type, are given together with expressions for the forces at the bases of the columns. The formulae relate to any vertical or horizontal load and to frames fixed or hinged at the bases. In *Tables 72* and *73* the corresponding formulae for special conditions of loading on frames of one bay are given.

Frames of the foregoing types are statically indeterminate, but a frame with a hinge at the base of each column and one at the ridge, i.e. a three-hinged frame, can be readily analysed. Formulae for the forces and bending moments are given in *Table 69* for three-hinged frames. Approximate expressions are also given for certain modified forms of these frames, such as when the ends of the columns are embedded in the foundations and when a tie-rod is provided at eaves level.

3.10.7 Finite elements

In conventional structural analysis, numerous approximations are introduced, although the engineer normally ignores the fact. Actual elements are considered as idealized one-dimensional members; deformations due to axial load and shear are assumed to be sufficiently small to be neglected; and so on.

In general, such assumptions are valid and the results obtained by analysis are sufficiently close to those that would be attained in the actual structure to be acceptable. However, when the sizes of members become sufficiently large in relation to the structure they form, the system of skeletal simplification breaks down. This occurs, for example, with the design of such elements as shear walls, deep beams and slabs of various types.

One method that has recently been developed to deal with such so-called *continuum* structures is that known as finite elements. The structure is subdivided arbitrarily into a set of individual elements (usually triangular or rectangular in shape) which are considered to be interconnected only at these extreme points (nodes). Although the resulting reduction in continuity might seem to indicate that the substitute system would be much more flexible than the original structure, if the substitution is undertaken carefully this is not so, since the adjoining edges of the elements tend not to separate and thus simulate continuity. A stiffness matrix for the substitute skeletal structure can now be prepared and analysed using a computer in a similar way to that already described above.

Theoretically, the choice of the pattern of elements may be thought to have a marked effect on the results obtained. However, although the use of a small mesh consisting of a large number of elements often increases the accuracy, it is normal for surprisingly good results to be obtained when using a rather coarse grid consisting of only a few large elements. Nevertheless, the finite-element method is one where previous experience in its application is of more than usual value.

For further information, see refs 6, 103 and 104: ref. 105 provides a useful introduction. The BASIC microcomputer programs provided in ref. 139 enable engineers to investigate and use elementary finite-element techniques for themselves by experimenting with the effects of different mesh spacings etc. on simple problems.

3.11 BENDING OF COLUMNS

3.11.1 External columns

Provision should be made for the bending moments produced on the columns due to the rigidity of the joints in monolithic beam-and-column construction of buildings.

The external columns of a building are subjected to a

greater bending moment than the internal columns (other conditions being equal), the magnitude of the bending moment depending on the relative stiffness of the column and beam and on the end conditions of the members. The two principal cases for exterior columns are when the beam is supported on the top of the column, as in a top storey, and when the beam is fixed to the column at an intermediate point, as in intermediate storeys. The second case is shown in the diagrams in *Table 65*. Since either end of the column or the end of the beam remote from the column can be hinged, fixed or partially restrained, there are many possible combinations.

For the first case the maximum reverse moment at the junction of the beam and column occurs when the far end of the beam is hinged and the foot of the column is fixed. The minimum reverse moment at the junction occurs when the beam is rigidly fixed at the far end and the column is hinged at the foot. Conditions in practice generally lie between these extremes, and with any condition of fixity of the foot of the column the bending moment at the junction decreases as the degree of fixity at the far end of the beam increases. With any degree of fixity at the far end of the beam the bending moment at the junction increases very slightly as the degree of fixity at the foot of the column increases.

The maximum reverse moment on the beam at the junction with the column in the second case occurs when the beam is hinged at the far end and the column is perfectly fixed at the top and the bottom as indicated in *Table 65*. With perfect fixity at the far end of the beam and hinges at the top and bottom of the column, as also shown in *Table 65*, the reverse moment on the beam at the junction is a minimum. Intermediate cases of fixity follow the following rules: any increase in fixity at the end of the beam decreases the bending moment at the junction; any decrease in fixity at either the top or the bottom of the column decreases the bending moment at the junction; and vice versa.

Formulae for the maximum and minimum bending moments are given in *Table 65* for a number of single-bay frames. The bending moment on the beam at the junction is divided between the upper and lower columns in the ratio of their stiffness factors K when conditions at the ends of the two columns are identical. When the end of one column is hinged and the other fixed, the ratio of the bending moments allocated to each column is in accordance with the expression

$$\frac{\text{bending moment on hinged portion}}{\text{bending moment on fixed portion}} = \frac{0.75K \text{ for hinged portion}}{K \text{ for fixed portion}}$$

3.12 COLUMNS IN BUILDING FRAMES

3.12.1 Internal columns

For the frames of ordinary buildings, the bending moments on the upper and lower internal columns can be computed from the formulae given in the lower part of *Table 65*; these expressions conform to the method described in clause 3.2.1.2.3 of BS8110 and clause 3.5.2 of CP110. When the spans are equal the value of M_{es} employed should be that which occurs when an imposed load is on only one of the adjacent spans. When the spans are unequal, the greatest bending moments on the column occur when the value of M_{es} (see *Table 65*) is greatest, which is generally when the longer beam is loaded with imposed + dead load while the shorter beam carries dead load only.

An alternative method of determining the moments in columns according to the Code requirements is to use the simplified sub-frame formulae given on *Table 68*. Then considering column SO, for example, if D_{SO} is the distribution factor for SO (i.e. $D_{SO} = K_{SO}/(\xi K_{RS} + K_{ST} + K_{SO} + K_{SP})$), and F'_S and F'_T are the out-of-balance fixed-end moments at S and T respectively for the particular loading condition considered, the moment in the column is given by the expression

$$D_{SO}\left(\frac{2D_{TS}F'_T + 4F'_S}{4 - D_{ST}D_{TS}}\right)$$

This moment is additional to any initial fixed-end moment acting on SO.

To determine the maximum moment in the column it may be necessary to examine the two separate simplified sub-frames in which each column is embodied at each floor level (i.e. a column at joint S, say, is part of the sub-frame comprising beams QR, RS and ST, and also part of that comprising beams RS, ST and TU). However, the maximum moments usually occur when the central beam of the sub-frame is the longer of the two beams adjoining the column being investigated, and this is the criterion specified in each Code.

Since they derive from an 'exact' analysis, these column moments may be redistributed as permitted by each Code, but this is normally not possible since, unless the ratio of moment to axial force is unusually high, the value of x/d for the column section is too great to permit any redistribution to be undertaken.

3.12.2 External columns

There is greater variation in the bending moments due to continuity between the beams and the external columns than is the case with internal columns. The lack of uniformity in the end conditions affects the bending moments determined by the simplified method described above more seriously than in the case of internal columns and thus the values obtained by simplified methods are more approximate, although they are still sufficiently accurate for designing ordinary buildings. The simplified formulae given on *Table 65* conform to clause 3.2.1.2.3 of BS8110 and clause 3.5.2 of CP110, while the alternative simplified sub-frame method described for internal columns may also be used.

3.12.3 Corner columns

A column at an external corner of a building is generally subjected to bending moments from beams in two directions at right angles. These bending moments can be calculated by considering two frames (also at right angles) independently, but practical methods of design depend on the relative magnitude of the bending moments and the direct load and the relevant limit-state condition. For the ultimate limit-state method see sections 22.2.3 and 22.2.4, and for the modular-ratio method see section 22.3.

3.12.4 Approximate methods

The methods hitherto described for evaluating the bending moments in column-and-beam construction with rigid joints involve a fair amount of calculation, including that of the moments of inertia of the members. In practice, and especially in the preparation of preliminary schemes, time is not always available to make these calculations, and therefore approximate methods are of value. Designs should be checked by more accurate methods.

For large columns and light beams, the effect on the column of the load on the beam is not great, and in such cases when preparing a design based on service stresses the difference between the permissible compressive stress for direct compression and for bending combined with direct compression is generally sufficient to enable the preliminary design of the column to be based on the direct load only. Where the effect of the beam on the column is likely to be considerable, and in order to allow a margin for the bending stresses in the column, the column can be designed provisionally for a direct load that has been increased to allow for the effects of bending, by the amounts shown in section 16.2 for the particular arrangement of beams supported by the column.

3.13 BENDING MOMENTS DUE TO WIND

In exposed structures such as water towers, bunkers and silos, and the frames of tall narrow buildings, the columns must be designed to resist the effects of wind. When conditions do not warrant a close analysis of the bending moments to which a frame is subjected due to wind or other horizontal forces, the methods described in the following and illustrated in *Table 74* are sufficiently accurate.

3.13.1 Braced columns

For braced columns (of the same cross-section) forming an open tower such as that supporting an elevated water tower, the expressions at (a) in *Table 74* give the bending moments and shearing forces on the columns and braces due to the effect of a horizontal force at the head of the columns. The increase or decrease of direct load on the column is also given.

In general, the bending moment on the column is the shearing force on the column multiplied by half the distance between the braces. If a column is not continuous or is insufficiently braced at one end, as at an unconnected foundation, the bending moment is twice this value.

The bending moment on the brace at an external column is the sum of the bending moments on the columns at the intersection with the brace. The shearing force on the brace is equal to the change of bending moment from one end of the brace to the other divided by the length of the brace. These shearing forces and bending moments are additional to those created by the dead weight of the brace and any external loads to which it may be subjected.

The overturning moment on the frame causes an additional direct load on the leeward column and a corresponding relief of load on the windward column, the maximum value of this direct load being approached at the foot of the column and being equal to the overturning moment divided by the distance between the centres of the columns.

The expressions in *Table 74* for the effects on the columns and for the bending moments on the braces apply whether the columns are vertical or at a slight inclination. If the columns are inclined, the shearing force on a brace is $2M_b$ divided by the length of the brace being considered.

3.13.2 Columns supporting massive superstructures

The case illustrated in (b) in *Table 74* is common in bunkers and silos where a superstructure of considerable rigidity is carried on comparatively short columns. If the columns are fixed at the base, the bending moment on a single column is $Fh/2J$, where J is the number of columns if they are all of the same size; the signification of the other symbols is given in *Table 74*.

If the columns are of different sizes, since each column is deflected the same amount, the total shearing force should be divided among the columns in any one line in proportion to their separate moments of inertia. If J_1 is the number of columns with moment of inertia I_1, J_2 the number of columns with moment of inertia I_2, etc., the total moment of inertia is $J_1I_1 + J_2I_2 + \text{etc.} = \sum I$. On any column having a moment of inertia I_j, the bending moment is $FhI_j/2\sum I$ as given in diagram (b) in *Table 74*. Alternatively, the total horizontal shearing force can be divided among the columns in the ratio of their cross-sectional area (thus giving uniform shearing stress), and with this method the formula for the bending moment on any column with cross-sectional area A_j is $FhA_j/2\sum A$, where $\sum A$ is the sum of the cross-sectional areas of all the columns resisting the total shearing force F.

3.13.3 Building frames

In the frame of a multistorey building, the effect of the wind may be small compared with that of other loads, and in this case it is sufficiently accurate to divide the horizontal shearing force on the basis that an external column resists half the shearing force on an internal column. If J_t is the total number of columns in one frame, in the plane of the lateral force F, the effective number of columns is $J_t - 1$ for the purpose of calculating the bending moment on an interior column, the two external columns being equivalent to one internal column; see diagram (c) in *Table 74*. In a building frame subjected to wind pressure, the pressure on each panel (or storey height) F_1, F_2, F_3 etc. is generally divided into equal shearing forces at the head and base of each storey height of columns. The shearing force at the base of any interior column, i storeys from the top, is $(\sum F + F_i/2)/(J_t - 1)$, where $\sum F = F_1 + F_2 + F_3 + \cdots + F_{i-1}$. The bending moment is the shearing force multiplied by half the storey height.

A bending moment and a corresponding shearing force are caused on the floor beams in the same way as on the braces of an open tower. At an internal column the sum of the bending moments on the two beams meeting at the column is equal to the sum of the bending moments at the base of the upper column and at the head of the lower column.

This method of analysis corresponds to the ultimate limit-state requirements of BS8110 and CP110 for carrying out the elastic analysis due to a lateral wind loading of $1.2W_k$ of a frame that provides lateral structural stability and is subjected to vertical and lateral loading, as described in *Table 1*.

3.14 EARTHQUAKE-RESISTANT STRUCTURES

Opinions may differ on whether structures to withstand the disruptive forces of earth tremors and quakes should be designed as rigid or flexible or semi-flexible. The effect of an earth tremor is equivalent to a horizontal thrust additional to the loads (but not wind effects) for which the building is commonly designed. There are codes for earthquake-resistant construction in several countries, and recent codes are more complex than earlier requirements. The simplest consideration, based on elastic design, is as follows.

The dead and imposed loads should be increased by 20% to allow for vertical movement. The magnitude of the horizontal thrust depends on the acceleration of the tremor, which may vary from less than $1\,m/s^2$ or $3\,ft/s^2$ in firm compact ground to over $4\,m/s^2$ or $12\,ft/s^2$ in alluvial soil and filling. A horizontal thrust equal to about one-tenth of the mass of the building seems to be sufficient for all but major shocks when the building does not exceed 6 m or 20 ft in height, and equal to one-eighth of the mass when the building is of greater height. The horizontal shearing force on the building at any level is one-eighth (or one-tenth) of the total weight of the structure (including imposed loads) above this level. The calculation of the bending moments and shearing forces on the columns and floor beams is, in this simple analysis, similar to that described for wind pressure on building frames in *Table 74*. In order that the structure acts as a unit, all parts must be effectively bonded together. Panel walls, finishes and ornaments should be permanently attached to the frame, so that in the event of a shock they will not collapse independently of the main structure. Separate column footings should be connected by ties designed to take a thrust or pull of say one-tenth of the load on the footing.

The satisfactory behaviour of structures that were designed to withstand arbitrary seismic forces and have since been subjected to severe earthquakes has been attributed to the following causes: yielding at critical sections, which increased the period of vibration and enabled greater amounts of input energy to be absorbed; the assistance of so-called non-structural partitions and the energy dissipated as they cracked; and the fact that the response was less than predicted owing to yielding of the foundations. It is uneconomical to design structures to withstand major earthquakes elastically, and hence present-day design procedures assume that the structure possesses sufficient strength and ductility to withstand such tremors by responding inelastically provided that the interconnections between members are designed specially to ensure adequate ductility.

A detailed discussion of the complexities of designing earthquake-resistant reinforced concrete structures in accordance with this philosophy is contained in ref. 28. The ACI code for reinforced concrete (ACI 318) contains requirements for seismic design: see ref. 29.

3.15 PROPERTIES OF MEMBERS OF A FRAME

3.15.1 End conditions

Since the results given by the more precise methods of frame analysis vary considerably with different degrees of restraint at the ends of the members, it is essential that the end conditions assumed should be reasonably obtained in the actual construction. Absolute fixity is difficult to attain unless the beam or column is embedded monolithically in a comparatively large mass of concrete. Embedment in a brick or masonry wall represents more nearly the condition of a hinge, and should be considered as such. The ordinary type of separate foundation, designed only for the limiting uniform ground pressure under the direct load on a column, should also be considered as a hinge at the foot of the column. A continuous beam supported on a beam or column is only partly restrained, and where the outer end of an end span is supported on a beam a hinge should be assumed. A column built on a pile-cap supported by two, three or four piles is not absolutely fixed but a bending moment can be developed if the resulting vertical reaction (upwards and downwards) and the horizontal thrust can be taken on the piles. A column can be considered as fixed if it is monolithic with a substantial raft foundation.

In two-hinged and three-hinged arches, hinged frames, and some types of girder bridges, where the assumption of a hinged joint must be fully realized, it is necessary to form a definite hinge in the construction. This can be done by inserting a steel hinge (or similar), or by forming a hinge within the frame. (See *Table 181*.)

3.15.2 Moments of inertia of reinforced concrete members

Three separate bases for calculating the moment of inertia of a reinforced concrete section are generally recognized; all are acknowledged in both BS8110 and CP110. They are as follows:

1. The entire concrete area may be considered including any concrete in tension but ignoring all reinforcement.
2. The entire concrete area may be considered together with the reinforcement which is allowed for on the basis of the modular ratio.
3. The area of concrete in compression only may be considered together with the reinforcement on the basis of the modular ratio (BS8110 recommends the use of a value of 15 unless a more accurate figure is available).

Method 3 gives what is usually known as the transformed moment of inertia. However, until the cross-section of the member has been determined, or assumed, the calculation of the moment of inertia in this way cannot be made with any precision. Moreover, the moment of inertia of an ordinary beam calculated on this basis changes considerably throughout its length, especially with a continuous or restrained beam in beam-and-slab construction, which acts as a T-beam at midspan but is designed as a rectangular beam towards the supports where reverse bending moments occur. It should be considered whether the probable tensile stresses at any time are sufficient to cause cracking, particularly with T-beams and L-beams if the flanges are in tension; although the beam may be designed on the assumption that the concrete has cracked and that the reinforcement resists all the tension due to bending, cracking may not take place owing to the comparatively large area of concrete in the flange.

Method 1 is clearly generally the simplest to apply and is often used but, as pointed out in the *Code Handbook*, both other methods are applicable when assessing the ability of an existing structure to carry revised loadings. When analysing single-bay monolithic frames where the ratio of beam span to column height exceeds three and the beam contains less than 1% of reinforcement, CP110 states that, in calculating the moments in the frame, the moments of inertia should be determined by method 3 (or the moments transferred to the columns should be limited). In such a case the *Code Handbook* suggests that it is more realistic to adopt method 2 and method 3 for the beams. Alternatively, it recommends that column moments calculated on the basis of method 2 should, in the case of single-bay frames, be increased by 10%.

Since early comparisons of moments of inertia are required in the design of frames, the errors due to approximations are of little importance. It is, however, important that the method of assessing the moment of inertia should be the same for all members in a single calculation. It is generally sufficient to compare the moments of inertia of the whole concrete areas alone for members that have somewhat similar percentages of reinforcement. Thus the ratio of the moment of inertia of a rectangular column to that of a rectangular beam is $b_c h_c^3/b_b h_b^3$, where b_c and h_c are the breadth and thickness of the column, and b_b and h_b are the breadth and depth of the beam.

In *Table 98* values of the moments of inertia for square, rectangular, octagonal and some other non-rectangular sections are given, calculated on the gross sections and ignoring the reinforcement (i.e. method 1). The moment of inertia and depth to the centroid of flanged beams when calculated on the same basis can be determined from the chart on *Table 101*; the breadth of the flange assumed for the purpose of calculating the moment of inertia should not exceed the maximum permissible width given at the bottom of *Table 91*. The particulars in *Table 98* exclude the effect of the reinforcement, but the data given in *Tables 99* and *100* for some regular cross-sections take the reinforcement into account, and thus give the moment of inertia as calculated in accordance with methods 2 and 3 above.

The alternative methods of assessing the ratio of the moments of inertia of two members given in the examples in section 16.1 show that approximate methods readily give comparative values that are accurate enough not only for trial calculations but also for final designs.

3.16 ARCHES

Arch construction in reinforced concrete occurs mainly in bridges but sometimes in roofs. The principal types of symmetrical concrete arch are shown in *Table 180*. An arch may be either a three-hinged arch, a two-hinged arch or a fixed-end arch (see the diagrams in *Table 75*), and may be symmetrical or unsymmetrical, right or skew, or a single arch or one of a series of arches mutually dependent upon each other. The following consideration is restricted to symmetrical and unsymmetrical three-hinged arches and symmetrical two-hinged and fixed-end arches; reference should be made to other publications for information on more complex types. Arch construction may comprise an arch slab (or vault) or a series of parallel arch ribs. The deck of an arch bridge may be supported by columns or transverse walls carried on an arch slab or ribs, in which case the structure may have open spandrels; or the deck may be below the crown of the arch either at the level of the springings (as in a bow-string girder) or at some intermediate level. A bow-string girder is generally considered to be a two-hinged arch with the horizontal component of the thrusts resisted by a tie which generally forms part of the deck. If earth or other filling is provided to support the deck, an arch slab and spandrel walls are required and the bridge is a closed or solid-spandrel structure.

3.16.1 Three-hinged arch

An arch with a hinge at each springing and with a hinge at the crown is statically determinate. The thrusts on the abutments, and therefore the bending moments and shearing forces on the arch itself, are not affected by a small movement of one abutment relative to the other. This type of arch is therefore used when there is a possibility of unequal settlement of the abutments.

For any load in any position the thrust on the abutments can be determined from the statical equations of equilibrium. For the general case of an unsymmetrical arch with a load acting vertically, horizontally or at an angle, the expressions for the horizontal and vertical components of the thrusts are given in the lower part of *Table 75*. For symmetrical arches the formulae for the thrusts given for three-hinged frames in *Table 69* are applicable, or similar formulae can be obtained from the general expressions in *Table 75*. The vertical component is the same as the vertical reaction for a freely supported beam. The bending moment at any section of the arch is the algebraic summation of the moments of the loads and reactions to the thrusts on one side of the section. There is no bending moment at a hinge. The shearing force is likewise the algebraic sum of the reactions and loads, resolved at right angles to the arch axis at the section considered, and acting on one side of the section. The thrust at any section is the sum of the reactions and loads, resolved parallel to the axis of the arch at the section, and acting on one side of the section.

The extent of the arch that should be loaded with imposed load to produce the maximum bending moment or shearing force or thrust at a given section is determined by drawing a series of influence lines. A typical influence line for a three-hinged arch and the formulae necessary to construct an influence line for unit load in any position are given in the upper part of *Table 75*.

3.16.2 Two-hinged arch

The hinges of a two-hinged arch are placed at the abutments and thus, as in a three-hinged arch, only thrusts are transmitted to the abutments, there being no bending moment on the arch at the springings. The vertical component of the thrust from a symmetrical two-hinged arch is the same as for a freely supported beam. Formulae for the thrusts and bending moments are given in *Table 75* and notes are given in section 17.1.

3.16.3 Fixed arch

An arch with fixed ends exerts a bending moment on the abutments in addition to the vertical and horizontal thrusts. Like a two-hinged arch and unlike a three-hinged arch, a fixed-end arch is statically indeterminate, and changes of temperature and the shrinkage of the concrete affect the stresses. As it is assumed in the general theory that the abutments are incapable of rotation or of translational movement, a fixed-end arch can only be used in such conditions.

Any section of a fixed-arch rib or slab is subjected to a bending moment and a thrust, the magnitudes of which have to be determined. The design of an arch is a matter of trial and adjustment since the dimensions and the shape of the arch affect the calculations, but it is possible to select preliminary sizes that reduce the repetition of arithmetical work to a minimum. The suggested method of determining the possible sections at the crown and springing as given in *Table 76*, and explained in section 17.2.1, is based on treating the fixed arch as a hinged arch, and estimating the size of the cross-sections by reducing greatly the maximum stresses.

The general formulae for thrusts and moments on a symmetrical fixed arch of any profile are given in *Table 76*, and notes on the application and modification of these formulae are given in section 17.2. The calculations involved in solving the general and modified formulae are tedious, but some labour is saved by preparing the calculations in tabulated form. One such form is that given in *Table 76*; this form is particularly suitable for open-spandrel arch bridges because the appropriate formulae, which are those in *Table 76*, do not assume a constant value of a_I, the ratio of the length of a segment of the arch to the mean moment of inertia of the segment.

For an arch of large span the calculations are made considerably easier and more accurate by preparing and using influence lines for the bending moment and thrust at the crown, the springing, and the first quarter-point. Typical influence lines are given in *Table 76*, and such diagrams can be constructed by considering the passage over the arch of a single concentrated unit load and applying the formulae for this condition. The effect of the dead load, and of the most adverse disposition of the imposed load, can be readily calculated from such diagrams. If the specified imposed load includes a moving concentrated load, such as a knife-edge load, influence lines are almost essential for determining the most adverse position, except in the case of the positive bending moment at the crown for which the most adverse position of the load is at the crown. The method of determining the data to establish the ordinates of the influence lines is given in the form in *Table 78*.

3.16.4 Fixed parabolic arches

In *Table 77* and in section 17.3 consideration is given to symmetrical fixed arches that can have either open or solid spandrels and can be either arch ribs or arch slabs. The method is based on that of Strassner as developed by H. Carpenter, and the principal assumption is that the axis of the arch is made to coincide with the line of pressure due to the dead load. This results in an economical structure and a simple method of calculation. The shape of the axis of the arch is approximately that of a parabola, and this method can therefore only be adopted when the designer is free to select the profile of the arch. The approximately parabolic form of arch may not be the most economical for large spans, although it is almost so, and a profile that produces an arch axis that coincides with the line of thrust for the dead load plus one-half of the imposed load may be more satisfactory. If the increase in thickness of the arch from the crown to the springing varies parabolically, only the bending moments and thrusts at the crown and springing need be investigated. The formulae for the bending moments and forces are given in section 17.3.1, and these include a series of coefficients, values of which are given in *Table 77*; an example of the application of the method is given in section 17.3. The component forces and moments are as in the following.

The thrusts due to the dead load are relieved somewhat by the effect of the compression causing elastic shortening of the arch. For arches with small ratios of rise to span, or for arches that are thick compared with the span, the stresses due to arch shortening may be excessive. This can be overcome by introducing temporary hinges at the crown and springings, which eliminate all bending stresses due to dead load. The hinges are filled with concrete after arch shortening and much of the shrinking of the concrete have taken place.

There are additional horizontal thrusts due to a rise of temperature or a corresponding counter-thrust due to a fall of temperature. A rise or fall of 16.7°C or 30°F is often used for structures in the UK, but careful consideration should be given to those factors that may necessitate an increase, or may justify a decrease, in the temperature range. The shrinking that takes place when concrete hardens produces counter-thrusts, and can be considered as equivalent to a fall of temperature; with the common sectional method of constructing arches the effect of shrinkage may be allowed for by assuming it to be equal to a fall of temperature of 8.3°C or 15°F.

The extent of the imposed load on an arch to produce the maximum stresses in the critical sections can be determined from influence lines, and the following are approximately correct for parabolic arches. The maximum positive bending moment at the crown occurs when the middle third of the arch is loaded; the maximum negative bending moment at a springing occurs when four-tenths of the span adjacent to the springing is loaded; the maximum positive bending moment at a springing occurs when the whole span is loaded except for the length of four-tenths of the span adjacent to the springing. In the expressions in *Table 77* the imposed load is expressed in terms of an equivalent uniformly distributed load.

When the corresponding normal thrusts and bending moments on a section have been determined, the area of reinforcement and the stresses at the crown and springing are calculated in accordance with the methods described in sections 5.13 or 5.14. All that now remains necessary is to determine the intermediate sections and the profile of the axis of the arch. If the dead load is uniform throughout (or practically so) the axis will be a parabola, but if it is not uniform the axis must be shaped to coincide with the line of pressure for dead load. The latter can be plotted by force-and-link polygons (as in ordinary graphic statics), the necessary data being the magnitudes of the dead load, the horizontal thrust due to dead load, and the vertical reaction (which equals the dead load on half the span) of the springing. The line of pressure, and therefore the axis of the arch, having been established, and the thicknesses of the arch at the crown and springing determined, the lines of the extrados and intrados can be plotted to give a parabolic variation of thickness between the two extremes.

Chapter 4
Materials and stresses

The properties of reinforcement and of the constituents of concrete are described in Regulations, Standards and Codes of Practice. Only those properties of reinforcement, cement and aggregate which concern the designer directly and influence ultimate and service stresses are dealt with in this chapter.

4.1 CONCRETE

4.1.1 Cement

Cements suitable for reinforced concrete are ordinary and rapid-hardening Portland cements, Portland blast-furnace cement, low-heat Portland cement, sulphate-resistant cement, super-sulphate cement, and high-alumina cement. Quick-setting cements are not used in ordinary construction. Calcium chloride is sometimes added to ordinary and rapid-hardening Portland cement to accelerate the initial set, either for concreting in cold weather or to enable the moulds or formwork to be removed earlier. Cements of different types should not be used together. Particulars of cements complying with British Standards and some other special cements are given in the following. The SI values are generally adopted equivalents of the imperial values given in the documents concerned.

Ordinary Portland cement (BS12). This is the basic Portland cement. The initial setting time must not be less than 45 minutes and the final setting time not more than 10 hours. The specific surface area must not be less than 2250 cm^2 per gram. The minimum compressive strengths of 1:3 mortar cubes are 15 N/mm^2 or 2200 lb/in^2 at 3 days and 23 N/mm^2 or 3400 lb/in^2 at 7 days. An alternative test on 100 mm or 4 in concrete cubes with a cement/aggregate ratio of about 1:6 (equivalent to 1:2:4), with aggregate from 19 mm or 3/4 in down, a water/cement ratio of 0.6, and a slump of 13 mm to 50 mm or 1/2 in to 2 in, is included. The strength of such cubes must be not less than 8.3 N/mm^2 or 1200 lb/in^2 at 3 days and 14 N/mm^2 or 2000 lb/in^2 at 7 days. According to the recommendations of CP114, the crushing strength of 150 mm or 6 in cubes of 1:2:4 nominal concrete in preliminary tests should be not less than 18.7 N/mm^2 or 2700 lb/in^2 at 7 days. It is possible that this strength might not be obtained if cubes tested in accordance with BS12 have only the minimum strength of 15 N/mm^2 or 2200 lb/in^2, but in this case the concrete would be acceptable as long as the strength of works cubes at 28 days is not less than 21 N/mm^2 or 3000 lb/in^2.

Rapid-hardening Portland cement (BS12). The principal physical difference between ordinary and rapid-hardening Portland cement is the greater fineness of the latter, which must have a specific surface area of not less than 3250 cm^2 per gram. The setting times are the same, but the minimum compressive strengths of mortar cubes are 21 N/mm^2 or 3000 lb/in^2 at 3 days and 28 N/mm^2 or 4000 lb/in^2 at 7 days. The minimum compressive strengths of concrete cubes are 12 N/mm^2 or 1700 lb/in^2 at 3 days and 17 N/mm^2 or 2500 lb/in^2 at 7 days. An optional tensile test at 1 day is included. The quicker hardening of this cement may enable formwork to be removed earlier.

Portland blast-furnace cement (BS146). The slag content must not exceed 65%. The setting times and the fineness are the same as for ordinary Portland cement. The minimum compressive strengths of mortar cubes are 11 N/mm^2 or 1600 lb/in^2 at 3 days, 21 N/mm^2 or 3000 lb/in^2 at 7 days and 35 N/mm^2 or 5000 lb/in^2 at 28 days, and of concrete cubes are 5.5, 11 and 22 N/mm^2 or 800, 1600 and 3200 lb/in^2 at these respective ages.

Sulphate-resistant cement (BS4027). This cement, as its name implies, is used for concrete liable to chemical attack by sea-water, acid ground-waters, and other medium-sulphate liquids. It is a mixture of blast-furnace slag and Portland cement clinker, has less free lime and has moderate low-heat properties.

Super-sulphated cement (BS4248). This cement is a mixture of blast-furnace slag, Portland cement clinker and calcium sulphate. It produces a slightly more workable concrete than with ordinary Portland cement at the same water/cement ratios, but it has a low heat of hydration and hence it only hardens slowly. Special care must be taken when it is used in cold weather. It also deteriorates rapidly in poor storage conditions (see clause 6.3.5 of CP110). Dense concrete with this cement is resistant to sulphates in all normal concentrations and to weak acids. It is expensive and difficult to obtain in some countries, including the UK.

High-alumina cement (BS915). This cement has extreme rapid-hardening properties owing mainly to the proportion of alumina being up to 40% compared with the 5% or thereabouts present in Portland cement; a minimum of 32% of alumina is required. The required fineness is between that of ordinary and rapid-hardening Portland cements. Initial setting must take place between 2 and 6 hours, and final setting within 2 hours after the initial set. The minimum compressive strengths of mortar cubes are 42 N/mm^2 or 6000 lb/in^2 at 1 day and 48 N/mm^2 or 7000 lb/in^2 at 3 days. High-alumina cement is more costly than Portland cement but it is immune from attack by sea-water and many corrosive liquids; because of its high early strength it is also used when saving time is important. Refractory concrete is made with this cement.

However, high-alumina cement concrete is subsequently subject to a phenomenon known as conversion, during which mineralogical and chemical changes occur when the metastable calcium aluminates produced during hydration convert to a more stable form. The concrete then becomes more porous and in vulnerable conditions substantial reductions in strength and durability may take place. For this and related reasons, the use of high-alumina cement in structural concrete (including all concrete in foundations) has at present been withdrawn from the Codes of Practice and related documents currently valid in the UK. For suitable guidance on the use of high-alumina cement concrete see ref. 30.

Low-heat Portland cement (BS1370). Low-heat Portland cement generates less heat during setting and hardening than do other cements, and thus reduces the risks of cracks occurring in large masses of concrete due to a reduction of tensile stresses during cooling. The development of strength is slower than that of other Portland cements, but in course of time the strengths may be equal. The minimum compressive strengths of mortar cubes are 7.5 N/mm^2 or 1100 lb/in^2 at 3 days, 14 N/mm^2 or 2000 lb/in^2 at 7 days and 28 N/mm^2 or 4000 lb/in^2 at 28 days. The strengths required from concrete cubes at these respective ages are 3.5, 7 and 14 N/mm^2 or 500, 1000 and 2000 lb/in^2. A high proportion of lime is not compatible with low heat of hydration, and therefore the permissible percentage of lime is less than for other Portland cements. The heat of hydration must not exceed 60 calories per gram at 7 days and 70 calories per gram at 28 days. The initial setting time must be not less than 1 hour and the final setting time not more than 10 hours. The specific surface must be not less than 3200 cm^2 per gram.

Low-heat Portland blast-furnace cement (BS4246). The composition of this cement is also a mixture of Portland cement clinker and blast-furnace slag and the behaviour of the product is similar to cements complying with BS146 and BS1370.

Portland pulverized-fuel-ash cement (BS6588). This cement is obtained by intergrinding the components forming ordinary Portland cement to BS12 with pulverized fuel ash (PFA) complying with BS3892: Part 1. When the proportion of PFA exceeds 25% some degree of resistance is provided to the action of weak acids and sulphates, and if the PFA content exceeds 30% the deleterious effects resulting from the reaction between alkalis and silica may be somewhat reduced.

Masonry cement (BS5224)

Other cements. Other cements used for special purposes but not at present covered by British Standards, although most have a base of Portland cement, include extra-rapid-hardening, ultra-high early strength, white and coloured, waterproofing and water-repellent, and hydrophobic.

4.1.2 Aggregates

Fine aggregate (sand) and coarse aggregate (stone) must be clean, inert, hard, non-porous and free from excessive quantities of dust, laminated particles and splinters. Gravels and crushed hard stone are the common materials for ordinary structural concrete. Broken brick is a cheap aggregate for plain concrete, generally of low strength. Clinker, foamed slag, expanded shale and clay, pellets of pulverized fuel ash, fire brick and pumice are used as aggregates for non-load-bearing and insulating concrete where great strength is not essential although structural lightweight concrete can be made with some of these materials (see BS8110 and CP110). Aggregates for reinforced concrete should comply with BS882, but air-cooled blast-furnace slag (BS1047), foamed blast-furnace slag (BS877), various lightweight aggregates (BS3797), crushed dense clay brick and tile, some proprietary forms of expanded shale or clay, and clean pumice may also be suitable.

The size and grading of aggregates vary with the nature and source of the material, and the requirements in this respect depend upon the type of structure. For buildings and most reinforced concrete construction, the fine aggregate should be graded from 5 mm or 3/16 in down to dust with not more than 3% passing a BS sieve no. 200. The coarse aggregate should be graded from 5 to 20 mm or 3/16 to 3/4 in, and between these limits the grading should be such as to produce a workable and dense concrete. The largest coarse aggregate should generally be 5 mm or 1/4 in less than the cover of concrete (except in slabs) or the bar spacing (although in certain circumstances both BS8110 and CP110 permit the distance between bars to be reduced to two-thirds of the maximum aggregate size), and should not exceed a quarter of the smallest dimension of the concrete member. For the ribs and top slab of hollow clay-block slabs, and for shell roofs and similar thin members, the largest aggregate is generally 10 mm or 3/8 in. In non-reinforced concrete larger aggregate, say 40 to 75 mm or $1\frac{1}{2}$ to 3 in, is permissible, and both BS8110 and CP110 permit aggregate having a nominal maximum aggregate size of 40 mm to be used for reinforced concrete work. In concrete in large piers of bridges and massive foundations or in concrete for filling large cavities or for kentledge, the use of hard stone 'plums' is common.

For concrete subject to attrition, such as roads and the floors of garages, factories and workshops, if a special finish is not applied, an angular aggregate and a coarse sand are preferable. For liquid-containing structures the aggregates should be selected to give as dense a concrete as possible.

4.1.3 Concrete mixes

The proportions in which the cement, fine aggregate and coarse aggregate are mixed may be expressed for convenience as volumetric ratios based on a unit volume of cement, for example, 1:2:4, meaning one part by volume of cement, two parts by volume of fine aggregate, and four parts by volume of coarse aggregate. Since it is important that the quantity of cement should be not less than that expected, the cement should be measured by weight. If Portland cement has a nominal weight of 1440 kg/m^3 or 90 lb/ft^3, 1:2:4 means 1440 kg of Portland cement to 2 m^3 of fine aggregate to 4 m^3 of coarse aggregate; or 90 lb of cement to 2 ft^3 of fine aggregate to 4 ft^3 of coarse aggregate. If the basis of a batch of concrete is a 50 kg or 1 cwt bag of cement, this mix is equivalent to 50 kg of cement to 0.07 m^3 of fine aggregate to 0.14 m^3 of coarse aggregate; or 112 lb of cement to 2.5 ft^3 of fine aggregate to 5 ft^3 of coarse aggregate.

Proportions of cement to aggregate. The proportion of cement to aggregate depends on the strength, impermeability and durability required. Experience shows that the equivalent of a 1:2:4 concrete is suitable for general construction in cost and strength. A nominal 1:3:6 concrete is suitable for non-reinforced construction or for concrete placed temporarily that will be cut away later. Workable mixes richer in cement than 1:2:4, for example $1:1\frac{1}{2}:3$ and 1:1:2, are stronger but more expensive owing to the higher proportion of cement. They are not generally economical for beams and slabs, although often so for heavily loaded columns or for members subjected to combined bending and direct thrust when the direct thrust predominates. Mixes richer than 1:1:2 contain so large a proportion of cement that, apart from the cost, shrinkage during hardening is excessive. Instead of using a rich mix it is generally more economical to obtain the necessary compressive strength by carefully grading the aggregates and controlling the amount of water.

In liquid-containing structures the nominal proportions should be not leaner than $1:1\frac{3}{5}:3\frac{1}{5}$. If the thickness of the concrete exceeds 450 mm or 18 in, nominal 1:2:4 concrete is permissible. Concrete having the proportions $1:1\frac{2}{3}:3\frac{1}{3}$ is generally used for precast piles, unprotected roof slabs and for concrete deposited under water, and in other places where a concrete of a better quality than 1:2:4 is required. For hollow-block floors and similar narrow-ribbed construction and for many precast products $1:1\frac{1}{2}:3$ concrete is often specified, but with smaller aggregate than is used for ordinary construction. The blinding layer on the bottom of an excavation may consist of concrete having the proportions of 1 part of Portland cement to 8 parts of combined aggregate.

Proportions of fine and coarse aggregates. The ratio between the amounts of fine and coarse aggregate necessarily depends on the grading and other characteristics of the materials in order that the volume of sand is sufficient to fill the voids in the coarse aggregate to produce a dense concrete. Until the material for a particular structure has been delivered to the site it is not possible to say what will be the exact grading of the sand or stone. Therefore this information is not always available when the specification is written. Several courses are open to the engineer when specifying the proportions for the concrete. The proportions of a particular sand and a particular stone with the properties of which the engineer is acquainted can be specified. Two or more independent sources of supply should be available within reasonable distance of the site. If the material is specified in this way, the permissible variations of the essential properties should be given. Another method is to specify the proportions of coarse and fine aggregates having definite gradings and leave it to the contractor to supply a material conforming to these requirements. Probably a better method is to specify a provisional ratio of fine to coarse material, and maximum and minimum sizes (with such percentages of intermediate sizes as necessary), and insert a provision to allow adjustment of the proportions after examination of the actual materials.

Generally the proportion of fine to coarse aggregate should be such that the volume of fine aggregate should be about 5% in excess of the voids in the coarse material. Since the volume of voids may be up to 45%, the common ratio of one part of fine to two parts of coarse aggregate, as in a 1:2:4 mix, is explainable. Such proportions, however, relate to dry materials. Whereas the water in a damp coarse aggregate does not appreciably affect the volume, the water in damp fine aggregate may increase the volume by 30% over the dry (or fully saturated) volume. The proportions specified should therefore apply to dry sand and must be adjusted on the site to allow for bulking due to dampness.

The ratio of 1:2 of fine (dry) to coarse aggregate should be altered if tests show that a denser and more workable concrete can be obtained by using other proportions. Permissible lower and upper limits are generally $1:1\frac{1}{2}$ and $1:2\frac{1}{2}$ respectively; thus for a nominal 1:2:4 concrete, the variation of the proportions may result in the equivalent extreme proportions of approximately $1:2\frac{1}{3}:3\frac{2}{3}$ and $1:1\frac{2}{3}:4\frac{1}{3}$.

Quantity of water. The strength and workability of concrete depend to a great extent on the amount of water used in mixing. There is an amount of water for certain proportions of given materials that produces a concrete of greatest strength. A smaller amount of water reduces the strength, and about 10% less may be insufficient to ensure complete setting of the cement and may produce an unworkable concrete. More than the optimum amount increases workability but reduces strength; an increase of 10% may reduce the strength by approximately 15%, while an increase of 50% may reduce the strength by one-half. With an excess of more than 50% the concrete becomes too wet and liable to separation. The use of an excessive amount of water not only produces low strength but increases shrinkage, and reduces density and therefore durability.

Some practical values of the water/cement ratio for structural reinforced concrete are about 0.45 for 1:1:2 concrete, 0.50 for $1:1\frac{1}{2}:3$ concrete, and 0.55 to 0.60 for 1:2:4 concrete.

Concrete compacted by efficient mechanical vibrators may generally contain less water than concrete compacted by tamping or rodding, thereby obtaining greater strength. Increased workability can be obtained by incorporating a plasticizing agent in the mix; the consequent reduction in the amount of water required results in a gain in strength.

A practical method of assessing the amount of water required is to make trial mixes and find the proportion of water which produces a concrete that is just plastic enough to be worked among and around the reinforcement bars. These trial mixes may also be used to determine the best ratio of fine to coarse aggregate. Several mixes are made with slightly differing amounts of fine and coarse aggregates in each, but with the same total volume of aggregate and weight of cement in each. The amount of water is adjusted to give the required workability. The mix that occupies the least volume, i.e. is the densest, will produce the best concrete. When the best mix has been determined, the slump may be determined and the slumps of subsequent batches checked. The slump test allows for the porosity and dampness of the aggregates but not for any variation in the grading, size or shape of the aggregate. A maximum slump for reinforced concrete is about 150 mm or 6 in, but a stiffer mix is often desirable and practicable; a slump of 25 mm or 1 in may be suitable if the reinforcement is not intricate or congested. For plain concrete in massive foundations, roads and dams, and similar work the concrete may not contain enough water to produce any slump, but sufficient water must be present to hydrate the cement and to enable the concrete to be properly consolidated by vibration or ramming.

Mixes per BS8110. Unlike its predecessors, BS8110 does not give specific information regarding the specifying of concrete mixes: instead, it refers users to BS5328 'Methods for specifying concrete'. Two basic types of concrete mixes are described in BS5328, namely *prescribed* and *designed* mixes. In addition, either type may be designated to produce either *ordinary* structural concrete, if the constituents consist solely of Portland cement, certain types of aggregate, and water, or *special* structural concrete if other constituents such as admixtures or other types of aggregate are included.

Prescribed mixes are similar in many respects to the standard mixes previously described in earlier Codes. With a prescribed mix it is the designer's task to specify mix proportions satisfying the necessary requirements regarding strength and durability; the manufacturer of the concrete merely produces a properly mixed concrete containing the correct proportions of constituents as specified in BS5328. Such mixes are designated by prefixing and suffixing the specified grade number (i.e. optimum 28 day compressive strength in N/mm^2) by the letters C and P respectively; e.g. C25P denotes an ordinary designed mix of grade 25.

Prescribed mixes other than those tabulated in BS5328 can be adopted if desired. In such a case the engineer must also specify the minimum cement content, the proportions of materials, the types of aggregate that may be used and the workability required: he must also arrange for strength tests to be made during construction to ensure that the mix he has prescribed meets the necessary requirements.

With a designed mix the onus is on the manufacturer of the concrete to select appropriate mix proportions to achieve the strength and workability specified; the engineer merely states the minimum cement content and any other requirements that may be necessary to achieve adequate durability. Prefixes C, F and IT (but with no corresponding suffix) denote the prescribed grades of designed mix. Thus IT2.5 indicates a designed mix having a specified characteristic indirect tensile strength of 2.5 N/mm^2. For designed mixes, the purchaser must specify the types of cement and aggregate permitted, and the required nominal maximum size of the aggregates. He is also free to specify additional optional requirements such as workability if so desired. Fifteen compressive strengths ranging from 2.5 to 60 N/mm^2 may be specified, three flexural strengths (3 to 5 N/mm^2), or three indirect tensile strengths (2 to 3 N/mm^2). The cement content of fresh, fully compacted reinforced concrete must also be not less than 240 kg/m^3.

Instead of a designed mix having a specified strength, the purchaser may alternatively specify a *special prescribed mix* where the required mix proportions in kilograms of each constituent are prescribed; such mixes are of particular value where properties other than strength are of paramount importance.

Mixes per CP110. The requirements regarding mix design given in CP110 are very similar to those in BS5328 and described above but preceded the appearance of the British Standard. The requirements for ordinary prescribed mixes tabulated in CP110 generally correspond to those in BS5328 but slightly richer aggregate/cement ratios should be adopted to conform to the desired grade.

Durability. The grade of concrete suitable for a particular structure should be selected to provide an appropriate degree of durability as well as strength. Durability depends on the conditions of exposure, on the grade of concrete and on the cement content of the mix: for this reason minimum cement contents for various conditions of exposure are specified in BS8110, CP110 and BS5337. However, greater cement contents increase the likelihood of thermal cracking; hence maximum values are also often specified. The amount of cover of concrete over the reinforcement also influences the durability of reinforced concrete. Details of the respective requirements of BS8110 and CP110 are given in *Table 139*.

4.2 PROPERTIES OF CONCRETE

4.2.1 Weight and pressure

The weight of ordinary concrete is discussed in section 9.1.1, and the weights of ordinary reinforced concrete, lightweight concrete and heavy concrete are given in *Tables 2* and *80*. A unit weight of 24 kN/m^3 or 150 lb/ft^3 is generally adopted in the structural design of reinforced concrete members, and this value is recommended in the *Joint Institutions Design Manual*.

In the design of formwork a weight of not less than 24 N/m^3 or 150 lb/ft^3 should be allowed for wet concrete. The horizontal pressure exerted by wet concrete is often assumed to be 22 kN/m^2 or 140 lb/ft^2 of vertical surface per metre or per foot of depth placed at one time, but for narrow widths, for drier concretes, and where the reinforcement is intricate, the increase in pressure for each metre or foot of depth is less: see also ref. 31.

Lightweight concrete. Concrete having a density less than that of concrete made with gravel or crushed stone is produced by using clinker, foamed slag, expanded clay and shale, vermiculite, pumice and similar lightweight materials. Some of these concretes do not have great strength at low density, but their low densities and high thermal insulation properties make them suitable for partitions and for lining walls and roofs. Concretes of medium weight with lightweight aggregates have sufficient strength for structural members, and BS8110 and CP110 give recommendations for their use. Some details of the various properties of different types of lightweight concrete are given in *Table 80*.

'No-fines' concrete is a form of lightweight concrete suitable for cast *in situ*, non-reinforced construction. It is generally ordinary gravel concrete with little or no aggregate less than 10 mm or 3/8 in, and has high thermal insulation properties.

Cellular or aerated concrete. Cellular (aerated or gas) concrete is a lightweight concrete made from a mixture of an aggregate (e.g. pulverized fuel ash, blast-furnace slag or fine sand), cement, a chemical admixture and water. The addition of aluminium powder to this mixture causes expansion and, after autoclaving, a lightweight concrete of cellular texture is produced. If the steel is suitably protected, the concrete can be reinforced.

Air-entrained concrete. Air is trapped in structural Portland-cement concrete with ordinary aggregates by adding resinous or fatty materials during mixing. Generally the amount of air entrained is about 5% (by volume). The results are decreases of about 3% in weight and up to 10% in strength, but a considerably increased resistance to frost and chemical attack and an improvement in workability.

4.2.2 Compressive strength

With given proportions of aggregates the compressive strength of concrete depends primarily upon age, cement content, and the cement/water ratio, an increase in any of these factors producing an increase in strength. The strengths of a range of concretes are given in *Tables 79* and *80*.

Compressive strengths vary from less than 10 N/mm^2 or 1500 lb/in^2 for lean concretes to more than 55 N/mm^2 or 8000 lb/in^2 for special concretes: the minimum characteristic strength of concrete made with dense aggregate, according to BS8110, is 25 N/mm^2 (about 3700 lb/in^2); for concrete made with lightweight aggregate (except for plain walls) it is 20 N/mm^2 (about 3000 lb/in^2). The relevant values according to CP110 are 20 N/mm^2 (about 3000 lb/in^2) for normal concrete and 15 kN/mm^2 (about 2300 lb/in^2) for concrete made with lightweight aggregate. The rate of increase of strength with age is almost independent of the cement content, and, with ordinary Portland-cement concrete, about 60% of the strength attained in a year is reached at 28 days; 70% of the strength at 12 months is reached in 2 months, and about 95% in 6 months. Characteristic strengths or permissible service stresses for design are generally based on the strength at 28 days. The strength at 7 days is about two-thirds of that at 28 days with ordinary Portland cement, and generally is a good indication of the strength likely to be attained: see *Table 79*.

Compression tests in the UK are made on 150 mm or 6 in cubes, which should be made, stored and tested in accordance with BS1881. For cubes made on the site, three should be cast from one batch of concrete. Identification marks should be made on the cubes. Two sets of three cubes each are preferable, and one set should be tested at 7 days and the other at 28 days. If only one set of three cubes is made, they should be tested at 28 days. The strengths of the cubes in any set should not vary by more than 15% of the average, unless the lowest strength exceeds the minimum required. The 7 day tests are a guide to the rate of hardening: the strength at this age for Portland-cement concrete should be not less than two-thirds of the strength required at 28 days.

In some countries cylinders or prisms are used for compressive tests. For ordinary concrete the compressive strength as measured on 150 mm or 6 in cylinders is about 85% of that as measured on 150 mm or 6 in cubes of ordinary concrete, although the ratio may be only two-thirds with high-strength concretes.

4.2.3 Tensile strength

The direct tensile strength of concrete is considered when calculating resistance to shearing force and in the design of cylindrical liquid-containing structures. The tensile strength does not bear a constant relation to the compressive strength, but is about one-tenth of the compressive strength. Because of the difficulty in applying a truly concentric pull, it is usual to measure the indirect tensile strength by crushing a concrete cylinder laterally.

The tensile resistance of concrete in bending is generally neglected in the design of ordinary structural members but is taken into account in the design of slabs and similar members in liquid-containing structures. The tensile resistance in bending is measured by the bending moment at failure divided by the section modulus, the result being termed the *modulus of rupture*.

4.2.4 Elastic properties

Notes on the elastic properties such as the modulus of elasticity, modular ratio and Poisson's ratio for plain and reinforced dense and lightweight concrete are given in section 18.1.

4.2.5 Thermal properties

The coefficient of thermal expansion is required in the design of chimneys, tanks containing hot liquids, and exposed or long lengths of construction, and provision must be made to resist the stresses due to changes of temperature or to limit the strains by providing joints. The thermal conductivity of concrete varies with the density and porosity of the material. Some coefficients of thermal expansion and conductivity are given in sections 18.1.7 and 18.1.8.

The nature of the aggregate is the principal factor in determining the resistance of concrete to fire, although the type of cement may affect this property to some extent. The resistance to fire of a reinforced concrete structure is affected considerably by the thickness of cover of concrete over the bars and, for a high degree of resistance, cover thicknesses in excess of those ordinarily specified should be provided, especially for floor and roof slabs and walls. Reference should be made to *Table 81*, which gives the requirements of BS8110, and to *Table 82*, which gives the corresponding data for CP110.

The Building Regulations also contain tables specifying minimum dimensions and cover thicknesses for prescribed fire resistance periods. Except in very rare instances these values are generally identical to or slightly less stringent than the corresponding requirements of CP110. Yet another set of values is provided in the joint report on fire resistance by the Institution of Structural Engineers and the Concrete Society (ref. 78): some details are given on *Table 84*.

According to the Building Regulations, the actual period of fire resistance needed depends on the size of the building and the use to which it is put: brief details are given on *Table 83*.

Aggregates that have been sintered are superior to other aggregates in their resistance to fire; also of high resistance, but less so than the foregoing, are limestone and artificial aggregates such as broken brick. The aggregates ordinarily used for structural concrete, such as crushed hard stone (excepting hard limestone, but including granite) and flint gravels, are inferior in resistance to fire although such aggregates produce the strongest concrete.

4.2.6 Shrinkage

Unrestrained concrete members exhibit progressive shrinking over a long period while they are hardening. For concrete that can dry completely and where the shrinkage is unrestrained, the linear coefficient is approximately 0.000 25 at 28 days and 0.000 35 at 3 months, after which shrinkage the change is less rapid until at the end of 12 months it may approach a maximum of 0.0005. The relationship between the percentage of shrinkage and time suggested in BS8110 and CP110 may be read from the appropriate diagrams on *Table 79*. In reservoirs and other structures where the concrete does not become completely dry, a maximum value of 0.0002 is reasonable. The *Code Handbook* suggests a value of 0.0003 for sections less than 250 mm in thickness and 0.000 25 otherwise, provided that the concrete is not made with aggregates prone to high shrinkage. More detailed information is given in ref. 32. A concrete rich in cement, or made with finely ground cement or with a high water content, shrinks more than a lean concrete or one with a low water content.

If a concrete member is restrained so that a reduction in length due to shrinkage cannot take place, tensile stresses are caused. A coefficient of 0.0002 may correspond to a stress of 3.5 N/mm^2 or 500 lb/in^2 when restrained; in such cases it is important to reduce or neutralize these stresses by using a strong concrete, by proper curing and by providing joints. Shrinkage is considered in the calculation of deflections and the design of fixed arches.

4.2.7 Creep

Creep is the slow deformation, additional to elastic contraction exhibited by concrete under sustained stress, and proceeds at a decreasing rate over many years. Characteristic values for creep, expressed in deformation per unit length, for 1:2:4 concrete loaded at 28 days with a sustained stress of 4 N/mm^2 or 600 lb/in^2 are 0.0003 at 28 days after loading, and 0.0006 at one year. Thus creep is of the same degree of magnitude as shrinkage, and appears to be directly proportional to the stress. The earlier the age of the concrete at which the stress is applied the greater is the creep, which also appears to be affected by the same factors as affect the compressive strength of the concrete; generally the higher the strength the less is the creep.

The effect of creep of concrete is not often considered directly in reinforced concrete design. It is, however, taken into account when calculating deflections according to the rigorous method described in BS8110 and CP110 (see *Table 136*), by modifying the elastic modulus of concrete. Values of the creep multiplier involved may be read from the graphs given on *Table 79*.

4.2.8 Reduction of bulk upon mixing

When the constituents of concrete are mixed with water and tamped into position, a reduction in volume to about two-thirds of the total volume of the dry unmixed materials takes place. The actual amount of reduction depends on the nature, dampness, grading and proportions of the aggregates, the amount of cement and water, the thoroughness of mixing, and the degree of consolidation. With so many variables it is impossible to assess exactly the amount of each material required to produce a unit volume of wet concrete when deposited in place.

4.2.9 Porosity and permeability

The porosity of concrete is the characteristic whereby liquids can penetrate the material by capillary action, and depends on the total volume of the spaces occupied by air or water between the solid matter in the hardened concrete. The more narrow and widely distributed these spaces are, the less easily can liquids diffuse in the concrete.

Permeability is the property of the concrete that permits a liquid to pass through the concrete owing to a difference in pressure on opposite faces. Permeability depends primarily on the size of the largest voids and on the size of the channels connecting the voids. Impermeability can only be approached by proportioning and grading the mix so as to make the number and sizes of the voids the least possible, and by thorough consolidation to ensure that the concrete is as dense as possible with the given proportions of the materials. Permeability seems to be a less determining factor than porosity when considering the effect on concrete of injurious liquids.

4.2.10 Fatigue

The effect of repeatedly applied loads, either compressive or tensile, or a frequent reversal of load, is to reduce the strength of concrete; this phenomenon is called fatigue. If the resultant stress is less than about half the strength, as is the case in compression on most concrete members, fatigue is not evident. When a stress exceeding half the strength of the unfatigued concrete is frequently caused, the strength of the concrete is progressively reduced, until it equals the stress due to the applied load, when the concrete fails. The number of repetitions of load to produce failure decreases the more nearly the stress due to the load equals the strength of the unfatigued concrete.

A relatively high frequency of repetition of stress would be ten times and upwards per minute. If intervals of time occur between successive applications of load, the effect of fatigue is delayed. The degree of fatigue differs for direct compression, direct tension, and bending. Since the tensile stress in concrete in bending more nearly approaches the strength than does the compressive stress, it is evident that fatigue due to tensile stress controls fatigue of concrete in bending.

Failure due to fatigue has been shown to be directly linked to the development and growth of microcracks (i.e. cracks too small to be seen by the naked eye.) If the growth of such cracking is inhibited, the concrete will be markedly more resistant to the effects of fatigue (or impact). This is the fundamental basis of fibre-reinforced concrete where short lengths of chopped steel, plastics or glass fibre are distributed randomly through the mix.

4.3 STRESSES IN CONCRETE

4.3.1 Characteristic strength

The characteristic strength of concrete is defined as the crushing strength of concrete cubes at 28 days below which not more than one-twentieth of the test results fall. If the distribution of test results about a mean strength f_m follows the normal (i.e. Gaussian) form, the characteristic crushing strength f_{cu} can be expressed in terms of the standard deviation s by the relationship

$$f_{cu} = f_m - 1.64s$$

where s is the positive square root of the variance. The variance is

$$\frac{1}{j}\sum_{i=1}^{j}(f_i - f_m)^2$$

where f_i is each individual test result and j is the total number of results. Thus

$$f_{cu} = f_m - 1.64\left[\frac{1}{j}\sum_{i=1}^{j}(f_i - f_m)^2\right]^{1/2}$$

Consequently, in order to achieve the required characteristic strength it is necessary to set out to achieve a 'target mean strength' that exceeds f_{cu} by what is known as the 'current margin'. The current margin is often either (1) $1.64s$ on tests on not less than 100 separate batches of similar concrete made within one year, but not less than $3.75\,\text{N/mm}^2$ for concrete of grade 20 and over; or (2) $1.64s$ on tests on not less than 40 separate batches of similar concrete made in more than 5 days but less than 6 months, but not less than $7.5\,\text{N/mm}^2$ for grade 20 concrete and over. For weaker concretes, the minimum standard deviation for conditions 1 and 2 should be $f_{cu}/6$ and $f_{cu}/3$ respectively. Until sufficient data have been accumulated to use these criteria, a current margin of $15\,\text{N/mm}^2$ for grade 20 concrete and over is recommended. For detailed information regarding mix design to achieve the desired characteristic strength, reference should be made to BS5328, CP110 and the *Code Handbook*.

Concrete grade. The grade of a concrete is defined as that number which indicates the characteristic compressive strength of concrete in N/mm^2, determined by cube tests made at 28 days. Thus a grade 25 concrete has a characteristic strength of $25\,\text{N/mm}^2$: this is the lowest grade that may be employed as reinforced concrete made with dense aggregate according to BS8110. The Code for water-containing structures (BS5337) only sanctions the use of concrete of grades 25 and 30 for reinforced concrete.

4.3.2 Design strengths

For ultimate limit-state analysis the design strength of concrete is determined by *dividing* the characteristic strength f_{cu} by the appropriate partial factor of safety for materials γ_m. However, in nearly all appropriate design formulae, including those in BS8110, CP110 and this book, the partial safety factor is embodied in the formula itself, so that the ultimate resistance of a section is related directly to the characteristic strength of the concrete. This generally simplifies the calculations, but if the effects of a less usual ultimate limit-state condition (e.g. due to excessive loading or local damage) are being investigated, the correct value of γ_m (i.e. 1.3 according to BS8110 and CP110) for this condition may be substituted instead of the normal value of γ_m for concrete of 1.5.

The requirements of BS5337, when limit-state design is adopted, correspond to those for CP110.

Strength in direct compression and in bending. According to both BS8110 and CP110, in all ultimate limit-state calculations for the design of sections such as beams, slabs and columns, involving the strength of concrete in direct compression or in compression in bending, the appropriate formulae require the direct use of the characteristic compressive strength. In the case of slender sections, e.g. columns, no adjustment to this value is made (as for example is done in permissible-service-stress design): instead, an additional moment related to the slenderness is taken into consideration (see section 5.15.1).

Strength in shear. BS8110 specifies that, for grade 25 concrete, the relationship between the maximum resistance to shear v_c of dense-aggregate concrete without special shearing reinforcement, the depth of section d and the proportion ρ of main reinforcement provided is given by the expression

$$v_c = 0.79(100\rho)^{1/3}(400/d)^{1/4}/\gamma_m$$

where γ_m is taken as 1.25, $100\rho \ngtr 3$ and $400/d \nless 1$. This relationship is shown graphically on *Table 142*. For other grades of concrete, v_c is proportional to $\sqrt[3]{(0.04f_{cu})}$, and the values of v_c obtained from the graph should be multiplied by the appropriate factor read from the adjoining scale. CP110 does not specify a direct relationship between the concrete strength and v_c but tabulates the results of many tests; these values are shown graphically on *Table 143*.

The shearing resistance of lightweight-aggregate concrete is markedly less than when dense aggregates are used. Both BS8110 and CP110 propose values that are 80% of the dense-concrete equivalents, and these are also shown on *Tables 142* and *143* respectively.

The limiting shearing resistance that may be adopted, even when reinforcement to resist shear is provided, is specified in BS8110 as the lesser of $0.85\sqrt{f_{cu}}$ or 5 N/mm², and of $0.68\sqrt{f_{cu}}$ or 4 N/mm² for normal and lightweight-aggregate concrete respectively. The equivalent values are not stated explicitly in CP110 but, for normal and lightweight-aggregate concrete, are found to correspond to $0.75\sqrt{f_{cu}}$ and $0.6\sqrt{f_{cu}}$ respectively, when $f_{cu} \nless 20$ N/mm².

Strength in torsion. Limiting values for the ultimate torsional strength of dense-aggregate concrete with or without special torsional reinforcement are given in BS8110: Part 2 and CP110. BS8110 specifies the use of the expressions $0.8\sqrt{f_{cu}}$ or 5 N/mm² whichever is the lesser, and $0.067\sqrt{f_{cu}}$ or 0.4 N/mm² whichever is the lesser, respectively; for lightweight-aggregate concrete the corresponding expressions are $0.64\sqrt{f_{cu}}$ or 4 N/mm², and $0.0536\sqrt{f_{cu}}$ or 0.32 N/mm², respectively. The limiting values given in CP110 are found to correspond to the expressions $0.75\sqrt{f_{cu}}$ and $0.15\sqrt{f_{cu}}$ respectively, as shown on *Table 143*. Lower values are applicable when lightweight-aggregate concrete is used and correspond to 80% of those given by the above expressions: these values are also indicated on *Table 143*.

Bond. The requirements of BS8110 and CP110 regarding bond are summarized and discussed in section 4.6.

Modification of strength with age. Values of the cube strengths of concretes having various characteristic strengths f_{cu} (at 28 days) of from 20 to 60 N/mm², at ages of from 7 days to one year, are given in BS8110 and CP110. Both Codes permit designs to be based either on f_{cu} or on the appropriate strength corresponding to the age at which the concrete will be loaded. The Code relationship between strength and age is illustrated graphically on *Table 79*.

Bearing on plain concrete. According to CP110 (clauses 5.5.5 and 5.5.7), bearing stresses due to ultimate loads beneath bearings should not exceed $0.6f_{cu}$ for grade 25 concrete and over, and $0.5f_{cu}$ otherwise, and may be assumed to disperse immediately.

4.3.3 Permissible service stresses

Compression due to bending. For modular-ratio or load-factor design the permissible service stress f_{cr} in concrete due to bending is generally assumed to be about one-third of the specified minimum crushing strength of works cubes at 28 days. The CPCP revision of CP114 suggests a relationship of $f_{cr} = 0.366f_{cu}$ for concrete grades from 15 to 60.

Direct compression. For members in direct compression, such as concentrically loaded columns, the permissible compressive stress f_{cc} is about 76% of the permissible compressive stress in bending; the CPCP recommendation is $f_{cc} = 0.275f_{cu}$. This stress is assumed to occur over the whole cross-sectional area of an ordinary column and on the cross-sectional area of the core of a column with helical binding.

Combined bending and direct force. When a member is subject to bending moment combined with a direct thrust, as in an arch or a column forming part of a frame, or is subjected to a bending moment combined with a direct pull, as in the walls of rectangular bunkers and tanks, and is designed according to the modular-ratio method, the same permissible compressive stress f_{cr} is used for the concrete as if the member were subjected to bending alone.

Tension. In the design of members subjected to bending the strength of the concrete in tension is commonly neglected, but in certain cases, such as structures containing liquids and in the consideration of shearing resistance, the tensile strength of the concrete is important. For suspension members which are in direct tension and where the cracking is not necessarily detrimental, the tensile strength of the concrete can be neglected and the reinforcement then resists the entire load. In a member that must be free from cracks of excessive width, such as the wall of a cylindrical container of liquids, the tensile stress in grade 25 concrete should not exceed 1.31 N/mm² in accordance with the alternative (i.e. working stress) design method prescribed in BS5337; a member in bending should be designed, as described in section 5.6, so that the tensile stress in the concrete does not exceed 1.84 N/mm². The corresponding tensile stresses in grade 30 concrete are 1.44 and 2.02 N/mm², as given in *Table 132*.

Overline railway bridges on lines on which steam locomotives may still run and similar structures where cracking may permit corrosive fumes to attack the reinforcement should also be designed with a limited tensile stress in the concrete (see section 5.2).

Shearing stresses. The permissible shearing stress v_d in a beam is about 10% of the maximum permissible compressive stress in bending, but if the diagonal tension due to the shearing force is resisted entirely by reinforcement the shearing stress should not exceed $4v_d$; a maximum stress of less than $4v_d$ is advisable in all but primary beams in buildings. The permissible shearing stresses per BS5337 are given in *Table 132*.

Bond. The permissible average-bond stress between concrete and plain round bars is slightly more than the shearing stress, and the local-bond stress f_{bsd} (see section 4.6.5) is about 50% greater than the average-bond stress. For deformed bars, the bond stresses may be increased by up to about 40%, according to CP114, in excess of the stress for plain round bars.

The CPCP revision of CP114 proposes permissible anchorage-bond stresses for type 2 deformed bars equal to $\sqrt{(f_{cu})}/3$, with permissible local-bond stresses that are 25% higher than these values.

Bearing on plain concrete. Plain concrete mixed in leaner proportion than 1:2:4 is used for filling under foundations and for massive piers and thick retaining walls. The bearing pressures on plain and reinforced concrete in piers and walls subjected to concentric or eccentric loads, and permissible local pressures as under bearings, are given in *Table 191*.

4.4 PROPERTIES OF REINFORCEMENT

4.4.1 Types of reinforcement

There are several types of steel reinforcement for concrete, the most common in the United Kingdom being plain round mild-steel bars and high-yield-stress deformed bars. These, and others, are covered by appropriate British Standards, the specified physical properties of which are given in *Table 85*. The British Standard reference numbers given in *Table 85* and the following are the metric editions of the standards which now supersede the previous standards in imperial units; the equivalents in the latter units given in *Table 85* are practical conversions.

Plain round hot-rolled mild-steel bars (BS4449). These have a minimum yield-point stress (i.e. characteristic stress) of 250 N/mm^2 (36 000 lb/in^2) upon which stress the permissible working stress depends. Because of the plain surface, the bond with the concrete is not so high as for deformed bars and therefore end anchorages, such as hooks and bends, may be required. Mild-steel bars are easily bent and are weldable.

Deformed mild-steel bars. These have higher bond qualities than plain round bars and are also specified in BS4449, but are not widely used at present.

Hot-rolled deformed (high-bond) high-yield-stress bars (BS4449). These are some of the most commonly used bars in the United Kingdom. The specified characteristic strength (i.e. the yield stress below which not more than 5% of the test results may fall) is 460 N/mm^2 for bars up to and including 16 mm in diameter, and 425 N/mm^2 for larger bars. This characteristic strength is considered to be achieved if not more than two results in forty consecutive tests to determine the yield stress fall below the specified strength *and* all the test results reach at least 93% of the specified strength.

Cold-worked bars (BS4461). These are usually mild-steel bars, the yield point of which has been eliminated by cold working, generally twisting under controlled conditions, resulting in a higher yield stress and consequently a higher permissible working stress. A common form of such bars are twisted square bars, the smaller sizes of which are truly square, while bars of intermediate and larger sizes have chamfered corners. Another form is a round deformed bar that has been twisted. The specified characteristic strength of cold-worked bars corresponds to that specified for hot-rolled deformed bars described above.

Fabric reinforcement (BS4483). This reinforcement is generally steel wire mesh, the wire complying with BS4482. Such fabrics are used mainly for reinforcing slabs, such as suspended and ground floor slabs, flat and shell roofs, roads and the like. There are four standard types of fabric, having the sizes and other properties given in *Table 91*, which are as follows. Square-mesh fabrics have wires of the same size and spacing in both directions. Oblong-mesh fabrics have transverse wires that are smaller and more widely spaced than the main longitudinal wires, the amount of transverse wires being less than that required as distribution steel in accordance with CP110. Standard structural fabrics also have oblong meshes but the transverse wires comply with the latter requirement. Wrapping fabrics are light fabrics used mainly for reinforcing the concrete casing steel stanchions and beams.

Special structural fabrics are also obtainable and these are generally made to specific requirements as to cross-sectional area in both directions. They are generally much heavier than standard fabrics and may incorporate bars instead of wires.

Other reinforcements are obtainable and may be proprietary materials or otherwise, such as high-grade twin bars and expanded metal. When expedient, such materials as old rails, disused wire ropes and light structural steelwork are used as reinforcement on occasion.

4.4.2 Areas, perimeters and weights

The data required by designers regarding cross-sectional areas, perimeters and weights of various types of reinforcement are given in *Tables 86* to *91* for bars of common metric and imperial sizes and for wires and fabric reinforcement of metric sizes. The data are given basically for plain round bars, but are also applicable to deformed and square bars since the standard nominal sizes of the latter are the diameters of plain round bars of the same cross-sectional areas.

For metric bars, *Table 86* gives the cross-sectional area per unit width of slab for bars of various sizes at specified spacings (values given in italics correspond to 'non-standard' spacings), the areas of numbers of bars from one to twenty, and the perimeters of from one to ten bars. Similar, but less extensive, information relating to bars of imperial sizes is provided on *Table 89*.

On *Table 87* the cross-sectional areas of various combinations of bars of metric sizes at recommended spacings are listed. The criterion adopted is that the bar diameters forming the combination must not differ by more than two sizes; for example with 10 mm bars, possible combinations are only with 6, 8, 12 or 16 mm bars. The values are tabulated so as to enable the particular combination providing an area satisfying a given value to be selected at a glance. A similar table giving cross-sectional areas of combinations of specific numbers of bars forms *Table 88*. Here, areas for all combinations of up to five bars of each size (or ten bars of the same size) are listed where the bar diameters do not differ by more than two sizes (i.e. for 20 mm bars, the possible combinations are with 12, 16, 25 or 32 mm bars only).

On *Table 90* the unit weight and weights of bars at specific spacings are given, and *Table 91* gives particulars of cross-sectional areas and weights of standard fabric reinforcements, together with particulars of single wires.

4.5 STRESSES IN REINFORCEMENT

4.5.1 Characteristic strength

The characteristic strength of the reinforcement is defined in BS8110 and CP110 as that value of yield or proof stress below which the values obtained from not more than one test in twenty fall. As in the case of concrete, with a Gaussian distribution of test results, this corresponds to a relationship between the characteristic strength of the reinforcement f_y and the mean yield strength f_m of

$$f_y = f_m - 1.64s$$

where s is the standard deviation. In the case of reinforcement, steel complying with the appropriate requirements of BS4449 and BS4461 has a characteristic strength of 250, 425 or 460 N/mm^2 (i.e. the characteristic strength corresponds to the minimum yield-point stress for the particular type of steel specified in these Standards).

4.5.2 Design strengths

Design strength in tension. The design strength of the reinforcement in tension f_{yd2} is determined by dividing the characteristic strength f_y by the appropriate partial safety factor for materials γ_m. Once again, however, certain design formulae, such as the simplified expressions for beams and slabs given in CP110, involve the direct use of f_y, the value of γ_m actually being embodied in the numerical values contained in the formulae. If ultimate limit-state analysis for local damage or excessive loading is being undertaken, therefore, an appropriate adjustment to cater for the differing value of γ_m may be made if desired.

With rigorous limit-state analysis from first principles, the design strength f_{yd2} is related not only to the characteristic strength but also to the strain in the reinforcement and hence, owing to the compatibility of strains in the concrete and steel, to the depth-to-neutral-axis factor x/d. This relationship is discussed in greater detail in section 5.3.1. Values of f_{yd2} for types of reinforcement having 'standard' and other values of f_y and various ratios of x/d may be calculated from the formulae on *Table 103* or read from the scales on *Table 104*.

Design strength in compression. While BS8110 permits a maximum design strength in compression f_{yd1} that is identical to that in tension f_{yd2} (i.e. f_y/γ_m), CP110 limits the maximum design strength in compression reinforcement f_{yd1} to $2000f_y/(2000\gamma_m + f_y)$. Thus if $f_y = 250$ N/mm^2 and $\gamma_m =$ 1.15, $f_{yd1}/f_y = 0.784$, and if $f_y = 460$ N/mm^2 and $\gamma_m = 1.15$, $f_{yd1}/f_y = 0.725$. With the simplified design expressions for beams, slabs and columns given in CP110, the varying relationship between f_{yd1} and f_y is simplified to a constant value of $f_{yd1} = 0.72f_y$, thus underestimating the true maximum design strength by up to a maximum of 8% (when mild-steel reinforcement is used).

With rigorous limit-state analysis using first principles, the design strength of the compression reinforcement f_{yd1} is related not only to the characteristic strength but also to the ratio of the depth of the steel from the compression face d' to the depth to the neutral axis x, owing to strain-compatibility requirements. Values of f_{yd1} for 'standard' and other types of reinforcement with various ratios of d'/d may be obtained from *Tables 103* and *104*.

Shearing reinforcement. In the design of shearing reinforcement using inclined bars, the same design strength (i.e. f_y/γ_m) may be used as in the corresponding tension reinforcement. Where reinforcement in the form of inclined bars or links is provided, however, the maximum characteristic strength therein is, according to CP110, limited to 425 N/mm^2.

Torsional reinforcement. In the design of longitudinal bars or links to resist torsion, the maximum characteristic strength in the reinforcement must not exceed 425 N/mm^2 to meet the requirements of CP110.

BS5337. When limit-state design procedures are adopted, the requirements of BS5337 correspond to those specified in CP110 and summarized above, except that in no case may f_y exceed 425 N/mm^2.

4.5.3 Permissible service stresses

Tension. The permissible basic service stresses in tension in mild-steel bars are frequently 140 N/mm^2 or 20 000 lb/in^2 in bars of diameter not greater than 40 mm or $1\frac{1}{2}$ in, and 125 N/mm^2 or 18 000 lb/in^2 in larger bars. The corresponding stress in high-yield bars is 55% of the yield stress but not more than 230 N/mm^2 or 33 000 lb/in^2 in bars of diameter not greater than 20 mm or 7/8 in, and not greater than 210 N/mm^2 or 30 000 lb/in^2 in larger bars. The revised version of CP114 drafted by the CPCP suggests limiting values of 140 and 250 N/mm^2 for mild-steel and high-yield bars in tension due to bending, and 140 and 200 N/mm^2 in tension due to shear.

Similar service stresses are generally acceptable in the design of retaining walls and foundations, and most industrial structures, although in the latter case consideration must be given to vibration, high temperatures, impact and other influences which may require the adoption of much lower service stresses. In liquid-containing structures, maximum tensile stresses of 85 N/mm^2 and 115 N/mm^2 are specified in BS5337 (see section 5.6 and *Table 121*), for class A and class B exposure when mild-steel bars are used and the alternative (working-stress) design method is employed or the section is designed to comply with 'deemed-to-satisfy' limit-state requirements. For deformed bars the corresponding limiting stresses are 100 N/mm^2 and 130 N/mm^2 for class A and class B exposure respectively. The tensile stress in bars near the face not in contact with the liquid also must not exceed the foregoing values, except in members not less than 225 mm thick, when the stress may be 125 N/mm^2 or even 140 N/mm^2 if deformed bars are used.

When deciding the tensile service stress suitable for the reinforcement in a part of a structure, modifying factors should be considered, but the factors that represent a variation in the strength of the concrete only must be disregarded except when the bond stress is affected.

The tensile service stress in the reinforcement in buildings can be increased by one-quarter when the increase is due solely to increased bending moments and forces caused by wind pressure; the CPCP version of CP114 limits the increased stress to 300 N/mm^2 or 43 500 lb/in^2.

Compression. The compressive stress in reinforcement depends on the compressive stress in the surrounding concrete if the modular-ratio theory of the action of reinforced concrete at service loads is applied. Since the strain of the two materials is equal as long as the bond is not destroyed, the stresses are proportional to the elastic moduli. Mild steel has a modulus of elasticity E_s of about 210×10^3 N/mm^2 or 30×10^6 lb/in^2 and, if the modulus of elasticity of concrete E_c is assumed, as is often the case, to be nominally 14×10^3 N/mm^2 or 2×10^6 lb/in^2, the compressive stress in the steel f_{sc} is fifteen times the compressive stress f_{cr} in the concrete, or generally $f_{sc} = \alpha_e f_{cr}$ if α_e is the modular ratio E_s/E_c. The value of α_e is considered in section 18.14. It is often convenient to calculate the compressive stress in the steel as additional to that in the concrete; i.e. as $f_{cr}(\alpha_e - 1)$. When this expression is used the resistance of the concrete can be calculated on the entire cross-sectional area, no deduction being necessary for the area of the bars.

In load-factor design, in the design of axially loaded columns generally, and in steel-beam theory, the compressive stresses in the main reinforcement are assumed to be independent of the stress in the adjoining concrete. For high-yield bars, the maximum stress is 55% of the yield stress but not more than 175 N/mm^2 or 25 000 lb/in^2. In the CPCP revision of CP114, limiting stresses of 120 and 215 N/mm^2 are suggested for mild-steel and high-yield bars respectively.

4.6 BOND BETWEEN CONCRETE AND REINFORCEMENT

4.6.1 Anchorage bond of tension reinforcement

For a bar to resist tensile forces effectively there must be a sufficient length of bar beyond any section to develop by bond between the concrete and the steel a force equal to the total tensile force in the bar at that section.

BS8110 and CP110 requirements. The minimum effective anchorage length required for bond or for overlap can be expressed in terms of the diameter ϕ of the bar. It can be shown (see section 18.3.1) that l/ϕ must be not less than $0.217 f_y/f_{bsa}$, where f_y is the characteristic strength of the reinforcement concerned and f_{bsa}, the ultimate anchorage-bond stress, depends on the type of steel used and the strength of the dense-aggregate concrete. Two types of deformed bars are recognized in BS8110 and CP110: bars of type 2 meet more stringent requirements and higher anchorage-bond stresses are allowed. According to BS8110, for type 1 deformed bars in tension f_{bsa} (termed f_{bu} in BS8110) $= 0.4\sqrt{f_{cu}}$. If plain round bars or type 2 deformed bars are used, the calculated values should be reduced by 30% and increased by 25% respectively. The limiting values of f_{bsa} given in CP110 do not appear at first sight to be linearly related to the concrete grade. However, closer examination indicates that the linear relationship employed has been masked when rounding off the tabulated values. The values for plain bars correspond closely with those resulting from the expression $(f_{cu} + 16)/30$, while those for type 1 deformed bars are 40% greater. For bars of type 2, anchorage-bond stresses 30% higher than those for type 1 may be adopted.

The foregoing relationship has been used to calculate the values of anchorage-bond length required for plain and deformed bars in tension and compression, and various values of f_{cu} are given (in terms of bar diameters) in *Table 92* for both normal and lightweight concretes. In *Table 93* the actual bond lengths required in millimetres are given for the three most commonly employed grades of dense concrete for the characteristic steel strengths specified in BS8110 and for various bar sizes: these lengths have been rounded to the 5 mm dimension above the exact length calculated. *Table 94* provides similar information relating to four concrete grades according to CP110 requirements.

If bars in contact are provided in groups of up to four, the bond achieved between the steel and the concrete is reduced. According to BS8110, in such situations the anchorage-bond length provided should be that for a single bar having an equivalent area; i.e. for a group comprising n bars of diameter d_1, provide for each bar forming the group the bond length necessary for a single bar of diameter $(d_1\sqrt{n})$. For example, the bond length required for a group of four 8 mm bars would be that needed for a single 16 mm bar. The corresponding requirement in CP110 is that the reduction may be considered by multiplying the sum of the effective perimeters of individual bars by $(6-j)/5$, where j is the number of bars forming the group. If all the bars are of equal size, the effect on the anchorage length required may be assessed simply by considering, instead of ϕ, a bar of diameter $5\phi/(6-j)$. For example, for a group of four 8 mm bars, an anchorage-bond length equivalent to that required for a 20 mm bar should be provided for each of the bars forming the group.

Where the calculated maximum tensile force in a bar is less than its design strength the anchorage-bond length provided may be reduced proportionately. Care should be taken, however, not to violate the requirements of the relevant Code regarding the curtailment of bars (see section 20.5.1).

According to BS8110, where two tension bars are lapped the overlap should be at least equal to the anchorage-bond length of the bar having the smaller diameter. In addition, where the lap is near the top of the section as cast and if the bar diameter exceeds one-half of the minimum cover, the lap length must be increased by 40%. The same increase should also be made at section corners where the bar diameter exceeds one-half of the minimum cover to either face or where the clear distance between adjoining laps is less than 75 mm (or six times the bar diameter if this is greater). If both conditions apply, the lap length should be doubled. Lap lengths corresponding to these multiples of the basic anchorage length are tabulated on *Table 93*.

CP110 requires that the overlap for plain bars should be at least equal to the anchorage-bond length of the bar having the smaller diameter, but not less than $25\phi + 150$ mm. For deformed bars of both types the overlap should be at least

25% longer than the anchorage-bond length of the smaller bar but not less than $25\phi + 150$ mm.

The bond between lightweight-aggregate concrete and steel is less strong than when dense aggregates are used. BS8110 recommends that with lightweight-aggregate concrete, bond stresses of four-fifths of the values adopted for normal-weight concrete should be employed for all types of bars, while CP110 requires that with lightweight aggregates, bond stresses of one-half and four-fifths of those for the corresponding grades of dense-aggregate concrete should be adopted for plain and deformed bars respectively. For grade 15 lightweight concrete the strengths should be 0.4 and 0.64 of those for dense-aggregate concrete of grade 20. These values are incorporated on the table forming *Table 92*.

4.6.2 Anchorages

If an anchorage is provided at the end of a bar in tension, the bond length required need not be so great as when no such anchorage is provided. An anchorage may be a semi-circular hook, a 45° hook, a right-angled bob or a mechanical anchorage. To obtain full advantage of the bond value of an anchorage, the hook or bend must be properly formed.

BS8110 and CP110 requirements. If r is the internal radius of a bend, the effective anchorage length (measured from the commencement of the bend to a point 4ϕ beyond the end) that is provided by a semi-circular hook is the lesser of 24ϕ or $8r$, and by a right-angled bob the lesser of 12ϕ (or 24ϕ according to CP110) or $4r$. The minimum radius of any bend must be at least twice that of the test bend guaranteed by the manufacturer, and must also be sufficient to ensure that the bearing stress within the bend does not exceed the permissible value. This requirement can be considered (see section 18.3.1) as a need to provide a minimum ratio of r/ϕ for given values of a_b/ϕ and f_{cu}/f_y, where a_b is the distance between bar centres perpendicular to the plane of bending: suitable ratios of r/ϕ meeting these requirements may be read from the appropriate chart on *Table 95* for dense-aggregate concrete. When lightweight-aggregate concrete is employed, the permissible bearing stress within the bend is somewhat lower, and appropriate ratios of a_b/ϕ and r/ϕ corresponding to this condition may be found by using the scales on the right-hand edges of the same charts.

If an appropriate end enchorage is provided, the bond length can be reduced accordingly. *Table 93* and *94* give details of the lengths required when anchorages are provided in the form of right-angled bobs and semi-circular hooks, having internal radii of 2ϕ and 3ϕ for bars of mild steel and high-yield steel respectively.

Mechanical anchorages. A mechanical anchorage can be a hook embracing an anchor bar (the internal diameter of the hook being equal to the diameter of the anchor bar); alternatively the end of the bar can be threaded and provided with a plate and nut. The size of the plate should be such that the compression on the concrete at, say, 7 N/mm^2 or 1000 lb/in^2 of the net area of contact (i.e. the gross area of the plate less the area of the hole in the plate) should be equal to the tensile resistance required.

4.6.3 Anchorage bond of compression reinforcement

BS8110 and CP110 requirements. According to both BS8110 and CP110, for bars in compression ultimate anchorage-bond stresses are permitted that are 25% higher than those for bars in tension. Whereas with BS8110 the maximum design strength of a bar in compression (f_{yd1}) is equal to that in tension (f_{yd2}), with CP110 the limiting design strength in compression is only about 85% of that in tension, so the maximum effective anchorage-bond length necessary is correspondingly smaller. Where compression bars are lapped the overlap should be at least the anchorage-bond length of the smaller bar (but not less than $20\phi + 150$ mm, according to CP110), although the appropriate anchorage-bond length is that for bars in compression, of course. Alternatively, square sawn ends of such bars may be butted together and held permanently in position by a mechanical sleeve or similar proprietary device.

4.6.4 Bars in liquid-containing structures

For liquid-containing structures the requirements of BS5337 regarding bond depend on whether limit-state design or the alternative (working-stress) design method is adopted. If limit-state design is used the limiting anchorage-bond stresses correspond to those for concrete grades 25 and 30 given in CP110 (see *Tables 92* and *94*). With working-stress design, the limiting anchorage-bond stresses are 0.9 and 1.0 N/mm^2 for grades 25 and 30 respectively if plain round bars are used. With deformed bars, these values may be increased by 40% (see *Table 132*).

Whichever design method is employed, BS5337 specifies that anchorage-bond stresses in horizontal bars in sections that are in direct tension should be reduced to 70% of normal values.

4.6.5 Local-bond stress

BS8110 requirements. BS8110 states that provided that the force in each bar is transmitted to the surrounding concrete by providing an adequate embedment length or end anchorage, the effects of local bond stresses may be ignored. (This view is not, however, shared by those responsible for preparing the CPCP revision to CP114.)

CP110 requirements. The ultimate local-bond stress f_{bs} resulting from the rapid variation of tensile stress in reinforcement in beams, slabs, foundations etc. should be investigated by applying the formulae in section 18.3.3. For dense-aggregate concrete with plain and type 1 deformed bars the resulting values must not exceed the limiting ultimate values given in CP110: for type 2 deformed bars the Code values may be increased by one-fifth. For plain bars the values given in the Code correspond closely to those resulting from the expression $(f_{cu} + 15)/20$, while those for type 1 deformed bars are 25% greater. The ultimate local-bond stresses for various values of f_{cu} are tabulated on *Table 92*.

With lightweight-aggregate concrete, f_{bs} must not exceed one-half and four-fifths of the values given in CP110 for dense-aggregate concrete when plain and deformed bars respectively are used: see *Table 92*.

4.7 DETAILS OF REINFORCEMENT

4.7.1 Length and size of bars

If attention is given to a number of points regarding the length and size of reinforcement bars, fixing the bars is facilitated and the construction is more efficient. As few different sizes of bars as possible should be used, and the largest size of bar consistent with good design should be used, thus reducing the number of bars to be bent and placed. Large bars are cheaper than small bars. The basic price is usually that of 16 mm or 5/8 in bars, all larger bars being supplied at this rate; smaller bars cost more for each size below 16 mm or 5/8 in.

Generally, the longest bar economically obtainable should be used, but regard should be paid to the facility with which a long bar can be transported and placed in position. Consideration should also be given to the greatest length that can be handled without being too whippy; these lengths are about 6 m for bars of 8 mm diameter and less, 8 m from 8 mm to 12 mm, 12 m for 16 mm, 18 m for 25 mm, and 20 m for bars over 30 mm. Corresponding limiting imperial values are 20 ft for bars of 5/16 in diameter and less, 25 ft from 5/16 in to 1/2 in, 40 ft for 5/8 in, 60 ft for 1 in, and 75 ft for bars over $1\frac{1}{4}$ in. The basic price only applies to bars up to 12 m or 40 ft long, and extras for greater lengths are charged. Bars up to 10 mm or 3/8 in can be obtained in long lengths in coils at ordinary prices and sometimes at lower prices. Over certain lengths it is more economical to lap two bars than to buy long bars, the extra cost of the increase in total length of bar due to overlapping being more than offset by the increased charge for long lengths. Long bars cannot always be avoided in long piles, but bars over 12 m or 40 ft require special vehicles which may result in delay and extra cost.

The total length of each bar should, where possible, be given to a multiple of 100 mm or 3 in and as many bars as possible should be of one length, thus keeping the number of different lengths of bars as small as practicable.

4.7.2 Bar-bending schedule

The method of giving bending dimensions and marking the bars should be uniform throughout the bar-bending schedules for any one structure. A system of bending dimensions is illustrated in *Tables 96* and *97* and conforms to BS4466, which also gives standard forms of bending schedules which are recommended to be adopted.

According to the Report of the Joint Committee of the Concrete Society and the Institution of Structural Engineers (ref. 33) a convenient method of allocating a reference number to an individual bar is to use a six-character number, the first three characters relating to the drawing number on which the bar is detailed, the next two characters corresponding to the schedule number, and the last character giving the revision letter.

4.7.3 Detailing

To avoid non-uniform presentation of the details of reinforcement, it is advisable to adopt a standard method and, in the United Kingdom, the method given in ref. 33 should be followed.

4.7.4 Concrete cover

To ensure adequate durability by providing proper protection to the reinforcement, and to employ a sufficient thickness of concrete around each bar to develop the necessary bond resistance between the steel and the concrete, it is necessary to provide an adequate cover of concrete over the bars. Also, unless grouped as permitted by BS8110 and CP110 (see *Table 139*), sufficient space must also be left between adjacent bars. To comply with the requirements of these Codes the minimum concrete cover should be as given on *Table 139*: it should be noted that these values relate to *all* reinforcement (i.e. including links etc.). BS5337 specifies that the minimum cover to all reinforcement must be not less than 40 mm, and that this value should be increased where the surface is liable to erosion, abrasion or contact with particularly aggressive liquid.

The cover provided to protect the reinforcement from the effects of exposure may be insufficient for adequate fire resistance. Details of minimum thicknesses of concrete cover to main bars to provide specified periods of fire resistance according to BS8110: Part 2 are given on *Table 81*.

Since much of the deterioration of reinforced concrete is due to the provision of insufficient cover to the bars, a designer should not hesitate to increase the minimum cover if it is thought desirable to do so. However, excessive thicknesses of cover are to be avoided since any increase will also increase the surface crack width.

4.7.5 Minimum spacing of bars

BS8110 and CP110 requirements regarding the minimum spacing between individual bars or groups of bars are summarized on *Table 139*.

In other cases the distance between two bars in any layer in a beam should normally be not less than the diameter of the bar, or 25 mm or 1 in, or the largest size of aggregate plus 6 mm or 1/4 in, whichever is the greater. The minimum clear distance between successive layers of bars in a beam should be 12 mm or 1/2 in and this distance should be maintained by providing 12 mm or 1/2 in spacer bars at 1 m or 3 ft centres throughout the length of the beam wherever two or more layers of reinforcement occur. Where the bars from transverse beams pass between reinforcement layers, spacer bars are unnecessary. If the bars in a beam exceed 25 mm or 1 in in diameter, it is preferable to increase the space between layers to about 25 mm or 1 in. If the concrete is to be compacted by vibration, a space of at least 75 mm or 3 in should be provided between groups of bars to allow a poker-type or similar vibrator to be inserted.

Chapter 5
Resistance of structural members

5.1 PROPERTIES OF CROSS-SECTIONS OF MEMBERS

The geometrical properties of plane figures, the shapes of which conform to those of the cross-sections of common reinforced concrete members, are given in *Table 98*. The data include areas, section moduli, moments of inertia, and radii of gyration. Curves to simplify the calculation of the moments of inertia of T-sections, which are also applicable to other flanged sections such as L-beams and inverted channels, are given in *Table 101*. These curves are suitable for cases when the amount of reinforcement provided need not be taken into account, as in the case when comparing moments of inertia (see section 16.1).

The data given in *Tables 99* and *100* apply to reinforced concrete members having rectilinear and polygonal cross-sections when the reinforcement is taken into account on the basis of the modular ratio. Two conditions are considered, namely when the entire section is subjected to stress, and when the concrete in tension in members subjected to bending is not taken into account. The data given for the former condition include the effective area, the position of the centroid, the moment of inertia, the section modulus and the radius of gyration. For the condition when a member is subjected to bending and the concrete is assumed to be ineffective in tension, the data provided include the position of the neutral axis, the lever-arm, and the moment of resistance. The corresponding general formulae for regular and irregular sections are given in Chapter 19.

5.2 DESIGN OF BEAMS AND SLABS

At the time of writing, three basic methods of designing reinforced concrete members are permitted by the Codes of Practice in current use in the UK, namely limit-state analysis, load-factor design and modular-ratio theory. Both the modular-ratio and the load-factor method are permitted by CP114; all design to both BS8110 and CP110 is undertaken on the basis of limit-state principles. All three methods employ certain common basic assumptions, e.g. that the distribution of strain across a section is linear and that the strength of concrete in tension is usually neglected, together with other assumptions that differ from method to method: these assumptions are summarized briefly in the following sections.

For many years the modular-ratio or elastic method has been used to prepare designs that are normally safe and reasonably efficient for many widely differing types of structures. The method is based on a consideration of the behaviour under service or working loads only, assuming that both steel and concrete behave perfectly elastically, and employing permissible stresses determined by dividing the material strength by an appropriate overall factor of safety.

Modular-ratio design has two principal shortcomings. Although the assumption that the concrete behaves elastically is not seriously incorrect within the range of stresses used in design this does not hold for higher stresses, with the result that at failure the distribution of stress over a section differs markedly from that under service loads. It is thus impossible to predict accurately the ratio between service loading and that causing collapse (i.e. the factor of safety) on the basis of modular-ratio design, and sections designed to behave similarly under working loads may have entirely different safety factors depending on the proportions, positioning and relative strengths of the materials provided. The second principal drawback of the method is that certain types of modular-ratio design, e.g. sections containing large amounts of compression steel, are uneconomic and impractical as the section as a whole will fail before the full resistance of its components is realized.

To overcome such shortcomings, the load-factor or ultimate-load method was introduced in the 1957 edition of CP114. With this method the resistance of a section is assessed as failure is approached. However, to avoid the necessity of employing both permissible service stresses and ultimate stresses in a single design document, the load-factor theory, as presented in CP114, was modified to enable the same permissible stresses employed in modular-ratio design to be used. This adjustment also avoided the need to analyse a structure for service loading when design was to modular-ratio principles and for ultimate loading when load-factor design was undertaken.

The familiarity resulting from the introduction of basic load-factor principles in 1957 was instrumental in making it possible to omit from CP110, published in 1972, any explicit reference to modular-ratio theory and to introduce a comprehensive design method, the limit-state theory, in which the requirements for strength and stability are expressed in terms of ultimate loads and ultimate stresses while satisfactory behaviour under service loads is also ensured. By introducing two partial safety factors, one relating to loads and the other to materials, uncertainties that arise in assessing values for these terms are kept separate and, as further statistical data become available, it will be possible to amend the values of γ used in design calculations without having to make major revisions to the Code.

Since the publication of CP110, other documents have appeared in which limit-state theory forms the design basis. The Code of Practice for bridges, BS5400, is conceived wholly in limit-state terms. In the document for water-containing structures (BS5337), however, the designer is given the choice of either following limit-state requirements (in which the limit-state of cracking plays a dominant role) based on those in CP110, or designing in accordance with modular-ratio theory. BS8110, the successor to CP110, which was published in 1985, is also written solely in terms of the limit-state method.

5.3 LIMIT-STATE METHOD: ULTIMATE LIMIT-STATE

When designing in accordance with limit-state principles as embodied in BS8110 and similar documents, each reinforced concrete section is first designed to meet the most critical limit-state and then checked to ensure that the remaining limit-states are not reached. For the majority of sections the critical condition to be considered is the ultimate limit-state, at which the strength of each section is assessed on the basis of conditions at failure. When the member has been designed to meet this limit-state it should be checked to ensure compliance with the requirements of the various serviceability limit-states, such as deflection and cracking, as described later. However, since certain serviceability requirements, e.g. the selection of an adequate ratio of span to effective depth to prevent excessive deflection and the choice of a suitable bar spacing to prevent excessive cracking occurring, clearly also influence the strength of the section, the actual design process actually involves the simultaneous consideration of requirements for various limit-states. Nevertheless the normal process in preparing a design is to ensure that the strength of each section at failure is adequate while also complying with the necessary requirements for serviceability.

5.3.1 Basic assumptions

In assessing the strength of any section at failure by rigorous limit-state analysis, the following four basic assumptions are laid down in BS8110 and CP110:

1. The resistance of the concrete in tension is ignored.
2. The distribution of strain across any section is linear, i.e. plane sections before bending remain plane after bending, and the strain at any point is proportional to its distance from the neutral axis.
3. The relationship between the stress and strain in the reinforcement is as shown in the diagrams on *Table 103*.
4. The relationship between the stress and strain in the concrete is as shown in the diagram on *Table 102*. Alternatively the distribution of stress in the concrete at failure may be satisfactorily represented by a uniform stress acting over most or all of the compression zone. In both cases the maximum strain at the compression face should be taken as 0.35% and the depth of the compression zone is limited to one-half of the effective depth of the section if tension steel only is provided.

Since the strain distribution across the compression zone is linear, the first of the two relationships in assumption 4 results in the consideration of a concrete 'stress-block' having a shape which consists of a combination of a rectangle and a parabola: it is hereafter referred to as the *parabolic-rectangular stress-block*. An interesting feature is that the relative areas contributed to the stress-block by the parabola and the rectangle depend on the concrete strength, and consequently the resulting expressions for the total compressive force in the concrete, the position of the centroid of compression, and the lever arm are rather complex. Data to facilitate the calculation of the shape, size etc. of this stress-block and to simplify the use of the stress–strain curve are given in *Table 102*: see also section 20.1.1.

The alternative assumption of a uniform distribution of stress in the concrete leads to a uniform rectangular stress-block. BS8110 proposes a stress of $4f_{cu}/9$ extending over a depth of $0.9x$ with a centroid at a depth of $0.45x$, while CP110 adopts a stress of $2f_{cu}/5$ extending to the neutral axis with a centroid that is located at one-half of the depth of the compression zone.

As a result of assumption 3 above, the design stress in the reinforcement depends on the corresponding strain in the steel. Since this is determined by the linear distribution of strain across the section being considered, which in turn is controlled by the maximum strain in the concrete and the position of the neutral axis, the strain and thus the stress in the steel are functions of the ratio of x/d. Thus, as explained in section 20.1.2, the maximum design stress f_{yd2} in the tension reinforcement can be directly related to f_y, γ_m and x/d, while the maximum design stress f_{yd1} in the compression reinforcement is related to $f_y, \gamma_m, x/d$ and d'/d. Then if the ratios x/d and d'/d are known or assumed, the corresponding design stresses f_{yd1} and f_{yd2} can be calculated for given values of f_y and γ_m by using the expressions given on *Table 103*; whereas, if the value of f_y corresponds to those given in BS8110 or CP110 and $\gamma_m = 1.15$, f_{yd1} and f_{yd2} can be read from the scales on *Table 104*.

5.3.2 Design methods using rigorous analysis

Position of neutral axis. A feature of the ultimate limit-state design procedure is that when rigorous analysis is employed the choice of the neutral-axis position is left to the designer, provided that, for sections reinforced in tension only, the depth to the neutral axis x must not exceed $d/2$. The correct choice of x is important for two principal reasons. Firstly, the amount of moment redistribution permitted by BS8110 and CP110 at a given section is related to x/d by the expression $x/d \ngtr (0.6 - \beta_{red})$, where β_{red} is the ratio of the reduction in resistance moment to the largest moment. Thus to achieve a 10% reduction in moment, x/d must not exceed 0.5; for the maximum permissible reduction of 30%, x/d must not exceed 0.3; and so on. Thus x/d should be selected to permit the required amount of moment redistribution to be achieved.

In addition, as previously described and as can easily be seen from *Table 103*, the ratio x/d also determines the strains and hence the corresponding design stresses in the tension and compression steel. For ratios of x/d below the limiting value of $805d'/(805 - f_y)d$ with BS8110 and $2.333d'/d$ with CP110, the strain in the compression steel is less than the limiting value, and the corresponding design stress f_{yd1} in this reinforcement must be reduced accordingly. For greater ratios of x/d both tension and compression steel work at their full design strength until x/d reaches a value of $805/(805 + f_y)$ with BS8110 and $805/(1265 + f_y)$ with CP110; at this point the critical strain in the tension steel is reached, and beyond it the design stress f_{yd2} must be reduced as indicated on the table to correspond to the limiting strain and hence the actual value of x/d.

It is clearly advantageous where possible to avoid providing reinforcement that is working at less than its maximum design value. It is usually equally clearly advantageous to make x as large as practicable since this means that, in sections reinforced in tension only, a given resistance moment can be provided with the minimum effective depth, whereas in sections with both tension and compression steel the greater the value of x the less the amount of compression steel required. Thus, unless the value of x/d is limited by the need to obtain a certain proportion of moment redistribution, it should normally be selected so that the corresponding strain in the tension reinforcement is at its limiting value (i.e. at points A and C on the stress–strain design curves for BS8110 and CP110, respectively). In sections reinforced in both tension and compression, it can be shown that such a choice usually minimizes the total reinforcement needed to provide a specified resistance moment with a section of given dimensions. A lesser value of x/d requires more compression steel but less tension reinforcement, while the decrease in compression steel required with a greater value of x/d is more than outweighed by the increase in tension reinforcement needed to work at the lower permissible stress: see the diagram and discussion in section 20.1.4.

Alternatively, with sections reinforced in tension only, it may be advantageous to adopt the maximum permissible value of x/d of 0.5 even if this involves reducing f_{yd2}. When designing to BS8110 requirements and where, with CP110, f_y does not exceed 345 N/mm^2, the corresponding limiting value of x/d to avoid reducing the design stress in the tension steel is not less than 0.5 and thus it is not necessary to reduce f_{yd2}. However, according to CP110, when f_y exceeds 345 N/mm^2 (i.e. for all types of steel described in clause 3.1.4.3 other than hot-rolled mild steel) the limiting value of x/d is less than 0.5, and if x is taken as $d/2$ the stress in the tension steel must be reduced accordingly. This situation thus resembles that in modular-ratio design where, for a given permissible concrete stress, the limiting value of M_d/bd^2 and thus the resistance moment of a particular section reinforced in tension only can be increased by decreasing the stress in the steel, although this expedient is 'uneconomic' in terms of the extra reinforcement that must be provided.

In such a section a slight design complication arises if the actual depth of section provided is greater than that theoretically needed, since this effectively reduces the x/d ratio. Thus to determine the true amount of tension steel necessary it is first desirable to recalculate the actual value of x/d in order to establish the corresponding design stress in the steel. While it is always safe to employ the value of f_{yd2} corresponding to the minimum effective depth and merely to adjust the amount of reinforcement necessary in proportion to the ratio of the minimum effective depth to that provided, it is more economical to recalculate x/d as described, and this is perhaps simpler if a uniform rectangular stress-block is adopted. The procedure is illustrated in the examples in section 20.1.

5.3.3 Simplified formulae for rectangular and flanged sections

As an alternative to rigorous limit-state analysis using basic principles, CP110 provides a series of simplified expressions for designing rectangular and flanged sections reinforced in tension only and rectangular beams with both tension and compression reinforcement, provided that d' does not exceed $d/5$. The formulae are based on the assumption of a rectangular concrete stress-block with a uniform concrete stress of $2f_{cu}/5$ and with a fixed depth to the neutral axis x of $d/2$ when compression reinforcement is provided, so that moment redistribution is limited to a maximum of 10% when these expressions are used.

An interesting feature, however, is that when using these expressions it is not necessary to reduce the design stress in the tension reinforcement even when x/d exceeds the value at which the strain in this reinforcement becomes less than $0.002 + f_y/230\,000$. Thus for sections reinforced in tension only, when adopting a rectangular concrete stress-block, the use of these simplified formulae occasionally leads to the need for slightly less reinforcement to resist a given moment than when a rigorous analysis is undertaken, in those cases where the limiting strain would otherwise require a reduction in the corresponding design stress. For example, with $f_y = 460$ N/mm^2, this would apply for values of M_u/bd^2f_{cu} of between 0.143 and 0.150, and with the greater value about 4.5% less reinforcement would be needed when using the simplified expressions. Since the CP110 simplified expressions are derived from the same fundamental assumptions, the resistance moment due to the concrete is near-identical whether these expressions or a rigorous analysis with a rectangular stress-block are employed; the only discrepancies result from some simplification in the numerical values in the expressions given in CP110.

BS8110 also provides (in clause 3.4.4.4) various design expressions. Unlike those in CP110, however, the BS8110 formulae are more strictly in accordance with rigorous analysis using a uniform rectangular concrete stress-block, and their use shows little saving in labour over the exact expressions given on *Table 105*.

5.3.4 Comparison between design methods

With rigorous limit-state analysis, the direct resistance in compression obtained when a uniform rectangular stress-block is assumed is $0.4f_{cu}bx$, and thus ranges from $10bx$ when f_{cu} is equal to 25 N/mm^2 to $20bx$ when f_{cu} equals

Concrete strength (N/mm^2)	Neutral-axis depth factor x/d	Resistance moment M_u			Percentage increase in M_u provided by (i)	
		(i) Parabolic-rectangular stress-block	(ii) BS8110 rectangular stress-block	(iii) CP110 rectangular stress-block	over (ii)	over (iii)
25	0.3	$2.607bd^2$	$2.595bd^2$	$2.550bd^2$	+0.5	+2.2
	0.6*	$4.389bd^2$	$4.380bd^2$	$4.200bd^2$	+0.2	+4.5
30	0.3	$3.101bd^2$	$3.114bd^2$	$3.060bd^2$	−0.4	+1.3
	0.6*	$5.231bd^2$	$5.256bd^2$	$5.040bd^2$	−0.5	+3.8
50	0.3	$5.015bd^2$	$5.190bd^2$	$5.100bd^2$	−3.4	−1.7
	0.6*	$8.516bd^2$	$8.760bd^2$	$8.400bd^2$	−2.8	+1.4

*Such a value can only be adopted if compression reinforcement is provided.

$50\,N/mm^2$. These values compare with resistances of $10.06bx$ and $19.26bx$ respectively when a parabolic-rectangular stress-block is assumed. It can in fact be shown that for values of f_{cu} of less than $28.14\,N/mm^2$ the choice of a parabolic-rectangular stress-block gives the greater direct resistance, whereas for higher values of f_{cu} the resistance due to a uniform rectangular stress-block is greater. Also, the depth to the centroid of a parabolic-rectangular stress-block varies between $0.455x$ and $0.438x$ as f_{cu} increases from 25 to $50\,N/mm^2$, compared with constant values of $0.45x$ and $0.5x$ for a uniform rectangular stress-block according to BS8110 and CP110 respectively.

The relationship between the moments of resistance provided by the alternative assumptions depends on the ratio of x/d selected, but typical comparative figures are as in the accompanying table. These values indicate that, while normally showing a slight advantage over the CP110 uniform rectangular distribution of stress, the choice of a parabolic-rectangular stress distribution in the concrete is most advantageous for lower values of f_{cu} and higher ratios of x/d. Perhaps more important when working to CP110 is the fact that, for a given applied ultimate moment, a parabolic-rectangular distribution of stress normally leads to the need for a lower x/d ratio and thus, if this ratio is greater than that corresponding to the critical strain in the tension reinforcement, to the need to reduce the design stress in the steel less severely than if a uniform rectangular stress-block is adopted. However, for other than simple rectangular sections the calculations with a parabolic-rectangular stress-block are often extremely complex and the choice of a uniform rectangular stress-block here is most desirable.

When designing sections reinforced in tension only to CP110, it is sometimes slightly advantageous and never disadvantageous to use the simplified Code expressions rather than to carry out a rigorous analysis with a uniform rectangular stress-block. However, a slight advantage, in terms of achieving an increased resistance moment and a slight reduction in steel, may be obtained by adopting a parabolic-rectangular stress-block, expecially with low values of f_{cu}.

It is shown later that the assumption of the CP110 uniform rectangular stress-block is particularly disadvantageous when considering sections subjected to combined bending and thrust where the latter predominates. This is because, when x equals h for example, the assumed shape of the parabolic-rectangular (and BS8110 uniform rectangular) stress-block still provides some resistance to bending, whereas in such a condition the CP110 stress-block does not. The purpose of the uniform rectangular stress-block is to provide a simple yet fairly accurate representation of the parabolic-rectangular distribution to use in calculations which would otherwise be unnecessarily complex (ref. 35); in BS8110 the correspondence has been considerably improved, while simplicity has been maintained, by employing a uniform stress of $0.67/\gamma_m$ over a depth of $0.9x$, as can be seen from the table in this section. The table also indicates that when working to BS8110 with concrete strengths of $30\,N/mm^2$ or greater it is more economical, as well as simpler, to employ a uniform rectangular rather than a parabolic-rectangular stress-block.

For sections reinforced in tension and compression, use of the appropriate CP110 simplified expressions is generally uneconomical, since a design stress of $0.72f_y$ is specified in the compression reinforcement as a simplification for $2000f_y/(2300+f_y)$, resulting in the need to provide much higher proportions of ρ' than when a rigorous analysis is employed. This simplification is particularly disadvantageous for low values of f_y: for $f_y = 250\,N/mm^2$, for example, the accurate expression for $f_{yd1} = 0.784f_y$, and thus nearly 9% more compression steel must be provided if the simplified expressions are used for design.

5.3.5 Design procedures and aids

Rectangular sections reinforced in tension only. When designing a rectangular section reinforced in tension only to resist a given ultimate moment, the normal procedure is to calculate the minimum effective depth needed but to provide a somewhat greater value of d based on the adoption of a convenient round figure for the overall section depth; the steel required is then calculated for this increased depth. With rigorous limit-state design this procedure may occasionally be slightly more complex than usual since with CP110. If f_y is greater than $345\,N/mm^2$ and d_{min} has been determined by adopting a value of x/d that exceeds that corresponding to the critical strain in the tension reinforcement, it is then necessary to recalculate the actual ratio of x/d

corresponding to the effective depth provided in order to determine the actual stress in the steel, before the area of reinforcement needed can be calculated. Thus for such sections the use of design charts is particularly advantageous since the necessary manipulations can be undertaken swiftly and simply.

The design charts in Part 3 of BS8110 and Part 2 of CP110 are based on the adoption of a parabolic-rectangular concrete stress-block with rigorous limit-state analysis. Those forming *Tables 110* and *111* of this book have been prepared using the BS8110 uniform rectangular stress-block with rigorous limit-state theory, while those provided on *Tables 112* to *114* employ the CP110 simplified expressions. All of these charts can only be used for the types of steel having the values of f_y set out in clauses 3.1.7.4 of BS8110 and 3.1.4.3 of CP110. For other values of f_y, the simplified expressions given in BS8110 and CP110 are the least trouble to apply, either in their original form or as rearranged on *Tables 105* and *106*: see also ref. 79. A similar chart to those given on *Tables 112* to *114* but catering for any value of f_y forms data sheet 12 in *Examples of the Design of Buildings*.

The ultimate moments of resistance and areas of steel required for slabs of various overall thicknesses are given in *Tables 115* and *116*. Those in *Table 115*, for values of f_{cu} of 25, 30 and 40 N/mm^2 and f_y of 250 and 460 N/mm^2, have been calculated using the BS8110 uniform rectangular stress-block and rigorous limit-state analysis: those forming *Table 116*, for values of f_{cu} of 20, 25 and 30 N/mm^2 and f_y of 250, 425 and 460 N/mm^2, have been calculated using the simplified design expression given in CP110.

Rectangular sections with tension and compression reinforcement. When both tension and compression reinforcement is provided, the dimensions of the section are normally predetermined or assumed and it is merely necessary to calculate the areas of steel required. Since with a rigorous analysis the choice of x/d is left to the designer unless controlled by the amount of redistribution required, a wide range of values of ρ and ρ' is usually possible, depending on the particular ratio of x/d selected.

Design curves based on a rigorous limit-state analysis with a parabolic-rectangular distribution of stress in the concrete are given in Part 3 of BS8110 and Part 2 of CP110, and enable ρ and ρ' corresponding to given values of M_u/bd^2 and x/d to be selected for a series of values of f_{cu}, f_y and d'/d. However, as illustrated in the examples in section 20.1, the design of such sections from basic principles or formulae is rather simpler than in the case of sections reinforced in tension only, and such methods may be found useful to avoid the complex interpolation that may be needed when sets of design charts are employed. Alternatively, *Tables 105* and *107* may be found useful for checking designs prepared by other means.

Design charts based on rigorous limit-state analysis with a uniform rectangular distribution of stress in the concrete are given in ref. 5.

Since they presuppose a ratio of x/d of 0.5, the CP110 simplified expressions lead to specific values of ρ and ρ' for given values of M_u/bd^2, f_{cu}, f_y and d'/d. The design charts forming *Tables 112* and *114* have been extended to give values for ρ and ρ' for sections reinforced in tension and compression for values of M_u/bd^2 of up to 6 when $d'/d = 0.1$: other ratios of d'/d can be catered for as described in the notes on the tables. As discussed above, the use of the CP110 simplified expressions is rather uneconomic, especially when providing large proportions of compression steel, but the inclusion of these data on the same design charts may be useful for preliminary design or checking purposes.

By setting a similar restriction of $x/d = 0.5$, similar curves for the design of doubly-reinforced sections according to rigorous limit-state analysis with the BS8110 uniform rectangular stress-block are included in *Tables 110* and *111*. These curves are only applicable when $d'/d = 0.1$, but other ratios of d'/d can be catered for as described in section 20.1.6. To design doubly-reinforced sections with other ratios of x/d it is simplest to use the design formulae given in *Table 105*.

Flanged and other sections. When designing flanged sections, the basic dimensions have usually already been decided. Three possible conditions may occur, as shown in the sketches at the bottom of *Table 109*. If the value of x corresponding to a given applied ultimate moment and calculated on the effective width of the flange is found to be less than the flange thickness h_f, the section may be designed for bending as a simple rectangular beam using the design methods and aids already described. However, if x exceeds h_f it is necessary to consider the assistance of the web section. If a parabolic-rectangular stress-block is assumed and $(1 - k_3)x$ exceeds h_f, the distribution of compressive stress over the flange area is uniform and is equal to $4f_{cu}/9$. However, if x is between h_f and $h_f/(1-k_3)$ the parabolic-rectangular diagram representing the compressive stress in the flange is truncated, as shown on *Table 109*. In this case the adoption of a rectangular stress-block is recommended, as such calculations with a parabolic-rectangular stress-block are unnecessarily complex: a suitable design procedure is outlined by the flow-chart forming *Table 109*.

The formulae for flanged beams given in clauses 3.4.4.4 and 3.4.4.5 of BS8110 are based on rigorous analysis with a uniform rectangular stress-block and, when x exceeds h_f, are only applicable where redistribution is limited to 10% (i.e. $x/d \geqslant 0.5$) and where compression steel is unnecessary. If these conditions are not met the design procedure outlined on *Table 108* must be adopted. Otherwise such sections can be designed using *Tables 110* and *111*, where limiting ratios of h_f/d corresponding to values of M_u/bd^2 and f_{cu} are plotted. Provided that the ratio of h_f/d read from the appropriate chart does not exceed the true value, the section acts as a rectangular beam: otherwise the procedure set out on *Table 108* must be employed.

The simplified expressions given in CP110 include formulae for flanged beams that give the maximum ultimate moment of resistance of the concrete section based on the assumption of a rectangular distribution of stress in the concrete over the depth of the flange only. These expressions may be rearranged to give limiting values of h_f corresponding to given values of M_u/bd^2 and f_{cu}, and as such they are incorporated on the design charts on *Tables 112–114*. Provided that the required ratio of h_f/d read from the charts for given values of M_u/bd^2 and f_{cu} does not exceed the actual ratio of h_f/d provided, the section acts as a rectangular beam and can be designed as such from these charts. If not, a rigorous limit-state analysis must be undertaken as outlined on *Table 109*.

Sections having other irregular sections can be designed most conveniently by employing a rigorous limit-state analysis with a rectangular concrete stress-block. A typical example of such a calculation is given in example 5 in section 20.1.

5.4 MODULAR-RATIO METHOD

The modular-ratio method is based on a consideration of the behaviour of the section under service loads only. The strength of the concrete in tension is neglected (except in certain cases in the design of liquid-containing structures) and it is assumed that for both concrete and reinforcement the relationship between stress and strain is linear (i.e. that the materials behave perfectly elastically). The distribution of strain across a section is also assumed to be linear (i.e. sections that are plane before bending remain plane after bending). Thus the strain at any point on a section is proportional to the distance of the point from the neutral axis and, since the relationship between stress and strain is linear, the stress is also proportional to the distance from the neutral axis. This gives a triangular distribution of stress in the concrete, ranging from zero at the neutral axis to a maximum at the compression face of the section. Assuming that no slipping occurs between the steel and the surrounding concrete, the strain in both materials at that point is identical and, since the modulus of elasticity E of a material is equal to the stress f divided by the strain ε, the ratio of the stresses in the materials thus depends only on the ratio of the elastic moduli of steel and concrete. This ratio is known as the modular ratio α_e. The value of E for steel is about 210×10^3 N/mm^2, but for concrete the value of E depends on several factors (see section 18.1.4) including the strength of the concrete. In some Codes of Practice a variable modular ratio depending on the concrete strength is recommended, but others, such as CP114 and BS5337, specify a fixed value irrespective of the strength of the concrete. Commonly adopted values of α_e are 15 for normal-weight concrete and 30 for lightweight concrete.

The internal resistance moment of a member is assumed to result from the internal resisting couple due to the compressive resistance of the concrete (acting through the centroid of the triangular distribution of compressive stress) and the tensile resistance of the tension reinforcement. The arm of this resisting couple, i.e. the distance between the lines of action of the resultant forces, is known as the lever-arm. Formulae for the position of the neutral axis, the lever-arm, the moments of resistance and the maximum stresses in rectangular and flanged sections (i.e. T-beams and L-beams) resulting from the foregoing principles are given in *Table 117*. For beams of other regular cross-sections, the expressions for the lever-arm and moments of resistance given in *Tables 99* and *100* are applicable. For a member of any general or irregular cross-section, the method of design described in section 20.2.10 may be used.

According to modular-ratio theory, for members reinforced in tension only, each of the ratios involving the depth to the neutral axis (i.e. x/d), the lever-arm (z/d), the proportion of reinforcement (ρ), the ratio of maximum stresses (f_{st}/f_{cr}) and the moments of resistance of the section in terms of the maximum stress in the concrete or steel (M_d/bd^2f_{cr} and M_d/bd^2f_{st}) may be expressed directly in terms of each other individual ratio and b, d and α_e only. The relevant formulae are sometimes complex and are therefore not given here, but may easily be derived from the formulae given in *Table 117*. These interrelationships are shown by the scales on the left-hand side of *Table 120* for any modular ratio. When the value of α_e is 15, the terms involved are somewhat simplified, and the corresponding interrelationships are shown by the scales on the right-hand side of *Table 120*.

5.4.1 Rectangular beams

Formulae 1(b) and 1(c) in *Table 117* apply to rectangular beams whether reinforced in tension only or in tension and compression, and give the depth-to-neutral-axis ratio x/d in terms of the proportions of tension and compression steel, i.e. ρ and ρ' respectively. For sections reinforced in tension only, values of x/d corresponding to various values of ρ, or conversely, may be read from the scales on *Table 120*.

The expressions for the lever-arm z when tension steel only or both tension and compression steel are provided are given by the formulae 3 and 3(a) in *Table 117*.

The moment of resistance of a rectangular beam reinforced in tension only is given by formulae 5 and 5(a), depending on whether the resistance to compression or tension determines the strength. Values of these moments of resistance (M_d/bd^2f_{cr} and M_d/bd^2f_{st} respectively) corresponding to various values of ρ, x, z or f_{st}/f_{cr} may be read from the scales on *Table 120*.

The moment of resistance in compression can be expressed conveniently in terms of a factor K_{conc} such that $M_d = K_{conc}bd^2$. Values of $K_{conc}(=M_d/bd^2)$ for various stresses with $\alpha_e = 15$ can be read from the charts on *Table 118* in SI units and on *Table 119* in imperial units. The corresponding values of ρ required can also be read from these charts.

A more detailed account of the various design aids provided and of their use is given in section 20.2.

When a sufficient depth or breadth of beam cannot be obtained to provide enough compressive resistance from the concrete alone, compression reinforcement must be provided. This extra reinforcement is not generally economical, although some concrete is saved by its use, but in some cases, such as at the support sections of continuous beams, the ordinary arrangement of the reinforcement provides compression reinforcement conveniently. The maximum amount of such reinforcement should not exceed $0.04bh$ in accordance with CP114 and compression reinforcement in excess of this amount should be neglected in calculating the resistance of the beam.

If the compressive resistance provided by the concrete is not neglected, the moment of resistance of a beam with compression reinforcement is the sum of the moments of resistance of the concrete and the compression reinforcement. The moment of resistance of the concrete is calculated as for a beam with tension reinforcement only, and the additional moment of resistance due to the compression reinforcement is as given by formula 5(b) in *Table 117*, in which x is based on formula 1(c). The maximum stresses due to a given bending moment are derived from formulae 11, in which z is based on the value of z calculated from formula 3(a) or approximately from 3(b), and x is determined from formula 1(c); note that formula 3(b) does not apply if ρ' is small compared with ρ.

The rational limit of application of the formulae for rectangular beams with compression reinforcement is when $A'_s = A_s$, and for this condition the moment of resistance is given by

$$M_d = \left[\frac{1}{2}\frac{x}{d}\left(1 - \frac{1}{3}\frac{x}{d}\right) + \rho'(\alpha_e - 1)\left(\frac{x - d'}{x}\right)\left(1 - \frac{d'}{d}\right)\right] f_{cr} b d^2$$

and the proportion of tension reinforcement, which is equal to the proportion of compression reinforcement, is given by

$$\rho = \rho' = \frac{1}{2}\frac{x}{d} \bigg/ \left[\frac{f_{st}}{f_{cr}} - (\alpha_e - 1)\left(\frac{x - d'}{x}\right)\right]$$

To prevent the compression reinforcement from buckling, links should be provided at a pitch not exceeding twelve times the diameter of the smallest bar in the compression reinforcement. The binders should be so arranged that each bar is effectively restrained.

5.4.2 Balanced design

In the design of a beam it is of course necessary to ensure that the permissible stresses in the steel and the concrete are not exceeded, but it is also desirable generally for the maximum stresses to be equal to the permissible stresses. When this condition is obtained, the design is considered to be *balanced*. There is, for each ratio of permissible stresses, a proportion of tension and compression (if provided) reinforcement which gives balanced design, and expressions for this amount are given in formulae 9 and 9(a) in *Table 117*. The percentage of reinforcement corresponding to the proportion for a given ratio of stresses is sometimes called the *economic* percentage, but this may be somewhat misleading since the relative amounts of steel and concrete in the most economical beam depend not only on the permissible stresses but also on the cost of the materials and formwork.

5.4.3 Steel-beam theory

If the amount of compression reinforcement required equals or exceeds the amount of tension reinforcement when using the formulae in *Table 117*, the beam may be designed by the steel-beam theory in which the compressive resistance provided by the concrete is neglected and $A_s = A'_s = M_d/(d - d')f_{st}$. When this method of design is adopted, the spacing of the links should not exceed eight times the diameter of the bars forming the compression reinforcement, and f_{st} should be equal to the permissible value of f_{sc}. The indiscriminate application of the steel-beam theory is not recommended. At first sight it might seem that a beam of any size can be designed to resist almost any bending moment irrespective of the compressive stress in the concrete. In fact, however, with a theoretical stress of 125 N/mm^2 in the reinforcement, the theoretical compressive stress in the surrounding concrete may exceed 8 N/mm^2, which for ordinary concrete leaves very little margin for accidental overloading, the differences between theoretical and actual bending moments and stresses, poor workmanship, and similar factors. Partial safeguards against unreasonable use of the steel-beam theory include the provision of a sufficient area of concrete to resist the shearing forces, the space required for the bars in the top and bottom of the beam, and the reduction of the lever-arm that results from the fact that the large numbers of bars needed require more than one layer of reinforcement in the top and bottom of the section.

5.4.4 Flanged beams

If a flanged section, such as a T-beam, an L-beam or an I-beam is constructed monolithically with the slab, the slab forms the compression flange of the beam if the bending moment is such that compression is induced in the top of the beam. If a slab extends an equal distance on each side of the rib, i.e. the beam is a T-beam, or if the slab extends on one side of the rib only, i.e. in the case of an L-beam (or an inverted L-beam), the breadth of slab assumed to form the effective compression flange should not exceed the least of the dimensions given in the lower part of *Table 91*.

There are two design conditions to consider, namely when the neutral axis falls within the thickness of the slab and when the neutral axis is below the slab. In the former case a flanged beam is dealt with in exactly the same way as a rectangular beam having a breadth b equal to the effective width of the flange. If the neutral axis falls below the slab, the small compressive resistance afforded by the concrete between the neutral axis and the underside of the slab is often neglected, and then the corresponding formulae in *Table 117* apply. Note the approximate expression for the lever-arm in formula 4(a); this value is usually sufficiently accurate for most T-beams and L-beams.

It is uncommon for beams with compression flanges to require compression reinforcement, but if this is unavoidable the same principles apply as for rectangular beams. The theoretical formulae for this case are too complex to be of practical value, although they may be of some use for I-beams, the design of which is described in section 20.2.11.

5.4.5 Beams with concrete effective in tension

In the design of liquid-containing structures and some other structures, the resistance to cracking of the concrete in the tension zone is important. Such members are therefore calculated taking the concrete as effective in tension. The corresponding formulae for rectangular and flanged beams are given in the lower part of *Table 91*.

5.4.6 Proportions and details of beams

The dimensions of beams are primarily determined from considerations of the moment of resistance and the resistance to shearing force, but beams having various ratios of depth to breadth may give the resistances required. In practice there are other factors that also affect the relative dimensions.

A rule for determining a trial section for a rectangular beam or T-beam designed by modular-ratio principles is that the total depth should be equal to about one-twelfth of the span. The breadth of a rectangular beam or the breadth of the rib of a T-beam is generally from one-third to equal to the total depth; for rectangular beams in buildings a reasonable breadth is one-half to two-thirds of the total depth; in industrial structures beams having proportions of breadth to depth of one-half to one-third are often convenient. The lower ratio in each case applies principally to T-beams. Much, however, depends upon the conditions controlling a structure, especially such factors as clearances below beams and the cross-sectional area required to give sufficient resistance to shearing. The breadth of the beams should also conform to the width of steel forms or timber commercially available. In buildings, the breadth of beams may have to conform to the nominal thicknesses of brick or block walls. If the ratio of the span to the breadth of a beam exceeds 30, the permissible compressive stress in the concrete must be reduced.

The breadth of the rib of a flanged beam is generally determined by the cross-sectional area required to resist the applied shearing force, but consideration must also be given to accommodating the tension reinforcement.

Various methods of designing sections or of determining the stresses induced therein, by using either charts, tables or formulae, are given in section 20.2, together with examples in the use of these tables.

5.4.7 Solid slabs

A slab is generally calculated for a strip 1 m or 1 ft wide; hence a slab is equivalent to a rectangular beam with $b = 1000$ mm or 12 in. The moment of resistance and the area of reinforcement required are then expressed per unit width. The formulae in *Table 117* for rectangular beams also apply to slabs but, as b is constant, the expressions may be modified to facilitate computation. For example, the effective depth and area of reinforcement required can both be expressed as simple functions of the applied bending moment.

Notes on the reinforcement of solid slabs are given in section 20.5.1. The use of compression reinforcement in slabs is unusual but, if provided, the calculation is the same as for a rectangular beam. Links or other means of preventing the compression bars from buckling should be provided at centres not exceeding twelve times the diameter of the compression bars; otherwise the bars in compression should be neglected when computing the resistance. Reinforcement to resist shearing is not generally necessary in slabs. Shearing stresses need not normally be considered unless the span is small and the load is large. The thickness of a slab should comply with the limiting span/effective-depth ratio requirements.

5.5 SERVICEABILITY LIMIT-STATES

The two principal controlling conditions corresponding to serviceability limit-state requirements according to BS8110 and CP110 are the prevention of excessive deflection and the prevention of excessive crack widths. To minimize the amount of calculation that would otherwise be necessary, both Codes provide various rules regarding serviceability; compliance with these requirements should ensure satisfactory behaviour under the loads corresponding to this limit-state. The simplified rules set out in these Codes may, however, be disregarded provided that the designer can produce appropriate detailed calculations to show that the resulting sections meet specified basic criteria for maximum deflection and maximum crack width: the same calculations are also necessary for those cases where the simplified requirements given in the Codes are not applicable. Methods of producing such calculations are described in Part 2 of BS8110 and Appendix A of CP110. These requirements are summarized on *Tables 136* and *138*.

It should be noted that, even if design in accordance with either Code is not being undertaken, compliance with the requisite requirements may be advantageous since the criteria presented represent the synthesis of a very great deal of research into these important aspects of the behaviour of reinforced concrete members.

5.5.1 Deflection

The deflection of reinforced concrete members cannot be predicted with any certainty. This fact is not particularly important where only comparative deflections are required since the indefinite numerical values offset each other to a large extent. If actual deflection values must be calculated, they may be estimated reasonably well by the careful use of the rigorous procedure set out in BS8110 and CP110.

In the past, deflections have been calculated approximately from the expression Fl^3K'/E_cI_c, where F is the total service load on the member, l is the span, E_c is the modulus of elasticity of concrete in compression, I_c is the equivalent moment of inertia of the section and K' is the deflection coefficient depending on the type of loading and the conditions at the supports of the member. Values of K' for various types of loading can be obtained from the formulae and curves on *Tables 23* to *28*. If all the terms are in units of millimetres and newtons, the resulting deflection will be in millimetres; if they are in units of inches and pounds, the deflection will be in inches.

An appropriate value of E_c may be read from the curves on *Table 79*; however, if a more accurate value can be obtained from tests on the concrete to be used, this should be employed. The moment of inertia should be expressed in concrete units and should be that at the point of maximum positive bending moment. In this instance, the moment of inertia should be computed for the whole area of the concrete within the effective depth, i.e. the area of the concrete between the neutral axis and the tension reinforcement should be included as well as that above the neutral axis. The areas of tension and compression steel should be considered by transforming them into an equivalent additional area of concrete by multiplying the area of the reinforcement by the effective modular ratio $(\alpha_e - 1)$, where $\alpha_e = 200/E_c$ in metric units or $30 \times 10^6/E_c$ in imperial units. The moment of inertia should be taken about the centroid of the transformed area and is approximately $(1 + 4\alpha_e\rho)bd^3/12(1 + \alpha_e\rho)$ for a rectangular section reinforced in tension only, the proportion of tension reinforcement being ρ. The corresponding expressions for rectangular beams with compression steel and for T-beams are those for I_g given on *Table 136*.

The rigorous procedure described in BS8110 and CP110

which is summarized on *Table 136*, consists of an extended complex version of the above calculation. Having determined the service moment and the properties of the transformed section, and taking a value of E_c of one-half of the instantaneous value read from the graph on *Table 79* or obtained elsewhere, the particular curvature being considered is calculated on the assumption that the section is both cracked and uncracked, and the more critical value is adopted. The total long-term curvature is then evaluated by adding and subtracting the instantaneous and long-term curvatures due to the total load and permanent load as shown on *Table 136*, the effects of creep and shrinkage also being taken into account. Finally the actual deflection is calculated by integrating the curvature diagram for the member twice or by using a deflection factor K. This factor represents the numerical coefficient relating to the curvature at the point where the deflection is calculated (i.e. at midspan for a freely supported or fixed span and at the free end in the case of a simple cantilever) divided by the numerical coefficient representing the maximum bending moment on the member (or the maximum positive moment in the case of a fixed member). Note that if the curvature is measured at midspan the resulting deflection given by this method is that at midspan. If the load is not arranged symmetrically on the span this will be slightly less than the maximum deflection, but the resulting difference is negligible.

Instead of calculating the total long-term curvature and then calculating the resulting deflection, it is possible to determine the maximum deflection by summing the individual deflections obtained for the various loading conditions. By so doing the difficulty of having to select a particular value of K to represent the total loading arrangement is avoided. However, where the same type of loading occurs throughout, the previous method is perhaps simpler to follow.

BS8110 requires that, for appearance purposes, any deflection should be limited to span/250 and also, in order to prevent damage to non-structural elements, deflections must not exceed span/500 or 20 mm for brittle materials and span/350 or 20 mm for non-brittle materials and finishes. Lateral deflections due to wind must not exceed storey height/500.

The two basic requirements of CP110 are that the long-term deflection (including all time-dependent effects such as creep and shrinkage as well as those of temperature) of each horizontal member below the supports must not exceed span/250, and that any deflection occurring after the construction of a partition or the application of a finish must not exceed span/350 or 20 mm.

The rigorous procedure for calculating deflections is described in considerable detail in *Examples of the Design of Buildings*, which includes charts to assist in the calculation of the sectional properties of rectangular and flanged beams and to facilitate the calculation of K-factors. Area-moment coefficients are required when investigating the effects of the rotation of cantilever supports, and further charts giving such coefficients are provided. The rigorous procedure is also discussed at some length in ref. 36.

As already described, compliance with the Code requirements for the serviceability limit-state of deflection for beams and slabs can be achieved either by providing detailed calculations or by observing limiting slenderness ratios. The latter procedure involves selecting a basic ratio of span to effective depth relating to the actual span and the support fixity conditions, which is then multiplied by factors due to the amount of and service stress in the tension reinforcement and to the amount of compression steel provided. For flat slabs, hollow-block, ribbed and voided slabs, and flanged beams, multiplication by a further factor is necessary; if lightweight concrete is used, yet another multiplier must be employed.

Since the initial span/effective-depth ratio is directly related to the span, it is possible to simplify the foregoing procedure slightly by tabulating the effective depth corresponding to a given span with given fixity conditions. This basic value of d is then adjusted as necessary by multiplying it by various factors. Such a procedure is described in greater detail in section 20.4.2 and, to facilitate the process, scales from which the various factors involved may be read are set out on *Table 137*. Since the amounts of reinforcement required are normally not known until well after an initial knowledge of the span/effective-depth ratio is needed, the use of a cyclic trial-and-adjustment design procedure is usually required.

5.5.2 Cracking

The prevention of excessive cracking is the second of the two principal criteria for the serviceability limit-states as considered in BS8110 and CP110. Except in particularly aggressive environments when more stringent restrictions are imposed, the Code specifies that the surface width of cracks should not generally exceed 0.3 mm. Beeby (ref. 37) has shown that cracking in the tension zone of a member subjected to bending is due to the interaction of two basic patterns of cracking, of which one is controlled by the initial height of the cracks and the other is controlled by the arrangement of, and proximity to, the reinforcing bars. These patterns can be represented by a hyperbolic relationship which, in a rearranged and considerably simplified form, is that given in Part 2 of BS8110 and Appendix A of CP110.

Basically, the calculation procedure is as follows. Having calculated the service bending moment, the appropriate modular ratio is determined by dividing E_s (200 N/mm^2 or 30×10^6 lb/in^2) by $E_c/2$ (the factor of one-half is introduced to allow for creep). The next step is to evaluate the neutral-axis depth and lever-arm of the cracked transformed concrete section and to use the appropriate expression on *Table 138* to determine the strain at the point being considered. It is now necessary to take into account the stiffening effect of the concrete in the tension zone in order to obtain the average strain which, when substituted into the basic width equation, gives the resulting width.

In normal design, calculations are only needed to check that the maximum surface crack widths do not exceed the limiting value of 0.3 mm. The criteria controlling cracking are such that across the tension face of a beam or slab the width of crack rises from a minimum directly above a bar to a maximum midway between bars or at an edge. Over the sides of a beam the width varies from a minimum at the level of the tension steel to zero at the neutral axis, attaining a maximum value at a depth of about one-third of the distance from the tension bars to the neutral axis. Thus in such cases the task of the designer is simplified merely to checking that the width of crack midway between bars on the tension face and at the critical level on the beam sides does not exceed 0.3 mm. These requirements can be expressed instead as limiting values of the clear spacing between bars s_b and the ratio $(d-x)/(h-x)$. If the actual values comply with these specified limits the required crack width will not be exceeded.

The operations necessary to undertake the foregoing calculations, together with the formulae required, are set out in flow-chart form on *Table 138*.

To avoid the need to undertake such calculations, rules which are summarized in section 20.5.1 and *Table 139* are given in BS8110 and CP110 to limit the maximum spacing of bars in beams and slabs. If these requirements are met, satisfactory compliance with serviceability limit-state requirements regarding cracking will be achieved. Greater bar spacings may often be adopted if desired, but these must then be substantiated by detailed calculations made as described above.

The basic crack-width formula given in CP110 embodies a 20% probability of the predicted width being exceeded. When preparing this Code it was considered simpler to combine this high probability with the use of characteristic loads (which themselves are considered only to have a 5% chance of occurring during the life of the structure and would thus be unlikely to occur often or long enough to influence corrosion or appearance) than to invoke the more logically correct combination of a 5% probability of the prescribed crack width being exceeded, with the need to consider yet another, and lower, set of loads.

The requirements for limiting crack widths presented in the Code for water-containing structures (BS5337) are basically similar to those in BS8110 and CP110, but are modified to reduce the likelihood of the prescribed width being exceeded from 20% to 5% because of the potential seriousness if such wide cracks should occur. The limiting crack widths are also reduced to 0.1 mm and 0.2 mm for exposure classes A and B respectively: see section 20.3.1. BS5337 does not sanction the alternative simplified rules for compliance regarding cracking by limiting bar spacing as given in BS8110 and CP110. In other words, if limit-state design in accordance with BS5337 is being undertaken, rigorous crack-width calculations must always be made.

The crack-width calculation procedure is discussed at some length in *Examples of the Design of Buildings*, where various charts are provided to facilitate the determination of the properties of cracked transformed sections and to check that cracks exceeding 0.3 mm in width do not form.

5.6 LIQUID-CONTAINING STRUCTURES

The principal UK document dealing with the design of liquid-containing structures, BS5337 'The structural use of concrete for retaining aqueous liquids', describes two fundamentally different design methods. The first is a development of the limit-state principles presented in BS8110 and CP110, but in which the serviceability limit-state of cracking now plays a dominant role. Rigorous calculations to determine probable maximum surface crack widths may be undertaken, but these may be avoided by complying instead with deemed-to-satisfy requirements. By following these requirements when investigating tension resulting from bending, it becomes unnecessary to calculate the anticipated crack widths, provided that the stress in the steel under working conditions is limited to specified conservative values. These same values *must* also be observed when designing members to resist direct tension only (i.e. in this case the crack-width calculation procedure is not applicable).

The width of cracks which occur in immature concrete due to restrained shrinkage and movements resulting from the heat generated by hydration must also be investigated.

In addition BS5337 presents alternative requirements for designing sections to specified working stresses using conventional modular-ratio theory. This part of the document is, in fact, merely a revised version of the design procedure given in CP2007 'The design of reinforced and prestressed concrete for the storage of water and other aqueous liquids', which BS5337 has superseded (the changes of title and of the document from a Code of Practice to a British Standard indicate no change of status) and the modifications have been made to correspond with the requirements of the current edition of CP114.

Throughout BS5337 only two concrete grades, namely 25 and 30, are considered. Provided that adequate durability and workability are assured, the lower grade should normally be employed, since the use of a richer mix will accentuate any problems that arise from early thermal cracking.

Three classes of exposure, A, B, and C, are defined. The most severe condition, class A, corresponds to exposure to a moist or corrosive atmosphere or to alternate wetting and drying (e.g. the roof and upper walls of a storage tank), and for reinforced concrete it restricts the maximum calculated width of crack at the surface of a member to 0.1 mm. Class B relates to surfaces in continuous or almost continuous contact with liquid (e.g. the lower walls of a liquid container) and corresponds to a maximum crack width of 0.2 mm. The final exposure condition, class C, is that considered in Appendix A of CP110 (i.e. for a maximum crack width of 0.3 mm). If a member is not greater than 225 mm in thickness, both faces must be designed for the same class of exposure, but for thicker members each face may be designed for the class of exposure to which it is subjected. Details of the calculation procedure necessary to evaluate the maximum surface width of cracks are given in section 20.3.1, and the strength, limiting stresses etc. permitted in the materials according to the various methods of analysis are summarized on *Tables 121* and *132*.

To prevent the formation of excessively wide cracks due to shrinkage, thermal movement and so on, secondary reinforcement must be provided near each face. However, if the slab thickness does not exceed 200 mm, the Standard permits the total reinforcement in each direction to be combined in a single layer. BS5337 specifies that nominal minimum amounts of 0.15% of deformed high-yield bars or 0.25% of plain mild steel (in terms of the gross cross-sectional area of the slab) must be provided in each direction near each face in slabs conforming to exposure classes A or B. For exposure class C the requirements of CP110 must be followed, i.e. a single layer of reinforcement having an area of not less than 0.12% of high-yield reinforcement or 0.15% of mild steel should be provided. An alternative procedure for calculating the amount of secondary reinforcement needed is also described. The Standard implies that the designer is free to choose between providing the nominal amounts or undertaking the rigorous calculations. However, ref. 26 makes it clear that the specified nominal amounts, although ensuring that wide cracks will not form, may not restrict the width of those cracks that do occur to the limits required by class A or B exposure. To ensure that these requirements are observed, the calculation procedure must be adopted. Further details are given in section 20.3.1.

Although BS5337 permits either deformed high-yield or mild-steel reinforcement to be used, the slight additional cost of the former is outweighed by its superior bonding properties and it should be employed wherever possible. The characteristic strength of reinforcement is restricted to 425 N/mm^2. Where a member is subjected to predominantly direct tension, research into certain types of failure has shown that the anchorage-bond stresses in horizontal bars should be restricted to 70% of normal values.

When analysing structures to be designed in accordance with BS5337, no moment redistribution is permitted. Moments should be determined by undertaking an elastic analysis.

An important point to note is that when undertaking a design in accordance with BS5337 the normal rules governing the maximum spacing of reinforcing bars, such as those set out in BS8110 or CP110 (see *Table 139*), do not apply. This means that if the stresses in the reinforcement are not restricted to the deemed-to-satisfy values, detailed analysis to determine the calculated surface crack widths *must* be undertaken, even in the case of exposure class C. However, closer investigation shows that in such circumstances cracking forms the limiting criterion in only a very few situations. Normally the resistance of a section is controlled by its strength in bending.

5.7 SHEARING

Much research has recently been undertaken in the hope of obtaining a better understanding of the behaviour of reinforced concrete when subjected to shearing forces. As a result of this research, which is still continuing, various theories have been put forward to explain the action of shearing forces after cracks have started to form and to give suitable methods for designing shearing reinforcement. One such theory, known as the truss-block method, is discussed in some detail in ref. 38, and an extensive general review of various theories of shearing is given in ref. 39.

Shearing forces produce diagonal tensile stresses in the concrete. If these stresses exceed some limiting tensile stress in the concrete, reinforcement in the form of either links or inclined bars or both must be provided to achieve the necessary resistance to shearing.

5.7.1 BS8110 and CP110 requirements

The method of designing shearing reinforcement given in BS8110 and CP110 thus involves the calculation of the average shearing stress v on a section due to ultimate loads, which is then compared with empirical limiting values of ultimate shearing stress v_c. These limiting values have been derived from test data and depend on the characteristic strength of the concrete and the amount of tension reinforcement present at the section being considered. If the limiting shearing stress is exceeded, reinforcement must be provided on the assumption that, for the purposes of resisting shearing, the member behaves as a pin-jointed truss or lattice girder in which the links or inclined bars forming the shearing reinforcement act as the tension members while the inclined compression in the concrete provides the corresponding compression member. The total shearing resistance at any section is thus the sum of the vertical components of all the tension bars and compression 'struts' cut by the section. To prevent failure occurring owing to the concrete crushing, an upper limit v_{max} to the shearing stress imposed on a section is also specified, irrespective of the amount of shearing reinforcement provided. Values of v_c and v_{max} may be read from *Tables 142* and *143* for normal-weight and lightweight concrete.

Although this so-called truss analogy offers a rather poor representation of the actual behaviour of the member after cracking has commenced, the designs that result from its adoption have been shown by tests to be conservative. Tests have also shown that the contribution of the concrete to the shearing strength of the section is not lost when v exceeds v_c; thus, according to both Codes, it is only necessary to provide sufficient shearing reinforcement to cater for the difference between the applied shearing force V and the shearing resistance ($v_c bd$) provided by the concrete.

5.7.2 Shearing reinforcement

The reinforcement provided to resist shearing forces is usually in the form of either vertical links or inclined bars. The ultimate resistance in shearing of such reinforcement, calculated in accordance with BS8110 and CP110 requirements, is given in *Table 145* for the values of f_y mentioned in the Codes: the resistances for other values of f_y are proportional. In some cases, such as beams subjected to vibration and impact, the stress in the reinforcement provided to resist shearing forces should be less than the normal maximum value, say two-thirds of the latter, and closely spaced links of small diameter should be used where possible.

In liquid-containing structures designed to BS5337 the permissible stress in shearing reinforcement should not exceed 85 or 100 N/mm^2 for plain and deformed bars with exposure class A, and 115 and 130 N/mm^2 respectively with exposure class B, if modular-ratio design is adopted. In such a case all shearing force has to be resisted by reinforcement and the shearing stress must not exceed 1.94 or 2.19 N/mm^2 for concrete grades 25 and 30 respectively, whatever the amount of reinforcement provided.

If the limit-state method described in the same document is adopted, the requirements for shearing reinforcement correspond to those in BS8110 or CP110. Thus reinforcement is necessary to withstand the difference between the shearing force applied to the sections and that resisted by the concrete alone.

Both BS8110 and CP110 recommend that, even when the

calculated shearing stress is less than that which can be resisted by the concrete alone, nominal shearing reinforcement should be provided (see section 21.1.1). Although a maximum limit of about four times the shearing strength of the concrete alone is permitted by both Codes, a limit of about 2.5 times the strength of the concrete is preferable for secondary beams that may be subjected to greater incidental loads, although the higher limit could be used for main beams in buildings (other than warehouses) where it appears unlikely that the full design load will occur.

Both BS8110 and CP110 permit the same characteristic strengths to be used for the design of shearing reinforcement as are used in bending, although according to CP110 the maximum value of f_y adopted should not exceed 425 N/mm^2 irrespective of the type of reinforcement employed.

Notes on the provision, resistance, spacing, size and shape of links according to BS8110 and CP110 are given in *Table 145* and in section 21.1.2; see also *Table 144*.

The principle assumed in evaluating the shearing resistance of inclined bars is that the bars form the tension members of a lattice, and notes on their arrangement as affecting the stresses therein are given on *Table 144* and in section 21.1.3. Note that, according to BS8110 and CP110 (and the related part of BS5337), not more than one-half of the shearing force to be resisted by reinforcement at any section can be carried by inclined bars, and links must be employed to resist the balance.

Inclined bars are frequently provided by bending up the main tension reinforcement, but in so doing an inspection must be made to ensure that the bar is not required to assist in providing the moment of resistance beyond the point at which the bar is bent. The points at which bars can be dispensed with as reinforcement to resist bending are given in *Table 141*, which applies to beams having up to eight bars as the principal tension reinforcement. Although a bar can be bent up at the points indicated, it is not implied that if it is not bent up it can be terminated at these points, since it may not have a sufficient bond length from the point of critical stress. This length depends on the rate of change of bending moment, and should be investigated in any particular beam.

When preparing designs, care must also be taken to ensure that the requirements of the Codes regarding detailing (see section 20.5.1) are not violated when bending up tension bars to act as shearing reinforcement.

5.8 TORSION

If the resistance or stiffness of a member in torsion is not taken into consideration when analysing a structure it is normally not necessary to design members for torsion, since adequate resistance will be provided by the nominal shearing reinforcement. However, if the torsional resistance of members is taken into account in a design, BS8110 recommends that the torsional rigidity CG of a section be determined by assuming a shear modulus G of $0.42E_c$ and a torsional constant C of one-half of the St Verant value for the plain concrete section: CP110 recommends a value of G of $0.4E_c$. The nominal shearing stress due to torsion v_t at any section may be found by assuming a plastic distribution of shearing stress, and an appropriate expression for rectangular sections is given in section 21.2.1, where details of the treatment of flanged sections are also summarized.

If v_t exceeds the limiting values of torsional shearing stress $v_{t\,min}$ set out in the Codes, torsional reinforcement consisting of a combination of closed rectangular links and longitudinal bars must be provided. The relevant design formulae are given in section 21.2.2, where the link reinforcement required is also expressed in terms of the link-reinforcement factor used in selecting normal shearing reinforcement. Thus *Table 145* can be used to select an appropriate arrangement of links.

To avoid premature crushing of the concrete, BS8110 and CP110 impose an upper limit v_{tu} on the sum of the stresses due to the direct shearing force and the torsional shearing force. Values of $v_{t\,min}$ and v_{tu} corresponding to various strengths of normal-weight and lightweight concrete may be read from *Tables 142* and *143*. Details of the arrangement of the reinforcement and a suitable design procedure are outlined in sections 21.2.2 and 21.2.3. For further information, reference should also be made to the comments given in the *Code Handbook* and to the specialist references quoted therein.

5.9 CURVED BEAMS (BOW GIRDERS)

Bow girders and beams that are not rectilinear in plan are subjected to torsional moments in addition to the normal bending moments and shearing forces. Beams forming a circular arc in plan may comprise part of a complete circular system supported on columns that are equally spaced, and each span may be equally loaded; such a system occurs in water towers, silos and similar cylindrical structures. The equivalent of these conditions also occurs if the circle is incomplete, as long as the appropriate negative bending moment can be developed at the end supports. This type of circular beam may occur in structures such as balconies.

On *Tables 146* and *147*, charts are given which enable the bending and torsional moments and shearing forces which occur in curved beams due to uniform and concentrated loads to be evaluated rapidly. The formulae on which the charts are based are given in sections 21.3.1 and 21.3.2 and on the tables concerned. The expressions for uniformly loaded beams have been developed from those given in ref. 40 and those for concentrated loads from ref. 41. In both cases the results have been recalculated to take into account the values of $G = 0.4E_c$ and $C = J/2$ recommended in CP110. (BS8110 recommends a slightly different value for G of $0.42E_c$.)

5.10 DEEP BEAMS

As the depth of a beam becomes greater in proportion to its span, the distribution of stress differs from that assumed for a 'normal' beam. In addition, the particular arrangement of the applied loads and of the supports has an increasing influence on this stress distribution. Thus if the ratio of clear span to depth is less than 2:3 for a freely-supported beam, or 2.5:4 for a continuous system, it should be designed as a deep beam.

No guidance on the design of such beams is given in BS8110 and CP110, but similar documents produced elsewhere deal with the subject. For example, both the American Concrete Institute and the Portland Cement Association (of America) have developed design methods, while the 1970 International Recommendations of the European Concrete Committee also include information on the design of deep beams (summarized in section 21.4.1), based on extensive experimental work by Leonhardt and Walther (ref. 42). Brief details of all these methods are given in ref. 43, where Kong, Robins and Sharp put forward their own empirical design method. The Swedish Concrete Committee has also produced recommendations that form the basis of the details given in ref. 34, while yet another method is contained in a comprehensive well-produced guide (ref. 44) issued by the Construction Industry Research and Information Association (which is based on developments of the work of Kong, Robins and Sharp).

The design proposals produced by Kong, Robins and Sharp and others are based on the results of several hundred tests and, unlike most other procedures, are also applicable to deep beams with web openings. Details of the method are presented on *Table 148* and in section 21.4.2.

5.11 COLUMNS: GENERAL CONSIDERATIONS

The imposed loads for which columns in buildings should be designed are the same as those for beams as given in *Table 6*, except that the concentrated loads do not apply. The imposed load on the floors supported by the columns may be reduced (see *Table 12*) when calculating the load on the column in accordance with the scale given for multistorey buildings. External columns in buildings, and internal columns under certain conditions, should be designed to resist the bending moments due to the restraint at the ends of beams framing into the columns and due to wind (see *Tables 65, 68* and *74*). An approximate method of allowing for the bending moment on a column forming part of a building frame is to design for a concentric load of K times the actual load, where K is as given in section 16.2 for different arrangements of beams framing into the column. These values have been evaluated for permissible-service-stress design but may also be applicable to limit-state methods: in any case so many factors affect the actual value of K that the tabulated values can only be approximate and the final design must be checked by more accurate calculation.

Reinforced concrete columns are generally either rectangular in cross-section with separate links, or circular or octagonal with helical binding. In some multistorey residential buildings columns that are L-shaped or T-shaped in cross-section are formed at the intersection of reinforced concrete walls. In most reinforced concrete columns the main vertical bars are secured together by means of separate links or binders. Rules for the arrangement of such links, the limiting amounts of main reinforcement etc. in accordance with BS8110 and CP110 are given in section 22.1.

So many variants enter into the design of a column that it is not easy to decide readily which combinations give the most economical member. For a short column carrying a service load exceeding 100 tonnes the following may apply, however.

Other factors being equal, the stronger the concrete the more economical is the column. For a square column the minimum amount of longitudinal reinforcement produces the cheapest member for a specified quantity of concrete. Also, for any concrete a square column is generally less costly than an octagonal column with helical binding. Taking eight designs to CP114 of columns to support service loads of 100 to 500 tonnes, the order of economy is generally as follows, the most economical design being the first: 1:1:2 concrete, square column with minimum vertical steel; 1:1:2 concrete, octagonal column with maximum volume of helical binding and minimum area of vertical steel; 1:$1\frac{1}{2}$:3 concrete, square column with minimum vertical steel; 1:$1\frac{1}{2}$:3 concrete, octagonal column with maximum volume of helical binding and minimum volume of vertical steel; 1:2:4 concrete, square column with minimum vertical steel; 1:2:4 concrete, octagonal column with maximum volume of helical binding and minimum volume of vertical steel; 1:2:4 concrete, octagonal column with maximum volume of helical binding and maximum volume of vertical steel; and 1:2:4 concrete, square column with maximum amount of vertical steel.

5.12 AXIALLY LOADED SHORT COLUMNS

The BS8110 and CP110 requirements for axial loading of short columns are as follows. For ultimate limit-state design of sections the characteristic dead and imposed loads must first be multiplied by the appropriate partial factors of safety for loads to obtain the required ultimate design loads. The values of characteristic strength f_{cu} and f_y of the concrete and reinforcement respectively are used directly in the design expressions given in BS8110 and CP110; the appropriate partial safety factors for materials are embodied in the numerical values given in the expressions. According to BS8110 the resistance of a section to pure axial load N_{uz} is $0.45 f_{cu} A_c + 0.87 f_y A_{sc}$; with CP110, $N_{uz} = 0.45 f_{cu} A_c + 0.75 f_y A_{sc}$, and values of N_{uz} can be read from the upper chart on *Table 168*. In practice, however, this ideal loading condition is virtually never achieved, and both Codes recommend the assumption for short braced columns that are axially loaded of an ultimate load N of $0.4 f_{cu} A_c + 0.75 f_y A_{sc}$ (according to BS8110) and $N = 0.4 f_{cu} A_c + 0.67 f_y A_{sc}$ (according to CP110). This expression, which corresponds to the introduction of a minimum eccentricity to cater for constructional tolerances of about $h/20$, is appropriate for a column supporting a rigid superstructure of very deep beams. When an approximately symmetrical beam arrangement is supported (i.e. the imposed loading is distributed uniformly and the maximum difference in the spans does not exceed 0.15 times the longer span) the ultimate load capacity N of the section of a short braced column is $0.35 f_{cu} A_c + 0.67 f_y A_{sc}$ (according to BS8110) and $0.35 f_{cu} A_c + 0.60 f_y A_{sc}$ (according to CP110), the further reduction in load-carrying capacity being to cater for the effects of asymmetrical imposed loading.

Ultimate loads on rectangular columns of various sizes which have been calculated according to these expressions are given in *Tables 149* and *150*. According to both Codes, A_c represents 'the area of concrete', but neither Code makes it clear whether this should be the net area of the section (i.e. that remaining after the area of concrete displaced by the reinforcement in compression is deducted) or the gross area of the section. In preparing the design charts for sections subjected to combined axial load and bending accompanying BS8110 and CP110, the common assumption is adopted that no deduction need be made for the small amount of concrete displaced by the reinforcement. With an eccentricity of load of $h/20$, the loads read from these design charts should correspond to those for a short braced column. However, if A_c is taken as the *net* area of concrete in this expression the resulting values are rather less than those given by the charts. Furthermore, since it is necessary to design short unbraced columns by using the Code design charts, it would appear an advantage to ignore the effect of any bracing and to design the column as unbraced using the Code charts! This is clearly illogical, and for uniformity it is preferable to take A_c as the gross concrete area. The maximum difference between the results obtained using the two differing assumptions occurs when the proportion of mild-steel reinforcement and the concrete grade are both as high as possible.

As is shown below, similar arguments are valid for taking A_c as the gross concrete area when designing slender columns and columns subjected to biaxial bending according to CP110.

Short unbraced columns not specifically subjected to bending must be designed as sections subject to an axial load acting at an eccentricity of $h/20$ (but not exceeding 20 mm according to BS8110): see section 22.1.1.

5.13 BENDING AND DIRECT FORCE ON SHORT COLUMNS: LIMIT-STATE METHOD

5.13.1 Combined uniaxial bending and thrust

The assumptions involved in the rigorous analysis of sections subjected to direct loading and bending about one axis at the ultimate limit-state are the same as those for members subjected to bending only, as set out in section 5.3.1. By resolving forces on a rectangular section vertically and by taking moments about the centre-line of the section, the following basic equations are obtained:

$$N = k_1xb + A'_{s1}f_{yd1} - A_{s2}f_{yd2}$$

$$M = k_1xb(\tfrac{1}{2}h - k_2x) + A'_{s1}f_{yd1}(\tfrac{1}{2}h - d') + A_{s2}f_{yd2}(d - \tfrac{1}{2}h)$$

where f_{yd1} and f_{yd2} are the appropriate design stresses in the reinforcement A'_{s1} and A_{s2} nearer and further from the action of the load respectively, k_1 and k_2 are factors depending on the shape assumed for the concrete stress-block (and possibly on f_{cu}), and x is the depth to the neutral axis. If x is greater than d, A_{s2} is in compression and negative values of f_{yd2} should be substituted in the foregoing expressions. With rigorous analysis the actual values of f_{yd1} and f_{yd2} depend on the actual value of x/h (and, of course, on f_y) and may be calculated from the expressions on *Table 103*.

If the shape of the concrete stress-block is assumed to be parabolic-rectangular the values of k_1 and k_2 depend on f_{cu} and may be either read from the scales or calculated from the expressions on *Table 102*. With the BS8110 uniform rectangular stress-block, $k_1 = 0.67f_{cu}/\gamma_m$, $k_2 = 0.5$ and the stress-block extends to a depth of only $0.9x$; with the CP110 uniform stress-block, $k_1 = 0.60f_{cu}/\gamma_m$, $k_2 = 0.5$ and the stress-block extends to the neutral axis.

As an alternative to rigorous analysis, CP110 permits the use of simplified formulae. These are based on the use of a rectangular stress-block and the assumption of a depth of concrete in compression of d_c, with the added restriction that d_c must not be less than $2d'$. The simplified formulae then correspond to the above equations but with $x = d_c$, $f_{yd1} = 0.72f_y$ and $f_{yd2} = f_{s2}$. With these formulae no direct correspondence between the design stresses in the reinforcement and the position of the neutral axis is assumed. It is thus necessary to adopt sensible values for f_{s2}: a useful relationship between f_y and f_{s2} for various ratios of d_c/h is suggested in the *Code Handbook* (see section 22.2.2).

Owing to the complex interrelationship between the variables involved, the foregoing equations are unsuitable for direct design purposes. Instead, they may be used to prepare sets of design charts or tables from which a section having the appropriate dimensional properties may be selected. The charts for rectangular sections provided in Part 3 of BS8110 and Part 2 of CP110 are derived from the equations for rigorous ultimate limit-state analysis with a parabolic-rectangular stress-block and $A'_{s1} = A_{s2} = A_{sc}/2$, with various values of f_{cu}, f_y and d/h $(= 1 - d'/h)$. Charts for circular sections derived from the same basic assumptions for ultimate limit-state analysis are given in Part 3 of CP110.

The charts for rectangular sections that form *Tables 151* to *156* are derived by using the same equations as those given in Part 3 of BS8110 and Part 2 of CP110, but the interrelated loads, moments and amounts of reinforcements are given in terms of f_{cu}. Each individual chart thus covers the full range of concrete grades. In addition, by using shaded zones to represent the various proportions of reinforcement it has been possible to incorporate the curves for mild steel and high-yield steel on the same charts. By interpolating between these limiting curves the designer is able to consider intermediate values of f_y.

In a similar manner the simplified expressions provided in Part 1 of CP110 may be used to prepare design charts that correspond to those in Part 2 of the Code. The charts given on *Tables 157* and *158* differ slightly (see section 22.2.2) as the basic expressions have been rearranged to cater for various ratios of f_y/f_{cu} and f_{s2}/f_y. Thus, unlike the charts in Part 2 of CP110, which only apply to single values of f_{cu} and f_y, these charts may be used for any practical combination of f_{cu} and f_y.

Charts for rectangular sections which are based on the assumption of a rectangular stress-block are given in *Examples of the Design of Buildings* and ref. 79.

In general the use of the simplified formulae in CP110 results in the need for more reinforcement than when the section is analysed rigorously, mainly because of the assumption of a fixed value of f_{yd2} of $0.72f_y$ instead of the relationship of $2000\,f_y/(2300 + f_y)$ permitted when rigorous analysis is used. Since this fixed relationship is most disadvantageous when f_y is low, the use of these expressions (and the charts based on them) is most uneconomical when mild steel is employed and when the applied moment is a minimum. In cases where it is thought that worthwhile savings may be made by utilizing rigorous analysis, and suitable design charts such as those in CP110 are not available, it is suggested that the charts on *Tables 157* and *158* may be used to obtain an approximate design and the resulting values of b, h and A_{sc} then substituted into the basic equations for rigorous analysis and refined by trial and adjustment. In the majority of cases, however, the resulting savings are unlikely to outweigh the additional work involved.

Requirements due to the limit-state of serviceability seldom influence the design of columns. Braced columns that are not slender (see below) need not be checked for deflection, and similar unbraced columns are deemed satisfactory if the average value of l_e/h for all columns at a certain level does not exceed 30. Excessive cracking in rectangular columns is unlikely if N/bh is greater than $f_{cu}/5$: if this is not so, and the section is subjected to bending, the axial load should be ignored and the section treated as a beam, using the appropriate criteria.

Unsymmetrically arranged reinforcement. In cases where the effects of bending are considerable and a reversal of bending is impossible, it may be worth while examining the effects of disposing the reinforcement unequally in the section, i.e. by providing more tension reinforcement to balance the assumption of a deeper concrete stress-block. On the other hand, if M/N is similar to $d - (h/2)$ the line of action coincides with the position of the compression steel: in such a case, no tension reinforcement is required theoretically. Design charts have been prepared which give the minimum amount and optimal arrangement of unsymmetrically disposed reinforcement to resist various combinations of M and N according to CP110: see ref. 85.

One possible method of designing such a section if appropriate tables are not available is as follows. When the resulting eccentricity of the load falls outside the line of A'_{s1} (i.e. A_{s2} is stressed in tension), CP110 permits the direct load N to be neglected and the section to be designed instead to resist a moment of $M + (d - h/2)\,N$. The amount of reinforcement required to resist this moment may then be reduced by $0.87N/f_y$. This stratagem actually corresponds to introducing equal and opposite forces N along the line of A_{s2}, the original direct load and the tensile force opposing it at a distance of $d - h/2$ giving rise to the additional moment, and the compressive 'opposing force' bringing about the reduction in the area of tension steel required. This method of design is not explicitly mentioned in BS8110, but there seems no reason why it should not be used. The method is illustrated in example 1 in section 22.2.

Although CP110 does not place restrictions on the actual method used to design the section for bending alone, it is clear that if rigorous analysis is used the value of x/d must be such that f_{yd2} is not less than $0.87\ f_y$. For maximum economy, the ratio chosen for x/d should be the maximum that may be adopted without reducing f_{yd2} below $0.87f_y$.

This method of design has the disadvantage that it is impossible to choose the relative proportions of steel near each face. If the resulting amounts are inconvenient and they are adjusted to achieve a more suitable arrangement, it may be difficult to be certain whether the strength of the resulting section is adequate.

Irregular sections. The design of an irregular section subjected to axial load and bending in order to meet ultimate limit-state requirements is bound to involve a considerable amount of trial and adjustment. The following procedure may, however, be found useful for short columns.

When the dimensions of the section are given or have been assumed, the section should be drawn to a convenient scale (say 1:10). A suitable arrangement of reinforcement should be decided upon, although the actual size of bars (assuming that these are all to be of the same diameter) need not be fixed at this stage. It is now necessary to select a position of the neutral axis. To obtain some approximate indication of a suitable ratio of x/h corresponding to the relative values of M and N given, it is suggested that a very rough calculation for a rectangular section having the same total area and ratio of overall dimensions as the section proposed be prepared. When M/bh^2f_{cu} and N/bhf_{cu} have been calculated, the charts in *Tables 157* and *158* are used to obtain a ratio of d_c/h that can be employed for x/h as a starting value. Next, calculate or measure the area of the concrete stress-block, i.e. the area of the section between the neutral axis and the compression face of the section in the case of CP110 or to a depth of $0.9x$ in the case of BS8110, and also the position of the centroid of this area. To determine the latter it may be necessary to divide the area into a number of convenient component parts or even strips and to take moments. Then if δA_{s1}, δA_{s2} etc. are the areas of these parts or strips and d_1, d_2 etc. are the distances of their individual centroids from the neutral axis, the distance of the centroid from the neutral axis $\bar{x}$ is $\sum(\delta A_{si}d_i)/\sum\delta A_{si}$.

The next step is to measure the distances of the individual reinforcing bars acting in tension below the neutral axis and thus to calculate the ratio x/a for each bar, where a is the distance of the bar from the compression face of the section. Knowing x/a, the design stress f_{yd2} in each bar can then be calculated from the relevant expressions given in *Tables 103*, and by multiplying these stresses by δA_s, where δA_s is the area of an individual bar, and summing, the total tensile force in the reinforcement can be found in terms of δA_s. The depth of the centroid of this reinforcement below the neutral axis should also be determined by summing the individual values of $a - x$ and dividing by the total number of bars. This part of the procedure is most conveniently undertaken tabularly as indicated in example 5 (for bending only) in section 20.1.

A similar summation should be made for the bars in compression, calculating a'/x (where a' is the depth of each bar of area $\delta A'_s$ below the compression face) and determining the corresponding value of f_{yd1} from *Table 103*. The height a_c of the centroid of this reinforcement above the neutral axis should also be found by summing the values of $x - a'$ for the individual bars and dividing by the number of bars.

Then, assuming a uniform stress of kf_{cu} over the rectangular concrete stress-block (where $k = 4/9$ with BS8110 and 2/5 with CP110), the two equations to be satisfied are

$$N = kf_{cu}A_c^* + K_1 - K_2$$
$$M = kf_{cu}A_c^*\bar{x} + K_1a_c + K_2a_t$$

where M, N and f_{cu} are given, A_c^* is the total area of the concrete stress-block, and $\bar{x}$, a_c and a_t are the distances from the neutral axis to the centroids of the stress-block, the compression steel and the tension steel respectively. K_1 and K_2 are the numerical summations (in terms of $\delta A_s'$ and δA_s) of the forces in the compression and tension reinforcement respectively. The two equations may be solved to obtain values of $\delta A_s'$ and δA_s, and appropriate bar sizes thus determined. If these sizes are impracticable, suitable adjustments should be made to the basic section dimensions or a different value of x tried, and the process repeated until a suitable section is achieved.

5.13.2 Combined uniaxial bending and tension

The analysis of sections subjected to combined bending and tension does not, in theory, differ from that for combined bending and thrust, and the above formulae can again be used provided the value of N is taken as negative. The appropriate expressions have been used to prepare the relevant sections of the curves shown on the charts for CP110 forming *Tables 153–156*.

In practice, the design of such sections will probably be determined by the prevention of excessively wide cracks. The formulae given in Appendix A of CP110 for calculating crack widths are only applicable to members subjected to bending only (as are those provided in BS5337), although BS8110 also outlies a procedure to adopt if tension extends over the entire section. The *Code Handbook* suggests an expression for calculating the crack width in a member subjected to pure tension: see Appendix 3 therein.

5.13.3 Biaxial bending

According to BS8110 short rectangular columns that are subjected to bending moments M_x and M_y about the two principal axes simultaneously with an axial load N may be designed as sections subjected to direct load with an increased bending moment about one axis only. If h' and b' are the distances from the compression face to the least compressed bars about the major and minor axes respectively, then when M_x/h' exceeds M_y/b' the section should be designed for the axial load N plus an increased moment M_x' of $M_x + \beta M_y h'/b'$ acting about the major axis; otherwise the section should be designed for N plus a moment M_y' of $M_y + \beta M_x b'/h'$ acting about the minor axis. In these expressions $\beta = 1 - (7N/6\,bhf_{cu})$, but must be not less than 0.3.

Although not stated in BS8110, these expressions only appear to be valid if all the reinforcing bars are located near the corners of the sections and thus contribute to the resistance to bending in both directions. If additional bars are provided, in important cases it may be worth while to assume a section size, steel arrangement, and position and angle of neutral axis and to carry out an analysis from first principles as for irregular sections in section 5.13.1. Computer analysis comes into its own in such circumstances.

CP110 permits short rectangular columns subjected to axial load together with moments about both principal axes to be considered as sections subjected to direct load and uniaxial bending about each individual axis in turn, provided that the resulting section meets the additional requirement that

$$\left(\frac{M_x}{M_{ux}}\right)^{\alpha_n} + \left(\frac{M_y}{M_{uy}}\right)^{\alpha_n} \leqslant 1.0$$

where M_{ux} and M_{uy} are the maximum moment capacities of the section provided, assuming the action of an axial load N and with bending about the individual axis being considered only; $1 \leqslant \alpha_n \leqslant 2$ and $\alpha_n = (2/3)\ (1 + 5N/2N_{uz})$, where N_{uz}, the resistance to pure axial load, can be read from *Table 159*. The resulting relationship between M_x/M_{ux}, M_y/M_{uy} and N/N_{uz} can be represented graphically by the lower chart on *Table 159*.

The foregoing requirements have been shown to lead to designs that conform to the basic stress and strain criteria laid down for ultimate limit-state analysis. Once again a direct design procedure is not strictly possible, and instead a trial-and-adjustment process is recommended. One possible procedure is outlined in example 2 in section 22.2. With this method suitable values are adopted for b and h and the ratios d'/b, d'/h, M_x/bh^2, M_y/b^2h and N/bh are calculated. Then, by assuming a convenient value for M_y/M_{uy} and thus obtaining M_{uy}/b^2h, the appropriate charts for the given cover ratio d'/b on *Tables 153–156* may be used to determine an appropriate value of ρ_y. Next the upper chart on *Table 159* can be employed to obtain N_{uz}/bh and thus N/N_{uz} may be calculated. Now with N/N_{uz} and the selected value of M_y/M_{uy}, the maximum corresponding value of M_x/M_{ux} can be read from the lower chart on *Table 159* and the required value of M_x/bh^2 may be evaluated. Use of the CP110 charts for the appropriate cover ratio d'/h with the given values of M_{ux}/bh^2 and N/bh will then give a value of ρ_x.

Now the actual value of ρ required will clearly lie somewhere between the values of ρ_x and ρ_y thus obtained, and a worthwhile estimate may be made by averaging the two values and perhaps rounding up slightly. Then with this new value of ρ, the charts on *Tables 153–156* and on *Table 159* may be employed to calculate the corresponding values of M_{ux}, M_{uy} and N_{uz}. These, together with the actual values of M_x, M_y and N, may then be substituted into the above expression to check that the section is satisfactory.

The foregoing procedure, which is described in more detail in example 2 in section 22.2, is only valid if the resulting bars (or groups of bars) are located near the corners of the section, and thus contribute to the resistance in both directions. A convenient design method, if this is not so, is described in *Examples of the Design of Buildings*.

To avoid the cumbersome procedure described above, Beeby (ref. 70) has suggested a simplified procedure in which, by making minimal simplifying assumptions, the calculations are little more than those required when uniaxial bending and thrust occurs: this is very similar to the method now specified in BS8110. Details are given in section 22.2.4.

It is recommended that N_{uz} is calculated on the assumption that A_c represents the gross (rather than the net) concrete area, as has been done when preparing the appropriate chart on *Table 159*. If this is so, the corresponding value of α_n is lower than if the alternative assumption were made, and thus the resulting values of $(M/M_u)^{\alpha_n}$ are increased. Therefore, for safety, it is preferable to adopt a higher rather than a lower value of N_{uz}.

5.14 BENDING AND DIRECT FORCE ON SHORT COLUMNS: MODULAR-RATIO METHOD

With modular-ratio analysis, the method of determining the magnitude and distribution of the service stresses induced across a section depends on the nature of the direct force and on the relative values of the force and the bending moment. There are three principal cases: (1) when the direct force is compressive and the resulting stresses are wholly compressive; (2) when the direct force is tensile and the resulting stresses are wholly tensile; and (3) when the direct force is either compressive or tensile and both compressive and tensile stresses result.

The effect of a bending moment M_d and a direct force N_d acting simultaneously is equivalent to that of a direct force N_d acting at a distance e from the centroid of the stressed area, where $e = M_d/N_d$. The eccentricity e is sometimes measured from the centroid of the concrete section and, except in case 3 if the eccentricity is small, the error involved by this approximation is small. In certain problems, the eccentricity of the load about one face of the section is known and, before the stresses can be calculated, this eccentricity must be converted to that about the centroid of the stressed area (or of the concrete section).

The value of e relative to the dimensions of the member determines into which of the three cases a particular problem falls. For problems in case 1, the maximum and minimum stresses are calculated by adding and subtracting respectively the stresses due to the direct force alone and to the bending moment alone. In this case the limit is reached when the tensile force produced by the bending moment alone (assuming the whole of the concrete and the reinforcement are fully effective) is equal to the compressive stress due to a concentric load N_z. For a rectangular section this limiting condition is reached when the value of e/h, where h is the total 'depth' of the section, is 0.167 for a section containing no reinforcement and rises to about 0.3 for sections with large percentages of reinforcement. As a small tensile stress may be permitted in the concrete in some cases, an upper limit for e/h may be about 0.5. If no tensile stress is permitted in the concrete, the limiting value of e is J/A_{tr}, where A_{tr} is the effective area of the transformed section expressed in concrete units and J is the section modulus of the transformed section (also expressed in concrete units) measured about the axis passing through the centroid of the equivalent section. Expressions for the effective area and the moment of inertia of reinforced concrete sections subjected to stress over the entire section are given on *Tables 99* and *100*. These expressions take into account the reinforcement; for preliminary approximate calculations it may not always be necessary to allow for the reinforcement, in which case the expressions in *Table 98* apply.

When N_d is a pull and the stresses are entirely tensile, the problem is one of case 2 when $e/(d - d')$ is less than 0.5, the tensile resistance of the concrete being entirely neglected.

When case 1 is applied to a problem in which N_d is a thrust, and an excessive tensile stress is produced in the concrete, or when case 2 is applied to a problem where N_d is tensile and compressive stresses are produced, the problem is one of case 3. Various methods of calculating the stresses for such a case have been devised. Any direct method is complex since exact analysis involves the solution of a cubic equation, and rapid computation without recourse to mechanical aids necessitates an impracticably large number of graphs or tables if account is to be taken of all the possible variations in the terms of the equation. In the method outlined in *Tables 160* and *161* the depth to the neutral axis is first assumed; this depth is later checked and adjusted.

For rectangular sections or sections capable of being reduced to equivalent rectangles, the notation is as indicated in *Table 161*; for an irregular section the notation is shown in *Table 160*. Where no compression reinforcement is provided, the term A'_s in the formulae is zero and simplifications consequently follow. An abstract of the methods of determining the stresses in a rectangular member subjected to a bending moment combined with a direct thrust is given in *Table 161* together with the values of some of the terms involved in the calculation. For values of e/h exceeding say 1.5, an approximate method can be used that gives the stresses with sufficient accuracy.

For rectangular members reinforced with equal amounts of 'tension' and 'compression' steel and resisting combinations of bending and direct thrust, the charts on *Tables 162* and *163* permit the direct design of suitable sections.

5.14.1 Combined bending and thrust on rectangular section

When e does not exceed $h/6$. In this case, with any amount of reinforcement, only compressive stresses are developed and the maximum and minimum values are given by the formula on *Table 161*. The expression for the section modulus is correct if $A_s = A'_s$ and is approximately correct otherwise. For more accurate expressions, see *Table 99*. The design of a section for this case involves the assumption of trial dimensions and reinforcement.

If $\alpha_e = 15$ and $A_s = A'_s$, the graphs given on *Tables 162* and *163* may be used directly. These are based on the assumption that the eccentricity is measured about the centre-line of the section, not the centroid of the stressed area.

When e is greater than $h/6$ and less than $h/2$. With no reinforcement, tension is developed in one face of the member when e exceeds $h/6$ but as the proportion of reinforcement is increased the ratio of e to h also increases before tensile stresses are developed. The limiting value of e/h depends on the amounts of A_s and A'_s and the relative values of d', d and h. Cases where e/h lies between 1/6 and 1/2 should first be calculated, as if e/h does not exceed 1/6, and if no tensile stress is shown to be developed, the stresses calculated by this method are the theoretical stresses. Even if a small tensile stress is developed, treatment as in the preceding section is generally justified as long as the tensile stress in the concrete for the worst combination of M_d and N_d does not exceed about one-tenth of the allowable compressive stress. If the tensile stress exceeds this amount the tensile resistance of the concrete should be ignored and the stresses calculated as in the following.

When e is greater than $h/2$ and less than $3h/2$. This is the general case, when tension in the concrete is ignored, and the method given in *Table 161* is applicable to members with or without compression reinforcement and with any value of d' and any modular ratio.

The first step is to select a trial position for the neutral axis by assuming a value of the depth-to-neutral-axis factor x/d, and then calculating the maximum stresses f_{cr} and f_{st} in the concrete and reinforcement respectively from the formulae given on *Table 161*, in which the expression for the factors and some numerical values for the factors are also given. The term $\bar{x}$ is the distance from the compressed edge of the section to the centroid of the stressed area. Since $\bar{x}$ may be very nearly equal to $h/2$, it is sufficiently accurate in the first trial calculation to assume this value, but for a second or final trial calculation $\bar{x}$ should be determined from the appropriate expression.

The value of x/d obtained by substituting the calculated values of f_{cr} and f_{st} in $x/d = \alpha_e f_{cr}/(\alpha_e f_{cr} + f_{st})$ should coincide with or be very nearly equal to the trial value of x/d. If in the first trial there is a difference between the two values of x/d, the factors β_1, β_2, β_3 and K_1 should be recalculated with a second trial value of x/d and the recalculated values of f_{cr} and f_{st} should give a satisfactory value of x/d. Values of x/d for various ratios of f_{st}/f_{cr} with differing modular ratios and values of β_2 and β_3 are given in *Table 161*, and values of x/d corresponding to any ratio of stresses can be read from the scales on *Table 120*.

When the member is reinforced in tension only, $\beta_3 = 0$ and the formulae for the stresses are $f_{cr} = N_d\beta_1/\beta_2 bd$ and $f_{st} = [(f_{cr}K_1/2) - N_d]/A_s$.

If a programmable calculator or a more sophisticated machine aid is available, the foregoing trial-and-adjustment procedure can be programmed automatically. The expression to be solved corresponds to that given by equations (20.3) or (20.4) (see section 20.3.1) but where, in the present case, N_d is negative.

For the special case of $\alpha_e = 15$ and $A_s = A'_s$, the stresses can be obtained approximately from the charts on *Tables 162* and *163*. Since these are based on the assumption that the eccentricity is measured from the centre-line of the section rather than the centroid of the stressed area, some error may be involved; in important cases the stresses should therefore be checked by applying the expressions given in *Table 161*.

A member that does not generally require compression reinforcement can be designed by first assuming a value for d (and therefore for h) and calculating the breadth required from $b = \beta_1 N_d/f_{cr}d\beta_2$, in which β_2 is calculated from the value of x/d corresponding to the permissible stresses f_{cr} and f_{st} or taken from *Table 161*. The area of tension reinforcement required is given by $[(f_{cr}K_1/2) - N_d]/f_{st}$. If the value of b thus obtained is unsuitable, another value of d may give suitable proportions. For a slab, b should be taken as 1000 mm or 12 in if N_d and M_d are given per metre or per foot width. If suitable proportions cannot be obtained in this way, a convenient section may be found by reducing the stress in the tension reinforcement, thereby increasing the area of concrete in compression, or by adding compression reinforcement, or by combining both methods.

If reinforcement is added to increase the compressive resistance, or if the member is such that ordinary design or other considerations require the provision of compression reinforcement (for example in columns, piles, the support section of beams, and members subject to the reversal of flexure), it is necessary to assume (or to determine from other considerations) suitable values of b as well as d. With these values, and with the ratio of the allowable stresses in tension reinforcement and concrete, the factors β_1, β_2, β_3 and K_1 can be calculated or read from *Table 161*. The amount of compression reinforcement required is given by

$$A'_s = \frac{d}{\beta_3(d-d')}\left(\frac{N_d\beta_1}{f_{cr}} - bd\beta_2\right)$$

and the amount of tension reinforcement required is given by

$$A_s = [f_{cr}(\tfrac{1}{2}K_1 + \beta_3 A'_s) - N_d]/f_{st}$$

In calculating β_1 the value of $\bar{x}$ may be assumed to be $h/2$, but in important members the stresses should be checked using the calculated value of $\bar{x}$.

If the calculated value of A'_s exceeds A_s, both values should be adjusted by reducing the tensile stress or by modifying the dimensions of the section.

When *e* is greater than 3*h*/2. When the eccentricity of the thrust is large compared with the dimensions of the member, the stresses are primarily determined by the bending moment, the thrust producing only a secondary modification. In this case the stresses should first be calculated for the bending moment acting alone as described in section 20.2. The resultant combined stresses can then be determined approximately by adding a stress f_c to the maximum compressive stress in the concrete and deducting $\alpha_c f_c$ from the tensile stress in the reinforcement, where f_c is given by the formula at the foot of *Table 161*.

Examples in the use of *Table 161* are given in section 22.3.2 and in the use of *Tables 162–165* after section 22.3.4.

5.14.2 Combined bending and thrust on annular section

Annular sections subjected to combined bending and thrust may be designed by using the charts given on *Tables 164* and *165*. These charts are prepared on the assumption that the individual reinforcing bars may be represented with little loss of accuracy by an imaginary ring of steel having the same total cross-sectional area and located at the midpoint of the section.

5.14.3 Combined bending and thrust on any section

Compressive stresses only. The first step in determining the stresses when the value of M_d/N_d is small is to evaluate the transformed area A_{tr} and the moment of inertia I_{tr} of the section about an axis passing through the centroid, as given by the expressions at the top of *Table 160*; an irregular section should be divided into a number of narrow strips as shown in the diagram. The maximum and minimum compressive stresses are obtained using the appropriate formulae in the table. The limit of this case occurs when f_{cr} (min) = 0. A small negative value of f_{cr} (min) may be permissible if this tensile stress does not exceed, say, one-tenth of the permissible compressive stress.

If the section is symmetrically reinforced and is rectangular (bending about a diagonal), circular, octagonal or has any of the symmetrical shapes given in *Table 98*, the area A and the modulus J_c of the concrete section can be obtained from the data given in the table. The additional area A_a and the additional modulus J_a due to the reinforcement are given by $A_a = (\alpha_e - 1)\sum \delta A_s$ and $J_a h = 2(\alpha_e - 1)\sum(h_c - \bar{x})^2 \ \delta A_s$, where δA_s is the area of a bar or group of bars placed at a distance of $(h_c - \bar{x})$ from the centroid of the section. Thus $A_{tr} = A + A_a$ and $J = J_c + J_a$, and the maximum and minimum compressive stresses in the concrete are given by

$$\frac{N_d}{A_{tr}} \pm \frac{M_d}{J}$$

The limit for this case occurs when $M_d/N_d = J/A_{tr}$. For other common sections the expressions for the effective area and section modulus in *Tables 99* and *100* may be used.

Compressive and tensile stresses. When the stress f_{cr} (min), determined as described above, is negative or exceeds the permissible tensile stress, or when e is so large compared with h that the simultaneous production of compressive and tensile stresses can be assumed at the outset, the total tension should be resisted by the reinforcement only. In this case it is necessary to select a trial position for the neutral axis, either after considering the maximum permissible stresses or otherwise, and to plot the axis on a diagram of the section drawn to scale, as indicated in the diagram in *Table 160*. Then the position of the centre of tension below the top edge of the section should be found. The next step is to divide the compression area above the neutral axis into a number of narrow horizontal strips. The depth h_s of each strip need not be the same, as any regularity in the shape of the section may suggest more convenient subdivisions. When the strips are all of equal depth, or when the section is symmetrical or hollow, simplifications should be readily perceived. For each strip the factors δA_{tr} and $(x - h_c)$ should be determined. The position of the centre of compression below the top edge can then be found. The distance h_c of the centroid of the stressed area below the compressed edge of the section can now be evaluated, and the maximum tensile and compressive stresses can be calculated from the formulae in *Table 160*. The value of x/d corresponding to these stresses should be compared with the assumed value and, if necessary, a second trial should be made. The values of a and δA_{tr} for individual bars or groups of bars and for individual compression strips are not affected by the value of x/d. An example of the application of this method is given at the bottom of *Table 160* and in section 22.3.1.

5.14.4 Combined bending and tension

Any section with e less than $z_s - \bar{x}_s$. If the distance between the centroids of the reinforcement near opposite faces of any member is z_s, and if e is measured about the centroid of the combined reinforcement, as shown on the diagram at the top of *Table 166*, then if e does not exceed $z_s - \bar{x}_s$ the stresses over the section are wholly tensile. The average stresses in the group of bars near the face closer to the line of action of N_d and in the group of bars near the face remote from the line of action of N_d are given by the formulae for f_{st1} and f_{st2} respectively. The maximum stress in a bar depends on the distance of the farthest bar in any group from the centroid of that group, and is given by the formula for $f_{st1\,max}$ in the table. The expressions for f_{st1} and f_{st2} can be rearranged to give the areas of reinforcement required for a specified permissible stress.

Simplified formulae are given in *Table 166* for this case for regular sections, such as rectangular sections in which the bars are in two rows only. Further simplifcations apply if the area of the bars in each row are equal, as also given in *Table 166*.

Rectangular section with e greater than $z_s - \bar{x}_s$ and less than $3h/2$. This is the general case, and the method of treatment is similar to that described previously for combined bending and direct thrust. Modifications are introduced to allow for the difference between a direct thrust and a direct pull, as given in the lower part of *Table 166*; the factors K_1, β_2 and β_3 can be obtained from *Table 161*.

When the section is reinforced in tension only, $\beta_3 = 0$ and the formulae for the maximum stresses are

$$f_{cr} = \frac{N_d \beta'_1}{bd\beta_2}$$

$$f_{st} = (\tfrac{1}{2} f_{cr} K_1 + N_d)/A_s$$

When designing a member to resist a bending moment and direct pull, a useful approximate method is as follows. If compression reinforcement is not likely to be required, assume values for d (and h) and determine the minimum breadth from $b = N_a\beta'_1/f_{cr}d\beta_2$, where f_{cr} is the permissible concrete stress and β_2 is calculated (or read from *Table 161*) from the value of x/d corresponding to the permissible stresses. If this value of b is unsatisfactory, d should be adjusted or compression steel provided. The area of tension reinforcement required is given by

$$A_s = (\tfrac{1}{2} f_{cr} K_1 + N_d)/f_{st}$$

For a singly-reinforced slab subject to a bending moment and a direct tension, such as the wall or floor of a tank or bunker, a simple approximate procedure is given at the foot of *Table 166*. Determine the eccentricity e_s of the line of action of the direct tension from the centre of the tension reinforcement. The total tension reinforcement required is then given by

$$\frac{N_d}{f_{st}}\left(\frac{e_s}{z} + 1\right).$$

The value of d (and h) is that required to resist the bending moments acting alone, and the value of the lever arm z is that corresponding to the ratio of the permissible stresses and should be read from *Table 120*.

In designing a member in which compression reinforcement is required, first assume or otherwise determine suitable values for b and d, and with these values and the maximum permissible stresses calculate the area of compression reinforcement from

$$A'_s = \frac{1}{\beta_3 z_s}\left(\frac{N_d \beta'_1}{f_{cr}} - bd\beta_2\right)$$

The area of tension reinforcement necessary is calculated from

$$A_s = [f_{ct}(\tfrac{1}{2}K_1 + \beta_3 A'_s) + N_d]/f_{st}$$

For this method the value of β'_1 can be based on $\bar{x} = h/2$, but in important members the stresses should be checked by using the calculated value of $\bar{x}$.

If it is necessary to reduce the amount of compression reinforcement, this can often be effected by reducing f_{st} and thus increasing x/d. Generally in problems involving bending and direct tension, the tensile force is the deciding factor, and a more economical member can be achieved by reducing the stress in the concrete.

Rectangular section with *e* greater than 3*h*/2. The determination of the approximate stresses in this case is similar to that described for the corresponding case of combined bending and direct thrust. The stresses are first computed for the bending moment acting alone. Next evaluate f_c from the expression for this case given near the bottom of *Table 166*. Deduct f_c from the stress in the concrete and add $\alpha_e f_c$ to the tensile stress in the reinforcement to obtain the maximum stresses in the concrete and the steel.

To design a member, such as a slab with tension reinforcement only, the following approximate method is applicable. The depth or thickness h, and the breadth b in the case of a beam, are determined for the bending moment acting alone. Evaluate the eccentricity e_s about the tension reinforcement. The area of tension reinforcement required is then given by substituting in the formula at the foot of *Table 166*, in which z is the lever-arm of the section designed for bending only.

Any section with tensile and compressive stresses. With the modification necessary to allow for N_d being a tensile instead of a compressive force, the method described for the corresponding case of combined bending moment and direct thrust can be applied to determine the stresses on any section that cannot be treated as rectangular. A trial position for the neutral axis is assumed and the part of the section above the neutral plane is divided into a number of narrow horizontal strips as in the diagram on *Table 166*. The values of S, a_t, $\bar{x}$, a_c, $(x - h_c)$ and δA_{tr} are determined and substituted in the formulae for the maximum stresses given in the table. If the value of x corresponding to these stresses is approximately equal to that assumed, the stresses are approximately the maximum stresses produced by the applied bending moment and direct tension. If the difference between the calculated and assumed values of x is too great, a second trial value must be chosen and the summations revised by taking in a greater or lesser number of strips to correspond to the revised value of x.

5.14.5 Position of neutral axis

The accuracy of the results obtained by some of the foregoing modular-ratio methods and the labour entailed at arriving at these results depends on the accuracy with which the position of the neutral axis is selected. From a consideration of the member and of the forces acting upon it, it is possible to assume a value of x that is very close to that corresponding to the calculated stresses. The maximum stresses for which the section has been designed may indicate a reasonable value of x for the first trial, or consideration can be given to the ratio of stresses for bending only, as determined by the proportion of tension reinforcement. The selected value of x should differ from the value for bending alone in accordance with the the following rules. For bending and compression, the value selected for x should be greater than the value for bending alone, the difference increasing as e/h or e/d decreases. For bending and tension, the selected value of x should be less than the value for bending only, the difference decreasing as e/h or e/d increases. If the difference between the first assumed value, say x_1, and the value corresponding to the calculated stresses, say x_s, is such that it is necessary to select another value, say x_2, intermediate between x_1 and x_s, the following considerations apply. For bending and compression, the value of x_2 should be nearer to x_s than it is to x_1. For bending and tension the value of x_2 should be nearer to x_1 than it is to x_s.

An automatic trial-and-adjustment procedure to determine x can be written if a programmable calculator or more sophisticated machine aid is available. The procedure involves the iterative solution of equations (20.3) or (20.4) (see section 20.3.1).

5.14.6 Biaxial bending

Some methods of estimating the stresses when a section is subjected to bending moments acting about two axes that are mutually at right angles simultaneously with a concentric compressive load are given in *Table 167*. The two cases considered are when the stresses are entirely compressive and when tensile and compressive stresses are produced. The method in the former case is accurate, but the method in the latter is approximate and is only valid if M_{dx} is much greater than M_{dy}. If M_{dx} and M_{dy} are more nearly equal, a semi-graphical method, which is only worth while for important members, can be applied by combining vectorially M_{dx} and M_{dy} to obtain the resultant moment M_r. A position of the neutral axis at right angles to the plane of action of M_r is then assumed and the procedure for an irregular section described on *Table 160* is followed.

5.14.7 Combination of stresses acting in different directions

If three stresses act on a square element of uncracked concrete the principal tensile and compressive stresses, mutually at right angles, are given by substituting in the general formulae in *Table 167*; the plane in which the principal tensile stress acts can also be established. The general formulae apply if a tensile stress acts normal to one face of the element, a tensile stress acts normal to an adjacent face, and a shearing force acts in the plane of the element. If either of the direct stresses is compressive, the sign of the appropriate term in the formula is changed. Formulae are also given for the cases in which one or both of the direct stresses are compressive or do not act.

5.15 SLENDER COLUMNS

If the ratio of the effective length of a column to the least radius of gyration exceeds about 50, the column is considered to be a slender or 'long' column. According to BS8110 and CP110 an additional moment related to the slenderness then has to be taken into account, while earlier documents introduce a factor that limits the load-carrying capacity of the section. For square and rectangular columns it is usually more convenient to calculate the slenderness ratio on the least lateral dimension of the section (provided that it has no re-entrant angles) than on the radius of gyration. Thus the limiting requirement in CP110 for a short rectangular column is a ratio of effective length to least lateral dimension of 12 for normal-weight concrete and 10 for lightweight concrete. In BS8110 the limiting ratios for normal-weight concrete are 15 and 10 for braced and unbraced columns respectively; for lightweight concrete the corresponding ratio for both types is 10.

5.15.1 BS8110 and CP110 requirements

The method advocated in BS8110 and CP110 is to assume that the capacity of the column to carry axial loading is undiminished, but to introduce an additional moment that is related to the slenderness of the section: the value of this moment may be determined by using the appropriate scales on *Table 168*. This additional moment αNh due to deflection may in turn be reduced by multiplying it by a factor K that is equal to the ratio of $(N_{uz} - N)$ to $(N_{uz} - N_{bal})$. The reason for the introduction of this factor is to take account of the fact that, as N increases beyond N_{bal}, the condition of the column more nearly approaches that corresponding to axial loading. The likelihood of incurring curvature and thus additional deflection owing to slenderness decreases accordingly, and so justifies a reduction in the additional moment.

The load N_{bal} occurs when a maximum compressive strain of 0.0035 in the concrete and a tensile strain of 0.002 in the outermost layer of tension steel are attained simultaneously. If $d' = h - d$, this situation occurs when $x = 7(h - d')/11$ and for any ratio of d'/h according to BS8110; and with CP110, provided that d'/h is not greater than $3/14(\simeq 0.214)$, the strain in the compression steel will have reached its limiting value of 0.002 also. Consequently, since the stress corresponding to this strain is $2000f_y/(2300 + f_y)$, if equal amounts of reinforcement are provided in both faces, the forces in the tension and compression steel balance each other. The resistance of the section to axial load is therefore that due to the concrete alone and is given by the relevant expression in section 22.4.1. This expression has been used to prepare the upper chart on *Table 168*. For simplicity BS8110 proposes that for rectangular sections reinforced symmetrically $N_{bal} = bdf_{cu}/4$. It should be noted that although the amount of reinforcement provided does not influence the value of N_{bal}, the position of the reinforcement does, since this determines the distribution of strain across the section and thus the depth of the concrete stress-block.

With CP110, if d'/h exceeds 0.214, N_{bal} should be determined by rigorous ultimate limit-state analysis from first principles.

Allen (ref. 36) was the first to point out that the values of K may be plotted directly on the design charts for members subjected to bending and direct thrust, and this has been done with the charts given in Part 3 of BS8110 and those forming the corresponding tables in this *Handbook*. They can easily be added to those given in Part 2 of CP110 as follows. Read N_{bal}/bh from the graph on *Table 168* for the values of f_{cu} and d/h corresponding to the chart being considered, and draw a horizontal line representing $K = 1$ across the chart for this value of N/bh. Next, calculate N_{uz}/bh from the expression $0.45f_{cu} + 0.06f_y$. Divide the height between the value thus obtained and that previously calculated for N_{bal}/bh into ten equal parts, marking along the curve representing $100\ A_{sc}/bh = 8$ the points where these divisions intersect the curve. Next, divide the height between $0.45f_{cu}$ and the value calculated for N_{bal}/bh into ten equal parts and mark the points where these vertical divisions intersect the curve representing $100A_{sc}/bh = 0$. Finally, join the corresponding points on each curve by straight lines, preferably in a distinctive coloured ink. The lines should be designated $K = 1$ (when $N/bh = N_{bal}/bh$) to $K = 0$ (which coincides with $M/bh^2 = 0$).

A suitable design procedure is thus as follows. Having selected or been given suitable dimensions for the section, the slenderness ratio is evaluated and the corresponding value of α read from the appropriate scale on *Table 168*. By calculating αNh, the modified ultimate design moment M_t is determined and a suitable trial section designed by using the charts in Part 3 of BS8110, Part 2 of CP110 or on *Tables 153–158*. For this trial section, the value of N_{bal}/bh can be read from the upper chart on *Table 168* and N_{uz}/bh can be found by using the upper chart on *Table 159*. These values of N_{bal}/bh and N_{uz}/bh are now used with the given value of N/bh to enter the lower chart on *Table 168* and thus obtain the corresponding value of K, which is then multiplied by αNh and added to M_i to obtain a revised value of M_t. The same trial-and adjustment procedure is repeated until the value of K stabilizes. This cyclic design procedure is discussed in more detail in section 22.4.1, and an example of its use is given following section 22.4.2. Full details of the background to the additional-moment concept, which has been introduced by the European Concrete Committee (CEB), are given in ref. 100. The method applies both when there is no initial moment on the section and when the section is already subject to direct load and uniaxial or biaxial bending.

Once again, the question must be considered as to whether A_c should be taken as the net or gross concrete area of the section when calculating N_{uz}. Since the design charts for sections subjected to bending and direct thrust given in BS8110 and CP110 and elsewhere make no allowance for the area of concrete displaced by the bars, it seems sensible to make the same assumption when calculating values of N_{uz} to be used in conjunction with these charts. Observe also that if N_{uz} is taken to be lower than its true value (as may be the case if A_c is taken as the net concrete area), the resulting value of K will be lower and thus will result in a lower additional moment being considered than should be the case. For these reasons it is recommended that A_c should be taken as the gross concrete area, as has been done on *Table 159*.

5.16 WALLS

Information concerning the design of reinforced concrete walls in accordance with BS8110 and CP110 is given in section 6.1.11. Both Codes also give design information for plain concrete walls, and the basic requirements for both types are compared in *Tables 170* and *171*.

5.17 DETAILING JOINTS AND INTERSECTIONS BETWEEN MEMBERS

It has long been realized that the calculated strength of a reinforced concrete member cannot be attained unless the reinforcement that it contains is detailed efficiently. Research by the Cement and Concrete Association and others has shown that this is even more true when considering the intersections between individual members. Unless the reinforcement linking intersecting wall faces is detailed correctly, for example, tests show that the actual strength of the joint is considerably lower than calculations indicate.

On *Tables 172* and *173* some details are given of the design recommendations that have emerged from the results of the research reported to date in this important field. Many of the design expressions are derived from actual test results, although the references listed often show that a reasonable theoretical explanation for the behaviour observed has subsequently been developed. Some of the research reported is still continuing and it is possible that these formulae may need to be modified in the light of future results. In certain instances, for example half-joints and corbels, design information provided in BS8110 and CP110 is included here and supplemented by information obtained elsewhere. In general, however, details primarily intended for precast concrete construction have been omitted as they fall outside the scope of this book.

Chapter 6
Structures and foundations

The loads and consequent bending moments and forces on the principal types of structural components, and the stresses in and resistances of such components, have been dealt with in the preceding chapters. In this chapter some complete structures, which are mainly assemblies or special cases of such components, and their foundations are considered.

6.1 BUILDINGS

A building may be constructed entirely of reinforced concrete, or one or more of the roof, floors, walls, stairs and foundations may be of reinforced concrete in conjunction with a steel frame. Alternatively, the interior and exterior walls may be of cast *in situ* reinforced concrete and support the floors and roof, the columns and beams being formed in the thickness of the walls. Again the entire structure, or parts thereof, may be built of precast concrete elements.

The design of the various parts of a building to comply with the relevant Codes and Standards forms the subject of *Examples of the Design of Buildings*. That book also includes illustrative calculations and drawings for a fairly typical six-storey multipurpose building. This section provides a brief guide to component design.

6.1.1 Stability

Although most reinforced concrete structures have a satisfactory degree of safety against instability under normal loading, BS8110 and CP110 recognize that with some of the combinations of loading prescribed in these Codes the resistance required to lateral loading is very low. For this reason, and to provide a certain amount of resistance to the possible effects of excessive loading or accidental damage, these codes contain special requirements regarding stability, including the provision of a system of continuous vertical and horizontal ties: details of these requirements are given in *Table 174*. To meet these requirements the same reinforcement that has already been provided to satisfy the normal structural requirements may be considered to account for the whole or part of the amount required, as the forces due to the abnormal loading are assumed to act independently of any other structural forces. The *Code Handbook* therefore considers that in many structures the reinforcement already provided for normal design purposes will also cover the requirements regarding stability with little modification; it suggests that normal design procedures should first be followed and the resulting design then checked to ensure that stability requirements are met, any adjustments being made as necessary.

Special care should be taken with detailing and the *Code Handbook* recommends that anchorage-bond stresses be increased by 15% to cater for the difference in the partial safety factors for materials when stressed normally and when stressed by the effects of abnormal loading. This might at first be thought to indicate that the anchorage-bond lengths, as read from *Tables 92–94*, may be reduced by two-fifteenths when considering such effects. However, BS8110 and CP110 permit the partial safety factor for materials to be reduced by 15% (i.e. from 1.5 to 1.3 for concrete and from 1.15 to 1.0 for steel) when considering abnormal loading. This, in effect, implies that the limiting stresses in the materials are increased accordingly so that identical bond lengths are required under both conditions.

6.1.2 Floors

Concrete floors may be of monolithic beam-and-slab construction (the slabs spanning in one or two directions), flat slabs, or ribbed or waffle slabs, or may be of precast concrete slabs supported on cast *in situ* or precast concrete beams. BS8110 and CP110 give recommendations for the design and construction of floors and flat roofs comprising hollow blocks, ribbed slabs, and precast concrete slabs.

6.1.3 Openings in slabs

The slabs around openings in floors or roofs should be strengthened with extra reinforcement, unless the opening is large compared with the span of the slab (for example, stair-wells or lift-wells) in which case beams should be provided around the opening. For small openings in solid slabs the cross-sectional area of the extra bars placed parallel to the principal reinforcement should be at least equal to the area of principal reinforcement interrupted by the opening. A bar should be placed diagonally across each corner of an opening.

The effect of an opening in the proximity of a concentrated load on the shearing resistance of a slab is dealt with in clause

3.7.7.7 of BS8110 and clause 3.4.5.2 of CP110 (the requirements differ slightly): see section 21.1.5.

Holes for pipes, ducts and other services should be formed when the floor is constructed and the cutting of such holes should not be permitted afterwards, unless this is done under the supervision of a competent engineer. It is therefore an advantage to provide, at the time of construction, a number of holes that can be used for electric conduits and small pipes, even when they are not required for the known services. Suitable positions are through floor slabs in the corners of rooms or corridors, and through the ribs of beams immediately below the slab.

6.1.4 Hollow-block slabs

If a floor or roof slab spans more than 3 m or 10 ft, it is often economical to provide a hollow-block slab, which is light in weight and requires less concrete than a solid slab. Such a floor comprises a topping from 30 to 90 mm or 1.25 to 3.5 in thick over concrete ribs. The ribs may be spaced at 150 to 1000 mm or 6 to 36 in centres, and may be from 60 to 125 mm or 2.5 to 5 in wide. The spaces between the ribs may be left open, but in order to simplify the formwork they may be filled with hollow blocks of burnt clay or lightweight concrete. The combined depth of the rib and slab is determined in the same way as the depth of a solid slab, and the thickness of the top slab is made sufficient to provide adequate compressive area. The width of the rib is primarily determined by the shearing force. Weights of solid and hollow slabs are given in *Table 2.* The principal requirements of BS8110 and CP110 are that the thickness of the top slab be not less than one-tenth of the clear distance between ribs or not less than 40 mm, whichever is greater. If the blocks are assumed to add to the strength of the construction and the clear distance between the ribs does not exceed 500 mm, the top slab should be not less than 30 mm thick, and this thickness may be reduced to 25 mm if the blocks are properly jointed. The distance between the centres of the ribs should not exceed 1.5 m. For resistance to shearing, the effective width of the rib is assumed to be the actual width plus the thickness of one wall of the block. The net depth of the rib (excluding topping) should not exceed four times the width.

In addition BS8110 requires that, where ribs contain one bar only, the bar is located in position by purpose-made spacers extending over the full rib width. Links are obligatory in ribs reinforced with more than one bar when the shearing stress exceeds $v_c/2$. CP110 specifies a minimum rib width of 65 mm; according to BS8110 this is determined by cover, fire resistance and bar spacing considerations.

6.1.5 Stairs

Structural stairs may be tucked away out of sight in a remote corner of a building or they may form a principal feature. In the former case they can be designed and constructed as simply and cheaply as possible, but in the latter it is worth while expending a great deal of time and trouble on the design. In contrast to a normal slab covering a large area, where a slight reduction in depth considerably increases the amount of reinforcement required and hence the cost, by making a stair as slender as possible the vast difference between clumsiness and grace may be attained if the thickness is visible. The extra steel needed to compensate for the reduction in the effective depth needed in this case is negligible when considering the cost of the whole building, and the improved appearance well warrants the extra expenditure and care in design and detailing.

Some of the types of stair that are possible are illustrated on *Table 175.* Various procedures have been developed for analysing the more common types, and some of these are described on this table and *Tables 176* and *177.* These theoretical procedures are based on the consideration of an idealized line structure and, when detailing the reinforcement for the resulting stair, bars must be also included to restrict the formation of cracks at the points of high stress concentration which inevitably occur. It is advantageous to provide a certain amount of steel in the form of small-diameter bars spaced reasonably closely throughout the stair. The 'three-dimensional' nature of the actual structure and the stiffening effect of the triangular tread areas (both of which are normally ignored when analysing the structure) lead to actual distributions of stress which differ from those calculated theoretically, and this must be remembered when detailing.

The types of stair illustrated on *Table 175* and others can now also be investigated by finite-element methods and similar procedures suitable for computer analysis, and with such methods it is often possible to take some account of the three-dimensional nature of the stair.

According to both BS8110 and CP110, stairs should be designed for ultimate loads of $1.4g_k$ and 1.6 or $1.0q_k$, as in the case of other structural members. They must also comply with the same serviceability requirements, although it is clearly well-nigh impossible to estimate accurately the likelihood of excess cracking or deflection occurring in more complex stairs, other than by carrying out large-scale tests.

Finally, it should be remembered that the prime purpose of a stair is to provide pedestrian access between the floors it connects. As such it is of vital importance regarding fire hazard and a principal design consideration must be to provide adequate fire resistance.

Simple straight flights of stairs can span transversely (i.e. across the flight) or longitudinally (i.e. in the direction of the flight). When spanning transversely, supports must be provided on both sides of the flight by either walls or stringer beams. In this case the waist or thinnest part of the stair construction need be only, say, 50 mm (or 2 in) thick, the effective lever-arm for resisting the bending moment being about one-half the maximum thickness from the nose to the soffit measured normal to the soffit. When the stair spans longitudinally the thickness required to resist bending determines the thickness of the waist.

The loads for which stairs should be designed are given in *Table 7.* The bending moments should be calculated from the total weight of the stairs and the total imposed load combined with the horizontal span. The stresses produced by the longitudinal thrust are small and are generally neglected in the design of simple systems. Unless circumstances otherwise dictate, a suitable shape for a step is a 175 mm (or 7 in) rise with a 250 mm (or 10 in) going, which with a 25 mm or (1 in) nosing or undercut gives a tread of 275 mm (or 11 in). Stairs in industrial buildings may be steeper: those in public buildings may be less steep. Optimum dimensions are given by the expression (2 × rise + going) = 600 mm.

Recommendations for the design of stairs and landings are given in BS8110 and CP110, and are amplified in the *Joint Institutions Design Manual.* BS5395 'Stairs' illustrates and describes various types of stairs.

6.1.6 Flat roofs

A flat reinforced concrete roof is designed similarly to a floor and may be a simple solid slab, or beam-and-slab construction, or a flat slab. In beam-and-slab construction the slab may be a solid cast *in situ* slab, a hollow-block slab, or a precast concrete slab. A watertight covering, such as asphalt or bituminous felt, is generally necessary, and with a solid slab some form of thermal insulation may be required. The watertight covering is sometimes omitted from a flat solid slab forming the roof of an industrial building, but in such a case the concrete should be particularly dense, and the slab should be not less than 100 mm (or 4 in) thick and should be laid to a slope of at least 1 in 40 to expedite the discharge of rainwater. Sodium silicate or tar, well brushed into the surface of the concrete, will improve the watertightness if there are no cracks in the slab.

For ordinary buildings the slab of a flat roof is generally built level and the slope for draining, often about 1 in 120, is formed by a mortar topping. The topping is laid directly on the concrete and below the asphalt or other watertight covering, and may form the thermal insulation if it is made of sufficient thickness and of lightweight concrete or other material having low thermal conductivity.

6.1.7 Sloping roofs

Planar slabs with a continuous steep slope are not common in reinforced concrete, except for mansard roofs; the covering of pitched roofs is generally metal or asbestos-cement sheeting, glass, wood-wool slabs, or other lightweight material. Such coverings and roof glazing require purlins for their support and, although the purlins are frequently of steel, reinforced concrete purlins, which may be either cast *in situ* or more commonly precast, are provided, especially if the roof structure is of reinforced concrete.

6.1.8 Precast concrete purlins

The size of a precast concrete purlin depends not so much on the stresses due to bending as on the deflection. Excessive deflection, although not necessarily a sign of structural weakness, may lead to defects in the roof covering. The shape of the purlin should be such that lightness is combined with resistance to bending, not only in a vertical plane but also in a direction parallel to the slope of the roof. An L-shape, which is often used, is efficient in these respects, but a wedge-shape is often less costly to make for small spans. The weight of a precast concrete purlin may be excessive for spans over 5 m or 15 ft. The dimensions depend on the span and the load, and for purlins spaced at 1.5 m or 4 ft 6 in centres and carrying ordinary lightweight roof sheeting and spanning 5 m or 15 ft, suitable sizes are 125 mm or 5 in for the width across the top flange and 200 mm or 8 in for the overall depth. For a span of 3 m or 10 ft the corresponding dimensions are 105 and 150 mm or 4.5 and 6 in, respectively.

For purlins on sloping roofs, the weights acting vertically and the wind pressure normal to the slope of the roof should be combined vectorially before computing the bending moment. The stresses should then be calculated with the neutral plane normal to the line of action of the resultant load. A semi-graphical method, as described in *Table 160*, is suitable for calculating the stresses.

The purlins may be supported on cast *in situ* or precast concrete frames or rafters. If the rafters are cast *in situ* the ends of the purlins can often be embedded in the rafters so as to obtain some fixity, which increases the stiffness of the purlin. If the rafters are of precast concrete, the type of fixing of the purlin is generally such that the purlin should be designed as freely supported.

6.1.9 Non-planar roofs

Roofs which are not planar, other than the simple pitched roofs considered in the foregoing, may be constructed in the form of a series of planar slabs (prismatic or hipped-plate construction), or as singly- or doubly-curved shells. Singly-curved shells such as segmental or cylindrical shells, are classified as *developable* surfaces. Such surfaces are less stiff than those formed by doubly-curved roofs and their equivalent prismatic counterparts, which cannot be 'opened up' into plates without some shrinking or stretching taking place.

If the curvature of a doubly-curved surface is generally similar in all directions, the surface is known as *synclastic*; a typical example is a dome, where the curvature is identical in all directions. If the shell curves in opposite directions over certain areas, the surface is termed *anticlastic* (i.e. saddle-shaped): the hyperbolic-paraboloidal shell is a well-known example and is the special case where such a doubly-curved shell is generated by two sets of straight lines. The elementary analysis of some of these structural forms is dealt with on *Table 178* and section 25.3, but reference should be made to specialized publications for more comprehensive analyses and more complex designs. Solutions for many particular types of shell have been produced, and in addition general methods have been developed for analysing forms of any shape by means of a computer.

Shells, like all indeterminate structures, are influenced by such secondary effects as shrinkage, temperature change, settlement and so on, and the designer must always bear in mind the fact that the stresses arising from these effects may modify quite considerably those calculated to occur due to normal dead and imposed loading.

In *Table 184* expressions are given for the forces in domed slabs such as are used for the bottoms and roofs of cylindrical tanks. In a building a domed roof generally has a much larger ratio of rise to span and, where the dome is part of a spherical surface and has an approximately uniform thickness throughout, the analysis given in *Table 178* applies. Shallow segmental domes and truncated cones are also dealt with in *Table 178*.

Cylindrical shell roofs. Segmental or cylindrical roofs are generally designed as shell structures. A thin curved slab acting as a shell is assumed to offer no resistance to bending and not to deform under applied distributed loads. Except near the edge and end stiffeners, it is subjected to only direct membrane forces, namely a direct force acting longitudinally in the plane of the slab, a direct force acting tangentially to the curve of the slab, and a shearing force. Formulae for these membrane forces are given in section 25.3.3. In practice, the boundary conditions due to the presence or absence of edge or valley beams, end diaphragms, continuity etc. affect the forces and displacements that would otherwise occur as a result of membrane action. Thus, as when analysing any indeterminate structure (such as a continuous beam system), the effects due to the various boundary restraints must be combined with the statically determinate stresses, which in this case arise from membrane action.

Shell roofs may be arbitrarily subdivided into 'short' (where the ratio of the length l of the shell to the radius r is less than about one-half), 'long' (where l/r exceeds 2.5) and 'intermediate'. For short shells the influence of the edge forces is slight in comparison with membrane action and the final stresses can normally be estimated quite accurately by considering the latter only. If the shell is long, membrane action is relatively insignificant and the stresses can be approximated by considering the shell to act as a beam with curved flanges, as described in section 25.3.3.

For preliminary analysis of intermediate shells, no equivalent short-cut method has yet been devised. The standard method of solution is described in various textbooks (for example refs 50 and 51). Such methods involve the solution of eight simultaneous equations if the shell or the loading is unsymmetrical, or four if symmetry is present, by matrix inversion or some other means. This normally requires the use of a computer, although a standard program exists for inverting and solving 4×4 matrices on a programmable pocket calculator, and the solution of such sets of simultaneous equations is very easy and rapid using even the simplest microcomputer. By making certain simplifying assumptions and providing tables of coefficients, Tottenham (ref. 52) has developed a popular simplified design method which is rapid and requires the solution of three simultaneous equations only.

J. D. Bennett has more recently developed an empirical method of designing long and intermediate shells, based on an analysis of the actual designs of more than 250 roofs. The method, which involves the use of simple formulae incorporating empirical constants, is summarized on *Table 179*. For further details see refs 53 and 54.

Buckling of shells. As already hinted, a major concern in designing any shell is the problem of buckling, since the loads at which buckling occurs, as established by tests, often differ from those predicted by theory. Ref. 131 indicates that for domes subtending angles of about 90°, the critical external pressure p at which buckling occurs, according to both theory and tests, is $0.3E(h/r)^2$, where E is the elastic modulus of concrete and h is the thickness and r the radius of the dome. For a shallow dome (span/rise $\simeq$ 10), $p = 0.15E(h/r)^2$. A factor of safety against buckling of 2 to 3 should be adopted. For synclastic shells having a radius ranging from r_1 to r_2, an equivalent dome with a radius of $r = \sqrt{(r_1 r_2)}$ may be considered.

For a cylindrical shell, buckling is unlikely if the shell is short. In the case of long shells, $p = 0.6E(h/r)^2$.

Anticlastic surfaces are more rigid than singly-curved shells and the buckling pressure for a saddle-shaped shell supported on edge stiffeners safely exceeds that of a cylinder having a curvature equal to that of the anticlastic shell at the stiffener. For a hyperbolic-paraboloidal surface with straight boundaries, the buckling load n obtained from tests is slightly more than $E(ch)^2/2ab$, where a and b are the lengths of the sides of the shell, c is the rise and h the thickness: this is only one-half of the value predicted theoretically.

6.1.10 Panel walls

Panel walls filling in a structural frame and not designed to carry loads (other than wind pressure) should be not less than 100 mm or 4 in thick (for constructional reasons), and should be reinforced with not less than 6 mm bars at 150 mm centres or 1/4 in bars at 6 in centres, or the equivalent in bars of other sizes but with a maximum spacing of not more than 300 mm or 12 in centres (or an equivalent fabric); this reinforcement should be provided in one layer in the middle of the wall. Bars 12 mm or 1/2 in or more in diameter should be placed above and at the sides of openings, and 12 mm or 1/2 in bars 1.25 m or 4 ft long should be placed across the corners of openings. The slab must be strong enough to resist the bending moments due to its spanning between the members of the frame. The connections to the frame must be strong enough to transfer the pressures on the panel to the frame either by bearing, if the panel is set in rebates in the members of the frame, or by the resistance to shearing of reinforcement projecting from the frame into the panel. A bearing is preferable since the panel is then completely free from the frame and therefore not subjected to secondary stresses due to deformation of the frame; nor is the connection between the panel and the frame subjected to tensile stresses due to contraction of the panel caused by shrinkage of the concrete or thermal changes. By setting the panel in a chase the connection is also made lightproof. If not rigidly connected to the frame, the panel or slab should be designed as a slab spanning in two directions without the corners being held down (see *Table 50*).

6.1.11 Load-bearing walls

BS8110 and CP110 give recommendations for the design of both reinforced and plain concrete load-bearing walls: some comparative details are given in *Table 171*. To be considered as a reinforced concrete wall the greater lateral dimension b of the member must exceed four times the lesser dimension h, otherwise it is considered to be a column. It must also contain at least $0.004bh$ of vertical reinforcement arranged in one or two layers; with a lesser proportion of steel the rules for plain concrete walls apply. BS8110 states that where tension occurs across the section, a layer of steel must be provided near each face and all bars must comply with the same spacing criteria adopted to control cracking that is specified for floor slabs. Reinforced concrete walls should also contain at least $0.0025bh$ of high-yield or $0.003bh$ of mild-steel reinforcement horizontally, the diameter of this steel being at least one-quarter of that of the vertical bars or 6 mm, whichever is the greater. If more than 0.02*bh* of vertical reinforcement is provided, links of at least one-quarter of the size of the largest main bar or 6 mm, whichever is the greater, must be employed. These links must be spaced at not more than twice the wall thickness horizontally and not more than twice the wall thickness or 16ϕ vertically. The distance from any vertical compression bar not enclosed by a link to the nearest restrained bar must not exceed 200 mm. Note that according to CP110 only, for fire-resistance purposes any wall containing less than 0.01*bh* of vertical reinforcement is classified as of plain concrete.

Load-bearing reinforced concrete walls may be short (termed 'stocky' in BS8110) or slender, and braced or unbraced. According to BS8110, walls of dense concrete having a ratio of effective height to minimum thickness of not more than 15 are considered to be short; the corresponding ratio for unbraced walls is 10. CP110 prescribes a limiting ratio of 12 for all normal-weight concrete walls. For walls of lightweight concrete both BS8110 and CP110 specify a limiting ratio of 10. If these ratios are exceeded the walls are considered to be slender and the procedure outlined for columns in section 5.15.1, whereby an additional moment is considered and the section is designed for direct load and bending, should be employed. If the structure of which the wall is part is laterally stabilized by walls or other means at right angles to the plane of the wall being investigated, it may be considered as braced; otherwise it is unbraced. This bracing or otherwise affects the effective height, which is assessed as for a column unless it carries freely supported construction, when the effective height is found in the same manner as that for a plain concrete wall. According to both Codes the limiting slenderness ratio for a braced wall is 40 if the amount of vertical reinforcement provided is not more than 0.01*bh*, and 45 otherwise: for an unbraced wall the limiting ratio is 30.

Walls that are axially loaded or that support an approximately symmetrical arrangement of slabs are designed using expressions corresponding to those for similar columns and given on *Table 171*. If the structural frame consists of monolithic walls and floors, the moments and axial forces in the walls may be determined by elastic analysis. Walls subjected to such moments and forces should be designed as equivalent columns by considering such effects over a unit length and determining the reinforcement necessary accordingly.

The minimum thickness of a reinforced concrete wall, as determined by fire-resistance considerations, is 75 mm, but sound or thermal insulation requirements or durability may necessitate a greater minimum thickness.

The requirements for plain concrete walls, which are treated in some detail in clause 3.9.4 of BS8110 and clause 5.5 of CP110, are only briefly summarized here. The definitions for short or slender and braced or unbraced walls given above also apply for plain concrete walls, but different criteria are used to determine the effective height of such a wall: this height depends on the lateral support provided. In no circumstances may the ratio of effective height to thickness exceed 30. Additional design information is given on *Table 171*.

Short braced and unbraced plain walls are deemed to carry an ultimate load determined by the wall thickness, the resultant eccentricity of load at right angles to the plane of the wall (with a minimum value of $h/20$), the characteristic strength of concrete, and a multiplying factor that depends upon the type of concrete used and the ratio of the clear height between supports to the length of the wall (see *Table 171*). To determine the ultimate load-carrying capacity of slender braced and of all unbraced walls, an additional eccentricity related to slenderness is taken into account together with the foregoing factors.

In addition to the requirements regarding direct force, the resistance of a plain concrete wall to horizontal shearing forces and to bearing stresses beneath concentrated loads such as are caused by girder or lintel supports must also be considered.

Minimum reinforcement. The minimum reinforcement in reinforced concrete load-bearing walls to BS8110 and CP110 is shown in the accompanying table. In this table, the area of reinforcement is given as a proportion of the cross-sectional area *bh* of wall. A_{sreq} is the total cross-sectional area of reinforcement needed in mm^2 per metre length or height of wall, taking account of bars near both faces of wall. If a single layer of bars is used to reinforce the wall, the given spacings

Minimum reinforcement in reinforced concrete load-bearing walls

Specified amount of reinforcement	0.0025*bh*		0.003*bh*		0.004*bh*	
Wall thickness (mm)	A_{sreq}(mm^2)	On each face	A_{sreq}(mm^2)	On each face	A_{sreq}(mm^2)	On each face
100	250	6@200	300	6@175	400	8@250
125	313	6@175	375	6@150	500	8@200
150	375	6@150	450	8@225	600	10@250
175	438	8@225	525	10@300	700	10@225
200	500	8@200	600	10@250	800	12@275
225	563	10@275	675	10@225	900	12@250
250	625	10@250	750	12@300	1,000	12@225

should be halved. The form '6 @ 200' denotes that a suitable arrangement would be 6 mm diameter bars at 200 mm centres.

It should be remembered that the minimum amounts of reinforcement recommended in BS8110 and CP110 may be insufficient to resist the effects of temperature and shrinkage. Also, the effect of the method of construction on the shrinkage stresses and the degree of exposure as it affects the probable thermal changes should be considered.

6.2 BRIDGES

As mentioned in section 2.4.6, the analysis and design of bridges is now so complex that it cannot be adequately covered in a book of this nature, and reference should be made to specialist publications. However, for the guidance of designers who may have to deal with structures having features in common with bridges, brief notes are given here on certain aspects of bridge design (e.g. loads, decks, piers, abutments etc.).

6.2.1 Types of bridges

A bridge may be one of two principal types, namely an arch bridge or a girder bridge, and either of these types may be statically determinate or statically indeterminate. Some basic types of bridges are illustrated in *Table 180*. A bowstring girder is a special type of arch, and a rigid-frame bridge can be considered as either a type of girder or an arch bridge.

The selection of the type in any particular instance depends principally on the situation, the span, the nature of the foundation, the materials to be used, and the clearance required. It may be that more than one type is suitable, in which case the economy of one over the others may be the deciding factor. If a bridge is fairly high above the railway, road or waterway, an arch is generally the most suitable if the ratio of the span to the rise does not greatly exceed ten and if the foundation is able to resist the inclined forces from the arch. If settlement of the foundation is probable, an arch provided with hinges can be used but the ratio of the span to that rise should not greatly exceed 5. For other conditions a girder bridge is more suitable.

The principal disadvantage of reinforced concrete as a structural material is its high self-weight. This makes it particularly unsuitable for structures comprised of members of which large areas are in tension, since over these areas the concrete thus does not contribute to the strength of the section. Generally speaking, reinforced concrete construction is thus unsuitable for girder bridges of any reasonable size since most of the resulting structure is required to support its own considerable self-weight. For such bridges, prestressed concrete or structural steel construction is considerably more efficient. However, either cast *in situ* or precast reinforced concrete is a viable alternative to prestressed concrete for the decks of such bridges, irrespective of the material forming the main structural members.

Since an arch section is largely or entirely in compression, reinforced concrete is here a principal material. In general, however, situations favouring arch construction are fewer than those favouring girder bridges, at least as far as the UK is concerned.

6.2.2 Loads

The imposed loads on road and railway bridges are described in section 2.4.6. Particulars of weights of typical road and rail vehicles, and some of the loading requirements of BS5400 and BS153: Part 3A, are given in *Tables 8* to *11*. Notes on the foregoing are given in sections 9.2.2, 9.2.3, 9.2.10 and 9.2.12.

6.2.3 Deck

The design of the deck of a reinforced concrete bridge is almost independent of the type of the bridge. Some typical cross-sections are given in *Table 180*. In the simplest case the deck is a reinforced concrete slab spanning between the abutments and bearing freely thereon, as in a freely supported type of bridge, or built monolithically therewith as in a rigid-frame bridge. This type of deck is suitable only for short spans. The more common case is for the main arches or girders to support a slab that spans transversely between these principal members. If the latter are widely spaced an economical deck is provided by inserting transverse beams or diaphragms and designing the slab to span in two directions. Such a system, termed a *grid* deck, is less popular than formerly, owing to the amount of workmanship involved in fabricating the transverse members.

For spans exceeding 15 m (50 ft) it is normal to reduce the self-weight of the section by incorporating cylindrical or rectangular void-formers at mid-thickness. With an increasing proportion of voids (usually more than 60% of the depth) the behaviour of the deck starts to alter and the construction is considered to be *cellular*. If the resulting deck is wide and shallow with numerous cells, it is termed *multicellular*: decks comprising only a few, very large cells (frequently with a wide top slab that cantilevers beyond the cellular structure below) are known as *box-girder* construction. Reinforced concrete is less likely to be used for cellular construction.

Beam-and-slab construction resembles grid construction but transverse members are not normally provided. The longitudinal beams may be closely spaced (a so-called *contiguous beam-and-slab* deck) or may be at 2 to 3.5 m (6 to 12 ft) centres (i.e. *spaced beam-and-slab* construction). In both cases a cast *in situ* slab usually spans between beams of precast prestressed concrete (or steel). One final form of construction may be encountered, particularly for footbridges. Here the ratio of length to width is so great that any loading causes the cross-section to displace bodily rather than to change in shape.

Apart from the final (beam) structure, which can be analysed simply as a continuous system, more complex procedures are required to analyse the deck. Four methods are in general use, namely grillage analysis, the load-distribution method, the finite-strip method and finite-plate elements. Of these, grillage analysis is the most widely used and probably the most versatile. The load-distribution and finite-strip methods are somewhat more restricted in application but offer other advantages. Finite-element methods are extremely complex and, although potentially very powerful, cannot as yet be considered a standard design tool. For details of all these methods specialist textbooks should be consulted, e.g. refs 56 to 58.

The underside of the deck of a bridge over a railway on which steam locomotives are still in use should have a flat soffit, thereby avoiding pockets in which smoke may collect. For such bridges the corrosion of the concrete by the smoke from steam locomotives has to be prevented. Smoke-guards may not entirely protect the structure. A dense concrete, free from cracks through which the fumes can reach and attack the steel reinforcement, is necessary. The cover of concrete should be greater than that provided in buildings, and the tensile stresses in the concrete should be calculated and limited in value as in liquid-containing structures.

A bridge less than 5 m or 15 ft wide is often economical if the slab spans transversely between two outer longitudinal girders. These girders may be the parapets of the bridge, but in general the parapets should not be used as principal structural members. If the width of the bridge exceeds 5 m or 15 ft, an economical design is produced by providing several longitudinal girders or arch ribs at about 6 ft or 2 m centres.

Footpaths are sometimes cantilevered off the principal part of the bridge. Water, gas, electrical and other services are generally installed in a duct under the footpaths.

6.2.4 Piers and abutments

The piers for girder bridges are generally subjected only to the vertical load due to the total loads on the girders; the abutments of girder bridges have to resist the vertical loads from the girders and the horizontal earth pressure on the back of the abutment. There may also be horizontal forces due to friction on bearings, braking, acceleration etc. Continuity between the girders and the abutments is assumed in rigid-frame bridges, and consequently the foregoing forces on the abutment must be combined with the bending moments and horizontal thrusts due to action as a frame.

The abutments of an arch bridge have to resist the vertical loads and the horizontal thrusts from the arch. Stability is obtained by constructing massive piers in plain concrete or masonry, or by providing tension and compression piles, or by a cellular reinforced concrete box filled with earth. Part of the horizontal thrust on the abutments will be resisted by the active earth pressure on the abutment, but in the case of fixed arches this pressure should be assumed to relieve the thrust from the arch only when complete assurance is possible that this pressure will always be effective. Adequate resistance to sliding should also be assured, and the buoyancy effect of foundations below water should be investigated.

Mid-river piers, if not protected by independent fenders, should be designed to withstand blows from passing vessels or floating debris, and should have cutwaters.

6.3 CULVERTS AND SUBWAYS

Concrete culverts are of rectangular (box), circular or similar cross-section and may be either cast *in situ* or precast.

6.3.1 Pipe culverts

For conducting small streams or drains under embankments, culverts can be constructed with precast reinforced concrete pipes, which must be strong enough to resist the vertical and horizontal pressures from the earth and other superimposed loads. The pipes should be laid on a bed of concrete and, where passing under a road, they should be surrounded with a thickness of reinforced concrete of at least 150 mm or 6 in. The culvert should also be reinforced longitudinally to resist bending due to unequal vertical earth pressure or unequal settlement. Owing to the uncertainty of the magnitude and disposition of pressures on circular pipes embedded in the ground, accurate analysis of the bending moments is impracticable. A basic guide is that the positive bending moments at the top and bottom of a circular pipe of diameter d and the negative bending moments at the ends of a horizontal diameter are $0.0625qd^2$, where q is the intensity of downward pressure on the top and of upward pressure on the bottom, assuming the pressures to be distributed uniformly on a horizontal plane.

6.3.2 Loads on culverts

The load on the top of a box or pipe culvert includes the weights of the earth and the top slab and the imposed load (if any).

Where a trench has been excavated in firm ground for the construction of a culvert and the depth from the surface of the ground to the roof of the culvert exceeds, say, three times the width of the culvert, it may be assumed that the maximum earth pressure on the culvert is that due to a depth of earth equal to three times the width of the culvert. Although a culvert passing under a newly filled embankment may be subjected to more than the full weight of the earth above, there is little reliable information concerning the actual load carried, and therefore any reduction in load due to arching of the ground should be made with discretion. If there is no filling and wheels or other concentrated loads can bear directly on the culvert, the load should be considered as carried on a certain length of the culvert. In the case of a box culvert, the length of the culvert supporting the load should be determined by the methods shown in *Tables 10, 11* and *56*. The concentration is modified if there is any filling above the culvert and, if the depth of filling is h_1, a concentrated load F can be considered as spread over an area of $4h_1^2$. When h_1 equals or slightly exceeds half the width of the culvert, the concentrated load is equivalent to a uniformly distributed load of $F/4h_1^2$ in units of force per unit area over a length of culvert equal to $2h_1$. For values of h_1 of less than half the width of the culvert, the bending moments will be between those due to a uniformly distributed load and those due to a central concentrated load.

The weights of the walls and top (and any load that is on them) produce an upward reaction from the ground. The weights of the bottom slab and the water in the culvert are carried directly on the ground below the slab and thus do not produce bending moments, although these weights must be taken into account when calculating the maximum pressure on the ground. The horizontal pressure due to the water in the culvert produces an internal triangular load or a trapezoidal load if the surface of the water outside the culvert is above the top, when there will also be an upward pressure on the underside of the top slab. The magnitude and distribution of the horizontal pressure due to the earth against the sides of the culvert can be calculated in accordance with the formulae given in *Tables 16–20*, consideration being given to the possibility of the ground becoming waterlogged with consequent increased pressures and the possibility of flotation.

6.3.3 Bending moments in box culverts

The bending moments can be calculated by considering the possible incidence of the loads and pressures. Generally there are only two conditions to consider: (1) culvert empty: full load and surcharge on the top slab, the weight of the walls, and maximum earth pressure on the walls; (2) culvert full: minimum load on the top slab, minimum earth pressure on the walls, weight of walls, maximum horizontal pressure from water in the culvert, and possible upward pressure on the top slab. In some circumstances these conditions may not produce the maximum positive or negative bending moments at any particular section, and the effect of every probable combination should be considered. The direct thrusts and tensions due to various loads should be combined with the bending moments to determine the maximum stresses.

The bending moments produced in monolithic rectangular culverts may be determined by considering the four slabs as a continuous beam of four spans with equal bending moments at the end supports but, if the bending of the bottom slab tends to produce a downward deflection, the compressibility of the ground and the consequent effect on the bending moments must be considered.

The loads on a box culvert can be conveniently divided as follows:

1. a uniformly distributed load on the top slab and an equal reaction from the ground below the bottom slab
2. a concentrated imposed load on the top slab and an equal reaction from the ground below the bottom slab
3. an upward pressure on the bottom slab due to the weight of the walls
4. a triangularly distributed horizontal pressure on each wall due to the increase in earth pressure in the height of the culvert
5. a uniformly distributed horizontal pressure on each wall due to pressure from the earth and any surcharge above the level of the roof of the culvert
6. the internal horizontal and possibly vertical pressures from water in the culvert

Formulae for the bending moments at the corners due to these various loads are given in *Table 186* and are applicable when the thicknesses of the top and bottom slabs are about equal, but may be equal to or different from the thicknesses of the walls. The limiting ground conditions should be noted.

6.3.4 Subways

A subway of rectangular cross-section is subjected to external earth pressures similar to those on a culvert, and the formulae in *Table 186* can be used for the purpose of calculating the bending moments. Internal pressures do not generally have to be considered.

6.4 BEARINGS, HINGES AND JOINTS

In the construction of frames and arches, hinges are necessary at points where it is assumed there is no bending moment. Bearings are necessary in some types of bridges to ensure statical determinacy. Some types of sliding and rocker bearings and hinges are illustrated in *Table 181*, and notes on these designs are given in section 25.4.1. Mechanical bearings have now been largely superseded by the introduction of polytetrafluoroethylene (PTFE).

Joints in monolithic concrete construction are required to allow free expansion and contraction due to changes of temperature and shrinking in such structures as retaining walls, reservoirs, roads and long buildings, and to allow unrestrained deformation of the walls of cylindrical containers when it is undesirable to transfer any bending moment or force from the walls to the bottom slab. Information and guidance on the provision of movement joints in buildings is given in section 8 of BS8110: Part 2; see also BS6093. Some designs of joints for various purposes are illustrated in *Table 182*, and notes on these designs are given in section 25.4.2. Joints in road slabs are illustrated in *Table 183*.

6.5 CONCRETE ROADS

A concrete road may be a concrete slab forming the complete road or may be a slab underlying bituminous macadam, granite setts, asphalt, wooden blocks or other surfacing. On the site of extensive works it is sometimes convenient to lay concrete roads before constructional work begins, these roads being the bases of permanent roads. A type of concrete road used for some motorways and similar main roads comprises a layer of plain cement-bound granular material (called 'dry-lean' concrete), the mix being about 1:18, with a bituminous surfacing. This section deals with the design of roads constructed using reinforced concrete only. For details of the preparation of the foundation (a very important aspect of the construction of a road) and methods of construction, reference should be made to other publications (refs 59, 60).

The design of concrete roads is based as much on experience as on calculation, since the combined effects of the expansion and contraction of the concrete due to moisture and temperature changes, of the weather, of foundation friction, of spanning over weak places in the foundation, of fatigue, and of carrying the loads imposed by traffic are difficult to assess. The provision of joints assists in controlling some of these stresses. The following notes give the basic principles only.

6.5.1 Stresses due to traffic

The stresses in a concrete road slab due to vehicles are greatest when a wheel is at an edge or near a corner of the slab, but considerably less when it is remote from an edge or corner; therefore, from the point of view of stresses due to traffic, it is desirable to reduce the number of joints and thereby reduce the number of effective edges and corners.

The empirical formulae derived originally by Westergaard for the calculation of the stresses are the basis of many subsequent attempts to reconcile the theoretical stresses with measured stresses; the formulae (first published in 1933) are given in a modified form in *Table 183* and have since been modified to apply to aircraft runways. See section 9.2.2 and *Table 8* for weights of vehicles.

6.5.2 Base

Except when the slab is laid on rock or similar non-deformable material, a sub-base must be provided; see ref. 59.

6.5.3 Slab

For all-concrete roads the concrete slab may be from 125 to 300 mm (or from 5 to 12 in) or more, depending on the amount of traffic and the type of soil. The thicknesses recommended in ref. 59 are given in *Table 183* for various intensities of traffic and types of soil as defined in the table. The thicknesses should be increased for particularly adverse conditions, such as for very heavy traffic on dockside roads on poor soil, for which a thickness of concrete of more than 300 mm or 12 in may be necessary. The concrete should not be leaner than $1:1\frac{2}{3}:3\frac{1}{3}$ unless special mixtures are designed to give a strong concrete with a lower cement content. For the wearing surface, rounded aggregates are not recommended and a hard crushed stone should be used. In districts where suitable crushed stone is costly an economical and durable slab can be formed by making the lower part of the slab of 1:2:4 concrete made with uncrushed gravel aggregate, and the upper part, to a depth of about 40 mm or 1.5 in, with $1:1\frac{1}{2}:3$ concrete made with crushed stone graded from 12 to 5 mm (or 1/2 to 3/16 in). Exposure to weather and abrasion from traffic subjects all-concrete roads to severe conditions, and all reasonable means of attaining a concrete of high quality should be taken.

6.5.4 Reinforcement

When a concrete road is laid on a firm and stable foundation, experience shows that reinforcement is not always necessary, but some engineers take the view that the provision of reinforcement is a precaution that justifies the cost. When mild-steel reinforcement is used the amount employed is generally between 3 to 5 kg/m^2 (6 to 10 lb/yd^2) provided in a single layer near the bottom or top of the slab; for roads subject to heavy traffic, reinforcement is provided near both top and bottom to give a total weight of 5 to 10 kg/m^2 (10 to 20 lb/yd^2).

For ordinary roads the reinforcement should be about 60 mm or 2.5 in from the top of the slab. The arrangement of the reinforcement depends on the width of the road and the spacing of the transverse joints. If the joints are at distances apart about equal to the width of the slab, the reinforcement should be arranged to give equal strength in both directions, but if the transverse joints are provided at long intervals to form panels that are, say, three or more times as long as they are wide, nine-tenths of the reinforcement should be parallel to the length of the road; for panels of intermediate proportions, ratios of between 0.5 and 0.9 of the total reinforcement should be placed longitudinally. Additional bars having a diameter of, say, 12 mm or 1/2 in should be provided in the top at the corners of the panels. For major roads and motorways, the recommendations given in ref. 59 should be followed: some requirements are collated in *Table 183*. According to this document the slab thickness, amount of reinforcement, joint spacing etc. depend on the amount of commercial traffic using the road. For further details see section 25.5.

6.5.5 Joints

Although some concrete roads have no transverse joints, the provision of such joints and, in wide roads, the provision of longitudinal joints may assist in reducing cracking. In the UK the common spacings of expansion and contraction joints were from 10 to 30 m or from 30 to 100 ft, but wider spacings are now recommended in ref. 59 and are given in *Table 183*, in which the recommended form of expansion joint is illustrated. In the centre of the slab, mild-steel dowel bars project horizontally from one panel into the next. One half of each bar is free to move and the other half is embedded in the concrete. Dowel bars prevent one panel rising relative to its neighbour, partially prevent warping and curling, and transfer a part of the load on one panel to the other, thereby reducing the stresses. The end of each day's concreting should coincide with a joint.

Simple dummy or other forms of contraction joints are provided at intervals between transverse expansion joints; a common form of such a joint is illustrated in *Table 183*. According to ref. 59, in a reinforced concrete slab two contraction joints should be formed between each expansion joint. The provision of dummy joints enables the slab to crack at intervals without being unsightly, irregular or injurious. It is normally necessary to provide dowel bars across contraction joints.

Longitudinal joints should be provided in roads so as to divide the road into strips not exceeding 4.5 m or 15 ft wide. A longitudinal joint may be a simple butt-joint, but some form of interlock is desirable to avoid one slab rising relative to the adjacent slab and to enable transfer of load to take place. Ref. 59 suggests that dowel bars 12 mm in diameter and 1 m long should be provided at 600 mm centres or 6 mm wires at 150 mm centres generally.

The joint shown in *Table 183* are typical. Similar and other designs are given in the publications of the Road Research Laboratory of the Department of Transport. For details of the groove size, depth of seal etc. see ref. 59.

6.6 TANKS

The weights of materials and the calculation of the horizontal pressure due to dry materials and liquids contained in tanks, reservoirs, bunkers, silos and other containers are given in *Tables 5, 16, 17, 18, 19* and *21*. This section and the next deal with the design of containers, and with the calculation of the forces and bending moments produced by the pressure of the contained materials. Where containers are required to be watertight, the recommendations given in BS5337 for reinforced concrete structures for the storage of water have been adopted. Containers are conveniently classified as *tanks* containing liquids, and *bunkers and silos* containing dry materials, each class being subdivided into cylindrical and rectangular structures.

6.6.1 Direct tension in the wall of a cylindrical tank

The wall of a cylindrical tank is primarily designed to resist direct tension due to the horizontal pressures of the contained materials, and, if q_{lp} per unit area is the pressure at any depth, the direct tension N in a horizontal ring of unit depth is $q_{lp}d/2$, where d is the internal diameter of the tank. Sufficient circumferential reinforcement must be provided to resist this tension; appropriate formulae are given in *Table 184*.

Tanks containing liquids may be designed to the limit-state criteria permitted by BS5337, where the restriction of crack widths due to characteristic loads to values of 0.1 or 0.2 mm for exposure classes A and B respectively forms, with the ultimate limit-state, a controlling condition. Alternatively, modular-ratio design may be employed provided that the limiting stresses in the materials are restricted to somewhat lower values than those that were permitted by CP114. For cylindrical tanks containing dry materials or for lined tanks containing liquids, limit-state design to BS8110 or CP110 or modular-ratio design may be employed, using the maximum design strength permitted. The lengths of laps in circumferential reinforcement must be sufficient to enable the calculated tensile stress in the reinforcement to be developed. Note that the code for water-containing structures (BS5337) restricts the anchorage-bond stress in such horizontal bars to only 70% of normal values, and this restriction should also be observed for tanks containing dry materials.

It is sometimes recommended that the thickness of the wall of a tank containing liquid should be not less than 100 mm or 4 in and not less than 2.5% of the depth of liquid plus 25 mm or 1 in.

6.6.2 Bending moments on the walls of cylindrical tanks

In addition to the horizontal tension in the wall of a cylindrical container, bending moments are produced by the restraint at the base of the wall. Unless a joint is made at the foot of the wall, as illustrated in *Table 182*, there is some continuity between the wall and the base slab which causes vertical deformation of the wall and reduces the circumferential tension. There are three principal factors, namely the magnitude of the bending moment at the base of the wall, the point at which the maximum circumferential tension occurs, and the magnitude of the maximum circumferential tension. Coefficients and formulae for determining these factors are given in *Table 184* and are derived from H. Carpenter's translation of Reissner's analysis: for a more detailed treatment of this method of analysis see ref. 93. The shape of the wall has some effect on the value of the coefficients, but the difference between the bending moments at the bases of walls of triangular or rectangular vertical section is so small that the common intermediate case of a trapezoidal section can be considered to be the same as a rectangular wall. The small error involved partly offsets the error of assuming perfect fixity at the junction of the wall and base.

The procedure is first to determine the maximum vertical bending moment and provide a wall having an equal moment of resistance at the bottom. The maximum circumferential tension and the height up the wall at which this occurs are next determined; a sufficient area of steel and thickness of concrete must be provided at this height to resist the maximum tension. Above this height the area of reinforcement can be uniformly decreased to a nominal amount, and below it the area of reinforcement can be maintained equal to that required for the maximum circumferential tension, although some reduction towards the bottom may be justified.

6.6.3 Octagonal tanks

If the wall of a tank forms, in plan, a series of straight sides instead of being circular, the formwork may be less costly but extra reinforcement or an increased thickness of concrete or both is necessary to resist the horizontal bending moments which are produced in addition to the direct tension. If the tank is a regular octagon the bending moment at the junction of adjacent sides is $ql^2/12$, where l is the length of side of the octagon. If the distance across the flats is d, the direct tension in each side is $qd/2$, and at the centre of each side the bending moment is $ql^2/24$. If the shape of the tank is not a regular octagon, but the lengths of the sides are alternately l_1 and l_2 and the corresponding thicknesses are d_1 and d_2, the bending moment at the junction of any two sides is

$$\frac{q}{12}\left[l_1^3 + l_2^3\left(\frac{d_1}{d_2}\right)^3\right]\Big/\left[l_1 + l_2\left(\frac{d_1}{d_2}\right)^3\right]$$

6.6.4 Walls of rectangular tanks

The bending moments and direct tensions on the walls of rectangular tanks are calculated in the same manner as described in section 6.7.2 for bunkers. For impermeable construction, however, limit-state or modular-ratio design in accordance with BS5337 should be undertaken. The consequent design charts, formulae etc. are given in *Tables 121–135*; these data apply to suspended bottoms of tanks as well as to walls.

The walls of large rectangular reservoirs generally span vertically and are monolithic with the roof and floor slab, the floor being generally laid directly on the ground. If the wall is considered as freely supported at the top and bottom, and if F is the total water pressure on the wall, the force at the top is $0.33F$ and at the bottom $0.67F$. If the wall is assumed to be freely supported at the top and fixed at the bottom, the forces are $0.2F$ and $0.8F$ at the top and bottom respectively. As neither of these conditions is likely to be obtained, a practical assumption is that the forces at the top and bottom are $0.25F$ and $0.75F$ respectively; the positive bending moment at about the midpoint of a wall of height h and the negative bending moment at the bottom are each equal to $0.0833Fh$. If the walls span vertically and horizontally, *Tables 53* and *61* apply.

6.6.5 Bottoms of elevated tanks

The type of bottom provided for an elevated cylindrical tank depends on the diameter of the tank and the depth of water. For small tanks a flat beamless slab is satisfactory, but beams are necessary for tanks from 3 to 8 m or 10 to 25 ft in diameter. Some appropriate designs are indicated in section 25.6.2, and notes on the designs, which include bottoms with beams and domed bottoms, and examples are given in sections 25.6.1 and 25.6.2.

According to BS5337, when considering the ultimate limit-state, the contained liquid must be treated as an imposed load and thus requires a partial safety factor of 1.6. The argument that this seems somewhat excessive (since it is clearly impossible to overload a fluid container to such an extent) has been countered (ref. 61) by the statement that the ultimate limit-state is seldom the controlling condition when designing beams and slabs to resist bending. This may be true but it clearly seems unnecessary to employ such a factor when considering the loads transferred to the supporting structure (i.e. columns, footings etc.). Certainly it seems reasonable to argue that the effect of the load resulting from the liquid in a tank consisting of a single compartment may be considered as a dead load when calculating the bending moments in the slabs and beams forming the bottom, since all spans must be loaded simultaneously.

6.6.6 Columns supporting elevated tanks

It is important that there should not be unequal settlement of the foundations of the columns supporting an elevated tank, and a raft should be provided if the nature of the ground is such that unequal settlement is likely. In addition to the bending moments and shearing forces due to the pressure of the wind on the tank, as described in *Table 14*, the wind force causes a thrust on the columns on the leeward side and a tension in the columns on the windward side; the values of the thrusts and tensions can be calculated for a group of columns from the expressions given in section 25.6.3.

6.6.7 Effects of temperature

For a tank containing a hot liquid, the design strengths should be lower than for other tanks, or the probable increases in stress due to the higher temperature should be calculated as described in section 6.8.3.

In the UK the effects of temperature due to weather variations are seldom sufficiently great to be considered in the design of the tank, but elsewhere it may be necessary to protect the tank of a water tower from extreme exposure to the sun. External linings of timber, brick or other material may be provided or the tank should be designed for the effects of the differences of temperature on opposite faces of the wall.

6.6.8 Joints

Permanent joints are provided in tanks, reservoirs and similar containers to allow for expansion and contraction due to changes of temperature or to shrinkage of the concrete, or to relieve parts of the structure from stresses due to indeterminate restraints that would otherwise be imposed by adjacent parts. Details of joints suitable for reservoirs, swimming pools and tanks are given in *Table 182*, and brief details of the spacing of such joints to comply with the requirements of BS5337 are given on *Table 121*.

6.6.9 Pipes

Pipes built into concrete tanks are sometimes made of non-ferrous alloy, since deterioration due to corrosion is much less than for ferrous metals and replacements that may affect the watertightness of the structure are obviated. Pipes built into the wall of a tank should have an additional intermediate flange cast in such a position that it will be buried in the thickness of the wall and thus form a water-bar.

6.6.10 Underground tanks

Underground or submerged tanks are subjected to external pressures due to the surrounding earth or water, which produce direct compression in the walls. The stress produced by this compression in the wall of a cylindrical tank is a maximum when the tank is empty, and is given by the expression in *Table 184*. Unless conditions are such that the permanence of the external pressure is assured, the relief to the tension provided by the compression should be disregarded in the calculation of the stresses in the tank when full. When empty, the structure should be investigated for flotation if it is submerged in a liquid or is in waterlogged ground.

Reservoirs with earth or other material banked up against the walls should be designed for earth pressure from outside with the tank empty. When the reservoir is full no reduction should be made to the internal pressure by reason of the external pressure, but in cases where the designer considers such reduction justified the amount of the reduction should be considerably less than the theoretical pressure calculated by the formulae for active pressures in *Tables 16–19*.

The earth on the roof of a reservoir should be considered as an imposed load, although it is ultimately a uniformly distributed load acting on all spans simultaneously. When the earth is being placed in position, conditions may occur whereby some spans are loaded and others are unloaded. Often, however, the designer can ensure that the earth is deposited in such a manner as to keep the bending moments to a minimum. Such a roof may often conveniently be designed as a flat slab in accordance with the requirements of BS8110 or CP110, or by permissible-stress theory, depending on whether the reservoir is being designed in accordance with the limit-state or modular-ratio methods permitted by BS5337.

6.7 BUNKERS AND SILOS

6.7.1 Properties of contained materials

The weights of materials commonly stored in bunkers are given in *Table 5*, and the pressures set up in relatively shallow containers due to these materials are dealt with in *Tables 16, 17* and *18*. In deep containers (silos) the increase of pressure with depth is no longer linear: see section 2.8.4.

When calculating the size of a structure of a specified capacity, the weight of the material should not be overrated and too small a value should not be assumed for the angle of repose. When calculating the weight to be carried on the bottom and the pressures to which the sides will be subjected, the weight should not be underestimated and the angle of internal friction should not be overestimated. Generally two assumptions are therefore necessary in designing a container; examples of these assumptions are given in *Table 17*.

Traditionally, silo design has been based on Janssen's theory with the introduction of an increased factor of safety to cover the lack of knowledge of actual unloading pressures. The advent of limit-state design and of more accurate methods of determining pressures now provides a basis for rationalizing silo design. However there is, to date, little published data on this topic. Where stored materials are sensitive to moisture the serviceability limit-state needs particular attention, especially with circular silos where the wall is subjected to hoop tension. The requirements of BS5337 may be applicable in certain circumstances.

Where granular materials are stored for long periods in structures that are subjected to fluctuations in temperature, increased pressures can develop from repeated cycles of wall expansion, consequent settlement of stored material, and wall contraction over long periods. The expansion of stored materials due to increases in moisture content can also develop high pressures.

6.7.2 Walls

The walls of bunkers and silos are designed to resist bending moments and tensions caused by pressure of the contained material. If the wall spans horizontally, it is designed for the bending moments and direct tension combined. If the wall spans vertically, horizontal reinforcement is provided to resist the direct tension and vertical reinforcement to resist the bending moments. In this case the horizontal bending moments due to continuity at corners should be considered, and it is generally sufficient if as much horizontal reinforcement is provided at any level at the corners as is required for vertical bending at this level; the amount of reinforcement provided for this purpose, however, need not exceed the amount of vertical reinforcement required at one-third of the height of the wall. The principal bending moment on walls spanning vertically is due to the triangularly distributed pressure from the contained material. Bending-moment coefficients for this distribution of load are given in *Tables 23–26* when the span is freely supported or fixed at one or both ends. The practical assumption described for the walls of rectangular reservoirs should be observed in this connection (see section 6.6.4).

For walls spanning horizontally the bending moments and forces depend on the number and arrangement of the compartments. For structures with several compartments, the intermediate walls act as ties between the outer walls, and in *Table 185* expressions are given for the negative bending moments on the outer walls of rectangular bunkers with various arrangements of intermediate walls or ties. The corresponding expressions for the reactions, which are a measure of the direct tensions in the walls, are also given. The positive bending moments can be readily calculated when the negative bending moments at the corners are known. An external wall is subject to maximum stresses when the adjacent compartment is filled, since it is then subjected simultaneously to the maximum bending moment and the maximum direct tension. An internal cross-wall is subjected to maximum bending moment when the compartment on one side of it is filled, and to maximum direct tension (but no bending moment) when the compartments on both sides of the wall are filled.

In small bunkers the panels of wall may be of such proportions that they span both horizontally and vertically, in which case *Table 53* should be used to calculate the bending moments since the pressure along the horizontal span is then uniformly distributed, while along the vertical span triangular distribution occurs.

In the case of an elevated bunker the whole load is generally transferred to the columns by the walls, and when the span exceeds twice the depth of the wall, the wall can be designed as a beam. Owing to the large moment of inertia of the wall (as a beam bending in a vertical plane) compared with that of the columns, the beam can be assumed to be freely supported but the heads of the columns under the corners of the bunker should be designed to resist a bending moment equal to, say, one-third of the maximum positive bending moment on the beam. If the provision of a sufficient moment of resistance so requires, a compression head can conveniently be constructed at the top of the wall, but there is generally ample space to accommodate the tension steel in the base of the wall. When the distance between the columns is less than twice the height of the wall the reinforcement along the base of the wall should be sufficient to resist a direct tension equal to one-quarter of the total load carried by the wall. The total load must include all other loads supported by the wall. These loads may be due to the roof or other superstructure or machines mounted above the bunker and to the weight of the wall.

The effect of wind on large structures should be calculated. In silos the direct compressive force on the leeward walls due to wind pressure is one of the principal forces to be investigated. The stress caused by the eccentric compression due to the proportion of the weight of the contents supported by friction on the walls of a silo must be combined with the stresses produced by wind pressure, and at the base or at the top of the walls there may be additional bending stresses due to continuity with the bottom or the covers or roof over the compartments.

If a wall is thicker at the bottom than at the top it may taper uniformly from bottom to top or the reduction in thickness may be made in steps. The formwork may be more costly for a tapered wall than for a stepped wall, especially for cylindrical containers. A stepped wall, however, may be subjected to high secondary stresses at each change of thickness, where also the daywork joints generally occur. Stepping on the outside is often objectionable as it provides ledges for the collection of dust. Stepping on the inside may interfere with the free flow of the contents when emptying the container.

The size and shape of a bunker depend on the purpose which it is to serve, and the internal dimensions are therefore generally specified by the owner. Typical calculations are given in the example in section 25.7 for a design in which the walls span horizontally. When the walls span horizontally, the reinforcement varies from a maximum at the bottom to a nominal amount at the top; the vertical reinforcement need only be sufficient to keep the horizontal bars in place, and generally 10 mm bars at 300 mm centres or 3/8 in bars at 12 in centres are satisfactory for this purpose. In the case of tall bunkers each lift of vertical reinforcement should not exceed about 3 m or 10 ft although, if continuously moving forms are used, the vertical bars should be only 1.2 to 1.8 m or 4 to 6 ft long.

All silos must be clearly marked with details of the materials which they are designed to contain, and with warnings against filling with other materials, eccentric filling, and changes in the unloading method.

6.7.3 Hopper bottoms

The design of sloping hopper bottoms in the form of inverted truncated pyramids consists of finding, for each sloping side, the centre of pressure, the intensity of pressure normal to the slope at this point, and the mean span. The bending moments at the centre and edge of each slope are then calculated. The horizontal direct tension is next computed and combined with the bending moment to determine the amount of horizontal reinforcement required. The direct tension acting in the line of the slope at the centre of pressure and the bending moment at this point are combined to find the reinforcement necessary in the underside of the slab at this point. At the top of the slope the bending moment and the component of the hanging-up force are combined to determine the reinforcement required in the upper face at the top of the slope.

The centre of pressure and the mean span can be found by inscribing on a normal plan of the sloping side a circle touching three of the sides. The diameter of this circle is the mean span and the centre is the centre of pressure. The total intensity of load normal to the slope at this point is the sum of the normal components of the vertical and horizontal pressures at the centre of pressure and the dead weight of the slab. Values for the pressure on an inclined slab are given in *Table 18*, and expressions for the bending moments and direct tensions along the slope and horizontally are given in *Table 186*. When using this method it should be remembered that, although the horizontal span of the sloping side is considerably reduced towards the outlet, the amount of reinforcement should not be reduced below that determined for the centre of pressure, since, in determining the bending moment based on the mean span, adequate transverse support from the reinforcement towards the base is assumed.

The hanging-up force in the direction of the slope has both a vertical and a horizontal component, the former being resisted by the walls acting as beams. The horizontal component, acting inwards, tends to produce horizontal bending moments on the beam at the top of the slope, but this inward force is opposed by a corresponding outward pressure from the contained material. The 'hip-beam' at the top of the hopper slope must be designed to withstand both the inward pull from the hopper bottom when the bottom is full and the silo above is only partially filled, and also the case where arching of the fill concentrates outward forces due to peak lateral pressure on to the beam during unloading. This is especially important in the case of mass-flow silos (see section 2.8.4).

6.8 CHIMNEYS

6.8.1 Maximum longitudinal service stresses

If the section is being designed on modular-ratio principles, the maximum service stresses on any horizontal plane of a chimney shaft should be investigated for the following conditions:

1. When subjected to direct load only, i.e. the weight of the concrete shaft and the lining, the maximum compressive service stress should not exceed the values for direct stress. For this purpose, the value of the modular ratio used in calculating the effect of the reinforcement can be assumed to be 15.
2. The stresses produced by combining the bending moment due to the wind with the maximum direct loads should be ascertained by using the design charts forming *Tables 164* and *165*. To the maximum compressive stress at the inner face of the wall should be added the stress f_{cT} due to the change of temperature, and to the maximum tensile stress in the reinforcement on the outer face should be added the stress f_{sT} due to the change of temperature, thereby giving approximately the maximum stresses. A method of calculating f_{sT} and f_{cT} is given in section 6.10. The maximum compressive stress in the concrete should not exceed the values for bending.

The various stresses are interrelated, and the addition of, say, the temperatures stresses to the combined bending and direct stresses may alter the basis of calculating these stresses by altering the position of the neutral plane, subjecting more of the concrete to tensile stresses which may cause cracking.

If limit-state design is employed, Pinfold has concluded (ref. 62) that temperature stresses of the magnitude normally encountered may generally be ignored in the longitudinal direction when investigating the ultimate limit-state. There is, however, some indication that the strength of concrete diminishes when subjected to high temperature for long periods, and it may be prudent to adopt a lower design strength than would otherwise be the case.

6.8.2 Transverse stresses

The preceding remarks deal solely with stresses normal to a horizontal plane. Stresses normal to a vertical plane are also produced both by wind pressure and by differences of temperature. In chimney shafts of ordinary dimensions the transverse bending moment resulting from wind pressure is generally negligible, but this is not necessarily so in tanks and cooling towers of large diameter. A uniform pressure of w_k per unit area produces a maximum bending moment of $w_k d^2/12$ on a unit height of a cylinder of external diameter d. This bending moment causes a compressive stress at the outer face of a wall normal to the line of the action of w_k and tension at the inner face. An equal bending moment, but of opposite sign, acts on the wall parallel to the line of action of w_k.

6.8.3 Dimensions

The height and internal sizes of a chimney are usually specified by the engineers responsible for the boiler installation. The reinforced concrete designer has to determine the thickness of, and the reinforcement in, the shaft. The two principal forces on the chimney are the wind pressure and the self-weight. At any horizontal section the cantilever bending moment due to the wind is combined with the direct force due to the weight of the chimney and lining above the section considered, to find the maximum stresses. Values for wind pressures on shafts are given in the 1958 edition of CP3, Chapter V. Part 2 of its 1972 successor does not cover chimneys, for which a BSI Draft for Development is in preparation. The section may be designed according to either limit-state or modular-ratio principles. Both procedures are discussed in detail in ref. 62, which provides series of charts for designing sections by both methods. If limit-state design is adopted, the sections may be evaluated by assuming an initial shaft thickness and amount of reinforcement and using the trial-and-adjustment procedure described in section 5.13.1. The charts for annual sections subjected to bending and thrust which form *Table 164* and *165* may be employed to design the sections if modular-ratio analysis is being undertaken. If this method is used, reduced design stresses should be adopted to resist the combination of bending moment and self-weight only, thereby leaving a margin to accommodate increases in the stresses due to a rise in temperature.

A difference in temperature between the two faces of a concrete wall produces a transverse bending moment equal to $T\varepsilon_c E_c I_c/h_c$ (see section 6.10 for notation employed). If the shaft is unlikely to be cracked vertically, the maximum stress is the concrete due to this bending moment is about $T\varepsilon_c E_c/2$, being compressive on the face subjected to the higher temperature and tensile on the opposite face.

6.9 INDUSTRIAL STRUCTURES

In addition to the ability of the various members to sustain the forces and moments to which they are subjected, there are other considerations peculiar to each type of industrial structure. Vibration must be allowed for in the substructures for crushing and screening plants. Provision against overstressing a reinforced concrete pit-head frame is obtained by designing for various conditions of working and accidental loading, as described in section 9.2.9. Watertightness is essential in slurry basins, coal draining bunkers, settling tanks and similar hydraulic structures, while airtightness is essential in gas purifiers and in airlock structures in connection with colliery work; the suction in airlocks is generally equivalent to a head of 125 to 250 mm or 5 to 10 in of water, that is, 1.25 to 2.9 N/m^2 or 26 to 60 lb/ft^2. The resistance of concrete to corrosion from fumes that are encountered in some industrial processes is one of the properties that makes the material particularly suitable for industrial construction, but protection of the concrete is needed with other fumes and some liquids. Provision should be made for expansion in structures in connection with steel-works, coke ovens, gas retorts and other structures where great heat is experienced. Boiler foundations, especially on clay, should be made sufficiently thick to prevent undue heating and drying out of the subsoil, or an insulating layer should be interposed between the foundation and the ground. Firing floors, coke-benches, and rolling-mill floors should be protected from extreme temperatures and abrasion by being covered with steel plates or bricks.

On floors where dust, rubbish or slime may collect, as in coal washeries, it is advantageous to make a fall in the top surface of 1 in 40 to facilitate the cleaning of the floors, but it must be ascertained that such a slope will not be inconvenient to the users of the floor; otherwise suitable channels must be provided to ensure that washing down will be effective.

Structures in mining districts should be designed for the possibility of subsidence of the ground upon which they stand. Thus raft foundations that have at any part equal resistance to negative and positive moments are commonly adopted for small structures. If isolated foundations are provided for long structures such as gantries, the longitudinal beams should be designed as if freely supported.

6.10 STRESSES DUE TO TEMPERATURE

The following consideration of stresses due to temperature can be applied to the walls of chimneys and tanks containing hot liquids, and other structures where there is a difference of temperature between the two concrete faces.

The first stage is to determine the change of temperature T through the concrete. The resistance to the transmission of heat through a wall of different materials, the successive thicknesses of which in metres or inches are h_1, h_2, h_3 etc., is given by

$$\frac{1}{k}=\frac{h_1}{k_1}+\frac{h_2}{k_2}+\frac{h_3}{k_3}+\cdots+a_i+a_a+a_o=\sum\frac{h}{k}+a_i+a_a+a_o$$

where k_1, k_2, k_3 etc. are the thermal conductivities of the various materials of which the wall is made, a_i and a_o represent the resistances at the internal and external faces respectively, and a_a is that due to a cavity in the wall. The conductivities are expressed in SI units in watts per metre per °C and in imperial units in Btu inches per square foot per hour per °F: 1 SI unit = 6.93 imperial units. The coefficient of heat transfer k is measured in watts per square metre per °C (or Btu per square foot per hour per °F) and the resistances a are in square metres per °C per watt (or Btu per square feet per hour per °F). Also 1 °C = 1.8 °F. The following data are in SI units, with imperial equivalents in parenthesis.

The thermal conductivity of 1:2:4 ordinary concrete at normal temperatures is about 1.5 (10) but may vary down to 1.1 (7.5) at high temperatures, the latter being also about the value for firebrick.

The value of a_o depends on the exposure, and a value of 0.09 m^2 °C/W (or 0.5) is a reasonable average value, although in sheltered positions facing south (in the northern hemisphere) the value may be 0.13 (or 0.75) and for conditions of severe exposure facing north it may be as low as 0.02 (or 0.1). In a chimney or in a tank containing hot liquid, there may be little difference between the temperature of the flue gas or liquid and the temperature of the face of the concrete or lining in contact with the gas or liquid. Hence a_i may often be neglected or, if some resistance at the internal face is expected, a value of 0.12 (or 0.7) may be used. The value of a_a depends on the amount of ventilation of the cavity; for an unventilated cavity it may be about 0.18 (or 1.0) and for a cavity with a moderate ventilation about 0.11 (or 0.65).

If the temperature of the flue gas or hot liquid is T_G °C and the external air temperature is T_A°C, the temperature T_1 on the warmer side of a concrete wall is given by

$$T_1 = T_G - \left(\sum\frac{h_x}{k_x} + a_i + a_o\right)(T_G - T_A)k$$

in which $\sum(h_x/k_x)$ is the summation of the factors $h_1/k_1, h_2/k_2$ etc. for the materials between the concrete face and the hot medium; a_o would be omitted if there were no cavity. The change of temperature T°C through a concrete wall h_c in thickness is $(T_G - T_A)kh_c/k_c$, where k_c is the conductivity of the concrete. Owing to the numerically indeterminate nature of many of the terms used in the calculation of T, extreme accuracy cannot be expected. Therefore only an approximate assessment of the stresses due to a difference in temperature is valid.

In an uncracked reinforced concrete wall, or in a cracked wall that is entirely in compression, the change in the compressive stress in the concrete due to a temperature difference of T°C is given by

$$f_{cT} = \pm 0.5T\varepsilon_c E_c$$

where ε_c is the coefficient of linear expansion of concrete, i.e. 0.000 01 per °C or 0.000 005 5 per °F, and E_c is the modulus of elasticity of concrete, i.e. 21 kN/mm^2 or 3×10^6 lb/in^2.

In a cracked wall subject to tension, the concrete being neglected except as a covering for the reinforcement, the change in stress in the reinforcement is

$$f_{sT} = \pm 0.5(1 - \alpha)T\varepsilon_s E_s$$

The term $(1 - \alpha)$ is such that $(1 - \alpha)h_c$ is the distance between the centres of the reinforcement on opposite faces of the wall; ε_s is the coefficient of linear expansion for steel, i.e. 0.000 011 per °C or 0.000 006 per °F; and E_s is the modulus of elasticity of steel, i.e. 210 kN/mm^2 or 30×10^6 lb/in^2.

If the wall subjected to temperature strains is already stressed in tension on one face and compression on the other, as may occur in the wall of a tank containing hot liquid, then to the service bending moment at any section a bending moment due to a change of temperature equal to $M_T = T\varepsilon_c E_c I_c/h_c$ should be algebraically added, where I_c is the moment of inertia of the section expressed in concrete units and ignoring the area of any concrete that may be cracked. In impermeable construction designed to prevent the concrete cracking, the value of I_c would be based on the whole thickness of concrete together with an allowance for the reinforcement with a modular ratio corresponding to the value assumed for E_c.

It should be noted that the bending moment M_T due to a change of temperature tends to produce compression on the face subjected to the higher temperature.

6.11 RETAINING WALLS

The characteristic weights of, and the methods of calculating the horizontal pressures due to, retained earth are given in *Tables 16–19*. This section deals with the design of retaining walls including the calculation of the forces and bending moments produced by the pressure of the retained material. When designing such structures in accordance with BS8110 and CP110 it should be remembered that all pressures etc. calculated by using the characteristic dead weights of materials represent *service* loads. Consequently, when designing sections according to ultimate limit-state considerations, the pressures etc. must be multiplied by the appropriate partial safety factors for loads to obtain ultimate bending moments and shearing forces. When considering pressures due to retained earth or surcharge, BS5400 recommends a partial safety factor for loads of 1.5 for ultimate limit-state calculations, but of only unity when considering relieving effects. BS5337 requires a partial safety factor of 1.6 to be adopted for retained or supported earth.

Normally, BS8110 suggests the adoption of partial safety factors for loads on earth-retaining and foundation structures that are similar to those used elsewhere. However, where detailed soils investigations have been made and possible interactions between the soil and the supporting structure carefully considered, Part 2 of BS8110 indicates that where clear limits can be defined for a particular value (e.g. water pressure) a 'worst credible' value, representing the extreme value which a designer believes is realistically possible, may be specified. In such a case a much lower partial safety factor for load, typically 1.2, may be adopted. For further details see clause 2.2.2.3 of BS8110:Part 2.

Other recommendations for the design of retaining walls, sheet-piled walls and the like are given in ref. 1.

6.11.1 Types of retaining walls

A retaining wall is essentially a vertical cantilever, and when it is constructed in reinforced concrete it can be a cantilevered slab, a wall with counterforts, or a sheet-pile wall. A cantilevered slab is suitable for walls of moderate heights and has a base projecting backwards under the filling, as at (b) in the diagram at the top of *Table 187*, or a base projecting forward as at (a). The former type is generally the more economical. The latter type is only adopted when for reasons relating to buildings or other adjacent property it is not permissible to excavate behind the stem of the wall. If excavation behind the wall is permitted, but to a limited extent only, a wall with a base projecting partly backwards and partly forwards as at (c) can be provided. Any length of base projecting backwards is advantageous as the earth supported on it assists in counterbalancing overturning effects. Appropriate dimensions for the base can be estimated with the aid of the graph on *Table 187*.

A wall provided with counterforts is suitable for a greater height than is economical for a simple slab wall. The slab spans horizontally between the vertical counterforts which are arranged as at (d). When the net height of the wall is great, it is sometimes more economical to adopt the type of wall shown at (e), where the slab spans vertically between horizontal beams which bear against counterforts. By graduating the spacing of the beams the maximum bending moment in each span of the slab can be equal and the slab kept the same thickness throughout. When the shearing stresses allow, the web of the counterfort can be perforated;

this saves concrete but complicates the formwork and reinforcement.

6.11.2 Pressures behind walls

The value of the horizontal pressure due to retained earth is often assumed to be $4.2h\,kN/m^2$ at a depth of h metres or $27h\,lb/ft^2$ at a depth of h feet below the level surface of the ground behind the wall. When the ground is compact a lower pressure is sometimes assumed, say, $3.5h\,kN/m^2$ or $22h\,lb/ft^2$, which corresponds to an angle of repose of 40° and a density of $1600\,kg/m^3$ or $100\,lb/ft^3$. These values should be increased or reduced when the surface of the ground behind the wall slopes upwards or downwards or when a superimposed load is supported. In ground that may become accidentally waterlogged, it is often advantageous to design for a nominal overall factor of safety of 4 against ground pressure, and of 2.5 against the possible water pressure; i.e. the equivalent pressure of the water alone after making allowance for the difference in factors of safety is $6.3h\,kN/m^2$ or $40h\,lb/ft^2$. In these expressions h is measured in metres where the pressure is in kN/m^2 and in feet where the pressure is in lb/ft^2.

6.11.3 Cantilevered retaining walls

The factors affecting the design of a cantilevered slab wall are usually considered per unit length of wall when the wall is of uniform height but, when the height varies, a length of say 3 m or 10 ft should be treated as a complete unit. For a wall with counterforts the length of a unit is the distance between two adjacent counterforts. The principal factors to be considered are stability against overturning, bearing pressure on the ground, resistance to sliding, and internal resistance to bending moments and shearing forces. Formulae for the bending moments, forces, dimensions and other factors relating to cantilevered-slab walls are given in *Table 187*, which includes a graph based on an idealized structure which aids the choice of the most suitable base shape and size. Notes on the use of this graph are given in section 25.8.

An appropriate overall factor of safety against overturning should be allowed, rotation being assumed to be about the lowest forward edge of the base. Ref. 63 states that a value of not less than 2 should be adopted; a value of 1.5 is not uncommon, however, and may be quite sufficient, especially for short-term conditions. Under the most adverse combination of vertical load and horizontal pressure, the maximum pressure on the ground should then not exceed that allowable.

To provide an overall factor of safety against forward movement of the wall as a whole the minimum total vertical load multiplied by a coefficient of friction should exceed the maximum horizontal pressure by a suitable margin. Again a factor of 2 is recommended in ref. 63, but a value of not less than 1.5 may suffice in appropriate circumstances. For dry sand, gravel, rock and other fairly dry soils a coefficient of 0.4 is often used, but for clay, the surface of which may become wet, the frictional resistance to sliding may be zero. In this case the resistance of the earth in front of the wall must provide the necessary resistance to sliding, which can be increased by providing a rib on the underside of the base as shown at (a), (b) and (c) in *Table 187*. A rib is essential if the depth of earth in front of the wall is shallow. The plane of failure due to shearing in front of the wall is a curve sweeping upwards from the lowest forward edge of the wall. The resistance of the earth in front of the wall is the passive resistance (see *Tables 16* and *19*). It is essential for the earth to be in contact with the front face of the base, as otherwise a small but undesirable movement of the wall must occur before the passive resistance can operate. In walls of the form shown at (a), where the vertical load is small compared with the horizontal pressure, a rib should be provided either immediately below the wall stem or at the forward edge of the base to increase the resistance to sliding. If the theoretical passive resistance is depended upon to provide the whole of the resistance to sliding, the overall factor of safety should be at least 2.

The foregoing movements of the wall, due to either overturning or sliding, are independent of the general tendency of the bank of a cutting to slip and to carry the retaining wall with it. The strength and stability of the retaining wall have no bearing on such failures; the precautions that must be taken to prevent the wall being carried away are outside the scope of the design of a retaining wall constructed to retain the toe of the bank, and become a problem in soil mechanics.

The safe moment of resistance of the stem of the wall should be equal to the bending moment produced by the pressure on the slab. In a cantilevered slab, the critical bending moment may be at the top of the splay at the base of the stem. The base slab should be made the same thickness as the bottom of the wall and equal reinforcement should be provided. The base slab and the stem of the wall should be tapered.

When a single splay only is provided at the base of the stem of a cantilevered-slab wall, the critical bending moment may be at the bottom of the splay instead of the top, since the increase in effective depth may not cause the moment of resistance to increase as rapidly as the bending moment increases. The effective depth should not be considered to increase more rapidly than is represented by a slope of 1:3 at each splay.

In walls with counterforts the slab, which spans horizontally, can also taper from the bottom upwards as the pressure and consequently the bending moments decrease towards the top. Fixity with the base slab near the bottom will produce a certain amount of vertical bending requiring vertical reinforcement near the back face of the slab near the bottom. The horizontal negative and positive bending moments can be assumed to be $q_{ep}l^2/12$, where q_{ep} is the intensity of horizontal pressure and l is the distance between the centres of adjacent counterforts. If horizontal beams are provided the slab is designed as a continuous slab spanning vertically, requiring reinforcement near the front face between the beams and near the back face at the beams.

Counterforts are designed as vertical cantilevers, the main tension reinforcement being in the back sloping face. Owing to the great width at the bottom, reinforcement to resist shear is seldom necessary, and when required it is generally most conveniently provided by horizontal links. Only in the case of very high walls are inclined bars necessary to provide resistance to shearing.

6.11.4 Expansion and contraction

Long walls should be provided with expansion joints, suitable designs for which are given in *Table 182*. To reduce the risk of cracking due to shrinkage of the concrete, sectional methods of construction should be specified. As a further precaution against contraction and temperature cracks appearing on the front face of a wall reinforced near the back face, a mesh of reinforcement consisting of 10 mm bars at 300 mm centres or 3/8 in bars at 12 in centres horizontally and vertically should be provided near the front face if the thickness of the wall exceeds 200 mm or 8 in.

6.11.5 Drainage behind walls

Sloping the base slab in front of and behind the wall not only economizes in concrete but also assists drainage, the provision for which is important, especially for a wall designed for a low pressure. Where the filling behind the wall is gravel or sand, a drain of clean loosely packed rubble should be provided along the base of the back of the wall; 75 to 150 mm (or 3 to 6 in) diameter weep-holes should be included at about 3 m or 10 ft centres. A weep-hole should be provided in every space between the counterforts, and the top surface of any intermediate horizontal beams should be given a slight slope away from the back of the wall. With backings of clay or other soil of low porosity, hand-packed rubble placed behind the wall for almost the whole height and draining to weep-holes assists effective drainage of the filling. The filling behind the wall should not be tipped from a height, but should be carefully deposited and consolidated in thin horizontal layers.

6.12 SHEET-PILE WALLS

When a satisfactory bearing stratum is not encountered at a reasonable depth below the surface in front of the earth to be retained, then a sheet-pile wall may be provided. Precast reinforced concrete sheet-piles are driven into the ground sufficiently far to obtain an anchorage for the vertical cantilever and security against sliding and spewing. This type of wall is particularly suitable for waterside works, and in the simplest form the sheet-piles simply cantilever out of the ground, the heads of the piles being generally stripped and bonded into a cast *in situ* capping beam.

Designs for typical sheet-piles and for the interlocked type of joint necessary to maintain alignment during driving are given in the lower part of *Table 193*, where shapes of the shoes for starting piles and following piles are also illustrated.

If the height of the wall and the pressure on the sheet-piles are such that an excessively thick pile is required, the provision of a tie at the level of the capping beam reduces the maximum bending moment. The tie can be constructed in reinforced concrete or it can be formed from a mild-steel bar anchored into the capping beam and wrapped with bituminized hessian to protect it from corrosion. The capping beam must be designed to span between the ties and to transfer the horizontal forces from the top of the sheet-piles to the ties. The end of the tie remote from the wall should be anchored behind the natural slope of the ground, behind one of the lines shown in the upper part of *Table 189*. The anchorage should be provided by a block of mass concrete, by a concrete wall, by a vertical concrete plate, or by an anchor-pile. Although the force in the tie is increased, bending moments on the sheet-piles can be further reduced by placing the tie at some point below the top of the wall, a horizontal beam being provided at the level of the tie. The provision of a tie reduces the depth to which it is necessary to drive the sheet-piles.

The results of research organized by CIRIA Steering Group for Waterfront Structures are presented in ref. 99. This report examines and contrasts various methods of designing quay walls in accordance with the UK, Danish and German Codes of Practice, and examines the resulting designs and their costs. It also describes an analytical method devised by P. W. Rowe which can be used to design cantilevered, anchored, fixed and strutted sheet-pile walls.

6.12.1 Cantilevered sheet-pile wall

The forces on a simple cantilevered sheet-pile wall are indicated in *Table 188*, where F_{h1} is the active pressure due to the filling and surcharge behind the wall and F_{h2} and F_{h3} are passive pressures producing the necessary restraint moment to resist the overturning effect of F_{h1}. The shaded diagram illustrates the probable variation of pressure, but the accompanying straight-line diagram is a practical approximation. The sheet-piles tend to rotate about the point X. The maximum bending moment on the sheet-piles occurs at some point D, and the distance l can be calculated approximately from the factors k'_1 given in the column headed 'free' in *Table 188* for different angles of repose of the ground in which the pile is embedded. The bending moment on the sheet-piles is $F_{h1}x$, the value of F_{h1} being conveniently represented by the area of the trapezium ABCD in *Table 188*; F_{h1} can be determined from *Table 18*. The distance x indicates the centroid of the area. The embedded length of the sheet-piles must be great enough to enable sufficient passive pressures to be produced, and the factors k'_2 (*Table 188*) enable this length to be calculated approximately.

The foregoing procedure, using the factors k'_1 and k'_2 given in *Table 188*, is suitable for the preparation of a preliminary design for a simple cantilevered sheet-pile wall. The final design should be checked by the formulae and procedure given in *Table 188*; the initial formula is derived by equating the forces acting behind the sheet-piles with those acting on the front of the sheet-piles, and by equating to zero the moments of these forces about E.

The value of q_{epa}, the increase in active pressure per unit of depth behind the wall, may be different at different depths if various classes of soil are encountered behind the wall and may be affected by waterlogged conditions. No general formula is serviceable under such conditions, and the designer should deal with such problems with caution and adopt safe values for the pressure factors. The two conditions which must be satisfied are that the algebraic sum of the horizontal forces must be zero and that the algebraic sum of the moments of these forces about the bottom of the sheet-piles must also be zero. The available theoretical passive resistance should be in excess of that required by a sufficient margin to allow for overestimating the passive resistance.

6.12.2 Sheet-pile wall with ties

When a tie is provided at the top of the wall the forces acting on the wall are as shown in *Table 189*; they are similar to those in *Table 188* except for the introduction of the horizontal force in the tie. It is not possible to determine the variations of the pressure with any precision, but the diagram shows the probable variation. It is therefore recommended that the following procedure be adopted for preliminary designs. The factor k_2' in the column headed 'hinged' in *Table 188* gives the minimum values for h' to produce sufficient restraint moment. The embedded length h' must, however, be not less than the minimum length required to resist forward movement of the toe and not less than the length required to prevent spewing. The wall will be stable if $1.5F_{h4}x \not> F_{h5}y$, where F_{h4} is the total active pressure on the whole depth of the wall as shown and F_{h5} is the total passive pressure in front of the wall. The values of F_{h4} and F_{h5} can be computed from the data in *Tables 16–18*. The factor of 1.5 is introduced in order to allow a margin between the theoretically calculated passive resistance and that actually required.

To prevent spewing in front of the wall the embedded length should not be less than $k_2^2 f_w/D$, where f_w is the intensity of vertical pressure (in units of force per unit length) at point E due to the earth and surcharge above this point, D is the unit weight of the earth in front of the wall, and k_2 is the pressure factor taken from *Table 16* or *18*.

The bending moment on the wall can be calculated by first determining l from the factors given in the column headed 'hinged' in *Table 188*. Each sheet-pile can be considered as a propped cantilever of span l built in at D and propped at A and subjected to a trapezoidal load represented by the area ABCD. This load can be divided into a uniformly distributed load and a triangularly distributed load, the bending-moment coefficients for which are given in *Table 26* where the reaction of the prop, which is the force in the tie, is also given. Since the security of this type of wall depends on the efficiency of the anchorage, no risk of underrating the force in the tie should be incurred; it is better to increase the force to be resisted from the value represented by the theoretical reactions to $0.5F_{h1}$. The value of this force should certainly not be less than $F_{h4} - 2F_{h5}/3$, which is the part of the outward active pressure not balanced by the reduced passive pressure. The forces in anchor-piles are given in the lower part of *Table 189*.

6.12.3 Sheet-pile wall with tie below head

In a wall as in *Table 189* it is assumed that the connection between the tie and the head of the wall is equivalent to a hinge, i.e. that the bending moment at A is zero. If the wall is extended above A, as shown, either by continuing the sheet-piles or by constructing a cast *in situ* wall, a bending moment is introduced at A equal to $F_{h6}z$, where F_{h6} is the total active pressure on the extended portion of the wall AF. This bending moment introduces a negative bending moment on the wall at A, but reduces the positive bending moment on the sheet-piles between D and A and also reduces the negative bending moment at D. If the bending moment at A is large enough to produce conditions amounting to complete fixity at A, then the span l can be calculated by the factors k_1' given in the column headed 'fixed' in *Table 188*. The factor k_2' in the same column gives the minimum embedded length h', but at the same time h' must be sufficient to prevent spewing and forward movement as already described. The equation for stability is given in *Table 189*. The force in the tie is $F_{h4} - (2F_{h5}/3) + F_{h6}$ or $(F_{h4}/2) + F_{h6}$, whichever is the greater. The bending moment on the wall is calculated from the pressure represented by the area of the trapezium ABCD, considering the beam as fixed at both ends and using the appropriate coefficients given in *Table 24*. When the bending moment at A is insufficient to provide complete fixity, the bending moments, forces, and values of l and h' are intermediate between those for hinged and fixed conditions at A.

A horizontal slab supported on king-piles, as is sometimes provided at A in the manner shown in the diagram at the bottom of *Table 189*, has a sheltering effect on the piles, since if the slab is carried far enough back it can completely relieve the wall below A from any active pressure due to the earth or surcharge above the level of A.

When a preliminary design has been prepared by the foregoing procedure, using the factors given in *Table 188* and the formulae in *Table 189*, the final design of the sheet-pile wall with anchored ties should be checked by one of the analytical or graphical methods given in textbooks on this subject.

6.12.4 Reduced bending moments on flexible walls

The pressures behind a flexible retaining wall adjust themselves in such a way that the bending moments on the wall are reduced. Stroyer suggested a formula applicable to reinforced concrete sheet-pile walls with ties. The reduction factors, which are not applicable to simple cantilevered walls, are given in *Table 188*.

6.13 FOUNDATIONS

The design of the foundations for a structure comprises three stages. The first is to determine from an inspection of the site the nature of the ground and, having selected the stratum upon which to impose the load, to decide the safe bearing pressure. The second stage is to select the type of foundation, and the suitability of one or more types may have to be compared. The third stage is to design the selected foundation to transfer and distribute the loads from the structure to the ground. Reference should be made to CP2004 'Foundations'.

6.13.1 Inspection of the site

The object of an inspection of the site is to determine the nature of the top stratum and of the strata below in order to detect any weak strata that may impair the load-carrying capacity of the stratum selected for the foundation. Generally the depth to which knowledge of the strata should be obtained should be not less than one and a half times the width of an isolated foundation or the width of a structure with closely spaced footings.

The nature of the ground can be determined by digging

trial holes, sinking bores or driving piles. A trial hole can be taken down to only a moderate depth, but enables the undisturbed soil to be examined, and the difficulty or otherwise of excavating and the need or otherwise of timbering and pumping to be determined. A bore can be taken very much deeper than a trial hole. A test pile does not indicate the type of soil it has been driven through, but the driving data combined with local information may give the necessary particulars. A test pile is useful in showing the thickness of the top crust or the depth below poorer soil at which a firm stratum lies. A sufficient number of any of these tests should be made until the engineer is satisfied that he is certain of the nature of the ground under all parts of the foundations.

Reference should be made to CP2001 'Site investigations'.

6.13.2 Safe bearing pressures on ground

The pressures that can be safely imposed on thick strata of soils commonly met with are in some districts the subject of by-laws. *Table 191* gives pressures recommended for preliminary design purposes in CP101 and CP2004, but these must be considered as maxima since several factors may necessitate the use of lower values. Permissible pressures may generally be exceeded by an amount equal to the weight of earth between the foundation level and adjacent ground level but, if this increase is allowed, any earth carried on the foundation must be included in the foundation load. For a soil of uncertain resistance a study of local existing buildings on the same soil may be useful, as may also be the results of a ground bearing test.

Failure of a foundation may be due to consolidation of the ground causing settlement, or rupture of the ground due to failure in resistance to shearing. The shape of the surface along which shearing failure occurs under a strip footing is an almost circular arc extending from one edge of the footing and passing under the footing and continued then as a tangent to the arc to intersect the ground surface at an angle depending on the angle of internal friction of the soil. The average safe resistance of soil therefore depends on the angle of internal friction of the soil, and on the depth of the footing below the ground surface. In a cohesionless soil the resistance to bearing pressure not only increases as the depth increases but is proportional to the width of the footing. In a cohesive soil there is also an increase in resistance to bearing pressure under wide footings, but it is less than in non-cohesive soils. Graphical solutions, such as that attributed to Krey, are sometimes used to find the bearing resistance under a footing of known width and depth. The theoretical formulae, based on Rankine's formula for a cohesionless soil and Bell's formula for clay, for the maximum bearing pressure on a foundation at a given depth, although giving irrational results in extreme cases, for practical cases give results that are well on the safe side. These formulae are given in *Table 191*.

Unless they bear on rock, foundations for all but single-storey buildings or other light structures should be taken down at least 1 m or 3 ft below the ground surface since, apart from the foregoing considerations, it is seldom that undisturbed soil which is sufficiently consolidated is reached at a shallower depth. In a clay soil a depth of at least 1.5 m or 5 ft is necessary in the UK to ensure protection of the bearing stratum from weathering.

6.13.3 Eccentric load

When a foundation is subjected to a concentric load, that is when the centre of gravity of the superimposed load coincides with the centroid of the foundation, the bearing pressure on the ground is for practical purposes uniform and its intensity is equal to the total applied load divided by the total area. When the load is eccentrically placed on the base the pressure is not uniformly spread, but varies from a maximum at the side nearer the centre of gravity of the load to a minimum at the opposite side, or to zero at some intermediate point. The variation of pressure between these two extremes depends on the magnitude of the eccentricity and is usually assumed to be linear. The maximum and minimum pressures are then given by the formulae in *Table 191*. For large eccentricities there may be a part of the foundation under which there is no bearing pressure. Although this state may be satisfactory for transient conditions (such as those due to wind), it is preferable for the foundation to the designed so that there is bearing pressure throughout under ordinary working conditions.

6.13.4 Blinding layer

For reinforced concrete footings or other construction where there is no mass concrete at the bottom forming an integral part of the foundation, the bottom of the excavation should be covered with a layer of lean concrete in order to provide a clean surface on which to place the reinforcement. The thickness of this layer depends upon the compactness and wetness of the bottom of the excavation, and is generally from 25 to 75 mm or 1 to 3 in. The safe compressive service stress in the concrete should be not less than the maximum bearing pressure on the ground.

6.13.5 Types of foundations

The most suitable type of foundation depends, primarily, on the depth at which the bearing stratum lies and the safe bearing pressure, which determines the area of the foundation. Data relating to common types of separate and combined reinforced concrete foundations, suitable for sites where the bearing stratum is near the surface, are given in *Table 191* and *192*. Some types of combined bases are also given in *Table 190*. In selecting a type of foundation suitable for a particular purpose, the type of structure should be considered. Sometimes it may have to be decided whether the risk of settlement can be taken in preference to providing a more expensive foundation. In the case of silos and fixed-end arches, the risk of unequal settlement of the foundation must be avoided at all costs, but for gantries and bases for large steel tanks a simple foundation can be provided and probable settlement allowed for in the design of the superstructure. In mining districts, where subsidence is reasonably anticipated, a rigid raft foundation should be provided for small structures in order that the structure may move as a whole; as a raft may not be economical for a large structure, the latter should be designed as a flexible structure or as a series of separate structures each of which, on independent raft foundations, can accommodate itself to movements of the ground without detriment to the structure as a whole.

6.13.6 Separate bases

The simplest form of foundation for a reinforced concrete column or steel stanchion is the common pyramidal base (*Table 191*). Such bases are suitable for concentric or slightly eccentric loads if the area exceeds about 1 m^2 or 10 ft^2. For smaller bases and those on rock or other ground of high bearing capacity, a rectangular block of plain concrete is probably more economical; the thickness of the block must be sufficient to enable the load to be transferred to the ground under the entire area of the base at an angle of dispersion through the block of not less than 45° to the horizontal.

To reduce the risk of unequal settlement, the sizes of separate bases for the columns of a building founded on a compressible soil should be in proportion to the dead load carried by each column. Bases for the columns of a storage structure should be in proportion to the total load, excluding the effects of wind. In all cases the pressure on the ground under any base due to the combined dead and imposed load, including wind load and any bending at the base of the column, must not exceed the safe bearing resistance of the ground.

In the design of a separate base the area of a concentrically loaded base (as in *Table 191*) is determined by dividing the maximum service (i.e. unfactored) load on the ground by the safe bearing resistance. The thickness of a footing of the common pyramidal shape is determined from a consideration of the resistance to shearing force and bending. The critical shearing stresses may be assumed to occur on a plane at a distance equal to the effective depth of the base from the face of the column. This assumption is in accordance with BS8110 although, if preferred, the condition at the column face may be considered while taking account of the enhanced design shear stress that may be adopted close to a support (see section 21.1.1): however, such enhancement only applies within a distance of $1.5d$ of the column face and the enhancement factor here is $1.5d/a_v$ where a_v is the distance of the point concerned to the column face. CP110 recommends the consideration of the critical shearing stress at a distance of one-and-a-half times the effective depth from the face of the loaded area. Both Codes also require the consideration of punching shear around the column perimeter, using the procedure for concentrated loads on slabs described in section 21.1.6, and both require that the maximum bending moment at any section shall be the sum of the moments of all the forces on one side of the section. The critical section for the bending moment on a base supporting a reinforced concrete column is at the face of the column, but for a base supporting a steel stanchion it is at the centre of the base. The appropriate formulae are given in *Table 191*. The moment of resistance of pyramidal bases cannot be determined with precision; the formulae are rational, but conservative.

Note that, according to BS8110 and the *Joint Institutions Design Manual*, if the width of the base exceeds $1.5(c + 3d)$, where c is the column width and d is the effective depth, the reinforcement required should be respaced such that two-thirds of the total amount is located within a strip $(c + 3d)$ wide and positioned centrally beneath the column. Care must be taken, however, that the remaining reinforcement still conforms to the minimum requirements.

When designing in accordance with BS8110 and CP110 it should be remembered that the maximum permissible bearing pressures employed represent service loads. Consequently, when designing the resulting sections for ultimate limit-state conditions these values must be multiplied by the appropriate partial safety factor for load (i.e. $1.4g_k$ or $1.6q_k$) corresponding to the load concerned to obtain the appropriate ultimate bending moments and shearing forces. To avoid complex calculations to determine the relative proportions of dead and imposed load it is almost always sufficiently accurate to adopt a uniform partial safety factor of 1.5 throughout. In cases of doubt the use of the remommended imposed-load partial safety factor of 1.6 for all loads will err on the side of safety. As regards serviceability considerations, according to both Codes it is not necessary to consider the limit-state of deflection when designing bases, but the limitations regarding the maximum spacing of tension bars (for zero redistribution) summarized in *Table 139* should be adhered to, although there is no need to provide bars in the sides of bases to control cracking.

If the size of the base relative to its thickness is such that the load from the column can be spread by dispersion at 45° over the entire area of the base, no bending moment need be considered and only nominal reinforcement need be provided. If the base cannot be placed centrally under the column, the pressure on the ground is not uniform but varies as shown in *Table 191*. The base is then preferably rectangular in plan and the modified formulae for bending resistance are given in *Table 191*. A special case of an independent base with the equivalent of eccentric loading is a chimney foundation.

A separate base may be subjected to moments and horizontal shearing forces in addition to a vertical concentric load. Such a base should be made equivalent to a concentrically loaded base by placing the base eccentrically under the column to such an extent that the eccentricity of vertical load offsets the equivalent of the moments and shearing forces. This procedure is impracticable if the moments and shearing forces can act either clockwise or anti-clockwise at different times, in which case the base should be provided centrally under the column and designed as an eccentrically loaded base complying with the two conditions.

6.13.7 Tied bases

Sometimes, as in the case of the bases under the towers of a trestle or gantry, the bases are in pairs and the moments and shearing forces act in the same sense on each base at the same time. In such conditions the bases can be designed as concentrically loaded and connected by a tie-beam which relieves them of effects due to eccentricity. Such a pair of tied bases is shown in *Table 192*, which also gives the formulae for the bending moment and other effects on the tie-beam.

6.13.8 Balanced foundations

When it is not possible to place an adequate base centrally under a column or other load owing to restrictions of the site, and when under such conditions the eccentricity would result in inadmissible ground pressures, a balanced foundation as shown in *Table 190* and *192* is provided. This case is common in the external columns of buildings on sites in built-up areas.

6.13.9 Combined bases

If the size of the bases required for adjacent columns is so large that independent bases would overlap, two or more columns can be provided with a common foundation. Suitable types for two columns are shown in *Table 192* for concentrically loaded bases and for a base that cannot be arranged relative to the columns so as to be concentrically loaded. It may be that, under some conditions of loading on the columns, the load on the combined base may be concentric, but under other conditions the load on the same base may be eccentric; alternative conditions must be taken into account. Some notes on combined bases are given in section 25.9.2.

6.13.10 Strip bases

When the columns or other supports of a structure are closely spaced in one direction, it is common to provide a continuous base similar to a footing for a wall. Particulars of the design of strip bases are given in *Table 192*. Some notes on these bases are given, in relation to the diagrams in *Table 190*, in section 25.9.2, together with an example.

6.13.11 Rafts

When the columns or other supports of a structure are closely spaced in both directions, or when the column loads are so high and the safe ground pressure so low that a group of independent bases almost or totally covers the space between the columns, a single raft foundation of one of the type shown in (a) to (d) in *Table 190* should be provided. Notes on these designs are given in section 25.9.4.

The analysis of a raft foundation supporting a series of symmetrically arranged equal loads is generally based on the assumption of uniformly distributed pressure on the ground, and the design is similar to an inverted reinforced concrete floor upon which the load is that portion of the ground pressure that is due to the symmetrically arranged loads only. Notes on the design of a raft when the columns are not symmetrically disposed are also given in section 25.9.4.

An example of the design of a raft foundation is included in *Examples of the Design of Buildings*.

6.13.12 Basements

A basement, a typical cross-section of which is shown at (e) in the lower part of *Table 190*, is partly a raft, since the weights of the ground floor over the basement, the walls and other structure above the ground floor, and the weight of the basement itself, are carried on the ground under the floor of the basement. For watertightness it is common to construct the wall and floor of the basement monolithically. In most cases the average ground pressure is low, but owing to the large span the bending moments are high and consequently a thick floor is required if the total load is assumed to be distributed uniformly over the whole area. Since the greater part of the load is transmitted through the walls of the basement, it is more economical to consider the load to be spread on a strip immediately under the walls if by so doing the ground pressure does not exceed the maximum allowable. The bending moment at the edge of the wall due to the cantilever action of this strip determines the thickness of the strip, and the remainder of the floor can generally be thinner.

Where basements are in water-bearing soils the effect of water pressure must be taken into account. The upward water pressure is uniform below the whole area of the basement floor, which must be capable of resisting the pressure less the weight of the slab. The walls must be designed to resist the horizontal pressure of the waterlogged ground. It is necessary to prevent the basement from floating. There are two critical stages. When the structure is complete the total weight of the basement and all superimposed dead loading must exceed the maximum upward pressure of the water by a substantial margin. When the basement only is complete, there must also be an excess of downward load. If these condition are not present, one of the following steps should be taken:

1. The level of the ground-water near the basement should be controlled by pumping or other measures.
2. Temporary vents should be formed in the floor or at the base of the walls of enable water freely to enter the basement, thereby equalizing the external and internal pressures. The vents should be sealed when sufficient dead load from the superstructure is obtained.
3. The basement should be temporarily flooded to a depth such that the weight of water in the basement, together with the dead load, exceeds the total upward force on the structure.

During the construction of the basement method 1 is generally the most convenient, but when the basement is complete method 3 is preferable on account of its simplicity. The designer should specify the depth of water required, a suitable rule for ascertaining this depth in a large basement being to provide 1 m for each metre head of ground-water less 1 m for each 400 mm thickness of concrete in the basement floor above the waterproof layer (or 1 ft for each 1 ft head less 1 ft for each 5 in thickness of concrete). The omission of the weights of the basement walls and any ground floor provides a margin of safety.

In view of the potential seriousness of an ingress of water, consideration should be given to designing a basement to meet the requirements of BS5337 'The structural use of concrete for retaining aqueous liquids'. This is essential if the adjoining ground is water bearing unless other means are adopted to seal the structure.

An informative guide to the design of waterproof basements, based on current BS Codes of Practice and experience by the authors, Coffin, Beckmann and Pearce, has been produced by CIRIA (ref. 101).

6.13.13 Foundation piers

When a satisfactory stratum is found at a depth of 1.5 to 5 m or 5 to 15 ft below the natural ground level, a suitable foundation can be made by building up piers from the low level to ground level, and commencing the construction of the columns or other supports on these piers at ground level. The piers are generally square in cross-section, and can be constructed in brick, masonry, or plain or reinforced concrete. The maximum bearing pressure of the construction on the top of the pier depends on the material of the pier. Safe pressures on plain concrete, brickwork and masonry, abstracted from CP111, are given in *Table 191*. CP110 limits the bearing stress in a plain concrete wall to $0.5f_{cu}$ except when due to ultimate loads that are purely local, where the ultimate stress may be increased to $0.6f_{cu}$. BS8110 specifies local limiting values of $0.6f_{cu}$ for grade 25 concrete and above, and $0.5f_{cu}$ otherwise.

The economical size of the pier is when the load it carries is sufficiently great to require a base to the pier equal in area to the smallest hole in which men can conveniently work; otherwise unnecessary excavation has to be taken out and refilled. For example, if a man can work in a hole 1 m or 3 ft square at a depth of 3 m or 10 ft, the total load would be 200 kN or 18 tons on a stratum capable of sustaining 200 kN/m^2 or 2 tons/ft^2.

Generally it is better to provide as few piers as possible and to transfer as much of the load as practicable on to each pier, thus making each pier of generous proportions. It may not be necessary to dig a hole larger than is required for the stem of the pier, if the ground at the bottom is firm enough to be undercut for a widening at the base.

Reinforced concrete columns can sometimes be taken down economically to moderate depths, but to avoid slender columns it is generally necessary to provide lateral support at ground level.

When piers are impracticable, either by reason of the depth at which a firm bearing stratum occurs or due to the nature of the ground requiring timbering or continuous pumping, piles are adopted.

6.13.14 Wall footings

When the load on a strip footing is uniformly distributed throughout its length, as in the general case of a wall footing, the principal bending moments are due to the transverse cantilever action of the projecting portion of the footing. If the wall is of concrete and is built monolithically with the footing, the transverse bending moment at the face of the wall is the critical bending moment. If the wall is of brick or masonry the maximum bending moment occurs under the centre of the wall. Expressions for these bending moments are given in *Table 192*. When the projection is less than the thickness of the base the transverse bending moments can be neglected, but in all cases the thickness of the footing should be such that the safe shearing stress is not exceeded.

Whether wall footings are designed for transverse bending or not, if the safe ground pressure is low, longitudinal reinforcement should be inserted to resist possible longitudinal bending moments due to unequal settlement and non-uniformity of the load. One method of providing the amount of longitudinal reinforcement required for unequal settlement is to design the footing to span over a cavity (or area of soft ground) from 1 to 1.5 m or 3 to 5 ft wide, according to the nature of the ground. The longitudinal bending moment due to non-uniform load is calculated in the same way as for combined footings.

6.13.15 Foundations for machines

The area of a concrete base for a machine or engine must be sufficient to spread the load on to the ground without exceeding the safe bearing pressure. It is an advantage if the shape of the base is such that the centroid of the bearing area coincides with the centre of gravity of the loads when the machine is working. This reduces the risk of unequal settlement. If vibration from the machine is transmitted to the ground the bearing pressure should be considerably lower than that generally assumed for the class of ground on which the base bears, especially if the ground is clay or contains a large proportion of clay. It is often essential that the vibration of the machine shall not be transmitted to adjacent structures either directly or through the ground. In such cases a layer of cork or similar insulating material should be placed between the concrete base carrying the machine and the ground. Sometimes the base is enclosed in a pit lined with insulating material. When transmission of vibration is particularly undesirable the base may stand on springs, or more elaborate damping devices may be installed. In all cases, however, the base should be separated from surrounding concrete ground floors.

With light machines the bearing pressure on the ground may not be the factor that decides the area of the concrete base, since the area occupied by the machine and its frame may require a base of larger area. The position of the holding-down bolts generally determines the width and length of the base, which should extend 150 mm or 6 in or more beyond the outer edges of holes left for the bolts.

The depth of the base must be such that the bottom is on a satisfactory bearing stratum and that there is sufficient thickness to accommodate the holding-down bolts. If the machine exerts an uplift on any part of the base, the dimensions of the base must be such that the part subjected to uplift has sufficient weight to resist the uplift with a suitable margin of safety. A single base should be provided under all the supports of one machine, and sudden changes in depth and width of the base should be avoided. This reduces any risk of fractures that might result in unequal settlements which may throw the machine out of alignment. If the load from the machine is irregularly distributed on the base, the dimensions of a plain concrete base should be sufficient to resist the bending moments produced therein without overstressing the concrete in tension. If there is any risk of overstressing the concrete in this way, or if the operation of the machine would be adversely affected by the cracking and deformation of the base, reinforcement should be provided to resist all tensile forces.

Reference should be made to CP2012 'Foundations for machinery': Part 1 'Foundations for reciprocating machines' which includes a bibliography and sets out, in an appendix, a step-by-step procedure for designing a reinforced concrete foundation for reciprocating machinery. Detailed advice on the design of reinforced concrete foundations to support vibrating machinery is given in ref. 64, which provides practical solutions for the design of raft, piled and massive foundations. Comprehensive information on the dynamics of machine foundations is included in ref. 65.

6.14 REINFORCED CONCRETE PILES

6.14.1 Precast concrete piles

Reinforced concrete piles are precast or cast *in situ*. Precast concrete piles have been driven in lengths exceeding 30 m or 100 ft, but if a length of more than 20 m or 60 ft is planned it is necessary to give special consideration to the design of the pile and of the lifting and driving plant. Piles less than 4.5 or 15 ft long may not be economical. For ordinary work, precast piles are generally square or octagonal in section and are 200 to 450 mm or 8 to 18 in wide. For support, piles depend either on direct bearing on a firm stratum or on frictional resistance in soft strata, or more often on a combination of both resistances. The safe load on a pile depends on the load that the pile can safely carry as a column and on the load that produces settlement or further penetration of the pile into the ground. So many factors affect the load causing settlement for any particular pile that calculated loads are not very reliable unless associated with loading tests on driven piles. Such tests are often inconvenient and expensive, and frequently an engineer has to rely on computed loads and a large factor of safety.

In the days when all piles were driven by simple falling ram or drop hammers, numerous empirical formulae were devised for calculating the safe bearing capacity of a pile. The expressions were based on the direct relationship which exists, when using such simple driving methods, between the measured movement of a pile of known weight due to a blow of given energy, and the bearing resistance achieved. Perhaps the most widely known of these formulae is that due to Hiley, which incorporates most of the variants occurring in pile driving such as the weight and the type of hammer, the fall of the hammer, the penetration per blow, the length of the pile, the type of helmet, the nature of the ground, and the material of which the pile is made. A modified form of this formula is given in *Table 193*, in which the constant c takes into account the energy absorbed in temporarily compressing the pile, the helmet and the ground. Since the quake of the ground below the pile shoe is included, it follows that the nature of the ground in which the toe of the pile is embedded affects the value of c, and the tabulated values apply to firm gravel; c must be increased if the pile is driven by a long dolly. The dimension $2c$ is a quantity that is measurable on a pile while being driven, since it represents the difference between the permanent penetration for one blow and the greatest instantaneous depression of the pile head as measured at the top of the helmet. The efficiency of the blow depends on the ratio of the weight of the pile (including the weight of the helmet, dolly, cushioning and the stationary parts of the hammer resting on the pile head) to the weight of the moving parts of the hammer. Values for the efficiency of the blow are given in *Table 193*, together with values of the effective fall which allow for the freedom or otherwise of the fall of the hammer. The resistance to driving as calculated by Hiley's formula is subject to a factor of safety of 1.5 to 3. If a pile is driven into clay or soils in which clay predominates, or into fine saturated sand, the resistance to further penetration may increase after the pile has been at rest for a while. This increase is due to the frictional resistance of the soil settling around the pile, but on clay may be in part offset by a reduction in the bearing resistance which takes place in the course of time. Impact formulae are not therefore very reliable for piles driven into clay, or for piles that are driven into sand with the assistance of a water-jet.

When piles are driven into soft ground and depend solely upon friction between the sides of the pile and the ground for their support, the safe load can only be estimated approximately by considering the probable frictional resistance offered by the strata through which the pile is driven and the probable bearing resistance of the ground under the toe of the pile. Formulae may be of little assistance in this case; a test load on an isolated pile or on a group of piles is the only satisfactory means of determining the settlement load.

A formula by which an estimate of the safe load on a pile driven entirely into clay can be derived is given in *Table 193*. An alternative formula is

$$\text{safe load} = \frac{1}{\gamma}[\tfrac{1}{2}A_sC + A(7.5C + D_sl)]$$

where C is the cohesive strength of the clay, D_s is the density of the clay, A is the cross-sectional area of the pile, A_s is the embedded surface area of the pile, l is the embedded length and γ is an overall factor of safety. The units used must be consistent throughout.

The foregoing 'dynamic' methods for calculating the ultimate bearing capacity of a pile are largely inapplicable when modern pile-driving equipment is used, and are of no help in predicting movement under working loads. Instead, so-called 'static' formulae founded on soil mechanics theory are now being developed to cover all types of piling, all driving methods and all ground conditions. As well as predicting ultimate bearing capacity, these techniques will indicate the possible load/deflection characteristics that may be expected. As yet no simple basic design method has been developed, but certain empirical procedures have been proposed. These are too complex to deal with adequately in this *Handbook* and reference should be made to Tomlinson (ref. 66) for further details.

The dynamic formulae mentioned above and given on *Table 193* are still of considerable use in predicting the stresses that arise in a pile during driving and which are thus used to design the pile.

Precast piles should be designed to withstand the stresses due to lifting, driving and loading, with appropriate overall factors of safety. Overstressing the concrete during handling and slinging can be guarded against by arranging the position and number of the points of suspension so that the stresses due to bending moments produced by the weight of the pile are within safe limits. For square piles of $1:1\frac{2}{3}:3\frac{1}{3}$ concrete and containing the normal amount of longitudinal steel the maximum bending moment due to bending about an axis parallel to one side of the section should not exceed, say, $0.4d^3$ N mm or $60d^3$ lb in, where d is the length of the side of the pile in millimetres or inches, if cracking is to be avoided.

The moment of resistance of a square pile bending about a diagonal is only about two-thirds of that when bending about an axis parallel to one of the sides. For this reason bending about a diagonal should be avoided where possible. If lifting holes are provided there is some assurance that the pile will not be lifted so as to bend about a diagonal. The lifting holes or the points of suspension should be arranged so that the smallest bending moments are experienced during lifting, and the positions for this condition for lifting at one or at two points are given in *Table 193*.

The greatest compressive stress in a pile is generally that due to the driving and occurs near the head. If driving is severe, helical links or binding should be provided at the top of the pile. Octagonal piles generally have helical links throughout their length.

Table 193 shows the reinforcement in a square precast reinforced concrete pile, in which helical links are provided at the head of the pile. The arrangement of the lifting holes and spacers is also indicated. For driving into clay, gravel or sand, a pile shoe having an overall taper of about 2 to 1, as shown, is generally satisfactory, but for other types of soil other shapes of shoe are necessary. If the pile has to be driven through soft material to bear on gravel overlying softer ground it is necessary to have a blunter shoe to prevent punching through the thin stratum. For friction piles driven into soft material throughout a shoe is not absolutely necessary, and a blunter end should be formed as shown in *Table 193*. When driving through soft material to a bearing on soft rock or stiff clay, the form of pile end shown for this case is satisfactory as long as driving ceases as soon as the firm stratum is reached or is only just penetrated. When driving down to hard rock, or where heavy boulders are anticipated, a special shoe or point as shown should be fitted.

Irrespective of the load a pile can carry before settlement occurs, the stresses produced by the load on the pile acting as a column should be considered. For calculating the reduction of load due to slenderness (see *Table 169*) the effective length of the pile can be considered as two-thirds of the length embedded in soft soil, or one-third of the length embedded in a fairly firm ground, plus the length of pile projecting above the ground. The end conditions of a pile are generally equivalent to one end fixed and one end hinged.

6.14.2 Arrangement of piles

In preparing plans of piled foundations attention must be given to the practicability of driving as well as to effectiveness for carrying loads. In order that each pile in a group shall carry an equal share of the load the centre of gravity of the group should coincide with the centre of the superimposed load. The clear distance between any two piles should generally be not less than 760 mm or 2 ft 6 in. As far as possible piles should be arranged in straight lines in both directions throughout any one part of a foundation, as this form reduces the amount of movement of the driving frame. The arrangement should also allow for driving to proceed in such a way that any displacement of earth due to consolidation in the piled area shall be free to take place in a direction away from the piles already driven.

6.14.3 Pile-caps

Pile-caps should be designed primarily for punching shear around the heads of the piles and around the column base and for the moment or force due to transferring the load from the column to the piles. According to BS8110 and CP110, pile-caps should also be designed to resist normal shearing forces, as in the case of beams carrying concentrated loads. The thickness of the cap must also be sufficient to provide adequate bond length for the bars projecting from the pile and for the dowel bars for the column.

If the thickness is such that the column load can all be transmitted to the piles by dispersion no bending moments need be considered, but generally when two or more piles are placed under one column it is necessary to reinforce the pile-cap for the moments or forces produced.

Two basic methods of analysing pile-caps are in common use. Firstly, the cap can be considered to behave as a short deep beam, transferring the load from column to piles by bending action. This method seems most appropriate for a two-pile cap. Alternatively, the pile-cap may be imagined to act as a space frame, the inclined lines of force linking the underside of the column to the tops of the piles being assumed to form compression members and the pile heads being linked together by reinforcement acting as horizontal tension members. This assumption appears particularly appropriate for analysing the more 'three-dimensional' pile-caps, such as those required for three or more piles. Both methods are specifically sanctioned by BS8110.

The size of the supported column is usually ignored, but Yan (ref. 67) has developed design expressions which take into account the fact that the load is transferred from the column over a not inconsiderable area.

Some research on the design and behaviour of pile-caps has been reported (ref. 69). This information has been incorporated into *Table 194*, which summarizes the information required to design caps for groups of two to five piles using the space-frame method. In conjunction with the preparation of a computer program to design pile-caps by the alternative beam method, Whittle and Beattie (ref. 68) have developed standardized arrangements and dimensions for caps for various numbers of piles. Details of these recommended patterns and sizes are also embodied in *Table 194*.

6.14.4 Loads on piles in a group

If the centre of gravity of the total load F_v on a group of n vertical piles is at the centre of gravity of the piles, each pile will be equally loaded, and will be subjected to a load F_v/n. If the centre of gravity of the load is displaced a distance e from the centre of gravity of the group of piles, the load on any one pile is

$$F_v\left(\frac{1}{n} \pm \frac{ea_1}{\sum a^2}\right)$$

where $\sum a^2$ is the sum of the squares of the distance of each pile measured from an axis passing through the centre of gravity of the group of piles, and at right angles to the line joining this centre of gravity to the centre of gravity of the applied load; a_1 is the distance of the pile considered from this axis, and is positive if it is on the same side of the axis as the centre of gravity of the load and negative if it is on the opposite side.

If the structure supported on the group of piles is subject to a bending moment M, which is transmitted to the foundations, the expression given for the load on any pile can be used by substituting $e = M/F_v$.

The total load that can be carried on a group of piles is not necessarily the safe load calculated for one pile multiplied by the number of piles, as allowance must be made for the overlapping of the zones of stress in the soil supporting the piles. The reduction due to this effect is greater in a group of piles that are supported mainly by friction. For piles supported entirely or almost entirely by bearing the maximum safe load on a group cannot greatly exceed the safe load on the area of the bearing stratum covered by the group.

6.14.5 Piles cast *in situ*

The following advantages are obtained with cast *in situ* piles, although all are not applicable to any one system.

The length of each pile conforms to the depth of the bearing stratum and no pile is too long or too short; cutting off surplus lengths or lengthening *in situ* is not therefore required. The top of a pile can be at any level below ground, and in some systems at any level above ground. The formation of an enlarged foot giving a greater bearing area is possible with some types of piles. With tube-driven or mandrel-driven piles it is possible to punch through a thin intermediate hard stratum. Boring shows the class of soil through which the pile passes and the nature of the bearing stratum can be observed. A bored pile may have little frictional resistance, but greater frictional resistance in soils such as compact gravels is obtained in tube-driven types where the tube is withdrawn. Bored piles have no ill-effect on adjacent piles or on the level of the ground due to consolidation of ground when several piles are driven in a constricted area. Boring piles is less noisy and is vibrationless; only a small headroom is required.

Some of the advantages of a precast pile over a cast *in situ* pile are that hardening of the concrete is unaffected by deleterious ground waters; that the pile can be inspected before being driven into the ground; that the size of the pile is not affected by water in the ground (this applies also to cast *in situ* types with a central core); and that the pile can be driven into ground that is below water.

In neither the precast pile nor the cast *in situ* pile is damage to, or faults in, the pile visible after it is driven or formed. The designer must consider the conditions of any problem, and select the pile which complies with the requirements.

6.14.6 Foundation cylinders

A rather more recent development is the foundation cylinder, which is in effect a large bored pile. Such cylinders, which may have a diameter of up to 3 m or 10 ft and be belled out at the bottom to, say, 4.5 m or 15 ft diameter, are most suitable for foundations in hard clay, and may be upwards of 30 m or 100 ft deep. The working loads are several thousand kilonewtons or several hundred tons.

6.14.7 Groups of inclined and vertical piles

Table 195 and the examples in section 25.10.2 relate to the loads on piles in a group that project above the ground, as in a wharf or jetty. For each probable condition of load the external forces are resolved into horizontal and vertical components F_h and F_v, the points of application of which are also determined. If the direction of action and position are opposite to those shown in the diagrams, the signs in the formulae must be changed. It is assumed that the piles are surmounted by a rigid pile-cap or superstructure. The effects on each pile when all the piles are vertical are based on a simple, but approximate, statical analysis. Since a pile offers little resistance to bending, structures with vertical piles only are not suitable when F_h predominates. The resistance of an inclined pile to horizontal force is considerable. In groups containing inclined piles, the bending moments and shearing forces on the piles are negligible. The ordinary theoretical analysis, upon which *Table 195* is based, assumes that each pile is hinged at the head and toe. Although this is not an accurate assumption, the theories which are based on it predict fairly well the behaviour of actual groups of piles.

Extensive information on the design of precast piles, the arrangement, analysis and design of groups of piles and the relative merits and disadvantages of precast and cast *in situ* piles is given in ref. 66.

6.15 WHARVES AND JETTIES

The loads, pulls, blows and pressures to which wharves and jetties and similar waterside and marine structures may be subjected are dealt with in section 2.6. Such structures may be a solid wall of plain or reinforced concrete, as are most dock walls and some quays, in which case the pressures and principles described in section 2.8 and in *Tables 16–20* and *187* for retaining walls apply. A quay or similar waterside wall is more often a sheet-pile wall, which is dealt with in *Tables 188* and *189*, or it may be an open-piled structure similar to a jetty. Piled jetties and the piles for such structures are considered in *Tables 193* and *195*. If the piles in a group containing inclined piles are arranged symmetrically, the summations in *Table 195* are simplified thus: $\sum_2 = 0$; $K = \sum_1 \sum_5$; $y_0 = -(\sum_4/\sum_5)$; $\sum_3$ is not required since $x_0 = 0.5x_n$. Three designs of the same typical jetty using different arrangements of piles are given in section 25.10.2.

Chapter 7
Electronic computational aids: an introduction

7.1 COMPUTING IN REINFORCED CONCRETE DESIGN

There can be little doubt that the advent of the computer has had a marked impact on the reinforced concrete design office, and it seems almost inevitable that this impact will increase rather than lessen in the immediate future. The increasing use of computers to aid structural analysis and design could be predicted confidently more than two decades ago (ref. 106). However, what was much less easy to foresee, even comparatively recently, was how developments in the equipment available and in the comparative costs of the hardware (the machines themselves) and the software (the programs required to solve actual problems) would alter the outlook.

A brief resumé of the development of computing may explain how and why things are as they are at present.

The first commercial electronic computers were, in present-day terms, large and expensive machines. The programs used to operate them had to be written in so-called machine code. This, in computer jargon, is the primitive language understood by the machine: in other words, the basic instructions by which a machine operates. Machine code differs from one model to another, and learning a particular code sufficiently well to program the machine being used was a difficult and time-consuming task. The preparation of actual computer programs was therefore normally entrusted to staff specially trained for this task.

To permit ordinary engineers and others to produce their own programs, special interpretative languages (e.g. Pegasus Ferranti Autocode) were developed. This interpretative language was read by and stored in the computer and automatically translated the commands in the individual program into machine code. These languages enabled programs incorporating simple easily understandable commands to be written. The advantage of simplicity was outweighed to some extent by the fact that the running time was vastly increased and extra restrictions were placed on the scope of the computer in terms of storage space and so on.

Nevertheless, in the early 1960s, work went ahead on the development of more advanced universal languages (the term 'universal' indicates that their use is not–hopefully–restricted to an individual machine or even a family of machines). Two that reached general acceptance in the field of science and engineering were FORTRAN and ALGOL. (These titles, like so many names in the world of computing, are acronyms and stand for, respectively, FORmula TRANslation and ALGOrithmic Language.) Many comprehensive present-day computer programs in the engineering field are written in (or in extended versions of) these computer 'languages', particularly the former.

One difficulty in using such high-level language (the height of level relates to the extent to which the language is oriented towards the user rather than the machine) is that a considerable amount of computer storage is required to store the interpretative program itself. This is a particular handicap with smaller equipment where storage restrictions are obviously more of a problem anyway. For this and other important reasons, simpler but more limited high-level languages have been developed. The best-known of these is undoubtedly BASIC (Beginners All-purpose Symbolic Instruction Code). Originally developed at Dartmouth College, New Hampshire, USA in 1964 for educational purposes, its simplicity and wide applicability have led to its becoming extremely popular for the writing of computer programs by non-specialists. A problem with BASIC is that it often varies slightly from machine to machine; in computer jargon there are various 'dialects', and a program written in one may not run on a computer designed to operate using only another (see section 7.6). By restricting the 'vocabulary' employed, such difficulties can usually be avoided, but the individual extensions which characterize the dialects permit short-cuts to be taken which reduce the pressure on storage space.

In the early years of computer development, it seemed likely that only the larger consulting engineers and similar organizations would be able to own their own machines. As a result the computer bureau developed, where the smaller user could either buy time to run his own programs on the bureau's machine or, more commonly, use programs owned and perhaps developed by the bureau itself to solve his problems. Even if so-called 'in-house' facilities were available within an engineering firm it was unlikely that the engineer would actually come into contact with the computer. In both of the above cases the more usual arrangement would be for an engineer to supply the necessary data to the computer staff who would then prepare the material in a form suitable for feeding into the machine and, at some later time, return the results to the engineer.

This method of operation has certain clear disadvantages. Firstly, the actual contact between man and machine is handled by someone who may have very little idea of the meaning of the data being processed. Errors may be input that would have been detected immediately if prepared by an engineer. The data may need to be modified in the light of the results being obtained, even perhaps before the computations are completed. The engineer would know this but the bureau personnel may not. Clearly the possibility of unnecessary delays occurring is high and, although the system is excellent for rigorously confirming the suitability of a tentative design that has already been prepared, it is less satisfactory for developing a design.

However, one development in the mind-1960s revolutionized the computer industry: the introduction of the microprocessor. By producing an entire complex circuit on a silicon 'chip' about 5 mm square and 0.1 mm in thickness using a lithographic etching process, extraordinary reductions in space and cost have become possible, since a single chip can now replace circuits which required up to 250 000 transistors.

The resulting developments have included the gradual but continual reductions in the size and expense of computers of equivalent power and the introduction of pocket calculators of increasing versatility. As described below, some of these latter devices can read, store and process complex programs that would have required a full-size computer a few years ago. Today's desktop machine is for more powerful than a machine which filled a room in the early 1960s. The resulting savings in space and operating power mean that, even with larger equipment, a standard 13 A power point will normally suffice compared with the special heavy-current electricity supply and air-conditioned rooms required for computing equipment until recently. It has been estimated that, by 1985, the performance/cost ratio of computers had increased by 10^6 compared with 1955 and 10^4 compared with 1965.

With the decrease in hardware costs have come sharp increases in software costs. Professional programming is now extremely expensive. The conclusions to be drawn from these facts are twofold. Firstly, there are clear advantages, financially as well as otherwise, to be gained if designers are willing and able to write their own computer programs. Secondly, it is most important to make every attempt to utilize the work already done by others. Particularly in those cases where a program is likely to be utilized repeatedly and the solution required is rather more than an *ad hoc* one, the user would be well advised to examine similar existing programs to which he can gain access to see if they can be adapted to suit his purpose. It may be worth making small compromises in order to save the great effort required to develop an efficient reliable program from scratch (ref. 116). Programming is both too expensive and too time-consuming an operation to duplicate work that has already been done well.

Owing to space limitations it is impossible to deal in detail with the various uses of computers in reinforced concrete design, and the present intention is to provide a more comprehensive treatment in a separate book. The following descriptions are therefore intended to give brief glimpses of a few representative examples of the use of computers to assist reinforced concrete design and an indication of future trends.

The Integraph system represents the current state of the art as regards the use of a purpose-designed computer system for engineering and architecture. Such a system, which handles many aspects of each project from initial conception to the preparation of final working drawings and schedules, invariably requires those engineers involved to reshape to some extent their individual working methods to meet the changed requirements brought about by such computerization.

In design offices maintaining more traditional practices, small individual desktop microcomputers can be provided for each section of three or four engineers, and these can be programmed to respond interactively as the design process proceeds. Two of the earliest established and most widely used systems are described below, together with a noteworthy more recent contender.

The application of these systems to the analysis and design of continuous-beam systems has been described in particular detail since it is thought that this is an individual facet of design that a reader can easily relate to his own experience. An authoritative and comprehensive independent review of a number of computer systems for analysing and designing continuous beams according to the requirements of CP110 has been published by the Design Office Consortium, now known as the Construction Industry Computing Association (CICA) (ref. 116). The CICA is a government-supported association which was set up to promote the use of computers and associated techniques in the building industry. No attempt is made here to summarize the conclusions of this excellent report since the entire document must be considered required reading for all designers interested in using computers for reinforced concrete design.

During the last decade dramatic developments have taken place in the personal microcomputer and programmable pocket calculator fields. Although a considerable amount of structural engineering software has been made available commercially for such machines, many designers prefer to prepare their own programs, and these matters are discussed in some detail.

For readers interested in developing their knowledge of the application of computers to reinforced concrete design and detailing, refs 106 to 124 and 133 to 136 provide background knowledge in this fragmentarily documented field.

7.2 INTERGRAPH

The Intergraph system shows what may be achieved when developing a dedicated computer graphics system for structural and architectural design. The system involves the use of individually configured workstations, equipped with computer terminals, printers and plotters, which are linked to VAX-based central processors which have been enhanced to handle graphics. This arrangement enables engineers and architects who may be based in locations that are many miles apart to access the structural data relating to a particular project simultaneously. Links to other types of mainframe computer are possible and the conversion of drawings created using different systems to Intergraph format can be arranged.

Civil and structural engineering is catered for by a number of software packages that are designed to operate using a central database of information relating to a single project, as well as exchanging information with each other. These packages include a structural modelling system which facilitates the rapid generation in three dimensional graphics of structural frameworks and the like, and stores the corresponding data in a non-graphical database. An analysis program (IRM) provides facilities for carrying out finite-element and frame analyses for a wide range of structures (including those comprising thin plates and shells) and can display the resulting forces and displacements using stress contours, exaggerated deformations etc., with members or regions subjected to critical values being highlighted in colour. An erection drawing package is also provided to create two-dimensional working layouts from the three-dimensional data that have been stored.

Separate program suites for interactive concrete and steel detailing are also available. The concrete detailing package currently supports four design codes: CP110 (with bar shapes to BS4466), the American ACI318–77 and AASHTO documents, and the French BAEL 83 code. Detailing is undertaken graphically. The materials grades and concrete cover are first specified. The designer then positions a reinforcing bar by selecting the chosen shape from a menu of those available which is displayed on the screen and locates this on a working plane on the three-dimensional outline displayed. If non-standard bar shapes are necessary, these can be created by the user and added to the menu. Next, by means of simple projection commands that cater for both equal and unequal spacings, the same bar is used to place all similar bars in a single action. Simultaneously, all the necessary information relating to the number, length, size, end anchorages etc. of the bars being detailed is stored in the database for later use when preparing bar-bending schedules and lists of materials required. The user is offered the option of displaying on the drawing either all the bars he has detailed, random bars only, or merely the central or end bars of each set.

The software includes facilities which ensure that reinforcing bars are positioned correctly and do not obstruct each other or clash with architectural features such as ducts. For example, appropriate distances between adjacent bars can be automatically enforced and the more comprehensive checking of an area can be specified by the user. Bars placed in curves, systems requiring bars of gradually increasing length, and the reinforcement of non-prismatic members are all supported.

Finally the software prepares two-dimensional working drawings from the three-dimensional model used for detailing and, in addition, any three-dimensional view of this model can be rotated and scaled according to requirements and included with the working plans and elevations. Facilities are also provided to slice the model arbitrarily at any selected point and to add the resulting cross-section to the drawings. This features enables representations of the most complex intersections between reinforcing bars to be produced rapidly and effortlessly.

7.3 DECIDE

The DECIDE (DEsk-top Computers In DEsign) system (ref. 114) was originally written by A. W. Beeby and H. P. J. Taylor in the mid 1970s, when they were both at the Cement and Concrete Association. Various versions of the suite of programs have been prepared for and implemented on a wide range of equipment from a desktop micro-computer to a bureau-operated IBM machine. The following description relates to the use of the system on an Olivetti P6060 minicomputer having 48 kilobytes (48K) of random-access memory (RAM) together with an operating system occupying 32K of read-only memory (ROM).

The version of DECIDE described is written in BASIC and can actually operate on a computer with a minimum of 16K of RAM. Covering all basic aspects of design in accordance with CP110 from structural analysis to bar curtailment, the aim is to provide the reinforced concrete designer with maximum flexibility. He can thus undertake his design in a similar way to that which he would adopt using normal hand methods, but interaction with the computer transfers the routine and tedious calculation to the machine.

The DECIDE system is made up of a number of individual modules, each of which consists of a separate program dealing with a specific design aspect. By so doing, the designer has a certain amount of freedom to choose the order in which he designs the structural members and can always return to a previous point in the design procedure if he is unhappy with his results, and restart the design process with a modified section or loading. When he is finally satisfied, the machine will provide printed output in a form suitable for passing on to a detailer or for submission to a checking authority.

The system will analyse either freely supported beams or arrangements of continuous beams. In the latter case, systems having up to seven spans (with end cantilevers, if desired) can be considered, with or without the interconnecting upper and lower columns. Alternatively, the beam system being considered can be analysed as a series of separate three-bay sub-frames as permitted by the Code. Whichever analytical method is adopted, the resulting moments can be redistributed in accordance with the Code requirements and the final bending moments and shearing forces stored on disk so that they may be detailed later on a span-by-span basis.

The next program module calculates the areas of reinforcement required to resist bending with a rectangular or flanged section. The program automatically takes account of the Code limitations on the depth to the neutral axis and the minimum permissible amount of reinforcement that may be provided. A further program checks the serviceability limit-states, the deflection being controlled by limiting span/effective-depth ratios and the maximum bar spacing being determined by the rigorous procedure outlined in the Code to restrict the surface crack widths to suitable values.

Curtailment of the reinforcement in accordance with the bending-moment information previously produced and to meet the Code requirements is next undertaken interactively, and a further program module calculates the shearing reinforcement required and checks that the limiting local-bond stresses are not exceeded. The remaining modules in the suite of beam-analysis programs are used to output data file contents, to sort such files after analysis in order to detail each individual span, to store data so that several different designs for a particular member may be prepared (and afterwards compared) without the need to input all the original data each time, to produce title blocks so that they appear on the printed output, and so on.

In addition, two further separate programs are provided for column design. The first calculates the steel areas required to resist direct load combined with bending about one or both axes in a symmetrically reinforced rectangular column, while the second analyses slender columns. A final program is included for designing two-way slabs, which calculates the bending moments at the ultimate limit-state and the resulting amounts of reinforcement required (taking into account the requirements regarding minima specified in the Code), checks the span/effective-depth ratio and the maximum bar spacing necessary to satisfy crack-width requirements, and also calculates the loads transferred from the slab to the various supporting beams. This program also permits the reinforcement over one support to be specified in advance if desired, the other moments (and hence steel areas) being adjusted accordingly to cater for this. The printed output from the computer can include rough but acceptable sketches of the bending-moment and shearing-force diagrams, if required.

7.4 OASYS

OASYS software was originally developed by the Ove Arup Partnership around 1980 specifically for the Hewlett-Packard 9845S desktop computer system. Since then the programs have been implemented on a number of other Hewlett-Packard systems including the HP80 series of personal computers and the more powerful HP9000 series 200. The more popular programs have also been converted into the Pascal language to run on the multi-user HP3000 system and other 9000 series 500 machines; their implementation on the HP150 Touchscreen desktop computer is currently in hand, as is the preparation of versions for Apricot and IBM-PC equipment.

The programs that have been produced include a large number of various aspects of structural analysis and design and others for surveying, drainage, roadworks, the thermal behaviour of sections etc. All of the programs can be purchased separately, but some are also available (at a substantial saving in cost) in four special packages, comprising systems for structural analysis, reinforced concrete design to CP110, civil engineering and building services respectively. The former includes programs for analysing plane, grid and portal frames, space frames and trusses, continuous beams, and finite-element analyses.

By arranging the printed output to be produced in A4 page lengths, each of which carries at the top the necessary information to identify the job and a section title, sheet number etc., this output may be divided into normal calculation pages for submission for approval or checking. The final sheets carry the input data (after correcting errors and editing), and the output is presented, where applicable, in graphical form.

Since the programs are conversational in style, the prompting information incorporated is almost completely self-explanatory and it is thus seldom necessary to refer to the comprehensive user manuals which are supplied with each program. To simplify input and save time, many standard values (e.g. $f_{cu} = 30\,\text{N/mm}^2$, $\gamma_c = 1.5$ for concrete and 1.15 for steel etc.) are input automatically by default unless different values are specified. Extensive facilities that are provided for copying selective items or whole blocks of data for future recall and editing save time and reduce the possibility of errors occurring. To trap errors introduced by inserting data in the wrong format (e.g. dimensions in millimetres instead of metres), all the programs incorporate a specially developed input routine which requests the data to be repeated if they do not fall within prescribed limits.

The CP110 design package contans programs for analysing and designing continuous beams, rectangular and irregular columns, and flat slabs (including checking the shearing resistance around the column heads), rigorously analysing deflections, designing foundations, and the statistical analysis of concrete cubes. Some idea of the sophistication of these programs can be gained by examining more closely the linked procedures for analysing and designing continuous beams. These programs analyse systems consisting of up to eight spans (together with the upper and lower storey-height columns) in accordance with CP110. The analysis program enables uniform, concentrated, triangular and trapezoidal loads arranged in either standard or non-standard patterns to be investigated. Non-prismatic spans having up to five values of moment of intertia may be considered, the appropriate subroutine dividing the length into twenty intervals and using numerical integration, as well as normal prismatic members. The program investigates a maximum of 56 different loads and nine loading cases in a single analysis, calculating the fixity moments and stiffnesses for slope deflection, inverting the resulting matrix and then considering the various combinations of load.

The resulting support moments may now be redistributed as permitted by the Code; the program displays the resulting moments and percentages of redistribution obtained after the maximum reductions of support moment have been made. These percentages, or lower values, may be selected, or alternatively it is possible to specify a desired support moment (i.e. that corresponding to a predesigned section) and the moment throughout the spans will be redistributed to correspond to these specified support values.

When this design stage is complete, the values of the bending-moment envelopes both before and after redistribution at one-tenth points across each span, together with details of the percentage redistribution of the shearing forces and the resulting values of β at these points, are printed. In addition, scale diagrams of the bending moments and shearing forces are plotted automatically.

The design program requires a uniform concrete section throughout each span and utilizes a single bar diameter for each particular area of steel specified. Within these constraints, the program calculates the areas of top and bottom steel required at midspan and at the supports according to the moment diagram and section dimensions. Bar sizes are then determined by an automatic optimizing procedure, taking into account local-bond requirements, bar spacing, the resulting number of layers etc. and searching through the range of diameters permitted. Shear reinforcement is selected in the same way. Dimensions for curtailing groups of main bars and links are selected according to prescribed rules that satisfy anchorage-bond requirements etc., and this information is printed out in a form which can be passed directly to the detailer. Finally the span/effective-depth ratio is checked to ensure that the limit-states of deflection criteria are satisfied. Subroutines are written into the program to ensure that, for example, the top reinforcement selected for the spans each side of a common support is composed of the same bars.

The complementary program for rectangular columns may be operated in either a design or an analysis mode. With the former, the steel required for a particular column subjected to up to ten different cases of loading can be determined. The analysis mode permits column sections containing various arrangements of up to fifty bars to be investigated to see whether they satisfy the requirements specified by CP110 for a maximum of ten loading cases. This procedure permits a single design to be selected that will satisfy the requirements of a number of columns supporting slightly different combinations of load and moment. Alternatively, the program will produce design charts plotting N against M_x and M_y (or M_x against M_y) for particular symmetrically reinforced rectangular columns.

Although the foregoing programs and the others comprising the suite permit a high degree of interactive design they also incorporate, as already stated, a large number of standard values (for example, ranges of bar diameters, cover dimensions, partial safety factors etc.) by default. In other words, these preselected values may be overwritten when desired. Thus much of the interactivity (which slows down the design process) may be omitted by accepting the optimized bar diameters, redistribution percentages etc. offered by the computer, but the procedures are so arranged that all such information is offered for acceptance or adjustment before the next design stage is undertaken.

7.5 CADS

An excellent example of what can be achieved using an IBM or compatible microcomputer with a minimum of 256K of random-access memory is the ANALYSE program developed by CADS of Broadstone, Dorset. The program for analysing two-dimensional structures can handle non-prismatic members, fixed, hinged, roller or spring supports, fixed or pinned joints, and any type of load and load combination.

Regular joint and member patterns can be program generated and sectional properties calculated automatically. Graphical screen displays provide a visual check on the geometry, member, joint and load numbering, supports and joint fixity. The moments, shearing and axial forces and deflections are also displayed graphically and a 'zoom' facility enables the forces or displacements to be displayed to a larger scale. Printed results, which are produced on titled and numbered A4 pages, can be generated selectively after they have first been viewed on-screen.

CADS also produce a similar program to analyse single-span or continuous systems of beams or slabs and produce reinforced concrete details to BS8110 requirements. This program consists of three independent modules which interlink when required to transfer common data. The analysis module takes specified arrangements of structure and loading together with prescribed partial safety factors, and produces moment and shear envelopes according to either the critical loading patterns required by BS8110 or the true worst conditions. These results, or alternatively data entered by the user, are then employed by the design module to determine the reinforcement to resist bending and shear, and information regarding the acceptability of the resulting span/effective-depth ratios is provided. A final module uses the results produced by the previous analyses to detail the reinforcement and offers either a totally automatic procedure or an interactive one. Further enhancements such as the automatic production of standard reinforcement details and bar schedules are in hand, as are the extension of these facilities to the design of two-way slabs, columns and walls to BS8110.

7.6 PROGRAMMABLE POCKET CALCULATORS AND MICROCOMPUTERS

The first programmable pocket calculators available in the UK were marketed by Hewlett-Packard and Texas Instruments in the early 1970s, and the capabilities of such machines rapidly increased. For example, the Hewlett-Packard HP65, which had the ability to store only 100 program steps, was succeeded scarcely two years later by the 224-step HP67. Indeed, unlike its predecessor the latter machine is capable of handling much longer programs, since it can be instructed to suspend operations while the magnetic card containing the next stage of the program is read. The data held in the various storage registers are unaffected by this operation. Conversely, a running program may be halted, if desired, while fresh data are loaded via the card reader to replace part or all of the information currently stored in these registers.

To give some idea of the sophistication that can be provided in a design routine contained on a single 224-step program card, it may be helpful to describe a program produced by the writer to design rectangular beams according to BS8110 and CP110 using rigorous limit-state analysis with a parabolic-rectangular concrete stress-block. The first stage of the program calculates the constants k_1, k_2 and k_3 (see section 20.1.1) for a given value of f_{cu}. During this part of the procedure, the calculation pauses in order for the machine to read automatically the data defining the bilinear or trilinear stress–strain diagram relating to the particular type of reinforcement used. Prerecorded cards giving the necessary data for values of f_y of 250, 425 and 460 N/mm^2 are kept immediately available, while supplementary programs have been prepared that will produce a data card carrying all the necessary information for any other value of f_y if this should be required.

The next step is to input the applied ultimate bending moment and the section breadth that the designer wishes to adopt. The machine then responds by displaying the maximum ratio of x/d that may be adopted without the need to restrict the design stress in the tension steel to less than its optimum value. The designer can choose at this stage whether to adopt this ratio or to overwrite it with another, and the calculator then determines the minimum effective depth of section that must now be adopted if tension reinforcement only is to be provided. If this depth is acceptable, or if the user prefers to adopt a greater value, the machine immediately evaluates the resulting area of tension steel required. However, if a shallower depth is chosen, the depth to the compression steel is requested and the calculator responds by displaying the previously chosen ratio of x/d. Once again, this may be accepted or overwritten as desired. The required areas of tension and compression steel are finally displayed. At any point in this design process, the user can go back and adjust his chosen values without the need to re-enter the basic information regarding the concrete and steel to be used and the moment applied. It is, furthermore, possible to consider the effect of altering the grade of concrete without reinserting the basic data relating to the reinforcement, and vice versa.

The HP65 and HP67 were so-called pocket calculators measuring 153 mm by 81 mm in size, although a larger desktop version of the latter, equipped with an integral near-silent thermal printer using paper 57 mm wide, was also marketed. Around 1980, Hewlett-Packard introduced a range of new hand-held calculators, the HP41 series. These, although basically similar in size to the calculators described above, have far more facilities and greater potential. Programs can be input either by a detachable card reader employing 71 mm by 11 mm magnetic cards, or by a miniature digital microcassette recorder, or via printed bar codes that are read using a light-pen. Two types of thermal printer (embodying sufficient preprogramming to permit quite complex graphical plotting, albeit on thermal paper only 57 mm in width!) are available, and the calculator can be integrated into a network of other devices. Among other purposes, it may thus act as a data-input device for a system that incorporates microcomputer processing.

The original HP41 calculator had a basic memory capacity of 448 memory bytes, but this could be increased fivefold by adding an additional memory module so as to provide for up to about 2000 program lines or 319 memory locations (or a combination of these facilities). Four sockets, to accommodate such modules or to attach peripheral equipment such as a printer, were provided, and HP also marketed plug-in read-only modules (ROMs) catering for specialized subjects such as stress analysis and mathematics. These ROMs have the advantage of providing readily available programs utilizing considerable amounts of calculator memory without employing any of the machine's own random-access memory (RAM), which is thus still available to store programs keyed in by the user or loaded via one of the input devices already mentioned. An important advantage of the HP41 over its predecessors was that the programs and data stored in the machine were not lost when it was switched off.

The structural engineering module incorporated the following programs: calculation of sectional properties; single-span, continuous-beam and continuous-frame analysis (including settlement of supports); steel and concrete column design; and concrete beam design. Unfortunately for UK users, the steel and concrete programs were to the US AISC and ACI318-77 design codes only.

A disadvantage of all the machines so far described is that, to utilize the limited memory to the full, programming has to be done in special relatively low-level languages somewhat similar to the assembly languages available on microcomputers. For this and other reasons (some of which were never clearly understood) programmable pocket calculators never achieved the same 'respectability' as a professional design tool in UK structural engineering offices as they did both on the Continent and in the USA.

The development and increased use of such devices was dealt a further blow in the 1970s by the introduction into the UK of so-called personal computers, such as the Commodore PET, the Tandy TRS-80 and the Apple II. Although these machines had pitifully small amounts of RAM by present-day standards (16K being the norm), this was far in excess of that commonly available in a calculator. A further advantage was that the computers could be programmed in BASIC (this language invariable being supplied with the machine in the form of a ROM chip), a language which, although considered by many computer professionals to have important limitations, is easily understood and learned by engineers.

Unlike the calculator manufacturers, the early microcomputer developers were not engineering-user oriented. Indeed, it was scarcely perceived at that time that the machines would be used for business purposes rather than home use. Consequently, virtually no professionally written engineering software was available initially for such computers. However, during the next few years, as systems developed in sophistication with increased memory capacities, as floppy-disk drives replaced the tediously slow process of loading programs from audiocasette tapes, and as graphics printers utilizing A4 paper became widely available, a number of organizations started to offer a range of structural engineering software. In many cases these were programs that had first been developed by firms of consultants for use in their own offices and were then offered for sale to help to recover some of the cost of development. Many of these pioneers fell by the wayside, but a few are still in existence.

Certain programmable calculator manufacturers (notably the Japanese companies Casio and Sharp) attempted to offer a viable alternative to the desktop personal computer by developing hand-held machines (optimistically described as 'pocket computers'!) running a cut-down version of BASIC and loading and saving programs via standard audiocassettes (or, in the case of the Sharp PC-1251, dictating-machine microcassettes). However, although quite ingenious structural engineering programs could be devised for these machines they did not halt the advance of the desktop computer.

Three important events from the computing point of view marked the first half of the decade that commenced in 1980, during which period a plethora of small computers were launched on an already well-saturated market and mostly sank without trace quite rapidly. Firstly, Clive Sinclair introduced his personal computers the ZX-80 and ZX-81 which, at rock-bottom prices (eventually less than £50), brought personal computing to the notice of a public that had hitherto ignored it. Sinclair's successor to these machines, the 64K RAM Spectrum (currently also available in a 128K version) is also used for 'serious' computing and some professional structural engineering software is still marketed for it. Secondly, in association with BBC-TV educational services, Acorn Computers developed the BBC-B microcomputer. This machine was widely purchased for schools and educational establishments and spawned a more respectable market for software. Again, a number of structural engineering programs have been written for this machine.

Finally came the entry into the microcomputer field of the computer giant IBM, which completed the move to respectability and rapidly led to a drastic decline of the minicomputer market. In truth, the design of the IBM-PC was far from innovative and did not represent particularly good value for money. However, it eliminated the worry that otherwise resulted from the rapid obsolescence of equipment purchased from other small manufacturers. Most of those responsible for authorizing the purchase of equipment (not necessarily the engineers who would actually be using the equipment concerned) had at least heard of IBM and were quite happy in the knowledge that, unlike many of its smaller brethren, the company would still be in business when support, repairs and upgrading were required.

For such reasons the initial sales of the IBM-PC considerably exceeded the most optimistic forecasts, and it soon became clear that the machine had set something of an industry standard (albeit a rather low-level one). In a field where, owing to differences between operating systems, microprocessors, disk drives and dialects of BASIC, programs developed for one system would almost invariably fail to operate on a different system without some (and often a considerable amount of) modification, the need for some sort of standard was long overdue (see section 7.1). As a result a new industry arose, the development by other manufacturers of so-called IBM-compatible or 'clone' microcomputers which, although differing sufficiently from the original to avoid breaching copyright, are nevertheless sufficiently similar to run most (and in some cases, nearly all) software developed for the IBM-PC itself.

This situation has led to the creation of a relatively large stable market for software, helped by the production of a wide range of peripheral devices by IBM and third-party suppliers. The availability of up to 640K memory and the attachment of a hard-disk drive (somewhat similar to a floppy-disk drive but holding 20 000K or more of material in semi-permanent form with the ability to load it to the computer much more rapidly) has encouraged the development of more professional software. Examples are versions of finite-element programs that were originally devised in the United States for aeronautical engineering using mainframe computers and are now available for microcomputers: these extremely powerful programs can also be used to solve plane frame problems.

7.7 WRITING MICROCOMPUTER SOFTWARE

Structural engineering software is frequently advertised on the products and services directory pages of technical journals such as *The Structural Engineer*, the *New Civil Engineer* and elsewhere. Prospective purchasers who contact the advertisers for further details are frequently discouraged by the high cost, which may be not much less than that of the computer system itself. Are such high charges justified? Can one not write perfectly adequate software oneself using BASIC?

The answer to the latter question is clearly yes, but there are a number of provisos. Computer programs normally consist of three main parts. During the first, the user inputs all the data required to solve the problem concerned, usually in response to prompts which are displayed on the screen. In the second section, the actual structural analysis and/or design calculations are undertaken. Finally, the results are displayed on the screen and perhaps printed.

It is usually not too difficult to write the program code for the second part of this process, and this is where the structural engineer is in his element. There are, broadly speaking, two main types of analytical procedure. The first may be termed a 'straight-through' problem. A typical example would be the analysis of a continuous beam, assuming that a non-iterative method of solution, such as one requiring the solution of simultaneous equations (probably by solving the corresponding matrix), were used. The necessary analytical procedure must be broken down into a series of successive steps, but is relatively straightforward and should present few problems.

The other main type of procedure is based on repetitive looping and is necessary where several of the variables controlling the behaviour of the element being analysed or designed are interdependent. For example, in the design of the reinforcement for a concrete column section of given dimensions to resist a specified load and applied moment it is necessary to know the position of the neutral axis, in order to determine the contribution of the concrete to the resistance of the section and to calculate the stresses in the steel. However, it is impossible to develop an expression that does not presuppose a knowledge of the area of steel required, from which the depth to the neutral axis may be calculated directly. It is thus necessary to assume a value for this unknown quantity, to use this to determine the strains and hence the stresses in the reinforcement, and thus to determine the direct load and moment that the section will resist. If these values do not correspond exactly with the applied forces, an adjustment is made to the neutral-axis position and the process repeated. As the calculated values approach their targets more closely the amount of incremental adjustment is reduced, until eventually the results are sufficiently close to be accepted. A subsidiary equation is then used to calculate the actual area of reinforcement needed.

With such problems a certain amount of expertise is required to establish the criteria to determine when exits should be made from a loop which will apply under all loading conditions, sizes of section and so on. Care must be taken to ensure that the values obtained by the looping procedure converge to the true result under all circumstances. This may be difficult to ensure where, for example, different combinations of load and moment on a section lead to different modes of behaviour that are modelled by different sets of equations (particularly where the equations are empirical and approximate rather than theoretical and exact) and perhaps where one looping procedure is located within another (such 'nested loops' occur, for example, in the design to CP110 of slender columns subjected to biaxial bending).

Checking that convergence does occur under every conceivable combination of circumstances is sometimes difficult, as many variables are frequently involved. Running very large numbers of problems is often the only means of testing the program comprehensively and this can prove both time-consuming and tedious if done manually. (Indeed the experienced programmer's claim that it takes five times as long to write the input/output routines as it does to write the program itself, and five times longer than that to test and 'debug' it, may not be too wild an exaggeration!)

One answer is to prepare a version of the program where some input values are written into the program by the user and the others are generated randomly (but within prescribed limits), and where the results are automatically stored on disk. The computer can then be set to run the program over and over again and left until the disk is full, when the hundred or more sets of values generated can be viewed extremely rapidly.

If difficulties arise because of the failure to exit from a loop, the foregoing procedure should be adjusted so that the results obtained as a result of correct program operation are *not* saved. The number of cycles of the loop should be counted automatically, and when this exceeds a prescribed limit (i.e. only in those circumstances where program operation would otherwise fail) the various variables involved should be automatically saved to disk, the current problem terminated and new input generated. An experienced programmer examining such data can often spot where the difficulty is arising quite quickly and, if he cannot pinpoint the difficulty from the results that have been accumulated, he can then use the data saved to rerun these particular problems manually and so locate the errors. The time taken to set up such an automated testing procedure is well worth spending when it is realized that a computer run of several hours may yield only a handful of problem cases, and to unearth these by setting up test problems manually might take weeks or months of effort.

This testing procedure can be further generalized by the use of the ONERR GOTO instruction provided in most versions of BASIC. If an error is detected that would otherwise cause the program to break down, this instruction redirects program operation to the line number (or label) following the GOTO. At this point a section of program code can be inserted directing *the input data only* to be stored to disk and program operation to be restarted. As before, the program to be tested is modified so that specific input variables are randomly generated and that it continuously recycles. A record should also be kept of the total number of individual problems solved. Having first ensured that all is working according to plan, the computer is now left to run undisturbed for as many hours as are available, or until the disk storing the data is full. (Beware: whereas in normal circumstances a DISK FULL error would halt program operation, with ONERR GOTO in control this will not happen, and thus a specific instruction must be provided to terminate operations when the disk is full.)

When the test is complete, the data saved to disk should be inspected and each set of input run manually using the original program to see exactly what the error is. It should be emphasized that this method of testing should only be used in conjunction with a rigorous program of manual testing: it is described in detail here only because it saves a great deal of time and is less well known than it should be.

If the resulting software may eventually be run on several different types of computer (as is normally the case when software is developed commercially) it may be advantageous to write this section of program code using only a subset of the range of BASIC instructions available for the particular machine on which the program is being developed; the subset is carefully chosen to ensure that the instructions are common to and (importantly but not always obviously) work identically in the versions of BASIC available for all makes of machine to be catered for. This technique of producing *machine-independent* program code may not utilize the more esoteric features of some of the sophisticated versions of BASIC that are now available, but saves a great deal of time and effort if the routines have to be implemented on a different type of computer at some future date.

The first and third parts of the overall plan outlined above (input and display) rely heavily on the particular types of computer and printer used; in other words, this program code is heavily *machine dependent*. However, if the input and output processes are carefully thought out and coded it is possible to use identical input and output procedures for a wide range of problems and programs.

It is these parts of a program that are frequently less rigorously prepared in user-written software. A producer of commercial software will probably have spent months or even years developing the user-interface software employed in his programs. It is normally standard procedure nowadays to check all input in two ways. Firstly, each keypress is monitored individually and rejected if it is invalid, for example if an alphabetical key is pressed when a numerical response is required. A full stop (representing a decimal point), the letter E (signifying exponent) and a minus sign will be accepted, but only one per entry and, in the case of the minus sign, only when it is the first response of a key sequence and/or follows E. Secondly, the resulting value may be checked against preset upper and lower limiting values. This helps to ensure that the user does not enter values in the wrong units (e.g. metres instead of millimetres or vice versa). For instance, the breadth of a concrete beam may be limited to the range 150 mm to 1000 mm and values input that fall outside these limits would be rejected.

More sophisticated programs make provision for the user to reset the limiting values supplied with the original program if he so wishes: he can thus tailor the program to his individual requirements. For example, limits applied by a bridge designer accustomed to large spans may differ somewhat from those applicable to the calculations undertaken by a floor specialist. The ability to override such validation procedures is also useful (although the responsibility for ensuring that all input is scrupulously checked now rests more firmly on the user). This is advantageous when dealing with the problem that arises when the occasional value falls outside the preset limits and avoids the need to reset these limits just for one particular case.

Unless he is very keen, the normal user may not have the time or patience to develop such complex input procedures. And there may be no need if the program is only to be used by its author or by experienced engineers who, if the results produced fall outside the range of possible values indicated by their past experience, will carefully recheck the input and employ an alternative means of analysis to confirm that the values produced by the computer are correct. However, problems may arise when such programs are operated by less experienced users with insufficient background to decide independently whether the computer-generated results are likely to be right.

Another problem with engineering is that, unlike that used on other types of business for word-processing, financial planning etc., the software to solve a particular type of structural problem may only be needed relatively infrequently. Then, when it is required, the engineer needs to remember or learn very quickly how the program works, both in terms of its operation on the screen and the limitations imposed by the theory employed in the program itself. For instance, almost all programs to analyse continuous beams assume that the beam is always in contact with all supports, and will give erroneous results if the loading on the beam is such that uplift can occur at any support. Many commercial programs incorporate some sort of 'help' facility so that pressing a certain key (or key sequence) will provide one or more screens of information or guidance, and this information is supplemented by a comprehensive manual. Both forms of documentation are not difficult to provide, but pressures on the user make it less likely that he will spend time producing these important items for programs that he has written himself.

Most programs actually include what amounts to a fourth part, consisting of the facility to change one or more input items and then recycle the analysis. Unless carefully written this can form the most error-prone part of the program, as certain variables must be re-initialized before a new cycle is commenced and others must not be. This recycling option is not infrequently tagged on as an extra facility after the main part of the program has been written and tested. As a result all sorts of curious errors creep in, some of which only become apparent after several cycles and when data items are changed in a specific sequence. Be warned!

7.7.1 Books containing program listings

A number of books are available from UK publishers containing listings of structural engineering programs in BASIC or FORTRAN: details of some of these, together with very brief notes on their contents, are given in refs 137–146. The BASIC programs can be implemented on most microcomputers having a minimum of 48K RAM (and often much less), though care should be taken if operating them on a different type of computer from that for which they were specifically written. For instance, the BASIC used on the Commodore PET interprets $-X^2$ as $-(X)^2$, whereas that used by the Apple II microcomputer understands it as $(-X)^2$.

The main weakness of such programs lies in the input/output routines provided. These are usually very basic, with no error-trapping facilities of any sort, no opportunity to review the input once it has been entered, and so on. This is understandable, since most computers have screen displays comprising different numbers of lines of text composed of different numbers of characters. Consequently, to make the best use of such programs the user should expect to have to spend some time rewriting the input routines to suit his own machine and requirements.

Similarly the output routines are normally minimal, with the results scrolling up and off the top of the screen, and no provision at all for printed output. There is also seldom any way of rerunning the program without re-entering all the input again. For the user to add such a facility is rather more difficult, since this requires some understanding of the program logic.

Given these limitations, and provided that the user is prepared to devote time and energy to tailoring the basic program code to his own particular requirements, such material can provide the basis for a useful set of computer routines for structural analysis and design.

To avoid considerable amounts of typing in of program code (with the consequent likelihood of errors) some publishers have marketed disks containing the programs listed in these books for popular makes of computer: where known, such details are mentioned in the appropriate reference. Prospective purchasers should note that while in some cases the disk versions of the programs have been modified to provide improved input and output facilities, in the others this has not been done. Thus if the programs are to be used for office design purposes (which normally implies a printed copy of the input data and results) the user may well have to add these facilities to the program himself.

7.7.2 Programming aids

Various software aids are available for users who wish to write their own programs, particularly if they use one of the more popular computers such as the IBM-PC or a compatible. One of the most useful is a generator that automatically produces the program code required during the data input and results output operations. Such a generator usually allows the user to first design one or more input screen displays, typing a character such as # in those positions where numerical values or alphabetical responses (e.g. job title) are to be entered. When the user has entered and positioned all the screen material to his liking, this information is automatically stored on disk. Next, at each position where input is required, details of the type of input are requested and numerical limits entered if appropriate; messages to be displayed if the input is inadmissible can also be specified. When this information is satisfactorily recorded, the software automatically generates the required program code, including all the necessary error-trapping routines. A similar procedure is used to display and/or print the required output information (often referred to in computing parlance as a 'report generator').

Such software can vastly simplify the task of writing input and output routines and can produce error-free program code very swiftly and simply. Unfortunately, however, most programs of this sort are actually designed to generate simple database programs (i.e. to keep names and addresses for mailing lists, staff records, invoicing etc.) and automatically incorporate facilities to sort sets of input data (comprising multiple records, each record consisting of a set of data items) alphabetically or numerically. These facilities are superfluous for engineering usage, where normally only a single 'record' will be input and sorting is not applicable. Nevertheless, if the user learns to manipulate and prune the generated code for his individual purpose, such a generator may still save much programming effort.

The other type of software aid increasinly in vogue is the spreadsheet, which should not, strictly speaking, be considered as a programming aid. This was originally developed for financial planning purposes, enabling the user to make projections of the likely result of alternative expenditure strategies and the like. However, more recent spreadsheets are not limited to financial analysis only but incorporate trigonometrical, logarithmic and other mathematical functions, as well as iteration, looping etc. It was thus not long before engineers were employing such programs for simple design calculations. A normal spreadsheet consists of a simple chequerboard or lattice where values in the 'cells' formed by the intersecting rows and columns relate in some way to the product of the variables represented by the rows and columns themselves. Often in financial calculations the columns represent different months or years while the rows indicate such items as gross income, overheads, expenditure, net profit etc.

In structural engineering calculations, often only a single column may be needed. The rows represent the data required, the intermediate calculations necessary, and the final results produced. On such a spreadsheet the individual cells contain the formulae required to determine the values indicated at the left-hand end of each row. Such a formula may, for instance, specify 'multiply the value five lines above (i.e. the section breadth) by the value immediately below that (the overall depth) by the value immediately below that (the concrete grade) by 0.4 and add this to the value two lines above' and so on. The advantage of such a program is that, once the input data are entered, all the remaining values are calculated automatically. Moreover, it is extremely easy to amend individual input items and observe the resulting effects. Problems of formatting the input and output on the screen and page are eliminated, as this is handled by the spreadsheet program itself; so is the rounding-off of output values to a specified number of decimal places where applicable.

In theory, spreadsheets can be used for quite complex structural analysis and a number of books and articles have indeed been written describing such applications. However, the mathematical functions and operators ideally needed for such calculations are not always available on the particular spreadsheet being employed and it may consequently be necessary to adopt cumbersome techniques to overcome such shortcomings. Such manipulations are rather like using a sledgehammer to crack a nut, and these problems would be better solved by employing a purpose-written program using BASIC or some similar language. However, for relatively simple problems such as the design of axially loaded short columns, pad foundations or earth pressure calculations, the use of spreadsheet programs may provide a labour-saving solution.

7.8 FUTURE DEVELOPMENTS

This *Handbook* is not the place for speculating on the future rôle of computers in life in general and reinforced concrete design in particular. However, some indication of possible trends may be both important and helpful.

Without doubt the area of computer production that is developing most rapidly is that involving small machines. At present, each year brings forth smaller and less expensive computers that are at least equal to, and often more powerful than, their predecessors. Already the cost of a suite of programs such as those for beam and frame analysis and for design to BS8110, and the rental of a suitable computer on which to run them, is less than a reinforced concrete designer's salary. Since the output produced by one good designer with such aid is equivalent to that achieved by several staff using conventional hand methods, it is clearly economical to utilize such equipment and programs.

Furthermore, experience with systems employing a large computer linked to a number of terminals on a time-sharing basis has shown that such arrangements sometimes operate rather slowly when used interactively. There is little doubt regarding the advantages of interactive design, particularly when the extent of interactivity can be modified as described above. It has also been suggested that the need to mount a possibly noisy terminal in an adjoining room has proved a disincentive to its use: certainly, whatever the reason, experience shows that an in-house system of the type discussed is sometimes used less often than might be expected.

It has been stated (ref. 114) that interactive design is an ideal procedure for a professional engineer, since it employs the skills and abilities that he has already learnt to their fullest advantage. The potential advantages of small computers are best exploited in an interactive situation, since the principal disadvantage of such machines is that their facilities for storing data are relatively limited and it may thus be impossible to store all the information required for later design at any one time if the structure being considered is large.

Small computers are normally designed on the assumption that the operator will wish to write at least some of the programs that he runs. The programming facilities are thus planned so that they are easy to use and employ a simple language, often some form of BASIC. It is therefore not difficult for any engineer to prepare simple programs which follow exactly the same steps as he does himself when using hand methods. Since computers are still viewed with distrust in some design offices there are great advantages in adopting this arrangement while their acceptance continues to grow. Because computers can handle complex procedures, this does not mean that such procedures must or even should necessarily be used. An engineer will be reassured if the procedure being followed corresponds sufficiently closely to the way that he would tackle the problem by hand to 'keep an eye' on the development of the design.

On the other hand, the reduction of the number of analytical methods of which an engineer requires knowledge, already referred to elsewhere in this *Handbook*, becomes even more valid here. A knowledge of a general method for solving space-frames will go a long way to analysing many varied types of structures, and the finite-element method is another procedure offering the promise of wide applicability in the future. If an engineer has a machine that will run pre-prepared general programs employing such methods, the skill he will most need to develop is that of arranging the data representing the structure that he is analysing in such a way that it produces an accurate representation of the behaviour being modelled.

The use of an individual machine by an individual engineer is being seen as increasingly important. It has been remarked (ref. 114) that it is surprising what a short distance an engineer will walk to use a computer. By giving each designer his own machine, it becomes a tool like a drawing board and slide rule (and even this *Handbook*!). Until recently, expense has prohibited this, but the void that once existed between the sophisticated hand-held calculator and the desktop computer is becoming increasingly filled with so-called personal machines that offer quite complex facilities for little more than £1000 and sometimes less. The use of such machines, first as glorified pocket calculators but gradually by making increasing use of their programming facilities, could smooth the way for the acceptance of the computer as an essential design-office feature.

Many of these machines have a storage capacity of up to 640K within the machine itself, and can also be linked to a secondary storage system within which programs and data are stored on floppy disks or on a hard-disk system. This system has considerable advantages over the storage of programs and data on compact cassettes (i.e. almost identical to audiocassettes), the method often adopted with extremely low-cost personal systems. Program and data storage and retrieval are reliable and virtually instantaneous, for example. The space required to store the operational program to analyse and redistribute the moments and shearing forces in a single-storey multibay system is typically in the order of 24K (irrespective of the number of bays), although sophisticated input and output routines may require much more memory.

Engineers should be encouraged to learn enough about programming to prepare their own programs, at least using a very simple language such as BASIC. (Books such as refs 122 and 123 enable this to be learnt very easily and the former, written by a civil and structural engineer, is particularly entertaining.) This should have three desirable results. The designer will obtain a better understanding of other programs that he meets and has to use. He will be able to tailor both his own and other programs to meet his particular needs, and establish a better and closer understanding of the equipment he is using. And finally he will perhaps gain fresh insights into design processes that have long been familiar. This could, in certain cases, lead to his adoption of newer machine-oriented approaches to solve old problems. At least, it may lead to a better understanding of the design processes and requirements embodied in Codes of Practice such as BS8110 and BS5337.

Perhaps the last words on this subject are best left to Professor Wright (ref. 120):

> The introduction of the computer into the world of... engineering is one of man's great technical steps forward, comparable to the discovery of fire, the starting of agriculture or the invention of a practical steam engine. We are at a very early stage in this process and are still experiencing many difficulties associated with the comparatively recent arrival of the computer. A slightly comparable situation occurred in the early days of the automobile which had to function on roads intended only for horses.... [The invention] had to function initially in an environment in no way designed or arranged for its use. The new device was able to function with initial success only in a limited number of favourable situations. However, as its use increased it led to the development of paved roads, traffic systems, service stations, a mass production industry, a licensing procedure, and finally to a restructuring of our whole way of life. Only then could the device be used to its full potential.

Up to the present, the computer has been functioning in an essentially unfavourable environment. Society and the computer have not yet had time to adapt to each other. The potentials and limitations of the computer and the ways of using it effectively are still very imperfectly understood. We are now, and in the next decade or two, living in a period of transition, where society and the computer are going through the painful and exciting process of adaptation to each other.

Part II

Chapter 8
Partial safety factors

Calculations made in accordance with the requirements of BS8110 and CP110 to determine the ability of a member (or assembly of members) to satisfy a particular limit-state are undertaken using design loads and design stresses. Such loads and stresses are determined from characteristic loads and characteristic material strengths by the application of partial safety factors which are specified in the Code concerned. At present, the characteristic dead and imposed loads G_k and Q_k are taken as the dead and imposed loads specified in Part 1 of BS6399, while the characteristic wind load W_k is as specified in Part 2 of CP3: Chapter V. Then

$$\text{design load} = F_k \gamma_f$$

where F_k is equal to G_k, Q_k or W_k as appropriate, and the partial safety factor γ_f for the appropriate limit-state being considered is as given on *Table 1*.

The characteristic strength f_k of concrete and reinforcement is defined as the strength below which not more than 5% of the test results fall. For further details regarding the determination of the former see section 4.3.1; the characteristic strength of reinforcement is normally prescribed for a given type. Then

$$\text{design strength} = f_k/\gamma_m$$

where f_k is equal to f_y or f_{cu} as appropriate, and the partial safety factor γ_m for the appropriate limit-state is as given on *Table 1*. Generally, however, design formulae and factors etc. incorporate the appropriate partial safety factor. Thus, when checking for the effects of less usual limit-states, care should be taken to ensure that the values of the partial safety factors embodied in any design expressions used are appropriate.

Bridges. Details of the partial safety factors specified for bridges in Part 2 of BS5400 are given on *Table 9*.

Water-containing structures. The partial safety factors to be adopted when designing water-containing structures to meet limit-state design requirements in BS5337 correspond to those specified in CP110 and set out on *Table 1*. Note that a partial safety factor for load of 1.6 must be considered when calculating the ultimate bending moment due to the action of water or earth on the structure, according to BS5337, whereas BS8110 permits partial safety factors of 1.4 for earth and water pressures.

Safety factors and simplified analytical methods

Limit-state **1**

Partial safety factors	Condition	Ultimate limit-state†: Dead load factor	Ultimate limit-state†: Imposed load factor	Ultimate limit-state†: Wind load factor	Serviceability limit-state: Dead load factor	Serviceability limit-state: Imposed load factor	Serviceability limit-state: Wind load factor	BS8110 only: Earth and water
Partial safety factor for loads γ_f	dead + imposed load	1.4 or 1.0*	1.6	—	1.0	1.0	—	1.4
	dead + wind load	1.4 or 1.0‡	—	1.4	1.0	—	1.0	1.4
	dead + imposed + wind load	1.2	1.2	1.2	1.0	0.8	0.8	1.2

Partial safety factor for materials γ_m	Material	For effects of excessive loads or damage	Otherwise	For calculations for deflections	For calculations for stresses or crack widths	Shear without:
	Concrete	1.3	1.5	1.0	1.3	Reinforcement = 1.25
	Reinforcement	1.0	1.15	1.0	1.0	Bond = 1.4
						Other ≮ 1.5

* Maximum loads of $(1.4G_k + 1.6Q_k)$ and minimum loads of $1.0G_k$ so arranged as to give most unfavourable arrangement of loading.
† To consider the probable effects of (*i*) excessive loading or (*ii*) localized damage, take $\gamma_f = 1.05$ and consider only loads likely to occur simultaneously for (*i*), or likely to occur before remedial measures are taken for (*ii*).
‡ 0.9 according to CP110.
Design load = characteristic load × partial safety factor for loads. γ_f Design strength = characteristic strength/partial safety factor for materials γ_m

SIMPLIFIED ARRANGEMENT FOR ANALYSING STRUCTURAL FRAMES

Basic arrangement of frame

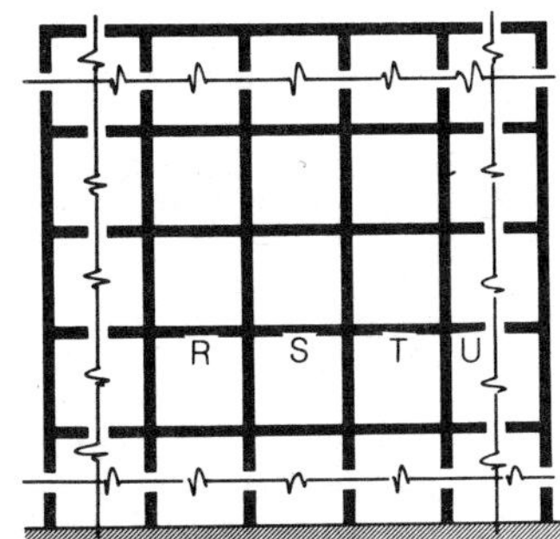

Frame subjected to vertical and lateral loads

Condition 1

Subdivide frame into single-storey systems as shown.

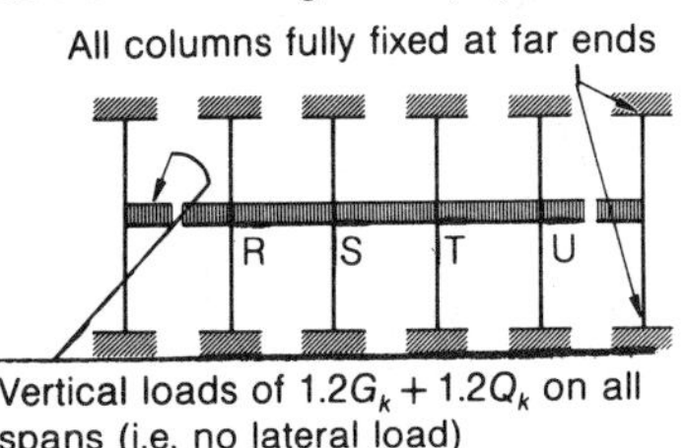

Analyse each individual system for single loading arrangement shown.

Condition 2

Lateral load of $1.2W_k$ throughout height of structure only (i.e. no vertical load)

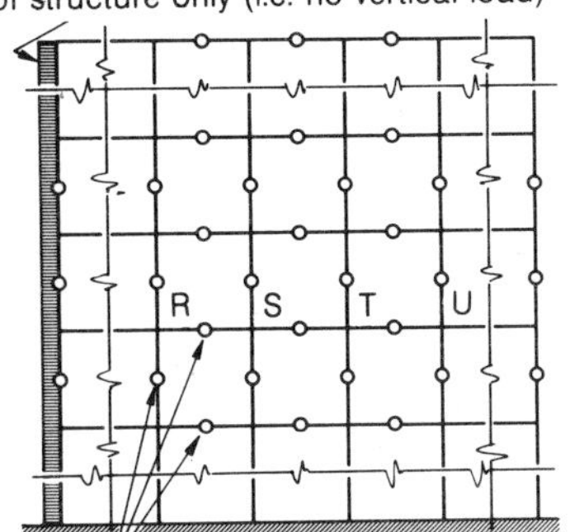

Points of contraflexure at midpoints of all members

Analyse the entire frame for the single loading arrangement shown.

Sum moments obtained under conditions 1 and 2, and compare with those obtained by considering vertical loads only. Design for maxima of these two sets of values.

Frame subjected to vertical loads only

Employ one of methods outlined below

Method 1

Subdivide frame into single-storey systems as shown.

All columns fully fixed at far ends
R S T U
Loading as specified

For maximum positive moment in span ST:
Loads of $1.4G_k + 1.6Q_k$ on one span ST and remaining alternate spans, and of $1.0G_k$ on all other spans.

For maximum negative moment at support S:
BS8110: loads of $1.4G_k + 1.6Q_k$ an all spans.
CP110: loads of $1.4G_k + 1.6Q_k$ on spans RS and ST, and of $1.0G_k$ on all other spans.

For maximum moment in columns at S:
Load of $1.4G_k + 1.6Q_k$ on one span adjoining S and of $1.0G_k$ on other span, such that unbalanced moment at support is a maximum.

Method 2

Subdivide frame into single-storey sub-frames as shown.

Loading as specifed
All columns fully fixed at far ends
R S T U
Assume one-half of true stiffness for outer beams

For maximum negative moment at support S:
BS8110: loads of $1.4G_k + 1.6Q_k$ on all spans.
CP110: loads of $1.4G_k + 1.6Q_k$ on spans RS and ST, and of $1.0G_k$ on span TU.

For maximum positive moment in span ST:
Loads of $1.4G_k + 1.6Q_k$ on span ST, and of $1.0G_k$ on spans RS and TU.

For maximum moment in columns at S:
(occurs when ST is longer of two beams adjoining column)
Loads of $1.4G_k + 1.6Q_k$ on span ST, and of $1.0G_k$ on spans RS and TU

(See *Table 68*)

Method 3

Subdivide frame into freely supported continuous-beam system at each floor as shown.

Loading as specifed below

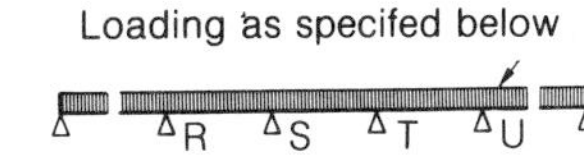

For maximum negative moment at support S:
BS8110: loads of $1.4G_k + 1.6Q_k$ on all spans.
CP110: loads of $1.4G_k + 1.6Q_k$ on spans RS and ST, and of $1.0G_k$ on all other spans.

For maximum positive moment in span ST:
Loads of $1.4G_k + 1.6Q_k$ on span ST and remaining alternate spans, and of $1.0G_k$ on all other spans.

For maximum moment in columns at S:
Subdivide frame into single-storey sub-frames as shown.
Load of $1.4G_k + 1.6Q_k$ on one span and of $1.0G_k$ on other span, such that unbalanced moment at support is a maximum.

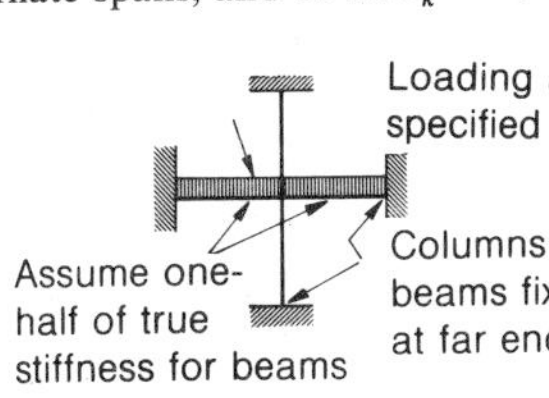

Chapter 9
Loads

In this chapter, unless otherwise stated, all the values given represent actual (i.e. service) forces, weights of materials etc. In carrying out limit-state calculations according to BS8110 or similar documents, such values must be multiplied by the appropriate partial safety factor for loads γ_f corresponding to the particular limit-state being investigated.

The weights and forces in *Tables 2* to *8* are given in SI and imperial values. Although unit weights of materials should strictly be given in terms of mass per unit volume (e.g. kg/m^3), the designer is usually only concerned with the forces that they impose on the structure; therefore, to avoid the need for repetitive conversion, unit weights are here expressed in terms of the force that they exert (e.g. kN/m^3). If required, conversion to the equivalent correct technical metric values can be made very simply by taking 1 newton as 0.102 kilograms. Most of the following SI values for loads have been determined by direct conversion of the corresponding imperial values. In almost all circumstances the resulting accuracy of the SI figures is largely fictitious and they could with advantage have been rounded off: however, this has not been done since it was thought that the resulting discrepancies between the imperial values and their SI equivalents might cause confusion.

9.1 DEAD LOAD

9.1.1 Weight of concrete

The primary dead load is usually the weight of the reinforced concrete. For design purposes this is sometimes assumed to be 22.6 kN/m^3 or 144 lb/ft^3 (one pound per linear foot for each square inch of cross-sectional area). The weight of reinforced concrete is rarely less than 23.6 kN/m^3 or 150 lb/ft^3, which is the minimum weight recommended in most codes of practice, but varies with the density of the aggregate and the amount of reinforcement. A convenient figure to consider in SI metric calculations is 24 kN/m^3: the value is recommended in the *Joint Institutions Design Manual.* Some typical weights of plain and reinforced concrete, solid concrete slabs, hollow clay-block slabs, concrete products, finishes, lightweight concretes and heavy concrete (as used for kentledge and nuclear-radiation shielding and made by using aggregates of great density, such as barytes, limonite, magnetite and other iron ores and steel shot or punchings) are given in *Table 2.*

9.1.2 Other structure materials and finishes

Dead loads include such permanent weights as those of the finishes and linings on walls, floors, stairs, ceilings and roofs; asphalt and other applied waterproofing layers; partitions; doors, windows, roof lights and pavement lights; superstructure of steelwork, masonry, brickwork or timber; concrete bases for machinery and tanks; fillings of earth, sand, puddled clay, plain concrete or hardcore; cork and other insulating materials; rail tracks and ballasting; refractory linings; and road surfacing. In *Table 3* the basic weights of structural and other materials including timber, stone, steelwork, rail tracks and various products are given. The average equivalent weights of steel trusses and various types of cladding as given in *Table 4* are useful in estimating the loads imposed on a concrete substructure. Rules for estimating the total weight of structural steelwork based on adding to the sum of the nominal weights of the members an allowance for cleats, connections, rivets, bolts and the like are given in *Table 3*; extra allowances should be made for stanchion caps, bases and grillages. The allowances permissible for welded steelwork are also given.

The weights of walls of various construction are also given in *Table 4*. Where concrete lintels support brick walls it is not necessary to consider the lintel as carrying the whole of the wall above it; it is sufficient to allow only for the triangular areas indicated in the diagrams in *Table 4*.

9.1.3 Partitions

The weights of partitions should be included in the dead loads of floors and it is convenient to consider such weights as equivalent uniformly distributed loads. The usual minimum load is 1 kN/m^2 or 20.5 lb/ft^2 of floor for partitions in offices and buildings of similar use, but this load is only sufficient for timber or glazed partitions. The material of which the partition is constructed and the storey height will determine the weight of the partition, and in the design of floors the actual weight and position of a partition, when known, should be allowed for when calculating shearing

Weights of concrete

2

	Type	Description		kN/m^3	lb/ft^3
Ordinary concrete (dense aggregates)	Non-reinforced plain or mass concrete	Nominal weight		22.6	144
		Aggregate : limestone		21.2 to 23.6	135 to 150
		: gravel		22.0 to 23.6	140 to 150
		: broken brick		19.6 (av.)	125 (av.)
		: other crushed stone		22.8 to 24.4	145 to 155
	Reinforced concrete	Nominal weight		23.6	150
		Reinforcement: 1%		22.6 to 24.2	144 to 154
		2%		23.1 to 24.7	147 to 157
		4%		24.0 to 25.6	153 to 163
			Thickness	kN/m^2	lb/ft^2
		Solid slabs (floors, walls etc.)	75 mm or 3 in	1.80	37.5
			100 mm or 4 in	2.40	50
			150 mm or 6 in	3.60	75
			250 mm or 10 in	6.00	125
			300 mm or 12 in	7.20	150
		Ribbed slabs	125 mm or 5 in	2.00	42
			150 mm or 6 in	2.15	45
			225 mm or 9 in	2.75	57
			300 mm or 12 in	3.35	70

	Aggregate or type	Compressive strength			
		N/mm^2	lb/in^2	kN/m^3	lb/ft^3
Lightweight concrete	Clinker (1:8)	2.1 to 6.2	300 to 900	10.2 to 14.9	65 to 95
	Pumice (1:6 semi-dry)	1.4 to 3.8	200 to 550	7.1 to 11.0	45 to 70
	Foamed blast-furnace slag	1.4 to 5.5	200 to 800	9.4 to 14.9	60 to 95
	ditto structural	13.8 to 34.5	2000 to 5000	16.5 to 20.4	105 to 130
	Expanded clay or shale	5.6 to 8.4	800 to 1200	9.4 to 11.8	60 to 75
	ditto structural	13.8 to 34.5	2000 to 5000	13.4 to 18.1	85 to 115
	Vermiculite (expanded mica)	0.5 to 3.5	70 to 500	3.9 to 11.0	25 to 70
	Pulverized fuel-ash (sintered)	2.8 to 6.9	400 to 1000	11.0 to 12.6	70 to 80
	ditto structural	13.8 to 34.5	2000 to 5000	13.4 to 17.3	85 to 110
	No-fines (gravel)	—	—	15.7 to 18.9	100 to 120
	Cellular (aerated or gas concrete)	1.4	200	3.9 (min.)	25 (min.)
	ditto structural	10.3 to 15.5	1500 to 2250	14.1 to 15.7	90 to 100
	Weights and compressive strengths of some proprietary concretes are given in *Table 80.*				

	Type	Description	kN/m^3	lb/ft^3
Special concretes etc.	Heavy concrete	Aggregates: barytes, magnetite, steel shot, punchings	31.5 (min.)	200 (min.)
			51.8	330
	Lean mixes	Dry-lean (gravel aggregate)	22.0	140
		Soil-cement (normal mix)	15.7	100
	Finishes etc.		N/m^2 per mm thick	lb/ft^2 per in thick
		Rendering, screed etc. } Granolithic, terrazzo }	18.9 to 23.6	10 to 12.5
		Glass-block (hollow) concrete	17.0 (approx.)	9 (approx.)
	Prestressed concrete	Weights as for reinforced concrete (upper limits)		
	Air-entrained concrete	Weights as for plain or reinforced concrete		
Construction with concrete products	Concrete block and brick walls	Blockwork: 200 mm or 8 in thick	kN/m^2	lb/ft^2
		Stone aggregates: solid	4.31	90
		hollow	2.87	60
		Lightweight aggregates: solid	2.63	55
		hollow	2.15	45
	Weights of walls of other thicknesses pro rata	Cellular (aerated gas)	1.15 to 1.53	24 to 32
		Brickwork: 120 mm or 4.5 in (nominal)	2.6	54
	Other products	Paving slabs (flags) 50 mm or 2 in thick	1.15	24
		Roofing tiles: plain	0.6. to 0.9	12.5 to 19
		interlocking	0.6	12.5

To convert values in kN to values in kg, multiply by 102.

Weights of constructional materials

3

Miscellaneous materials

Material	kN/m³	lb/ft³
Concrete	See *Table 2*	
Brickwork, plaster etc.	See *Table 4*	
Tarmacadam	22.6	144
Macadam (waterbound)	25.1	160
Snow: compact	2.4 to 8.0	15 to 50
: loose	0.8 to 1.9	5 to 12
Vermiculite (aggregate)	0.8	5
Terracotta	20.8	132
Glass	26.7	170
Cork: granular	1.2	7.5
compressed	3.8	24

Material	N/m²	lb/ft²
Clay floor tiles	575	12
Pavement lights	1200	25
Damp-proof course	48	1
	N/m² per mm thickness	lb/ft² per in thickness
Felt (insulating)	1.9	1
Paving slabs (stone)	26.4	14
Granite setts	28.3	15
Asphalt	22.6	12
Rubber paving	15.1	8
Polyvinylchloride	19 (av.)	10 (av.)
Glass-fibre (forms)	1.9	1

Timber

Material	kN/m³	lb/ft³
General	7.9 (av.)	50 (av.)
Douglas fir	4.7	30
Yellow pine, spruce	4.7	30
Pitch pine	6.6	42
Larch, elm	5.5	35
Oak (English)	7.1 to 9.4	45 to 60
Teak	6.3 to 8.6	40 to 55
Jarrah	9.4	60
Greenheart	10.2 to 11.8	65 to 75
Quebracho	12.6	80

Material	N/m² per mm	lb/ft² per in
Wooden boarding and blocks: softwood	4.7	2.5
hardwood	7.5	4
Hardboard	10.4	5.5
Chipboard	7.5	4
Plywood	6.1	3.25
Blockboard	4.7	2.5
Fibreboard	2.8	1.5
Wood-wool	5.7	3
Plasterboard	9.4	5
Weather boarding	3.8	2

Stone and other materials

Material	kN/m³	lb/ft³
Natural stone (solid)		
Granite	25.1 to 28.7	160 to 183
Limestone: Bath stone	20.4	130
marble	26.7	170
Portland stone	22.0	140
Sandstone	22.0 to 23.6	140 to 150
Slate	28.3	180

Material	kN/m³	lb/ft³
Stone rubble (packed)	22.0	140
Quarry waste	14.1	90
Hardcore (consolidated)	18.9	120
All-in aggregate	19.6	125
Crushed rock, gravel, sand, coal etc. (granular materials)	See *Table 17*	
Clay, earth etc. (cohesive)	See *Table 17*	

Metals, steel construction etc.

Material	kN/m³	lb/ft³
Iron: cast	70.7	450
wrought	75.4	480
Ore: general	23.6	150
(crushed) Swedish	36.1	230
Steel (see also below)	77.0	490
Copper: cast	85.6	545
wrought	87.7	558
Brass	83.3	530
Bronze	87.7	558
Aluminium	27.2	173
Lead	111.0	707
Zinc (rolled)	70.0	446
	g/mm² per metre	lb/in² per foot
Steel bars	7.85	3.4

Structural steelwork: riveted	Net weight of member + 10% for cleats, rivets, bolts etc.
welded	+ 1.25% to 2.5 for welds etc.
Rolled sections: beams	+ 2.5%
stanchions	+ 5% (extra for caps and bases)
Plate-web girders	+ 10% for rivets or welds, stiffeners etc.
Roof trusses and wall-framing	See *Table 4*

	N/m	lb/ft
Steel stairs: industrial type 1 m or 3 ft wide	820	56
Steel tubes: 50 mm or 2 in bore	45 to 60	3 to 4
Gas piping: 20 mm or 0.75 in	18	1.25

		kN/m of track	lb/ft of track
Rail tracks, standard gauge main lines	Bull-head rails, chairs, transverse timber (softwood) sleepers etc.	2.4	165
	Flat-bottom rails, transverse prestressed concrete sleepers etc.	4.1	280
	Add for electric third rail	0.5	35
	Add for crushed stone ballast	25.5	1750
		kN/m²	lb/ft²
	Overall average weight: rails, connections, sleepers, ballast etc.	7.2	150
		kN/m of rail	lb/ft of rail
	Bridge rails, longitudinal timber sleepers etc.	1.1	75

To convert values in kN to values in kg, multiply by 102.

Weights of roofs and walls

Roofs — Cladding

(Weights per m² or per ft² of slope of roof)	N/m²	lb/ft²
Patent glazing (with lead-covered astragals)	290	6
ditto including steel purlins etc.	380	8
Slates or tiles, battens, steel purlins etc.	670 to 860	14 to 18
ditto with boarding, felt etc.	800 to 1100	17 to 23
Corrugated asbestos or steel sheeting, steel purlins etc.	380 to 480	8 to 10
Reinforced concrete slabs, concrete tiles etc.	See *Table 2*	

Roofs — Roof trusses

Approximate weights of steel roof trusses in N/m² or lb/ft² of plan area of roof	Span of trusses		Spacing of trusses: 3.0 m	4.5 m	10 ft	15 ft
	7.5 m	25 ft	95	72	2	1.5
	9 m	30 ft	120	72	2.5	1.5
	12 m	40 ft	132	84	2.75	1.75
	15 m	50 ft	144	108	3	2.25
	18 m	60 ft	203	144	4.25	3
	25 m	80 ft	239	168	5	3.5

Walls and components of walls — Brickwork and blockwork

Concrete blocks and bricks	See *Table 2*	
	N/m² per mm thick	lb/ft² per in thick
Hollow clay blocks	11.3 (av.)	6 (av.)
Common clay blocks	18.9	10
Engineering clay bricks	22.6	12
Refractory bricks	11.3	6
Sand-lime (and similar) bricks	19.8	10.5

Plaster

	N/m²	lb/ft²
Gypsum: two-coat 12 mm or 0.5 in thick	215	4.5
plasterboard 12 mm or 0.5 in thick	108	2.25
Lath and plaster (two-faced including studding)	480	10

Sheeting etc.

	N/m²	lb/ft²
Corrugated steel or asbestos-cement sheeting (including bolts, sheeting rails etc.)	430	9
Steel wall framing (for sheeting or brick panels)	240 to 335	5 to 7
ditto with brick panels and windows	2400	50 (av.)
ditto with steel or asbestos-cement sheeting	720	15 (av.)
Windows (industrial type: metal or wooden frames)	240	5 (av.)
Doors (ordinary industrial type: wooden)	380	8

Partitions on solid slabs — Equivalent uniformly distributed dead load

h_p thickness of partition in millimetres or inches
w_p weight of partition in kN/m or lb/ft
w_e equivalent uniformly distributed load in kN/m² or lb/ft²

Position not known:

Per BS6399: Part 1	kN/m²	lb/ft²
Additional uniformly distributed load	$0.33w_p$	$0.10w_p$
ditto minimum for office floors	1	20.5

Position known:

Partition normal to span

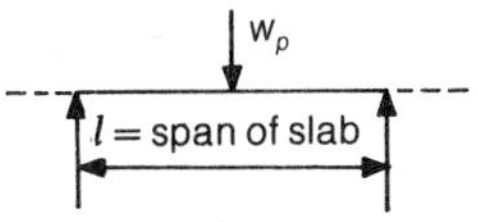

Freely supported	$w_e = 2\frac{w_p}{l}$ (maximum)
Continuous over both supports	$w_e = \frac{3}{2}\frac{w_p}{l}$ (minimum)

Partition parallel to span of slab (based on BS8110)

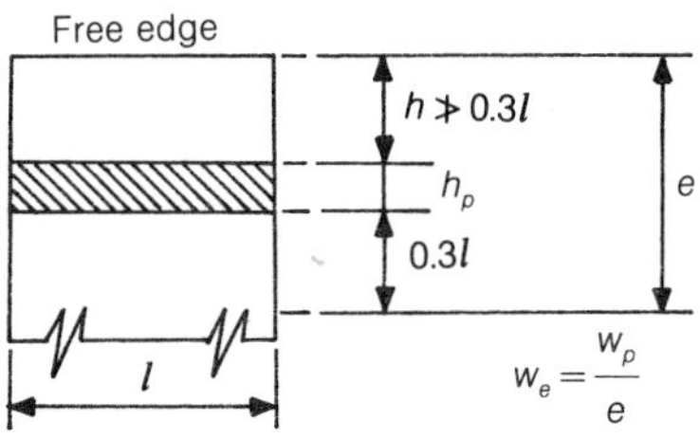

metres	feet
$e = \frac{h_p}{1000} + 0.3l + h$	$e = \frac{h_p}{12} + 0.3l + h$
$e_{max} = \frac{h_p}{1000} + 0.6l$	$e_{max} = \frac{h_p}{12} + 0.6l$
$e_{min} = 1$ m	$e_{min} = 3$ ft

Lintels

Load on lintels supporting brickwork (or similarly bonded walls)

Shading denotes extent of wall considered to be supported by lintel

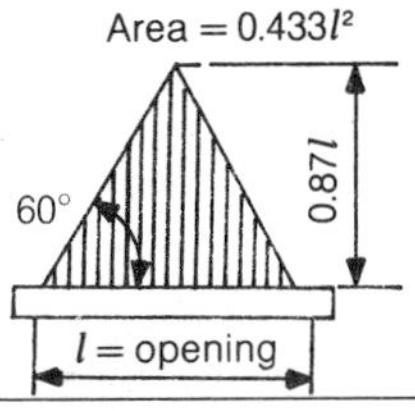

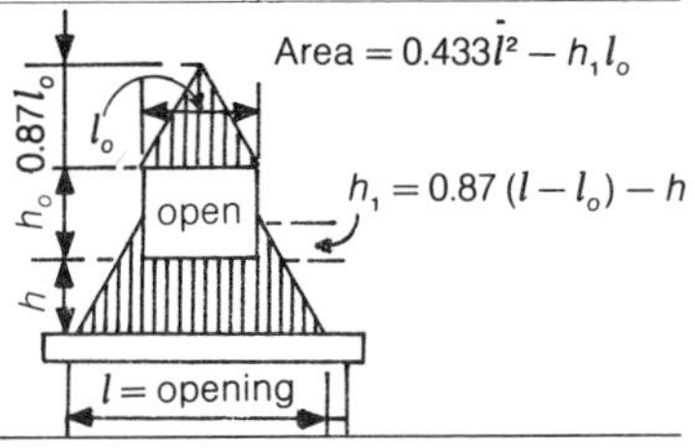

To convert values in N to values in kg, divide by 9.81.

forces and bending moments on the slab and beams. Expressions are given in *Table 4* for the equivalent uniformly distributed load if the partition is at right angles to the direction of the span of the slab and is placed at the middle of the span, or if the partition is parallel to the direction of the span. According to BS6399: Part 1, the equivalent uniformly distributed load per unit area of floor for partitions, the positions of which are not known, should be not less than the fractions of the weight as given in *Table 4*.

In the case of brick or similarly bonded partitions some relief of loading on the slab occurs owing to arching action of the partition if it is continuous over two or more beams, but the presence of doorways or other openings destroys this relieving action.

The uniformly distributed load on a beam due to partitions can be considered as the proportion of the total weight of the partitions carried by the beam adjusted to allow for non-uniform incidence.

9.2 IMPOSED LOADS

Imposed loads on structures include the weights of stored solid materials and liquids (see *Table 5*) and the loads imposed by vehicles and moving equipment, the weights of some of which are given in *Tables 8–12*.

9.2.1 Imposed loads on buildings

The data given in *Table 6*, 7 and *12* comply with BS6399: Part 1. The arrangement of the floor and roof classification has been altered for convenience of reference and comparison.

Units. Loads are specified in the Code in terms of an exact number of kilonewtons (kN) but the equivalent loads in pounds are also given as in *Tables 6* and 7. Equivalents for kN, lb and kg are given in Appendix C. A convenient conversion is that 102 kg = 1 kN.

Concentrated loads. The tabulated loads are assumed to be concentrated on an area 300 mm or 12 in square unless otherwise specified (e.g. roof cladding). Concentrated loads on sloping roofs act vertically on a 300 mm or 12 in square measured in the plane of the roof.

Concentrated loads do not apply if the floor construction is capable of lateral distribution (e.g. a solid reinforced concrete slab).

Roof loads. Uniformly distributed imposed loads on roofs include snow but not wind, and are given per m^2 or ft^2 of area in plan.

Fixed seating. 'Fixed seating' implies that it is improbable that the seats would be removed and the floor used for any other purpose than that specified.

Reduction of imposed loads. Under certain circumstances, the imposed loads on beams supporting floors of large areas and on columns or similar supports in multi-storey buildings can be reduced. The conditions of applicability and the amount of the reductions are given in *Table 12*.

Foundations. The reductions in *Table 12* apply also (with the stipulated limitations) to foundations.

Warehouses. For imposed loads on the floors of warehouses and other stores see *Table 5*.

9.2.2 Weights and dimensions of road vehicles

The data given in *Table 8* relating to heavy motor vehicles, trailers, public-service vehicles and load locomotives are abstracted from 'The Motor Vehicles (Construction and Use) Regulations 1978' (issued on behalf of the Department of Transport). As there are many varieties of vehicle, only the maximum loads and dimensions permissible are given. In general the Regulations apply to vehicles registered recently; vehicles registered earlier may have greater dimensions and weights. The specified limits vary with age, and for details the document itself should be consulted.

Information relating to types of vehicles not covered by the foregoing document may be obtained from The Motor Vehicles (Authorization of Special Types) General Order 1973.

9.2.3 Standard imposed loads for road bridges

Normal load (HA). The uniformly distributed load applicable to the 'loaded length' of a bridge or a structural member forming part of a bridge may be selected from *Tables 9, 10* and *11* as appropriate. The loaded length is the length of member that should be considered to be carrying load in order to produce the most severe effects. Influence lines may be needed to determine the loaded lengths for continuous spans and arches.

The imposed load is considered in two parts: (1) the uniform load which varies with the loaded length; and (2) an invariable knife-edge load of 40 kN/m or 2700 lb/ft of width in the case of BS153, and 120 kN per lane in the case of BS5400. This knife-edge load must be so positioned as to have the most adverse effect. In certain circumstances an alternative single nominal wheel load of 100 kN so arranged that it exerts an effective pressure of 1.1 N/mm^2 over a circular or square contact area may be considered, according to BS5400.

Abnormal load (HB or HC). The arrangement of HB loading that must be considered is as shown in *Tables 9–11*. For information regarding HC loading see section 2.4.6.

9.2.4 Footbridges and footpaths

The loads given in *Table 11* for footbridges between buildings and footpaths at ground-floor level of buildings are abstracted from BS6399: Part 1. The requirements of BS5400: Part 2 for foot and cycle-track bridges are given in *Table 9*.

9.2.5 Garages

Floors of car-parking structures to be used for the parking of ordinary motor cars (not exceeding 25 kN or 2.5 tons in weight) should be designed for a uniformly distributed

Weights of stored materials

5

		kN/m³	lb/ft³		kN/m³	lb/ft³
Liquids and semi-liquids	Acids: acetic	10.4	66	Mineral oils:		
	nitric	15.1	96	naphtha	7.4	47
	sulphuric	18.1	115	paraffin (kerosene)	7.9	50
	Alcohol (commercial)	7.9	50	petrol (gasoline)	6.9	44
	Ammonia	8.8	56	petroleum oil	8.6	55
	Beer: in bulk	10.0	64	Pulp (wood)	7.1	45
	bottled (in cases)	4.6	29	Slurry: cement	14.1	90
	in barrels	5.5	35	clay	11.9	76
	Benzine, benzol	8.6	55	clay-chalk	15.7	100
	Bitumen (prepared)	13.7	87	Sewage	9.7 to 11.8	62 to 75
	Methylated spirit	8.2	52	Tar, pitch	11.8	75
	Linseed oil	8.8	56	Turpentine	8.5	54
	Milk	10.2	65	Water: fresh	9.81	62.4
				sea	10.05	64
				Wine: in bulk	9.7	62
				bottled (in cases)	5.8	37
Solid and packed materials	Brewer's grains (wet)	5.5	35	Lime (slaked): dry	5.5	35
	Bricks (stacked)	17.3	110	wet	14.9	95
	Clinker	9.4 to 10.2	60 to 65	Paper: packed	9.4	60
	Cotton (in bales)	2.4 to 5.5	15 to 35	waste (pressed)	5.5	35
	Flour: in bulk	7.1	45	Salt: dry	9.4	60
	in sacks	6.3	40	loose	14.1	90
	Hay (pressed in bales)	1.3	8	Sawdust	2.4	15
	Hops (in sacks)	1.7	10.5	Slag: basic	17.3	110
	Ice	9.0	57	crushed	9.4 to 14.1	60 to 90
				foamed	6.3	40
				Sugar (loose)	7.9	50
				Tea (in chests)	4.4	28

Imposed loads on floors BS6399: Part 1		Uniformly distributed		Concentrated	
		kN/m²	lb/ft²	kN	lb
	Type (printing works)	12.5	261	9.0	2023
	Books (on trucks)	4.8 per m height but 15.0 minimum	30.6 per ft height but 313 minimum	7.0	1575
	Cold store	5.0 per m height but 15.0 minimum	31.8 per ft height but 313 minimum	9.0	2023
	Paper store (printing works) Stationery store	4.0 per m height	25.5 per ft height	9.0	2023
	Other storage (warehouse, industrial, retail)	2.4 per m height	15.3 per ft height	7.0	1575

Granular materials in liquids — Intensity of pressure on bottom of containers

Notation

D_l unit weight (density) of liquid (N/m³ or lb/ft³) $= 9807$ N/m³ or 62.4 lb/ft³ for water

h_0 depth of liquid above top of submerged material (m or ft)

h thickness of layer of submerged granular material (m or ft)

D_m unit weight (density) of granular material in solid (N/m³ or lb/ft³)

β volume fraction of voids in unit volume of dry granular material

q_v intensity of vertical pressure on bottom of container in N/m² or lb/ft²

$H = h_o + h$

If materials float in liquid ($D_m < D_l$): $q_v = D_l H$

If materials sink in liquid ($D_m > D_l$): $q_v = D_l h_0 + (D_l \alpha_v) h$ where $\alpha_v = \frac{D_m}{D_l}(1 - \beta) + \beta$

Materials submerged in water: values of $(D_l \alpha_v)$

Materials	$D_l = 9807$ N/m³				$D_l = 62.4$ lb/ft³			
	D_m	Percentage of voids $= 100\beta$			D_m	Percentage of voids $= 100\beta$		
	N/m³	30	40	50	lb/ft³	30	40	50
Coal (crushed) etc.	12 570	11 750	11 500	11 200	80	75	73	71
Stone (crushed), sand etc.	25 140	20 600	19 000	17 500	160	131	121	111

To convert values in kN to values in kg, multiply by 102.

Imposed loads on floors

6

Type of building		Use of floor	Uniformly distributed		Concentrated	
General	Particular		kN/m^2	lb/ft^2	kN	lb
Residential premises	Domestic: self-contained dwelling units	All rooms, including bedrooms, kitchens, laundries etc.	1.5	31.3	1.4	315
	Hotels, motels, hospitals	Bedrooms (including hospital wards)	2.0	41.8	1.8	405
	Boarding houses, hostels, residential clubs, schools, colleges, institutions	Bedrooms (including dormitories)	1.5	31.3	1.8	405
Places of public assembly or access	Public halls Theatres, cinemas Assembly areas in clubs, school, colleges Grandstands Sports halls (indoors)	With fixed seating	4.0	83.6	nil	nil
		Without fixed seating	5.0	104.5	3.6	809
	Dance halls, gymnasia		5.0	104.5	3.6	809
	Drill halls		5.0	104.5	9.0	2023
	Churches, classrooms	Including chapels etc.	3.0	62.7	2.7	607
	Library reading rooms	Without book storage	2.5	52.2	4.5	1011
		With book storage	4.0	83.6		
	Museums, art galleries		4.0	83.6	4.5	1011
	Hotels (see also residential)	Bars, vestibules	5.0	104.5	nil	nil
	Banking halls		3.0	62.7		
	Shops	Display and sale	4.0	83.6	3.6	809
Commercial and industrial premises	Offices	General	2.5	52.2	2.7	607
		Filing and storage spaces	5.0	104.5	4.5	1011
		Computer rooms etc.	3.5	73.1		
	Theatres, cinemas, TV and radio studios etc. (see also places of assembly)	Stages: in theatres etc.	7.5	157	4.5	1011
		in colleges and gymnasia	5.0	104.5	3.6	809
		Grids	2.5	52.2	nil	nil
		Fly galleries (uniformly distributed over width)	4.5 per m	308 per ft		
		Projection rooms	5.0	104.5		
		Sports halls (indoor) equipment area	2.0	41.8	1.8	405
	Work places, factories etc.	Utility rooms, X-ray rooms, operating theatres (hospitals)	2.0	41.8	4.5	1011
		Laundries: residential buildings (excl. domestic)	3.0	62.7		
		non-residential (excl. equipment) Kitchens (communal) inc. normal equipment	3.0	62.7		
		Laboratories (incl. equipment)	3.0	62.7	4.5	1011
		Light workrooms (no storage)	2.5	52.2	1.8	405
		Workshops, factories	5.0	104.5	4.5	1011
		Foundries	20.0	418	nil	nil
		Printing works (see also *Table 5*)	12.5	261	9.0	2023
		Machinery halls (circulation spaces)	4.0	83.6	4.5	1011

7

Imposed loads on other parts of buildings

	Description of loaded member (excluding floors)		Uniformly distributed kN/m²	Uniformly distributed lb/ft²	Concentrated kN	Concentrated lb
Ancillary areas	Corridors, hallways, passages etc.	Subject to crowds (including in libraries)	4.0	83.6	4.5	1012
		Loads exceeding crowds (e.g. trolleys etc.)	5.0	104.5	4.5	1012
		In grandstands	5.0	104.5	4.5	1012
	Stairs and landings	In self-contained dwelling units	1.5	31.3	1.4	315
		In boarding houses, hostels, residential clubs etc.	3.0	62.7	4.5	1011
		In grandstands	5.0	104.5	4.5	1011
		Other	4.0	83.6	4.5	1011
	Miscellaneous	Dressing rooms (in colleges, gymnasia, theatres etc.)	2.0	41.8	1.8	405
		Toilets	(2.0)	(41.8)	nil	nil
		Balconies (concentrated loads are per unit length and act at edge)	Sf	Sf	1.5	103
		Catwalks (concentrated load acts at 1 m or 3 ft centres)	nil	nil	1.0	225
		Motor rooms, fan rooms etc. (including weight of machines)	7.5	157	4.5	1012
		Boiler rooms	7.5	157	(4.5)	(1012)
External areas	Footpaths, plazas, terraces etc.	Possible use by vehicles	5.0	104.5	9.0	2023
		Pedestrians only	4.0	83.6	4.5	1012
		Pavement lights	5.0	104.5	9.0	2023
	Driveways, vehicle ramps	Excluding garages for vehicles ≯ 2.5 tons	5.0	104.5	9.0	2023
Roofs	With access	Flat or slope ≯ 10°	1.5	31.3	1.8	405
	Without access (except for cleaning and repair)	Flat ($A = 0°$)	0.75	15.7	0.9	202
		Sloping: for slopes between 30° and 75°, $W_L = \frac{75° - A°}{60} W_R$, $W_R = 1\ \text{kN/m}^2 = 20.9\ \text{lb/ft}^2$; A ≯ 30°	0.75	15.7	0.9	202
		A = 37.5°	0.625	13.1	nil	nil
		A = 45°	0.50	10.4	nil	nil
		A = 52.5°	0.375	7.8	nil	nil
		A = 60°	0.25	5.2	nil	nil
		A ≮ 75°	nil	nil	nil	nil
	Roof cladding, ceilings etc.	Cladding (excluding glazing): concentrated load on 125 mm or 5 in square, A ≯ 45°	nil	nil	0.9	202
		A > 45°	nil	nil	nil	nil
		Ceiling (concentrated load on any joist); Hatch covers (except glazing); Ribs of skylights and frames	nil	nil	0.9	202
	Curved roofs	Divide arc into odd number (≮ 5) of segments	Imposed load on each segment = load on roofs having the same average slope (A_1, A_2 etc.) as the segment			
			kN/m	lb/ft		
Parapets and balustrades	Light access stairs, gangways etc.	≯ 600 mm or 2 ft wide	0.22	15	Loads act horizontally at level of handrail or coping	
		> 600 mm or 2 ft wide	0.36	24.7		
	Other stairs, landings, balconies, etc.	Domestic and private	0.36	24.7		
		Others	0.74	50.7		
		Balconies with fixed seating close to barrier	1.5	103		
		Stairs, landings etc. in theatres, cinemas, concert halls, stadia etc.	3.0	206		
		Footways or pavements	1.0	69		
		Pavements adjacent to sunken areas	3.0	206		

Sf imposed load to be same as that on floor to which access is given characteristic load and an alternative concentrated characteristic load as given in *Table 11*. For the parking of heavier vehicles and for repair workshops, greater loading and the most adverse arrangement of actual wheel loads must be taken into account.

9.2.6 Overhead travelling cranes

To allow for vibration, acceleration and deceleration, slipping of slings, and impact of wheels, maximum static wheel loads (see *Table 12* for typical loads) of simple electric overhead travelling cranes should be increased by 25%. Braking or travelling under power produces in the rail-beam a horizontal thrust which is transferred to the supports. The traversing of the crane and load produces a horizontal thrust transversely to the rail-beam. Therefore the additional forces acting on the supporting structure when the crane is moving are (a) a horizontal force acting transversely to the rail and equal to 10% of the weight of the crab and the load lifted, it being assumed that the force is equally divided between the two rails; (b) a horizontal force acting along each rail and equal to 5% of the greatest static wheel load that can act on the rail. The forces (a) and (b) are not considered to act simultaneously, but the effect of each must be combined with that of the increased maximum vertical wheel loads.

For a crane operated by hand, the vertical wheel loads need be increased by only 10%; for force (a) the proportion of the weight of crab and load can be 5%. Force (b) is the same for hand as for electrically operated cranes.

The foregoing requirements are in accordance with BS6399: Part 1. Gantry cranes other than simple types should be considered individually.

9.2.7 Structures supporting lifts

The effect of acceleration must be considered in addition to the static loads when calculating the load due to lifts and similar machinery. If a net static load of F_d is subject to an acceleration of a metres per second per second (m/s^2) the load on the supporting structure is approximately $F_m = F_d \times (1 + 0.098a)$. If a is in ft/s^2, $F_m = F_d(1 + 0.03a)$ approximately. The average acceleration of a passenger lift may be about 0.6 m/s^2 or 2 ft/s^2, but the maximum acceleration will be considerably greater. An equivalent load of $2F_d$ should be taken as the minimum to allow for dynamic effects. The load for which the supports of a lift and similar structures are designed should be related to the total load on the ropes. If the latter is F_m and the ropes have an overall factor of safety of 10, the service load on the supports should be not less than $2.5F_m$ to ensure that a structure, if designed for a nominal overall factor of safety of 4, is as strong as the ropes.

The requirements of BS2655 (see *Table 12*) are that the supporting structure should be designed for twice the total load suspended from the beams when the lift is at rest. Reinforced concrete beams should be designed for this load with an overall factor of safety of 7, and the deflection under this load should not exceed 1/1500 of the span.

9.2.8 Industrial plant

Typical static weights of screening plant, conveyors and conveyor gantries are given in *Table 12* (in SI and imperial units). The supports for such machines and for all industrial machinery should be designed for the static weight plus an allowance for dynamic effects; i.e. vibration, impact etc.

9.2.9 Pit-head frames

A pit-head frame of the type that is common at coal mines and similar may be subjected to the following loads. (These notes do not apply to the direct vertical winding type of pit-head tower.)

Dead loads. The dead loads include the weights of (1) the frame and any stairs, housings, lifting beams etc. attached to it; (2) winding pulleys, pulley-bearings, pedestals etc.; (3) guide and rubbing ropes plus 50% for vibration.

Imposed loads. The imposed loads are the resultants of the tensions in the ropes passing over the pulleys and (unless described otherwise) are transmitted to the frame through the pulley bearings and may be due to the following conditions. (a) Retarding of descending cage when near the bottom of the shaft; this force is the sum of the net weight of the cage, load and rope, and should be doubled to allow for deceleration, shock and vibration. (b) Force due to overwinding the cage which is then dropped on to the overwind platform; this force acts only on the platform (and not at the pulley bearings) and is the sum of the net weights of the cage and attachments and the load in the cage, which sum should be doubled to allow for impact. (c) Force causing rope to break due to cage sticking in shaft or other causes; the force in the rope just before breaking is the tensile strength of the rope. (d) Tension in rope when winding up a loaded cage.

Combined loads. For a frame carrying one pulley, the conditions to be designed for are the total dead load combined with either imposed load (a), (b), (c) or (d). Generally condition (c) gives the most adverse effects, but it is permissible in this case to design using service stresses of say, double the ordinary permissible service stresses because of the short duration of the maximum force. The procedure would be to design the frame for service dead load plus half of force (c) and adopt the ordinary service stresses. If the frame carries two pulleys, the conditions to be investigated are: dead load plus (a) on one rope and (d) on the other (this is the ordinary working condition); dead load plus (a) on one rope and overwind (b) on the other; and dead load plus (a) on one rope and breaking force (c) on the other rope (this is generally the worst case: force (c) can be halved as explained for a single-pulley frame).

The weights of the ropes, cages etc. and the strength of the ropes would be obtained for any particular pit-head frame from the mining authorities, and they vary too greatly for typical values to be of any use.

9.2.10 Railway bridges

As stated in section 2.4.6, standard railway loading throughout Europe (including the UK) consists of two types, RU and RL. The former, which is illustrated in *Table 9*, covers all combinations of main-line locomotives and rolling stock. RL

Weights of vehicles

8

Railway rolling stock

Steam locomotives

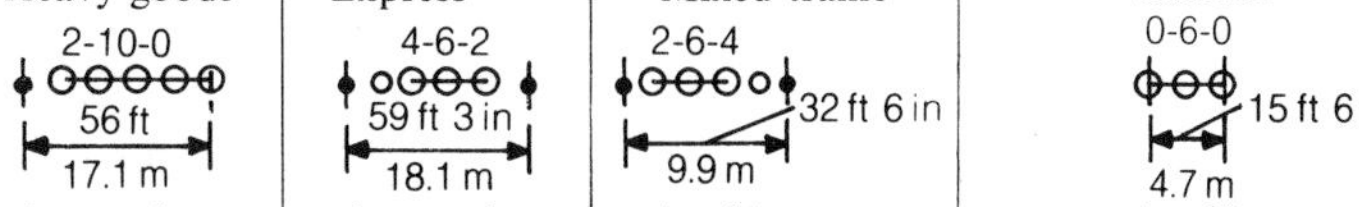

Type		Heavy goods 2-10-0, 56 ft, 17.1 m, plus tender	Express 4-6-2, 59 ft 3 in, 18.1 m, plus tender	Mixed traffic 2-6-4, 32 ft 6 in, 9.9 m (tank)	Shunter 0-6-0, 15 ft 6 in, 4.7 m (tank)
Total weight engine + tender	kN tons	1385 139	1564 157	867 87	558 56
Maximum axle load	kN tons	154 15.5	219 22	179 18	189 19

Diesel and diesel-electric locomotives

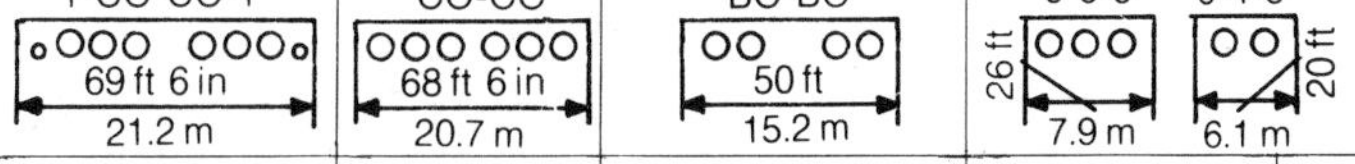

Type		Express 1-CO-CO-1, 69 ft 6 in, 21.2 m	Express CO-CO, 68 ft 6 in, 20.7 m	Mixed traffic BO-BO, 50 ft, 15.2 m	Shunters 0-6-0, 26 ft, 7.9 m	Shunters 0-4-0, 20 ft, 6.1 m
Total weight	kN	1320 to 1380	1000 to 1280	680 to 770	300 to 550 (500 standard)	220 to 360
	tons	132 to 138	100 to 128	68 to 77	30 to 55 (50 standard)	22 to 36
Maximum axle load	kN tons	≯200 ≯20	170 to 220 17 to 22	170 to 200 17 to 20	100 to 170 10 to 17	110 to 180 11 to 18

Open mineral wagons

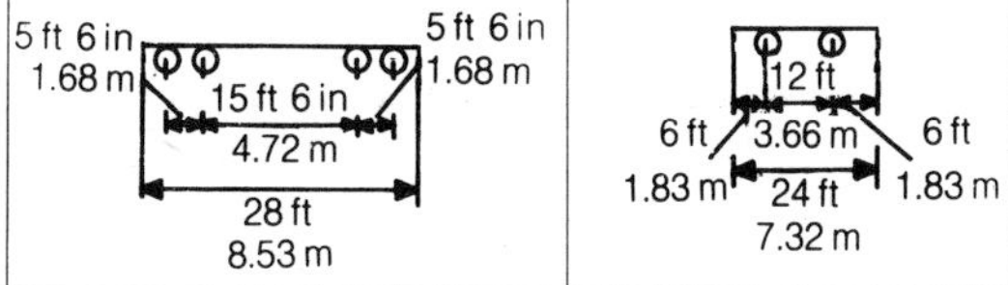

Type		560 kN 56 ton ore wagons: 5 ft 6 in 1.68 m, 15 ft 6 in 4.72 m, 28 ft 8.53 m	240 kN 24 ton wagons: 12 ft 3.66 m, 6 ft 1.83 m, 24 ft 7.32 m	Colliery tubs and mine cars ‡ 610 mm or 690 mm (2 ft or 2 ft 3 in) gauge. Minimum turning radius 3.66 m or 12 ft
Overall width		2.74 m 9 ft 11 in	2.44 m 8 ft	1.07 m 3 ft 6 in
Total weight	kN tons	850 85	350 35	7.5 to 15 0.75 to 1.5
Maximum axle load	kN tons	212 21.25	175 17.5	3.75 to 7.5 0.375 to 0.75

Data apply to standard gauge rolling stock on British Railways except ‡ (steam locomotives not now in general use)
Maximum axle load ≯200 kN or 20 tons on rails weighing 500 kg/m or 95–100 lb/yd, or ≯225 kN or 22.5 tons for multicylinder locomotives.

Road vehicles

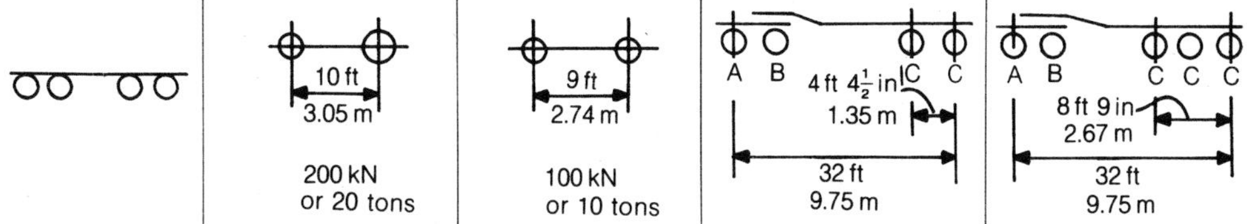

Type of vehicle		Street tram car (eight wheeled)	Road rollers: Steam, 10 ft 3.05 m, 200 kN or 20 tons	Road rollers: Diesel, 9 ft 2.74 m, 100 kN or 10 tons	Articulated tipping lorries: Tractor (A, B) Trailer (C, C), 4 ft 4½ in 1.35 m, 32 ft 9.75 m	Articulated tipping lorries: Tractor (A, B) Trailer (C, C, C), 8 ft 9 in 2.67 m, 32 ft 9.75 m
Axle loads		Driving / Pony	Roller / Driving wheels	Roller / Driving wheels	A / B / C	A / B / C
	kN	75 / 37	80 / 120	50 / 50	60 / 80 / 80	60 / 80 / 60
	tons	7.5 / 3.75	8 / 12	5 / 5	6 / 8 / 8	6 / 8 / 6
Total weight laden	kN tons	224 22.5	200 20	100 10	300 30	320 32
Overall width		—	2.74 m 9 ft	1.68 m 5 ft 6 in	2.44 m 8 ft	2.44 m 8 ft
Gauge		1.435 m 4 ft 8½ in	1.75 m 5 ft 9 in driving wheels	1.37 m 4 ft 6 in driving wheels	—	—

Department of Transport regulations — Maximum dimensions and axle loads

Width

Vehicle	m	ft	in
Locomotive	2.75	9	0¼
Heavy motor car and other vehicles	2.50	8	2½
Trailer	2.30*	7	6*

* Unless drawn by locomotive, heavy motor car or tractor: otherwise projection on either side of drawing vehicle not greater than 300 mm or 12 in

Length

Vehicle	m	ft	in
Rigid vehicle	11.0	36	1
Articulated*	13.0	42	7¾
Trailers*	7.0	22	11½
Vehicle and trailer*	18.0	59	0¾

* No specified limit if constructed and normally used to carry indivisible loads of exceptional length

Axle loads

Description	kN	tons
One-wheel axle	45(50)	4.5(5)
Single two-wheel axle	(90(100)	9(10)

Weights in brackets apply if wheels are fitted with twin tyres at not less than 300 mm or 12 in centres.

VALUES OF PARTIAL FACTOR OF SAFETY CORRESPONDING TO LOADING CONDITION 1

Type of loading			Limit-state considered*	
			Ultimate	Serviceability
Dead load	From structural elements	Steelwork	1.05 (1.10) [1.00]	1.00
		Concrete	1.15 (1.20) [1.00]	1.00
	From all materials other than structural elements		1.75 {1.20}	1.20 {1.00}
	Earth pressure	Due to retained material and/or surcharge	1.50	1.00
		Due to relieving effects	1.00	—
Imposed load	On highway bridges	Due to HA loading alone	1.50	1.20
		Due to HB loading with or without HA loading	1.30	1.10
	On footbridges and cycle track bridges		1.50	1.00
	On railway bridges		1.40	1.00

*Increased values indicated thus (1.10) apply when dead loads are not properly assessed.
Reduced values indicated thus [1.00] apply where these cause a more severe total effect.
Reduced values indicated thus {1.20} may be adopted only where approved by appropriate authority.

IMPOSED LOADS

			Loading	Notes
Highway bridges	HA	Basic	Uniform load as follows: Loaded length l (m): / Load (kN/m of lane): Up to 30 — 30 30 to 379 — $151\,(1/l)^{0.475}$ More than 379 — 9 *PLUS* a knife-edge load of 120 kN per lane	No dispersal of load beneath contact area may be considered Knife-edge load arranged to have most severe effect
		Alternative	Single 100 kN load having circular (340 mm dia.) or square (300 mm) contact area transmitting effective pressure of 1.1 kN/mm²	Loads may be dispersed as indicated on *Table 10*
	HB		Due to vehicle as follows: 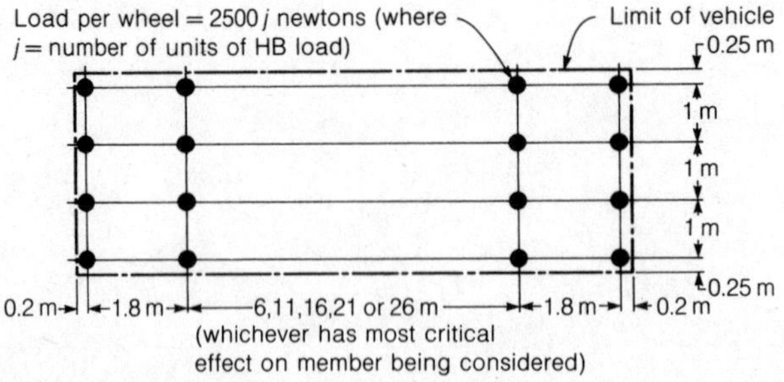 Load per wheel = 2500 j newtons (where j = number of units of HB load) Limit of vehicle 0.25 m, 1 m, 1 m, 1 m, 0.25 m 0.2 m, 1.8 m, 6, 11, 16, 21 or 26 m (whichever has most critical effect on member being considered), 1.8 m, 0.2 m	Loads may be dispersed as indicated on *Table 10* 1 unit represents 4 tonnes gross laden weight of vehicle
	HC		See section 2.4.6	
Footbridges and cycle track bridges			Loaded length l (m): / Load (kN/m²): Upto 30 — 5 Exceeding 30 — $25(1/l)^{0.475}$*	*But not less than 1.5 kN/m²
Railway bridges (RU loading)			Due to train of loads as follows: 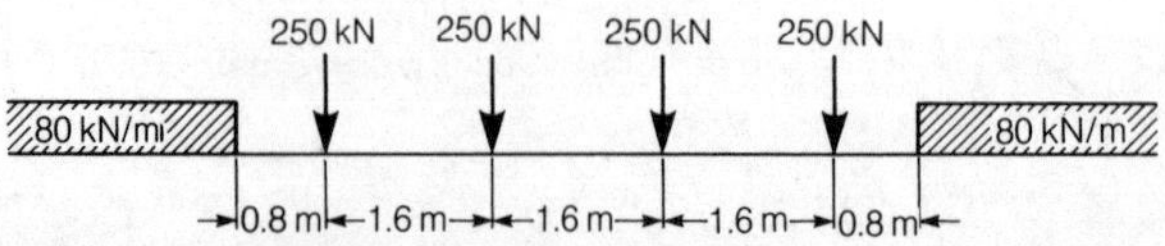 80 kN/m, 250 kN, 250 kN, 250 kN, 250 kN, 80 kN/m 0.8 m, 1.6 m, 1.6 m, 1.6 m, 0.8 m	

Note: for details of loads due to wind, braking, traction, lurching, nosing, centrifugal force etc. see BS5400

Loads on bridges: BS5400—2

FORMULAE FOR DISPERSAL OF LOAD

Material	Shape of loaded area	Formula
Concrete slab	Square	$f = \dfrac{2500j}{[\sqrt{(2500j/1.1)} + 2h']^2}$
	Circular	$f = \dfrac{10000j}{[\sqrt{(10000j/1.1\pi)} + 2h']^2\pi}$
Asphalt etc. surfacing	Square	$f = \dfrac{2500j}{[\sqrt{(2500j/1.1)} + h']^2}$
	Circular	$f = \dfrac{10000j}{[\sqrt{(10000j/1.1)} + h']^2\pi}$

Notation

f pressure in N/mm²

h' depth below surface at which load is applied in mm

j number of units of HB load (to consider alternative HA load, take $j = 4$)

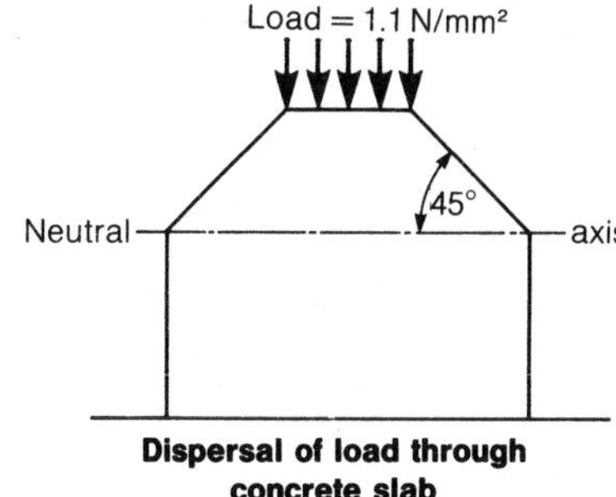

Dispersal of load through concrete slab

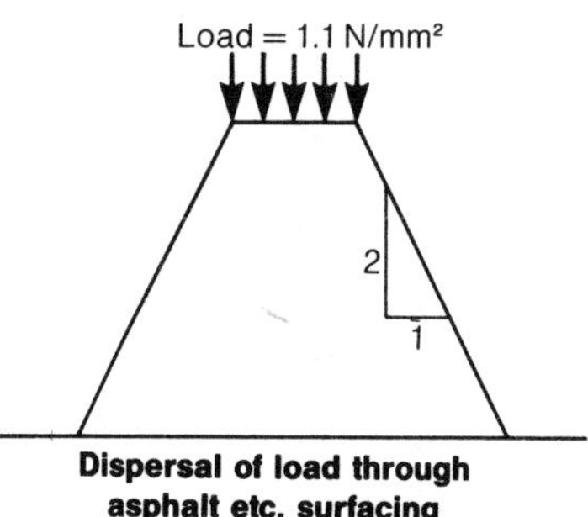

Dispersal of load through asphalt etc. surfacing

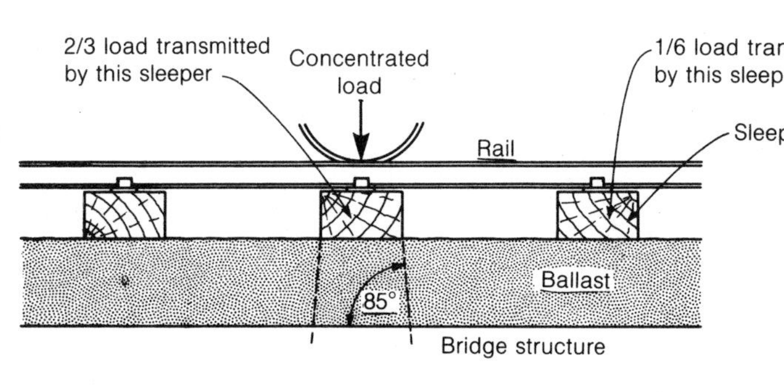

Dispersal of concentrated load beneath sleepers

DETERMINATION OF LANE ARRANGEMENT

Total carriageway width	Lane arrangement
Up to 4.6 m	Divide each carriageway by 3 m. Loading on any fractional lane is proportional to that on a complete lane.
Exceeding 4.6 m	Divide each carriageway into least possible integral number of lanes of equal width by dividing by 3.8 m and rounding up to next whole number.

SURCHARGE ON RETAINING STRUCTURE

HA load	10 kN/m²
HB load	$(j-5)/2$ kN/m² where j = number of units of HB load
RU load	50 kN/m² on areas occupied by tracks

DISPOSITION OF LOADS IN BANDS

	Loading arrangement			
	1	2	3	4
	HA only	HB with or without HA		
First lane	HA	HB	HB {HA / HA}	HB {HA / HA/3}
Second lane	HA	HA		
Third lane (if any)	HA/3	HA/3	HA/3	HA
Any other lanes	HA/3	HA/3	HA/3	HA/3

Notes:

1. Actual lanes designated first, second etc. should be chosen so as to induce most severe conditions (but if HB load straddles two lanes, these must adjoin).
2. Where HB loading occurs, no HA load need be considered in that lane within a distance of 2.5 m from the limits of the HB vehicle.
3. HB {HA / HA} indicates HB load straddling adjoining lanes with remainder of both lanes loaded with full HA loading.
   HB {HA / HA/3} indicates HB load straddling both lanes with remainder of one lane loaded with full HA load and other with HA/3 load.

loading is less severe and is only applicable for rapid-transit passenger systems where main-line equipment cannot operate: brief details of this loading are given in section 2.4.6.

In addition to the primary loads considered above, secondary live loading due to dynamic effects (such as impact and oscillation), nosing, lurching, centrifugal force, acceleration and braking must be taken into account. For details reference should be made to clause 8 of BS5400: Part 2.

9.2.11 Aircraft runways

The design of a pavement for an aircraft runway or apron depends on the amount, frequency and distribution of loading from the aircraft, the flexural strength of the slab, the support provided by the subgrade and the particular type of facility (e.g. runway, apron etc.) being designed. In current design practice, the loading data produced by the aircraft manufacturers are used to prepare design charts giving the resulting flexural stresses in slabs of various thicknesses by means of computer programs or influence charts: for further details see ref. 132.

Designers of such pavements must anticipate future as well as present loading requirements.

Experience obtained from designing runways for heavy US military aircraft which are supported on isolated groups of up to four wheels (the gross tyre weight of a B52 bomber exceeds 22 680 kg) has confirmed the validity of current design methods. However, it seems possible that future heavier aircraft may utilize undercarriage arrangements in which larger numbers of wheels act together, with additional increases in the tyre contact area. The deflection of, and support provided beneath, slabs carrying such large loaded areas then become increasingly important and may require greater consideration in future.

For information, some details regarding the Boeing 747, the largest commercial aircraft currently operating, are as follows: overall width 59.64 m; length 70.51 m; height 19.33 m; gross weight at take-off 371 945 kg; capacity up to 550 passengers; undercarriage consists of sixteen wheels arranged as four 4-wheel bogies; maximum weight per tyre 20 640 kg.

9.2.12 Dispersion of wheel loads

Rules for the dispersion of road and rail wheel loads on concrete slabs are shown on *Tables 10* and *11*. Note that the requirements of BS5400 (*Table 10*) differ from those that have been generally adopted in the past (*Table 11*).

9.2.13 Effects of wind

The data in *Tables 13* to *15* are based on BS3: Chapter V: Part 2: 1972, and a description of the use of these tables is given in section 2.7.

Imposed loads from vehicles

Road bridges. Standard loading per BS153: Part3A (metric and imperial versions)

Loaded length (m)	Equivalent HA uniform loading (kN/m²)	HA uniform loading for reinforced concrete slabs on steel beams: Longitudinal (kN/m²)	Transverse (kN/m²)	Loaded length (ft)	Equivalent HA uniform loading (lb/ft²)	HA uniform loading for reinforced concrete slabs on steel beams: Longitudinal (lb/ft²)	Transverse (lb/ft²)
1.0	106.2	106.2	94.0	3	2420	2420	2270
1.5	59.8	59.8	37.8	4	1700	1700	1180
2.0	42.2	35.7	24.2	5	1225	1225	770
2.5	33.9	24.0	18.4	6	966	885	580
3.0	28.2	19.5	15.0	7	828	655	460
3.5	24.1	16.4	12.9	8	725	520	390
4.0	21.6	14.0	11.4	9	644	452	340
4.5	19.0	12.1	10.6	10	580	400	310
5.0	16.4	11.3	10.5	12	487	325	260
5.5	13.7	10.7	10.5	14	421	270	230
6.0	11.0	10.5	10.5	16	355	240	220
6.5 to 23	10.5	10.5	10.5	18	288	225	220
25	10.3	10.3	10.3	20 to 75	220	220	220
30	9.6	9.6	9.6	80	216	216	216
50	7.6	7.6	7.6	100	200	200	200
100	5.3	5.3	5.3	200	142	142	142

Wheel loads

Twin wheels

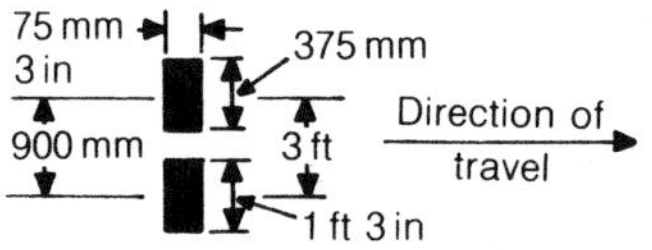

Load on each contact area = 112.5 kN or 11.25 tons

HB abnormal loading

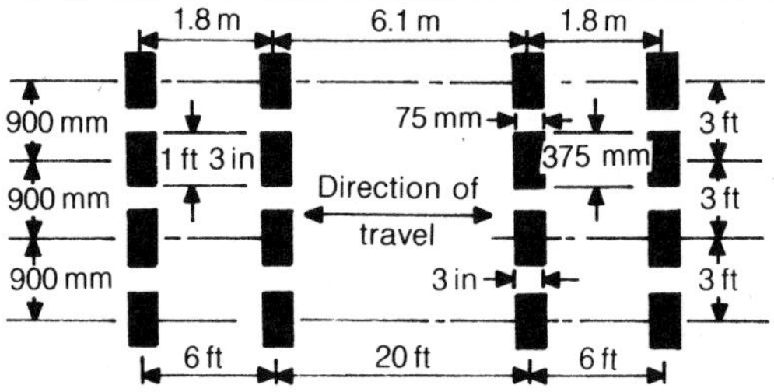

Load on each contact area = 112.5 kN or 11.25 tons

Dispersion at 45° is allowed from each contact area. Specified loads include an allowance for impact. With HB and twin-wheel loading, stresses permissible may be increased by 25%.

	Imposed loads per BS6399: Part 1 Concentrated load usually assumed to act on 300 mm or 12 in square	Uniformly distributed kN/m²	Uniformly distributed lb/ft²	Concentrated kN	Concentrated lb
Footbridges					
Footbridges between buildings	Loading from crowds only	4.0	83.5	4.5	1012
	Loading exceeding crowds (e.g. trolleys etc.)	5.0	104.5	4.5	1012
	Grandstands	5.0	104.5	4.5	1012
Garages					
Floors, ramps, driveways etc.	Parking only: vehicles ≯ 25 kN or 2.5 tons	2.5	52.2	9.0	2023
	Parking of vehicles > 25 kN or 2.5 tons Repair workshops	5.0	104.5	9.0	2023
Footpaths					
At ground floors of buildings	Pedestrian traffic only	4.0	83.5	4.5	1012
	No obstruction to vehicular traffic	5.0	104.5	9.0	2023
Road bridges DTp	Where vehicles can mount footpath	Concentrated load of 40 kN or 4 tons (including impact) in any position			

Dispersion of wheel loads

Wheels on concrete slab

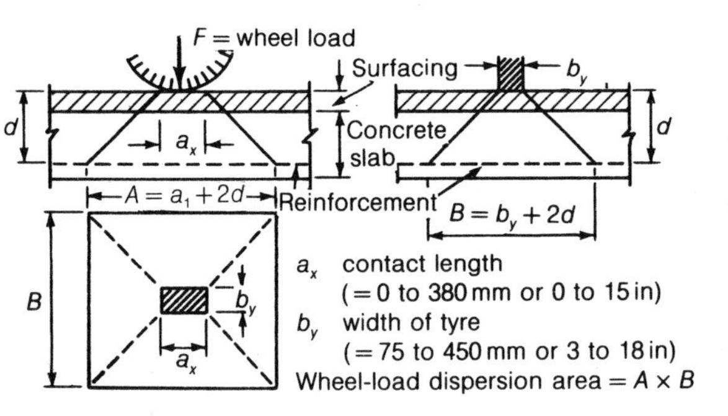

a_x contact length (= 0 to 380 mm or 0 to 15 in)
b_y width of tyre (= 75 to 450 mm or 3 to 18 in)
Wheel-load dispersion area = $A \times B$

Wheels on ballasted rail tracks on concrete slab

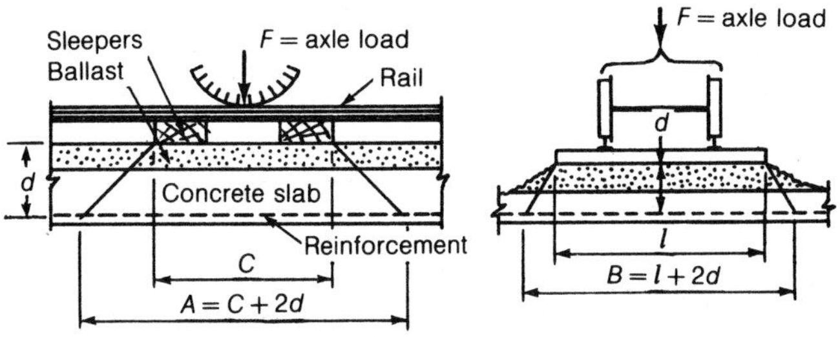

C overall width (two sleepers)
l length of sleeper
Axle-load dispersion area = $A \times B$

Imposed loads: miscellaneous data

			1	2	3	4	5 to 10	More than 10
Reduction of uniformly distributed imposed loads specified on *Tables 6* and *7* (per BS6399:Part 1)	Columns Piers Walls Foundations	Number of floors (including roof) supported by member	1	2	3	4	5 to 10	More than 10
		Reduction of load on all floors	0	10%	20%	30%	40%	50% max.
	Beams	Single span supporting not less than 40 m^2 or 430 ft^2 at same general level	Reduce load by 5% for each 40 m^2 or 430 ft^2 supported. Maximum reduction = 25%					
		This reduction or reduction for columns etc. can be made, whichever gives the greatest reduction						
	Applicability	Reductions apply to all buildings except warehouses and other stores, garages and office areas used for storage or filing Applicable also to factories, workshops etc. Design for imposed load not less than 5 kN/m^2 or 104 lb/ft^2 provided the reduced load is not less than 5 kN/m^2 or 104 lb/ft^2 No reduction is to be made for machinery or other particular loads						

MISCELLANEOUS IMPOSED LOADS

Overhead travelling cranes

Lifting capacity		Minimum wheelbase or ≯ $l/5$		Maximum static load on pair of wheels kN: Span l of crane (m)				Maximum static load on pair of wheels tons: Span l of crane (ft)				Height H		End clearance E		Notes
kN	tons	m	ft in	9	12	15	18	30	40	50	60	m	ft in	mm	in	
20	2	1.8	6 0	55	60	70	—	5.5	6	7	—	1.7	5 6	200	8	Tabulated data are typical and may vary due to make and use of crane
50	5	2.5	8 6	—	115	130	140	—	11.5	13	14	1.8	6 0	230	9	
100	10	3.0	10 0	—	180	200	215	—	18	20	21.5	2.0	6 9	240	9.5	
200	20	3.2	10 6	—	310	330	355	—	31	33	35.5	2.3	7 6	280	11	
300	30	3.6	12 0	—	460	480	510	—	46	48	51	2.6	8 6	300	12	
500	50	4.0	13 0	—	700	720	810	—	70	72	81	3.1	10 3	360	14	

			Operation: Electric	Operation: Hand
Allowances for dynamic effects on crane beams and supports BS6399: Part 1	Increased vertical load to be considered to act at same time as either transverse or longitudinal horizontal force		Electric	Hand
	Vertical load	Increase static wheel load by	25%	10%
	Forces acting horizontally at rail level	Transverse to rail: proportion of weights of crab plus load	10%	5%
		Longitudinally (along rail): proportion of max. static wheel loads	5%	5%

Lifts

Beams and supports BS 2655	Design load: weight of all machinery on beams plus twice max. suspended loads Factor of safety of beams (based on strength of materials) = 7 Deflection of beams ≯ $\frac{\text{span}}{1500}$

Industrial plant

Type of plant	Use/construction	kN/m	lb/ft
Belt conveyors	For cement, grain, coal, crushed stone etc.	2.5 to 4.1	168 to 280
Conveyor gantries	Steel framing, corrugated sheeting, wooden floor	8.2 to 9.8	560 to 672
		kN/m^2	lb/ft^2
Screening plant	Shaker type for coal (including steel supports)	8.0	168

Wind velocities and pressures

13

Characteristic wind pressure

W_k $0.613 V_s^2$ N/m^2
where:

V_s design wind speed in m/s $= V S_1 S_2 S_3$

V basic wind speed in m/s (read from adjoining map)

S_1 multiplying factor relating to topology

S_2 multiplying factor relating to height above ground and wind braking

S_3 multiplying factor related to life of structure

Relation between design wind speed V_s and characteristic wind pressure w_k

V_s (m/s)	w_k (N/m^2)
10	61
12	88
14	120
16	157
18	199
20	245
22	297
24	353
26	414
28	481
30	552
32	628
34	709
36	794
38	885
40	981
42	1080
44	1190
46	1300
48	1410
50	1530
52	1660
54	1790
56	1920
58	2060
60	2210
62	2360
64	2510
66	2670
68	2830
70	3000

Values of factor S_1

S_1 may generally always be taken as unity except in the following cases:
On sites adversely affected by very exposed hill slopes and crests where wind acceleration is known to occur: $S_1 = 1.1$
On sites in enclosed steep-sided valleys completely sheltered from winds: $S_1 = 0.9$

Values of factor S_3

S_3 is a probability factor relating the likelihood of the design wind speed being exceeded to the probable life of the structure. A value of unity is recommended for general use and corresponds to an excessive speed occurring once in fifty years.

Values of factors S_2

Structure		Topo-graphical factor	Height of structure h (m)														
			5	10	15	20	30	40	50	60	80	100	120	140	160	180	200
Cladding etc.		1	0.88	1.00	1.03	1.06	1.09	1.12	1.14	1.15	1.18	1.20	1.22	1.24	1.25	1.26	1.27
		2	0.79	0.93	1.00	1.03	1.07	1.10	1.12	1.14	1.17	1.19	1.21	1.22	1.24	1.25	1.26
		3	0.70	0.78	0.88	0.95	1.01	1.05	1.08	1.10	1.13	1.16	1.18	1.20	1.21	1.23	1.24
		4	0.60	0.67	0.74	0.79	0.90	0.97	1.02	1.05	1.10	1.13	1.15	1.17	1.19	1.20	1.22
Maximum vertical or maximum horizontal dimension	≯ 50 m	1	0.83	0.95	0.99	1.01	1.05	1.08	1.10	1.12	1.15	1.17	1.19	1.20	1.22	1.23	1.24
		2	0.74	0.88	0.95	0.98	1.03	1.06	1.08	1.10	1.13	1.16	1.18	1.19	1.21	1.22	1.24
		3	0.65	0.74	0.83	0.90	0.97	1.01	1.04	1.06	1.10	1.12	1.15	1.17	1.18	1.20	1.21
		4	0.55	0.62	0.69	0.75	0.85	0.93	0.98	1.02	1.07	1.10	1.13	1.15	1.17	1.19	1.21
	> 50 m	1	0.78	0.90	0.94	0.96	1.00	1.03	1.06	1.08	1.11	1.13	1.15	1.17	1.19	1.20	1.21
		2	0.70	0.83	0.91	0.94	0.98	1.01	1.04	1.06	1.09	1.12	1.14	1.16	1.18	1.19	1.21
		3	0.60	0.69	0.78	0.85	0.92	0.96	1.00	1.02	1.06	1.09	1.11	1.13	1.15	1.17	1.18
		4	0.50	0.58	0.64	0.70	0.79	0.89	0.94	0.98	1.03	1.07	1.10	1.12	1.14	1.16	1.18

Notes

h is height (in metres) above general level of terrain to top of structure or part of structure. Increase to be made for structures on edge of cliff or steep hill.

Topographical factors

1. open country with no obstructions
2. open country with scattered wind-breaks
3. country with many wind-breaks; small towns; suburbs of large cities
4. city centres and other environments with large and frequent obstructions.

Wind pressures on structures—1

EXTERNAL PRESSURE COEFFICIENT C_{pe} FOR ROOFS OF CLAD BUILDINGS

Pitched roofs

h Height to eaves or parapet

b Lesser horizontal dimension of building

$a = h$ or $0.15b$, whichever is the lesser

Where no local coefficients are given, overall coefficients apply

Overall coefficients

Building height ratio	$h \not> b/2$				$b/2 < h \not> 3b/2$				$3b/2 < h \not> 6b$			
	Wind at right angles to building		Wind parallel to building		Wind at right angles to building		Wind parallel to building		Wind at right angles to building		Wind parallel to building	
Slope of roof (deg.)	Windward slope	Leeward slope	Windward half	Leeward half	Windward slope	Leeward slope	Windward half	Leeward half	Windward slope	Leeward slope	Windward half	Leeward half
0	−0.8	−0.4	−0.8	−0.4	−0.8	−0.6	−1.0	−0.6	−0.7	−0.6	−0.9	−0.7
5	−0.9	−0.4	−0.8	−0.4	−0.9	−0.6	−0.9	−0.6	−0.7	−0.6	−0.8	−0.8
10	−1.2	−0.4	−0.8	−0.6	−1.1	−0.6	−0.8	−0.6	−0.7	−0.6	−0.8	−0.8
20	−0.4	−0.4	−0.7	−0.6	−0.7	−0.5	−0.8	−0.6	−0.8	−0.6	−0.8	−0.8
30	0	−0.4	−0.7	−0.6	−0.2	−0.5	−0.8	−0.8	−1.0	−0.5	−0.8	−0.7
40	—	—	—	—	—	—	—	—	−0.2	−0.5	−0.8	−0.7
45	+0.3	−0.5	−0.7	−0.6	+0.2	−0.5	−0.8	−0.8	—	—	—	—
50	—	—	—	—	—	—	—	—	+0.2	−0.5	−0.8	−0.7
60	+0.7	−0.6	−0.7	−0.6	+0.6	−0.5	−0.8	−0.8	+0.5	−0.5	−0.8	−0.7

Local coefficients

Slope of roof (deg.)	Area				Area				Area			
	A	B	C	D	A	B	C	D	A	B	C	D
0	−2.0	−2.0	−2.0	—	−2.0	−2.0	−2.0	—	−2.0	−2.0	−2.0	—
5	−1.4	−1.2	−1.2	−1.0	−2.0	−2.0	−1.5	−1.0	−2.0	−2.0	−1.5	−1.0
10	−1.4	−1.4	—	−1.2	−2.0	−2.0	−1.5	−1.2	−2.0	−2.0	−1.5	−1.2
20	−1.0	—	—	−1.2	−1.5	−1.5	−1.5	−1.0	−1.5	−1.5	−1.5	−1.2
30	−0.8	—	—	−1.1	−1.0	—	—	−1.0	−1.5	—	—	—
40	—	—	—	—	—	—	—	—	−1.0	—	—	—
45	—	—	—	−1.1	—	—	—	—	—	—	—	—
50	—	—	—	—	—	—	—	—	—	—	—	—
60	—	—	—	−1.1	—	—	—	—	—	—	—	—

Monopitch roofs

h height to lower eaves

b lesser horizontal dimension of building

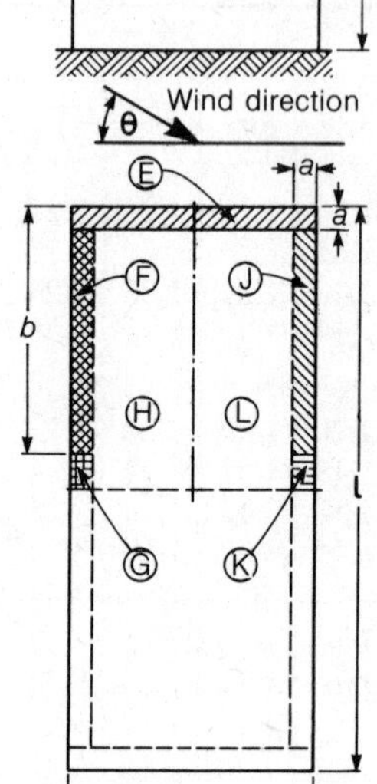

$a = h$ or $0.15b$, whichever is the lesser

Overall coefficients

Slope of roof (deg.)	Area H (values of θ in degrees)					Area L (values of θ in degrees)				
	0	45	90*	135	180	0	45	90*	135	180
5	−1.0	−1.0	−1.0(−0.5)	−0.9	−0.5	−0.5	−0.9	−1.0(−0.5)	−1.0	−1.0
10	−1.0	−1.0	−1.0(−0.5)	−0.8	−0.4	−0.5	−0.8	−1.0(−0.5)	−1.0	−1.0
15	−0.9	−1.0	−1.0(−0.5)	−0.6	−0.3	−0.5	−0.7	−1.0(−0.5)	−1.0	−1.0
20	−0.8	−1.0	−0.9(−0.5)	−0.5	−0.2	−0.5	−0.6	−0.9(−0.5)	−1.0	−1.0
25	−0.7	−1.0	−0.8(−0.5)	−0.3	−0.1	−0.5	−0.6	−0.8(−0.5)	−0.9	−0.9
30	−0.5	−1.0	−0.8(−0.5)	−0.1	0	−0.5	−0.6	−0.8(−0.5)	−0.6	−0.6

Local coefficients

Slope of roof (deg.)	Area				
	E	F	G	J	K
5	−2.0	−2.0	−1.5	−2.0	−1.5
10	−2.0	−2.0	−1.5	−2.0	−1.5
15	−2.0	−1.8	−0.9	−1.8	−1.4
20	−2.0	−1.8	−0.8	−1.8	−1.4
25	−2.0	−1.8	−0.7	−0.9	−0.9
30	−2.0	−1.8	−0.5	−0.5	−0.5

*First value applies to length of $b/2$ from windward end of roof: second value (in brackets) applies to remainder.

Outline of basic procedure for determining wind force

1. Calculate characteristic wind pressure w_k as indicated on *Table 13*.
2. Determine appropriate external and internal pressure coefficients from *Table 14* or *Table 15* (top and centre).
3. Total wind force F on area A of structure as a whole $= w_k A(C_{pe1} - C_{pe2})$, where C_{pe1} and C_{pe2} are external pressure coefficients on windward and leeward faces respectively.

   Total wind force F on area A of particular face of structure $= w_k A C_{pe}$.

   Total wind force F on cladding element $= w_k A\ (C_{pe} - C_{pi})$, where C_{pe} and C_{pi} are external and internal pressure coefficients respectively.

To obtain total force on entire structure, divide structure into parts, determine force on each part by steps 1–3 and then sum results vectorially. Consider appropriate value of h for each individual part (but for approximate analysis, use of single value of w_k corresponding to height to top of building errs on side of safety).

Alternatively, first calculate characteristic wind pressure. Next, obtain value of force coefficient C_f from *Table 15* (bottom). Then total wind force on area $A = w_k A C_f$. For greater accuracy, subdivide structure and sum individual results vectorially as before.

These procedures are described in more detail in section 2.7.2.

Wind pressures on structures—2

VALUES OF EXTERNAL PRESSURE COEFFICIENT C_{pe} ON RECTANGULAR STRUCTURE WITH FLAT ROOF

	$h \leqslant b/2$	$b/2 < h \leqslant 3b/2$	$3b/2 < h \leqslant 6b$
$b < l \leqslant 3b/2$	↓ wind +0.70 −0.50 −0.50 −0.20	↓ wind +0.70 −0.60 −0.60 −0.25	↓ wind +0.80 −0.80 −0.80 −0.25
$3b/2 < l \leqslant 4b$	↓ wind +0.70 −0.60 −0.60 −0.25	↓ wind +0.70 −0.70 −0.70 −0.30	↓ wind +0.70 −0.70 −0.70 −0.40
$b < l \leqslant 3b/2$	wind → −0.50 +0.70 −0.20 −0.50	wind → −0.60 +0.70 −0.25 −0.60	wind → −0.80 +0.80 −0.25 −0.80
$3b/2 < l \leqslant 4b$	wind → −0.50 +0.70 −0.10 −0.50	wind → −0.50 +0.70 −0.10 −0.50	wind → −0.50 −0.80 −0.10 −0.50
Cladding: $b < l \leqslant 3b/2$	−0.8	−1.1	−1.2
Cladding: $3b/2 < l \leqslant 4b$	−1.0	−1.1	−1.2

h height of structure
l greater length in plan
b lesser length in plan

TYPICAL VALUES OF INTERNAL PRESSURE COEFFICIENTS C_{pi} ON CLADDING

	All four faces impermeable	Two opposite faces permeable Two opposite faces impermeable
Wind on impermeable face	−0.3	−0.3
Wind on permeable face	—	+0:2

VALUES OF TOTAL FORCE COEFFICIENT C_f FOR SECTIONS OF VARIOUS SHAPES

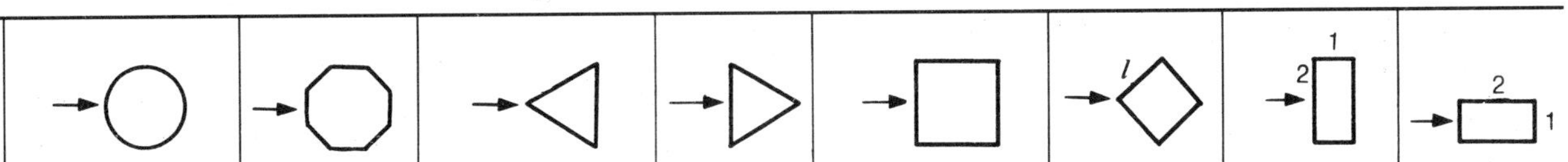

Shape		$V_s b \nless 6$ smooth surface	$V_s b < 6$ all and $V_s b \nless 6$ rough surface		$b = 48r$	$b = 12r$	Between $b = 48r$ and $b = 12r$	$b = 6r$ $V_s b \nless 10$	$b = 6r$ $V_s b < 10$	$l = 48r$ and $l = 12r$	$b = 12r$	$b = 6r$
h/b ratio	$\ngtr 1$	0.5	0.7	1.0	0.7	0.8	1.2	0.5	0.8	0.9	0.9	0.5
	$\ngtr 2$	0.5	0.7	1.1	0.8	0.8	1.2	0.5	0.8	0.9	1.0	0.5
	5	0.5	0.8	1.2	0.9	1.0	1.4	0.5	0.9	1.1	1.1	0.5
	10	0.5	0.9	1.2	1.0	1.1	1.6	0.6	1.0	1.2	1.2	0.6
	20	0.6	1.0	1.3	1.1	1.2	1.7	0.6	1.0	1.3	1.5	0.6
	∞	0.6	1.2	1.4	1.3	1.4	2.1	0.6	1.3	1.6	1.9	0.7

b, h, l breadth, height and length of side of section considered
r radius of corners of section

w_k characteristic wind pressure
V_s characteristic wind speed

Chapter 10

Pressures due to retained materials

In this chapter, unless otherwise stated, the unit weights given are characteristic values and the pressures etc. resulting from the formulae are in terms of service loads. Thus if limit-state methods are to be used to design the resulting structural sections, these characteristic loads must be multiplied by the appropriate partial safety factor for loads for the particular limit-state being considered.

10.1 GRANULAR MATERIALS

Tables 16–19 are discussed in section 2.8.1.

10.1.1 Effect of ground-water

If ground-water occurs at a depth h_w below the top of the wall, the intensity of horizontal pressure is $k_2\ Dh$ when h does not exceed h_w. When h is greater than h_w the pressure is given by

$$q = k_2 D h_w = (k_2 D_2 + D_w)(h - h_w)$$

where D_2 is the buoyant unit weight of the soil (about 60% of the drained unit weight D) and D_w is the unit weight of water (9.81 kN/m^3 or 62.4 lb/ft^3).

For a dry granular material with level fill, the passive resistance is

$$q_p = \left(\frac{1 + \sin\theta}{1 - \sin\theta}\right) Dh = \frac{Dh}{k_2}$$

as given in *Table 16*; values of k_2 are given in *Table 18*. This expression also applies to drained soil above ground-water level. For saturated soil below this level the passive resistance is given by

$$q_p = \frac{Dh_w}{k_2} + \left(\frac{D_2}{k_2} + D_w\right)(h - h_w)$$

The symbols have the same significance as in *Tables 17* and *18*; h_w is the depth to ground-water.

10.1.2 Active pressure normal to inclined surfaces

The intensity of pressure normal to the slope of an inclined surface, such as a hopper bottom loaded with coal, grain, sand, stone or other granular material, at a depth h below the level surface of the filling is

$$Dh(k_2 \sin^2\theta_1 + \cos^2\theta_1)$$

where θ_1 is the angle between the horizontal and the sloping surface. Values of k_2 and of $k_4 = k_2 \sin^2\theta_1 + \cos^2\theta_1$ for various angles θ from 30° to 45° are given in *Table 18*.

10.1.3 Surcharge on granular material

Non-level filling. As is seen from the factors in *Table 18*, the slope of the surface of the filling behind the wall has a marked effect on the theoretical pressures. For practical purposes any alteration of the shape of the surface beyond the point B in the diagrams in *Table 20*, or any additional loading beyond this point, has little or no effect upon the pressure on the wall. The general formulae in *Table 16* allow for any slope between the limits OB and OB_1 in diagram (d) on *Table 20*.

When the surface of the filling is not a uniform slope, special consideration is required. In the common cases depicted in *Table 20* the magnitude of the active horizontal pressure on the wall is between that when the surface is level and that when the surface slopes upwards at the maximum angle. On the diagrams empirical expressions for the increase of pressure due to these intermediate conditions are given. The total pressure on the wall is increased above that for a level surface by an amount proportional to the mean increase in the head of the material. These surcharges give no pressure at the top of the wall, and the centre of total pressure is assumed to act at one-third of the way up the wall.

Load imposing on filling. When the filling behind a wall is level but liable to self-retaining loads, such as stacked materials, traffic or buildings, the total imposed load should be converted into an equivalent head of the same material as that retained by the wall, and the pressure intensity on the back of the wall increased uniformly throughout the depth of the wall. In this case there is a positive intensity of pressure at the top of the wall; these conditions are illustrated in *Table 20*.

Slope beyond natural angle of repose. A type of surcharge not dealt with in the foregoing is shown in diagram (f)

Horizontal pressures due to retained materials

16

Dry granular materials

Active pressures

Intensity of pressure normal to back of wall at depth h: $q = kDh\sin^2\beta$

Total pressure normal to back of wall of height h_1: $F = \frac{1}{2}kDh_1^2\sin\beta$
Values of k for various conditions are given below.

Total pressure on back of wall: $F_1 = F\sec\mu$

Angle between line of action of F_1 and back of wall $= (90-\mu)^\circ$

Force parallel to back of wall: $F_\mu = F\tan\mu = F_1\sin\mu$

When friction on back of wall is neglected ($\mu = 0$): $F_1 = F$; $F_\mu = 0$;
F_1 acts at right angles to back of wall

Notation

- D weight of retained material
- ϕ angle of slope of bank of retained material (in degrees)
- θ angle of internal friction of material retained (in degrees)
- μ angle of friction between material and concrete wall (in degrees)

Friction on back of wall	Slope of bank of retained material	Inclined outwards	Inclined inwards	Vertical
		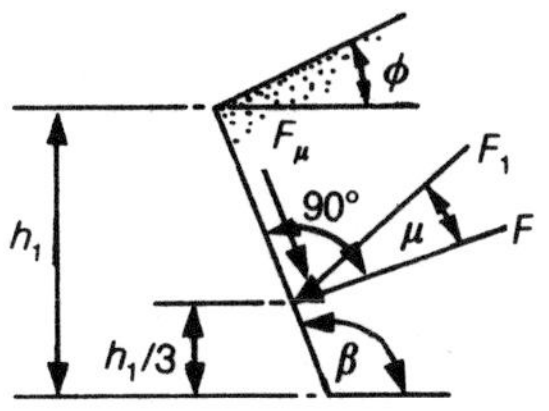	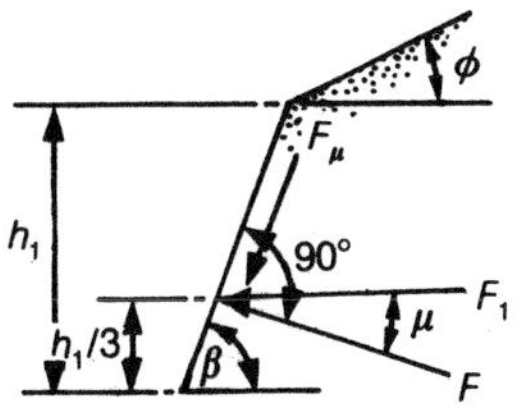	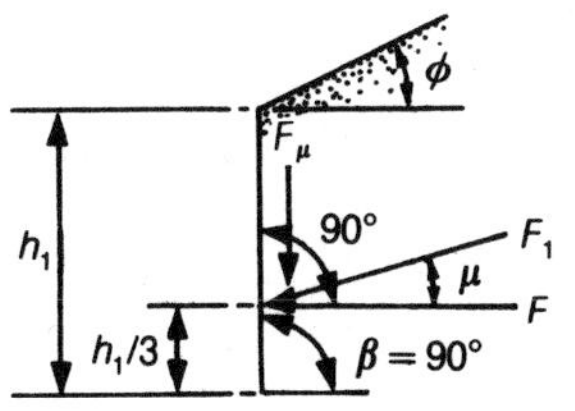
$\mu = 0$	Any slope ϕ	$k = \left[\dfrac{\sin(\beta-\theta)}{(\alpha+1)\sin\beta}\right]^2 \dfrac{1}{\sin^2\beta}$	$\alpha = \sqrt{\left[\dfrac{\sin\theta\sin(\theta-\phi)}{\sin\beta\sin(\beta-\phi)}\right]}$	$k = \left(\dfrac{\cos\theta}{\alpha+1}\right)^2$ $\alpha = \sqrt{[\sin^2\theta - \frac{1}{2}\tan\phi\sin 2\theta]}$
$\mu = 0$	$\phi = \theta$ (max.)	$k_1 = \left[\dfrac{\sin(\beta-\theta)}{\sin\beta}\right]^2 \dfrac{1}{\sin^2\beta}$		$k_1 = \cos^2\theta$
$\mu = 0$	$\phi = 0$ (level)	$k_2 = \left[\dfrac{\sin(\beta-\theta)}{\sin\theta+\sin\beta}\right]^2 \dfrac{1}{\sin^2\beta}$		$\boldsymbol{k_2 = \dfrac{1-\sin\theta}{1+\sin\theta}}$
$\mu = 0$	$\phi = -\theta$ (min.)	$k_3 = \left[\dfrac{\sin(\beta-\theta)}{(\alpha+1)\sin\beta}\right]^2 \dfrac{1}{\sin^2\beta}$	$\alpha = \sqrt{\left[\dfrac{2\sin^2\theta\cos\theta}{\sin\beta\sin(\beta+\theta)}\right]}$	$k_3 = \left[\dfrac{\cos\theta}{1+\sqrt{(2)}\sin\theta}\right]^2$
μ taken into account	Any slope ϕ	$k = \left[\dfrac{\sin(\beta-\theta)}{(\alpha+1)\sin\beta}\right]^2 \dfrac{\cos\mu}{\sin(\mu+\beta)\sin\beta}$ $\alpha = \sqrt{\left[\dfrac{\sin(\theta+\mu)\sin(\theta-\phi)}{\sin(\mu+\beta)\sin(\beta-\phi)}\right]}$		$k = \left(\dfrac{\cos\theta}{\alpha+1}\right)^2$ $\alpha = \sqrt{\left[\dfrac{\sin(\theta+\mu)\sin(\theta-\phi)}{\cos\mu\cos\phi}\right]}$
μ taken into account	$\phi = \theta$ (max.)	$k_1 = k$	$\alpha = 0$	$k_1 = \cos^2\theta$
μ taken into account	$\phi = 0$ (level)	$k_2 = k$	$\alpha = \sqrt{\left[\dfrac{\sin(\theta+\mu)\sin\theta)}{\sin(\mu+\beta)\sin\beta}\right]}$	$k_2 = k$ $\alpha = \sqrt{[\sin\theta(\sin\theta+\cos\theta\tan\mu)]}$
μ taken into account	$\phi = -\theta$ (min.)	$k_3 = k$	$\alpha = \sqrt{\left[\dfrac{\sin(\theta+\mu)\sin 2\theta}{\sin(\mu+\beta)\sin(\beta+\theta)}\right]}$	$k_3 = k$ $\alpha = \sqrt{[2\sin\theta(\sin\theta+\cos\theta\tan\mu]}$

Passive resistance

Intensity of horizontal passive resistance against vertical wall at depth $h(\phi = 0)$: $q_p = \dfrac{Dh}{k_2} = \left(\dfrac{1+\sin\theta}{1-\sin\theta}\right)Dh$

Cohesive soils

Active pressures

Intensity of horizontal pressure at depth h on vertical wall ($\phi = 0$):

$$q_2 = \left(\frac{1-\sin\theta}{1+\sin\theta}\right)Dh - 2C\sqrt{\left(\frac{1-\sin\theta}{1+\sin\theta}\right)} = k_2Dh - 2C\sqrt{k_2}$$

C is a cohesion factor, equal to the shearing strength of unloaded soil

Passive resistance

Intensity of horizontal passive resistance against vertical wall at depth $h(\phi = 0)$ retaining ordinary saturated clay:

$$q_p = \frac{Dh}{k_2} + \frac{2C}{k_2}$$

Other notation as for granular materials

Units

The foregoing formulae are applicable to any consistent set of units.

17 Pressures due to materials

Properties of granular materials

Retained cohesionless soils etc.	Angle of internal friction θ	Weight kN/m³ In bulk D	Weight kN/m³ Moist (drained) D_3	Weight lb/ft³ In bulk D	Weight lb/ft³ Moist (drained) D_3
Gravel: common ($\mu = 30°$)	35° to 45°	17.3 to 22.0	—	110 to 140	—
Shingle: loose	40°	18.1	—	115	—
sandy: compact	40° to 45°	20.4	—	130	—
loose	35° to 40°	18.9	—	120	—
Sand ($\mu = 30°$)					
fine: dry	30° to 35°	15.7	—	100	—
wet	0° to 30°	18.1 to 18.9	—	115 to 120	—
well graded: compact	40° to 45°	17.3 to 18.9	18.9 to 22.0	110 to 120	120 to 140
loose	35° to 40°	15.7 to 17.3	17.3 to 18.9	100 to 110	110 to 120
uniform:					
fine or silty: compact	35° to 40°	15.7 to 17.3	17.3 to 21.2	100 to 110	110 to 135
loose	30° to 35°	14.1 to 15.7	15.7 to 17.3	90 to 100	100 to 110
coarse or medium: compact	35° to 40°	15.7 to 17.3	18.9 to 20.4	100 to 110	120 to 130
loose	30° to 35°	14.1 to 15.7	16.5 to 18.9	90 to 100	105 to 120
Crushed rock:					
granite	35° to 45°	15.7 to 20.4	—	100 to 130	—
basalt, dolerites		17.3 to 22.0	—	110 to 140	—
limestone, sandstone		12.5 to 18.9	—	80 to 120	—
Broken chalk		9.4 to 12.5	—	60 to 80	—

Contained granular materials	Pressure calculations θ	Pressure calculations D kN/m³	Pressure calculations D lb/ft³	Capacity calculations Angle of repose	Capacity calculations D kN/m³	Capacity calculations D lb/ft³
Coal: dry unwashed ($\mu = 35°$)	40°	9.1	58	45°	7.1	45
washed	40°	9.0	56	45°	7.1	45
wet (15% moisture)	25°	9.0	56	45°	7.1	45
fine	20°	9.0	56	40°	7.1	45
slurry	0° to 20°	9.8	62.5	40°	7.9	50
anthracite	27°	8.2	52	40°	7.1	45
Coke, breeze etc.	40°	5.5	35	45°	4.7	30
Shale: broken	30°	20.4	130	35°	15.7	100
colliery dirt	35°	11.0	70	45°	9.4	60
Grain: wheat ($\mu = 24°$)	25°	7.9	50	25°	7.9	50
maize ($\mu = 23°$)	27.5°	7.1	45	25°	7.1	45
barley ($\mu = 24.5°$)	27°	6.3	40	25°	6.3	40
oats ($\mu = 25°$)	28°	4.7	30	25°	4.7	30
Cement: static fine ($\mu = 30°$)	10°	14.1	90	15°	13.2	84
coarse ($\mu = 30°$)	18°	14.1	90	20°	14.1	90
air-agitated	0°	11.8	75	—	11.8	75
Ashes ($\mu = 40°$)	35°	9.4	60	45°	6.3	40
Broken brick	35°	15.7	100	45°	11.0	70

Values of $D_l\alpha = D_l\left\{1 + k_2\left[\frac{D_m}{D_l} - (1-\beta)\right]\right\}$

Horizontal pressure of granular materials submerged in water	θ approximately when submerged	$D_l = 9.81$ kN/m³: D_m (solid) kN/m³	Percentage of voids ($= 100\beta$) 30%	40%	50%	$D_l = 62.4$ lb/ft³: D_m (solid) lb/ft³	Percentage of voids 30%	40%	50%
Coal (crushed)	35°	12.5	11.30	11.60	11.87	80	72	74	76
Stone (crushed)	35°	25.0	14.72	15.00	15.25	160	94	96	97
Sand	0°	25.0	27.94	28.92	29.90	160	179	185	191

$$q_2 = D_l h_o + (D_l\alpha)h$$

For k_2 see *Table 18*

$$\alpha = 1 + k_2\left[\frac{D_m}{D_l} - (1-\beta)\right]$$

Properties of cohesive soils

Type of soil	Saturated unit weight D kN/m³	Saturated unit weight D lb/ft³	Angle of internal friction θ	Cohesion C kN/m²	Cohesion C lb/ft²
Clay: very stiff boulder	19 to 22	120 to 140	16°	170	3600
hard shaly			—	> 140	> 3000
stiff			7°	70 to 140	1500 to 3000
firm	17.5 to 20.5	110 to 130	6°	35 to 70	750 to 1500
moderately firm	17.5 to 19	110 to 120	5°	50	1100
soft	15.5 to 19	100 to 120	4°	18 to 35	375 to 750
very soft			3°	< 18	< 375
Puddle clay: soft			3°	32	675
very soft			0°	21	450
Sandy clay: stiff	15.5	100		70 to 140	1500 to 3000
firm				35 to 70	750 to 1500
Silt	19	120		< 35	< 750

Type of soil	Bulk unit weight D kN/m³	Bulk unit weight D lb/ft³	Angle of internal friction θ	Cohesion
Clay: dry	17.3	110	30°	Determine by test
damp (well drained)	18.1	115	45°	
wet	18.9	120	15°	
gravelly	19.6	125	35°	
Earth: top soil	13.4	85	(35°)	In absence of test results, apply formulae for saturated clay with $\theta = 0°$
common	15.7	100	(35°)	
dry	14.2	90	30°	
moist	15.7	100	45° to 50°	
very wet	16.5	105	17°	
punned	15.7	100	65° to 75°	
Peat: dry	4.7	30	15° to 45°	
wet	9.4	60		

18 Pressures due to granular materials

Vertical walls

Active pressures (friction between material and face of wall or surface neglected)

Angle of internal friction of contained or retained material (approximate angle of repose)

Angle θ	Equivalent slope	Maximum positive surcharge: $q_1 = k_1 Dh$; $k_1 = \cos^2\theta$	Level fill: $q_2 = k_2 Dh$; $k_2 = \left[\frac{1-\sin\theta}{1+\sin\theta}\right]$	Maximum negative surcharge: $q_3 = k_3 Dh$; $k_3 = \left[\frac{\cos\theta}{1+\sin\theta\sqrt{2}}\right]^2$
5°	1 in 11.43	0.992	0.840	0.787
10°	1 in 5.67	0.970	0.704	0.625
11°18′	1 in 5	0.962	0.672	0.589
14°02′	1 in 4	0.941	0.610	0.522
15°	1 in 3.73	0.933	0.589	0.500
18°26′	1 in 3	0.900	0.519	0.430
20°	1 in 2.75	0.883	0.490	0.401
25°	1 in 2.14	0.821	0.406	0.322
26°34′	1 in 2	0.800	0.382	0.300
30°	1 in 1.73	0.750	0.333	0.257
33°41′	1 in 1.5	0.692	0.286	0.217
35°	1 in 1.43	0.671	0.271	0.205
40°	1 in 1.19	0.587	0.217	0.161
45°	1 in 1	0.500	0.172	0.125
50°	1 in 0.84	0.413	0.132	0.095
55°	1 in 0.7	0.329	0.099	0.071
60°	1 in 0.58	0.250	0.072	0.051
65°	1 in 0.47	0.179	0.049	0.034
70°	1 in 0.36	0.117	0.031	0.022
80°	1 in 0.18	0.030	0.008	0.005

Inclined surfaces

Intensity of pressure normal to surface

$q_n = k_4 Dh + g_s \cos\theta_1$

$q_h = k_2 Dh$

D unit weight of material

g_s weight per unit area of inclined slab

Values of k_4 are tabulated below.

$k_4 = k_2 \sin^2\theta_1 + \cos^2\theta_1$

Angle θ	Inclination of surface θ_1°: 30°	35°	40°	45°	50°	55°	60°	65°
30°	0.833	0.781	0.725	0.667	0.609	0.553	0.500	0.452
32°30′	0.825	0.770	0.711	0.650	0.590	0.531	0.476	0.426
35°	0.818	0.760	0.699	0.635	0.572	0.511	0.453	0.401
37°30′	0.811	0.751	0.687	0.622	0.556	0.492	0.432	0.378
40°	0.804	0.743	0.677	0.609	0.541	0.475	0.413	0.357
42°30′	0.798	0.735	0.667	0.597	0.527	0.459	0.395	0.338
45°	0.793	0.727	0.658	0.586	0.514	0.444	0.379	0.320

Notes on vertical walls

Tabulated factors apply only to intensity of active horizontal pressures of granular (cohesionless) material retained or contained by reinforced concrete walls, sheet-piles, and the like (not heavy gravity walls).

Unit weights (weight per unit volume):

D unit weight of retained or contained material ($= D_1, D_2$ or D_3)

D_1 unit weight of dry soil if there is no water in the ground, or weight of contained material

D_2 buoyant unit weight of soil below ground-water level ($= 0.6\,D_1$ approx.)

D_3 unit weight of moist (drained) soil above ground-water level in *Table 20* for the case where the angle of the slope of the surface exceeds the natural angle of repose, as occurs by protecting a bank of earth with turf or stone pitching. For such a case it is suggested that the weight of earth above the angle of repose, represented by the triangle BOC, should be considered as a load operating at the top of the wall. The magnitude of the resultant horizontal thrust T and increase in pressure would be as shown in *Table 20*, and each section of the wall should be designed for the extra moment due to T.

Concentrated load. A single concentrated load imposed on the filling behind a wall can be dealt with approximately by dispersion. With an angle of dispersion of 45°, as indicated in diagram (c) in *Table 20*, the intensity of active horizontal pressure additional to the pressure due to the filling is given by the appropriate formulae in *Table 20*.

10.2 MATERIALS IMMERSED OR FLOATING IN LIQUIDS

10.2.1 Materials heavier than liquid

With granular material, of which the specific gravity exceeds that of the liquid in which it is just fully immersed, the intensity of horizontal active pressure on the vertical wall of the container is given by the modified formula of Terzaghi and Peck:

$$q = D_l h\left\{1 + k\left[\frac{D_m}{D_l} - (1-\beta)\right]\right\} + D_l h_0 = D_l(h_0 + \alpha h)$$

where

$$\alpha = 1 + k\left[\frac{D_m}{D_l} - (1-\beta)\right]$$

where D_l is the weight per unit volume of the liquid, D_m is the weight per unit volume of the solid material, β is the ratio of the volume of the voids in a given volume of the dry material, k is the horizontal pressure factor depending on the slope of the surface of the material and the angle of repose of the dry material (that is, factors k_1, k_2 or k_3 in *Table 18*), and h is the depth from the top of the submerged material to the level at which the pressure is being calculated. If the surface of the liquid is at a distance h_0 above the top of the submerged material, there is an additional pressure of $D_l h_0$. The total intensity of pressure at any depth $h_0 + h$ below the surface of the liquid is $D_l(h_0 + h\alpha)$.

If the material is immersed in water, D_l is equal to 9.81 kN/m^3 or 62.4 lb/ft^3.

The above expressions apply to materials such as coal or broken stone, whose angle of repose is not materially affected by submergence. It is advisable to reduce the value of the angle of repose to about 5° below that for the dry material when determining the value of k for the submerged material. In calculating k for such material it can be assumed that the angle of repose and the angle of internal friction are identical.

For a material such as sand, which has a definite angle of repose when dry but none when saturated, k is unity when submerged.

The values of αD_l for unit depth for crushed coal, broken stone and sand, when immersed in water and with a level surface, are given in *Table 17*.

10.2.2 Materials lighter than liquid

If the specific gravity of the material is less than that of the liquid, the intensity of horizontal pressure at any depth h below the surface of the liquid in which the material floats is $D_l h$. Therefore, if stored in water, the horizontal pressure on the walls of the container is equal to the simple hydrostatic pressure of $9.81h$ kN/m^2 or $62.4h$ lb/ft^2.

10.3 SILOS

The information provided on *Table 21* is abstracted from DIN1055.

The ratio $k = q_h/q_v$ is assumed constant throughout h_1. During filling k is approximately equal to k_2, and DIN1055 recommends a value of 0.5; during discharge a value of 1 is recommended. As a result of these differing values of k and also since θ' differs, the values of q_h, q_v and q that occur during emptying differ from those which occur during filling. The particular conditions that give rise to the maximum values are indicated in the central part of the table on *Table 21*.

For the reasons discussed in section 2.8.4, special care must be taken when selecting appropriate values of D and θ for silo calculations.

Effects likely to increase loads. Moisture may alter the angle of friction θ' between the contained material and the wall. If this is possible, actual values of θ' must be determined.

Since loads may increase when 'bridges' that have formed in the contained material collapse, the vertical load on the compartment floor should be taken as twice that due to q_v, but not more than Dh. If experience has shown that such bridging effects do not occur in the particular material being stored, this increase in load need not be considered.

Effects likely to decrease loads. Owing to the proximity of a compartment floor, the horizontal pressure during discharge is reduced over a height of $1.2d$ (but not more than $0.75h_1$) above the outlet. Over this height q_h may be assumed to vary linearly, as shown in the diagram on *Table 21*.

Example. Calculate (i) the horizontal service pressures at various depths in a 6 m diameter cylindrical silo having a filled depth of 18 m and containing wheat during filling and during emptying. Also calculate (ii) the vertical pressure on the bottom.

(i) For wheat, $D = 8400$ N/m^3 and $\theta = 25°$. Thus $\theta'_f = 0.75\theta = 18.75°$ and $\theta'_e = 0.6\theta = 15°$. $r = (1/4) \times 6 = 1.5$ m.

Thus at an infinite depth, during filling,

$$q_h = \frac{Dr}{\tan\theta'_f} = \frac{8400 \times 1.5}{0.340} = 37.1 \text{ kN/m}^2$$

and during emptying

$$q_h = \frac{Dr}{\tan\theta'_e} = \frac{8400 \times 1.5}{0.268} = 47.0 \text{ kN/m}^2$$

19 Pressures due to cohesive soils

	Type of soil	Formulae giving intensity (in force per unit area) of horizontal pressure at depth h
Active pressures on vertical wall	Clay (partially saturated) and silt $\theta > 0°$	$h_0 = \frac{2C}{D}\sqrt{\left(\frac{1}{k_2}\right)}$ Above ground-water level: $h \ngtr h_0$: $q_2 = D_w h$ $h > h_0 \ngtr h_w$: $q_2 = k_2 Dh - 2C\sqrt{k_2}$ (this is Bell's formula) Below ground-water level: $h > h_0 > h_w$: $q_2 = k_2 Dh_w + (k_2 D_2 + D_w)(h - h_w) - 2C\sqrt{k_2}$
	Fissured clay	$h_0 = \frac{2C_s}{D}\sqrt{\left(1 + \frac{C_w}{C_s}\right)}$ $h \ngtr h_0 \ngtr H/2$ (where $H \nless 3$ m or 10 ft): $q_2 = D_w h$ $h > h_0$: $q_2 = Dh - 2C_s\sqrt{\left(1 + \frac{C_w}{C_s}\right)}$
	Non-fissured clay $\theta = 0°$	$h_0 = \frac{2C_h}{D}\sqrt{\left(1 + \frac{C_w}{C_h}\right)}$ $h \ngtr h_0 \ngtr H/2$ (where $H \nless 3$ m or 10 ft): $q_2 = D_w h$ $h > h_0$: $q_2 = Dh - 2C_h\sqrt{\left(1 + \frac{C_w}{C_h}\right)}$
	Formulae apply to reinforced concrete walls, sheet piles etc. (not to heavy gravity walls)	
Passive resistance	Clay (partially saturated) and silt $\theta > 0°$	With water level below ground level in front of wall: $h_p \ngtr h_w$: $q_p = \frac{Dh_p}{k_2} + \frac{2C}{\sqrt{k_2}}$ $h_p > h_w$: $q_p = \frac{Dh_w}{k_2} + \left(\frac{D_2}{k_2} + D_w\right)(h_p - h_w) + \frac{2C}{\sqrt{k_2}}$
		With water level above ground level in front of wall: $h_p \ngtr h_w$: $q_p = D_w h_p$ $h_p > h_w$: $q_p = \frac{D_2}{k_2}(h_p - h_w) + D_w h_p + \frac{2C}{\sqrt{k_2}}$
	Non-fissured clay $\theta = 0°$	$q_p = Dh_p + \frac{2C_h}{\sqrt{k_2}}$

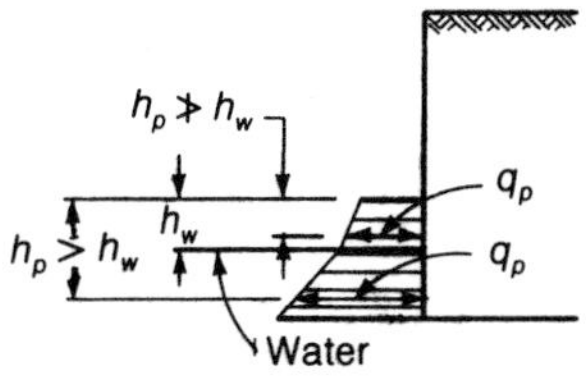

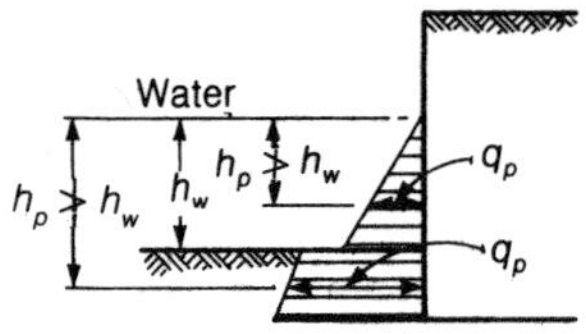

Notation

Active pressures

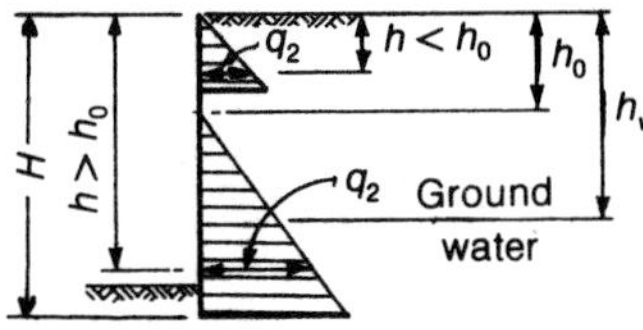

Unit weights:

- D unit weight of saturated clay or unit bulk weight of earth
- D_w unit weight of water = 9.81 kN/m³ or 62.4 lb/ft³
- D_2 buoyant unit weight = $0.6D$ approx.

Cohesion (force per unit area):

- C cohesion at no load on clay
- C_s cohesion of softened clay
- C_h cohesion at depth h
- C_w cohesion between clay and wall $= C_h$ but not greater than 47.9 kN/m² or 1000 lb/ft²

$k_2 = \frac{1 - \sin\theta}{1 + \sin\theta}$ (see *Table 18*)

θ angle of internal friction

Passive resistance

During filling, reference depth $h_0 = 2r/\tan\theta'_f = 3/0.340 = 8.82$ m, and during emptying $h_0 = r/\tan\theta'_e = 1.5/0.268 = 5.60$ m. However, when emptying, q_h decreases linearly below a depth of $18 - (6 \times 1.2) = 10.8$ m from the top of the silo.

At 3 m depth during filling, $h/h_0 = 3/8.82 = 0.340$ and thus $\xi = 1 - e^{-0.340} = 0.288$. Then $q_h = 37.1 \times 0.288 = 10.70\,\mathrm{kN/m^2}$.

By undertaking similar calculations, a table of q_h against h can be built up. During emptying, the value of q_h reaches a maximum of $40.2\,\mathrm{kN/m^2}$ at a depth of 10.8 m, and this then decreases linearly to the value of $32.3\,\mathrm{kN/m^2}$ which occurs at a depth of 18 m during filling.

(ii) During filling,

$$q_v = 2\,Dr/\tan\theta'_f = 2 \times 8400 \times 1.5/0.340 = 74.1\,\mathrm{kN/m^2}$$

but if bridging is likely to occur this value should be doubled to $148.2\,\mathrm{kN/m^2}$ (i.e. just below the upper-bound value of $151.2\,\mathrm{kN/m^2}$) when calculating the load on the compartment floor. During discharge,

$$q_v = Dr/\tan\theta'_e = 8400 \times 1.5/0.268 = 47.0\,\mathrm{kN/m^2}$$

Pressures due to surcharge

20

Vertical wall   Granular material: unit weight = D Friction on back of wall neglected

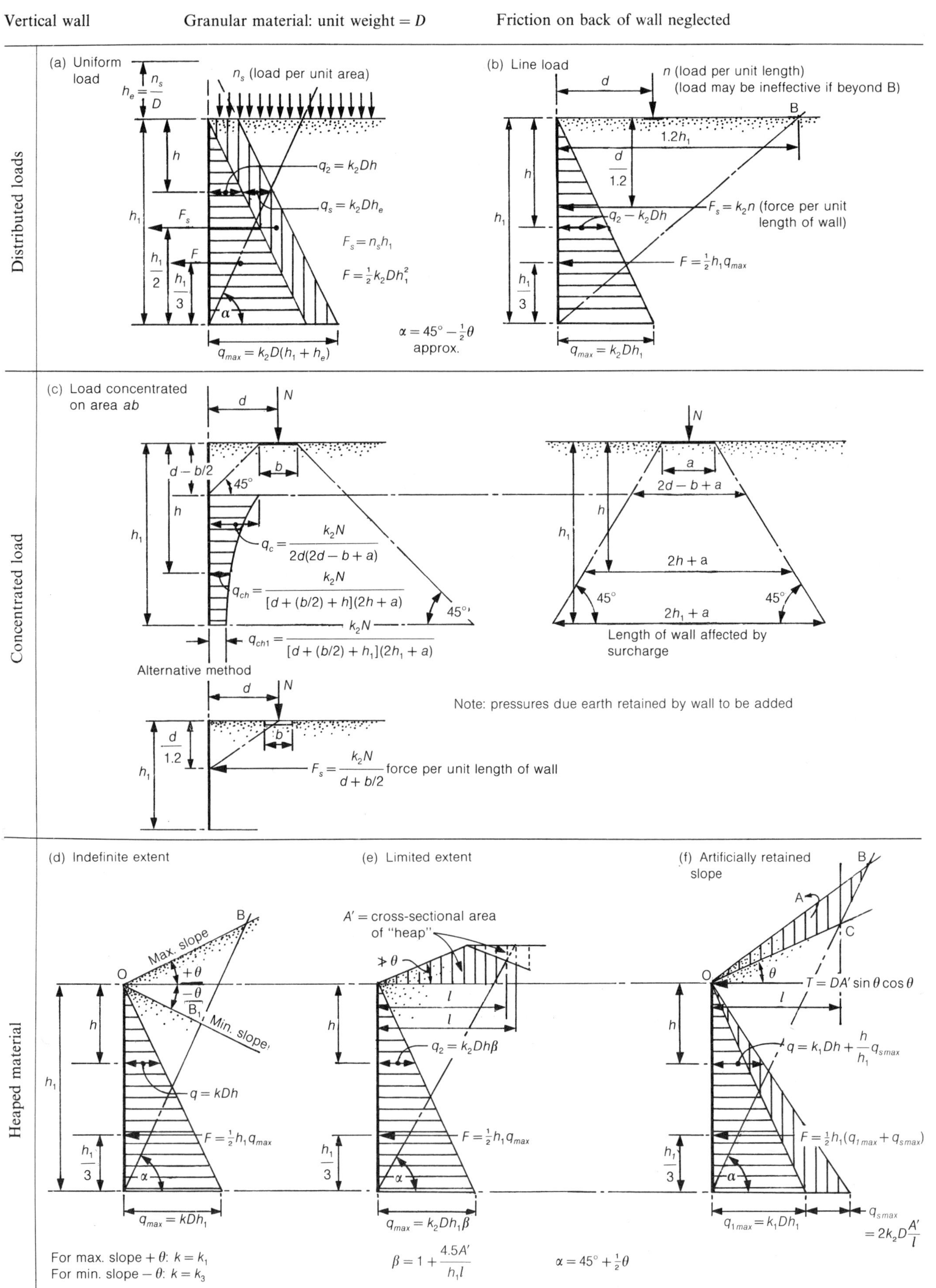

For values of k_1, k_2 and k_3 see *Table 18*.

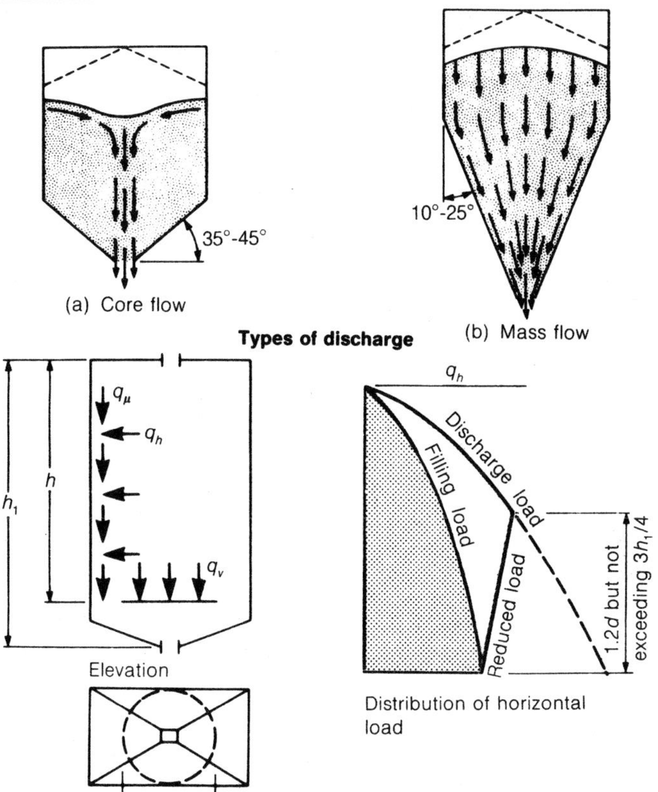

Notation

- D unit weight of contained material (given here in terms of equivalent force)
- θ angle of internal friction of contained material (in degrees)
- d width of container
- h_1 overall depth of container
- h depth to point considered measured from mean surface level of contained material if container is filled to capacity (see sketches) and then levelled

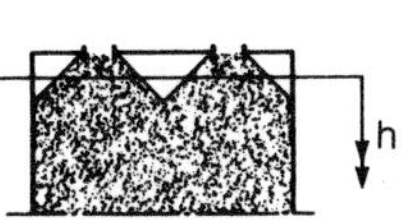

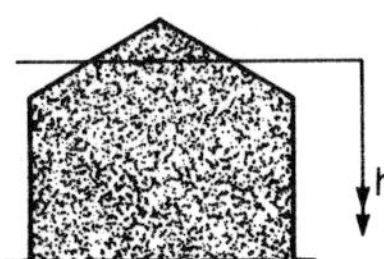

- θ' angle of friction between contained material and concrete wall (in degrees) $= \tan^{-1}(q_\mu/q_h)$
- q_h horizontal pressure at depth $h = kq_v$
- q_v vertical pressure at depth h
- q_μ vertical load per unit area supported by wall friction
- r hydraulic radius = (internal plan area of container A)/(internal plan perimeter of container u). For containers square, circular or regularly polygonal in plan, $r = d/4$. For wedge-shaped containers, substitute square container having equal area.

Properties of contained materials

Material	D(N/m^3)	θ
Wheat	8400	25
Maize	8400	25
Barley	7500	25
Oats	6300	25

Janssen's formula: $q_h = \dfrac{Dr}{\tan\theta'}(1 - e^{-hk\tan\theta'/r})$;

if $1/\psi = e^{-hk\tan\theta'/r}$ the common logarithm of $\psi = hk\tan\theta'/2.3026r$

Data for calculating internal forces

			During filling	During emptying
Angle of friction (in degrees) between contained material and wall	For grain sizes between 0.06 and 0.2 mm, use linear interpolation	Granular material (grain size > 0.2 mm)	$\theta'_f = 0.75\theta$	$\theta'_e = 0.60\theta$
		Powdered material (grain size < 0.06 mm)	$\theta'_f = \theta$	$\theta'_e = \theta$
Critical maximum loads per unit area arising from specified conditions	Infinite depth	Granular material	$q_{v\,max}, q_{\mu\,max}$	$q_{h\,max}, q_{\mu\,max}$
		Powdered material	$q_{v\,max}, q_{h\,max}, q_{\mu\,max}$	$q_{h\,max}, q_{\mu\,max}$
	Finite depth	Granular and powdered material	$q_{v\,max}$	$q_{h\,max}, q_{\mu\,max}$
Expressions giving maximum load per unit area	At infinite depth	$q_{h\,max} =$	$\dfrac{Dr}{\tan\theta'_f}$	$\dfrac{Dr}{\tan\theta'_e}$
		$q_{v\,max} =$	$\dfrac{2Dr}{\tan\theta'_f}$	$\dfrac{Dr}{\tan\theta'_e}$
		$q_{\mu\,max} =$	Dr	Dr
	At finite depth	Reference depth $h_0 =$	$\dfrac{2r}{\tan\theta'_f}$	$\dfrac{r}{\tan\theta'_e}$
		Multiply values of q_h, q_v and q_μ given by above expressions by ξ, where $\xi = 1 - e^{-(h/h_0)}$. Values of ξ for given ratios of h/h_0 may be read from scale below.		

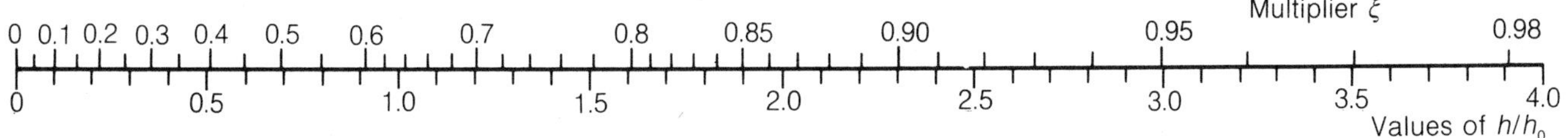

Chapter 11

Cantilevers and beams of one span

Formulae and coefficients on tables in this chapter give service moments and shearing forces corresponding to unfactored characteristic loads. To obtain ultimate moments and shearing forces for limit-state design, all loads must be multiplied by partial safety factor for loads γ_f appropriate to the particular limit-state being considered.

11.1 BEAMS FIXED AT BOTH ENDS

The bending moment on a beam fixed at both ends is derived from the principle that the area of the bending-moment diagram due to the same load imposed on a freely supported beam of equal span (the 'free-moment' diagram) is equal to the area of the restraint-moment diagram; also the centroids of the two diagrams are in the same vertical line. The shape of the free-moment diagram depends upon the characteristics of the imposed load, but the restraint-moment diagram is a trapezium. For loads symmetrically disposed on the beam the centroid of the free-moment diagram is above the midpoint of the span, and thus the restraint-moment diagram is a rectangle, giving a restraint bending moment at each support equal to the mean height of the free-moment diagram.

The amount of shearing force in a beam with one or both ends fixed is calculated from the variation of the bending moment. The shearing force resulting from the restraint moment alone is constant throughout the beam, and equals the difference between the two end moments divided by the span, that is, the rate of change of the restraint moment. This shearing force is algebraically added to the shearing force due to the imposed load considering the beam to be freely supported; that is, the reaction at a support is the sum (or difference) of the restraint-moment shearing force and the free-moment shearing force. For a symmetrically loaded beam with both ends fixed the restraint moment at each end is the same, and the shearing forces are identical with those for the same beam freely supported; the reactions both equal one-half of the total load on the beam.

11.1.1 Fixed-end-moment coefficients

The charts in *Tables 30* and *31* give the load factors (i.e. fixed-end-moment coefficients) C_{AB} and C_{BA} due to partial uniformly and triangularly distributed loads on a span. Nearly all complex loading arrangements can be broken down into a combination of these loading shapes and the corresponding coefficients found by superposition in the manner indicated in the example below. The lower chart on *Table 31* gives load factors for trapezoidal loading, such as occurs on a beam supporting the longer side of a slab spanning in two directions. In addition, by using the appropriate values of $\alpha = 1 - \beta$, the coefficients relating to the beam supporting the short side of a two-way slab may also be found. The equations from which the charts have been plotted are as follows:

Partial uniform load:

$$C_{AB} = Fl\left(\frac{1}{12} + \frac{1}{4}\alpha^3 - \frac{5}{12}\alpha^2 + \frac{1}{12}\alpha - \frac{1}{4}\alpha^2\beta + \frac{1}{6}\alpha\beta + \frac{1}{4}\alpha\beta^2 + \frac{1}{12}\beta + \frac{1}{12}\beta^2 - \frac{1}{4}\beta^3\right)$$

Partial triangular load (load decreasing from left to right):

$$C_{AB} = Fl\left(\frac{1}{10} + \frac{2}{5}\alpha^3 - \frac{7}{10}\alpha^2 + \frac{1}{5}\alpha - \frac{3}{10}\alpha^2\beta + \frac{4}{15}\alpha\beta + \frac{1}{5}\alpha\beta^2 + \frac{1}{30}\beta - \frac{1}{30}\beta^2 - \frac{1}{10}\beta^3\right)$$

$$C_{BA} = Fl\left(\frac{1}{15} - \frac{2}{5}\alpha^3 + \frac{1}{5}\alpha^2 + \frac{2}{15}\alpha + \frac{3}{10}\alpha^2\beta + \frac{1}{15}\alpha\beta - \frac{1}{5}\alpha\beta^2 - \frac{1}{30}\beta - \frac{2}{15}\beta^2 + \frac{1}{10}\beta^3\right)$$

Trapezoidal load:

$$C_{AB} = Fl\left(\frac{1}{6} - \frac{1}{10}\alpha^4 + \frac{1}{3}\alpha^3 - \frac{1}{3}\alpha^2 + \frac{1}{10}\beta^4 - \frac{1}{6}\beta^3\right)\Big/(2 - \alpha - \beta)$$

Note that if the triangular load slopes in the opposite direction to that indicated, factors α and β should be transposed, and the resulting coefficients given by the upper and lower charts on *Table 30* are respectively C_{BA} and C_{AB} instead of C_{AB} and C_{BA}. To obtain values of C_{BA} from the charts on *Table 31*, transpose α and β.

Example. Determine the load factors C_{AB} and C_{BA} for the beam shown in the accompanying diagram (a) by (i) using the charts for partial uniform and triangular loading and (ii) using the chart for trapezoidal loading.

Bending moments and shearing forces: basic data

BASIC RELATIONSHIPS

At any section:

Shearing force $V = \sum \left[\begin{array}{l} \text{loads and reactions on} \\ \text{one side of section} \end{array} \right] = \text{rate of change of } M$

Bending moment $M = \sum \left[\begin{array}{l} \text{moments of loads and reactions} \\ \text{on one side of section} \end{array} \right] = \text{rate of change of } EI\theta$

Slope $\theta = \int \dfrac{M}{EI} = \text{rate of change of } a$

Deflection (elastic) $a = \int \theta$

I moment of inertia of member at section
E elastic modulus of material

DIAGRAMS OF BENDING MOMENT AND SHEARING FORCE DUE TO UNIFORM LOADING

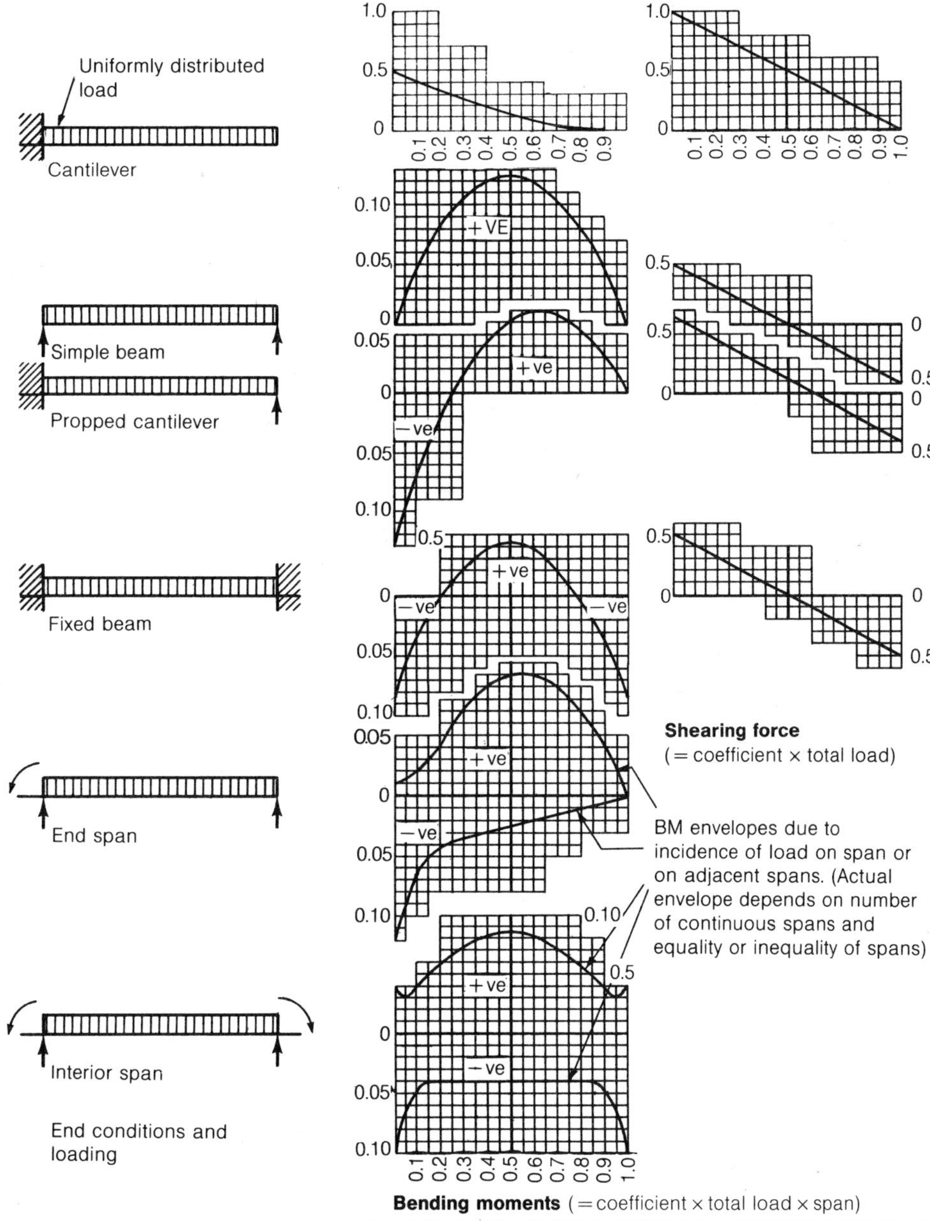

CRITICAL LOADING FOR CONTINUOUS BEAMS: incidence of imposed load

To produce maximum positive bending moment on span ST:

To produce maximum negative bending moment at support S:

CP110: loads on spans RS and ST only need be taken into account.
BS8110: consider load extending over *all* spans.
For service-load design, consider a service dead load of g_k and a service imposed load of q_k.
For ultimate-limit-state design, consider an 'ultimate dead load' of g_k and an 'ultimate imposed load' of $(0.4g_k + 1.6q_k)$.

PARTIAL UNIFORM LOAD

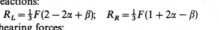

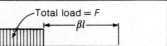

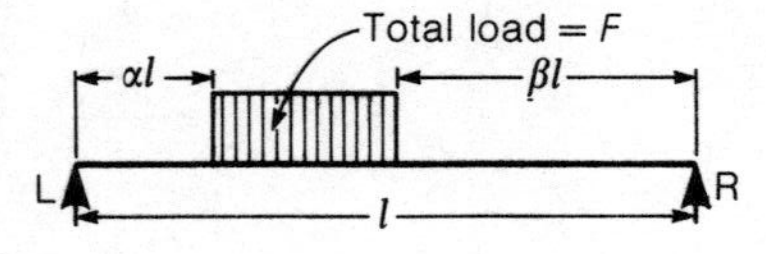

Reactions:

$R_L = \frac{1}{2}F(1-\alpha+\beta)$; $R_R = \frac{1}{2}F(1+\alpha-\beta)$

Shearing forces:

when $x<\alpha$: $V_x = \frac{1}{2}F(1-\alpha+\beta)$

when $\alpha<x<(1-\beta)$: $V_x = F\left[\frac{1}{2}(1-\alpha+\beta)+\frac{(\alpha-x)}{(1-\alpha-\beta)}\right]$

when $x>(1-\beta)$: $V_x = -\frac{1}{2}F(1+\alpha-\beta)$

Bending moments:

when $x<\alpha$: $M_x = \frac{1}{2}Flx(1-\alpha+\beta)$

when $\alpha<x<(1-\beta)$: $M_x = \frac{1}{2}Fl\left[x(1-\alpha+\beta)-\frac{(x-\alpha)^2}{(1-\alpha-\beta)}\right]$

when $x>(1-\beta)$: $M_x = \frac{1}{2}Fl(1-x)(1+\alpha-\beta)$

$M_{x\,max} = \frac{1}{8}(1+\alpha+\beta)(1+\alpha-\beta)\times(1-\alpha+\beta)Fl$ at $\frac{1}{2}(1+\alpha^2-\beta^2)l$

Deflections:

when $x<\alpha$: $a_x = -\frac{Fl^3(1-\alpha+\beta)}{24EI}[(1+2\alpha-\alpha^2-\beta^2)x-2x^3]=a_1$

when $\alpha<x<(1-\beta)$: $a_x = a_1-\frac{Fl^3(x-\alpha)^4}{24EI(1-\alpha-\beta)}$

when $x>(1-\beta)$: use formula for a_1, transpose α and β and substitute $(1-x)$ for x

PARTIAL TRIANGULAR LOAD

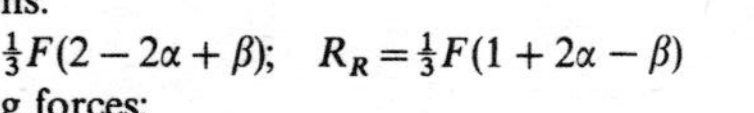

Reactions:

$R_L = \frac{1}{3}F(2-2\alpha+\beta)$; $R_R = \frac{1}{3}F(1+2\alpha-\beta)$

Shearing forces:

when $x<\alpha$: $V_x = \frac{1}{3}F(2-2\alpha+\beta)$

when $\alpha<x<(1-\beta)$: $V_x = -F\left[\frac{1}{3}(1+2\alpha-\beta)-\frac{(1-x-\beta)^2}{(1-\alpha-\beta)^2}\right]$

when $x>(1-\beta)$: $V_x = -\frac{1}{3}F(1+2\alpha-\beta)$

Bending moments:

when $x<\alpha$: $M_x = \frac{1}{3}Flx(2-2\alpha+\beta)$

when $\alpha<x<(1-\beta)$: $M_x = \frac{1}{3}Fl\left[(1+2\alpha-\beta)(1-x)-\frac{(1-x-\beta)^3}{(1-\alpha-\beta)^2}\right]$

when $x>(1-\beta)$: $M_x = \frac{1}{3}Fl(1-x)(1+2\alpha-\beta)$

Deflections:

when $x<\alpha$:

$$a_x = -\frac{Fl^3x(2-2\alpha+\beta)}{162EI}\left[9(1+x)(1-x)-(2-2\alpha+\beta)^2-(1-\alpha-\beta)^2\left\{\frac{3}{2}-\frac{(1-\alpha-\beta)}{5(2-2\alpha+\beta)}\right\}\right]=a_1$$

when $\alpha<x<(1-\beta)$:

$$a_x = a_1-\frac{Fl^3(x-\alpha)^4}{60EI(1-\alpha-\beta)}\left\{5-\frac{(x-\alpha)}{(1-\alpha-\beta)}\right\}$$

when $x>(1-\beta)$:

$$a_x = -\frac{Fl^3(1-x)(1+2\alpha-\beta)}{162EI}\left[9x(2-x)-(1+2\alpha-\beta)^2-(1-\alpha-\beta)^2\left\{\frac{3}{2}+\frac{(1-\alpha-\beta)}{5(1+2\alpha-\beta)}\right\}\right]$$

TRAPEZOIDAL LOAD

Total load = F

Reactions:

$R_L = R_R = \frac{1}{2}F$

Shearing forces:

when $x<\alpha$: $V_x = \frac{1}{2}F\left[1-\frac{x^2}{\alpha(1-\alpha)}\right]$

when $\alpha<x\leqslant\frac{1}{2}$: $V_x = \frac{1}{2}F\frac{(1-2x)}{(1-\alpha)}$

Bending moments:

when $x<\alpha$: $M_x = \frac{1}{6}Flx\left[3-\frac{x^2}{\alpha(1-\alpha)}\right]$

when $\alpha<x\leqslant\frac{1}{2}$: $M_x = \frac{1}{6}Fl\left[\frac{3x(1-x)-\alpha^2}{(1-\alpha)}\right]$

$M_{x\,max} = (3-4\alpha^2)/\{24(1-\alpha)\}Fl$ at midspan

Deflections:

when $x<\alpha$: $a_x = -(Fl^3x/24EI)[(1+\alpha-\alpha^2)-2x^2+\{x^4/5\alpha(1-\alpha)\}]$

when $\alpha<x\leqslant\frac{1}{2}$: $a_x = -[Fl^3/\{24EI(1-\alpha)\}]\times[\{1-2\alpha^2+x(1-x)\}x(1-x)+(\alpha^4/5)]$

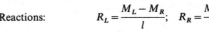

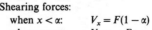

$a_{x\,max} = -(4\alpha^2-5)^2Fl^3/\{1920(1-\alpha)EI\}$ at midspan

CONCENTRATED LOAD

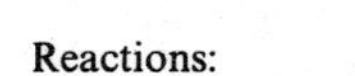
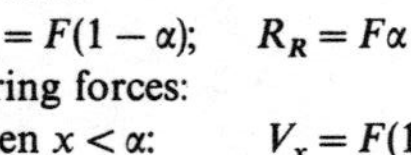
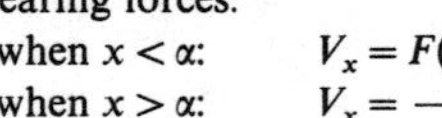
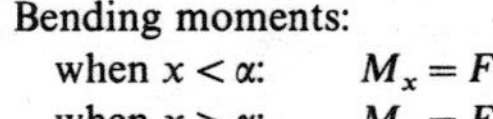

Reactions:

$R_L = F(1-\alpha)$; $R_R = F\alpha$

Shearing forces:

when $x<\alpha$: $V_x = F(1-\alpha)$

when $x>\alpha$: $V_x = -F\alpha$

Bending moments:

when $x<\alpha$: $M_x = Fl(1-\alpha)x$

when $x>\alpha$: $M_x = Fl\alpha(1-x)$

$M_{x\,max} = Fl\alpha(1-\alpha)$ beneath load

Deflections:

when $x<\alpha$: $a_x = (Fl^3(1-\alpha)x/6EI)[\alpha(2-\alpha)-x^2]$

when $x>\alpha$: $a_x = -(Fl^3\alpha(1-x)/6EI)[x(2-x)-\alpha^2]$

when $\alpha\leqslant\frac{1}{2}$: $a_{x\,max} = -Fl^3\alpha(1-\alpha^2)^{3/2}/9\sqrt{(3)}EI$ at $\sqrt{[(1-\alpha^2)/3]}\,l$ from R.

SUPPORT MOMENTS

Reactions: $R_L = \frac{M_L-M_R}{l}$; $R_R = \frac{M_R-M_L}{l}$

Shearing force: $V_x = \frac{M_L-M_R}{l}$

Bending moments: $M_x = M_L(1-x)+M_Rx$

Deflections: $a_x = -[x(1-x)l^2/6EI][(2-x)M_L+(1+x)M_R]$

For notes see *Table 25*.

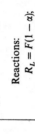

24 Moments, shears, deflections: special cases for beams

	Freely supported span	Fully fixed span
Uniform load	Reactions: $R_L = R_R = \frac{1}{2}F$ Shearing forces: $V_x = F(\frac{1}{2} - x)$ Bending moments: $M_L = M_R = 0$ $M_x = \frac{1}{2}x(1-x)Fl$ $M_{x\,max} = \frac{1}{8}Fl$ at $\frac{1}{2}l$ Slopes: $\theta_L = \theta_R = \pm Fl^2/24EI$ Deflections: $a_x = -(Fl^3x/24EI)(1-x)(1+x-x^2)$ $a_{x\,max} = -5Fl^3/384EI$ at midspan	Reactions: $R_L = R_R = \frac{1}{2}F$ Shearing forces: $V_x = F\left(\frac{1}{2} - \frac{x}{l}\right)$ Bending moments: $M_L = M_R = -\frac{1}{12}Fl$ $M_x = \frac{1}{2}Fl[x(1-x) - \frac{1}{6}]$ $M_{x\,max} = \frac{1}{24}Fl$ at midspan Slopes: $\theta_L = \theta_R = 0$ Deflections: $a_x = -Fl^3x^2(1-x)^2/24EI$ $a_{x\,max} = -Fl^3/384EI$ at midspan
Triangular load	*Apex at left-hand end* Reactions: $R_L = \frac{2}{3}F; \quad R_R = \frac{1}{3}F$ Shearing forces: $V_x = (F/3)(2 - 6x + 3x^2)$ Bending moments: $M_L = M_R = 0$ $M_x = \frac{1}{3}Flx(1-x)(2-x)$ $M_{x\,max} = 2Fl/9\sqrt{3}$ at $(1 - 1/\sqrt{3})l$ from L Slopes: $\theta_L = -2Fl^2/45EI; \quad \theta_R = +7Fl^2/180EI$ Deflections: $a_x = -x(1-x)(2-x)(4+6x-3x^2)Fl^3/180EI$ $a_{x\,max} \simeq -Fl^3/76.7EI$ at $x \simeq 0.4807l$ from L	*Apex at left-hand end* Reactions: $R_L = \frac{7}{10}F; \quad R_R = \frac{3}{10}F$ Shearing forces: $V_x = (F/10)(7 - 20x + 10x^2)$ Bending moments: $M_L = -Fl/10 \quad M_R = -Fl/15$ $M_x = (Fl/30)(10x^3 - 30x^2 + 21x - 3)$ $M_{x\,max} \simeq Fl/23.32$ at $(1 - \sqrt{0.3})l$ from L Slopes: $\theta_L = \theta_R = 0$ Deflections: $a_x = -(Fl^3/60EI)x^2(1-x)^2(3-x)$ $a_{x\,max} \simeq -Fl^3/382EI$ at $x \simeq 0.4753l$ from L
Central concentrated load	Reactions: $R_L = R_R = \frac{1}{2}F$ Shearing forces: when $x < \frac{1}{2}$: $V_x = \frac{1}{2}F$ when $x > \frac{1}{2}$: $V_x = -\frac{1}{2}F$ Bending moments: $M_L = M_R = 0$ $M_{x\,max} = \frac{1}{4}Fl$ at midspan Slopes: $\theta_L = -Fl^2/16EI; \quad \theta_R = +Fl^2/16EI$ Deflections: when $x \leqslant \frac{1}{2}$: $a_x = -(Fl^3/48EI)x(3-4x^2)$ $a_{x\,max} = -Fl^3/48EI$ at midspan	Reactions: $R_L = R_R = \frac{1}{2}F$ Shearing forces: when $x < \frac{1}{2}$: $V_x = \frac{1}{2}F$ when $x > \frac{1}{2}$: $V_x = -\frac{1}{2}F$ Bending moments: $M_L = M_R = -\frac{1}{8}Fl$ when $x \leqslant \frac{1}{2}$: $M_x = (Fl/8)(4x-1)$ when $x \geqslant \frac{1}{2}$: $M_x = (Fl/8)(3-4x)$ $M_{x\,max} = \frac{1}{8}Fl$ at midspan Slopes: $\theta_L = \theta_R = 0$ Deflections: when $x \leqslant \frac{1}{2}$: $a_x = -(Fl^3/48EI)x^2(3-4x)$ $a_{x\,max} = -Fl^3/192EI$ at midspan

For notes see *Table 25*.

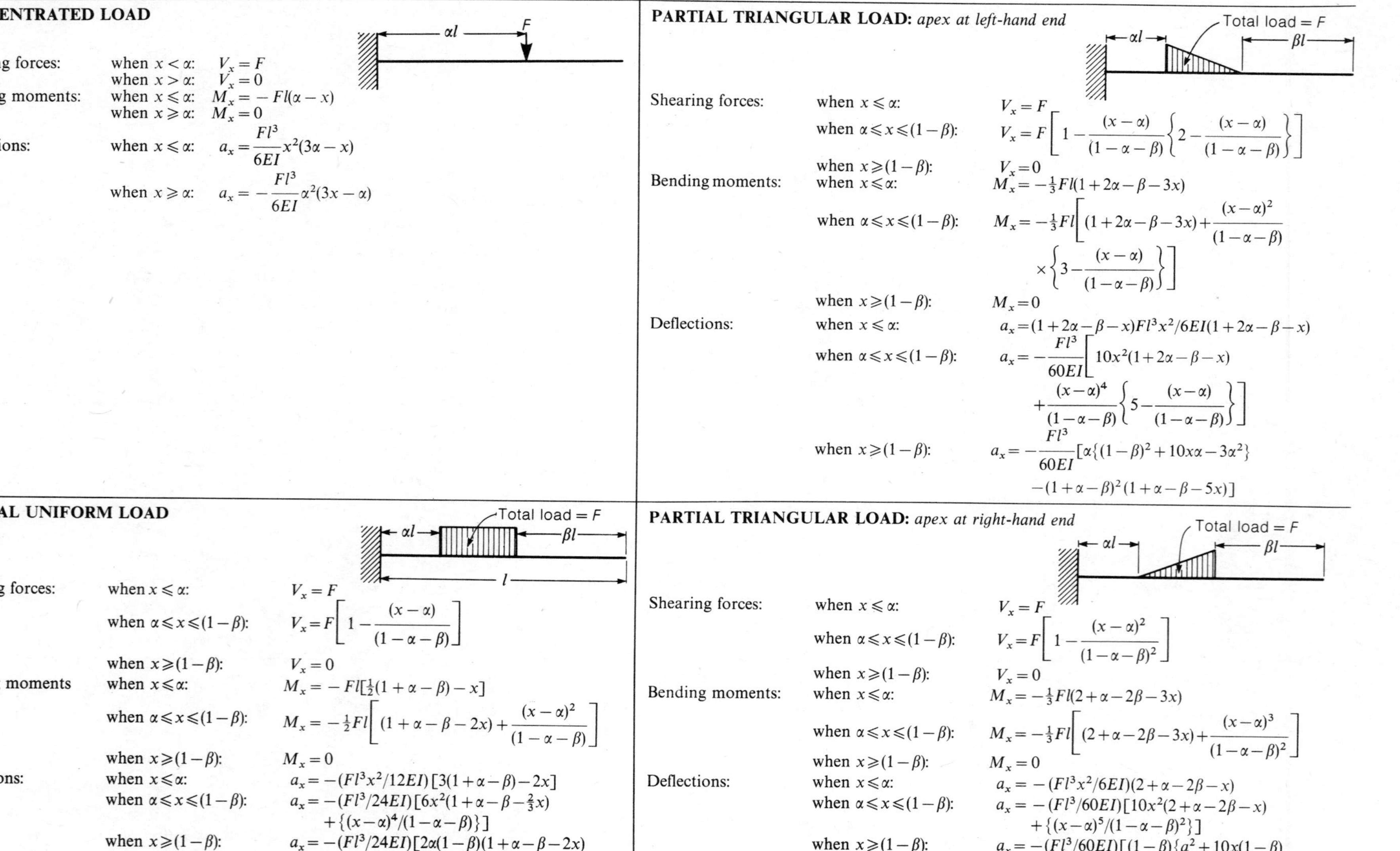

CONCENTRATED LOAD

Shearing forces: when $x < \alpha$: $V_x = F$
when $x > \alpha$: $V_x = 0$

Bending moments: when $x \leqslant \alpha$: $M_x = -Fl(\alpha - x)$
when $x \geqslant \alpha$: $M_x = 0$

Deflections: when $x \leqslant \alpha$: $a_x = \dfrac{Fl^3}{6EI}x^2(3\alpha - x)$

when $x \geqslant \alpha$: $a_x = -\dfrac{Fl^3}{6EI}\alpha^2(3x - \alpha)$

PARTIAL TRIANGULAR LOAD: *apex at left-hand end*

Shearing forces: when $x \leqslant \alpha$: $V_x = F$

when $\alpha \leqslant x \leqslant (1-\beta)$: $V_x = F\left[1 - \dfrac{(x-\alpha)}{(1-\alpha-\beta)}\left\{2 - \dfrac{(x-\alpha)}{(1-\alpha-\beta)}\right\}\right]$

when $x \geqslant (1-\beta)$: $V_x = 0$

Bending moments: when $x \leqslant \alpha$: $M_x = -\frac{1}{3}Fl(1+2\alpha-\beta-3x)$

when $\alpha \leqslant x \leqslant (1-\beta)$: $M_x = -\frac{1}{3}Fl\left[(1+2\alpha-\beta-3x) + \dfrac{(x-\alpha)^2}{(1-\alpha-\beta)} \times\left\{3 - \dfrac{(x-\alpha)}{(1-\alpha-\beta)}\right\}\right]$

when $x \geqslant (1-\beta)$: $M_x = 0$

Deflections: when $x \leqslant \alpha$: $a_x = (1+2\alpha-\beta-x)Fl^3x^2/6EI(1+2\alpha-\beta-x)$

when $\alpha \leqslant x \leqslant (1-\beta)$: $a_x = -\dfrac{Fl^3}{60EI}\left[10x^2(1+2\alpha-\beta-x) + \dfrac{(x-\alpha)^4}{(1-\alpha-\beta)}\left\{5 - \dfrac{(x-\alpha)}{(1-\alpha-\beta)}\right\}\right]$

when $x \geqslant (1-\beta)$: $a_x = -\dfrac{Fl^3}{60EI}[\alpha\{(1-\beta)^2 + 10x\alpha - 3\alpha^2\} - (1+\alpha-\beta)^2(1+\alpha-\beta-5x)]$

PARTIAL UNIFORM LOAD

Shearing forces: when $x \leqslant \alpha$: $V_x = F$

when $\alpha \leqslant x \leqslant (1-\beta)$: $V_x = F\left[1 - \dfrac{(x-\alpha)}{(1-\alpha-\beta)}\right]$

when $x \geqslant (1-\beta)$: $V_x = 0$

Bending moments when $x \leqslant \alpha$: $M_x = -Fl[\frac{1}{2}(1+\alpha-\beta) - x]$

when $\alpha \leqslant x \leqslant (1-\beta)$: $M_x = -\frac{1}{2}Fl\left[(1+\alpha-\beta-2x) + \dfrac{(x-\alpha)^2}{(1-\alpha-\beta)}\right]$

when $x \geqslant (1-\beta)$: $M_x = 0$

Deflections: when $x \leqslant \alpha$: $a_x = -(Fl^3x^2/12EI)[3(1+\alpha-\beta) - 2x]$

when $\alpha \leqslant x \leqslant (1-\beta)$: $a_x = -(Fl^3/24EI)[6x^2(1+\alpha-\beta-\frac{2}{3}x) + \{(x-\alpha)^4/(1-\alpha-\beta)\}]$

when $x \geqslant (1-\beta)$: $a_x = -(Fl^3/24EI)[2\alpha(1-\beta)(1+\alpha-\beta-2x) - (1+\alpha-\beta)^2(1+\alpha-\beta-4x)]$

PARTIAL TRIANGULAR LOAD: *apex at right-hand end*

Shearing forces: when $x \leqslant \alpha$: $V_x = F$

when $\alpha \leqslant x \leqslant (1-\beta)$: $V_x = F\left[1 - \dfrac{(x-\alpha)^2}{(1-\alpha-\beta)^2}\right]$

when $x \geqslant (1-\beta)$: $V_x = 0$

Bending moments: when $x \leqslant \alpha$: $M_x = -\frac{1}{3}Fl(2+\alpha-2\beta-3x)$

when $\alpha \leqslant x \leqslant (1-\beta)$: $M_x = -\frac{1}{3}Fl\left[(2+\alpha-2\beta-3x) + \dfrac{(x-\alpha)^3}{(1-\alpha-\beta)^2}\right]$

when $x \geqslant (1-\beta)$: $M_x = 0$

Deflections: when $x \leqslant \alpha$: $a_x = -(Fl^3x^2/6EI)(2+\alpha-2\beta-x)$

when $\alpha \leqslant x \leqslant (1-\beta)$: $a_x = -(Fl^3/60EI)[10x^2(2+\alpha-2\beta-x) + \{(x-\alpha)^5/(1-\alpha-\beta)^2\}]$

when $x \geqslant (1-\beta)$: $a_x = -(Fl^3/60EI)[(1-\beta)\{a^2 + 10x(1-\beta) - 3(1-\beta)^2\} - (1+\alpha-\beta)^2(1+\alpha-\beta-5x)]$

KEY TO SIGN CONVENTION FOR *TABLES* 23 TO 26

	Reaction	Shearing force	Bending moment	Slope	Deflection
Positive					
Negative					

F total load
x distance of point considered from left-hand support in terms of l

Members with fixed ends
To determine deflection, moment etc. for member with one or both ends fixed or continuous, first calculate deflection, moment etc. for freely supported span. Next, determine deflection, moment etc. throughout span due to action of support moments only. Lastly, obtain final values of deflection, moment etc. by summing foregoing results algebraically.

Slope
To determine slope at any point, distance xl from left-hand support, differentiate expression for deflection with respect to x.

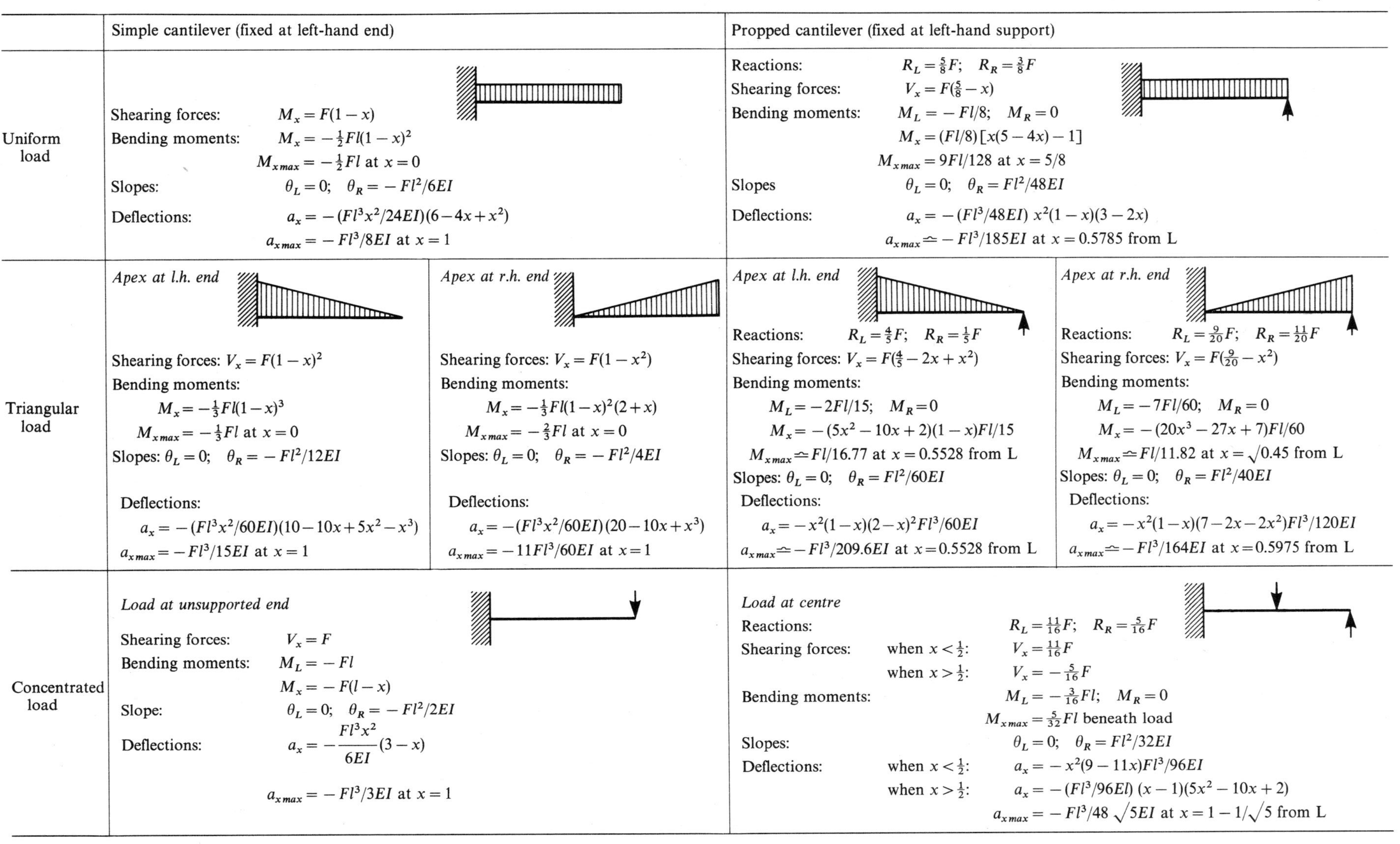

<table>
<tr><th></th><th colspan="2">Simple cantilever (fixed at left-hand end)</th><th colspan="2">Propped cantilever (fixed at left-hand support)</th></tr>
<tr><td>Uniform load</td><td colspan="2">Shearing forces: $M_x = F(1-x)$
Bending moments: $M_x = -\frac{1}{2}Fl(1-x)^2$
$M_{x\,max} = -\frac{1}{2}Fl$ at $x=0$
Slopes: $\theta_L = 0$; $\theta_R = -Fl^2/6EI$
Deflections: $a_x = -(Fl^3x^2/24EI)(6-4x+x^2)$
$a_{x\,max} = -Fl^3/8EI$ at $x=1$</td><td colspan="2">Reactions: $R_L = \frac{5}{8}F$; $R_R = \frac{3}{8}F$
Shearing forces: $V_x = F(\frac{5}{8}-x)$
Bending moments: $M_L = -Fl/8$; $M_R = 0$
$M_x = (Fl/8)[x(5-4x)-1]$
$M_{x\,max} = 9Fl/128$ at $x = 5/8$
Slopes $\theta_L = 0$; $\theta_R = Fl^2/48EI$
Deflections: $a_x = -(Fl^3/48EI)\,x^2(1-x)(3-2x)$
$a_{x\,max} \simeq -Fl^3/185EI$ at $x = 0.5785$ from L</td></tr>
<tr><td>Triangular load</td><td>Apex at l.h. end
Shearing forces: $V_x = F(1-x)^2$
Bending moments:
$M_x = -\frac{1}{3}Fl(1-x)^3$
$M_{x\,max} = -\frac{1}{3}Fl$ at $x=0$
Slopes: $\theta_L = 0$; $\theta_R = -Fl^2/12EI$
Deflections:
$a_x = -(Fl^3x^2/60EI)(10-10x+5x^2-x^3)$
$a_{x\,max} = -Fl^3/15EI$ at $x=1$</td><td>Apex at r.h. end
Shearing forces: $V_x = F(1-x^2)$
Bending moments:
$M_x = -\frac{1}{3}Fl(1-x)^2(2+x)$
$M_{x\,max} = -\frac{2}{3}Fl$ at $x=0$
Slopes: $\theta_L = 0$; $\theta_R = -Fl^2/4EI$
Deflections:
$a_x = -(Fl^3x^2/60EI)(20-10x+x^3)$
$a_{x\,max} = -11Fl^3/60EI$ at $x=1$</td><td>Apex at l.h. end
Reactions: $R_L = \frac{4}{5}F$; $R_R = \frac{1}{5}F$
Shearing forces: $V_x = F(\frac{4}{5}-2x+x^2)$
Bending moments:
$M_L = -2Fl/15$; $M_R = 0$
$M_x = -(5x^2-10x+2)(1-x)Fl/15$
$M_{x\,max} \simeq Fl/16.77$ at $x = 0.5528$ from L
Slopes: $\theta_L = 0$; $\theta_R = Fl^2/60EI$
Deflections:
$a_x = -x^2(1-x)(2-x)^2Fl^3/60EI$
$a_{x\,max} \simeq -Fl^3/209.6EI$ at $x = 0.5528$ from L</td><td>Apex at r.h. end
Reactions: $R_L = \frac{9}{20}F$; $R_R = \frac{11}{20}F$
Shearing forces: $V_x = F(\frac{9}{20}-x^2)$
Bending moments:
$M_L = -7Fl/60$; $M_R = 0$
$M_x = -(20x^3-27x+7)Fl/60$
$M_{x\,max} \simeq Fl/11.82$ at $x = \sqrt{0.45}$ from L
Slopes: $\theta_L = 0$; $\theta_R = Fl^2/40EI$
Deflections:
$a_x = -x^2(1-x)(7-2x-2x^2)Fl^3/120EI$
$a_{x\,max} \simeq -Fl^3/164EI$ at $x = 0.5975$ from L</td></tr>
<tr><td>Concentrated load</td><td colspan="2">Load at unsupported end
Shearing forces: $V_x = F$
Bending moments: $M_L = -Fl$
$M_x = -F(l-x)$
Slope: $\theta_L = 0$; $\theta_R = -Fl^2/2EI$
Deflections: $a_x = -\dfrac{Fl^3x^2}{6EI}(3-x)$
$a_{x\,max} = -Fl^3/3EI$ at $x=1$</td><td colspan="2">Load at centre
Reactions: $R_L = \frac{11}{16}F$; $R_R = \frac{5}{16}F$
Shearing forces: when $x < \frac{1}{2}$: $V_x = \frac{11}{16}F$
when $x > \frac{1}{2}$: $V_x = -\frac{5}{16}F$
Bending moments: $M_L = -\frac{3}{16}Fl$; $M_R = 0$
$M_{x\,max} = \frac{5}{32}Fl$ beneath load
Slopes: $\theta_L = 0$; $\theta_R = Fl^2/32EI$
Deflections: when $x < \frac{1}{2}$: $a_x = -x^2(9-11x)Fl^3/96EI$
when $x > \frac{1}{2}$: $a_x = -(Fl^3/96EI)\,(x-1)(5x^2-10x+2)$
$a_{x\,max} = -Fl^3/48\sqrt{5}EI$ at $x = 1-1/\sqrt{5}$ from L</td></tr>
</table>

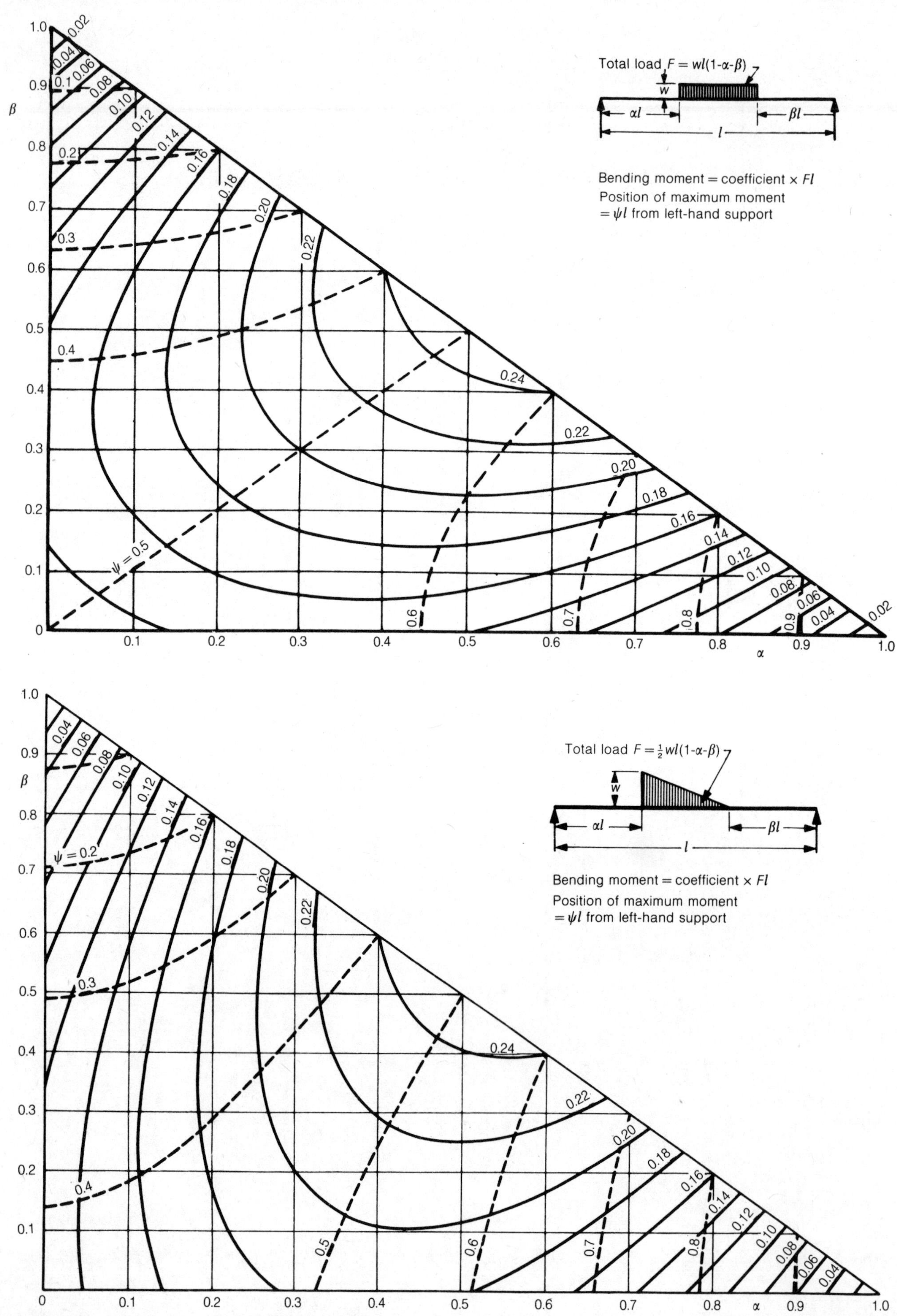
Total load $F = wl(1-\alpha-\beta)$
w
αl
βl
l
Bending moment = coefficient × Fl
Position of maximum moment
= ψl from left-hand support
$\psi = 0.5$
α
β
Total load $F = \frac{1}{2}wl(1-\alpha-\beta)$
w
αl
βl
l
Bending moment = coefficient × Fl
Position of maximum moment
= ψl from left-hand support
$\psi = 0.2$
α
β

Freely supported beams: maximum deflections

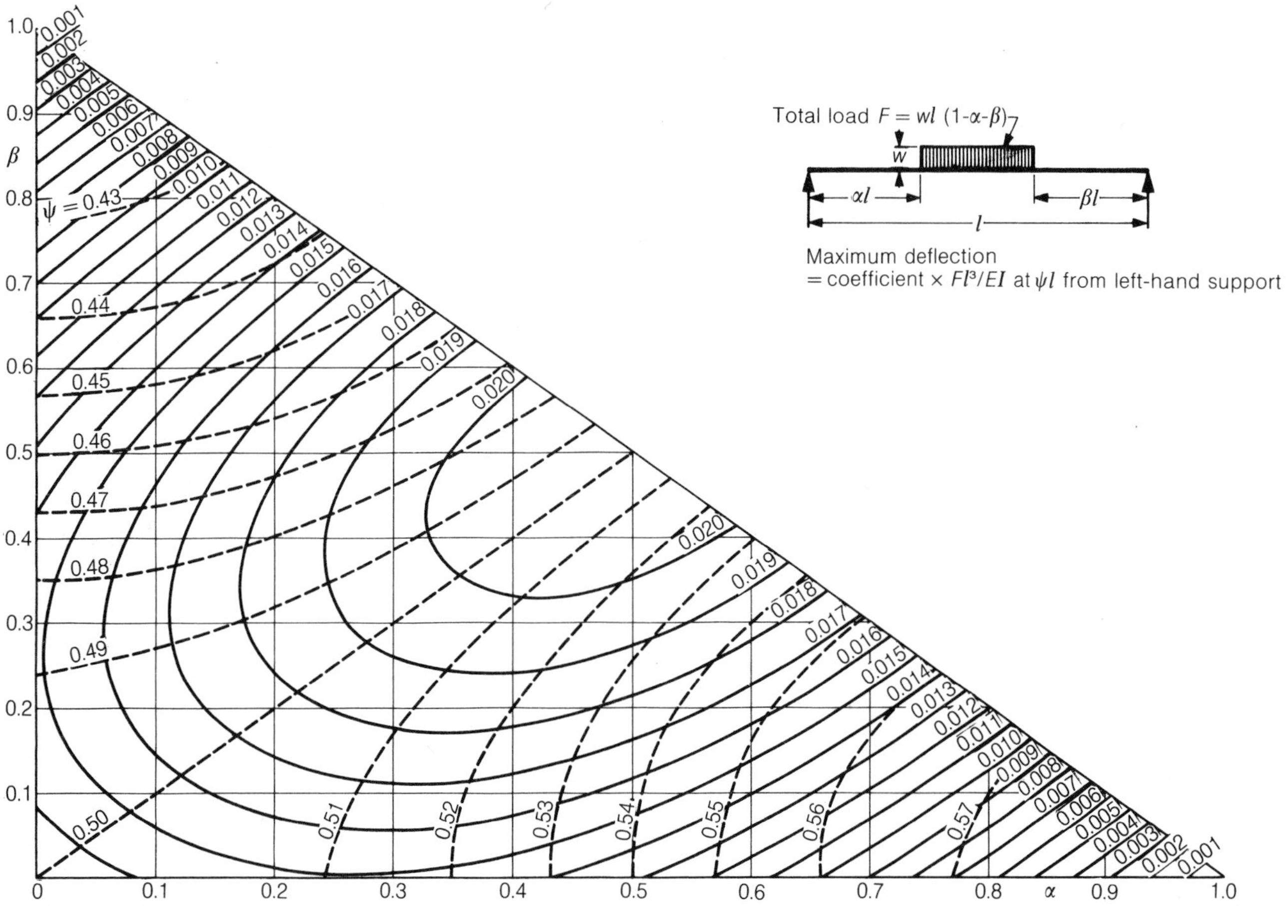
Total load $F = wl\,(1-\alpha-\beta)$
w
αl
βl
l
Maximum deflection
= coefficient × Fl^3/EI at ψl from left-hand support
ψ = 0.43
β
α

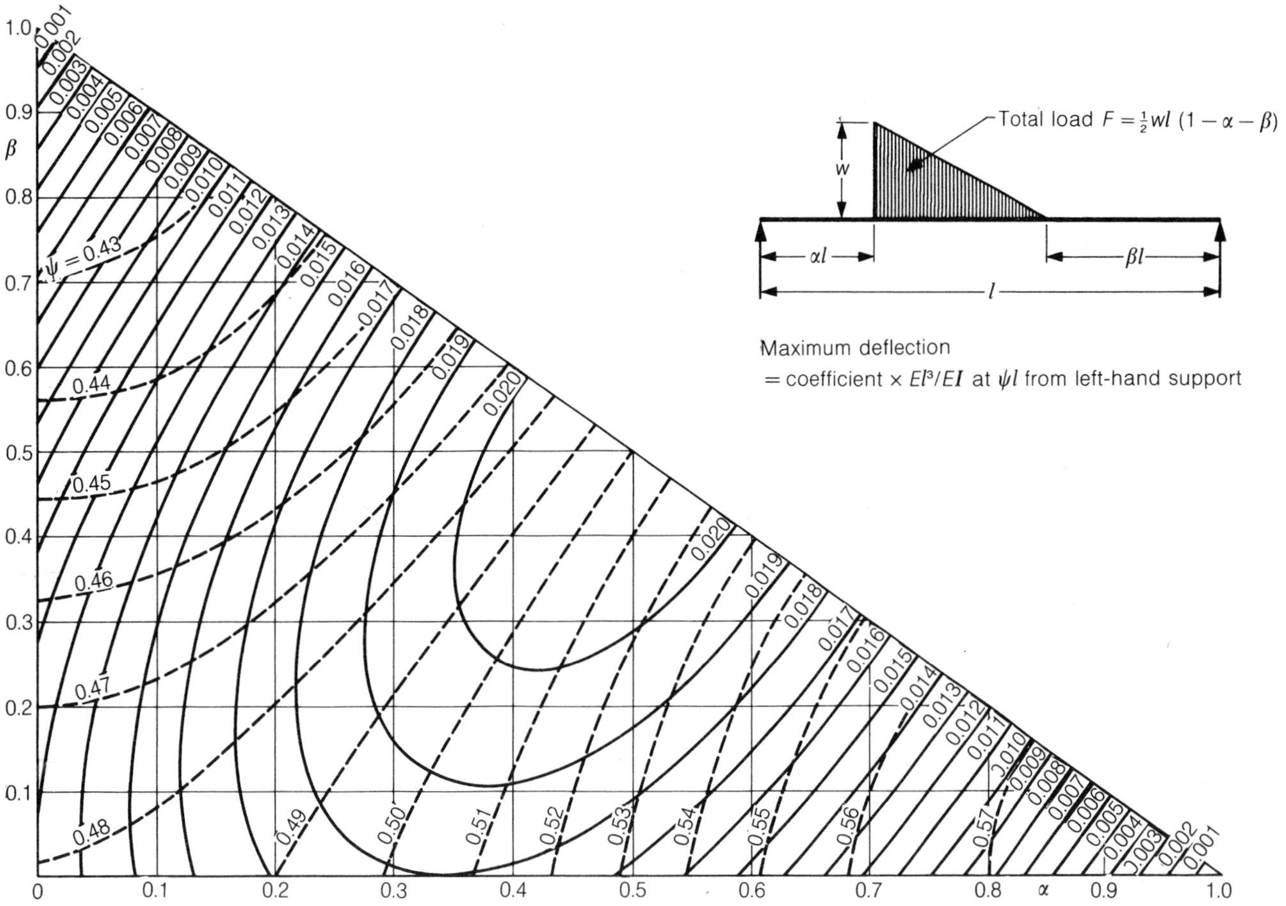
Total load $F = \frac{1}{2}wl\,(1-\alpha-\beta)$
w
αl
βl
l
Maximum deflection
= coefficient × El^3/EI at ψl from left-hand support
ψ = 0.43
β
α

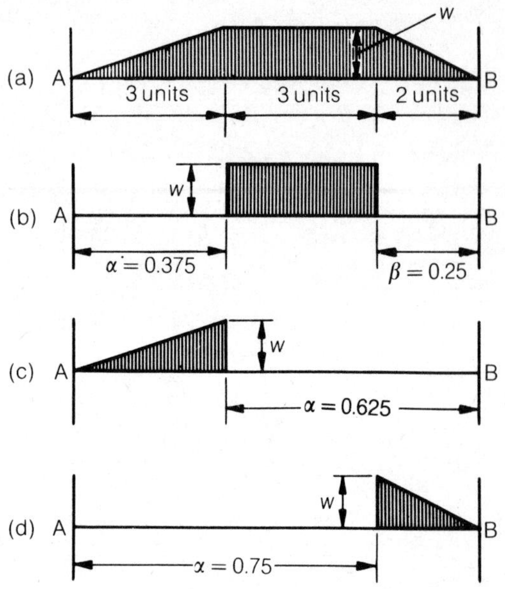

(i) The loading shown in diagram (a) can be subdivided into the three separate arrangements shown in diagrams (b), (c) and (d).

To obtain C_{AB}:

For the uniform load, $\alpha = 0.375$ and $\beta = 0.25$ thus $C_{AB} = 0.104W = 0.0390wl$ (since $W = 0.375wl$).
For the right-hand triangular load, $\alpha = 0.75$ and $\beta = 0$: thus $C_{AB} = 0.025W = 0.0031wl$ (since $W = 0.25wl/2$).
For the left-hand triangular load, $\alpha = 0.625$ and $\beta = 0$: thus $C_{AB} = 0.130W = 0.0244wl$ (since $W = (1/2)0.375wl$).
Thus total $C_{AB} = 0.0390 + 0.0031 + 0.0244 = 0.0665wl$.

Similarly, to obtain C_{BA}:

For the uniform load, $\alpha = 0.25$ and $\beta = 0.375$: $C_{BA} = 0.129W = 0.0489wl$.
For the left-hand triangular load, $\alpha = 0.625$ and $\beta = 0$: $C_{BA} = 0.049W = 0.0092wl$.
For the right-hand triangular load, $\alpha = 0.75$ and $\beta = 0$: $C_{BA} = 0.110W = 0.0138wl$.
Thus total $C_{BA} = 0.0489 + 0.0092 + 0.0138 = 0.0719wl$.

(ii) With $\alpha = 0.375$ and $\beta = 0.25$, $C_{AB} = 0.097W = 0.0667wl$. With $\alpha = 0.25$ and $\beta = 0.375$, $C_{BA} = 0.104W = 0.0719wl$.

Fixed-end-moment coefficients: general data

The fixed-end-moment coefficients C_{AB} and C_{BA} can be used as follows.

1. To obtain bending moments at supports of single-span beams fixed at both ends (see *Table 24*)

$$M_{AB} = -C_{AB}l_{AB} \qquad M_{BA} = -C_{BA}l_{AB} \qquad \text{With symmetrical load } M_{AB} = M_{BA}$$

2. For continuous beams: moment-distribution methods (see *Table 40*)

Fixed-end moments (i.e. span-load factors) are $FEM_{AB} = C_{AB}l_{AB}$ $\quad FEM_{BA} = C_{BA}l_{AB}$ $\quad$ With symmetrical load $FEM_{AB} = FEM_{BA}$

3. Framed structures (see *Table 65*) Loading factors $P(=F_{AB})$ and $Q(=F_{BA})$ have the following values:

$$F_{AB} = C_{AB}l_{AB} \qquad F_{BA} = C_{BA}l_{AB} \qquad \text{With symmetrical load } F_{AB} = F_{BA} = A_{AB}/l_{AB} = C_{AB}l_{AB}$$

4. Portal frames (see *Tables 70–73*) and **Method of fixed points** (see *Table 41*)

$$D = \frac{\text{area of free BM diagram}}{\text{loaded span}}\left[= \frac{A}{l} \text{ or } \frac{A}{l/2} \text{ or } \frac{A}{h} \text{ or } \frac{A}{\psi h}\right] = \frac{C_{AB}+C_{BA}}{2}l_{AB}; \qquad z = \frac{C_{AB}+2C_{BA}}{3(C_{AB}+C_{BA})}$$

Distance from left-hand or lower support to centroid of free BM diagram $= z \times$ span

Unsymmetrical loading

Loading (beam A–B, span l_{AB})	Fixed-end-moment coefficients C_{AB}	C_{BA}
F_1, F_2, F_3 at $\alpha_1 l$, $\alpha_2 l$, $\alpha_3 l$; Any number of loads	$\sum\alpha(1-\alpha)^2F$	$\sum\alpha^2(1-\alpha)F$
F at αl	$\alpha(1-\alpha)^2F$ or read values from *Table 30*	$\alpha^2(1-\alpha)F$
F(total), uniform, αl, βl	Read values from *Table 31* or use formula in section 11.1.1	
F(total), triangular, αl, βl	Read values from *Table 30* or use formulae in section 11.1.1.	
F(total), trapezoidal, αl, βl	Read values from *Table 31* or use formulae in section 11.1.1	
M at αl	$\frac{M}{l}(3\alpha-1)(\alpha-1)$	$\frac{M\alpha}{l}(2-3\alpha)$

Symmetrical loading

Loading (beam A–B, span l_{AB})	Fixed-end-moment coefficients $C_{AB} = C_{BA}$
F/j F/j F/j F/j; Any number of loads (j) equally spaced	$\frac{(j+2)}{12(j+1)}F$ j – factor: 1 – $0.125F$ 2 – $0.111F$ 3 – $0.104F$ 4 – $0.100F$
$0.5F$ $0.5F$; αl, αl	$\frac{\alpha}{2}(1-\alpha)F$
$\frac{1}{2}\alpha l$, $\frac{1}{2}\alpha l$; $\frac{1}{2}l$; F(total)	$\frac{1}{8}\left(1-\frac{\alpha^2}{3}\right)F$
F(total), uniform over l	$\frac{1}{12}F$
F(total), triangular	$\frac{5}{48}F$
F(total), Parabolic	$\frac{1}{10}F$
F(total), trapezoidal, αl, αl	$\frac{(1+\alpha-\alpha^2)}{12}F$
M, M; αl, αl	$\frac{M}{l}(1-2\alpha)$

Other loadings can generally be considered by combining tabulated cases, thus:

 = plus 

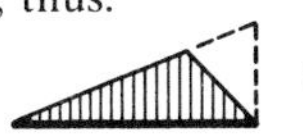 = 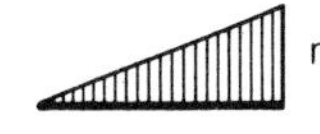 minus 

Fixed-end-moment coefficients: partial triangular loads

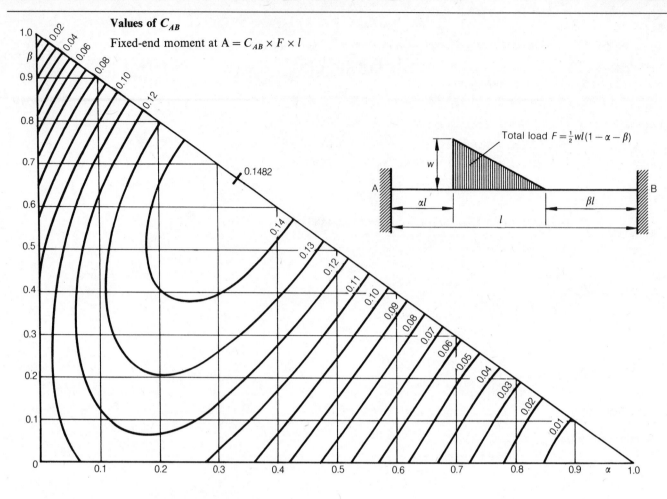

Values of C_{AB}

Fixed-end moment at A $= C_{AB} \times F \times l$

Total load $F = \frac{1}{2}wl(1 - \alpha - \beta)$

Values of C_{BA}

Fixed-end moment at B $= C_{BA} \times F \times l$

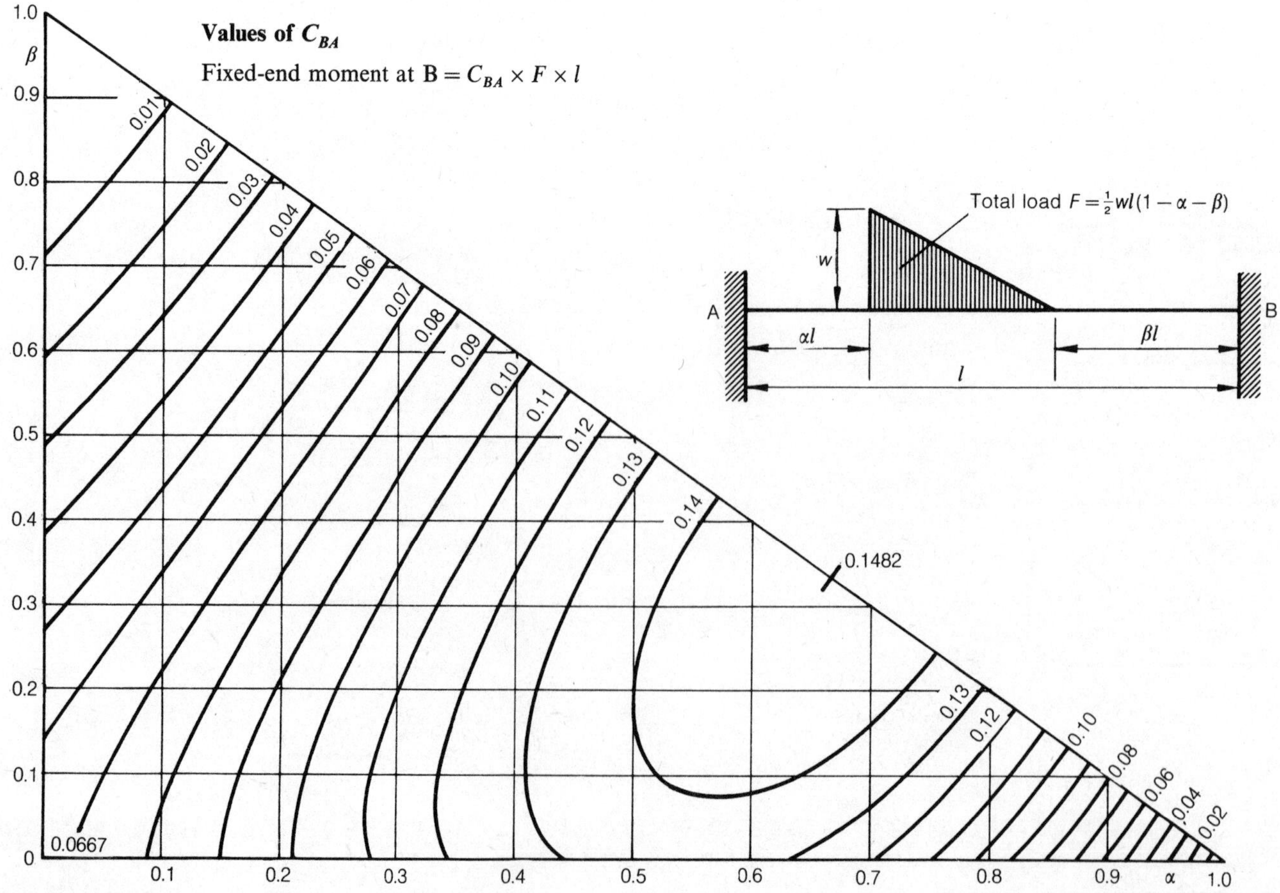

Total load $F = \frac{1}{2}wl(1 - \alpha - \beta)$

Fixed-end-moment coefficients: partial uniform and trapezoidal loads

Values of C_{AB} for partial uniform load

Fixed-end moment at A $= C_{AB} \times F \times l$
To evaluate fixed-end moment at B, transpose α and β to determine C_{BA}: then $FEM_{BA} = C_{BA} \times F \times l$

Total load $F = wl(1 - \alpha - \beta)$

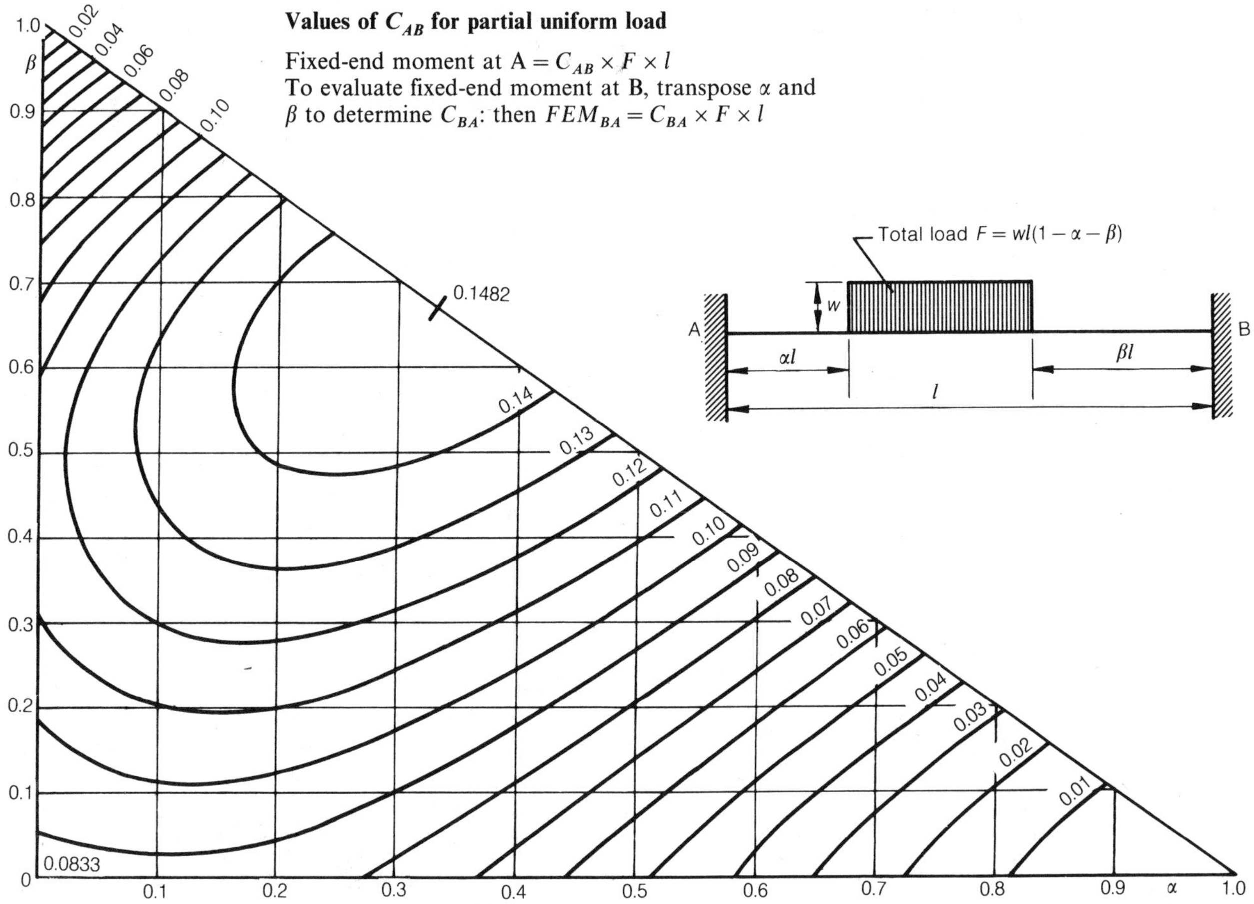

Values of C_{AB} for trapezoidal load

Fixed-end moment at A $= C_{AB} \times F \times l$
To evaluate fixed-end moment at B, transpose α and β to determine C_{BA}: then $FEM_{BA} = C_{BA} \times F \times l$

Total load $F = \frac{1}{2}wl(2 - \alpha - \beta)$

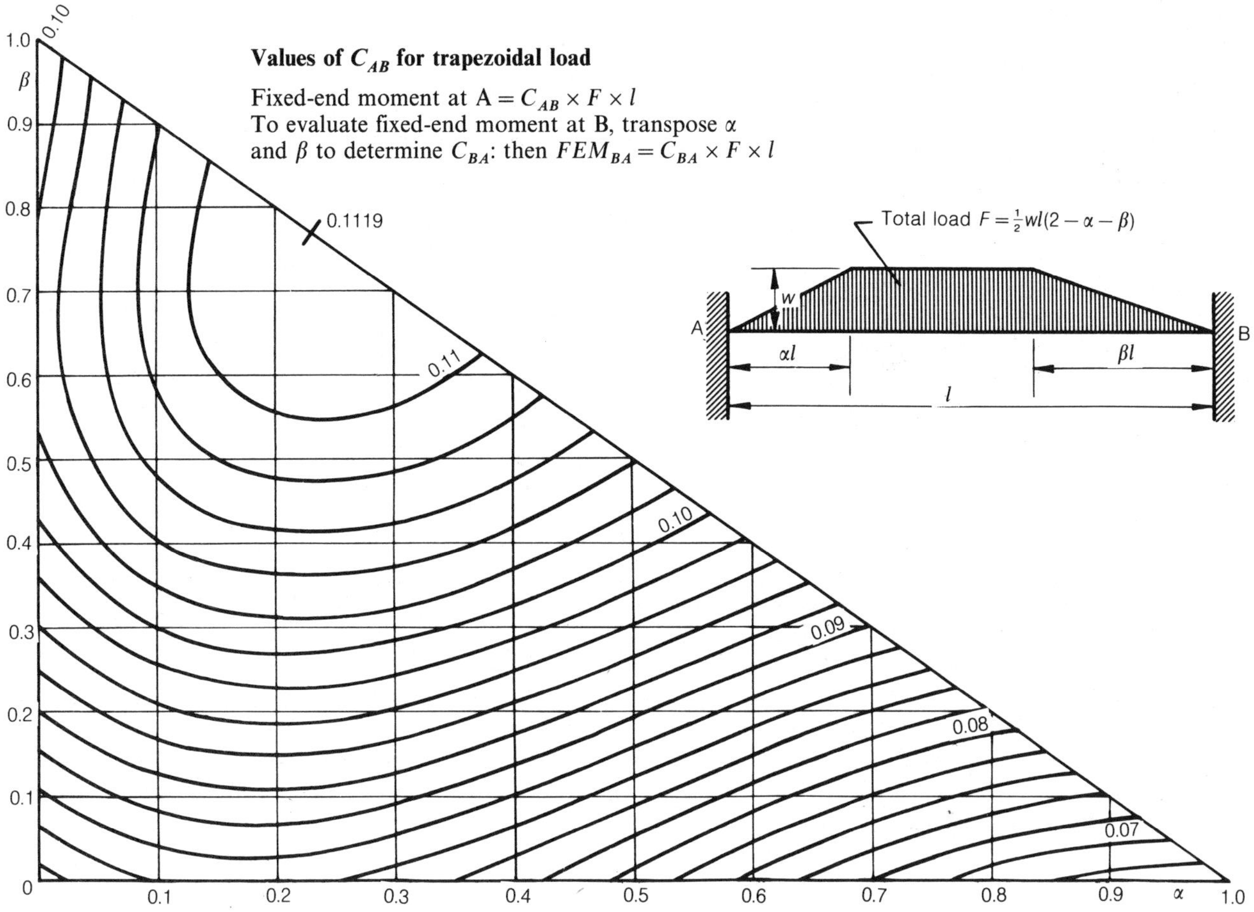

Chapter 12
Continuous beams

Unless otherwise stated, formulae and coefficients on tables in this chapter give service bending moments and shearing forces corresponding to unfactored characteristic loads. To obtain ultimate moments and shearing forces for limit-state design, all loads must be multiplied by the partial safety factor for loads appropriate to the particular limit-state being considered.

Some general notes on the analysis of systems of continuous beams are given in the introduction to Chapter 3.

12.1 MAXIMUM BENDING MOMENTS

12.1.1 Incidence of imposed load to produce maximum bending moments

The values of the bending moments at the support and in the span depend upon the incidence of the imposed load, and for equal spans or with spans approximately equal the dispositions of imposed load illustrated in *Table 22* give the maximum positive bending moment at midspan, and the maximum negative bending moment at a support. Both BS8110 and CP110 require a less severe incidence of imposed load to be considered when determining the maximum negative moment over any support. According to CP110 only the spans immediately on either side of the support under consideration need be loaded. This affects only the coefficients for four or more continuous spans and the reduction is commonly much less than 5%.

According to BS8110 the maximum support moments that need to be considered are those which occur when all spans are loaded with dead and imposed load.

When undertaking limit-state design according to the requirements of BS8110 or CP110, the spans carrying the maximum load to produce the critical condition at the section under consideration should support a total load of $1.4g_k + 1.6q_k$, while the spans carrying the minimum load should support a load of only $1.0g_k$, where g_k and q_k are the characteristic dead and imposed ultimate loads respectively. These requirements are met most simply by analysing the system for a 'dead load' of $1.0g_k$ over all spans and for an 'imposed load' of $0.4g_k + 1.6q_k$ acting only on those spans that will cause the maximum moment to be induced at the section being considered. As required by CP110 the latter are, for maximum support moments, the spans on each side of the support only; for maximum span moment they are the span under consideration and all alternate spans.

Since, to determine the maximum positive moment according to BS8110, the span currently being considered and all alternate spans must carry imposed load, the maximum positive moments throughout the system can be determined by considering two loading systems only, the first with imposed load on all odd-numbered spans and the second with this load on all even-numbered spans. Also, since this Code requires all spans to carry imposed load when determining the maximum support moments, the latter condition can be considered by summing the results obtained from the two loading conditions to obtain the maximum positive moments.

12.1.2 Positive and negative bending moments in the span

When the negative bending moments at the supports of a continuous beam have been determined, the positive bending moments on a loaded span can be determined graphically or, in the case of a uniformly distributed load, by means of the expressions in *Table 32*.

Beams and slabs, such as those in bridge decks, where the ratio of imposed load to dead load is high, should be designed for a possible negative bending moment occurring at midspan. Formulae for the approximate evaluation of this bending moment, which apply if the lengths of adjacent spans do not differ by more than 20% of the shorter span, are given in *Table 32*. These formulae make some allowance for the torsional restraint of the supports.

12.1.3 Shearing forces

The variation of shearing force on a continuous beam is determined by first considering each span as freely supported and algebraically adding the rate of change of restraint moment for the span considered. Formulae for calculating the component and resultant shearing forces are given in *Table 32*. The shearing force due to the load can be determined from statics. The shearing force due to the restraint moments is constant throughout the span.

Continuous beams and slabs: general data

Shearing forces

Due to load

$$V'_T = \frac{z_0}{l_{ST}} F$$

$$V'_S = -\frac{l_{ST} - z_0}{l_{ST}} F = -(F - V'_T)$$

Due to end restraint

$$V_M = \frac{M_{ST} - M_{TS}}{l_{ST}}$$

Resultant shearing forces

$$V_S = V'_S + V_M$$

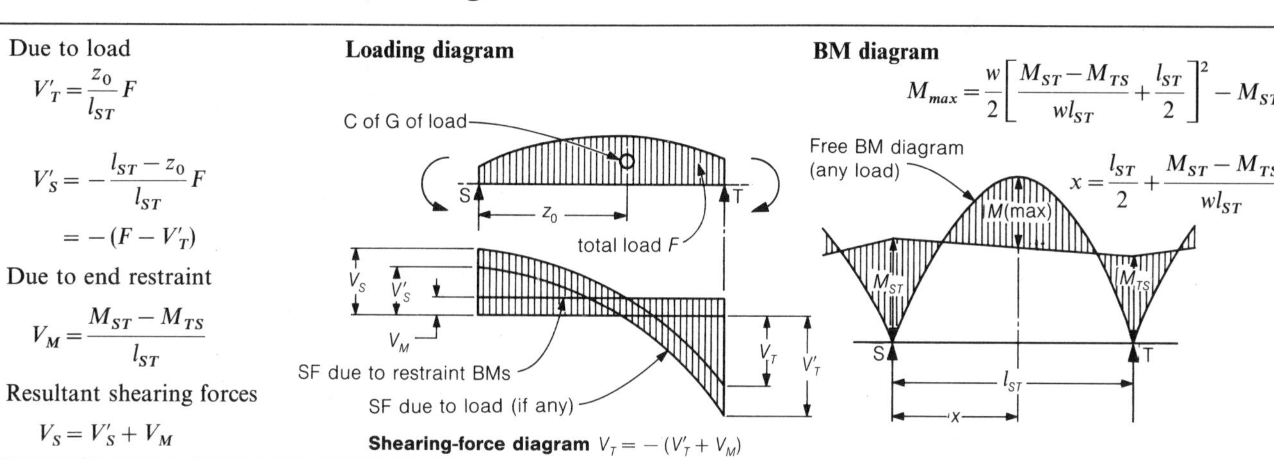

$$M_{max} = \frac{w}{2}\left[\frac{M_{ST} - M_{TS}}{wl_{ST}} + \frac{l_{ST}}{2}\right]^2 - M_{ST}$$

$$x = \frac{l_{ST}}{2} + \frac{M_{ST} - M_{TS}}{wl_{ST}}$$

Approximate bending-moment coefficients

Uniformly distributed load on equal spans (applicable to three or more spans)

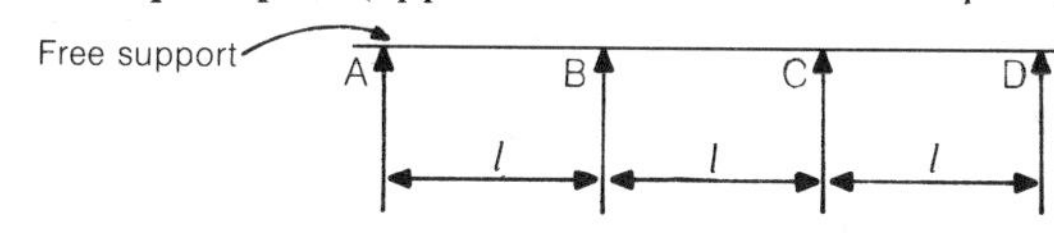

Bending moment = coefficient × total load × l

Coefficients apply also to unequal spans if inequality does not exceed 15% of the longest span.

	Beams	Slabs	Beams and slabs			Slabs only. Monolithic with end support A (nominally freely supported). Coefficients for total load		
	BS8110 $q_k \ngtr g_k$ Total load	BS8110 $q_k \ngtr g_k$ Total load	CP110 $q_k \ngtr g_k$ Total load	Commonly used coefficients: Dead load g_k	Commonly used coefficients: Imposed load q_k	Without splays	With splays	Minimum proportions of splays
End span AB about midspan	+1/11.1	+1/11.6	+1/11	+1/12	+1/10	+1/10	+1/12	
Penultimate support B	−1/9.1	−1/11.6	−1/9	−1/10	−1/9	−1/10	−1/9	
Interior span BC etc. about midspan	+1/14.3	+1/16.0	+1/14	+1/24	+1/12	+1/12	+1/16	
Interior supports C etc.	−1/12.5	−1/16.0	−1/10	−1/12	−1/9	−1/12	−1/10	
End support A	—	—	—	—	—	−1/24	−1/16	

Effect on equal spans of moments applied at end supports

		Bending moment applied at A only				Equal bending moments applied at A and K			
Number of spans		2	3	4	5	2	3	4	5
Bending moment	M_A	−1.000	−1.000	−1.000	−1.000	−1.000	−1.000	−1.000	−1.000
	M_B	+0.250	+0.267	+0.268	+0.268	+0.500	+0.200	+0.286	+0.263
	M_C	—	—	−0.071	−0.072	—	—	−0.143	−0.053
	M_H	—	—	—	+0.019	—	—	—	−0.053
	M_J	—	−0.067	+0.018	−0.005	—	+0.200	+0.286	+0.263
	M_K	0	0	0	0	−1.000	−1.000	−1.000	−1.000
Shearing force	V_{AR}	+1.250	+1.267	+1.268	+1.268	+1.500	+1.200	+1.286	+1.263
	V_{BL}	−1.250	−1.267	−1.268	−1.268	−1.500	−1.200	−1.286	−1.263
	V_{BR}	−0.250	−0.333	−0.339	−0.340	−1.500	0	−0.429	−0.316
	V_{CL}	—	—	+0.339	+0.340	—	—	+0.429	+0.316
	V_{CR}	—	—	+0.089	+0.091	—	—	—	0
	V_{HL}	—	—	—	−0.091	—	—	—	0
	V_{HR}	—	—	—	−0.024	—	—	+0.429	+0.316
	V_{JL}	—	+0.333	−0.089	+0.024	—	0	−0.429	−0.316
	V_{JR}	—	+0.067	−0.018	+0.005	—	−1.200	−1.286	−1.263
	V_{KL}	+0.250	−0.067	+0.018	−0.005	+1.500	+1.200	+1.286	+1.263

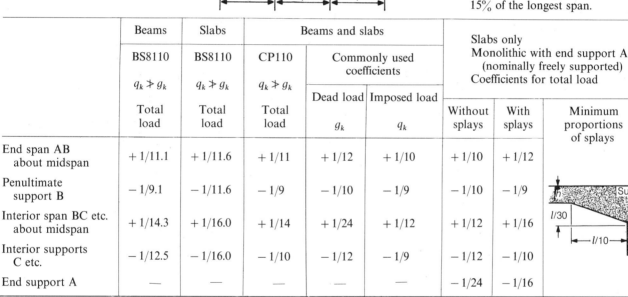

Key:

A B K

A B J K

A B C J K

A B C H J K

Adjustment to bending moment = M-coefficient × applied bending moment

$$\text{Adjustment to shearing force} = \frac{V\text{-coefficient} \times \text{applied bending moment}}{\text{span}}$$

Continuous beams: moments from equal loads on equal spans—1

Load	All spans loaded (e.g. dead load): support moments	All spans loaded (e.g. dead load): span moments	Imposed load (sequence of loaded spans to give max. bending moment): support moments	Imposed load (sequence of loaded spans to give max. bending moment): span moments
Uniformly distributed	0.125	0.070, 0.070	0.125	0.096, 0.096
	0.100, 0.100	0.080, 0.025, 0.080	0.117, 0.117	0.101, 0.075, 0.101
	0.107, 0.071, 0.107	0.077, 0.036, 0.036, 0.077	[0.107] [0.071] [0.107] (0.116) (0.107) (0.116) 0.121, 0.107, 0.121	0.099, 0.081, 0.081, 0.099
	0.105, 0.079, 0.079, 0.105	0.078, 0.033, 0.046, 0.033, 0.078	[0.105] [0.079] [0.079] [0.105] (0.116) (0.106) (0.106) (0.116) 0.120, 0.111, 0.111, 0.120	0.100, 0.079, 0.086, 0.079, 0.100
0.1*l* / 0.1*l*	0.136	0.077, 0.077	0.136	0.105, 0.105
	0.109, 0.109	0.088, 0.028, 0.088	0.127, 0.127	0.111, 0.083, 0.111
	0.117, 0.078, 0.117	0.085, 0.040, 0.040, 0.085	[0.117] [0.078] [0.117] (0.127) (0.117) (0.127) 0.131, 0.117, 0.131	0.109, 0.089, 0.089, 0.109
	0.115, 0.086, 0.086, 0.115	0.086, 0.037, 0.051, 0.037, 0.086	[0.115] [0.086] [0.086] [0.115] (0.126) (0.116) (0.116) (0.126) 0.131, 0.121, 0.121, 0.131	0.110, 0.087, 0.094, 0.087, 0.110
0.2*l* / 0.2*l*	0.145	0.084, 0.084	0.145	0.114, 0.114
	0.116, 0.116	0.095, 0.032, 0.095	0.135, 0.135	0.120, 0.090, 0.120
	0.124, 0.083, 0.124	0.092, 0.045, 0.045, 0.092	[0.124] [0.083] [0.124] (0.135) (0.124) (0.135) 0.140, 0.124, 0.140	0.118, 0.096, 0.096, 0.118
	0.122, 0.092, 0.092, 0.122	0.093, 0.041, 0.056, 0.041, 0.093	[0.122] [0.092] [0.092] [0.122] (0.135) (0.123) (0.123) (0.135) 0.139, 0.129, 0.129, 0.139	0.119, 0.095, 0.102, 0.095, 0.119
0.3*l* / 0.3*l*	0.151	0.090, 0.090	0.151	0.121, 0.121
	0.121, 0.121	0.102, 0.036, 0.102	0.141, 0.141	0.128, 0.097, 0.128
	0.130, 0.086, 0.130	0.098, 0.050, 0.050, 0.098	[0.130] [0.086] [0.130] (0.140) (0.130) (0.140) 0.146, 0.130, 0.146	0.126, 0.103, 0.103, 0.126
	0.127, 0.096, 0.096, 0.127	0.099, 0.046, 0.062, 0.046, 0.099	[0.127] [0.096] [0.096] [0.127] (0.140) (0.129) (0.129) (0.140) 0.145, 0.135, 0.135, 0.145	0.127, 0.102, 0.109, 0.102, 0.127

Continuous beams: moments from equal loads on equal spans—2

Load	Spans	All spans loaded (e.g. dead load): above line (supports)	All spans loaded: below line (spans)	Imposed load (sequence of loaded spans to give max. bending moment): above line (supports)	Imposed load: below line (spans)
0.4l — 0.4l	2	0.155	0.094, 0.094	0.155	0.127, 0.127
0.4l — 0.4l	3	0.124, 0.124	0.107, 0.040, 0.107	0.145, 0.145	0.134, 0.102, 0.134
0.4l — 0.4l	4	0.133, 0.089, 0.133	0.103, 0.054, 0.054, 0.103	[0.133] (0.144) 0.149, [0.089] (0.133) 0.133, [0.133] (0.144) 0.149	0.132, 0.109, 0.109, 0.132
0.4l — 0.4l	5	0.131, 0.098, 0.098, 0.131	0.104, 0.050, 0.066, 0.050, 0.104	[0.131] (0.144) 0.149, [0.098] (0.132) 0.138, [0.098] (0.132) 0.138, [0.131] (0.144) 0.149	0.133, 0.107, 0.115, 0.107, 0.133
0.5l — 0.5l	2	0.156	0.095, 0.095	0.156	0.129, 0.129
0.5l — 0.5l	3	0.125, 0.125	0.108, 0.042, 0.108	0.146, 0.146	0.136, 0.104, 0.136
0.5l — 0.5l	4	0.134, 0.089, 0.134	0.104, 0.056, 0.056, 0.104	[0.134] (0.145) 0.151, [0.089] (0.134) 0.134, [0.134] (0.145) 0.151	0.134, 0.111, 0.111, 0.134
0.5l — 0.5l	5	0.132, 0.099, 0.099, 0.132	0.105, 0.051, 0.068, 0.051, 0.105	[0.132] (0.145) 0.150, [0.099] (0.133) 0.139, [0.099] (0.133) 0.139, [0.132] (0.145) 0.150	0.135, 0.109, 0.117, 0.109, 0.135
Concentrated at midspan	2	0.188	0.156, 0.156	0.188	0.203, 0.203
Concentrated at midspan	3	0.150, 0.150	0.175, 0.100, 0.175	0.175, 0.175	0.213, 0.175, 0.213
Concentrated at midspan	4	0.161, 0.107, 0.161	0.170, 0.116, 0.116, 0.170	[0.161] (0.174) 0.181, [0.107] (0.161) 0.161, [0.161] (0.174) 0.181	0.210, 0.183, 0.183, 0.210
Concentrated at midspan	5	0.158, 0.118, 0.118, 0.158	0.171, 0.112, 0.132, 0.112, 0.171	[0.158] (0.174) 0.179, [0.118] (0.160) 0.167, [0.118] (0.160) 0.167, [0.158] (0.174) 0.179	0.211, 0.181, 0.191, 0.181, 0.211
Concentrated at third points	2	0.167	0.111, 0.111	0.167	0.139, 0.139
Concentrated at third points	3	0.133, 0.133	0.122, 0.033, 0.122	0.156, 0.156	0.144, 0.100, 0.144
Concentrated at third points	4	0.143, 0.095, 0.143	0.119, 0.056, 0.056, 0.119	[0.143] (0.155) 0.160, [0.095] (0.143) 0.144, [0.143] (0.155) 0.160	0.143, 0.111, 0.111, 0.143
Concentrated at third points	5	0.140, 0.105, 0.105, 0.140	0.120, 0.050, 0.061, 0.050, 0.120	[0.140] (0.155) 0.159, [0.105] (0.142) 0.148, [0.105] (0.142) 0.148, [0.140] (0.155) 0.159	0.144, 0.108, 0.115, 0.108, 0.144

Bending moment = (coefficient) × (total load on one span) × (span)
Bending moment coefficients:
above line apply to negative bending moment at supports
below line apply to positive bending moment in span
Coefficients apply when all spans are equal (or shortest $\not>$ 15% less than longest). Loads on each loaded span are equal. Moment of inertia same throughout all spans.
Bending moments is square brackets (imposed load) apply if all spans are loaded (i.e. BS8110 requirements).
Bending moments coefficients in curved brackets (imposed load) apply if two spans only are loaded (i.e. CP110 requirements).

12.1.4 Approximate bending-moment coefficients

The bending-moment coefficients in *Table 32* apply to beams or slabs (spanning in one direction) continuous over three or more spans. The coefficients given for end spans and penultimate supports assume that the beam or slab is nominally freely supported on the end support. The BS8110 and CP110 coefficients, which are for total load only, are only valid when $g_k \nless q_k$; they correspond approximately to the values that were given in CP114 when $g_k = q_k$. The coefficients given for slabs only, without splays, are values commonly assumed and apply to the total load on a slab spanning in one direction; they take into account the fact that the slab is partially restrained at the end supports because of monolithic construction. If the slab is provided with splays, of sizes not less than indicated in the diagram, the positive bending moments are reduced and the negative bending moments increased; suitable coefficients are also given in *Table 32*.

12.2 CONTINUOUS BEAMS: COEFFICIENTS FOR EQUAL SPANS

12.2.1 Moments and shears from equal loads on equal spans

The coefficients on *Tables 33* and *34* giving the bending moments at the supports due to incidental imposed load apply to the condition where, in addition to the two spans immediately adjoining the support being considered, all the remaining alternate spans are loaded. The coefficients corresponding to the condition where only the two spans immediately adjoining the support are loaded (i.e. that specified in CP110 are shown in curved brackets ( ) and those relating to imposed load covering all spans (i.e. BS8110 requirements) are shown in square brackets [ ].

The coefficients in *Table 35* give the shearing forces at each of the supports due to similar arrangements of loading.

Example 1. Calculate the maximum service bending moments at the centre of the end and central spans and at the penultimate and interior supports on a beam that is continuous over five equal 5 m spans if the dead service load is 20 kN/m and the imposed service load is 20 kN/m.

(i) From *Table 33* (using coefficients for all alternate spans loaded) the service bending moments are as follows:

Penultimate support:
- Dead load: $0.105 \times 20 \times 5^2 =$ 52.5 kN m (negative)
- Imposed load: $0.120 \times 20 \times 5^2 =$ 60.0 kN m (negative)
- Total = 112.5 kN m (negative)

Interior support:
- Dead load: $0.079 \times 20 \times 5^2 =$ 39.5 kN m (negative)
- Imposed load: $0.111 \times 20 \times 5^2 =$ 55.5 kN m (negative)
- Total = 95.0 kN m (negative)

Middle of end span:
- Dead load: $0.078 \times 20 \times 5^2 =$ 39.0 kN m (positive)
- Imposed load: $0.100 \times 20 \times 5^2 =$ 50.0 kN m (positive)
- Total = 89.0 kN m (positive)

Middle of central span:
- Dead load: $0.046 \times 20 \times 5^2 =$ 23.0 kN m (positive)
- Imposed load: $0.086 \times 20 \times 5^2 =$ 43.0 kN m (positive)
- Total = 66.0 kN m (positive)

(ii) By means of *Table 32*, using the coefficients suggested in BS8110. Ratio of imposed to dead service load = 20/20 = 1. Total service load = 20 + 20 = 40 kN/m. The service bending moments are as follows:

- Penultimate support: $40 \times 5^2/9.1 =$ 109.9 kN m (negative)
- Interior support: $40 \times 5^2/12.5 =$ 80.0 kN m (negative)
- Middle of end span: $40 \times 5^2/11.1 =$ 90.1 kN m (positive)
- Middle of interior span: $40 \times 5^2/14.3 =$ 69.9 kN m (positive)

Example 2. Solve, by means of *Tables 33* and *34*, example 1 in section 12.7.

Service bending moment at penultimate support on a beam continuous over four spans:

- Dead service load: $0.107 \times 15 \times 5^2 =$ 40.0 kN m (negative)
- Imposed service load: $0.181 \times 50 \times 5 =$ 45.3 kN m (negative)
- Total = 85.3 kN m (negative)

Example 3. Calculate the maximum ultimate bending moments on a beam continuous over five equal 5 m spans with characteristic dead and imposed loads of 10 kN/m and 20 kN/m respectively, according to the requirements of CP110.

Since $g_k = 10$ kN/m and $q_k = 20$ kN/m, it is necessary to consider a 'dead load' of $10 \times 1.0 = 10$ kN/m and an 'imposed load' of $(10 \times 0.4) + (20 \times 1.6) = 36$ kN/m. Then from *Table 33* (using the coefficients for only those spans adjoining the supports under consideration being loaded) the ultimate bending moments are as follows:

Penultimate support:
- Dead load: $0.105 \times 10 \times 5^2 =$ 26.3 kN m (negative)
- Imposed load: $0.116 \times 36 \times 5^2 =$ 104.4 kN m (negative)
- Total = 130.7 kN m (negative)

Interior support:
- Dead load: $0.079 \times 10 \times 5^2 =$ 20.0 kN m (negative)
- Imposed load: $0.106 \times 36 \times 5^2 =$ 96.3 kN m (negative)
- Total = 116.3 kN m (negative)

Middle of end span:
- Dead load: $0.078 \times 10 \times 5^2 =$ 19.5 kN m (positive)
- Imposed load: $0.100 \times 36 \times 5^2 =$ 90.0 kN m (positive)
- Total = 109.5 kN m (positive)

Middle of central span:
- Dead load: $0.046 \times 10 \times 5^2 =$ 11.5 kN m (positive)
- Imposed load: $0.086 \times 36 \times 5^2 =$ 77.4 kN m (positive)
- Total = 88.9 kN m (positive)

12.2.2 Bending moment diagrams

The bending-moment diagrams and coefficients given in *Tables 36* and *37* apply to beams that are continuous over two, three, or four or more equal spans for the special

Continuous beams: shears from equal loads on equal spans

Load	Spans	All spans loaded (e.g. dead load)	Imposed load (sequence of loaded spans to give max. shearing force)
Uniformly distributed	2	0.375 0.625 0.625 0.375	0.438 0.625 0.625 0.438
	3	0.400 0.500 0.600 0.600 0.500 0.400	0.450 0.583 0.617 0.617 0.583 0.450
	4	0.393 0.536 0.464 0.607 0.607 0.464 0.536 0.393	0.446 0.603 0.571 0.621 0.621 0.571 0.603 0.446
	5	0.395 0.526 0.500 0.474 0.605 0.605 0.474 0.500 0.526 0.395	0.447 0.598 0.591 0.576 0.620 0.620 0.576 0.591 0.598 0.447
Triangularly distributed	2	0.344 0.656 0.656 0.344	0.422 0.656 0.656 0.422
	3	0.375 0.500 0.625 0.625 0.500 0.375	0.437 0.605 0.646 0.646 0.605 0.437
	4	0.366 0.545 0.455 0.634 0.634 0.455 0.545 0.366	0.433 0.628 0.589 0.651 0.651 0.589 0.628 0.433
	5	0.369 0.532 0.500 0.468 0.631 0.631 0.468 0.500 0.532 0.369	0.434 0.622 0.614 0.595 0.649 0.649 0.595 0.614 0.622 0.434
Concentrated at midspan	2	0.313 0.688 0.688 0.313	0.406 0.688 0.688 0.406
	3	0.350 0.500 0.650 0.650 0.500 0.350	0.425 0.625 0.675 0.675 0.625 0.425
	4	0.339 0.554 0.446 0.661 0.661 0.446 0.554 0.339	0.420 0.654 0.607 0.681 0.681 0.607 0.654 0.420
	5	0.342 0.540 0.500 0.460 0.658 0.658 0.460 0.500 0.540 0.342	0.421 0.647 0.636 0.615 0.679 0.679 0.615 0.636 0.647 0.421
Concentrated at third-points	2	0.333 0.667 0.667 0.333	0.417 0.667 0.667 0.417
	3	0.367 0.500 0.633 0.633 0.500 0.367	0.433 0.611 0.656 0.656 0.611 0.433
	4	0.357 0.548 0.452 0.643 0.643 0.452 0.548 0.357	0.429 0.637 0.595 0.661 0.661 0.595 0.637 0.429
	5	0.360 0.535 0.500 0.465 0.640 0.640 0.465 0.500 0.535 0.360	0.430 0.631 0.621 0.602 0.659 0.659 0.602 0.621 0.631 0.480

For any trapezoidal load.

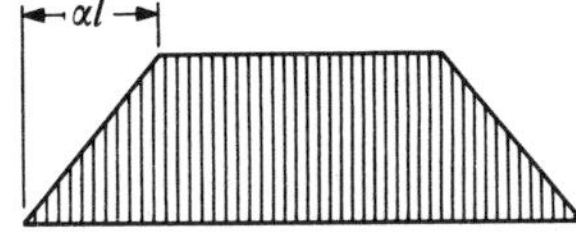

SF coefficient $= (k - \frac{1}{2})(1 + \alpha - \alpha^2) + \frac{1}{2}$ where k is SF coefficient for uniform load, read from above table.
E.g. if $\alpha = 0.5$, coefficient at central support of two-span beam is $(0.625 - 0.5)(1 + 0.5 - 0.25) + 0.5 = 0.656$.

Two spans		Three spans	
Dead load (all spans loaded)	Imposed load	Dead load (all spans loaded)	Imposed load

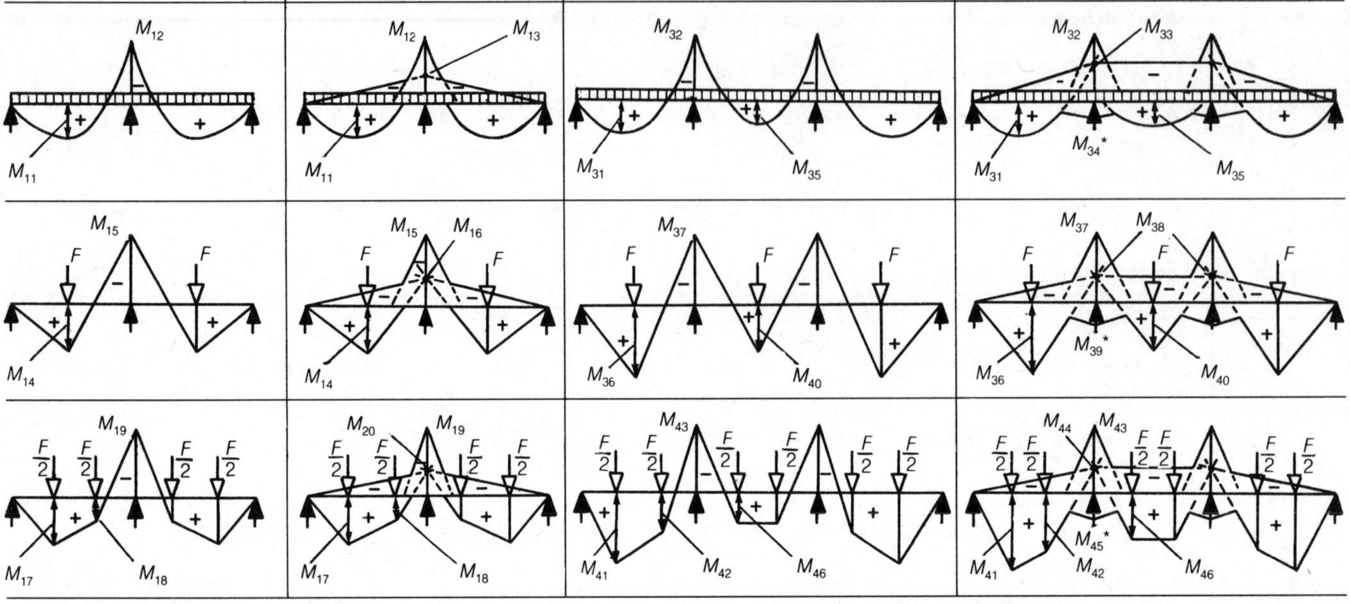

Equal total load F on each loaded span
Bending moment = coefficient × F × span
Diagrams are symmetrical but are not drawn to scale

Moments indicated thus * do not result from loading arrangement prescribed in Codes, which give zero positive moment at all supports.

Values below indicated thus[11] give maximum percentage reduction of span moment due to imposed load possible when support moments have already been reduced by full 30%.

			Dead load (all spans loaded)			Imposed load			Imposed load		
			BS8110 and CP110			BS8110			CP110		
Redistribution			nil	10%	30%	nil	10%	30%	nil	10%	30%
Two spans	Uniform loads	M_{11}	+ 0.070	+ 0.075	+ 0.085	+ 0.096	+ 0.086	+ 0.085[11]	+ 0.096	+ 0.086	+ 0.085[11]
		M_{12}	− 0.125	− 0.113	− 0.088	− 0.125	− 0.113	− 0.088	− 0.125	− 0.113	− 0.088
		M_{13}	—	—	—	− 0.063	− 0.085	− 0.088	− 0.063	− 0.085	− 0.088
	Central point loads	M_{14}	+ 0.156	+ 0.166	+ 0.184	+ 0.203	+ 0.183	+ 0.184[9]	+ 0.203	+ 0.183	+ 0.184[9]
		M_{15}	− 0.188	− 0.169	− 0.131	− 0.188	− 0.169	− 0.131	− 0.188	− 0.169	− 0.131
		M_{16}	—	—	—	− 0.094	− 0.134	− 0.131	− 0.094	− 0.134	− 0.131
	Third-point loads	M_{17}	+ 0.111	+ 0.117	+ 0.128	+ 0.139	+ 0.125	+ 0.128[8]	+ 0.139	+ 0.125	+ 0.128[8]
		M_{18}	+ 0.056	+ 0.067	+ 0.089	+ 0.111	+ 0.100	+ 0.089[20]	+ 0.111	+ 0.100	+ 0.089[20]
		M_{19}	− 0.167	− 0.150	− 0.117	− 0.167	− 0.150	− 0.117	− 0.167	− 0.150	− 0.117
		M_{20}	—	—	—	− 0.083	− 0.125	− 0.117	− 0.083	− 0.125	− 0.117
Three spans	Uniform loads	M_{31}	+ 0.080	+ 0.084	+ 0.093	+ 0.101	+ 0.091	+ 0.092[13]	+ 0.101	+ 0.091	+ 0.087[13]
		M_{32}	− 0.100	− 0.090	− 0.070	− 0.100	− 0.090	− 0.070	− 0.117	− 0.106	− 0.082
		M_{33}	—	—	—	− 0.050	− 0.074	− 0.070	− 0.050	− 0.074	− 0.082
		M_{34}*	—	—	—	0.000	0.000	0.000	+ 0.017	+ 0.015	+ 0.012
		M_{35}	+ 0.025	+ 0.035	+ 0.055	+ 0.075	+ 0.068	+ 0.055[27]	+ 0.075	+ 0.068	+ 0.053[30]
	Central point loads	M_{36}	+ 0.175	+ 0.183	+ 0.198	+ 0.213	+ 0.191	+ 0.198[7]	+ 0.213	+ 0.191	+ 0.189[11]
		M_{37}	− 0.150	− 0.135	− 0.105	− 0.150	− 0.135	− 0.105	− 0.175	− 0.158	− 0.123
		M_{38}	—	—	—	− 0.075	− 0.118	− 0.105	− 0.075	− 0.118	− 0.123
		M_{39}*	—	—	—	0.000	0.000	0.000	+ 0.025	+ 0.023	+ 0.018
		M_{40}	+ 0.100	+ 0.115	+ 0.145	+ 0.175	+ 0.158	+ 0.145[17]	+ 0.175	+ 0.158	+ 0.128[27]
	Third-point loads	M_{41}	+ 0.122	+ 0.127	+ 0.136	+ 0.144	+ 0.130	+ 0.136[6]	+ 0.144	+ 0.130	+ 0.130[10]
		M_{42}	+ 0.078	+ 0.087	+ 0.104	+ 0.122	+ 0.110	+ 0.105[14]	+ 0.122	+ 0.110	+ 0.094[23]
		M_{43}	− 0.133	− 0.120	− 0.093	− 0.133	− 0.120	− 0.093	− 0.156	− 0.140	− 0.109
		M_{44}	—	—	—	− 0.067	− 0.110	− 0.093	− 0.067	− 0.110	− 0.109
		M_{45}*	—	—	—	+ 0.000	0.000	0.000	+ 0.022	+ 0.020	+ 0.016
		M_{46}	+ 0.033	+ 0.047	+ 0.073	+ 0.100	+ 0.090	+ 0.074[26]	+ 0.100	+ 0.090	+ 0.070[30]

Continuous beams: bending moment diagrams—2

End span and penultimate span and support of infinite system		Internal span and support of infinite system	
Dead load (all spans loaded)	Imposed load	Dead load (all spans loaded)	Imposed load
M_{51}, M_{52}, M_{55}	M_{51}, M_{52}, M_{53}, M_{54}*, M_{55}	M_{71}, M_{72}	M_{71}, M_{72}, M_{73}, M_{74}*
M_{56}, M_{57}, M_{60}	M_{56}, M_{57}, M_{58}, M_{59}*, M_{60}	M_{75}, M_{76}	M_{75}, M_{76}, M_{77}, M_{78}*
M_{61}, M_{62}, M_{63}, M_{66}, M_{67}	M_{61}, M_{62}, M_{63}, M_{64}, M_{65}, M_{66}, M_{67}	M_{79}, M_{80}	M_{79}, M_{80}, M_{81}, M_{82}*

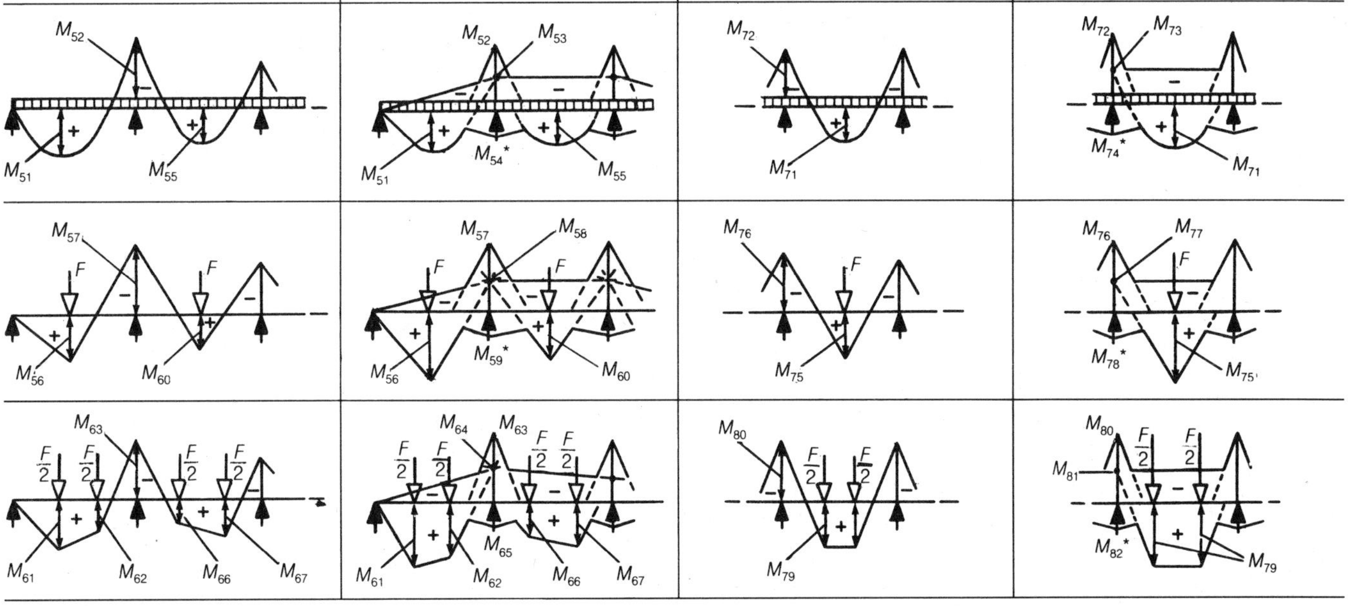

Equal total load F on each loaded span
Bending moment = coefficient × F × span
Diagrams are symmetrical but are not drawn to scale

Moment indicated thus * do not result from loading arrangement prescribed in Codes, which give zero positive moment at all supports.
Values below indicated thus(12) give maximum percentage reduction of span moment due to imposed load possible when support moments have already been reduced by full 30%.

			Dead load (all spans loaded)			Imposed load			Imposed load		
			BS8110 and CP110			BS8110			CP110		
Redistribution			nil	10%	30%	nil	10%	30%	nil	10%	30%
End span, and penultimate support and span of infinite system	Uniform loads	M_{51}	+ 0.078	+ 0.082	+ 0.091	+ 0.100	+ 0.090	+ 0.091(9)	+ 0.100	+ 0.090	+ 0.088(12)
		M_{52}	− 0.106	− 0.095	− 0.074	− 0.106	− 0.095	− 0.074	− 0.116	− 0.104	− 0.081
		M_{53}	—	—	—	− 0.053	− 0.076	− 0.074	− 0.054	− 0.076	− 0.081
		M_{54}*	—	—	—	0.000	0.000	0.000	+ 0.014	+ 0.013	+ 0.010
		M_{55}	+ 0.034	+ 0.043	+ 0.061	+ 0.079	+ 0.071	+ 0.061(23)	+ 0.079	+ 0.071	+ 0.056(30)
	Central point loads	M_{56}	+ 0.171	+ 0.178	+ 0.194	+ 0.210	+ 0.189	+ 0.195(7)	+ 0.210	+ 0.189	+ 0.189(10)
		M_{57}	− 0.159	− 0.143	− 0.111	− 0.159	− 0.143	− 0.111	− 0.174	− 0.157	− 0.122
		M_{58}	—	—	—	− 0.079	− 0.122	− 0.111	− 0.079	− 0.122	− 0.122
		M_{59}*	—	—	—	0.000	0.000	+ 0.000	+ 0.021	+ 0.019	+ 0.015
		M_{60}	+ 0.113	+ 0.127	+ 0.154	+ 0.181	+ 0.163	+ 0.153(15)	+ 0.181	+ 0.163	+ 0.145(30)
	Third-point loads	M_{61}	+ 0.120	+ 0.124	+ 0.134	+ 0.143	+ 0.129	+ 0.134(7)	+ 0.143	+ 0.129	+ 0.130(9)
		M_{62}	+ 0.072	+ 0.082	+ 0.101	+ 0.119	+ 0.107	+ 0.100(16)	+ 0.119	+ 0.107	+ 0.094(21)
		M_{63}	− 0.141	− 0.127	− 0.099	− 0.141	− 0.127	− 0.099	− 0.155	− 0.140	− 0.109
		M_{64}	—	—	—	− 0.071	− 0.114	− 0.099	− 0.072	− 0.114	− 0.109
		M_{65}*	—	—	—	0.000	0.000	0.000	+ 0.019	+ 0.017	+ 0.013
		M_{66}	+ 0.038	+ 0.051	+ 0.077	+ 0.103	+ 0.092	+ 0.077(25)	+ 0.103	+ 0.092	+ 0.072(30)
		M_{67}	+ 0.051	+ 0.062	+ 0.086	+ 0.109	+ 0.098	+ 0.086(21)	+ 0.109	+ 0.098	+ 0.076(30)
Internal span and support of infinite system	Uniform loads	M_{71}	+ 0.042	+ 0.050	+ 0.067	+ 0.083	+ 0.075	+ 0.067(20)	+ 0.083	+ 0.075	+ 0.058(30)
		M_{72}	− 0.083	− 0.075	− 0.058	− 0.083	− 0.075	− 0.058	− 0.106	− 0.095	− 0.074
		M_{73}	—	—	—	− 0.042	− 0.050	− 0.067	− 0.042	− 0.050	− 0.067
		M_{74}*	—	—	—	0.000	0.000	0.000	+ 0.028	+ 0.025	+ 0.020
	Central point loads	M_{75}	+ 0.125	+ 0.138	+ 0.163	+ 0.188	+ 0.169	+ 0.162(13)	+ 0.188	+ 0.169	+ 0.139(26)
		M_{76}	− 0.125	− 0.113	− 0.088	− 0.125	− 0.113	− 0.088	− 0.159	− 0.143	− 0.111
		M_{77}	—	—	—	− 0.063	− 0.081	− 0.088	− 0.063	− 0.081	− 0.111
		M_{78}*	—	—	—	0.000	0.000	0.000	+ 0.043	+ 0.038	+ 0.030
	Third-point loads	M_{79}	+ 0.055	+ 0.067	+ 0.089	+ 0.111	+ 0.100	+ 0.089(20)	+ 0.111	+ 0.100	+ 0.078(30)
		M_{80}	− 0.111	− 0.100	− 0.078	− 0.111	− 0.100	− 0.078	− 0.141	− 0.127	− 0.099
		M_{81}	—	—	—	− 0.055	− 0.067	− 0.078	− 0.055	− 0.067	− 0.089
		M_{82}*	—	—	—	0.000	0.000	0.000	+ 0.038	+ 0.034	+ 0.027

conditions of a uniform moment of inertia throughout all spans and with equal dead, imposed or total load on each loaded span. They are equally applicable to the requirements for an elastic analysis using service loads, in which case the dead and imposed loads considered should be g_k (or G_k) and q_k (or Q_k) respectively, or those for an elastic analysis using ultimate loads as specified in BS8110 or CP110. In the latter case the value of dead load considered should be $1.0g_k$ (or $1.0G_k$) and the value of 'imposed load' should be $(0.4g_k + 1.6q_k)$ (or $0.4G_k + 1.6Q_k$).

For convenience, the appropriate coefficients, both before adjustment and after various amounts and methods of redistribution have been employed, are tabulated against location reference symbols indicated on the diagrams. For example, M_{12} is the coefficient corresponding to the maximum moment at the central support of a two-span beam, while M_{13} is the coefficient giving the moment that occurs at this support when the moment in the adjoining span is a maximum. Thus, by means of the coefficients given, the appropriate envelope of maximum moments can be sketched.

The types of loads considered are a uniformly distributed load throughout each span, a central concentrated load, and equal concentrated loads positioned at the third-points. The coefficients may also be used to determine the support moments resulting from various combinations of the foregoing types by calculating the moments resulting from each individual type of load and summing them.

Maximum span moments resulting from uniform loading, obtained by summing the individual maximum values due to dead and imposed load separately, will be approximate only since each of the maximum values occurs at a slightly different position. However, maxima thus determined err on the side of safety.

12.3 REDISTRIBUTION OF MOMENTS

As explained in section 3.2.2, both BS8110 and CP110 permit the theoretical distribution of moments in a continuous system given by an elastic analysis to be adjusted if required, although the actual adjustment process permitted differs in the two documents. In general, the common method of redistribution is to reduce the critical moments by the percentage permitted and then to re-establish the other values, determining the particular bending-moment diagram being investigated by a consideration of equilibrium between internal forces and external loads.

An important point to note is that in general each particular combination of loading can be considered separately. Thus with imposed loads it is possible to reduce both the maximum span and maximum support moments provided that the increased value of the support moment corresponding to the loading condition that gives rise to the (reduced) maximum span moment does not exceed the reduced value of the support moment corresponding to the loading condition giving the maximum support moment.

When redistributing moments care must be taken not to violate the principles of statics, i.e. that equilibrium between internal forces and external loads is maintained. For example, where the end support of a continuous system resists a cantilever moment, this moment cannot be reduced by redistribution under any circumstances.

12.3.1 Code requirements

CP110 actually states that a redistribution giving a *reduction* of moment of up to 30% of the *maximum* moment on a member may be made *at any section* provided that the corresponding section is designed using the 'rigorous' limit-state design procedure described in section 5.3.2; that the maximum x/d ratio adopted in this design is limited to correspond to the degree of redistribution adopted; and that the spacing of the reinforcement provided conforms to the limitations set out in *Table 139*. (Note that there is no corresponding restriction on the maximum percentage *increase* of moment allowed.) However, CP110 also requires that the ultimate resistance moment provided at any section is also at least 70% of the maximum ultimate moment occurring at that section before redistribution. In effect, the redistribution process alters the positions of the points of contraflexure, and the purpose of this requirement is to ensure that at such points on the diagram of redistributed moments (at which, of course, no reinforcement to resist bending is theoretically required), sufficient steel is provided to limit cracking due to the moments that actually occur at these points as a result of service loading. This matter is discussed more fully in the *Code Handbook* and ref. 71. This requirement actually means that it is not possible to reduce the moment at any point by more than 30% of the value before redistribution *at that point*; since this is more stringent than the limit of 30% of the maximum moment, the latter requirement is actually superfluous and has been omitted from the related section in BS8110.

In the 30%-adjustment coefficients for dead load given on *Tables 36* and *37*, the support moments have been reduced by 30% and the span moments increased accordingly to correspond to these adjusted values. For the imposed-load coefficients, the support moments have first been reduced by the full 30% permitted and the span moments then reduced to the maximum possible extent concomitant with the restriction that the corresponding (increased) support moment due to this loading condition must not exceed the reduced support moment due to the maximum-support-moment condition. In certain cases, this limits the percentage decrease of span moment possible, and in such cases the actual percentage possible is indicated in parentheses next to the coefficient value. This figure enables the maximum ratio of x/d at this section to be determined. However, it should be remembered that this percentage relates to the *imposed-load* condition only, and when considering the combined effects of dead and imposed loads the controlling value is the adjustment to the *total* load.

For example, in a two-span beam supporting equal dead and imposed loads and with the usual partial safety factors, the span moments are increased by about 21% to permit a 30% reduction at the support under the dead load, but reduced by about 11% under the imposed load. Taking the 'weighting' due to the safety factors into account, the resulting adjustment actually represents a reduction of span moment of about 2.5%. In any particular case, of course, the actual figure depends on the ratio of dead to imposed load and the particular values of the moment coefficients concerned. Clearly the simplest method of determining the actual percentage of redistribution made is therefore to

Continuous beams: moment redistribution

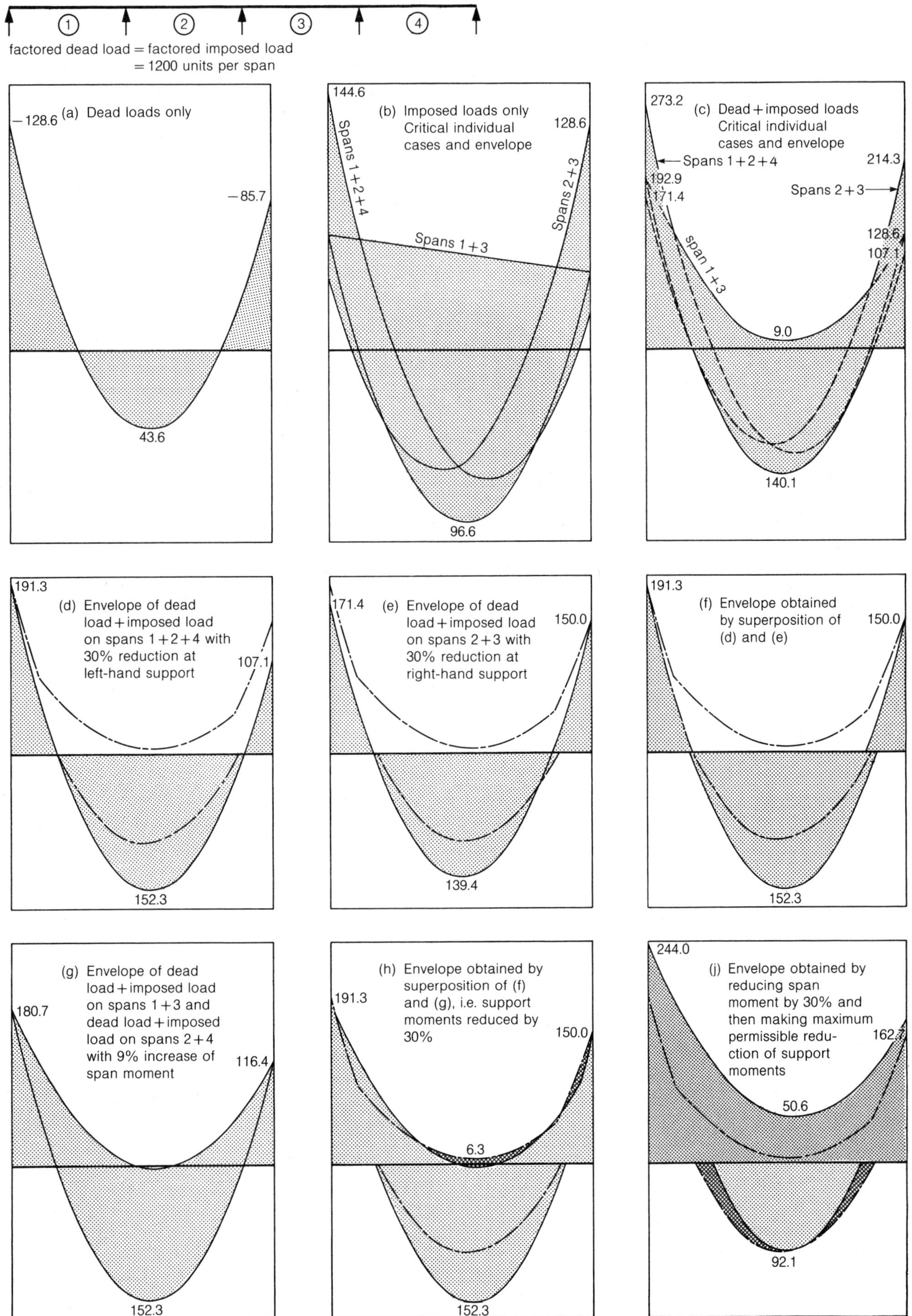

①
②
③
④
factored dead load = factored imposed load
= 1200 units per span
−128.6
(a) Dead loads only
−85.7
43.6
144.6
(b) Imposed loads only
Critical individual
cases and envelope
128.6
Spans 1+2+4
Spans 2+3
Spans 1+3
96.6
273.2
(c) Dead + imposed loads
Critical individual
cases and envelope
Spans 1+2+4
214.3
192.9
171.4
Spans 2+3
span 1+3
128.6
107.1
9.0
140.1
191.3
(d) Envelope of dead
load + imposed load
on spans 1+2+4 with
30% reduction at
left-hand support
107.1
152.3
171.4
(e) Envelope of dead
load + imposed load
on spans 2+3 with
30% reduction at
right-hand support
150.0
139.4
191.3
(f) Envelope obtained
by superposition of
(d) and (e)
150.0
152.3
(g) Envelope of dead
load + imposed load
on spans 1+3 and
dead load + imposed
load on spans 2+4
with 9% increase of
span moment
180.7
116.4
152.3
(h) Envelope obtained by
superposition of (f)
and (g), i.e. support
moments reduced by
30%
191.3
150.0
6.3
152.3
244.0
(j) Envelope obtained by
reducing span
moment by 30% and
then making maximum
permissible redu-
ction of support
moments
162.7
50.6
92.1

evaluate the span moments with the aid of the moment coefficients provided both before and after adjustment. Thus for the two-span beam supporting equal dead and imposed loads, if $g = q$ and making the full 30% reduction of moment at the support:

maximum span moment before adjustment

$$\simeq 0.070 \times 1.0gl^2 + 0.096 \times (1.6 + 0.4)ql^2 = 0.262gl^2$$

maximum span moment after adjustment

$$\simeq 0.085 \times 1.0gl^2 + 0.085 \times (1.6 + 0.4)ql^2 = 0.255gl^2$$

Thus the percentage adjustment $= -(0.262 - 0.255) \times 100/0.262 \simeq -2.5\%$: the corresponding maximum allowable ratio of x/d at midspan would be 0.575.

The analysis and redistribution procedure is illustrated on *Table 38*, where an internal span of a system of four equal spans is examined. When loaded with a factored dead load on each span only, the moment diagram for the span being considered (span 2) is as shown in diagram (a). The moment diagrams illustrating the effects of the four arrangements of factored imposed load which give the critical moments at the supports and in the span are shown in diagram (b), and diagram (c) shows the envelope obtained by combining dead with critical imposed loading. (Note that the vertical scale of diagrams (c) to (j) differs from that of (a) and (b).) A further diagram may now be drawn in which the values are only 70% of the envelope forming diagram (c): this '70% envelope', which is shown by chain lines on the subsequent diagrams, indicates the values below which the moment at any point may not be reduced as a result of redistribution.

Now assume that the aim is to reduce the support moments as much as is permitted. If the moment diagram for imposed load on spans 1, 2 and 4 only is combined with that for dead load, and the left-hand support moments are reduced by 30%, diagram (d) will be obtained. Similarly, combining dead loading with imposed load on spans 2 and 3 only and reducing the right-hand support moment by 30% gives diagram (e). It may be thought that this moment could be reduced by 30% of the *maximum* moment on the span (i.e. that at the left-hand support), in other words by $273.2 \times 0.3 = 82$ kN m to 132.3 kN m, since both Codes permit this. However, there is no point is so doing, as the adjusted moment at this point then becomes less than 70% of the value before redistribution, which neither Code permits. If diagrams (d) and (e) are now combined, the moment envelope shown in diagram (f) is obtained.

The next step is to examine on diagram (c) the curves representing the combination of dead load with imposed load on spans 2 and 4 only and dead load with imposed load on spans 1 and 3 only. The former combination results in a span moment of 140.1 kN m; it is desirable to increase this value to 152.3 kN m (i.e. to correspond to the maximum span value on diagram (f)) by making a redistribution of about 9%, since this reduces accordingly the corresponding support moments and thus the hogging moments which occur when imposed loading occupies spans 1 and 3 only. (The fact that these maximum values may occur at slightly different points across the span may safely be ignored.)

By combining diagrams (f) and (g) the final moment diagram which results from all these redistribution operations is as shown in diagram (h). Note that within the portions of the envelope shown hatched the redistributed moments are less than 70% of the values before adjustment and the envelope must therefore be enlarged to include these areas. As regards the area near midspan, the nominal steel which would normally be provided in the top of the member to support the shear reinforcement is often sufficient to cater for this additional moment, while within a distance of about one-quarter of the span from the support the maximum moments actually result from a combination of partial imposed load on the span being investigated, together with full loading on other spans. Since this loading condition is not considered in either BS8110 or CP110, the extended 70% envelope probably represents the true envelope of maximum moments after redistribution quite well.

To clarify the explanation, it has been assumed in the foregoing description that, when each maximum support moment is redistributed, the moment at the opposite end of the span is not altered. However, the maximum positive moment at midspan may be further reduced by *increasing* the moments at the opposite ends of the spans when reducing the maximum support moments.

For example assume that, when the moment at the left-hand support is reduced to 191.3 kN m, the right-hand support moment is increased by 42.9 kN m to that which will occur when the maximum possible reduction (i.e. to 150 kN m) is made at this point. Next assume that the right-hand support moment is reduced by 30% to 150 kN m and the left-hand support moment is increased to 191.3 kN m (i.e. by 19.9 kN m). Now the lines representing the redistributed moments due to these two conditions coincide and give a corresponding positive moment near midspan of about 130 kN m.

It is now possible to increase the support moments which correspond to the loading arrangement that produces the maximum midspan moment until this maximum value is also reduced to 130 kN m. However, one problem that may arise if such a substantial reduction of moment is made at midspan is that the hogging moment that occurs across the span when it is carrying dead load only is increased accordingly (in the case considered above, for example, from 6.3 kN m to about 30 kN m); this may be an unwelcome factor, particularly where the ratio of imposed to dead load is high.

Of course, the chief criterion may not be to reduce the support moments as much as possible. For example, in the case of an upstand beam it may be preferable to minimize the span moments, which may otherwise be excessive and require large amounts of compression reinforcement. The envelope shown in diagram (j) on *Table 38* has been obtained in a similar manner to that given in diagram (h), but here the span moment has been reduced by the maximum amount possible to obtain 70% of the original value. After this has been done, it has been found possible to reduce the left and right support moments substantially (by about 11% and 24% respectively) since these maximum values arise from different combinations of dead and imposed load to that causing the maximum span moment. Again, over the area shown hatched on the diagram, the redistributed moments are less than 70% of the values before adjustment and the

Continuous beams: three-moment theorem

39

General equation

Deformation

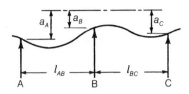

Bending moments (both spans loaded)

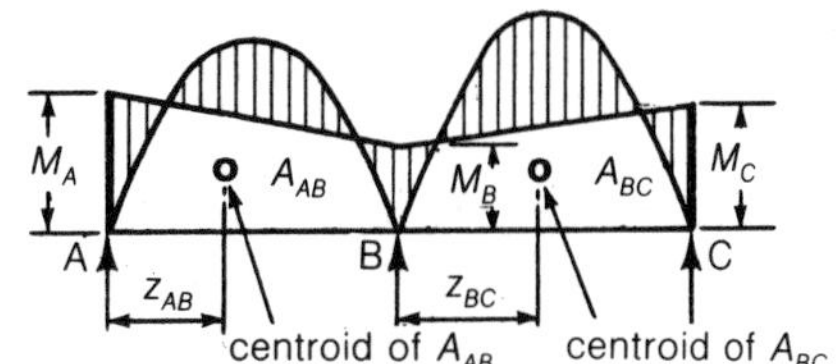

$$M_A\frac{l_{AB}}{I_{AB}}+2M_B\left(\frac{l_{AB}}{I_{AB}}+\frac{l_{BC}}{I_{BC}}\right)+M_C\frac{l_{BC}}{I_{BC}}=6E\left[\frac{a_B-a_A}{l_{AB}}-\frac{a_C-a_B}{l_{BC}}\right]-6\left[\frac{A_{AB}z_{AB}}{I_{AB}l_{AB}}+\frac{A_{BC}(l_{BC}-z_{BC})}{I_{BC}l_{BC}}\right]$$

Special cases

Rigid supports:

$$M_A\frac{l_{AB}}{I_{AB}}+2M_B\left(\frac{l_{AB}}{I_{AB}}+\frac{l_{BC}}{I_{BC}}\right)+M_C\frac{l_{BC}}{I_{BC}}=-6\left[\frac{A_{AB}z_{AB}}{I_{AB}l_{AB}}+\frac{A_{BC}(l_{BC}-z_{BC})}{I_{BC}l_{BC}}\right]=-6(\theta_{BA}-\theta_{BC})$$

Rigid supports, uniform moment of inertia:

$$M_Al_{AB}+2M_B(l_{AB}+l_{BC})+M_Cl_{BC}=-6\left[\frac{A_{AB}z_{AB}}{l_{AB}}+\frac{A_{BC}(l_{BC}-z_{BC})}{l_{BC}}\right]$$

Uniformly distributed load (w per unit length on both spans), *rigid supports, uniform moment of inertia*:

$$M_Al_{AB}+2M_B(l_{AB}+l_{BC})+M_Cl_{BC}=-\frac{w}{4}(l_{AB}^3+l_{BC}^3)$$

Non-uniform moment of inertia

Graphical method

Treat each consecutive pair of spans thus:

On the spans drawn to scale, construct the free-moment curves and the moment of inertia curves. Divide the ordinates of the former by those of the latter to enable the curves of (free bending moment/I) to be drawn.

Find A_{AB}, the area under the (free bending moment/I) curve for span l_{AB} and position of centroid G_1, and A_{BC}, the area under the (free bending moment/I) curve for span l_{BC} and position of centroid G_2.

Set up AD, BE and CF to a suitable scale to represent any assumed values of the moments at A, B and C respectively. Connect DB, AE, EC and BF.

Let

$$M_A=K_A\text{AD} \qquad M_B=K_B\text{BE} \qquad M_C=K_C\text{CF}$$

Divide the ordinates of DBF and AEC by the ordinates of the moment of inertia curve to give the curves AHC and GBJ. Find

- A_V area under curve GB and position of centroid G_V
- A_X area under curve AH and position of centroid G_X
- A_Y area under curve HC and position of centroid G_Y
- A_U area under curve BJ and position of centroid G_U

Substitute in

$$(A_{AB}z_1+K_AVA_V+K_BXA_X)\frac{1}{l_{AB}}=-(A_{BC}z_2+K_CA_UW+K_BA_YY)\frac{1}{l_{BC}}$$

Unknowns are K_A, K_B and K_C, and requisite number of equations follow from consecutive pairs of spans and end support conditions.

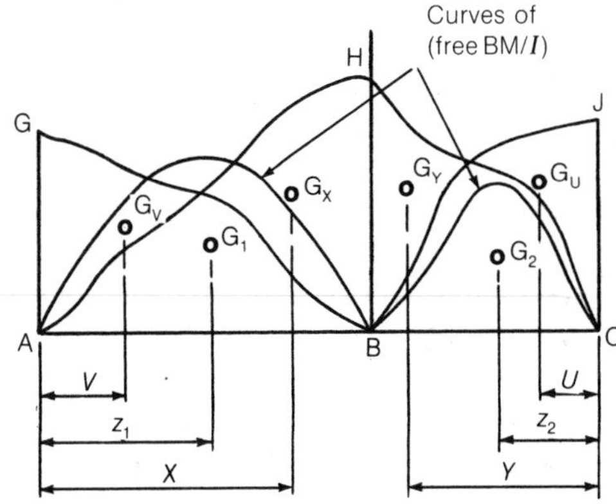

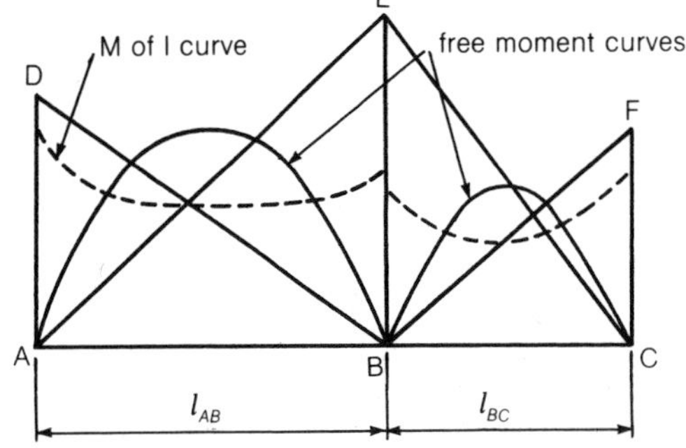

Approximate method	Ratio of I_S:I_C		0.25	0.50	0.75	1.25	1.50
Calculate bending moments for uniform moment of inertia and increase or decrease by the appropriate percentage tabulated.	both ends fixed	midspan	+55%	+26%	+7%	−6%	−13%
		support	−28%	−15%	−5%	+3%	+4%
I_S = moment of inertia at support	one fixed	midspan	+27%	+13%	+6%	$-2\frac{1}{2}$%	−10%
I_C = moment of inertia at midspan	one free	support	−40%	−20%	−8%	+5%	+13%

final moment envelope must be extended to include these areas.

Beeby discusses moment redistribution in some detail in ref. 71, particularly when considering systems of beams analysed in conjunction with adjoining columns. In such cases he shows that it is important to consider the effect on the column sections of redistributing the moments that arise when alternate spans are loaded. To ensure that the final plastic hinges that may form in any postulated collapse mechanism are those in the columns, it is recommended that there should be no adjustment to the moment diagram that results when the span in question carries dead load only while both adjoining spans carry maximum load, and that the column sections should be designed to resist either the redistributed or non-redistributed unbalanced moments, whichever are greater.

In view of the many factors involved, Beeby concludes that it is difficult to produce rules to indicate whether to redistribute the moments in any particular case and if so by how much, these decisions being matters of individual engineering judgement. A useful proposal is to design a suitable section to meet the requirements at a number of supports and to calculate the resulting resistance moment first, and then to redistribute the moment diagram as necessary to obtain these calculated support moments. Finally, design the beams at midspan to resist the resulting redistributed moments at these points and check that none of the requirements of BS8110 or CP110 has been violated.

If the simplified formulae for limit-state design given in CP110 are to be used to design the sections, the maximum amount of redistribution permitted is 10%. In the 10%-adjustment coefficients for dead load given in *Tables 36* and *37*, the support moments have been reduced by 10% and the span moments increased correspondingly. In the corresponding coefficients for imposed load, both maximum span and maximum support moments have been reduced by this figure, the foregoing complication not arising with this lower percentage of redistribution.

Redistribution is also limited to only 10% in structural frames at least five storeys high where lateral stability is provided by the frame.

12.4 THREE-MOMENT THEOREM

12.4.1 General method

Formulae in general and special cases are given in *Table 39*; the values of the factors A/Il and z for use in these formulae are given in *Table 29*.

When known factors relating to the load, span, moment of inertia and relative levels of the supports are substituted in the general formula, an equation with three unknown support bending moments is obtained for each pair of spans; that is, for n spans, $n-1$ equations are obtained containing $n+1$ unknowns (the moments at $n+1$ supports). The two excess unknowns represent the bending moments at the end supports and, if these bending moments are known or can be assumed, the bending moments at the intermediate supports can be determined. At a freely supported end the bending moment is zero. For a perfectly fixed end the support bending moments can be determined if an additional span is considered continuous at the fixed end; this additional span must be identical in all respects with the original end span except that the load should produce symmetry about the original end support with the load on the original end span. The bending moment at the new end support is considered to be equal to that at the original penultimate support, and thus an additional equation is obtained without introducing another unknown.

When the bending moments at the supports have been calculated, the diagram of the support bending moments is combined with the diagram of the 'free moments' and the resulting bending moments are obtained.

Example. Determine by the theorem of three moments the service bending moments at the supports of the slabs in the diagram, assuming continuity over supports. (This represents a tank with a sloping bottom BC and walls AB and CD of unequal heights.)

From *Table 39* the appropriate formula modified for spans AB and BC (span $l_1 = l_{AB}$ and $l_2 = l_{BC}$) is

$$M_A\frac{l_1}{I_1} + 2M_B\left(\frac{l_1}{I_1} + \frac{l_2}{I_2}\right) + M_C\frac{l_2}{I_2} = -6\left(\frac{A_1 z_1}{I_1 l_1} + \frac{A_2(l_2 - z_2)}{I_2 l_2}\right) \tag{12.1}$$

and for spans BC and CD (span l_2 = span l_{BC} and $l_3 = l_{CD}$)

$$M_B\frac{l_2}{I_2} + 2M_C\left(\frac{l_2}{I_2} + \frac{l_3}{I_3}\right) + M_D\frac{l_3}{I_3} = -6\left(\frac{A_2 z_2}{I_2 l_2} + \frac{A_3(l_3 - z_3)}{I_3 l_3}\right) \tag{12.2}$$

For span AB: $l_1/I_1 = 3.0/0.0052 = 577\,\text{m}^{-3}$; $A_1/l_1 = 50 \times 3.0^2/24 = 18.7\,\text{kN m}$ per metre width; $z_1 = 3.0 \times 8/15 = 1.6\,\text{m}$. Hence

$$A_1 z_1/I_1 l_1 = 18.7 \times 1.6/0.0052 = 5770\,\text{kN/m}^2$$

For span BC: $l_2/I_2 = 4.5/0.0078 = 577\,\text{m}^{-3}$; $A_2/l_2 = 75 \times 4.5^2/12 = 126\,\text{kN m}$ per metre width; $z_2 = 4.5/2 = 2.25\,\text{m}$.

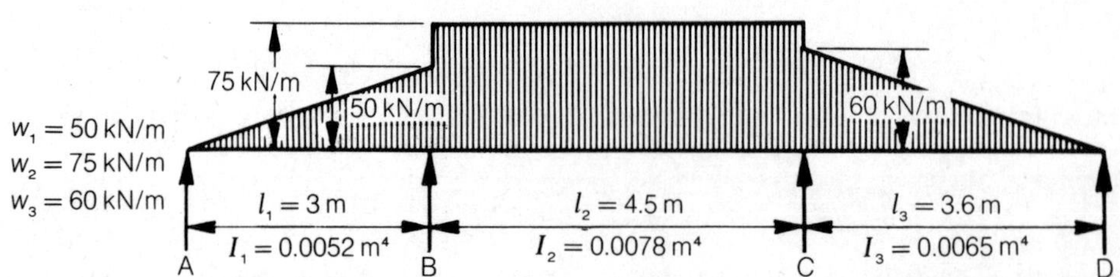

Continuous beams: moment distribution methods

HARDY CROSS MOMENT DISTRIBUTION

1. Consider each member to be fixed at ends: calculate *fixed-end moments* (*FEMs*) due to external loads on individual members by means of *Tables 29* to *31*.
2. Where members meet, sum of bending moments must equal zero for equilibrium; i.e. at B, $M_{BA} + M_{BC} = 0$. Since ΣFEM (i.e. $FEM_{BA} + FEM_{BC}$) is unlikely to equal zero, a balancing moment of $-\Sigma FEM$ must be introduced at each support to achieve equilibrium.
3. Distribute this balancing moment between members meeting at a joint in proportion to their relative stiffnesses $K = I/l$ by multiplying $-\Sigma FEM$ by *distribution factor D* for each member (e.g. at B, $D_{BA} = K_{AB}/(K_{AB} + K_{BC})$ etc. so that $D_{BA} + D_{BC} = 1$. At a free end, $D = 1$; at a fully fixed end, $D = 0$.
4. Applying a moment at one end of member induces moment of one-half of magnitude and of same sign at opposite end of member (termed *carry-over*). Thus distributed moment $-\Sigma FEM \times D_{BA}$ at B of AB produces a moment of $-(1/2)\Sigma FEM \times D_{BA}$ at A, and so on.
5. These carried-over moments produce further unbalanced moments at supports (e.g. moments carried over from A and C give rise to further moments at B). These must again be redistributed and the carry-over process repeated.
6. Repeat cycle of operations described in steps 2 to 5 until unbalanced moments are negligible. Then sum values obtained each side of support.

Various simplifications can be employed to shorten analysis. The most useful is that for dealing with system which is freely supported at end. If stiffness considered for end span when calculating distribution factors is taken as only three-quarters of actual stiffness, and one-half of fixed-end moment at free support is added to *FEM* at other end of span, the span may then be treated as fixed and no further carrying over from free end back to penultimate support takes place.

30 kN/m — Uniform moment of inertia — A –6 m– B –9 m– C –12 m– D –8 m– E

	A	B		C		D		E
Distribution factors	1	$\frac{3}{5}$	$\frac{2}{5}$	$\frac{4}{7}$	$\frac{3}{7}$	$\frac{2}{5}$	$\frac{3}{5}$	0
Fixed-end moments	0	0	−203	+203	0	0	0	0
First distribution	0	+122	+81	−116	−87	0	0	0
1st carry-over	+61	0	−58	+40	0	−43	0	0
2nd distribution	−61	+35	+23	−23	−17	+17	+26	0
2nd carry-over	+17	−30	−12	+12	+9	−9	0	+13
3rd distribution	−17	+25	+17	−12	−9	+4	+5	0
3rd carry-over	+13	−9	−6	+8	+2	−4	0	+3
4th distribution	−13	+9	+6	−6	−4	+2	+2	0
Summations	0	+152	−152	+106	−106	−33	+33	+16

PRECISE MOMENT DISTRIBUTION

1. Calculate *fixed-end moments* (*FEMs*) as for Hardy Cross moment distribution.
2. Determine *continuity factors* for each span of system from general expression

$$\phi_{n+1} = 1\bigg/\left[2 + \frac{K_{n+1}}{K_n}(2 - \phi_n)\right]$$

where ϕ_n is continuity factor for previous span and K_n and K_{n+1} are stiffnesses of two spans. Work from left to right along system. If left-hand support (A in example below) is free, take $\phi_{AB} = 0$ for first span: if A is fully fixed, $\phi_{AB} = 0.5$. (Intermediate fixity conditions may be assumed if desired, by interpolation.) Repeat the foregoing procedure starting from right-hand end and working to left (to obtain continuity factor ϕ_{BA} for span AB, for example).
3. Calculate *distribution factors* (*DFs*) at junctions between spans from general expression

$$DF_{AB} = \frac{1 - 2\phi_{AB}}{1 - \phi_{AB}\phi_{BA}}$$

where ϕ_{AB} and ϕ_{BA} are continuity factors obtained in step 2. Note that these distribution factors do not correspond to those used in Hardy Cross moment distribution. Check that, at each support, $\Sigma DF = 1$.
4. Distribute the balancing moments $-\Sigma FEM$ introduced at each support to provide equilibrium for the unbalanced *FEMs* by multiplying by the distribution factors obtained in step 3.
5. Carry over the distributed balancing moments at the supports by multiplying them by the continuity factors obtained in step 2 *by working in opposite direction*. For example, the moment carried over from B to A is obtained by multiplying the distributed moment at B by ϕ_{AB} and so on. This procedure is illustrated in example below. Only a single carry-over operation in each direction is necessary.
6. Sum values obtained to determine final moments.

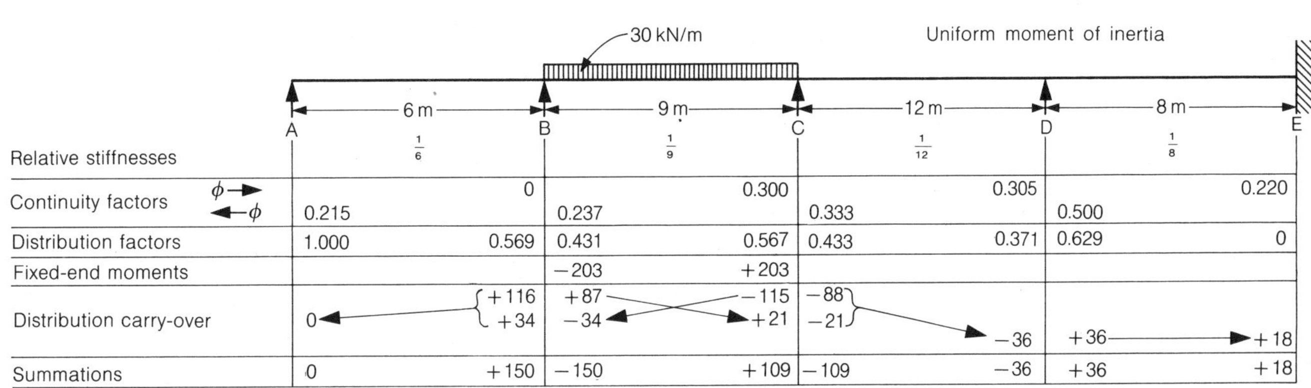

30 kN/m — Uniform moment of inertia — A –6 m– B –9 m– C –12 m– D –8 m– E

	A	B		C		D		E
Relative stiffnesses		$\frac{1}{6}$		$\frac{1}{9}$		$\frac{1}{12}$		$\frac{1}{8}$
Continuity factors $\phi\rightarrow$		0		0.300		0.305		0.220
Continuity factors $\leftarrow\phi$	0.215		0.237		0.333		0.500	
Distribution factors	1.000	0.569	0.431	0.567	0.433	0.371	0.629	0
Fixed-end moments			−203	+203				
Distribution carry-over	0	+116 +34	+87 −34	−115 +21	−88 −21	−36	+36	+18
Summations	0	+150	−150	+109	−109	−36	+36	+18

Hence

$$A_2z_2/I_2l_2 = 126 \times 2.25/0.0078 = 36\,510\,\text{kN/m}^2$$

For span CD: $l_3/I_3 = 3.6/0.0065 = 554\,\text{m}^{-3}$; $A_3/l_3 = 60 \times 3.6^2/24 = 32.4\,\text{kN m}$ per metre width; $l_3 - z_3 = 3.6 \times 8/15 = 1.92\,\text{m}$. Hence

$$A_3(l_3 - z_3)/I_3l_3 = 32.4 \times 1.92/0.0065 = 9570\,\text{kN/m}^2$$

If the slab is freely supported at A and D, $M_A = M_D = 0$. Substituting known values in (12.1) and (12.2):

$$2M_B(577 + 577) + 577M_C = -6(5770 + 36\,510) \quad (12.3)$$

$$577M_B + 2M_C(577 + 554) = -6(36\,510 + 9570) \quad (12.4)$$

Thus

$$2308M_B + 577M_C = -253\,680 \quad (12.5)$$

$$577M_B + 2262M_C = -276\,480 \quad (12.6)$$

Now multiplying (12.6) by $2308/577 = 4$:

$$2308M_B + 9048M_C = 1\,105\,920 \quad (12.7)$$

Subtracting (12.5) from (12.7), $8471\,M_C = 852\,240$:

$$M_C = 100.6\,\text{kN m per metre width}$$

Substituting in (12.5):

$$M_B = -253\,680 - (-577 \times 100.6)/2308$$
$$= 84.8\,\text{kN m per metre width}$$

12.4.2 Non-uniform moment of inertia

When the moment of inertia is practically uniform throughout each span of a series of continuous spans, but differs in one span relative to another, the general expressions for the theorem of three moments given in *Table 39* are applicable as in the example above. When the moment of inertia varies irregularly within the length of each span, the semi-graphical method given in *Table 39* can be used. The moments of inertia of common reinforced concrete sections are given in *Tables 98–101*.

If the moment of inertia varies in such a way that it can be represented by an equation, the theorem of three moments can be used if M/I is substituted for M and if the area of the M/I diagram is used instead of the area of the free-moment diagram. The solution of the derived simultaneous equations then gives values of the support bending moment divided by I, enabling a complete M/I diagram for the beam to be constructed. From this the bending moment at any section is readily obtained by multiplying the appropriate ordinate of the M/I diagram by the moment of inertia at the section.

When circumstances do not permit the foregoing methods to be used, the bending moments can be calculated on the assumption of a uniform moment of inertia, and an approximate adjustment can be made for the effect of the neglected variation. An increase in the moment of inertia near a support causes an increase in the negative bending moment at that support and a consequent decrease in the positive bending moments in the adjacent spans, and vice versa. As a guide in making the adjustment the approximate factors given in *Table 39* represent a percentage addition to, or deduction from, the calculated moments.

12.5 FIXED POINTS

One graphical method of determining the bending moments on a continuous beam is given in *Table 41*. The basis of the method is that there is a point (termed the 'fixed point') adjacent to the left-hand support of any span of a continuous system at which the bending moment is unaffected by any alteration in the bending moment at the right-hand support. A similar point occurs near the right-hand support, the bending moment at this point being unaffected by alteration in the bending moment at the left-hand support. When a beam is rigidly fixed at a support the 'fixed point' is one-third of the span from that support; when freely supported the fixed point coincides with the support. For intermediate conditions of fixity the 'fixed point' is between these extremes. In two continuous spans, l_1 and l_2, if the distance from the left-hand (or right-hand) support to the adjacent fixed point is p_1, then the distance p_2 from the left-hand (or right-hand) support of span l_2 to the adjacent fixed point is

$$p_2 = \frac{l_2^2(l_1 - p_1)}{3(l_1 + l_2)(l_1 - p_1) - l_1^2}$$

Alternatively p_2 can be found from p_1 by the graphical construction shown in *Table 41*. By combining the free-moment diagram with the position of the fixed points for a span, as described in *Table 41*, the resultant negative and positive bending moments throughout the system, due to the load on this span, can be determined. By treating each span separately the envelopes of the maximum possible bending moments throughout the system can be drawn.

12.6 CHARACTERISTIC POINTS

Another semi-graphical method of analysing continuous beams is outlined on *Table 42*. Here it is first necessary to calculate the positions of so-called characteristic points, from which the graphical construction given can be used to find the support-moment line.

On *Table 42* the method, which was developed by Claxton Fidler (ref. 72), is given for a beam system having a constant moment of inertia only, but both this and the graphical construction illustrated, which is due to Osterfeld (ref. 73), can also be extended to systems of beams that have non-uniform moments of inertia and where the supports yield (see ref. 74).

12.7 SUPPORT-MOMENT-COEFFICIENT METHOD

12.7.1 Analytical procedure

The factors in *Table 43* apply to the calculation of the support moments for beams with uniform moment of inertia and continuous over two, three or four equal or unequal spans, and carrying almost any type or arrangement of imposed and dead loads, provided that the load on each individual span is arranged symmetrically. (In theory, the method can be extended to any type of loading but only at the expense of increasing algebraic complexity.)

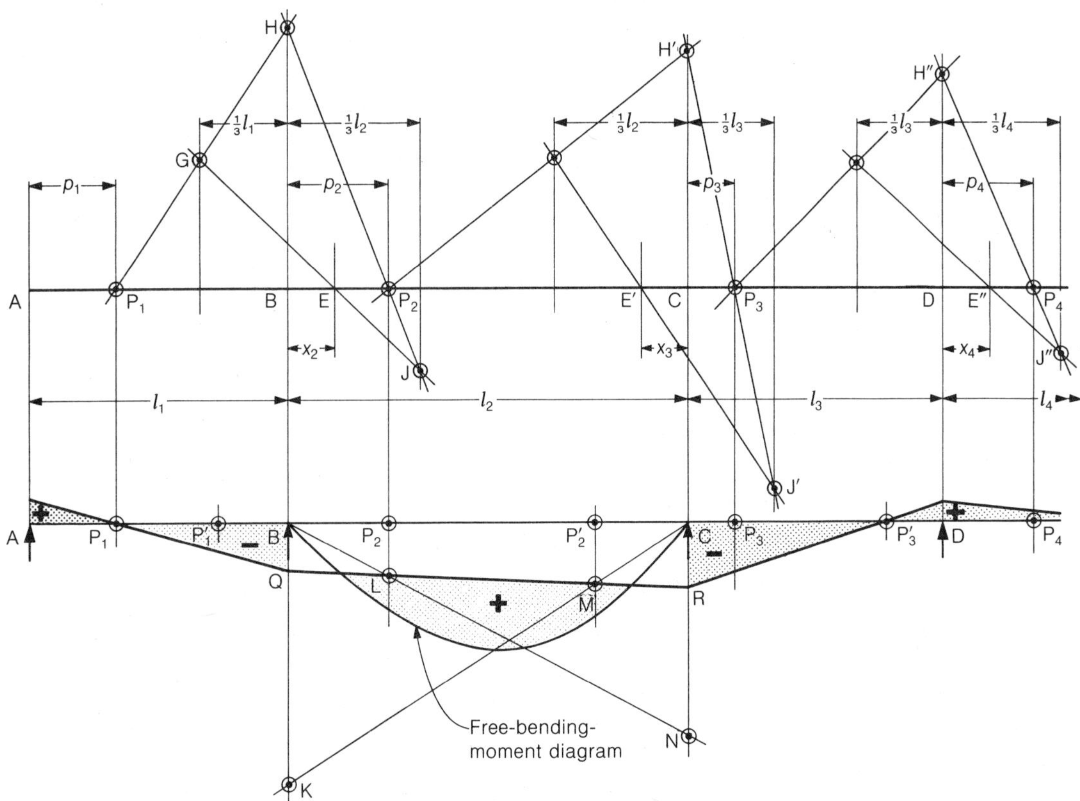

Graphical method

To determine the position of the fixed points (sketch (a))

Draw the beam ABCD... to scale.

Plot the position of the fixed point P_1 in left-hand part of span AB. If the beam is freely supported at A, P_1 is at A. If the beam is fixed at A, $P_1 = 0.333l_1$.

Set up verticals through the third-points of each span.

Set off BE $= x_2 = 0.333(l_2 - l_1)$; CE′ $= x_3 = 0.333(l_3 - l_2)$; DE″ $= x_4 = 0.333(l_4 - l_3)$ etc., and set up verticals through E, E′, E″ etc. (If $l_{n+1} < l_n$, x is negative and should be set off on left-hand side of support, for example as x_3.)

Draw GEJ at any convenient angle through E. Join P_1G and produce to intersect vertical through B at H. Join HJ, intersecting BC at P_2 which is the fixed point in the left-hand part of span BC.

Repeat the construction in spans CD, DE etc., working to the right-hand end of the beam, thereby establishing the left-hand fixed points P_3, P_4 etc.

Commence at the extreme right-hand support, and repeat the construction working to the left-hand end of the beam, thus establishing the position of the right-hand fixed points P'_1, P'_2, P'_3 etc.

To determine the bending moments (sketch (b))

Draw the beam ABCD... to scale and mark the positions of the fixed points P_1, P'_1, P_2, P'_2 etc.

Set up BK and CN to some convenient scale at the supports of the loaded span, where BK $= 6A_2z_2/l_2^2$ and CN $= 6A_2(l_2 - z_2)/l_2^2$ etc.

For any symmetrical load: BK = CN $= 3A_2/l_2$.
For uniform load: BK = CN $= Fl_2/4$.
For central concentrated load: BK = CN $= 3Fl_2/8$.
For any single concentrated load at distance αl_2 from B:
BK $= \alpha(1 - \alpha^2)Fl_2$
CN $= \alpha(1 - \alpha)(2 - \alpha)Fl_2$

where A_2 = area of free-moment diagram; z_2 = distance of centroid of A_2 from B; F = total load on span.

Join KC and BN; draw line QR through intersections with verticals through P_2 and P'_2 at L and M.

Complete bending moment diagram (shown shaded) by drawing QP_1 produced, RP'_3 etc.

Repeat for other loaded spans and combine diagrams to give total bending moments.

Algebraical method

To determine the positions of the fixed points

(i) *Unequal spans*:

If the distance of the left-hand fixed point in the end span AB is p_1, the position of the left-hand fixed point in span BC is

$$p_2 = \frac{l_2^2(l_1 - p_1)}{3(l_1 + l_2)(l_1 - p_1) - l_1^2}$$

or generally

$$p_{n+1} = \frac{l_{n+1}^2(l_n - p_n)}{3(l_n + l_{n+1})(l_n - p_n) - l_n^2}$$

(ii) *Equal spans* ($l_1 = l_2 = l_3$ etc. $= l$):

Distance of fixed points:	p_1	p_2	p_3	p_4 etc.
Beam freely supported at A:	0	$0.200l$	$0.211l$	$0.211l$
Beam fixed at A:	$0.333l$	$0.222l$	$0.212l$	$0.211l$

To determine the support bending moments

With load on span l_2:

$$QB = \frac{p_2[CN - p'_2(CN + BK)]}{(l_2 - p_2 - p'_2)}$$

and

$$CR = \frac{p'_2[BK - p_2(CN + BK)]}{(l_2 - p_2 - p'_2)}$$

where BK and CN are obtained from expressions given earlier. For values of A/l and z see *Table 29*.

The basis of the method is that the load on any span of a given system can be divided into one or more of the types shown in *Table 43*. A given beam system can be divided into a series of identical systems each with only one span loaded with one type of load. Each of these loads produces a bending moment at each support, the total bending moment at any support being the algebraic sum of the moments due to each type of load. When the support moments are known, the midspan moments can be calculated or determined graphically therefrom.

For equal spans the bending moment at any support due to any one span loaded with any one type of load is given by

$$M_s = \text{load factor } (\alpha) \times \text{support-moment coefficient } (Q) \times \text{total load } (F) \times \text{span } (l)$$

The total moment at any support is $\sum M_s$.

For unequal spans the method is similar to that for equal spans, except for the introduction of the moment multiplier U, which varies with the support being treated and for the particular span loaded, and depends on the ratio that each span bears to the basic span. Thus for unequal spans $M_s = U\alpha QFl$.

If one type of load extends equally over all spans of a system of equal spans, the beam need not be divided into separately loaded spans, as the values of Q tabulated for this condition apply.

12.7.2 Alternative method

The factors given in *Table 43* can also be used to prepare graphs that permit even more rapid analysis of the support moments for symmetrically loaded spans of systems that are continuous over two or three spans and which have their outer ends freely supported. Such graphs form *Tables 44* and *45*.

For a three-span system supporting a uniform load, it is necessary to calculate factors α and β which represent the ratios of the stiffnesses of the left-hand and right-hand outer spans to that of the central span. Then, by means of the three graphs, values of the related coefficients k_1, k_2 and k_3 are read off. These, when multiplied by the span length and total load thereon and summed as shown on *Tables 44* and *45*, give the resulting moments at the left-hand internal support. (Note that *coefficients* k_1 to k_3 read from *Tables 44* and *45* are not directly related to *ratios* k_1 to k_3 employed on *Table 43*.) Finally, by transposing α and β, further coefficients k'_1, k'_2 and k'_3 can be read from the graphs and used to obtain the right-hand internal support moment. If the loads are not uniformly distributed, they should be multiplied by the appropriate load factor given on *Table 43*.

The graphs can also be employed to solve two-span systems with fixed or freely supported outer supports, as indicated on the table.

Examples of the use of *Tables 43* to *45* are given below.

Example 1. Find the maximum service bending moment at the penultimate support of a beam that is continuous over four equal 5 m spans carrying a uniform load of 15 kN/m; an imposed load of 50 kN can occur at the centre of one or more of the spans simultaneously.

The maximum bending moment occurs when the first, second and fourth spans are loaded with the concentrated load. Dividing the total load into single-span loads gives the results shown in the table below.

It can be seen from the table that these results are for the critical conditions, since if the third span is also loaded a positive bending moment is introduced that reduces the total negative bending moment.

Example 2. A continuous system consisting of spans of 6 m, 12 m and 8 m respectively, freely supported at the outer ends, carries a uniform load of 100 kN/m plus a concentrated load of 500 kN at the centre of the 12 m span. Determine the moments at the internal supports.

Analytical method. $k_1 = 6/12 = 0.5$ and $k_2 = 8/12 = 0.667$. Thus $x = 1.5$ and $y = 1.667$, so that $H = 5/9 = 0.556$. Then, for the left-hand span, $U_B = 0.347$ and $U_C = 0.417$; for the central span, $U_B = 1.296$ and $U_C = 1.111$; and for the right-hand span, $U_B = 0.741$ and $U_C = 0.556$. Thus

For M_B:

From left-hand span:

$$-0.0667 \times 0.347 \times 600 \times 12 = -166.7$$

From central span:

$$-0.05 \times 1.296(1200 + 500 \times 1.5)12 = -1516.7$$

From right-hand span:

$$+0.0167 \times 0.741 \times 800 \times 12 = +118.5$$

$$M_B = -1564.8 \text{ kN m}$$

Load F		Span	Load factor α	Support-moment coefficient Q	Product αQF
Uniform:	15 × 5 = 75 kN	All spans	1.00	−0.107	−8.03
Concentrated:	50 kN	1st span	1.50	−0.067	−5.00
Concentrated:	50 kN	2nd span	1.50	−0.049	−3.68
Concentrated:	50 kN	4th span	1.50	−0.004	−0.30
				$\sum\alpha QF =$	−17.01

Service bending moment $= l\sum\alpha QF = -17.01 \times 5 = 85$ kN m (negative).

Continuous beams: characteristic-points method

42

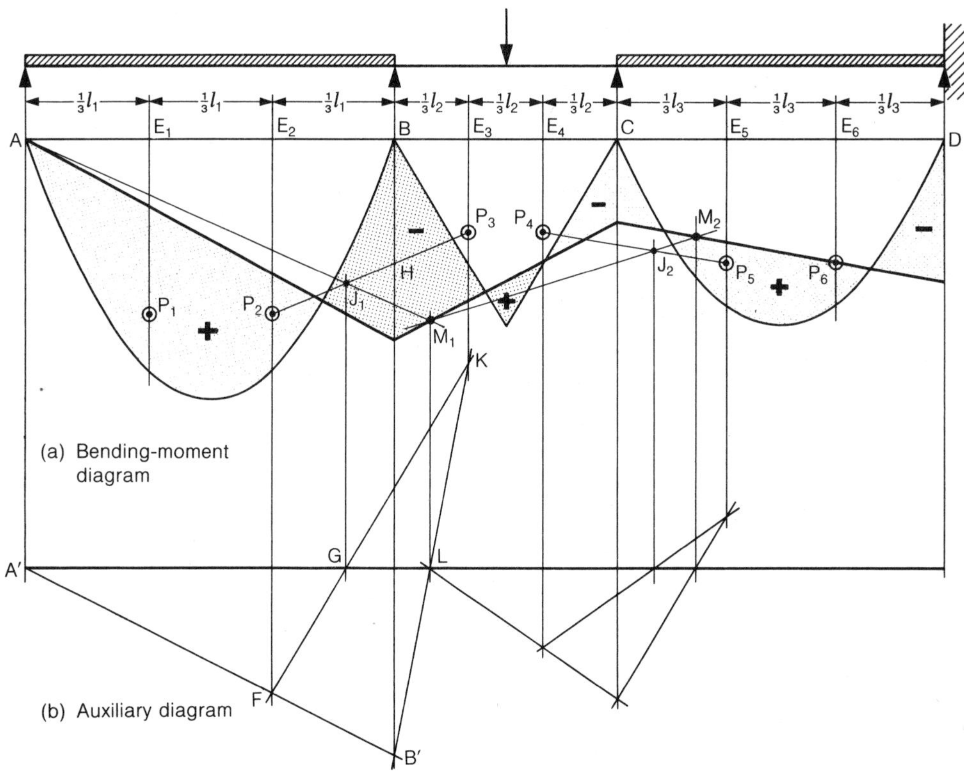

(a) Bending-moment diagram

(b) Auxiliary diagram

To determine the positions of the characteristic points

Draw the beam A, B, C etc. and plot the free-bending-moment diagrams to suitable scales.

Construct verticals through the third-points of each span, e.g. E_1P_1 and E_2P_2 for span AB, such that distance $E_1P_1 = 2Ax/l_1^2$, where A is the area of the free-bending-moment diagram for span AB and x is the distance of the centroid of this diagram from A. Similarly, $E_2P_2 = 2Ax'/l_1^2$, where x' is the distance of the centroid from B, and so on. Repeat for the remaining spans.

Points P_1, P_2, P_3 etc. obtained in this way are known as the *characteristic points.*

Standard cases

No load on span: $E_1P_1 = E_2P_2 = \text{zero}$

Uniform load: $E_1P_1 = E_2P_2 = \frac{2}{3} \times$ maximum bending-moment ordinate

Central concentrated load:

$E_1P_1 = E_2P_2 = \frac{1}{2} \times$ maximum bending-moment ordinate

Concentrated load at distance αl from A:

$E_1P_1 = \frac{2}{3}(2-\alpha) \times$ maximum bending-moment ordinate

$E_2P_2 = \frac{2}{3}(1+\alpha) \times$ maximum bending-moment ordinate

To determine the bending moments

Firstly, considering spans AB and BC only, join P_2P_3 to intersect the vertical through B at H. Set out J_1 such that $P_2J_1 = P_3H$ (or $P_2H = P_3J_1$). J_1 is termed the *intersection point* for this pair of spans. Repeat for the other pairs of adjoining spans to obtain J_2 etc.

Now construct an auxiliary diagram (diagram (b)) by projecting downwards, commencing from a known point on the line of fixing moments (point A in the example). Draw a new horizontal baseline to intersect a vertical through A at A′. Erect a vertical from B to B′ and draw A′B′ at any convenient angle to intersect a vertical through P_2 at F. Join F to G, where the vertical through intersection point J_1 meets the new baseline, and project to intersect a vertical through P_3 at K. Now join K to B′ to cut the baseline at L and erect a vertical from L, cutting the projection of a line joining A to J_1 at M_1. M_1 is now one point on the line of final support moments.

Repeat the construction, starting at point L to obtain points M_2 etc. For any continuous-beam system fully fixed at one end (e.g. D in the present example), the support-moment line passes through the characteristic point adjacent to that support (i.e. P_6 in this case). For any system freely supported at one end, the moment is zero at that end, of course.

In the example, the support-moment line passes through points A, M_1, M_2 and P_6, and this information is sufficient to construct the diagram. Alternatively, the construction could be made working from right to left and commencing from point P_6 (since the support-moment line must pass through this point).

The support-moment line may alternatively be obtained algebraically or by a trial-and-adjustment procedure sometimes known as the 'pin-and-string' method. Plot the bending-moment diagrams for the individual freely supported spans forming the system and calculate and plot the characteristic points P_1, P_2 etc. Determine the positions of the intersection points as described above. Now insert pins at points A and D and at trial values of the support moments at B and C and pass a thread weighted at the ends, over A and D and below the other points to represent the trial base line. Then, by moving the positions of the pins up and down to adjust the moments at B and C, alter the position of the thread until a line joining points R_2 and R_3 (where the thread intersects verticals through the third-points) intersects the line joining P_2 and P_3, and so on at each other support. When this condition is achieved, the thread represents the support-moment line.

For M_C:

From left-hand span:

$+0.0167 \times 0.417 \times 600 \times 12 \quad = +\quad 50.0$

From central span:

$-0.05 \times 1.111(1200 + 500 \times 1.5)12 = -1300.0$

From right-hand span:

$-0.0667 \times 0.556 \times 800 \times 12 \quad = -\quad 355.6$

$M_C = -1605.6\,\text{kN m}$

Alternative method. From the graphs on *Tables 44* and *45*, if $\alpha = 0.5$ and $\beta = 0.667$, $k_1 = 0.046$, $k_2 = 0.065$ and $k_3 = 0.018$. Also if $\alpha' = 0.667$ and $\beta' = 0.5$, $k'_1 = 0.056$, $k'_2 = 0.056$ and $k'_3 = 0.014$. Then

$$M_B = -k_1F_1l_1 - k_2F_2l_2 + k_3F_3l_3$$
$$= -0.046 \times 6^2 \times 100 - 0.065$$
$$\times (12^2 \times 100 + 12 \times 500 \times 1.5) + 0.018 \times 8^2 \times 100$$
$$= -1571.4\,\text{kN m}$$
$$M_C = +k'_3F_1l_1 - k'_2F_2l_2 - k'_1F_3l_3$$
$$= 0.014 \times 6^2 \times 100 - 0.056$$
$$\times (12^2 \times 100 + 12 \times 500 \times 1.5) - 0.056 \times 8^2 \times 100$$
$$= -1618.4\,\text{kN m}.$$

These values differ by less than 1% from the exact values obtained by calculation.

Continuous beams: unequal prismatic spans and loads

43

Divide given beam system into a number of similar systems each having one span loaded with a particular type of load. To find the bending moment at any support due to any one of these loads, evaluate the following factors for the particular support and type of load:

- F total load on span being considered
- α load factor (= unity for distributed load)
- Q support moment coefficient
- U moment multiplier (= unity for equal spans)

Moment at support $= \alpha QU \times F \times$ base span l

Ratios of remaining spans to base span $= k_1, k_2, k_3$

Type of load	Load factor $= \alpha$	Max. free bending moment
	1.00	$0.125\,Fl$
	1.25	$0.167\,Fl$
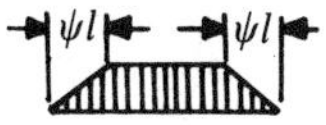 ψl ψl	$1+\psi-\psi^2$	$\dfrac{3-4\psi^2}{24(1-\psi)}Fl$
 = =	1.50	$0.250\,Fl$
 = = =	1.33	$0.167\,Fl$
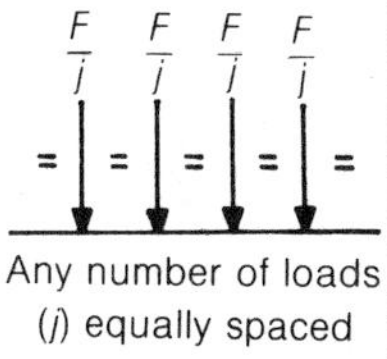 $\frac{F}{j}$ $\frac{F}{j}$ $\frac{F}{j}$ $\frac{F}{j}$ = = = = = Any number of loads (j) equally spaced	$\dfrac{2+j}{1+j}$	Even number of loads: $\dfrac{1}{8}\left(\dfrac{2+j}{1+j}\right)Fl$ Odd number of loads: $\dfrac{1}{8}\left(\dfrac{1+j}{j}\right)Fl$

No. of spans	Loaded span	Equal spans Support moment coefficients Q_A	Q_B	Q_C	Unequal spans Moment multipliers $= U$	
2	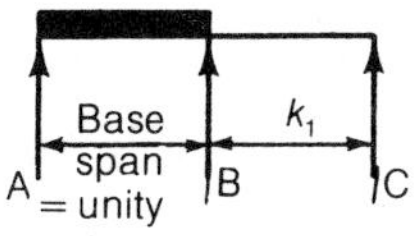 Base span = unity, k_1; A, B, C	—	−0.0625	—	$U_B = \dfrac{2}{1+k_1}$	
		—	−0.0625	—	$U_B = \dfrac{2k_1^2}{1+k_1}$	
	Both spans loaded with identical load	—	−0.1250	—	See note below	
3	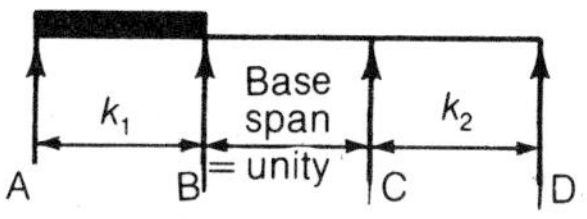 k_1, Base span = unity, k_2; A, B, C, D	—	−0.0667	+0.0167	$U_B = 0.5yU_C$ $U_C = 3k_1^2 H$	$x = k_1 + 1$ $y = k_2 + 1$ $H = \dfrac{5}{4xy-1}$
		—	−0.0500	−0.0500	$U_B = H(y+k_2)$ $U_C = H(x+k_1)$	
	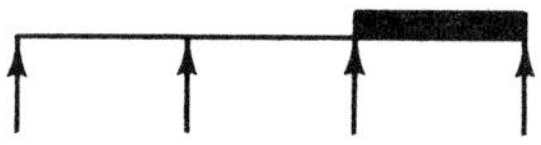	—	+0.0167	−0.0667	$U_B = 3k_2^2 H$ $U_C = 0.5xU_B$	
	All spans loaded with identical load	—	−0.1000	−0.1000	For two, three, or four unequal spans loaded simultaneously, determine bending moment for each span loaded separately and add	
4	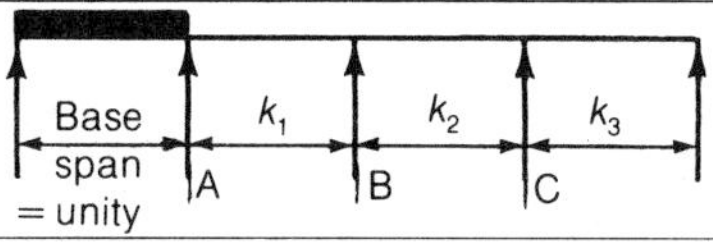 Base span = unity, k_1, k_2, k_3; A, B, C	−0.0670	+0.0179	−0.0045	$U_A = (2/15x)(14 + k_1 H_1 z)$ $U_B = zH_1$ $U_C = 2k_2 H_1$	$x = k_1 + 1$ $y = k_1 + k_2$ $z = k_2 + k_3$ $Y = \dfrac{1}{4xyz - k_1^2 z - k_2^2 x}$ $H_1 = 14k_1 Y$ $H_2 = 14k_1^2 Y(x+1)/3$ $H_3 = 14k_2^2 Y(k_3+z)/3$ $H_4 = 14k_3^2 Y$
		−0.0491	−0.0536	+0.0134	$U_A = (6/11x)k_1 \times [(14k_1/3) - U_B]$ $U_B = zH_2$ $U_C = 2k_2 H_2$	
		+0.0134	−0.0536	−0.0491	$U_A = 2k_1 H_3$ $U_B = xH_3$ $U_C = (6/11z)k_2 \times [(14k_2/3) - U_B]$	
	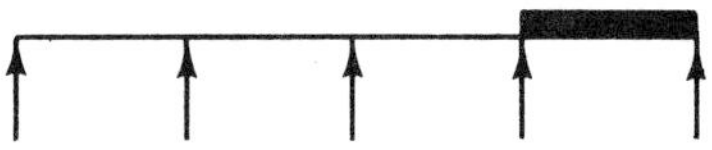	−0.0045	+0.0179	−0.0670	$U_A = 2k_1 H_4 k_2$ $U_B = xH_4 k_2$ $U_C = 2H_4(4xy - k_1^2)/15$	
	All spans loaded with identical load	−0.1071	−0.0714	−0.1071	See note above	

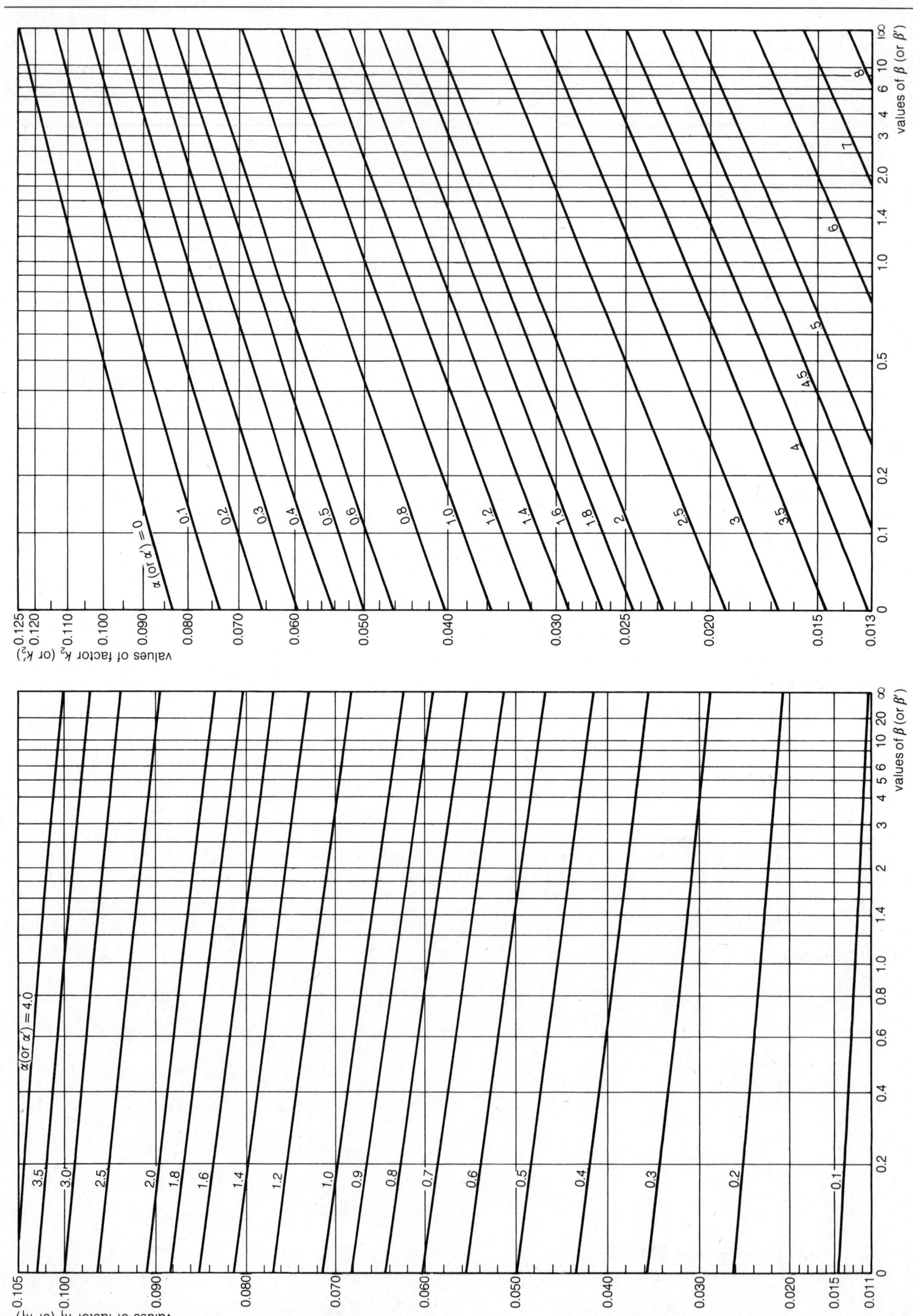

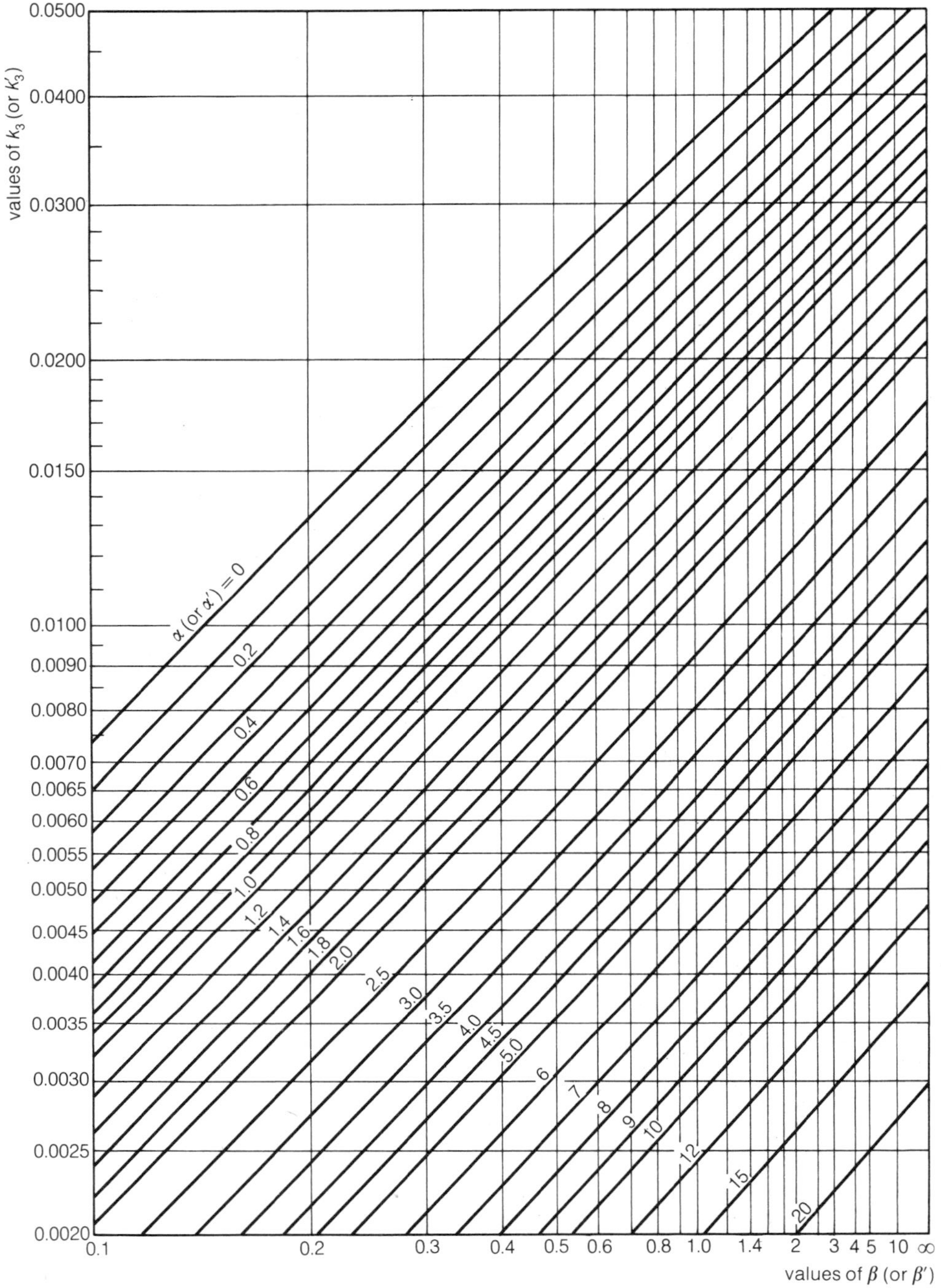

values of k_3 (or k_3')
0.0500
0.0400
0.0300
0.0200
0.0150
0.0100
0.0090
0.0080
0.0070
0.0065
0.0060
0.0055
0.0050
0.0045
0.0040
0.0035
0.0030
0.0025
0.0020
α (or α') = 0
0.2
0.4
0.6
0.8
1.0
1.2
1.4
1.6
1.8
2.0
2.5
3.0
3.5
4.0
4.5
5.0
6
7
8
9
10
12
15
20
0.1
0.2
0.3
0.4
0.5
0.6
0.8
1.0
1.4
2
3 4 5 10 ∞
values of β (or β')

CALCULATION PROCEDURE

Total load = F_1
Total load = F_2
Total load = F_3
K
L
R
S
I_1
K_1
I_2
K_2
I_3
K_3
l_1
l_2
l_3

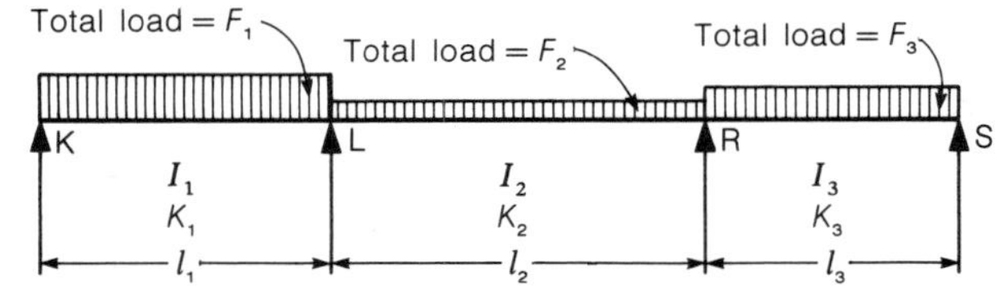

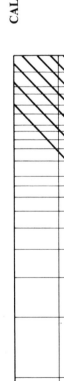

Three-span beam: freely supported at K and S

1. With $\alpha = \dfrac{K_2}{K_1} = \dfrac{l_1 I_2}{l_2 I_1}$ and $\beta = \dfrac{K_2}{K_3} = \dfrac{l_3 I_2}{l_2 I_3}$

   read off values of k_1, k_2 and k_3 from appropriate charts.

2. With $\alpha' = \dfrac{K_2}{K_3} = \dfrac{l_3 I_2}{l_2 I_3}$ and $\beta' = \dfrac{K_2}{K_1} = \dfrac{l_1 I_2}{l_2 I_1}$

   read off values of k_1', k_2' and k_3' from appropriate charts.

3. Then $M_L = -k_1 F_1 l_1 - k_2 F_2 l_2 + k_3 F_3 l_3$
   $M_R = +k_3' F_1 l_1 - k_2' F_2 l_2 - k_1' F_3 l_3$

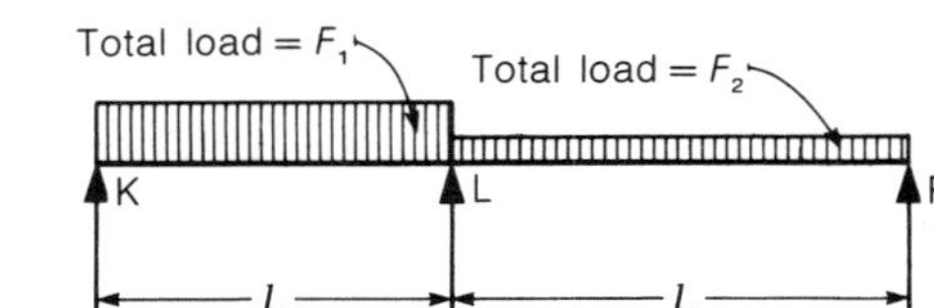

Total load = F_1
Total load = F_2
K
L
R
l_1
l_2

Two-span beam: freely supported at K and R

1. With $\alpha = \dfrac{K_2}{K_1} = \dfrac{l_1 I_2}{l_2 I_1}$ and taking $\beta = \infty$,

   read off values of k_1 and k_2 from appropriate charts.

2. Then $M_L = -k_1 F_1 l_1 - k_2 F_2 l_2$

Two-span beam: freely supported at K; fixed at R

1. With $\alpha = \dfrac{K_2}{K_1} = \dfrac{l_1 I_2}{l_2 I_1}$ and taking $\beta = 0$,

   read off values of k_1 and k_2 from appropriate charts.

2. With $\beta' = \dfrac{K_2}{K_1} = \dfrac{l_1 I_2}{l_2 I_1}$ and taking $\alpha' = 0$,

   read off values of k_2' and k_3' from appropriate charts.

3. Then $M_L = -k_1 F_1 l_1 - k_2 F_2 l_2$
   $M_R = -k_2' F_2 l_2 + k_3' F_1 l_1$

Chapter 13
Influence lines for continuous beams

To determine the bending moments at any of the critical sections in a system of continuous beams due to a train of loads in any given position, the procedure is as follows:

1. Draw the beam system to a convenient linear scale.
2. With the ordinates tabulated in *Tables 46, 47, 48* or *49*, construct the influence line (for unit load) for the section being considered, selecting a convenient scale for the bending moment.
3. Plot on this diagram the train of loads in what is considered to be the most adverse position.
4. Tabulate the value of ordinate × load for each load.
5. Algebraically add the values of ordinate × load to give the resultant bending moment at the section considered.
6. Repeat for other positions of load to ensure that the most adverse position has been assumed.

The following example shows the direct use of the tabulated influence lines for calculating the service bending moments on a beam that is continuous over four spans and is subjected to concentrated loads in specified positions.

Example. Determine the service bending moments at the penultimate left-hand support of a system of four spans having a constant moment of inertia and freely supported at the end supports when subjected to a central load of 100 kN (or 10 tons) on the first and third spans from the left-hand end. The end spans are 8 m (or 20 ft) long and the interior spans 12 m (or 30 ft) in length: the span ratio is thus 1:1.5:1.5:1.

SI units

With load on first span (ordinate c):
Bending moment $= -(0.082 \times 100 \times 8)$ $= -65.6$ kN m

With load on third span (ordinate m):
Bending moment $= +(0.035 \times 100 \times 8)$ $= +28.0$ kN m

Net service bending moment at penultimate support $= -37.6$ kN m

Imperial units

With load on first span (ordinate c):
Bending moment
$= -(0.082 \times 10 \times 2240 \times 20)$ $= -36\,800$ lb ft

With load on third span (ordinate m):
Bending moment
$= +(0.035 \times 10 \times 2240 \times 20)$ $= +15\,700$ lb ft

Net service bending moment at penultimate support $= -21\,100$ lb ft

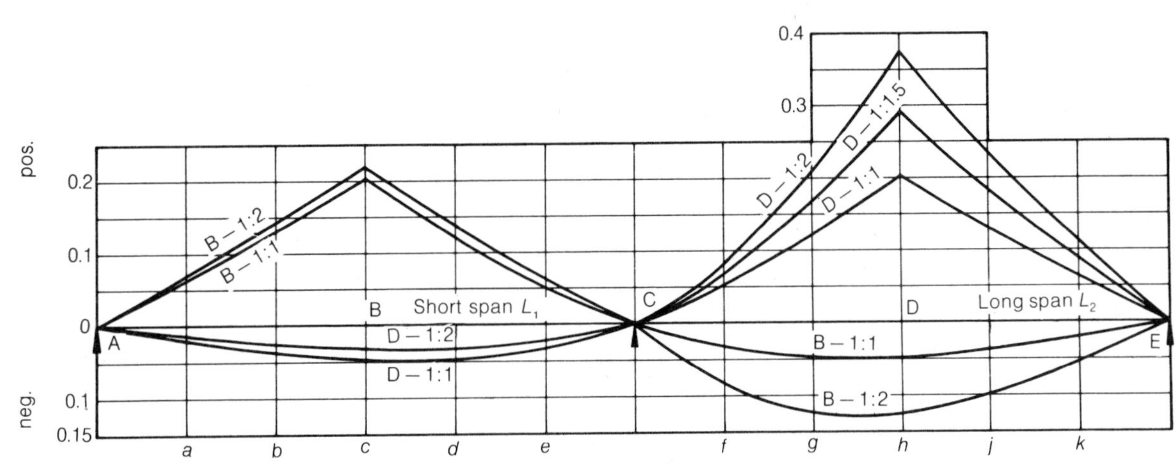

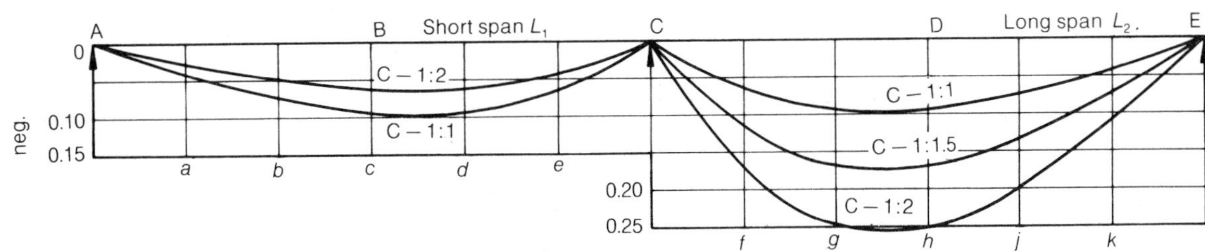

Section	Ratio of spans $L_1:L_2$	Ordinates									
		Shorter span					Longer span				
		a	*b*	*c*	*d*	*e*	*f*	*g*	*h*	*j*	*k*
Shorter span midspan B	1:1 1:1.5 1:2	0.063 0.067 0.070	0.130 0.137 0.142	0.203 0.213 0.219	0.121 0.130 0.136	0.052 0.058 0.062	0.032 0.058 0.085	0.046 0.083 0.124	0.047 0.084 0.125	0.037 0.067 0.099	0.020 0.037 0.054
Central support C	1:1 1:1.5 1:2	0.041 0.032 0.027	0.074 0.059 0.049	0.094 0.075 0.063	0.093 0.074 0.062	0.064 0.051 0.042	0.064 0.115 0.170	0.093 0.167 0.247	0.094 0.169 0.250	0.074 0.133 0.198	0.041 0.073 0.108
Longer span midspan D	1:1 1:1.5 1:2	0.020 0.016 0.014	0.037 0.030 0.025	0.047 0.038 0.031	0.046 0.037 0.031	0.032 0.025 0.021	0.052 0.067 0.082	0.121 0.167 0.210	0.203 0.291 0.375	0.130 0.183 0.235	0.063 0.088 0.113

Unequal spans
Data enable influence lines to be drawn for the bending moments produced by a single unit load moving over two unequal spans.

Ordinates for intermediate ratios of spans can be interpolated.

Equal spans
Influence lines marked 1:1 can be used directly (diagram of a succession of loads must be drawn to the same linear scale).

Bending moment due to load F concentrated at any point.
= (ordinate of appropriate influence line)
× (shorter span L_1) × F

Continuous beams: influence lines: three spans

Three spans (equal or symmetrical inequality)

Influence lines for bending moments
at midspan B of end span AC
and midspan D of central span CC′

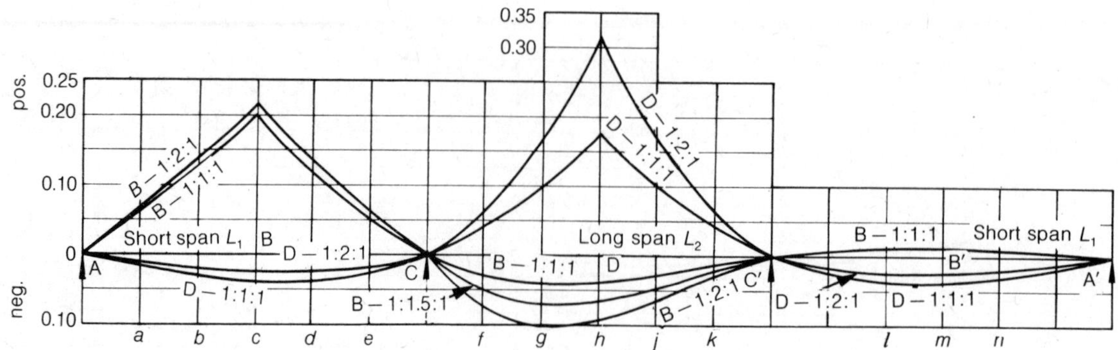

Influence lines for bending moments
at interior support C

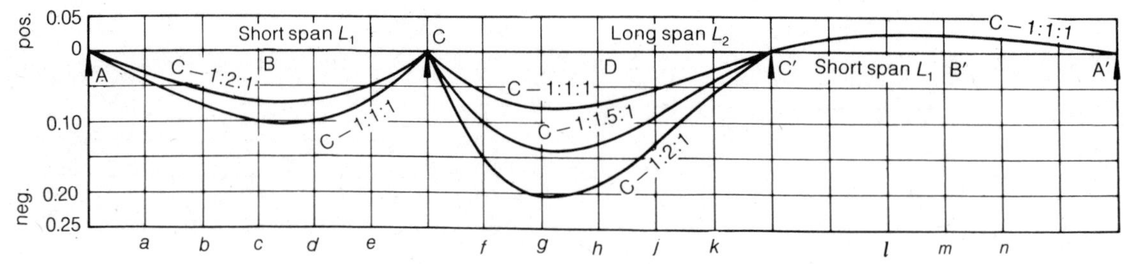

Section	Ratio of spans $L_1:L_2:L_1$	Ordinates												
		End span AC					Central span CC′					End span C′A′		
		a	*b*	*c*	*d*	*e*	*f*	*g*	*h*	*j*	*k*	*l*	*m*	*n*
Midspan B of end span AC	1:1:1	0.062	0.127	0.200	0.117	0.050	0.029	0.040	0.038	0.027	0.013	0.012	0.013	0.010
	1:1.5:1	0.066	0.134	0.209	0.126	0.056	0.051	0.070	0.065	0.046	0.021	0.012	0.012	0.010
	1:2:1	0.068	0.139	0.215	0.132	0.060	0.075	0.102	0.094	0.065	0.029	0.012	0.012	0.009
Interior support C	1:1:1	0.043	0.079	0.100	0.099	0.068	0.057	0.079	0.075	0.054	0.026	0.025	0.025	0.020
	1:1.5:1	0.036	0.065	0.082	0.081	0.056	0.102	0.139	0.130	0.092	0.042	0.024	0.025	0.020
	1:2:1	0.030	0.056	0.070	0.069	0.048	0.151	0.204	0.188	0.129	0.058	0.023	0.023	0.019
Midspan D of central span CC′	1:1:1	0.016	0.030	0.038	0.037	0.025	0.042	0.100	0.175	0.100	0.042	0.037	0.038	0.030
	1:1.5:1	0.013	0.023	0.029	0.028	0.020	0.053	0.135	0.245	0.135	0.053	0.028	0.029	0.023
	1:2:1	0.010	0.019	0.023	0.023	0.016	0.063	0.167	0.313	0.167	0.063	0.023	0.023	0.019

Unequal spans
Data enable influence lines to be drawn for bending moments produced by a single unit load moving over three unequal spans.

Ordinates for intermediate ratio of spans can be interpolated.

Equal spans
Influence lines marked 1:1:1 can be used directly (diagram of a succession of loads must be drawn to the same linear scale).

Bending moment due to load F concentrated at any point =(ordinate of appropriate influence line) $\times$(end span L_1) $\times F$

Continuous beams: influence lines: four spans

Four spans (equal or symmetrical inequality)

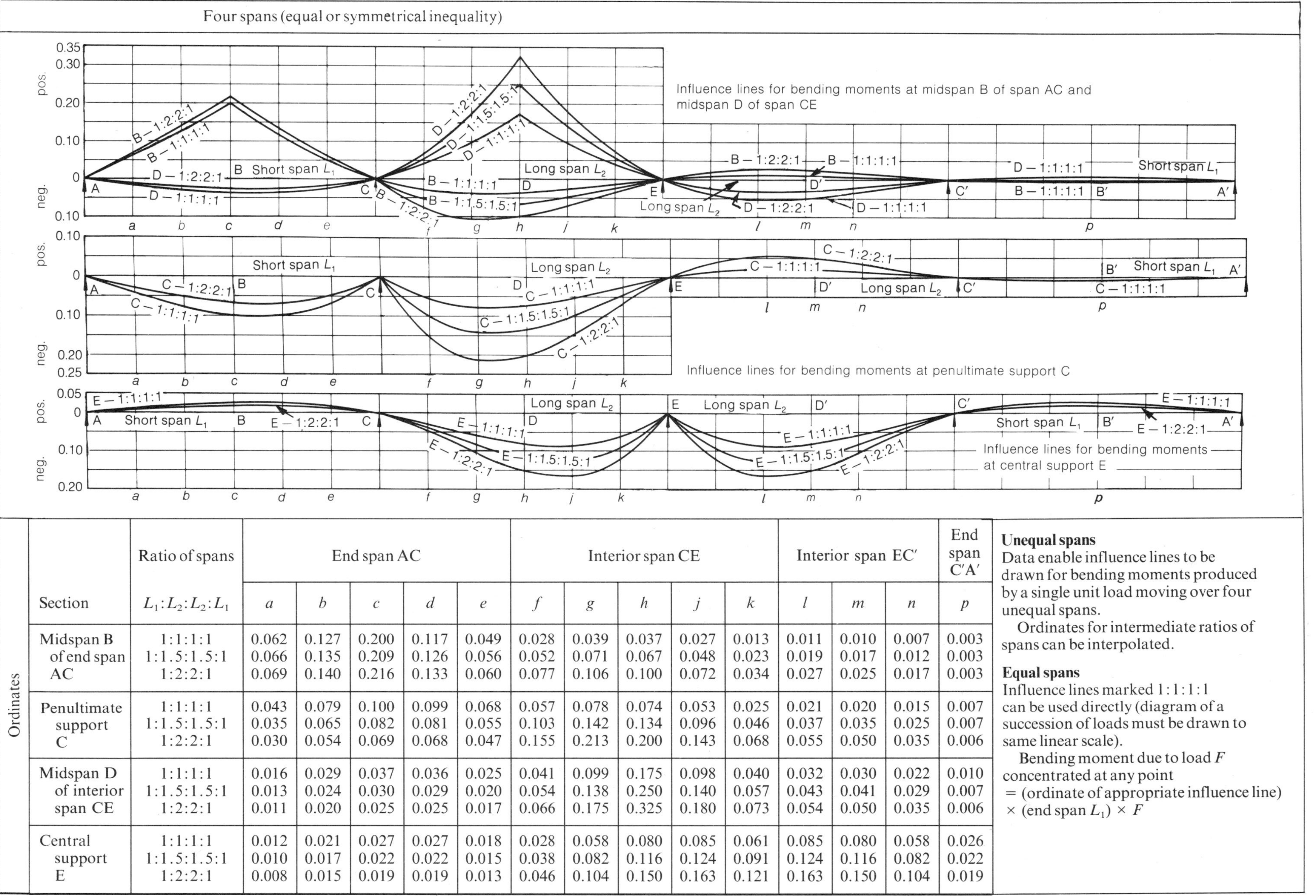

Section	Ratio of spans $L_1:L_2:L_2:L_1$	End span AC *a*	*b*	*c*	*d*	*e*	Interior span CE *f*	*g*	*h*	*j*	*k*	Interior span EC′ *l*	*m*	*n*	End span C′A′ *p*
Midspan B of end span AC	1:1:1:1	0.062	0.127	0.200	0.117	0.049	0.028	0.039	0.037	0.027	0.013	0.011	0.010	0.007	0.003
	1:1.5:1.5:1	0.066	0.135	0.209	0.126	0.056	0.052	0.071	0.067	0.048	0.023	0.019	0.017	0.012	0.003
	1:2:2:1	0.069	0.140	0.216	0.133	0.060	0.077	0.106	0.100	0.072	0.034	0.027	0.025	0.017	0.003
Penultimate support C	1:1:1:1	0.043	0.079	0.100	0.099	0.068	0.057	0.078	0.074	0.053	0.025	0.021	0.020	0.015	0.007
	1:1.5:1.5:1	0.035	0.065	0.082	0.081	0.055	0.103	0.142	0.134	0.096	0.046	0.037	0.035	0.025	0.007
	1:2:2:1	0.030	0.054	0.069	0.068	0.047	0.155	0.213	0.200	0.143	0.068	0.055	0.050	0.035	0.006
Midspan D of interior span CE	1:1:1:1	0.016	0.029	0.037	0.036	0.025	0.041	0.099	0.175	0.098	0.040	0.032	0.030	0.022	0.010
	1:1.5:1.5:1	0.013	0.024	0.030	0.029	0.020	0.054	0.138	0.250	0.140	0.057	0.043	0.041	0.029	0.007
	1:2:2:1	0.011	0.020	0.025	0.025	0.017	0.066	0.175	0.325	0.180	0.073	0.054	0.050	0.035	0.006
Central support E	1:1:1:1	0.012	0.021	0.027	0.027	0.018	0.028	0.058	0.080	0.085	0.061	0.085	0.080	0.058	0.026
	1:1.5:1.5:1	0.010	0.017	0.022	0.022	0.015	0.038	0.082	0.116	0.124	0.091	0.124	0.116	0.082	0.022
	1:2:2:1	0.008	0.015	0.019	0.019	0.013	0.046	0.104	0.150	0.163	0.121	0.163	0.150	0.104	0.019

Ordinates

Unequal spans
Data enable influence lines to be drawn for bending moments produced by a single unit load moving over four unequal spans.

Ordinates for intermediate ratios of spans can be interpolated.

Equal spans
Influence lines marked 1:1:1:1 can be used directly (diagram of a succession of loads must be drawn to same linear scale).

Bending moment due to load F concentrated at any point = (ordinate of appropriate influence line) × (end span L_1) × F

INFLUENCE LINES FOR BENDING MOMENTS AT MIDSPAN AND AT THIRD-POINT OF INTERIOR SPAN AND AT INTERIOR SUPPORT

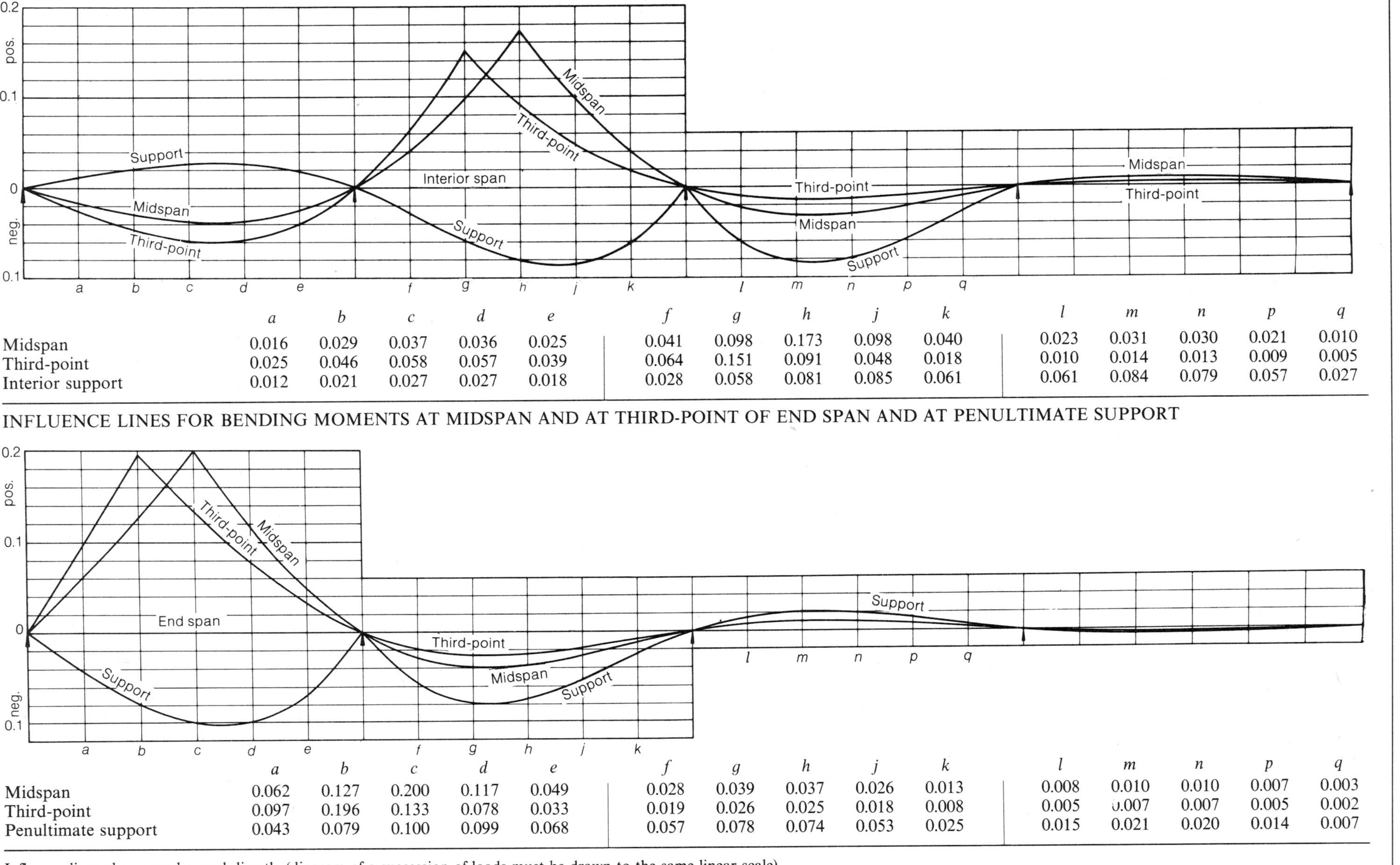

	a	*b*	*c*	*d*	*e*	*f*	*g*	*h*	*j*	*k*	*l*	*m*	*n*	*p*	*q*
Midspan	0.016	0.029	0.037	0.036	0.025	0.041	0.098	0.173	0.098	0.040	0.023	0.031	0.030	0.021	0.010
Third-point	0.025	0.046	0.058	0.057	0.039	0.064	0.151	0.091	0.048	0.018	0.010	0.014	0.013	0.009	0.005
Interior support	0.012	0.021	0.027	0.027	0.018	0.028	0.058	0.081	0.085	0.061	0.061	0.084	0.079	0.057	0.027

INFLUENCE LINES FOR BENDING MOMENTS AT MIDSPAN AND AT THIRD-POINT OF END SPAN AND AT PENULTIMATE SUPPORT

	a	*b*	*c*	*d*	*e*	*f*	*g*	*h*	*j*	*k*	*l*	*m*	*n*	*p*	*q*
Midspan	0.062	0.127	0.200	0.117	0.049	0.028	0.039	0.037	0.026	0.013	0.008	0.010	0.010	0.007	0.003
Third-point	0.097	0.196	0.133	0.078	0.033	0.019	0.026	0.025	0.018	0.008	0.005	0.007	0.007	0.005	0.002
Penultimate support	0.043	0.079	0.100	0.099	0.068	0.057	0.078	0.074	0.053	0.025	0.015	0.021	0.020	0.014	0.007

Influence lines above can be used directly (diagram of a succession of loads must be drawn to the same linear scale).
Bending moment due to load F concentrated at any point = (ordinate of appropriate influence line) × (span) × F
Ordinates for end span and penultimate support of four equal spans can be used for five or more spans with reasonable accuracy.

Chapter 14
Slabs spanning in two directions

14.1 LOADS AND STRESSES

Various methods, based on elastic and collapse considerations, are used to design slabs spanning in two directions. The data for single freely supported two-way slabs given in BS8110 and CP110 derive from an elastic analysis, while those for continuous series of slabs relate to collapse conditions. In both cases the load per unit area considered should be the total ultimate load $n = 1.4g_k + 1.6q_k$, and the design of the sections to resist the resulting ultimate moments should be undertaken using ultimate-limit-state methods and employing characteristic strengths f_{cu} and f_y for the concrete and reinforcement respectively.

Note that the sections so obtained must also be checked to ensure compliance with the appropriate Code requirements regarding slenderness, bar spacing, shear and fire resistance.

14.2 RECTANGULAR PANELS FREELY SUPPORTED ALONG ALL EDGES WITH UNIFORM LOAD

14.2.1 No restraint at corners

For a rectangular panel freely supported along all four edges and for which no provision is made at the corners to prevent them lifting or to resist torsion, the Grashof and Rankine method is applicable. The normal free bending moment in each direction due to a service load $w = g_k$ is multiplied by reduction coefficients $\alpha_{x2} = k^4/(k^4 + 1)$ and $\alpha_{y2} = 1 - \alpha_{x2}$, the resulting midspan moments being calculated from the formulae $M_{dx} = \alpha_{x2}(wl_x^2/8)$ and $M_{dy} = \alpha_{y2}(wl_y^2/8)$. Values of α_{x2} and α_{y2} are given in *Table 50*. The limit of application of this method is often taken to be when the length of the slab is twice the width, i.e. $k = 2$. Beyond this limit, the slab is considered to span across the short direction only, the bending moment per unit width thus being $wl_x^2/8$.

The same method and coefficients are employed for the identical condition in BS8110 and CP110. The appropriate coefficients, which are identical in both documents, correspond to α_{x1} and α_{y1} (where $\alpha_{x1} = \alpha_{sx}$ in the Code notation and $\alpha_{y1} = \alpha_{sy}/k^2$) on *Tables 51* and *52*. Then the ultimate bending moments M_{sx} and M_{sy} are given by $M_{sx} = \alpha_{x1} n l_x^2$ and $M_{sy} = \alpha_{y1} n l_y^2$, where $n = 1.4g_k + 1.6q_k$.

14.2.2 Restraint at corners

When the corners of the slab are prevented from lifting and torsional restraint is provided, the simple Grashof and Rankine method is inappropriate. A more exact elastic analysis, assuming a value of Poisson's ratio of zero, gives the reduction coefficients α_{x3} and α_{y3} tabulated in *Table 50*. The resulting service bending moments at midspan are then $M_{dx} = \alpha_{x3}(wl_x^2/8)$ and $M_{dy} = \alpha_{y3}(wl_y^2/8)$.

Alternatively, Marcus's method may be used. Here the Grashof and Rankine coefficients are multiplied by a further factor ξ_1, which depends on the fixity at each slab edge; for a slab freely supported along all four edges, $\xi_1 = 1 - 0.833k^2/(1 + k^4)$. The midspan service bending moments per unit width are then $M_{dx} = \xi_1\alpha_{x2}(wl_x^2/8)$ and $M_{dy} = \xi_1\alpha_{y2}(wl_y^2/8)$.

Marcus's method and exact elastic analysis with Poisson's ratio equal to zero give near-identical bending moments. If Poisson's ratio is taken as 0.2, the midspan service bending moments per unit width are $M_{dx} = \xi_1\alpha_{x2}(wl_x^2/8)(1 + 0.2/k^2)$ and $M_{dy} = \xi_1\alpha_{y2}(wl_y^2/8)(0.2 + 1/k^2)$. Alternatively, the appropriate coefficients can be obtained from the curves on *Table 55* for $a_x/l_x = a_y/l_y = 1$, for a slab completely covered with a load of intensity $w = F_d/l_x l_y$.

Bending-moment coefficients for this case, derived as described below, are also given in BS8110 and CP110, and correspond to the curves for β_{x1} and β_{y1} and β_{x2} and β_{y2} on the top left-hand diagrams on *Tables 51* and *52* respectively.

14.3 RECTANGULAR PANELS FIXED ALONG ALL EDGES WITH UNIFORM LOAD

If a panel is completely fixed along all four edges, the service bending moments resulting from an elastic analysis are as follows:

Short span l_x:
  Support $M_{dx} = -\alpha_{x3}(wl_x^2/8)$
  Span $M_{dx} = +0.8 \times$ support M_{dx}
Long span l_y:
  Support $M_{dy} = -\alpha_{y3}(wl_y^2/8)$
  Span $M_{dy} = +0.8 \times$ support M_{dy}

where the values of α_{x3} and α_{y3} are as given in *Table 50*.

Alternatively, Marcus's method may again be used to

Two-way slabs: rectangular panels: uniform load: elastic analyses

Ratio of spans k	Condition along all edges: Free. Corners not held down		Free or fixed. Corners held down		Free (Marcus)	Fixed (Marcus)
	α_{x2}	α_{y2}	α_{x3}	α_{y3}	ξ_1	ξ_2
1.0	0.500	0.500	0.300	0.300	0.583	0.861
1.05	0.549	0.451	0.330	0.271	0.585	0.862
1.1	0.594	0.406	0.360	0.246	0.591	0.864
1.15	0.636	0.364	0.389	0.222	0.599	0.866
1.2	0.675	0.325	0.418	0.202	0.610	0.870
1.25	0.709	0.291	0.446	0.183	0.622	0.874
1.3	0.741	0.259	0.474	0.166	0.635	0.878
1.4	0.793	0.207	0.526	0.137	0.663	0.888
1.5	0.835	0.165	0.575	0.114	0.691	0.897
1.6	0.868	0.132	0.621	0.095	0.718	0.906
1.75	0.904	0.096	0.682	0.073	0.754	0.918
2.0	0.941	0.059	0.768	0.048	0.804	0.935
2.5	0.975	0.025	0.892	0.023	0.870	0.957
3.0	0.988	0.012	0.972	0.012	0.909	0.970

Ratio of spans $k = \dfrac{\text{long span}}{\text{short span}} = \dfrac{l_y}{l_x}$ Uniform service load $= w$ per unit area

Freely supported along all four edges:
Corners not held down:

$$M_x = +\alpha_{x2}(wl_x^2/8); \quad M_y = +\alpha_{y2}(wl_y^2/8) = M_x/k^2$$

Corners held down:

$$M_x = +\alpha_{x3}(wl_x^2/8); \quad M_y = +\alpha_{y3}(wl_y^2/8)$$

Corners held down (Marcus's method):

$$M_x = +\xi_1\alpha_{x2}(wl_x^2/8); \quad M_y = +\xi_1\alpha_{y2}(wl_y^2/8) = M_x/k^2$$

Fixed along all four edges:
Corners held down (Marcus's method):

$$M_x = +\xi_2\alpha_{x2}(wl_x^2/24); \quad M_y = +\xi_2\alpha_{y2}(wl_y^2/24) = M_x/k^2$$

$$M_{x1} = M_{x3} = -\alpha_{x2}(wl_x^2/12);$$

$$M_{y2} = M_{y4} = -\alpha_{y2}(wl_y^2/12) = M_{x1}/k^2$$

Continuity (or fixity) along one or more edges (BS8110 and CP110)

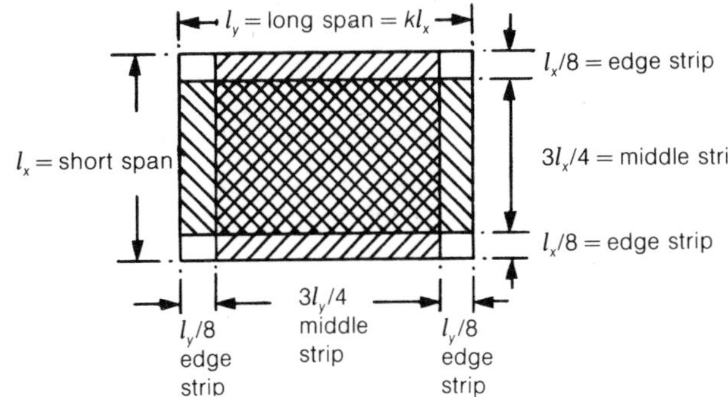

Conditions: corners held down
torsional resistance provided
No main reinforcement required in edge strips to resist bending moment parallel to edges of panel.

CP110 requirements:
If $k \not> 2$, the adjoining arrangement applies.
If $k > 2$, the panel should be designed to span in one direction only.

n = total ultimate load

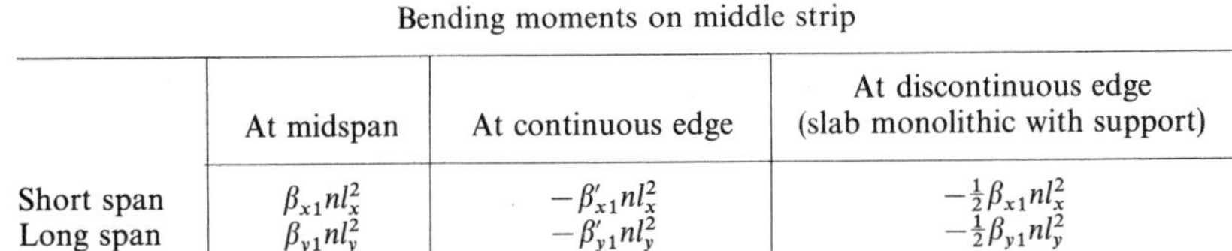

Bending moments on middle strip

	At midspan	At continuous edge	At discontinuous edge (slab monolithic with support)
Short span	$\beta_{x1}nl_x^2$	$-\beta'_{x1}nl_x^2$	$-\frac{1}{2}\beta_{x1}nl_x^2$
Long span	$\beta_{y1}nl_y^2$	$-\beta'_{y1}nl_y^2$	$-\frac{1}{2}\beta_{y1}nl_y^2$

Values given by expressions are *ultimate* moments.
For BS8110 values of β_{x1}, β'_{x1}, β_{y1} and β'_{y1} see *Table 51*; for CP110 values see *Table 52*.

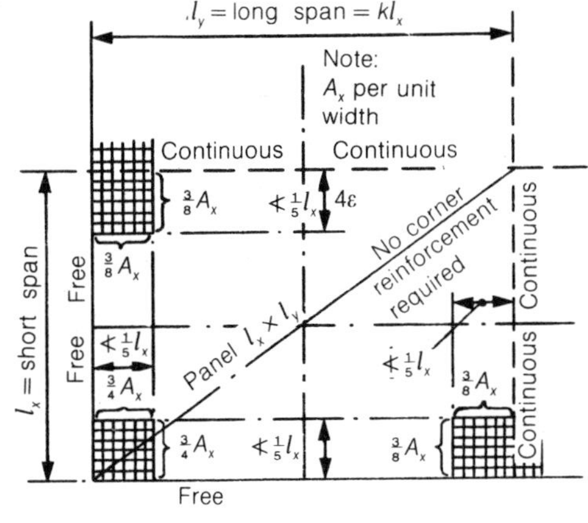

Main reinforcement

BS8110 requirements

Span:
$\not< 0.5A_s$ should extend $(d/2) + 12\phi$ beyond face of support at which slab is discontinuous; remainder to within $0.08l$ of support face (ϕ = diameter).
$\not< 0.3A_s$ should extend $(d/2) + 12\phi$ beyond face of support over which slab is continuous; remainder to within $0.15l$ of support face.

Support:
$\not< 0.2A_s$ should extend throughout span; $\not< 0.6A_s$ should extend to $0.25l$ from face of continuous support. All steel must extend $0.15k$ or 45ϕ, whichever is greater, beyond face of support.
In top at discontinuous support, provide one-half of steel area employed at midspan extending a minimum distance of $0.15l$ or 45ϕ beyond face of support.

CP110 requirements

$\not< A_s/2$ should extend to support; remainder to $0.1l$ from support.

With torsional restraint

Span:
$\not< A_s/2$ should extend to 50 mm from discontinuous edge; remainder to $0.15l$ from edge.
$\not< A_s/2$ should extend to $0.15l$ from continuous edge; remainder to $0.25l$ from edge.

Support:
$\not< A_s/2$ should extend to $0.3l$ from continuous edge; remainder to $0.15l$ from edge.
At discontinuous support A_{sreq} depends on fixity; generally $A_s/2$ provided at midspan extending $0.1l$ into span will suffice.

Corner reinforcement for torsional resistance

BS8110 and CP110 (see adjoining diagram)

A_x and A_y = cross-sectional area (per unit width) of reinforcement for positive BM at midspan of short and long spans respectively

$\frac{3}{4}A_x$ and $\frac{3}{8}A_x$ = cross-sectional area of corner reinforcement in each direction in each of two layers (one near top face of slab; one near bottom face): in² per ft or mm² per m

If $A_y > A_x$ substitute $\frac{3}{4}A_y$ and $\frac{3}{8}A_y$ for $\frac{3}{4}A_x$ and $\frac{3}{8}A_x$

analyse the slab. The appropriate additional multiplying factor $\xi_2 = 1 - 0.277k^2/(1 + k^4)$ and values of this coefficient, together with the Grashof and Rankine reduction coefficients α_{x2} and α_{y2}, are given in *Table 50*. The appropriate formulae are then as follows:

Short span l_x:
Support $M_{dx} = -\alpha_{x2}(wl_x^2/12)$
Span $M_{dx} = +\xi_2\alpha_{x2}(wl_x^2/24)$
Long span l_y:
Support $M_{dy} = -\alpha_{y2}(wl_y^2/12)$
Span $M_{dy} = +\xi_2\alpha_{y2}(wl_y^2/24)$

14.4 CODE METHOD FOR RECTANGULAR PANELS WITH UNIFORM LOAD

For the conditions common in reinforced concrete construction, i.e. with continuity over the supports along some edges and discontinuity at the other edges, the method recommended in BS8110 and CP110 is applicable. In this method provision is made at the discontinuous edges for the possible restraining moment due to the slab being cast monolithically with reinforced concrete beams supporting the panel or with concrete encasing steel beams, or due to embedment in a brick or masonry wall; if the restraint is of such magnitude that full fixity or conditions of continuity exist, the slab should be considered as continuous rather than discontinuous at the edge concerned.

14.4.1 BS8110 and CP110 requirements

The ultimate bending moments given in Table 3.15 of BS8110 and Table 13 of CP110, which are based on modified yield-line analysis, correspond to the curves for β_{x1} and β'_{x1}, β_{y1} and β'_{y1} in the diagrams on *Tables 51* and *52* respectively. (Actually β_{x1} and $\beta'_{x1} = \beta_{sx}$ in the Code notation, and β_{y1} and $\beta'_{y1} = \beta_{sy}/k^2$.) Details of their derivation are given in section 3.5.3; see also note on other methods in section 14.6. The resulting ultimate bending moments are then given by the following expressions:

Short span:
Support $M_{sx} = -\beta'_{x1}nl_x^2$
Span $M_{sx} = +\beta_{x1}nl_x^2$
Long span:
Support $M_{sy} = -\beta'_{y1}nl_y^2$
Span $M_{sy} = +\beta_{y1}nl_y^2$

where $n = 1.4g_k + 1.6q_k$. At a discontinuous edge where the slab is monolithic with the support a value of M_s of one-half of that at midspan in the same direction should be taken. The resulting sections should be designed using limit-state methods.

When $k > 2$, the slab should be designed to span in one direction only.

Part 1 of BS8110 gives (Equations 16–18) equations from which the coefficients β may be calculated. However, because the exact constants have been rounded to more-convenient values in these expressions, some of the resulting coefficients differ slightly from those on Table 3.15 of BS8110.

Example 1. Determine the bending moments on a rectangular slab freely supported on all four sides (corners not held down) and subjected to loads of $g_k = 4\,\text{kN/m}^2$ and $q_k = 6\,\text{kN/m}^2$ when $l_x = 3.0\,\text{m}$ and $l_y = 3.75\,\text{m}$. Thus $k = l_y/l_x = 1.25$.

(i) From *Table 50* the Grashof and Rankine coefficients are $\alpha_{x2} = 0.709$ and $\alpha_{y2} = 0.291$. The service load $w = 4 + 6 = 10\,\text{kN/m}^2$. The service bending moments per metre width are as follows:

Midspan on short span:
$M_{dx} = 0.709 \times (1/8) \times 10 \times 3.0^2 = 7.98\,\text{kN m}$
Midspan on long span:
$M_{dy} = 0.291 \times (1/8) \times 10 \times 3.75^2 = 5.12\,\text{kN m}$

(ii) From *Table 51* (or *Table 52*), using the coefficients α_{x1} and α_{y1} corresponding to the BS8110 and CP110 condition of 'corners not held down', the ultimate load $n = (1.4 \times 4 + 1.6 \times 6) = 15.2\,\text{kN/m}^2$. The ultimate bending moments per metre width are as follows:

Midspan on short span:
$M_{sx} = 0.089 \times 15.2 \times 3.0^2 = 12.18\,\text{kN m}$
Midspan on long span:
$M_{sy} = 0.036 \times 15.2 \times 3.75^2 = 7.70\,\text{kN m}$

Example 2. Find the bending moments in the panel in example 1 if it is constructed monolithically with the supports, but is discontinuous along all edges (i.e. it is nominally freely supported but with corners held down and torsional restraint provided).

(i) From *Table 50*, using 'exact' coefficients $\alpha_{x3} = 0.446$ and $\alpha_{y3} = 0.183$. The service bending moments per metre width are:

Midspan on short span:
$M_{dx} = 0.446 \times (1/8) \times 10 \times 3.0^2 = 5.02\,\text{kN m}$
Midspan on long span:
$M_{dy} = 0.183 \times (1/8) \times 10 \times 3.75^2 = 3.22\,\text{kN m}$

(ii) From *Table 51*, using the appropriate BS8110 coefficients (curves in top left-hand corner). The ultimate bending moments per metre width are:

Short span:
Middle strip at midspan:
$M_{sx} = 0.078 \times 15.2 \times 3.0^2 = +10.67\,\text{kN m}$
Middle strip at edge:
$M_{sx} = -10.67/2 = -5.34\,\text{kN m}$
Long span:
Middle strip at midspan:
$M_{sy} = 0.036 \times 15.2 \times 3.75^2 = +7.70\,\text{kN m}$
Middle strip at edge:
$M_{sy} = -7.70/2 = -3.85\,\text{kN m}$

(iii) From *Table 52*, using the appropriate CP110 coefficients (curves in top left-hand corner). The ultimate bending moments per metre width are:

Short span:
Middle strip at midspan:
$M_{sx} = 0.075 \times 15.2 \times 3.0^2 = +10.26\,\text{kN m}$

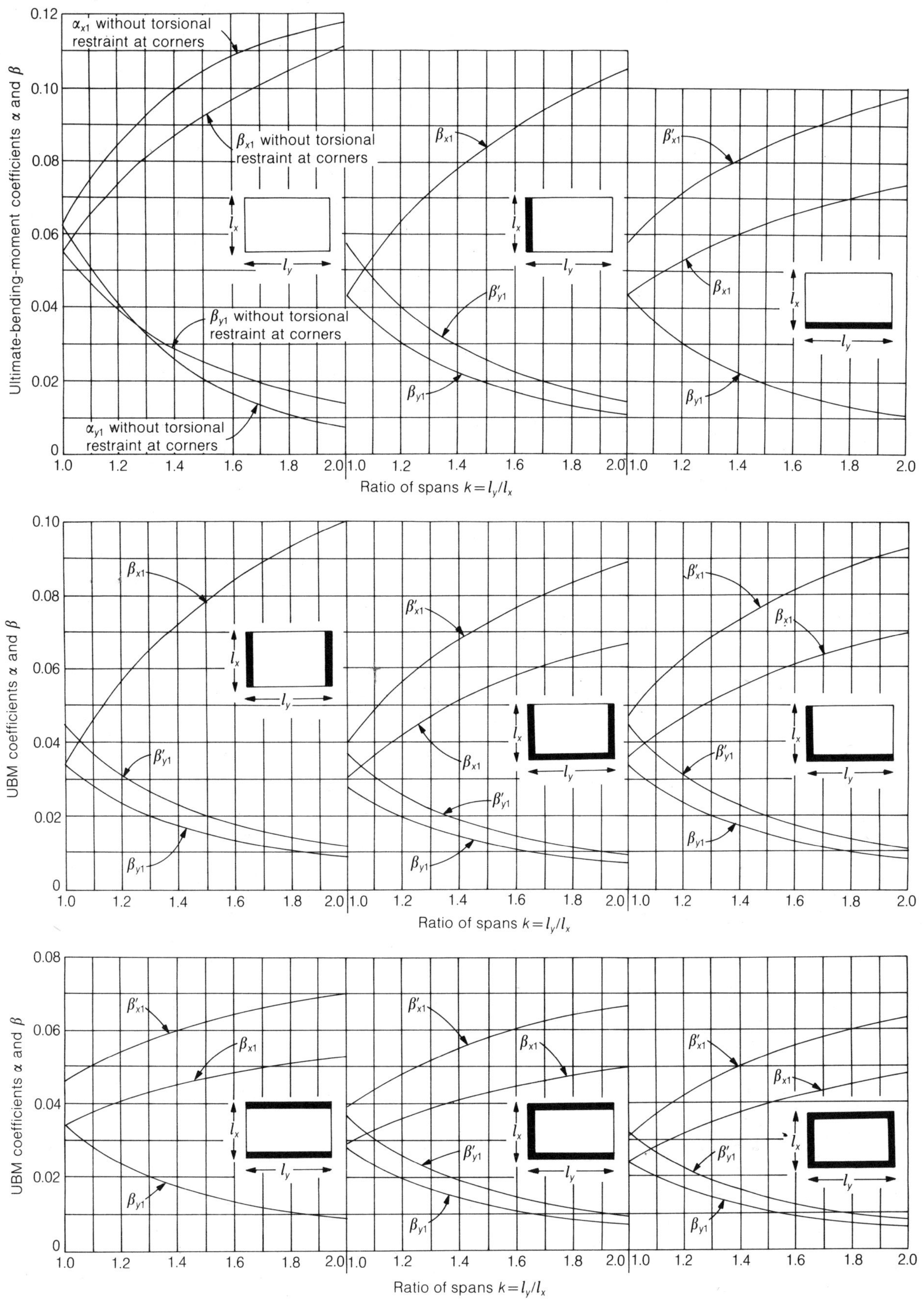

edge which is discontinuous or which is cast monolithically with support

edge which is continuous

Bending-moment coefficients β_{x1} and β'_{x1} apply to maximum positive and negative bending moments respectively on short span l_x.

Bending-moment coefficients β_{y1} and β'_{y1} apply to maximum positive and negative bending moments respectively on long span l_y.

Middle strip at edge:
$M_{sx} = -10.26/2 \quad = -5.13\,\mathrm{kN\,m}$
Long span:
Middle strip at midspan:
$M_{sy} = 0.036 \times 15.2 \times 3.75^2 = +7.70\,\mathrm{kN\,m}$
Middle strip at edge:
$M_{sy} = -7.70/2 \quad = -3.85\,\mathrm{kN\,m}$

Example 3. Determine the bending moments in the panel of example 1 if it is nominally freely supported along one long side only and continuous over the other three supports.

(i) Using the BS8110 coefficients given in *Table 51*, with $w = 10\,\mathrm{kN/m^2}$. The ultimate bending moments per metre width are:

Short span:
Middle strip at midspan:
$M_{sx} = 0.045 \times 15.2 \times 3.0^2 \quad = +6.16\,\mathrm{kN\,m}$
Middle strip at continuous edge:
$M_{sx} = -0.059 \times 15.2 \times 3.0^2 \quad = -8.07\,\mathrm{kN\,m}$
Middle strip at 'free' edge:
$M_{sx} = -6.16/2 \quad = -3.08\,\mathrm{kN\,m}$
Long span:
Middle strip at midspan:
$M_{sy} = 0.018 \times 15.2 \times 3.75^2 \quad = +3.85\,\mathrm{kN\,m}$
Middle strip at edge:
$M_{sy} = -0.024 \times 15.2 \times 3.75^2 = -5.13\,\mathrm{kN\,m}$

(ii) Using the CP110 coefficients given in *Table 52*, with $n = 15.2\,\mathrm{kN/m^2}$. The ultimate bending moments per metre width are:

Short span:
Middle strip at midspan:
$M_{sx} = 0.041 \times 15.2 \times 3.0^2 \quad = +5.61\,\mathrm{kN\,m}$
Middle strip at continuous edge:
$M_{sx} = -0.054 \times 15.2 \times 3.0^2 \quad = -7.39\,\mathrm{kN\,m}$
Middle strip at 'free' edge:
$M_{sx} = -5.61/2 \quad = -2.81\,\mathrm{kN\,m}$
Long span:
Middle strip at midspan:
$M_{sy} = 0.018 \times 15.2 \times 3.75^2 \quad = +3.85\,\mathrm{kN\,m}$
Middle strip at edge:
$M_{sy} = -0.024 \times 15.2 \times 3.75^2 = -5.13\,\mathrm{kN\,m}$

Example 4. The following example illustrates the use of the limiting case (when $a_x l_x = a_y/l_y = 1$) of Pigeaud's curves for concentrated loads. With the same data and conditions as in example 2 above, from *Tables 54* and *55*, $\alpha_{x4} = 0.045$ and $\alpha_{y4} = 0.025$. $F_d = 10 \times 3.0 \times 3.75 = 112.5\,\mathrm{kN}$. Then, assuming $v = 0$, the service bending moments at midspan are:

Short span: $M_{dx} = 0.045 \times 112{\cdot}5 = +5.1\,\mathrm{kN\,m}$
Long span: $M_{dy} = 0.025 \times 112.5 = +2.8\,\mathrm{kN\,m}$

Alternatively, considering an ultimate load of $F_u = 15.2 \times 3.0 \times 3.75 = 171\,\mathrm{kN}$ and adopting a value of v of 0.2, the ultimate bending moments at midspan are:

Short span: $M_{sx} = (0.045 + 0.2 \times 0.025)171 = +8.55\,\mathrm{kN\,m}$
Long span: $M_{sy} = (0.2 \times 0.045 + 0.025)171 = +5.81\,\mathrm{kN\,m}$

If the panel is continuous over all four edges, allowances for continuity must be made as indicated in the notes and examples relating to *Tables 54* and *55* given below.

14.5 CONCENTRATED LOADS

Additional comments on *Tables 54, 55* and *56* are given in section 3.7.1.

14.5.1 Poisson's ratio

The bending-moment formulae given apply when Poisson's ratio v is 0.2, which is the value recommended in BS8110 and CP110 when considering serviceability conditions. If Poisson's ratio is assumed to be zero, the terms $0.2\alpha_{x4}$ and $0.2\alpha_{y4}$ in the formulae should be omitted.

If bending moments corresponding to a different value of Poisson's ratio are required, they may be calculated from the expressions given on *Table 54*.

14.5.2 Units

The factors α_{x4} and α_{y4} given are non-dimensional. Thus if F is given in kilonewtons the resulting moments are in kN m per metre width; if F is in kilograms the moments are in kg m per metre width; and if F is in pounds the moments are in lb ft per foot width.

14.5.3 Square panels

If $a_x = a_y$, the resulting bending moment is the same in both directions and is $F(\alpha_{x4} + 0.2\alpha_{y4})$. The limiting case $a_x/l = a_y/l = 1$ occurs when the load extends over the entire panel.

For other cases, i.e. when a_x and a_y are not equal, α_{x4} is the coefficient for the bending moment in the direction of a_x, and α_{y4} is the bending moment in the direction of a_y. The coefficient α_{x4} is based on the selected direction of a_x; for coefficient α_{y4}, reverse a_x and a_y as illustrated in example 1 below.

Example 1. Square panel with $k = 1$.

If $a_x/l = 0.8$ and $a_y/l = 0.2$, $\alpha_{x4} = 0.072$; for $a_x/l = 0.2$ and $a_y/l = 0.8$, $\alpha_{y4} = 0.103$. Then the bending moments per unit width are:

On span in direction of a_x: $F[0.072 + (0.2 \times 0.103)] = 0.093F$
On span in direction of a_y: $F[0.103 + (0.2 \times 0.072)] = 0.118F$

Example 2. The footpath of a bridge spans 2 m between a parapet beam and a main longitudinal beam and is monolithic with both beams. The imposed load can be either $5\,\mathrm{kN/m^2}$ distributed uniformly, or a load of 40 kN from a wheel whose contact area is 300 mm by 75 mm. With the latter load the permissible service stresses may be increased by 50%, i.e. at ordinary working stresses the wheel load can be assumed to be about 27 kN.

(i) Assume a 150 mm slab; then total uniform service load = $5 + 3.5 = 8.5\,\mathrm{kN/m^2}$. With continuity at both supports, the service bending moment at midspan and at each support is $(1/12) \times 8.5 \times 2.15^2 = 3.3\,\mathrm{kN\,m}$ per metre width.

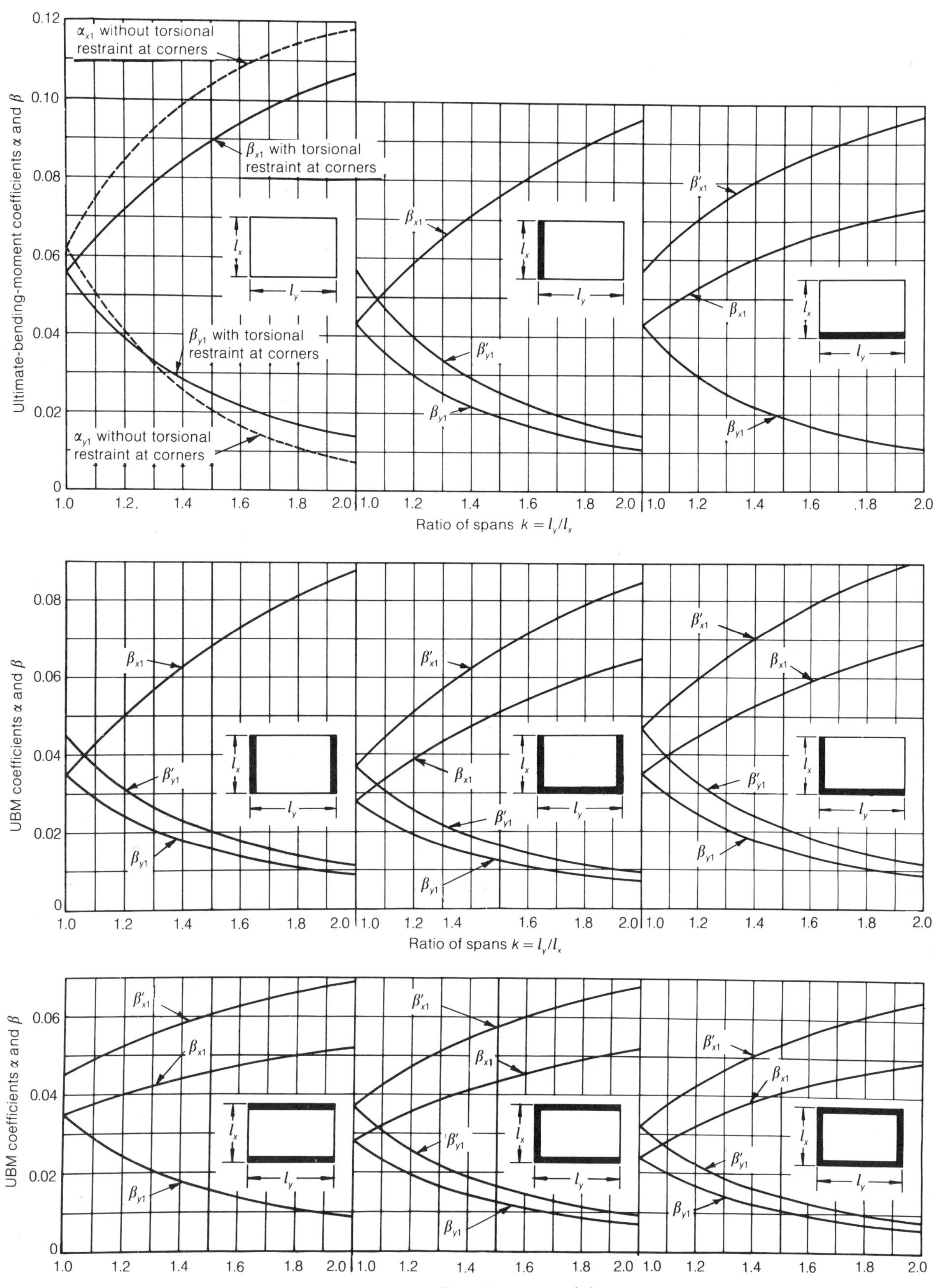

edge which is discontinuous or which is cast monolithically with support

edge which is continuous

Bending-moment coefficients β_{x1} and β'_{x1} apply to maximum positive and negative bending moments respectively on short span l_x.

Bending-moment coefficients β_{y1} and β'_{y1} apply to maximum positive and negative bending moments respectively on long span l_y.

(ii) The contact area of 300 mm by 75 mm at the wheel can be increased to 550 mm by 330 mm (see *Table 11*), the depth to the reinforcement being about 125 mm.

The slab spans mainly in one direction and thus the curves in the lower right-hand corner of *Table 55* apply. With $a_x/l_x = 0.33/2.15 = 0.15$ and $a_y/l_x = 0.55/2.15 = 0.26$, the curves give $\alpha_{x4} = 0.23$ and $\alpha_{y4} = 0.12$. Then free transverse service bending moment $= 27[0.23 + (0.2 \times 0.12)] + [(1/8) \times 3.5 \times 2.15^2] = 6.86 + 2.02 = 8.88$ kN m per metre width.

Allow for continuity (partial fixity) by reducing the free bending moment due to the dead load by one-third, and that due to the imposed load by 20%; the transverse bending moment is then $(0.8 \times 6.86) + (2/3)2.02 = 6.84$ kN m per metre width. This exceeds the service moment in case (i); therefore case (ii) controls the design.

Longitudinal service bending moment $= 27[(0.2 \times 0.23) + 0.12] = 4.48$ kN m per metre width.

Allowing a 20% reduction for continuity, the net service bending moment is about 3.6 kN m per metre width. This bending moment determines the amount of longitudinal reinforcement needed which, however, should not be less than that required under the DTp requirements.

(iii) Another method of design is to calculate the transverse service bending moment due to the concentrated load by estimating the width of slab assumed to carry the load, from the formula

$$\tfrac{2}{3}(l_x + a_x) + a_y = 0.67(2.15 + 0.33) + 0.55 = 2.20 \text{ m}$$

Then load carried by 1 m width of slab $= 27/2.2 = 12.3$ kN. Thus the free transverse service bending moment $= (1/4)12.3[2.15 - (1/2)0.33] = 6.08$ kN m per metre width; introducing a 20% reduction for continuity, the net bending moment (after adding 1.33 kN m per metre width due to the dead load) is 6.20 kN m per metre width, which differs little from the value calculated by means of *Table 55*.

(iv) A further method is an adaptation of the technique described in BS8110. From the left-hand diagram at the bottom of *Table 56*, $b_e = 0.55 + [2.4 \times (1/2) \times 2.15 \times (1 - 1/2)] = 1.84$ m. Then the free service bending moment (with symmetrical load) is given by

$$\frac{27}{4 \times 1.84}[2.15 - (\tfrac{1}{2} \times 0.33)] = 7.28 \text{ kN m per metre width}$$

Making the usual reductions for continuity, the net bending moment is $(0.8 \times 7.28) + (2/3)2.02 = 7.16$ kN m per metre width, which slightly exceeds that found by the preceding methods.

Example 3. A panel of a deck slab of a bridge is 3.75 m long by 3.0 m wide and is supported on all four sides, being fully continuous over all supports. Calculate the maximum bending service moments due to a load of 200 kN symmetrically placed at the centre of the panel, the contact area being 75 mm by 600 mm.

Assume a slab 200 mm in thickness ($d = 175$ mm) with 50 mm of tarmacadam. Then the loaded area, allowing for dispersion down to the reinforcement, is 0.525 m by 1.05 m. Then $k = l_y/l_x = 3.75/3.0 = 1.25$; $a_x/l_x = 0.525/3.0 = 0.175$; and $a_y/l_y = 1.05/3.75 = 0.28$. From *Table 54*, $\alpha_{x4} = 0.19$ and $\alpha_{y4} = 0.12$. Allow a reduction of 20% for continuity.

For the uniform dead load of about 7 kN/m^2 with $k = 1.25$, from *Table 56*, $\alpha_{x3} = 0.45$ and $\alpha_{y3} = 0.17$. Alternatively, the service bending moments due to dead load can be calculated from *Table 54* for the condition $k = 1.25$, $a_x/l_x = a_y/l_y = 1$; this method is adopted here, the appropriate values of α_{x4} and α_{y4} being approximately 0.05 and 0.03 respectively.

Then the service bending moments in kN m per metre width are as follows:

Midspan and supports of shorter span:
Concentrated load:
$200[0.19 + (0.2 \times 0.12)] \times 0.8 = 34.24$
Uniform load:
$7 \times 3.75 \times 3.0[0.05 + (0.2 \times 0.03)] \times 0.8 = 3.53$
Total $= 37.77$

Midspan and supports of longer span:
Concentrated load:
$200[0.12 + (0.2 \times 0.19)] \times 0.8 = 25.28$
Uniform load:
$7 \times 3.75 \times 3.0[0.03 + (0.2 \times 0.05)] \times 0.8 = 2.52$
Total $= 27.80$

Example 4. Find the service bending moments due to the same concentrated imposed load if it is against one of the longer sides of the panel but is symmetrical on the span l_y. Thus $a_{x1} = 0.525$ m; $x = (l_x/2) - a_x = 0.975$ m; $a_y/2 = 0.525$ m. Assume that the panel in example 3 is not continuous over two of its adjacent sides but is monolithic with the supporting beams on these two sides; continuity exists over the supports on the two remaining sides (case (f) in *Table 56*, giving $k_1 = 1$). Adopt the procedure for case IV, in *Table 56*.

(i) $a_x = 2(0.525 + 0.975) = 3.0$ m; $a_y = 1.05$ m; $a_x/l_x = 3.0/3.0 = 1$; $a_y/l_y = 1.05/3.75 = 0.28$. From *Table 54*, with $k = 1.25$, $\alpha_{x4} = 0.073$ and $\alpha_{y4} = 0.063$; these are the factors for a load of $2F(a_{x1} + x)/a_{x1}$ on an area of $2(a_{x1} + x)$ by a_y. $a_{x1} + x = 0.525 + 0.925 = 1.5$ m. Then $\alpha_{x4}(a_{x1} + x) = 0.073 \times 1.5 = 0.109$; $\alpha_{y4}(a_{x1} + x) = 0.063 \times 1.5 = 0.095$. These are the corresponding basic service bending moments divided by $2F/a_{x1}$.

(ii) $a_x = 2 \times 0.975 = 1.95$ m; $a_y = 1.05$ m; $a_x/l_x = 1.95/3.0 = 0.65$; $a_y/l_y = 1.05/3.75 = 0.28$. From *Table 54*, $\alpha_{x4} = 0.10$ and $\alpha_{y4} = 0.088$; these are the factors for a load of $2Fx/a_{x1}$ on an area of $2x$ by a_y symmetrically disposed at the centre of the panel. Then $\alpha_{x4}x = 0.10 \times 0.975 = 0.098$; $\alpha_{y4}x = 0.088 \times 0.975 = 0.086$. These are the corresponding basic service bending moments divided by $2F/a_{x1}$.

(iii) Now $\alpha_{x4} = 0.109 - 0.098 = 0.011$; $\alpha_{y4} = 0.095 - 0.086 = 0.009$; these are the basic bending-moment factors for a total load of $2F(a_{x1} + x)/a_{x1} - 2Fx/a_{x1} = 2F$ on two symmetrically disposed areas of a_{x1} by a_y (as in case II). The case under consideration, case IV, is one-half of case II; thus the immediately preceding bending-moment factors α_{x4} and α_{y4} must be multiplied by $(1/2)2F/a_{x1} = F/a_{x1}$ to give

Two-way slabs: triangularly distributed loads: elastic analyses

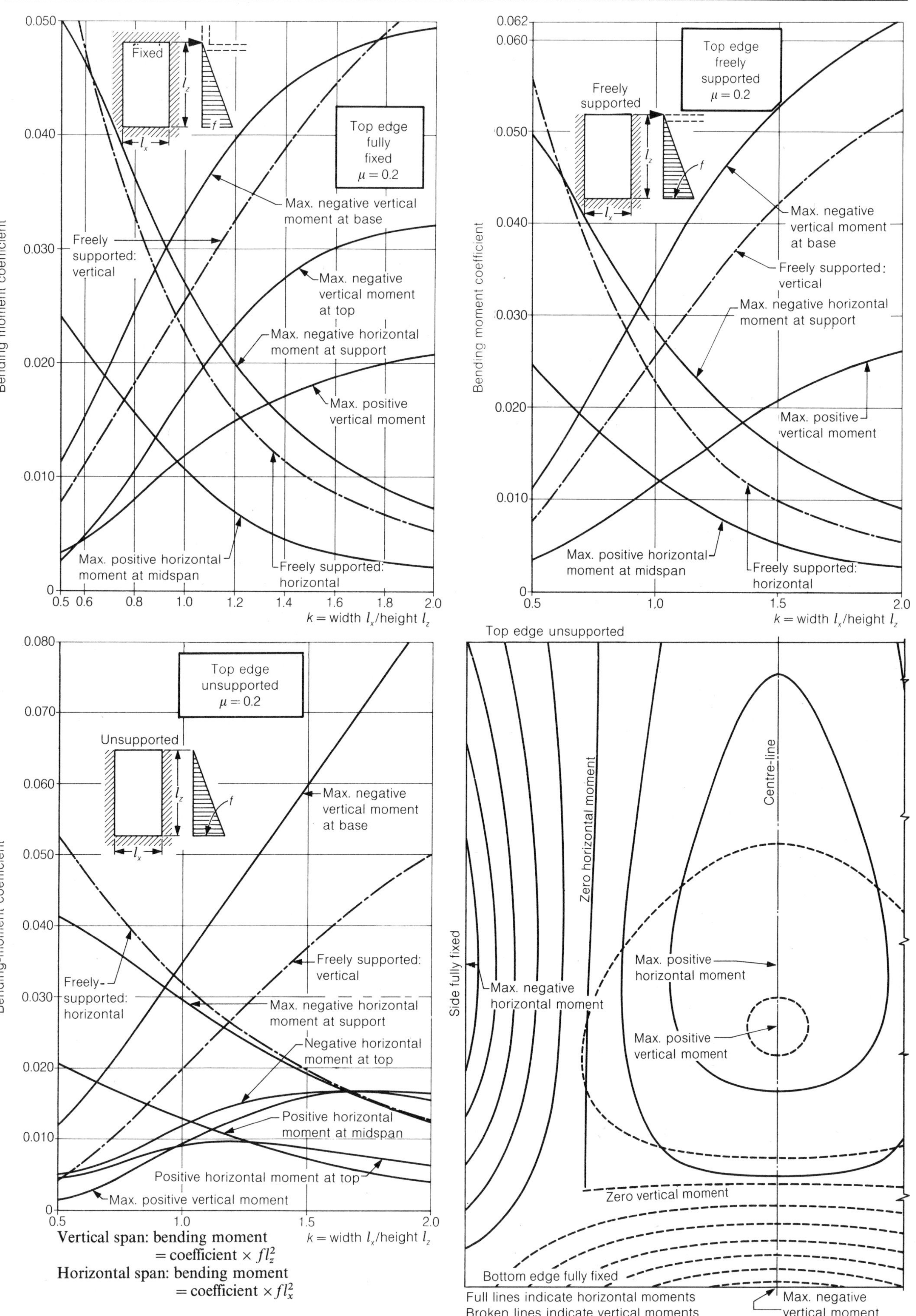

Vertical span: bending moment $= \text{coefficient} \times fl_z^2$

Horizontal span: bending moment $= \text{coefficient} \times fl_x^2$

the basic bending-moment factors for the specified load. $F/a_{x1} = 200/0.525 = 382$ kN/m.

Then the free bending moments per metre width are:

Short span:

$$M_x = F(\alpha_{x4} + 0.2\alpha_{y4})/a_{x1}$$
$$= 382[0.011 + (0.2 \times 0.009)] = 4.89 \text{ kN m}$$

Long span:

$$M_y = F(0.2\alpha_{x4} + \alpha_{y4})/a_{x1}$$
$$= 382[(0.2 \times 0.011) + 0.009] = 4.28 \text{ kN m}$$

The maximum service bending moments per metre width for the imposed load, allowing for continuity by using the factors given in *Table 56*, are:

Shorter span:
- Midspan: $+0.85 \times 4.89 = +4.16$ kN m
- Inner support: $-0.95 \times 4.89 = -4.65$ kN m
- Outer support: $-0.25 \times 4.89 = -1.23$ kN m

Longer span:
- Midspan: $+0.85 \times 4.28 = +3.64$ kN m
- Inner support: $-0.95 \times 4.38 = -4.07$ kN m
- Outer support: $-0.25 \times 4.28 = -1.07$ kN m

The service bending moments due to the uniformly distributed dead load must be added to these values.

14.6 OTHER METHODS

Both BS8110 and CP110 also permit other analytical techniques to be employed. Elastic analyses such as those of Pigeaud and Westergaard may be adopted, and thus again the coefficients for α_{x3} and α_{y3} given in *Table 50* may be utilized. Alternatively an analysis by yield-line theory or the Hillberborg strip method may be undertaken (see below). Whatever analytical method is used, the resulting sections must be designed by limit-state principles to resist the ultimate bending moments induced.

14.7 YIELD-LINE ANALYSIS

As mentioned in section 3.5.2, yield-line theory is too complex a subject to deal with adequately in the space available in this *Handbook*. The following notes are thus intended merely to introduce the designer to the basic concepts, methods and problems. For further information see refs 17 to 24.

The application of yield-line theory to the design of rectangular slabs subjected to triangularly distributed loads is dealt with in section 14.9.2.

14.7.1 Basic principles

When loaded excessively, a reinforced concrete slab commences to crack at those points where the ratio of the applied moment to the resistance provided is greatest. As the load increases the concrete continues to crack and the steel to yield, so that the cracks eventually extend to the slab corners, thus dividing it into several individual areas, as shown in diagrams (i) to (iii) on *Table 58*, separated by so-called yield lines. Any further increase in load will then cause the slab to collapse. In the design process the load which causes the formation of the entire system of yield lines is calculated and, by applying a suitable factor of safety, the resistance moment that must be provided in order to withstand a specified load is determined.

For a slab of a given shape, it is usually possible to postulate different modes of failure, the critical mode depending on the support conditions, the dimensions, and the proportion of steel provided in each direction. For example, if the slab shown in diagram (i)(a) is reinforced sufficiently strongly in the direction of the shorter span compared to that in the longer direction, this mode of failure will be prevented and that shown in diagram (i)(b) will occur instead. Similarly, if the slab with one edge unsupported shown in diagrams (ii) is loaded uniformly, pattern (b) will only occur if the ratio of longer to shorter side (or ratio of longer to shorter 'reduced side length': see section 14.7.6) exceeds $\sqrt{2}$; otherwise pattern (a) will occur.

All these patterns may be modified by the formation of corner levers: see section 14.7.9.

14.7.2 Rules for postulating yield-line patterns

Viable yield-line patterns must comply with the following rules:

1. All yield lines must be straight.
2. A yield line can only change direction at an intersection with another yield line.
3. The yield line separating two slab elements must pass through the intersection of their axes of rotation. (Note: this may be at infinity.)
4. All reinforcement intercepted by a yield line is assumed to yield at the line.

14.7.3 Methods of analysis

Two basic methods of yield-line analysis have been developed. These are commonly referred to as the 'work' or 'virtual work' method and the 'equilibrium' method. The former method involves equating, for the yield-line pattern postulated, the work done by the external loads on the various areas of the slab to obtain a virtual displacement, to the work done by the internal forces in forming the yield lines. When the yield pattern is adjusted to its critical dimensions the ratio of the ultimate resistance to the ultimate load reaches its maximum, and when analysing a slab algebraically this situation can be ascertained by differentiating the expression representing the ratio and equating the differential to zero in order to establish the critical dimensions. Then by resubstituting these values into the original expression, a formula giving the ultimate resistance required for a slab of given dimensions and loading can be derived.

The so-called equilibrium method is not really a true equilibrium method (which would give a lower-bound solution) but a variant of the work method, and it also gives an upper-bound solution. The method has the great advantage that the resulting equations give sufficient information themselves to eliminate the unknown variables and thus differentiation is unnecessary. There are also other advan-

Two-way slabs: rectangular panels: concentric concentrated loads—1

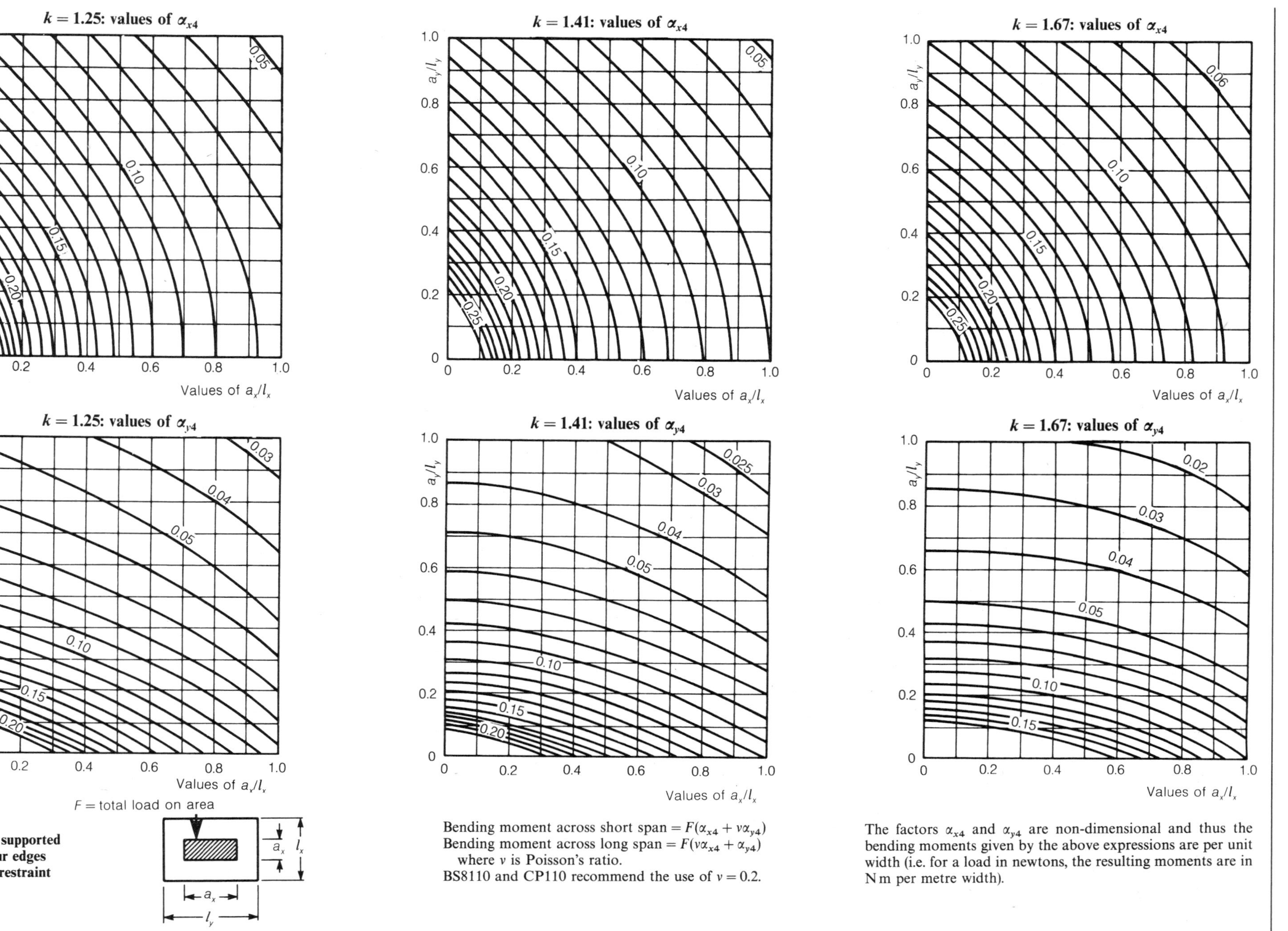

Slabs freely supported along all four edges with corner restraint
$k = l_y/l_x$

Bending moment across short span $= F(\alpha_{x4} + \nu\alpha_{y4})$
Bending moment across long span $= F(\nu\alpha_{x4} + \alpha_{y4})$
where ν is Poisson's ratio.
BS8110 and CP110 recommend the use of $\nu = 0.2$.

The factors α_{x4} and α_{y4} are non-dimensional and thus the bending moments given by the above expressions are per unit width (i.e. for a load in newtons, the resulting moments are in N m per metre width).

tages, but the method is generally more limited in scope and it is not described here: for details see refs 20 and 21.

14.7.4 Virtual-work method

As explained above, this method consists of equating the virtual work done by the external loads in producing a given virtual displacement at some point on the slab, to the work done by the internal forces along the yield lines in rotating the slab elements. To demonstrate the principles involved, an analysis will be given of the simple freely supported rectangular slab supporting a uniform load and reinforced to resist equal moments M each way shown in diagram (i)(a) on *Table 58*. Here, due to symmetry, yield line OO′ is clearly midway between AB and CD. Similarly $\alpha = \beta$, and thus only one dimension is unknown.

Consider first the external work done. The work done by an external load on an individual slab element is equal to the area of that element times the displacement of its centroid times the load. Thus for the triangular element ADO having a displacement δ at O,

$$\text{work done} = \tfrac{1}{2} \times l_x \times \alpha l_y \times \tfrac{1}{3}\delta n = \tfrac{1}{6} l_x l_y \alpha \delta n$$

Similarly, for the trapezoidal area ABOO′ with displacement δ at O and O′,

$$\begin{aligned}\text{work done} &= [2 \times \tfrac{1}{2} \times \tfrac{1}{2} l_x \times \alpha l_y \times \tfrac{1}{3}\delta + l_y(1 - 2\alpha) \times \tfrac{1}{2} l_x \times \tfrac{1}{2}\delta]n \\ &= \tfrac{1}{12}(3 - 4\alpha) l_x l_y \delta n\end{aligned}$$

Thus, since the work done on BCO′ is the same as that done on ADO, and the work done on CDOO′ is the same as that on ABOO′, the total external work done on the entire slab is

$$\tfrac{1}{3} l_x l_y \alpha \delta n + \tfrac{1}{6}(3 - 4\alpha) l_x l_y \delta n = \tfrac{1}{6}(3 - 2\alpha) l_x l_y \delta n$$

The internal work done in forming the yield lines is obtained by multiplying the moment along the yield line by the length of the line concerned and multiplying by the rotation. A useful point to note is that where a yield line is formed at an angle to the direction of the principal moments, instead of considering its true length and rotation it is possible and usually simpler to consider instead the components in the direction of the principal moments. For example, for yield line AO, instead of considering the actual length AO and the rotation at right angles to AO, consider length $l_x/2$ and the rotation about AB plus length αl_y and the rotation about AD.

Thus considering the component of the yield line along AOO′B about AB, the length of the line is l_y, the moment is M and the rotation is $\delta/(l_x/2)$. Thus

$$\text{work done} = 2Ml_y\delta/l_x$$

Similarly, for the yield line along DOO′C, the work done is again $2Ml_y\delta/l_x$. (Length OO′ appears to have been considered twice. This is because the actual rotation between the elements separated by this length is double that which occurs over the remaining length.)

Now, considering the component of the yield line AOD about AD,

$$\text{work done} = l_x M \times \delta/\alpha l_y$$

Since the work done on yield line BOC is similar, the total internal work done on the slab is

$$2\delta(2Ml_y/l_x + Ml_x/\alpha l_y)$$

and by equating the internal and external work done,

$$\tfrac{1}{6}(3 - 2\alpha) l_x l_y \delta n = 2\delta\left(\frac{2Ml_y}{l_x} + \frac{Ml_x}{\alpha l_y}\right)$$

or

$$M = \frac{n}{12} l_x^2 \left[\frac{3\alpha - 2\alpha^2}{2\alpha + (l_x/l_y)^2}\right]$$

To determine the critical value of αl_y the quotient in square brackets must be differentiated and equated to zero. As Jones (ref. 20) has pointed out, when using the well-known relationship

$$\frac{\mathrm{d}y}{\mathrm{d}x} = \left(v\frac{\mathrm{d}u}{\mathrm{d}x} - u\frac{\mathrm{d}v}{\mathrm{d}x}\right)\Big/ v^2 = 0$$

simply as a means of maximizing $y = u/v$, it is most convenient to rearrange it as

$$\frac{u}{v} = \frac{\mathrm{d}u/\mathrm{d}x}{\mathrm{d}v/\mathrm{d}x}$$

Thus, for the present example,

$$\frac{3\alpha - 2\alpha^2}{2\alpha + (l_x/l_y)^2} = \frac{3 - 4\alpha}{2}$$

This leads to a quadratic, the positive root of which is

$$\alpha = \frac{1}{2}\left\{\sqrt{\left[\left(\frac{l_x}{l_y}\right)^4 + 3\left(\frac{l_x}{l_y}\right)^2\right]} - \left(\frac{l_x}{l_y}\right)^2\right\}$$

which gives, when resubstituted in the original equation,

$$M = \tfrac{1}{24} n l_x^2 \left\{\sqrt{\left[3 + \left(\frac{l_x}{l_y}\right)^2\right]} - \frac{l_x}{l_y}\right\}^2$$

14.7.5 Line and concentrated loads

Concentrated and line loads are easier to deal with than uniform loads. When considering the external work done, the contribution of a concentrated load is obtained by multiplying the load by the relative deflection of the point at which it is applied. In the case of a line load the external work done over a given slab area is obtained by multiplying the portion of the load carried on that area by the relative deflection at the centroid of the load.

Yield lines tend to pass beneath heavy concentrated or line loads since this maximizes the external work done by such loads. Where concentrated loads act in isolation, so-called circular fans of yield lines tend to form: this behaviour is complex and reference should be made to specialized textbooks for details (refs 17, 19, 21).

14.7.6 Affinity theorems

Section 14.7.4 illustrates the work involved in analysing the simplest freely supported slab with equal reinforcement in each direction (i.e. so-called *isotropic* reinforcement). If different steel is provided each way (i.e. the slab is *orthotropically* reinforced), or if continuity or fixity exists along one or more edges, the formula needs modifying accordingly.

Two-way slabs: rectangular panels: concentric concentrated loads—2

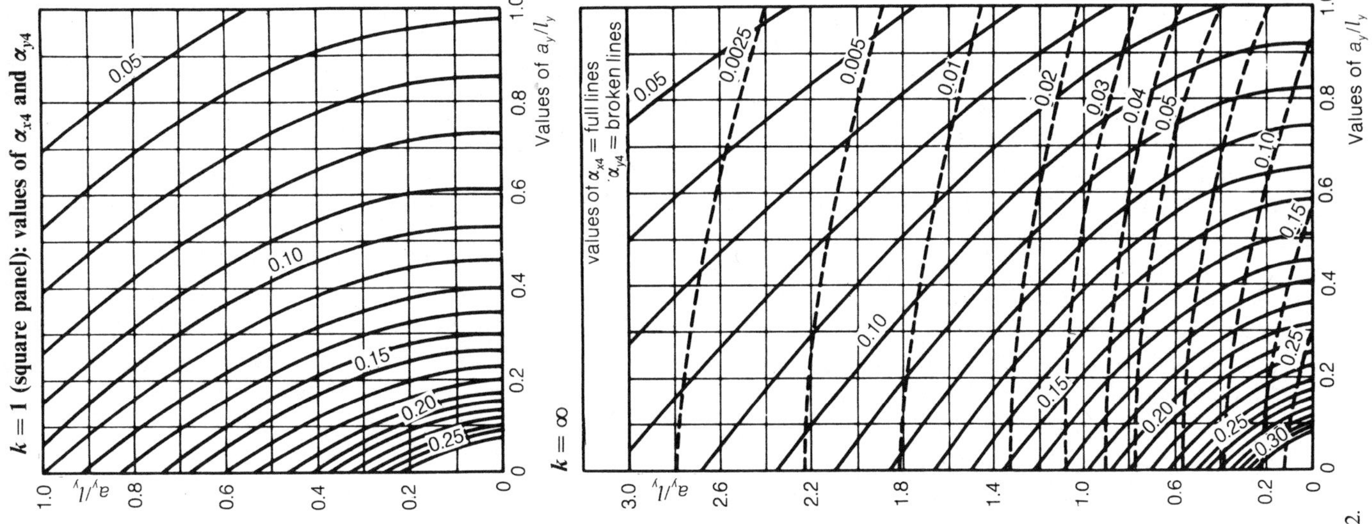

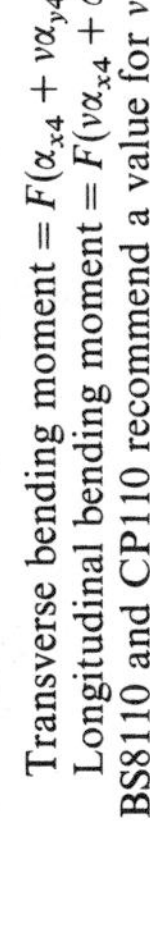

Transverse bending moment = $F(\alpha_{x4} + \nu\alpha_{y4})$
Longitudinal bending moment = $F(\nu\alpha_{x4} + \alpha_{y4})$
BS8110 and CP110 recommend a value for ν of 0.2.

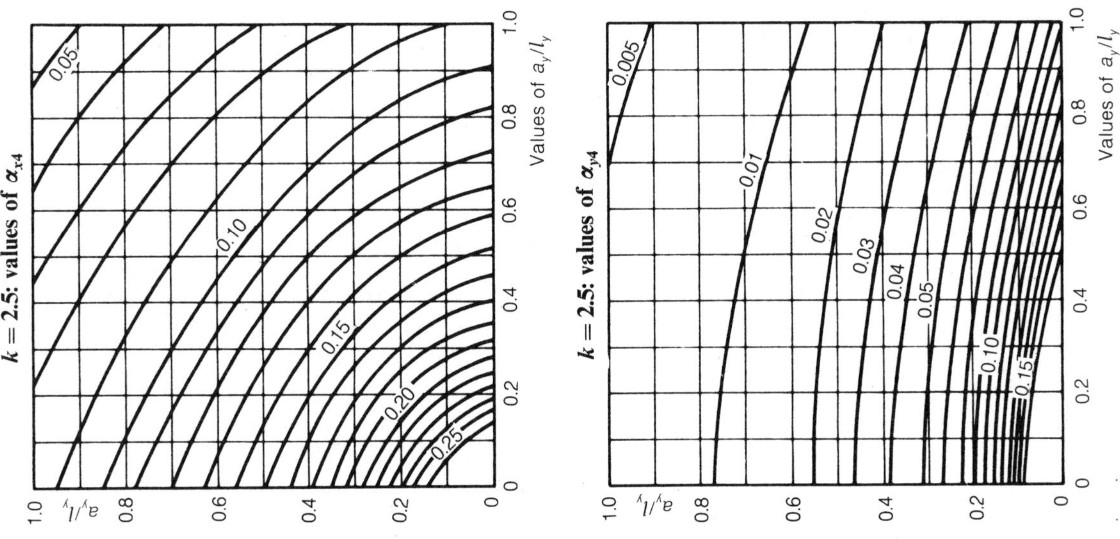

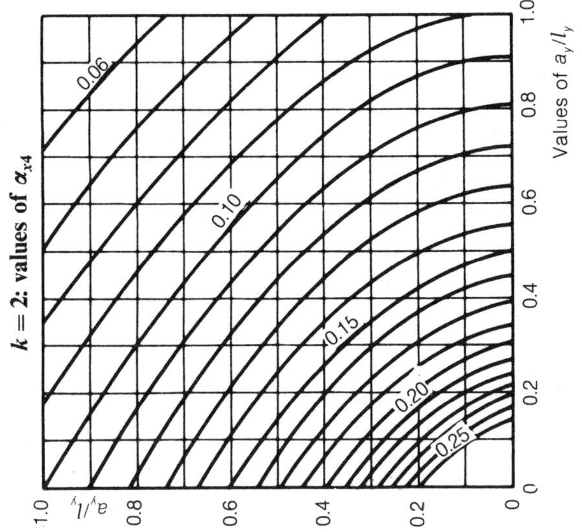

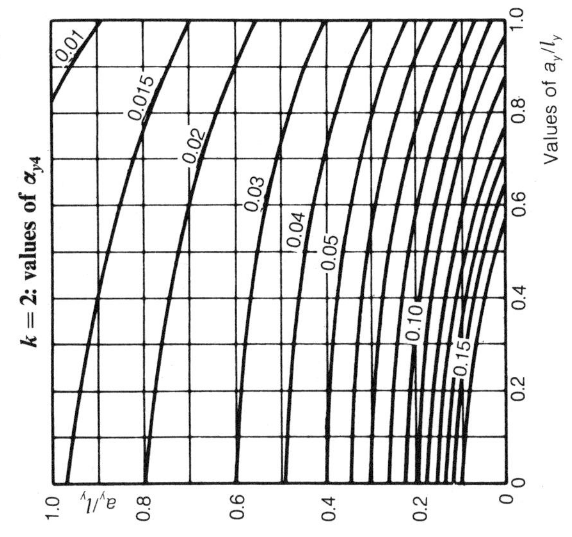

To avoid the need for a vast number of design formulae covering all conceivable conditions it is possible to transform most slabs with fixed or continuous edges and orthotropic reinforcement into their simpler freely supported isotropic equivalents by using the following affinity theorems: skew slabs can be transformed similarly into rectangular slabs.

1. If an orthotropic slab is reinforced as shown in diagram (iv)(a) on *Table 58*, it can be transformed into the simpler isotropic slab shown in diagram (iv)(b). All loads and dimensions in the direction of the principal co-ordinate axis remain unchanged, but in the affine slab the distances in the direction of the secondary co-ordinate axis are obtained by dividing the true values by $\sqrt{\mu}$ and the total corresponding loads are obtained by dividing the original total loads by $\sqrt{\mu}$. (The latter requirement means that the intensity of a uniformly distributed load per unit area remains unchanged by the transformation since both the area and the total load on that area are divided by $\sqrt{\mu}$.)

   Similarly a skew slab reinforced as shown in diagram (v)(a) can be transformed into the isotropic slab shown in diagram (v)(b) by dividing the original total loads by $\sin\psi$. (As before, this requirement means that the intensity of a uniformly distributed load per unit area remains unchanged by the transformation.)

   These rules can be combined when considering skew slabs with differing reinforcement in each direction; for details see ref. 23, article 6.
2. By considering the reduced side lengths l_{xr} and l_{yr}, an orthotropic slab which is continuous over one or more supports (such as that shown in diagram (vi)(a) or *Table 58*) can be transformed into the simpler freely supported isotropic slab shown in diagram (vi)(b).

For example, for an orthotropic slab with fixed edges, reinforced for a positive moment M and negative moments i_2M and i_4M in span direction l_x and for positive moment μM and negative moments $\mu i_1 M$ and $\mu i_3 M$ in direction l_y:

$$M = \frac{nl_x^2}{6[\sqrt{(1+i_2)}+\sqrt{(1+i_4)}]^2} \times \left[\sqrt{\left\{3+\frac{[\sqrt{(1+i_1)}+\sqrt{(1+i_3)}]^2\mu l_x^2}{[\sqrt{(1+i_2)}+\sqrt{(1+i_4)}]^2 l_y^2}\right\}} - \frac{[\sqrt{(1+i_1)}+\sqrt{(1+i_3)}]\sqrt{(\mu)}l_x}{[\sqrt{(1+i_2)}+\sqrt{(1+i_4)}]l_y}\right]$$

Now if

$$l_{xr} = \frac{2l_x}{\sqrt{(1+i_2)}+\sqrt{(1+i_4)}}$$

$$l_{yr} = \frac{2l_y}{[\sqrt{(1+i_1)}+\sqrt{(1+i_3)}]\sqrt{\mu}}$$

then

$$\frac{l_{xr}}{l_{yr}} = \left(\frac{\sqrt{(1+i_1)}+\sqrt{(1+i_3)}}{\sqrt{(1+i_2)}+\sqrt{(1+i_4)}}\right)\sqrt{(\mu)}\left(\frac{l_x}{l_y}\right)$$

and

$$M = \tfrac{1}{24}nl_{xr}^2\left\{\sqrt{\left[3+\left(\frac{l_{xr}}{l_{yr}}\right)^2\right]}-\frac{l_{xr}}{l_{yr}}\right\}^2$$

This is identical to the expression derived above for the freely supported isotropic slab but with l_{xr} and l_{yr} substituted for l_x and l_y. This relationship is represented by the scale provided on *Table 58*, from which values of M/nl_x^2 corresponding to ratios of l_y/l_x can be read directly.

The validity of the above analysis is based on the assumption that $l_{yr} > l_{xr}$. If this is not so, the yield pattern will be as shown in diagram (i)(b) on *Table 58*, and l_{xr} and l_{yr} should be transposed.

The following example illustrates the analysis involved.

Example. Design the slab in diagram (vii) to support an ultimate load n per unit area assuming that the relative moments of resistance are as shown.

since $l_x = 4$ m, $i_2 = 3/2$ and $i_4 = 0$,

$$l_{xr} = \frac{2\times 4}{\sqrt{(1+3/2)}+1} = 3.10\,\text{m}$$

Since $l_y = 6$ m, $\mu = 1/2$, $\mu i_1 = 1/2$ and $\mu i_3 = 0$,

$$l_{yr} = \frac{2\times 6}{[\sqrt{(2)}+1]\sqrt{(1/2)}} = 7.03\,\text{m}$$

Thus

$$M = \tfrac{1}{24}nl_{xr}^2\left\{\sqrt{\left[3+\left(\frac{l_{xr}}{l_{yr}}\right)^2\right]}-\frac{l_{xr}}{l_{yr}}\right\}^2$$

$$= \frac{n}{24}\times 3.10^2\left\{\sqrt{\left[3+\left(\frac{3.10}{7.03}\right)^2\right]}-\frac{3.10}{7.03}\right\}^2$$

$$= 0.726n$$

14.7.7 Superposition theorem

A problem which may occur when designing a slab to resist a combination of uniform, line and concentrated loads, some of which may not always occur, is that the critical pattern of yield lines may well differ for differing combinations of loads. Also it is not theoretically possible to add the ultimate moments obtained when considering the various loads individually, since these moments may occur as a result of different critical yield patterns. However, Johansen has established the superposition theorem:

The sum of the ultimate moments for a series of loads is greater than or equal to the ultimate moments due to the sum of the loads.

In other words, if the ultimate moments corresponding to the yield-line patterns for each load considered individually are added together, the resulting value is equal to or greater than that of the system as a whole. This theorem is demonstrated in ref. 23, article 4.

14.7.8 Empirical virtual-work analysis

A principal advantage of collapse methods of design is that they can be applied simply to solve problems such as slabs that are irregularly shaped or loaded or that contain large openings. The analysis of such slabs using elastic methods is in comparison quite arduous, even if sophisticated calculating equipment is available.

Two-way slabs: rectangular panels: eccentric concentrated loads

56

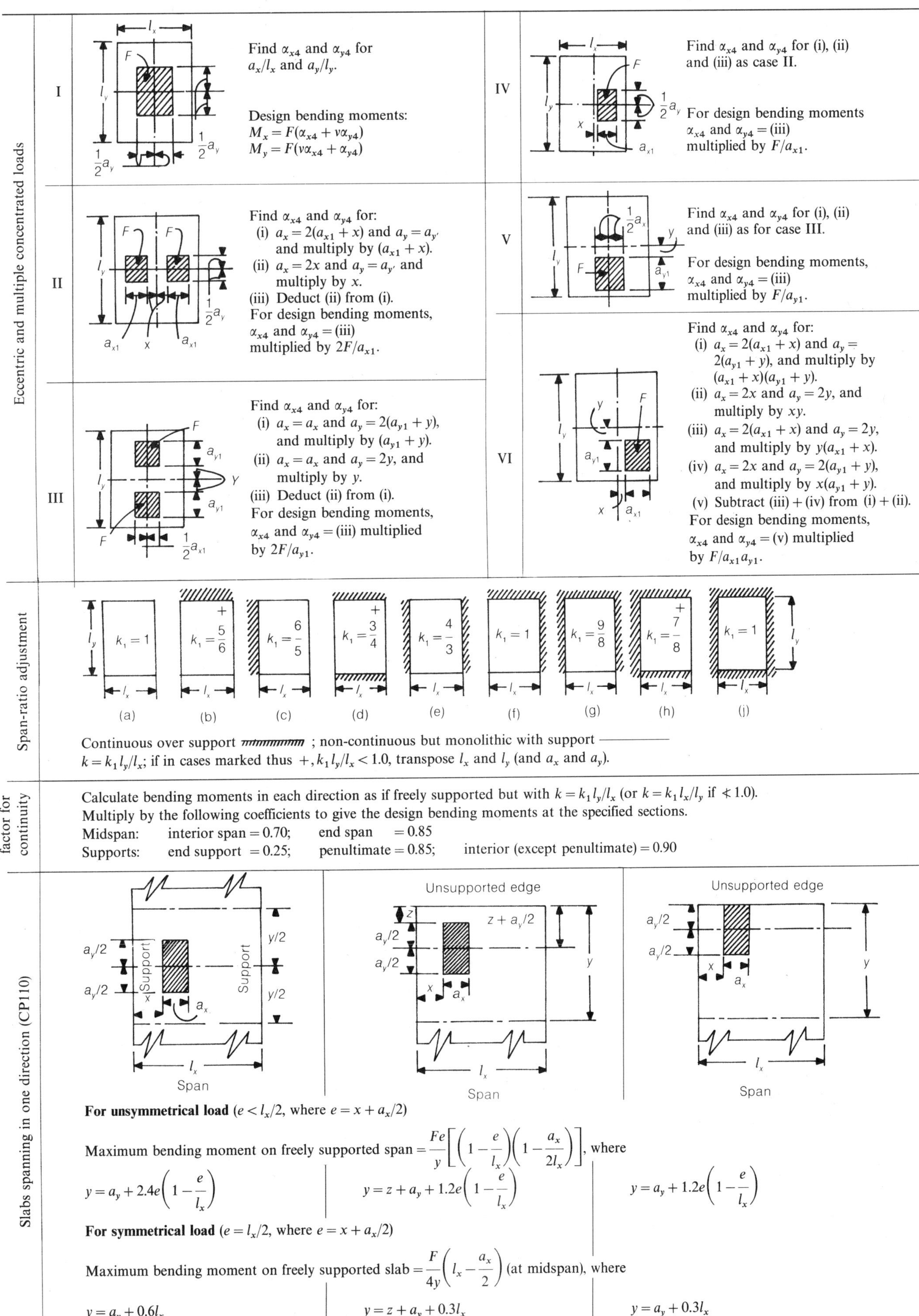

Eccentric and multiple concentrated loads

I

Find α_{x4} and α_{y4} for a_x/l_x and a_y/l_y.

Design bending moments:
$M_x = F(\alpha_{x4} + \nu\alpha_{y4})$
$M_y = F(\nu\alpha_{x4} + \alpha_{y4})$

II

Find α_{x4} and α_{y4} for:
(i) $a_x = 2(a_{x1} + x)$ and $a_y = a_{y'}$ and multiply by $(a_{x1} + x)$.
(ii) $a_x = 2x$ and $a_y = a_{y'}$ and multiply by x.
(iii) Deduct (ii) from (i).
For design bending moments, α_{x4} and α_{y4} = (iii) multiplied by $2F/a_{x1}$.

III

Find α_{x4} and α_{y4} for:
(i) $a_x = a_x$ and $a_y = 2(a_{y1} + y)$, and multiply by $(a_{y1} + y)$.
(ii) $a_x = a_x$ and $a_y = 2y$, and multiply by y.
(iii) Deduct (ii) from (i).
For design bending moments, α_{x4} and α_{y4} = (iii) multiplied by $2F/a_{y1}$.

IV

Find α_{x4} and α_{y4} for (i), (ii) and (iii) as case II.

For design bending moments α_{x4} and α_{y4} = (iii) multiplied by F/a_{x1}.

V

Find α_{x4} and α_{y4} for (i), (ii) and (iii) as for case III.

For design bending moments, α_{x4} and α_{y4} = (iii) multiplied by F/a_{y1}.

VI

Find α_{x4} and α_{y4} for:
(i) $a_x = 2(a_{x1} + x)$ and $a_y = 2(a_{y1} + y)$, and multiply by $(a_{x1} + x)(a_{y1} + y)$.
(ii) $a_x = 2x$ and $a_y = 2y$, and multiply by xy.
(iii) $a_x = 2(a_{x1} + x)$ and $a_y = 2y$, and multiply by $y(a_{x1} + x)$.
(iv) $a_x = 2x$ and $a_y = 2(a_{y1} + y)$, and multiply by $x(a_{y1} + y)$.
(v) Subtract (iii) + (iv) from (i) + (ii).
For design bending moments, α_{x4} and α_{y4} = (v) multiplied by $F/a_{x1}a_{y1}$.

Span-ratio adjustment

(a) $k_1 = 1$; (b) $k_1 = \frac{5}{6}$ +; (c) $k_1 = \frac{6}{5}$; (d) $k_1 = \frac{3}{4}$ +; (e) $k_1 = \frac{4}{3}$; (f) $k_1 = 1$; (g) $k_1 = \frac{9}{8}$; (h) $k_1 = \frac{7}{8}$ +; (j) $k_1 = 1$

Continuous over support ////////; non-continuous but monolithic with support ————

$k = k_1 l_y/l_x$; if in cases marked thus +, $k_1 l_y/l_x < 1.0$, transpose l_x and l_y (and a_x and a_y).

B.M. reduction factor for continuity

Calculate bending moments in each direction as if freely supported but with $k = k_1 l_y/l_x$ (or $k = k_1 l_x/l_y$ if $\nless 1.0$).
Multiply by the following coefficients to give the design bending moments at the specified sections.

Midspan: interior span = 0.70; end span = 0.85
Supports: end support = 0.25; penultimate = 0.85; interior (except penultimate) = 0.90

Slabs spanning in one direction (CP110)

For unsymmetrical load ($e < l_x/2$, where $e = x + a_x/2$)

Maximum bending moment on freely supported span $= \frac{Fe}{y}\left[\left(1 - \frac{e}{l_x}\right)\left(1 - \frac{a_x}{2l_x}\right)\right]$, where

$y = a_y + 2.4e\left(1 - \frac{e}{l_x}\right)$ | $y = z + a_y + 1.2e\left(1 - \frac{e}{l_x}\right)$ | $y = a_y + 1.2e\left(1 - \frac{e}{l_x}\right)$

For symmetrical load ($e = l_x/2$, where $e = x + a_x/2$)

Maximum bending moment on freely supported slab $= \frac{F}{4y}\left(l_x - \frac{a_x}{2}\right)$ (at midspan), where

$y = a_y + 0.6l_x$ | $y = z + a_y + 0.3l_x$ | $y = a_y + 0.3l_x$

If F is in kN and dimensions are in m, bending moments are in kN m per metre width
If F is in lb and dimensions are in ft, bending moments are in lb ft per foot width

To solve such 'one-off' problems it is clearly unrealistic to develop standard algebraic design formulae. The following empirical trial-and-adjustment technique which involves directly applying virtual-work principles is easy to master and can then be applied to solve complex problems. The method is best illustrated by working through a simple example, the one selected being the same as that considered above. For such a standard problem there is, of course, no need to employ trial-and-adjustment procedures. They are only used here to illustrate the method. A more complicated example is given in ref. 23, article 1, on which the description of the method is based.

In addition to the fundamental principles of virtual work discussed in section 14.7.4, the present method depends on the additional principle that if all yield lines (other than those along the supports) are positive and if none of them meets an unsupported edge except at right angles, then shearing or torsional forces cannot occur at the yield lines and an individual virtual-work balance for each slab area demarcated by the yield lines can be taken.

Example. Consider the slab shown in diagram (vii) on *Table 58*, which is continuous over two adjacent edges, freely supported at the others, and subjected to a uniform load n per unit area. The ratios of the moments of resistance provided over the continuous edges and in the secondary direction to that in the principal direction are as shown.

is $4n(1/3) = 4n/3$. Now since O is displaced by unity, the rotation of this slab area about the support is $1/\alpha l_y = 1/2$. The moment of $M/2$ across the positive yield line exerts a total moment of $(M/2)4 = 2M$ on the slab, and the negative moment of $M/2$ at the support also exerts a total moment of $(M/2)4 = 2M$. Thus the total internal work done in rotating the slab is $(2M + 2M)(1/2) = 2M$. By equating the internal and external work done on A, $2M = 4n/3$, i.e. $M/n = 2/3$.

Similarly, for area C, $M/n = 1/3$.

Area B is conveniently considered by dividing it into a rectangle (shown shaded) plus two triangles, and calculating the work done on each part separately. The centre of gravity of the rectangle is displaced by 1/2 when the displacement at O is unity. Thus

Work done by load on triangles $= 3 \times 2.5 \times (1/2) \times n = 3.75n$

Work done by load on triangles $= 2.5 \times (2 + 1) \times (1/2) \times (1/3) \times n = 1.25n$

Total work done $= 3.75n + 1.25n = 5n$

Since the rotation is 1/2.5, the work done by the moments is $(1.5M + M) \times 6/2.5 = 6M$. Thus the virtual-work ratio here is $M/n = 5/6 = 0.833$.

Likewise for area D, $M/n = 0.750$.

It is simplest to set out the calculations in tabular form as follows:

Area	External work done		Internal work done		Balance M/n
A	$(1/2) \times 2 \times 4 \times (1/3) \times n$	$= 1.333n$	$4[(M/2) + (M/2)]/2.000 =$	$2.000M$	0.667
B	$[(3 \times 2.5 \times 1/2) + 2.5(2 + 1)(1/2) \times (1/3)]n =$	$5.000n$	$6[(3M/2) + M]/2.500$	$= 6.000M$	0.833
C	$(1/2) \times 1 \times 4 \times (1/3) \times n$	$= 0.667n$	$4 \times (M/2)/1.000$	$= 2.000M$	0.333
D	$[(3 \times 1.5 \times 1/2) + 1.5(2 + 1)(1/2) \times (1/3)]n =$	$3.000n$	$6 \times M/1.500$	$= 4.000M$	0.750
Totals		$= 10.000n$		$= 14.000M$	0.714

The step-by-step trial and adjustment procedure is as follows:

1. Postulate a likely yield-line pattern.
2. Give a virtual displacement of unit at some point and calculate the relative displacement of other yield-line intersection points. In the example given, if O is given unit displacement, the displacement at O′ is also unity since OO′ is parallel to the axes of rotation of the adjoining slab areas.
3. Choose reasonable arbitrary values for the dimensions that must be determined to define the yield-line pattern. Thus, in the example, αl_y is initially taken as 2 m, βl_y as 1 m and ξl_x as 2.5 m.
4. Calculate the actual work done by the load n per unit area and the internal work done by the moments of resistance M for each individual part of the slab and thus obtain ratios of M/n for each part.

For example, on slab area A, the total load is $(1/2) \times 2 \times 4 \times n = 4n$. Since the centre of gravity of this area moves through a distance of 1/3, the work done by the load on A

5. Also sum the individual values of internal and external work done by the various slab areas and thus obtain a ratio of $\sum M/\sum n$ for the entire slab. Thus in the example, $\sum M/\sum n = 0.714$. This ratio will be lower than the critical value unless the dimensions chosen arbitrarily in step 3 happen to be correct.
6. Now by comparing the overall ratio obtained for $\sum M/\sum n$ with those due to each individual part it is possible to see how the arbitrary dimensions may be adjusted so that the ratios for the individual parts become approximately equal to each other and to that of the slab as a whole.

For example, for A an examination of the equations giving the internal and external work done shows that M/n is proportional to $(\alpha l_y)^2$. Thus, to increase M/n from 0.667 to 0.714, αl_y must be increased to $\sqrt{(0.714/0.667)} \times 2 = 2.071$. Similarly for C, βl_y must be increased by $\sqrt{(0.714/0.333)} \times 1 = 1.462$.

Now since αl_y and βl_y are fixed, the only variable affecting B is ξl_x. Recalculating the external work done using the

Two-way slabs: non-rectangular panels: elastic analysis

Trapezium

$l_x < l_y$

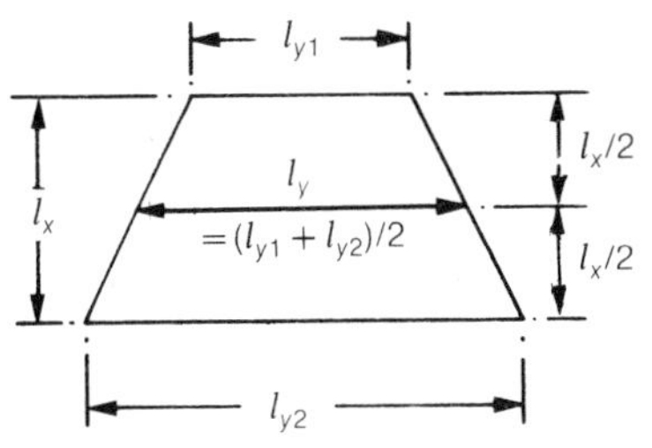

Calculate bending moments as for rectangular panel with $k = l_y/l_x$

$l_x < l_y$

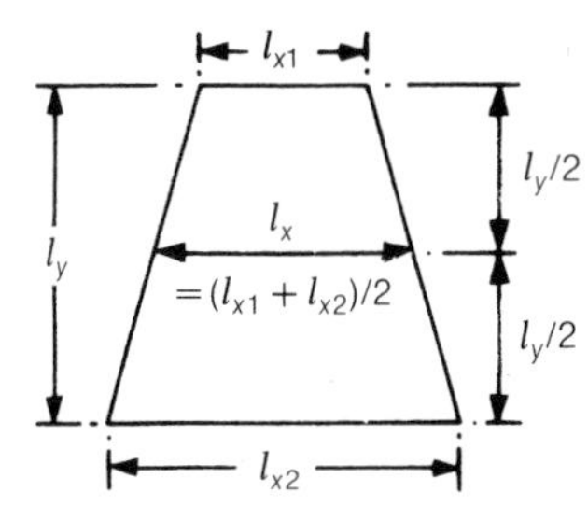

If l_{y1} is small compared with l_{y2} or l_{x1} is small compared with l_{x2} } apply rules for triangular panel

Isosceles triangle

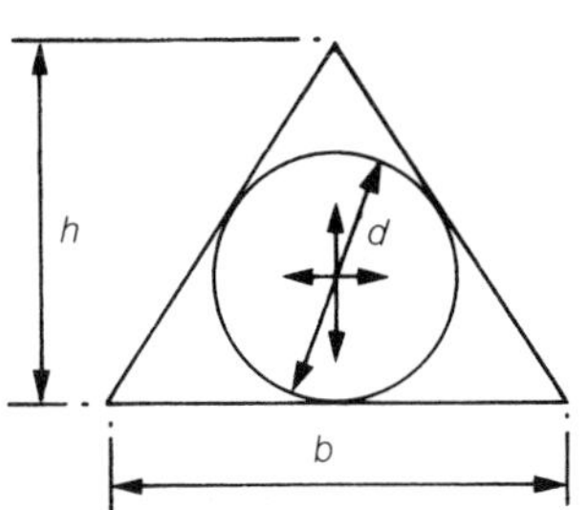

$$d = \text{diameter of inscribed circle} = \frac{2bh}{b + \sqrt{(b^2 + 4h^2)}}$$

Freely supported along all edges (corners restrained):

Bending moment (in two directions at centre of circle) $= +wd^2/16$

Continuous along all sides:

Bending moment (in two directions at centre of circle) $= +wd^2/30$

Bending moment (at sides) $= -wh^2/30$

w is intensity of uniformly distributed load (or intensity of pressure at centre of circle if pressure varies uniformly).
These expressions are valid for values of $v \ngtr 0.2$.

Regular polygon

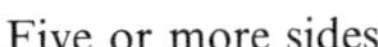

Five or more sides

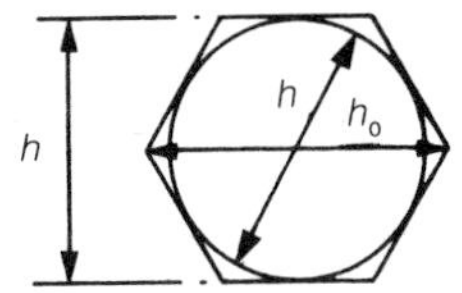

h diameter of inscribed circle = distance across flats
h_0 diameter of circumscribed circle = distance across corners
h_1 $(h + h_0)/2 = 1.077h$ for hexagon
$1.041h$ for octagon
Calculate bending moments as for circle of diameter h_1

Circle (diameter = h)

	Freely supported edge	Clamped edge
Concentric concentrated load F uniformly distributed over small area of diameter d	Beneath loaded area $M_r = M_t \ngtr \frac{F}{4\pi}\left[1 + (1+v)\ln\frac{h}{d}\right]$ Beneath unloaded area $M_r = -\frac{F}{4\pi}(1+v)\ln\xi$ $M_t = \frac{F}{4\pi}[(1-v) - (1+v)\ln\xi]$	Beneath loaded area $M_r = M_t \ngtr \frac{F}{4\pi}(1+v)\ln\frac{h}{d}$ Beneath unloaded area $M_r = \frac{F}{4\pi}\left[\left(\frac{d}{2\xi h}\right)^2(1-v) - (1+v)\ln\xi - 1\right]$ $M_t = \frac{F}{4\pi}\left[\left(\frac{d}{2\xi h}\right)^2 v(1-v) - (1+v)\ln\xi - v\right]$
Uniformly distributed load w over entire panel	$M_r = \frac{wh^2}{64}(3+v)(1-\xi^2)$ $M_t = \frac{wh^2}{64}[(3+v) - (1+3v)\xi^2]$	$M_r = \frac{wh^2}{64}[(1+v) - (3+v)\xi^2]$ $M_t = \frac{wh^2}{64}[(1+v) - (1+3v)\xi^2]$

Notes

Reinforcement to resist positive bending moments to be provided in two directions mutually at right angles.

M_r moment in radial direction
M_t moment in tangential direction
v Poisson's ratio
ξ $\dfrac{\text{distance of point considered from slab centre}}{\text{radius of slabs}}$

For slab continuous at edge, average moments obtained by considering freely supported slab and slab with clamped edge.
If $d <$ half the thickness of slab t, substitute $d' = \sqrt{(1.6d^2 + t^2)} - 0.675t$ for d in above formulae.

corrected values of αl_y and βl_y,

$$(1/2) \times 2.467 \times 2.5 \times n + (1/2) \times (2.071 + 1.462) \times 2.5 \times (1/3) \times n = 4.556n$$

Therefore, since the work done by the moments remains unchanged, the revised ratio of M/n is $4.556/6 = 0.759$. Since M/n is again proportional to $(\xi l_x)^2$, the corrected value of ξl_x is $\sqrt{(0.714/0.759)} \times 2.5 = 2.424$.

7. Recalculate the individual values of internal and external work done and draw up another table:

Area	External work done	Internal work done	Balance M/n
A	$(1/2) \times 2.071 \times 4 \times (1/3) \times n = 1.381n$	$4[(M/2)+(M/2)]/2.071 = 1.931M$	0.715
B	$[(2.467 \times 2.424 \times 1/2) + (2.424 \times 3.533 \times (1/2) \times (1/3))]n = 4.418n$	$6[(3M/2)+M]/2.424 = 6.188M$	0.714
C	$(1/2) \times 1.462 \times 4 \times (1/3) \times n = 0.975n$	$4 \times (M/2)/1.462 = 1.368M$	0.713
D	$[(2.467 \times 1.576 \times 1/2) + (1.576 \times 3.533 \times (1/2) \times (1/3))]n = 2.872n$	$6 \times M/1.576 = 3.807M$	0.754
Totals	$= 9.646n$	$= 13.294M$	0.726

8. Repeat this cyclic procedure until reasonable agreement between the ratios of M/n is obtained. This then gives the value of M for which reinforcement must be provided corresponding to a load n. In the example, the ratios given by the second cycle are quite satisfactory. Note that, although some of the dimensions originally guessed were not particularly accurate, the resulting error in M/n was only about 1.5%, indicating that the actual load-carrying capacity of the slab is not greatly influenced by the accuracy of the arbitrary dimensions.

Concentrated loads and line loads occurring at boundaries between slab areas should be divided equally between the areas that they adjoin, and their contribution to the external work done assessed as described in section 14.7.5.

As in all yield-line theory, the above analysis is only valid if the pattern of yield lines considered is the critical one. If reasonable alternatives are possible, both patterns should be investigated to determine which is critical.

14.7.9 Corner levers

Tests and elastic analyses of slabs show that the negative moments along the edges reduce to zero near the corners and increase rapidly away from these points. In slabs that are fixed or continuous at their edges, negative yield lines thus tend to form across the corners and, in conjunction with pairs of positive yield lines, result in the formation of additional triangular slab elements known as corner levers, as shown in diagram (i)(a) on *Table 59*. If the slab is freely supported a similar mechanism is induced, causing the corner to lift (diagram (i)(b)). If these mechanisms are substituted for the original yield lines running into the corners of the slab, the overall strength of the slab is correspondingly decreased, the amount of this decrease depending principally on the various factors listed on *Table 59*.

For a corner having an included angle of not less than 90°, the reduction of strength is unlikely to exceed 8 to 10%. Such cases can therefore be treated quite simply by neglecting corner-lever action, increasing the amount of main reinforcement slightly, and providing top steel at the corners to restrict cracking. The recommendations of the Swedish Code of Practice (see ref. 34) for this reinforcement are shown in diagram (ii) on *Table 59*.

For acute-angled corners, the decrease in strength is more serious. For a triangular slab ABC where no corner angle is less than 30°, Johansen (ref. 18) suggests dividing the calculated strength without corner lever action by a factor k, where k is given by the approximation

$$k = (7.4 - \sin A - \sin B - \sin C)/4$$

Thus for an equilateral triangle, $k \simeq 1.2$.

The determination mathematically of the true critical dimensions of an individual corner lever involves much complex trial and adjustment. Fortunately this is unnecessary, as Jones and Wood (ref. 21) have devised a direct design method that establishes corner levers having dimensions which are such that the resulting adjustment in strength is similar to that due to the true mechanisms. This design procedure is summarized in the lower part of *Table 59* and illustrated by the example below.

The formulae derived by Jones and Wood and on which the graphs on *Table 59* are based are as follows:

With fixed edges:

$$k_1 = \sec(\theta/2)\left[\sqrt{\{6(1+i)\}}\left\{\frac{1}{K_1 \sin^2(\theta/2)} - 1\right\}\right]$$

$$k_2 = \frac{k_1}{\cos(\theta/2) - \cot\psi \sin(\theta/2)}$$

where $K_1 = \sqrt{[4 + 3\cot^2(\theta/2)]} - 1$ and $\cot\psi = (K_1 - 1)\tan(\theta/2)$.

With freely supported edges:

$$k_1 = \sqrt{(2/3)}\sec(\theta/2)[\sqrt{(K_2)} - 2\sqrt{(1+i)}]$$

$$k_2 = \frac{k_1}{\cos(\theta/2) - \cot\psi \sin(\theta/2)}$$

where $K_2 = 4 + i + 3\cot^2(\theta/2)$ and $\cot\psi = [\sqrt{\{K_2(1+i)\}} - (2+i)]\tan(\theta/2)$.

Example. Calculate the resistance of the 5 m square slab with fixed edges shown on *Table 59*.

The negative resistance-moment coefficient i of 1 at the fixed

Two-way slabs: yield-line theory: general information

58

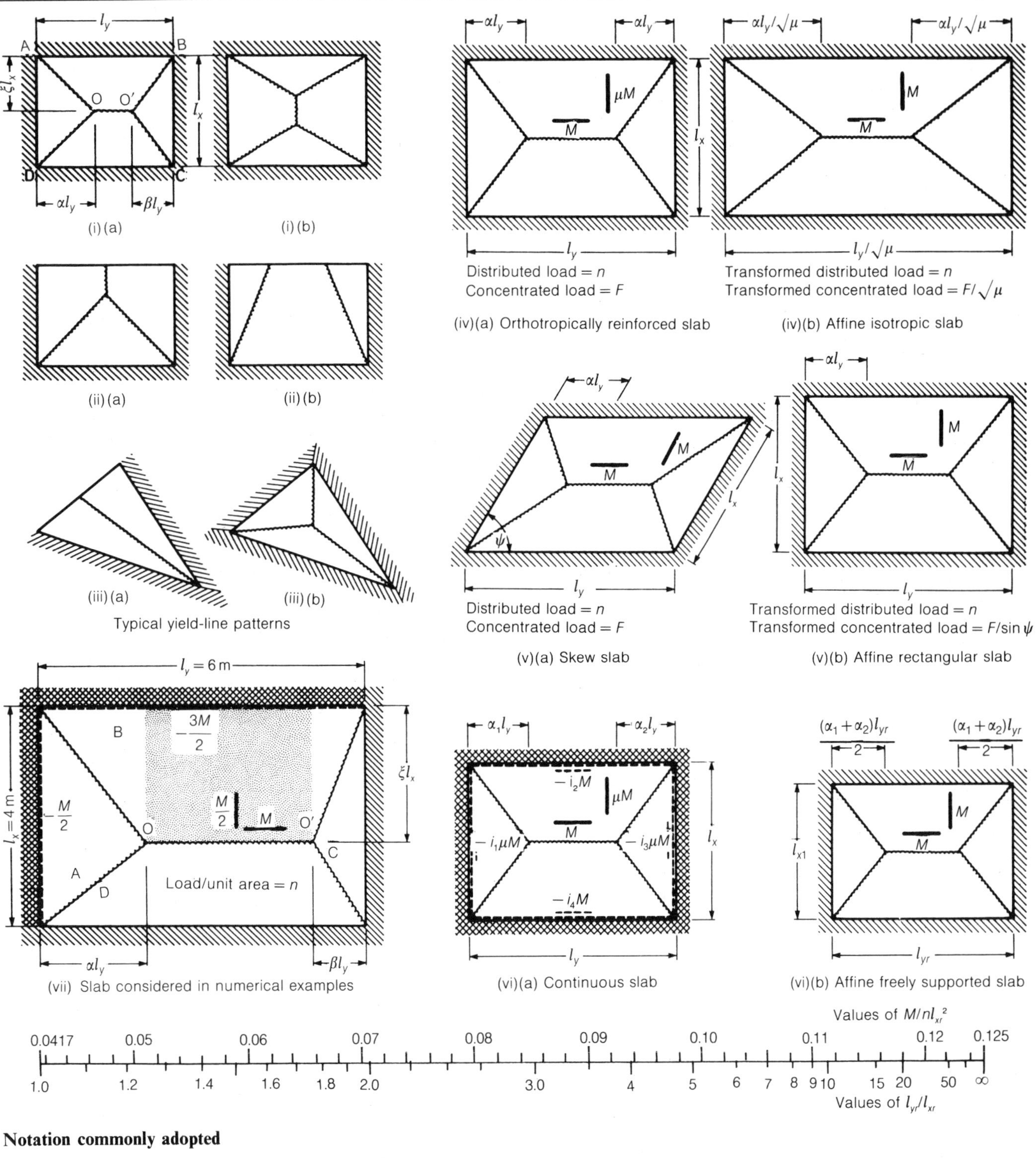

Notation commonly adopted

positive yield line
negative yield line
unsupported slab edge
freely supported slab edge
fixed or continuous slab edge

M, μM: values and direction of positive resistance moments provided in slab (which act at right angles to direction in which line is drawn). Thus as shown here, resistance (in plane of page) is M vertically and μM horizontally

iM, $i\mu M$: value and direction of negative resistance moments

M	principal positive resistance moment
μ	ratio of secondary to principal resistance moment
i_1, i_2, i_3 etc.	ratios of negative resistance moments at supports to positive resistance moment
l_x, l_y	lesser and greater side lengths of slab
l_{xr}, l_{yr}	reduced side lengths
ψ	angle of skew of slab
n	distributed ultimate load
F	concentrated ultimate load

edges gives reduced side lengths of $l/\sqrt{(1+i)} = 5/\sqrt{2} = 3.54$ m. Then, for a square slab (ignoring, for the moment, the formation of corner levers) the resistance moment $M = 0.0417nl_r^2 = 0.521n$. Now, from the appropriate graph on *Table 59*, with $i = 1$ and $\theta = 90°$, read off $k_1 = 1.1$ and $k_2 = 4.2$. Thus $a_1 = 1.1\sqrt{0.521} = 0.794$ and $a_2 = 4.2\sqrt{0.521} = 3.032$.

Plotting these values on a diagram of the slab it is now possible to recalculate the revised ultimate resistance required. If the deflection of the centre of the slab is unity, the relative deflection at the inner corners of the levers is $3.032/3.536 = 0.858$. Thus the revised virtual-work expression is

$$4 \times 2M\left[\frac{3.412}{2.5} + \frac{0.794\sqrt{(2)} \times 0.858}{2.471}\right]$$
$$= [\tfrac{1}{3} \times 5^2 - 4 \times \tfrac{1}{2} \times 0.794^2 \times \tfrac{1}{3} \times 0.858]n$$

or $14.036M = 7.973n$, so that $M = 0.568n$.

Note that this is 9% greater than the uncorrected value; in other words, the load supported by a square slab having a specified moment of resistance is actually 9% less than that calculated when corner levers are not taken into account.

14.7.10 Hillerborg's simple strip method

Moments in slab. According to lower-bound (i.e. equilibrium) theory, the load acting on a slab is supported by two bending moments and a torsional moment. In the simple strip method, the torsional moment is chosen as zero and thus the load (or part load) at any point is considered to be carried by a moment in one of two principal directions. Thus in diagram (i) on *Table 60*, the load n on the shaded areas is considered to be supported by the slab spanning in direction l_y only. The remaining area is supported by the slab spanning in direction l_x only. The designer can select an infinite number of ways of apportioning the load, each of which will lead to a different arrangement of reinforcement while still fulfilling the collapse criteria. However, the loading arrangement selected should also be such that the resulting design is simple, economical and behaves well regarding deflection and cracking under working loads.

Some possible ways of dividing the load on a freely supported rectangular slab are shown in diagrams (i) to (iv) on *Table 60*, the notation adopted being given on the table. Perhaps the most immediately obvious arrangement is that shown in diagram (i); Hillerborg originally suggested that θ may be taken as 45° where both adjacent edges are freely supported. However, in ref. 22 he recommends that θ should be made equal to $\tan^{-1}(l_y/l_x)$, as shown in diagram (i). The disadvantage of the load distribution shown is that the moment (and thus the steel theoretically required) varies across strips 2 and 3. Since it is impracticable to vary the reinforcement continuously, the usual procedure is to calculate the total moment acting on the strip, to divide by the width to obtain the average, and to provide uniform reinforcement to resist this moment. To avoid the need to integrate across the strip to obtain the total moment, Hillerborg recommends calculating the moment along the centre-line of the strip considered and multiplying this value by the correction factor

$$1 + \frac{(l_{max} - l_{min})^2}{3(l_{max} + l_{min})^2}$$

where l_{max} and l_{min} are the maximum and minimum loaded lengths of the strip. Strictly speaking, averaging the moments as described violates the principles on which the method is based and this stratagem should only be adopted where the factor of safety will not be seriously impaired. If the width of the strip over which the moments are to be averaged is appreciable, it is better to subdivide it and to calculate the average moment for each separate part.

An alternative arrangement that avoids the need to average the moments across the strips is that shown in diagram (ii). This has the disadvantages that six different types of strip (and thus six different reinforcement arrangements) must be considered, and that in strip 6 no moment theoretically occurs. Such a strip must contain distribution steel and so this design is perhaps less economical.

So far, the load at any point is assumed to be supported in one direction only. In diagram (iii), however, the loads on the corner areas are so divided that one-half is carried in each direction. Hillerborg (ref. 22) states that this extremely simple and practical arrangement never requires more than 10% of extra steel than the theoretically exact but less practical solution (diagram (i)) when l_y/l_x is between 1.1 and 4. An additional sophistication that can be arranged is to so determine the proportion of load in each direction in the two-way spanning areas that the resulting steel area across the shorter span corresponds to the minimum distribution steel which has to be provided. Details of this and similar stratagems are given in ref. 22.

Diagram (iv) illustrates yet another arrangement that may be considered. By dividing the corner areas into triangles and averaging the moments over these widths as described above, Hillerborg shows that the moments in the side strips are reduced to two-thirds of the moments given by the arrangement in diagram (iii).

Load on supporting beams. A feature of Hillerborg's method is that the boundaries between the different load-carrying areas also define the manner in which the loads are transferred to the supporting beams. For example, in diagram (i) the beams in direction l_x support triangular areas of slab giving maximum loads of $nl_x^2/2l_y$ at their centres.

14.8 SHEARING FORCE ON RECTANGULAR PANEL WITH UNIFORM LOAD

BS8110 includes coefficients that enable the loads transferred to the supporting beams from two-way slabs designed using the Code bending-moment coefficients to be calculated, as shown graphically in *Table 62*. These unit loads (which correspond to the shearing force per unit width acting on the slab at right angles to the edge) are considered to act along a central length of the supporting beam in question equal to three-quarters of the span.

The maximum shearing forces at the edges of a panel spanning in two directions and carrying a uniformly distributed load are, according to Pigeaud, approximately $wl_x/3$

Two-way slabs: yield-line theory: corner levers

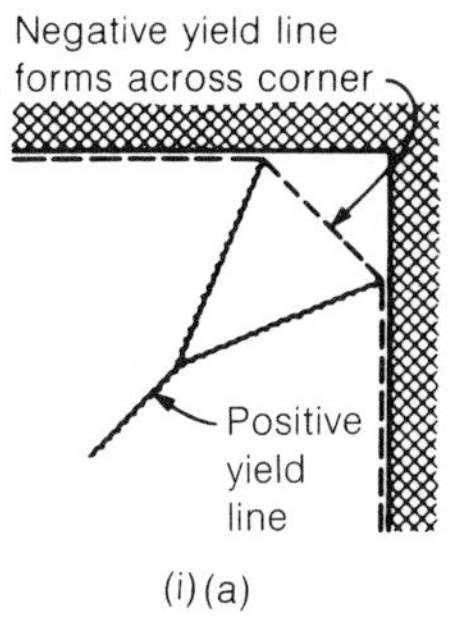

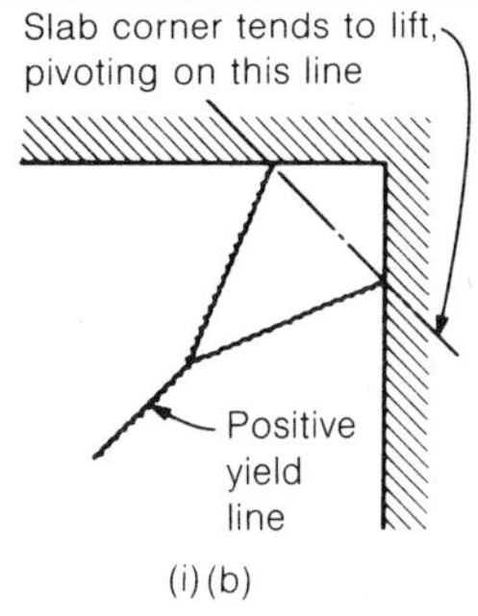

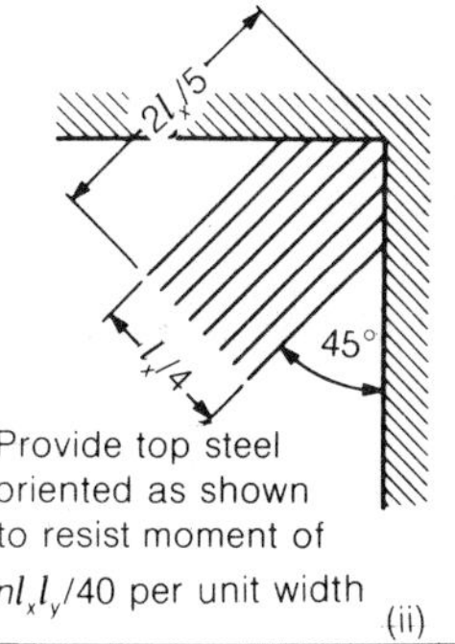

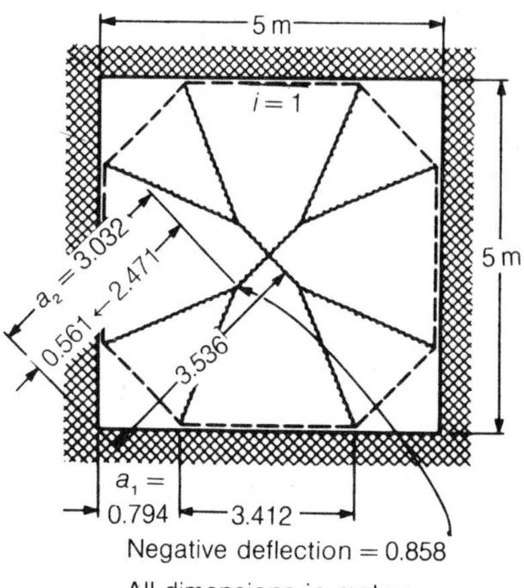

Formation of corner levers (and also circular fans)		
More likely with:	Less likely with:	
Heavy concentrated loads Acute-angled corners Fixed or continuous edges Unsupported edges (particularly where opposite corners) No top steel in corners	Distributed loads only Obtuse-angled corners Freely supported edges No unsupported edges Top steel in corners	Individual conditions listed are additive. Thus corner levers are most likely to form if several or all factors apply. However, heavy loads is most influential cause.

Design procedure for corner levers

1. Establish the ultimate resistance of the slab without taking corner levers into account.
2. With known values of the corner angle θ and the negative reinforcement factor i, calculate distances a_1 and a_2 by means of the accompanying graphs.
3. Using these dimensions, plot the corner levers on a diagram of the yield lines. If the calculated value of a_2 exceeds the distance XX on the diagram, adopt the length given by the original yield-line pattern.
4. Recalculate the revised ultimate resistance moment for the slab using the new node points established in this way, by means of virtual work.

This procedure is illustrated in the example in section 14.7.9.

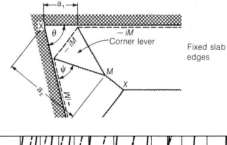

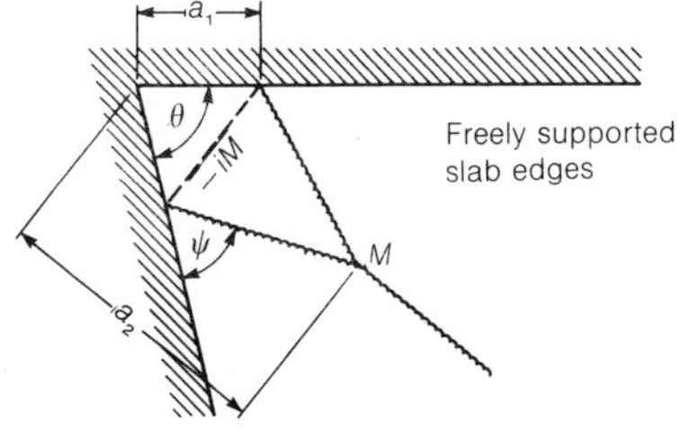

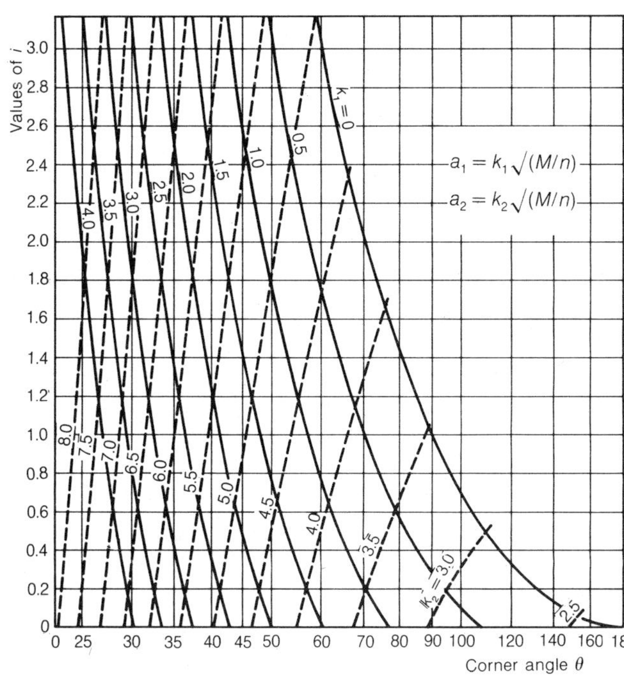

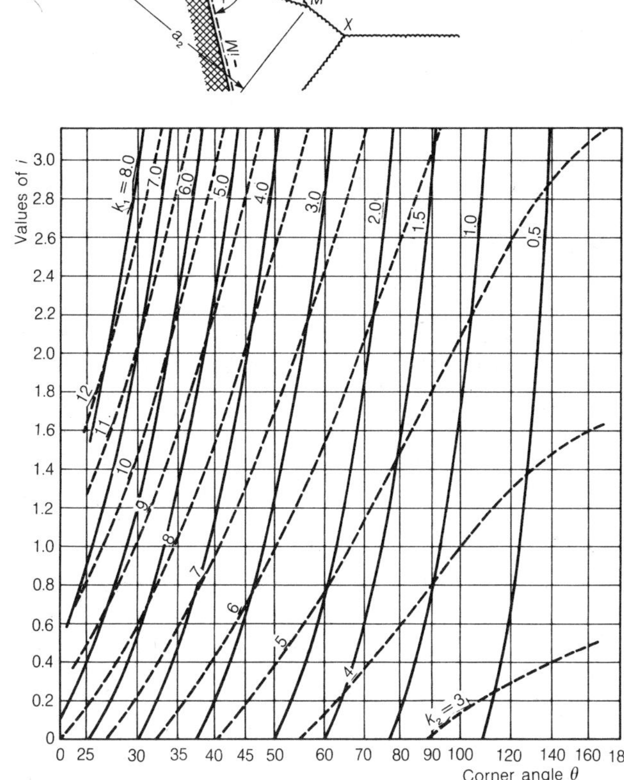

at the middle of the short edge and $wl_xk/(2k+1)$ at the middle of the long edge. The same values are applicable to a panel fixed or continuous along all four edges, but for other conditions the distribution of shearing force, the stresses due to which are rarely critical, must be adjusted on the principle that the shearing force is slightly greater at an edge at which there is continuity or fixity than at an opposite freely supported edge.

14.9 RECTANGULAR PANELS WITH TRIANGULARLY DISTRIBUTED LOADS

14.9.1 Elastic analysis

The intensity of pressure on the walls of containers is normally uniform at any given level, but vertically it may vary linearly from zero at or near the top to a maximum f at the bottom. The curves given on *Table 53* enable the probable critical service bending moments on vertical and horizontal strips of unit width to be calculated when the slab is fully fixed or freely supported or unsupported along the top edge.

In all cases it is assumed that the slab is fully fixed along the two vertical edges and along the bottom edge. This assumption may be reasonably true when the span and stiffness of the adjoining areas of wall and floor are similar to that being considered, but in other circumstances some rotation of the supports may take place. The condition may then tend to approach that of a freely supported slab, which is the corresponding limiting condition. On *Table 53* the corresponding curves for the maximum horizontal and vertical bending moment when the slab is freely supported at the bottom and sides (and also at the top in the case of a slab fixed along all edges) are shown on the charts for slabs with fixed edges, by means of chain lines. These enable the designer, having some idea of the amount of fixity at the bottom and sides of the slab, to estimate the probable resulting increase in the midspan moments.

The curves are based on the results of elastic analyses tabulated in ref. 13, and suitably adjusted for a value of Poisson's ratio of 0.2. To consider a different value of Poisson's ratio, the equation given on *Tables 54* and *55* for Pigeaud's method may be used.

If the ratio of width to height is less than 0.5 the bending moments should be calculated on the assumption that the slab spans entirely horizontally. If this ratio k exceeds 2, the slab should be assumed to span entirely vertically. In either case, the amount of reinforcement that must be provided at right angles to meet the minimum requirements of the Code is normally sufficient to resist any moment in that direction.

At a nominally freely supported top edge, resistance to a negative bending moment equal to two-thirds of the positive bending moment on the vertical span should be provided.

It is advantageous, wherever possible, to provide 45° splays at the internal corners of containers, and it should be noted that the critical negative bending moments may not necessarily occur at the edges of the splays.

A trapezoidally distributed pressure can be considered by adding the bending moments due to the triangularly distributed load given by the curves on *Table 53* to the bending moments due to a uniformly distributed load (obtained from *Tables 50* or *52*). The resulting negative moments are accurate but the positive moments are only approximate.

In designing sections to resist the foregoing moments, the bending moments on the horizontal span must be combined with the direct tension due to service loads, as described on *Table 166*.

The final diagram on *Table 53* illustrates a typical distribution of vertical and horizontal moments in a half-slab subjected to a triangularly distributed load, where the bottom and side edges are fully fixed and the top edge is unsupported. The actual values and distribution of the bending moments in each direction depend on the ratio of vertical to horizontal span, but the general distribution is basically similar in all cases.

In addition to the foregoing methods of determining the bending moments due to triangularly distributed loads, which are based on elastic analyses, an analysis of conditions at collapse may be made by utilizing the yield-line method or the strip method: see below and *Table 61*.

Example. Find the maximum service bending moments in a wall panel of a rectangular tank that can be considered as freely supported along the top edge and fixed along the bottom edge and along the two vertical sides. The height l_z of the panel is 2.5 m and the horizontal span l_x is 3.75 m. The intensity of pressure is 25 kN/m^2 along the bottom edge, decreasing to zero at the top edge.

Ratio of spans $k = l_x/l_z = 3.75/2.5 = 1.5$. From *Table 53* the bending moments are thus as follows:

Maximum negative moment on vertical span (at midpoint along bottom of panel) $= -0.053 \times 2.5^2 \times 25 = -8.3$ kN m per metre width

Maximum positive moment on vertical span (at a height of about 0.45 from the base) $= +0.021 \times 2.5^2 \times 25 = \pm 3.3$ kN m per metre width

Maximum negative moment on horizontal span (at a height of about $3l_z/7$ along vertical edges) $= -0.015 \times 3.75^2 \times 25 = -5.3$ kN m per metre height

Maximum positive moment on horizontal span (at about midheight and midspan) $= +0.005 \times 3.75^2 \times 25 = +1.8$ kN m per metre height

If the panel is assumed to be freely supported along all the edges, the corresponding maximum positive vertical and horizontal bending moments will be $+0.042 \times 2.5^2 \times 25 = +6.6$ kN m per metre and $+0.009 \times 3.75^2 \times 25 = +3.2$ kN m per metre. Thus, if the actual fixity along the base and sides is about halfway between the limiting conditions of fully fixed and freely supported, the maximum bending moments vertically and horizontally may rise to about $(3.3 + 6.6)/2 = 5$ kN m per metre width and $(1.8 + 3.2)/2 = 2.5$ kN m per metre height respectively.

14.9.2 Yield-line method

A feature of collapse methods of designing two-way slabs is that the designer is free to choose the ratio between the moments in each direction and between the positive and negative moment in each direction. However, if the triangu-

Two-way slabs: Hillerborg's simple strip theory

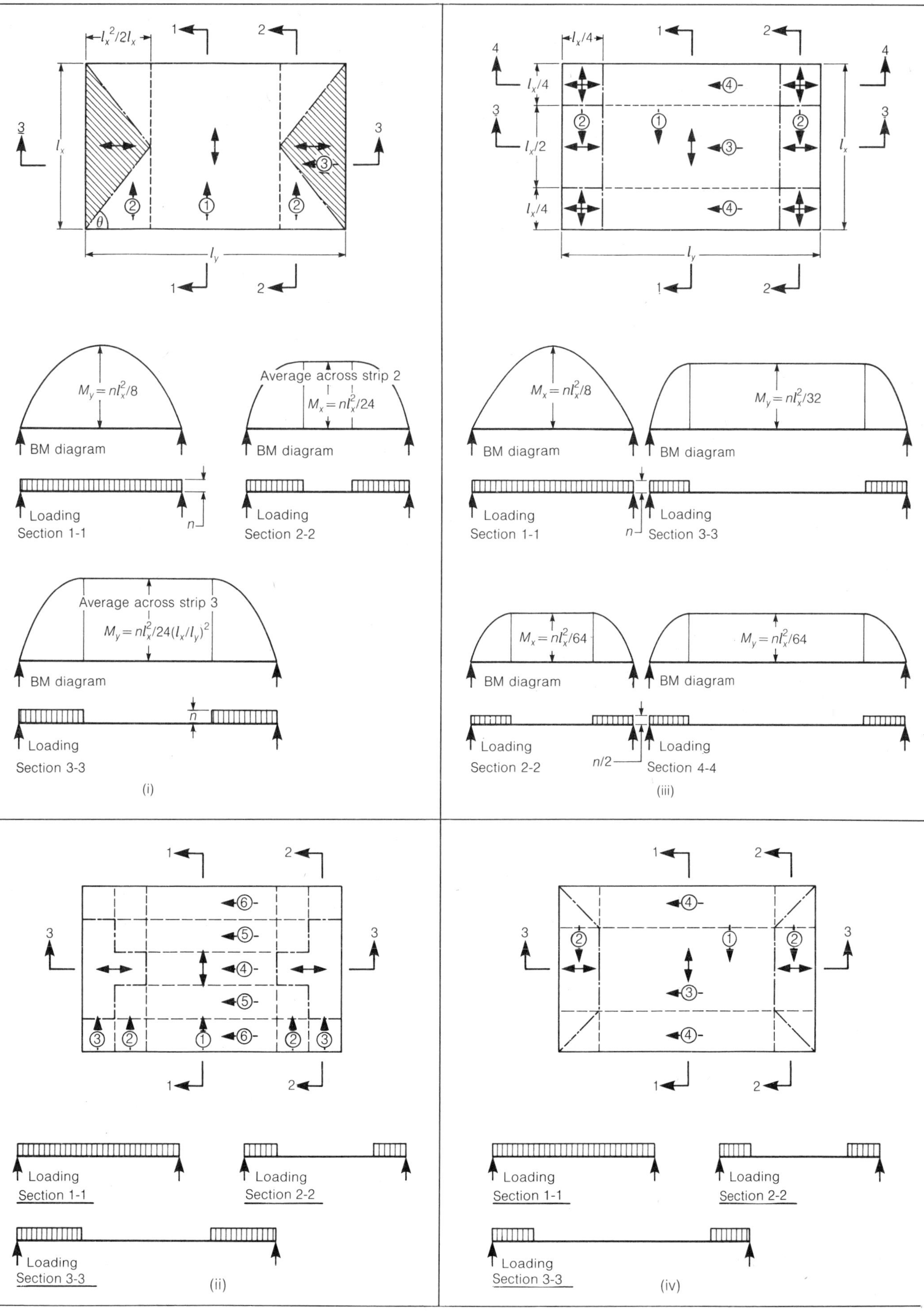

---- boundary between individual strips

—·— boundary between load-carrying areas of slab

-①▶ reference number of strip spanning in direction shown

◀▶ direction in which load over area indicated is supported

larly distributed load results from the storage of liquid it is more important than ever to ensure that the choice of these ratios is such that the formation of cracks under service loading is minimized. This is achieved if the ratios selected correspond approximately to those given by elastic analysis.

The following design procedure is thus suggested:

1. Determine the proportion of the horizontal moments at midspan M_{hm} and at the supports M_{hs}, and the vertical moment at the base M_{vs}, to the vertical moment at midspan M_{vm} from the appropriate chart on *Table 53*.
2. Then if $i_4 = M_{vs}/M_{vm}$, $\mu = M_{hm}/M_{vm}$ and $\mu i_1 = \mu i_3 = M_{hs}/M_{vm}$, determine μ, $i_1(=i_3)$ and i_4.
3. Calculate l_{yr} from

$$l_{yr} = \frac{2l_y}{\sqrt{(1+i_1)}+\sqrt{(1+i_3)}}$$

and, if the slab is supported at the top edge, calculate l_{xr} from

$$l_{xr} = \frac{2l_x}{\sqrt{(1+i_2)}+\sqrt{(1+i_4)}}$$

4. Finally, with f, l_x (or l_{xr}), l_{yr} and i, determine M from the scale on *Table 58* if the slab is supported at the top edge and from the chart on *Table 61* otherwise.

This procedure is illustrated below.

Top edge of slab supported. In ref. 18 Johansen shows that the total moments resulting from yield-line analysis for triangularly loaded slabs correspond to those obtained when the slab is loaded uniformly with the same total load (i.e. considering a uniform load of one-half the maximum triangular load f). Thus the design expressions in section 14.7.6 and the scale given on *Table 58* for uniformly loaded slabs can again be used. As before, if the edges of the slab are restrained, the reduced side lengths l_{xr} and l_{yr} should be calculated and substituted into the formula instead of the actual side lengths l_x and l_y.

Top edge of slab unsupported. For the case where the top edge of the slab is unsupported, Johansen (ref. 18) derives the following 'exact' formulae for the two possible modes of failure.

For failure mode 1:

$$M = \frac{fl_x^2}{12k}$$

where

$$4k^2\left[1+i_4+\left(\frac{l_x}{l_{yr}}\right)^2\right] - 4k\left[i_4(1+i_4)+2(2+3i_4)\left(\frac{l_x}{l_{yr}}\right)^2\right] + i_4^2\left[1+i_4\left(\frac{l_x}{l_{yr}}\right)^2\right] = 0$$

By solving the quadratic in k and substituting values of l_{yr}/l_x, the corresponding values of M/fl_x^2 may be found.

For failure mode 2:

$$M = \frac{fl_{yr}^2}{96}(6-8\xi+3\xi^2)$$

$$M = \frac{fl_{xr}^2}{12}(2-\xi)\xi^2$$

By solving these equations simultaneously, values of M for various ratios of l_{xr}/l_{yr} may be obtained.

The results of these calculations can be plotted graphically as shown on *Table 61*, from which coefficients of M/fl_x^2 corresponding to given values of l_{yr}/l_x and i_4 may be read. The chain line on the chart indicates the values at which the failure mode changes.

Example. Find the ultimate moments in a wall panel of a rectangular tank that is unsupported along the top edge and fully fixed along the remaining sides. The height of the panel is 2.5 m and the horizontal span is 3.75 m. The pressure at the bottom edge is 25 kN/m^2, decreasing to zero at the top.

With a ratio of spans of $3.75/2.5 = 1.5$, from *Table 53* the service bending moments per metre would be as follows:

$$M_{vs} = -0.060 \times 2.5^2 \times 25 = -9.38\,\text{kN m}$$
$$M_{vm} = +0.016 \times 2.5^2 \times 25 = +2.50\,\text{kN m}$$
$$M_{hs} = -0.019 \times 3.75^2 \times 25 = -6.68\,\text{kN m}$$
$$M_{hm} = +0.075 \times 3.75^2 \times 25 = +2.64\,\text{kN m}$$

The most suitable values for μ, i_1, i_3 and i_4 are thus as follows: $i_4 = 9.38/2.5 = 3.75$; $\mu = 2.64/2.5 = 1.06$; and $i_1 = i_3 = 6.68/2.64 = 2.53$. Thus $l_{yr} = 2 \times 3.75/[2\sqrt{(1+2.53)}] = 2.0$ m and $l_{yr}/l_x = 2.0/2.5 = 0.8$. From the chart on *Table 61* with $l_{yr}/l_x = 0.8$ and $i_4 = 3.75$, $M/fl_x^2 = 0.012$. Therefore, with a maximum ultimate load f of $25 \times 1.6 = 40$ kN/m^2,

$$M = 0.012 \times 40 \times 2.5^2 = 3.0\,\text{kN m per metre}$$

so that $M_{vm} = 3.0$ kN m per metre, $M_{vs} = 3.0 \times 3.75 = -11.25$ kN m per metre, $M_{hm} = 3.0 \times 1.06 = 3.18$ kN m per metre and $M_{hs} = 3.0 \times 1.06 \times 2.53 = -8.05$ kN m per metre.

In designing sections to resist these moments, remember that the horizontal bending moments must be combined with direct (i.e. bursting) tensile forces.

14.10 BEAMS SUPPORTING RECTANGULAR PANELS

Beams supporting slabs spanning in two directions are subjected to loading from the slab that is distributed approximately triangularly on the beam along each shorter edge l_x and trapezoidally on the beam along each longer edge l_y, as shown in the diagrams in *Table 63*. For the calculation of the ultimate bending moments only on the beams, if the span of a beam is equal to the length (or width) of the panel, and the beam supports one panel only, the equivalent total uniformly distributed ultimate loads on the beams supporting a panel which is freely supported along all four edges or is subjected to the same degree of restraint along all four edges are as follows:

Short-span beam: $\frac{1}{3}nl_x$

Long-span beam: $\frac{1}{2}nl_x\left(1-\frac{1}{3k^2}\right)$

where $n(=1.4g_k+1.6q_k)$ is the intensity of total uniformly

Yield-line theory

Top edge fixed

Determine moments from expressions for uniformly loaded slab (see section 14.7.6).

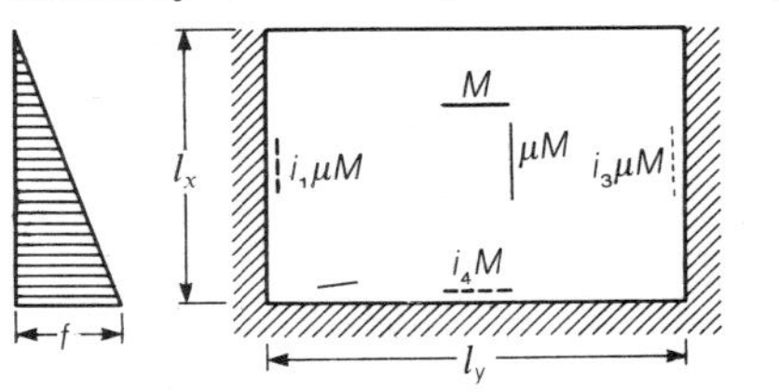

Top edge unsupported

Read M/fl_x^2 corresponding to given values of i_4 and l_{yr}/l_x from accompanying graph.

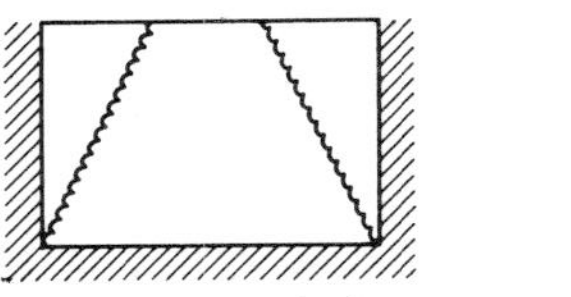
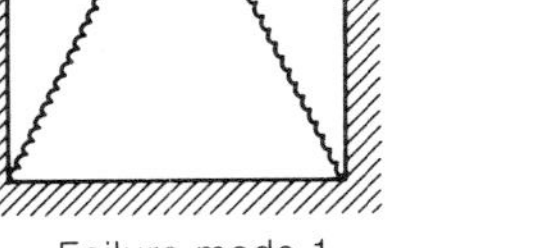

Failure mode 1

Failure mode 2

Simple strip theory: top edge fixed or freely supported

If $l_y > l_x$, assuming vertical and horizontal loads are apportioned as shown, if $x/l_x < 3/4$ (note: x is measured in terms of l_x throughout):

Moment on vertical strip 2-5:

$$M_{2-5} = \tfrac{1}{6} f l_x^2 x(1-x)(2-x) + i_2 x + i_4(1-x)$$

Maximum positive moment occurs at

$$x = 1 - \sqrt{\left[\frac{1}{3} - \frac{2(i_2 - i_4)}{fl_x^2}\right]}$$

from bottom of wall.

Moment on vertical strips 1-4 and 3-6:

$$M_{3-6} = (1/480) f l_x^2 (80x^2 - 144x + 67)x + (1/4)[i_2 x + i_4(1-x)]$$

Maximum positive moment occurs at

$$x = \frac{3}{5} - \sqrt{\left[\frac{97}{1200} - \frac{1}{2}\frac{(i_2 - i_4)}{fl_x^2}\right]}$$

from bottom of wall.

Design procedure: Assume suitable values for all support moments and for horizontal span moments M_{1-2-3} and M_{4-5-6}. Next calculate k_1 and k_2 and thus evaluate vertical span moments $M_{1-4}(=M_{3-6})$ and M_{2-5} and the positions at which these occur.

Top edge fixed or freely supported

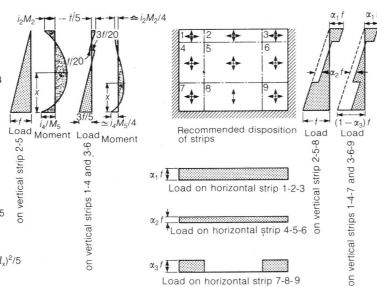

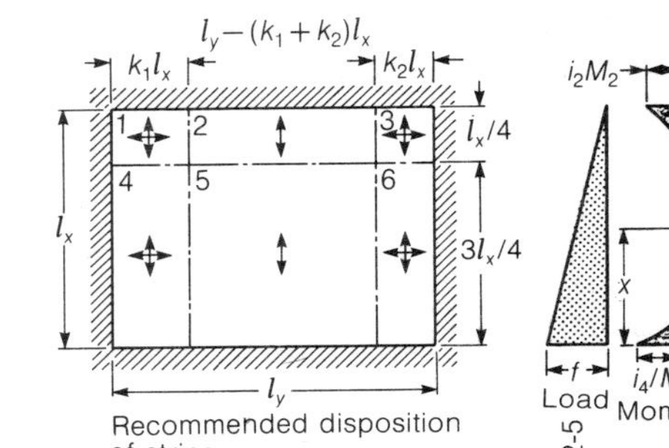

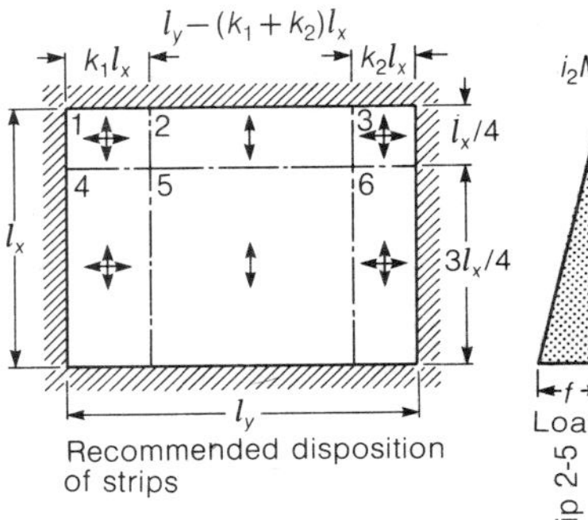

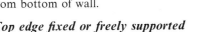

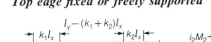

Recommended disposition of strips

Load on horizontal strip 1-2-3

Load on horizontal strip 4-5-6

Moment on horizontal strip 4-5-6

Top edge unsupported

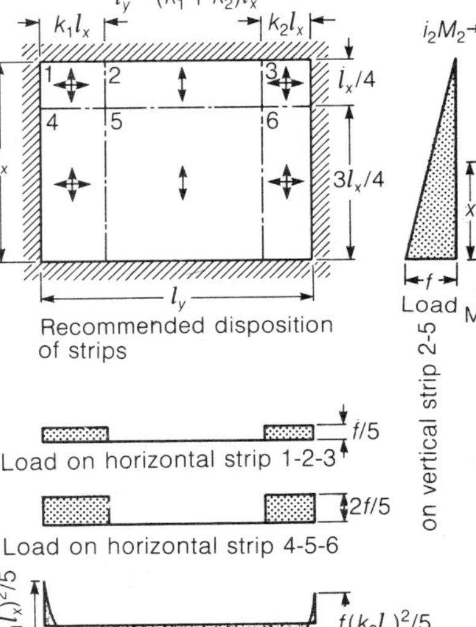

Recommended disposition of strips

Load on horizontal strip 1-2-3

Load on horizontal strip 4-5-6

Load on horizontal strip 7-8-9

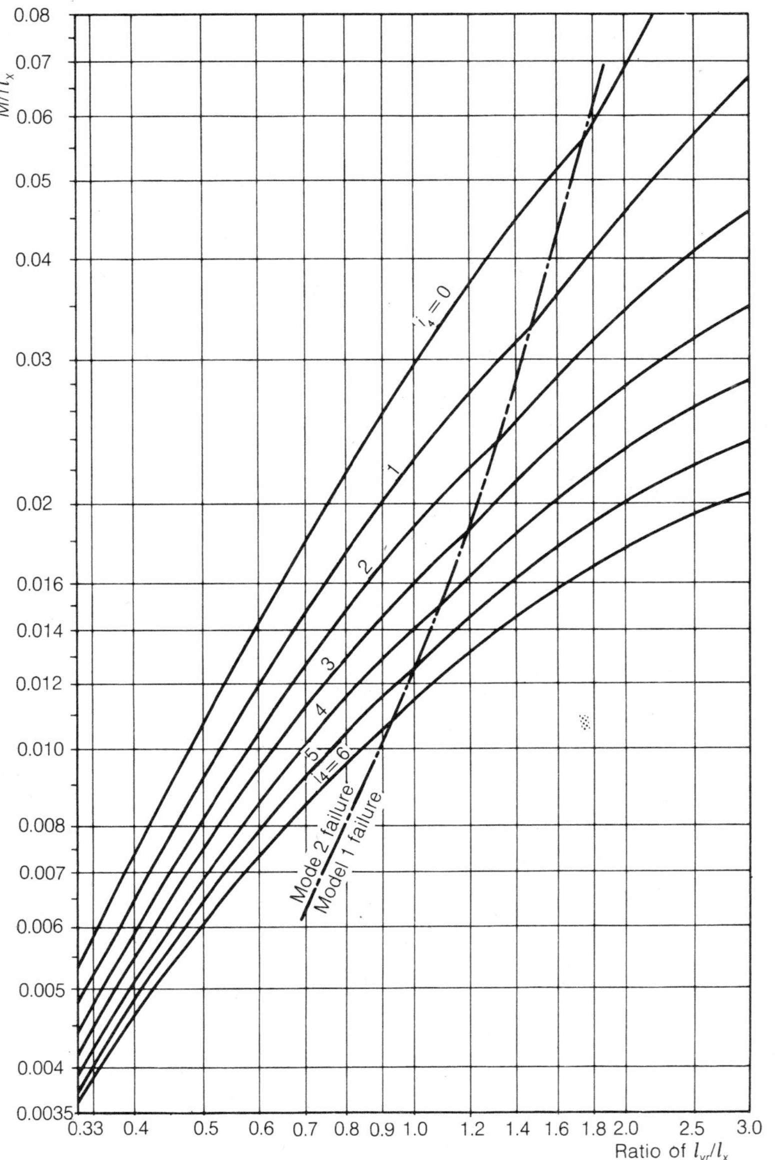
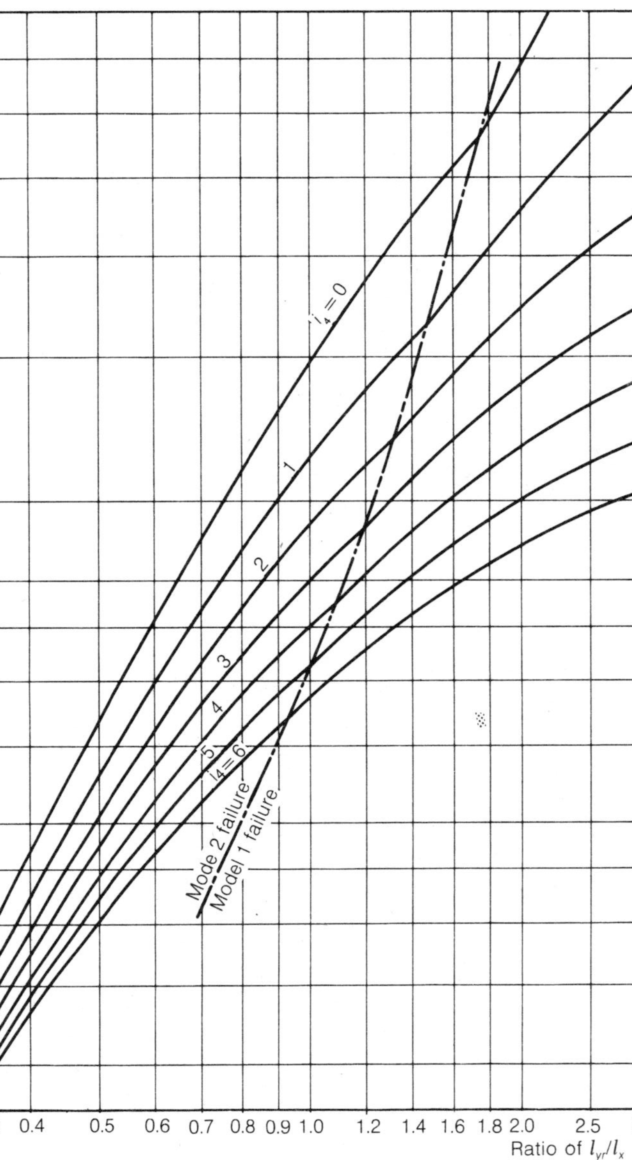

distributed ultimate load and $k = l_y/l_x$. If a beam supports two identical panels, one on either side, the foregoing equivalent loads are doubled. If a beam supports more than one panel in the direction of its length, the distribution of the load is in the form of two or more triangles (or trapeziums), and the foregoing formulae do not apply; in such case, however, it is accurate enough to assume that the total ultimate load on the beam is uniformly distributed.

If an analysis under service loads is being made, the total uniformly distributed service load $w(= g_k + q_k)$ should be substituted for n in the appropriate expressions.

BS8110 provides coefficients that enable the determination of the load transferred to the supporting beams from two-way slabs having torsional restraint and designed using the bending moment coefficients given in this Code. These coefficients are shown graphically in *Table 62*.

14.11 NON-RECTANGULAR PANELS

Additional notes regarding *Table 57* are given in section 3.8.

14.11.1 Units

If the uniform load w or n is in kN/m^2 and all dimensions are in metres, the resulting bending moments are in kN m per metre. Similarly, with loads in lb/ft^2 or kg/m^2 and dimensions in feet or metres, the resulting moments are in lb ft per foot or kg m per metre.

In the case of a circle the following units apply:

14.11.2 Yield-line method

For details of the yield-line method applied to polygonal slabs (including triangular, trapezoidal, circular and annular panels) see ref. 18.

14.12 FLAT SLABS: EMPIRICAL METHOD

The following notes and the data in *Table 64* comply with the recommendations for the empirical method (termed the simplified method in BS8110) of flat-slab design described in BS8110 and CP110. If all the limitations mentioned are not met, the structure should be analysed by the alternative continuous-frame method permitted by both codes.

14.12.1 Limitations of method

According to both Codes, the system must comprise at least three rows of rectangular panels of approximately constant thickness and equal span in each direction. CP110 stipulates specifically that $l_2 \nless 0.75 l_1$, that lengths and/or widths of adjoining panels should not differ by more than 15% of the greater length or width, and that end spans must not exceed those of internal panels. According to BS8110, the length of any drop to be taken into account must be not less than one-third of the smaller span of the panel: the corresponding requirement in CP110 states that the length must be not less than one-third of the panel length in that direction. The drop width at non-continuous edges (measured from the column centre-line) should be at least one-half that of the

	kN and m	*kg and m*	*ft and lb*
Average positive bending moment across a diameter	kN m per m of diameter	kg m per m of diameter	ft lb per ft of diameter
Alternative maximum positive bending moment at centre	kN m per m at centre	kg m per m at centre	ft lb per ft at centre
Negative bending moment around edge	kN m per m of circumference	kg m per m of circumference	ft lb per ft of circumference

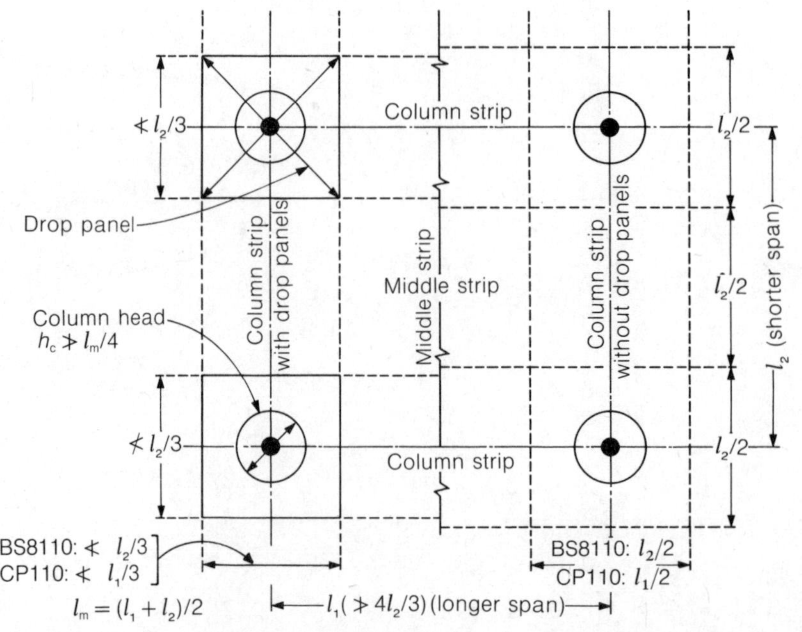

Two-way slabs: rectangular panels: loads on beams: BS8110 coefficients

62

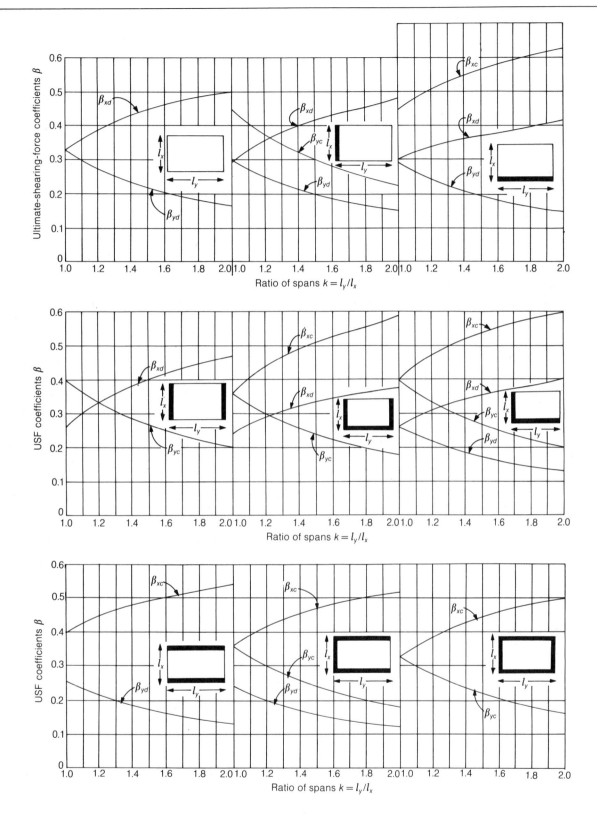

——— edge which is discontinuous or which is cast monolithically with support

▬▬▬ edge which is continuous

These coefficients only apply to rectangular panels consisting of solid slabs spanning in two directions at right angles carrying uniform loads only and designed using coefficients provided on *Table 51*.

Coefficients β_{xc} and β_{xd} apply to shearing force acting on short span l_x at continuous edge and discontinuous edge respectively. Load per unit length transferred from slab to supporting beam (i.e. spanning in direction l_y) $= \beta_x n l_x$.

Coefficients β_{yc} and β_{yd} apply to shearing force acting on long span l_y at continuous edge and discontinuous edge respectively. Long per unit length transferred from slab to supporting beam (i.e. spanning in direction l_x) $= \beta_y n l_y$.

Load is considered to be transferred from slab to beam over central length of 0.75*l* as shown below.

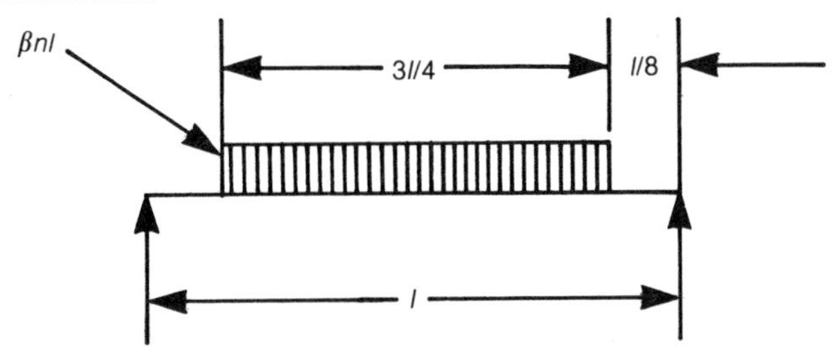

adjoining panel. All lateral forces must be resisted by shear walls or bracing.

14.12.2 Panel thickness

The minimum slab thickness must comply with the normal span/effective-depth limitations adopted to restrict deflection, as described on *Table 137*; in addition, CP110 specifies a minimum thickness of 125 mm. Unlike the corresponding situation with two-way slabs, when calculating permissible span/effective-depth ratios, BS8110 requires such calculations to be based on the *longer* of the two panel dimensions. If drops having widths in each direction of at least one-third of the span in that direction are provided, the values given by *Table 137* can be adopted directly, but otherwise the minimum thicknesses obtained from this table must be multiplied by a further factor of 1.11.

14.12.3 Bending moments

The total positive and negative bending moments on each of the various strips are some fraction of a basic bending moment $\alpha n l_2(l_1 - 2h_c/3)^2$, where n is the total ultimate load per unit area. Values of α according to both codes are given in *Table 64*, and substitution in the above formula gives the total basic bending moment on a particular strip of width l_2.

Adjustment of bending moments. If the width of the drop panel is less than one-half of the panel width, the total bending moment on the middle strip should be increased in proportion to the increased width of the middle strip, and the additional bending moment should be deducted from the total for the corresponding column strip. This adjustment ensures that the total bending moments along the principal axes are unaltered. In edge panels the bending moments should be increased as described on *Table 64*.

14.12.4 Columns

The diameter of the column head h_c (*Table 64*) should not exceed $l_m/4$, and the angle between the slope of the head and the vertical should not exceed 45°. The diameter h_c of the head is that at a distance of 40 mm below the underside of the slab. If the head is not circular, h_c should be the diameter of the circle having an equivalent area. Exterior columns should be provided with as much as possible of the head prescribed for interior columns.

Columns should be designed for bending moments calculated using the appropriate coefficients given on *Table 64*, these moments being divided between upper and lower columns in proportion to their stiffnesses.

14.12.5 Shearing forces

BS8110 requirements. According to BS8110 the critical consideration regarding shear for flat-slab structures is that of punching around the column head, and the requirements of this Code regarding the analysis and design necessary are summarized on *Table 64*.

CP110 requirements. When using the empirical method of flat-slab design, the critical conditions for shearing should be investigated using the procedure for concentrated loads described in section 21.1.6 and *Table 143* (considering the column head as a concentrated load acting upwards). Thus the shearing stresses should be investigated at a distance of 1.5 times the thickness of the drop (if provided) or of the slab (if no drop is provided) from the perimeter of the column head, and also at a distance of 1.5 times the thickness of the slab beyond the edge of the drop if a drop is provided, with all the panels adjoining the column carrying a total ultimate load of $n = 1.4g_k + 1.6q_k$.

If the resulting shearing stress exceeds 0.8 times the value of $\xi_s v_c$ given by *Table 143*, steel to resist shearing must be provided. Further sections at distances of 0.75 times the relevant slab thickness should then be progressively investigated and reinforced until the shearing stress induced does not exceed the shearing resistance (i.e. $0.8\xi_s v_c d \times$ perimeter) provided by the slab section (see section 21.1.6). Note the introduction here of the factor of 0.8, which does not apply in the normal case of a slab supporting a concentrated load, dealt with in section 21.1.6. This factor is introduced solely to take into account the seriousness of shearing failure around a column head.

Two-way slabs: rectangular panels: loads on beams: common coefficients

Panels supported along four edges

$k > 1$: $R_1 = R_3 = \frac{1}{4}wl_x^2$

$R_2 = R_4 = \frac{1}{2}(k - \frac{1}{2})wl_x^2$

$\alpha = \beta = 1/2k$

$k = 1$: $R_1 = R_2 = R_3 = R_4 = \frac{1}{4}wl_x^2$

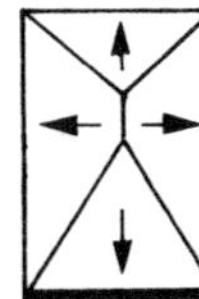

$k \nless 4/3$: $R_1 = \frac{1}{4}wl_x^2$ (min.) $\quad \alpha = 1/2k$ (min.)

$R_2 = R_4 = \frac{1}{2}(k - \frac{2}{3})wl_x^2$

$R_3 = \frac{5}{12}wl_x^2$ (max.) $\quad \beta = 5/6k$ (max.)

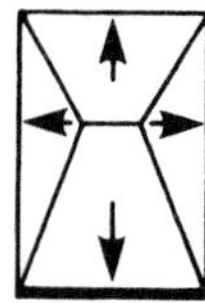

$k \leqslant 4/3$: $R_1 = \frac{3}{5}R_3$ approx. (min.) $\quad \alpha = 3/8$ (min.)

$\beta = 5/8$ (max.)

$R_2 = R_4 = \frac{3}{16}k^2wl_x^2 \quad \psi = \xi = 3k/8$

$R_3 = \frac{5}{8}k(1 - \frac{3}{8}k)wl_x^2$ approx. (max.)

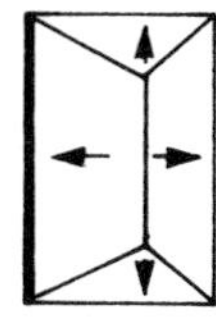

$R_1 = R_3 = \frac{3}{16}wl_x^2$

$R_2 = \frac{3}{5}R_4$ (min.)

$R_4 = \frac{5}{8}(k - \frac{3}{8})wl_x^2$ (max.)

$\alpha = \beta = 3/8k \quad \psi = \frac{5}{8}$ (max.)

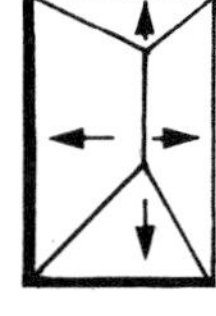

$R_1 = \frac{3}{16}wl_x^2$ (min.) $\quad \alpha = 3/8k$ (min.)

$R_2 = \frac{3}{5}R_4$ (min.) $\quad \beta = 5/8k$ (max.)

$R_3 = \frac{5}{16}wl_x^2$ (max.) $\quad \psi = 5/8$ (max.)

$R_4 = \frac{5}{8}(k - \frac{1}{2})wl_x^2$ (max.)

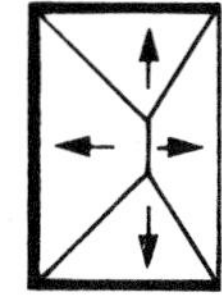

$k \nless 5/4$: $R_1 = R_3 = \frac{5}{16}wl_x^2 \quad \alpha = \beta = 5/8k$

$R_2 = \frac{3}{5}R_4$ (min.) $\quad \psi = 5/8$ (max.)

$R_4 = \frac{5}{8}(k - \frac{5}{8})wl_x^2$ (max.)

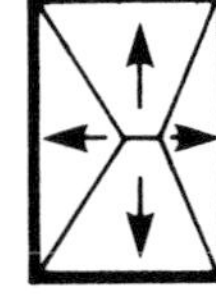

$k \leqslant 5/4$: $R_1 = R_3 = \frac{1}{2}k(1 - \frac{2}{5}k)wl_x^2 \quad \alpha = \beta = 1/2$

$R_2 = \frac{3}{20}k^2wl_x^2$ (min.)

$R_4 = \frac{1}{4}k^2wl_x^2$ (max.) $\quad \psi = k/2$

$\xi = 3k/10$

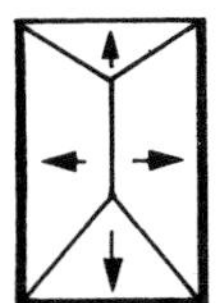

$R_1 = \frac{3}{20}wl_x^2$ (min.) $\quad \alpha = 3/10k$ (min.)

$R_2 = R_4 = \frac{1}{2}(k - \frac{2}{5})wl_x^2$

$R_3 = \frac{1}{4}wl_x^2$ (max.) $\quad \beta = 1/2k$ (max.)

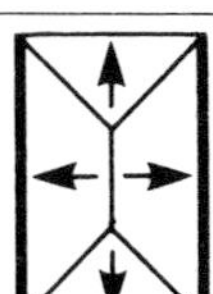

$R_1 = R_3 = \frac{3}{20}wl_x^2$ (min.)

$R_2 = R_4 = \frac{1}{2}(k - \frac{3}{10})wl_x^2$ (max.)

$\alpha = \beta = 3/10k$ (min.)

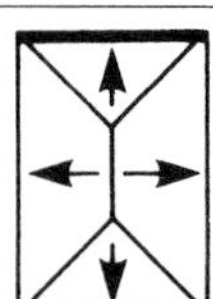

$k \nless 5/3$: $R_1 = R_3 = \frac{5}{12}wl_x^2$ (min.)

$R_2 = R_4 = \frac{1}{2}(k - \frac{5}{6})wl_x^2$ (max.)

$\alpha = \beta = 5/6k$ (min.)

Panels unsupported along one edge

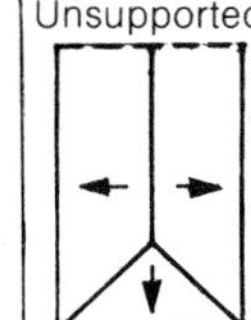

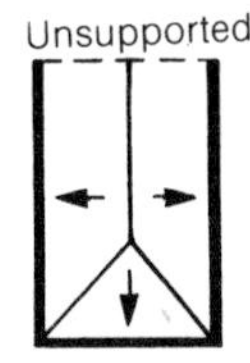

$R_1 = 0$

$R_2 = R_4 = \frac{1}{2}(k - \frac{1}{4})wl_x^2$

$R_3 = \frac{1}{4}wl_x^2$

$\beta = 1/2k$

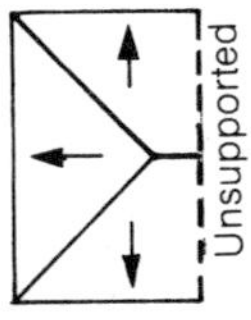

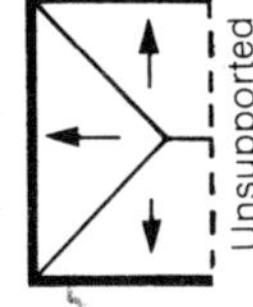

$k \ngtr 2$: $R_1 = R_3 = \frac{1}{2}k(1 - \frac{1}{4}k)wl_x^2$

$R_2 = 0$

$R_4 = \frac{1}{4}k^2wl_x^2$

$\psi = k/2$

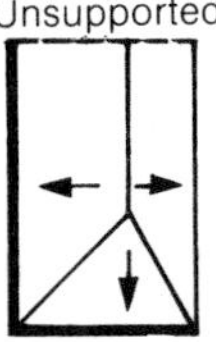

$R_1 = 0 \quad \beta = 5/8k$

$R_2 = \frac{3}{5}R_4$ (min.) $\quad \psi = 5/8$

$R_3 = \frac{5}{16}wl_x^2$

$R_4 = \frac{5}{8}(k - \frac{5}{16})wl_x^2$ (max.)

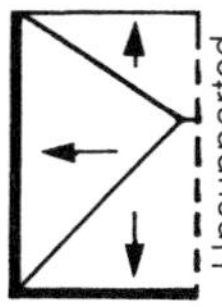

$k \ngtr 8/5$: $R_1 = \frac{3}{5}R_3$ (min.) $\quad R_2 = 0$

$R_3 = \frac{5}{8}k(1 - \frac{5}{16}k)wl_x^2$ (max.)

$R_4 = \frac{5}{16}k^2wl_x^2 \quad \alpha = 3/8k$ (min.)

$\psi = 5k/8$ (max.)

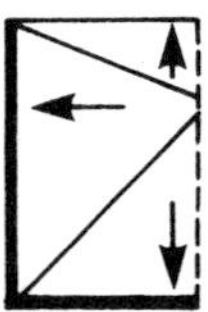

$k \geqslant 8/5$: $R_1 = \frac{3}{10}wl_x^2$ (min.) $\quad R_2 = 0$

$R_3 = \frac{1}{2}wl_x^2$

$R_4 = (k - \frac{4}{5})wl_x^2$ (max.)

$\alpha = 3/5k \quad \beta = 1/k$

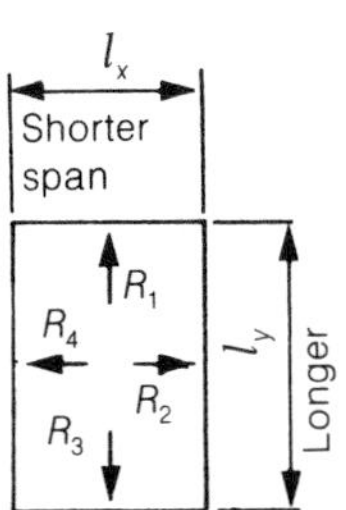

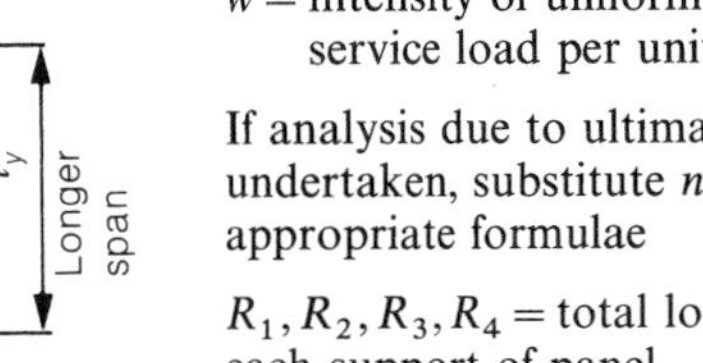

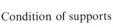

$k = \dfrac{l_y}{l_x} = \dfrac{\text{longer span}}{\text{shorter span}}$

w = intensity of uniformly distributed service load per unit area

If analysis due to ultimate loads is undertaken, substitute n for w in appropriate formulae

R_1, R_2, R_3, R_4 = total load carried by each support of panel

Condition of supports

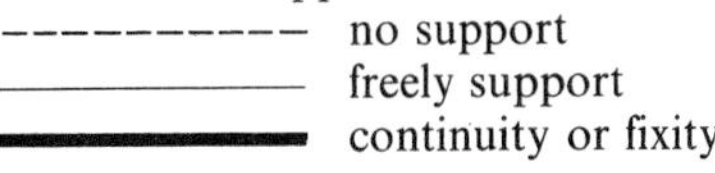

Loads marked (min.) apply if panel is entirely freely supported along edge indicated: if partially restrained, load will be slightly greater than given and load marked (max.) on opposite edge will be correspondingly reduced.

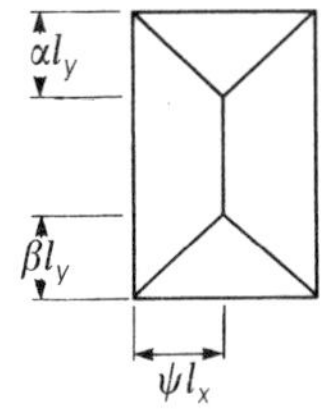

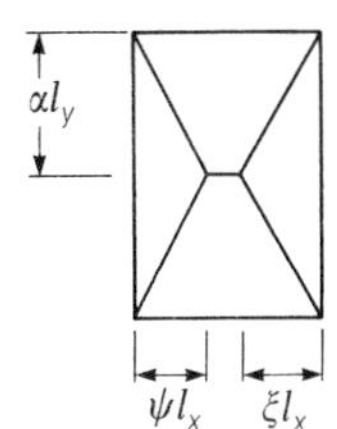

Chapter 15
Frame analysis

Unless otherwise stated, the formulae and coefficients on tables in this chapter give service bending moments and shearing forces corresponding to unfactored characteristic loads. When undertaking elastic analyses to obtain ultimate moments and shearing forces for limit-state design according to BS8110 or similar documents, the design loads considered must be those obtained by multiplying these characteristic loads by the partial safety factor for loads γ_f appropriate to the particular limit-state being investigated.

15.1 SLOPE-DEFLECTION METHOD

The principles of the slope-deflection method of analysing a restrained member are that the difference in slope between any two points in the length of the member is equal to the area of the M/EI diagram between these two points; and that the distance of any point on the member from a line drawn tangentially to the elastic curve at any other point, the distance being measured normal to the initial position of the member, is equal to the moment (taken about the first point) of the M/EI diagram between these two points. In the foregoing, M represents the bending moment, E the modulus of elasticity of the material, and I the moment of inertia of the member. The bending moments at the ends of a member subject to the deformation and restraints shown in the diagram at the top of *Table 65* are given by the corresponding formulae, which are derived from a combination of the basic principles and which are given in the general form and in the special form for members on non-elastic supports.

The symbol K is the stiffness factor, I/l; the stiffness is proportional to EK, a term in the formulae, but as E is assumed to be constant the term which varies in each member is K. The terms F_{AB} and F_{BA} relate to the load on the member. When there is no external load the factors F_{AB} and F_{BA} are zero, and when the load is symmetrically disposed on the member $F_{AB} = F_{BA} = A/l$. Values of F_{AB}, F_{BA} and A/l are given in *Table 29*.

The conventional signs for slope-deflection analyses are: an external restraint moment acting clockwise is positive; a slope is positive if the rotation of the tangent to the elastic line is clockwise; a deflection in the same direction as a positive slope is positive.

Example. Establish the formulae for the bending moments in a column CAD into which is framed a beam AB. The beam is hinged at B and the column is fixed at C and D (see diagram in *Table 65*). The beam only is loaded. Assume there is no displacement of the joint A.

From the general formulae given on *Table 65*:

$$M_{AB} = 3EK_{AB}\theta_A - (F_{AB} + F_{BA}/2)$$
$$M_{AC} = 4EK_{AC}\theta_A$$
$$M_{AD} = 4EK_{AD}\theta_A$$

Therefore

$$M_{AB} + M_{AC} + M_{AD} = E\theta_A(3K_{AB} + 4K_{AC} + 4K_{AD}) - (F_{AB} + F_{BA}/2) = 0$$

Thus

$$E\theta_A = \frac{F_{AB} + F_{BA}/2}{3K_{AB} + 4K_{AC} + 4K_{AD}}$$
$$M_{AC} = \frac{4K_{AC}(F_{AB} + F_{BA}/2)}{3K_{AB} + 4K_{AC} + 4K_{AD}}$$
$$M_{AD} = M_{AC}K_{AD}/K_{AC}$$
$$M_{AB} = -(M_{AC} + M_{AD})$$
$$M_{CA} = 2EK_{AC}\theta_A = M_{AC}/2$$
$$M_{DA} = M_{AD}/2$$

For symmetrical loading:

$$F_{AB} + F_{BA}/2 = 1.5A_{AB}/l_{AB}$$
$$M_{AC} = \frac{6K_{AC}}{3K_{AB} + 4K_{AC} + 4K_{AD}} \frac{A_{AB}}{l_{AB}}$$

15.2 CONTINUOUS BEAMS AS MEMBERS OF A FRAME

In many buildings it is often unnecessary to consider the interaction of the columns and beams more accurately than by applying one of the various simplified methods of analysis. One convenient method is that recommended in BS8110 and CP110 (the second method on *Table 68*), in which the simplified sub-frame shown in the diagrams on

Flat slabs

			Moment at interior support	Moment in interior span	Column supports: Moment at penultimate support	Column supports: Moment in end span	Column supports: Moment at outer support	Wall supports: Moment at penultimate support	Wall supports: Moment in end span	Wall supports: Moment at outer support	Total moments transferred to columns: Internal	Total moments transferred to columns: External
Column strip	with drops		*a*	*b*	*c*1	*d*1*	*e*1	*c*2	*d*2	*e*2	*f*	*g*
		BS8110	−0.04125	0.03905	−0.04725	0.04565	−0.03000	−0.04725	0.04565	−0.01500	0.02200	0.04000
		CP110	−0.06250	0.02500	−0.06250	0.03125	−0.05625	−0.09000	0.04500	−0.00750	0.03125§	0.05063
	without drops		*h*	*j*	*k*1	*l*1*	*m*1	*k*2	*l*2	*m*2	*n*	*p*
		BS8110	−0.04125	0.03905	−0.04725	0.04565	−0.03000	−0.04725	0.04565	−0.01500	0.02200	0.04000
		CP110	−0.05750	0.02750	−0.05750	0.03500	−0.05125	−0.08250	0.05000	−0.00750	0.02875§	0.04613
Middle strip	with drops		*q*	*r*	*s*1	*t*1	*u*1	*s*2	*t*2	*u*2		
		BS8110	−0.01375	0.03195	−0.01575	0.03735	−0.01000	−0.01575	0.03735	−0.00500		
		CP110	−0.01875	0.01875	−0.01875	0.02375	−0.01250	−0.02750	0.03250	−0.00750		
	without drops		*v*	*w*	*x*1	*y*1	*z*1	*x*2	*y*2	*z*2		
		BS8110	−0.01375	0.03195	−0.01575	0.03735	−0.01000	−0.01575	0.03735	−0.00500		
		CP110	−0.02000	0.02000	−0.02000	0.02500	−0.01250	−0.03000	0.03500	−0.00750		

Values of bending-moment coefficients α

§At penultimate supports, these coefficients should be multiplied by 1.44 if edge of slab is supported on walls.

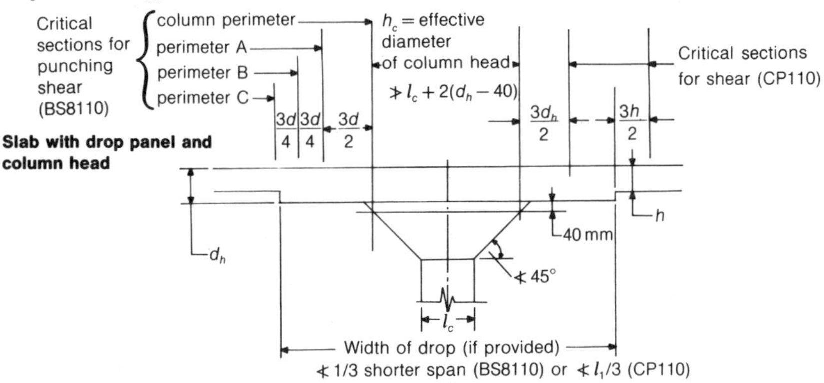

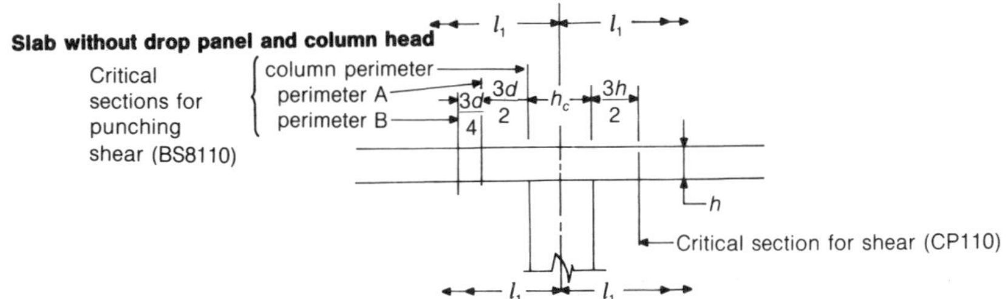

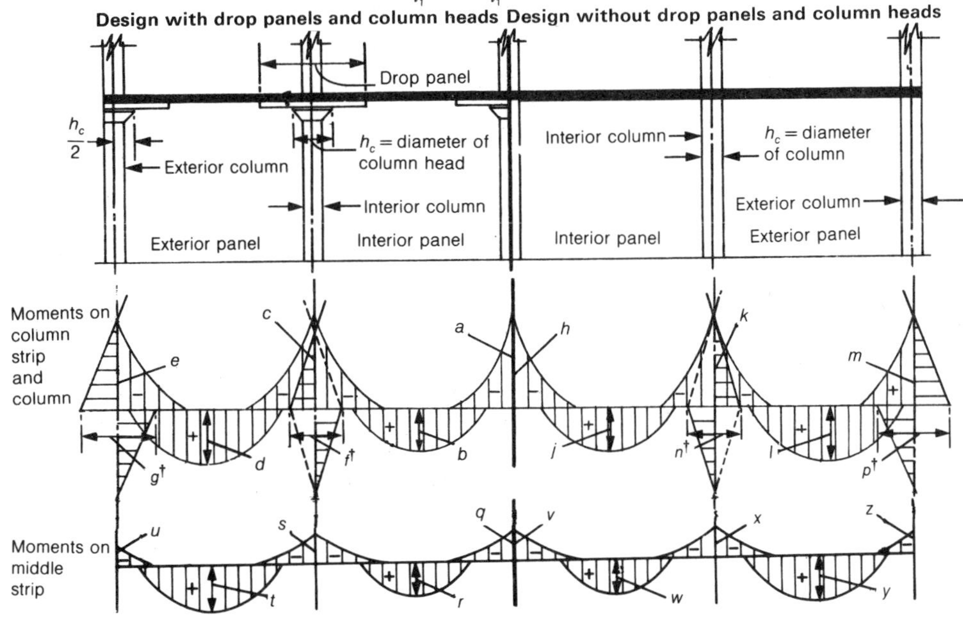

*If moment calculated using this coefficient exceeds that which may be transferred to columns from column strip at edge of slab, as calculated below, the edge moments must be reduced as required and the positive moments in the end span increased accordingly.

Total bending moment on strip of width l_2:

$$M_{ds} = \alpha n l_2 (l_1 - \tfrac{2}{3} h_c)^2$$

- n total ultimate load per unit area $= 1.4 g_k + 1.6 q_k$
- l_1 distance between column centres in direction of span
- l_2 distance between column centres at right angles to l_1

Transfer of moment from slab to edge and corner columns

Maximum moment transferred to columns via column strip at slab edge $= 0.15 b_e d^2 f_{cu}$, where b_e is effective breadth of column strip and d is effective depth of top steel in strip. Where column is near or at slab edge, $b_e = x + y$, where x is length in contact with slab of innermost column face and y = one-half sum of lengths also in contact with slab, of column faces at right angles. (Where column is inset from slab edge, y = distance from edge to face x. b_e must not exceed width of column strip for internal panel.

†Divided between upper and lower columns in proportion to stiffnesses. Figures indicate appropriate values of α.
Suffix 1 coefficients (i.e. c_1, k_1 etc.) apply where edge of slab is supported on columns: suffix 2 coefficients (i.e. c_2, k_2 etc.) apply where edge of slab is supported on masonry or other walls.

BS8110 design procedure to resist punching shear

1. Calculate effective shear force at column perimeter $V_{eff} = kV_t$, where V_t is shear force transferred from slab, and $k = 1.15$ for internal columns, 1.25 for corner columns and edge columns where moment acts parallel to free edge, and 1.4 for edge columns where moment acts at right angles to free edge.
2. Determine $v_{max} = V_{eff}/u_0 d$, where u_0 is effective length of column perimeter (i.e. after allowing for holes, etc). v_{max} must not exceed limits shown on *Table 142*.
3. Determine $v = (V_{eff} - V_r)/ud$, where u is effective length of perimeter A and V_r is load acting within perimeter being considered. If $v < v_c$, no steel to resist punching is required and further analysis is unnecessary. Otherwise provide vertical links $A_{sv} = V_{diff} ud/0.87 f_{yv}$, where $V_{diff} = (v - v_c)$ or 0.4, whichever is greater. Space links evenly along this perimeter and another $3d/4$ nearer column at $\not> 3d/2$ centres. Shear steel must not be used where slab thickness is less than 250 mm.
4. Repeat step 3 for perimeters B, C etc. until $v < v_c$. When assessing steel required at perimeter currently being considered, links already provided when investigating previous perimeter may be taken into account.

Table 68 is analysed on the assumption that the remote ends of the beams and columns forming the three-span sub-frame are fixed. Therefore for any internal span ST, the ends of the beams at R and U, the ends of the lower columns at O and X, and the ends of the upper columns at P and Y are assumed to be fixed. In addition, the stiffnesses of the two outer beams RS and TU are taken as one-half of their true values. For fixed-end moments due to normal (i.e. downward-acting) loads, positive numerical values should be substituted into the tabulated expressions. If the resulting sign of the support moment is negative, tension across the top face of the beam is indicated.

15.2.1 Internal spans

By slope-deflection methods it can be shown that

$$M_{ST} = -F_{ST} + K_{ST}(\theta_{ST} + \theta_{TS}/2)$$
$$M_{TS} = -F_{TS} - K_{ST}(\theta_{TS} + \theta_{ST}/2)$$

where

$$\theta_{ST} = \frac{(K_{ST}/2)(F_{TS} - F_{TU}) - \sum K_T(F_{SR} - F_{ST})}{\sum K_S \sum K_T - K_{ST}^2/4}$$

$$\theta_{TS} = \frac{(K_{ST}/2)(F_{SR} - F_{ST}) - \sum K_S(F_{TS} - F_{TU})}{\sum K_S \sum K_T - K_{ST}^2/4}$$

$$\sum K_S = \zeta K_{RS} + K_{SO} + K_{SP} + K_{ST}$$
$$\sum K_T = K_{ST} + K_{TX} + K_{TY} + \zeta K_{TU}$$

and ζ is a factor representing the ratio of the assumed stiffness to the actual stiffness for the span concerned (i.e. here $\zeta = 1/2$).

By eliminating θ_{ST} and θ_{TS} and rearranging, the following basic formulae are obtained:

$$M_{ST} = -F_{ST} + \frac{D_{ST}}{4 - D_{ST}D_{TS}}\left[2D_{TS}\left(\frac{1}{D_{ST}} - 1\right) \times (F_{TU} - F_{TS}) + (4 - D_{TS})(F_{ST} - F_{SR})\right]$$

$$M_{TS} = -F_{TS} - \frac{D_{TS}}{4 - D_{ST}D_{TS}}\left[2D_{ST}\left(\frac{1}{D_{TS}} - 1\right) \times (F_{ST} - F_{SR}) + (4 - D_{ST})(F_{TU} - F_{TS})\right]$$

These formulae, which are 'exact' within the limitations of the fixity conditions of the sub-frame, represent the case of all spans loaded, such as results for example due to the condition of dead load only on an interior span. When working to BS8110, maximum bending moments at both supports S and T occur when the imposed load extends across all three spans. However, to comply with CP110, to produce the greatest bending moments at support S due to imposed load only it is necessary to load spans RS and ST only. Similarly, to obtain maximum values at support T, the imposed load should cover spans ST and TU only. To produce the maximum bending on the span ST due to imposed load, only this span should carry the load. The appropriate formulae for these conditions are also given in *Table 68*. To comply with the requirements of both Codes, when undertaking an elastic analysis under ultimate load conditions the dead load considered should be $1.0g_k$ and the 'imposed load' should be $(0.4g_k + 1.6q_k)$. In other circumstances, e.g. for elastic analysis under service-load conditions, values of $1.0g_k$ and $1.0q_k$ are applicable.

As an alternative to the foregoing, where dead and imposed loads are considered separately, it may be advantageous to consider both dead and imposed loads in a single operation by evaluating the basic formulae with appropriate fixed-end-moment values corresponding to dead + imposed load on the above-mentioned spans and dead load only on the other. To comply with CP110, for example, to obtain the maximum support moments at S, the fixed-end moments F_{SR}, F_{ST} and F_{TS} should be calculated for a load of $1.4g_k + 1.6q_k$, while F_{TU} should be evaluated for a load of $1.0g_k$ only. This method is illustrated in the example below.

In accordance with both Codes, the moments derived from these calculations may be redistributed by up to 30% if so desired. It should be emphasized that, although the diagrams on *Table 68* and in the example below illustrate uniform loads only, the method and formulae are equally applicable to any type of loading, provided that the correct fixed-end-moment coefficients, obtained from *Tables 29, 30* or *31*, are used.

15.2.2 End spans

The formulae for any interior span ST are rewritten to apply to an end span AB by substituting A, B, C etc. for S, T, U etc.; A is the end support, and there is no span corresponding to RS. The modified stiffness and distribution factors are given in *Table 68*, together with the formulae for all spans loaded, and also the formulae for the maximum bending moments at the supports due to imposed load and for the bending moments at the supports for the arrangement of imposed load resulting in the maximum bending moment in the end span AB.

When the bending moments M_{ST} and M_{TS} (or M_{AB} and M_{BA}) at the supports are known, the positive and negative moments in the spans are obtained by combining the diagram of free bending moments due to the loads with the diagram of the corresponding support moments.

15.2.3 Columns and adjoining spans

The outer members of the sub-frame are assumed to be fully fixed at their further ends. Thus, for a member such as RS, the slope-deflection equation is

$$M_{SR} = K_{RS}\theta_{SR}$$

Since the rotation of all the members meeting at a joint is equal, $\theta_{SR} = \theta_{ST}$. Thus, by eliminating θ_{SR} and rearranging,

$$M_{SR} = -F_{SR} - \frac{D_{SR}}{4 - D_{ST}D_{TS}} \times [2D_{TS}(F_{TU} - F_{TS}) + 4(F_{ST} - F_{SR})]$$

Similarly,

$$M_{TU} = -F_{TU} + \frac{D_{TU}}{4 - D_{ST}D_{TS}} \times [2D_{ST}(F_{ST} - F_{SR}) + 4(F_{TU} - F_{TS})]$$

65

Framed structures: basic data

Basic formulae (slope deflection)

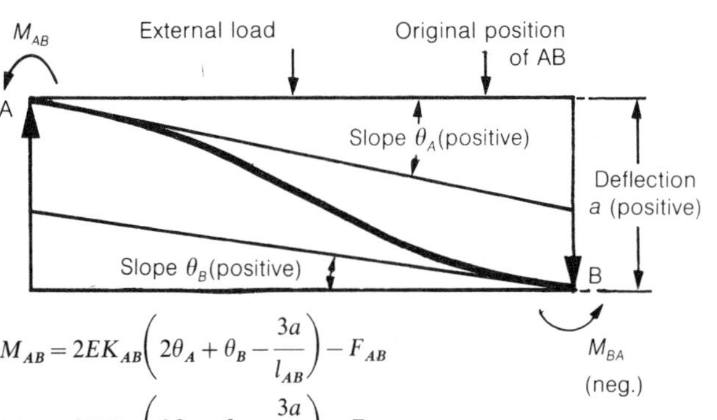

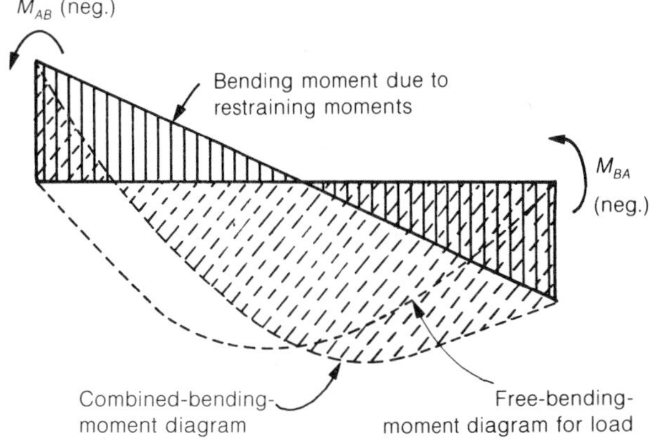

$$M_{AB}=2EK_{AB}\left(2\theta_A+\theta_B-\frac{3a}{l_{AB}}\right)-F_{AB}$$

$$M_{BA}=2EK_{AB}\left(2\theta_B+\theta_A-\frac{3a}{l_{AB}}\right)+F_{BA}$$

Notation

The suffixes AB relate to joint or support A of any member AB
The suffixes BA relate to joint or support B of any member AB
} Similarly for other members BC, AC etc

l_{AB}	length of member AB
I_{AB}	moment of inertia ("concrete units") of AB
K_{AB}	stiffness factor of AB $=I_{AB}/l_{AB}$
E	modulus of elasticity for concrete
θ_A	slope of deformed member AB at A. With no load on AB, $F_{AB}=F_{BA}=0$

$$F_{AB}=\frac{2A_{AB}}{l_{AB}^2}(2l_{AB}-3Z_{AB})$$

$$F_{BA}=\frac{2A_{AB}}{l_{AB}^2}(3Z_{AB}-l_{AB})$$

For symmetrical load on AB $F_{AB}=F_{BA}=A_{AB}/l_{AB}$

A_{AB}	area of free-bending-moment diagram for load on AB
Z_{AB}	distance from A to centroid of free-bending-moment diagram for load on AB

Slope-deflection general formulae non-elastic supports

	A, B (both simply supported)	A fixed, B simply supported	A fixed, B fixed	A simply supported, B hinged (free)	A fixed, B hinged (free)
M_{AB}	$2EK_{AB}(2\theta_A+\theta_B)-F_{AB}$	$2EK_{AB}\theta_B-F_{AB}$	$-F_{AB}$	$3EK_{AB}\theta_A-(F_{AB}+\frac{1}{2}F_{BA})$	$-(F_{AB}+\frac{1}{2}F_{BA})$
M_{BA}	$2EK_{AB}(2\theta_B+\theta_A)+F_{BA}$	$4EK_{AB}\theta_B+F_{BA}$	$+F_{BA}$	Zero	Zero

Exterior columns

	D, F, A, B, C, E (fixed); Symmetrical load	D, F, A, B, C, E (pinned); Symmetrical load	D, A, C, B; $\beta=F_{AB}$; Any load — or D, A, B, C; $\beta=F_{AB}+\frac{1}{2}F_{BA}$; Any load	D, A, B, C; $\beta=F_{AB}+\frac{1}{2}F_{BA}$; Any load; Condition for max. M_{AB}	D, A, B, C; Any load; Condition for min. M_{AB}
M_{AC}	$\dfrac{2K_{AC}}{2K_{AC}+2K_{AD}+K_{AB}}\dfrac{A_{AB}}{l_{AB}}$	$\dfrac{3K_{AC}}{3K_{AC}+3K_{AD}+2K_{AB}}\dfrac{A_{AB}}{l_{AB}}$	$\dfrac{K_{AC}\beta}{K_{AC}+K_{AD}+K_{AB}}$	$\dfrac{4K_{AC}\beta}{4K_{AC}+4K_{AD}+3K_{AB}}$	$\dfrac{3K_{AC}F_{AB}}{3K_{AC}+3K_{AD}+4K_{AB}}$

$$M_{AD}=\frac{K_{AD}}{K_{AC}}M_{AC}\qquad M_{AB}=-(M_{AC}+M_{AD})$$

If fixed at C: $M_{CA}=0.5M_{AC}$ etc.
at hinges: bending moment $=0$

Bending moment in external columns of building frames

$$M_{AC}=\frac{K_{AC}}{K_{AC}+K_{AD}+\zeta K_{AB}}F_{AB}$$

$$M_{AD}=\frac{K_{AD}}{K_{AC}}M_{AC}\qquad M_{AB}=-(M_{AC}+M_{AD})$$

For frames of one bay width only $\zeta=1/2$
For frames of more than one bay width $\zeta=1$
For top storey (e.g. roof beam and top storey column): $K_{AD}=0$

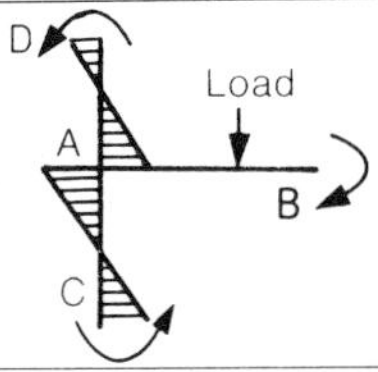

Interior columns

Load D Load
E A B
C

$$M_{AC}=\frac{K_{AC}}{K_{AC}+K_{AD}+K_{AB}+K_{AE}}M_{es}$$

$$M_{AD}=\frac{K_{AD}}{K_{AC}}M_{AC}$$

(M_{AB} and M_{AE} are in all cases less than bending moment assuming knife-edge support for beam EAB at A.)

$M_{es}=$ either F_{AB} (for dead + imposed load) $-F_{AE}$ (for dead load only)

or F_{AE} (for dead + imposed load) $-F_{AB}$ (for dead load only)

whichever is the greater.

This method is recommended in CP110, when a simplified sub-frame analysis (see Table 68) is undertaken, and in BS8110, when the adjoining beams are analysed as a continuous system on knife-edge supports. In each case, when determining the column moments using the formula shown here, the far ends of the beams should be considered fixed and their stiffnesses taken as one-half of the true values.

Note: For values of F_{AB} and F_{BA} see *Table 29*.

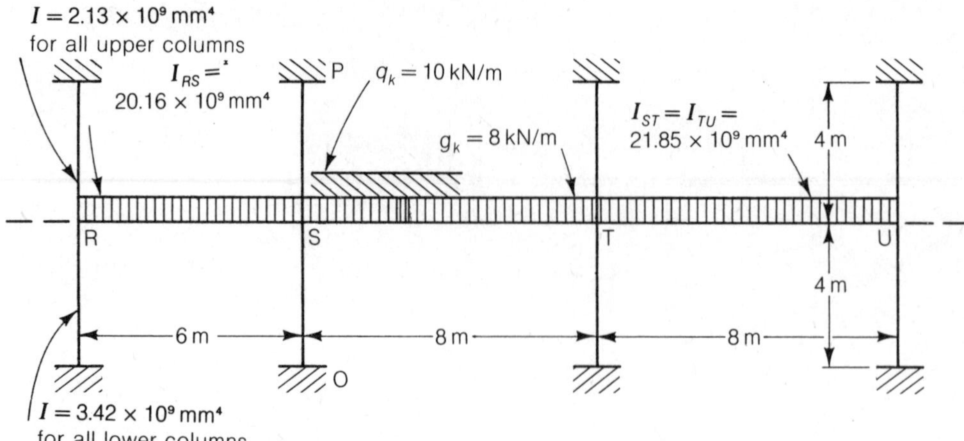

The expressions giving the moments in the columns are similar to the foregoing but F_{SR} and F_{TU} should be replaced by the initial fixed-end moment in the column concerned (normally zero) and the appropriate distribution factor for the column should be substituted for D_{SR} or D_{TU}.

Example. Determine the critical ultimate bending moments in beam ST of the system shown in the accompanying figure, which represents part of a multistorey frame, using the simplified method of elastic analysis permitted by BS8110 and CP110. The dead and imposed characteristic loads g_k and q_k are 8 and 10 kN/m respectively, and the moments of inertia of the members comprising the frame are as shown (calculated on the gross concrete section).

Stiffnesses

$$\tfrac{1}{2}K_{RS} = \frac{0.5 \times 20.16 \times 10^9}{6 \times 10^3} = 1.68 \times 10^6\,\text{mm}^3$$

$$K_{ST} = \frac{21.85 \times 10^9}{8 \times 10^3} = 2.73 \times 10^6$$

$$\tfrac{1}{2}K_{TU} = \tfrac{1}{2}K_{ST} = 0.5 \times 2.73 \times 10^6 = 1.37 \times 10^6$$

For upper columns: $$K = \frac{2.13 \times 10^9}{4 \times 10^3} = 0.53 \times 10^6$$

For lower columns: $$K = \frac{3.42 \times 10^9}{4 \times 10^3} = 0.86 \times 10^6$$

Distribution factors. If the foregoing stiffnesses are divided throughout by 10^6, then

$$D_{ST} = \frac{2.73}{2.73 + 1.68 + 0.53 + 0.86} = 0.471$$

$$D_{TS} = \frac{2.73}{2.73 + 1.37 + 0.53 + 0.86} = 0.497$$

Support-moment equations

$$M_{ST} = -F_{ST} + \frac{0.471\{2 \times 0.497[(1/0.471) - 1](F_{TU} - F_{TS}) + (4 - 0.497)(F_{ST} - F_{SR})\}}{4 - (0.471 \times 0.497)}$$

$$= -F_{ST} + 0.125[1.116(F_{TU} - F_{TS}) + 3.503(F_{ST} - F_{SR})]$$

$$M_{TS} = -F_{TS} - \frac{0.497\{2 \times 0.471[(1/0.497) - 1](F_{ST} - F_{SR}) + (4 - 0.471)(F_{TU} - F_{TS})\}}{4 - (0.471 \times 0.497)}$$

$$= -F_{TS} - 0.132[0.953(F_{ST} - F_{SR}) + 3.529(F_{TU} - F_{TS})]$$

Fixed-end moments. For dead load only:

$$F_{RS} = F_{SR} = \tfrac{1}{12}g_k l_{RS}^2 = 0.0833 \times 8 \times 6^2 = 24\,\text{kN m}$$

$$F_{ST} = F_{TS} = F_{TU} = F_{UT} = \tfrac{1}{12}g_k l_{ST}^2$$

$$= 0.0833 \times 8 \times 8^2 = 42.7\,\text{kN m}$$

For dead + imposed load:

$$F_{RS} = F_{SR} = \tfrac{1}{12}(1.4g_k + 1.6q_k)l_{RS}^2$$

$$= 0.0833(1.4 \times 8 + 1.6 \times 10)6^2 = 81.6\,\text{kN m}$$

$$F_{ST} = F_{TS} = F_{TU} = F_{UT} = 0.0833(1.4 \times 8 + 1.6 \times 10)8^2$$

$$= 145.1\,\text{kN m}$$

Maximum moments on beams

(i) *At S*

BS8110 requirements The maximum ultimate support moment at S occurs when all spans carry dead + imposed load. Then

$$M_{ST} = -145.1 + 0.125 \times [1.116(145.1 - 145.1) + 3.503(145.1 - 81.6)]$$

$$= -145.1 + 27.81 = -117.3\,\text{kN m}$$

CP110 requirements The maximum ultimate support moment at S occurs when spans RS and ST carry dead + imposed load and span TU carries dead load only. Then

$$M_{ST} = -145.1 + 0.125 \times [1.116(42.7 - 145.1) + 3.503(145.1 - 81.6)]$$

$$= -145.1 + 13.5 = -131.6\,\text{kN m}$$

(ii) *At T*

BS8110 requirements The maximum ultimate support moment at T occurs when all spans carry dead + imposed load. Then

$$M_{TS} = -145.1 - 0.132 \times [0.953(145.1 - 81.6) + 3.529(145.1 - 145.1)]$$

$$= -145.1 - 8.0 = -153.1\,\text{kN m}$$

Framed structures: moment-distribution method: no sway

HARDY CROSS MOMENT DISTRIBUTION

The procedure is basically identical to that when analysing continuous-beam systems (see *Table 40*).

1. At each junction of beams and columns, *distribution factors D* are determined for each member (e.g. at B, $D_{BA} = K_{AB}/K_{AB} + K_{BC} + K_{BU} + K_{BL}$ etc.), so that $D_{BA} + D_{BC} + D_{BU} + D_{BL} = 1$.
2. The total balancing moment $-\sum FEM$ introduced at each support to obtain joint equilibrium is then distributed between the members meeting at that support by multiplying by these distribution factors, and the resulting moments are carried over to the opposite ends of the members, as described on *Table 40*.
3. Any columns considered pinned at their far ends are best treated as 'equivalent fixed-end members', as described on *Table 40*.

The procedure is illustrated in the following example (UC upper column; LC lower column).

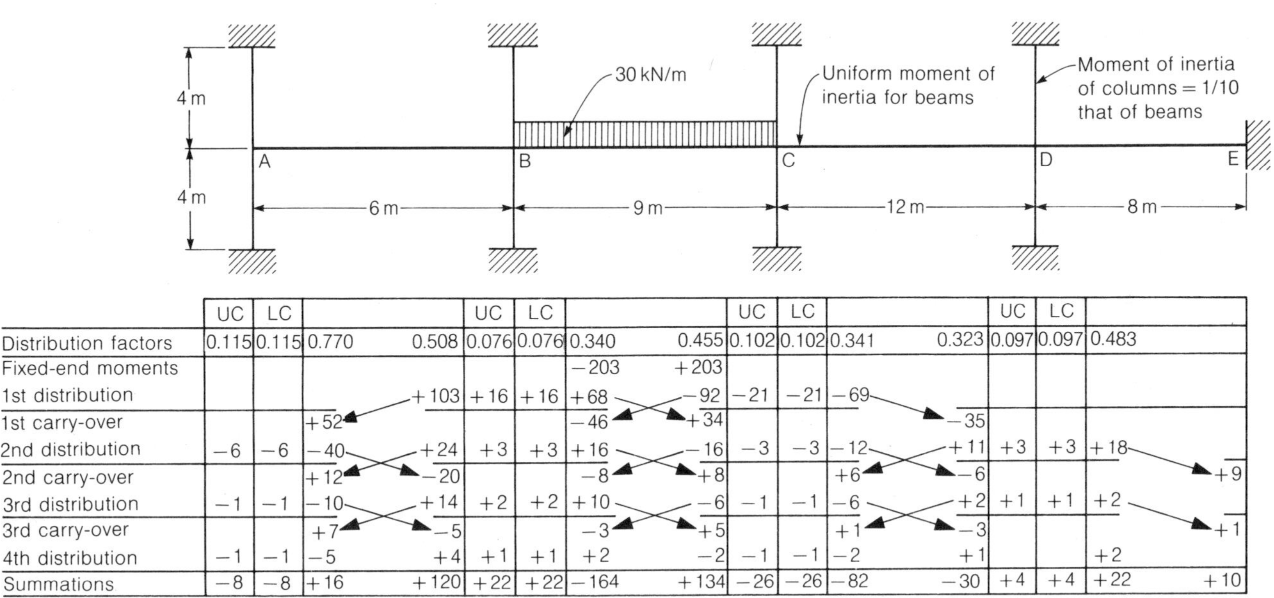

	UC	LC			UC	LC			UC	LC			UC	LC		
Distribution factors	0.115	0.115	0.770	0.508	0.076	0.076	0.340	0.455	0.102	0.102	0.341	0.323	0.097	0.097	0.483	
Fixed-end moments							−203	+203								
1st distribution				+103	+16	+16	+68	−92	−21	−21	−69					
1st carry-over			+52				−46	+34				−35				
2nd distribution	−6	−6	−40	+24	+3	+3	+16	−16	−3	−3	−12	+11	+3	+3	+18	
2nd carry-over			+12	−20			−8	+8			+6	−6				+9
3rd distribution	−1	−1	−10	+14	+2	+2	+10	−6	−1	−1	−6	+2	+1	+1	+2	
3rd carry-over			+7	−5			−3	+5			+1	−3				+1
4th distribution	−1	−1	−5	+4	+1	+1	+2	−2	−1	−1	−2	+1			+2	
Summations	−8	−8	+16	+120	+22	+22	−164	+134	−26	−26	−82	−30	+4	+4	+22	+10

PRECISE MOMENT DISTRIBUTION

The procedure differs only slightly from that for continuous-beam systems described in *Table 40*.

1. Calculate fixed-end moments as before.
2. Determine continuity factors for each span from general expression

$$\phi_{n+1} = 1 \Bigg/ \left\{ 2 + \frac{K_{n+1}}{\Sigma[K_n/(2-\phi_n)]} \right\}$$

   where ϕ_{n+1} and K_{n+1} are continuity factor and stiffness of span being considered, and $\sum[K_n/(2-\phi_n)]$ is sum of values of $K_n/(2-\phi_n)$ of all *remaining* members meeting at joint. If far end of column is fully fixed, $K_n/(2-\phi_n) = 2K_n/3$, since $\phi_n = 1/2$: if far end is pinned, $K_n/(2-\phi_n) = K_n/2$. As for continuous-beam system, work along system from left to right and then repeat procedure working from right to left.
3. Calculate *distribution factors* (*DF*s) at joints from general expression (given here for member BC at joint B)

$$DF_{BC} = \frac{1 - 2\phi_{BC}}{1 - \phi_{BC}\phi_{CB}}$$

   where ϕ_{BC} and ϕ_{CB} are continuity factors given by step 2. Unlike continuous beam, sum of distribution factors each side of support will not equal unity, due to action of columns. At support B say, sum of distribution factors for columns is $1 - DF_{BA} - DF_{BC}$. Then obtain distribution factor for each column by dividing total column distribution factor in proportion to stiffness of columns.
4. Carry over moments at supports as follows. Multiply distributed balancing moment at left-hand end of member by continuity factor obtained by working *from right to left* and carry over this value to right-hand end. At this point, balance carried-over moment by dividing an equal moment of opposite sign between remaining members meeting at that point in proportion to their values of $K_{LR}/(2-\phi_{RL})$. Thus, in example, moment of −30 kN m carried over from C to D is obtained by multiplying −81.1 kN m by 0.368. This moment is balanced at D by moments of 4 kN m (i.e. 30 × 0.0167/0.1167) in each column and 22 kN m (i.e. 30 × 0.0833/0.1167) in beam DE.
5. Undertake one complete carry-over operation working from left to right and then from right to left from each joint at which fixed-end moment occurs and sum results to obtain final moments on system. (Note: analysis may be further shortened by combining distribution and carry-over operations: see ref. 11.)

For details of structure and loading see diagram above

UC upper column LC lower column

	UC	LC			UC	LC			UC	LC			UC	LC		
Relative stiffnesses	1/40	1/40	1/6		1/40	1/40	1/9		1/40	1/40	1/12		1/40	1/40	1/8	
Continuity factors $\phi \rightarrow$				0.143				0.344				0.353				0.287
Continuity factors $\leftarrow \phi$			0.271				0.301				0.368				0.500	
Distribution factors	0.128	0.128	0.744	0.476	0.089	0.089	0.346	0.443	0.110	0.110	0.337	0.302	0.100	0.100	0.498	
Fixed-end moments							−203	+203								
Distribution				+97	+18	+18	+70	−90	−22	−22	−69					
Carry-over	−8	−8	+16	+23	+4	+4	−31	+21	−4	−4	−13	−30	+4	+4	+22	+11
Summations	−8	−8	+16	+120	+22	+22	−164	+134	−26	−26	−82	−30	+4	+4	+22	+11

CP110 requirements The maximum ultimate support moment at T occurs when spans ST and TU carry dead + imposed load and span RS carries dead load only. Then

$$M_{TS} = -145.1 - 0.132 \times [0.953(145.1 - 24.0) + 3.529(145.1 - 145.1)] = -145.1 - 15.2 = -160.3\,\mathrm{kN\,m}$$

(iii) *Span ST*

BS8110 and CP110 requirements The maximum ultimate moment in span ST occurs when span ST carries dead + imposed load and spans RS and TU carry dead load only. Then

$$M_{ST} = -145.1 + 0.125 \times [1.116(42.7 - 145.1) + 3.503(145.1 - 24.0)] = -145.1 + 38.7 = -106.4\,\mathrm{kN\,m}$$

$$M_{TS} = -145.1 - 0.132 \times [0.953(145.1 - 24.0) + 3.529(42.7 - 145.1)] = -145.1 + 32.5 = -112.6\,\mathrm{kN\,m}$$

The maximum ultimate span moment is then approximately

$$1.5F_{ST} - 0.5(M_{ST} + M_{TS}) = (1.5 + 145.1) - 0.5(106.4 + 112.6) = 217.6 - 109.5 = 108.1\,\mathrm{kN\,m}$$

Maximum moments on column. Consider, for example, the columns at S. The maximum ultimate moment will be transmitted to the column when the span on one side of the column carries its maximum load and the span on the other side carries its minimum load. This corresponds to case (iii) considered above. Then if $D_{SO} = 0.86/5.80 = 0.148$ and $D_{SP} = 0.53/5.80 = 0.091$ are the distribution factors for the lower and upper columns and M_{SO} and M_{SP} are the resulting ultimate moments in these columns, respectively,

$$M_{SO} = -\frac{0.148}{4 - (0.471 \times 0.497)} \times [2 \times 0.497(145.1 - 42.7) + 4(145.1 - 24.0)] = 23.1\,\mathrm{kN\,m}$$

$$M_{SP} = -\frac{0.091}{4 - (0.471 \times 0.497)} \times [2 \times 0.497(145.1 - 42.7) + 4(145.1 - 24.0)] = 14.2\,\mathrm{kN\,m}$$

Alternatively, if CP110 applies, the simplified method permitted in clause 3.5.2 and illustrated on *Table 65* may be employed. Then, using the foregoing notation,

$$\sum K_S = \tfrac{1}{2}K_{RS} + \tfrac{1}{2}K_{ST} + K_{SO} + K_{SP} = (1.68 + 1.37 + 0.53 + 0.86)10^6 = 4.44 \times 10^6$$

and, with a maximum unbalanced fixing moment at S of $145.1 - 24.0 = 121.1\,\mathrm{kN\,m}$,

$$M_{SO} = 121.1 \times \frac{0.86}{4.44} = 23.5\,\mathrm{kN\,m}$$

$$M_{SP} = 121.1 \times \frac{0.53}{4.44} = 14.5\,\mathrm{kN\,m}$$

As will be seen, in the present case the results given by the two methods are almost identical.

Framed structures: moment-distribution methods: sway

NAYLOR'S METHOD FOR SINGLE-BAY FRAMES

1. Consider only one-half of frame as shown. Assuming firstly that loads are applied only horizontally at floor levels, calculate fixed-end moments. Fixed-end moment at each end of each column forming storey = (1/4) × sum of horizontal forces above floor being considered × height of storey (see example).
2. Calculate distribution factors as for normal Hardy Cross moment distribution but assuming stiffness of each horizontal member is six times actual stiffness.
3. Carry out conventional Hardy Cross moment distribution but carrying-over moments equal in value to distributed balancing moments but of *opposite sign*. Procedure is illustrated in example.
4. If interpanel loading occurs, distribute moments in two stages. Firstly, undertake normal Hardy Cross moment distribution for complete frame using distribution factors obtained with true stiffnesses of beams and columns. Secondly, to cater for effects of sway, undertake second distribution using modified distribution factors and carry over as described in steps 1 to 3 above. Sum results obtained from both distributions to obtain final moments.

Effects of side-sway due to unsymmetrical vertical loads on beams may be considered in a similar manner. Firstly, calculate fixed-end moments FEM_{LR} and FEM_{RL} at left-hand (L) and right-hand (R) ends of beam due to given loads. Then analyse structure for fixed-end moments of $(FEM_{LR} + FEM_{RL})/2$ at L and R by normal Hardy Cross method and for fixed-end moments of $(FEM_{LR} - FEM_{RL})$ at L and R respectively as described above. Lastly, sum results obtained by both distributions to obtain final moments.

	A		B			C
Modified stiffness		1	12		1	12
Distribution factors		1/14	6/7	1/14	1/13	12/13
Fixed-end moments	−80.0	−80.0		−40.0	−40.0	
1st distribution		+8.6	+102.8	+8.6	+3.1	+36.9
1st carry-over	−8.6			−3.1	−8.6	
2nd distribution		+0.2	+2.7	+0.2	+0.7	+7.9
2nd carry-over	−0.2			−0.7	−0.2	
3rd distribution		+0.1	+0.5	+0.1		+0.2
Summations	−88.8	−71.1	+106.0	−34.9	−45.0	+45.0

For details of structure and loadings see diagram below

HARDY CROSS MOMENT DISTRIBUTION

1. Assuming firstly that loads are applied only horizontally at floor levels, determine number of degrees of sway freedom of structure (e.g. frame considered in example has two degrees of freedom, as shown in sketches).
2. Assuming that degree of freedom (i.e. sway of upper storey in example given) gives rise to fixed-end moments of unity at ends of upper columns, distribute these moments by conventional Hardy Cross distribution procedure. Consider one-half of frame only, as shown in example, and adopt stiffness for beams of 1.5 times actual stiffness.
3. Repeat procedure to obtain separate distributions of fixed-end moments of unity, corresponding to sway due to each degree of freedom to be considered.
4. Now values of moments obtained from steps 2 and 3 represent effects of applying arbitrary horizontal forces causing sway. To determine actual values of unknown forces $F_1, F_2, \ldots, F_n$ required it is necessary to set up n simultaneous equations relating horizontal force acting above level considered to internal shearing force acting on columns at that level. The internal shearing forces are obtained by multiplying the arbitrary distributed moments by the unknown forces and dividing by storey height. Thus, in example given, simultaneous equation corresponding to shearing forces in upper storey is

$$(1/4) \times 2[-(0.708 + 0.683)F_1 + (0.191 + 0.076)F_2] = -40$$

i.e. $-0.696F_1 + 0.133F_2 = -40$.
Similarly, for lower storey,

$$(1/4) \times 2[+(0.178 + 0.089)F_1 - (0.899 + 0.797)F_2] = -80$$

i.e. $+0.133F_1 - 0.848F_2 = -80$. These equations yield $F_1 = +77.83$ and $F_2 = +106.55$.

5. To obtain final moments, multiply moments obtained by distributing each arbitrary fixed-end moment by the appropriate force concerned and sum. For example, final moment in column at base $= +0.089 \times 77.83 - 0.899 \times 106.55 = -88.8$ kN m.
6. If interpanel loading is applied, distribute fixed-end moments corresponding to this loading throughout frame using normal Hardy Cross moment distribution and assuming no sway occurs, and sum resulting moments obtained and those due to sway analysis to obtain final moments.

Note: precise moment distribution can also be used to solve frames subjected to sway: see ref. 10.

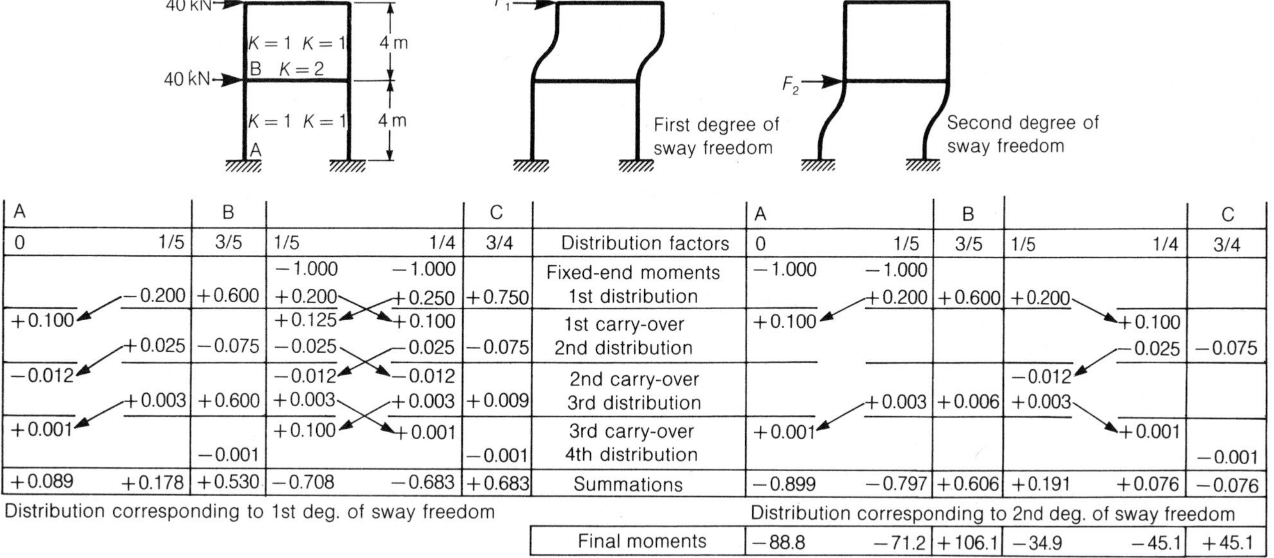

A	B		B	C	C	
0	1/5	3/5	1/5	1/4	3/4	Distribution factors
			−1.000	−1.000		Fixed-end moments
	−0.200	+0.600	+0.200	+0.250	+0.750	1st distribution
+0.100			+0.125	+0.100		1st carry-over
	+0.025	−0.075	−0.025	−0.025	−0.075	2nd distribution
−0.012			−0.012	−0.012		2nd carry-over
	+0.003	+0.600	+0.003	+0.003	+0.009	3rd distribution
+0.001			+0.100	+0.001		3rd carry-over
		−0.001			−0.001	4th distribution
+0.089	+0.178	+0.530	−0.708	−0.683	+0.683	Summations

Distribution corresponding to 1st deg. of sway freedom

	A	B		B	C	C
Distribution factors	0	1/5	3/5	1/5	1/4	3/4
Fixed-end moments	−1.000	−1.000				
1st distribution		+0.200	+0.600	+0.200		
1st carry-over	+0.100				+0.100	
2nd distribution					−0.025	−0.075
2nd carry-over				−0.012		
3rd distribution		+0.003	+0.006	+0.003		
3rd carry-over	+0.001				+0.001	
4th distribution						−0.001
Summations	−0.899	−0.797	+0.606	+0.191	+0.076	−0.076
Final moments	−88.8	−71.2	+106.1	−34.9	−45.1	+45.1
	A	B				C

Distribution corresponding to 2nd deg. of sway freedom

Framed structures: BS8110 and CP110 simplified sub-frame

	BS8110 requirement	CP110 requirement			Stiffness factors (K) and distribution factors (D)
End span AB	*Dead load* All spans loaded *Imposed load* Maximum bending moment at both supports	*Dead load* All spans loaded *Imposed load* Maximum bending moment at right-hand support	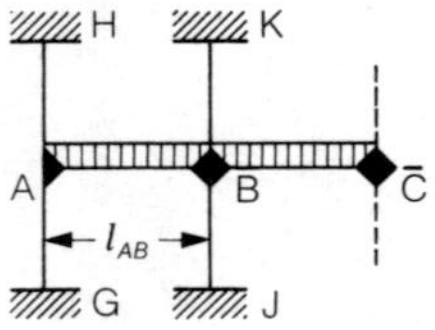	$M_{AB} = -F_{AB} + \frac{D_{AB}}{4 - D_{AB}D_{BA}}\left[2D_{BA}\left(\frac{1}{D_{AB}} - 1\right) \times (F_{BC} - F_{BA}) + (4 - D_{BA})F_{AB}\right]$ $M_{BA} = -F_{BA} - \frac{D_{BA}}{4 - D_{AB}D_{BA}}\left[2D_{AB}\left(\frac{1}{D_{BA}} - 1\right) \times F_{AB} + (4 - D_{AB})(F_{BC} - F_{BA})\right]$	$K_{AB} = \frac{I_{AB}}{l_{AB}}$ $K_{AG} = \frac{I_{AG}}{l_{AG}}$ $K_{BC} = \frac{I_{BC}}{l_{BC}}$ $K_{BJ} = \frac{I_{BJ}}{l_{BJ}}$
	Imposed load Bending moments at supports to produce maximum moments in span and in columns	*Imposed load* Maximum bending moment at left-hand support *Imposed load* Bending moments at supports to produce maximum moments in span and in columns	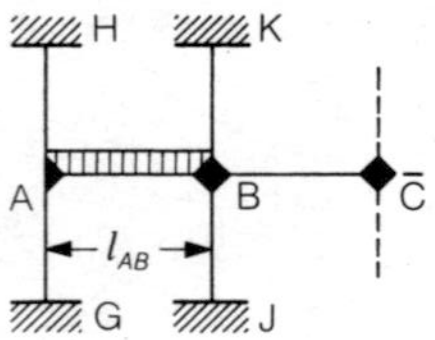	$M_{AB} = -F_{AB} + \frac{D_{AB}}{4 - D_{AB}D_{BA}}\left[-2D_{BA}\left(\frac{1}{D_{AB}} - 1\right) \times F_{BA} + (4 - D_{BA})F_{AB}\right]$ $M_{BA} = -F_{BA} - \frac{D_{BA}}{4 - D_{AB}D_{BA}}\left[2D_{AB}\left(\frac{1}{D_{BA}} - 1\right) \times F_{AB} - (4 - D_{AB})F_{BA}\right]$	$K_{AH} = \frac{I_{AH}}{l_{AH}}$ $D_{AB} = \frac{K_{AB}}{K_{AB} + K_{AG} + K_{AH}}$ $K_{BK} = \frac{I_{BK}}{l_{BK}}$ $D_{BA} = \frac{K_{AB}}{K_{AB} + \zeta K_{BC} + K_{BJ} + K_{BK}}$
	Dead load All spans loaded *Imposed load* Maximum bending moment at both supports	*Dead load* All spans loaded	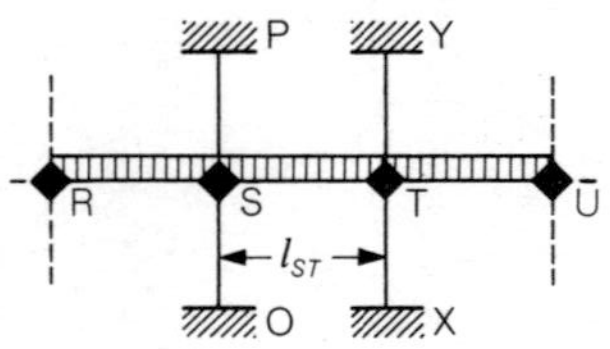	$M_{ST} = -F_{ST} + \frac{D_{ST}}{4 - D_{ST}D_{TS}}\left[2D_{TS}\left(\frac{1}{D_{ST}} - 1\right) \times (F_{TU} - F_{TS}) + (4 - D_{TS})(F_{ST} - F_{SR})\right]$ $M_{TS} = -F_{TS} - \frac{D_{TS}}{4 - D_{ST}D_{TS}}\left[2D_{ST}\left(\frac{1}{D_{TS}} - 1\right) \times (F_{ST} - F_{SR}) + (4 - D_{ST})(F_{TU} - F_{TS})\right]$	$K_{RS} = \frac{I_{RS}}{l_{RS}}$ $K_{ST} = \frac{I_{ST}}{l_{ST}}$ $K_{TU} = \frac{I_{TU}}{l_{TU}}$

Interior span ST		*Imposed load* Maximum bending moment at left-hand support		$M_{ST} = -F_{ST} + \frac{D_{ST}}{4-D_{ST}D_{TS}}\left[-2D_{TS}\left(\frac{1}{D_{ST}}-1\right) \times F_{TS} + (4-D_{TS})(F_{ST}-F_{SR})\right]$ $M_{TS} = -F_{TS} - \frac{D_{TS}}{4-D_{ST}D_{TS}}\left[2D_{ST}\left(\frac{1}{D_{TS}}-1\right) \times (F_{ST}-F_{SR}) - (4-D_{ST})F_{TS}\right]$	$K_{SO} = \frac{I_{SO}}{l_{SO}}$ $K_{SP} = \frac{I_{SP}}{l_{SP}}$ $K_{TX} = \frac{I_{TX}}{l_{TX}}$ $K_{TY} = \frac{I_{TY}}{l_{TY}}$
		Imposed load Maximum bending moment at right-hand support		$M_{ST} = -F_{ST} + \frac{D_{ST}}{4-D_{ST}D_{TS}}\left[2D_{TS}\left(\frac{1}{D_{ST}}-1\right) \times (F_{TU}-F_{TS}) + (4-D_{TS})F_{ST}\right]$ $M_{TS} = -F_{TS} - \frac{D_{TS}}{4-D_{ST}D_{TS}}\left[2D_{ST}\left(\frac{1}{D_{TS}}-1\right) \times F_{ST} + (4-D_{ST})(F_{TU}-F_{TS})\right]$	$D_{ST} = \frac{K_{ST}}{\zeta K_{RS} + K_{ST} + K_{SO} + K_{SP}}$ $D_{TS} = \frac{K_{ST}}{K_{ST} + \zeta K_{TU} + K_{TX} + K_{TY}}$
	Imposed load Bending moments at supports to produce maximum moments in span and in columns	*Imposed load* Bending moments at supports to produce maximum moments in span and in columns		$M_{ST} = -F_{ST} + \frac{D_{ST}}{4-D_{ST}D_{TS}}\left[-2D_{TS}\left(\frac{1}{D_{ST}}-1\right) \times F_{TS} + (4-D_{TS})F_{ST}\right]$ $M_{TS} = -F_{TS} - \frac{D_{TS}}{4-D_{ST}D_{TS}}\left[2D_{ST}\left(\frac{1}{D_{TS}}-1\right) \times F_{ST} - (4-D_{ST})F_{TS}\right]$	

Note: to comply with simplified requirements for analysing frames supporting vertical loading only given in BS8110 and CP110, take $\zeta = 1/2$.

Notation: F_{AB} etc. numerical value of fixed-end moment (negative) at A etc. due to load on AB etc. l_{AB} etc. length of member AB etc. I_{AB} etc. moment of inertia of member AB etc.

Chapter 16
Framed structures

16.1 RATIO OF MOMENTS OF INERTIA OF MEMBERS OF FRAMES

In the formulae for the elastic bending moments on members of framed structures, only the relative stiffness factors of adjoining members are required; i.e. the relative moments of inertia are needed. The following examples, in which a value of α_e of 15 has been assumed, indicate the relative accuracy and complexity of various methods of comparison.

Example 1. Find the ratio of the moments of inertia of the column in diagram (b) and the beam in diagram (a).

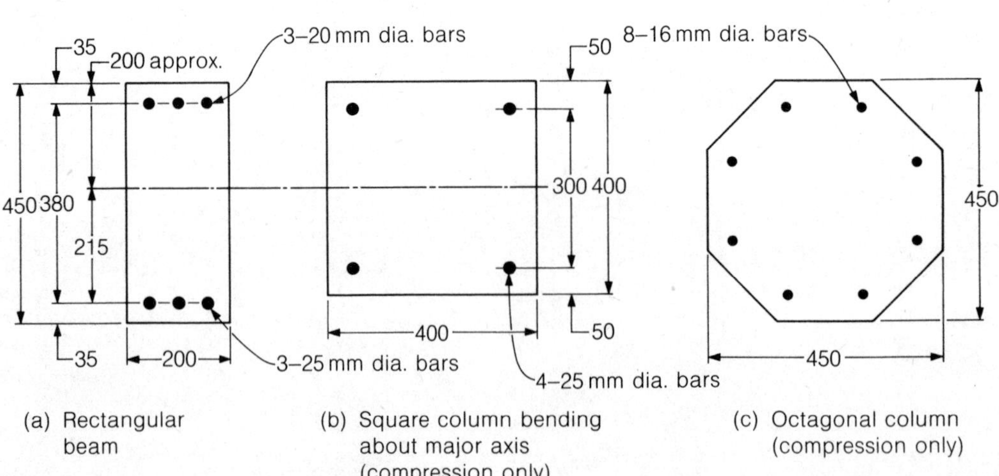

(a) Rectangular beam
(b) Square column bending about major axis (compression only)
(c) Octagonal column (compression only)

(i) Considering complete concrete areas only (i.e. method 1 in section 3.15.2): $I_c/I_b = 400^4/(200 \times 450^3) = 1.41$.

(ii) Considering stressed concrete areas only (i.e. method 3 in section 3.15.2):

Column:

Concrete: $0.083 \times 400^4 = 2.12 \times 10^9\,\text{mm}^4$

Reinforcement: $14 \times 1963 \times 150^2 = 0.62 \times 10^9\,\text{mm}^4$

$I_c = 2.74 \times 10^9\,\text{mm}^4$

Beam:

Concrete: $0.33 \times 200 \times 200^3 = 0.53 \times 10^9\,\text{mm}^4$

Tension reinforcement:

$15 \times 1473 \times 210^2 = 0.97 \times 10^9\,\text{mm}^4$

Compression reinforcement:

$14 \times 943 \times 160^2 = 0.34 \times 10^9\,\text{mm}^4$

$I_b = 1.84 \times 10^9\,\text{mm}^4$

Thus $I_c/I_b = 2.74 \times 10^9/(1.84 \times 10^9) = 1.49$ (compared with 1.41 for method 1).

Example 2. Find the ratio of the moments of inertia of the beam in (a) and the column in (c).

(i) Complete concrete areas only: from *Table 98* the moment of inertia of an octagonal section is $0.055h^4$. Therefore

$$I_c/I_b = \frac{0.055 \times 450^4}{0.083 \times 200 \times 450^3} = 1.49$$

(ii) Stressed areas only: I_c (by calculation similar to that in example 1) $= 2.60 \times 10^9\,\text{mm}^4$. I_b as calculated in example 1 $= 1.84 \times 10^9\,\text{mm}^4$. Thus $I_c/I_b = 2.60 \times 10^9/(1.84 \times 10^9) = 1.41$ (compared with 1.49).

16.2 COLUMNS IN BUILDINGS: APPROXIMATE METHOD

For preliminary calculations when designing the columns in a multistorey building frame (*Table 74*) using limiting-service-stress methods it is often convenient to design them for resistance to direct load only and to allow for the effects of bending either (1) by decreasing the maximum design

Framed structures: three-hinged portal frames

69

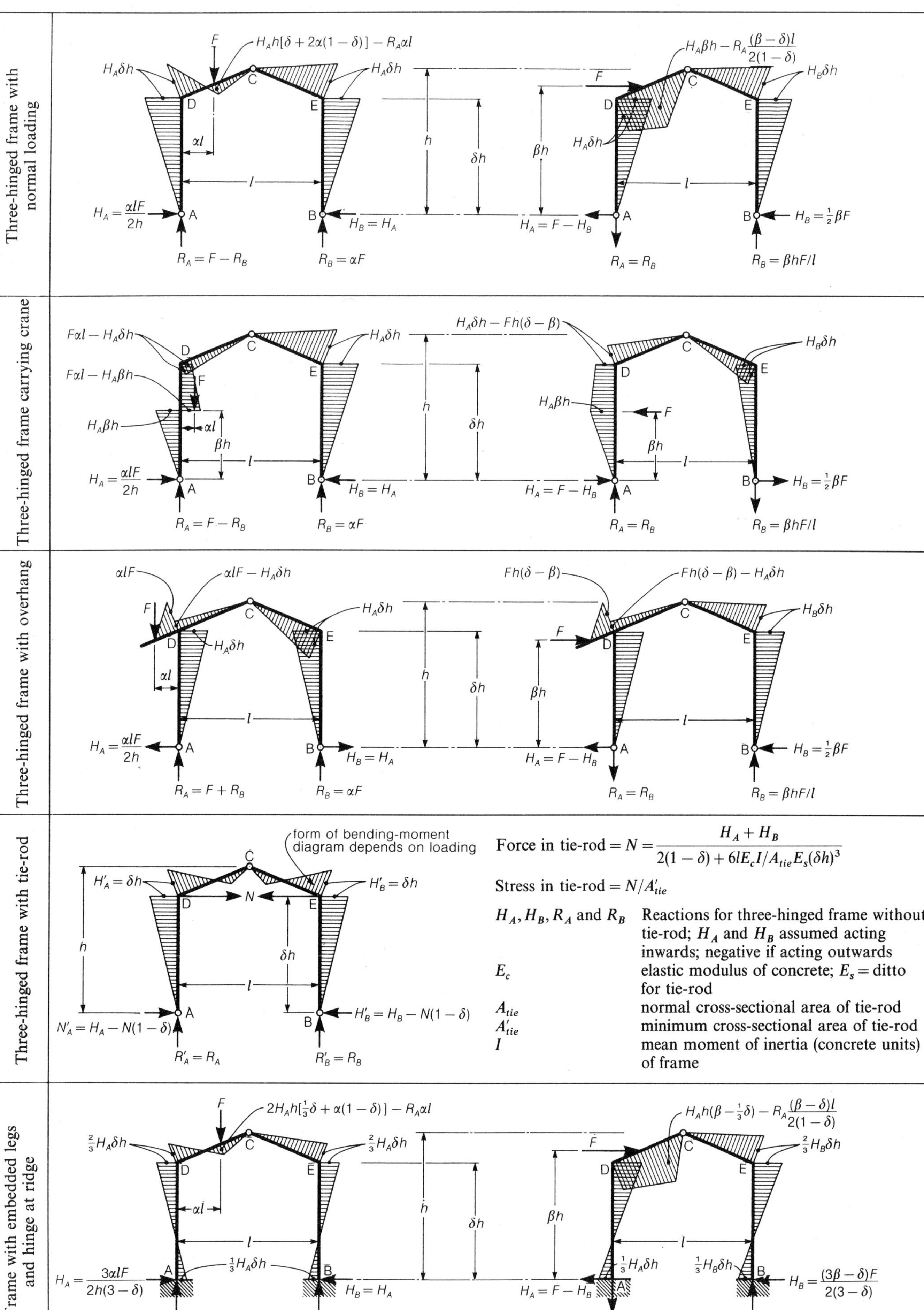

stresses or (2) by increasing the load to a value that is equivalent to that producing the same stresses as would occur if the actual applied load and bending moment were combined. The factors K given in the accompanying table apply to method 2 and have been found satisfactory when applied to most normal building frames when using elastic design. Equivalent direct load $= K \times$ load based on static reactions. The diagrams indicate the arrangement of beams supported by the column.

Storey	Top	Next to top	Lower
╋	1.0	1.0	1.0
┻	4.5	2.0	1.4
┛	6.0	2.3	1.8

Example. Find the approximate elastic bending moments and forces in the columns of a gantry (see (a) in *Table 74*); the vertical design load on each pair of columns is 1000 kN and the horizontal design wind load is 50 kN. The height of the columns is 16 m braced at top and bottom and with intermediate braces at 4 m centres; the columns are 6 m apart at the base.

Thus $F = 50$ kN; vertical load on each column $= (1/2) \times 1000 = 500$ kN; $h = 16$ m; $h_1 = 4$ m; $l = 6$ m.

Bending moment on columns at junction with brace: $(1/4) \times 50 \times 4 \times 10^3 = 50$ kN m. Bending moment in brace at junction with columns: $2 \times 50 = 100$ kN m. Shearing force on brace (constant throughout length) $= 2 \times 100/6 = 33.3$ kN.

The vertical load on the leeward column is $500 + (50 \times 16)/6 = 633.3$ kN plus the dead load of the column and half of the braces. The vertical load on the windward column is $500 - (50 \times 16)/6 = 366.7$ kN plus the dead load of the column and half of the braces.

Frame form	Loading	Reactions and bending moments: Fixed feet		Hinged feet
	$D = A/l$	$H_A = 3D/k_1 h$ $R_D = \alpha F - 2k'_2 D$ $M_A = \left(\frac{1}{k_1} - k'_2\right)D$ $M_B = H_A h - M_A$	$M_C = H_A h - M_D$ $M_D = \left(\frac{1}{k_1} + k'_2\right)D$ $k'_2 = 3(1 - 2z_1)/k_2$	$H_A = 3D/k_3 h$ $R_D = \alpha F$ $M_A = M_D = 0$ $M_B = M_C = H_A h$
	$D = A/l$	$H_D = \frac{1}{2}\alpha F + \frac{3D}{k_1 h}(k_5 z_1 - k_6)$ $C_1 = \frac{D}{k_1}[k_3(1 - z_1) - Kz_1]$ $C_2 = \frac{1}{2k_2}[F\alpha h k_4 + 6KD]$ $R_D = (M_B + M_C)/l$	$M_A = C_1 + C_2$ $M_B = h(H_D - \alpha F) + M_A$ $M_C = H_D h - M_D$ $M_D = C_1 - C_2$	$H_D = \frac{1}{2}\alpha F + \frac{3Kz_1 D}{k_3 h}$ $R_D = F\alpha h/l$ $M_A = M_D = 0$ $M_B = h[H_A - F(1 - \alpha)]$ $M_C = H_D h$
$K = \frac{I_{BC} h}{I_{AB} l}$ $k_1 = K + 2$ $k_2 = 6K + 1$ $k_3 = 2K + 3$ $k_4 = 3K + 1$ $k_5 = 2K + 1$ $k_6 = K + 1$	⊗	$H_A = \frac{3F\alpha l}{2k_1 h}[2K\beta(1 - \beta) + \beta(2 - \beta)]$ $R_D = \frac{6F\alpha K\beta}{k_2}$ $M_A = \frac{F\alpha l}{2k_1 k_2}\{k_2[3k_6(1 - \beta)\beta + 2k_1(\beta - 1)] + \beta(k_2 - k_1)\}$ $M_B = \frac{F\alpha l}{2k_1 k_2}[3(\beta k_2 - k_5) + 13]K\beta$ $M_C = \frac{F\alpha l}{2k_1 k_2}[3(\beta k_2 - 3k_5) - 5]K\beta$ $M_D = \frac{F\alpha l}{2k_1 k_2}\{k_2[3k_6(1 - \beta) + 1] + k_1\}\beta$		$H_A = \frac{3F\alpha l}{2hk_3}[(1 - \beta^2)K + 1]$ $R_D = \alpha F$ $M_A = M_D = 0$ $M_B = F\alpha l - H_A h$ $M_C = H_A h$

Notes for *Tables 70 and 71*

Formulae (except X and Y) apply to any type of loading and give numerical values of reactions and moments; see loading diagrams for direction of action.

Centre of gravity of total load F is at αl or αh. Centroid of free-bending-moment diagram is at $z_1 l$, $z_1 h$, $z_1 \psi h$ or $\frac{1}{2}z_1 l$ from left-hand support (vertical loads) or lower support (horizontal loads)

$$D = \frac{\text{area of free-bending-moment diagram}}{\text{loaded length}} = \frac{A}{l}, \frac{A}{l/2}, \frac{A}{h} \text{ or } \frac{A}{\psi h}; \text{ see } \textit{Table 29}.$$

Framed structures: gable frames: general cases

Frame form	Loading	Reactions and bending moments: Fixed feet	Hinged feet
$K=\dfrac{I_{BC}h}{I_{AB}\sqrt{[(l/2)^2+(\psi h)^2]}}$ $k_4=3K+1$ $k_7=K+3+\psi(3+\psi)$ $k_8=2K+6+3\psi+\alpha\psi(3+2\psi)$ $k_9=2K+6+3\psi$ $k_{10}=3K+\psi(4K+1)$ $k_{11}=K-\psi+2z_1\psi(1+K)$ $k_{12}=K(K+4+6\psi)+\psi^2(4K+1)$ $k_{13}=K+\psi(2K+1)$ $k_{14}=K-\psi(3+2\psi)+3z_1\psi(2+K+\psi)$ $k_{15}=(K+4+3\psi)K$ $k_{16}=\dfrac{3(1-z_1)D}{3K+1}$ $k_{17}=K+2+\psi-2z_1(K+1)$ $k_{18}=2(K+3)+2\psi(\psi+3)-3z_1(K+2)-3z_1\psi$	$D=A/(l/2)$ $R_A=F-R_E$	$H_A=\dfrac{\frac{1}{2}F\alpha lk_{10}+3k_{11}D}{hk_{12}}$ $\quad R_E=F\alpha-\dfrac{k_{16}}{l}$ $M_A=\dfrac{\frac{1}{2}F\alpha lk_{13}+Dk_{14}}{k_{12}}-\frac{1}{2}k_{16}$ $\quad M_B=H_Ah-M_A$ $M_C=\frac{1}{2}(F\alpha l+M_A+M_E)-H_Ah(1+\psi)$ $\quad M_D=H_Ah-M_E$ $M_E=\dfrac{\frac{1}{2}F\alpha lk_{13}+Dk_{14}}{k_{12}}+\frac{1}{2}k_{16}$	$H_A=\dfrac{F\alpha l(3+2\psi)+6(1+z_1\psi)D}{4hk_7}$ $R_E=\alpha F$ $M_A=M_E=0$ $M_B=M_D=H_Ah$ $M_C=\frac{1}{2}F\alpha l-H_Ah(1+\psi)$
	$D=A/\psi h$ $H_A=F-H_E$ $R_A=R_E$	$H_E=\dfrac{Fh(k_{15}+\alpha k_{10})+6k_{11}D}{2hk_{12}}$ $\quad R_E=\dfrac{1}{l}[Fh(1+\alpha)-M_E-M_A]$ $M_A=\dfrac{1}{k_{12}}\left[\dfrac{Fh\psi}{2}(1-\alpha)k_{13}-Dk_{14}\right]+\dfrac{Fh(3\psi+2)+6(1-z_1)D}{4k_4}$ $M_B=H_Ah-M_A$ $M_C=\frac{1}{2}[Fh(1+\alpha)-M_A+M_E]-H_Eh(1+\psi)$ $\quad M_D=H_Eh-M_E$ $M_E=\dfrac{1}{k_{12}}\left[\dfrac{Fh\psi}{2}(1-\alpha)k_{13}-Dk_{14}\right]-\dfrac{Fh(3\psi+2)+6(1-z_1)D}{4k_4}$	$H_E=\dfrac{Fhk_8+6(1+z_1\psi)D}{4hk_7}$ $R_E=Fh(1+\alpha)/l$ $M_A=M_E=0$ $M_B=H_Ah$ $M_C=\frac{1}{2}Fh(1+\alpha)-H_Eh(1+\psi)$ $M_D=H_Eh$
	$D=A/h$ $H_A=F-H_E$ $R_A=R_E$	$H_E=\dfrac{1}{2hk_{12}}(F\alpha hk_{15}-6Kk_{17}D)$ $\quad R_E=(F\alpha h-M_E-M_A)/l$ $M_A=\dfrac{1}{k_{12}}(\frac{1}{2}F\alpha h\psi k_{13}+Kk_{18}D)+\dfrac{1}{4k_4}[F\alpha h(3K+2)+6KD]$ $M_B=h(F\alpha-H_E)-M_A$ $\quad M_C=\frac{1}{2}(F\alpha h-M_A+M_E)-H_Eh(1+\psi)$ $M_D=H_Eh-M_E$ $M_E=\dfrac{1}{k_{12}}(\frac{1}{2}F\alpha h\psi k_{13}+Kk_{18}D)-\dfrac{1}{4k_4}[F\alpha h(3K+2)+6KD]$	$H_E=\dfrac{F\alpha hk_9+6Kz_1D}{4hk_7}$ $R_E=F\alpha h/l$ $M_A=M_E=0$ $M_B=h(F\alpha-H_E)$ $M_C=\frac{1}{2}F\alpha h-H_Eh(1+\psi)$ $M_D=H_Eh$
	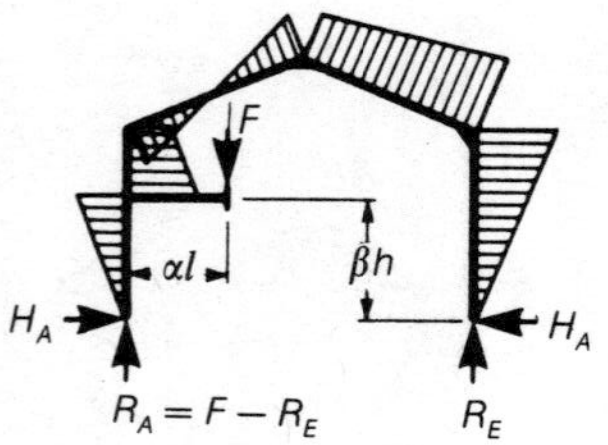 (Y) $R_A=F-R_E$		$H_A=\dfrac{3F\alpha l[K(1-\beta^2)+2+\psi]}{4hk_7}$ $R_E=\alpha F$ $\quad M_A=M_E=0$ $M_B=F\alpha l-H_Ah$ $M_C=\frac{1}{2}F\alpha l-H_Ah(1+\psi)$ $M_D=H_Ah$ when also hinged at C: $H_A=\dfrac{F\alpha l}{2h(1+\psi)}$ and $M_C=0$ All other expressions are unaltered

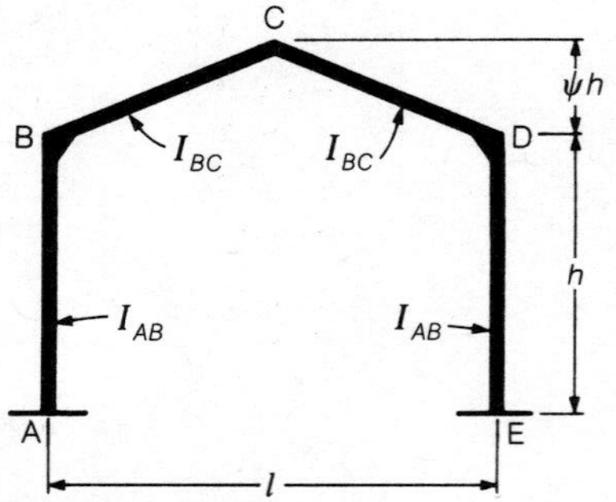

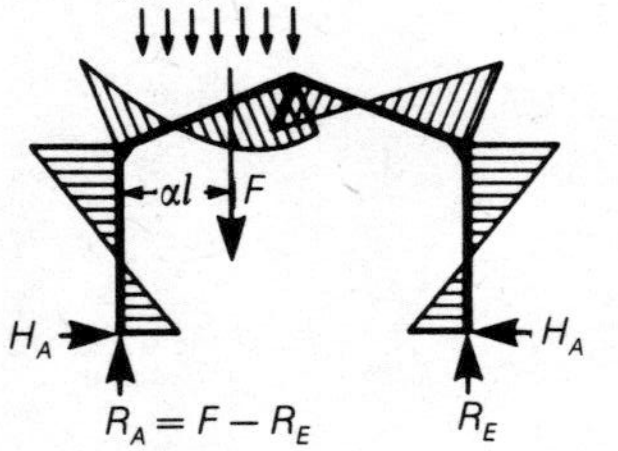

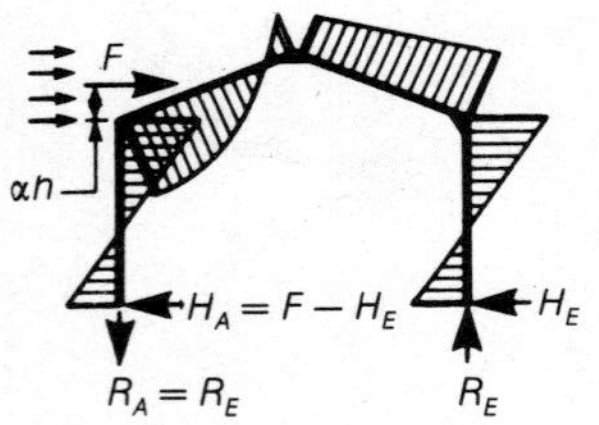

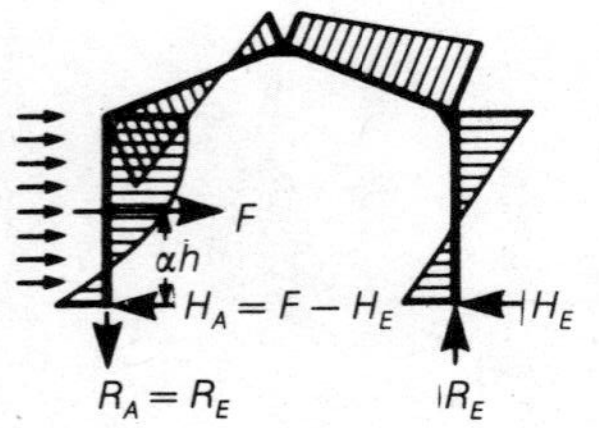

Frame form	Loading	Reactions and bending moments: Fixed feet		Hinged feet
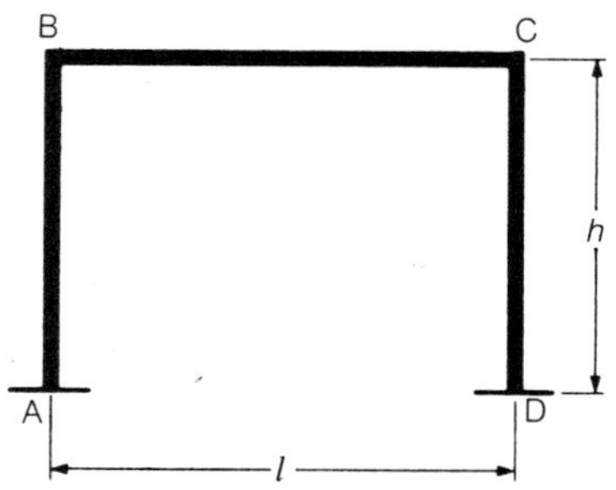	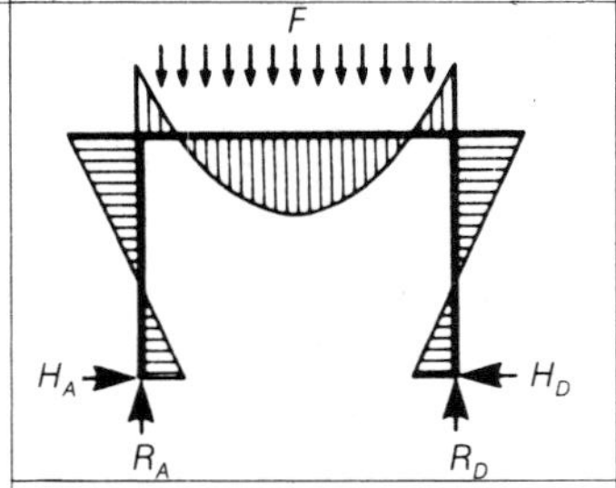	$H_A = H_D = \frac{Fl}{4hk_1}$ $R_A = R_D = \frac{1}{2}F$	$M_A = M_D = \frac{Fl}{12k_1}$ $M_B = M_C = \frac{Fl}{6k_1}$	$H_A = H_D = \frac{Fl}{4hk_3}$ $R_A = R_D = \frac{1}{2}F$ $M_A = M_D = 0$ $M_B = M_C = H_A h = \frac{Fl}{4k_3}$
	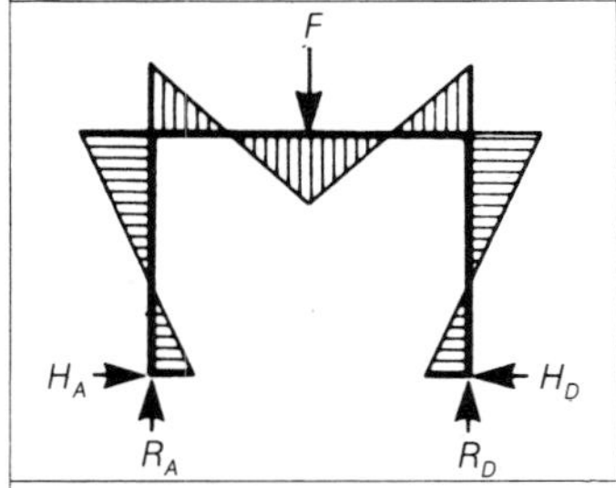	$H_A = H_D = \frac{3Fl}{8hk_1}$ $R_A = R_D = \frac{1}{2}F$	$M_A = M_D = \frac{Fl}{8k_1}$ $M_B = M_C = \frac{Fl}{4k_1}$	$H_A = H_D = \frac{3Fl}{8hk_3}$ $R_A = R_D = \frac{1}{2}F$ $M_A = M_D = 0$ $M_B = M_C = H_A h = \frac{3Fl}{8k_3}$
	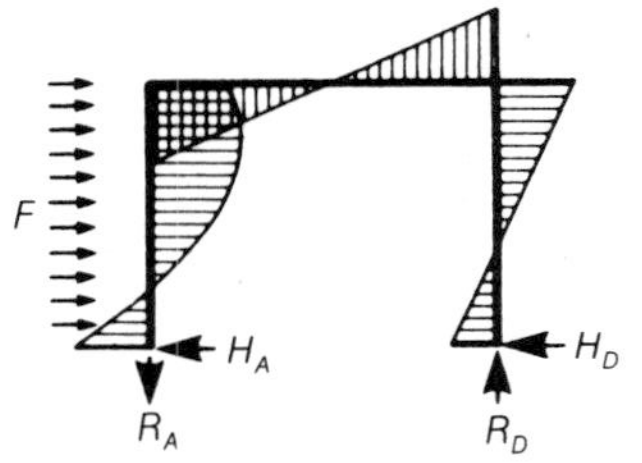	$H_A = F - H_D$ $H_D = \frac{Fk_3}{8k_1}$ $R_A = -\frac{FhK}{lk_2} = -R_D$ $M_A = \frac{Fh}{4}\left[\frac{K+3}{6k_1} + \frac{4K+1}{k_2}\right]$	$M_B = h(H_A - \frac{1}{2}F) - M_A$ $M_C = H_D h - M_D$ $M_D = \frac{Fh}{4}\left[\frac{K+3}{6k_1} - \frac{4K+1}{k_2}\right]$	$H_A = \frac{F}{8}\left(\frac{6k_3 - K}{k_3}\right)$ $H_D = F - H_A$ $R_D = -R_A = \frac{Fh}{2l}$ $M_A = M_D = 0$ $M_B = h(\frac{1}{2}F - H_D) = \frac{3Fhk_1}{8k_3}$ $M_C = H_D h = \frac{Fh}{8}\left(\frac{2k_3 + K}{k_3}\right)$
$F =$ total load $I_{AB} = I_{CD}$ $K = \frac{I_{BC}h}{I_{AB}l}$ $k_1 = K + 2$ $k_2 = 6K + 1$ $k_3 = 2K + 3$ $k_4 = 3K + 1$	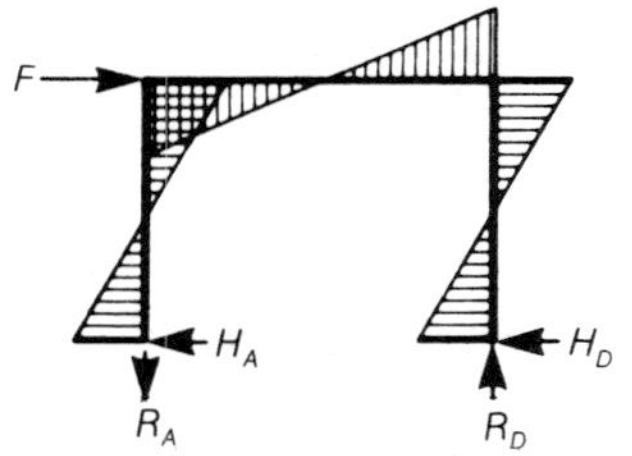	$H_A = H_D = \frac{1}{2}F$ $R_A = -R_D = -\frac{3FhK}{lk_2}$	$M_A = M_D = \frac{Fhk_4}{2k_2}$ $M_B = M_C = \frac{3FhK}{2k_2}$	$H_A = H_D = \frac{1}{2}F$ $R_D = -R_A = \frac{Fh}{l}$ $M_A = M_D = 0$ $M_B = M_C = \frac{1}{2}Fh$

Note: formulae give numerical values of reactions and bending moments; see diagrams for direction of action.

Chapter 17
Arches

Throughout this chapter elastic analyses are undertaken employing characteristic loads and service stresses. If the resulting sections are to be designed in accordance with limit-state methods, the design loads employed must be determined by multiplying the characteristic values by the partial safety factor for loads appropriate to the particular limit-state considered.

17.1 TWO-HINGED ARCH

The diagram in *Table 75* shows that there is no bending moment at the springings of a two-hinged arch. The vertical component of the thrust at the springings is the same as for a freely supported beam; the horizontal component H is as given by the formula in *Table 75*, in which M_x is the bending moment on a section at a distance x from the crown considering the arch as a freely supported beam; i.e. M_x is as given by the corresponding expression in *Table 75*.

The summations $\sum M_x y a_I$ and $\sum y^2 a_I$ are taken over the whole length of the arch. The formula for H allows for the elastic contraction of the arch. A is the average equivalent area of the arch rib or slab; a is the length of a short segment of the axis of the arch or slab; the ordinates of a are x and y as shown in *Table 75*. If I is the moment of inertia of the arch at x, then $a_I = a/I$. The bending moment at any section is $M_d = M_x - Hy$.

The procedure is to divide the axis of the arch into an even number of segments and to calculate the value of H. The calculation can be facilitated by tabulating the successive steps. The total bending moment need only be determined generally for the crown ($x = 0, y = y_c$) and the first quarter-point ($x = 0.25l$). The bending moment M_c at the crown is the bending moment for a freely supported beam minus Hy_c. For the maximum positive bending moment at the crown the sum of the values of M_c for all elements of dead load is added to the values of M_c for only those elements of imposed load that give positive values of M_c. For the maximum negative bending moment at the crown the sum of the values of M_c for all elements of dead load is added to the values of M_c for only those elements of imposed load that give negative values of M_c. The bending moment at the first quarter-point is the bending moment for a freely supported beam minus Hy_q, where y_q is the vertical ordinate of the first quarter-point. The bending moment is combined with the normal component of H.

For an arch having large span it is worth while drawing the influence lines ($F = 1$) for the bending moments at the crown and at the first quarter-point.

17.2 FIXED ARCH

17.2.1 Approximate determination of thickness

The diagram at the top of *Table 76* shows the method. Draw a horizontal line through the crown C and find G, the point of intersection with the vertical through the centre of gravity of the total load on half the span of the arch. Set off GT equal to the dead load on the half-span, drawn to a convenient scale; draw a horizontal through T to intersect GS produced at R. Draw RK perpendicular to GR, and GK parallel to the tangent to the arch axis at S. With the same unit of weight used in drawing GT, scale off TR, which equals H_c, and GK, which equals H_s. If f_{cc} is the maximum allowable compressive stress in the concrete, h_c is the thickness of the arch at the crown, h_s the thickness of the arch at the springing, and b the assumed breadth of the arch (1 m or 12 in for a slab), then approximately $h_c = 1.7H_c/f_{cc}b$, and $h_s = 2H_s f_{cc} b$.

The method applies to spans of from 12 to 60 m (40 to 200 ft) and span/rise ratios of between 4 and 8. The method does not depend on knowing the profile of the arch (except for solid-spandrel earth-filled arches, where the dead load is largely dependent on the shape of the arch), but the span and rise must be known. With d_c and d_s thus approximately determined, the thrusts and bending moments at the crown, springing, and quarter-points can be determined and the stresses on the assumed sections calculated. If this calculation shows the sections to be unsuitable, other dimensions must be assumed and the calculations reworked.

17.2.2 Stresses in arch of any profile

The following method is suitable for determining the stresses in any symmetrical fixed arch if the dimensions and shape of the arch are known, or assumed, and if the shape of the arch must conform to a specified profile. Reference should be made to section 3.16.3 for general comments on this method.

On half the arch drawn to scale, as in *Table 76*, plot the arch axis. Divide the half-arch into a number k of segments

Framed structures: gable frames: special cases

Frame form	Loading	Reactions and bending moments: Fixed feet	Hinged feet
F = total load $I_{AB} = I_{DE}$ $I_{BC} = I_{CD}$ $K = \dfrac{I_{BC}h}{I_{AB}\sqrt{(l/2)^2 + (\psi h)^2}}$ $k_1 = K + 2$ $k_4 = 3K + 1$ $k_7 = K + 3 + \psi(3 + \psi)$ $k_9 = 2K + 3(2 + \psi)$ $k_{10} = 3K + \psi(4K + 1)$ $k_{12} = K(K + 4 + 6\psi) + \psi^2(4K + 1)$ $k_{13} = K + \psi(2K + 1)$ $k_{15} = K(K + 4 + 3\psi)$ $k_{19} = 8(K + 3) + 5\psi(4 + \psi)$ $k_{20} = K + 3 + 2\psi$ $k_{21} = 2K(K + 4 + 5\psi) + \psi^2(5K + 1)$ $k_{22} = 2(10K + 3) + \psi(9K + 6) + \psi^2$		$H_A = H_E = \dfrac{Fl}{8h}\left[\dfrac{4K + \psi(5K + 1)}{k_{12}}\right]$ $M_B = M_D = H_A h - M_A$ $R_A = R_E = \frac{1}{2}F$ $M_C = H_A h(1 + \psi) - \frac{1}{8}Fl - M_A$ $M_A = M_E = \dfrac{Fl}{48}\left[\dfrac{K(8 + 15\psi) + \psi(6 - \psi)}{k_{12}}\right]$	$H_A = H_E = \dfrac{Fl}{32h}\left(\dfrac{8 + 5\psi}{k_7}\right)$ $R_A = R_E = \frac{1}{2}F$ $M_A = M_E = 0$ $M_B = M_D = H_A h$ $M_C = H_A h(\psi + 1) - \dfrac{Fl}{8}$
		$H_A = H_E = \dfrac{Fl}{4h}\left(\dfrac{k_{10}}{k_{12}}\right)$ $M_B = M_D = H_A h - M_A$ $R_A = R_E = \frac{1}{2}F$ $M_C = H_A h(1 + \psi) - \frac{1}{4}Fl - M_A$ $M_A = M_E = \dfrac{Fl}{4}\left(\dfrac{k_{13}}{k_{12}}\right)$	$H_A = H_E = \dfrac{Fl}{8h}\left(\dfrac{3 + 2\psi}{k_7}\right)$ $R_A = R_E = \frac{1}{2}F$ $M_A = M_E = 0$ $M_B = M_D = H_A h$ $M_C = H_A h(1 + \psi) - \frac{1}{4}Fl$
	F(total) = $wh(1 + \psi)$	$H_E = \dfrac{wh}{4k_{12}}(Kk_{20} + \psi k_{21})$ $H_A = F - H_E$ $R_E = -R_A = \dfrac{wh^2}{8lk_4}[4K(1 + 3\psi) + \psi^2(12K + 5)]$ $M_A = \dfrac{wh^2}{24}\left\{\left[\dfrac{K(K + 6 + 15\psi) + \psi^2 k_{22}}{k_{12}}\right] + \dfrac{12k_5 + \psi[12(3K + 2) + 3\psi]}{2k_4}\right\}$ $M_B = H_A h - M_A - \frac{1}{2}wh^2$ $M_C = H_E h(1 + \psi) - \frac{1}{2}lR_E - M_E$ $M_D = H_E h - M_E$ $M_E = \dfrac{wh^2}{24}\left\{\left[\dfrac{K(K + 6 + 15\psi) + \psi^2 k_{22}}{k_{12}}\right] - \dfrac{12k_5 + \psi[12(3K + 2) + 3\psi]}{2k_4}\right\}$	$H_E = \dfrac{wh}{16k_7}(2k_9 + K + \psi k_{19})$ $H_A = wh(1 + \psi) - H_E$ $R_E = -R_A = \dfrac{wh^2}{2l}[1 + \psi(2 + \psi)]$ $M_A = M_E = 0$ $M_B = H_A h - \frac{1}{2}wh^2$ $M_C = H_E h(1 + \psi) - \frac{1}{2}R_E l$ $M_D = H_E h$
		$H_A = H_E = \frac{1}{2}F$ $M_B = M_D = H_A h - M_A$ $R_E = -R_A = \dfrac{1}{l}[Fh(1 + \psi) - 2M_E]$ $M_C = 0$ $M_A = M_E = \dfrac{Fh}{4}\left(\dfrac{3K + 2}{2K + 1}\right)$	$H_A = H_E = \frac{1}{2}F$ $R_E = -R_A = \dfrac{1}{l}[Fh(1 + \psi)]$ $M_A = M_E = 0$ $M_B = M_D = \frac{1}{2}Fh$ $M_C = 0$
		$H_E = \dfrac{FK}{2}\left(\dfrac{k_{15}}{k_{12}}\right)$ $H_A = F - H_E$ $M_B = H_E h - M_A$ $R_E = -R_A = \dfrac{3Fh}{2l}\left(\dfrac{K}{3K + 1}\right)$ $M_C = H_E h(1 + \psi) - \frac{1}{2}lR_E - M_E$ $M_D = H_E h - M_E$ $M_A = \dfrac{Fh}{2}\left(\dfrac{\psi k_{13}}{k_{12}} + \dfrac{k_4 + 1}{2k_4}\right)$ $M_E = \dfrac{Fh}{2}\left(\dfrac{\psi k_{13}}{k_{12}} - \dfrac{k_4 + 1}{2k_4}\right)$	$H_E = \dfrac{Fk_9}{4k_7}$ $R_E = -R_A = \dfrac{Fh}{l}$ $H_A = F - H_E$ $M_A = M_E = 0$ $M_B = H_A h$ $M_D = H_E h$ $M_C = H_E h(1 + \psi) - \frac{1}{2}Fh$

Note: formulae give numerical values of reactions and bending moments; see diagrams for direction of action.

such that each segment has the same ratio a_I of length a to mean moment of inertia I based on the thickness of the arch measured normal to the axis, allowance being made for the reinforcement; $a_I = a/I$.

The ordinates x and y about the axis of the arch at the crown are determined by measurement to the centre of the length of each segment, Calculate the dead load and the imposed load separately on each segment. Assume each load acts at the centre of the length of each segment. In an open-spandrel arch, the dead and imposed loads are concentrated on the arch at the positions of the columns; these positions should be taken as the centre of the segments, but it may not then be possible to maintain a constant value of a_I and the value of a_I for each segment must be calculated; the general formulae in *Table 76* are then applicable.

For constant values of a_I, the effects at the crown are as follows:

$$H_c = \frac{k\sum M_1 y - \sum y \sum M_1}{2[k\sum y^2 - (\sum y)^2]}$$

$$R_c = \sum M_1 x / 2\sum x^2$$

$$M_c = (\sum M_1 - 2H_c \sum y)/2k$$

The summations are taken over one-half of the arch. The term M_1 is the moment at the centre of the segment of all loads between the centre of the segment and the crown. Summations are also made for the loads on the other half of the arch, for which R_c is negative.

Owing to the elastic shortening of the arch resulting from H_c:

$$H_{c1} = \frac{H_c k \sum (a/A)}{a_I[k\sum y^2 - (\sum y)^2]}$$

$$M_{c1} = -H_{c1} a \sum y/k$$

in which A is the cross-sectional area of the segment calculated on the same basis as I.

Owing to a rise $(+T)$ or a fall $(-T)$ in temperature:

$$H_{c2} = \frac{\pm T\lambda l_1 k E_c}{2a_I[k\sum y^2 - (\sum y)^2]}$$

$$M_{c2} = -H_{c2}\sum y/k$$

in which l_1 is the length of the arch axis. Arch shortening due to H_{c2} is neglected. Shrinkage of the concrete is equal to a fall of 8.3°C (15°F).

The procedure for applying the foregoing formulae is to calculate $(H_c - H_{c1})$, R_c and $(M_c - M_{c1})$ for the dead load. Calculate separately H_{c2} and M_{c2} for a rise and fall of temperature of 16.7°C (or any other amount considered suitable) and separately due to shrinkage. Then calculate $(H_c - H_{c1})$ and $(M_c - M_{c1})$ for the imposed load (reduced to an equivalent uniform load) which, for the purpose of finding the maximum bending moment at the crown (and the horizontal thrust), should be considered as operating on the segments in the middle third of the arch. (By considering the effect of the imposed load on one segment more and one segment less than those in the middle third, the number of segments that should be loaded to give the maximum positive bending moment due to imposed load at the crown can be determined.) With the imposed load on only those segments that are unloaded when calculating the maximum positive bending moment, the maximum negative bending moment at the crown due to the imposed load is obtained. These maximum bending moments are then each combined with the bending moments due to dead load and arch shortening, and with the bending moments due to a change in temperature and shrinkage, in such a way that the absolute maximum and minimum values are obtained. The corresponding thrusts are also calculated and are combined with the appropriate bending moments to determine the stresses at the crown.

The bending moment at the springing due to a load at a point between the springing and the crown of the arch and at a distance αl from the springing (where l is the span of the arch) is

$$M_s = (M_c - M_{c1}) + (H_c - H_{c1})y_c + \tfrac{1}{2}lR_c - F\alpha l$$

where y_c is the rise of the arch. For the dead load the values determined for the crown are substituted in this expression, with the term $F\alpha l$ replaced by $\sum F[(l/2) - x]$. To give the maximum negative bending moment at the springing, the imposed load is considered as acting only on those segments in the part of the arch extending 0.4 of the span from the support. (As before, the effect of the imposed load on one more and one less segment should be determined to ensure that the most adverse disposition of loading has been considered.) By loading only those segments that are unloaded when finding the maximum negative bending moment, the maximum positive bending moment is obtained. These maximum moments are each combined with the bending moments due to dead load, temperature and shrinkage to give the most adverse combination, and the stresses at the springing are obtained by combining the bending moments and normal thrusts.

Thrust normal to the section at the springing:

$$N_s = (H_c - H_{c1})\cos\theta + R_s \sin\theta.$$

Vertical component of thrust at springing: R_s = total load on half-arch giving the appropriate value of $(H_c - H_{c1})$ minus R_c corresponding to $(H_c - H_{c1})$.

Shearing force at crown = maximum value of R_c due to any combination of dead and imposed load.

Shearing force at springing $= (H_c - H_{c1})\sin\theta + R_s\cos\theta$; the values of $(H_c - H_{c1})$ are those due to the incidence of dead load plus imposed load that gives the maximum value for the shearing force, which is generally when the imposed load extends over the whole arch.

Quarter-point ($x_q = l/4$ from the crown). Bending moment due to a single load F placed between the crown and the section at a distance of $(x_q - x_1)$ from the section:

$$M_q = M_c + H_c y_q + R_c x_q - F(x_q - x_1)$$

The procedure is then similar to the analysis of the section at the springing.

17.3 FIXED PARABOLIC ARCH

See section 3.16.4 for comments on the analysis of a fixed parabolic arch using the data in *Table 77*. The formulae and bases of the coefficients are given below.

Framed structures: effects of lateral loads

(a) Open braced tower

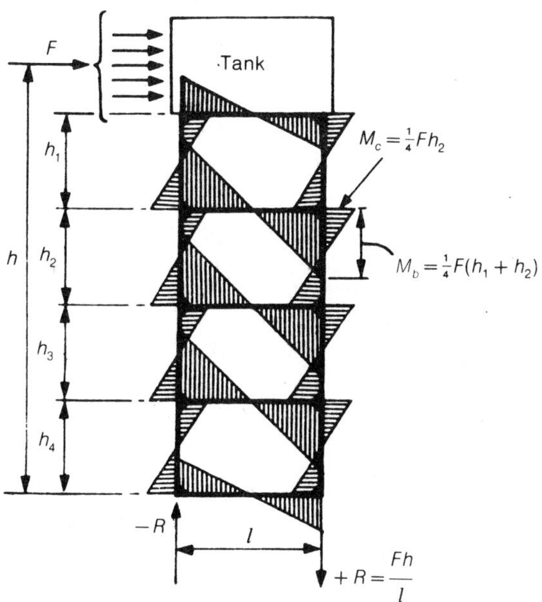

Shearing forces:

on column: $V_c = \frac{1}{2}F$

on brace: $V_b = 2M_b/l$

Assumption: both columns of same size and vertical or nearly vertical.

(b) Substructure of silo (or similar structure)

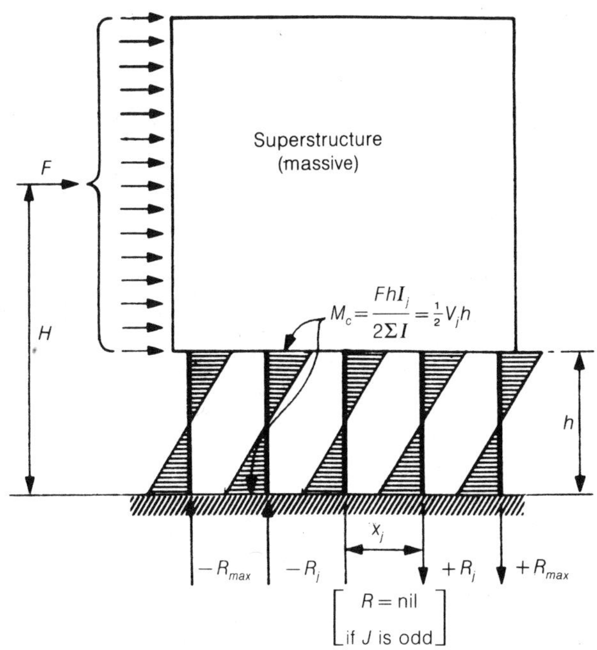

$$R_j = \frac{FHx_j}{\Sigma x^2}$$

I_j moment of inertia of any column j (columns of different sizes.)

J total number of columns supporting superstructure

Shearing force on column j: $V_j = FI_j/\Sigma I$

If all columns are same size: $M_c = Fh/2J$

(c) Frame of multistorey building

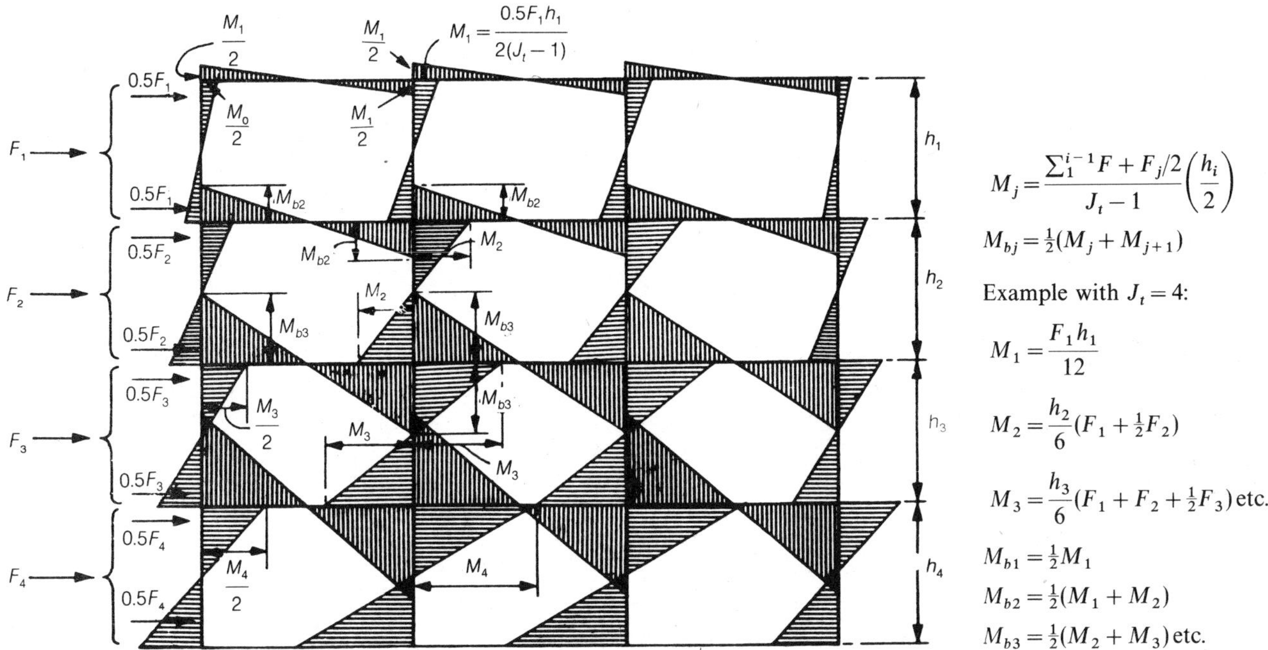

$$M_j = \frac{\Sigma_1^{i-1}F + F_j/2}{J_t - 1}\left(\frac{h_i}{2}\right)$$

$$M_{bj} = \tfrac{1}{2}(M_j + M_{j+1})$$

Example with $J_t = 4$:

$$M_1 = \frac{F_1h_1}{12}$$

$$M_2 = \frac{h_2}{6}(F_1 + \tfrac{1}{2}F_2)$$

$$M_3 = \frac{h_3}{6}(F_1 + F_2 + \tfrac{1}{2}F_3) \text{ etc.}$$

$$M_{b1} = \tfrac{1}{2}M_1$$

$$M_{b2} = \tfrac{1}{2}(M_1 + M_2)$$

$$M_{b3} = \tfrac{1}{2}(M_2 + M_3) \text{ etc.}$$

Assumption: exterior column subjected to half shearing force on interior column.

J_t total number of columns in frame

Note: explanations of the effects of wind forces (or other lateral loads) on the types of structures illustrated in *Table 74* are given in section 3.13.

17.3.1 Dead load and elastic contraction

Horizontal thrust due to dead load alone $H = k_1 gl^2/y_c$, where g is the dead load per unit length at the crown, l is the span and y_c the rise of the arch axis. Coefficient k_1 depends on the dead load at the springing, which varies with the rise/span ratio and type of structure, i.e. whether the arch is open spandrel or solid spandrel, or whether the dead load is uniform throughout the span.

Elastic contraction is produced by the thrust along the arch axis (assuming rigid abutments). The counter-thrust H_1, while slightly reducing the thrust due to the dead load, renders this thrust eccentric and produces a positive bending moment at the crown and a negative bending moment at each springing. If h is the thickness of the arch at the crown,

$$H_1 = -k_2\left(\frac{h}{y_c}\right)^2 H$$

in which the coefficient k_2 depends on the relative thicknesses at the crown and springing.

Owing to dead load and arch shortening, the resultant thrusts H_c and H_s at the crown and springing respectively acting parallel to the arch axis at these points are

$$H_c = H - H_1$$

$$H_s = \frac{H}{\cos\theta} - H_1\cos\theta$$

in which θ is the angle between the horizontal and the tangent to the arch axis at the springing. Values of $\cos\theta$ are given in *Table 77*.

Bending moments due to the eccentricity of H_c and H_s are $M_c = k_3 y_c H_1$ and $M_s = (k_3 - 1)y_c H_1$.

17.3.2 Effect of change of temperature

Additional horizontal thrust due to a rise in temperature or the corresponding counter-thrust due to a fall in temperature is given by

$$H_2 = \pm k_4\left(\frac{h}{y_c}\right)^2 hT$$

in which T is the rise or fall in temperature in degrees centigrade. If h and y_c are in metres, H_2 is in kN per metre width of arch. The values of k_4 in *Table 77* are based on the assumption of an elastic modulus for concrete E_c of $20\,\text{kN/mm}^2$ ($2.9\times10^6\,\text{lb/in}^2$) and a coefficient of linear expansion λ of 12×10^{-6} per degree centigrade (6.7×10^{-6} per degree Fahrenheit). If other metric values of E_1 and λ_1 are employed, k_4 should be multiplied by $4.17\times10^3 E_1\lambda_1$. If imperial values of T, E_2 and λ_2 are employed, k_4 should be multiplied by $0.6E_2\lambda_2$. At the crown the increase or decrease in normal thrust due to the change of temperature is H_2 and the bending moment is $-k_3 y_c H_2$, account being taken of the sign of H_2. The normal thrust at the springing due to a change of temperature is $H_2\cos\theta$, and whether the thrusts due to dead load etc. are increased or decreased thereby depends on the sign of H_2. At the springing the bending moment is $(1-k_3)y_c H_2$, the sign being the same as that of H_2.

17.3.3 Shrinkage of concrete

Shrinkage can be considered to be equivalent to a fall of temperature of 8.3°C (15°F).

17.3.4 Imposed load

The intensity of uniform load equivalent to the specified imposed load is q per unit length.

Maximum positive bending moment at crown $= k_5 ql^2$; horizontal thrust $= k_6 ql^2/y_c$.
Maximum negative bending moment at springing $= k_7 ql^2$; horizontal thrust $= k_8 ql^2/y_c$; vertical reaction $= k_9 ql$.
Maximum positive bending moment at springing $= k_{10} ql^2$; horizontal thrust $= k_{11} ql^2/y_c$; vertical reaction $= k_{12} ql$.
If H and R are the corresponding horizontal thrust and vertical reaction, normal thrust at the springing $= H\cos\theta + R\sqrt{(1-\cos^2\theta)}$.

17.3.5 Dimensions of arch

The line of pressure, and therefore the arch axis, can now be plotted as described in section 3.16.4. The thicknesses of the arch at the crown and the springing having been determined, the lines of the extrados and intrados can be plotted to give a parabolic variation of thickness between the two extremes. Thus the thickness normal to the axis of the arch at any point is given by $[(h_s - h)\alpha + h]$ where α has the following values: if the ratio of the distance of the point from the springing, measured along the axis of the arch, to half the length of the axis of the arch is 1/4, the value of α is 0.563; if the ratio is 1/2, α is 0.250; and if the ratio is 3/4, α is 0.063; i.e. $\alpha = (1 - \text{ratio})^2$.

17.3.6 Units

Factors k_1 to k_3 and k_5 to k_{12} are non-dimensional. Factor k_4 is given in metric units, but analysis in imperial values is possible by using the conversion factor given above. For example, if $E_2 = 2\times10^6\,\text{lb/in}^2$ and $\lambda_2 = 6.7\times10^{-6}$, k_4 (imperial) $= 0.6\times2\times6.7\times k_4$ (metric) and the resulting value of H_2 is in pounds per foot width if h and y_c are in feet and T is in degrees Fahrenheit.

Example. Design a fixed arch slab for an open-spandrel bridge, using *Table 77*.

Selected values

Span: 50 m measured horizontally between the intersection of the arch axis and the abutment.
Rise: 7.5 m, being the rise of the axis of the arch within the 50 m span.
Thickness of arch slab: 900 mm at springings; 600 mm at crown.
Dead load: $12\,\text{kN/m}^2$, excluding the weight of the arch slab.
Imposed load: $15\,\text{kN/m}^2$.
Temperature range: ± 8.3°C. $E_c = 20\,\text{kN/mm}^2$. $\lambda = 12\times10^{-6}$.
Shrinkage: equivalent to a fall in temperature of 8.3°C.

Arches: three-hinged and two-hinged arches

Three-hinged arch **Influence line for section at x**

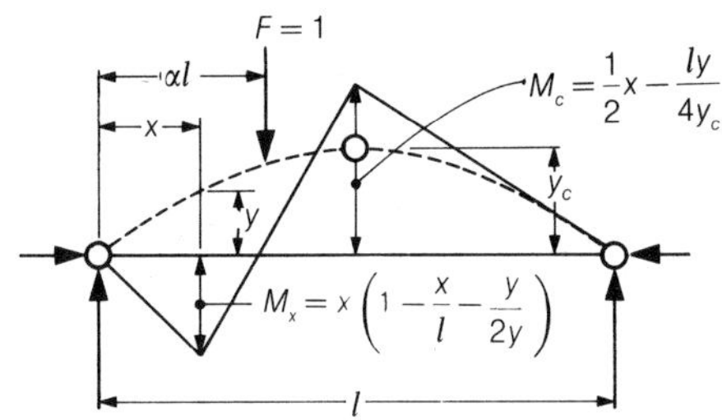

Types of arches

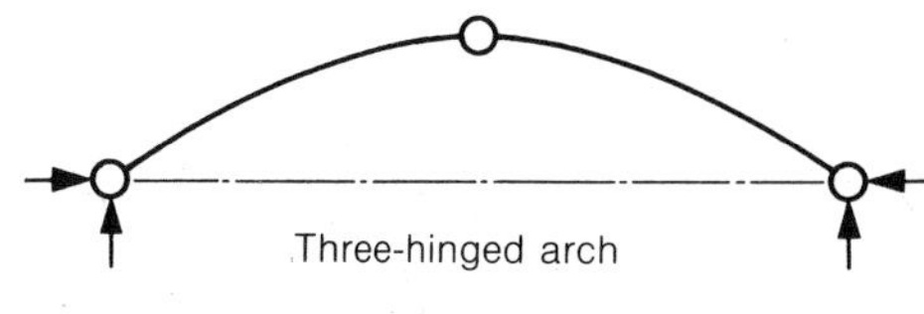

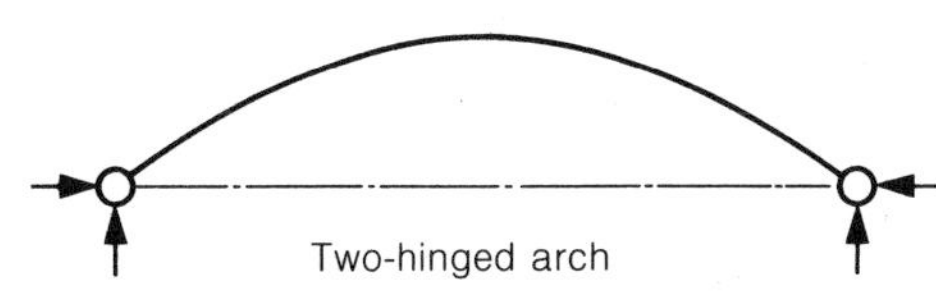

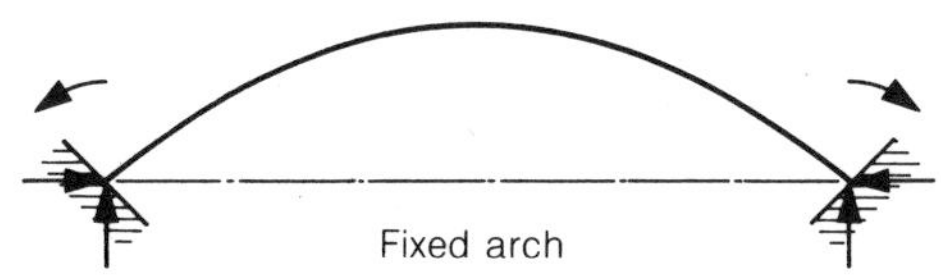

Two-hinged arch

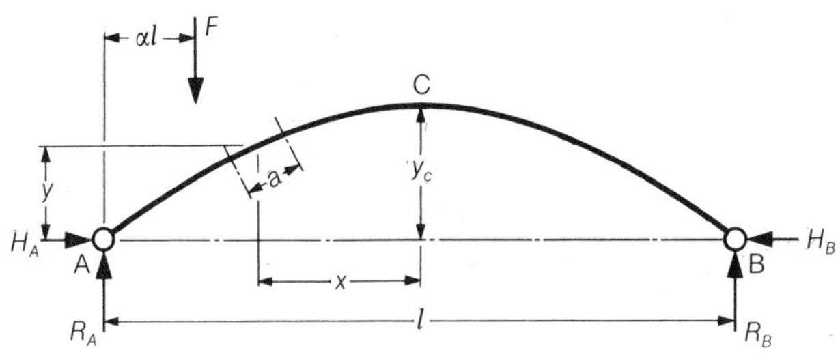

Bending moment at x: $M_x = F\alpha l\left(\frac{x}{l} + \frac{1}{2}\right)$

Horizontal thrust: $H_A = H_B = \dfrac{\Sigma M_x y a_I}{(\Sigma y^2 a_I) + l/A}$

Unsymmetrical three-hinged arches **General case**

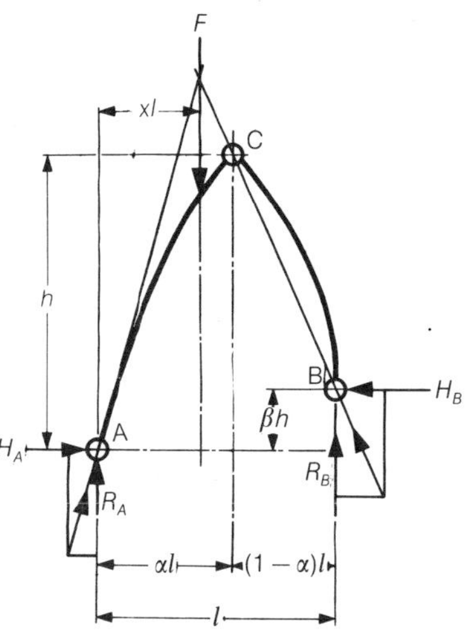

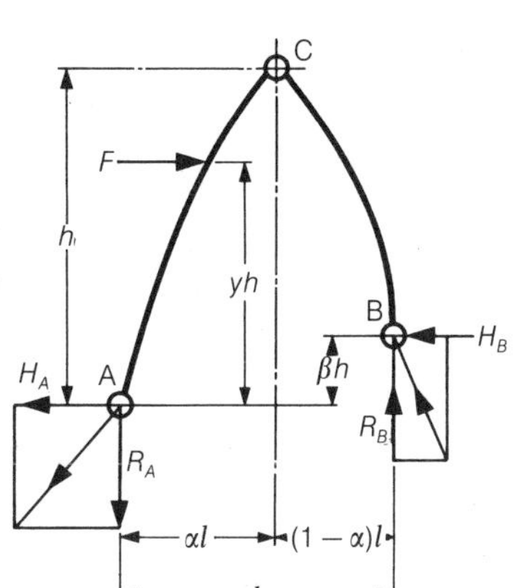

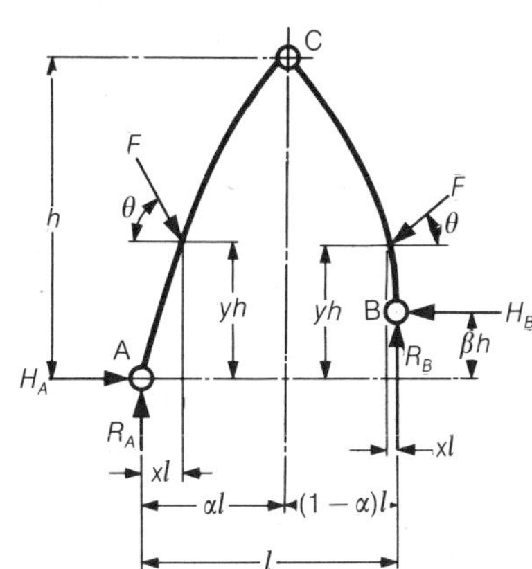

Reaction formulae for general case:

$$R_A = \sum_A^C\left[1 - \frac{(1-\beta)x}{1+\alpha\beta}\right]F\sin\theta + \frac{1}{1-\alpha\beta}\sum_B^C xF\sin\theta + \frac{h}{(1-\alpha\beta)l}\left[\sum_B^C (y-\beta)F\cos\theta - (1-\beta)\sum_A^C yF\cos\theta\right]$$

$$R_B = \frac{1-\beta}{1-\alpha\beta}\sum_A^C xF\sin\theta + \sum_B^C\left[1 - \frac{x}{1-\alpha\beta}\right]F\sin\theta + \frac{h}{(1-\alpha\beta)l}\left[(1-\beta)\sum_A^C yF\cos\theta - \sum_B^C (y-\beta)F\cos\theta\right]$$

$$H_A = \frac{l}{(1-\alpha\beta)h}\left[(1-\alpha)\sum_A^C xF\sin\theta + \alpha\sum_B^C xF\sin\theta\right] + \frac{\alpha}{(1-\alpha\beta)}\sum_B^C (y-\beta)F\cos\theta - \sum_A^C\left[1 - \frac{(1-\alpha)y}{(1-\alpha\beta)}\right]F\cos\theta$$

$$H_B = \frac{l}{(1-\alpha\beta)h}\left[(1-\alpha)\sum_A^C xF\sin\theta + \alpha\sum_B^C xF\sin\theta\right] + \frac{1-\alpha}{(1-\alpha\beta)}\sum_A^C yF\cos\theta - \sum_B^C\left[1 - \frac{(y-\beta)\alpha}{(1-\alpha\beta)}\right]F\cos\theta$$

Note: see section 17.1 for explanation of symbols in, and notes on, the formulae for two-hinged arches.

Geometrical properties

$$\frac{\text{thickness at springing}}{\text{thickness at crown}} = \frac{h_s}{h} = \frac{900}{600} = 1.5$$

$$\frac{\text{rise}}{\text{span}} = \frac{y_c}{l} = \frac{7.5}{50} = 0.15$$

Angle of inclination of arch axis (from *Table 77*): $\cos\theta = 0.82$.

Dead load at crown

12000 N/m² plus weight of 600 mm slab (= 14 200 N/m² at 23.6 kN/m³); $g = 12\,000 + 14\,200 = 26\,200$ N/m².

A strip of slab 1 m wide is considered. The coefficients are taken from *Table 77* and substituted in the formulae in section 17.3.4.

Horizontal thrusts due to dead load etc.

Dead load ($k_1 = 0.140$):	
$H = 0.140 \times 26\,200 \times (50^2/7.5)$	$= +1\,220\,000$ N/m
Arch shortening ($k_2 = 1.39$):	
$H_1 = -1.39(0.6/7.5)^2 \times 1\,220\,000$	$= -$ 10 900 N/m
Change of temperature ($k_4 = 422 \times 10^3$):	
$H_2 = \pm 422 \times 10^3(0.6/7.5)^2 \times 0.6 \times 8.3$	$= \pm$ 13 500 N/m
Shrinkage: as for fall in temperature:	$= -$ 13 500 N/m

Crown: maximum positive bending moment

	Bending moment N m per m	*Thrust* N/m
Dead load and arch shortening:		
$H_c = 1\,220\,000 - 10\,900$		+1 209 100
($k_3 = 0.243$): $M_c = 0.243 \times 7.5 \times 10\,900$	+ 19 900	
Fall in temperature: thrust H_2 as above:		− 13 500
$M_c = 0.243 \times 7.5 \times 13\,500$	+ 24 600	
Shrinkage: as for fall in temperature:	+ 24 600	− 13 500
Imposed load: thrust ($k_6 = 0.064$):		
$H = 0.064 \times 15\,000 \times (50^2/7.5)$		+ 320 000
($k_5 = 50 \times 10^{-4}$): $M_c = 0.005 \times 15\,000 \times 50^2$	+187 500	
Totals	+256 600	+1 502 100

Springing: maximum negative bending moment

Dead load and arch shortening:		
$H_s = (1\,220\,000/0.82) - 10\,900 \times 0.82$		+1 479 000
$M_s = (1 - 0.243) \times 7.5 \times 10\,900$	− 62 000	
Fall in temperature: thrust $= -13\,500 \times 0.82$		− 11 100
$M_s = -0.757 \times 7.5 \times 13\,500$	− 76 600	
Shrinkage: as for fall in temperature:	− 76 600	− 11 100
Imposed load:		
($k_8 = 0.038$): $H = 0.038 \times 15\,000 \times (50^2/7.5) = 190\,000$ N/m		
($k_9 = 0.352$): $R = 0.352 \times 15\,000 \times 50 = 264\,000$ N/m		
Normal thrust $= (190\,000 \times 0.82) + 264\,000\sqrt{(1 - 0.82^2)}$		+ 306 900
($k_7 = 0.020$); $M_s = 0.02 \times 15\,000 \times 50^2$	−750 000	
Totals	−965 200	+1 763 700

Springing: maximum positive bending moment

Dead load and arch shortening as before:	− 62 000	+1 479 000
(rise in temperature and shrinkage neutralize each other)		
Imposed load: ($k_{11} = 0.089$):		
$H = 0.089 \times 15\,000 \times (50^2/7.5) = 445\,000$ N/m		
($k_{12} = 0.151$): $R = 0.151 \times 15\,000 \times 50 = 113\,300$ N/m		
Normal thrust $= (445\,000 \times 0.82) + 113\,300\sqrt{(1 - 0.82^2)}$		+ 429 700
($k_{10} = 0.023$): $M_s = 0.023 \times 15\,000 \times 50^2$	+862 500	
Totals	+ 800 500	+1 908 700

The corresponding bending moments and thrusts should be combined to determine the maximum stresses and reinforcement at the crown and springing.

Arches: fixed-end arches

Determination of trial sizes: Approximate method

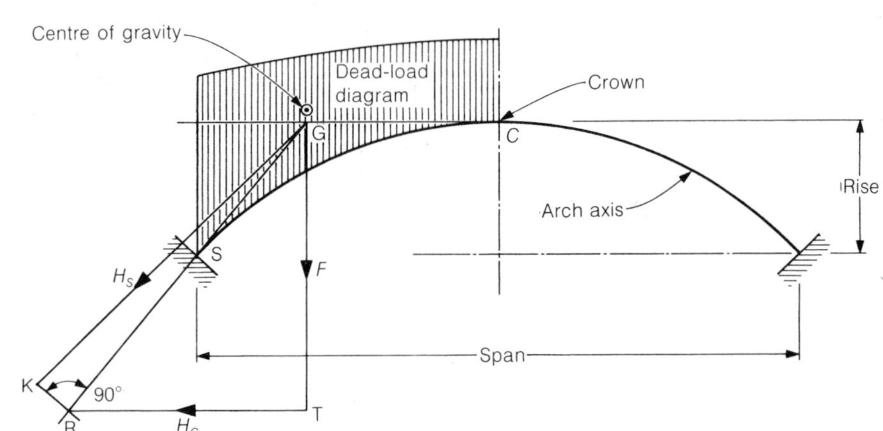

Notation and typical influence lines

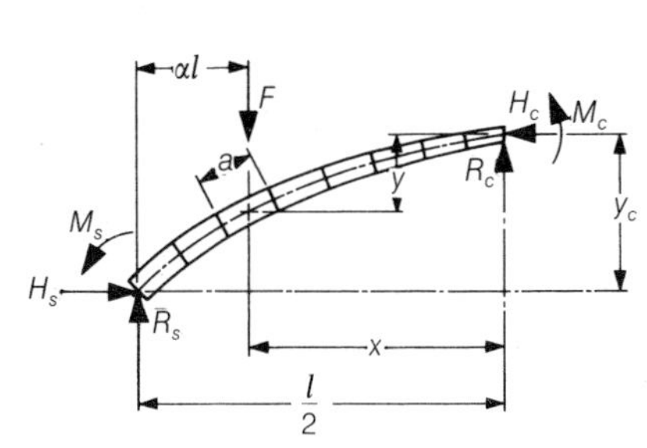
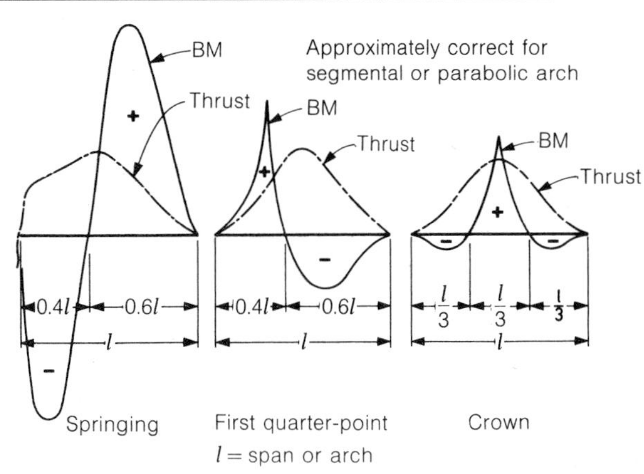

T rise or fall of temperature
λ coefficient of linear expansion per degree C

General formulae

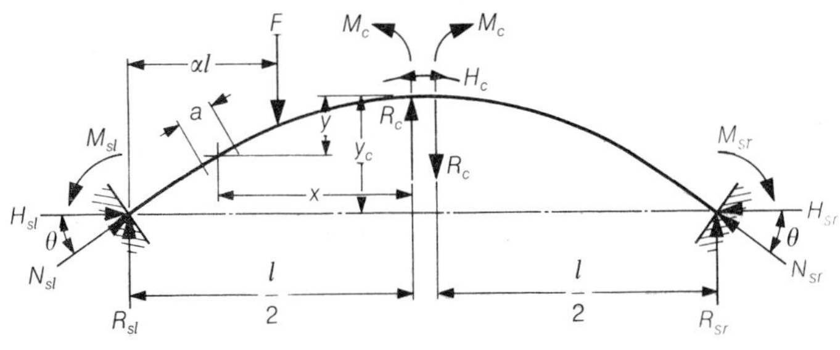

$$M_f = [x - l(\tfrac{1}{2} - \alpha)]F$$
$$a_I = a/I$$
$$a_A = a/A$$

Load F on left-hand side: $H_c = \dfrac{\Sigma a_I \Sigma M_f y a_I - \Sigma y a_I \Sigma M_f a_I}{2[\Sigma a_I \Sigma y^2 a_I - (\Sigma y a_I)^2]}$ $\quad M_c = \dfrac{\Sigma M_f a_I - 2H_c \Sigma y a_I}{2\Sigma a_I}$ $\quad R_c = \dfrac{\Sigma M_f x a_I}{2\Sigma x^2 a_I}$

Temperature and shrinkage: $H_{c2} = \dfrac{(\pm T)\lambda l E_c \Sigma a_I}{2[\Sigma a_I \Sigma y^2 a_I - (\Sigma y a_I)^2]}$ $\quad M_{c2} = -\dfrac{H_{c2}\Sigma y a_I}{\Sigma a_I}$

Arch shortening: $H_{c1} = -\dfrac{\Sigma a_A \Sigma a_I (H_c + H_{c2})}{\Sigma a_I \Sigma y^2 a_I - (\Sigma y a_I)^2}$ $\quad M_{c1} = -\dfrac{H_{c1}\Sigma y a_I}{\Sigma a_I}$

Summations are taken over left-hand half of arch: note that summations involving M_f include only segments within αl.

At crown: net thrust $H_c^* = H_c + H_{c1} + H_{c2}$ (note signs of H and M)
net bending moment $M_c^* = M_c + M_{c1} + M_{c2}$

At springings: $M_{sl} = M_c^* + H_c^* y_c + \tfrac{1}{2} l R_c - F\alpha l$ $\quad R_{sl} = F - R_c$
$M_{sr} = M_c^* + H_c^* y_c - \tfrac{1}{2} l R_c$ $\quad R_{sr} = R_c$; $H_{sl} = H_{sr} = H_c^*$
$N_{sl} = H_{sl}\cos\theta + R_{sl}\sin\theta$ $\quad N_{sr} = H_{sr}\cos\theta + R_{sr}\sin\theta$

At any section x_q from crown: in left-hand half: $M_q = M_c^* + H_c^* y_q + R_c x_q - F[x_q - l(\tfrac{1}{2} - \alpha)]$
(include term for F only if within x_q)
$H_q = H_c^*$ $\quad R_q = R_c - F$
in right-hand half: $M_{qr} = M_c^* + H_c^* y_q - R_c x_q$ $\quad H_{qr} = H_c^*$ $\quad R_{qr} = R_c$

Note: for an explanation of the approximate method of determining the size of a fixed arch, see section 17.2.1.

Chapter 18
Concrete and reinforcement

18.1 PROPERTIES OF CONCRETE

18.1.1 Compressive strength

The compressive strengths f_{cu} of concretes made with the same cement and cured and tested under the same conditions have been shown by Feret to comply approximately with the expression

$$f_{cu} = \alpha_1 \left(\frac{B_c}{B_c + B_w + B_v} \right)^2$$

in which B_c, B_w and B_v are respectively the net volumes of cement, water and voids in a unit volume of mixed concrete; i.e. if B_a is the net volume of aggregate in a unit volume of mixed concrete, $B_c + B_a + B_w + B_v = 1$. The coefficient α_1 is a numerical factor determined from tests and depends on the nature of the materials.

18.1.2 Tensile strength

The ratio of the direct tensile strength f_{cut} to the compressive strength f_{cu} varies from 0.05 to more than 0.1, the relation being very approximately of the form $f_{cut} = \alpha_2 (f_{cu})^\beta$, where β is between 0.5 and 1. A formula derived by Feret is $f_{cut} = \alpha_3 \sqrt{(f_{cu})} - \alpha_4$. Coefficients α_3 and α_4 are obtained by testing and depend on the nature of the cement, the type, grading and maximum size of aggregate, the amount of water, the conditions of curing, and the method of testing employed.

The draft Unified Code (ref. 77) gives values of indirect tensile strength at 28 days for concretes having various crushing strengths. These correspond approximately to the expression

$$\text{indirect tensile strength} = \frac{2}{3} + \frac{f_{cu}}{15} - \frac{f_{cu}^2}{2600}$$

A very simple approximate relationship which has been suggested (ref. 75) is

$$\text{indirect tensile strength} = 0.5\sqrt{f_{cu}}$$

18.1.3 Flexural strength (modulus of rupture)

For the values obtained for various concretes to be comparable, the test pieces must be of standard dimensions, say $100 \times 100 \times 400$ mm or $4 \times 4 \times 16$ in. If such a specimen is supported over a span of 300 mm or 12 in with a centrally applied load, the modulus of rupture $f_{cur} = 0.004\,25F$ N/mm^2 or $0.281\,25F$ lb/in^2, where F is the load in kg or lb that causes the test piece to break. Factors that contribute to a high compressive strength f_{cu} also lead to an increase in the modulus of rupture. The relation of f_{cur} to f_{cu} is given by Feret as approximately

$$f_{cur} = \alpha_5 \sqrt{(f_{cu})} - \alpha_6$$

where α_5 and α_6 are parameters affected by the same conditions that affect α_3 and α_4 for direct tensile strength.

Data for estimating the flexural strength f_{cuf} at 28 days from a specified crushing strength given in the draft Unified Code correspond closely to the relationship

$$f_{cuf} = \frac{1}{2} + \frac{f_{cu}}{10} - \frac{f_{cu}^2}{2000}$$

The flexural strength of a concrete is about 1.5 times the cylinder splitting strength.

18.1.4 Modulus of elasticity

The modulus of elasticity of concrete E_c increases with increases in cement content, age, repetition of stress and various other factors, actual values ranging between 500 and 1600 times the compressive strength. Thus E_c for a 1:2:4 concrete may average 24 kN/mm^2 or 3.5×10^6 lb/in^2.

For serviceability limit-state calculation purposes, ranges of probable values for the short-term static modulus of elasticity E_c corresponding to various values of f_{cu}, for use if actual experimental values are not available, are given in BS8110: Part 2 and CP110 on which the mean curve and range (shaded area) for normal-weight concrete shown on *Table 79* are based. Both mean and range values differ between documents. The BS8110 mean values are calculated from the expression

$$E_c = 20 + f_{cu}/5$$

The BS8110 values relate specifically to the elastic modulus at 28 days, but the value at any age t can be assessed from the expression

Arches: fixed parabolic arches

Type		Uniform dead load				Open spandrel				Solid spandrel			
Rise/span		0.10	0.15	0.20	0.25	0.10	0.15	0.20	0.25	0.10	0.15	0.20	0.25
Inclination of axis of arch at springing: cos θ		0.930	0.848	0.781	0.709	0.918	0.820	0.740	0.650	0.893	0.764	0.665	0.565
Horizontal thrust due to dead load: values of k_1	—	0.125	0.125	0.125	0.125	0.135	0.140	0.144	0.148	0.160	0.176	0.190	0.204
Horizontal thrust due to arch shortening: values of k_2	h_s/h												
	1.25	1.10	1.07	1.03	0.99	1.13	1.08	1.03	1.00	1.19	1.13	1.08	1.00
	1.50	1.42	1.37	1.32	1.25	1.44	1.39	1.33	1.27	1.53	1.48	1.42	1.33
	1.75	1.68	1.63	1.58	1.53	1.73	1.68	1.63	1.58	1.86	1.82	1.76	1.69
Moments due to arch shortening, temperature change and eccentricity of thrust: values of k_3	1.25	0.284	0.293	0.300	0.307	0.279	0.280	0.281	0.282	0.255	0.261	0.265	0.270
	1.50	0.248	0.253	0.258	0.263	0.240	0.243	0.247	0.251	0.224	0.226	0.228	0.230
	1.75	0.223	0.227	0.231	0.235	0.218	0.220	0.222	0.224	0.200	0.200	0.200	0.200
Horizontal force due to temperature change: values of k_4	1.25	321	305	293	280	326	311	294	276	343	319	300	274
	1.50	432	413	396	380	441	422	401	381	472	448	422	394
	1.75	538	518	497	477	552	532	510	484	592	566	542	520
Horizontal thrusts due to imposed load	k_6	0.059	0.059	0.059	0.059	0.062	0.064	0.065	0.066	0.070	0.074	0.077	0.080
	k_8	0.039	0.039	0.039	0.039	0.038	0.038	0.037	0.037	0.037	0.035	0.033	0.032
	k_{11}	0.086	0.086	0.086	0.086	0.088	0.089	0.090	0.092				
	h_s/h												
	1.25									0.093	0.097	0.098	0.100
	1.50									0.095	0.098	0.101	0.103
	1.75									0.097	0.100	0.104	0.106
Vertical reactions due to imposed load	k_9	0.358	0.358	0.358	0.358	0.354	0.352	0.350	0.349	0.342	0.337	0.330	0.321
	k_{12}	0.149	0.149	0.149	0.149	0.150	0.151	0.153	0.155	0.160	0.164	0.170	0.177
Bending moments due to imposed load: Values of $k_5 \times 10^4$	h_s/h												
	1.25	48	49	51	52	52	54	57	60	60	69	77	84
	1.50	45	46	46	47	48	50	52	54	56	62	68	75
	1.75	42	43	43	44	44	46	48	50	52	58	63	68
Bending moments due to imposed load: Values of k_7	1.25	0.019	0.019	0.018	0.018	0.018	0.018	0.017	0.017	0.017	0.015	0.014	0.014
	1.50	0.021	0.021	0.020	0.020	0.020	0.020	0.019	0.018	0.018	0.017	0.016	0.015
	1.75	0.022	0.022	0.022	0.022	0.022	0.021	0.020	0.020	0.020	0.018	0.017	0.016
Bending moments due to imposed load: Values of k_{10}	1.25	0.019	0.019	0.018	0.018	0.020	0.021	0.021	0.021	0.024	0.025	0.025	0.026
	1.50	0.021	0.020	0.020	0.020	0.022	0.023	0.023	0.023	0.026	0.027	0.028	0.028
	1.75	0.022	0.022	0.022	0.022	0.024	0.025	0.025	0.025	0.029	0.030	0.031	0.031

Note: see section 17.3 for formulae in which coefficients k_1, k_2 etc. should be substituted, as shown in the example in that section.

$$E = E_c(2 + 3f_{cut}/f_{cu28})/5$$

If actual values of the dynamic elastic modulus E_{cq} can be obtained for the concrete in question, E_c may be estimated from these figures by using the relation (in kN/mm^2)

$$E_c = (5E_{cq}/4) - 19$$

proposed for normal-weight concrete in both Codes: this relationship does *not* apply to lightweight-aggregate concrete. Both Codes state that the value obtained from this expression will generally be within $4\,kN/mm^2$ of the true value. CP110 also suggests a method of obtaining values of E_c for lightweight-aggregate concrete by multiplying the values given therein for normal-weight mixes by $189 \times 10^{-9}D_c^2$, where D_c is the density of the mix in kg/m^3. This relation forms the basis of the curves on the chart for values of D_c of from 1400 to $2200\,kg/m^3$. The corresponding relationship suggested in Part 2 of BS8110 requires the value of elastic modulus obtained for the equivalent normal-weight concrete to be multiplied by $174 \times 10^{-9}D_c^2$. These values are indicated on the appropriate chart on *Table 79*. The expressions provided in BS8110 are derived from BRS research described in ref. 76.

When combined with a modulus of elasticity for steel E_s of $200\,kN/mm^2$ or $30 \times 10^6\,lb/in^2$, a modular ratio ($\alpha = E_s/E_c$) of 8.5 is obtained. The generally accepted arbitrary value for the modular ratio is now taken as 15 (i.e. corresponding to a fixed value E_c of $14\,kN/mm^2$ or $2 \times 10^6\,lb/in^2$) for concretes of all proportions, and is recommended in BS8110 in the absence of better information (although a value of α_e of 30 was suggested in CP114 for stiffness calculations when lightweight-aggregate concrete is used). This fixed ratio compensates in part for the errors involved in considering reinforced concrete as a theoretically elastic substance, and for the neglect of any tensile resistance of the concrete in bending. The modular ratio applies within only the range of service stresses and plays no part in ultimate limit-state or load-factor design.

When calculating sectional properties etc. for serviceability limit-state calculations for BS8110 and CP110, the modular ratio should be determined by dividing the elastic modulus for steel of $200\,kN/mm^2$ by one-half of the value of E_c corresponding to the grade of concrete being used: see *Table 79*. (The factor of one-half is introduced to cater for creep.) For long-term calculations of deflections, additional allowance for creep must be made when calculating the modular ratio: see *Table 79*.

With BS5337, the same procedure applies if limit-state design is being undertaken. For the concrete grades 25 and 30 permitted for reinforced concrete construction, the corresponding modular ratios are thus 15.4 and 14.3 respectively. The use of a constant value of 15 often simplifies the calculations and introduces no significant error. For the alternative (i.e. elastic-strain) design method, a constant value of α_e of 15 is specified.

18.1.5 Creep and shrinkage

Some notes on creep and shrinkage are given in sections 4.2.6 and 4.2.7.

18.1.6 Poisson's ratio

Poisson's ratio v, which enables the secondary stress that occurs normal to and as a result of a primary stress to be calculated, has a value of 0.15 to 0.3 for concrete, although in many cases this effect can safely be ignored. For example, CP114 suggested the assumption of $v = 0$ when undertaking purely theoretical elastic analyses of two-way slabs. For serviceability calculations, BS8110 and CP110 recommend the adoption of a value of 0.2. Tests on lightweight concretes have given values of 0.18 to 0.22. The omission of a consideration of Poisson's ratio affects the calculated stresses in ordinary slabs spanning in two directions (more seriously where the panels are almost square) and the analyses of the stresses in shells and in road slabs.

18.1.7 Temperature coefficients

The coefficient of linear expansion and contraction due to temperature change increases with an increase in the cement content and depends on the type of aggregate employed, varying from 7 to 12×10^{-6} per °C (4 to 7×10^{-6} per °F). A coefficient of 10×10^{-6} per °C (5.5×10^{-6} per °F), which is about the same as that of mild steel, is commonly used.

18.1.8 Thermal conductivity

The average value of thermal conductivity k of normal-weight 1:2:4 gravel concrete at normal temperatures is 1.44 watts per metre per °C difference in temperature between the two faces. The corresponding imperial value is 10 British thermal unit inches per square foot per hour per °F (where $1\,W/m°C = 6.93\,Btu\,in/ft^2$ hour °F). Corresponding values for various types of lightweight concrete are given in *Table 80*.

18.1.9 Fire resistance

According to BS8110, CP110 and similar documents, the resistance to fire of reinforced concrete construction depends primarily on the type of aggregate, the thickness of the various parts comprising the member, and the cover of concrete over the reinforcement, and is expressed by the number of hours of effective fire resistance, as established by tests made in accordance with BS476 'Fire tests on building materials and structures'. The material embodied in CP110 is extensive and the data presented in *Table 82* summarize the principal details relating to normal-weight concrete made with siliceous or calcareous aggregate.

Since the publication of these documents, a joint committee of the Institution of Structural Engineers and The Concrete Society has produced ref. 78, which takes account of more recent research in both the UK and elsewhere. The aim of this report is to encourage the design of structures that behave in a stable manner when exposed to fire, from the early stages of cracking and local damage, through the yielding of the reinforcement, to the occurrence of large displacements including suspension effects. The report emphasizes the importance of accepting and anticipating the local damage that will probably occur during the early stages of heating and recommends that the reinforcement is suitably anchored to resist this.

Arches: computation chart for fixed arch

CALCULATION CHART FOR FIXED-ENDED SYMMETRICAL ARCH

Dimensional properties													Unit load at A (crown)				Unit load at B				Unit load at C etc.		
Seg. no.	x	y	h_x	a	A	I_x	$a_I = a/I$	$a_I x$	$a_I x^2$	$a_I y$	$a_I y^2$	$a_A = a/A$	M_f $(=x)$	$M_f a_I$ $= a_I x$	$M_f a_I x$ $= a_I x^2$	$M_f a_I y$ $= a_I xy$	M_f	$M_f a_I$	$M_f a_I x$	$M_f a_I y$	C	D	E
																					Sub-headings as B		
1	√	√	√	√	√	√	√	√	√	√	√	√	√	—	—	√	—	—	—	—	—	—	—
2	√	√	√	√	√	√	√	√	√	√	√	√	√	—	—	√	√	√	√	√	—	—	—
3	√	√	√	√	√	√	√	√	√	√	√	√	√	—	—	√	√	√	√	√	√		—
4	√	√	√	√	√	√	√	√	√	√	√	√	√	—	—	√	√	√	√	√	√	√	—
5 etc.	√	√	√	√	√	√	√	√	√	√	√	√	√	—	—	√	√	√	√	√	√	√	√
Summations on left-hand half of arch						$\sum_0^{0.5l} =$	S_s	S_{1A}	S_{2A}	S_{sy}	S_{sy2}	S_{sA}		S_{1A}	S_{2A}	S_{3A}	$\sum_0^{\alpha l} =$	S_{1B}	S_{2B}	S_{3B}	Totals similar to B		

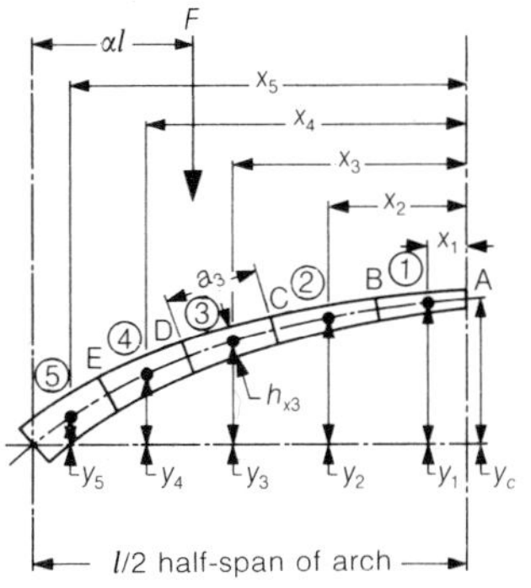

F
αl
x_5 x_4 x_3 x_2 x_1
a_3
E ④ D ③ C ② B ① A
⑤
h_{x3}
y_5 y_4 y_3 y_2 y_1 y_c
$l/2$ half-span of arch

Denominator (den.)
$$= (S_s \times S_{sy2}) - (S_{sy})^2$$

Horizontal thrust at crown
$$H_c = \frac{(S_s \times S_3) - (S_{sy} \times S_1)}{2 \times \text{denominator}}$$

Bending moment at crown
$$M_c = \frac{S_1 - (2H_c \times S_{sy})}{2S_s}$$

Shearing force at crown and springing
$R_c = S_2/2S_{2A}$: $R_s = 1 - R_c$

Ordinates of influence lines

Unit load at		A (crown) $\alpha = 0.5$	B $(\alpha = \surd)$	C $(\alpha = \surd)$	D etc. $(\alpha = \surd)$
1	$S_s \times S_3$	√	√	√	√
2	$S_{sy} \times S_1$	√	√	√	√
3	(1)–(2)	√	√	√	√
4	$H_c = (3)/(2 \times \text{den.})$	√	√	√	√
5	$2(4) \times S_{sy}$	√	√	√	√
6	$S_1 - (5)$	√	√	√	√
7	$M_c = (6)/2S_s$	√	√	√	√
8	$R_c = S_2/(2S_{2A})$	√	√	√	√
9	$R_s = 1 - (8)$	√	√	√	√
10	(4) or H_{c2}	√	√	√	√
11	$(10) \times S_{sA} \times S_s$	√	√	√	√
12	$H_{c1} = -(11)/\text{den.}$	√	√	√	√
13	$M_{c1} = -(12) \times S_{sy}/S_s$	√	√	√	√
14	$[(4) - (12)] \times y_c$	√	√	√	√
15	$(7) - (13)$	√	√	√	√
16	$(14) + (15)$	√	√	√	√
17	$\frac{1}{2}l \times (8)$	√	√	√	√
18	$M_{sl} = (16) + (17) - F\alpha l$	√	√	√	√
19	$M_{sr} = (16) - (17)$	√	√	√	√

Temperature and shrinkage
$$H_{c2} = \pm \frac{T\lambda l E_c S_s}{2 \times \text{denominator}}$$
$$M_{c2} = -H_{c2} S_{sy}/S_s$$

Arch shortening:
Horizontal thrust at crown
$$H_{c1} = -\frac{S_{sA} \times S_s \times (H_c \text{ or } H_{c2})}{\text{denominator}}$$
BM at crown
$$M_{c1} = -H_{c1} S_{sy}/S_s$$

Bending moments at springings:
Left-hand support: $M_{sl} = M_c^* + H_c^* y_c + R_c \frac{1}{2}l - F\alpha l$
Right-hand support: $M_{sr} = M_c^* + H_c^* y_c - R_c \frac{1}{2}l - M_f$
(M_f is zero when load is on left-hand half of arch)
$H_c^* = H_c - (H_{c1}$ due to $H_c)$
$M_c^* = M_c - (M_{c1}$ for H_{c1} due to $H_c)$

Bending moment at quarter-point: repeat similar to foregoing with corresponding formulae

Dead loads (effects calculated from influence lines)

Segment	Loads			At crown								M_{sl} at springing				Quarter point	Imposed loads
	Arch: $24 \times 10^3 \times ah_x$	Fill and other dead load	Total dead load ($\frac{1}{2}$ arch)	H_c		H_{c1}		M_c		M_{c1}		LH segments		RH segments			
				Ordinate	Product	Ordinate	Product	Ordinate	Product	Ordinate	Product	Ordinate	Product	Ordinate	Product	Repeat for M_q	Maximum thrusts, shearing forces and bending moments due to imposed loads are calculated from the influence lines for the most adverse position of loads.
1	√	√	√	√	√	√	√	√	√	√	√	√	√	√	√		
2	√	√	√	√	√	√	√	√	√	√	√	√	√	√	√		
3	√	√	√	√	√	√	√	√	√	√	√	√	√	√	√		
4	√	√	√	√	√	√	√	√	√	√	√	√	√	√	√		
5 etc.	√	√	√	√	√	√	√	√	√	√	√	√	√	√	√		
		$\Sigma =$	F_g	$\Sigma H_c =$	√	$\Sigma H_{c1} =$	√	$\Sigma M_c =$	√	$\Sigma M_{c1} =$	√	$\Sigma M_{sl} =$	√	$\Sigma M_{sr} =$	√		
$R_s = F_g$ $R_c = 0$				Total $H_c^* = 2(\Sigma H_c - \Sigma H_{c1}) =$ √				Total $M_c^* = 2(\Sigma M_c - \Sigma M_{c1}) =$ √				Net $M_s = \Sigma M_{sl} \pm \Sigma M_{sr} =$ √					

Resultant thrusts, bending moments and shearing forces due to dead and imposed loads are calculated by substituting in formulae.

Note: Factors in this chart are non-dimensional except for weight of segments. If dimensions are in feet, substitute $150ah_x$ for $24 \times 10^3 ah_x$. See also section 3.16.

For most structures where the fire resistance periods required are not excessive, the above objectives can be achieved simply by proportioning the members suitably and detailing them carefully. In such cases compliance with the requirements of the report can be achieved by observing specified minimum dimensions and cover thicknesses: details of these basic requirements are summarized on *Table 84*. Alternatively, the document describes an analytical procedure which may be used to demonstrate the appropriateness of alternative designs, or actual fire-resistance tests may be undertaken instead.

BS8110 provides (in Section 4 of Part 2) extensive information concerning fire resistance. Three methods of determining the resistance of an individual element or combination of elements are described: (1) the use of tabulated data derived from Building Research Establishment work (ref. 147) and supplemented by international test data; (2) the results of fire-resistance tests; and (3) a calculation method (inapplicable to columns, walls etc.). The tabulated data in BS8110: Part 2, from which the information presented in *Table 81* has been summarized, has also been used to produce the shortened and simplified data relating to dense-aggregate concrete only, which forms clause 3.3.6 of BS8110: Part 1.

The degree of resistance required depends on the size of a building and on the use to which it is to be put, and is specified in many by-laws. For example, Part E of the Building Regulations 1976 deals with structural fire precautions. In this document eight separate types of usage (designated as purpose groups, PGs) are recognized. For each purpose group, maximum limits to the floor area of each individual storey, to the height and to the cubic capacity are specified. If the overall values relating to the building being considered exceed any of these limits, the structure must be subdivided into *compartments*, each individual compartment being separated from its fellows by walls or floors or both that have the required periods of fire resistance. Note that groups PG1 and PG4 have no corresponding size limits.

Details of the minimum periods of fire resistance corresponding to the limiting dimensions in each purpose group are summarized in *Table 83*: for further details reference must be made to the Building Regulations themselves.

18.1.10 Lightweight concretes

A wide range of lightweight concretes of various types, with densities of from below 300 kg/m^3 or 19 lb/ft^3 upwards, can now be obtained. Brief details of the principal materials employed and the range of unit weight, compressive strength, thermal conductivity and elastic modulus that may be achieved, are summarized in *Table 80*; for more detailed information reference should be made to specialist literature. Additional data on unit weight are given on *Table 2*.

Both BS8110 and CP110 give specific information regarding those matters where the design of structural lightweight-aggregate concrete differs from that of normal-weight concrete; such data are summarized in the related design sections of this book.

18.2 STRESSES IN CONCRETE

18.2.1 Design strengths

When using the limit-state method of design as embodied in BS8110 and CP110, the concrete grade, which represents the numerical value (in N/mm^2) of the characteristic compressive strength of the mix as determined by 28 day cube tests, is used directly in all design calculations involving the compressive strength of the material. For details of the relationship between the value of concrete grade and the ultimate resistances of the mix in shearing and torsion, with or without appropriate reinforcement, and in bond, reference should be made to the tables concerned. For example, see *Table 143* for the ultimate shearing and torsional resistances of normal-weight and lightweight concrete and *Table 92* for the ultimate local- and average-bond strengths of normal-weight and lightweight concrete. Other design data relating to mixes emanating from BS8110 and CP110 (e.g. the increase of strength with age, the relationship between strength and elastic modulus etc.) are included on *Table 79*.

18.2.2 Slender members

To ensure lateral stability, both BS8110 and CP110 set limits to the ratio of the clear distance between lateral restraints l_r to the dimensions of the section. For a freely supported or continuous beam l_r should not exceed $60b_c$ if b_c/d exceeds 0.24, or $250b_c^2/d$ otherwise, where b_c is the breadth of the compression face midway between restraints. For a cantilever restrained at the support only, l_r should not exceed $25b_c$ if b_c/d exceeds 0.25, or $100b_c^2/d$ otherwise. Beams carrying any axial load should be considered as columns and, if the slenderness ratio exceeds the permissible limit for short columns, the additional-moment design technique outlined in sections 22.4.1 and 22.4.2 should be employed. For upstand beams the *Code Handbook* recommends that slabs attached to the tensile zone provide effective lateral restraint if $h_f \nless 0.1d$ and $h - h_f \ngtr 10b$, where b, d and h relate to the upstand beam (h_f is the flange thickness).

18.3 BOND

This section gives BS8110 and CP110 requirements for bond.

18.3.1 Anchorage bond

To ensure adequate end anchorage, the bond stress obtained by dividing the force in a bar by the contact area between the concrete and reinforcement (given by the effective bar perimeter multiplied by the effective anchorage length) must not exceed empirical limiting values. Thus for tension reinforcement (and compression according to BS8110)

$$f_{bsa} \leqslant \frac{f_y}{\gamma_m} \frac{\pi\phi^2}{4} \frac{1}{\pi\phi l}$$

where f_{bsa} is the limiting ultimate anchorage-bond stress and l is the effective anchorage length. Rearranging this expression gives

$$l/\phi \geqslant 0.217 f_y/f_{bsa}$$

Concrete: properties per BS8110 and CP110

Increase of strength with time (both Codes)

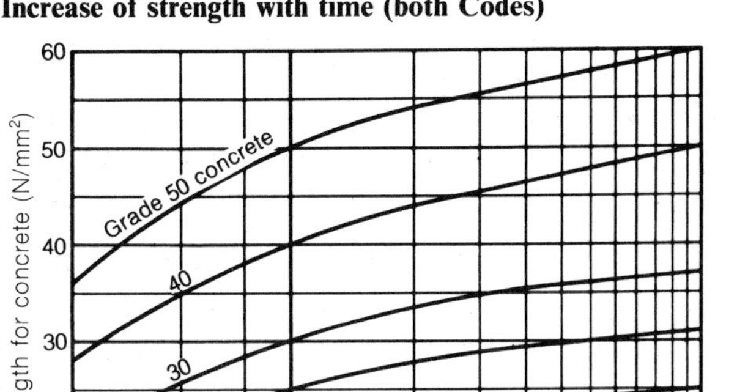

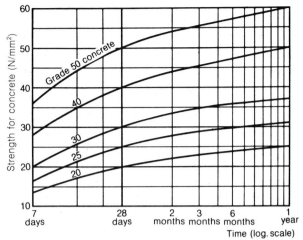

Coefficient ρ_0 (CP110)

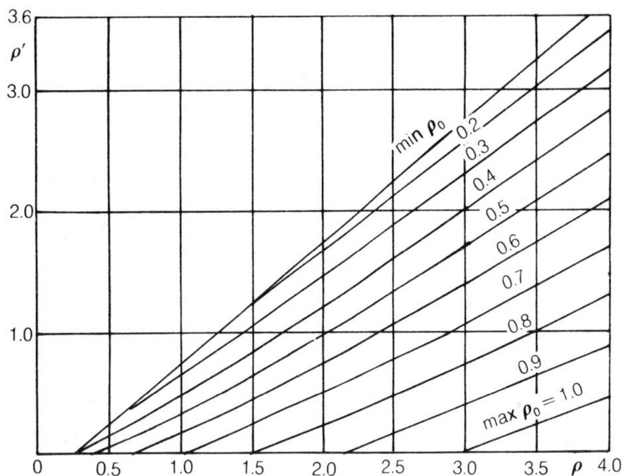

Creep coefficients (BS8110)

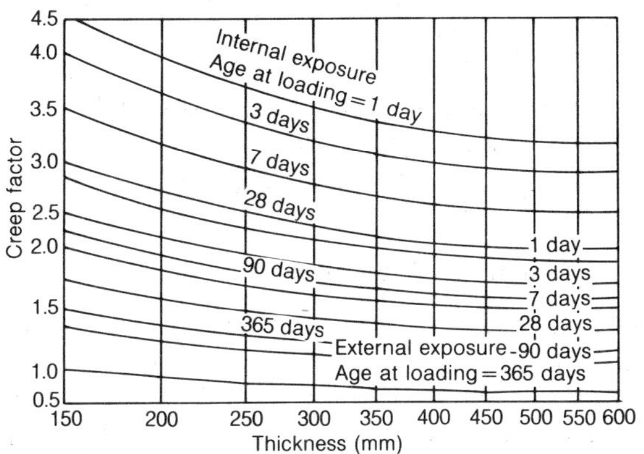

Creep multiplier (CP110)

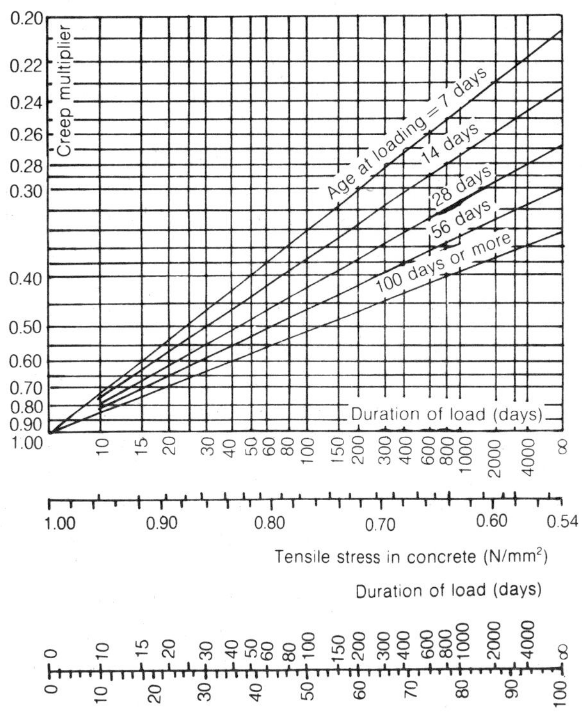

Shrinkage coefficients (BS8110)

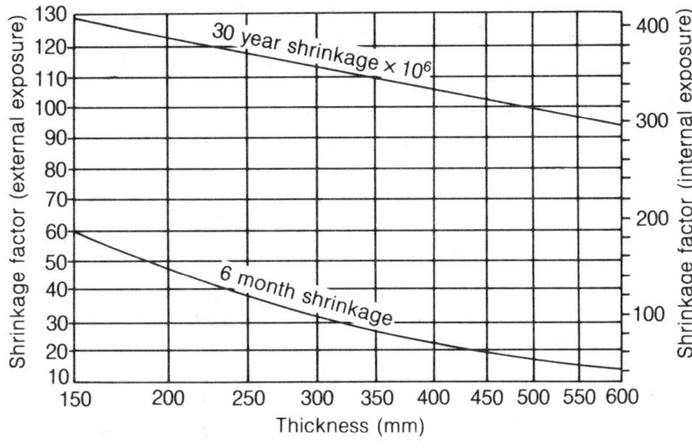

Variation of modulus of elasticity with strength and density of concrete

BS8110 recommendations

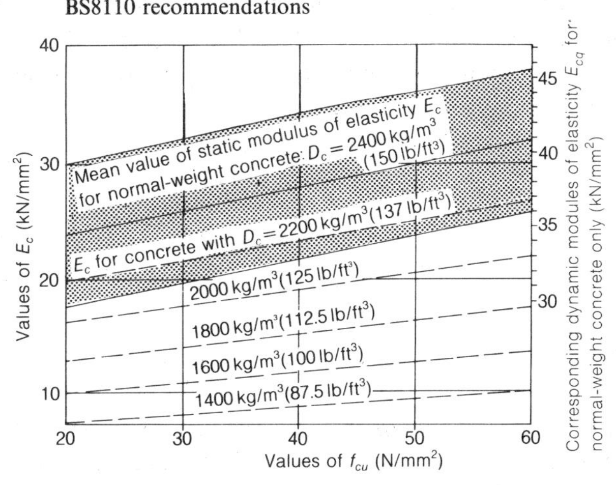

CP110 recommendations

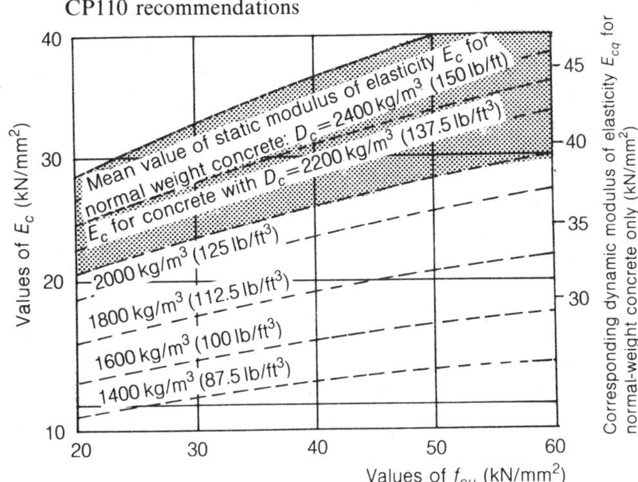

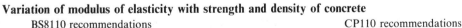

For bars in compression according to CP110

$$f_{bsa} \leqslant \frac{2000 f_y}{2000\gamma_m + f_y} \frac{\pi\phi^2}{4} \frac{1}{\pi\phi l}$$

which can be rearranged as

$$l/\phi \geqslant 500 f_y/[f_{bsa}(2300 + f_y)]$$

The values on the chart on *Table 92* give limiting ratios of l/ϕ corresponding to the grade of dense-aggregate concrete and the type of reinforcement employed. The BS8110 values are calculated from the equation and coefficients given in clause 3.12.8.4 of this Code, while those relating to CP110 have been prepared by fitting a first-degree curve to the values given in this document, by means of least-squares methods.

These lengths are derived on the assumption that the stresses in the bars at the point from which the anchorage-bond length is being measured are equal to the maximum possible values of f_{yd1} and f_{yd2} respectively. If the maximum stress at this point is less, then the bond length provided may be reduced accordingly, but care should be taken to ensure that the Code requirements regarding detailing are met.

Both Codes require account to be taken of the reduction in anchorage provided when groups of bars are in contact. BS8110 states that where two or more bars are in contact, a single 'effective size' bar should be considered having an area equal to the sum of the areas of the bars in contact. Thus four 16 mm bars in contact would require the same anchorage bond length as one 32 mm bar.

According to CP110, if groups of up to four bars are used, the effective perimeter of each group in withstanding bond stress may be found by multiplying the sum of the individual bar perimeters by a factor $0.2(6-j)$, where j is the number of bars in the group. If all the bars are of the same size the effects of this reduction may for simplicity be considered instead by simply increasing the diameter of the bars to $\phi/(1.2-0.2j)$. Thus, with a group of three 12 mm bars, an anchorage-bond length equal to that required for a 20 mm bar should be provided for each bar forming the group.

The bond resistance of lightweight-aggregate concrete is appreciably less than that of normal-weight concrete, and CP110 recommends the adoption of anchorage-bond stresses of 0.5 and 0.8 times those for normal-weight concrete with plain and with deformed bars respectively, the values for grade 15 concrete being taken as 80% of those for grade 20 concrete. BS8110 recommends values of 80% of those for normal-weight concrete throughout. These assumptions have been used to obtain the appropriate values for lightweight concrete on *Table 92*.

Both Codes recognize two types of deformed bars. Plain twisted-square or chamfered-square bars having a pitch of twist not exceeding eighteen times the nominal size are classified as type 1: bars having transverse ribs spaced at not more than $4\phi/5$ and with the requisite mean area specified by the Code are of type 2. When the latter are used, ultimate anchorage-bond stresses are permitted that are 25% greater than those allowed for type 1 bars according to BS8110 and 30% greater according to CP110. Performance tests may be used to classify other forms of deformed bars as type 1 or type 2.

The anchorage length determined in the foregoing may be reduced by providing hooks or bobs at the ends of bars. The effective anchorage distance provided by such a bend (measured from the start of bending to a point 4ϕ beyond the end) is the lesser of 24ϕ or $8r$ for a semi-circular hook and the lesser of 24ϕ or $4r$ for a right-angled bob, where ϕ is the bar diameter and r is the internal radius of the bend. Since the actual length of bar needed for a semi-circular hook is $\pi r + 4\phi$, if $r = 3\phi$, the actual reduction in the length of bar necessary if a semi-circular hook is provided is 10ϕ; if r is greater or less than 3ϕ this saving is reduced. However, if the bar carries stress beyond the bend, the bearing stress inside the bend must not exceed the limiting value indicated below and this further criterion places an additional restriction on the radius of bend required.

The actual bond lengths in millimetres according to BS8110 and CP110 requirements are given on *Tables 93* and *94* respectively for four commonly used grades of normal-weight concrete, for mild-steel and high-yield bars of various sizes. The lengths have been rounded to the 5 mm dimension above the exact length required. The lengths are given for straight bars and also for bars with right-angled bobs and semi-circular hooks having internal radii of 2ϕ and 3ϕ for mild-steel and high-yield bars respectively.

18.3.2 Bearing inside bends

In bars that are stressed beyond a distance of 4ϕ past the end of a bend, the stress within the bend is given by $F_{bt}/r\phi$, where F_{bt} is the tensile force in the bar (i.e. area of bar × actual stress in bar) and for normal-weight concrete must not exceed $kf_{cu}/(1 + 2\phi/a_b)$, where a_b is the distance between bar centres perpendicular to the plane of bending. According to BS8110, for normal-weight concrete $k = 2$; CP110 proposes a value of k of 1.5. Near a surface, $a_b = \phi$ plus cover. If a bundle of bars is used, ϕ is the size of a bar of equivalent area. Thus if $F_{bt} = (\pi\phi^2/4)f_y/1.15$,

$$\frac{\pi\phi^2 f_y}{4.6r\phi} \leqslant \frac{kf_{cu}}{1 + 2\phi/a_b}$$

or

$$\frac{a_b}{\phi} \geqslant 2\Big/\left[\frac{4.6k}{\pi}\left(\frac{r}{\phi}\right)\frac{f_{cu}}{f_y} - 1\right]$$

Values of r/ϕ corresponding to given ratios of a_b/ϕ and f_{cu}/f_y are plotted on the charts on *Table 95*, thus enabling a suitable radius of bend to be determined quickly.

For lightweight concrete, $k = 4/3$ according to BS8110 and $k = 1$ according to CP110. Appropriate values of r/ϕ corresponding to this condition are also plotted on the chart on *Table 95*.

18.3.3 Local bond

According to CP110, the local-bond stress that results from rapid variations in tensile stress over short distances is given by the expression

$$f_{bs} = \left(V \pm \frac{M}{d}\tan\theta_s\right)\frac{1}{d\sum u_s}$$

where V is the ultimate shearing force, M is the ultimate moment, d is the effective depth, θ_s is the angle between top

Concrete: typical properties of lightweight concretes

Type	Principal aggregate	Density		28 day cube strength	
		kg/m^3	lb/ft^3	N/mm^2	lb/in^2
Insulating lightweight aggregate concrete	vermiculite	400–560	25–35	0.70–1.23	100–175
	perlite	400–640	25–40	1.40–4.83	200–690
	wood particles	640–1200	40–75	1.75–12.25	250–1750
Structural lightweight aggregate concrete	Leca	1000–1500	65–95	7.0–16.0	1000–2250
	Aglite	1600–1700	100–105	21.0–31.5	3000–4500
	Solite	1600–1650	100–105	21.0–42.0	3000–6000
	Lytag	1600–1800	100–115	21.0–31.5	3000–4500
	foamed slag	1800–2000	115–125	16.0–31.5	2250–4500
Autoclaved aerated concrete		400–880	25–55	1.80–6.00*	250–850*
Foamed cast *in situ* concrete		290–1440	18–90	0.50–9.80	60–1400
Aerated lightweight-aggregate concrete		800–1280	50–80	8.4–28.0	1200–4000
No-fines concrete		1900–2000	120–125	7.0–14.5	1000–2100

Type	Principal aggregate	Thermal conductivity k		Modulus of elasticity	
		W/m °C	Btu in/ft^{2}h °F	MN/mm^2	lb/in^2 × 10^{-6}
Insulating lightweight aggregate concrete	vermiculite	0.094–0.158	0.65–1.10		
	perlite	0.098–0.155	0.67–1.08		
	wood particles	0.202–0.288	1.40–2.00		
Structural lightweight aggregate concrete	Leca	0.288–0.591	200–4.10	0.011–0.018	1.5–2.5
	Aglite	0.461–0.663	3.20–4.60	0.014–0.018	2.0–2.5
	Solite			0.011–0.018	1.5–2.5
	Lytag	0.562–0.721	3.90–5.00	0.014–0.018	2.0–2.5
	foamed slag	0.534–0.620	3.70–4.30	0.014–0.021	2.0–3.0
Autoclaved aerated concrete		0.120–0.210	0.80–1.50	0.0012–0.0032†	0.17–0.45†
Foamed cast *in situ* concrete		0.080–0.550	0.60–3.80	0.0014–0.0098	0.2–1.4
Aerated lightweight-aggregate concrete		0.170–0.330	1.20–2.30	0.0032–0.0180	0.45–2.50
No-fines concrete		0.860–0.940	6.00–6.50		

* Saturated compressive strengths

† Corresponding to density values of 400 to 800 kg/m^3

Data compiled from Nesbit, J.K. (1966) Structural lightweight-aggregate concrete. London, Concrete Publications Ltd. and Nesbit, J.K. (1970) An introduction to lightweight concrete. London, Cement and Concrete Association, 4th edn.

Aggregate manufacturers' data

Fire resistance: BS8110 requirements

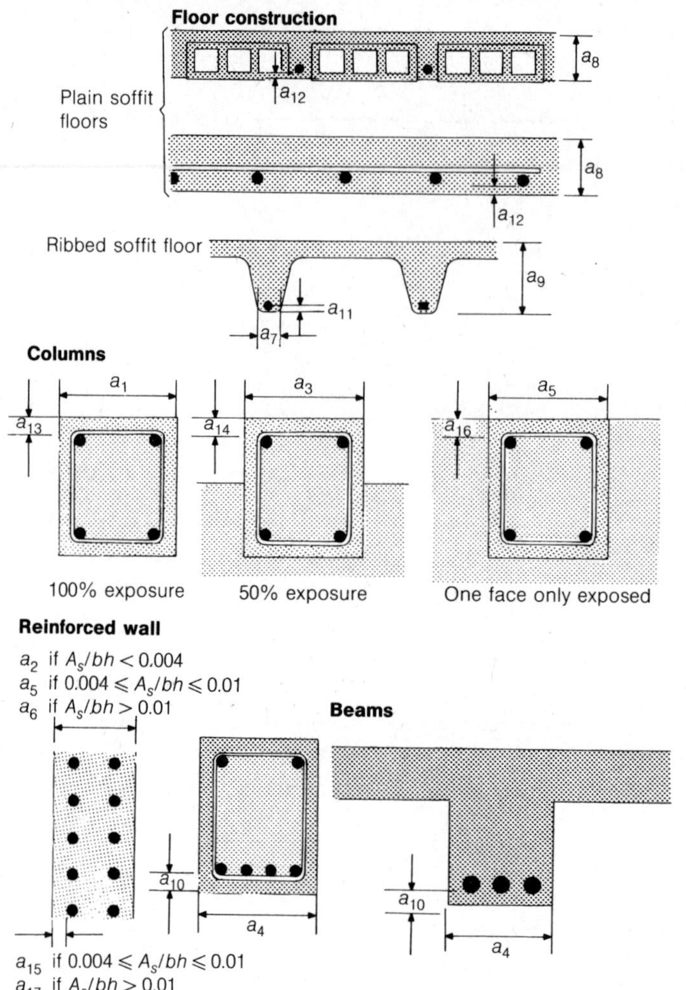

Minimum dimension in millimetres

Type of concrete	Normal-weight aggregate							Lightweight aggregate					Notes
Fire period (hours)	0.5	1	1.5	2	3	4	0.5	1	1.5	2	3	4	
a_1	150	200	250	300	400	450	150	160	200	240	320	360	
a_2	150	150	175	—	—	—	—	—	—	—	—	—	
a_3	125	160	200	200	300	350	125	130	160	185	250	275	
a_{4F}	80	120	150	200	240	280	80	100	130	160	200	250	
a_{4C}	80	80	120	150	200	240	60	80	90	110	150	200	
a_5	100	120	140	160	200	240	100	100	115	130	160	190	3
a_6	75	75	100	100	150	180	—	—	—	—	—	—	
a_{7F}	75	90	110	125	150	175	60	75	85	100	125	150	
a_{7C}	75	80	90	110	125	150	70	75	80	90	100	125	
a_{8FC}	75	95	110	125	150	170	70	90	105	115	135	150	
a_{9FC}	70	90	105	115	135	150	70	85	95	100	115	130	
a_{10F}	20	30	40	50	70	80	15	20	35	45	55	65	1, 2
a_{10C}	20	20	35	50	60	70	15	20	25	35	45	55	1, 2
a_{11F}	15	25	35	45	55	65	15	25	30	35	45	55	1, 2
a_{11C}	15	20	25	35	45	55	15	20	25	30	35	45	1, 2
a_{12F}	15	20	25	35	45	55	15	15	20	25	35	45	1, 2
a_{12C}	15	20	20	25	35	45	15	15	20	20	25	35	1
a_{13}	20	25	30	35	35	35	20	20	25	35	35	35	1
a_{14}	20	25	25	25	30	35	20	20	25	25	30	30	1
a_{15}	25	25	25	25	25	25	10	20	20	25	25	25	1
a_{16}	20	25	25	25	25	25	10	20	20	25	25	25	1
a_{17}	15	15	25	25	25	25	—	—	—	—	—	—	1

Subscripts F and C denote values for freely supported and continuous spans respectively.

Notes

1. 'Average cover' dimensions illustrated are nominal values to main reinforcement, evaluated by multiplying area of each bar by its distance from the nearest exposed face and then dividing the resulting summation by the total steel area. Compliance with 'minimum cover' requirements related to durability and concrete grade etc. must also be observed.
2. Where actual cover to outermost steel exceeds 40 mm for normal-weight concrete or 50 mm for lightweight concrete, spalling may occur and special measures must be taken to prevent this in those cases where the member would be endangered if this should happen.
3. Lightweight values are for a concrete density of 1.2 tonnes per cubic metre. For concretes having densities of between this value and that of normal-weight concrete (i.e. 2.4 t/m^3) the required minimum thickness may be interpolated.
4. Additional protection can be achieved by applying a finish of mortar, gypsum, plaster, vermiculite etc (see BS8110; Part 2: clause 4.2.4)
5. Values of average cover tabulated relate specifically to members having the minimum widths set out above. For wider members the average cover dimension may be decreased as follows:

Minimum increase in width in mm	Decrease in cover in mm	
	Normal-weight concrete	Lightweight concrete
25	5	5
50	10	10
100	15	15
150	15	20

Fire resistance: CP110 requirements

Floor construction (A = gross section)

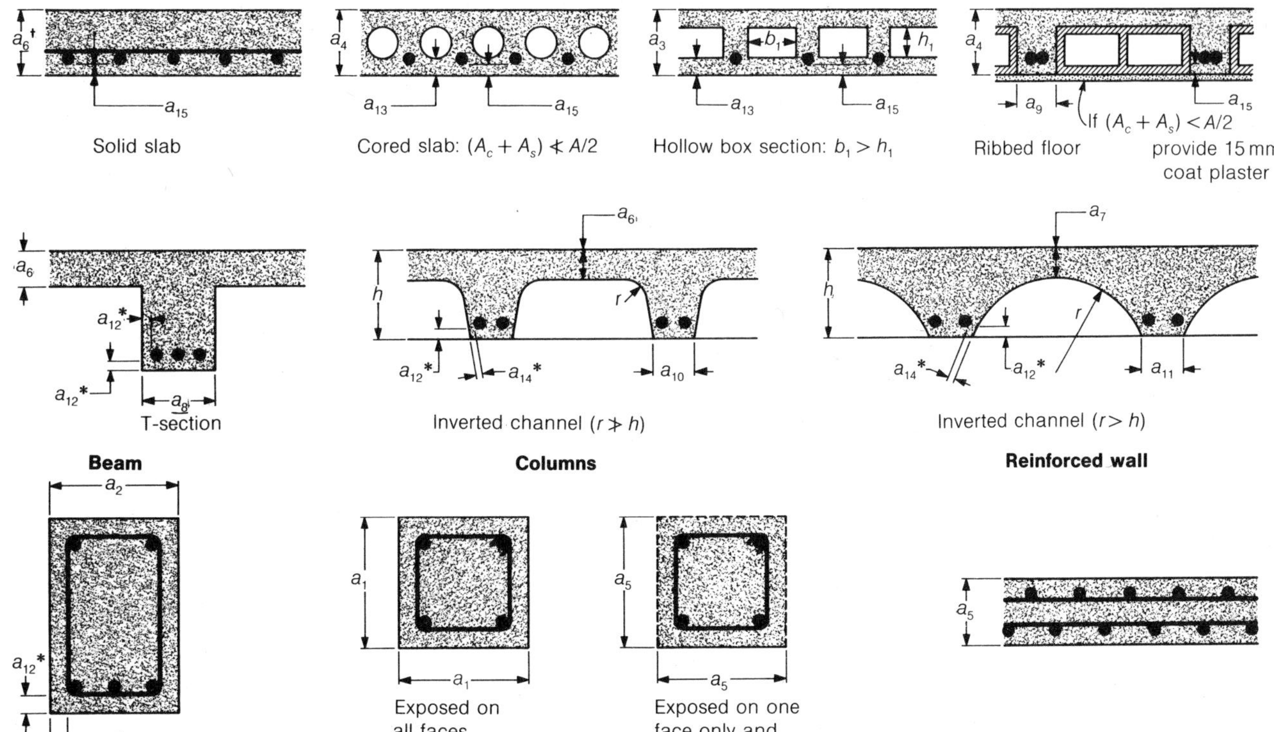

Dimension	Minimum dimension in millimetres to give fire resistance of						Protective ceiling treatment group (see note below)	See also note
	0.5 hour	1 hour	1.5 hours	2 hours	3 hours	4 hours		
a_1	150	200	250	300	400	450	—	1
a_2	80	110	140	180	240	280	—	1
a_3	105	130	155	180	205	230	1 & 3	2
a_4	100	110	140	160	175	190	1 & 3	2
a_5	75	75	100	100	150	180	—	1
a_6	90	100	125	125	150	150	2 & 3	2
a_6†	100	100	125	125	150	150	1 & 3	2
a_7	65	75	100	100	150	150	2 & 3	2
a_8	60	75	90	115	140	150	2 & 3	
a_9	50	70	80	90	100	125	1 & 3	
a_{10}	30	40	45	60	70	75	2 & 3	
a_{11}	25	35	40	50	60	70	2 & 3	
a_{12}	15	25	35	45	55	65	2 & 3	3,4,5
a_{13}	20	25	30	40	40	50	1 & 3	
a_{14}	10	15	20	25	30	40	2 & 3	5
a_{15}	15	15	20	20	25	25	1 & 3	5

Notes

1. Dimensions are for siliceous-aggregate concrete, and certain reductions are possible where cement, gypsum, vermiculite gypsum or sprayed asbestos plaster is provided as protection, or where lightweight aggregates are employed. See CP110. Supplementary reinforcement of not less than 0.5 kg/m^2 is required when cover to all bars exceeds 40 mm.
2. These dimensions include non-combustible screeds and finishes.
3. Dimensions indicated thus * require supplementary reinforcement of not less than 0.5 kg/m^2 when cover to all bars exceeds 40 mm.
4. Cover to beam reinforcement (main bars) may be reduced when protective coating as described in note 1 is provided.
5. 'Average cover' dimensions, evaluated by multiplying area of each bar by its distance from nearest exposed face and then dividing resulting summation by total area. Compliance with 'minimum cover' requirements related to concrete grade and durability must also be ensured.

Protective ceiling treatment

Additional fire resistance can be provided for floor construction by employing a protective finish or ceiling. The necessary minimum thickness of treatment to give the desired increase in resistance should be as tabulated below.

Group treatment	Minimum thickness in mm to give additional resistance of				
	0.5 hour	1 hour	1.5 hours	2 hours	3 hours
1 Soffit finish of vermiculite/gypsum plaster or sprayed asbestos	10	10	15	15	25
2 Suspended ceiling of vermiculite/gypsum plaster or sprayed asbestos an expanded metal	10	10	10	10	15
3 Suspended ceiling of gypsum/sand or cement/sand on expanded metal	10	10	15	20	25

Fire resistance: Building Regulations requirements

(i) Purpose group	(ii) Type of accommodation	(iii) Number of floors	(iv) Maximum dimensions (dash indicates no limit specified): Height (m)	(v) Floor area (m²)	(vi) Capacity (m³)	(vii) Minimum fire resistance in hours: Ground or upper storey	(viii) Basement (including floor over)
PG1	Private dwelling house	1	—	—	—	0.5	—
		2 or 3	—	—	—	0.5	1
		4	—	250	—	1	1
		any	—	—	—	1	1.5
PG2	Institution	1	—	3000	—	0.5	—
		> 1	28	2000	—	1	1.5
			—	2000	—	1.5	2
PG3	Other residential building	1	—	3000	—	0.5	—
		2	—	500	—	0.5	1
		3	—	250	—	1	1
		any	28	3000	8500	1	1.5
			—	2000	5500	1.5	2
PG4	Office	1	—	3000	—	0.5	—
			—	—	—	1	—
		> 1	7.5	250	—	0.5	1
			7.5	500	—	0.5	1
			15	—	3500	1	1
			28	500	14000	1	1.5
			—	—	—	1.5	2
PG5	Shop	1	—	2000	—	0.5	—
			—	3000	—	1	—
			—	—	—	2	—
		> 1	7.5	150	—	0.5	1
			7.5	500	—	0.5	1
			15	—	3500	1	1
			28	1000	7000	1	2
			—	2000	7000	2	4
PG6	Factory	1	—	2000	—	0.5	—
			—	3000	—	1	—
			—	—	—	2	—
		> 1	7.5	250	—	0.5	1
			7.5	—	1700	0.5	1
			15	—	4250	1	1
			28	—	8500	1	2
			28	—	28000	2	4
			—	2000	5000	2	4
PG7	Other place of assembly	1	—	3000	—	0.5	—
			—	—	—	1	—
		> 1	7.5	250	—	0.5	1
			7.5	500	—	0.5	1
			15	—	3500	1	1
			28	1000	7000	1	1.5
			—	—	7000	1.5	2
PG8	Storage and general use	1	—	500	—	0.5	—
			—	1000	—	1	—
			—	3000	—	2	—
			—	—	—	4	—
		> 1	7.5	150	—	0.5	1
			7.5	300	—	0.5	1
			15	—	1700	1	1
			15	—	3500	1	2
			28	—	7000	2	4
			28	—	21000	4	4
			—	1000	—	4	4

Notes

1. The period of fire resistance specified in columns (vii) or (viii) of the table must be provided for all elements forming a structure (or part) which has a maximum dimension that does not exceed the limiting values specified in columns (iv), (v) and (vi).
2. If any dimension of the structure being considered exceeds the greatest maximum value specified for the appropriate group, the structure must be divided into individual *compartments*, each of which is separated from its neighbours by walls and/or floors having the required period of fire resistance.
3. *Height* is measured from the mean level of the adjoining ground to the top of the walls or parapet, or to half the vertical height of a pitched roof, whichever is greater. *Floor area* is measured within enclosing walls if such walls are provided and to outer edge of floor otherwise. *Volume* is calculated from the floor area limits specified above, to the top of the lowest floor, and the soffit of the roof or uppermost ceiling.
4. If an approved sprinkler system is installed, the limits in columns (v) and (vi) of the table may be doubled.
5. Compartment walls dividing areas of building of PG2 or PG3 from other areas and walls common to adjoining buildings require a period of fire resistance of not less than 1 hour.
6. The general requirements set out in the table are modified in a few individual cases. For details of such cases and extra requirements pertaining to external, separating and compartment walls, compartment floors, protected shafts, stairs etc., reference should be made to Part E of the Building Regulations themselves.

Fire resistance: IStructE/Concrete Society requirements

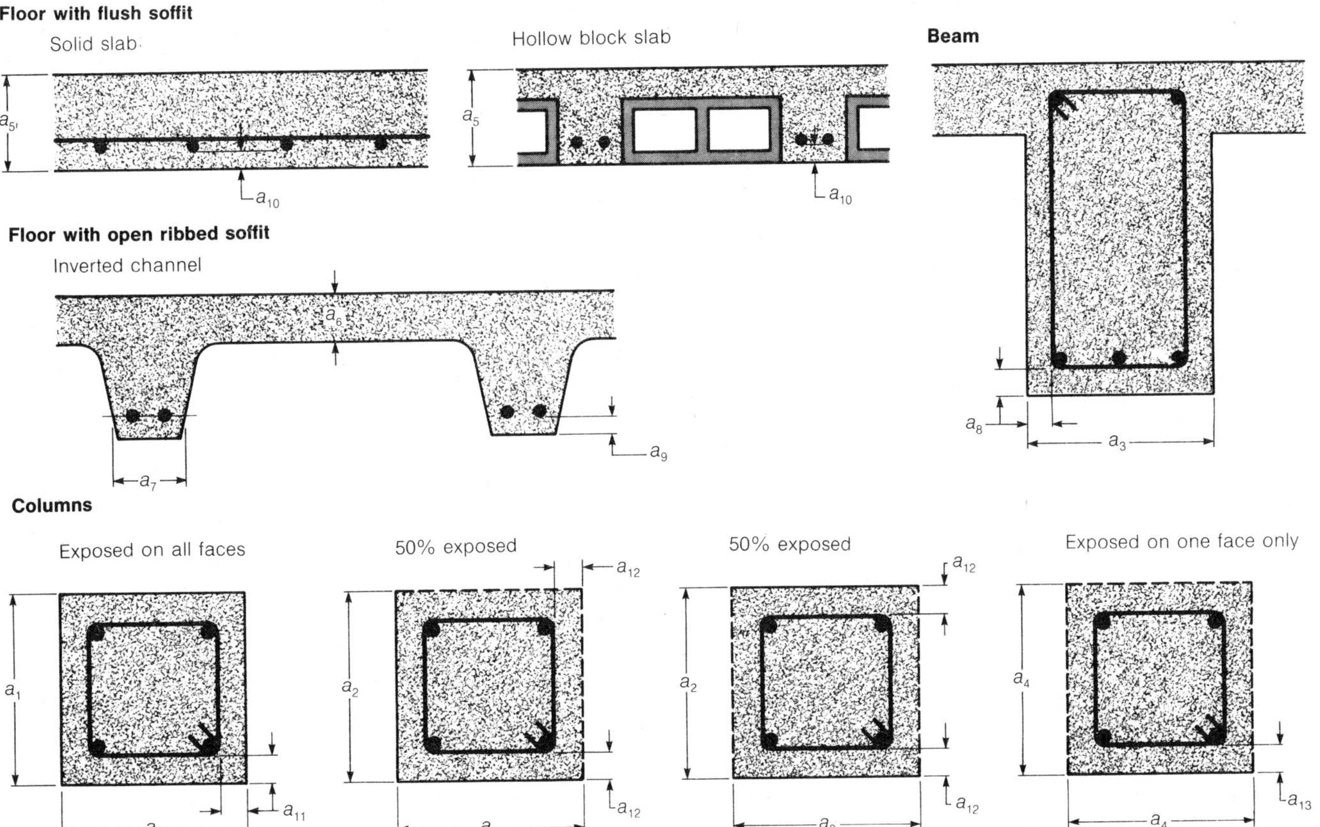

Reinforced wall

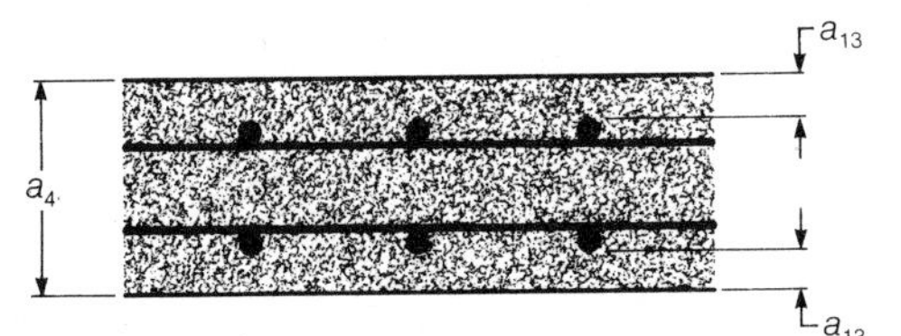

Notes

Cover Dimensions a_8 to a_{13} relate to *average* cover c. If several layers of bars have areas A_1, A_2 etc. and covers c_1, c_2 etc., then

$$c = (A_1c_1 + A_2c_2 \ldots / A_1 + A_2 \ldots) = \Sigma Ac/\Sigma A$$

When $c_1 < c_2$, bars A_1 do not contribute to ultimate resistance when considering effects of high temperature.

Thickness Dimension a_{10} relates to effective thickness = actual thickness + non-combustible finish. If hollow blocks etc, are used, effective thickness = actual thickness $\times \sqrt{k}$, where k is proportion of solid material per unit width.

Width Width is measured at level of lowest reinforcement layer.

Minimum dimension in millimetres to give stated period of fire resistance

Dimension	Normal-weight concrete						Lightweight concrete					
	0.5 hour	1 hour	1.5 hours	2 hours	3 hours	4 hours	0.5 hour	1 hour	1.5 hours	2 hours	3 hours	4 hours
a_1	150	200	250	300	410	450	150	160	200	240	320	360
a_2	125	160	200	200	300	350	125	130	160	185	250	275
a_{3F}	80	120	150	200	240	280	80	100	130	160	200	250
a_{3C}	80	80	120	150	200	240	60	80	90	110	150	200
a_4	100	120	140	160	200	240	100	100	115	130	160	190
a_5	75	95	110	125	150	170	70	90	105	115	135	150
a_6	70	90	105	115	135	150	70	85	95	100	115	130
a_{7F}	75	90	110	125	150	175	60	75	85	100	125	150
a_{7C}	75	80	90	110	125	150	70	75	80	90	100	125
a_{8F}	20	30	40	60	70	80	15	20	35	45	55	65
a_{8C}	20	20	35	50	60	70	15	20	25	35	45	55
a_{9F}	15	25	35	45	55	65	15	25	30	35	45	55
a_{9C}	15	20	25	35	45	55	15	20	25	30	35	45
a_{10F}	15	20	25	35	45	55	15	15	20	25	35	45
a_{10C}	15	20	20	25	35	45	15	15	20	20	25	35
a_{11}	20	25	30	35	35	35	20	20	25	35	35	35
a_{12}	20	25	25	25	30	35	20	20	25	25	30	30
a_{13}	20	25	25	25	25	25	10	20	20	25	25	25

Subscripts F and C denote values for freely supported and continuous spans respectively, where these differ.

A system may only be considered continuous if adequate end fixity is provided.

and bottom faces of the beam, and $\sum u_s$ is the sum of the effective perimeters of the tension reinforcement at the section under consideration. The positive sign applies when the bending moment decreases as d increases, such as at a haunch at the end of a freely supported beam. The negative sign applies when M increases as d increases, such as occurs at the haunch at an interior support of a continuous beam. If the beam is of uniform depth h (i.e. the top and bottom faces are parallel), $f_{bs} = V/d\sum u_s$. The resulting value of f_{bs} for normal-weight concrete must not exceed the empirical values given in Table 21 of CP110. With lightweight concrete, f_{bs} must not exceed 0.5 and 0.8 of these values when plain and deformed bars respectively are used.

The foregoing expressions for f_{bs} correspond to the more commonly used expressions employed elsewhere, but for convenience the term $z\sum u_s$ has here been replaced by $d\sum u_s$ and the limiting values of f_{bs} adjusted accordingly to account for this. Limiting values of local-bond stress corresponding to the type (e.g. normal or lightweight) and grade of concrete and type of reinforcement employed can be read from *Table 92*. These values have been interpolated from those given in the Code by least-squares curve fitting.

Positions at which local-bond considerations may be critical include the support faces of freely supported members, the stopping-off points of tension bars and the points of contraflexure. According to CP110, however, the two latter situations do not need to be considered if the anchorage-bond stresses in the bars continuing beyond the point concerned do not exceed 80% of the permissible values.

When groups of up to four bars are employed, the effective perimeter of each bar is reduced by 20% for every bar added to the group. Thus if u_s is the full effective perimeter of an individual bar and $\sum_e u_s$ is the effective perimeter of a group of similarly sized bars, for a two-bar group $\sum_e u_s = 1.6u_s$; for a three-bar group, $\sum_e u_s = 1.8u_s$; and for a four-bar group, $\sum_e u_s = 1.6u_s$.

Perimeters of groups of metric bars are tabulated on *Table 86*.

Neither BS8110 nor the *Joint Institutions Design Manual* require local bond stresses to be specifically investigated, specifying merely that sufficient anchorage-bond length must be provided.

18.3.4 BS5337 requirements

The requirements of BS5337 regarding bond depend on the basis of design adopted. If limit-state design is employed, the requirements correspond to those of CP110. If the alternative (working-stress) method is adopted, the limiting stresses are as given on *Table 132*. Whichever method is chosen, the anchorage-bond stresses in horizontal bars in sections that are in direct tension are restricted to 70% of normal values.

18.4 CONCRETE COVER TO REINFORCEMENT

18.4.1 BS8110 and CP110 requirements

The minimum thickness of concrete cover over the reinforcement is determined by considerations of adequate fire resistance and durability. Data regarding fire resistance are given on *Tables 81* to *84* and requirements in respect of durability are set out on *Table 139*. Then the minimum cover provided should be the larger of the values given by these requirements, or equal to the diameter of the bar concerned, whichever is the greater. If bars are arranged in bundles of three of more, the diameter considered should be that of a single bar of an equivalent area to the bundle.

18.4.2 Liquid-containing structures

BS5337 requires a cover of 40 mm to all reinforcement. This should be increased where the liquid in contact is particularly aggressive or where erosion or abrasion may occur. Excessive cover should be avoided, however, since the surface crack width will increase with any increase in cover provided.

Reinforcement: properties and stresses 85

Type of reinforcement			Min. specified tensile strength (N/mm²)	Specified characteristic strength f_y(N/mm²)		Typical limiting stresses in permissible-stress design (N/mm²)	
Type of bar		Size (mm)		B58110	CP 110	Tension	Compression
Plain round hot-rolled mild-steel bars	BS4449	all	250	250	250	140	120
Deformed hot-rolled high-yield bars	BS4449	$\ngtr 16$ > 16	460 425	460 460	460 425	250 250	215 215
Cold-worked bars	BS4461	$\ngtr 16$ > 16	460 425	460 460	460 425	250 250	215 215
Hard drawn mild-steel wire	BS4482	$\ngtr 12$	485	485	485	250	—

BS8110 requirements

Unless a lower value is necessary to limit deflection or cracking, design to BS8110 is based on the values of characteristic strength shown above. Details of the relationship between this characteristic strength f_y and the appropriate design yield stresses f_{yd1} and f_{yd2} in the compression and tension reinforcement respectively are given in *Tables 103* and *104* and the accompanying notes. For ultimate bond stresses to BS8110 see *Table 92.*

CP110 requirements

Unless a lower value is necessary to limit deflection or cracking, design to CP110 is based on the values of characteristic strength shown above. Details of the relationship between this characteristic strength f_y and the appropriate design yield stresses f_{yd1} and f_{yd2} in the compression and tension reinforcement respectively are given in *Tables 103* and *104* and the accompanying notes. For ultimate bond stresses to CP 110 see *Table 92.*

BS5337 requirements

Limit-state design method When considering the ultimate limit-state, the requirements correspond to those of CP110. When considering the limit-state of cracking, the requirements are as given in *Table 121.*
Alternative (*modular-ratio*) *method* Permissible working stresses are as tabulated on *Table 132.*

See Table 91 for details of fabrics made from hard drawn wire.

Values of typical limiting stresses in permissible-stress design are those recommended in the revision of CP 114 produced by the Campaign for Practical Codes of Practice.

Reinforcement: metric bar data

Cross-sectional areas of bars at specific spacings

Bar spacing in millimetres (non-preferred spacings shown in italics)	6	8	10	12	16	20	25	32	40	50
	Bar size in millimetres									
75	376	670	1047	1507	2680	4188	6544	—	—	—
80	*353*	*628*	*981*	*1413*	*2513*	*3926*	*6135*	—	—	—
90	*314*	*558*	*872*	*1256*	*2234*	*3490*	*5454*	—	—	—
100	282	502	785	1130	2010	3141	4908	8042	—	—
110	*257*	*456*	*713*	*1028*	*1827*	*2855*	*4462*	*7311*	—	—
120	*235*	*418*	*654*	*942*	*1675*	*2617*	*4090*	*6702*	*10471*	—
125	226	402	628	904	1608	2513	3926	6433	10053	—
130	*217*	*386*	*604*	*869*	*1546*	*2416*	*3775*	*6186*	*9666*	—
140	*201*	*359*	*560*	*807*	*1436*	*2243*	*3506*	*5744*	*8975*	—
150	188	335	523	753	1340	2094	3272	5361	8377	13090
160	*176*	*314*	*490*	*706*	*1256*	*1963*	*3067*	*5026*	*7853*	*12272*
175	161	287	448	646	1148	1795	2804	4595	7180	11220
180	*157*	*279*	*436*	*628*	*1117*	*1745*	*2727*	*4468*	*6981*	*10908*
200	141	251	392	565	1005	1570	2454	4021	6283	9817
220	*128*	*228*	*356*	*514*	*913*	*1427*	*2231*	*3655*	*5711*	*8925*
225	125	223	349	502	893	1396	2181	3574	5585	8727
240	*117*	*209*	*327*	*471*	*837*	*1308*	*2045*	*3351*	*5235*	*8181*
250	113	201	314	452	804	1256	1963	3216	5026	7854
275	102	182	285	411	731	1142	1784	2924	4569	7140
300	94	167	261	376	670	1047	1636	2680	4188	6545

Number of bars

Number of bars	6	8	10	12	16	20	25	32	40	50
1	28.3	50.3	78.5	113.1	201.1	314.2	490.9	804.2	1257	1963
2	56.5	100.5	157.1	226.2	402.1	628.3	981.7	1608	2513	3927
3	84.8	150.8	235.6	339.3	603.2	942.5	1473	2413	3770	5890
4	113.1	201.1	314.2	452.4	804.2	1257	1963	3217	5027	7854
5	141.4	251.3	392.7	565.5	1005	1571	2454	4021	6283	9817
6	169.6	301.6	471.2	678.6	1206	1885	2945	4825	7540	11781
7	197.9	351.9	549.8	791.7	1407	2199	3436	5630	8796	13744
8	226.2	402.1	628.3	904.8	1608	2513	3927	6434	10053	15708
9	254.5	452.4	706.9	1018	1810	2827	4418	7238	11310	17671
10	282.7	502.7	785.4	1131	2011	3142	4909	8042	12566	19635
11	311.0	552.9	863.9	1244	2212	3456	5400	8847	13823	21598
12	339.3	603.2	942.5	1357	2413	3770	5890	9651	15080	23562
13	367.6	653.5	1021	1470	2614	4084	6381	10455	16336	25525
14	395.8	703.7	1100	1583	2815	4398	6872	11259	17593	27489
15	424.1	754.0	1178	1696	3016	4712	7363	12064	18850	29452
16	452.4	804.2	1257	1810	3217	5027	7854	12868	20106	31416
17	480.7	854.5	1335	1923	3418	5341	8345	13672	21363	33379
18	508.9	904.8	1414	2036	3619	5655	8836	14476	22619	35343
19	537.2	955.0	1492	2149	3820	5969	9327	15281	23876	37306
20	565.5	1005	1571	2262	4021	6283	9817	16085	25133	39270

Perimeters of specific numbers of bars

Number of bars	6	8	10	12	16	20	25	32	40	50
1	18.8	25.1	31.4	37.6	50.2	62.8	78.5	100.5	125.6	157.1
2	37.6	50.2	62.8	75.3	100.5	125.6	157.0	201.0	251.3	314.2
3	56.5	75.3	94.2	113.0	150.7	188.4	235.6	301.5	376.9	471.2
4	75.3	100.5	125.6	150.7	201.0	251.3	314.1	402.1	502.6	628.3
5	94.2	125.6	157.0	188.4	251.3	314.1	392.6	502.6	628.3	785.4
6	113.0	150.7	188.4	226.1	301.5	376.9	471.2	603.1	753.9	942.5
7	131.9	175.9	219.9	263.8	351.8	439.8	549.7	703.7	879.6	1100
8	150.7	201.0	251.3	301.5	402.1	502.6	628.3	804.2	1005	1257
9	169.6	226.1	282.7	339.2	452.3	565.4	706.8	904.7	1130	1414
10	188.4	251.3	314.1	376.9	502.6	628.3	785.3	1005	1256	1571

Areas are given in square millimetres: perimeters in millimetres.

For additional notes see *Table 89*.

Reinforcement: combinations of metric bars at specific spacings

Cross-sectional area	Bar arrangement	Cross-sectional area	Bar arrangement	Cross-sectional area	Bar arrangement	Cross-sectional area	Bar arrangement
94	6@300	425	10/12@225		12/16@150	2454	25@200
102	6@275	427	6/10@125	1047	10@ 75	2485	20/32@225
113	6@250	429	8/10@150		20@300	2513	20@125
125	6@225	448	10@175	1068	12/20@200	2576	16/20@100
130	6/8@300	452	12@250	1089	8/12@ 75	2590	25/32@250
141	6@200	466	8/12@175	1118	10/16@125	2680	16@ 75
142	6/8@275		10/16@300	1130	12@100		32@300
157	6/8@250	479	10/12@200	1142	20@275	2683	20/25@150
161	6@175	502	8@100	1144	16/20@225	2767	16/25@125
167	8@300		12@225	1148	16@175	2796	20/32@200
174	6/8@225	508	10/16@275	1153	16/25@300	2804	25@175
178	6/10@300	515	8/10@125	1220	12/20@175	2848	12/20@ 75
182	8@275		6/8@ 75	1256	12/16@125	2878	25/32@225
188	6@150	523	12/16@300		20@250	2924	32@275
194	6/10@275		10@150	1258	16/25@275	3141	20@100
196	6/8@200	534	6/10@100	1277	10/12@ 75	3195	20/32@175
201	8@250	544	8/12@150	1288	16/20@200	3216	32@250
213	6/10@250	547	10/12@175	1340	16@150	3220	20/25@125
214	8/10@300	559	10/16@250	1341	20/25@300	3237	25/32@200
223	8@225	565	12@200	1383	16/25@250	3272	25@150
224	6/8@175	571	12/16@275	1396	20@225	3434	16/20@ 75
226	6@125	621	10/16@225	1398	10/16@100	3459	16/25@100
234	8/10@275	628	12/16@250	1424	12/20@150	3574	32@225
237	6/10@225		10@125	1463	20/25@275	3700	25/32@175
251	8@200	638	10/12@150	1472	16/20@175	3728	20/32@150
257	8/10@250	644	8/10@100	1507	12@ 75	3926	25@125
261	6/8@150	646	12@175	1537	16/25@225	4021	32@200
	10@300	653	8/12@125	1570	12/16@100	4025	20/25@100
267	6/10@200	670	8@ 75		20@200	4188	20@ 75
272	8/12@300		16@300	1608	16@125	4317	25/32@150
282	6@100	698	12/16@225	1610	20/25@250	4473	20/32@125
285	10@275	699	10/16@200	1636	25@300	4595	32@175
286	8/10@225	712	6/10@ 75	1709	12/20@125	4612	16/25@ 75
287	8@175		12/20@300	1717	16/20@150	4908	25@100
297	8/12@275	731	16@275	1729	16/25@200	5180	25/32@125
305	6/10@175	753	12@150	1784	25@275	5361	32@150
314	6/8@125	766	10/12@125	1788	20/25@225	5366	20/25@ 75
	10@250	776	12/20@275	1795	20@175	5592	20/32@100
319	10/12@300	785	12/16@200	1864	10/16@ 75	6433	32@125
322	8/10@200		10@100		20/32@300	6475	25/32@100
326	8/12@250	798	10/16@175	1963	25@250	6544	25@ 75
335	8@150	804	16@250	1976	16/25@175	7456	20/32@ 75
348	10/12@275	816	8/12@100	2010	16@100	8042	32@100
349	10@225	854	12/20@250	2012	20/25@200		
356	6/10@150	858	8/10@ 75	2033	20/32@275		
363	8/12@225	858	16/20@300	2060	16/20@125		
368	8/10@175	893	16@225	2094	12/16@ 75		
376	6@ 75	897	12/16@175		20@150		
	12@300	904	12@125	2136	12/20@100		
383	10/12@250	932	10/16@150	2158	25/32@300		
392	6/8@100	936	16/20@275	2181	25@225		
	10@200	949	12/20@225	2236	20/32@250		
402	8@125	958	10/12@100	2300	20/25@175		
408	8/12@200	1005	16@200	2306	16/25@150		
411	12@275	1030	16/20@250	2354	25/32@275		

Cross-sectional areas of metric bars in mm^2 per m width 10@75 etc. denotes 10 mm bars at 75 mm centres etc. 10/16@75 etc. denotes 10 mm and 16 mm bars alternately at 75 mm centres etc. Only combinations of bars not differing by more than two sizes and spaced at multiples of 25 mm are tabulated. All areas are rounded to value in mm^2 below exact value.

For additional notes see *Table 89*.

Reinforcement: areas of combinations of metric bars

Cross-sectional area	Bar arrangement	Cross-sectional area	Bar arrangement	Cross-sectional area	Bar arrangement	Cross-sectional area	Bar arrangement
113	1/12		1/12 + 5/16	1809	9/16	3041	2/20 + 3/32
201	1/16	1118	4/16 + 1/20	1822	5/12 + 4/20	3043	5/20 + 3/25
226	2/12		1/20 + 1/32	1859	3/16 + 4/20	3057	3/16 + 5/25
314	1/20	1119	2/20 + 1/25	1874	2/16 + 3/25	3081	3/25 + 2/32
	1/12 + 1/16	1130	10/12	1884	6/20	3082	2/20 + 5/25
339	3/12	1143	3/12 + 4/16	1910	3/12 + 5/20	3141	10/20
402	2/16		1/16 + 3/20	1922	1/20 + 2/32	3179	5/20 + 2/32
427	1/12 + 1/20	1168	5/12 + 3/16	1924	3/20 + 2/25	3216	4/32
	2/12 + 1/16		2/12 + 3/20	1947	5/16 + 3/20	3220	4/20 + 4/25
452	4/12	1182	1/16 + 2/25	1963	4/25		
490	1/25	1193	5/12 + 2/20	1972	2/16 + 5/20	3258	5/25 + 1/32
515	1/12 + 2/16	1206	6/16	1987	5/16 + 2/25		4/16 + 5/25
	1/16 + 1/20	1231	2/12 + 5/16	2010	10/16	3355	3/20 + 3/32
540	2/12 + 1/20		3/16 + 2/20	2023	4/12 + 5/20	3394	2/25 + 3/32
	3/12 + 1/16						
565	5/12	1256	4/12 + 4/16	2060	4/16 + 4/20	3436	7/25
603	3/16		4/20		4/20 + 1/32	3459	5/16 + 5/25
628	2/12 + 2/16	1281	3/12 + 3/20	2061	5/20 + 1/25	3531	1/20 + 4/32
	2/20		4/16 + 1/25	2075	3/16 + 3/25	3534	5/20 + 4/25
		1295	1/20 + 2/25	2099	1/25 + 2/32	3571	4/25 + 2/32
			1/25 + 1/32				
653	3/12 + 1/20	1319	5/16 + 1/20	2100	2/20 + 3/25	3669	4/20 + 3/32
	4/12 + 1/16	1344	3/12 + 5/16	2136	5/12 + 5/20	3707	1/25 + 4/32
678	6/12		2/16 + 3/20	2164	1/16 + 4/25	3711	4/20 + 5/25
691	1/16 + 1/25	1369	1/12 + 4/20	2173	3/16 + 5/20	3845	2/20 + 4/32
			5/12 + 4/16	2199	7/20	3885	3/25 + 3/32
716	1/12 + 3/16	1383	2/16 + 2/25	2236	2/20 + 2/32	3926	8/25
	2/16 + 1/20	1394	4/12 + 3/20	2238	4/20 + 2/25	3983	5/20 + 3/32
741	1/12 + 2/20	1407	7/16	2261	5/16 + 4/20	4021	5/32
	3/12 + 2/16	1432	4/16 + 2/20	2276	3/25 + 1/32	4025	5/20 + 5/25
			2/20 + 1/32		4/16 + 3/25		
766	4/12 + 1/20	1433	3/20 + 1/25	2277	1/20 + 4/25	4062	5/25 + 2/32
	5/12 + 1/16	1457	1/16 + 4/20	2365	2/16 + 4/25	4159	3/20 + 4/32
791	7/12		4/12 + 5/16	2375	4/16 + 5/20	4198	2/25 + 4/32
804	4/16	1472	3/25		5/20 + 1/32	4335	1/20 + 5/32
	1/32	1482	2/12 + 4/20	2412	3/32	4376	4/25 + 3/32
805	1/20 + 1/25	1496	5/16 + 1/25	2415	3/20 + 3/25	4417	9/25
829	1/16 + 2/20	1507	5/12 + 3/20	2454	5/25	4473	4/20 + 4/32
	2/12 + 3/16	1545	3/16 + 3/20	2477	5/16 + 3/25	4512	1/25 + 5/32
854	2/12 + 2/20	1570	5/20	2513	8/20	4649	2/20 + 5/32
	4/12 + 2/16		5/12 + 5/16	2550	3/20 + 2/32	4,689	3/25 + 4/32
879	5/12 + 1/20	1584	3/16 + 2/25	2552	5/20 + 2/25	4787	5/20 + 4/32
892	2/16 + 1/25	1595	3/12 + 4/20	2566	3/16 + 4/25	4825	6/32
904	8/12	1608	8/16	2576	5/16 + 5/20	4867	5/25 + 3/32
917	1/12 + 4/16		2/32	2590	2/25 + 2/32	4908	10/25
	3/16 + 1/20	1610	2/20 + 2/25	2591	2/20 + 4/25	4963	3/20 + 5/32
942	3/12 + 3/16	1633	5/16 + 2/20	2655	1/16 + 5/25	5002	2/25 + 5/32
	3/20	1658	2/16 + 4/20	2726	1/20 + 3/32	5180	4/25 + 4/32
967	5/12 + 2/16	1673	1/16 + 3/25	2729	4/20 + 3/25	5277	4/20 + 5/32
	3/12 + 2/20	1683	1/12 + 5/20	2767	4/25 + 1/32	5493	3/25 + 5/32
981	2/25	1709	4/12 + 4/20		4/16 + 4/25		
1005	5/16	1746	3/20 + 1/32	2768	1/20 + 5/25	5592	5/20 + 5/32
1017	9/12		4/16 + 3/20	2827	9/20	5629	7/32
1030	2/12 + 4/16	1747	4/20 + 1/25	2856	2/16 + 5/25	5671	5/25 + 4/32
	2/16 + 2/20	1771	1/16 + 5/20	2865	4/20 + 2/32	5984	4/25 + 5/32
1055	1/12 + 3/20	1785	4/16 + 2/25	2903	1/25 + 3/32	6433	8/32
	4/12 + 3/16		2/25 + 1/32	2905	3/20 + 4/25	6475	5/25 + 5/32
1080	4/12 + 2/20	1795	1/20 + 3/25	2945	6/25	7238	9/32
1094	3/16 + 1/25	1796	2/12 + 5/20	2968	5/16 + 4/25	8042	10/32

Cross-sectional areas of metric bars in mm^2. 4/16+3/25 etc. denotes combination of four 16 mm bars plus three 25 mm bars etc. Only combinations of up to five bars of two diameters differing by not more than two sizes (or ten bars of a single size) are considered. All areas are rounded to value in mm^2 below exact value.

For additional notes see *Table 89*.

Reinforcement: imperial bar data

CROSS-SECTIONAL AREAS OF SPECIFIC NUMBERS OF BARS (AND PERIMETERS)

Size in inches	Number of bars 1	2	3	4	5	6	7	8	9	10	Perimeter in inches
$\frac{1}{4}$	0.049	0.098	0.147	0.196	0.245	0.295	0.344	0.393	0.442	0.491	0.785
$\frac{5}{16}$	0.077	0.153	0.230	0.307	0.383	0.460	0.537	0.614	0.690	0.767	0.982
$\frac{3}{8}$	0.110	0.221	0.331	0.442	0.552	0.663	0.773	0.884	0.994	1.104	1.178
$\frac{7}{16}$	0.150	0.301	0.451	0.601	0.752	0.902	1.052	1.203	1.353	1.503	1.374
$\frac{1}{2}$	0.196	0.393	0.589	0.785	0.982	1.178	1.374	1.571	1.767	1.963	1.571
$\frac{5}{8}$	0.307	0.614	0.920	1.227	1.534	1.841	2.148	2.454	2.761	3.068	1.963
$\frac{3}{4}$	0.442	0.884	1.325	1.767	2.209	2.651	3.093	3.534	3.976	4.418	2.356
$\frac{7}{8}$	0.601	1.203	1.804	2.405	3.007	3.608	4.209	4.811	5.412	6.013	2.749
1	0.785	1.571	2.356	3.142	3.927	4.712	5.498	6.283	7.069	7.854	3.142
$1\frac{1}{8}$	0.994	1.988	2.982	3.976	4.970	5.964	6.958	7.952	8.946	9.940	3.534
$1\frac{1}{4}$	1.227	2.454	3.682	4.909	6.136	7.363	8.590	9.818	11.04	12.27	3.927
$1\frac{1}{2}$	1.767	3.534	5.301	7.068	8.835	10.60	12.37	14.14	15.90	17.67	4.712
2	3.142	6.283	9.425	12.57	15.71	18.85	21.99	25.13	28.27	31.42	6.283

Areas are given in square inches.

CROSS-SECTIONAL AREAS OF BARS AT SPECIFIC SPACINGS

Bar size in inches	Bar spacing in inches 3	3.5	4	4.5	5	5.5	6	7	7.5	8	9	10.5	12
$\frac{1}{4}$	0.196	0.168	0.147	0.131	0.118	0.107	0.098	0.084	0.079	0.074	0.065	0.056	0.049
$\frac{5}{16}$	0.307	0.263	0.230	0.205	0.184	0.167	0.153	0.131	0.123	0.115	0.102	0.088	0.077
$\frac{3}{8}$	0.442	0.379	0.331	0.295	0.265	0.241	0.221	0.189	0.177	0.166	0.147	0.126	0.110
$\frac{7}{16}$	0.601	0.515	0.451	0.401	0.361	0.328	0.301	0.258	0.241	0.225	0.200	0.172	0.150
$\frac{1}{2}$	0.785	0.673	0.589	0.524	0.471	0.428	0.393	0.337	0.314	0.295	0.262	0.224	0.196
$\frac{5}{8}$	1.227	1.052	0.920	0.818	0.736	0.669	0.614	0.526	0.491	0.460	0.409	0.351	0.307
$\frac{3}{4}$	1.767	1.515	1.325	1.178	1.060	0.964	0.884	0.757	0.707	0.663	0.589	0.505	0.442
$\frac{7}{8}$	2.405	2.062	1.804	1.604	1.443	1.312	1.203	1.031	0.962	0.902	0.802	0.687	0.601
1	3.142	2.693	2.356	2.094	1.885	1.714	1.571	1.346	1.257	1.178	1.047	0.898	0.785
$1\frac{1}{8}$	—	3.408	2.982	2.651	2.386	2.169	1.988	1.704	1.590	1.491	1.325	1.136	0.994
$1\frac{1}{4}$	—	—	3.681	3.272	2.945	2.677	2.454	2.104	1.963	1.841	1.636	1.402	1.227
$1\frac{1}{2}$	—	—	—	4.712	4.241	3.856	3.534	3.029	2.827	2.651	2.356	2.020	1.767

Cross-sectional areas of imperial bars in in^2 per foot width.

Notes

These notes also apply to *Tables 86, 87* and *88.*

Plain round bars

The cross-sectional areas (A_s) tabulated are basically for plain round bars (where size = diameter = ϕ). If number of bars = k,

$$A_s = \tfrac{1}{4}\pi\phi^2 k.$$

If spacing (or pitch) = s (in inches or millimetres),

$$A_s = \frac{12}{s} \times 0.7854\phi^2 = \frac{9.425}{s}\phi^2 \text{ in}^2/\text{ft}$$

or

$$A_s = \frac{1000}{s} \times 0.7854\phi^2 = \frac{785.4}{s}\phi^2 \text{ mm}^2/\text{m}$$

Deformed (high-bond) bars

The cross-sectional areas tabulated also apply to deformed (high-bond) bars if the specified size (effective diameter) of the bar is the diameter of a circle having the same cross-sectional area.

Twisted square bars

The cross-sectional areas tabulated apply to small non-chamfered and larger chamfered twisted square bars if the specified size is based on 'round area' but do not apply if based on 'square area'.

Perimeters

Tabulated perimeters apply to plain round bars only ($u = \pi\phi$).

Reinforcement: weights at specified spacings and unit weights

Weights of metric (millimetre) bars in kilograms per square metre

Size (mm)	Weight per m (kg)	Length per tonne (m)	Spacing of bars in millimetres									
			75	100	125	150	175	200	225	250	275	300
6	0.222	4505	2.960	2.220	1.776	1.480	1.269	1.110	0.987	0.888	0.807	0.740
8	0.395	2532	5.267	3.950	3.160	2.633	2.257	1.975	1.756	1.580	1.436	1.317
10	0.616	1623	8.213	6.160	4.928	4.107	3.520	3.080	2.738	2.464	2.240	2.053
12	0.888	1126	11.84	8.880	7.104	5.920	5.074	4.440	3.947	3.552	3.229	2.960
16	1.579	633	21.05	15.79	12.63	10.53	9.023	7.895	7.018	6.316	5.742	5.263
20	2.466	406	32.88	24.66	19.73	16.44	14.09	12.33	10.96	9.864	8.967	8.220
25	3.854	259	51.39	38.54	30.83	25.69	22.02	19.27	17.13	15.42	14.01	12.85
32	6.313	158	—	63.13	50.50	42.09	36.07	31.57	28.06	25.25	22.96	21.04
40	9.864	101	—	—	78.91	65.76	56.37	49.32	43.84	39.46	35.87	32.88

Basic weight = 0.007 85 kg/mm^2 per metre
Weight per metre = 0.006 165 ϕ^2 kg
Weight per mm^2 at spacing s(mm) = 6.165 ϕ^2/s kg
ϕ = diameter of bar in millimetres

Spacing of bars in inches

Weights of imperial (inch) bars in pounds per square foot

Size (in)	Weight per foot (lb)	Length per ton (ft)	Spacing of bars in inches												
			3	3.5	4	4.5	5	5.5	6	7	7.5	8	9	10.5	12
$\frac{1}{4}$	0.1669	13421	0.668	0.572	0.501	0.445	0.401	0.364	0.334	0.286	0.267	0.250	0.223	0.191	0.167
$\frac{5}{16}$	0.2608	8590	1.043	0.894	0.782	0.695	0.626	0.569	0.522	0.447	0.417	0.391	0.348	0.298	0.261
$\frac{3}{8}$	0.3755	5965	1.502	1.287	1.127	1.001	0.901	0.819	0.751	0.644	0.601	0.563	0.501	0.429	0.376
$\frac{7}{16}$	0.5111	4383	2.044	1.752	1.533	1.363	1.227	1.115	1.022	0.876	0.818	0.767	0.681	0.584	0.511
$\frac{1}{2}$	0.6676	3355	2.670	2.289	2.003	1.780	1.602	1.457	1.335	1.144	1.068	1.001	0.890	0.763	0.668
$\frac{5}{8}$	1.0431	2147	4.712	3.576	3.129	2.782	2.503	2.276	2.086	1.788	1.669	1.565	1.391	1.192	1.043
$\frac{3}{4}$	1.5021	1491	6.008	5.150	4.506	4.006	3.605	3.277	3.004	2.575	2.403	2.253	2.003	1.717	1.502
$\frac{7}{8}$	2.0445	1096	8.178	7.010	6.133	5.452	4.907	4.461	4.089	3.505	3.271	3.067	2.726	2.337	2.044
1	2.6704	839	10.68	9.155	8.011	7.121	6.409	5.826	5.341	4.578	4.273	4.006	3.560	3.052	2.670
$1\frac{1}{8}$	3.3797	663	—	11.59	10.14	9.012	8.111	7.374	6.759	5.794	5.407	5.069	4.506	3.862	3.380
$1\frac{1}{4}$	4.1724	537	—	—	12.52	11.13	10.01	9.103	8.345	7.153	6.676	6.259	5.563	4.768	4.172
$1\frac{1}{2}$	6.0083	373	—	—	—	16.02	14.42	13.11	12.02	10.30	9.613	9.012	8.011	6.867	6.008

Basic weight = 3.4 lb/in^2 per foot
Weight per foot = 2.6704 ϕ^2 lb
Weight per ft^2 at spacing s (in) = 32.044ϕ^2/s lb
ϕ = diameter of bar in inches

Plain round bars

The weights tabulated are basically for plain round bars.

Deformed (high-bond bars)

The weights tabulated apply to deformed (high-bond) bars of uniform cross-sectional area if the specified size (effective diameter) of the bars is the diameter of a circle of the same cross-sectional area.

Twisted square bars

The weights tabulated apply to small non-chamfered and larger chamfered twisted square bars if the specified size is based on 'round area' but do not apply if based on 'square area'.

Reinforcement: fabrics and wire

—	Type of fabric	Size of mesh mm × mm	BS ref. no.	Weight (kg/m²)	Main wires: Size (mm)	Main wires: Cross-sectional are (mm²/m)	Transverse wires: Size (mm)	Transverse wires: Cross-sectional area (mm²/m)	Notes
Fabrics	Square mesh	200 × 200	A98†	1.54	5	98	5	98	
			A142*	2.22	6	142	6	142	
			A193*	3.02	7	193	7	193	
			A252	3.95	8	252	8	252	
			A393	6.16	10	393	10	393	
	Structural	100 × 200	196†	3.05	5	196	7	193	
			B283*	3.73	6	283			
			B385*	4.53	7	385			
			B503	5.93	8	503	8	252	
			B785	8.14	10	785			
			B1131	10.90	12	1131			
	Long mesh	100 × 400	C283	2.61	6	283	5	49	
			C385*	3.41	7	385			
			C503	4.34	8	503			
			C636	5.55	9	636	6	71	
			C785	6.72	10	785			
	Wrapping	100 × 100	D49	0.77	2.5	49	2.5	49	Stock sheets 2.4 m × 1.2 m
		200 × 200	D98	1.54	5	98	5	98	

Notes: Wire of grade 460 complying with requirements of BS4449, 4461 or 4482 must be used, except for wrapping fabric, for which grade 250 wire will suffice. In practice, the majority of fabric is produced from cold hard-drawn steel wire to BS4482.

Preferred sizes:
Sheets: 2.4 m wide
4.8 m log

Rolls: 2.4 m wide
48 m
(indicated thus*)
or 72 m
(indicated thus†)

Wire													
Size	SWG no.	6g	5g	4g	3g	2g	1g	1/0g	2/0g	3/0g	4/0g	5/0g
	in	0.192	0.212	0.232	0.252	0.276	0.300	0.324	0.348	0.372	0.400	0.432
	mm	4.9	5.4	5.9	6.4	7.0	7.6	8.2	8.8	9.5	10.2	11.0
Cross-sectional area	in²	0.029	0.035	0.042	0.050	0.060	0.071	0.082	0.095	0.109	0.126	0.146
	mm²	19	23	27	32	39	46	53	61	70	81	95

Rectangular and flanged beams: miscellaneous data

Flanged beams

T-beams and L-beams
The effective width of flange b_e should not exceed the least of the following dimensions:

CP110 requirements:
1. $(b_w + l_e/5)$ for T-beam or $(b_w + l_e/10)$ for L-beam (l_e = length of flange in compression)
2. actual width of flange

CP114 requirements:
1. $l/3$ for T-beam or $l/6$ for L-beam
2. $(b_w + 12h_f)$ for T-beam or $(b_w + 4h_f)$ for L-beam
3. distance between centres of adjacent beams

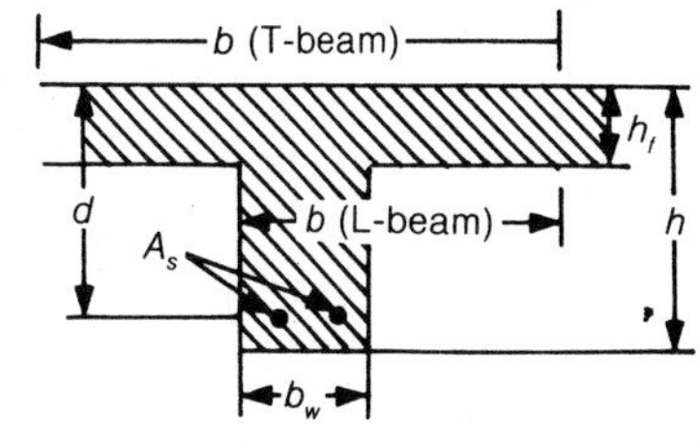

Formulae for beams when concrete is effective in tension

	Rectangular beams: Tension reinforcement only	Rectangular beams: Tension and compression reinforcement	Flanged beams
Effective area A_{tr}	$bh + (\alpha_e - 1)A_s$	$bh + (\alpha_e - 1)(A'_s + A_s)$	$b_w h + (b - b_w)h_f + (\alpha_e - 1)A_s$
Depth to neutral axis x	$\left[\frac{bh^2}{2} + (\alpha_e - 1)A_s d\right]\frac{1}{A_{tr}}$	$\left[\frac{bh^2}{2} + (\alpha_e - 1)(A_s d + A'_s d')\right]\frac{1}{A_{tr}}$	$[b_w h^2 + (b - b_w)h_f^2 + 2(\alpha_e - 1)A_s d]\frac{1}{2A_{tr}}$
Moment of inertia I	$\frac{1}{3}b[x^3 + (h-x)^3] + (\alpha_e - 1)(d-x)^2 A_s$	$\frac{1}{3}b[x^3 + (h-x)^3] + (\alpha_e - 1)[A_s(d-x)^2 + A'_s(x-d')^2]$	$\frac{1}{3}b_w[x^3 + (h-x)^3] + (\alpha_e - 1)(d-x)^2 A_s + (b - b_w)[\frac{1}{12}h_f^2 + (x - \frac{1}{2}h_f)^2]h_f$

Section modulus	$J_0 = I/x$	$J_h = I/(h-x)$
Maximum stresses	$f_{cr} = M_d/J_0$	$f_{ct} = M_d/J_h$
Moments of resistance	Moment of resistance in compression $= J_0 f_{cr}$	Moment of resistance in tension $= J_h f_{ct}$

Reinforcement bond: BS8110 and CP110 requirements—1

NORMAL-WEIGHT CONCRETE

Concrete grade (N/mm²)	Anchorage-bond length l required in terms of bar diameter ϕ														Ultimate local-bond stress (N/mm²) (CP110 only)		
	Tension							Compression									
	BS8110 requirements		CP110 requirements					BS8110 requirements		CP110 requirements					Plain bars	Deformed bars	
	$f_y=250$	460 Type 2	250	425 Type 1	425 Type 2	460 Type 1	460 Type 2	250	460 Type 2	250	425 Type 1	425 Type 2	460 Type 1	460 Type 2		Type 1	Type 2
20	For bond lengths for type 1 deformed bars add 25% to values for type 2 bars		44.7	54.3	41.8	58.8	45.2	For bond lengths for type 1 deformed bars add 25% to values for type 2 bars		32.3	36.7	28.2	39.2	30.1	1.7	2.1	2.6
21			43.6	52.9	40.7	57.3	44.1			31.4	35.7	27.5	38.2	29.4	1.8	2.2	2.6
22			42.5	51.6	39.7	55.9	43.0			30.7	34.8	26.8	37.2	28.6	1.8	2.3	2.7
23			41.5	50.4	38.7	54.5	41.9			29.9	34.0	26.2	36.3	27.9	1.9	2.3	2.8
24			40.5	49.2	37.8	53.2	40.9			29.2	33.2	25.5	35.5	27.3	1.9	2.4	2.9
25	38.9	40.1	39.6	48.0	36.9	52.0	40.0	31.1	31.8	28.5	32.4	24.9	34.6	26.7	2.0	2.5	3.0
26	38.1	39.3	38.7	46.9	36.1	50.8	39.1	30.5	31.2	27.9	31.7	24.4	33.8	26.0	2.0	2.5	3.0
27	37.4	38.5	37.8	45.9	35.3	49.7	38.2	29.9	30.6	27.3	31.0	23.8	33.1	25.5	2.1	2.6	3.1
28	36.7	37.8	37.0	44.9	34.5	48.6	37.4	29.4	30.0	26.7	30.3	23.3	32.4	24.9	2.1	2.6	3.2
29	36.1	37.2	36.2	43.9	33.8	47.6	36.6	28.9	29.5	26.1	29.7	22.8	31.7	24.4	2.2	2.7	3.3
30	35.5	36.6	35.4	43.0	33.1	46.6	35.6	28.4	29.0	25.6	29.0	22.4	31.0	23.9	2.2	2.8	3.3
31	34.9	36.0	34.7	42.1	32.4	45.6	35.1	27.9	28.6	25.0	28.4	21.9	30.4	23.4	2.3	2.8	3.4
32	34.4	35.4	34.0	41.3	31.8	44.7	34.4	27.5	28.1	24.5	27.9	21.5	29.8	22.9	2.3	2.9	3.5
33	33.8	34.9	33.4	40.5	31.2	43.8	33.7	27.1	27.7	24.1	27.3	21.0	29.2	22.5	2.4	3.0	3.6
34	33.3	34.3	32.7	39.7	30.6	43.0	33.1	26.7	27.3	23.6	26.8	20.6	28.6	22.0	2.4	3.0	3.6
35	32.9	33.9	32.1	39.0	30.0	42.2	32.5	26.3	26.9	23.2	26.3	20.2	28.1	21.6	2.5	3.1	3.7
36	32.4	33.4	31.5	38.3	29.4	41.4	31.9	25.9	26.5	22.7	25.8	19.9	27.6	21.2	2.5	3.1	3.8
37	32.0	32.9	30.9	37.6	28.9	40.6	31.3	25.6	26.1	22.3	25.4	19.5	27.1	20.8	2.6	3.2	3.9
38	31.5	32.5	30.4	36.9	28.4	39.9	30.7	25.2	25.8	21.9	24.9	19.2	26.6	20.5	2.6	3.3	3.9
39	31.1	32.1	29.9	36.2	27.9	39.2	30.2	24.9	25.5	21.5	24.5	18.8	26.1	20.1	2.7	3.3	4.0
40	30.7	31.7	29.3	35.6	27.4	38.6	29.7	24.6	25.1	21.2	24.0	18.5	25.7	19.8	2.7	3.4	4.1

LIGHTWEIGHT-AGGREGATE CONCRETE

Concrete grade (N/mm^2)	Anchorage-bond length l required in terms of bar diameter ϕ — Tension: BS8110 requirements $f_y = 250$	Tension: BS8110 requirements 460 Type 2	Tension: CP110 requirements 250	Tension: CP110 425 Type 1	Tension: CP110 425 Type 2	Tension: CP110 460 Type 1	Tension: CP110 460 Type 2	Compression: BS8110 requirements 250	Compression: BS8110 requirements 460 Type 2	Compression: CP110 requirements 250	Compression: CP110 425 Type 1	Compression: CP110 425 Type 2	Compression: CP110 460 Type 1	Compression: CP110 460 Type 2	Ultimate local-bond stress (N/mm^2) (CP110 only): Plain bars	Deformed bars Type 1	Deformed bars Type 2
15	For bond lengths for type 1 deformed bars add 25% to values for type 2 bars		111.7	84.8	65.2	91.8	70.6	For bond lengths for type 1 deformed bars add 25% to values for type 2 bars		80.6	57.2	44.0	61.1	47.0	0.7	1.4	1.7
16			106.4	80.8	62.1	87.4	67.2			76.7	54.5	41.9	58.2	44.8	0.7	1.4	1.8
17			101.6	77.1	59.3	83.4	64.2			73.2	52.0	40.0	55.6	42.8	0.8	1.5	1.9
18			97.2	73.7	56.7	79.8	61.4			70.1	49.7	38.3	53.2	40.9	0.8	1.6	2.0
19			93.1	70.7	54.4	76.5	58.8			67.1	47.4	36.7	50.9	39.2	0.8	1.6	2.1
20	54.3	55.9	89.4	67.9	52.2	73.5	56.5	43.4	44.4	64.5	45.8	35.3	49.0	37.7	0.9	1.7	2.1
21	52.9	54.6	87.1	66.1	50.9	71.6	55.1	42.4	43.3	62.8	44.6	34.4	47.7	36.7	0.9	1.8	2.1
22	51.7	53.3	85.0	64.5	49.6	69.8	53.7	41.4	42.3	61.3	43.5	33.5	46.5	35.8	0.9	1.8	2.2
23	50.6	52.1	82.9	62.9	48.4	68.1	52.4	40.5	41.4	59.8	42.5	32.7	45.4	34.9	0.9	1.9	2.2
24	49.5	51.0	80.9	61.4	47.3	66.5	51.2	39.6	40.5	58.4	41.5	31.9	44.3	34.1	1.0	1.9	2.3
25	48.5	50.0	79.1	60.0	46.2	64.9	50.0	38.8	39.7	57.0	40.5	31.2	43.3	33.3	1.0	2.0	2.4
26	47.6	49.0	77.3	58.6	45.1	63.5	48.8	38.1	38.9	55.7	39.6	30.5	42.3	32.5	1.0	2.0	2.4
27	46.7	48.1	75.5	57.3	44.1	62.1	47.8	37.4	38.2	54.5	38.7	29.8	41.4	31.8	1.0	2.1	2.5
28	45.9	47.2	73.9	56.1	43.2	60.7	46.7	36.7	37.5	53.3	37.9	29.1	40.5	31.1	1.1	2.1	2.5
29	45.1	46.4	72.3	54.9	42.2	59.4	45.7	36.0	36.8	52.2	37.1	28.5	39.6	30.5	1.1	2.2	2.6
30	44.3	45.6	70.8	53.8	41.4	58.2	44.8	35.4	36.2	51.1	36.3	27.9	38.8	29.8	1.1	2.2	2.7
31	43.6	44.9	69.4	52.7	40.5	57.0	43.9	34.9	35.6	50.0	35.5	27.4	38.0	29.2	1.1	2.3	2.7
32	42.9	44.2	68.0	51.6	39.7	55.9	43.0	34.3	35.1	49.0	34.8	26.8	37.2	28.6	1.2	2.3	2.8
33	42.2	43.5	66.7	50.6	38.9	54.8	42.1	33.8	34.5	48.1	34.2	26.3	36.5	28.1	1.2	2.4	2.8
34	41.6	42.9	65.4	49.6	38.2	53.7	41.3	33.3	34.0	47.2	33.5	25.8	35.8	27.5	1.2	2.4	2.9
35	41.0	42.3	64.2	48.7	37.5	52.7	40.6	32.8	33.5	46.3	32.9	25.3	35.1	27.0	1.2	2.5	3.0
36	40.4	41.7	63.0	47.8	36.8	51.7	39.8	32.3	33.1	45.4	32.3	24.8	34.5	26.5	1.3	2.5	3.0
37	39.9	41.1	61.8	46.9	36.1	50.8	39.1	31.9	32.6	44.6	31.7	24.4	33.9	26.0	1.3	2.6	3.1
38	39.4	40.6	60.7	46.1	35.5	49.9	38.4	31.5	32.2	43.8	31.1	23.9	33.2	25.6	1.3	2.6	3.1
39	38.9	40.0	59.7	45.3	34.9	49.0	37.7	31.1	31.8	43.0	30.6	23.5	32.7	25.1	1.3	2.7	3.2
40	38.4	39.5	58.6	44.5	34.3	48.2	37.1	30.7	31.4	42.3	30.0	23.1	32.1	24.7	1.4	2.7	3.3

ANCHORAGE BOND: MINIMUM LENGTHS IN MILLIMETRES FOR NORMAL-WEIGHT CONCRETE

Diam. of bar (mm)	Min. 12ϕ (mm)	Min. lap 15ϕ or 300 mm	Type of anchorage	$f_{cu} = 25\ \text{N/mm}^2$				$f_{cu} = 30\ \text{N/mm}^2$				$f_{cu} = 40\ \text{N/mm}^2$			
				$f_y = 250\ \text{N/mm}^2$	$f_y = 460\ \text{N/mm}^2$ Plain	Type 1	Type 2	$f_y = 250\ \text{N/mm}^2$	$f_y = 460\ \text{N/mm}^2$ Plain	Type 1	Type 2	$f_y = 250\ \text{N/mm}^2$	$f_y = 460\ \text{N/mm}^2$ Plain	Type 1	Type 2
			Tension 0°	235	430	300	240	215	395	275	220	185	340	240	190
			90°	185	360	230	170	165	320	205	150	140	270	170	120
6	75	300	180°	140	285	160	100	120	250	130	80	90	195	95	50
			1.4 × lap	330	600	420	340	300	550	385	310	260	475	335	270
			2 × lap	470	860	600	480	430	785	550	440	370	680	475	380
			Compression	190	345	240	195	175	315	220	175	150	275	190	155
			Tension 0°	315	575	400	320	285	525	370	295	250	455	320	255
			90°	250	480	305	225	220	430	270	200	185	360	225	160
8	100	300	180°	185	380	210	130	160	330	175	105	120	260	125	65
			1.4 × lap	435	800	560	450	400	735	515	410	345	635	445	355
			2 × lap	625	1145	800	640	570	1045	735	585	495	905	635	510
			Compression	250	460	320	255	230	420	295	235	200	365	255	205
			Tension 0°	390	715	500	400	355	655	460	370	310	565	400	320
			90°	310	595	380	280	275	535	340	250	230	445	280	200
10	120	300	180°	230	475	260	160	195	415	220	130	150	325	160	80
			1.4 × lap	545	1000	700	560	500	915	640	515	430	795	555	445
			2 × lap	780	1430	1000	800	710	1305	915	735	615	1130	795	635
			Compression	315	575	400	320	285	525	370	290	250	455	320	255
			Tension 0°	470	860	600	480	430	785	550	440	370	680	475	380
			90°	370	715	455	335	330	640	405	295	275	535	335	240
12	145	300	180°	275	570	310	190	235	495	260	155	180	390	190	95
			1.4 × lap	655	1200	840	675	600	1100	770	615	520	950	665	535
			2 × lap	935	1715	1200	960	855	1565	1100	880	740	1360	950	760
			Compression	375	690	480	385	345	630	440	350	295	545	380	305
			Tension 0°	625	1145	800	640	570	1045	735	585	495	905	635	510
			90°	495	955	605	445	440	855	540	395	365	715	445	315
16	195	300	180°	370	760	415	255	315	660	350	205	240	520	250	125
			1.4 × lap	870	1600	1120	900	795	1465	1025	820	690	1265	890	710
			2 × lap	1245	2290	1600	1280	1135	2090	1465	1170	985	1810	1265	1015
			Compression	500	915	640	510	455	835	585	465	395	725	510	405

1. Minimum stopping-off length = 12ϕ or d, whichever is greater.
2. In beams only, where sufficient links to meet nominal requirements are not provided, employ anchorage bond length corresponding to plain bars, irrespective of actual type provided.
3. Minimum lap in tension: 15ϕ or 300 mm, whichever is greater, *or* anchorage length of smaller bar.
   (i) Where lap occurs at top of section as cast and size of lapped bars exceeds half the minimum cover, multiply lap length by 1.4.
   (ii) Where lap occurs near section corner and size of lapped bars exceeds half the minimum cover to either face, or where clear distance between adjacent bars is less than 75 mm or six times size of lapped bars, whichever is greater, multiply lap length by 1.4.
   Where conditions (i) and (ii) both apply, multiply lap length by 2.0. Minimum lap in compression: 15ϕ or 300 mm, whichever is greater, *or* 1.25 times anchorage length of smaller bar.
4. All lengths are rounded to 5 mm value above calculated figure.

Diam. of bar (mm)	Min. 12ϕ (mm)	Min. lap 15ϕ or 300 mm	Type of anchorage	$f_{cu} = 25\ N/mm^2$ $f_y =$ 250 N/mm²	$f_y = 460\ N/mm^2$ Plain	Type 1	Type 2	$f_{cu} = 30\ N/mm^2$ $f_y =$ 250 N/mm²	$f_y = 460\ N/mm^2$ Plain	Type 1	Type 2	$f_{cu} = 40\ N/mm^2$ $f_y =$ 250 N/mm²	$f_y = 460\ N/mm^2$ Plain	Type 1	Type 2
			Tension 0°	780	1430	1000	800	710	1305	915	735	615	1130	795	635
			90°	620	1190	760	560	550	1065	675	495	455	890	555	395
20	240	300	180°	460	950	520	320	390	825	435	255	295	650	315	155
			1.4 × lap	1090	2000	1400	1120	995	1830	1280	1025	860	1585	1110	890
			2 × lap	1555	2860	2000	1600	1420	2610	1830	1465	1230	2260	1585	1265
			Compression	625	1145	800	635	570	1045	735	580	495	905	635	505
			Tension 0°	975	1790	1250	1000	890	1635	1145	915	770	1415	990	795
			90°	775	1490	950	700	690	1335	845	615	570	1115	690	495
25	300	375	180°	575	1190	650	400	490	1035	545	315	370	815	390	195
			1.4 × lap	1360	2500	1750	1400	1245	2285	1600	1280	1075	1980	1385	1110
			2 × lap	1945	3575	2500	2000	1775	3265	2285	1830	1535	2825	1980	1585
			Compression	780	1430	1000	795	710	1305	915	725	615	1130	795	630
			Tension 0°	1245	2290	1600	1280	1135	2090	1465	1170	985	1810	1265	1015
			90°	990	1905	1215	895	880	1705	1080	785	730	1425	885	630
32	385	480	180°	735	1520	830	510	625	1320	695	405	475	1040	500	245
			1.4 × lap	1740	3200	2240	1795	1590	2925	2045	1640	1375	2530	1775	1425
			2 × lap	2485	4575	3200	2560	2270	4175	2925	2340	1965	3615	2530	2025
			Compression	995	1830	1280	1020	910	1670	1170	930	790	1450	1015	805
			Tension 0°	1555	2860	2000	1600	1420	2610	1830	1465	1230	2260	1585	1265
			90°	1235	2380	1520	1120	1100	2130	1350	985	910	1780	1105	785
40	480	600	180°	915	1900	1040	640	780	1650	870	505	590	1300	625	305
			1.4 × lap	2175	4000	2800	2240	1985	3655	2560	2045	1720	3165	2215	1775
			2 × lap	3110	5715	4000	3200	2840	5220	3655	2925	2460	4520	3165	2530
			Compression	1245	2290	1600	1270	1135	2090	1465	1160	985	1810	1265	1005
			Tension 0°	1945	3575	2500	2000	1775	3265	2285	1830	1535	2825	1980	1585
			90°	1545	2975	1900	1400	1375	2665	1685	1230	1135	2225	1380	985
50	600	750	180°	1145	2375	1300	800	975	2065	1085	630	735	1625	780	385
			1.4 × lap	2720	5000	3500	2800	2485	4565	3200	2560	2150	3955	2770	2215
			2 × lap	3885	7145	5000	4000	3545	6525	4565	3655	3070	5650	3955	3165
			Compression	1555	2860	2000	1590	1420	2610	1830	1450	1230	2260	1585	1255

5. Values for hooks correspond to internal radii of 2ϕ for mild-steel bars and 3ϕ for high-yield steel bars. Bars must extend a minimum distance of 4ϕ beyond bend.
6. Lengths tabulated correspond to maximum design stress in steel of $f_y/1.15$ in tension and compression. For lower design stresses at point beyond which anchorage is to be provided, determine length required from no-hook value no pro rata basis. Then, if hook is provided, subtract * length equal to difference between appropriate value given on table.
7. 0°, 90° and 180° indicate no hook, right-angled hook or bob, and standard hook, respectively.
8. For lightweight-aggregate concrete multiply no-hook length by 1.25. Then, if hook is provided, subtract length equal to difference between appropriate values given on table.

Chapter 19
Properties of reinforced concrete sections

In sections 19.1 and 19.2, formulae containing summation sign $\sum$ apply to irregular sections only (see accompanying figures (a) and (b)). Formulae containing integration sign $\int$ apply to regular sections only (figure (c)) in which b_s is a mathematical function of h_c.

19.1 ENTIRE SECTION SUBJECTED TO STRESS

Effective area:

$$A_{tr} = \sum_{0}^{h} [b_s h_s + (\alpha_e - 1)\delta A'_s]$$

$$= \left[\int_0^h b_s \, dh_c\right] + (\alpha_e - 1)(A'_s + A_s)$$

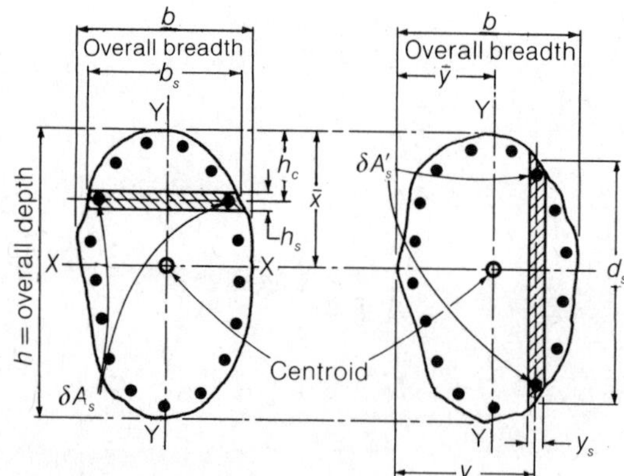

(a) Irregular section

Entire section subjected to stress.

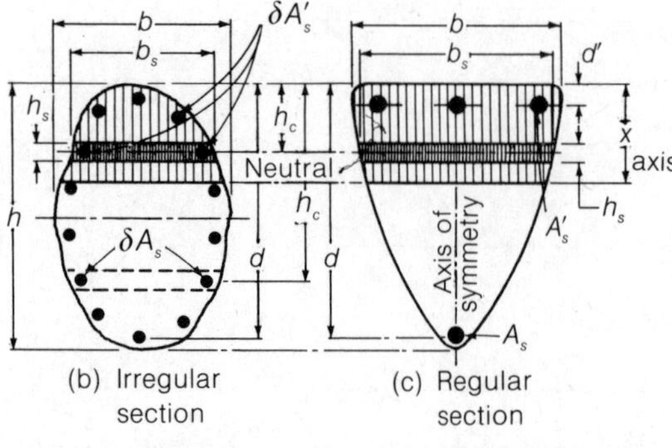

(b) Irregular section

b_s independent of h_c

(c) Regular section

b_s is a mathematical function of h_c

Sections subjected to bending only.

Position of centroid:

$$\bar{x} = \frac{1}{A_{tr}}\left\{\sum_{0}^{h} h_c[b_s h_s + (\alpha_e - 1)\delta A'_s]\right\}$$

$$= \frac{1}{A_{tr}}\left\{\left[\int_0^h h_c b_s \, dh_c\right] + (\alpha_e - 1)(A'_s d' + A_s d)\right\}$$

$$\bar{y} = \frac{1}{A_{tr}}\left\{\sum_{0}^{h} y_c[d_s y_s + (\alpha_e - 1)\delta A'_s]\right\}$$

$$= \tfrac{1}{2}b \text{ (for symmetrical section)}$$

Moments of inertia about axes through centroid:

$$I_{XX} = \sum_{0}^{h} [b_s h_s + (\alpha_e - 1)\delta A'_s](\bar{x} - h_c)^2$$

$$= \left[\int_0^b b_s(\bar{x} - h_c)^2 \, dh_c\right]$$

$$+ (\alpha_e - 1)[A'_s(\bar{x} - d')^2 + A_s(d - \bar{x})^2]$$

$$I_{YY} = \sum_{0}^{b} [d_s y_s + (\alpha_e - 1)\delta A'_s](\bar{y} - y_c)^2$$

Radius of gyration:

$$i_X = \sqrt{(I_{XX}/A_{tr})} \qquad i_Y = \sqrt{(I_{YY}/A_{tr})}$$

Modulus of section:

$$J_{(h_c=0)} = I_{XX}/\bar{x} \qquad J_{(h_c=h)} = I_{XX}/(h - \bar{x})$$

$$J_{(y_c=0)} = I_{YY}/\bar{y} \qquad J_{(y_c=b)} = I_{YY}/(b - \bar{y})$$

19.2 SECTION SUBJECTED TO BENDING ONLY

Strip compression and tension factors:

$$\delta K_c = (x - h_c)[b_s h_s + (\alpha_e - 1)\delta A'_s] \qquad \delta K_t = (h_c - x)\delta A_s$$

Total compression factor:

$$K_c = \sum_{0}^{x} \delta K_c = \left[\int_0^x (x - h_c) b_s \, dh_c\right] + (\alpha_e - 1)(x - d')A'_s$$

Total tension factor:

$$K_t = \sum_{x}^{d} \delta K_t = (d - x)A_s$$

ANCHORAGE BOND: MINIMUM LENGTHS IN MILLIMETRES FOR NORMAL-WEIGHT CONCRETE

Diam. of bar (mm)	Minimum[1] 12ϕ (mm)	Minimum lap[2] Tension (mm)	Minimum lap[2] Comp. (mm)	Type of hook		$f_{cu} = 20$ N/mm² $f_y = 250$	$f_{cu} = 20$ N/mm² $f_y = 425/460$ Type 1	$f_{cu} = 20$ N/mm² $f_y = 425/460$ Type 2	$f_{cu} = 25$ N/mm² $f_y = 250$	$f_{cu} = 25$ N/mm² $f_y = 425/460$ Type 1	$f_{cu} = 25$ N/mm² $f_y = 425/460$ Type 2	$f_{cu} = 30$ N/mm² $f_y = 250$	$f_{cu} = 30$ N/mm² $f_y = 425/460$ Type 1	$f_{cu} = 30$ N/mm² $f_y = 425/460$ Type 2	$f_{cu} = 40$ N/mm² $f_y = 250$	$f_{cu} = 40$ N/mm² $f_y = 425/460$ Type 1	$f_{cu} = 40$ N/mm² $f_y = 425/460$ Type 2
6	75	300	270	Tension	0	275	355	275	235	320	245	220	275	210	175	235	180
					90°	225	285	200	185	245	175	170	205	140	125	160	110
					180°	180	210	130	140	175	100	125	130	70	80	90	35
				Compression		200	240	185	175	210	165	155	190	145	130	160	125
8	100	350	310	Tension	0	365	475	365	315	425	325	290	365	280	230	310	240
					90°	300	375	270	250	330	230	230	270	185	165	215	145
					180°	235	280	170	185	230	135	165	175	90	105	120	45
				Compression		265	320	245	235	280	215	210	250	190	175	210	165
10	120	400	350	Tension	0	455	590	455	390	530	405	365	455	350	290	385	300
					90°	375	470	335	310	410	285	285	335	230	210	265	180
					180°	295	350	215	230	290	165	205	215	110	130	145	60
				Compression		330	400	310	290	350	270	260	310	240	215	265	205
12	145	450	390	Tension	0	545	710	545	470	635	490	435	550	420	345	465	360
					90°	450	565	400	370	490	345	340	405	280	250	320	215
					180°	355	420	255	275	345	200	245	260	135	155	175	70
				Compression		395	480	370	350	420	325	310	375	285	260	315	245
16	195	550	470	Tension	0	725	945	725	625	845	650	580	730	560	460	620	475
					90°	600	750	535	495	655	460	455	540	370	330	425	285
					180°	470	560	340	370	460	265	325	345	180	205	235	90
				Compression		525	635	490	465	560	430	415	495	380	345	420	325
20	240	650	550	Tension	0	910	1090	840	780	975	750	725	840	650	575	715	550
					90°	750	850	600	620	735	510	565	600	410	415	475	310
					180°	590	610	360	460	495	270	405	360	170	255	235	70
				Compression		655	745	575	580	650	500	520	580	445	430	490	375
25	300	775	650	Tension	0	1135	1360	1050	975	1220	940	910	1050	810	720	890	685
					90°	935	1060	750	775	920	640	710	750	510	520	590	385
					180°	735	760	450	575	620	340	510	450	210	320	290	85
				Compression		820	930	715	725	815	625	645	725	560	535	610	470
32	385	950	790	Tension	0	1450	1740	1340	1245	1560	1200	1160	1345	1035	920	1140	875
					90°	1195	1360	955	990	1175	815	905	960	650	660	755	495
					180°	940	975	570	735	790	430	650	580	270	405	370	110
				Compression		1050	1190	915	925	1040	800	830	925	715	685	780	600

Notes

1. Minimum stopping-off length = 12ϕ or d, whichever is greater.
2. Minimum lap in tension: the greater of $25\phi + 150$ mm *or* anchorage length of smaller bar (mild steel) *or* 1.25 times anchorage length of smaller bar (high-yield steel). Minimum lap in compression: the greater of $20\phi + 150$ mm *or* anchorage length of smaller bar.
3. 250 indicates mild steel. 425/460 indicates high-yield bars.
4. All lengths rounded to 5 mm value above exact figure.
5. Values for hooks correspond to internal radius of 2ϕ for mild-steel bars and 3ϕ for high-yield steel bars.
6. Bar must extend a minimum distance of 4ϕ beyond bend.
7. Lengths given correspond to maximum design stresses in steel of $0.87f_y$ in tension and $2000f_y/(2300 + f_y)$ in compression. For lower design stresses at point beyond which anchorage is to be provided, determine length required from no-hook value on pro rata basis. Then if hook is provided, subtract length equal to difference between appropriate values given in table.

Position of neutral axis:

General: value of x satisfying formula $K_c - \alpha_e K_t = 0$

In terms of maximum stresses: $x = \dfrac{d}{1 + f_{st}/\alpha_e f_{cr}}$

Lever-arm:

$$z = \frac{\sum_x^d h_c \delta K_t}{K_t} - \frac{\sum_0^x h_c \delta K_c}{K_c}$$

$$= d - \left\{ \left[\int_0^x h_c(x - h_c) h_s \, dh_c \right] + (\alpha_e - 1)(x - d') A'_s d' \right\} \Big/ K_c$$

Moment of resistance (compression)

$$\frac{z f_{cr}}{x} K_c$$

Moment of resistance (tension):

$$\frac{z \alpha_e f_{cr}}{x} K_t = z f_{st} A_s$$

19.3 COMMON SECTIONS

For properties of common reinforced concrete sections see *Tables 99* and *100*.

For properties of sections subjected to stress over entire section but neglecting reinforcement, omit terms δA_s, A_s, $\delta A'_s$ and A'_s from the foregoing formulae. The properties of some common sections for this condition are given in *Table 98*.

The moment of inertia of T- and L-sections may be determined from the chart on *Table 101* on which values of I in terms of b_w and h are given for various ratios of b_w/b and h_f/h. This chart, which is similar to one that first appeared in ref. 48, has been calculated from the expression

$$I = K b_w h^3 = \left\{ \frac{\left[\left(\frac{h_f}{h} \right)^3 \left(\frac{b}{b_w} - 1 \right) + 1 \right]}{3} - \frac{\left[\left(\frac{h_f}{h} \right)^2 \left(\frac{b}{b_w} - 1 \right) + 1 \right]^2}{4 \left[\left(\frac{h_f}{h} \right) \left(\frac{b}{b_w} - 1 \right) + 1 \right]} \right\} b_w h^3$$

This chart also includes curves giving the depth to the centroid, the resulting values having been calculated from the relationship

$$\frac{x}{h} = \left[\left(\frac{h_f}{h} \right)^2 \left(\frac{b}{b_w} - 1 \right) + 1 \right] \Big/ 2 \left[\left(\frac{h_f}{h} \right) \left(\frac{b}{b_w} - 1 \right) + 1 \right]$$

MINIMUM INTERNAL RADII FOR ANCHORAGES PER BS8110

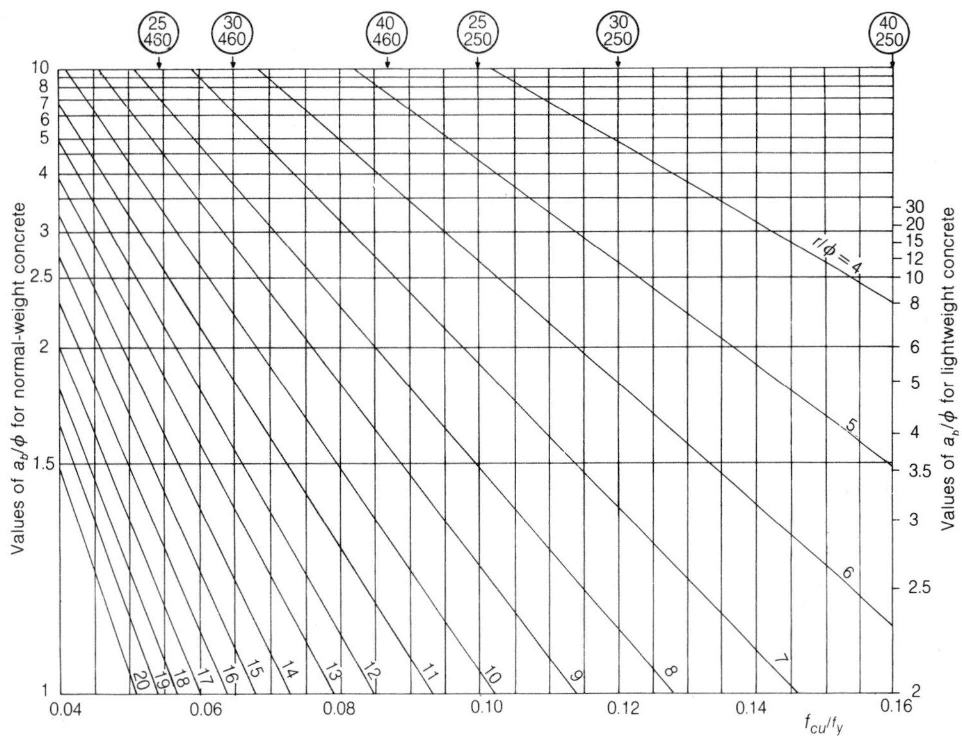

MINIMUM INTERNAL RADII FOR ANCHORAGES PER CP110

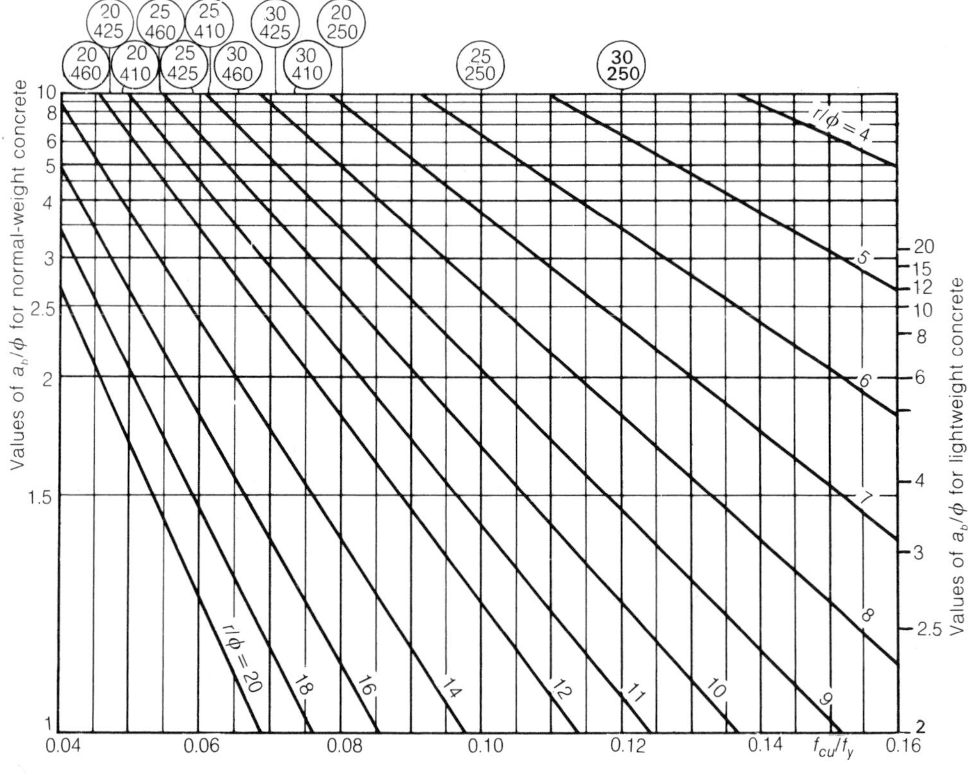

ϕ bar diameter
r internal radius of bend

a_b distance between centres of bars or groups of bars, measured perpendicular to plane of bend

Reinforcement: bending to BS4466—1

Shape code	Method of measuring bending dimensions	Total length of bar	Sketch to be given in schedule
20	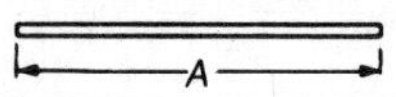	A	Straight
* 32	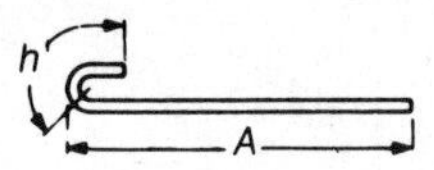	$A+h$	
* 33	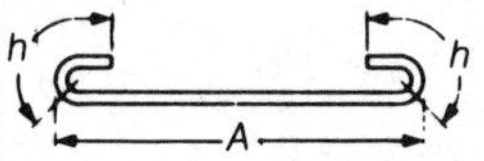	$A+2h$	
* 34	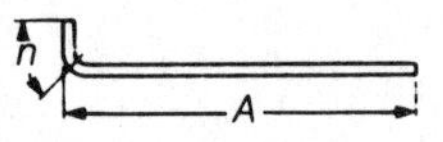	$A+n$	
* 35	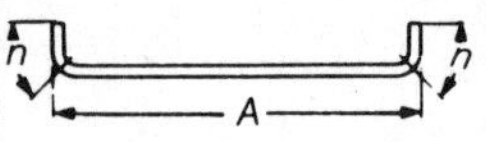	$A+2n$	
* 37	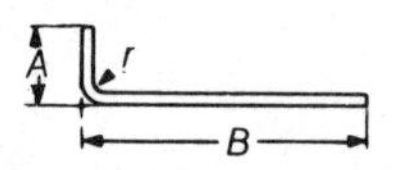	If r is non-standard use shape code 51 $A+B-(\frac{1}{2}r+d)$	
* 38	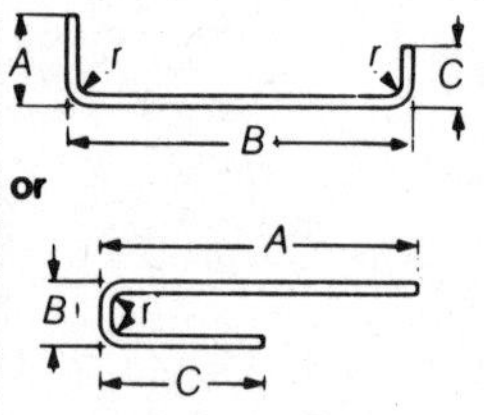 or	$A+B+C-2(\frac{1}{2}r+d)$ $A+B+C-2(\frac{1}{2}r+d)$	or
39	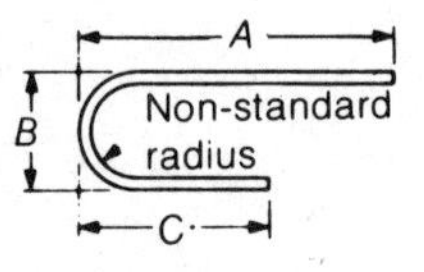 Non-standard radius	$A+0.57B+C-\frac{1}{2}\pi d$	
* 41	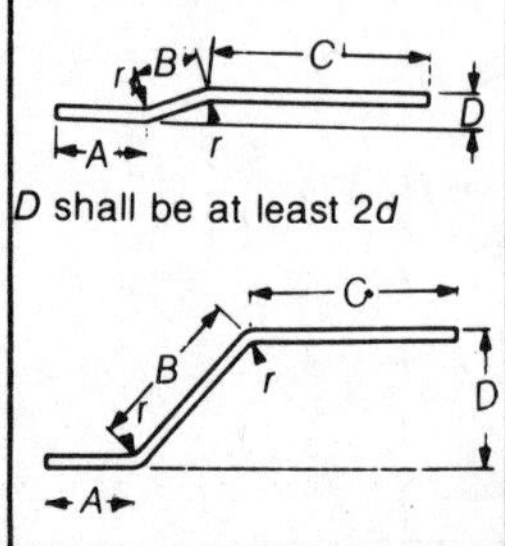 D shall be at least $2d$	If angle with horizontal is 45· or less $A+B+C$	or
42	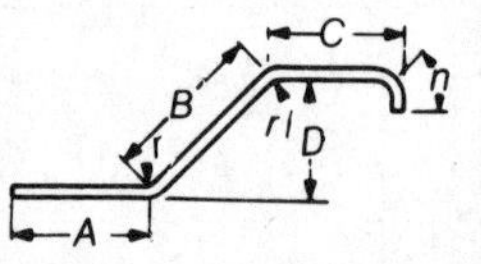	If angle with horizontal is 45° or less $A+B+C+n$	
* 43	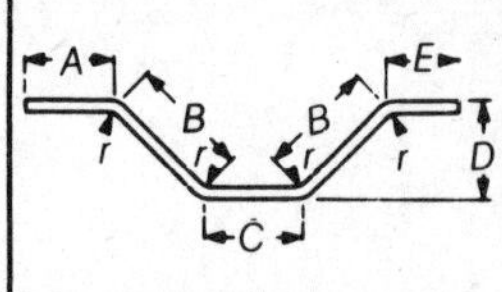	If angle with horizontal is 45° or less $A+2B+C+E$	
45	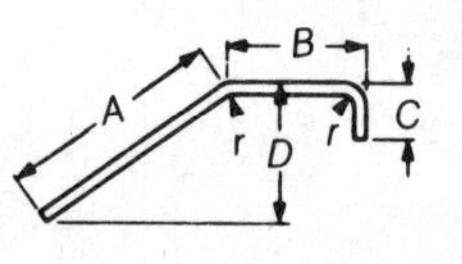	$A+B+C-(\frac{1}{2}r+d)$	
48	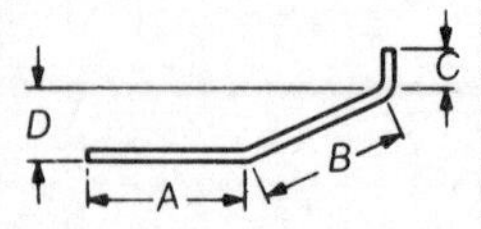	$A+B+C$	
* 51	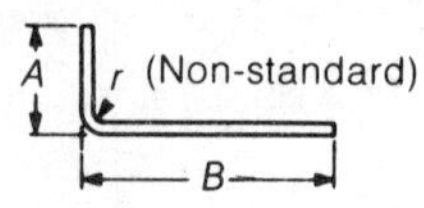 (Non-standard)	If r is standard use shape code 37 $A+B-(\frac{1}{2}r+d)$	
52	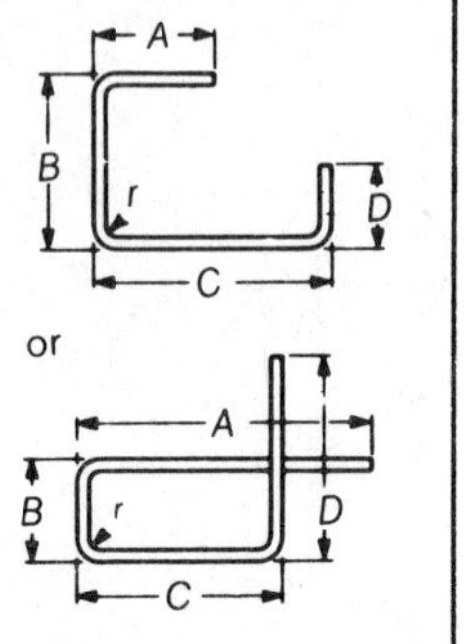 or	$A+B+C+D-3(\frac{1}{2}r+d)$	or
53	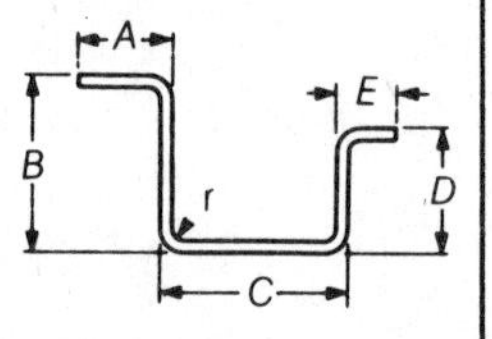	$A+B+C+D+E-4(\frac{1}{2}r+d)$	
54	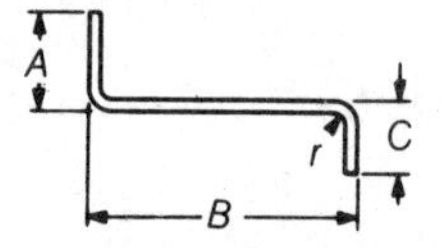	$A+B+C-2(\frac{1}{2}r+d)$	
58	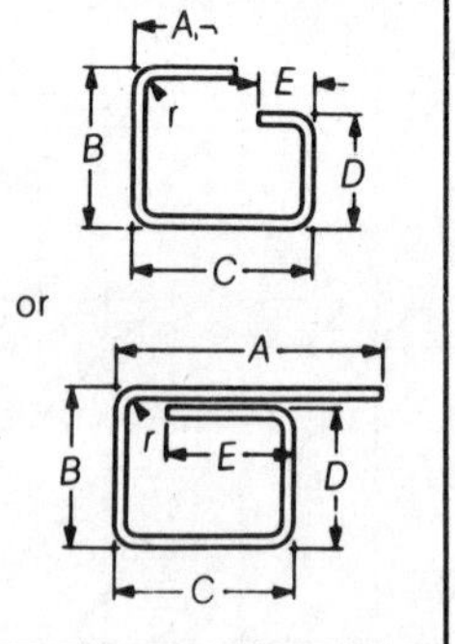 or	$A+B+C+D+E-4(\frac{1}{2}r+d)$	or
* 60	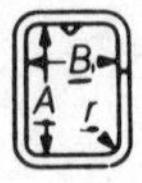	$2(A+B)+20d$	
62	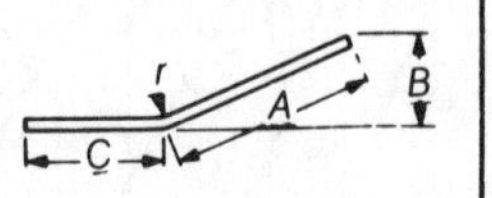	If angle with horizontal is 45° or less $A+C$	
65	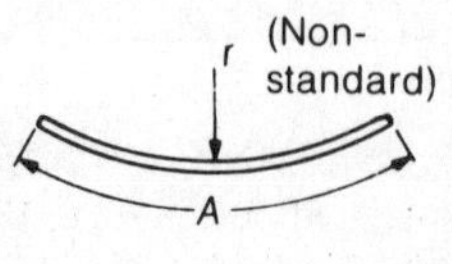 (Non-standard)	A *See also note 4*	

For notes see *Table 97*.

Reinforcement: bending to BS4466—2

Shape code	Method of measuring bending dimensions	Total length of bar	Sketch to be given in schedule
72	See also note 1	$2A+B+25d$	
73	See also notes 1 & 2	$2A+B+C+10d$	C(ID)
74	See also note 1	$2A+3B+20d$	
* 81		$2A+3B+22d$	A(ID)
* 83	Isometric view	$A+2B+C+D-4(\frac{1}{2}r+d)$	B(OD), C(OD), Isometric view
85	Non-standard radius	$A+B+0.57C+D$ $\frac{1}{2}r-2.57d$	
86		where B is not greater than $A/5$ $\frac{C}{B}\pi(A+d)+8d$ Where d is size of bar	Helix A internal dia. B pitch of helix C overall height of helix Dimensions (mm)
99	All other shapes		A dimensioned sketch of the shape must be given on the schedule

Notes

1. If the dimension shown is not internal, use shape code 99.
2. Generally the position of the dimensions in the sketch indicates whether a dimension is internal or external. If the shape is such that there may be doubt as to which is the inside of the bar, arrows should be shown in the bending schedule or the dimension must be marked with the suffix OD (outside dimension) or ID (inside dimension).
3. ϕ diameter of bar
   r radius of bend (standard unless otherwise stated)
   h hook allowance
   n bend allowance

   Hook and bend allowances, standard radii of bends, and values of $(r/2)+\phi$ with standard radii are as follows.

Bar diameter (mm)	$(r/2)+\phi$ Mild steel (mm)	$(r/2)+\phi$ High-yield steel (mm)	Critical min. radius (shape 65) (m)
6	12	18	2.40
8	16	24	2.75
10	20	30	3.50
12	24	36	4.25
16	32	48	7.50
20	40	60	14.00
25	50	100	30.00
32	64	128	43.00
40	80	160	58.00
50	100	200	—

4. For critical radii of bars of this shape, see above table.

* Indicates 'preferred shape' in BS4466.

Dimensions of binders, links etc. are inside dimensions. Radii at corners to be half diameter of bar enclosed by binder etc. (to be stated if non-standard)

	Allowances for links			
Dia.	10ϕ	20ϕ	22ϕ	25ϕ
mm	mm	mm	mm	mm
6	60	120	140	150
8	80	160	180	200
10	100	200	220	250
12	120	240	270	300
in	in	in	in	in
$\frac{1}{4}$	$2\frac{1}{2}$	5	$5\frac{1}{2}$	$6\frac{1}{2}$
$\frac{5}{16}$	$3\frac{1}{2}$	$6\frac{1}{2}$	7	8
$\frac{3}{8}$	4	$7\frac{1}{2}$	$8\frac{1}{2}$	$9\frac{1}{2}$
$\frac{1}{2}$	5	10	11	$12\frac{1}{2}$

Chapter 20
Design of beams and slabs

20.1 ULTIMATE LIMIT-STATE DESIGN: BS8110 AND CP110 REQUIREMENTS

The basic assumptions relating to the ultimate limit-state design of beam and slab sections in accordance with BS8110 and CP110 are outlined in section 5.3.1. As usual, the tensile strength of the concrete is neglected and strains are evaluated on the assumption that plane sections before bending remain plane after bending. To consider conditions at failure, stresses in the reinforcement are then derived from these strains by using the short-term stress–strain design curves on *Table 103*. For the stress in the concrete, alternative assumptions are permitted by both codes. The short-term stress–strain design curve for normal concrete shown on *Table 102* may be employed, and this leads to the assumption of a distribution of stress in the concrete at failure of the form of a combined paraboloid and rectangle as shown. Owing to the form of the basic data governing the shape of the stress–strain curve, the relative proportions of the parabolic and rectangular parts of the concrete stress-block vary as the concrete strength f_{cu} changes. Thus the total compressive resistance provided by the concrete is not linearly related to f_{cu} and the position of the centroid of the stress-block changes slightly as f_{cu} is adjusted.

Alternatively, an equivalent rectangular distribution of stress in the concrete may be assumed, as shown on *Table 102* (the assumptions regarding shape differ between BS8110 and CP110). In the following, basic expressions for determining the shape and properties of these stress distributions are derived and employed to produce suitable design aids and formulae.

In addition to the foregoing rigorous analysis, which may be used for sections of any shape, CP110 also provides simplified formulae for designing rectangular beams and slabs. These are discussed in greater detail below.

20.1.1 Parabolic-rectangular concrete stress-block

From the basic data on the short-term design stress-strain curve for normal concrete, the strain at the interface between the parabolic and linear portions of the curve is given by

$$\varepsilon_0 = \frac{4}{3 \times 5500}\sqrt{\frac{f_{cu}}{\gamma_m}} = \frac{1}{4125}\sqrt{\frac{f_{cu}}{\gamma_m}}$$

When $\gamma_m = 1.5$, $\varepsilon_0 = \sqrt{(f_{cu})}/5052.07$. Over the parabolic curve,

$$\text{stress} = 5500 \times \text{strain}\left(\sqrt{\frac{f_{cu}}{\gamma_m}} - \frac{4125}{2} \times \text{strain}\right)$$

If k_3 is the ratio of the distance between the neutral axis and ε_0 to the depth to the neutral axis x (i.e. $k_3\,x$ is as shown in the top left-hand diagram on *Table 102*), then

$$k_3 = \frac{\varepsilon_0}{0.0035} = \frac{4}{3 \times 5500 \times 0.0035}\sqrt{\frac{f_{cu}}{\gamma_m}} = \frac{1}{14.44}\sqrt{\frac{f_{cu}}{\gamma_m}}$$

When $\gamma_m = 1.5$, $k_3 = \sqrt{(f_{cu})}/17.682$.

The 'volume' of the concrete stress-block (of uniform width b) is now

$$\tfrac{2}{3}bx\frac{f_{cu}}{\gamma_m}(1 - \tfrac{1}{3}k_3) = k_1 bx$$

where

$$k_1 = \frac{2}{3}\frac{f_{cu}}{\gamma_m} - \frac{8}{27 \times 5500 \times 0.0035}\sqrt{\left(\frac{f_{cu}}{\gamma_m}\right)^3}$$

When $\gamma_m = 1.5$, $k_1 = 0.445\,f_{cu} - 0.00838\sqrt{(f_{cu})^3}$

The depth of the centroid of this concrete stress-block from the top of the stressed section is given by

$$\{[\tfrac{1}{2} - \tfrac{1}{3}k_3(1 - \tfrac{1}{4}k_3)]/[1 - \tfrac{1}{3}k_3]\}x$$

$$= \left\{\left[6 - \frac{4}{14.44}\sqrt{\left(\frac{f_{cu}}{\gamma_m}\right)} + \left(\frac{1}{14.44}\right)^2\frac{f_{cu}}{\gamma_m}\right]\Big/\left[12 - \frac{4}{14.44}\sqrt{\left(\frac{f_{cu}}{\gamma_m}\right)}\right]\right\}x$$

$$= k_2 x$$

Then lever-arm $= d - k_2 x$. When $\gamma_m = 1.5$,

$$k_2 = \frac{1876 - 70.73\sqrt{(f_{cu})} + f_{cu}}{3752 - 70.73\sqrt{(f_{cu})}}$$

Resistance moment of concrete section $= k_1 bx(d - k_2 x)$.

For values of f_{cu} between 20 and 40 N/mm^2, the corresponding coefficients k_1, k_2 and k_3 can be read from the scales on *Table 102*. For frequently used concrete grades, values of M_u/bd^2 corresponding to different ratios of x/d are also tabulated. These expressions and values for k_1 and k_2 are valid for simple rectangular sections only: for more

Geometric properties of uniform sections

Section	Area A	Section modulus J_c	Second moment of area I	Radiation of gyration i
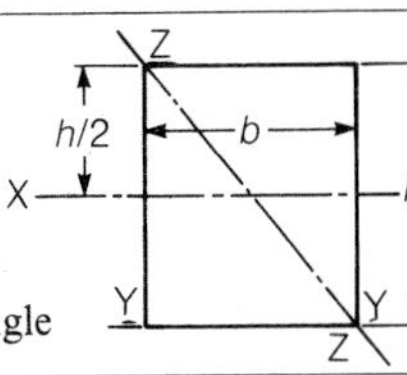 Rectangle	bh	About XX: $\frac{1}{6}bh^2$ About ZZ: $\frac{1}{6}\frac{b^2h^2}{\sqrt{(b^2+h^2)}}$	About XX: $\frac{1}{12}bh^3$ About YY: $\frac{1}{3}bh^3$ About ZZ: $\frac{1}{6}\frac{b^3h^3}{(b^2+h^2)}$	About XX: $h/\sqrt{12} = 0.2887h$
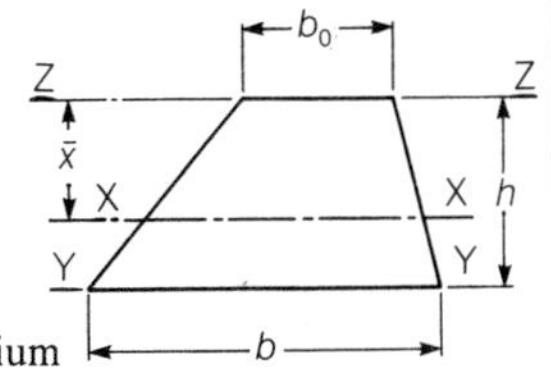 Trapezium	$\frac{1}{2}h(b_0+b)$	About XX to b_0: $\frac{(b^2+4bb_0+b_0^2)h^2}{12(b+2b_0)}$ To b: $I_{xx}/(h-\bar{x})$ where $\bar{x} = \frac{1}{3}h\left(\frac{2b+b_0}{b+b_0}\right)$	About XX: $\frac{(b^2+4bb_0+b_0^2)h^3}{36(b+b_0)}$ About YY: $I_{xx} + A(h-\bar{x})^2$ About ZZ: $I_{xx} + A(\bar{x})^2$	About XX: $\sqrt{\frac{I_{xx}}{A}}$
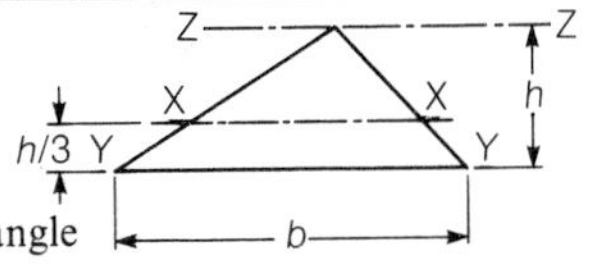 Triangle	$\frac{1}{2}bh$	About XX to apex: $\frac{1}{24}bh^2$ About XX to base: $\frac{1}{12}bh^2$	About XX: $\frac{1}{36}bh^3$ About YY: $\frac{1}{12}bh^3$ About ZZ: $\frac{1}{4}bh^3$	About XX: $h/\sqrt{18} = 0.2357h$
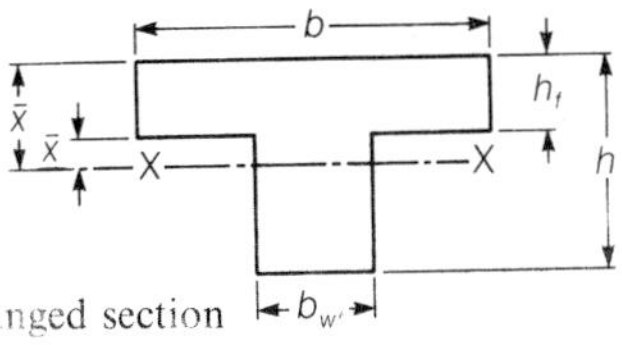 Flanged section	$bh_f + b_w(h-h_f)$	About XX: $\frac{I_{xx}}{\bar{x}}$ or $\frac{I_{xx}}{h-\bar{x}}$ $\bar{x} = \frac{h_f^2(b-b_w)+h^2b_w}{2[h_f(b-b_w)+hb_w]}$	About XX: $\frac{1}{3}[b\bar{x}^3 + b_w(h-\bar{x})^3 - (\bar{x}')^3(b-b_w)]$ where $\bar{x}' = \bar{x} - h_f$	About XX: $\sqrt{\frac{I_{xx}}{A}}$
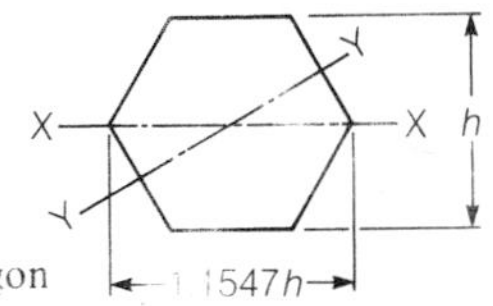 Hexagon (1.1547h)	$0.8660h^2$ (side $= 0.5774h$)	About XX: $0.1203h^3$ About YY: $0.1042h^3$	About XX or YY: $0.0601h^4$	About XX or YY: $0.2635h$
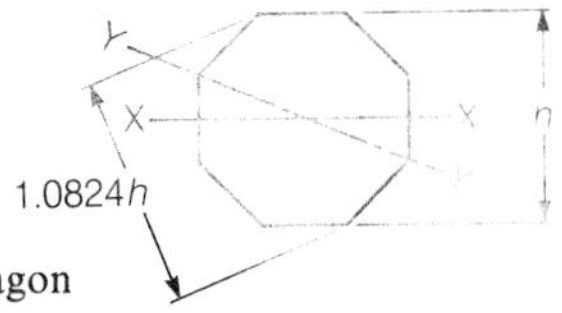 Octagon (1.0824h)	$0.8284h^2$ (side $= 0.4142h$)	About XX: $0.1095h^3$ About YY: $0.1011h^3$	About XX or YY: $0.0547h^4$	About XX or YY: $0.2570h$
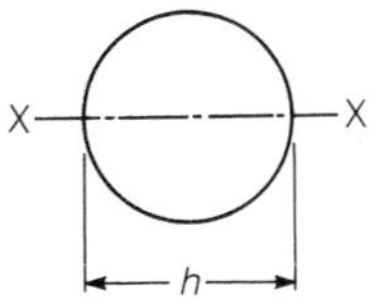 Circle	$0.7854h^2 = \frac{\pi}{4}h^2$	About XX: $\frac{1}{32}\pi h^3 = 0.0982h^3$	About XX: $\frac{1}{64}\pi h^4 = 0.0491h^4$	About XX: $0.2500h$
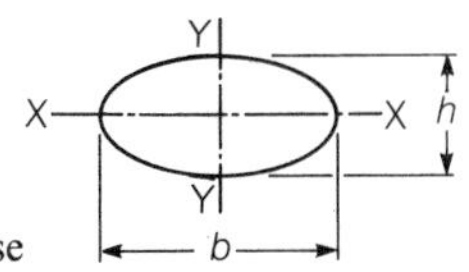 Ellipse	$\frac{1}{4}\pi bh = 0.7854bh$	About XX: $\frac{1}{32}\pi bh^2 = 0.0982bh^2$	About XX: $\frac{1}{64}\pi bh^3 = 0.0491bh^3$	About XX: $0.2500h$
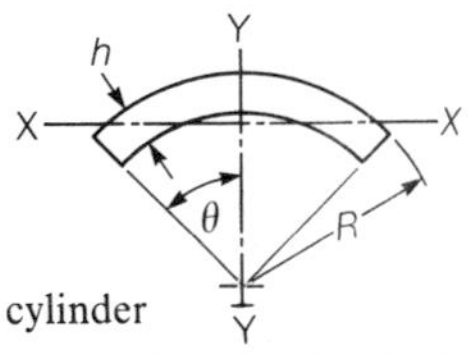 Sector of cylinder	$\theta h(2R-h)$	About XX to top: I_{xx}/y_t^* About XX to bottom: I_{xx}/y_b^*	About XX: I_{xx}^* About YY: I_{yy}^*	About XX: $\sqrt{\frac{I_{xx}}{A}}$

(For approx. formulae for shell roof design, see *Table 179*)

$$y_t^* = R\left\{1 - \frac{2\sin\theta}{3\theta}\left(1 - \frac{h}{R} + \frac{1}{2-(h/R)}\right)\right. \qquad y_b^* = R\left[\frac{2\sin\theta}{3\theta(2-(h/R))} + \left(1-\frac{h}{R}\right)\frac{2\sin\theta - 3\theta\cos\theta}{3\theta}\right]$$

About XX: $$I_{xx}^* = R^3h\left\{\left[1 - \frac{3h}{2R} + \left(\frac{h}{R}\right)^2 - \frac{1}{4}\left(\frac{h}{R}\right)^3\right]\left[\theta + \sin\theta\cos\theta - \frac{2\sin^2\theta}{\theta}\right] + \frac{h^2\sin^2\theta}{3R^2\theta(2-(h/R))}\left[1 - \frac{h}{R} + \frac{1}{6}\left(\frac{h}{R}\right)^2\right]\right\}$$

About YY: $$I_{yy}^* = R^3h\left\{\left[1 - \frac{3h}{2R} + \left(\frac{h}{R}\right)^2 - \frac{1}{4}\left(\frac{h}{R}\right)^3\right][\theta - \sin\theta\cos\theta]\right\}$$

	Entire cross-section subjected to stress	Bending only with concrete ineffective in tension compression zone at top (as drawn)
Notation (additional to data on diagrams) Geometrical properties are expressed in equivalent concrete units	A_{tr} effective area $\bar{x}$ position of centroid from top edge I_{XX} moment of inertia about centroidal axis Modulus of section: For top edge: $J_0 = \dfrac{I_{XX}}{\bar{x}}$ For bottom edge: $J_h = \dfrac{I_{XX}}{h-\bar{x}}$ } unless expressed otherwise Radius of gyration: $i = \sqrt{\dfrac{I_{XX}}{A_{tr}}}$	Distance of neutral axis below top edge $= x$ Related to maximum stresses: $x = d \bigg/ \left(1 + \dfrac{f_{st}}{\alpha_e f_{cr}}\right)$ Lever-arm $= z$ Compression-reinforcement factor $K_1 = A'_s(\alpha_e - 1)\left(\dfrac{x-d'}{x}\right)$ Moment of resistance: M_d (compression) $= zK_2 f_{cr}$ M_d (tension) $= zA_s f_{st}$ } unless expressed otherwise
Rectangle	$A_{tr} = bh + (\alpha_e - 1)(A_s + A'_s)$ $\bar{x} = \dfrac{1}{A_{tr}}[\tfrac{1}{2}bh^2 + (\alpha_e - 1)(A_s d + A'_s d')]$ $= \tfrac{1}{2}h$ if $A_s = A'_s$ $I_{XX} = \tfrac{1}{3}b[\bar{x}^3 + (h-\bar{x})^3] + (\alpha_e - 1)[A_s(d-\bar{x})^2 + A'_s(\bar{x}-d')^2]$ $= \tfrac{1}{12}bh^3 + 2A_s(\alpha_e - 1)(\tfrac{1}{2}h - d')^2$ if $A_s = A'_s$	$x = \sqrt{\left\{\left[\alpha_e\dfrac{A_s}{b} + (\alpha_e - 1)\dfrac{A'_s}{b}\right]^2 + 2\left[\alpha_e\dfrac{A_s}{b} + (\alpha_e - 1)\dfrac{A'_s}{b}\dfrac{d'}{d}\right]\right\}}$ $- \left[\alpha_e\dfrac{A_s}{b} + (\alpha_e - 1)\dfrac{A'_s}{b}\right]$ $z = \dfrac{1}{K_2}[\tfrac{1}{2}bx(d - \tfrac{1}{3}x) + K_1(d-d')]$ $\quad K_2 = \tfrac{1}{2}bx + K_1$ If $A'_s = 0$, $z = d - \tfrac{1}{3}x$ and $M_d(\text{compression}) = \tfrac{1}{2}bxzf_{cr} = K_{conc}bd^2$
Square A_{si} at each corner	$A_{tr} = h^2 + 4(\alpha_e - 1)A_{si}$ About axis XX: $\bar{x} = \tfrac{1}{2}h$ $I_{XX} = \tfrac{1}{12}h^4 + 4A_{si}(\alpha_e - 1)(\tfrac{1}{2}h - d')^2$ $J_0 = J_h = \dfrac{2I_{XX}}{h}$ About diagonal axis YY: $\bar{y} = 0.707h$ $I_{YY} = \tfrac{1}{12}h^4 + 2A_{si}(\alpha_e - 1)(\tfrac{1}{2}h - d')^2$ $J_0 = J_h = \dfrac{2\sqrt{(2)}I_{YY}}{h}$	About axis XX: formulae as for rectangular section with $A_s = A'_s = 2A_{si}$ and $b = h$. About diagonal axis YY: $x \not> 0.707h$ $z = \dfrac{1}{K_2}\left[\dfrac{x^2}{3\sqrt{2}}\left(d\sqrt{2} - \dfrac{4x}{9}\right) + A_{si}(\alpha_e - 1)\left(\dfrac{x - d'\sqrt{2}}{x}\right)(h - 2d')\sqrt{2}\right]$ $K_2 = \dfrac{x^2}{3\sqrt{2}} + A_{si}(\alpha_e - 1)\left(\dfrac{x - d'\sqrt{2}}{x}\right)$ $\quad A_s = A_{si}$
Trapezium	$A_{tr} = \tfrac{1}{2}(b + b_0)h + (\alpha_e - 1)(A_s + A'_s)$ $\bar{x} = \dfrac{1}{A_{tr}}\left[\dfrac{h^2}{6}(b + 2b_0) + (\alpha_e - 1)(A_s d + A'_s d')\right] = \dfrac{h}{3}\left(\dfrac{b + 2b_0}{b + b_0}\right)$ approx. $I_{XX} = \left[\dfrac{(b+b_0)^2 + 2bb_0}{b + b_0}\right]\dfrac{h^3}{36} + (\alpha_e - 1)[A_s(d-\bar{x})^2 + A'_s(\bar{x}-d')^2]$	$z = \dfrac{1}{K_2}\left\{\tfrac{1}{2}x\left[b(d - \tfrac{1}{3}x) - \dfrac{x}{3h}(b - b_0)\left(d - \dfrac{4x}{9}\right)\right] + K_1(d-d')\right\}$ $K_2 = \tfrac{1}{2}x\left[b - \dfrac{x}{3h}(b - b_0)\right] + K_1$
Triangle	$A_{tr} = \tfrac{1}{2}bh + (\alpha_e - 1)(A_s + A'_s)$ $\bar{x} = \dfrac{1}{A_{tr}}[\tfrac{1}{6}bh^2 + (\alpha_e - 1)(A_s d + A'_s d')] = \tfrac{1}{3}h$ approx. $I_{XX} = \dfrac{bh^3}{36} + (\alpha_e - 1)[A_s(d-\bar{x})^2 + A'_s(\bar{x}-d')^2]$	$z = \dfrac{1}{K_2}\left\{\dfrac{bx}{2}\left[(d - \tfrac{1}{3}x) - \dfrac{x}{3h}\left(d - \dfrac{4x}{9}\right)\right] + K_1(d-d')\right\}$ $K_2 = \tfrac{1}{2}bx\left(1 - \dfrac{x}{3h}\right) + K_1$

I-section

$$A_{tr} = bh_f + b_0h_0 + b_w(h - h_f - h_0) + (\alpha_e - 1)(A_s + A_s')$$

$$\bar{x} = \frac{1}{2A_{tr}}[(b - b_w)h_f^2 + (b_0 - b_w)(2h - h_0)h_0 + b_wh^2 + 2(\alpha_e - 1)(A_sd + A_s'd')]$$

$$I_{XX} = \tfrac{1}{3}[b\bar{x}^3 - (b - b_w)(\bar{x} - h_f)^3 + b_0(h - \bar{x})^3 - (b_0 - b_w)(h - \bar{x} - h_0)^3] + (\alpha_e - 1)[A_s'(\bar{x} - d')^2 + A_s(d - \bar{x})^2]$$

If $x \ngtr h_f$: use formulae for rectangle

If $x > h_f$:

$$z = \frac{1}{K_2}\left[\tfrac{1}{2}bx(d - \tfrac{1}{3}x) - \frac{1}{6x}(b - b_w)(x - h_f)(3d - 2h - x) - K_1(d - d')\right]$$

$$K_2 = \frac{1}{2}\left[bx - \frac{1}{x}(b - b_w)(x - h_f)\right] + K_1$$

T- and L-sections

$$A_{tr} = bh_f + b_w(h - h_f) + (\alpha_e - 1)A_s$$

$$\bar{x} = \frac{1}{2A_{tr}}[bh_f^2 + b_w(h - h_f)(h + h_f) + 2A_sd(\alpha_e - 1)]$$

$$I_{XX} = \tfrac{1}{3}[b\bar{x}^3 - (b - b_w)(\bar{x} - h_f)^3 + b_w(h - \bar{x})^3] + (\alpha_e - 1)A_s(d - \bar{x})^2$$

If $x \ngtr h_f$: use formulae for rectangle

If $x > h_f$: $x \simeq \dfrac{(1/2)bh_f^2 + A_s\alpha_e d}{bh_f + A_s\alpha_e}$

$$z = d - \left(\frac{3x - 2h_f}{2x - h_f}\right)\frac{h_f}{3} = d - \tfrac{1}{2}h_f \text{ approx.}$$

$$M_d\ (\text{compression}) = (2x - h_f)\frac{zf_{cr}bh_f}{2x}$$

Octagon

A_{si} at each corner.

$d = h - d'$ $\quad d' = \frac{1}{2}h - 0.462h_1$

$$A_{tr} = 0.828h^2 + 8A_{si}(\alpha_e - 1)$$

$$\bar{x} = \tfrac{1}{2}h$$

$$I_{XX} = 0.055h^4 + 4A_{si}(\tfrac{1}{2}h_1)^2(\alpha_e - 1)$$

$$J_0 = J_h = 0.109h^3 + 4A_{si}\frac{(h_1/2)^2}{h}(\alpha_e - 1)$$

$$z = \frac{1}{K_2}\left[0.207hx\left(h - \frac{x}{8}\right) + K_3 + 2A_{si}(\alpha_e - 1)\left(\frac{x - d'}{x}\right)(d - d')\right]$$

$$K_2 = 0.207hx + K_4 + 2A_{si}(\alpha_e - 1)\left(\frac{x - d'}{x}\right)$$

If $x \ngtr 0.29h$: $K_3 = K_4\left(d - \dfrac{4x}{9}\right)$ $\qquad K_4 = \frac{1}{3}x^2$

If $x > 0.29h$:

$$K_3 = K_4\left[d - 0.195h\left(\frac{x - 0.22h}{x - 0.195h}\right)\right] \qquad K_4 = \frac{0.086h^2}{x}(x - 0.195h)$$

Circle and annulus

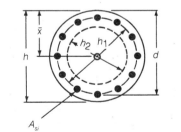

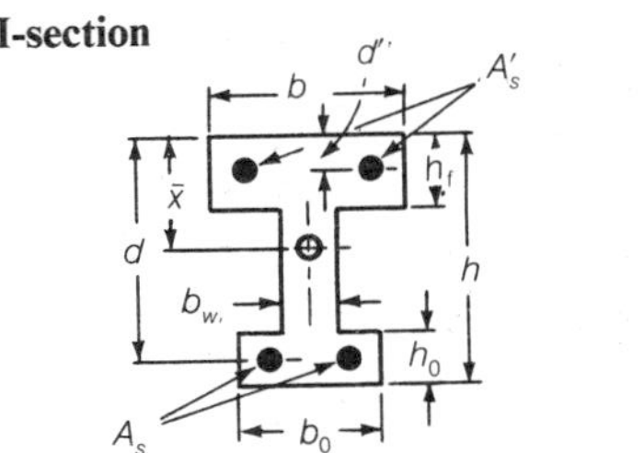

a = depth of individual bar from top of section

For annulus:

$$A_{tr} = 0.7854(h^2 - h_2^2) + (\alpha_e - 1)\Sigma A_{si}$$

$$\bar{x} = 0.5h$$

$$I_{XX} = \tfrac{1}{64}\pi(h^4 - h_2^4) + (\alpha_e - 1)\tfrac{1}{2}(\tfrac{1}{2}h_1)^2\Sigma A_{si}$$

$$J_0 = J_h = \frac{\pi}{32h}(h^4 - h_2^4) + (\alpha_e - 1)\frac{(h_1/2)^2}{h}\Sigma A_{si}$$

For circle: use above formulae with $h_2 = 0$

For circle:

$$M_d(\text{compression}) = M_d(\text{tension}) = [K_5(a_t - a_c) + K_6(a_t - a_t')]f_{cr}$$

$$K_5 = \left(\frac{h^2}{4x} - \frac{h - x}{3}\right)\sqrt{[(h - x)x]} + \frac{h^2}{8x}(h - 2x)\sin^{-1}\left(\frac{h - 2x}{h}\right)$$

$$K_6 = \frac{\alpha_e - 1}{x}\Sigma_0^x(x - a)A_{si}$$

$$a_t = \frac{\Sigma_x^d(a - x)aA_{si}}{\Sigma_x^d(a - x)A_{si}} \qquad a_t' = \frac{\Sigma_0^x(x - a)aA_{si}}{\Sigma_0^x(x - a)A_{si}}$$

$$a_c = \frac{1}{K_5}\left\{\left[\frac{2}{3}x^2 - \frac{7}{12}h\left(x + \frac{h}{4}\right) + \frac{5}{32x}h^3\right]\sqrt{[(h - x)x]} + \tfrac{1}{2}\sqrt{[(h - x)^3x^3]} + \frac{h^3}{8x}(\tfrac{5}{8}h - x)\sin^{-1}\left(\frac{h - 2x}{h}\right)\right\}$$

For annulus: if $x \ngtr (h - h_2)/2$ use above formulae; otherwise use graphical method complex shapes the necessary formulae may be obtained by evaluating appropriate volume integrals.

Rectangular concrete stress-block according to BS8110

Compressive resistance of stress-block $= 0.402 f_{cu} bx$.
Depth of centroid from top of stressed section $= 0.45x$.
Lever-arm of section $= d - 0.45x$.
Resistance moment of concrete section $= 0.402 f_{cu} bx(d - 0.45x) = M_u$.

Thus

$$\frac{M_u}{bd^2 f_{cu}} = 0.402\frac{x}{d}\left(1 - 0.45\frac{x}{d}\right)$$

Values of $M_u/bd^2 f_{cu}$ relating to various values of x/d can be read from *Table 102*.

Rectangular concrete stress-block according to CP110

Compressive resistance of stress-block $= 2f_{cu}bx/5$.
Depth of centroid from top of stressed section $= x/2$.
Lever-arm of section $= d - x/2$.
Resistance moment of concrete section $= (2f_{cu}bx/5)(d - x/2) = M_u$.

Thus

$$\frac{M_u}{bd^2 f_{cu}} = \frac{1}{5}\frac{x}{d}\left(2 - \frac{x}{d}\right)$$

Values of $M_u/bd^2 f_{cu}$ relating to various values of x/d can be read from *Table 102*.

20.1.2 Reinforcement: relationship between stress and strain according to BS8110

The short-term stress–strain curve for reinforcement is defined by the following expressions:

Stress at A:

$$f_A = f_y/\gamma_m$$

Strain at A:

$$\varepsilon_A = f_y/200\,000\gamma_m$$

For bar reinforcement having the specified characteristic strengths f_y given in Table 3.1 of BS8110 (i.e. 250 and 460 N/mm^2), values of stress and strain which determine the shape of the stress–strain curve may be read from *Table 103*.

Stress for a given strain. For a given value of strain, the corresponding stress in the reinforcement can be determined from the expression

$$f_x = 200\,000\varepsilon_x$$

when the strain at the point considered is less than the strain at point A.

Stress for a given neutral-axis depth. The strains ε_s and ε'_s in the tension and compression reinforcement respectively are related to the depth to the neutral axis x by the expressions

$$\varepsilon'_s = 0.0035\left(1 - \frac{d'}{x}\right) = 0.0035\left(1 - \frac{d'}{d}\frac{d}{x}\right)$$

$$\varepsilon_s = 0.0035\left(\frac{d}{x} - 1\right)$$

Hence the design stress f_{yd} in the reinforcement can conveniently be related directly to the depth-to-neutral-axis factor x/d. Then, by simply comparing the actual value of x/d adopted for a particular section with the limiting value occurring at point A on the reinforcement stress–strain curve, the corresponding value of f_{yd} can be ascertained without having to calculate the strains concerned. The values of x/d and f_{yd} derived from the short-term design stress–strain curve in *Table 103* are as follows.

For compression reinforcement:

When $\dfrac{x}{d} \leqslant \dfrac{700\gamma_m}{(700\gamma_m - f_y)}\left(\dfrac{d'}{d}\right)$: $f_{yd} = 700\left(\dfrac{d}{x}\right)\left(\dfrac{x}{d} - \dfrac{d'}{d}\right)$

Otherwise: $f_{yd} = f_y/\gamma_m$

For tension reinforcement:

When $\dfrac{x}{d} \leqslant \dfrac{700\gamma_m}{(700\gamma_m + f_y)}$: $f_{yd} = f_y/\gamma_m$

Otherwise: $f_{yd} = 700\left(\dfrac{d}{x} - 1\right)$

When $\gamma = 1.15$ for reinforcement, appropriate values of x/d at point A on the stress–strain curve and expressions for f_{yd} for normal values of f_y and also for the general case are tabulated in *Table 103*.

20.1.3 Reinforcement: relationship between stress and strain according to CP110

The expressions that give the values of stress and strain which determine the shape of the short-term design stress–strain curve for reinforcement are as follows:

Stress at A: $f_A = 0.8f_y/\gamma_m$
Strain at A: $\varepsilon_A = 0.8f_y/200\,000\gamma_m$
Stress at B: $f_B = 2000f_y/(2000\gamma_m + f_y)$
Strain at B: $\varepsilon_B = 0.002$
Stress at C: $f_C = f_y/\gamma_m$
Strain at C: $\varepsilon_C = 0.002 + f_y/200\,000\gamma_m$

For bar reinforcement having the specified characteristic strength f_y tabulated in clause 3.1.4.3 of CP110, values of stress and strain at the points which determine the shape of the stress–strain curve are set out in *Table 103*.

Stress for a given strain. For a given value of strain, the corresponding stress in the reinforcement can be obtained from the stress–strain curve.

When the strain at the point under consideration is less than the strain at point A on the stress–strain curve, the stress at point X considered is $f_x = 200\,000\varepsilon_x$. When the strain at the point under consideration is greater than the strain at point A but less than the strain at point C, the stress at X is

$$f_x = \frac{(\text{strain at X} - \text{strain at A})}{(\text{strain at C} - \text{strain at A})} \times (\text{stress at C} - \text{stress at A}) + \text{stress at A}$$

Properties of flanged sections

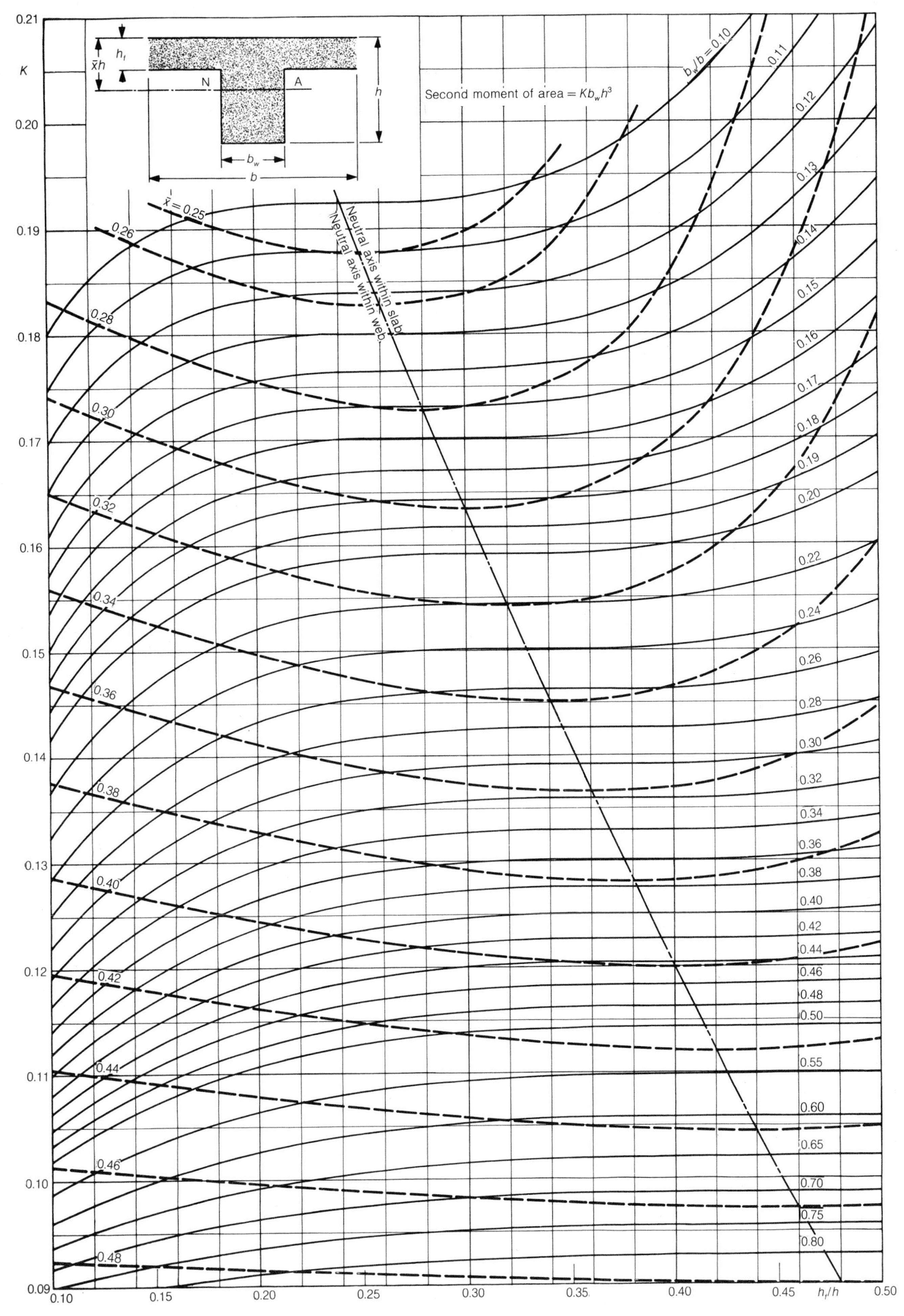

$$= (100\varepsilon_x + 0.8)\frac{2000 f_y}{2000\gamma_m + f_y}$$

$$= k_4\varepsilon_x + k_5$$

Values of k_4 and k_5 for reinforcement having specified characteristic strengths tabulated in clause 3.1.4.3 of CP110 are given in *Table 103*.

Stress for a given neutral-axis depth. Since the strains ε_s and ε_s' in the tension and compression reinforcement respectively are related to the depth to the neutral axis by the expressions

$$\varepsilon_s' = 0.0035\left(1 - \frac{d'}{x}\right) = 0.0035\left(1 - \frac{d'}{d}\frac{d}{x}\right)$$

$$\varepsilon_s = 0.0035\left(\frac{d}{x} - 1\right)$$

the design yield stress f_{yd} in the reinforcement can conveniently be related directly to the depth-to-neutral-axis factor x/d. Then, by simply comparing the actual value of x/d adopted for a particular section with the limiting values occurring at points A, B and C on the reinforcement stress–strain curve, the corresponding value of f_{yd} can be ascertained without the need to evaluate the strains concerned. The values of x/d and f_{yd} derived from the short-term design stress–strain curve for reinforcement shown on *Table 103* are as follows.

For compression reinforcement:

When $\dfrac{700\gamma_m}{(700\gamma_m - 0.8 f_y)}\left(\dfrac{d'}{d}\right) \geqslant \dfrac{x}{d}$:

$$f_{yd} = 700\left(\frac{d}{x}\right)\left(\frac{x}{d} - \frac{d'}{d}\right)$$

When $\dfrac{700\gamma_m}{(700\gamma_m - 0.8 f_y)}\left(\dfrac{d'}{d}\right) \leqslant \dfrac{x}{d} \leqslant \dfrac{7}{3}\left(\dfrac{d'}{d}\right)$:

$$f_{yd} = \frac{d}{x}\left(2300\frac{x}{d} - 700\frac{d'}{d}\right) \times \frac{f_y}{2000\gamma_m + f_y}$$

When $\dfrac{x}{d} \geqslant \dfrac{7}{3}\left(\dfrac{d'}{d}\right)$:

$$f_{yd} = \frac{2000 f_y}{2000\gamma_m + f_y}$$

For tension reinforcement:

When $\dfrac{700\gamma_m}{1100\gamma_m + f_y} \geqslant \dfrac{x}{d}$:

$$f_{yd} = f_y/\gamma_m$$

When $\dfrac{700\gamma_m}{1100\gamma_m + f_y} \leqslant \dfrac{x}{d} \leqslant \dfrac{700\gamma_m}{700\gamma_m + 0.8 f_y}$:

$$f_{yd} = \left(700\frac{d}{x} - 900\right) \times \frac{f_y}{2000\gamma_m + f_y}$$

When $\dfrac{x}{d} \geqslant \dfrac{700\gamma_m}{700\gamma_m + 0.8 f_y}$:

$$f_{yd} = 700\left(\frac{d}{x} - 1\right)$$

When $\gamma_m = 1.15$ for reinforcement, appropriate values of x/d at points A, B and C on the stress–strain curve and expressions for f_{yd} for normal values of f_y and also for the general case are given in *Table 103*.

For values of f_y of 250, 425 and 460 N/mm^2, the values of f_{yd1} corresponding to various ratios of $d'/x = (d'/d)(d/x)$ and of f_{yd2} corresponding to various ratios of x/d can conveniently be read directly from the appropriate scales provided on *Table 104*. The points on these scales marked 'scale changes' indicate points A on the trilinear stress–strain curves for reinforcement specified in CP110 and shown in *Table 103*.

20.1.4 Design methods: rigorous analysis

Position of neutral axis. With the limit-state design method the choice of the value of x, the depth to the neutral axis of the section, is left to the designer, subject to the restriction that $x/d \not> 1/2$ for sections reinforced in tension only. As explained in more detail in section 5.3.2, since the choice of x/d controls the strains and hence the stresses in the tension and compression reinforcement, it is usually advantageous to select that value of x/d which corresponds to the limiting strain at which the design stress in the tension reinforcement is a maximum, since this minimizes the total amount of reinforcement required. This can be seen from the accompanying diagram, which has been prepared from a typical CP110 design chart (ref. 79) for beams with tension and compression reinforcement employing rigorous limit-state analysis with a rectangular concrete stress-block. The bold line indicates the resistance moment provided by a total proportion of reinforcement of $0.002bdf_{cu}$ for various ratios of x/d, and shows clearly that in the present case the maximum resistance corresponds to a value of x/d of 0.531, which in turn corresponds to an offset strain of 0.2% in the tension reinforcement.

With BS8110, if normal partial safety factors apply, the limiting ratios of x/d at which the design stress in the tension steel is at its maximum value are 0.763 and 0.636 when $f_y = 250$ and 460 N/mm^2 respectively. For sections reinforced in tension only, the x/d ratio is limited to 0.5, and this ratio should be adopted unless redistribution reequirements (see section 5.3.2) determine the maximum ratio that may be adopted. Where compression steel is needed, if redistribution requirements allow, the total steel needed is minimized if the foregoing ratios are employed.

However, if compression steel is to be used, BS8110 specifies that a minimum of 0.2% must be provided in rectangular sections and in flanged sections where the web is in compression, and of 0.4% in other flanged sections. There is thus no point in adopting a ratio of x/d such that the resulting amount of compression steel falls below these percentages, and other considerations also indicate that it is perhaps less than wise in normal circumstances to adopt x/d ratios greater than 0.6.

Concrete stress-block data

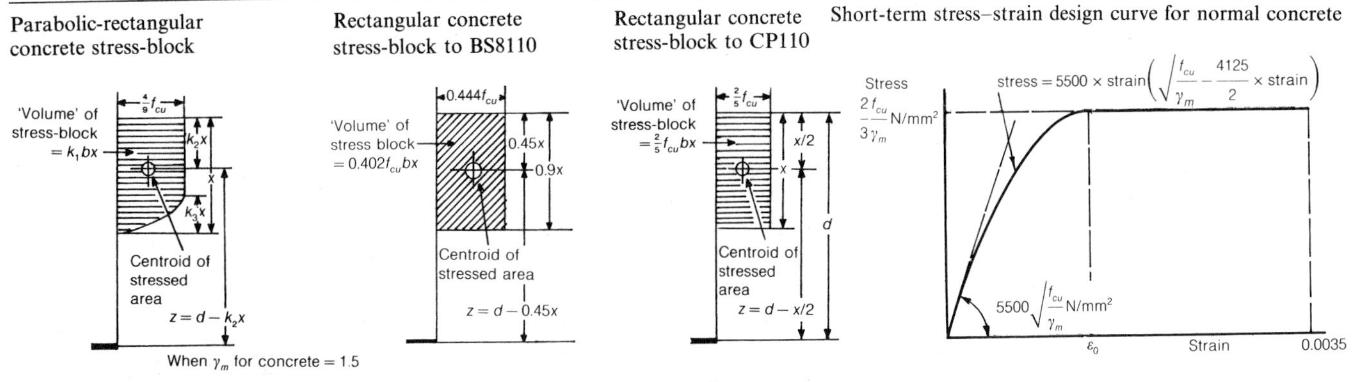

Stress-block factors

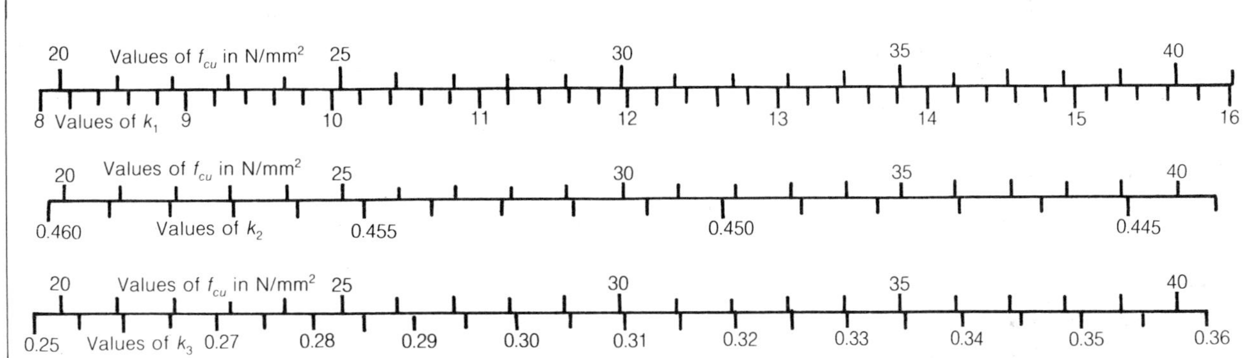

Resistance-moment and lever-arm factors for particular concrete strengths and x/d ratios

	Parabolic-rectangular stress-block										Uniform stress block	
	f_{cu} in N/mm²										BS8110	CP110
	20		25		30		40		50			
x/d	M_u/bd^2	z/d	M_u/bd^2	z/d	M_u/bd^2	z/d	M_u/bd^2	z/d	M_u/bd^2	z/d	M_u/bd^2f_{cu}	M_u/bd^2f_{cu}
0.467	2.983	0.785	3.699	0.788	4.405	0.789	5.792	0.793	7.149	0.795	—	—
0.476	3.028	0.781	3.754	0.783	4.471	0.785	5.880	0.788	7.258	0.791	—	—
0.531	3.268	0.756	4.054	0.758	4.830	0.760	6.355	0.764	7.850	0.726	—	—
0.02	0.161	0.991	0.199	0.991	0.237	0.991	0.310	0.991	0.382	0.991	0.008	0.008
0.04	0.320	0.982	0.395	0.982	0.470	0.982	0.615	0.982	0.757	0.982	0.016	0.016
0.06	0.475	0.972	0.587	0.973	0.698	0.973	0.914	0.973	1.125	0.974	0.023	0.023
0.08	0.627	0.963	0.776	0.964	0.922	0.964	1.208	0.964	1.487	0.965	0.031	0.031
0.10	0.777	0.954	0.961	0.954	1.142	0.955	1.496	0.956	1.842	0.956	0.038	0.038
0.12	0.923	0.945	1.142	0.945	1.357	0.946	1.779	0.947	2.190	0.947	0.046	0.045
0.14	1.066	0.936	1.319	0.936	1.568	0.937	2.056	0.938	2.531	0.939	0.053	0.052
0.16	1.207	0.926	1.493	0.927	1.775	0.928	2.327	0.929	2.865	0.930	0.060	0.059
0.18	1.344	0.917	1.663	0.918	1.977	0.919	2.593	0.920	3.193	0.921	0.066	0.066
0.20	1.478	0.908	1.829	0.909	2.175	0.910	2.853	0.911	3.514	0.912	0.073	0.072
0.22	1.610	0.899	1.992	0.900	2.369	0.901	3.108	0.902	3.828	0.904	0.080	0.078
0.24	1.738	0.890	2.151	0.891	2.559	0.892	3.357	0.893	4.136	0.895	0.086	0.084
0.26	1.863	0.880	2.307	0.882	2.744	0.883	3.601	0.884	4.437	0.886	0.092	0.090
0.28	1.986	0.871	2.459	0.873	2.925	0.874	3.839	0.876	4.731	0.877	0.098	0.096
0.30	2.105	0.862	2.607	0.863	3.101	0.865	4.071	0.867	5.018	0.868	0.104	0.102
0.32	2.221	0.853	2.751	0.854	3.274	0.856	4.298	0.858	5.298	0.860	0.110	0.108
0.34	2.335	0.844	2.892	0.845	3.441	0.847	4.519	0.849	5.572	0.851	0.116	0.113
0.36	2.445	0.834	3.029	0.836	3.605	0.838	4.735	0.840	5.839	0.842	0.121	0.118
0.38	2.553	0.825	3.163	0.827	3.764	0.828	4.945	0.831	6.099	0.833	0.127	0.123
0.40	2.657	0.816	3.292	0.818	3.919	0.819	5.150	0.822	6.353	0.825	0.132	0.128
0.42	2.758	0.807	3.418	0.809	4.070	0.810	5.349	0.813	6.600	0.816	0.137	0.133
0.44	2.857	0.798	3.541	0.800	4.216	0.801	5.542	0.804	6.839	0.807	0.142	0.137
0.46	2.952	0.788	3.660	0.791	4.358	0.792	5.730	0.796	7.073	0.798	0.147	0.142
0.48	3.045	0.779	3.775	0.781	4.496	0.783	5.913	0.787	7.299	0.790	0.151	0.146
0.50	3.134	0.770	3.886	0.772	4.629	0.774	6.089	0.778	7.519	0.781	0.156	0.150
0.52	3.221	0.761	3.994	0.763	4.758	0.765	6.261	0.769	7.732	0.772	0.160	0.154
0.54	3.304	0.752	4.098	0.754	4.883	0.756	6.426	0.760	7.938	0.763	0.164	0.158
0.56	3.384	0.743	4.199	0.745	5.003	0.747	6.586	0.751	8.137	0.754	0.168	0.161
0.58	3.462	0.733	4.296	0.736	5.119	0.738	6.741	0.742	8.330	0.746	0.172	0.165
0.60	3.536	0.724	4.389	0.727	5.231	0.729	6.890	0.733	8.516	0.737	0.176	0.168

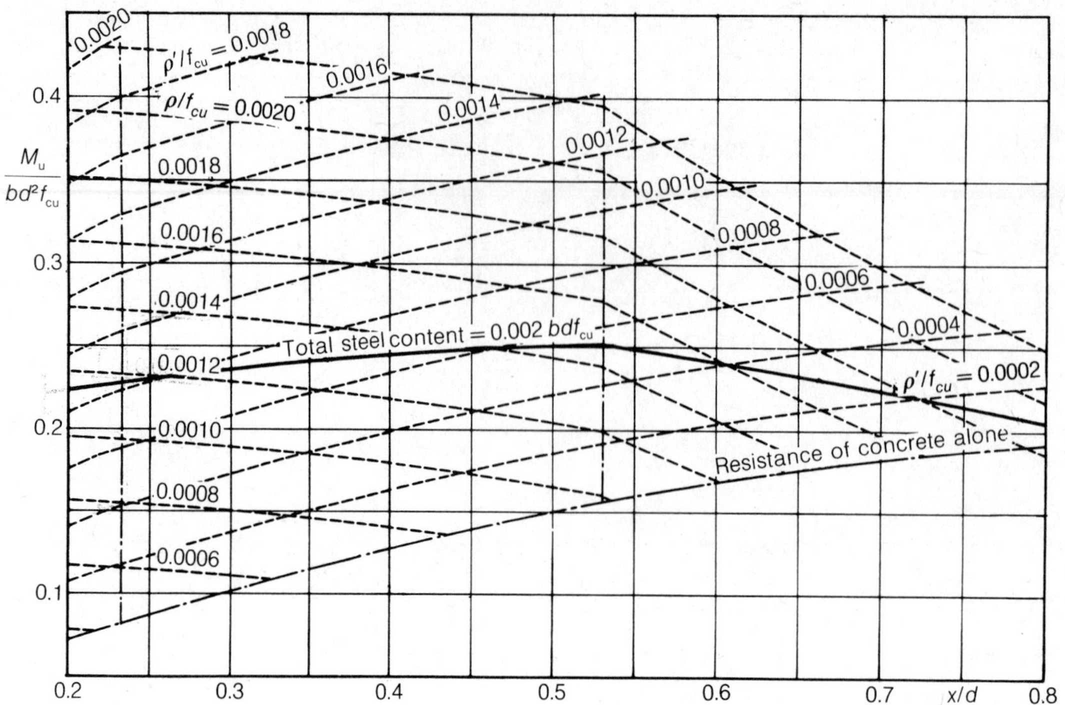

For design to CP110, with reinforcement having the limiting values of f_y prescribed in Table 3 of that Code, the ratios of x/d corresponding to an offset strain of 0.2% in the tension reinforcement are set out in *Table 104* and the formula for calculating the limiting value of x/d for any other type is given on *Table 103*. Alternatively, for sections reinforced in tension only, to obtain the minimum depth of section x/d may be taken at its maximum value of 1/2, although if $f_y > 345\ \mathrm{N/mm^2}$ this will require a reduction in the design stress f_{yd2} in the reinforcement.

Rectangular beams and slabs. Formulae giving M_u, d_{min}, ρ and ρ' relating to various values of x/d for rectangular sections reinforced in tension only or with both tension and compression reinforcement, obtained from rigorous analysis when either a parabolic-rectangular or a uniform rectangular stress-block is employed, are given in *Tables 105*, *106* and *107* (upper). In these formulae the appropriate values of f_{yd1} and f_{yd2} can be read or calculated from *Table 103* or *104*. The values of k_1, k_2 and k_3 for use with the expressions for a parabolic-rectangular stress-block and the relationship between x/d and M_u/bd^2f_{cu} for use in the formulae for a uniform rectangular stress-block can be read from *Table 102*.

Flanged sections. With a flanged section of given dimensions and subjected to given ultimate loading, if the resulting value of x evaluated on the effective width of flange is less than the flange thickness h_f, as shown in diagram (b) at the foot of *Table 109*, the section can be considered as a normal rectangular beam of width b from the point of view of bending and the methods of design previously described can be used. If x exceeds h_f, however, the resistance of the web of the section must also be taken into account. If the depth to the neutral axis is such that $(1-k_3)x$ exceeds h_f the interface between the parabolic and horizontal portions of the curve defining the concrete stress-block will fall below the underside of the flange and thus the entire flange area will be subjected to a uniform stress of $4f_{cu}/9$ (diagram (c) at the foot of *Table 109*). However, if $(1-k_3)x$ does not exceed h_f (diagram (d)) the parabolic part of the stress-block is truncated across the flange width. In such a case the calculations using a parabolic-rectangular stress-block become so complex that it is clearly much simpler to employ a uniform rectangular stress-block instead. The design procedure to be adopted in such a case, according to both Codes, is set out in *Table 109*, which also indicates the method of determining the amount of compression steel necessary when this is required.

20.1.5 Design methods: simplified formulae

As an alternative to rigorous analysis, both Codes give formulae for designing rectangular and flanged sections which are based on the use of a uniform rectangular concrete stress-block with further simplifications, although when such formulae are used the amount of moment redistribution permitted is limited to 10% only. The CP110 formulae, which cannot be used for sections with compression reinforcement when $d'/d > 0.2$, are based on the assumption of the same uniform rectangular concrete stress-block employed in rigorous limit-state analysis but with a fixed value of x/d of 0.5 when both tension and compression reinforcement is provided. When sections are reinforced in tension only an expression for the lever-arm z is given, which depends on the proportion of reinforcement provided but must not exceed $0.95d$. Since with a uniform rectangular stress-block $z = d - x/2$, the value of x/d here effectively ranges from 0.1 to 0.5 as ρ increases.

Note that when using the CP110 simplified expressions it is unnecessary to reduce the design stress in the tension reinforcement even though the critical value of x/d may be exceeded. This is clearly advantageous when designing sections reinforced in tension only, and for values of x/d close to 0.5, when $f_y > 345\ \mathrm{N/mm^2}$, the use of these

Reinforcement: basic data

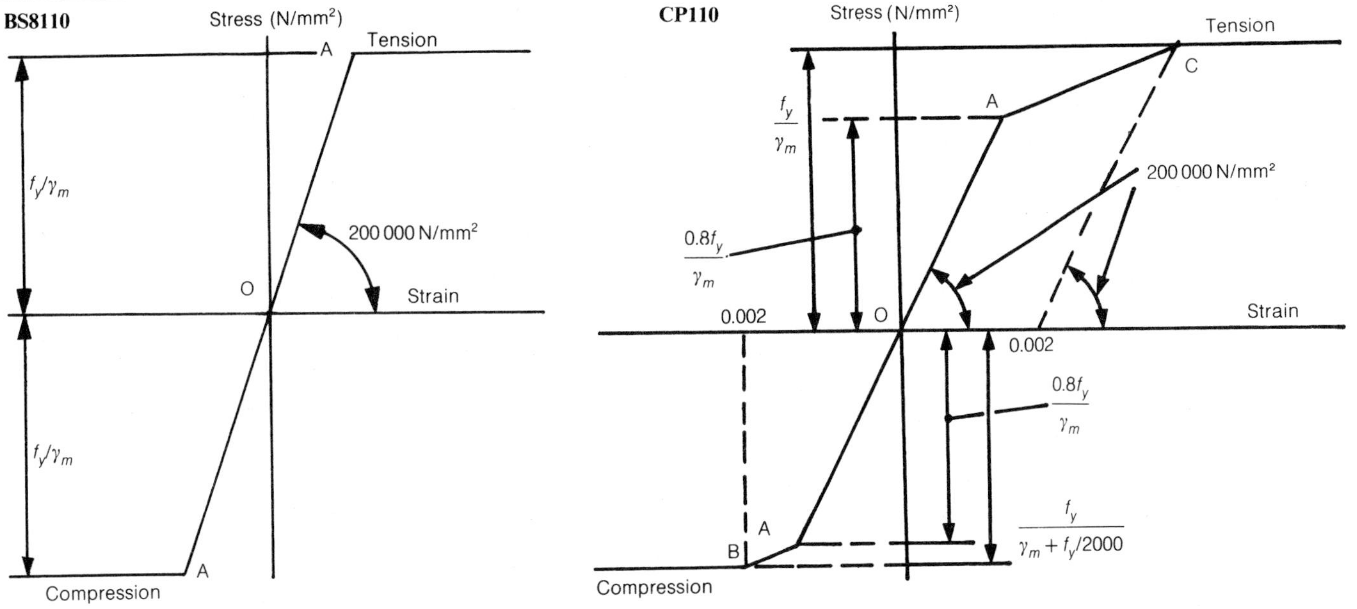

f_A, f_B, f_C stress in reinforcement at points A, B and C on stress/strain curves, in N/mm²
$\varepsilon_A, \varepsilon_B, \varepsilon_C$ strain in reinforcement at points A, B and C on stress/strain curves.
f_{yd1}, f_{yd2} design stresses in compression and tension reinforcement respectively at any point on stress/strain curve, in N/mm².

If partial safety factor for steel $\gamma_m = 1.15$, values of f_{yd1} corresponding to given ratios of d'/x, and f_{yd2} corresponding to given ratios of x/d, for any value of f_{yd2} can be calculated by using the expressions in the table. Alternatively, if $f_y = 250$, 425 (CP110 only) or 460 N/mm², f_{yd1} and f_{yd2} can be read from the appropriate scales on *Table 104*. Values of k_4 and k_5 given in table are in N mm². For column sections, to obtain values of x/h at A, B and C, multiply values of x/d given in table by appropriate ratio of d/h.

BS8110			Values of f_y in N/mm²		
			Any value	250	460
Compression reinforcement	Between O and A	f_{yd1}	$700\left(1-\frac{d\,d'}{x\,d}\right)$	$700\left(1-\frac{d'}{x}\right)$	$700\left(1-\frac{d'}{x}\right)$
	At A	f_A	$f_y/1.15$	217.4	400.0
		ε_A	$f_y/230\,000$	0.001 09	0.002 00
		x/d	$\frac{805}{805-f_y}\left(\frac{d'}{d}\right)$	$1.450d'/d$	$2.333d'/d$
Tension reinforcement	Between O and A	f_{yd2}	$700\left(\frac{d}{x}-1\right)$	$700\left(\frac{d}{x}-1\right)$	$700\left(\frac{d}{x}-1\right)$
	At A	f_A	$f_y/1.15$	217.4	400.0
		ε_A	$f_y/230\,000$	0.001 09	0.002 00
		x/d	$\frac{805}{805+f_y}$	0.763	0.636

CP110			Values of f_y in N/mm²			
			Any value	250	425	460
Compression reinforcement	Between O and A	f_{yd1}	$700\left(1-\frac{d\,d'}{x\,d}\right)$	$700\left(1-\frac{d'}{x}\right)$	$700\left(1-\frac{d'}{x}\right)$	$700\left(1-\frac{d'}{x}\right)$
	At A	f_A	$0.696f_y$	173.9	295.7	320.0
		ε_A	$3.48\times10^{-6}f_y$	0.000 87	0.001 48	0.001 60
		x/d	$\frac{805}{805-0.8f_y}\left(\frac{d'}{d}\right)$	$1.331d'/d$	$1.731d'/d$	$1.842d'/d$
	Between A and B	f_{yd1}	$\left(2300-700\frac{d'}{x}\right)\frac{f_y}{2300+f_y}$	$225.5-68.63\frac{d'}{x}$	$358.7-109.2\frac{d'}{x}$	$383.3-116.7\frac{d'}{x}$
	At B	f_B	$\frac{2000f_y}{2300+f_y}$	196.1	311.9	333.3
		ε_B	0.002	0.002	0.002	0.002
		x/d	$7d'/3d$	$2.333d'/d$	$2.333d'/d$	$2.333d'/d$
Tension reinforcement	At C	f_C	$f_y/1.15$	217.4	369.6	400.0
		ε_C	$0.002+\frac{f_y}{230\,000}$	0.003 09	0.003 85	0.004 00
		x/d	$\frac{805}{1265+f_y}$	0.531	0.476	0.467
	Between C and A	f_{yd2}	$\left(700\frac{d}{x}+900\right)\frac{f_y}{2300+f_y}$	$68.63\frac{d}{x}+88.24$	$109.2\frac{d}{x}+140.4$	$116.7\frac{d}{x}+150.0$
	At A	f_A	$0.696f_y$	173.9	295.7	320.0
		ε_A	$3.48\times10^{-6}f_y$	0.000 87	0.001 48	0.001 60
		x/d	$\frac{805}{805+0.8f_y}$	0.801	0.703	0.686
	Between O and A	f_{yd2}	$700\left(\frac{d}{x}-1\right)$	$700\left(\frac{d}{x}-1\right)$	$700\left(\frac{d}{x}-1\right)$	$700\left(\frac{d}{x}-1\right)$
	(see section 20.1.3	k_4	$200\,000f_y/(2300+f_y)$	19 608	31 193	33 333
		k_5	$1600f_y/(2300+f_y)$	156.9	249.5	266.7

simplified expressions results in the provision of slightly less reinforcement than is necessary when rigorous analysis is employed; if a uniform rectangular stress-block is adopted, the resulting resistance moment of the concrete is, not surprisingly, identical.

Suitable design formulae for rectangular and flanged sections derived from the simplified expressions presented in CP110 are given in the lower part of *Table 107*.

20.1.6 BS8110 design methods and aids

Rectangular beams and slabs reinforced in tension only. Design charts resulting from a rigorous limit-state analysis and assuming a parabolic-rectangular stress-block are included in Part 3 of BS8110.

The design charts forming *Tables 110* and *111* are based on the assumption of a uniform rectangular concrete stress-block. The appropriate formulae in *Table 105* can be rearranged to give

$$\frac{M_u}{bd^2}(\max) = 0.155\,775 f_{cu}$$

$$\frac{M_u}{bd^2} = \frac{f_y \rho}{1.15}\left(1 - \frac{0.45 f_y \rho}{0.4623 f_{cu}}\right) \qquad \text{when } z < 0.95d$$

$$\frac{M_u}{bd^2} = \tfrac{19}{23} f_y \rho \qquad \text{when } z = 0.95d$$

and the design charts have been produced by substituting appropriate values. Their use is illustrated in the examples that follow.

Such sections can also be designed on rigorous limit-state principles with either a parabolic-rectangular or a uniform rectangular concrete stress-block, either from first principles or by using the formulae given on *Table 105*; examples are given below.

Table 115 gives the ultimate resistance moments M_u and the proportion of reinforcement ρ required, together with a typical suitable arrangement of steel for solid slabs of various thicknesses reinforced in tension only, when $f_{cu} = 25$, 30 and 40 N/mm² and $f_y = 250$ or 460 N/mm². These values have been determined using a uniform rectangular concrete stress-block. If the true effective depth provided differs from that shown, after taking account of the concrete cover and bar diameter actually adopted, the corresponding values of M_u and ρ should be recalculated from the basic factors given.

Rectangular sections with tension and compression reinforcement. Design charts based on rigorous limit-state analysis with a parabolic-rectangular stress-block are included in Part 3 of BS8110.

Values of ρ and ρ' for sections reinforced in compression and with $d'/d = 0.1$ have been included on the charts on *Tables 110* and *111*. The charts have been produced by assuming a ratio of x/d of 0.5 and using the expressions for a uniform rectangular stress-block, which can be rearranged to give

$$\frac{M_u}{bd^2} = 0.155\,775 f_{cu} + \frac{f_y \rho'}{1.15}\left(1 - \frac{d'}{d}\right)$$

$$\frac{M_u}{bd^2} = 0.201 f_{cu}\left(\frac{d'}{d} - 0.225\right) + \frac{f_y \rho'}{1.15}\left(1 - \frac{d'}{d}\right)$$

The use of the charts is illustrated below.

For values of d'/d other than 0.1 the amount of compression steel required can be determined by multiplying the value of ρ' given by the curves by the correction factor read from the scale at the side of each chart. The correct amount of tension steel required can then be found by adding or subtracting (depending on whether d' is greater or less than $0.1d$ respectively) the *adjustment* made to the amount of compression steel. Note that, with compression steel, these charts only apply if $x/d = 0.5$.

Both the charts in this book and those in BS8110 only apply for values of f_y of 250 and 460 N/mm². For other values of f_y, sections can alternatively be designed using rigorous limit-state analysis with either a parabolic-rectangular or a uniform rectangular distribution of stress in the concrete, either from first principles or by using the formulae given in *Table 105* as illustrated below.

Flanged and other sections. If, for a flanged section, x falls within the flange depth, the section may be considered as rectangular with a breadth equal to the flange width, and the design methods and aids described above may be used. On *Tables 110* and *111* broken lines indicate the ratios of h_f/d corresponding to the situation where x coincides with the underside of the flange.

As explained earlier, if a parabolic-rectangular stress-block is adopted the flange area is subjected to a uniform stress of $0.45 f_{cu}$ when x exceeds $h_f/(1 - k_3)$. This situation occurs when x exceeds about $1.4h_f$ with grade 25 concrete and about $1.56h_f$ with grade 40 concrete: in other words, if h_f is less than about $0.36d$ and $0.32d$ with grade 20 and grade 40 concretes respectively, and x reaches its limiting value of $d/2$ when tension steel only is provided.

Thus, if h_f is less than these limiting values, the maximum moment that a flanged section can resist without compression steel being needed can be calculated by adding the resistance of $(1/2)k_1(1 - k_2)b_w d^2$ provided by the web section to the resistance of $0.45 f_{cu}(b - b_w)(d - h_f/2)$. If this is insufficient, compression reinforcement must be provided. Otherwise the section can be designed as follows.

Check whether the resistance of the flange section alone will suffice (i.e. whether x is less than h_f) and, if so, design as a simple beam with a width equal to that of the flange. If not, assume a depth x of $d/2$, calculate the resistance moment provided by the web section alone from the expression $M_u = (1/2)k_1(1 - k_2)b_w d^2$ and subtract this from the applied moment to obtain M_1. This value of M_1 can then be used to determine the 'average' stress over the width $(b - b_w)$ from the expression $f_{av} = M_1/h_f(b - b_w)(d - h_f/2)$. The total area of tension steel required to balance the compression in the concrete is then obtained from the expression

$$A_s = \frac{0.575}{f_y}[k_1 b_w d + 2 f_{av}(b - b_w)h_f]$$

This method is approximate but gives results that err on the side of safety.

A suitable procedure for designing flanged sections by rigorous limit-state analysis with a uniform rectangular distribution of concrete stress is set out in *Table 108*. Clause 3.4.4.5 of BS8110 gives design formulae for flanged

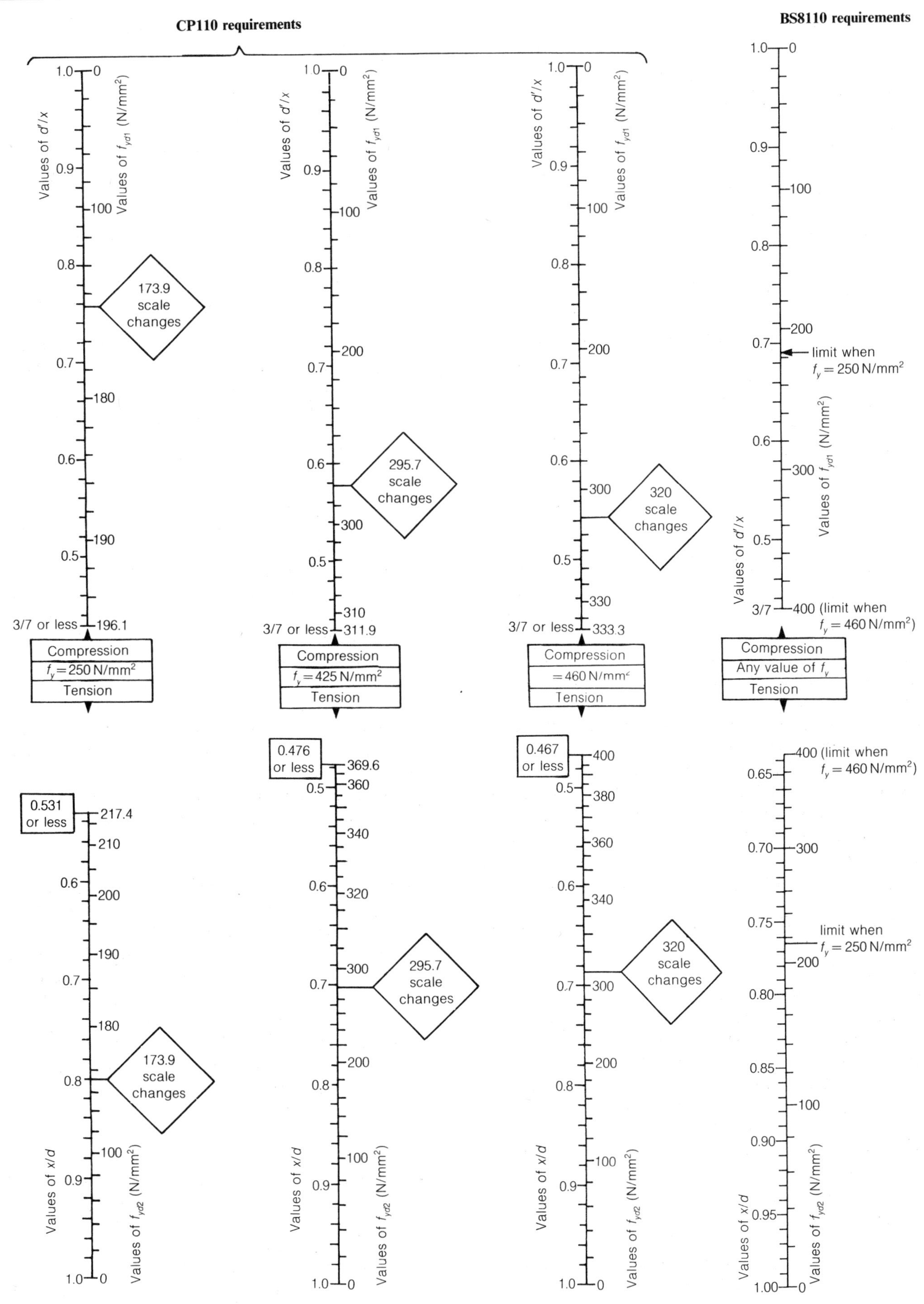

Note: the relationships shown on this table are only applicable if the partial safety factor for reinforcement $\gamma_m = 1.15$

sections assuming a uniform rectangular stress-block. These simplified expressions assume an x/d ratio of 1/2, and they thus cannot be used where a redistribution of moment of more than 10% is required.

Sections of other non-rectangular shapes can be analysed using rigorous limit-state analysis with a uniform rectangular concrete stress-block by means of basic principles. The procedure is less complex than might at first appear and is illustrated in the final example below. It is impracticable to adopt a parabolic-rectangular concrete stress-block for such sections unless suitable sets of design charts or an appropriate computer routine is available.

20.1.7 CP110 design methods and aids

Rectangular beams and slabs reinforced in tension only. Design charts resulting from a rigorous limit-state analysis and assuming a parabolic-rectangular stress-block are included in Part 2 of CP110.

The design charts on *Tables 112–114* have been prepared from the simplified formulae given in clause 3.3.5.3 of CP110. These can be rearranged to give

$$\frac{M_u}{bd^2}(\max) = 0.15 f_{cu}$$

$$\frac{M_u}{bd^2} = 0.87 f_y \rho \left(1 - \frac{1.1 f_y \rho}{f_{cu}}\right) \qquad \text{when } z < 0.95d$$

$$\frac{M_u}{bd^2} = 0.8265 f_y \rho \qquad \text{when } z = 0.95d$$

and the design charts have been produced by substituting appropriate values. Their use is self-evident and is illustrated in the examples that follow.

Such sections can also be designed by rigorous limit-state analysis with either a parabolic-rectangular or a uniform rectangular stress-block, either from first principles or by using the formulae on *Tables 106* and *107*; a similar but more general chart covering any value of f_y is provided in *Examples of the Design of Buildings*. Alternatively the rearranged CP110 simplified expressions given on *Table 107* may be used. Examples of all these methods are also given below.

Table 116 gives values of the ultimate resistance moment M_u and the proportion of reinforcement ρ required, together with a typical suitable arrangement of reinforcement for solid slabs of various thicknesses reinforced in tension only, when $f_{cu} = 20$, 25 or 30 N/mm^2 and f_y is one of the three values specified in clause 3.1.4.3 of CP110. These data have been calculated using the simplified expressions in CP110. A similar table but calculated using a parabolic-rectangular concrete stress-block is given in *Examples of the Design of Buildings*. If the actual effective depth provided, after taking the concrete cover needed and the bar diameter required into account, differs from that tabulated, the corresponding values of M_u and ρ should be recalculated from the basic factors given.

Rectangular sections with tension and compression reinforcement. Design charts based on rigorous limit-state analysis with a parabolic-rectangular stress-block are included in Part 2 of CP110.

Values of ρ and ρ' for sections reinforced in tension and compression and having $d'/d = 0.1$, with values of M_u/bd^2 of up to 6, have been included on the design charts on *Tables 112–114* using the simplified expressions in CP110. These can be rearranged to give

$$\frac{M_u}{bd^2} = 0.15 f_{cu} + 0.72 f_y \rho' \left(1 - \frac{d'}{d}\right)$$

$$\frac{M_u}{bd^2} = 0.05 f_{cu} \left(4\frac{d'}{d} - 1\right) + 0.87 f_y \rho' \left(1 - \frac{d'}{d}\right)$$

from which the data given on the charts have been prepared. Their use is illustrated in the examples that follow.

The discontinuity in the charts that occurs where the curves for ρ intersect the line giving $M_u/bd^2 = 0.15 f_{cu}$ (i.e. corresponding to the maximum moment of resistance of the concrete section alone) results from the fact that the resistance moments given by the simplified expressions in the Code for tension reinforcement and for tension and compression reinforcement (with $\rho' = 0$) differ slightly for identical values of ρ.

For values of d'/d other than 0.1 the amount of compression steel required can be determined by multiplying the value of ρ' given by the curves by the correction factor read from the scale at the side of the chart. The true amount of tension steel required can then be found by multiplying the adjustment to the compression reinforcement by 0.83 and adding or subtracting this amount from the value for tension reinforcement given by the chart, according to whether d' is greater than or less than $0.1d$.

Both the charts in CP110 and those in this book only apply for the specific values of f_y given. For these and other values of f_y, sections can alternatively be designed using a rigorous limit-state analysis with a parabolic-rectangular or rectangular distribution of concrete stress, either from first principles or by utilizing the formulae on *Tables 106* and *107*, or the rearranged CP110 simplified expressions may be applied directly. Examples of all these methods are given below.

Flanged and other sections. If, for a flanged section, $x \not> h_f$ the section may be designed as a plain rectangular section and the same design methods and aids employed.

As explained in section 20.1.4, if a parabolic-rectangular stress-block is adopted the flange area is subjected to a uniform stress of $4f_{cu}/9$ when x exceeds $(1 - k_3)h_f$. This occurs when x exceeds about $4h_f/3$ with grade 20 concrete and $3h_f/2$ with grade 40 concrete: in other words, if h_f is less than $3d/8$ and $d/3$ with grade 20 and grade 40 concretes respectively, and x reaches its limiting value of $d/2$.

Thus when designing, if h_f is less than these limiting values, the maximum moment that a flanged section can resist without the assistance of compression steel can be calculated by adding to the resistance of the web section of $(1/2)k_1(1 - k_2)b_w d^2$ the resistance provided by the flange section of $(4/9)f_{cu}(b - b_w)(d - h_f/2)$. If this is insufficient, compression reinforcement must be provided. Otherwise the section can be designed as follows.

Check whether the resistance of the flange width alone will suffice (i.e. whether x does not exceed h_f) and, if so, design as a simple beam of width b. If not, assume a depth

	Condition	Parabolic-rectangular concrete stress-block	Uniform rectangular concrete stress-block
Tension reinforcement only	For any value of x/d	$\frac{M_u}{bd^2}=k_1\left(\frac{x}{d}\right)\left(1-k_2\frac{x}{d}\right)$ $\rho=\frac{1.15k_1}{f_y}\left(\frac{x}{d}\right)$ $\quad d_{min}=\sqrt{\left[M_u\Big/bk_1\left(1-k_2\frac{x}{d}\right)\frac{x}{d}\right]}$ If d provided exceeds d_{min}: $\rho=\frac{0.575k_1}{f_yk_2}\left[1-\sqrt{\left(1-4\frac{k_2}{k_1}\frac{M_u}{bd^2}\right)}\right]$	$\frac{M_u}{bd^2}=0.402f_{cu}\left(\frac{x}{d}\right)\left(1-0.45\frac{x}{d}\right)$ $\rho=0.4623\frac{f_{cu}}{f_y}\left(\frac{x}{d}\right)$ $\quad d_{min}=\sqrt{\left[M_u\Big/0.402bf_{cu}\left(1-0.45\frac{x}{d}\right)\frac{x}{d}\right]}$ If d provided exceeds d_{min}: $\rho=\frac{0.4623f_{cu}}{0.9f_y}\left[1-\sqrt{\left(1-\frac{3M_u}{0.67bd^2f_{cu}}\right)}\right]$
	When $x/d=1/2$	$\frac{M_u}{bd^2}=\frac{1}{2}k_1(1-\frac{1}{2}k_2)$ $\rho=\frac{0.575k_1}{f_y}$ $\quad d_{min}=\sqrt{\left[\frac{2M_u}{bk_1(1-k_2/2)}\right]}$ If d provided exceeds d_{min}: $\rho=\frac{0.575k_1}{f_yk_2}\left[1-\sqrt{\left(1-4\frac{k_2}{k_1}\frac{M_u}{bd^2}\right)}\right]$	$\frac{M_u}{bd^2}=\frac{12.462f_{cu}}{80}\simeq0.156f_{cu}$ $\rho=0.231\,15\frac{f_{cu}}{f_y}$ $\quad d_{min}\simeq\sqrt{\left(\frac{M_u}{0.156bf_{cu}}\right)}$ If d provided exceeds d_{min}: $\rho=0.514\frac{f_{cu}}{f_y}\left[1-\sqrt{\left(1-\frac{3M_u}{0.67bd^2f_{cu}}\right)}\right]$
Tension and compression reinforcement	For any ratio of x/d	$\frac{M_u}{bd^2}=k_1\left(\frac{x}{d}\right)\left(1-k_2\frac{x}{d}\right)+\rho'f_{yd1}\left(1-\frac{d'}{d}\right)$ $\rho'=\left[\frac{M_u}{bd^2}-k_1\left(\frac{x}{d}\right)\left(1-k_2\frac{x}{d}\right)\right]\Big/f_{yd1}\left(1-\frac{d'}{d}\right)$ or $\quad A'_s=\frac{M_u-k_1bx(d-k_2x)}{f_{yd1}(d-d')}$ $\quad$ or $\quad A_s=\frac{k_1}{f_{yd2}}bx+A'_s\left(\frac{f_{yd1}}{f_{yd2}}\right)$ $\rho=\frac{k_1}{f_{yd2}}\left(\frac{x}{d}\right)+\rho'\left(\frac{f_{yd1}}{f_{yd2}}\right)$	$\frac{M_u}{bd^2}=0.402f_{cu}\left(\frac{x}{d}\right)\left(1-0.45\frac{x}{d}\right)+\rho'f_{yd1}\left(1-\frac{d'}{d}\right)$ $\rho'=\left[\frac{M_u}{bd^2}-0.402f_{cu}\left(\frac{x}{d}\right)\left(1-0.45\frac{x}{d}\right)\right]\Big/f_{yd1}\left(1-\frac{d'}{d}\right)$ or $\quad A'_s=\frac{M_u-0.402f_{cu}bx(d-0.45x)}{f_{yd1}(d-d')}$ $\quad$ or $\quad A_s=0.402\frac{f_{cu}}{f_{yd2}}bx+A'_s\left(\frac{f_{yd1}}{f_{yd2}}\right)$ $\rho=0.402\frac{f_{cu}}{f_{yd2}}\left(\frac{x}{d}\right)+\rho'\left(\frac{f_{yd1}}{f_{yd2}}\right)$
	When x/d attains limiting ratio to avoid reducing stress in tension reinforcement	When $f_y=250\,\mathrm{N/mm^2}$ $\quad x/d=0.763$ $\frac{M_u}{bd^2}=0.763k_1(1-0.763k_2)+217.4\rho'\left(1-\frac{d'}{d}\right)$ $\rho'=\left[\frac{M_u}{bd^2}-0.763k_1(1-0.763k_2)\right]\Big/217.4\left(1-\frac{d'}{d}\right)$ or $\quad A'_s=\frac{M_u-0.763k_1bd^2(1-0.763k_2)}{217.4(d-d')}$ $\rho=0.003\,51k_1+\rho'$ $\quad A_s=0.003\,51k_1bd+A'_s$ When $f_y=460\,\mathrm{N/mm^2}$ $\quad x/d=0.636$ $\frac{M_u}{bd^2}=0.636k_1(1-0.636k_2)+400\rho'\left(1-\frac{d'}{d}\right)$ $\rho'=\left[\frac{M_u}{bd^2}-0.636k_1(1-0.636k_2)\right]\Big/400\left(1-\frac{d'}{d}\right)$ or $\quad A'_s=\frac{M_u-0.636k_1bd^2(1-0.636k_2)}{400(d-d')}$ $\rho=0.001\,59k_1+\rho'$ $\quad A_s=0.001\,59k_1bd+A'_s$	When $f_y=250\,\mathrm{N/mm^2}$ $\quad x/d=0.763$ $\frac{M_u}{bd^2}=0.2014f_{cu}+217.4\rho'\left(1-\frac{d'}{d}\right)$ $\rho'=\left[\frac{M_u}{bd^2}-0.2014f_{cu}\right]\Big/217.4\left(1-\frac{d'}{d}\right)$ or $\quad A'_s=\frac{M_u-0.2014bd^2f_{cu}}{217.4(d-d')}$ $\rho=0.001\,41f_{cu}+\rho'$ $\quad A_s=0.001\,41bd^2f_{cu}+A'_s$ When $f_y=460\,\mathrm{N/mm^2}$ $\quad x/d=0.636$ $\frac{M_u}{bd^2}=0.1826f_{cu}+400\rho'\left(1-\frac{d'}{d}\right)$ $\rho'=\left[\frac{M_u}{bd^2}-0.1826f_{cu}\right]\Big/400\left(1-\frac{d'}{d}\right)$ or $\quad A'_s=\frac{M_u-0.1826bd^2f_{cu}}{400(d-d')}$ $\rho=0.000\,64f_{cu}+\rho'$ $\quad A_s=0.000\,64bd^2f_{cu}+A'_s$

Condition	Parabolic-rectangular concrete stress-block	Uniform rectangular concrete stress-block
For any value of x/d	$\frac{M_u}{bd^2}=k_1\left(\frac{x}{d}\right)\left(1-k_2\frac{x}{d}\right)$ $\rho=\frac{k_1}{f_{yd2}}\left(\frac{x}{d}\right)$ $d_{min}=\sqrt{\left[M_u\Big/bk_1\left(1-k_2\frac{x}{d}\right)\frac{x}{d}\right]}$ If d provided exceeds d_{min}: $\rho=\frac{1}{2f_{yd2}}\frac{k_1}{k_2}\left[1-\sqrt{\left(1-4\frac{k_2}{k_1}\frac{M_u}{bd^2}\right)}\right]$	$\frac{M_u}{bd^2}=\frac{1}{5}f_{cu}\left(\frac{x}{d}\right)\left(2-\frac{x}{d}\right)$ $\rho=\frac{2}{5}\frac{f_{cu}}{f_{yd2}}\left(\frac{x}{d}\right)$ $d_{min}=\sqrt{\left[5M_u\Big/bf_{cu}\left(2-\frac{x}{d}\right)\frac{x}{d}\right]}$ If d provided exceeds d_{min}: $\rho=\frac{2}{5}\frac{f_{cu}}{f_{yd2}}\left[1-\sqrt{\left(1-\frac{5}{f_{cu}}\frac{M_u}{bd^2}\right)}\right]$
When $x/d=1/2$	$\frac{M_u}{bd^2}=\frac{1}{2}k_1(1-\frac{1}{2}k_2)$ $d_{min}=\sqrt{\left[\frac{2M_u}{bk_1(1-k_2/2)}\right]}$ When $f_y\leqslant 345\,\text{N/mm}^2$ $\rho=0.575\frac{k_1}{f_y}$ If d provided exceeds d_{min}: $\rho=\frac{0.575}{f_y}\frac{k_1}{k_2}\left[1-\sqrt{\left(1-4\frac{k_2}{k_1}\frac{M_u}{bd^2}\right)}\right]$ When $f_y\geqslant 345\,\text{N/mm}^2$ $\rho=\frac{(2300+f_y)}{4600f_y}k_1$ If d provided exceeds d_{min}: calculate $\frac{x}{d}=\frac{1}{2k_2}\left[1-\sqrt{\left(1-4\frac{k_2}{k_1}\frac{M_u}{bd^2}\right)}\right]$ then $\rho=\frac{k_1}{f_{yd2}}\left(\frac{x}{d}\right)$ where f_{yd2} is that corresponding to value of x/d found	$\frac{M_u}{bd^2}=\frac{3}{20}f_{cu}$ $d_{min}=\sqrt{\frac{20M_u}{3bf_{cu}}}$ When $f_y\leqslant 345\,\text{N/mm}^2$ $\rho=0.23\frac{f_{cu}}{f_y}$ If d provided exceeds d_{min}: $\rho=0.46\frac{f_{cu}}{f_y}\left[1-\sqrt{\left(1-\frac{5}{f_{cu}}\frac{M_u}{bd^2}\right)}\right]$ When $f_y\geqslant 345\,\text{N/mm}^2$ $\rho=\frac{(2300+f_y)}{11\,500f_y}f_{cu}$ If d provided exceeds d_{min}: calculate $\frac{x}{d}=1-\sqrt{\left(1-\frac{5}{f_{cu}}\frac{M_u}{bd^2}\right)}$ then $\rho=\frac{2}{5}\frac{f_{cu}}{f_{yd2}}\left(\frac{x}{d}\right)$ where f_{yd2} is that corresponding to value of x/d found
When x/d is the lesser of: *either* limiting ratio to avoid reducing design stress in tension reinforcement; *or* 1/2	When $f_y\leqslant 345\,\text{N/mm}^2$ The expressions for M_u/bd^2, d_{min} and ρ correspond to those when $x/d=1/2$ above When $f_y\geqslant 345\,\text{N/mm}^2$ $\frac{M_u}{bd^2}=\frac{805}{1265+f_y}k_1\left(1-\frac{805}{1265+f_y}k_2\right)$ $d_{min}=\sqrt{\left[M_u\Big/bk_1\left(\frac{805}{1265+f_y}\right)\left(1-\frac{805}{1265+f_y}k_2\right)\right]}$ $\rho=\frac{925.75}{(1265+f_y)f_y}k_1$ If d provided exceeds d_{min}: calculate $\frac{x}{d}=\frac{1}{2k_2}\left[1-\sqrt{\left(1-4\frac{k_2}{k_1}\frac{M_u}{bd^2}\right)}\right]$ then $\rho=\frac{k_1}{f_{yd2}}\left(\frac{x}{d}\right)$ where f_{yd2} is that corresponding to value of x/d found	When $f_y\leqslant 345\,\text{N/mm}^2$ The expressions for M_u/bd^2, d_{min} and ρ correspond to those when $x/d=1/2$ above When $f_y\geqslant 345\,\text{N/mm}^2$ $\frac{M_u}{bd^2}=\frac{(277\,725+322f_y)}{(1265+f_y)^2}f_{cu}$ $d_{min}=\sqrt{\left[\frac{(1265+f_y)^2M_u}{bf_{cu}(277\,725+322f_y)}\right]}$ $\rho=\frac{370.3}{(1265+f_y)f_y}f_{cu}$ If d provided exceeds d_{min}: calculate $\frac{x}{d}=1-\sqrt{\left(1-\frac{5}{f_{cu}}\frac{M_u}{bd^2}\right)}$ then $\rho=\frac{2}{5}\frac{f_{cu}}{f_{yd2}}\left(\frac{x}{d}\right)$ where f_{yd2} is that corresponding to value of x/d found

Condition	Parabolic-rectangular concrete stress-block	Uniform rectangular concrete stress-block
	$\frac{M_u}{bd^2} = k_1\left(\frac{x}{d}\right)\left(1 - k_2\frac{x}{d}\right) + \rho' f_{yd1}\left(1 - \frac{d'}{d}\right)$	$\frac{M_u}{bd^2} = \frac{1}{5}f_{cu}\left(\frac{x}{d}\right)\left(2 - \frac{x}{d}\right) + \rho' f_{yd1}\left(1 - \frac{d'}{d}\right)$
For any ratio of x/d	$\rho' = \left[\frac{M_u}{bd^2} - k_1\left(\frac{x}{d}\right)\left(1 - k_2\frac{x}{d}\right)\right] \Big/ f_{yd1}\left(1 - \frac{d'}{d}\right)$ or $A'_s = \frac{M_u - k_1 bx(d - k_2 x)}{f_{yd1}(d - d')}$ $\rho = \frac{k_1}{f_{yd2}}\left(\frac{x}{d}\right) + \rho'\left(\frac{f_{yd1}}{f_{yd2}}\right)$ or $A_s = \frac{k_1}{f_{yd2}}bx + A'_s\left(\frac{f_{yd1}}{f_{yd2}}\right)$	$\rho' = \left[\frac{M_u}{bd^2} - \frac{1}{5}f_{cu}\left(\frac{x}{d}\right)\left(2 - \frac{x}{d}\right)\right] \Big/ f_{yd1}\left(1 - \frac{d'}{d}\right)$ or $A'_s = \frac{M_u - f_{cu}bx(2 - x)/5}{f_{yd1}(d - d')}$ $\rho = \frac{2}{5}\frac{f_{cu}}{f_{yd2}}\left(\frac{x}{d}\right) + \rho'\left(\frac{f_{yd1}}{f_{yd2}}\right)$ or $A_s = \frac{2}{5}\frac{f_{cu}}{f_{yd2}}bx + A'_s\left(\frac{f_{yd1}}{f_{yd2}}\right)$
When x/d attains limiting ratio to avoid reducing stress in tension reinforcement	$\frac{M_u}{bd^2} = \frac{805}{1265 + f_y}k_1\left(1 - \frac{805}{1265 + f_y}k_2\right) + \rho'\left(\frac{2000f_y}{2300 + f_y}\right)\left(1 - \frac{d'}{d}\right)$ $\rho' = \left(\frac{2300 + f_y}{2000f_y}\right)\left[\frac{M_u}{bd^2} - \frac{805}{1265 + f_y}k_1\left(1 - \frac{805}{1265 + f_y}k_2\right)\right] \Big/ \left(1 - \frac{d'}{d}\right)$ $\rho = \frac{925.75}{(1265 + f_y)f_y}k_1 + \rho'\left(\frac{2300}{2300 + f_y}\right)$	$\frac{M_u}{bd^2} = \frac{277\,725 + 322f_y}{(1265 + f_y)^2}f_{cu} + \rho'\left(\frac{2000f_y}{2300 + f_y}\right)\left(1 - \frac{d'}{d}\right)$ $\rho' = \left(\frac{2300 + f_y}{2000f_y}\right)\left[\frac{M_u}{bd^2} - \frac{277\,725 + 322f_y}{(1265 + f_y)^2}f_{cu}\right] \Big/ \left(1 - \frac{d'}{d}\right)$ $\rho = \frac{370.3}{(1265 + f_y)f_y}f_{cu} + \rho'\left(\frac{2300}{2300 + f_y}\right)$

Simplified CP110 formulae for limit-state design

Rectangular sections

Tension reinforcement only: maximum resistance moment occurs when $x/d = 1/2$. Then

$$\frac{M_u}{bd^2} = \frac{3}{20}f_{cu} \qquad d_{min} = \sqrt{\frac{20M_u}{3bf_{cu}}} \qquad \rho = 0.23f_{cu}/f_y, \text{ where } A_s = \rho bd$$

If value of d provided is greater than d_{min},

$$\rho = \frac{1}{2.2}\frac{f_{cu}}{f_y}\left[1 - \sqrt{\left(1 - \frac{5.06M_u}{f_{cu}bd^2}\right)}\right] \quad \text{if} \quad \frac{M_u}{bd^2} \not< \frac{1653}{44\,000}f_{cu}; \quad \text{otherwise} \quad \rho = \frac{1}{0.8265f_y}\frac{M_u}{bd^2}$$

For a given value of ρ which is less than $0.2314f_{cu}/f_y$,

$$\frac{M_u}{bd^2} = 0.87f_y\rho\left(1 - \frac{1.1f_y\rho}{f_{cu}}\right) \quad \text{if} \quad \rho \not< \frac{f_{cu}}{22f_y}; \quad \text{otherwise} \quad \frac{M_u}{bd^2} = 0.8265f_y\rho$$

Tension and compression reinforcement

$$\frac{M_u}{bd^2} = \frac{3}{20}f_{cu} + 0.72f_y\rho'\left(1 - \frac{d'}{d}\right) \qquad \rho' = \left[\frac{M_u}{bd^2} - \frac{3}{20}f_{cu}\right] \Big/ 0.72f_y\left(1 - \frac{d'}{d}\right) \qquad \rho = 0.23\frac{f_{cu}}{f_y} + 0.828\rho'$$

The term $0.72f_y$ in the foregoing equations is a simplification of the expression $2000f_y/(2300 + f_y)$.

Flanged sections

Tension reinforcement only:

Maximum resistance moment occurs when $x = h_f$. Then

$$\frac{M_u}{bd^2} = \frac{1}{5}f_{cu}\frac{h_f}{d}\left(2 - \frac{h_f}{d}\right) \qquad \rho = 0.46\left(\frac{h_f}{d}\right)\frac{f_{cu}}{f_y}$$

If the value of M_u/bd^2 acting on the section is less then that given by the foregoing expression, use formulae for rectangular section with tension reinforcement only.

If the value of M_u/bd^2 acting on the section exceeds that given by the foregoing expression, the section must be analysed using the 'basic principles' formulae on *Table 109*.

x of $d/2$, calculate the resistance moment of the web section alone from the expression $M_u = (1/2)k_1(1-k_2)b_w d^2$ and subtract this from the applied moment to obtain M_1. This value of M_1 can then be used to determine an 'average' stress over the width $(b-b_w)$ from the expression $f_{av} = M_1/h_f(b-b_w)(d-h_f/2)$. The total area of tension steel to balance the compression in the concrete is then given by the expression

$$A_s = \frac{0.575}{f_y}[k_1 b_w d + 2f_{av}(b-b_w)h_f]$$

This method is approximate but gives results that err on the side of safety. A suitable procedure for designing flanged sections by a rigorous limit-state analysis with a uniform rectangular concrete stress distribution is set out in *Table 109*.

CP110 provides simplified expressions for the ultimate moment of resistance of flanged sections, based on the assumption of a rectangular distribution of stress in the concrete over the depth of the flange only. This can be rearranged to give

$$\frac{M_u}{bd^2} = \frac{2}{5}f_{cu}\frac{h_f}{d}\left(1-\frac{h_f}{2d}\right)$$

and by substituting appropriate values of h_f/d and f_{cu} the broken lines on the charts on *Tables 112–114* have been obtained. For given values of M_u/bd^2 and f_{cu} they enable the corresponding limiting ratio of h_f/d to be determined. If the ratio of h_f/d provided exceeds this limiting value the section acts as a rectangular beam and may be designed as such. Otherwise a rigorous analysis is necessary.

Sections of other non-rectangular shapes can be analysed conveniently using a rigorous limit-state analysis with a rectangular stress-block by means of basic principles. The procedure, which is perhaps less complex than might at first appear, is illustrated in the final example of the following. The adoption of a parabolic-rectangular stress-block for analysing such sections is inadvisable unless sets of design charts, such as those for circular columns in Part 3 of CP110, are available.

In the design examples that follow, two basic rectangular beams are first analysed by various design methods, the aim being to illustrate the computational procedures involved and to indicate the relative amount of work required. The remaining examples illustrate particular advantages (or shortcomings) of the application of individual methods to rectangular, flanged and other sections.

Example 1. Design a rectangular beam (using high-yield tension reinforcement only) to withstand an ultimate bending moment of 61 kN m, if $f_{cu} = 30\,\text{N/mm}^2$.

Rigorous analysis with parabolic-rectangular stress-block. From first principles, or from *Table 102*, read values of $k_1 = 11.96$ and $k_2 = 0.4513$ corresponding to $f_{cu} = 30\,\text{N/mm}^2$. Assuming $b = 200$ mm and an initial neutral-axis depth of $d/2$, the total compressive force in the concrete $= 11.96 \times 200 \times 0.5d$ and the depth to the centroid of the stress-block $= 0.4513 \times 0.5d$, so that the lever-arm $z = (1 - 0.4513 \times 0.5)d$. Now the maximum moment of resistance of the concrete alone is

$$M_u = (1 - 0.4513 \times 0.5)d \times 11.96 \times 200 \times 0.5d = 926d^2$$

Thus

$$\text{minimum permissible } d = \sqrt{\left(\frac{61 \times 10^6}{926}\right)} = 257\,\text{mm}$$

Adopting an actual value of d of 265 mm (i.e. $h = 300$ mm), the expression for the total compressive force in the concrete becomes $11.96 \times 200 \times 265x/d$ and the lever-arm is now $z = (1 - 0.4513x/d)265$. Thus the moment of resistance of the concrete is

$$M_u = 61 \times 10^6 = 11.96 \times 200 \times 265 \times x/d(1 - 0.4513x/d)265$$

so that $75.81(x/d)^2 - 168.0x/d + 61 = 0$, from which $x/d = 0.46$. Now total tension in the reinforcement = total compression in the concrete $= 11.96 \times 200 \times 265 \times 0.46 = 290\,000$ N. With BS8110, $f_y = 460\,\text{N/mm}^2$, so that

$$A_{s\,req} = 290\,000 \times 1.15/460 = 725\,\text{mm}^2$$

Provide four 16 mm bars.

With CP110, for bars exceeding 12 mm, $f_y = 425\,\text{N/mm}^2$, and since x/d is less than the limiting value of 0.476 for $f_y = 425\,\text{N/mm}^2$, there is no reduction of design stress in the reinforcement, so that

$$A_{s\,req} = 290\,000 \times 1.15/425 = 785\,\text{mm}^2$$

Provide three 20 mm bars.

The procedure is considerably shortened if the formulae on *Tables 105* and *106* are used. Then

$$d_{min} = \sqrt{\left(\frac{2 \times 61 \times 10^6}{200 \times 11.96(1 - 0.5 \times 0.4513)}\right)} = 257\,\text{mm}$$

Since d provided (265 mm) exceeds d_{min}, calculate

$$\frac{x}{d} = \frac{1}{2k_2}\left[1 - \sqrt{\left(1 - 4\frac{k_2}{k_1}\frac{M_u}{bd_2}\right)}\right]$$

$$= \frac{1}{2 \times 0.4513}\left[1 - \sqrt{\left(1 - 4\frac{0.4513 \times 61 \times 10^6}{11.96 \times 200 \times 265^2}\right)}\right]$$

$$= 0.458$$

With BS8110, $f_y = 460\,\text{N/mm}^2$ and

$$\rho = \frac{k_1 \times 1.15}{f_y}\frac{x}{d} = \frac{11.96 \times 1.15 \times 0.458}{460} = 0.0137$$

and

$$A_{s\,req} = 0.0137 \times 200 \times 265 = 725\,\text{mm}^2$$

Provide four 16 mm bars.

With CP110, since $f_y = 425\,\text{N/mm}^2$ and true x/d is less than 0.476, no reduction in the full design stress is required. Then

$$\rho = \frac{k_1 \times 1.15}{f_y}\frac{x}{d} = \frac{11.96 \times 1.15 \times 0.458}{425} = 0.0148$$

and

$$A_{s\,req} = 0.0148 \times 200 \times 265 = 786\,\text{mm}^2$$

Provide three 20 mm bars.

The values given on *Table 102* simplify the calculations

Assume, if not already known, suitable values for b, b_w, h_f and d.

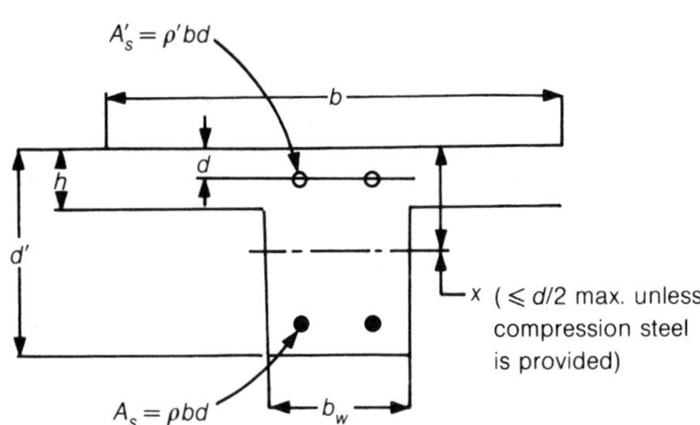

Evaluate $M_u/bd^2 f_{cu}$, where M_u is the ultimate applied bending moment.

Evaluate $\dfrac{x}{d} = 1 - \sqrt{\left(1 - \dfrac{3M_u}{0.67bd^2 f_{cu}}\right)}$

Values of x/d corresponding to values of $M_u/bd^2 f_{cu}$ can be read from *Table 102*.

Is $\dfrac{x}{d} \leqslant \dfrac{h_f}{0.9d}$?

Yes: Section acts as a normal rectangular beam and

$$\rho = 0.4623\frac{f_{cu}}{f_y}\left(\frac{x}{d}\right)$$

No: Section acts as a flanged beam.

Evaluate
$$\frac{x}{d} = \frac{1}{0.9}\left\{1 - \sqrt{\left[1 - \frac{3}{0.67}\left(\frac{M_u}{bd^2 f_{cu}}\right)\frac{b}{b_w} + \left(\frac{b}{b_w} - 1\right)\frac{h_f}{d}\left(2 - \frac{h_f}{d}\right)\right]}\right\}$$

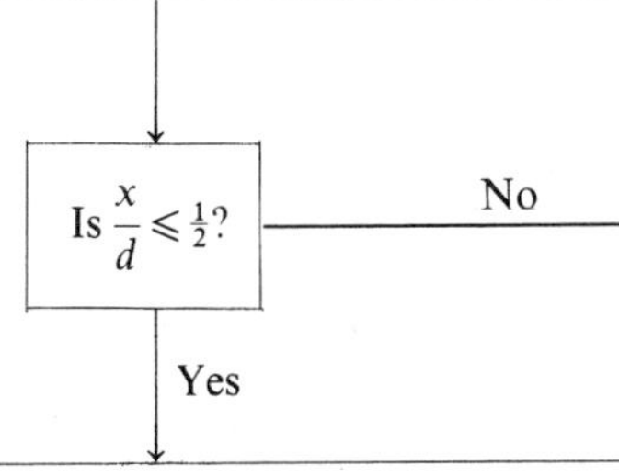

Is $\dfrac{x}{d} \leqslant \tfrac{1}{2}$?

No: Compression reinforcement must be provided. Select revised value of x/d between h_f/d and value already calculated. Then

$$\rho' = \frac{M_u}{bd^2} - \frac{0.67 f_{cu}}{3}\left[\frac{h_f}{d}\left(2 - \frac{h_f}{d}\right)\left(1 - \frac{b_w}{b}\right) + 0.9\frac{b_w}{b}\cdot\frac{x}{d}\left(2 - 0.9\frac{x}{d}\right)\right]\Bigg/ f_{yd1}\left(1 - \frac{d'}{d}\right)$$

and

$$\rho = \frac{1.34}{3}\cdot\frac{f_{cu}}{f_{yd2}}\left[0.9\frac{b_w x}{bd} + \left(1 - \frac{b_w}{b}\right)\frac{h_f}{d}\right] + \rho'\left(\frac{f_{yd1}}{f_{yd2}}\right)$$

where f_{yd1} and f_{yd2} correspond to the particular ratio of x/d adopted.

Yes:

$$\rho = \frac{1.541}{3}\frac{f_{cu}}{f_y}\left[0.9\frac{b_w x}{bd} + \left(1 - \frac{b_w}{b}\right)\frac{h_f}{d}\right]$$

If $x/d = 1/2$ then

$$\rho = \frac{1.541}{3}\frac{f_{cu}}{f_y}\left[\frac{b_w}{b}\left(0.45 - \frac{h_f}{d}\right) + \frac{h_f}{d}\right]$$

and

$$\frac{M_u}{bd^2 f_{cu}} = \frac{0.67}{3}\left[\frac{h_f}{d}\left(2 - \frac{h_f}{d}\right)\left(1 - \frac{b_w}{b}\right) + 0.6975\frac{b_w}{b}\right]$$

For this condition, values of $M_u/bd^2 f_{cu}$ corresponding to various ratios of h_f/d and b_w/b can be read from the adjacent chart.

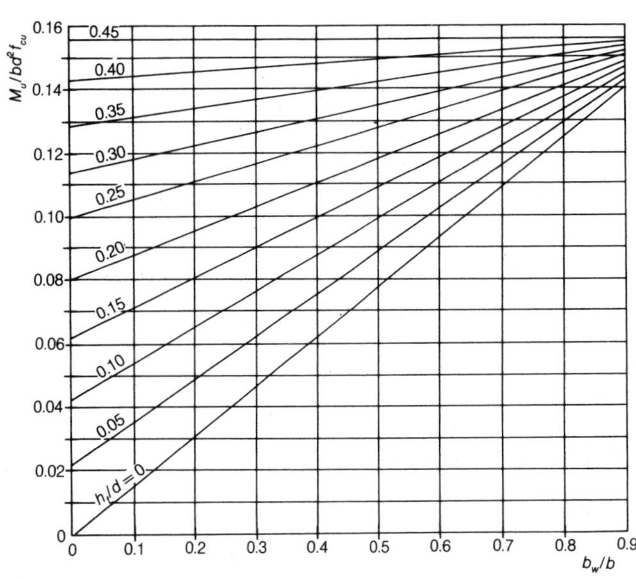

Parabolic-rectangular stress-block

The possible types of behaviour according to BS8110 requirements are identical to those shown at the bottom of *Table 109*.

still further. Having obtained d_{min} and chosen an actual value of d of 265 mm, $M_u/bd^2 = 61 \times 10^6/(200 \times 265^2) = 4.34$. From the values tabulated on *Table 102*, the corresponding values of x/d and z/d are 0.460 and 0.792 respectively. Then with BS8110,

$$A_s = \frac{61 \times 10^6 \times 1.15}{265 \times 0.792 \times 460} = 726\,\text{mm}^2$$

With CP110, since $x/d < 0.476$, no reduction in the full design stress in the steel is needed and thus

$$A_s = \frac{61 \times 10^6 \times 1.15}{265 \times 0.792 \times 425} = 786\,\text{mm}^2$$

Reference to the curve for $100A'_s/bd = 0$ on charts 6 to 8 of BS8110: Part 3 confirms that when $M_u/bd^2 = 4.35$,

$$A_{s\,req} = 0.0137 \times 200 \times 265 = 726\,\text{mm}^2$$

and to that on charts 35 to 38 of CP110: Part 2 confirms that, when $M_u/bd^2 = 4.35$,

$$A_{s\,req} = 0.015 \times 200 \times 265 = 795\,\text{mm}^2$$

Rigorous analysis with uniform rectangular stress-block to BS8110. From first principles, assuming a value of b of 200 mm and an initial ratio of x/d of 1/2, the total compressive force in the concrete $= 0.67/1.5 \times 30 \times 200 \times 0.9 \times 0.5d$. With a lever-arm of $(1 - 0.5 \times 0.5 \times 0.9)d$, the maximum moment of resistance of the concrete alone is

$$M_u = 0.67/1.5 \times 30 \times 200 \times 0.9 \times 0.5 \times 0.775d^2 = 934.6d^2.$$

Thus

$$d_{min} = \sqrt{\left(\frac{61 \times 10^6}{934.6}\right)} = 256\,\text{mm}$$

Adopting a value of d of 265 mm, the total compressive force in the concrete is $0.67/1.5 \times 30 \times 200 \times 265 \times 0.9x/d$ and the lever-arm z is $(1 - 0.45x/d)265$, so that the moment of resistance of the concrete is

$$M_u = 61 \times 10^6 = 0.67/1.5 \times 30 \times 200 \times 265 \times 0.9 \times x/d \times (1 - 0.45x/d) \times 265$$

giving $76.22(x/d)^2 - 169.4(x/d) + 61 = 0$, from which $x/d = 0.452$. Then since the total tension in the reinforcement = total compression in the concrete $= 0.67/1.5 \times 30 \times 200 \times 265 \times 0.9 \times 0.452 = 289\,000$ N,

$$A_{s\,req} = 289\,000 \times 1.15/460 = 723\,\text{mm}^2$$

Again the process is considerably shortened by using the formulae on *Table 105*. With $b = 200$ mm,

$$d_{min} = \sqrt{\left(\frac{M_u}{0.156bf_{cu}}\right)} = \sqrt{\left(\frac{61 \times 10^6}{0.156 \times 200 \times 30}\right)} = 256\,\text{mm}$$

Then, since the actual value of d provided (= 265 mm) exceeds d_{min}, for a value of M_u/bd^2f_{cu} of $61 \times 10^6/200 \times 265 \times 30 = 0.145$, the corresponding value of x/d of 0.452 can be read from the appropriate column on *Table 102*. Thus

$$\rho = 0.402\frac{f_{cu}}{f_{yd2}}\frac{x}{d} = 0.402 \times 30 \times 0.452 \times 1.15/460 = 0.0136$$

$$A_{s\,req} = 0.0136 \times 200 \times 265 = 723\,\text{mm}^2$$

Alternatively the curves on *Table 111* may be used. With $b = 200$ m,

$$d_{min} = \sqrt{\left(\frac{61 \times 10^6}{4.67 \times 200}\right)} = 255\,\text{mm}$$

If $h = 300$ mm and $d = 265$ mm, $M_u/bd^2 = 61 \times 10^6/200 \times 265^2 = 4.35$ and the corresponding value of ρ read from the curves is 0.0136. Thus

$$A_{s\,req} = 0.0136 \times 200 \times 265 = 723\,\text{mm}^2$$

Rigorous analysis with uniform rectangular stress-block to CP110. From first principles, assuming a value of b of 200 mm and an initial ratio of x/d of 1/2, the total compressive force in the concrete $= (2/5) \times 30 \times 200 \times 0.5d$. With a lever-arm $z = 3d/4$, the maximum moment of resistance of the concrete alone

$$M_u = \tfrac{2}{5} \times 30 \times 200 \times 0.5 \times 0.75d^2 = 900d^2$$

Thus

$$\text{minimum permissible } d = \sqrt{\left(\frac{61 \times 10^6}{900}\right)} = 260\,\text{mm}$$

Adopting a value of d of 265 mm, the total compressive force in the concrete is $0.4 \times 30 \times 200 \times 265x/d$ and the lever-arm z is $(1 - 0.5x/d)265$ so that the moment of resistance of the concrete is

$$M_u = 61 \times 10^6 = 0.4 \times 30 \times 200 \times 265 \times x/d(1 - 0.5x/d)265$$

giving $84.27(x/d)^2 - 168.5x/d + 61 = 0$, so that $x/d = 0.475$. Since this is less than the critical value of 0.476 there is no need to reduce the design stress in the reinforcement. Total tension in the reinforcement = total compression in the concrete $= 0.4 \times 30 \times 200 \times 265 \times 0.475 = 302\,000$ N, so that

$$A_{s\,req} = 302\,000 \times 1.15/425 = 817\,\text{mm}^2$$

Again, the process is considerably shortened by using the formulae on *Table 106*. With $b = 200$ mm,

$$d_{min} = \sqrt{\left(\frac{20M_u}{3bf_{cu}}\right)} = \sqrt{\left(\frac{20 \times 61 \times 10^6}{3 \times 200 \times 30}\right)} = 260\,\text{mm}$$

Then since the actual value of d provided (265 mm) exceeds d_{min}, for a value of M_u/bd^2f_{cu} of 0.145, the corresponding value of $x/d = 0.475$ can be read from the appropriate column on *Table 102*. Thus

$$\rho = \frac{2}{5}\frac{f_{cu}}{f_{yd2}}\frac{x}{d} = 0.4 \times 30 \times 0.475 \times 1.15/425 = 0.0154$$

and

$$A_{s\,req} = 0.0154 \times 200 \times 265 = 817\,\text{mm}^2$$

Design charts for CP110 simplified equations. From the curves on *Table 113*, the maximum value of M_u/bd^2 of the concrete alone = 4.5. Assume that $b = 200$ mm. Then

$$\text{minimum permissible } d = \sqrt{\left(\frac{61 \times 10^6}{200 \times 4.5}\right)} = 260\,\text{mm}$$

Say $h = 300$ mm, so that with 15 mm cover, 10 mm max. links and 20 mm max. bars, $d = 265$ mm. Then $M_u/bd^2 = 61 \times 10^6/200 \times 265^2 = 4.35$, and the corresponding value of

Uniform rectangular stress-block

Assume, if not already known, suitable values for b, b_w, h_f and d.

↓

Evaluate M_u/bd^2f_{cu}, where M_u is the ultimate applied bending moment.

↓

Evaluate $\dfrac{x}{d} = 1 - \sqrt{\left(1 - \dfrac{5M_u}{bd^2f_{cu}}\right)}$

Values of x/d corresponding to values of M_u/bd^2f_{cu} can be read from *Table 102*.

↓

Is $\dfrac{x}{d} \leqslant \dfrac{h_f}{d}$?

Yes → Section acts as a normal rectangular beam and $\rho = \dfrac{2}{5}\dfrac{f_{cu}}{f_{yd2}}\left(\dfrac{x}{d}\right)$, where f_{yd2} corresponds to the particular ratio of x/d found.

No ↓

Section acts as a flanged beam.

Evaluate $\dfrac{x}{d} = 1 - \sqrt{\left[1 - 5\left(\dfrac{M_u}{bd^2f_{cu}}\right)\dfrac{b}{b_w} + \left(\dfrac{b}{b_w} - 1\right)\left(2 - \dfrac{h_f}{d}\right)\dfrac{h_f}{d}\right]}$

↓

Is $\dfrac{x}{d} \leqslant \frac{1}{2}$?

No → Compression reinforcement must be provided. Select revised value of x/d between h_f/d and value already calculated. Then

$$\rho = \frac{2}{5}\frac{f_{cu}}{f_{yd2}}\left[\frac{b_w x}{bd} + \left(1 - \frac{b_w}{b}\right)\frac{h_f}{d}\right] + \rho'\left(\frac{f_{yd1}}{f_{yd2}}\right)$$

where f_{yd1} and f_{yd2} correspond to particular ratio of x/d adopted.

Yes ↓

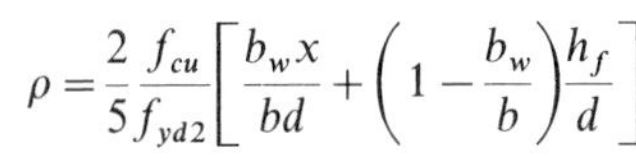

$$\rho = \frac{2}{5}\frac{f_{cu}}{f_{yd2}}\left[\frac{b_w x}{bd} + \left(1 - \frac{b_w}{b}\right)\frac{h_f}{d}\right]$$

where f_{yd2} corresponds to the particular ratio of x/d found. If $x/d = 1/2$ then

$$\rho = \frac{2}{5}\frac{f_{cu}}{f_{yd2}}\left[\frac{b_w}{b}\left(\frac{1}{2} - \frac{h_f}{d}\right) + \frac{h_f}{d}\right]$$

$$\frac{M_u}{bd^2f_{cu}} = \frac{1}{5}\left[\frac{h_f}{d}\left(2 - \frac{h_f}{d}\right)\left(1 - \frac{b_w}{b}\right) + \frac{3b_w}{4b}\right]$$

For this condition, values of M_u/bd^2f_{cu} corresponding to various ratios of h_f/d and b_w/b can be read from the adjacent chart.

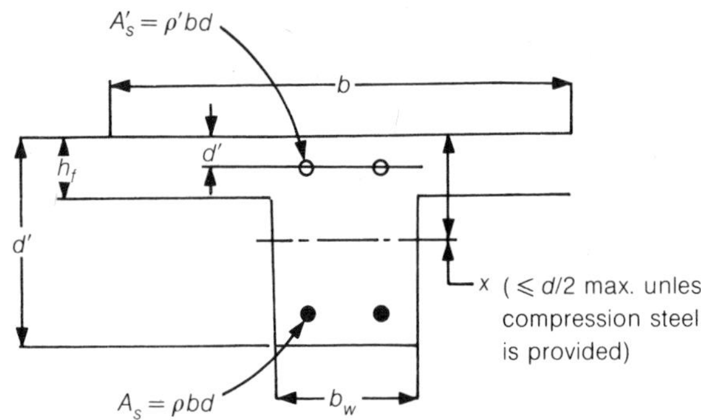

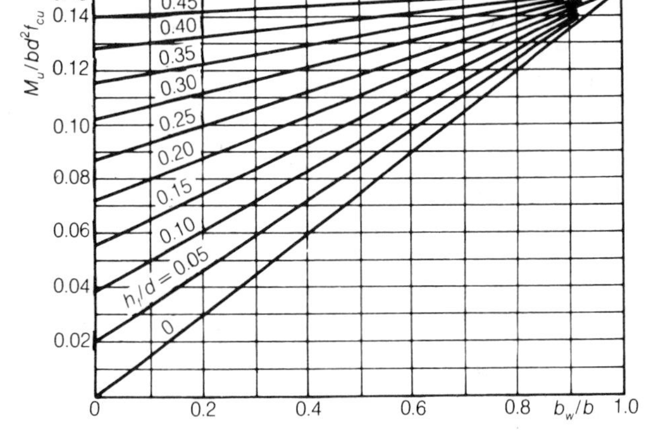

Parabolic-rectangular stress-block

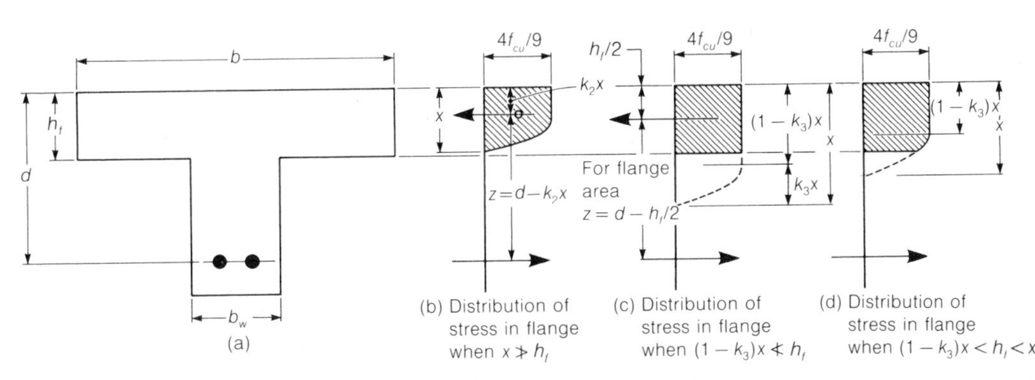

(a)

(b) Distribution of stress in flange when $x \ngtr h_f$

(c) Distribution of stress in flange when $(1 - k_3)x \nless h_f$

(d) Distribution of stress in flange when $(1 - k_3)x < h_f < x$

Case (b)
Design as slab of width b with parabolic-rectangular stress distribution.

Case (c)
Design as beam of width b_w, plus slab of width $b - b_w$ with uniform rectangular stress distribution of $4f_{cu}/9$.

Case (d)
No simple design method available.

ρ read from the curves is 0.0155. Thus

$$A_{s\,req} = 0.0155 \times 200 \times 265 = 822\,\text{mm}^2$$

Provide three 20 mm bars.

Rearranged formulae for CP110 simplified equations. From formulae on *Table 107*, maximum value of M_u/bd^2 of concrete alone $= 3f_{cu}/20 = 4.5$. Assume $b = 200$ mm. Then minimum permissible $d = 260$ mm as already obtained. Now with an actual value of d of 265 mm as before,

$$A_{s\,req} = \frac{1}{2.2}\frac{f_{cu}}{f_y}\left[1 - \sqrt{\left(1 - \frac{5.06M_u}{f_{cu}bd^2}\right)}\right]bd$$

$$= \frac{30 \times 200 \times 265}{2.2 \times 425}\left[1 - \sqrt{\left(1 - \frac{5.06 \times 61 \times 10^6}{30 \times 200 \times 265^2}\right)}\right]$$

$$= 821\,\text{mm}^2$$

Provide three 20 mm bars as before.

Example 2. Design a rectangular beam with $b = 200$ mm, $d = 300$ mm, $f_{cu} = 25\,\text{N/mm}^2$ and using high-yield reinforcement to resist an ultimate bending moment of 100 kN m.

Rigorous analysis with parabolic-rectangular stress-block. From first principles, from the scales provided on *Table 102*, read off values of $k_1 = 10.06$ and $k_2 = 0.4553$ corresponding to $f_{cu} = 25\,\text{N/mm}^2$.

With BS8110, since no corresponding redistribution of moment is specified (with would otherwise restrict the maximum ratio of x/d that may be adopted), take $x/d = 0.636$ corresponding to the limiting strain in the tension steel, as this will minimize the total amount of reinforcement required. (In fact in the present example, since a minimum area of compression steel of 402 mm² (i.e. two 16 mm bars) would need to be provided for practical requirements, it is clearly advantageous to adopt a lower ratio of x/d. This would increase the area of compression steel theoretically required to match that actually provided, and reduce the area of tension steel. For example, with $x/d = 0.4$, $A'_{s\,req} = 391\,\text{mm}^2$ and $A_{s\,req} = 994\,\text{mm}^2$.) Then

$$k_1bx = 10.06 \times 200 \times 0.636 \times 300 = 384\,000\,\text{N}$$
$$k_2x = 0.4553 \times 0.636 \times 300 = 86.9\,\text{mm}$$

so that $z = 300 - 86.9 = 213.1$ mm. Thus the moment of resistance of the concrete alone is $384\,000 \times 213.1 = 81.8 \times 10^6$ N mm. The design stress in the compression steel is $460/1.15 = 400\,\text{N/mm}^2$, so that

$$A'_{s\,req} = \frac{100 \times 10^6 - 81.8 \times 10^6}{400(300 - 40)} = 175\,\text{mm}^2$$

Provide two 16 mm bars.

The design stress in the tension reinforcement is also 400 N/mm², so that

$$A_{s\,req} = \frac{384\,000}{400} + \frac{100 \times 10^6 - 81.8 \times 10^6}{400(300 - 40)} = 1135\,\text{mm}^2$$

Provide four 20 mm bars.

With CP110, to avoid having to reduce the stress in the tension reinforcement, take $x/d = 0.476$ corresponding to limiting strain, since this will minimize the total amount of reinforcement required. Then

$$k_1bx = 10.06 \times 200 \times 0.476 \times 300 = 287\,300\,\text{N}$$
$$k_2x = 0.4553 \times 0.476 \times 300 = 65.0\,\text{mm}$$

so that $z = 300 - 65.0 = 235.0$ mm. Thus the moment of resistance of the concrete alone $= 287\,300 \times 235.0 = 67.5 \times 10^6$ N mm. From *Table 104* the design stress in the compression reinforcement is 311.9 N/mm², so that

$$A'_{s\,req} = \frac{100 \times 10^6 - 67.5 \times 10^6}{311.9(300 - 40)} = 401\,\text{mm}^2$$

Provide two 16 mm bars.

The design stress in the tension reinforcement is 369.6 N/mm², so that

$$A_{s\,req} = \frac{287\,300}{369.6} + \frac{100 \times 10^6 - 67.5 \times 10^6}{369.6(300 - 40)} = 1116\,\text{mm}^2$$

Provide four 20 mm bars.

Alternatively, using the BS8110 formulae on *Table 105*,

$$\rho' = \frac{\left[\dfrac{100 \times 10^6}{200 \times 300^2} - 10.06 \times 0.636(1 - 0.4553 \times 0.636)\right]}{400(1 - 40/300)}$$

$$= 0.0029$$

and

$$A'_{s\,req} = 0.0029 \times 200 \times 300 = 175\,\text{mm}^2$$

Also

$$\rho = \frac{10.06}{400} \times 0.636 + 0.0029 = 0.0189$$

and

$$A_{s\,req} = 0.0189 \times 200 \times 300 = 1135\,\text{mm}^2$$

Using the CP110 formulae at the top of *Table 107*,

$$\rho' = \frac{\left[\dfrac{100 \times 10^6}{200 \times 300^2} - 10.06 \times 0.476(1 - 0.4553 \times 0.476)\right]}{311.9(1 - 40/300)}$$

$$= 0.0067$$

and

$$A'_{s\,req} = 0.0067 \times 200 \times 300 = 400\,\text{mm}^2$$

Also

$$\rho = \frac{10.06}{369.6} \times 0.476 + 0.0067 \times \frac{311.9}{369.6} = 0.0186$$

and

$$A_{s\,req} = 0.0186 \times 200 \times 300 = 1116\,\text{mm}^2$$

Interpolation between charts 6 and 7 of Part 3 of BS8110 confirms that, when $M_u/bd^2 = 100 \times 10^6/200 \times 300^2 = 5.56$ and $x/d = 0.636$,

$$A_s = 0.019 \times 200 \times 300 = 1140\,\text{mm}^2$$
$$A'_s = 0.003 \times 200 \times 300 = 180\,\text{mm}^2$$

Similarly, interpolation between charts 32 and 33 of Part 2

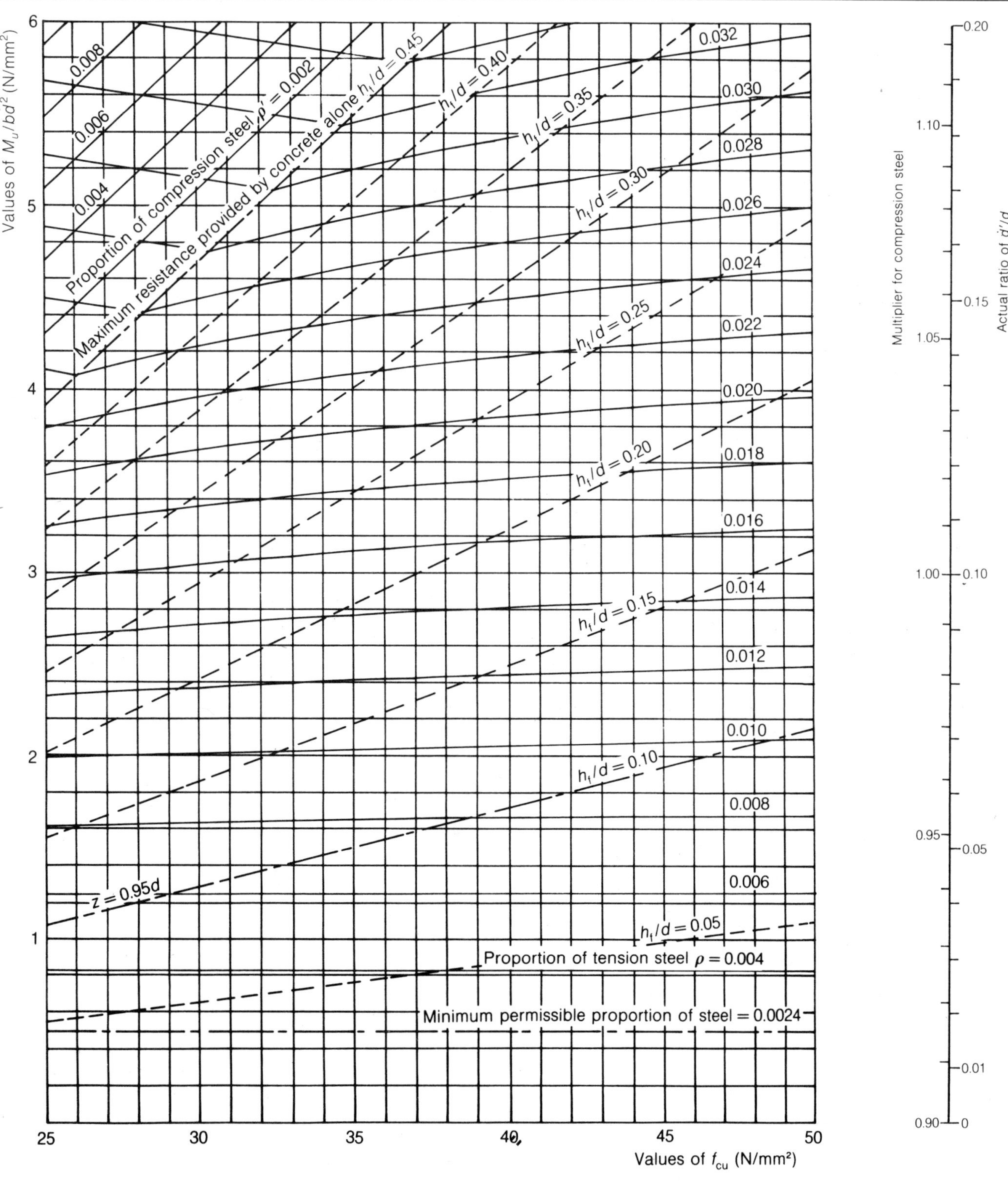

$A_s = \rho bd \qquad A'_s = \rho' bd$

Curves are based on rigorous analysis using BS8110 uniform rectangular concrete stress-block (clause 3.4.4.1).

Basic design procedure

Slabs and rectangular beams: ignore curves for h_f/d and select a value of ρ corresponding to intersection of given values of M_u/bd^2 and f_{cu}.

For doubly-reinforced beams with $d' = 0.1d$, read ρ' and ρ directly.

For doubly-reinforced beams with $d' \neq 0.1d$, determine ρ' and ρ from curves on chart. Multiply ρ' by coefficient relating to actual ratio of d'/d read from scale at side of chart. Then add or subtract to ρ (depending whether actual ratio of d'/d is greater or less than 0.1) the *adjustment* made to ρ'.

Flanged beams: with b = breadth of flange, calculate value of M_u/bd^2 and at intersection with chosen f_{cu} read off limiting value of h_f/d. If actual value of h_f/d exceeds limiting value, follow procedure for rectangular sections outlined above. If otherwise, adopt procedure set out on *Table 108*.

of CP110 confirms that with $M_u/bd^2 = 5.56$ and $x/d = 0.476$,

$$A_s = 0.0186 \times 200 \times 300 = 1116\,\text{mm}^2$$
$$A_s' = 0.0067 \times 200 \times 300 = 402\,\text{mm}^2$$

Rigorous analysis with BS8110 uniform rectangular stress-block. From first principles, assuming a value of b of 200 mm and a ratio of x/d of 0.636 as above, the total compressive force provided by the concrete $= 0.67/1.5 \times 25 \times 200 \times 0.636 \times 0.9 \times 300 = 383\,000$ N, and $z = 300 - 0.5 \times 0.9 \times 0.636 \times 500 = 214.1$ mm. The moment of resistance of the concrete alone is thus $383\,000 \times 214.1 = 82.1 \times 10^6$ N mm. Then, since the design stress in the compression reinforcement is $460/1.15 = 400\,\text{N/mm}^2$,

$$A_{s\,req}' = \frac{100 \times 10^6 - 82.1 \times 10^6}{400(300 - 40)} = 172\,\text{mm}^2$$

The design stress in the tension reinforcement is also $400\,\text{N/mm}^2$, so that

$$A_{s\,req} = \frac{383\,000}{400} + 172 = 1130\,\text{mm}^2$$

With the formulae on *Table 105*,

$$\rho' = \frac{\left[\dfrac{100 \times 10^6}{200 \times 300^2} - 0.402 \times 25 \times 0.636 \times (1 - 0.45 \times 0.636)\right]}{400(1 - 40/300)}$$
$$= 0.0029$$

and

$$A_{s\,req}' = 0.0029 \times 200 \times 300 = 172\,\text{mm}^2$$

Also

$$\rho = 0.402 \times 25 \times 0.636/400 + 0.0029 = 0.0189$$

and

$$A_{s\,req} = 0.0189 \times 200 \times 300 = 1130\,\text{mm}^2$$

Rigorous analysis with CP110 uniform rectangular stress-block. Analysis from first principles is similar to that shown above but with $0.4f_{cu}$ instead of k_1 and 0.5 instead of k_2.

Alternatively, using the formulae at the top of *Table 107*,

$$\rho' = \frac{\left[\dfrac{100 \times 10^6}{200 \times 300^2} - 0.2 \times 25 \times 0.476(2 - 0.476)\right]}{311.9(1 - 40/300)}$$
$$= 0.0071$$

and

$$A_{s\,req}' = 0.0071 \times 200 \times 300 = 428\,\text{mm}^2$$

Also

$$\rho = 0.4 \times \frac{25 \times 0.476}{369.6} + 0.0071 \times \frac{311.9}{369.6} = 0.0189$$

and

$$A_{s\,req} = 0.0189 \times 200 \times 300 = 1134\,\text{mm}^2$$

Design charts for CP110 simplified equations. From the curves on *Table 113*, for $M_u/bd^2 = 100 \times 10^6/200 \times 300^2 = 5.56$ and $f_{cu} = 25\,\text{N/mm}^2$, $\rho = 0.0190$ and $\rho' = 0.0066$. Thus

$$A_{s\,req} = 0.0190 \times 200 \times 300 = 1138\,\text{mm}^2$$
$$A_{s\,req}' = 0.0066 \times 200 \times 300 = 393\,\text{mm}^2$$

These values apply when $d'/d = 0.1 = 30$ mm. The actual value of d' is say $20 + 10 + 10 = 40$ mm, so that the true ratio of $d'/d = 40/300 = 0.133$. Thus the actual value of A_s' required (taking correction factor from scale at side of chart) is

$$A_s' = 393 \times 1.04 = 409\,\text{mm}^2$$

Provide two 20 mm bars.

The actual value of A_s required is

$$A_s = 1138 + (409 - 393)0.83 = 1151\,\text{mm}^2$$

Provide four 20 mm bars.

Formulae for CP110 simplified equations

$$\rho = \left[\frac{100 \times 10^6}{200 \times 300^2} - 0.15 \times 25\right] \Big/ 0.72 \times 425(1 - 40/300)$$
$$= 0.0068$$

Thus

$$A_{s\,req}' = 0.0068 \times 200 \times 300 = 409\,\text{mm}^2$$

Provide two 20 mm bars.

$$\rho' = 0.23 \times \frac{25}{425} + 0.828 \times 0.0068 = 0.0192$$

Thus

$$A_{s\,req} = 0.0192 \times 200 \times 300 = 1150\,\text{mm}^2$$

Provide four 20 mm bars.

Example 3. Design a rectangular section with $b = 200$ mm and $d = 300$ mm to permit a moment redistribution of 30% and to resist an ultimate bending moment of 90 kN m, with $f_{cu} = 27.5\,\text{N/mm}^2$ and $f_y = 350\,\text{N/mm}^2$, according to CP110.

Since moment redistribution is limited to 10% when the simplified formulae provided in clause 3.3.5.3 of CP110 are employed, it is necessary to undertake a rigorous analysis. Furthermore, since the values of f_y and f_{cu} are 'non-standard', it is not possible to employ the design charts in CP110: Part 2 without complex interpolation.

From the scales on *Table 102*, read values of $k_1 = 11.0$ and $k_2 = 0.4533$ corresponding to $f_{cu} = 27.5\,\text{N/mm}^2$. To achieve a 30% redistribution of moment, the maximum permissible value of $x/d = 0.3$. Then since the lower limiting value of x/d to avoid the need to reduce the strain in the compression reinforcement is $7d'/3d = 7 \times 400/3 \times 300 = 0.311$ and the actual value of x/d adopted is less than this, the stress in the compression steel must be reduced. With $x/d = 0.3$, *Table 103* indicates that

$$f_{yd1} = \frac{d}{x}\left(2300\frac{x}{d} - 700\frac{d'}{d}\right)\frac{f_y}{2300 + f_y}$$
$$= \frac{1}{0.3}\left(2300 \times 0.3 - \frac{700 \times 40}{300}\right)\frac{350}{2300 + 350}$$
$$= 262.7\,\text{N/mm}^2$$

and, since there is no reduction of stress in the tension steel,

$$f_{yd2} = 0.87f_y = 304.3\,\text{N/mm}^2$$

Now from the formulae at the top of *Table 107*,

BS8110 design chart for beams and slabs: $f_y = 460\,\text{N/mm}^2$

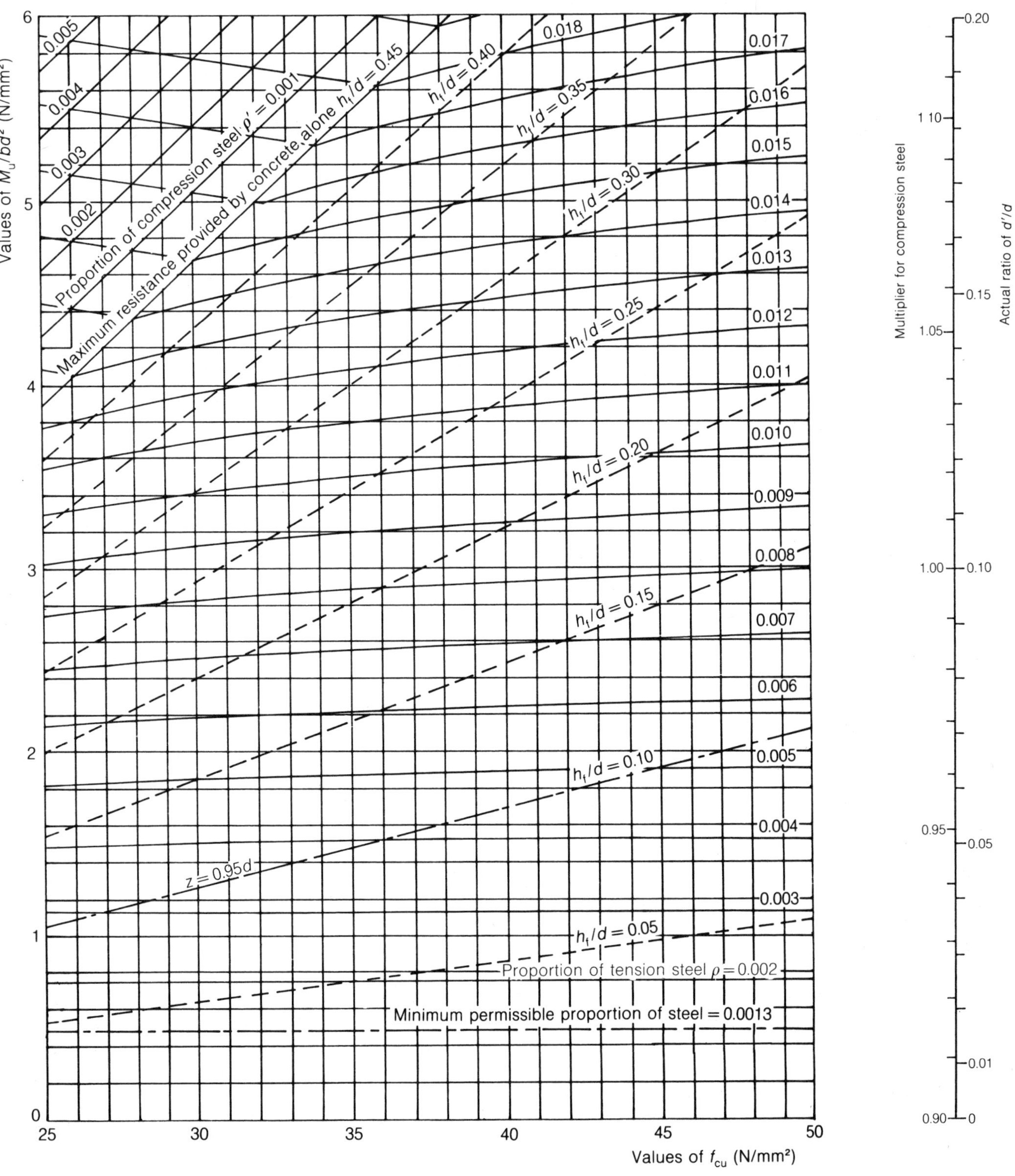

$A_s = \rho bd \qquad A'_s = \rho' bd$

Curves are based on rigorous analysis using BS8110 uniform rectangular concrete stress-block (clause 3.4.4.1).

Basic design procedure

Slabs and rectangular beams: ignore curves for h_f/d and select a value of ρ corresponding to intersection of given values of M_u/bd^2 and f_{cu}.

For doubly-reinforced beams with $d' = 0.1d$, read ρ' and ρ directly.

For doubly-reinforced beams with $d' \neq 0.1d$, determine ρ' and ρ from curves on chart. Multiply ρ' by coefficient relating to actual ratio of d'/d read from scale at side of chart. Then add or subtract to ρ (depending whether actual ratio of d'/d is greater or less than 0.1) the *adjustment* made to ρ'.

Flanged beams: with b = breadth of flange, calculate value of M_u/bd^2 and at intersection with chosen f_{cu} read off limiting value of h_f/d. If actual value of h_f/d exceeds limiting value, follow procedure for rectangular sections outlined above. If otherwise, adopt procedure set out on *Table 108*.

$$\rho' = \frac{\left[\dfrac{90 \times 10^6}{200 \times 300^2} - 11.0 \times 0.3(1 - 0.4533 \times 0.3)\right]}{262.7\left(1 - \dfrac{40}{300}\right)}$$

$$= 0.0094,$$

so that

$$A'_{s\,req} = 0.0094 \times 200 \times 300 = 566\,\text{mm}^2$$

Provide two 20 mm bars.

Also

$$\rho = \frac{11.0 \times 0.3}{304.3} + 0.0094 \times \frac{262.7}{304.3} = 0.019$$

so that

$$A_{s\,req} = 0.019 \times 200 \times 300 = 1138\,\text{mm}^2$$

Provide four 20 mm bars.

Example 4. Check the resistance of the section and design suitable high-yield reinforcement if a flanged beam of grade 25 concrete, with $b = 960$ mm, $b_w = 200$ mm, $h_f = 125$ mm and $h = 375$ mm, is to withstand ultimate moments of (i) 310 kN m and (ii) 340 kN m.

BS8110 requirements ($f_y = 460\,\text{N/mm}^2$)

(i) $M_u = 310$ kN m. Adopting a rectangular stress-block, first determine the ratio of x/d on the assumption that $h_f > 0.9x$. Then, from the values on *Table 102* and assuming an effective depth of 315 mm, since $M_u/bd^2f_{cu} = 310 \times 10^6/(960 \times 315^2 \times 25) = 0.130$, $x/d = 0.393$. The depth of the stress block is thus $0.9 \times 0.393 = 0.354$ and, since this is less than $125/315 = 0.397$, the section acts as a simple rectangular slab having a width of 960 mm. Thus the total compression in the concrete $= (4/9) \times 0.9 \times 0.393 \times 960 \times 315 \times 25 = 1\,190\,000$ N and

$$A_{s\,req} = 1\,190\,000/(460/1.15) = 2975\,\text{mm}^2$$

Provide three 32 mm plus two 20 mm bars.

(ii) $M_u = 340$ kN m. Again, assume first that h_f exceeds $0.9x$. Then if $d = 315$ mm, $M_u/bd^2f_{cu} = 340 \times 10^6/(960 \times 315^2 \times 25) = 0.143$ and the corresponding ratio of x/d (read from *Table 102*) is 0.48, so that the depth of the stress block is $0.432d$. Since this exceeds $125/315 = 0.397$, the section now acts as a flanged beam (*Table 108*) and the recalculated ratio of x/d is thus

$$\frac{1}{0.9}\left\{1 - \sqrt{\left[1 - \frac{3}{0.67}\left(\frac{M_u}{bd^2f_{cu}}\right)\frac{b}{b_w} + \left(\frac{b}{b_w} - 1\right)\left(2 - \frac{h_f}{d}\right)\frac{h_f}{d}\right]}\right\}$$

$$= \frac{1}{0.9}\left\{1 - \sqrt{\left[1 - \frac{3 \times 340 \times 10^6 \times 960}{0.67 \times 960 \times 315^2 \times 25 \times 200} + \left(\frac{960}{200} - 1\right)\left(2 - \frac{125}{315}\right)\frac{125}{315}\right]}\right\} = 0.455$$

As this is less than 1/2, compression steel is not required The area of tension steel needed is given by

$$\frac{1.541}{3}\frac{f_{cu}}{f_y}[0.9b_w x + (b - b_w)h_f]$$

$$= \frac{1.541 \times 25}{3 \times 460}[0.9 \times 200 \times 0.455 \times 315 + (960 - 200) \times 125]$$

$$= 3372\,\text{mm}^2$$

Provide three 32 mm plus two 25 mm bars.

CP110 requirements ($f_y = 460\,\text{N/mm}^2$)

(i) $M_u = 310$ kN m. Assume a rectangular stress-block and first calculate the value of x/d on the assumption that h_f exceeds x. From *Table 102*, with an effective depth of 315 mm, as $M_u/bd^2f_{cu} = 310 \times 10^6/(960 \times 315^2 \times 25) = 0.130$, the corresponding ratio of x/d is 0.41. Since this exceeds $h_f/d = 125/315 = 0.397$, the section acts as a flanged beam (*Table 109*). The recalculated value of x/d is

$$1 - \sqrt{\left[1 - \left(\frac{5M_u}{bd^2f_{cu}}\right)\frac{b}{b_w} + \left(\frac{b}{b_w} - 1\right)\left(2 - \frac{h_f}{d}\right)\frac{h_f}{d}\right]}$$

$$= 1 - \sqrt{\left[1 - \frac{5 \times 310 \times 10^6 \times 960}{960 \times 315^2 \times 25 \times 200} + \left(\frac{960}{200} - 1\right)\left(2 - \frac{125}{315}\right)\frac{125}{315}\right]} = 0.458$$

Since this is less than the limiting value of x/d of 0.476 for $f_y = 425\,\text{N/mm}^2$, no reduction in the design stress in the tension reinforcement is necessary. Thus

$$\rho = \frac{2}{5}\frac{f_{cu}}{f_{yd2}}\left[\frac{b_w}{b}\frac{x}{d} + \left(1 - \frac{b_w}{b}\right)\frac{h_f}{d}\right]$$

$$= \frac{0.4 \times 25}{369.6}\left[\frac{200 \times 0.458}{960} + \left(1 - \frac{200}{960}\right)\frac{125}{315}\right] = 0.0111$$

Then

$$A_{s\,req} = 0.0111 \times 315 \times 960 = 3352\,\text{mm}^2$$

Provide three 32 mm plus two 25 mm bars.

(ii) $M_u = 340$ kN m. First calculate the value of x/d on the assumption that h_f exceeds x. From *Table 102*, with an effective depth of 315 mm, since $M_u/bd^2f_{cu} = 340 \times 10^6/(960 \times 315^2 \times 25) = 0.143$, the corresponding ratio of x/d is 0.465. Since this exceeds $h_f/d = 125/315 = 0.397$, the section must act as a flanged beam (*Table 109*). Attempting to recalculate x/d from the expression

$$\frac{x}{d} = 1 - \sqrt{\left[1 - \left(\frac{5M_u}{bd^2f_{cu}}\right)\frac{b}{b_w} + \left(\frac{b}{b_w} - 1\right)\left(2 - \frac{h_f}{d}\right)\frac{h_f}{d}\right]}$$

leads to the futile attempt to find the square root of a negative quantity. Thus to achieve a rational value for x, compression steel must be provided. Adopting a ratio of x/d of 0.5, the resistance moment provided by the flanged concrete section alone is

$$\frac{M_u}{bd^2f_{cu}} = \frac{1}{5}\left[\frac{h_f}{d}\left(2 - \frac{h_f}{d}\right)\left(1 - \frac{b_w}{b}\right) + \frac{3b_w}{4b}\right]$$

so that

$$M_u = \tfrac{25}{5}[125(2 \times 315 - 125)(960 - 200) + \tfrac{3}{4} \times 200 \times 315^2] = 314.3 \times 10^6\,\text{N mm}$$

CP110 design chart for beams and slabs: $f_y = 250\,\text{N/mm}^2$

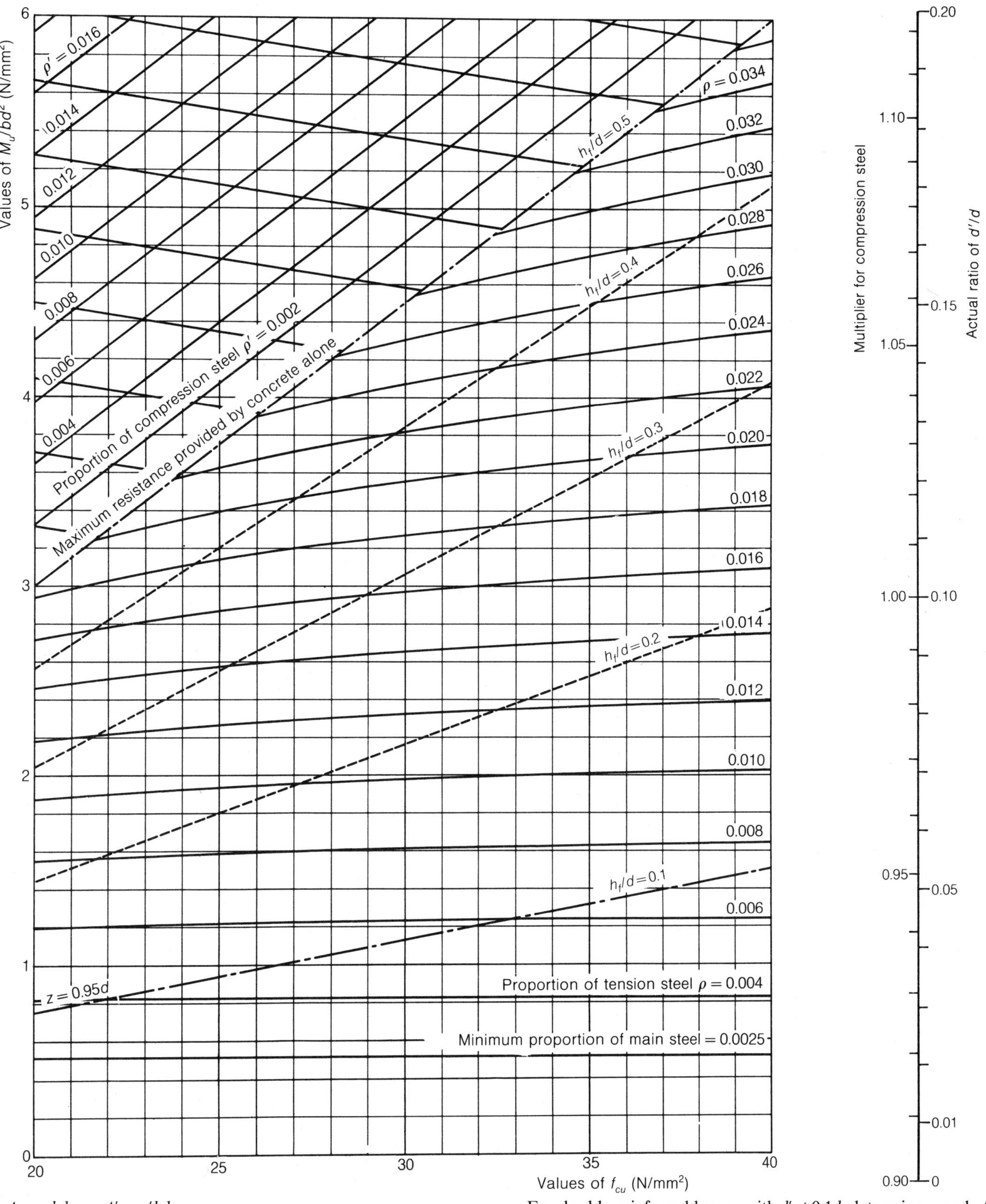

$A_s = \rho bd \qquad A'_s = \rho' bd$

Curves are based on simplified formulae given in clause 3.3.5.3 of CP110.

Basic design procedure

Slabs and rectangular beams: ignore curves for h_f/d and select a value of ρ corresponding to intersection of given values of M_u/bd^2 and f_{cu}.

For doubly-reinforced beams with $d' = 0.1d$, read ρ' and ρ directly.

For doubly-reinforced beams with $d' \neq 0.1d$, determine ρ and ρ' from curves on chart. Multiply ρ' by coefficient relating to actual ratio of d'/d read from scale at side of chart. Then add or subtract to ρ (depending on whether actual ratio of d'/d is greater or less than 0.1), 0.83 times the *adjustment* made to ρ'.

Flanged beams: with b = breadth of flange, calculate value of M_u/bd^2 and at intersection with chosen f_{cu} read off limiting value of h_f/d. If actual ratio of h_f/d exceeds limiting value, follow procedure for rectangular sections outlined above. If otherwise, adopt procedure set out on *Table 109*.

1	2	3	4	5	6	7	8
Bar	Distance from neutral axis $a-x$(mm)	Number of bars	(2) × (3)	x/a	f_{yd2}	Area of bars $\delta A_s \times (3)$	(6) × (7)
1	475	1	475	0.500	217.4	δA_s	$217.4\delta A_s$
2	441	2	882	0.519	217.4	$2\delta A_s$	$413.8\delta A_s$
3	343	2	686	0.581	217.4	$2\delta A_s$	$434.8\delta A_s$
4	197	2	394	0.707	217.4	$2\delta A_s$	$434.8\delta A_s$
5	25	2	50	0.950	36.8	$2\delta A_s$	$73.6\delta A_s$
Σ		9	2487				$1595.4\delta A_s$

Thus the resistance moment required from the compression bars is

$$340 \times 10^6 - 314.3 \times 10^6 = 25.7 \times 10^6 \text{ N mm}$$

If $d' = 60$ mm, $d - d' = 255$ mm and $f_{yd1} = 311.9$ N/mm². Thus

$$A'_{s\,req} = 25.7 \times 10^6/(255 \times 311.9) = 323 \text{ mm}^2$$

Since $x/d = 0.5$, $f_{yd2} = 359$ N/mm². Then

$$A_{s\,req} = \frac{2}{5}\frac{f_{cu}}{f_{yd2}}[b_w x + (b - b_w)h_f] + A'_s\frac{f_{yd1}}{f_{yd2}}$$

$$= \frac{0.4 \times 25}{359}(200 \times \tfrac{1}{2} \times 315 + 760 \times 125) + \frac{323 \times 311.9}{359}$$

$$= 3804 \text{ mm}^2$$

Provide four 32 mm plus two 20 mm bars.

It is of interest to compare the foregoing results with those obtained from rigorous analysis with a parabolic-rectangular stress-block, the designs being prepared on a computer using an iterative procedure. The parabolic-rectangular stress-block designs to BS8110 require steel areas of 2998 mm² and 3381 mm² respectively (i.e. almost identical amounts to those needed with a uniform rectangular stress-block). However, the areas of tension steel required with a parabolic-rectangular stress-block, when working to CP110, are 3245 mm² and 3675 mm² respectively (i.e. about 3.5% less than those necessary with a uniform rectangular stress-block). Since the resistance moment provided by the concrete section alone is greater, no compression steel is necessary to resist either applied moment.

Example 5. The following example illustrates the application of rigorous analysis with a rectangular concrete stress-block to non-rectangular sections. The annular section shown in the accompanying figure is to be used as a pipe bridge. If the ultimate applied moment is 600 kN m, design suitable reinforcement, assuming that sixteen bars positioned as shown are to be provided, when $f_{cu} = 25$ N/mm² and $f_y = 250$ N/mm², according to BS8110 requirements.

For simplicity, take $x/d = 0.5$ and neglect any resistance provided by the bars that are in compression. Then $x = (1/2) \times 950 = 475$ mm, so depth of stress block $= 0.9 \times 475 = 427.5$ mm. With $\theta = 2\cos^{-1}(72.5/450) = 161.5°$, the area of concrete in compression is approximately

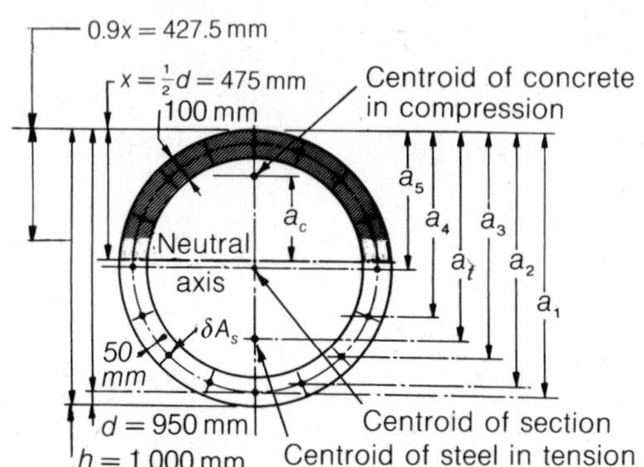

$$\tfrac{1}{2}(r_1^2 - r_2^2)(\theta - \sin\theta) = \tfrac{1}{2} \times 900 \times 100 \times 2.5 = 112\,500 \text{ mm}^2$$

The total direct compression in the concrete is $(4/9)f_{cu}A_c = (4/9) \times 25 \times 112\,500 = 1\,250\,000$ N. Thus the distance of the centre of compression from the neutral axis is

$$\frac{4(r_1^3 - r_2^3)\sin^3\tfrac{1}{2}\theta}{3(r_1^2 - r_2^2)(\theta - \sin\theta)} = \frac{4 \times 61 \times 10^6 \times 0.9613}{3 \times 90\,000 \times 2.5} = 347.5 \text{ mm}$$

The force in the bars is determined as in the above table. The design stress in each individual bar is calculated by determining the ratio of x/a for the bar in question and then applying the relevant expression for f_{yd2} on *Table 103* (where $a = d$). Thus by summation the total force provided by the bars $= 1595.4\delta A_s$ and, for this to balance the total compressive force provided by the concrete, it is necessary for δA_s to equal $1\,250\,000/1595.4 = 783$ mm²; thus 32 mm bars will provide a steel area comfortably in excess of that required. Since the depth of the centroid of the tension reinforcement below the neutral axis (i.e. $a_t - x) = 2487/9 = 276$ mm, the total resistance moment of the section is $1\,250\,000 \times (347 + 276) = 779 \times 10^6$ N mm, which is satisfactory.

This method of taking account of the resistance contributed by reinforcement well away from the tension flange is also particularly useful when considering the contribution of bars provided in the sides of deep rectangular sections to limit cracking (see section 20.5.1).

20.2 MODULAR-RATIO METHOD: DESIGN PROCEDURES

20.2.1 Singly-reinforced sections

According to modular-ratio theory, the resistance moment of a section M_d reinforced in tension only is

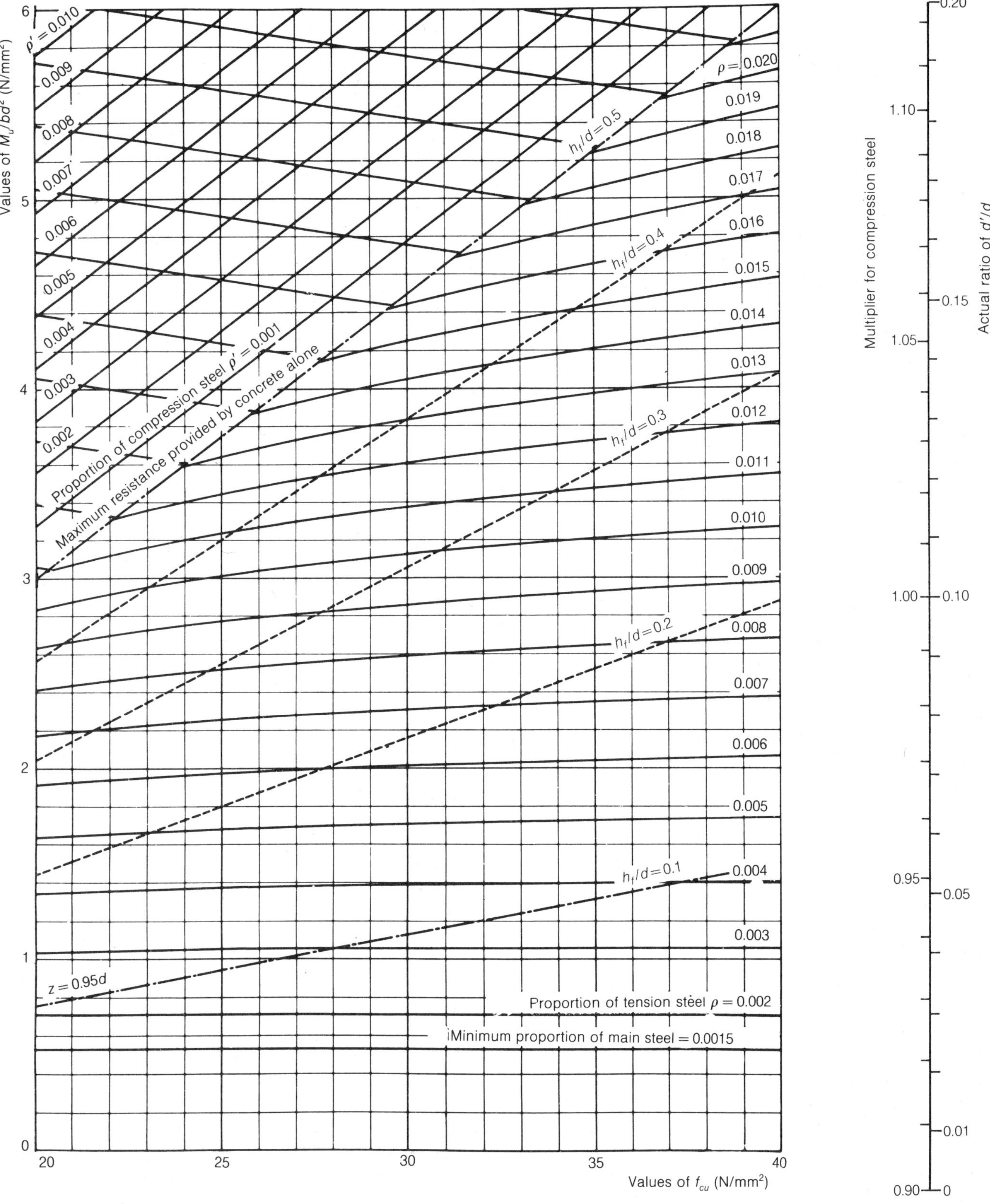

$A_s = \rho bd \qquad A'_s = \rho' bd$

Curves are based on simplified formulae given in clause 3.3.5.3 of CP110.

Basic design procedure

Slabs and rectangular beams: ignore curves for h_f/d and select a value of ρ corresponding to intersection of given values of M_u/bd^2 and f_{cu}.

For doubly-reinforced beams with $d' = 0.1d$, read ρ' and ρ directly.

For doubly-reinforced beams with $d' \neq 0.1d$, determine ρ and ρ' from curves on chart. Multiply ρ' by coefficient relating to actual ratio of d'/d read from scale at side of chart. Then add or subtract to ρ (depending on whether actual ratio of d'/d is greater or less than 0.1) 0.83 times the *adjustment* made to ρ'.

Flanged beams: with b = breadth of flange, calculate value of M_u/bd^2 and at intersection with chosen f_{cu} read off limiting value of h_f/d. If actual ratio of h_f/d exceeds limiting value, follow procedure for rectangular sections outlined above. If otherwise, adopt procedure set out on *Table 109*.

$$\tfrac{1}{2}bxzf_{cr} = A_s z f_{st}$$

This may be expressed as

$$\frac{M_d}{bd^2} = \frac{1}{2}\left(\frac{x}{d}\right)\left(1 - \frac{x}{3d}\right)f_{cr} = \rho f_{st}\left(1 - \frac{x}{3d}\right)$$

where

$$x = \frac{1}{1 + f_{st}/\alpha_e f_{cr}} d$$

The curves on *Tables 118* and *119* relate values of f_{cr}, f_{st}, ρ and M_d/bd^2 in metric and imperial units and thus, if any two of these quantities are known, the remaining two terms can be read off immediately from the same intersection point. The use of these charts is illustrated in the examples at the end of this section.

20.2.2 Coefficients

A feature of the modular-ratio theory is that, for a given modular ratio, each of the individual quantities ρ, x/d, z/d, $M_d/bd^2 f_{cr}$, $M_d/bd^2 f_{st}$ and f_{st}/f_{cr} relating to a particular rectangular section reinforced in tension only is directly and independently related to each other quantity. This interrelationship is expressed graphically by the scales on *Table 120*. The scales on the left of the central bold rule, which are applicable to any modular ratio, relate corresponding values of x/d, $M_d/bd^2 f_{cr}$, $\alpha_e M_d/bd^2 f_{st}$, $\alpha_e f_{cr}/f_{st}$, $\alpha_e \rho$ and z/d, while the scales to the right of the rule, which are only applicable when $\alpha_e = 15$, relate the simplified terms x/d, $M_d/bd^2 f_{cr}$, $M_d/bd^2 f_{st}$, f_{st}/f_{cr}, ρ and z/d.

The scales, which are not alignment charts in the strict sense of the term, are used as follows. A horizontal straight-edge, whose alignment can be checked by ensuring that the values on the scales for x/d, which are duplicated at each side of each set of scales, are identical, is laid across the chart and the required values corresponding to the given data are read from the appropriate scales. Examples of the use of this table are given at the end of this section.

20.2.3 To design a rectangular beam to resist a given bending moment with given stresses

Method 1 ($\alpha_e = 15$). For the given stresses, read off the appropriate values of M_d/bd^2 and ρ from the curves on *Tables 118* and *119*. Calculate the value of bd^2 required and select suitable values of b and d from considerations of shear and slenderness. The area of tension steel required is ρbd.

Method 2 ($\alpha_e = 15$). Read off from the scales on the right-hand side of *Table 120* the appropriate values of $M_d/bd^2 f_{cr}$ (or $M_d/bd^2 f_{st}$) and ρ corresponding to the given ratio of permissible stresses. Thus knowing M_d and f_{cr}, determine the value of bd^2 required and choose appropriate values of b and d from shear and slenderness considerations. The area of tension steel required is ρbd.

Method 3 (any value of modular ratio). Read off from the scales on the left-hand side of *Table 120* the appropriate values of $M_d/bd^2 f_{cr}$, $\alpha_e M_d/bd^2 f_{st}$ and $\alpha_e \rho$ corresponding to the given ratio $\alpha_e f_{cr}/f_{st}$. Thus knowing M_d, α_e and f_{cr}, determine the value of bd^2 required and select suitable values of b and d from considerations of shear and slenderness. The area of tension steel required is ρbd.

20.2.4 To determine the stresses in a rectangular beam subjected to a given bending moment

Method 1 ($\alpha_e = 15$). Determine M_d/bd^2 and ρ from the data given, and read off the corresponding values of f_{cr} and f_{st} from the curves on *Tables 118* and *119*.

Method 2 ($\alpha_e = 15$). Determine ρ from the data given and, from the scales on the right-hand side of *Table 120*, read off the corresponding values of $M_d/bd^2 f_{cr}$ and $M_d/bd^2 f_{st}$. Then knowing M_d, b and d, calculate f_{cr} and f_{st}.

Method 3 (any value of modular ratio). Determine $\alpha_e \rho$ from the data given and from the scales on the left-hand side of *Table 120*, read off the corresponding values of $M_d/bd^2 f_{cr}$ and $\alpha_e M_d/bd^2 f_{st}$. Then knowing M_d, α_e, b and d, calculate f_{cr} and f_{st}.

20.2.5 To determine the moment of resistance of a rectangular beam with given maximum stresses

Method 1 ($\alpha_e = 15$). From the curves on *Tables 118* and *119* read off the values of M_d/bd^2 corresponding to the intersections between the curves for ρ and f_{cr}, and ρ and f_{st}, respectively. The lesser of these two values gives the moment of resistance of the section.

Method 2 ($\alpha_e = 15$). Determine ρ from the data given, and read off the corresponding value of f_{st}/f_{cr} from the scales on the right-hand side of *Table 120*. If this is *greater* than the ratio of the permissible stresses then the moment of resistance of the reinforcement controls the strength of the section; by reading off the appropriate value of $M_d/bd^2 f_{st}$ and substituting the known values of b, d and f_{st}, the value of M_d can be obtained. If f_{st}/f_{cr} is less than the permissible ratio the concrete stress is the limiting factor; by reading off the corresponding value of $M_d/bd^2 f_{cr}$ and substituting, M_d can be found.

Alternatively, merely calculate both $M_d/bd^2 f_{cr}$ and $M_d/bd^2 f_{st}$ by substituting the maximum permissible stresses for f_{cr} and f_{st} respectively and select the *lower* of the two values of M_d thus obtained.

Method 3 (any value of modular ratio). Follow the procedure outlined in method 2 immediately above, but using the corresponding scales on the left-hand side of *Table 120*, i.e. those for $\alpha_e f_{cr}/f_{st}$, $M_d/bd^2 f_{cr}$ and $\alpha_e M_d/bd^2 f_{st}$ corresponding to the given value of $\alpha_e \rho$.

20.2.6 To design a rectangular beam with compression reinforcement

Method 1 ($\alpha_e = 15$). With given or selected values of b and d, calculate M_{conc} from the value of M_d/bd^2 obtained from the curves on *Tables 118* or *119* for the appropriate permissible

CP110 design chart for beams and slabs: $f_y = 460\,N/mm^2$

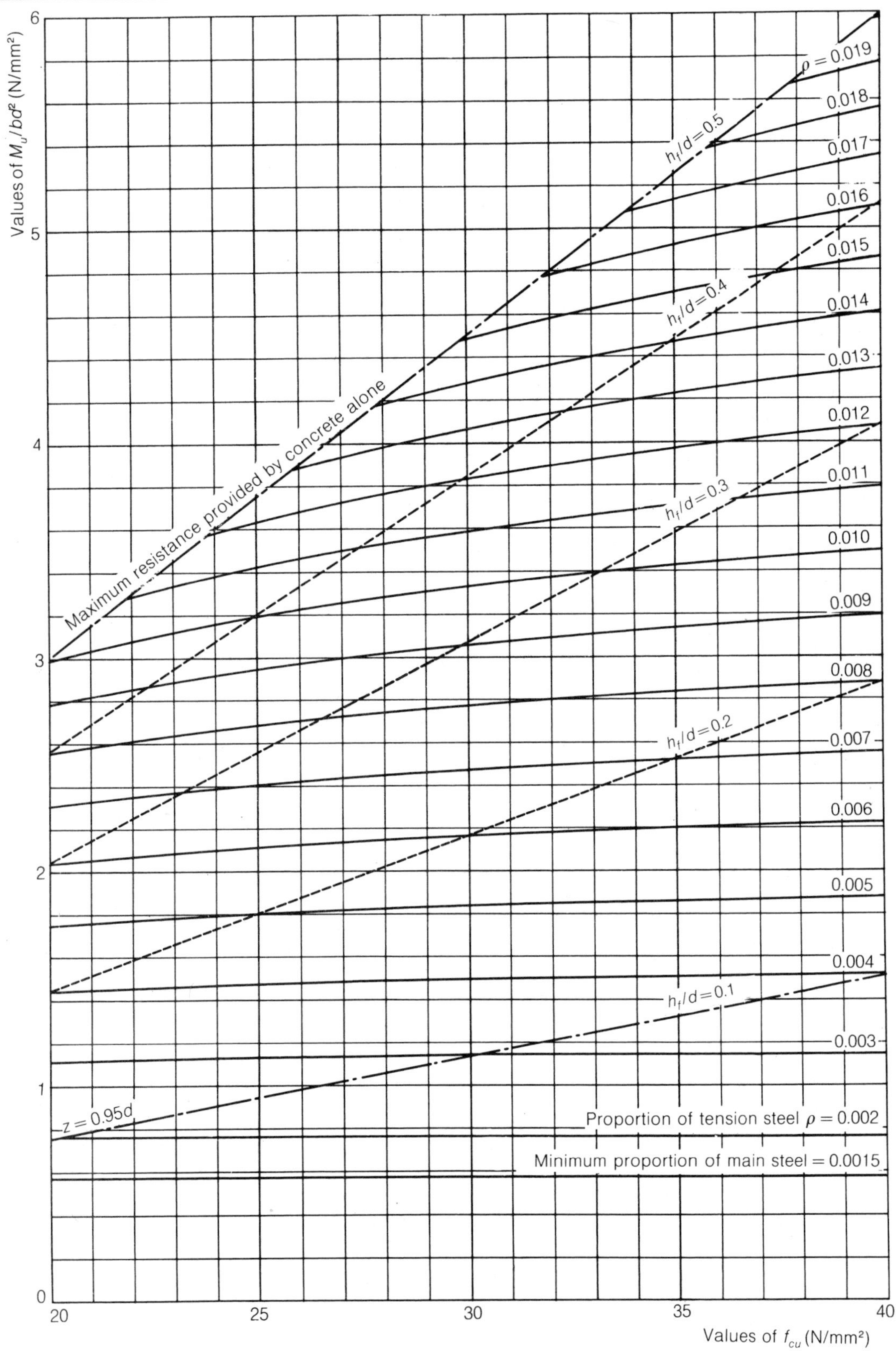

$A_s = \rho bd \qquad A'_s = \rho' bd$

Curves are based on simplified formulae given in clause 3.3.5.3 of CP110.

Basic design procedure

Slabs and rectangular beams: ignore curves for h_f/d and select a value of ρ corresponding to intersection of given values of M_u/bd^2 and f_{cu}.

Flanged beams: with b = breadth of flange, calculate value of M_u/bd^2 and at intersection with chosen f_{cu} read off limiting value of h_f/d. If actual ratio of h_f/d exceeds limiting value, follow procedure for rectangular sections outlined above. If otherwise, adopt procedure set out in *Table 109*.

Solid slabs to BS8110: resistance and reinforcement

Limit-state
ULTIMATE VALUES **115**

f_y	f_{cu}	Basic factors	Thickness h of slab in millimetres									
			75	100	125	150	175	200	225	250	275	300
250	25	Eff. depth d	44	67	87	112	124	149	174	190	215	240
		$M_u = 3.894d^2$	7,500	17,400	29,800	49,200	59,800	86,400	117,900	140,500	180,000	224,300
		$A_s = 23.115d$	1,018	1,549	2,023	2,601	2,867	3,445	4,023	4,392	4,970	5,548
		Arrangement	12@100	16@125	25@225	25@175	32@275	32@225	32@175	40@275	40@250	40@225
	30	Eff. depth d	49	70	87	112	124	140	165	190	215	240
		$M_u = 4.673d^2$	11,200	22,800	35,700	59,100	71,800	91,500	127,200	168,700	216,000	269,100
		$A_s = 27.738d$	1,360	1,942	2,428	3,121	3,440	3,884	4,577	5,271	5,964	6,658
		Arrangement	12@75	20@150	25@200	25@150	32@225	40@300	40@250	40@225	40@200	40@175
	35	Eff. depth d	47	70	87	99	124	140	165	190	215	240
		$M_u = 5.452d^2$	12,000	26,700	41,700	53,400	83,800	106,800	148,400	196,800	252,000	314,000
		$A_s = 32.361d$	1,521	2,266	2,832	3,204	4,013	4,531	5,340	6,149	6,958	7,767
		Arrangement	16@125	20@125	25@150	32@250	32@200	40@275	40@225	40@200	40@175	40@150
	40	Eff. depth d	47	70	87	99	115	140	165	190	215	240
		$M_u = 6.231d^2$	13,700	30,500	47,700	61,000	82,400	122,100	169,600	224,900	288,000	358,900
		$A_s = 36.984d$	1,739	2,589	3,237	3,662	4,254	5,178	6,103	7,027	7,952	8,877
		Arrangement	16@100	20@100	25@150	32@200	40@275	40@225	40@200	40@175	40@150	40@125
460	25	Eff. depth d	45	69	92	115	137	162	187	199	224	249
		$M_u = 3.894d^2$	7,800	18,500	32,900	51,500	73,600	102,800	136,900	154,200	195,400	241,400
		$A_s = 12.563d$	566	867	1,156	1,445	1,728	2,042	2,356	2,500	2,815	3,129
		Arrangement	10@125	12@125	16@150	20@200	25@275	25@225	25@200	32@300	32@275	32@250
	30	Eff. depth d	50	72	95	112	137	162	174	199	224	249
		$M_u = 4.673d^2$	11,600	24,200	42,100	59,100	88,300	123,400	141,400	185,000	234,400	289,700
		$A_s = 15.075d$	754	1,086	1,433	1,696	2,073	2,450	2,624	3,000	3,377	3,754
		Arrangement	10@100	16@175	20@200	25@275	25@225	25@200	32@300	32@250	32@225	32@200
	35	Eff. depth d	54	72	95	112	137	149	174	199	224	240
		$M_u = 5.452d^2$	15,800	28,200	49,200	69,000	103,000	121,000	165,000	215,900	273,500	314,000
		$A_s = 17.588d$	950	1,267	1,671	1,979	2,419	2,621	3,061	3,500	3,940	4,222
		Arrangement	12@100	16@150	20@175	25@225	25@200	32@300	32@250	32@225	32@200	40@275
	40	Eff. depth d	54	72	95	112	124	149	174	199	215	240
		$M_u = 6.231d^2$	18,100	32,300	56,200	78,800	95,800	138,300	188,600	246,700	288,000	358,900
		$A_s = 20.100d$	1,086	1,448	1,910	2,262	2,493	2,995	3,498	4,000	4,322	4,825
		Arrangement	12@100	16@125	20@150	25@200	32@300	32@250	32@225	32@200	40@275	40@250
Distribution steel		Mild steel $A_s = 2.4h$	180	240	300	360	420	480	540	600	660	720
		Arrangement	6@125*	8@200	10@250	12@300	12@250	12@225	12@200	12@175	12@150	16@275
		High-yield steel $A_s = 1.3h$	98	130	163	195	228	260	293	325	358	390
		Arrangement	6@125*	6@200	6@150	8@250	8@200	10@300	10@250	10@225	10@300	12@275

M_u ultimate moment of resistance in N m (or kN mm) per metre width of slab reinforced in tension only

A_s area of tension reinforcement in mm^2 per metre width of slab

Diameter and spacing given (e.g. 12@150 denotes 12 mm bars at 150 mm centres) are possible arrangements of tension reinforcement.

Arrangement tabulated is that requiring minimum area of reinforcement.

If combination of actual cover and bar size adopted gives a different effective depth, calculate M_u and A_s from basic factors given.

Cover assumed: 25 mm or bar diameter for $f_{cu} = 25\ \text{N/mm}^2$; 20 mm or bar diameter for $f_{cu} = 30\ \text{N/mm}^2$; 15 mm or bar diameter for $f_{cu} = 40\ \text{N/mm}^2$ (rounded to 5 mm dimension above).

*Indicates spacing determined by restriction that it must not exceed $3d$.

Solid slabs to CP110: resistance and reinforcement

Limit-state
ULTIMATE VALUES

116

f_y	f_{cu}	Basic factors	Thickness h of slab in millimetres									
			75	100	125	150	175	200	225	250	275	300
250	20	Eff. depth d	44	67	90	112	137	162	187	212	237	262
		$M_u = 3.00d^2$	5,800	13,500	24,300	37,600	56,300	78,700	104,900	134,800	168,500	206,000
		$A_s = 18.40d$	809	1,230	1,660	2,060	2,520	2,980	3,440	3,900	4,360	4,820
		Arrangement	12@125	16@150	20@175	25@225	25@175	25@150	25@125	25@125	25@100	25@100
	25	Eff. depth d	49	70	95	112	137	162	187	212	237	262
		$M_u = 3.75d^2$	9,000	18,400	33,800	47,000	70,400	98,400	131,100	168,500	210,600	257,400
		$A_s = 23.00d$	1,130	1,610	2,190	2,580	3,150	3,730	4,300	4,880	5,450	6,030
		Arrangement	12@100	20@175	20@125	25@175	25@150	25@125	25@100	25@100	25@75	25@75
	30	Eff. depth d	54	70	95	112	137	162	187	212	237	249
		$M_u = 4.50d^2$	13,100	22,000	40,600	56,400	84,500	118,100	157,400	202,200	252,800	279,000
		$A_s = 27.6d$	1,490	1,930	2,620	3,090	3,780	4,470	5,160	5,850	6,540	6,870
		Arrangement	12@75	20@150	20@100	25@150	25@125	25@100	25@75	25@75	25@75	32@100
425	20	Eff. depth d				115	140	165	190	212	237	262
		$M_u = 3.00d^2$				39,700	58,800	81,700	108,300	134,800	168,500	206,000
		$A_s = 10.82d$				1,250	1,520	1,790	2,060	2,290	2,570	2,840
		Arrangement				20@250	20@200	20@175	20@150	25@200	25@175	25@150
	25	Eff. depth d				120	145	162	187	212	237	262
		$M_u = 3.75d^2$				54,000	78,800	98,400	131,100	168,500	210,600	257,400
		$A_s = 13.53d$				1,620	1,960	2,190	2,530	2,870	3,210	3,540
		Arrangement				20@175	20@150	25@200	25@175	25@150	25@150	25@125
	30	Eff. depth d				120	137	162	187	212	237	262
		$M_u = 4.50d^2$				64,800	84,500	118,100	157,400	202,200	252,800	308,900
		$A_s = 16.24d$				1,950	2,220	2,630	3,040	3,440	3,850	4,250
		Arrangement				20@150	25@200	25@175	25@150	25@125	25@125	25@100
460	20	Eff. depth d	46	69	92	117	142	167	192	217		
		$M_u = 3.00d^2$	6,350	14,300	25,400	41,100	60,500	83,700	110,600	141,300		
		$A_s = 10.00d$	460	690	920	1,170	1,420	1,670	1,920	2,170		
		Arrangement	8@100	12@150	16@200	16@150	16@125	16@100	16@100	16@75		
	25	Eff. depth d	50	74	97	122	147	172	197			
		$M_u = 3.75d^2$	9,370	20,500	35,300	55,800	81,000	110,900	145,500			
		$A_s = 12.50d$	625	925	1,210	1,530	1,840	2,150	2,460			
		Arrangement	10@125	12@100	16@150	16@125	16@100	16@75	16@75			
	30	Eff. depth d	54	72	97	122	147	172				
		$M_u = 4.50d^2$	13,100	23,300	42,300	67,000	97,200	133,100				
		$A_s = 15.00d$	810	1,080	1,460	1,830	2,210	2,580				
		Arrangement	12@125	16@175	16@125	16@100	16@75	16@75				
Distribution steel		Mild steel $A_s = 1.5h$	113	150	188	225	263	300	338	375	413	450
		Arrangement	6@200*	8@300	8@250	8@200	10@275	10@250	10@225	12@300	12@250	12@250
		High-yield steel $A_s = 1.2h$	90	120	150	180	210	240	270	300	330	360
		Arrangement	6@200*	6@225	8@300	8@275	8@225	8@200	10@275	10@250	10@225	12@300

M_u ultimate moment of resistance in Nm (or kN mm) per metre width of slab reinforced in tension only

A_s area of tension reinforcement in mm² per metre width of slab

Diameter and spacing given (e.g. 12 @ 150 denotes 12 mm bars at 150 mm centres) are possible arrangements of tension reinforcement.

If combination of actual cover and bar size adopted gives a different effective depth, calculate M_d and A_s from basic factors given.

Cover assumed: 25 mm or bar diameter for $f_{cu} = 20$ N/mm²; 20 mm or bar diameter for $f_{cu} = 25$ N/mm²; 15 mm or bar diameter for $f_{cu} = 30$ N/mm^s (rounded to 5 mm dimension above).

*Indicates spacing determined by restriction that it must not exceed $5d$.

stresses. From the scales on the right-hand side of *Table 120* read off the value of x/d for the given ratio of f_{st}/f_{cr}. The required moment of resistance to be provided by the compression reinforcement is $M_{add} = M_d - M_{conc}$. Substitute in formula 7(a) in *Table 117* to find A_s', the area of compression reinforcement required. The total area of tension reinforcement necessary is the sum of the area required to balance the resistance of the concrete, which is given by the steel ratio ρ on the charts, and the area required to balance the resistance of the compression steel, which is $M_{add}/(d-d')f_{st}$. Alternatively, apply formula 7(b) in *Table 117*, employing the value for z/d obtained from the scales on the right-hand side of *Table 120*.

If A_s' is greater than A_s, modify the values of b and d (or use materials offering higher stresses) if possible.

Method 2 (any value of modular ratio). With known values of f_{cr}, f_{st} and α_e, and given or selected values of b and d, read from the scales on the left-hand side of *Table 120* the values of $x/d, z/d, \alpha_e\rho$ and M_d/bd^2f_{cr} corresponding to the given value of $\alpha_e f_{cr}/f_{st}$, and evaluate the corresponding numerical values of x, z and M_{conc}. Then calculate $M_{add} = M_d - M_{conc}$ and follow the procedure outlined for method 1 above; the area of tension steel required to balance the resistance of the concrete is determined from the value of $\alpha_e\rho$ read from the scales on *Table 120*, and the area required to balance the resistance of the compression steel is $M_{add}/(d-d')f_{st}$.

20.2.7 To determine the stresses in a rectangular beam with compression reinforcement

Determine x/d from formula 1(c) in *Table 117* and z from formula 3(a) (or approximately from formula 3(b)). Substitute in formula (11) to obtain the maximum stresses.

20.2.8 To find the moment of resistance of a given rectangular section with compression reinforcement (any value of modular ratio)

Determine x/d from formula 1(c) in *Table 117* and z from formula 3(a) or 3(b) for the known values of ρ' and ρ. Substitute with the permissible values of f_{cr} and f_{st} in formulae 5(b) and 5(c) and thus calculate the two values of M_d. The smaller of the two moments thus obtained is the safe moment of resistance.

20.2.9 To design a T-beam (or L-beam) to resist a given bending moment with given maximum stresses (any value of modular ratio)

The slab thickness h_f, the effective depth d, the breadth of rib b_w and the maximum effective width of flange b are generally known since they are determined from considerations other than the bending moment on the beam. From the scales on the left- or right-hand sides of *Table 120* as appropriate, determine the value of x/d corresponding to the given ratio $\alpha_e f_{cr}/f_{st}$ or f_{st}/f_{cr}. If x does not exceed h_f, proceed as for a rectangular beam. If x exceeds h_f, find z from formula (4) and A_s from formula (8) (first equality) on *Table 117*. Finally check the breadth of flange required from formula 8(a).

For approximate calculations, z is given by formula 4(a) on *Table 117* and A_s by formula (8) (second equality), and b is checked from formula 8(b).

20.2.10 Beams having an irregular cross-section (any value of modular ratio)

Such beams can be designed using the following semi-graphical method. Draw the cross-section to scale as shown in the accompanying diagram, and assume a position for the neutral axis. Divide the area above the neutral axis into strips parallel to this axis. With irregular figures the depth h_s of each strip should be equal, but any regularity in the shape of the cross-section may suggest the choice of positions for the boundaries of the strips such that the shape of each strip forms a common geometrical figure. The area A_s is the area of each individual bar, or of a number of bars, each of which is at the same distance a from the lowest bar or bars. The measurements to be taken from the diagram are (1) A_s and the corresponding distance a; and (2) b, h_s and h_c for each of the strips above the neutral axis. The following summations are required and are best made in tabular form:

$$S_1 = \sum A_s(d-x-a)$$
$$S_2 = \sum A_s(d-x-a)a$$
$$S_3 = \sum (bh_s)(x-h_c)$$
$$S_4 = \sum (bh_s)(x-h_c)h_c$$

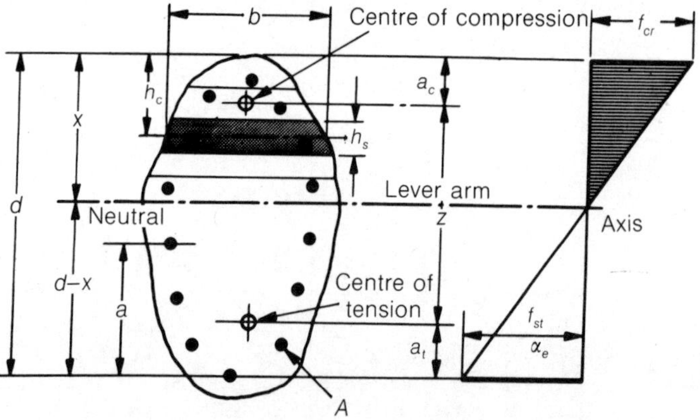

The product bh_s is the area of each strip above the neutral axis, and if a strip contains any reinforcement A_s' the corresponding value of bh_s should be increased by $(\alpha_e - 1)A_s'$.

The position of the centre of tension above the lowest bar or group of bars is $a_t = S_2/S_1$. The position of the centre of compression below the top edge of the section is $a_c = S_4/S_3$. The lever-arm $z = d - a_c - a_t$. Having determined numerical values for the foregoing terms, substitute them in the following expressions to determine the maximum compressive stress in the concrete and the maximum tensile stress in the steel:

$$f_{cr} = xM_d/zS_3$$
$$f_{st} = f_{cr}(d-x)S_3/xS_1$$

where M_d is the applied bending moment.

The assumed depth to the neutral axis can now be checked by substituting in formula (1) on *Table 117*. If the difference between the assumed and calculated values of x is greater than the depth of an individual strip h_s, a second trial value

Rectangular and flanged beams: design formulae

Modular ratio $\alpha_e = E_s/E_c$

f_{cr}, f_{st} actual or permissible stresses in concrete and tension reinforcement, depending on context

M_d resistance moment or applied moment depending on context

$\rho = A_s/bd$

$\rho' = A'_s/bd$

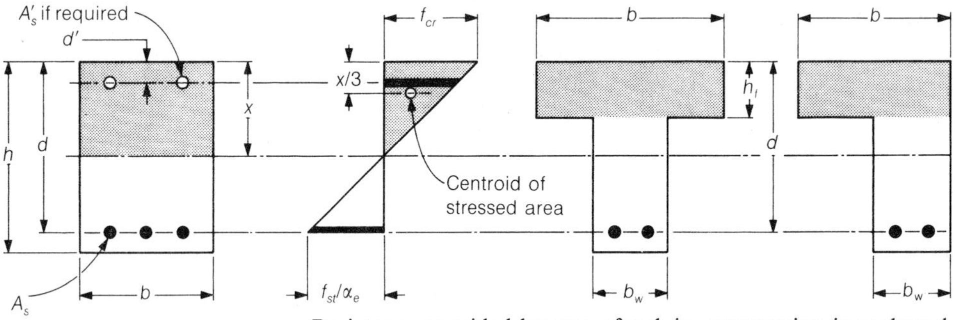

A'_s if required; d'; x; $x/3$; f_{cr}; h; d; A_s; b; f_{st}/α_e; Centroid of stressed area; b; h_f; d; b_w; b; b_w

Resistance provided by area of web in compression is neglected

Depth to neutral axis

Rectangular section

1 $x = \dfrac{1}{1 + f_{st}/\alpha_e f_{cr}} d$ or **1(a)** $\dfrac{x}{d} = \dfrac{\alpha_e f_{cr}}{f_{st} + \alpha_e f_{cr}}$

Tension reinforcement only

1(b) $x = \dfrac{\alpha_e A_s}{b}\left[\sqrt{\left(1 + \dfrac{2bd}{A_s \alpha_e}\right)} - 1\right]$ or $\dfrac{x}{d} = \alpha_e \rho\left[\sqrt{\left(1 + \dfrac{2}{\alpha_e \rho}\right)} - 1\right]$

Tension and compression reinforcement

1(c) $\dfrac{x}{d} = \sqrt{\left\{[\alpha_e\rho + (\alpha_e - 1)\rho']^2 + 2\left[\alpha_e\rho + (\alpha_e - 1)\dfrac{d'}{d}\rho'\right]\right\}} - [\alpha_e\rho + (\alpha_e - 1)\rho']$

Flanged section ($x > h_f$)

2 $x = \dfrac{\alpha_e d A_s + \frac{1}{2}bh_f^2}{\alpha_e A_s + bh_f}$

2(a) $\dfrac{x}{d} = \dfrac{\alpha_e \rho + (h_f/d)^2/2}{\alpha_e \rho + (h_f/d)}$

Lever-arm

Rectangular section

Tension reinforcement only

3 $z = d - \frac{1}{3}x$

Tension and compression reinforcement

3(a) $z = \dfrac{(x^2/2)(d - x/3) + \rho'(\alpha_e - 1)(x - d')(d - d')d}{(x^2/2) + \rho'(\alpha_e - 1)(x - d')d}$

3(b) $= d - \frac{1}{6}x - \frac{1}{2}d'$ approx.

Flanged section

4 $z = d - \frac{1}{3}h_f\left(\dfrac{3x - 2h_f}{2x - h_f}\right)$

4(a) $z = d - \frac{1}{2}h_f$ approx.

Moment of resistance M_d

Rectangular section

Tension reinforcement only

5 $M_d = \frac{1}{2}x(d - \frac{1}{3}x)bf_{cr} = K_{conc}bd^2$ where $K_{conc} = \dfrac{x}{2d}\left(1 - \dfrac{x}{3d}\right)f_{cr}$

5(a) $M_d = \dfrac{z}{d}\rho f_{st}bd^2 = zA_{st}f_{st}$

Tension and compression reinforcement

5(b) $M_d = \left[\frac{1}{2}x(d - \frac{1}{3}x) + \rho'(\alpha_e - 1)\left(1 - \dfrac{d'}{x}\right)(d - d')d\right]bf_{cr}$

5(c) $M_d = \dfrac{z}{d}\rho f_{st}bd^2 = zA_{st}f_{st}$

Flanged section

6 $M_d = (2x - h_f)(d - \frac{1}{2}h_f)\dfrac{f_{cr}bh_f}{2x}$

6(a) $M_d = \frac{1}{2}(d - \frac{1}{3}h_f)f_{cr}bh_f$ approx.

6(b) $M_d = A_s(d - \frac{1}{2}h_f)f_{st}$ approx.

Design (M_d = applied moment)

Rectangular section

Tension reinforcement only

7 $d = \sqrt{\dfrac{M_d}{K_{conc}b}}$ $\quad K_{conc} = \dfrac{M_d}{bd^2}$ $\quad A_s = \dfrac{M_d}{zf_{st}}$

Tension and compression reinforcement

7(a) $A'_s = \dfrac{\text{applied bending moment} - K_{conc}bd^2}{(\alpha_e - 1)(1 - d'/x)(d - d')f_{cr}}$

7(b) $A_s = \left(\dfrac{K_{conc}bd^2}{z} + \dfrac{\text{applied bending moment} - K_{conc}bd^2}{d - d'}\right)\dfrac{1}{f_{st}}$

Flanged section

8 $A_s = \dfrac{M_d}{zf_{st}} = \dfrac{M_d}{(d - h_f/2)f_{st}}$ approx.

8(a) $b \nless \dfrac{2M_d x}{(2x - h_f)(d - h_f/2)h_f f_{cr}}$

8(b) or $b \nless \dfrac{2M_d}{h_f z f_{cr}}$ approx.

Proportion of tension reinforcement required for 'balanced' design

$\rho_{bal} = \dfrac{A_s}{bd}$

Rectangular section

Tension reinforcement only

9 $\rho_{bal} = \dfrac{1}{2}\left(\dfrac{x}{d}\right)\dfrac{f_{cr}}{f_{st}}$

Tension and compression reinforcement

9(a) $\rho_{bal} = \left[\dfrac{1}{2}\left(\dfrac{x}{d}\right) + \rho'(\alpha_e - 1)\left(1 - \dfrac{d'}{x}\right)\right]\dfrac{f_{cr}}{f_{st}}$

Flanged section

10 $\rho_{bal} = \dfrac{h_f}{2x}\left(2\dfrac{x}{d} - \dfrac{h_f}{d}\right)\dfrac{f_{cr}}{f_{st}}$

Maximum stresses

11 $f_{st} = \dfrac{M_d}{zA_{st}}$ $\quad f_{cr} = \left(\dfrac{x}{d - x}\right)\dfrac{f_{st}}{\alpha_e}$

12 Ratio of stresses $\dfrac{f_{st}}{f_{cr}} = \alpha_e\left(\dfrac{d}{x} - 1\right)$

of x between the two foregoing values should be assumed and the procedure repeated. The adjustment to the summations is easily made because the distances h_c and a_t are measured from the outer edges of the 'effective' section, and thus the adjustment merely consists of adding or deducting one or more strips and including or excluding one or more areas A_s of steel below the neutral axis.

20.2.11 I-beams (any value of modular ratio)

The formulae required for the design of an I-section beam are as follows (see accompanying diagram). The area of tension reinforcement is

$$A_s = (\tfrac{1}{2}x + \beta_1 d - \beta_2 d) b f_{cr}/f_{st}$$

The resistance-moment factor is given by

$$\frac{M_d}{bd^2} = K_{conc} + \left[\beta_1\left(1 - \frac{d'}{d}\right) - \tfrac{1}{3}\beta_2\left(3 - \frac{2h_f}{d} - \frac{x}{d}\right)\right] f_{cr}$$

in which

$$\beta_1 = \frac{(\alpha_e - 1)\rho'(x - d')}{x}$$

$$\beta_2 = \frac{(1 - b_w/b)(x - h_f)^2}{2xd}$$

and K_{conc} is the resistance-moment factor of the concrete alone.

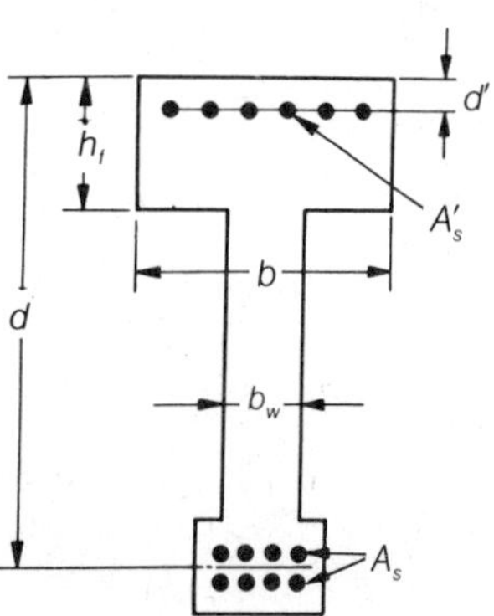

The method of designing a beam to resist a given moment M_d is first to determine the neutral-axis depth x for the permissible stresses given by using the scales in *Table 120* or the formulae in *Table 117*. The resistance-moment factor K_{conc} for the concrete section is obtained also from *Table 117* or *120* or from the curves on *Tables 118* and *119*. Assume, if not given, suitable dimensions for b, d, b_w, h_f and d'. Calculate β_2 from the foregoing formula. The value of β_1 required is then

$$\beta_1 = \left[\frac{M_d}{bd^2 f_{cr}} - \frac{K_{conc}}{f_{cr}} + \tfrac{1}{3}\beta_2 \frac{(3d - 2h_f - x)}{d}\right]\frac{d}{(d - d')}$$

The cross-sectional area of compression reinforcement required is

$$A'_s = \frac{\beta_1 xbd}{(\alpha - 1)(x - d')}$$

A_s is calculated from the formula given above. Then with $z = M_d/A_s f_{st}$, the shearing stress $v_d = V_d/b_w z$.

Example 1. Design a rectangular beam (using tension reinforcement only) to resist a bending moment of 90 000 N m, if $f_{st} = 140\,\text{N/mm}^2$ (mild steel), $f_{cr} = 7\,\text{N/mm}^2$ and $\alpha_e = 15$.

Method 1 (*Table 118 applies*) With a breadth $b = 300$ mm and an overall depth h of 550 mm, assuming 25 mm cover, $d = 512$ mm. Thus $M_d/bd^2 = 90\,000 \times 10^3/(300 \times 512^2) = 1.144$. Then from the curves on *Table 118* and with $f_{st} = 140\,\text{N/mm}^2$, $f_{cr} = 6.45\,\text{N/mm}^2$ and $\rho = 0.0095$. Thus $A_s = 0.0095 \times 300 \times 512 = 1460\,\text{mm}^2$: three 25 mm bars will suffice.

Method 2 (*Table 120 applies*) Ratio of permissible stresses $= f_{st}/f_{cr} = 140/7 = 20$. From *Table 120* the corresponding values of $M_d/bd^2 f_{cr}$ and ρ are 0.184 and 0.0108 respectively. Then, since $90\,000 \times 10^3/7bd^2 = 0.184$, the value of bd^2 required $= 90\,000 \times 10^3/(7 \times 0.184) = 69.9 \times 10^6\,\text{mm}^3$, and with $b = 300$ mm, $d = 483$ mm. Then $A_s = 0.0108 \times 483 \times 300 = 1564\,\text{mm}^2$; say five 20 mm bars.

Example 2. Determine the reinforcement required in the following rectangular beams if the bending moment is 90 000 N m, $f_{st} = 140\,\text{N/mm}^2$, $f_{cr} = 7\,\text{N/mm}^2$ and $\alpha_e = 15$.

(i) Overall depth $h = 450$ mm and breadth $b = 250$ mm. Assume $d = 400$ mm. This section can resist a moment of $206 \times 250 = 51\,500$ N m with $A'_s = 0$, and $456 \times 250 = 114\,000$ N m with $A'_s = A_s$; therefore compression reinforcement is required. The moment of resistance required from A'_s is $90\,000 - 51\,500 = 38\,500$ N m. With $f_{st}/f_{cr} = 140/7 = 20$, the corresponding value of x/d (from *Table 120*) is 0.428. Thus $x = 0.428 \times 400 = 171$ mm and, from the formula in *Table 117* (assuming $d' = 50$ mm), $f_{sc} = (171 - 50) \times (15 - 1) \times 7/171 = 69\,\text{N/mm}^2$. Since $d - d' = 400 - 50 = 350$ mm, $A'_s = 38\,500 \times 10^3/69 \times 350 = 1590\,\text{mm}^2$, which is provided by four 25 mm bars in the top of the section. $A_s = (4.29 \times 250) + 38\,500 \times 10^3/(140 \times 350) = 1072 + 785 = 1858\,\text{mm}^2$, which is also provided by four 25 mm bars in the bottom of the section. With 40 mm of cover and 25 mm bars, the actual effective depth provided is $450 - 40 - 12.5 = 397.5$ mm, which is sufficiently close to the value of 400 mm assumed.

(ii) Overall depth = 400 mm and breadth $b = 250$ mm. Assume $d = 350$ mm. The bending moment per mm width = $90\,000/250 = 360$ N m per mm width, which is near enough the resistance of a section with $d = 350$ mm and $A'_s = A_s$. The reinforcement required is $8.09 \times 250 = 2023\,\text{mm}^2$ ($A'_s = A_s$), which may be provided by three 32 mm bars (from *Table 86*) top and bottom. The actual effective depth with a cover of 32 mm is $400 - 32 - 16 = 352$ mm, compared with the assumed value of 350 mm. $d - d' = 352 - 32 - 16 = 304$ mm, and thus $(d - d')/d = 304/350 = 0.87$ compared with the assumed value of 0.9.

20.2.12 Solid slabs

When $\alpha_e = 15$, a solid slab can be designed by using the curves on *Tables 118* and *119*. If M_d, d, f_{cr} and f_{st} are given, calculate M_d/bd^2 (by adopting a value of b of 1 m or 12 in). By inspecting the points where this value intersects the

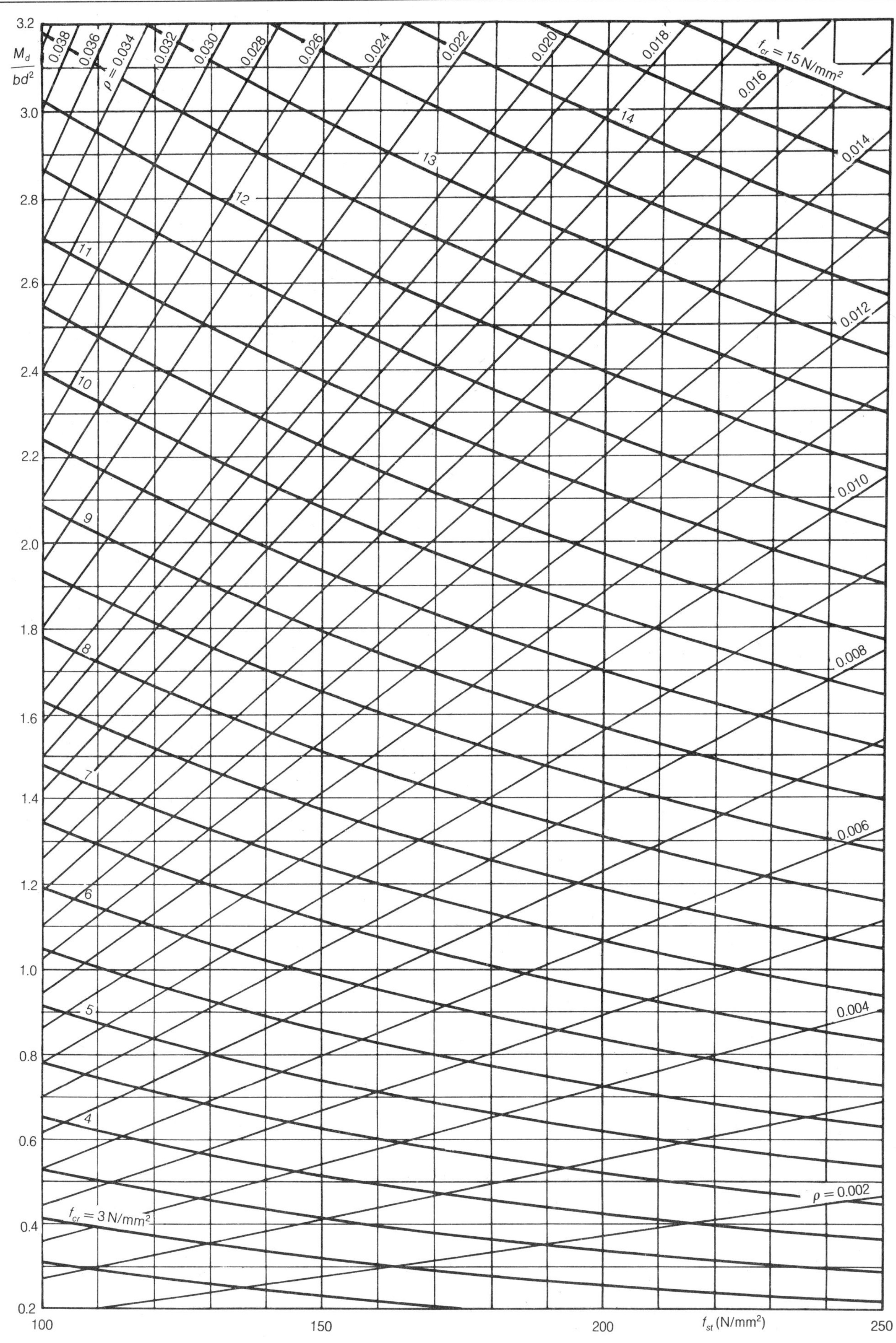
M_d/bd^2
3.2
3.0
2.8
2.6
2.4
2.2
2.0
1.8
1.6
1.4
1.2
1.0
0.8
0.6
0.4
0.2
100
150
200
250
f_{st} (N/mm^2)
$f_{cr} = 15$ N/mm^2
14
13
12
11
10
9
8
7
6
5
4
$f_{cr} = 3$ N/mm^2
0.038
0.036
$\rho = 0.034$
0.032
0.030
0.028
0.026
0.024
0.022
0.020
0.018
0.016
0.014
0.012
0.010
0.008
0.006
0.004
$\rho = 0.002$

curves representing the limiting values of f_{cr} and f_{st}, the actual stress in the understressed material can be determined and the corresponding value of ρ (and thus A_s) required can be ascertained.

If d is unknown, determine the values of $K = M_d/bd^2$ and ρ corresponding to the limiting stresses f_{cr} and f_{st}. Then $d = \sqrt{(M_d/bK)}$ and $A_s = \rho bd$.

To check the resistance of a given section, calculate $\rho = A_s/bd$ and determine the two values of M_d/bd^2 where ρ intersects the curves for the limiting values of f_{cr} and f_{st}. The lesser of these two values then gives the safe resistance moment for the section.

For values of modular ratio other than 15, the same procedures can be followed using the scales for $\alpha_e f_{cr}/f_{st}$, $M_d/bd^2 f_{cr}$ and $\alpha_e M_d/bd^2 f_{st}$ on the left-hand side of *Table 120* instead of the curves on *Tables 118* and *119*.

20.3 LIQUID-CONTAINING STRUCTURES

General notes on the requirements of BS5337 'The structural use of concrete for retaining aqueous liquids' are given in section 5.6. The basic requirements of the Standard are as summarized below, where details are also given of the design aids provided on *Tables 121–135*.

20.3.1 Limit-state design

Partial safety factors. The recommended partial safety factors for loads and materials correspond to those required by BS8110 and given on *Table 1*. Note that for both earth and aqueous liquids the full partial safety factor for load of 1.6 must be considered.

Ultimate limit-state

Concrete and reinforcement Only concrete grades 25 or 30 may be employed, and f_y must not exceed 425 N/mm^2. With these provisos, the data, formulae etc. given on *Tables 102–116* for design to BS8110 and CP110 still apply.

Shearing resistance The data given on *Table 143* for values of f_{cu} of 25 and 30 N/mm^2 for design to CP110 still apply.

Bond resistance The requirements of the Standard correspond to those given in CP110, except that the anchorage-bond stresses in horizontal bars for sections that are predominantly in direct tension are reduced to 70% of the normal values. Other than in this particular case, therefore, the information given on *Tables 92–94* still applies. For convenience, anchorage-bond lengths required in terms of the bar diameter for concrete grades 25 and 30 and for various types of bar are set out on *Table 121*.

Limit-state of deflection. Where necessary, the design should be checked to ensure that excessive deflection does not occur. Rigorous analysis (*Table 136*) may be undertaken, or the simplified rules given on *Table 137* may be followed. These are based on the consideration of the action of a uniform load on a section of uniform thickness. In the case of a tank wall cantilevering from the base the load may be distributed triangularly and/or the section may taper: either condition will influence the deflection. To cater for such effects the scales on *Table 121* provide further multipliers which should be used in addition to those given on *Table 137*. (These factors have been obtained by calculating the moment of area of the resulting M/I diagram about the free end of the cantilever.)

As discussed in section 14.9.1, the coefficients given for a cantilever assume that no rotation occurs at the support. If rigidity at the junction with the floor of the tank is not assured, some allowance should be made for possible rotation.

Limit-state of cracking. Three basic conditions regarding cracking must be considered: for mature concrete, tension from bending and direct tension; and for immature concrete, shrinkage and movement.

Mature concrete: cracking due to tension resulting from bending

Rigorous analysis The calculation procedure that must be followed corresponds to that given in Appendix A3 of CP110 and summarized on *Table 138*. However, to reduce from 1 in 5 to 1 in 20 the probability of the width of any crack exceeding the calculated value, the coefficients in the appropriate formula have been adjusted. The modified expression is thus

$$\text{design surface crack width} = 9a_{cr}\varepsilon_m \Bigg/ \left[2 + 5\left(\frac{a_{cr} - c_{min}}{h - x}\right)\right] \tag{20.1}$$

where ε_m is the average strain in the member at the level at which the crack width is being calculated, a_{cr} is the distance between the point considered and the surface of the nearest longitudinal bar, and c_{min} is the minimum cover to the tension reinforcement.

Assuming that a bar arrangement has already been selected to resist a service moment M_d, the basic calculation procedure is thus as follows:

1. Calculate the neutral-axis depth x and the lever-arm z corresponding to the given proportion of reinforcement $\rho = A_s/bd$ with a modular ratio of 15, from the formulae on *Table 117* or the right-hand scales on *Table 120*. (Since the values of elastic modulus for concrete grades 25 and 30 are given in CP110 as 26 and 28 kN/mm^2 respectively, and E_s for steel is 200 × 10^6 kN/mm^2, the exact modular ratios are 15.4 and 14.3 respectively: the use of an approximate value of 15 is convenient and satisfactory for most purposes. Alternatively the scales on the left-hand side of *Table 120* may be used.)
2. Calculate the average surface strain ε_1 in the member at the point being considered from the expression
$$\varepsilon_1 = \frac{M_d}{A_s z E_s}\frac{(a' - x)}{(d - x)}$$
where a' is the distance from the compression face of the member to the point being considered.
3. The foregoing value of ε_1 is now modified to take into account the stiffening effect of the concrete in tension, to obtain the average strain ε_m at the level at which the crack width is being calculated, using the expression
$$\varepsilon_m = \varepsilon_1 - \frac{0.0007 b_t h(a' - x)}{A_s(h - x) f_{st}}$$

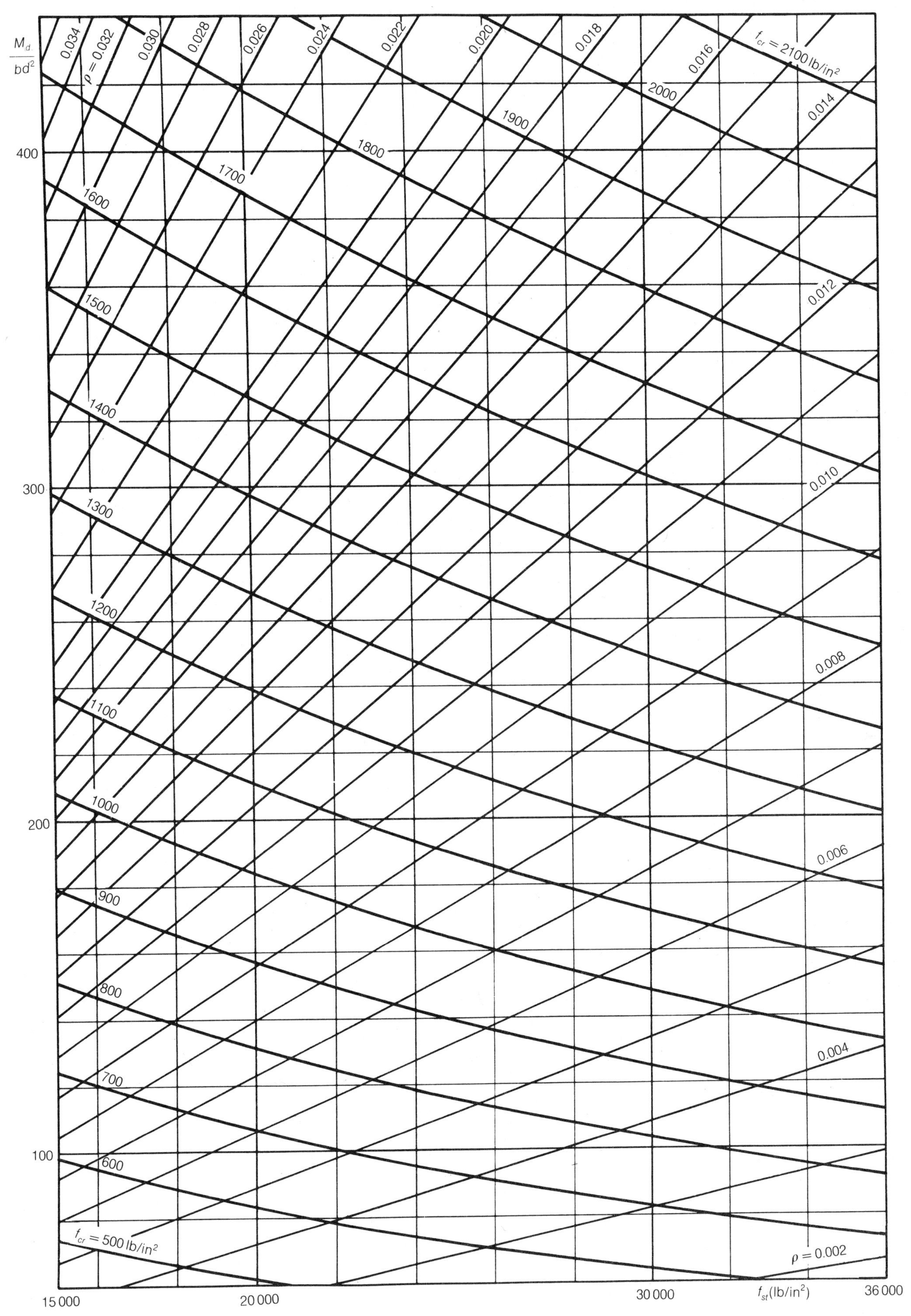
$\frac{M_d}{bd^2}$
400
300
200
100
0.034
$\rho = 0.032$
0.030
0.028
0.026
0.024
0.022
0.020
0.018
0.016
0.014
0.012
0.010
0.008
0.006
0.004
$\rho = 0.002$
$f_{cr} = 2100$ lb/in^2
2000
1900
1800
1700
1600
1500
1400
1300
1200
1100
1000
900
800
700
600
$f_{cr} = 500$ lb/in^2
15 000
20 000
30 000
f_{st}(lb/in^2)
36 000

where b_t is the width of the member at the level of the centroid of the tension steel.

4. Now, provided the strain in the tension steel does not exceed $0.8f_y/E_s$, expression (20.1) may be used to calculate the anticipated surface width of crack.

Deemed-to-satisfy requirements To avoid undertaking the foregoing calculations, the crack widths may be considered satisfactory if the stress in the steel under working loads does not exceed the appropriate limiting values given on *Table 121*.

Note that, as these values correspond to those specified for modular-ratio design, this method of complying with the requirements for the serviceability limit-state of cracking involves exactly the same calculations that are needed with modular-ratio design (see section 20.3.2).

Mature concrete: cracking due to direct tension. The formulae for calculating crack widths given above have not proved entirely satisfactory when considering members subjected to direct tension, and BS5337 therefore recommends that the deemed-to-satisfy requirements that the steel stress under working loads does not exceed the limiting values set out on *Table 121* be adhered to instead.

Immature concrete: cracking due to restrained shrinkage and movements due to heat generated by hydration. Although BS5337 specifies nominal minimum amounts of secondary reinforcement, these will not necessarily restrict the width of any cracks that form to the limits required for class A or class B exposure. To ensure that these criteria are met the design procedure specified in Appendix B of the Standard must be followed. In this appendix the ratio ρ_{crit} of the minimum steel area needed to distribute cracking in terms of the gross concrete section is calculated from the expression f_{ct}/f_y, where f_{ct} is here the direct tensile strength of immature concrete, which may be taken (at 3 days) as 1.15 N/mm² for grade 25 and 1.30 N/mm² for grade 30 concrete. If at least this amount of steel is provided, the likely maximum spacing of cracks s_{max} is given by the expression

$$s_{max} = \frac{f_{ct}}{f_b}\frac{\phi}{2\rho_1}$$

in which the ratio of f_{ct} to the average bond strength f_b may be taken as 1 for plain bars, 0.8 for type 1 deformed bars and 0.67 for type 2 deformed bars.

BS5337 then offers a series of options (listed on *Table 121*) covering differing combinations of minimum steel ratio and joint spacing. These range from providing a small amount of steel in the form of widely spaced high-strength bars together with closely spaced movement joints, to the use of a rather larger amount of steel in the form of closely spaced small-diameter high-bond bars with no movement joints at all.

Since the Standard was prepared, new evidence has been obtained that suggests that options 3, 4 and 5 in BS5337 should be superseded by a new option (designated 3 N on *Table 121*). The necessary amendment will almost certainly be incorporated into the next revision of BS5337.

To control cracking due to shrinkage and thermal movement, the most efficient position for the reinforcement provided for this purpose is as near the surface as possible concomitant with the need to provide adequate cover. It may therefore be desirable to detail the section in such a way that this steel passes outside that provided to resist bending, despite the resulting reduction in the effective depth of the latter.

Analysis. Three principal conditions need to be considered: (1) when a member is subjected to bending only; (2) when a member is subjected to direct tension only; and (3) when a member is subjected to combined bending and tension.

Case 1: bending only. If the thickness of the member is more than 225 mm and the face in contact with the liquid is in compression, the section need only be designed to meet the joint requirements of the ultimate limit-state and the limit-state of cracking corresponding to exposure class C; otherwise the governing requirements are the ultimate limit-state together with the limiting crack width corresponding to exposure class A or B as appropriate. The calculations to determine the strength of the section (i.e. at the ultimate limit-state) should be made according to CP110 using either rigorous analysis or the simplified Code formulae described in section 20.1.5. The calculations to determine the crack widths follow the CP110 procedure outlined on *Table 138*, except that the formulae given above are substituted for those given in Appendix A of CP110 where appropriate.

If given arrangements of bar diameter ϕ and spacing s are considered in sections of various thicknesses h and with cover c, it is possible to calculate the ultimate resistance moment of the resulting section and also the service resistance moment at which the maximum surface width of crack attains the prescribed limit. The results of these calculations can then be plotted to produce the graphs which form *Tables 122–131*. Each individual graph on these tables represents a particular combination of bar diameter, cover and limiting crack width, and the charts included here are abstracted from the more complete series provided in ref. 80.

As can be seen, over the upper area of each chart (where the proportion of steel provided is low), the resistance of the section is controlled by the ultimate limit-state. Since the resistance moments on the graphs are service (i.e. unfactored) values, the calculated ultimate moments have been divided by the appropriate partial load factor of 1.6. The upper limit of this area of the charts corresponds to the minimum proportion of 0.15% of high-yield bars that is permitted by BS5337.

Over the lower area of each chart, the resistance of the section is controlled by cracking. Although BS5337 permits the adoption of a maximum concrete stress of $0.45f_{cu}$ (i.e. 11.1 N/mm²), when considering ultimate limit-state conditions it seems reasonable to restrict the maximum concrete stresses in serviceability calculations to a lower value, say $f_{cu}/2.73$ (i.e. 9.15 N/mm² for grade 25 concrete), which is the limiting value given in the modular-ratio section of BS5337 for compression due to bending, or even to $f_{cu}/3$. Lines corresponding to concrete stresses of $4f_{cu}/9$ and $f_{cu}/3$ are included on each chart, and the curve representing $f_{cu}/2.73$ can be interpolated approximately by eye.

As the proportion of steel decreases, the stress in the reinforcement rises. Although the Standard places no specific

Modular-ratio coefficients

For any value of α_e

Scale	Values
x/d	0.65, 0.60, 0.55, 0.50, 0.45, 0.40, 0.35, 0.30, 0.25, 0.20, 0.15, 0.10, 0.05, 0
$\frac{M_d}{bd^2 f_{cr}}$	0.25, 0.24, 0.23, 0.22, 0.21, 0.20, 0.19, 0.18, 0.17, 0.16, 0.15, 0.14, 0.13, 0.12, 0.11, 0.10, 0.09, 0.08, 0.07, 0.06, 0.05, 0.04, 0.03, 0.02, 0.01, 0
$\frac{\alpha_e M_d}{bd^2 f_{st}}$	0.4, 0.3, 0.20, 0.15, 0.10, 0.09, 0.08, 0.07, 0.06, 0.05, 0.04, 0.03, 0.02, 0.01, 0
$\alpha_e f_{cr}/f_{st}$	1.9, 1.8, 1.7, 1.6, 1.5, 1.4, 1.3, 1.2, 1.1, 1.0, 0.9, 0.8, 0.7, 0.6, 0.5, 0.4, 0.3, 0.2, 0.1, 0
$\alpha_e \rho$	0.6, 0.5, 0.4, 0.3, 0.20, 0.15, 0.10, 0.09, 0.08, 0.07, 0.06, 0.05, 0.04, 0.03, 0.02, 0.01, 0
z/d	0.79, 0.80, 0.81, 0.82, 0.83, 0.84, 0.85, 0.86, 0.87, 0.88, 0.89, 0.90, 0.91, 0.92, 0.93, 0.94, 0.95, 0.96, 0.97, 0.98, 0.99, 1.00
x/d	0.65, 0.60, 0.55, 0.50, 0.45, 0.40, 0.35, 0.30, 0.25, 0.20, 0.15, 0.10, 0.05, 0

For $\alpha_e = 15$

Scale	Values
x/d	0.65, 0.60, 0.55, 0.50, 0.45, 0.40, 0.35, 0.30, 0.25, 0.20, 0.15, 0.10, 0.05, 0
$\frac{M_d}{bd^2 f_{cr}}$	0.25, 0.24, 0.23, 0.22, 0.21, 0.20, 0.19, 0.18, 0.17, 0.16, 0.15, 0.14, 0.13, 0.12, 0.11, 0.10, 0.09, 0.08, 0.07, 0.06, 0.05, 0.04, 0.03, 0.02, 0.01, 0
$\frac{M_d}{bd^2 f_{st}}$	0.03, 0.02, 0.015, 0.010, 0.009, 0.008, 0.007, 0.006, 0.005, 0.004, 0.003, 0.002, 0.0010, 0.0008, 0.0006, 0.0004, 0.0002, 0
f_{st}/f_{cr}	8, 9, 10, 12, 14, 16, 18, 20, 25, 30, 40, 50, 60, 70, 80, 90, 100, 150, 200, 300, 400, 500, 600, 800, 1000, ∞
ρ	0.04, 0.03, 0.02, 0.015, 0.010, 0.009, 0.008, 0.007, 0.006, 0.005, 0.004, 0.003, 0.002, 0.0010, 0.0008, 0.0006, 0.0004, 0.0002, 0
z/d	0.79, 0.80, 0.81, 0.82, 0.83, 0.84, 0.85, 0.86, 0.87, 0.88, 0.89, 0.90, 0.91, 0.92, 0.93, 0.94, 0.95, 0.96, 0.97, 0.98, 0.99, 1.00
x/d	0.65, 0.60, 0.55, 0.50, 0.45, 0.40, 0.35, 0.30, 0.25, 0.20, 0.15, 0.10, 0.05, 0

restriction on this calculated stress, some authorities (ref. 61) have suggested that, until greater experience is gained, it may be prudent to adopt values that do not greatly exceed those employed in current design to date. (On the other hand, of course, it may presumably be argued that experience cannot be gained unless some designers, at least, decide to adopt higher stresses!)

Using these charts, the design procedure becomes extremely simple. Knowing the service moment of resistance M_d and limiting crack width required, the bar diameter and cover are chosen and the appropriate chart is selected. The designer can then either select a convenient bar spacing and read off the slab thickness, or vice versa. If the working stress in the steel is a controlling factor, the point at which the permitted value intersects the curve for M_d then gives both the section thickness and the reinforcement spacing.

Charts are provided for grade 25 concrete and deformed high-yield bars ($f_y = 425\ \text{N/mm}^2$), these being thought to be the most frequently employed combination of materials, with cover thicknesses of 40 mm and 60 mm. For other depths of cover, interpolation may be used. Although the charts have been designed for use for slabs (i.e. where $b = 1000$ mm), they can also be used to design beams by increasing the moment on the beam pro rata. For example a beam 250 mm wide and resisting a service moment of 50 kN m may be considered as a slab resisting a moment of $50 \times 1000/250 = 200$ kN mm. If the chart shows that the resulting section requires, say 20 mm bars at 110 mm centres, this can be converted back to the need to provide $250/110 = 2.27$ bars; i.e. three would be required in this case. The charts corresponding to other bar diameters should also be tried, so as to achieve the most economic arrangement.

By making certain simplifying assumptions, Threlfall (ref. 81) has shown that, provided the overall depth of the section does not exceed ten times the distance from the bar surface to the furthest point on the tensile face of the section (i.e. $a_{cr\,max}$), the maximum crack width on the side of the beam will be less than that on the tensile face. Thus if the bar arrangement adopted limits the crack width on the tensile face to the limiting value, these limiting requirements are also met at the sides of the beam. Threlfall also shows that if the cover to the bars is at least 50 mm (and it is unlikely to be less in a beam, since the minimum prescribed cover to all steel including links is 40 mm), the corresponding overall depth of beam must be at least 750 mm. For beams whose depth exceeds 750 mm, BS8110 and CP110 require additional longitudinal bars to be provided near the side faces to restrict cracking (see section 20.5.1).

Case 2: tension only. As already mentioned, in this case the formulae for calculating crack widths are not entirely satisfactory, and such sections should be so designed that the deemed-to-satisfy allowable steel stresses are not exceeded. The design procedure is then identical to that adopted in modular-ratio design and further details are given in section 20.3.2.

Case 3: combined bending and tension. As with case 1, if the thickness of the member exceeds 225 mm and the face in contact with the liquid is in compression, the section need only be designed to meet the ultimate limit-state requirements together with those giving a maximum surface crack width of 0.3 mm (i.e. exposure class C). If the member is not more than 225 mm thick or if the tensile face is in contact with the liquid or both of these requirements are met, the design method adopted depends on whether the stress over the section is entirely tensile or whether both tension and compression occur.

Tension over entire section It is simplest to consider that this condition occurs when $M_d/N_d < d - h/2$. In actual fact, of course, the true criterion is when $M_d/N_d = h/2$, but the former limit permits the criterion to be based on whether the stress in any 'compression steel' provided is tensile or compressive. If tension occurs over the entire section, reinforcement near each face must be provided. Once more, the formulae given in BS5337 for calculating crack widths do not apply and the steel must be designed to meet the deemed-to-satisfy requirements. The areas of reinforcement required are thus as follows:

$$A_s = \frac{1}{2f_{st}}\left(N + \frac{M}{d - h/2}\right)$$

$$A'_s = \frac{1}{2f_{st}}\left(N - \frac{M}{d - h/2}\right)$$

Tension and compression occur In this situation the controlling requirements are the ultimate limit-state together with the limiting of crack widths to meet the requirements of class A or B exposure, as appropriate. The simplest design procedure now is to reverse the method described in clause 3.5.3.3(3) of CP110. Firstly, ignore the axial tension and design the section to resist the reduced moment of $M_d - N_d(d - h/2)$ and then increase the area of steel provided by N_d/f_{st}. If the charts provided for case 1 are used, the value of f_{st} should be that corresponding to the appropriate intersection point.

Adding extra steel in this way invalidates the calculations made when preparing the charts, and it is now necessary to check the maximum surface crack width. Assuming that a calculator capable of being programmed to solve an equation by repeated iteration is available, the most convenient procedure is probably as follows.

Resolving the forces acting on the section axially,

$$N_d = f_{st}\left[A_s - A'_s\left(\frac{\alpha_e - 1}{\alpha_e}\right)\left(\frac{x - d'}{d - x}\right) - \frac{bx^2}{2\alpha_e(d - x)}\right] \tag{20.2}$$

and taking moments about the centre-line of the section,

$$M_d = f_{st}\left[A_s(d - \tfrac{1}{2}h) + A'_s(\tfrac{1}{2}h - d')\left(\frac{\alpha_e - 1}{\alpha_e}\right)\left(\frac{x - d'}{d - x}\right) + \frac{bx^2(3h - 2x)}{12\alpha_e(d - x)}\right]$$

If these expressions are rearranged to eliminate f_{st}, the following equation is obtained:

$$M_d\left[A_s - A'_s\left(\frac{\alpha_e - 1}{\alpha_e}\right)\left(\frac{x - d'}{d - x}\right) - \frac{bx^2}{2\alpha_e(d - x)}\right]$$
$$- N_d\left[A_s(d - \tfrac{1}{2}h) + A'_s(\tfrac{1}{2}h - d')\left(\frac{\alpha_e - 1}{\alpha_e}\right)\left(\frac{x - d'}{d - x}\right)\right.$$

BS5337: Basic data

Options for controlling cracking in immature concrete

Option	Method of control	Spacing of movement joints	Min. steel ratio	Notes
1	Continuous construction	None	ρ_{crit}	Provide closely spaced small-diameter high-bond bars
2	Semi-continuous construction	Either partial contraction joints at 7.5 m centres or complete contraction joints at 15 m centres	ρ_{crit}	Provide closely spaced small-diameter bars but less steel than for option 1
3	Moderate joint spacing with controlled cracking	Not greater than $2s_{max}$ or greater than $4w/\varepsilon$	ρ_{crit}	Avoid using small-diameter bars which limit joint spacing
4	Close joint spacing with controlled cracking	Not greater than $1.25s_{max}$ or greater than $s_{max} + (w/\varepsilon)$	$2\rho_{crit}/3$ but $\nless 0.2\%$	Provide large-diameter bars at spacing of about 300 mm to give minimum steel ratio only
5	Close joint spacing designed for no cracking	Not greater than s_{max}	$2\rho_{crit}/3$ but $\nless 0.2\%$	As for option 4
3N	Close joint spacing with controlled cracking (this option does not yet form part of BS5337 but will supersede options 3, 4 and 5)	(a) With complete joints only: $\ngtr 4.8\,\text{m} + (w/\varepsilon)$ (b) With alternate partial and complete joints: $\ngtr (s_{max}/2) + 2.4\,\text{m} + (w/\varepsilon)$ (c) With partial joints only: $\ngtr s_{max} + (w/\varepsilon)$	$2\rho_{crit}/3$	Avoid using small-diameter bars which limit joint spacing with options 3N(b) and 3N(c)
ε $\varepsilon_{cs} + \varepsilon_{te} - 0.0001$ ε_{cs} estimated shrinkage strain ε_{te} estimated total thermal contraction w prescribed maximum crack width s_{max} calculated maximum crack spacing (see section 20.3.1)			If thickness exceeds 200 mm, $\nless \rho_{crit}/3$ required near each face	

Deflection multipliers for tapered cantilevers

*These multiplying factors must be used in conjunction with those given on *Table 137*

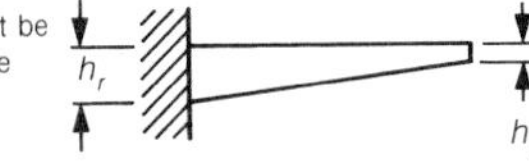

Multiplier for uniformly distributed load

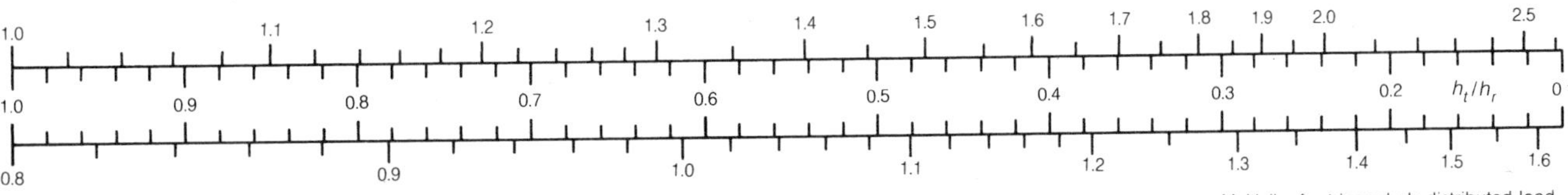

Multiplier for triangularly distributed load

Limit-state criteria

Material	Reinforcement			Concrete			
Limit-state being considered	Ultimate	Serviceability: Class of exposure A	Serviceability: Class of exposure B	Ultimate	Serviceability: Class of exposure A	B	C
Plain mild-steel bars	250	85	115	Strength in direct compression and in compression due to bending: as grade number	0.1	0.2	0.3
Deformed high-yield bars	425	100	130				
Criterion	Strength in N/mm²	Maximum allowable stress in N/mm²		Strength in N/mm²	Max. allowable crack width in mm, due to direct tension or to bending in regions of max. tensile strain		

Anchorage bond: lengths required in terms of diameters

Concrete grade	25			30		
Type of reinforcement	Plain	Deformed type 1	Deformed type 2	Plain	Deformed type 1	Deformed type 2
In tension: horizontal bars in direct tension	55.5	69.5	53.5	51.8	60.0	46.2
In tension: otherwise	38.9	48.7	37.5	36.3	42.0	32.3
In compression	28.9	32.5	25.0	25.8	28.9	22.3

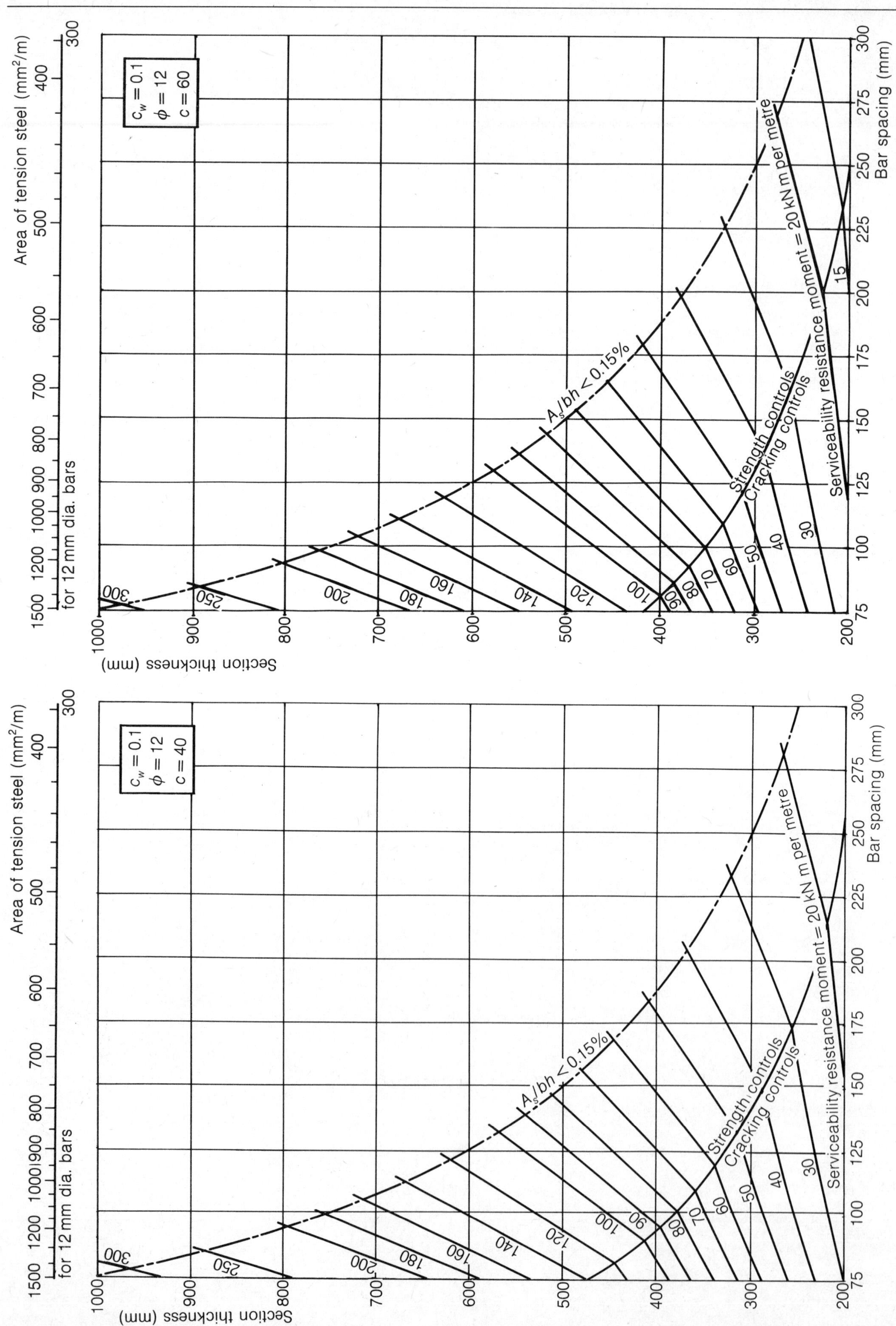
Area of tension steel (mm²/m)
for 12 mm dia. bars
Section thickness (mm)
Bar spacing (mm)
$c_w = 0.1$
$\phi = 12$
$c = 60$
$A_s/bh < 0.15\%$
Strength controls
Cracking controls
Serviceability resistance moment = 20 kN m per metre
$c_w = 0.1$
$\phi = 12$
$c = 40$
$A_s/bh < 0.15\%$
Strength controls
Cracking controls
Serviceability resistance moment = 20 kN m per metre

BS5337: design charts for singly-reinforced rectangular sections—2

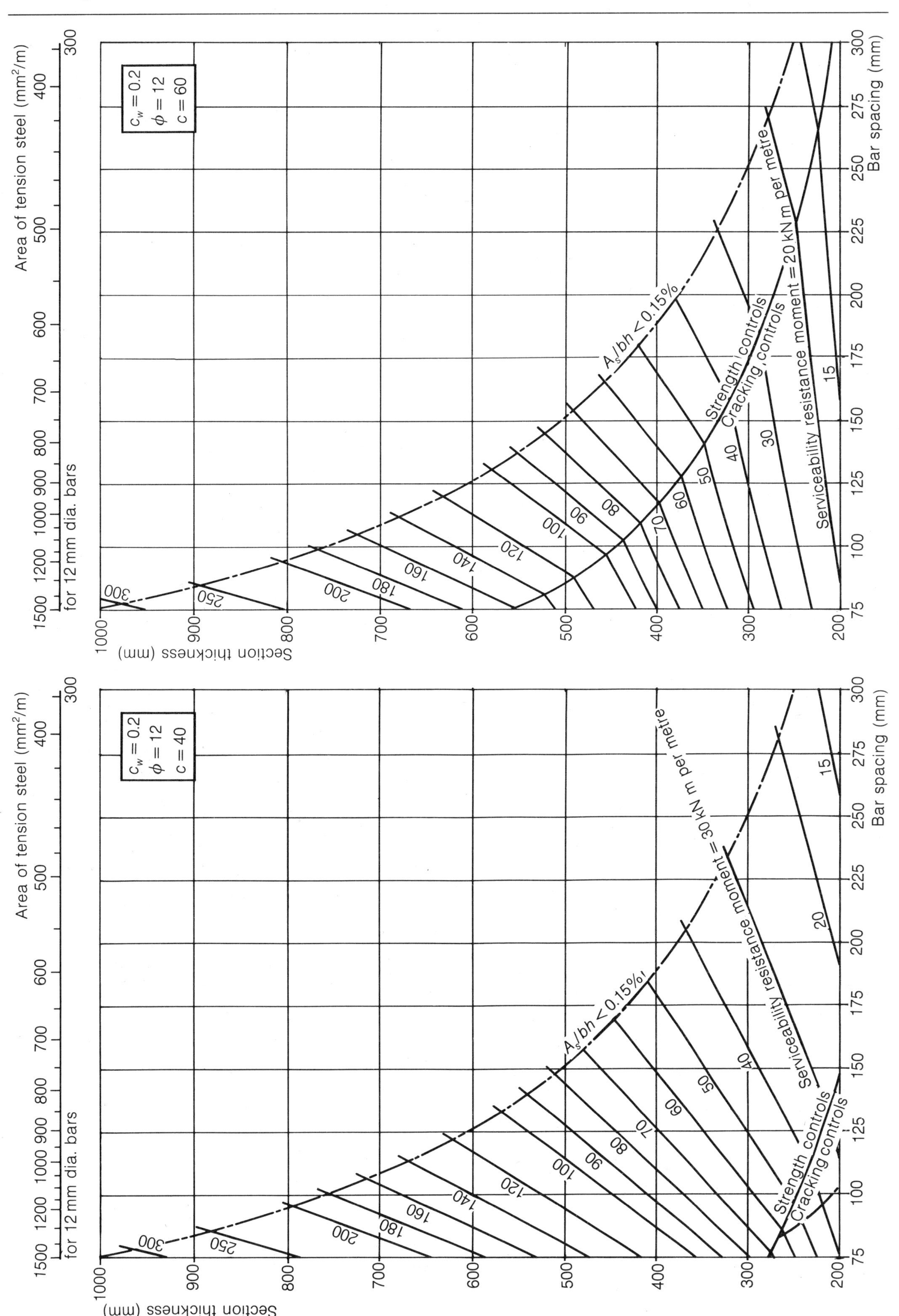

BS5337: design charts for singly-reinforced rectangular sections—3

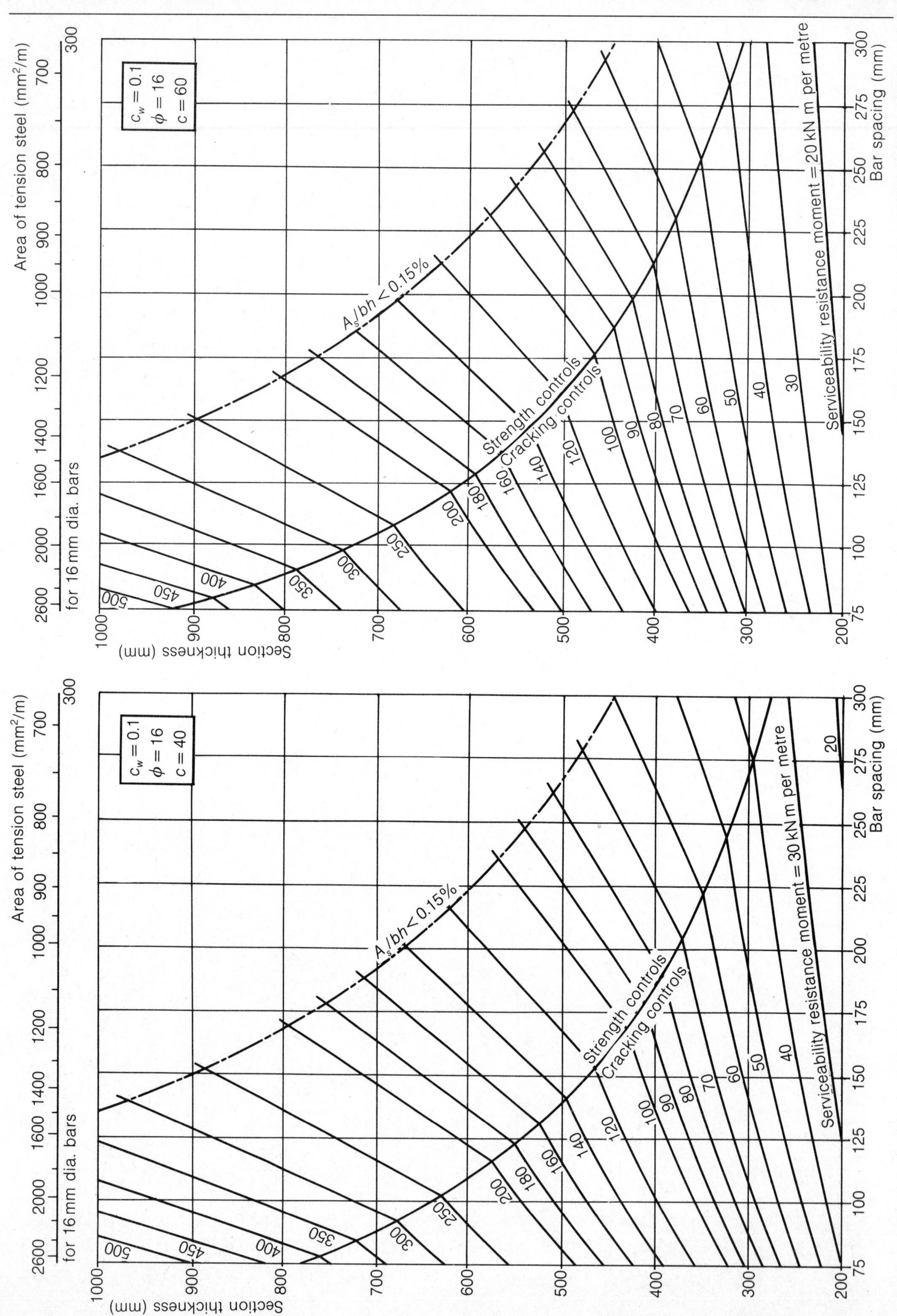

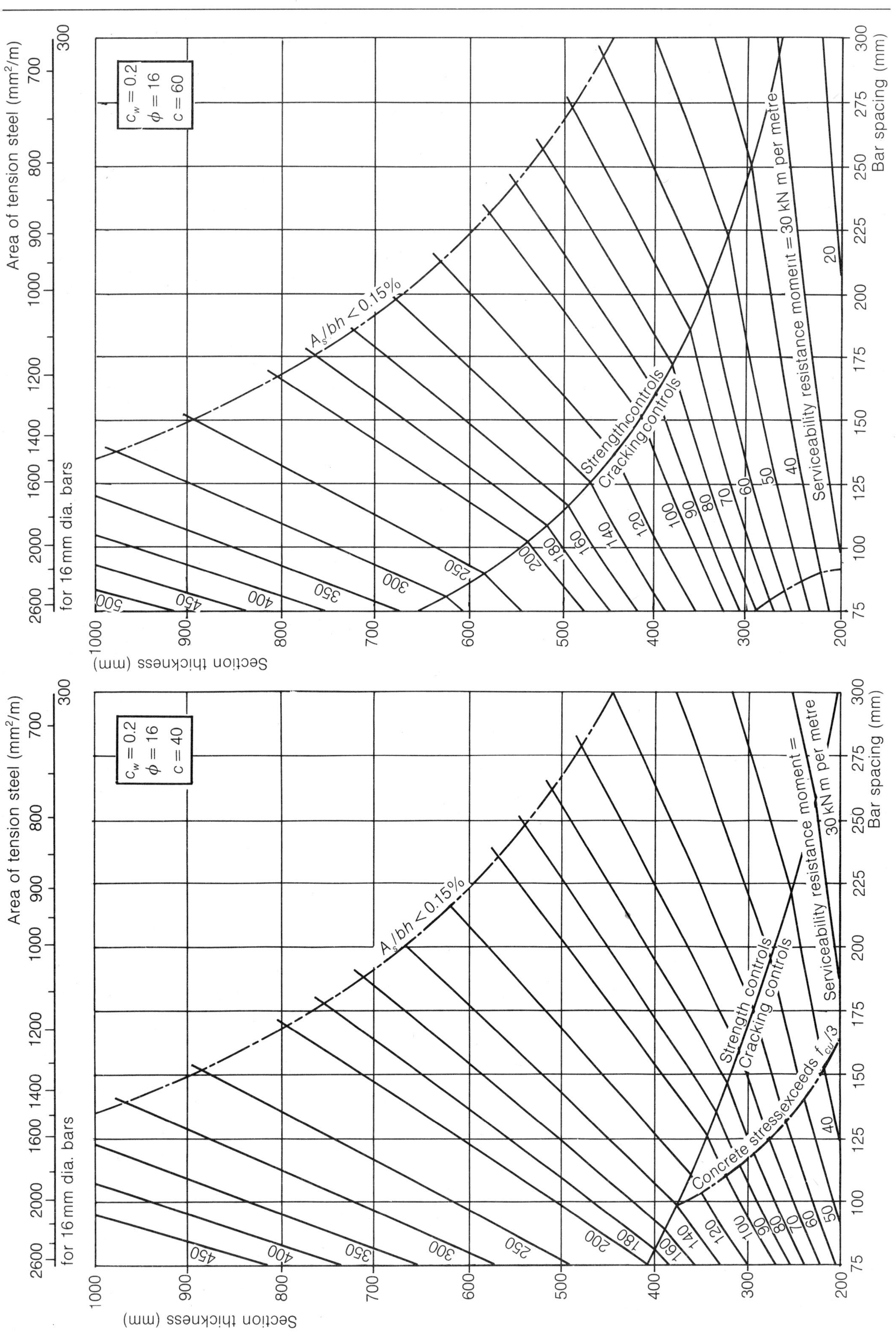

$c_w = 0.2$
$\phi = 16$
$c = 60$
Area of tension steel (mm²/m)
for 16 mm dia. bars
Section thickness (mm)
Bar spacing (mm)
$A_s/bh < 0.15\%$
Strength controls
Cracking controls
Serviceability resistance moment = 30 kN m per metre
$c_w = 0.2$
$\phi = 16$
$c = 40$
Area of tension steel (mm²/m)
for 16 mm dia. bars
Section thickness (mm)
Bar spacing (mm)
$A_s/bh < 0.15\%$
Strength controls
Cracking controls
Concrete stress exceeds $f_{cu}/3$
Serviceability resistance moment = 30 kN m per metre

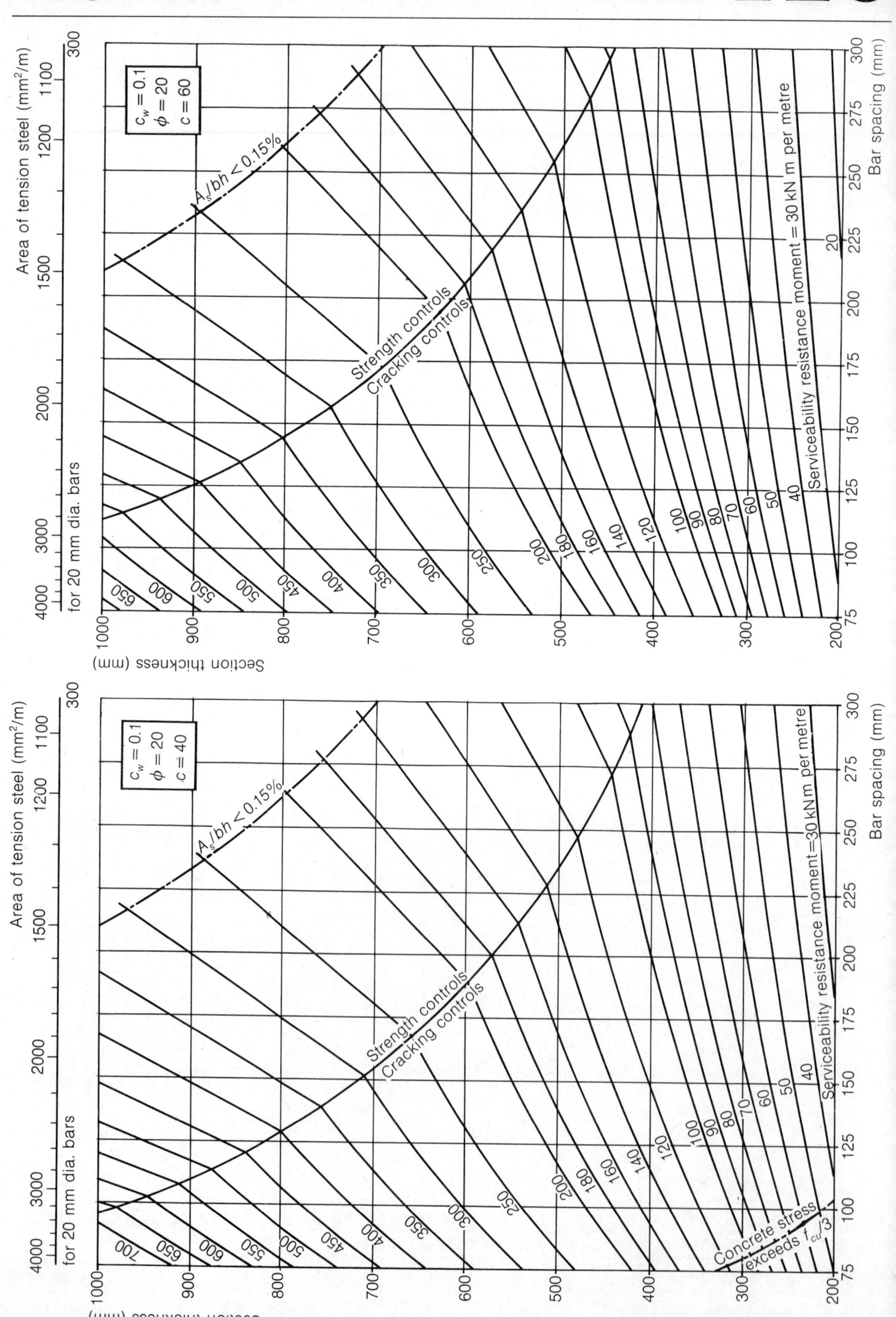
$c_w = 0.1$
$\phi = 20$
$c = 60$
Area of tension steel (mm²/m)
for 20 mm dia. bars
Section thickness (mm)
Bar spacing (mm)
$A_s/bh < 0.15\%$
Strength controls
Cracking controls
Serviceability resistance moment = 30 kN m per metre
$c_w = 0.1$
$\phi = 20$
$c = 40$
Area of tension steel (mm²/m)
for 20 mm dia. bars
Section thickness (mm)
Bar spacing (mm)
$A_s/bh < 0.15\%$
Strength controls
Cracking controls
Serviceability resistance moment=30 kNm per metre
Concrete stress exceeds $f_{cu}/3$

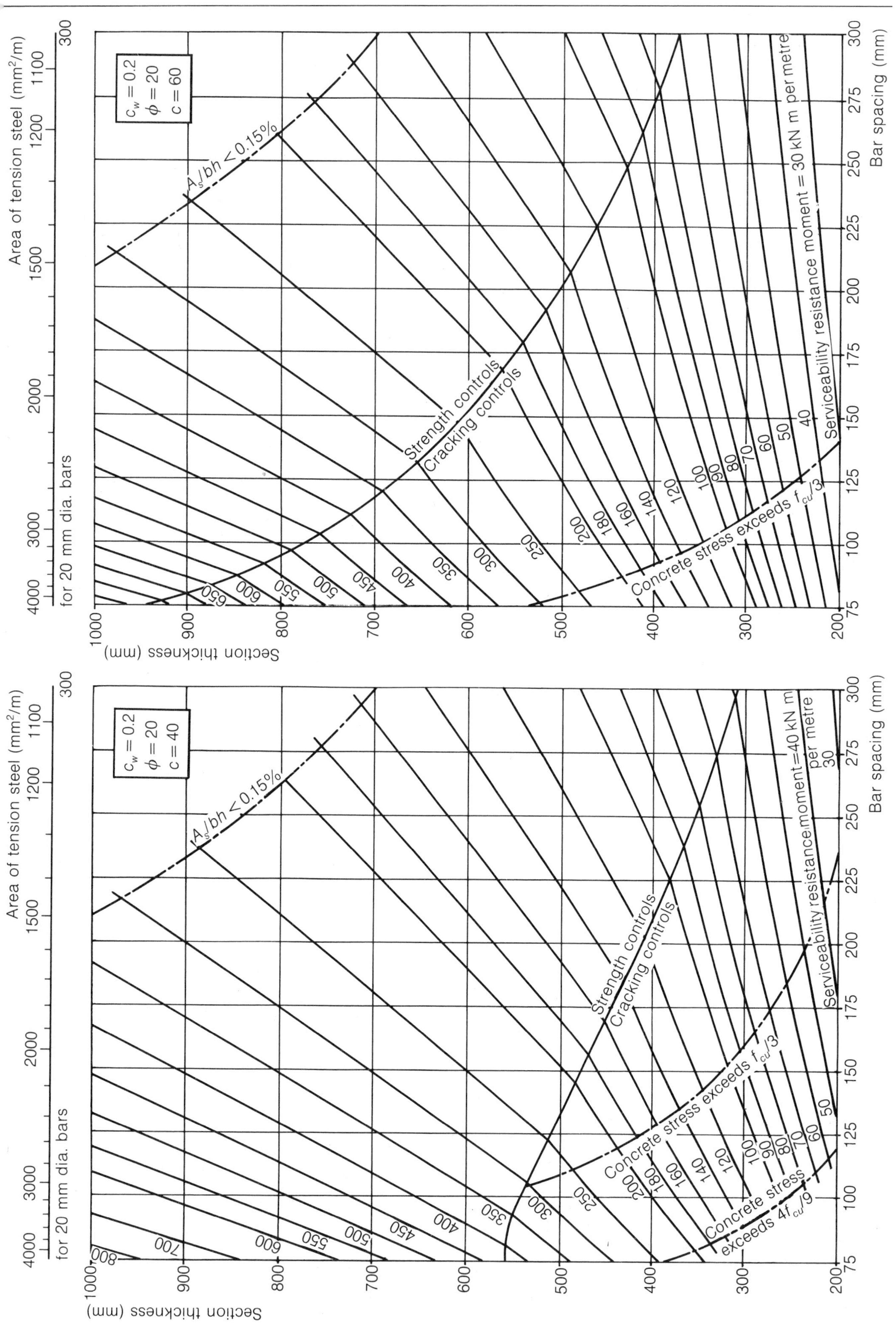

Area of tension steel (mm²/m)
for 20 mm dia. bars
Section thickness (mm)
Bar spacing (mm)
$c_w = 0.2$
$\phi = 20$
$c = 60$
$A_s/bh < 0.15\%$
Strength controls
Cracking controls
Concrete stress exceeds $f_{cu}/3$
Serviceability resistance moment = 30 kN m per metre
$c_w = 0.2$
$\phi = 20$
$c = 40$
$A_s/bh < 0.15\%$
Strength controls
Cracking controls
Concrete stress exceeds $f_{cu}/3$
Concrete stress exceeds $4f_{cu}/9$
Serviceability resistance moment = 40 kN m per metre

BS5337: design charts for singly-reinforced rectangular sections—7

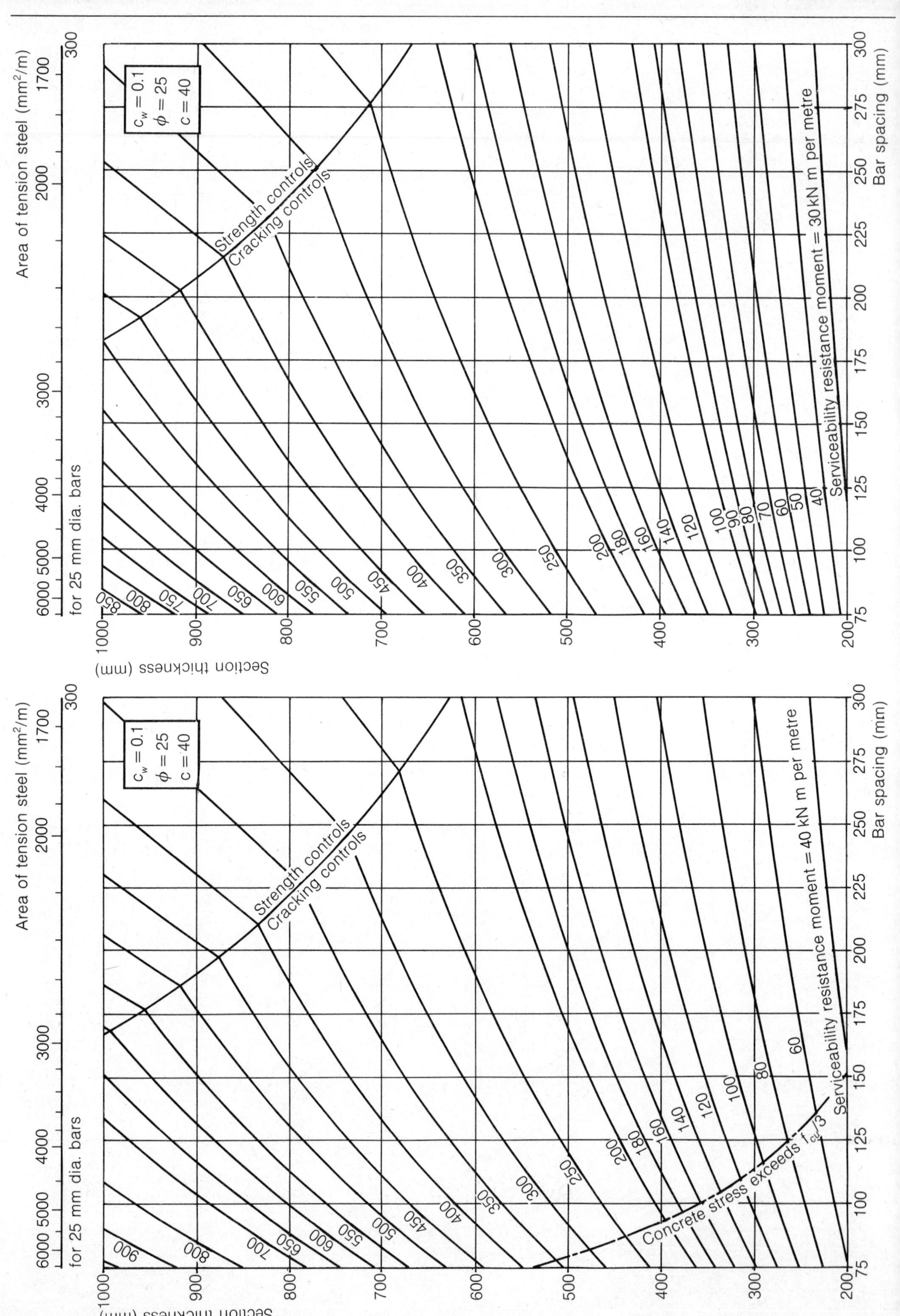

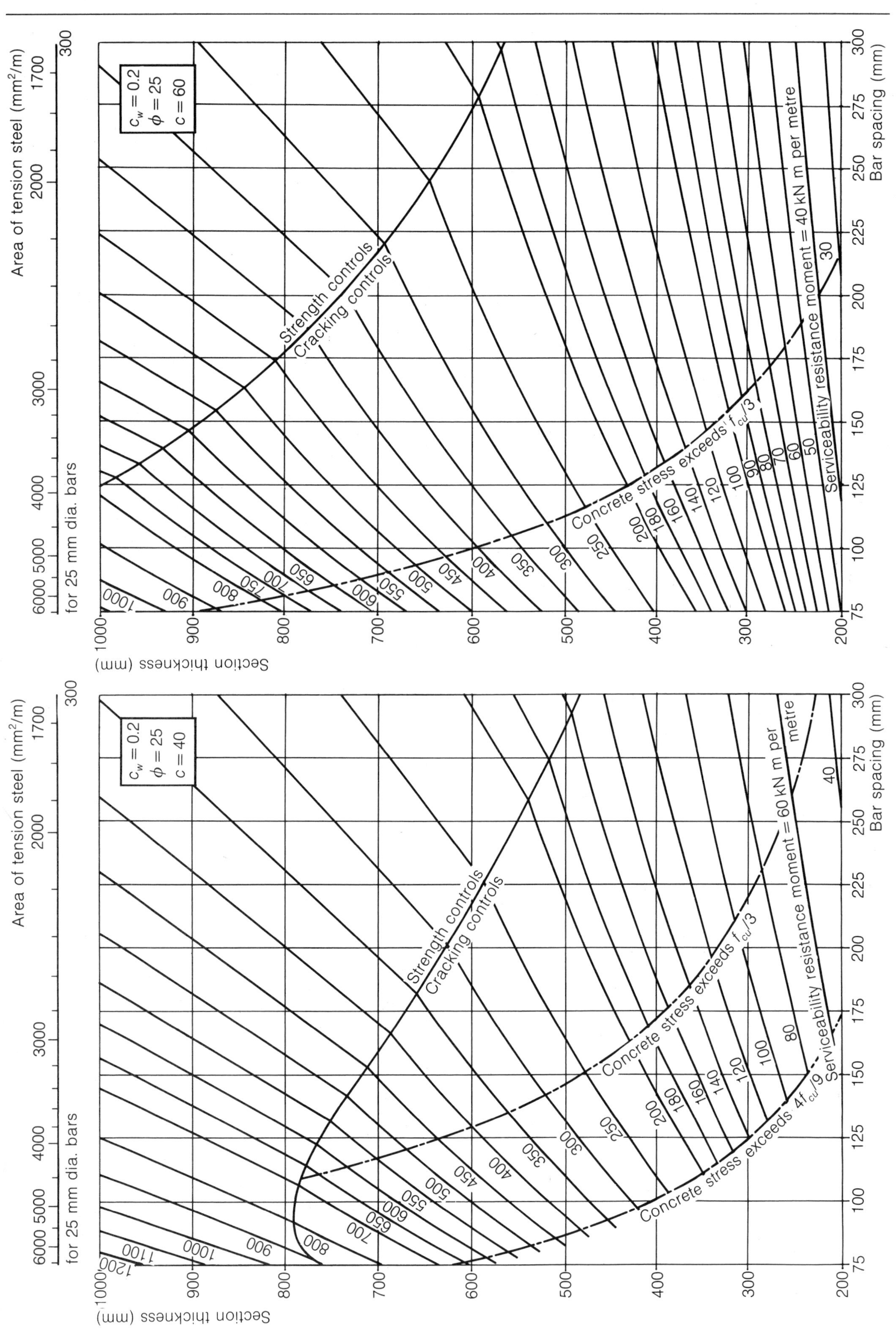
Area of tension steel (mm²/m)
for 25 mm dia. bars
Section thickness (mm)
Bar spacing (mm)
$c_w = 0.2$
$\phi = 25$
$c = 60$
Strength controls
Cracking controls
Concrete stress exceeds $f_{cu}/3$
Serviceability resistance moment = 40 kN m per metre
$c_w = 0.2$
$\phi = 25$
$c = 40$
Serviceability resistance moment = 60 kN m per metre
Concrete stress exceeds $4f_{cu}/9$

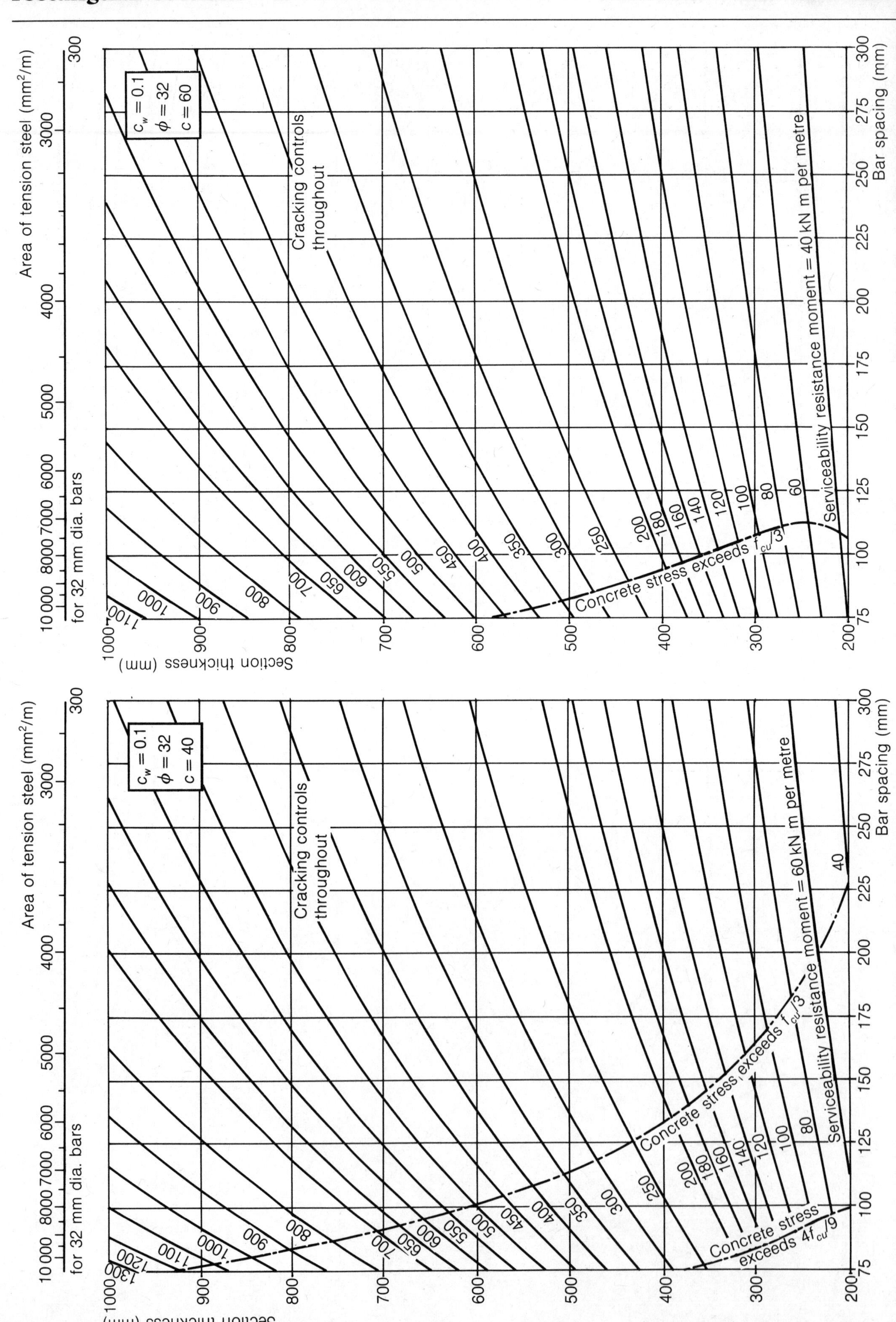

$c_w = 0.1$
$\phi = 32$
$c = 60$
Cracking controls throughout
Serviceability resistance moment = 40 kN m per metre
Concrete stress exceeds $f_{cu}/3$
Area of tension steel (mm²/m)
for 32 mm dia. bars
Section thickness (mm)
Bar spacing (mm)
$c_w = 0.1$
$\phi = 32$
$c = 40$
Cracking controls throughout
Serviceability resistance moment = 60 kN m per metre
Concrete stress exceeds $f_{cu}/3$
Concrete stress exceeds $4f_{cu}/9$
Area of tension steel (mm²/m)
for 32 mm dia. bars
Section thickness (mm)
Bar spacing (mm)

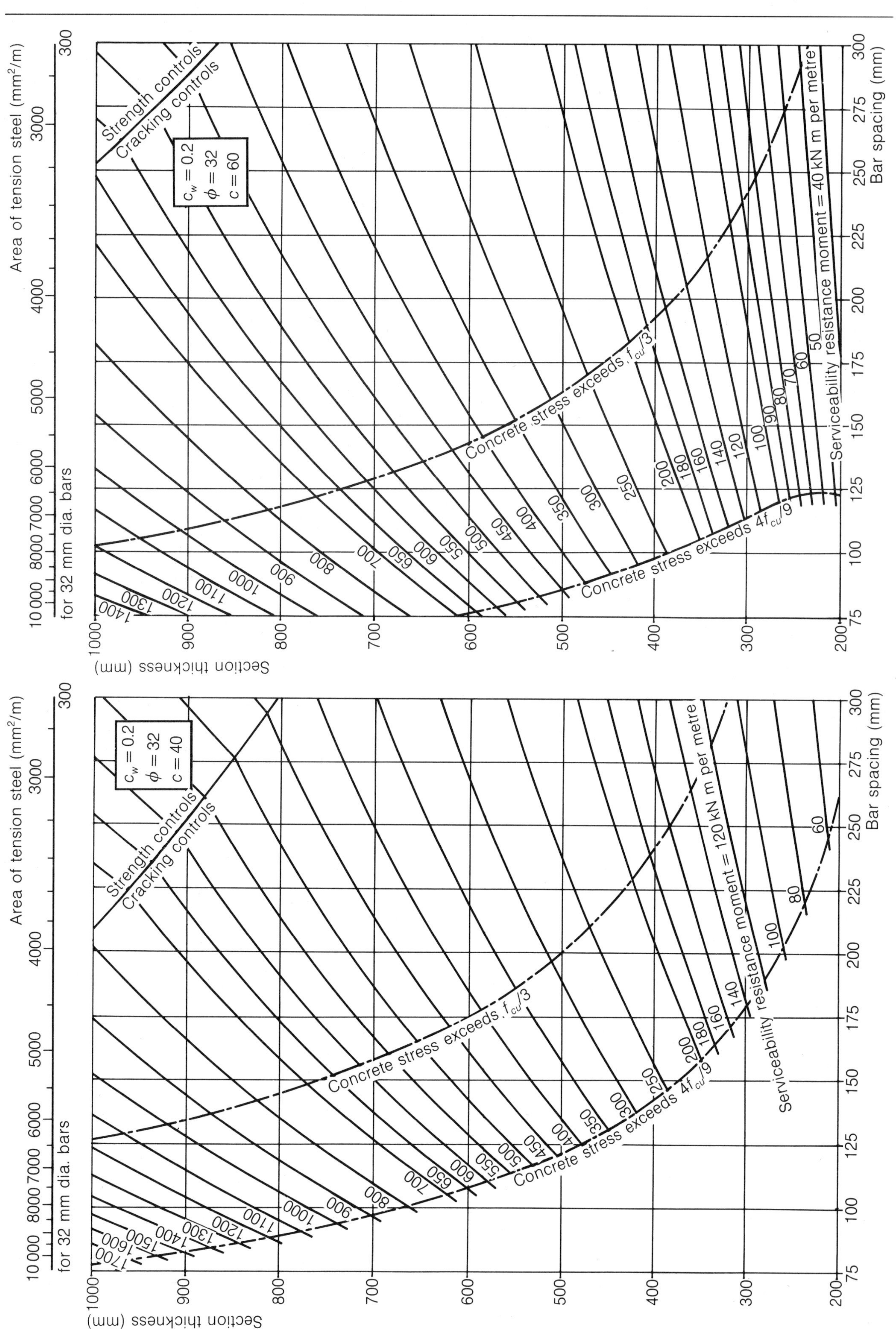

Area of tension steel (mm²/m)
for 32 mm dia. bars
Section thickness (mm)
Bar spacing (mm)
Strength controls
Cracking controls
c_w = 0.2
φ = 32
c = 60
Concrete stress exceeds f_cu/3
Concrete stress exceeds 4f_cu/9
Serviceability resistance moment = 40 kN m per metre
Area of tension steel (mm²/m)
for 32 mm dia. bars
Section thickness (mm)
Bar spacing (mm)
Strength controls
Cracking controls
c_w = 0.2
φ = 32
c = 40
Concrete stress exceeds f_cu/3
Concrete stress exceeds 4f_cu/9
Serviceability resistance moment = 120 kN m per metre

$$+\frac{bx^2(3h-2x)}{12\alpha_e(d-x)}\bigg]=0 \qquad (20.3)$$

Further, if (as in the present case) no compression steel is present, equation (20.3) simplifies to

$$M_d\left[A_s-\frac{bx^2}{2\alpha_e(d-x)}\right]-N_d\left[A_s(d-\tfrac{1}{2}h)+\frac{bx^2(3h-2x)}{12\alpha_e(d-x)}\right]=0 \qquad (20.4)$$

Now, by substituting the known values, equation (20.3) or (20.4) can be solved by repeated iteration to obtain x, which can then be resubstituted into equation (20.2) to obtain f_{st}. Finally, with these known values, expressions (20.1) etc. can be solved to determine the calculated surface crack width. The procedure is illustrated in example 4 below.

20.3.2 Modular-ratio design

Modular-ratio design is the alternative to limit-state analysis for liquid-containing structures.

Permissible stresses. The permissible stresses in the concrete and reinforcement are summarized at the top of *Table 132*. A modular ratio of 15 is specified in BS5337.

Deflection. Deflections should be checked by using the same simplified procedure described for limit-state design (see section 20.4.2).

Analysis. As with limit-state design, three principal conditions need consideration: (1) when a member is subjected to bending only; (2) when a member is subjected to direct tension only; and (3) when a member is subjected to combined bending and tension. The formulae corresponding to each case are given on *Tables 132* and *133*.

Case 1: bending only. Members subjected to bending which are not more than 225 mm in thickness, or where the face in contact with the liquid is in tension, or both, must first be designed to restrict cracking by limiting the tensile stress in the concrete to the value prescribed. The section is analysed on the assumption that the concrete resists both tension and compression, these calculations determining or confirming the dimensions of the member. The amount of reinforcement necessary is now calculated by means of a further analysis in which the concrete is assumed to have no strength in tension. The term *balanced design* may be used to indicate the condition where the dimensions of the member are just sufficient to ensure that the tensile stress in the concrete is equal to the maximum allowable value f_{ct} and that the proportion ρ_1 of steel provided is just sufficient to ensure that the strength of the section is equal to the applied moment M_d. By rearranging the appropriate formulae on *Table 132* it is possible to obtain expressions corresponding to the balanced design situation. For slabs that are reinforced in tension only, curves giving values of M_d/bh^2 and ρ_1 for specified values of f_{st}, d/h and concrete grade are given on *Table 132*. If a lower proportion of reinforcement than that corresponding to balanced design is preferred, the amount required can be calculated from the expression $A_s = M_d/zf_{st}$. The lever-arm z in this formula actually depends on the amount of reinforcement provided, but a simple and convenient approximation for design purposes is $z \simeq d - h/10$.

If tension and compression steel is provided, similar formulae to those given on *Table 132* can be derived. In such a case, balanced design values can be obtained by interpolating between the curves for $A'_s = 2A_s$ and $A'_s = 0$ on *Tables 134* and *135*, taking N_d/bh as equal to zero.

If the thickness of the member is more than 225 mm and if the face in contact with the liquid is in compression, the section should be designed to meet the normal requirements of CP114.

Case 2: direct tension only. Planar members subjected to direct tension without bending are uncommon; a curved slab such as the wall of a cylindrical tank is the more common case. As in case 1, the two design conditions are that the tensile stress f_{ct} in the concrete must not exceed the prescribed value, in order to prevent extensive cracks forming, and that sufficient reinforcement must be provided to ensure the strength of the section. The procedure is outlined on *Table 133*.

Case 3: combined bending and tension. Two conditions may occur: when the face in contact with the liquid is in tension, and when the reverse situation occurs. If the maximum tensile strain is in the face further from the liquid and the member is greater than 225 mm in thickness, it should be designed in accordance with the requirements of CP114. Otherwise the formulae controlling the strength and resistance to cracking of the section are as given on *Table 133*, and the zones over which the particular formulae are applicable are indicated on the accompanying typical interaction diagram. In case 3, the balanced design condition may be considered to be formed by the boundary between zones 2 and 3 on this diagram, and the formulae give on the table can be employed to prepare balanced-design charts giving N_d/bh and M_d/bh^2 for various combinations of ρ_1, A'_s/A_s, d/h, f_{st} and the concrete grade. Typical charts form *Tables 134* and *135*: these are taken from the more complete series provided in ref. 80.

The foregoing charts may be used for design as follows. Select the pair of charts corresponding to the given value of f_{st} and, with a chosen ratio of A'_s/A_s and value of b, by using a trial value of h calculate N_d/bh and M_d/bh^2. Interpolate between the charts according to the ratio of A'_s/A_s chosen, to check whether the intersection of these values corresponds to the ratio of d/h to be adopted. If not, adjust h (and/or b and A'_s/A_s) and repeat the procedure: see example 4 below.

If the resulting amount of steel needed is greater than desired, a lower proportion may be used provided that the section dimensions are increased accordingly. Since this adjustment corresponds to reducing the values of N_d/bh and M_d/bh^2, the interaction diagram shows that the intersection point now falls within zone 3 and thus the resistance of the section is controlled by the strength of the reinforcement in tension. Assuming that programmable aid is available, the simplest design procedure at this stage is to substitute trial values of b, h, A_s and A'_s into expression (20.3) and thus obtain the value of x by repeated iteration. Then f_{st} can be found from expression (20.2). If this value is too great, one or more

	Concrete				Reinforcement			
	Modular ratio $\alpha_e = 15$		Grade 25	Grade 30	Minimum cover of concrete = 40 mm		Class of exposure A	Class of exposure B
Permissible stresses (N/mm²)	Resistance to cracking f_{ct}	In direct tension	1.31	1.44	Plain bars (minimum proportion of reinforcement near *each* face $\rho_1 = \frac{A_s}{bh} \nless 0.0025$)	In compression	125	125
		In tension due to bending	1.84	2.02		In direct tension, In tension due to bending, In shear	85	115
		In shear	1.94	2.19				
	Strength (increase bond stresses by 40% if deformed bars are used)	In direct compression	6.95	8.37	Deformed bars (minimum proportion of reinforcement near *each* face $\rho_1 = \frac{A_s}{bh} \nless 0.0015$)	In compression	140	140
		In compression due to bending	9.15	11.00		In direct tension, In tension due to bending, In shear	100	130
		In shear.	0.77	0.87				
		Anchorage bond	0.90	1.00				
		Local bond	1.36	1.49				

Case 1
Bending only

(a) Tensile stress at face in contact with liquid

Tension reinforcement only (i.e. reinforcement provided near compression face may be ignored)

Resistance to cracking: determines thickness h.

$$h \nless \sqrt{\frac{M_d}{K_{dc} b}} \quad \text{where} \quad K_{dc} = \frac{f_{ct}}{1-\beta}\left[\tfrac{1}{3} - (1-\beta)\beta + 14\rho_1\left(\frac{d}{h} - \beta\right)^2\right] \quad \text{and} \quad \beta = \frac{(1/2) + 14\rho_1(d/h)}{1 + 14\rho_1}$$

Substitute assumed or given values of ρ_1 and d/h to obtain K_{dc} and β.

Moment of resistance $M_{dc} = K_{dc} bh^2$.

Design for strength: determines reinforcement A_s required.

$$A_s \nless \frac{M_d}{f_{st} z} \quad \text{where} \quad z = d - \tfrac{1}{3}x \quad \text{and} \quad \frac{x}{d} = \sqrt{[(15\rho)^2 + 30\rho]} - 15\rho \qquad \rho = \rho_1\left(\frac{h}{d}\right)$$

Moment of resistance $M_{ds} = K_{ds} bh^2$ where $K_{ds} = \rho_1 f_{st} z/h$.

Balanced design: charts below give values of ρ_{bal} and $K_{bal} = K_{dc} = K_{ds}$ for balanced design.

βh, d, h, f_{ct}, f_{cr}, x, f_{st}/α_e

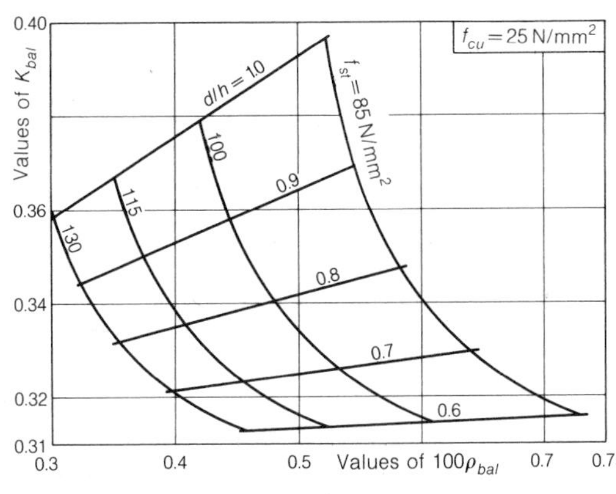

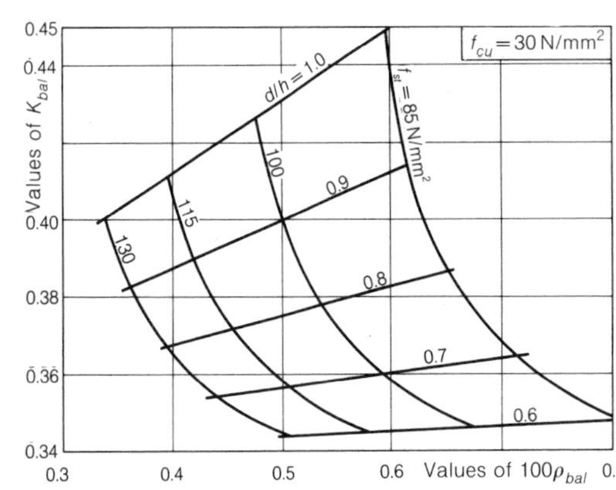

Normal design procedure
1. Assume values for h and d and read K_{bal} from appropriate chart above.
2. Calculate $K = M_d/bh^2$.
3. If $K < K_{bal}$, calculate $A_s = M_d/zf_{st}$ where a convenient approximation for z is $z \simeq d - h/10$.

Tension and compression reinforcement: use charts given on *Tables 134* and *135* with $N_d/bh = 0$.

Case 1
Bending only

(b) Tensile stress at face remote from liquid

(i) $h < 225$ mm: apply case 1(a)

(ii) $h \nless 225$ mm
Design for strength only:

$$d \nless \sqrt{\frac{M_d}{K_{conc} b}} \qquad A_s = \frac{M_d}{f_{st} z} \qquad \rho_1 = \frac{A_s}{bh}$$

Value for K_{conc} depends on f_{cr} and f_{st}.

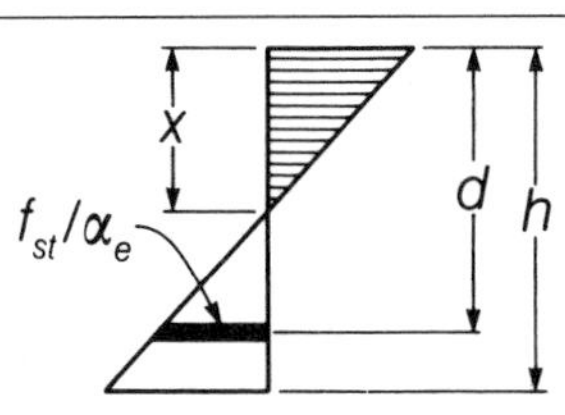

Stresses: given d and ρ_1 or A_s. Obtain x/d and z/d as case 1(a). Actual $f_{st} = M_d/A_s z$ and actual $f_{cr} = (f_{st} x)/(15(d-x))$

of the trial values must be increased and the iterative process repeated until the resulting value of f_{st} is satisfactory, taking care that in the process the proportion of steel provided does not exceed the balanced value.

It will be seen from the balanced-design charts that there is very little advantage to be gained by providing compression steel to increase the strength of a section (adding equal compression reinforcement to a singly-reinforced section increases its resistance to bending by about 10% typically). However, according to the requirements of BS5337 some reinforcement must be provided near the compression face of thicker sections, and the charts enable the contribution of this steel to be taken into account.

An alternative design method is first to ignore the axial force and to modify the moment accordingly as described for the corresponding limit-state case, finally providing extra steel to resist the additional axial force along the line of the reinforcement. However, this method does not check the tensile stress in the uncracked concrete section and it is therefore necessary to solve the zone 2 equations given on *Table 133* simultaneously by iteration to obtain f_{ct}. The procedure is described in more detail in example 4 below.

All the following examples assume the use of grade 25 concrete and deformed high-yield bars to meet the requirements of exposure class B.

Example 1. Design a tank wall to resist a service bending moment of 50 kN m per metre. No tensile force occurs.

Limit-state design. Assuming 40 mm cover to 20 mm bars, from the appropriate chart on *Table 127* a suitable section would have a thickness h of 300 mm with 20 mm bars at 300 mm centres ($A_s = 1047\ \text{mm}^2/\text{m}$).

Modular-ratio design. Assume a ratio of d/h of 0.85. Then with $f_{st} = 130\ \text{N/mm}^2$, the corresponding balanced-design values read from the curves on *Table 132* are $M_d/bh^2 = 0.337$ and $\rho = 0.34\%$. Thus

$$h = \sqrt{\left(\frac{50 \times 10^6}{0.337 \times 10^3}\right)} = 386\ \text{mm}; \qquad \text{say } 400\ \text{mm}$$

$$A_s = \frac{0.34 \times 386 \times 10^3}{100} = 1310\ \text{mm}^2/\text{m}$$

Provide 20 mm bars at 225 mm centres ($A_s = 1396\ \text{mm}^2/\text{m}$).

Example 2. Design a tank wall to resist a direct tensile force of 330 kN/m. No bending moment occurs.

Since the entire section is in tension, crack-width calculations cannot be made and the section must be designed using the alternative deemed-to-satisfy limiting stresses. For balanced design,

$$h = \frac{N_d}{b}\left[\frac{1}{f_{ct}} - \frac{(\alpha_e - 1)}{f_{st}}\right] = \frac{330 \times 10^3}{10^3}\left[\frac{1}{1.31} - \frac{14}{130}\right] = 217\ \text{mm}$$

Provide a 225 mm slab. Then

$$A_{s\,req} = 330 \times 10^3/130 = 2538\ \text{mm}^2/\text{m}$$

Provide 16 mm bars at 150 mm centres in each of two rows, one near each face.

Example 3. Design a tank wall to resist a service bending moment of 7.5 kN m per metre together with an axial tensile force of 175 kN/m.

Assume that $h = 300$ mm and $d = 300 - 40 - 10 = 250$ mm. Thus $d - h/2 = 250 - 150 = 100$ mm. Since this is greater than $M_d/N_d = 7.5 \times 10^3/175 = 43$ mm, the entire section is considered to be subject to tensile stresses only. Once again, the crack-width formulae do not apply and the section must be designed using the deemed-to-satisfy procedure. The areas of reinforcement required are as follows:

$$A_s = \frac{1}{2 \times 130}\left[175 \times 10^3 + \frac{7.5 \times 10^6}{100}\right] = 962\ \text{mm}^2$$

$$A_s' = \frac{1}{260}\left[175 \times 10^3 - \frac{7.5 \times 10^6}{100}\right] = 385\ \text{mm}^2$$

Provide 20 mm bars at 300 mm centres ($A_s = 1047\ \text{mm}^2/\text{m}$) and 12 mm bars at 300 mm centres ($A_s' = 377\ \text{mm}^2/\text{m}$) respectively.

It is now necessary to check the maximum tensile stress in the concrete. This is given by the expression.

$$f_{ct} = \frac{N_d}{A_{tr}} + \frac{M_d(h - \bar{x})}{I_{xx}}$$

where

$$A_{tr} = bh + (\alpha_e - 1)(A_s + A_s')$$

$$\bar{x} = \frac{1}{A_{tr}}[\tfrac{1}{2}bh^2 + (\alpha_e - 1)(A_s d + A_s' d')]$$

$$I_{xx} = \tfrac{1}{12}bh^3 + (\alpha_e - 1)[A_s(d - \bar{x})^2 + A_s'(\bar{x} - d')^2]$$

In the present case, $A_{tr} = 320 \times 10^3\ \text{mm}^2$, $\bar{x} = 153$ mm and $I_{xx} = 2.44 \times 10^9\ \text{mm}^4$. Thus

$$f_{ct} = \frac{175 \times 10^3}{320 \times 10^3} + \frac{7.5 \times 10^6(300 - 153)}{2.44 \times 10^9} = 1.0\ \text{N/mm}^2$$

which is satisfactory. Note that it is almost always possible to adopt the approximation $\bar{x} = h/2$. Then

$$f_{ct} \simeq \frac{N_d}{A_{tr}} + \frac{6M_d h}{bh^3 + 12(\alpha_e - 1)(d - h/2)^2(A_s + A_s')}$$

If this approximation is made in the present example, $f_{ct} \simeq 1.01\ \text{N/mm}^2$, the difference being insignificant.

Example 4. Design a tank wall to resist a service bending moment of 110 kN m per metre together with an axial tensile force of 92.5 kN/m. Assume that $h = 400$ mm and $d = 400 - 40 - 10 = 350$ mm. Thus $d - h/2 = 350 - 200 = 150$ mm. Since this is less than $M_d/N_d = 110 \times 10^6/92.5 \times 10^3 = 1190$ mm, both tension and compression occur across the section.

Limit-state design. Combining the bending moment and the tensile force, the modified moment becomes $110 \times 10^6 - 92.5 \times 10^3(350 - 200) = 96.2 \times 10^6$ N mm per metre. Reference to the appropriate chart on *Table 127* shows that a section 400 mm in thickness and reinforced with 20 mm bars at 250 mm centres will suffice. Next, additional steel must be provided to resist the axial force of 92.5×10^3 N. Since calculation shows that the stress in this reinforcement f_{st} is

Case 2

Concentric tensile force only

Design for strength: determines reinforcement A_s. $A_s = \dfrac{N_d}{f_{st}}$ or $\rho_1 = \dfrac{N_d}{f_{st} bh}$

Resistance to cracking: determines thickness h. $h \nless \left[\dfrac{N_d}{f_{ct}} - (\alpha_e - 1)A_s\right]\dfrac{1}{b}$

For balanced design: $h = \dfrac{N_d}{b}\left[\dfrac{1}{f_{ct}} - \dfrac{(\alpha_e - 1)}{f_{st}}\right]$

$A_s = \rho_1 bh$ (if more than one row of bars, A_s = total of all rows)

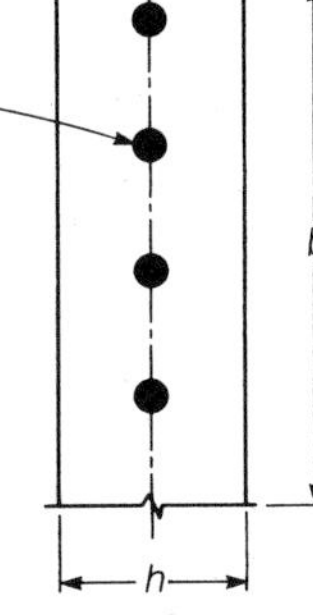

Case 3

Tensile force combined with bending.
(a) Tensile stress at face in contact with liquid

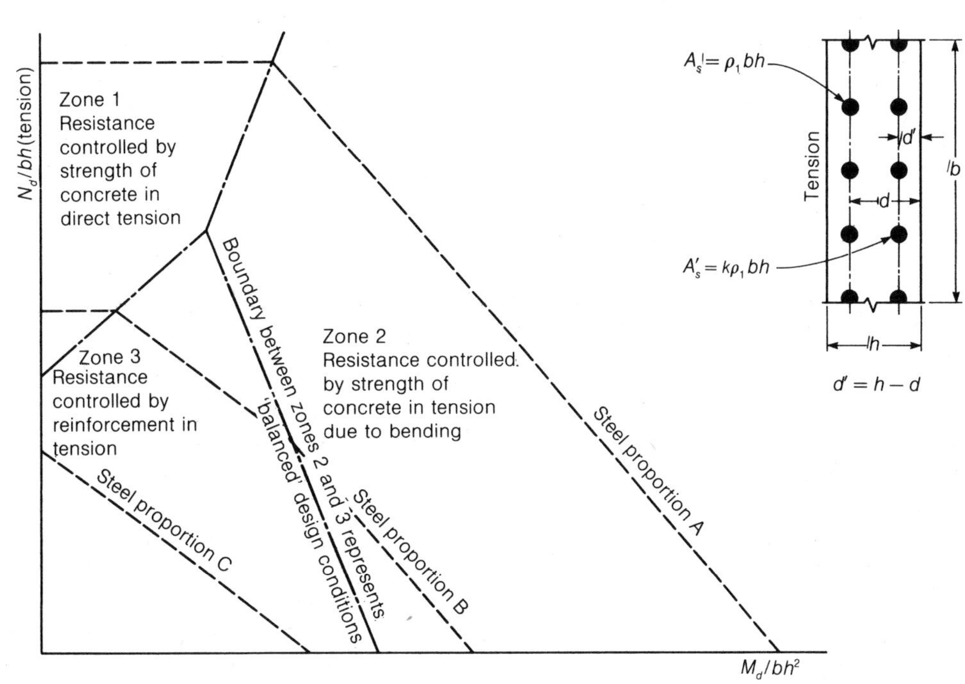

Interaction diagram:

In zone 1: $N_d = f_{ct}[bh + (\alpha_e - 1)A_s]$

In zone 2: $N_d = \dfrac{f_{ct}}{(h - x)}\{bh(\tfrac{1}{2}h - x) + A_s(\alpha_e - 1)(d - x) - k(x - d')]\}$

$$M_d = \frac{f_{ct}}{(h - x)}\{\tfrac{1}{12}bh^3 + A_s(\alpha_e - 1)(d - \tfrac{1}{2}h)[(d - x) + k(x - d')]\}$$

In zone 3: $N_d = f_{st}\left\{A_s\left[1 - k\left(\dfrac{\alpha_e - 1}{\alpha_e}\right)\left(\dfrac{x - d'}{d - x}\right)\right] - \dfrac{bx^2}{2\alpha_e(d - x)}\right\}$

$$M_d = f_{st}\left\{A_s(d - \tfrac{1}{2}h)\left[1 + k\left(\frac{\alpha_e - 1}{\alpha_e}\right)\left(\frac{x - d'}{d - x}\right)\right] + \frac{bx^2(3h - 2x)}{12\alpha_e(d - x)}\right\}$$

(If $x < d'$, omit the term $(\alpha_e - 1)/\alpha_e$.)
For balanced design (i.e. boundary between zones 2 and 3), read values of N_d/bh and M_d/bh^2 corresponding to given values of f_{ct}, f_{st}, d'/h and A_s/bh from charts on *Tables 134* and *135*.

Case 3

Tensile force combined with bending.
(b) Tensile stress at face remote from liquid

(i) $h < 225$ mm: adopt case 3(a)

(ii) $h \nless 225$ mm

Given or assuming d and h: $d \nless \sqrt{\dfrac{M_d}{K_{conc} b}}$ where value of K_{conc} is appropriate to f_{st} and f_{cc}.

$e_1 = e + \tfrac{1}{2}h - d$ $\qquad A_s = \dfrac{N_d}{f_{st}}\left(1 + \dfrac{e_1}{0.83d}\right)$

If d, h and A_s are given, substitute in $\dfrac{N_d}{A_s}\left(1 + \dfrac{e_1}{0.83d}\right) \ngtr f_{st}$ for this condition.

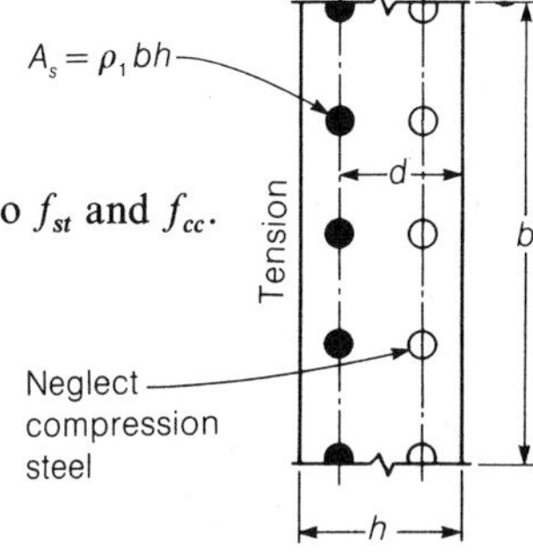

250 N/mm^2, the amount of steel required is $92.5 \times 10^3/250 = 370$ mm^2. Thus the total area of reinforcement needed is $1257 + 370 = 1627$ mm^2/m. Bars of 20 mm at 175 mm centres will provide 1795 mm^2/m. If the foregoing values are substituted into expressions (20.2) and (20.3), the iteration process gives values of x and f_{st} of 101 mm and 221 N/mm^2 respectively. Thus

$$\varepsilon_1 = \frac{f_{st}}{E_s}\left(\frac{h-x}{d-x}\right) = \frac{221}{200 \times 10^3}\left(\frac{400-101}{350-101}\right) = 0.001\,33$$

and $\varepsilon_m = 0.001\,33 - 0.7 \times 400/(1795 \times 221) = 0.000\,62$. Now since $a_{cr} = \sqrt{(50^2 + 87.5^2)} - 10 = 90.8$ mm,

$$\text{design surface crack width} = 9 \times 90.8 \times 0.000\,62 \Big/ \left[2 + 5\left(\frac{90.8-40}{400-101}\right)\right] = 0.178 \text{ mm}$$

which is satisfactory.

Modular-ratio design. Try a section thickness of 500 mm. Then $M_d/bh^2 = 110 \times 10^6/10^3 \times 500^2 = 0.440$ and $N_d/bh = 92.5 \times 10^3/10^3 \times 500 = 0.185$. The intersection of these values exceeds the line for $d/h - 1$ on the appropriate chart in ref. 80 and is therefore unacceptable. Increasing h to 600 mm, $M_d/bh^2 = 0.306$ and $N_d/bh = 0.154$, and the intersection point falls where $d/h = 0.72$, which is clearly too low. If intermediate values of h are tried, the balanced design situation will be found to occur where $h = 585$ mm, $M_d/bh^2 = 0.321$ and $N_d/bh = 0.158$. Then $d/h = 0.91$ and $\rho_1 = 0.003\,65$, so that

$$A_{s\,req} = 0.00365 \times 585 \times 10^3 = 2135 \text{ mm}^2/\text{m}$$

A convenient practical wall thickness would be 600 mm, and if this thickness were adopted the area of steel provided could be reduced on the basis

$$\text{actual } A_{s\,req} \simeq \text{theoretical } A_s \times d_{min}/d_{prov}$$

Thus in the present case

$$A_s \simeq 2135 \times 535/550 = 2077 \text{ mm}^2/\text{m}$$

Provide 20 mm bars at 150 mm centres ($A_s = 2094$ mm^2/m).

An alternative design method is to combine the axial force and moment by modifying the latter, as described earlier. If this is done, assuming a thickness of 600 mm with $d = 600 - 40 - 10 = 550$ mm, the modified moment becomes $110 \times 10^6 - 92.5 \times 10^3(550 - 300) = 86.8 \times 10^6$ N mm per metre. From the scales on *Table 120* with $M_d/bd^2f_{st} = 86.8 \times 10^6/10^3 \times 550^2 \times 130 = 0.002\,21$, $\rho = 0.002\,38$, so that $A_{s\,req} = 0.002\,38 \times 550 \times 10^3 = 1309$ mm^2/m. The additional steel required to resist the axial force is $92.5 \times 10^3/130 = 711$ mm^2/m, so that the total area of steel needed is 2020 mm^2/m.

This alternative method takes no account of the tensile stress in the concrete. This must now be checked, either by substituting all known values into the equations for M_d and N_d for zone 2 on *Table 133* and using iteration to determine f_{ct}, or by calculating the actual values of M_d/bh^2 and N_d/bh and checking that these do not exceed the balanced values given by the appropriate chart, corresponding to the intersection point for the ratio of d/h and value of ρ_1 adopted.

20.4 DEFLECTIONS

The recommendations in BS8110 and CP110 regarding deflections are designed to meet the appropriate requirements of the limit-state of serviceability. Either suitable dimensions may be assumed and the resulting deflection estimated by rigorous analysis as outlined in Part 2 of BS8110 and Appendix A of CP110, or a simplified method may be adopted in which a limiting span/effective-depth ratio is evaluated.

20.4.1 Rigorous analysis

The procedure to be adopted if rigorous calculations are to be prepared, to demonstrate that the resulting deflections do not exceed the limits prescribed, is summarized in *Table 136*: see also section 5.5.1. The method is discussed and illustrated in some detail in *Examples of the Design of Buildings*, where suitable design aids are also provided.

20.4.2 Simplified method

The following design procedure, which complies with the Code requirements, involves determining the basic effective depth corresponding to a given span and given fixity conditions. This minimum value of d is then adjusted by multiplying it by coefficients that depend on the various factors which control deflection. Values of d corresponding to the length and type of span can be read from the scales at the top of *Table 137*. If necessary, this value is then modified by multiplying it by factors that depend on the proportions of tension and compression reinforcement and on the service stress f_s in the tension reinforcement. (With BS8110, the tension factor is found indirectly by taking account of the ultimate applied moment.) Further modifications may be necessary for flanged sections or if lightweight concrete is used: details are given below. The value of d finally obtained from this procedure is the *minimum* that may be used: the actual effective depth employed must equal or exceed this value.

The multiplier for the amount and service stress in the tension reinforcement and that for the amount of compression steel can be read from the respective scales on *Table 137*. Since the amounts of tension and compression reinforcement clearly cannot be determined with certainty until well after a knowledge of the effective depth is required, it is thus clear that with depths approaching critical values the design procedure becomes a matter of trial and adjustment; an interim value of d is used initially to design the section, and the resulting values of ρ and ρ' are then employed to check that the value of d adopted is permissible. BS8110 recommends that the service stress is estimated from the equation

$$f_s = \tfrac{5}{8} f_y \frac{A_{s\,req}}{A_{s\,prov}} \frac{1}{\beta_b}$$

where $A_{s\,req}$ and $A_{s\,prov}$ are the areas of tension steel required and provided at the middle of a freely supported or continuous span and at the support of a cantilever, respectively, and β_b is the actual moment of resistance provided at midspan, as given by the diagram of redistributed maximum moments, divided by the maximum calculated moment at midspan before redistribution. If the amount of

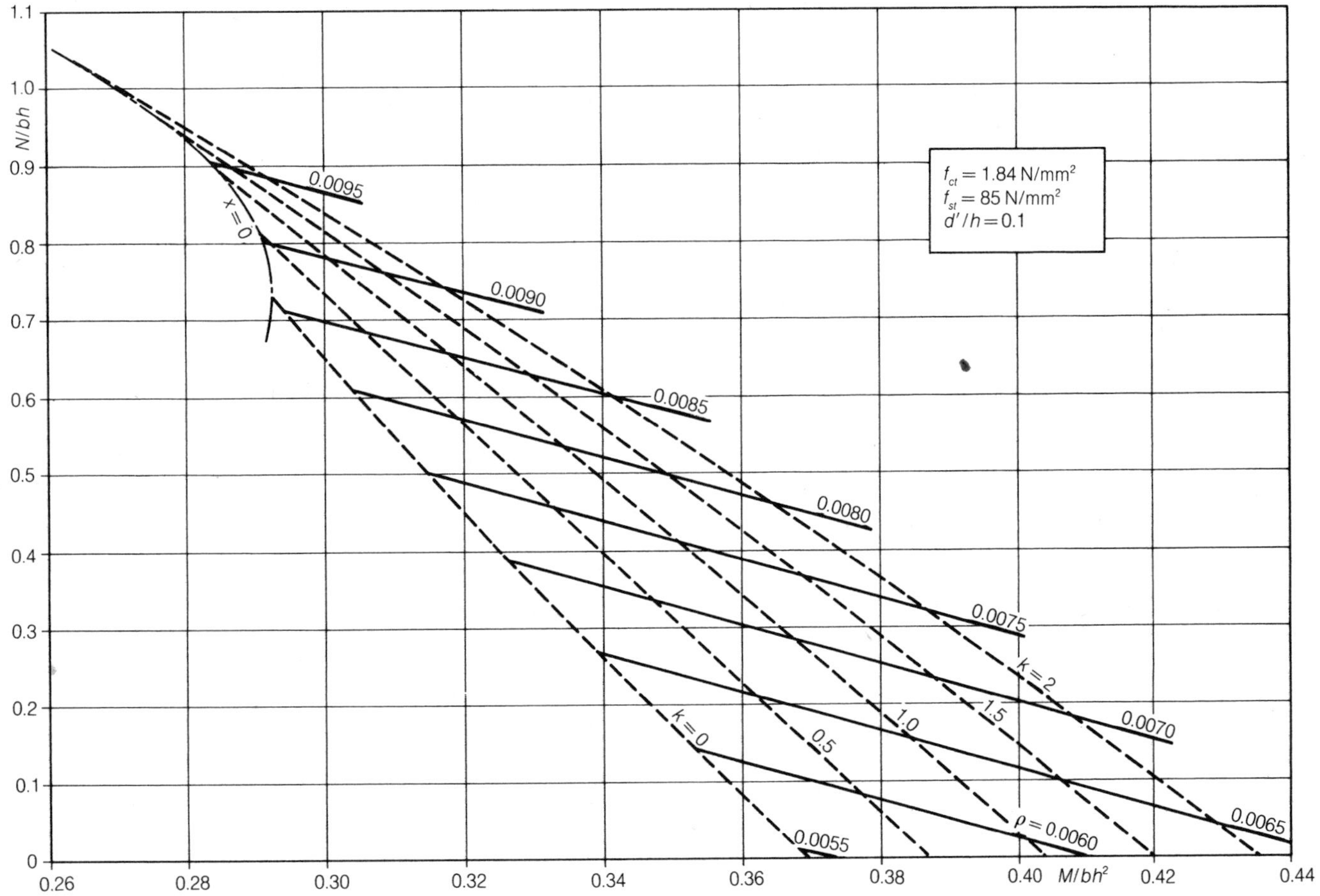

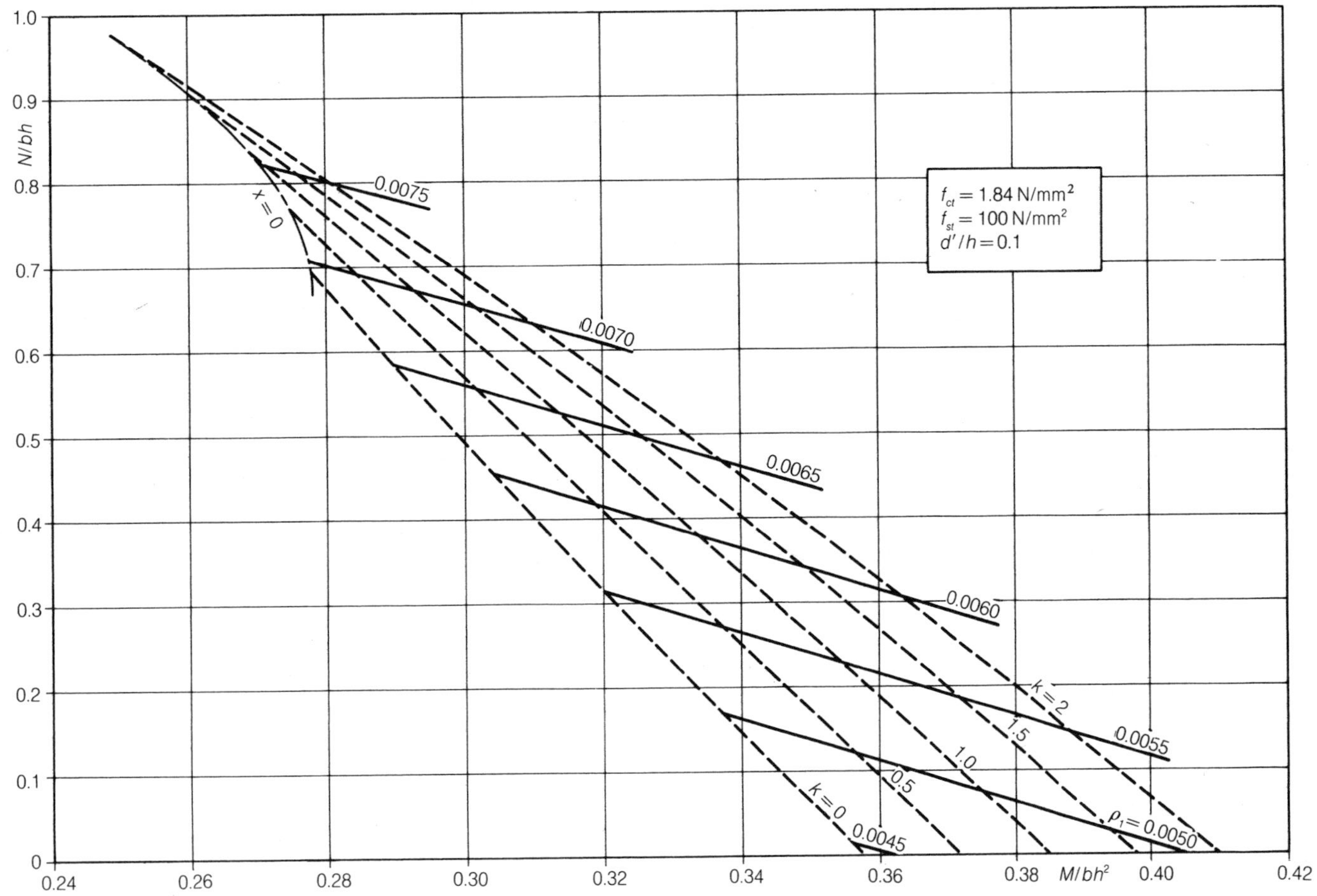

Note: tension steel required $= \rho_1 bh$. Compression steel required $= k\rho_1 bh$.

redistribution undertaken is unknown but the ultimate moment provided at midspan clearly exceeds the calculated elastic moment due to ultimate loads, f_s may be taken as $5f_y/8$. In such a case the tension-reinforcement multiplier is directly related to f_y and ρ, and the scale given for f_y can be used rather than that for f_s.

Where the slabs span in two directions the same design procedure and limiting conditions apply; the shorter span and the amount of reinforcement provided in this direction are considered to control the design.

For flat-slab designs the minimum effective depths obtained by the foregoing procedure can be used directly in cases where each panel has a total width of drop of at least one-third of the corresponding span in each direction. If this is not the case, the final effective depth should be multiplied by 1.11.

For flanged sections the design procedure is as already described, but the effective depth calculated should be multiplied by a further factor α, where $\alpha = 5/4$ when $b_w/b \leqslant 0.3$ and $\alpha = 7/(5 + 2b_w/b)$ when $0.3 \leqslant b_w/b \leqslant 1$. The multiplier can also be read from the appropriate scale on *Table 137*. The same requirement applies to hollow-block, ribbed or voided construction, but when blocks are employed b_w may be assumed to include the walls of the hollow blocks adjoining the rib. If the floor is voided or is constructed of I- or box-shaped units, an equivalent effective value of b_w may be determined by assuming that all the material below the top flange forms a rectangular rib of the same depth and having an equivalent area.

20.4.3 Lightweight concrete

For lightweight concrete beams the foregoing requirements apply but the final value of effective depth should be multiplied by 1.18. For slabs, deflections may be calculated from basic principles using the values of E_c obtained from the chart on *Table 79*. Alternatively, appropriate limiting effective depths can be determined by the procedure already described. However, if the characteristic imposed load q exceeds $4\,\text{kN/m}^2$, the final effective depth should again be increased by multiplying by 1.18.

20.4.4 Tapered cantilevers and/or triangularly distributed loads

If a cantilever, which is either of uniform section or tapers towards the tip, supports a uniformly distributed or triangularly distributed load, the effect of the change of section and loading can be taken into account by multiplying the minimum permissible value of d obtained as described above by a further multiplying factor, the value of which can be read from the appropriate scale on *Table 121*.

20.5 REINFORCEMENT IN BEAMS AND SLABS

20.5.1 Arrangement, curtailment and spacing of bars

BS8110 and CP110 requirements. General recommendations for bar curtailment are given in both Codes. Except at end supports, each bar should extend a distance of d or 12ϕ, whichever is the greater, beyond the point at which the resistance provided by the remaining bars is equal to that required. Also, unless a full anchorage-bond length is provided, or $v_c \nless 2v$ or the area of steel provided by the continuing bars is not less than twice $A_{s\,req}$ at the point where the bars stop, no reinforcing bar should terminate in the tension zone. At a free support each tension bar must be provided with either an effective anchorage equal to 12ϕ beyond the centre-line of the support or $12\phi + d/2$ beyond the face of the support (no bend commencing before the support centre-line or at a distance of less than $d/2$ from the support face, respectively). If at the support face the actual shear stress is less than $v_c/2$, according to BS8110, or the actual local-bond stress is less than one-half of the appropriate ultimate value of local-bond stress read from *Table 92*, according to CP110, a straight length of bar must be provided equal to either 1/3 of the support width or 30 mm, whichever is the greater, beyond the centre-line of the support.

For one-way slabs and beams supporting substantially uniform loads, both Codes also give alternative simplified rules for bar curtailment that are summarized diagrammatically on *Table 140*. Basic requirements for two-way slabs are summarized on *Table 50*. For the requirements for flat slabs see section 3.9.2.

Recommendations regarding the minimum spacing of bars are given in both Codes and are summarized on *Table 139*. In addition, to ensure acceptable crack widths, both Codes suggest rules to determine the maximum spacing of tension bars in beams and slabs subjected to normal exposure conditions. The maximum clear horizontal distance between adjacent bars (or pairs or groups of bars) s_b should not exceed the values shown on the chart on *Table 139*. These spacings are calculated from the expression

$$\text{clear spacing } s_b \text{ in millimetres} \ngtr 75\,000\beta_b/f_y \quad \text{or} \quad 300$$

where β_b is the ratio of the resistance moment provided at midspan to that required. In CP110 the tabulated values are rounded off to the nearest 5 mm above those calculated from this expression, and these tabulated values are indicated by the black circles on the chart. The clear horizontal distance from the corner of a beam to the face of the first bar should not exceed one-half of the appropriate tabulated distance.

If h exceeds 750 mm, longitudinal bars at not more than 250 mm centres should be provided in the side faces of the beam for a height of $2h/3$ from the tension face. These bars, which should be not less than $(s_b b/f_y)^{1/2}$ in size, where b is the breadth of section at the point considered, may be assumed to assist in providing the resistance of the section; their contribution may be calculated by using the method in section 20.1.7. Bars having diameters of less than 0.45 times that of the maximum bar size should be ignored, except where provided in the sides of beams to control cracking. The foregoing rules also apply to slabs except that, when $h \ngtr 200$ mm (or 250 mm if $f_y \ngtr 425\,\text{N/mm}^2$), the spacing need not be checked provided that the clear distance between bars does not exceed $3d$. When $\rho_1 (= A_s/bd) < 0.005$, the maximum given spacing may be doubled, while if $0.005 \leqslant \rho_1 \leqslant 0.01$ the maximum allowable spacing may be increased to $s_b(3 - 200\rho_1)$. In all cases the maximum spacing may be

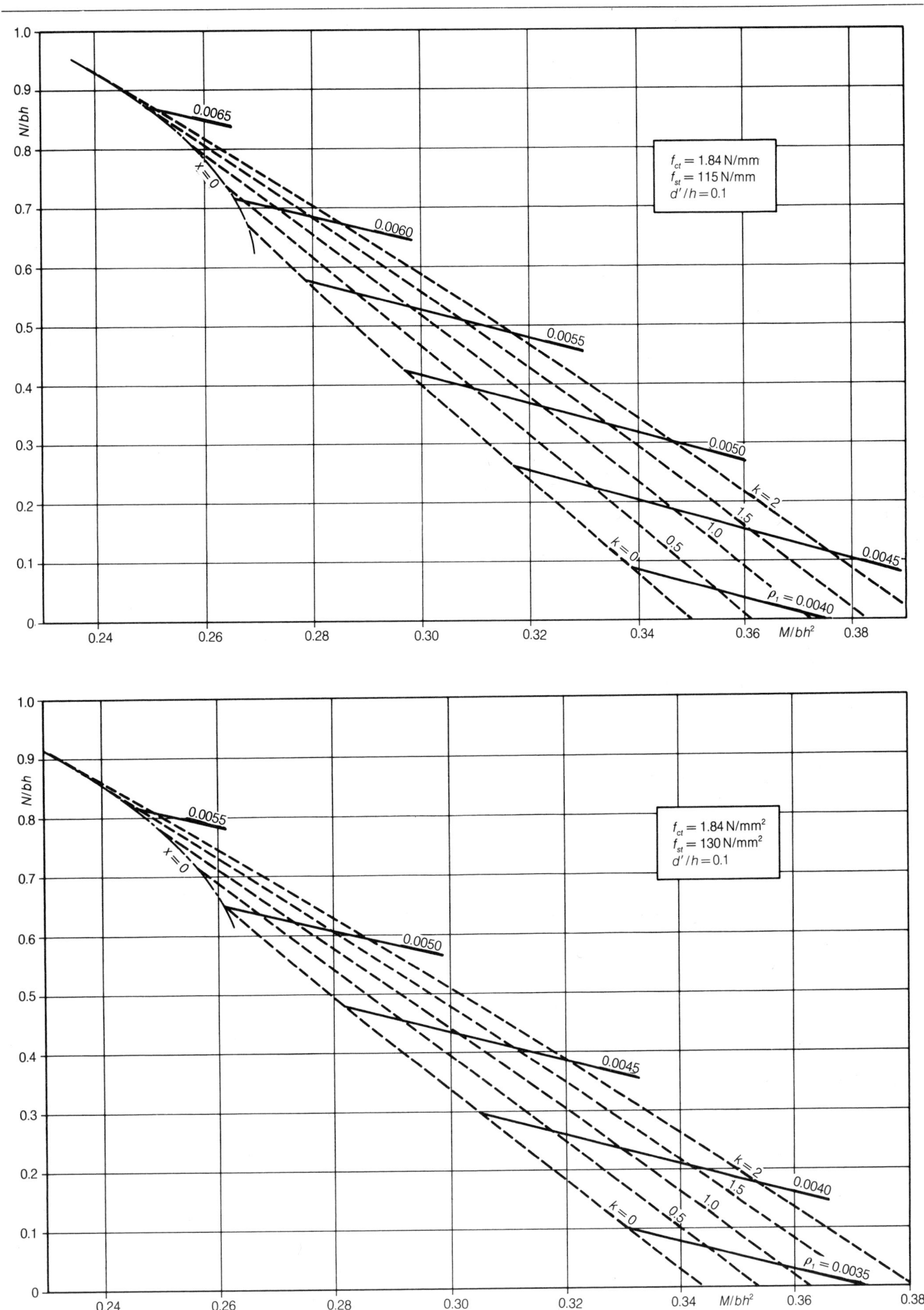

Note: tension steel required $-\rho_1 bh$. Compression steel required $-k\rho_1 bh$.

FORMULAE FOR DEFLECTION: properties of transformed sections

Cracked section

Rectangular section
(and flanged section where $x \leqslant h_f$)

$$\frac{x}{d} = \sqrt{\left\{[\alpha_e\rho + (\alpha_e - 1)\rho']^2 + 2\left[\alpha_e\rho + (\alpha_e - 1)\rho'\frac{d'}{d}\right]\right\}} - [\alpha_e\rho + (\alpha_e - 1)\rho']$$

$$\frac{I_e}{bd^3} = \frac{1}{3}\left(\frac{x}{d}\right)^3 + \alpha_e\rho\left(1 - \frac{x}{d}\right)^2 + (\alpha_e - 1)\rho'\left(\frac{x}{d} - \frac{d'}{d}\right)^2$$

Flanged section
(where $x > h_f$)

$$\frac{x}{d} = \left\{\sqrt{\left\{\left[\alpha_e\rho + (\alpha_e - 1)\rho' + \left(1 - \frac{b_w}{b}\right)\frac{h_f}{b}\right]^2 + 2\left[\alpha_e\rho + (\alpha_e - 1)\rho'\frac{d'}{d} + \frac{1}{2}\left(1 - \frac{b_w}{b}\right)\left(\frac{h_f}{d}\right)^2\right]\frac{b_w}{b}\right\}} - \left[\alpha_e\rho + (\alpha_e - 1)\rho' + \left(1 - \frac{b_w}{b}\right)\frac{h_f}{d}\right]\right\}\frac{b}{b_w}$$

$$\frac{I_e}{bd^3} = \frac{1}{3}\left[\left(\frac{x}{d}\right)^3 - \left(1 - \frac{b_w}{b}\right)\left(\frac{x}{d} - \frac{h_f}{d}\right)^3\right] + \alpha_e\rho\left(1 - \frac{x}{d}\right)^2 + (\alpha_e - 1)\rho'\left(\frac{x}{d} - \frac{d'}{d}\right)^2$$

where $\rho = A_s/bd$ and $\rho' = A_s'/bd$.

Uncracked section

Rectangular section

$$\frac{x}{h} = \left[1 + 2(\alpha_e - 1)\left(\rho_1\frac{d}{h} + \rho_1'\frac{d'}{h}\right)\right] \Big/ 2[1 + (\alpha_e - 1)(\rho_1 + \rho_1')]$$

$$\frac{I_g}{bh^3} = \frac{1}{3}\left[\left(\frac{x}{h}\right)^3 + \left(1 - \frac{x}{h}\right)^3\right] + (\alpha_e - 1)\left[\rho\left(\frac{d}{h} - \frac{x}{h}\right)^2 + \rho'\left(\frac{x}{h} - \frac{d'}{h}\right)^2\right]$$

Flanged section

$$\frac{x}{h} = \left[\frac{b_w}{b} + \left(1 - \frac{b_w}{b}\right)\left(\frac{h_f}{h}\right)^2 + 2(\alpha_e - 1)\left(\rho_1\frac{d}{h} + \rho_1'\frac{d'}{h}\right)\right] \Big/ 2\left[\frac{b_w}{b} + \frac{h_f}{h}\left(1 - \frac{b_w}{b}\right) + (\alpha_e - 1)(\rho_1 + \rho_1')\right]$$

$$\frac{I_g}{bh^3} = \frac{1}{3}\left[\left(\frac{x}{h}\right)^3 + \frac{b_w}{b}\left(1 - \frac{x}{h}\right)^3 - \left(1 - \frac{b_w}{b}\right)\left(\frac{x}{h} - \frac{h_f}{h}\right)^3\right] + (\alpha_e - 1)\left[\rho_1\left(\frac{d}{h} - \frac{x}{h}\right)^2 + \rho_1'\left(\frac{x}{h} - \frac{d'}{h}\right)^2\right]$$

where $\rho_1 = A_s/bh$ and $\rho_1' = A_s'/bh$.

CALCULATION PROCEDURE

Calculate moments and forces		Undertake elastic analysis with working (i.e. service) loads. No redistribution permitted.	Carry out analysis using sectional properties of cracked transformed sections (see formulae on opposite page) to determine stiffnesses etc., taking any axial loads into account. Take E_c as one-half of instantaneous value (see *Table 79*).
Calculate curvatures assuming section is both uncracked and cracked and adopt greater value (usually latter condition is critical)		Cracked section	Uncracked section
	Assumptions	1. Concrete in compression and steel behave elastically. 2. Tensile stress in concrete f_{ct} varies linearly from zero at neutral axis to 1 N/mm^2 (instantaneous) and 0.55 N/mm^2 (long term) at centroid of steel. 3. Linear distribution of strain across section. 4. Elastic modulus of steel $E_s = 200$ kN/mm^2. 5. Short-term elastic modulus of concrete is as shown in *Table 79*; for long-term modulus, divide short-term modulus by $(1+\phi)$ where ϕ is creep coefficient (for suitable value of ϕ see ref. 32 or *Table 79*).	1. Concrete and steel behave elastically in both tension and compression. 2. Assumption 3 to 5 for cracked section also apply.
		Determine properties of transformed section from formulae given on opposite page.	
		Cracked section Calculate curvature $(1/r)$ from $\dfrac{1}{r} = \dfrac{f_c}{xE_c} = \dfrac{f_s}{(d-x)E_s}$ using a successive approximation procedure, where f_c and f_s are the design service stresses in concrete and steel respectively. *Uncracked section* Calculate curvature $(1/r)$ from $1/r = M/E_cI$.	
	Determine long-term curvature	1. Calculate instantaneous curvature $(1/r_{it})$ due to total load. 2. Calculate instantaneous curvature $(1/r_{ip})$ due to 'permanent load' (permanent load = dead load + partitions and finishes + proportion of imposed load, ranging from 1/4 for domestic and office buildings to >3/4 for storage buildings). 3. Calculate long-term curvature $(1/r_{tp})$ due to permanent load (i.e. with long-term elastic modulus). 4. Calculate curvature due to shrinkage $(1/r_{cs})$. According to BS8110, $1/r_{cs} = \varepsilon_{cs}\alpha_e S_s/I$, where $\alpha_e = 200\,000(1+\phi)/E_c$,	S_s is the first moment of area of the reinforcement about the centroid of either the cracked or uncracked section, as appropriate, and I is the moment of inertia of either the cracked or gross section. According to CP110, $1/r_{cs} = \varepsilon_{cs}\rho_0/d$, where reinforcement coefficient ρ_0 may be read from *Table 79*. Values of free shrinkage strain ε_{cs} are given in ref. 32. (*Code Handbook* suggests $\varepsilon_{cs} = 0.0003$ for sections less than 250 mm thick and 0.000 25 otherwise.) 5. Then total long-term curvature $\dfrac{1}{r_{tt}} = \dfrac{1}{r_{tp}} + \dfrac{1}{r_{it}} + \dfrac{1}{r_{cs}} - \dfrac{1}{r_{ip}}$
Calculate deflection	Basic method	Plot diagram of curvature $1/r$ along member and integrate twice using Simpson's rule or Newmark's numerical method (ref. 129) to obtain deflection.	
	Alternative simplified method	Calculate deflection a from $a = Kl^2/r_b$, where l is effective span, $1/r_b$ is curvature at midspan for freely supported or continuous member and at support for cantilever and K is coefficient depending on type of loading and support conditions: K is obtained by dividing numerical coefficient	relating to deflection at point being considered by maximum bending moment on member: values of K for selected loadings are given in *Code Handbook* or may be calculated for any load from data on *Tables 23* to *28*.

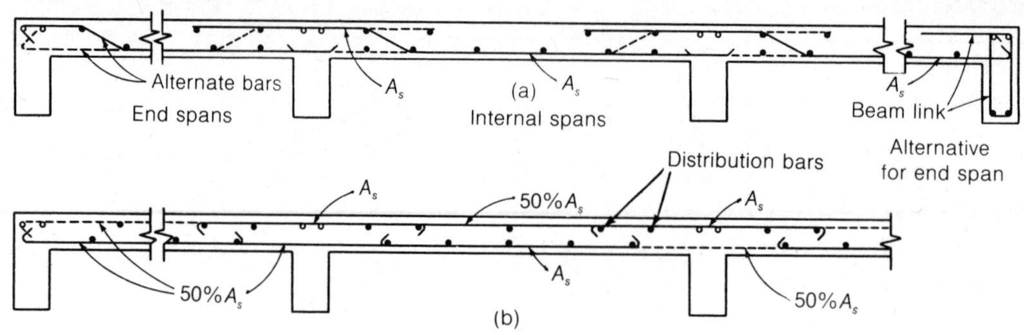

increased if desired by multiplying the given value of s_b by the ratio $A_{s\,prov}/A_{s\,req}$ according to CP110; for more detailed information see *Table 139*.

Alternatively, both Codes permit these limiting spacings to be exceeded if it can be shown by calculation that the resulting surface crack widths do not generally exceed the limiting values specified. The calculation procedure that must be followed to undertake such calculations is illustrated by the flow chart that forms *Table 138*. Details and examples of the calculations required are included in *Examples of the Design of Buildings*.

Curtailment of bars: general. The positions at which some of the main tension bars near the bottom of a beam can be terminated or bent up can be estimated from the data in *Table 140*. The positions indicated by the coefficients k_1, k_2 and k_3 are those at which specific bars are no longer required as tension reinforcement. These coefficients have been calculated on the assumption that the span concerned is either freely supported or is a member of a system of approximately equal spans all of which are loaded with similar uniform loads.

Details of the general requirements of BS8110 and CP110 regarding bar curtailment are summarized near the top of this table, and a formula is also given by which the curtailment points for tension and compression bars can be calculated for uniformly loaded spans when the two support moments differ.

Main bars. Various typical arrangements for the main reinforcement in slabs are illustrated in the above diagram. Ordinary floor slabs are generally detailed as in the design in diagram (a). When the imposed load is so large compared with the dead load that reinforcement against negative bending moments is required in the middle of the span, the design in diagram (b) is suitable. Hooks or similar end anchorages are not generally necessary on bars in slabs, except at the outer supports of end spans. In design (b), hooks should be provided if the bars end in the tension zone.

The spacing of the main bars in a slab should not exceed three times the effective depth of the slab. For slabs spanning in two directions, the spacing of the bars in either direction should not exceed three times the effective depth, and the bars across the shorter span should at midspan be under, and at the supports over, the bars at right angles to this span.

The spacing of the secondary bars must not exceed $3d$ according to BS8110 and $5d$ according to CP110.

20.5.2 Limiting amounts of reinforcement

According to BS8110 the minimum amount of main tension reinforcement provided in a rectangular beam or slab should be $0.0024bh$ with mild steel and $0.0013bh$ with high-yield steel. In slabs this minimum proportion must be provided in each direction. Similar minimum amounts of steel (but calculated using the web breadth) apply for flanged sections where the web is in tension and where the web breadth is at least 40% of that of the flange; however, if in such a case the ratio of web breadth to flange breadth is less, the specified minimum amounts are increased to $0.0032bh$ and $0.0018bh$ respectively. Where the web is in compression (i.e. over a continuous support), minimum amounts of $0.0048bh$ (mild steel) and $0.0026bh$ (high-yield steel) for a T-beam and $0.0036bh$ and $0.002bh$ respectively for an L-beam are stipulated. Additionally, a steel area of 0.0015 times the longitudinal cross-sectional area of the flange (irrespective of the type of reinforcement used) must be provided over the top and across the full effective width of the flange near the top face in order to resist the horizontal shearing force. Although not specified in the Code, for good practice the spacing of these bars should not exceed three times the effective depth and they should extend an average distance of at least six times the slab thickness on each side of the beam, the bar ends being staggered. Bars provided for other purposes (i.e. as support steel in a system of continuous slabs) may suffice, provided that the area of steel provided is sufficient.

BS8110 also requires that if compression steel is needed to resist the ultimate applied moment, irrespective of the type of steel used, minimum proportions of $0.002bh$ should be provided in rectangular sections and in flanged sections where the web is in compression (the calculation here being based on the web breadth), and of $0.004bh_f$ (this calculation being based on the flange breadth and thickness) in flanged beams where the web is in tension.

In no case should the amount of either tension or compression steel exceed $0.04bh$.

According to CP110 the minimum amount of main tension reinforcement provided in a beam or slab should be $0.0025bd$ when using mild-steel reinforcement or $0.0015bd$ when high-yield reinforcement is employed. For T-, L-, I- or box-sections the value of b should be the average breadth below the top flange. For secondary reinforcement in slabs the minimum area of steel provided should be $0.0015bh$ when this reinforcement is of mild steel and $0.0012bh$ when it is

Deflection: BS8110 and CP110 simplified requirements

DESIGN PROCEDURE

1. Read, from the appropriate scale below, the basic effective depth corresponding to the given length of span and fixity.

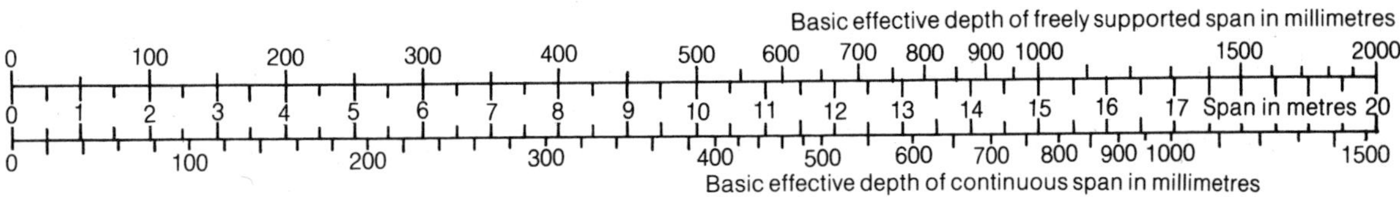

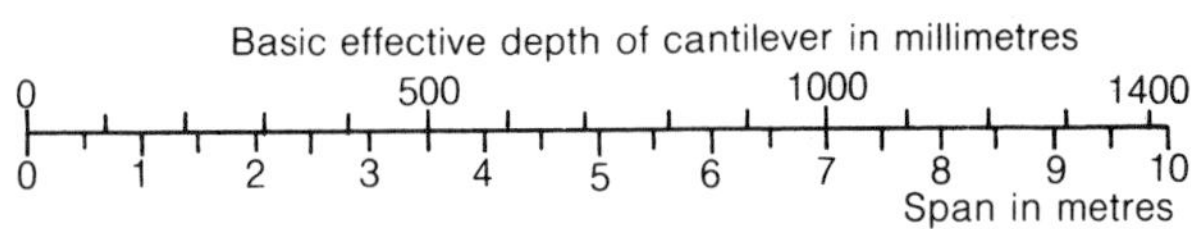

For cantilevers spanning more than 10 m, the minimum effective depth must be justified by rigorous analysis.

2.

BS8110 only:

Multiply the basic effective depth by the coefficient from the graph below relating to the ultimate applied moment and the service stress in the tension reinforcemnt.

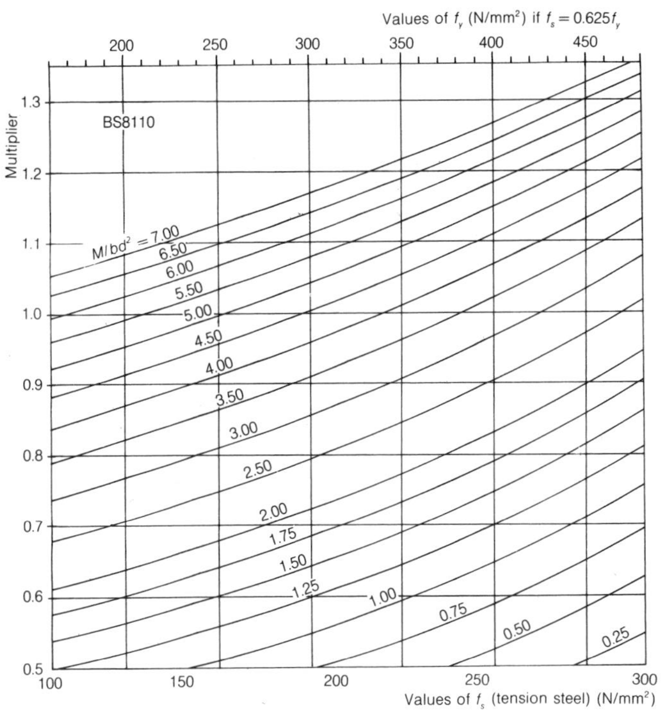

CP110 only:

Multiply the basic effective depth by the coefficient from the graph below relating to the proportion of and service stress in the tension reinforcement.

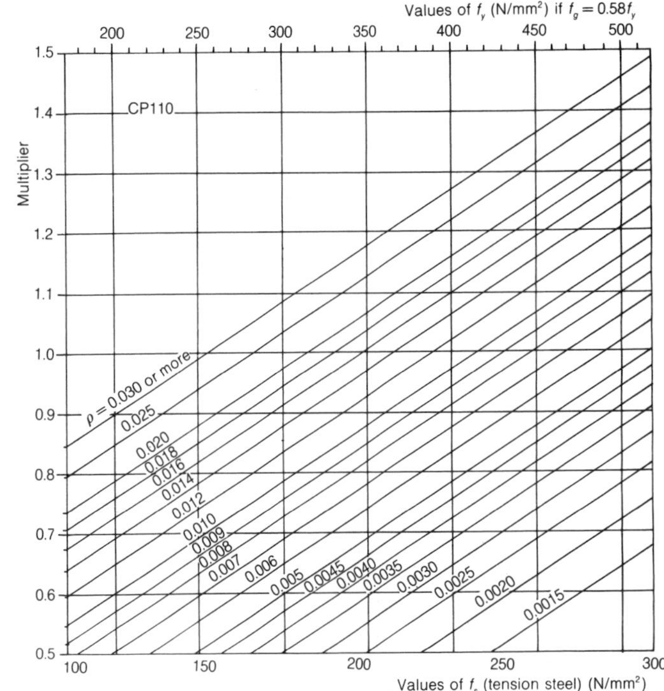

3. Multiply the modified effective depth by the coefficient from the scale below relating to the proportion of compression reinforcement (if any)

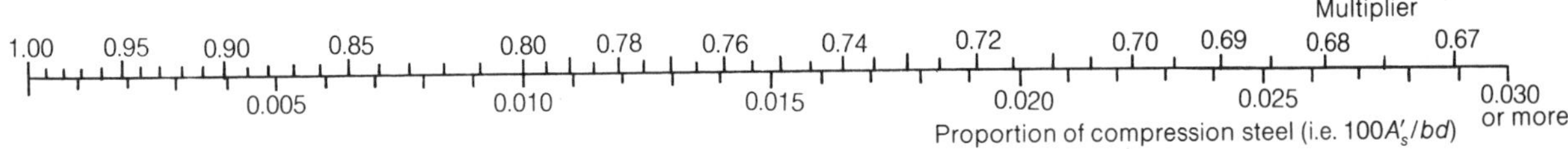

4. For flanged sections (including hollow-block similar floors), multiply the modified effective depth by the coefficient from the scale below, relating to the web width divided by the effective flange width.

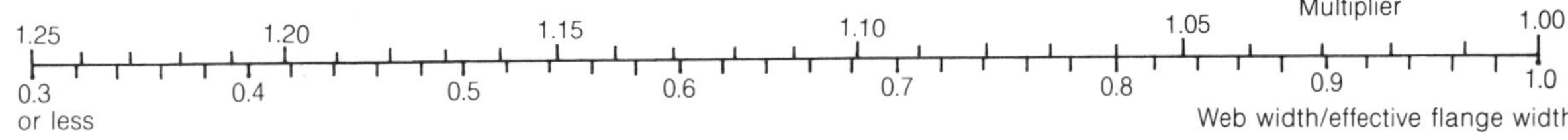

5. For flat slabs not having a width of drop panel in both directions of at least one-third of the total width or length in that direction, multiply the modified effective depth by a further factor of 1.11.

6. Lightweight-aggregate concrete only: for slabs supporting a characteristic imposed load of more than 4 kN/m² and for all beams of lightweight-aggregate concrete, multiply the modified effective depth by a further factor of 1.18.

of high-yield steel. In addition, an area of steel of not less than 0.003 times the longitudinal cross-sectional area of the flange must be provided over the top and across the full effective flange width of all flanged beams. For good practice, the spacing of these bars should not exceed three times the effective depth and they should extend an average distance of at least six times the slab thickness on each side of the beam, the ends of the bars being staggered.

In no case should the maximum area of tension reinforcement or of compression reinforcement provided in a beam exceed $0.04bh$.

Fabricated meshes do not always have sufficiently large transverse bars or wires to provide the foregoing minimum amounts, and any deficiency must be made up by providing an additional sheet or by wiring extra bars to the main fabric reinforcement. There is, however, a range of standard fabrics (see *Table 91*) that have sufficient transverse wires to comply with the requirements of CP110.

Start → Determine moment M_s at section concerned from elastic analysis with service loads → Determine instantaneous value of elastic modulus of concrete E_c from *Table 79* → Calculate $\alpha_e = 400/E_c$

Evaluate x and z (using the following expressions if required)

Rectangular section (and flanged section where $x \leqslant h_f$):

$$\frac{x}{d} = \sqrt{\left\{[\alpha_e\rho + (\alpha_e - 1)\rho']^2 + 2\left[\alpha_e\rho + (\alpha_e - 1)\rho'\frac{d'}{d}\right]\right\}} - [\alpha_e\rho + (\alpha_e - 1)\rho']$$

$$\frac{z}{d} = \left[3\left(\frac{x}{d}\right)^2 - \left(\frac{x}{d}\right)^3 + 6(\alpha_e - 1)\rho'\left(\frac{x}{d} - \frac{d'}{d}\right)\left(1 - \frac{d'}{d}\right)\right] \Big/ \left[3\left(\frac{x}{d}\right)^2 + 6(\alpha_e - 1)\rho'\left(\frac{x}{d} - \frac{d'}{d}\right)\right]$$

Flanged section (where $x > h_f$):

$$\frac{x}{d} = \left\{\sqrt{\left\{\left[\alpha_e\rho + (\alpha_e - 1)\rho' + \left(1 - \frac{b_w}{b}\right)\frac{h_f}{d}\right]^2 + 2\left[\alpha_e\rho + (\alpha_e - 1)\rho'\frac{d'}{d} + \frac{1}{2}\left(1 - \frac{b_w}{b}\right)\left(\frac{h_f}{d}\right)^2\right]\frac{b_w}{b}\right\}} - \left[\alpha_e\rho + (\alpha_e - 1)\rho' + \left(1 - \frac{b_w}{b}\right)\frac{h_f}{d}\right]\right\}\frac{b_w}{b}$$

$$\frac{z}{d} = \left\{\frac{b_w}{b}\left[3\left(\frac{x}{d}\right)^2 - \left(\frac{x}{d}\right)^3\right] + 2\left(1 - \frac{b_w}{b}\right)\left(\frac{x}{d} - \frac{h_f}{2d}\right)\left[3 - \frac{h_f}{d}\left(3\frac{x}{d} - 2\frac{h_f}{d}\right)\Big/\left(2\frac{x}{d} - \frac{h_f}{d}\right)\right] \times \frac{h_f}{d} + 6(\alpha_e - 1)\rho'\left(\frac{x}{d} - \frac{d'}{d}\right)\left(1 - \frac{d'}{d}\right)\right\} \Big/ \left\{3\frac{b_w}{b}\left(\frac{x}{d}\right)^2 + 6\left(1 - \frac{b_w}{b}\right) \times \left(\frac{x}{d} - \frac{h_f}{2d}\right)\frac{h_f}{d} + 6(\alpha_e - 1)\rho'\left(\frac{x}{d} - \frac{d'}{d}\right)\right\}$$

In these expressions, $\rho = A_s/bd$ and $\rho' = A_s'/bd$.

Check stress in tension steel $f_s \ngtr 0.8f_y$ from $f_s = M_s/A_s z$

GENERAL CASE: TO CALCULATE CRACK WIDTH

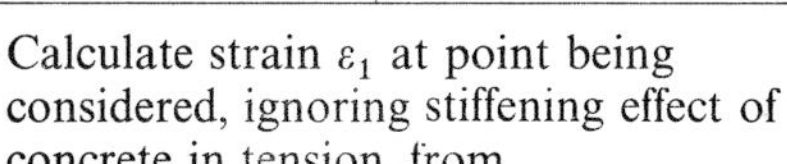

Calculate strain ε_1 at point being considered, ignoring stiffening effect of concrete in tension, from

$$\varepsilon_1 = \frac{f_s}{2 \times 10^5}\left(\frac{a' - x}{d - x}\right)$$

where a' = distance of point considered from compression face

Calculate average strain ε_m at point being considered from BS8110 requirements:

$$\varepsilon_m = \varepsilon_1 - \frac{b_t(a' - x)(h - x)}{600\,000\,A_s(d - x)}$$

CP110 requirements:

$$\varepsilon_m = \varepsilon_1 - \frac{0.0012\,b_t h(a' - x)}{A_s f_y(h - x)}$$

Then design surface crack width

$$= 3a_{cr}\varepsilon_m \Big/ \left[1 + 2\left(\frac{a_{cr} - c_{min}}{h - x}\right)\right]$$

where a_{cr} = distance of point considered from face of nearest longitudinal bar.
Negative value indicates section is uncracked

TO CHECK CRACK WIDTH DOES NOT EXCEED 0.3 mm

Calculate strain ε_h at tensile face (ignoring stiffening effect of concrete in tension) from

$$\varepsilon_h = \frac{f_s}{2 \times 10^5}\left(\frac{h - x}{d - x}\right)$$

Calculate average strain ε_{mh} (taking stiffening into account) from BS8110 requirements:

$$\varepsilon_m = \varepsilon_1 - \frac{b_t(h - x)^2}{600\,000\,A_s(d - x)}$$

CP110 requirements:

$$\varepsilon_m = \varepsilon_1 - \frac{0.0012\,b_t h}{A_s f_y}$$

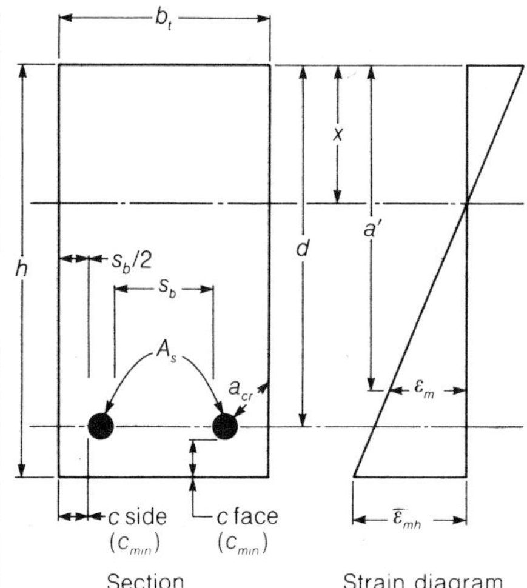

AT TENSILE FACE OF BEAM OR SLAB

Maximum clear spacing between bars

$$s_b \ngtr 2\sqrt{[(a_{cr} - c_{face})(a_{cr} + c_{face} + \phi)]}$$

where

$$a_{cr} = \frac{(1/2)(h - x) - c_{face}}{5\,\varepsilon_{mh}(h - x) - 1}$$

AT SIDE OF BEAM

$$\left(\frac{d - x}{h - x}\right) \nless \frac{0.15\left[1 + 2\frac{(a_{cr} - c_{side})}{(h - x)}\right]}{a_{cr}\varepsilon_{mh}}$$

where

$$a_{cr} = \sqrt{[(m_{min} + \tfrac{1}{2}\phi)^2 + \tfrac{1}{9}(d - x)^2]} - \tfrac{1}{2}\phi$$

Chapter 21
Resistance to shearing and torsional forces

21.1 SHEARING RESISTANCE

21.1.1 BS8110 and CP110 requirements

The ultimate stress v in a section of uniform depth is calculated from

$$v = \frac{V}{bd}$$

where V is the shearing force due to ultimate load.

In beams the ultimate resistance to shearing of the concrete alone v_c (i.e. without the assistance of shearing reinforcement) is determined by the concrete grade and the proportion of longitudinal reinforcement provided at, and extending a distance of at least d beyond, the section being considered. At supports the entire tension steel present may be taken into account provided that the Code requirements regarding the curtailment and termination of bars (see *Table 141*) are strictly observed. A graphical representation of the values of v_c for normal-weight 25 grade concrete corresponding to ρ and f_{cu} given in BS8110 forms the chart at the top of *Table 142*. To use this chart with other grades of concrete, the values of v_c obtained therefrom should be multiplied by the appropriate factor read from the scale beneath. The corresponding data from CP110 form the chart at the top of *Table 143*, on which proportions of ρ between those given in CP110 have been interpolated.

Lightweight concretes have a much lower resistance than normal-weight concrete to shearing, and in clause 5.4 of Part 2 of BS8110 and clause 3.12 of CP110 corresponding values of v_c for such concretes are tabulated. These data are also represented graphically on the charts on *Tables 142* and *143*, the appropriate values being those given in brackets.

According to BS8110, with effective depths of less than 400 mm the concrete shearing resistance v_c increases as d is reduced, as indicated on *Table 142*. CP110 specifies that in a slab having an overall thickness h of less than 300 mm, shearing reinforcement is unnecessary where $v \leqslant \xi_s v_c$, where the multiplication factor $\xi_s = 1.6 - 0.002h$ when $300 \geqslant h \geqslant 150$ mm. Values of ξ_s corresponding to h can be read from the appropriate table on *Table 143*. For slabs for which $h < 200$ mm, shearing reinforcement is undesirable, but for thicker slabs reinforcement must be provided as described below.

Within a distance of twice the effective depth from the support, BS8110 permits v_c to be increased to $2\,dv_c/a_v$, where a_v is the distance from the face of the support, provided that the enhanced value of v_c at the support face does not exceed v_{max}. A similar enhancement may be adopted within a distance of twice the effective depth from a concentrated load.

If $v > v_c$, reinforcement either in the form of links only or as a combination of links and inclined bars must be provided to resist the shearing forces due to ultimate load less the resistance provided by the concrete itself (i.e. $V - v_c bd$, or $V - \xi_s v_c bd$ in the case of slabs designed to CP110). However, even when suitable reinforcement is provided the maximum shearing stress on a section must in no circumstances exceed v_{max}, values of which depend on the grade and type of concrete concerned. For normal-weight and lightweight concretes appropriate values of v_{max} according to BS8110 and CP110 may be read from *Tables 142* and *143* respectively. It will be observed that in the case of CP110 the values for slabs are only one-half of those for beams: although not stated in this Code, it seems reasonable to assume that a section greater than 300 mm in thickness may be considered as a beam for the purpose of this requirement.

In flat-slab design the foregoing procedure should be followed, but if v exceeds v_c (or $\xi_s v_c$ in the case of CP110) shearing reinforcement must be provided in the slab as described below. Note that, as described in clause 3.7.6.2 of BS8110 and clause 3.6.2 of CP110, the shearing force V to be resisted may exceed the true value.

21.1.2 Reinforcement: links

The shearing resistance of vertical links is given by

$$\frac{0.87 f_{yv} A_{sv} d}{s_v} = K_u d$$

where A_{sv} is the cross-sectional area of both vertical legs of the link, f_{yv} is the characteristic stress in the link reinforcement and s_v is the spacing of the links. According to BS8110 and CP110, f_{yv} must not exceed 460 N/mm^2 and 425 N/mm^2 respectively. Values of the link resistance factor K_u for various types, sizes and spacing of link reinforcement can be read from *Table 145*, and the total shearing resistance of such a system may be rapidly assessed by multiplying the

Crack-width criteria: simplified requirements

Limit-state **139**

Notes
Bold lines on chart represent expression for maximum spacing given in BS8110 and *Code Handbook* from which values tabulated in CP110 (indicated by black circles) have been derived.
According to CP110 only, in particularly aggressive conditions, chart only applies when $f_y \not> 300\,\text{N/mm}^2$.

For beams
1. Read off maximum spacing $s_{b\,max}$ corresponding to given f_y and percentage redistribution of moment at section,
2. According to CP110 only, if desired, increase maximum spacing to $s_{b\,max} \times A_{s\,prov}/A_{s\,req}$.

For slabs subject to normal exposure, foregoing rules apply but according to CP110 only:
1. If $\rho_1 \leqslant 0.005$, maximum spacing may be increased to $2s_{b\,max}$; or
2. If $0.005 < \rho_1 \leqslant 0.01$, maximum spacing may be increased to $s_{b\,max} \times (3 - 200\rho_1)$, where $\rho_1 = A_s/bh$.
According to BS8110, if $\rho \leqslant 0.01$ maximum spacing may be increased to $s_{b\,max}(3 - 200\rho)$, where $\rho = A_s/bd$.
In no case may clear spacing exceed 750 mm.

Minimum spacing required for bars or groups of bars
Individual bars or pairs one above the other:
Minimum horizontal spacing required $= h_{agg} + 5$ mm. Minimum vertical spacing required $= 2h_{agg}/3$
Pairs of bars side by side:
Minimum spacing required in each direction $= h_{agg} + 5$ mm
Groups of more than two bars:
Minimum spacing required in each direction $= h_{agg} + 15$ mm
h_{agg}: maximum size of coarse aggregate
In all cases horizontal spaces between bars or groups should be vertically in line.

For slabs, if actual percentage of redistribution is unknown, adopt;

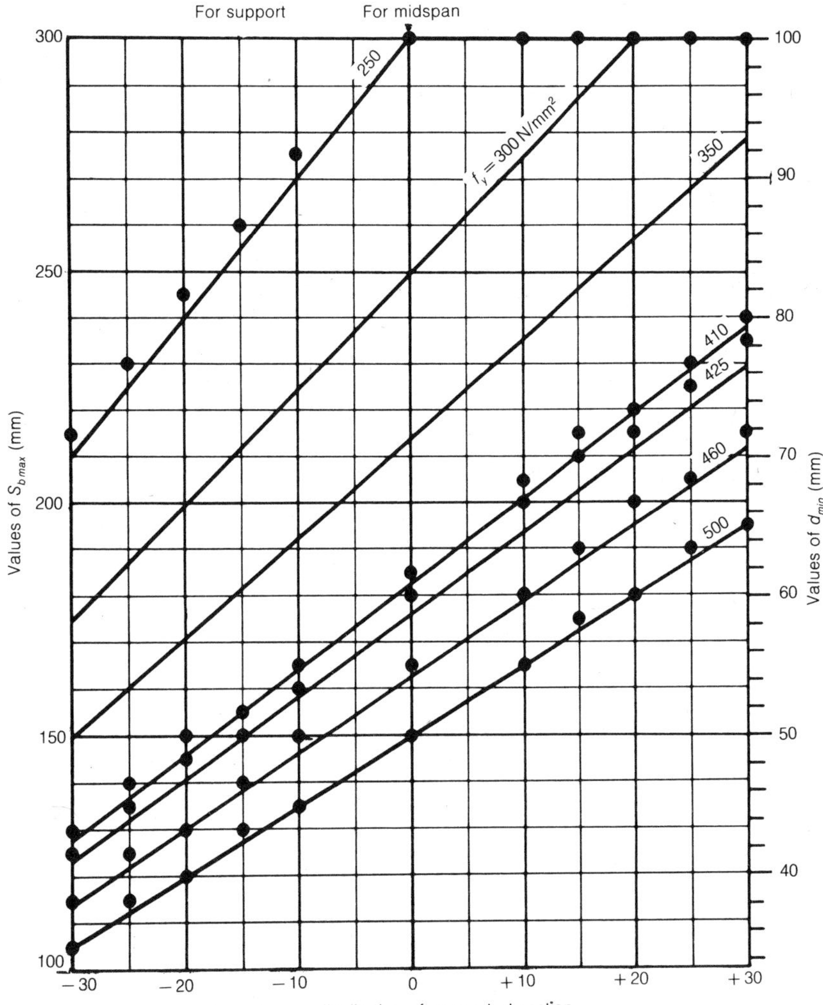

Nominal cover to all reinforcement in millimetres

Exposure rating	Code	Typical conditions	Code	Minimum concrete grade				
			BS8110 CP110	C30* 20	C35* 25	C40* 30	C45* 40	C50 50
Mild	Both	Complete protection from weather or from aggressive conditions	BS8110 CP110	25 25	20 20	$15^{\dagger}$ 15	$15^{\dagger}$ 15	$15^{\dagger}$ 15
Moderate	Both	Protected from heavy rain and from freezing while saturated Continuously under water In contact with non-aggressive soil Subject to condensation	BS8110 CP110	— —	35 40	30 30	25 25	20 20
Severe	Both CP110	Exposed to heavy rain, alternate wetting and drying, occasional freezing while wet, severe condensation Corrosive fumes	BS8110 CP110	— —	— 50	40 40	30 30	25 25
....	CP110	Exposed to deicing salt	CP110	—	—	$50^{\ddagger}$	$40^{\ddagger}$	25
Very severe	BS8110 CP110	Exposed to sea-water spray, severe freezing while wet, deicing salt, corrosive fumes Exposure to sea or acidic water and with abrasion	BS8110 CP110	— —	— —	$50^{\S}$ —	$40^{\S}$ 60	30 50
Extreme	BS8110	Exposed to abrasion (e.g. sea with shingle, acidic flowing water, machinery or vehicles)	BS8110	—	—	—	$60^{\S}$	50

—denotes grade of concrete unsuitable for given conditions
*BS8110 permits these grades to be reduced to C25, C30, C35 and C40 if a 'systematic checking regime is established to ensure compliance with limits on free-water/cement ratio and cement content'.
†Increase to 20 mm if max. aggregate size exceeds 15 mm
‡Grade of concrete suitable only if air-entrained mix is used
§Air-entrained mix must be used if concrete is subjected to freezing while wet

BS8110 also specifies limits for maximum free-water/cement ratio and minimum cement content corresponding to nominal cover values.

appropriate value of K_u by the effective depth of the member. The resistance of link arrangements having other values of f_{yv} are directly proportional to those tabulated. When the shearing resistance of the concrete alone exceeds v, the spacing of the links can be increased to provide nominal resistance only. However, according to BS8110, in beams this spacing should not exceed three-quarters of the effective depth longitudinally and d laterally. BS8110 further specifies that no longitudinal tension bar must be further than 150 mm (measured at right angles to the direction of span) from a vertical leg of a link. CP110 specifies maximum spacings of individual link legs in beams of $3d/4$ longitudinally and laterally, although it permits the spacing in slabs to be increased to that of the effective depth.

Apart from beams of minor importance such as small lintels and the like, where they may be omitted altogether if $v < v_c/2$, nominal links should always be provided in beams. According to CP110 such links should be equal to a minimum cross-sectional area of 0.2% of that of the beam at the level of the tension steel if mild-steel links are provided and 0.12% if high-yield steel is used. Thus for mild steel $b_{t\,max} = A_{sv}/0.002\,s_v$, and for high-yield steel $b_{t\,max} = A_{sv}/0.0012\,s_v$. Appropriate values of $b_{t\,max}$ corresponding to various combinations of A_{sv}, f_{yv} and s_v can be read from *Table 145*, and it is only necessary to ensure that the value of b_t for the section concerned does not exceed that value of b_t given in this table to confirm that the corresponding arrangement of links is adequate as regards nominal reinforcement.

BS8110 does not specify minimum percentages of nominal links as such: instead it requires sufficient links to be provided to give a design shear resistance of 0.4 N/mm^2. However, if $K_u d = 0.4 b_t d$ then $b_t = K_u/0.4$, and thus this requirement can be similarly be expressed as a limiting breadth b_t corresponding to various combinations of A_{sv}, f_{yv} and s_v. To ensure compliance with this Code requirement it is simply necessary to check that the actual breadth of the section does not exceed the appropriate value of b_t given in *Table 145*.

21.1.3 Reinforcement: inclined bars

BS8110 and CP110 permit up to one-half of the shearing resistance provided by the reinforcement at any section to be contributed by inclined bars. These bars are assumed to act as the tension members of one or more single systems of lattice girders, the corresponding compression 'struts' being formed by the surrounding concrete. Each system provides a shearing resistance at any vertical section of 0.87 $f_{yv}A_{sv}\sin\theta$ over length l, where f_{yv} is the characteristic strength of the bar reinforcement, A_{sv} is the area of this reinforcement and θ is the inclination of the bar; according to BS8110 and CP110, f_{yv} should not exceed 460 N/mm^2 and 425 N/mm^2 respectively. Care must be taken to ensure compliance with the Code requirements regarding anchorage and bearing at the bends.

The ultimate resistance of one or two single systems of different types of bar of from 16 mm to 40 mm in size and inclined at 30° and 45° are given in *Table 144*. For other stresses, the resistances provided are directly proportional to these stresses.

21.1.4 Design procedure

To calculate the shearing resistance of any section the value of v_c corresponding to the grade of concrete and the amount of longitudinal reinforcement provided is read from the graph on *Table 142* or *143* (modified in the case of slabs designed in accordance with CP110 by the appropriate factor ξ_s; or, if BS8110 applies and the section concerned is within $2d$ of the face of the support, by $2d/a_v$) and multiplied by bd. This resistance of the concrete alone is added to the shearing resistance provided by the links, obtained by multiplying the value of K_u for the links read from *Table 145* by the effective depth d, and the resistance provided by any inclined bars; the value for each system of such bars as given in this table is multiplied by the number of systems provided.

To design a member, first evaluate V/bd. If this is less than v_c (enhanced if the design is to BS8110 and the section considered is within $2d$ of the support face by multiplying by $2d/a_v$) no reinforcement is required to resist the shearing force but nominal links should be provided in beams. If v exceeds v_c, decide from inspection whether links only or a combination of links and inclined bars should be provided. If links alone are to be used the value of K_u required is $(V - v_c bd)/d$ (or $(v - v_c)b$) and a suitable type, size and spacing of links giving this value of K_u should be selected from *Table 145*. If inclined bars are to be used the maximum resistance that they can provide is limited to $(V - v_c bd)/2$. Having selected a suitable arrangement of one or more systems giving a resistance of $V_i \leqslant (V - v_c bd)/2$, the balance of the shearing force of $V - v_c bd - V_i$ must be resisted by links. The resistance provided by inclined bars and links can be adjusted to provide a convenient arrangement of steel by deciding which bars can be bent up from the reinforcement near the bottom of the beam and introducing extra inclined bars as necessary. Links are then added to increase the resistance to that required, but care must be taken to limit the value of V_i to $(V - v_c bd)/2$ as described. In the case of slabs less than 300 mm in thickness designed to CP110, v_c should be multiplied by ξ_s in all of the above expressions.

In important members it is advisable to plot the shearing-resistance diagram for the entire beam on the same base and to the same scale as the shearing-force diagram to ensure that the resistance provided exceeds the force. However, for most beams it is generally sufficient to determine the point at which no reinforcement to resist shearing force is required and to calculate the steel required at the point of maximum shear. Between these two points the reinforcement can usually be allocated by judgement.

21.1.5 Concentrated loads on beams

According to CP110, if at any support the distance a_v from the support to the nearer edge of a concentrated load that causes more than 7/10 of the total shearing force at that support is less than $2d$, the shearing resistance v_c of the concrete alone (obtained from the graph on *Table 143*) may be increased to $2dv_c/a_v$, providing that the resulting value does not exceed the maximum permissible shearing stress in beams, read from the appropriate scales on the same tables. In such a case all the main reinforcement must extend

Rectangular beams and slabs: detailing per BS8110 and CP110

140

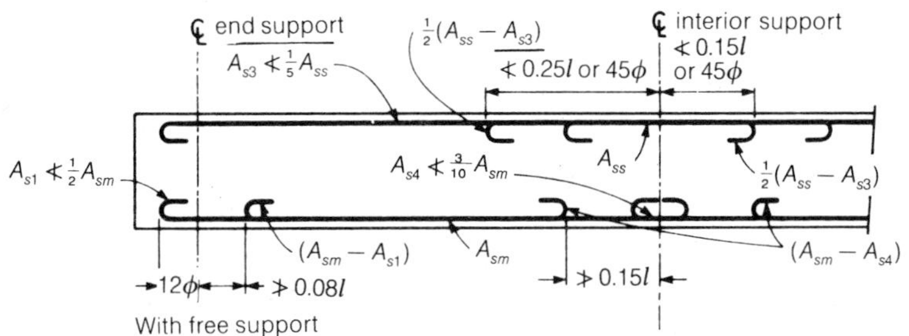

℄ end support

$A_{s1} \nless \frac{1}{2}A_{sm}$

$\ngtr 0.1l$ $(A_{sm} - A_{s1})$

Monolithic with supporting member (according to CP110 only)

Continuous beam

BS8110: spans approximately equal.
CP110: $q \ngtr g$ and designed using values given by Code coefficients.

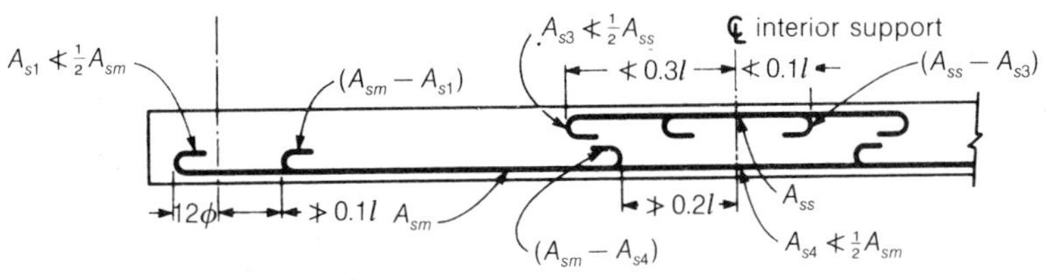

With free support

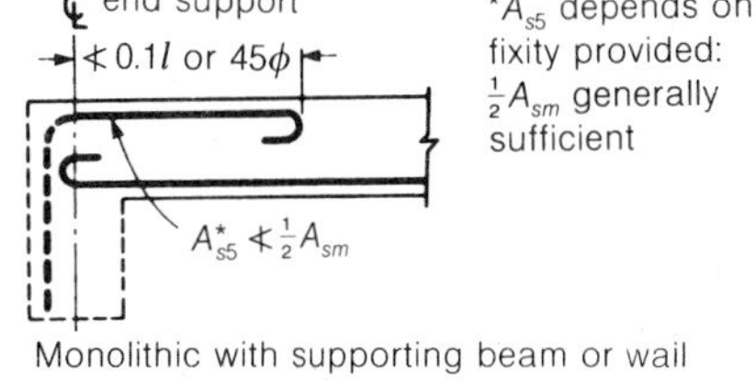

Monolithic with supporting beam or wail

Continuous slab

CP110: $q \ngtr g$ and designed using values given by Code coefficients.

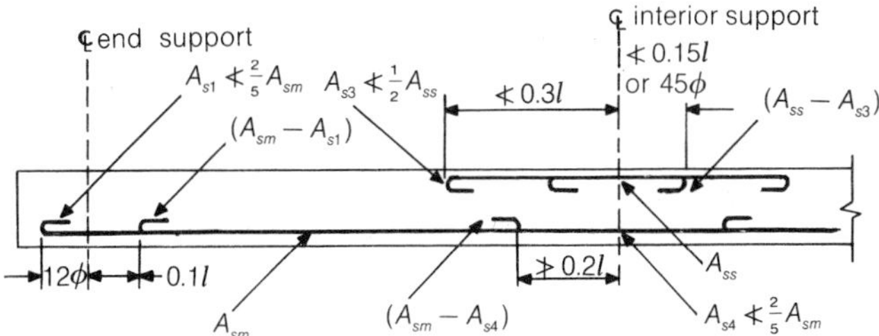

Continuous slab

BS8110: spans approximately equal with simplified load arrangement.

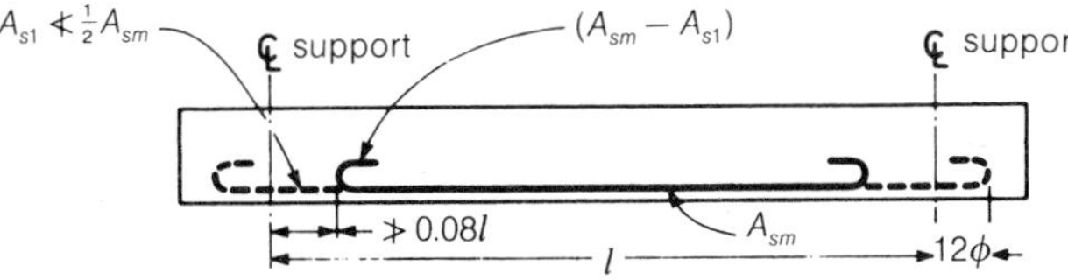

Freely supported beam or slab

BS8110 and CP110

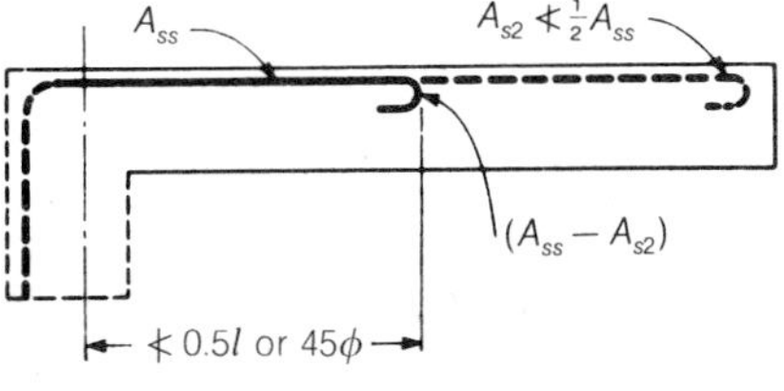

Cantilevered beam or slab

Anchorages must comply with either of the following requirements

The simplified requirements illustrated are in accordance with clauses 3.12.10.2 and 3.12.10.3 of BS8110 and clauses 3.11.7.2 and 3.11.7.3 of CP110 and apply to members supporting substantially uniform loads.

If A_{sm} is the area of tension steel required in the bottom of the member at midspan, and A_{ss} is the area of tension steel required in the top of the member over a support, then A_{s1} to A_{s5} are the areas of tension reinforcement required at various points, in terms of A_{sm} and A_{ss}, and terminating at the positions indicated.

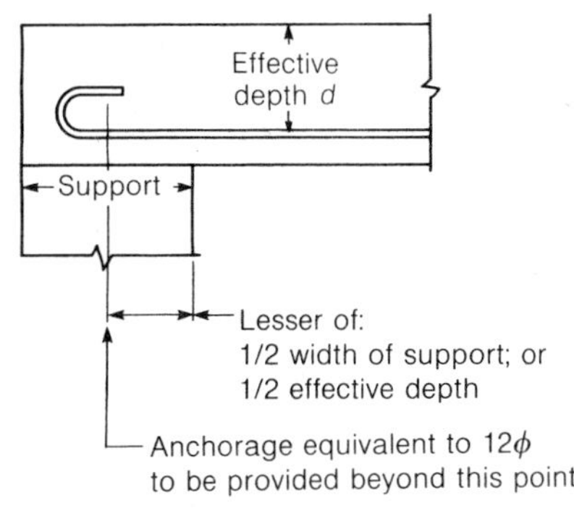

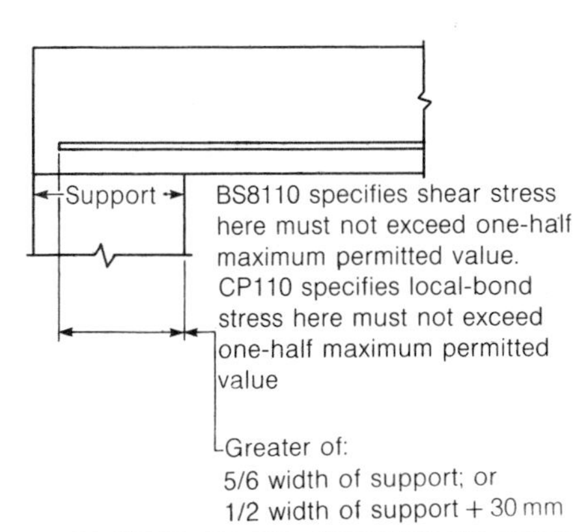

to the support in question and have an anchorage length equivalent to 20ϕ. If $a_v < 3d/5$, horizontal links should normally be provided in cantilevered beams and corbels. More extensive information on the design of such corbels is given in the sections of BS8110 and CP110 dealing with precast concrete: the typical detail given on *Table 172* is based on these recommendations and is compiled from information given in refs 82 and 83.

The increase in shearing resistance close to a support described above is also permitted in BS8110, where it is not solely restricted to the support of concentrated loads.

21.1.6 Concentrated loads on slabs

BS8110 requires that the punching shear which results due to the action of concentrated loads on slabs is treated in a similar manner to that occurring around the heads of columns supporting flat slabs. Details of the design procedure required in such cases according to BS8110 are summarized at the foot of *Table 64*.

The analytical method described in CP110 is similar but the position and shape of the critical shear perimeter differ. According to CP110, where a solid slab is subjected to a concentrated load N, the critical perimeter for shear is located at a distance of $3h/2$ from the edge of the load, as shown in the accompanying sketch (a). The length of this critical perimeter u_{crit} is thus $u + 3\pi h$, where u is the perimeter of the loaded area itself. The value of v_c for the slab should be determined from *Table 143*, the appropriate value of ρ used being the average for both slab directions and considering all tension reinforcement within a strip of width $(a + 6h)$, where a is the width of the loaded area in the direction considered, which extends a distance d beyond the section being considered. Then if

$$\xi_s v_c \geqslant \frac{N}{(u + 3\pi h)d}$$

no shear reinforcement is required. If $h \nless 200$ mm and

$$\xi_s v_c < \frac{N}{(u + 3\pi h)d} < v_{max}$$

where v_{max} is the maximum permissible shearing stress in slabs, shear reinforcement having a total area of

$$A_{sv} = \frac{N - v_c(u + 3\pi h)d}{0.87 f_{yv}} \quad \text{or} \quad \frac{0.4(u + 3\pi h)d}{0.87 f_{yv}}$$

whichever is the greater, should be provided along the critical perimeter and an equal amount parallel to and at a distance of $3h/4$ within it. Similar assessments should also be undertaken at progressive distances of $3h/4$ outwards from the load and appropriate amounts of shear reinforcement provided as described where $v > \xi_s v_c$. Vertical or inclined links not exceeding $3h/4$ apart with both ends passing around the main slab reinforcement should form any shear reinforcement required. To achieve satisfactory anchorage it is also recommended that the diameter of such links should not exceed $h/25$ if vertical or $h/20$ if inclined at 45°.

Because of difficulties in assembling and positioning the inclined links it is normal to prefabricate cages, sometimes known as 'shear hats', as illustrated in diagram (b). Links are the only type of such reinforcement considered in BS8110 and CP110, but other regulations (such as the ACI Code) permit the use of certain assemblies of rolled steel sections: see ref. 29.

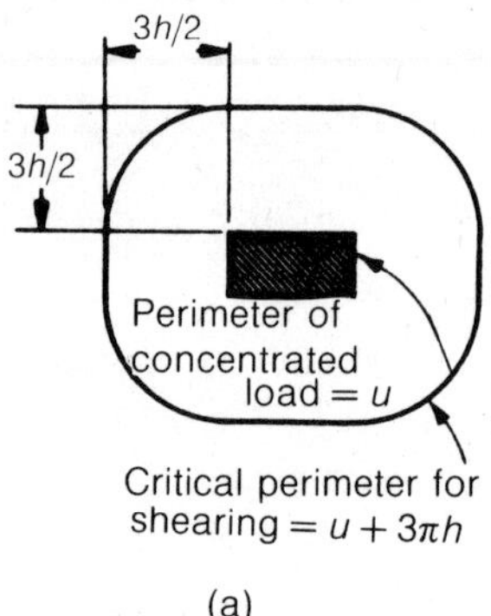

(a)

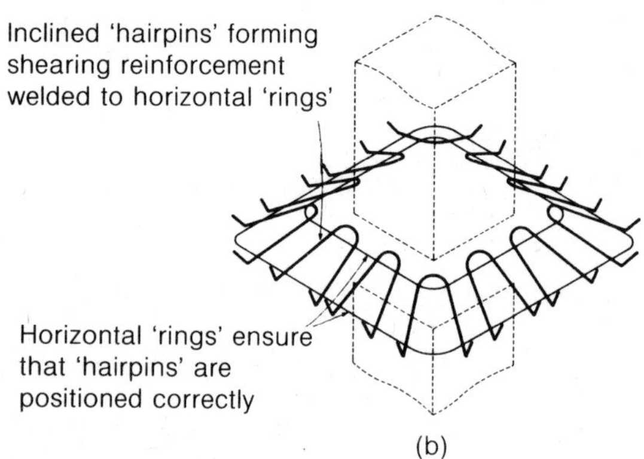

(b)

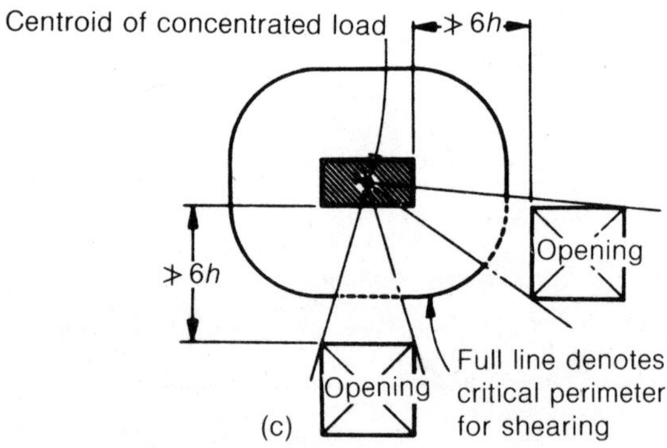

(c)

When an opening occurs in the slab within a distance of $6h$ from the edge of the concentrated load, the shearing resistance of the portion of the critical perimeter that lies within the angle subtended by the opening (see sketch (c)) should be neglected in the foregoing calculations. Regan (ref. 84) suggests that the Code requirement is conservative.

The foregoing analysis assumes that the shearing force is distributed uniformly around the critical perimeter. If this force results from markedly eccentric loading at an internal column this will not be so, and Regan suggests that the shearing force v_c should accordingly be multiplied by $1 + 12.5\ (M/Vl)$. This expression corresponds to that given in clause 3.6.2 of CP110, where it is introduced to make further allowance for the reduction in strength that may occur when large moments combined with high shearing forces are transmitted to internal columns.

Rectangular beams and slabs: curtailment of bars

Curtailment procedure

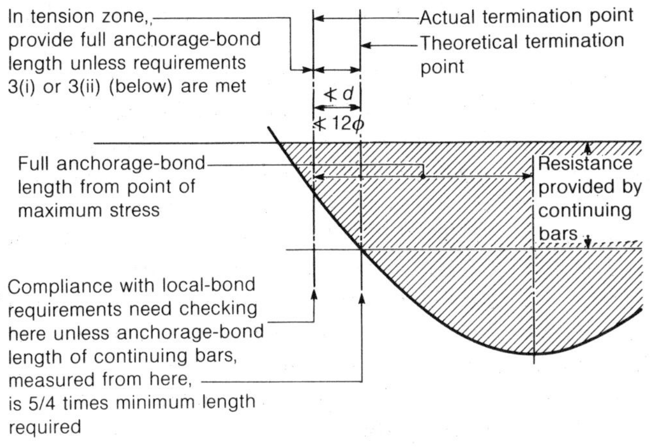

Procedure

1. Sketch bending-moment envelope.
2. Determine theoretical termination point by calculating resistance provided by reinforcement not being terminated and plotting on diagram.
3. Minimum distance to termination point is now as follows: in compression zone, either d or 12ϕ, whichever is greater; in tension zone, either d or 12ϕ, whichever is greater. In addition, full anchorage length must be provided beyond theoretical termination point unless, at *actual* termination point,

either (i) continuing reinforcement provides at least twice the area theoretically required

or (ii) shear capacity provided is at least twice that theoretically required.

General case for uniform load and unequal support moments

Coefficients k and k' corresponding to curtailment points P for a given span moment M_k can be calculated from the expression

$$\frac{k}{k'} = K \mp \sqrt{\left(K^2 - \frac{2(M_L + M_k)}{nl^2}\right)}$$

where

$$K = \tfrac{1}{2} + \left(\frac{M_L - M_R}{nl^2}\right)$$

and n is load per unit length. (To calculate curtailment points over negative areas of diagram, take M_k as negative quantity.)

Coefficients for uniform load and single or approximately equal continuous spans

Position P at which bars in the bottom of beams can be stopped or bent up.	Coefficient	Order of stopping-off or bending-up bars	Number of bars at midspan 1	2	3	4	5	6	7	8
Maximum distance from support P is kl.	k_1	1st	0	0.146	0.211	0.250	0.276	0.296	0.311	0.323
If bar is not bent up at P, a sufficient bond length beyond P must be provided.		2nd		0	0.092	0.146	0.184	0.211	0.233	0.250
In case of continuous spans, coefficients calculated by assuming imposed load only acts on infinite system of equal spans.		3rd			0	0.067	0.113	0.146	0.173	0.194
		4th				0	0.053	0.092	0.122	0.146
		5th					0	0.044	0.077	0.105
		6th						0	0.037	0.067
		7th							0	0.032
		8th								0
	k_2	1st	0.106	0.237	0.295	0.329	0.353	0.370	0.384	0.395
		2nd		0.106	0.188	0.237	0.270	0.295	0.314	0.329
		3rd			0.106	0.165	0.206	0.237	0.260	0.279
		4th				0.106	0.153	0.188	0.215	0.237
		5th					0.106	0.144	0.175	0.199
		6th						0.106	0.139	0.165
		7th							0.106	0.134
		8th								0.106
	k_3	1st	0	0.131	0.189	0.224	0.247	0.265	0.278	0.289
		2nd		0	0.082	0.131	0.164	0.189	0.208	0.224
		3rd			0	0.060	0.101	0.131	0.154	0.173
		4th				0	0.047	0.082	0.109	0.131
		5th					0	0.039	0.069	0.094
		6th						0	0.033	0.060
		7th							0	0.029
		8th								0
	k_4	1st	0.092	0.211	0.264	0.296	0.317	0.333	0.346	0.356
		2nd		0.092	0.167	0.211	0.242	0.264	0.282	0.296
		3rd			0.092	0.146	0.184	0.211	0.233	0.250
		4th				0.092	0.135	0.167	0.191	0.211
		5th					0.092	0.127	0.155	0.177
		6th						0.092	0.122	0.146
		7th							0.092	0.118
		8th								0.092

21.2 TORSIONAL RESISTANCE

21.2.1 BS8110 and CP110 requirements

With the exception of a different suggested relationship between the shear modulus G and the elastic modulus E_c, and different relationships between $v_{t\,min}$ and v_{tu} and the concrete grade, the requirements of BS8110 and CP110 regarding torsion are identical. Where torsional stresses must be taken into account the ultimate shearing stress v_t due to torsion on a rectangular section is given by

$$v_t = \frac{2T}{h_{min}^2(h_{max} - h_{min}/3)}$$

where h_{max} and h_{min} are the greater and lesser dimensions of the section and T is the ultimate torsional moment. For more complex sections, such as T-, L- or I-beams, it is recommended that the section be subdivided into its component rectangles in such a way that the summation of the values of $h_{min}^3 h_{max}$ for each of the individual rectangles is as great as possible. This situation is normally achieved by arranging the subdivision in such a way that the length of the widest individual rectangle is as great as possible (see example 2 below). Each component rectangle is now considered to be subjected to a moment of

$$\frac{h_{min}^3 h_{max} \text{ for the rectangle considered}}{\sum h_{min}^3 h_{max} \text{ for the whole section}} \times T$$

If the resulting stress for any individual rectangle is less than $v_{t\,min}$ it is unnecessary to reinforce that rectangle to resist torsion unless it is of major importance. Limiting values of $v_{t\,min}$ for normal-weight and lightweight concretes can be read from *Table 143*.

21.2.2 Reinforcement

If v_t exceeds $v_{t\,min}$ for any component rectangle, the entire torsional moment on that rectangle must be resisted by a combination of links and longitudinal bars that are additional to those already required to resist bending and direct shear. The system of link reinforcement A_{sv} provided should be such that

$$T \leqslant 0.8 x_1 y_1 \frac{0.87 f_{yv} A_{sv}}{s_v} = 0.8 x_1 y_1 K_u$$

where x_1 and y_1 are the lesser and greater dimensions of the link, and K_u is the shearing reinforcement factor corresponding to a particular size and spacing of links and can be read from *Table 145*: f_{yv} should not exceed 425 N/mm^2. Thus to comply with the Code requirements here it is merely necessary to evaluate $K_u = T/0.8x_1y_1$ and to select a link arrangement corresponding to K_u from the table.

The additional longitudinal reinforcement A_{sl} required should be such that

$$A_{sl} \geqslant \frac{(x_1 + y_1)}{0.87 f_{yl}} \frac{0.87 f_{yv} A_{sv}}{s_v} = \frac{x_1 + y_1}{0.87 f_{yl}} K_u$$

where $0.87\,f_{yl}$ is the design yield stress in this longitudinal reinforcement: f_{yl} should not exceed 425 N/mm^2. Again, to meet the Code requirements it is only necessary to multiply the value of K_u giving the link system necessary by $(x_1 + y_1)/0.87\,f_{yl}$ and to select a suitable bar arrangement corresponding to this area of steel.

The maximum permissible spacing of the links, which must be of the closed type, is either x_1, $y_1/2$ or 200 mm, whichever is the least, and these links should be detailed in such a way that the individual component rectangles of the section are bound together. At least four longitudinal bars, one in each link corner, must be provided and the maximum clear distance between them is limited to 300 mm, while the aim should be to distribute the longitudinal reinforcement around each rectangle as evenly as possible. Alternatively, where the longitudinal torsional reinforcement required coincides with bars already provided to resist bending, the additional requirement may be met by appropriately increasing the sizes of the bars used. Although not stated in either Code, the same procedure may presumably also be followed with the link reinforcement, the requirements for direct and torsional shearing being evaluated separately and summed, and a suitable system meeting the overall requirements chosen, taking care that the system selected meets all the individual requirements for both conditions regarding spacing etc. If this procedure is adopted, note that since $K_u \propto A_{sv}/s_v$, it is only necessary to calculate K_u for direct shearing and torsional shearing separately, to add these figures and to select an arrangement from *Table 145* corresponding to the total. Note also that the amount of A_{sl} required is that equivalent to the value of K_u for the torsional link reinforcement only.

Under no circumstances may the shearing stress on any component rectangle due to the combination of torsional and direct shearing (i.e. $v + v_t$) exceed the limiting value of ultimate torsional shearing stress v_{tu} specified. For normal-weight and lightweight concrete, values of v_{tu} corresponding to the concrete grade may be read from *Table 143*. Furthermore, in sections where the greater link dimension y_1 is less than 550 mm, v_t must never exceed $v_{tu}y_1/550$.

21.2.3 Design procedure

The design of direct and torsional shearing reinforcement should be undertaken simultaneously where necessary. At this stage in the design the section dimensions, the amount of main tension steel provided and the values of T and V will generally be known. Evaluate $v = V/bd$ for the section and, by comparison with v_c, determine whether shearing reinforcement is required. If so, calculate $v_c bd$ and decide on the amount of shearing force V_i (up to $(V - v_c bd)/2$) to be supported by inclined bars. Next divide the balance of the shearing force by d (i.e. $(V - V_i - v_c bd)/d$) to obtain the value of K_u required for direct shearing resistance from the link system.

The next step is to allocate the correct proportion α of the torsional moment T to each component rectangle forming the section as described, and to evaluate v_t for each individual rectangle, checking that $v + v_t \leqslant v_{tu}$ or, if $y_1 < 550$ mm, $v_t \leqslant v_{tu} y_1/550$. Where $v_t > v_{t\,min}$, evaluate $\alpha T/0.8x_1y_1$ to obtain K_u for torsion. By multiplying this figure by $(x_1 + y_1)/0.87\,f_{yl}$, determine the amount and hence a suitable arrangement of longitudinal torsional reinforcement to reinforce the rectangle. Finally, sum the values of K_u obtained for direct and torsional shearing separately and

Shearing resistance of concrete without shearing reinforcement

Resistances are in N/mm². First value relates to normal-weight concrete. Second value (i.e. that in brackets) relates to lightweight-aggregate concrete.

Values given are for concrete with characteristic strength of 25 N/mm². For other grades of concrete, multiply value of v_c obtained from chart by multiplier read from scale below.

Proportion of longitudinal reinforcement to be considered is that which extends a distance at least equal to effective depth beyond point being considered, except at supports where total area of tension steel may be taken into account provided that BS8110 requirements regarding curtailment and anchorage are met.

At junction between beam and column where beam is assumed simply supported but where nominal top steel is provided to limit cracking, v_c may be determined according to area of bottom steel at support if anchorage provided complies with Code requirements for detailing freely supported end. Otherwise v_c must be determined from top steel which extends from face into support a distance equal to three times effective depth.

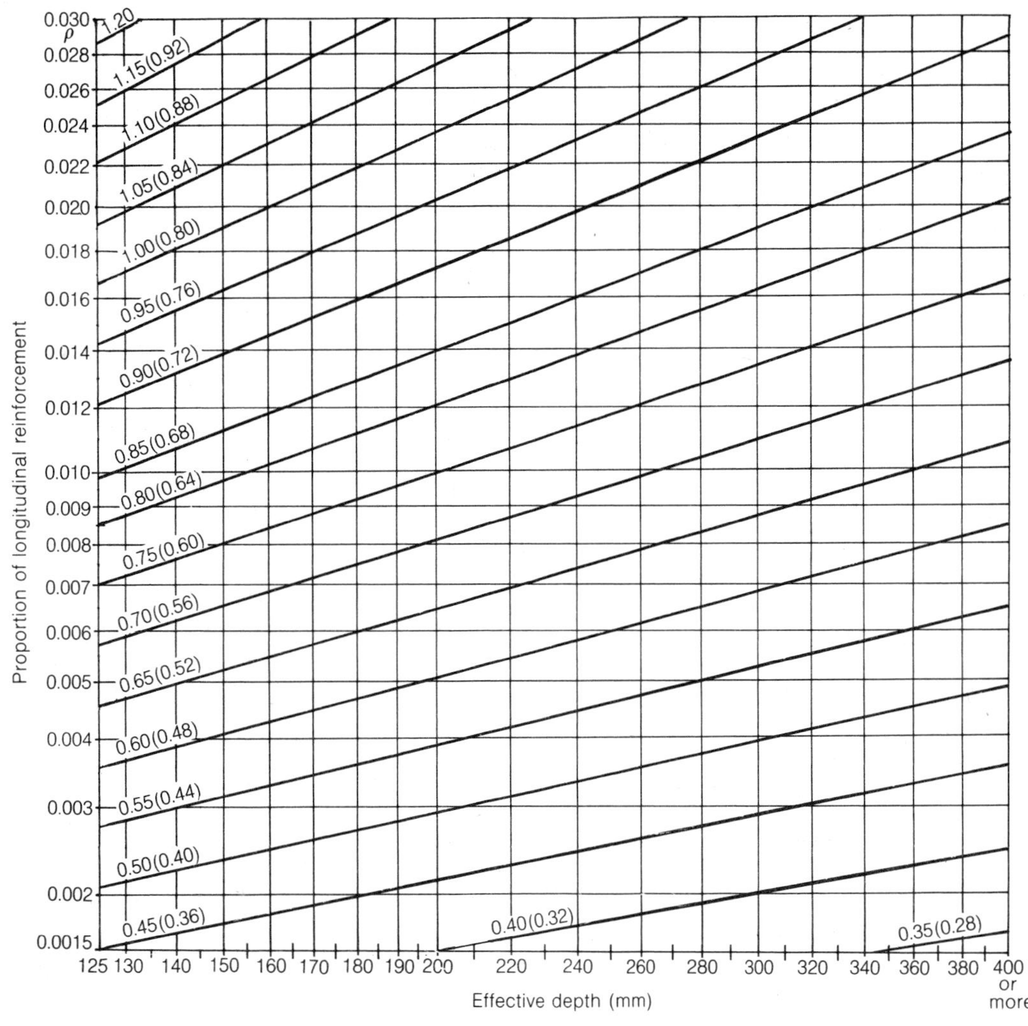

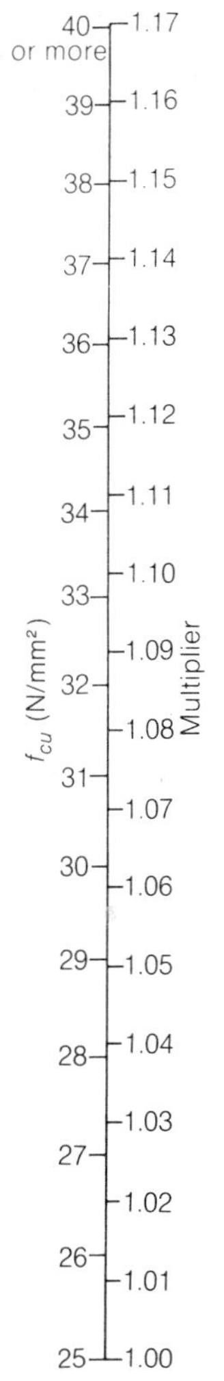

Shearing and torsional resistance of reinforced section (N/mm²)

Concrete grade	Normal-weight concrete: Maximum shearing stress	Normal-weight concrete: Maximum torsional stresses $v_{t\,min}$	Normal-weight concrete: Maximum torsional stresses v_{tu}	Lightweight-aggregate concrete: Maximum shearing stress	Lightweight-aggregate concrete: Maximum torsional stresses $v_{t\,min}$	Lightweight-aggregate concrete: Maximum torsional stresses v_{tu}
20	—	—	—	2.82	0.24	2.86
21	—	—	—	2.89	0.25	2.93
22	—	—	—	2.95	0.25	3.00
23	—	—	—	3.02	0.26	3.07
24	—	—	—	3.09	0.26	3.14
25	4.00	0.34	4.00	3.15	0.27	3.20
26	4.08	0.34	4.08	3.21	0.27	3.26
27	4.16	0.35	4.16	3.27	0.28	3.33
28	4.23	0.35	4.23	3.33	0.28	3.39
29	4.31	0.36	4.31	3.39	0.29	3.45
30	4.38	0.37	4.38	3.45	0.30	3.51
31	4.45	0.37	4.45	3.51	0.30	3.56
32	4.53	0.38	4.53	3.56	0.30	3.62
33	4.60	0.38	4.60	3.62	0.30	3.68
34	4.66	0.39	4.66	3.67	0.31	3.73
35	4.73	0.40	4.73	3.73	0.32	3.79
36	4.80	0.40	4.80	3.78	0.32	3.84
37	4.87	0.41	4.87	3.83	0.33	3.89
38	4.93	0.41	4.93	3.88	0.33	3.95
39	5.00	0.42	5.00	3.93	0.34	4.00
40	5.00	0.42	5.00	3.98	0.34	4.00

select a suitable arrangement of link reinforcement from *Table 145* meeting the various requirements regarding spacing and the like.

This design procedure is illustrated in example 1 below.

Example 1. A rectangular section with $b=200$ mm and $h=350$ mm is subjected to a torsional moment of 8.5 kN m and a shearing force of 100 kN. Design suitable shear reinforcement if $f_{cu}=25$ N/mm^2, $f_{yu}=f_{yl}=410$ N/mm^2 and the main tension reinforcement consists of three 20 mm bars.

Assuming the use of 8 mm links with 20 mm cover and the possibility of 25 mm bars, $d=350-20-8-12.5=309$ mm say. Also $x_1=200-(2\times 20)-8=152$ mm and $y_1=350-(2\times 20)-8=302$ mm. Now $v=100\times 10^3/309\times 200=1.62$ N/mm^2. Since $\rho=942.5/(309\times 200)=0.0152$ and $f_{cu}=25$ N/mm^2, the resistance to shearing of the concrete alone $v_c(=0.77$ N/mm$^2)$ is less than v, so that shearing reinforcement would be necessary even if no torsional moment were present. Assuming that it is decided not to provide inclined bars, the shearing resistance required from the link reinforcement is therefore $100\,000-(0.77\times 309\times 200)=52\,400$ N. Thus K_u required is $52\,400/309=170$.

The torsional stress on the rectangular section is

$$v_t=\frac{2\times 8.5\times 10^6}{200^2[350-(1/3)200]}=1.50\ \text{N/mm}^2$$

and since this exceeds the value of $v_{t\,min}$ corresponding to $f_{cu}=25$ N/mm^2 of 0.33, torsional reinforcement is also necessary. However, since $v+v_t=1.62+1.50=3.12$ N/mm^2 is less than the limiting value of v_{tu} of 3.75, and also since, as y_1 $(=302)<550$ mm, v_t $(=1.50)$ is less than $v_{tu}y_1/550=3.75\times 302/550=2.06$, the section is feasible. Now K_u for torsional links is $T/0.8x_1y_1=8.5\times 10^6/(0.8\times 152\times 302)=231$, and thus the area of longitudinal torsional reinforcement needed

$$A_{sl}=231\times(302+152)/(0.87\times 410)=295\ \text{mm}^2$$

In the compression area of the section provide two 10 mm bars and in the tension area increase the two outer bars from 20 mm to 25 mm in size. Finally, the total value of $K_u=231+170=401$ and a system of 8 mm links at 85 mm centres will be adequate to meet the requirements regarding spacing etc.

Example 2. An L-shaped section having $b=600$ mm, $b_w=200$ mm, $h=350$ mm and $h_f=150$ mm is subjected to a torsional moment of 3 kN m. Determine the proportion of the moment to be resisted by each component rectangle and decide what reinforcement, if any, is required.

If the rectangle containing the web is made as long as possible,

$$\sum h_{min}^3 h_{max}=(200^3\times 350)+(150^3\times 400)=4.15\times 10^9$$

while if the length of the rectangle containing the flange is maximized,

$$\sum h_{min}^3 h_{max}=(150^3\times 600)+(200^3\times 200)=3.625\times 10^9$$

Thus the former case is the critical one. Then the proportion of the torsional moment resisted by the web is $200^3\times 350/(4.15\times 10^9)=0.675$. Thus for the web rectangle,

$$v_t=\frac{2\times 0.675\times 3\times 10^6}{200^2[350-(1/3)200]}=0.36\ \text{N/mm}^2$$

For the flange rectangle,

$$v_t=\frac{2\times 0.325\times 3\times 10^6}{150^2[400-(1/3)150]}=0.25\ \text{N/mm}^2$$

Consequently, if $f_{cu}=25$ N/mm^2 say, $v_{t\,min}=0.33$ and the web rectangle requires reinforcement since $v_t>v_{t\,min}$. However, since $v_t<v_{t\,min}$ for the rectangular flange, only nominal (but nevertheless fairly substantial) torsional reinforcement is essential here.

21.3 BEAMS CURVED IN PLAN

21.3.1 Concentrated loads

If a beam LR (see *Table 146*) curved in plan is subjected to a concentrated load F such that the angle between the radii through the point of application F of F and the centre-line O of the beam is ψ_0, the following expressions apply at any point X between F and L (i.e. $\psi_0\leqslant\psi$):

$$M=M_0\cos\psi-T_0\sin\psi+V_0r\sin\psi-Fr\sin(\psi-\psi_0)$$

$$T=M_0\sin\psi+T_0\cos\psi+V_0r(1-\cos\psi)-Fr[1-\cos(\psi-\psi_0)]$$

$$V=-V_0+F$$

where M_0, T_0 and V_0 are respectively the bending moment, the torsional moment and the shearing force at midspan, r is the radius of curvature in plan and ψ is the angle defining the position of X, as shown in the diagram on *Table 146*.

If X is between F and O (i.e. X′, $\psi\leqslant\psi_0$), the terms containing F are equal to zero. If X is between O and R (i.e. X″), the signs of the terms containing $\sin\psi$ should also be reversed.

Now by writing $M_0=K_1Fr$, $T_0=K_2Fr$ and $V_0=K_3F$,

$$K_1=\frac{k_1}{k_2}$$

$$K_2=\frac{k_3k_8-k_5k_6}{k_4k_8-k_5k_7}$$

$$K_3=\frac{k_4k_6-k_3k_7}{k_4k_8-k_5k_7}$$

where

$$k_1=\tfrac{1}{4}(K-1)\sin\psi_0(\sin 2\theta-\sin 2\psi_0)-\tfrac{1}{2}(K-1)\cos\psi_0(\sin^2\theta-\sin^2\psi_0)-\tfrac{1}{2}(K+1)(\theta-\psi_0)\sin\psi_0-K(\cos\theta-\cos\psi_0)$$

$$k_2=(K+1)\theta-\tfrac{1}{2}(K-1)\sin 2\theta$$

$$k_3=K(\sin\theta-\sin\psi_0)-\tfrac{1}{4}(K-1)\cos\psi_0(\sin 2\theta-\sin 2\psi_0)-\tfrac{1}{2}(K+1)(\theta-\psi_0)\cos\psi_0-\tfrac{1}{2}(K-1)\sin\psi_0(\sin^2\theta-\sin^2\psi_0)$$

$$k_4=\tfrac{1}{2}(K-1)\sin 2\theta+(K+1)\theta$$

$$k_5=2K\sin\theta-(K+1)\theta-\tfrac{1}{2}(K-1)\sin 2\theta$$

Shearing and torsional stresses to CP110

Limit-state ULTIMATE VALUES **143**

Shearing resistance of concrete without shearing reinforcement

Resistances are in N/mm^2. First value relates to normal-weight concrete. Second value (i.e. that in brackets) relates to lightweight-aggregate concrete.

Proportion of longitudinal reinforcement to be considered is that which extends a distance at least equal to effective depth beyond point being considered, except at supports where total area of tension steel may be taken into account providing that Code anchorage requirements are met.

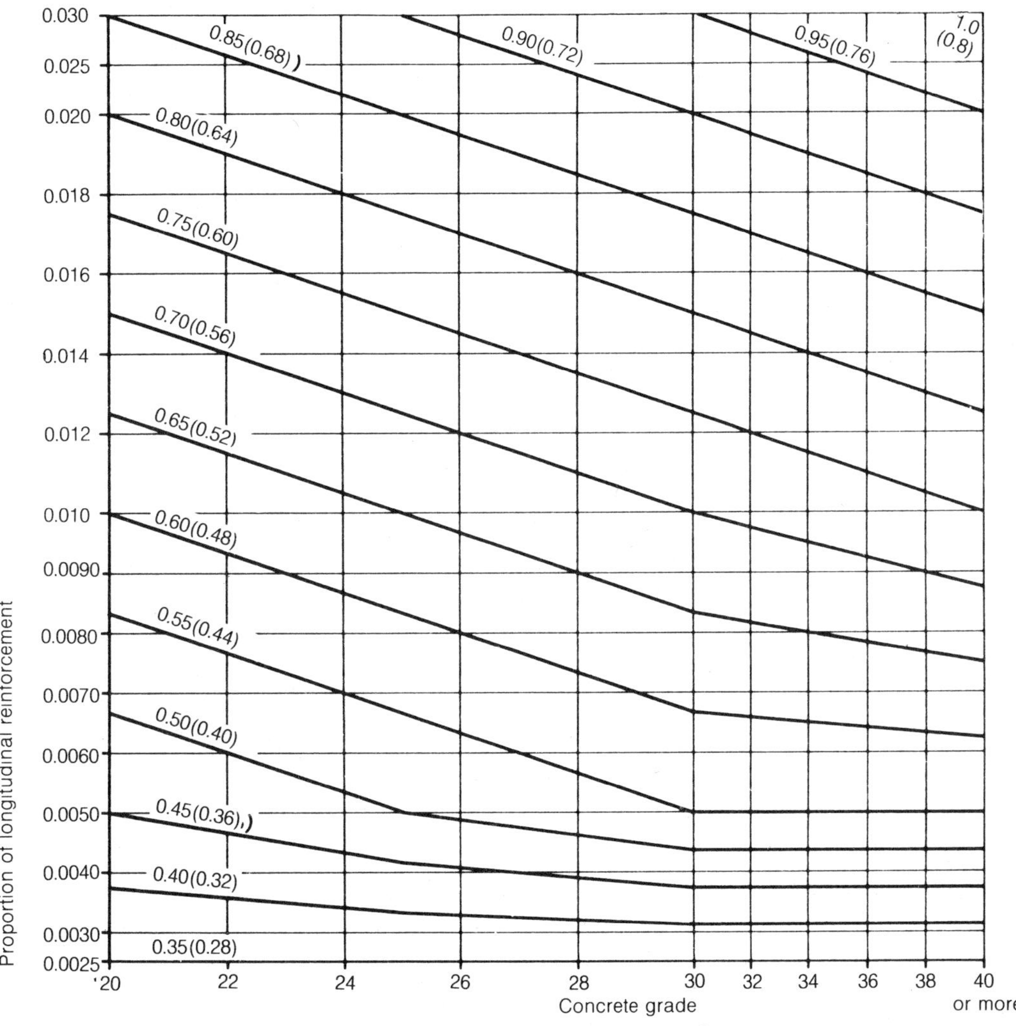

Shearing and torsional resistance of reinforced section (N/mm^2)

Concrete grade	Normal-weight concrete				Lightweight concrete			
	Maximum shearing stress		Maximum torsional stresses		Maximum shearing stress		Maximum torsional stresses	
	in beams	in slabs	$v_{t\,min}$	v_{tu}	in beams	in slabs	$v_{t\,min}$	v_{tu}
15	—	—	—	—	2.30	1.15	0.15	2.00
16	—	—	—	—	2.38	1.19	0.17	2.14
17	—	—	—	—	2.46	1.23	0.19	2.27
18	—	—	—	—	2.53	1.27	0.20	2.41
19	—	—	—	—	2.61	1.30	0.22	2.54
20	3.35	1.68	0.30	3.35	2.68	1.34	0.24	2.68
21	3.43	1.72	0.31	3.43	2.75	1.37	0.25	2.75
22	3.52	1.76	0.31	3.52	2.81	1.41	0.25	2.81
23	3.60	1.80	0.32	3.60	2.88	1.44	0.26	2.88
24	3.67	1.84	0.33	3.67	2.94	1.47	0.26	2.94
25	3.75	1.87	0.33	3.75	3.00	1.50	0.27	3.00
26	3.82	1.91	0.34	3.82	3.06	1.53	0.27	3.06
27	3.89	1.95	0.35	3.89	3.12	1.56	0.28	3.12
28	3.96	1.98	0.35	3.96	3.17	1.59	0.29	3.17
29	4.03	2.02	0.36	4.03	3.23	1.61	0.29	3.23
30	4.10	2.05	0.37	4.10	3.28	1.64	0.30	3.28
32	4.24	2.12	0.38	4.24	3.39	1.70	0.30	3.39
34	4.37	2.19	0.39	4.37	3.50	1.75	0.31	3.50
36	4.50	2.25	0.40	4.50	3.60	1.80	0.32	3.60
38	4.63	2.31	0.41	4.63	3.70	1.85	0.33	3.70
40 or more	4.75	2.38	0.42	4.75	3.80	1.90	0.34	3.80

Slab modifying factor

Overall slab thickness (mm)	Value of ξ_s
150	1.30
160	1.28
170	1.26
180	1.24
190	1.22
200	1.20
210	1.18
220	1.16
230	1.14
240	1.12
250	1.10
260	1.08
270	1.06
280	1.04
290	1.02
300	1

Multiply the value of v_c obtained from the chart by the value of ξ_s corresponding to the slab thickness adopted.

$$k_6 = \tfrac{1}{4}(K-1)\cos\psi_0(\sin 2\theta - \sin 2\psi_0) + K(\theta - \psi_0)$$
$$+ \tfrac{1}{2}(K+1)\cos\psi_0(\theta - \psi_0)$$
$$+ \tfrac{1}{2}(K-1)\sin\psi_0(\sin^2\theta - \sin^2\psi_0)$$
$$- K(1+\cos\psi_0)(\sin\theta - \sin\psi_0)$$
$$+ K\sin\psi_0(\cos\theta - \cos\psi_0)$$

$$k_7 = k_5$$

$$k_8 = \tfrac{1}{2}(K-1)\sin 2\theta - 4K\sin\theta + (3K+1)\theta$$

The graphs provided on *Table 146* enable the factors K_1, K_2 and K_3 corresponding to various values of θ, ψ_0 and h/b to be read directly.

21.3.2 Uniform load

For a curved beam supporting a uniformly distributed load over the entire span, owing to symmetry the torsional moment (and also the shearing force) at midspan is zero. Thus, by integrating the foregoing formulae, the bending and torsional moments at any point X along the beam are given by the expressions

$$M = M_0\cos\psi - nr^2(1-\cos\psi)$$
$$T = M_0\sin\psi - nr^2(\psi - \sin\psi)$$

If $M_0 = K_4nr^2$, where

$$K_4 = 4\frac{(1+K)\sin\theta - K\theta\cos\theta}{2\theta(1+K) + \sin 2\theta(1-K)} - 1$$

these expressions may be rearranged to give the bending and torsional moments at the supports and the maximum positive torsional moment in the span in terms of non-dimensional factors K_4, K_5, K_6 and K_7, as shown on *Table 147*. These factors may be read from the graphs given on that table.

Example 1. A bow girder 450 mm deep and 450 mm wide has a radius of 4 m and subtends an angle of 90°. The ends are rigidly fixed and the total load is 200 kN uniformly distributed. Determine the maximum moments.

From *Table 147*, with $b/h = 1$ and $\theta = 45°$, $K_4 = +0.086$, $K_5 = -0.23$, $K_6 = -0.0175$ and $K_7 = +0.023$, $\psi_1 = 23°$ and $\psi_2 = 40°$.

$$n = \frac{200 \times 10^3}{\pi \times 2 \times 4 \times (1/4)} = 31\,800 \text{ N/m}$$

Then

maximum positive bending moment (at midspan)

$$= K_4nr^2 = +0.086 \times 31\,800 \times 4^2 = 43\,800 \text{ N m}$$

maximum negative bending moment (at supports)

$$= K_5nr^2 = -0.23 \times 31\,800 \times 4^2 = -117\,000 \text{ N m}$$

Zero bending moment occurs at $\psi_1 = 23°$.

maximum negative torsional moment (at supports)

$$= K_6nr^2 = -0.0175 \times 31\,800 \times 4^2 = -8900 \text{ N m}$$

maximum positive torsional moment (at point of contraflexure)

$$= K_7nr^2 = +0.023 \times 31\,800 \times 4^2 = 11\,700 \text{ N m}$$

Zero torsional moment occurs at $\psi_2 = 40°$.

Example 2. If the curved beam in example 1 supports a concentrated load of 200 kN at an angle of 15° from the left-hand support (i.e. 30° from midspan), calculate the moments and shearing forces induced at midspan and the supports.

If $\theta = 45°$, $h/b = 1$, and $\psi = 30°$, $K_1 = 0.015$, $K_2 = -0.0053$ and $K_3 = 0.067$ from the graphs on *Table 146*.

Thus, at midspan,

$$M_0 = 0.015 \times 200 \times 10^3 \times 4 = 12\,000 \text{ N m}$$
$$T_0 = -0.0053 \times 200 \times 10^3 \times 4 = -4240 \text{ N m}$$
$$V_0 = 0.067 \times 200 \times 10^3 = 13\,400 \text{ N}$$

At left-hand support,

$$M = M_0\cos 45° - T_0\sin 45° + V_0r\sin 45° - Fr\sin(45° - 30°)$$
$$= 12\,000 \times 0.707 - (-4240 \times 0.707)$$
$$+ 13\,400 \times 4 \times 0.707 - 200 \times 10^3 \times 4 \times 0.259$$
$$= -158\,000 \text{ N m}$$

$$T = M_0\sin 45° + T_0\cos 45° + V_0r(1-\cos 45°)$$
$$- Fr(1-\cos 15°)$$
$$= 12\,000 \times 0.707 + (-4240 \times 0.707)$$
$$+ 13\,400 \times 4(1-0.707) - 200 \times 10^3 \times 4(1-0.966)$$
$$= -6070 \text{ N m}$$

$$V = V_0 - F = 13\,400 - 200 \times 10^3 = -186\,000 \text{ N}$$

At right-hand support,

$$M = M_0\cos 45° + T_0\sin 45° - V_0r\sin 45°$$
$$= 12\,000 \times 0.707 + (-4240 \times 0.707)$$
$$- 13\,400 \times 4 \times 0.707$$
$$= -32\,400 \text{ N m}$$

$$T = M_0\sin 45° + T_0\cos 45° + V_0r(1-\cos 45°)$$
$$= -12\,000 \times 0.707 + (-4240 \times 0.707)$$
$$+ 13\,400 \times 4(1-0.707)$$
$$= 4220 \text{ N m}$$

$$V = 13\,400 \text{ N}$$

21.4 DEEP BEAMS

21.4.1 European Concrete Committee recommendations

When the ratio of span l (between centres of supports) to overall depth h is less than 2 in the case of a freely supported beam or 2.5 for a continuous beam, the 1970 CEB international recommendations are as follows.

Main longitudinal reinforcement. Design to resist greatest moment, adopting lever arm of $3l/5$ when $l/h \leqslant 1$ and $(l+2h)/5$ when $1 \leqslant l/h < 2$. Use many small-diameter uncurtailed bars securely anchored at supports and distributed over a depth of $(5h - l)/20$ from soffit.

Web reinforcement. Provide mesh of vertical links and horizontal U-bars, giving total proportion of 0.25% of mild

Shearing reinforcement: arrangements of links and inclined bars

Links

Links in rectangular beam

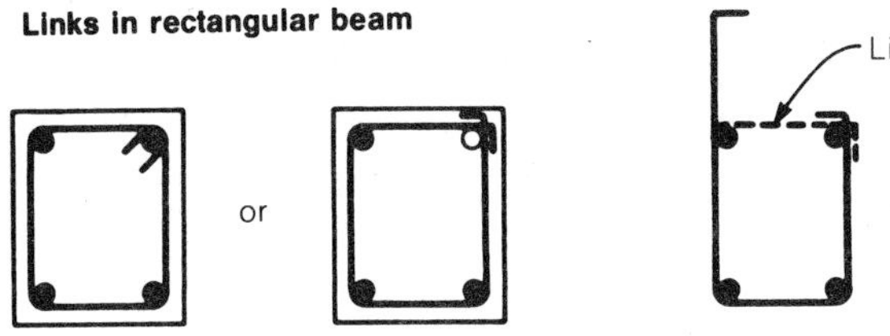

or

Link bent down

Links in T-beams

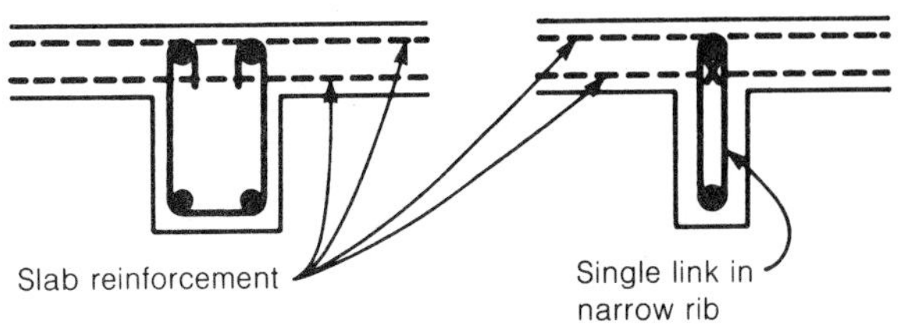

Slab reinforcement

Single link in narrow rib

Links in L-beams

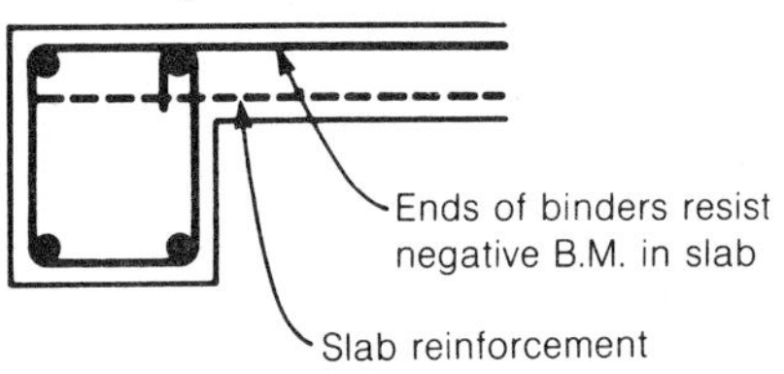

Ends of binders resist negative B.M. in slab

Slab reinforcement

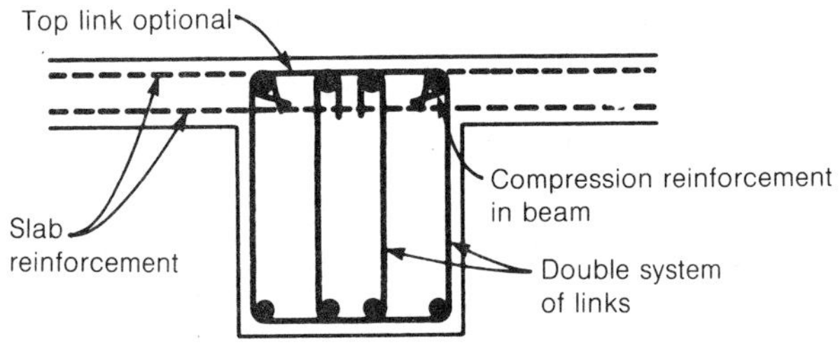

Top link optional

Slab reinforcement

Compression reinforcement in beam

Double system of links

Inclined bars

Equal stress f_{st} in straight and inclined parts

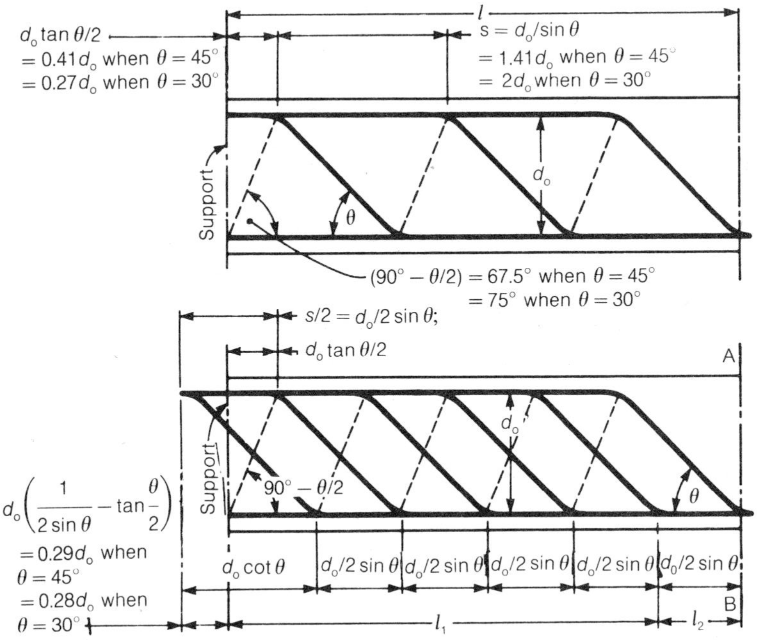

$d_o \tan \theta/2$
$= 0.41 d_o$ when $\theta = 45°$
$= 0.27 d_o$ when $\theta = 30°$

l

$s = d_o/\sin\theta$
$= 1.41 d_o$ when $\theta = 45°$
$= 2 d_o$ when $\theta = 30°$

Support

d_o

θ

$(90° - \theta/2) = 67.5°$ when $\theta = 45°$
$= 75°$ when $\theta = 30°$

$s/2 = d_o/2 \sin\theta$;

$d_o \tan\theta/2$

A

Support

$90° - \theta/2$

$d_o\left(\frac{1}{2\sin\theta} - \tan\frac{\theta}{2}\right)$
$= 0.29 d_o$ when $\theta = 45°$
$= 0.28 d_o$ when $\theta = 30°$

$d_o \cot\theta$ | $d_o/2 \sin\theta$ | $d_o/2 \sin\theta$ | $d_o/2 \sin\theta$ | $d_o/2 \sin\theta$ | $d_o/2 \sin\theta$

B

l_1 l_2

Reduced stress in inclined parts
For common arrangement of bars

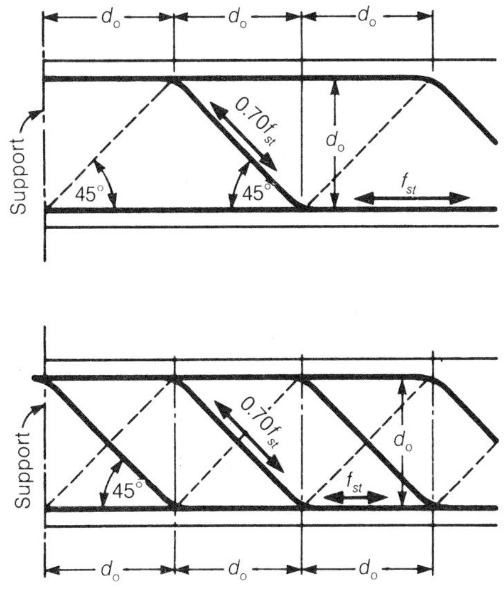

d_o d_o d_o

$0.70 f_{st}$

$45°$ $45°$

f_{st}

Support

Bar size in mm	Ultimate resistance when $\theta = 30°$						Ultimate resistance when $\theta = 45°$					
	$f_y = 250$ N/mm²		$f_y = 425$ N/mm²		$f_y = 460$ N/mm²*		$f_y = 250$ N/mm²		$f_y = 425$ N/mm²		$f_y = 460$ N/mm²*	
	single system	double system	single system	double system	single system	double system	single system	double system	single system	double system	single	double
16	21.9	43.7	37.2	74.2	40.2	80.5	30.9	61.8	52.6	105.1	56.9	113.8
20	34.2	68.3	58.1	116.2	62.9	125.7	48.3	96.6	82.1	164.3	88.9	177.8
25	53.4	106.8	90.8	181.5	98.2	196.4	75.5	151.0	128.3	256.7	138.9	277.8
32	87.5	174.9	148.7	297.7	160.9	321.9	123.7	247.7	210.3	420.5	227.6	455.2
40	136.7	273.3	232.3	464.6	251.5	502.9	193.3	386.5	328.6	657.1	355.6	711.2

*BS8110 only.

Bars in deep beams

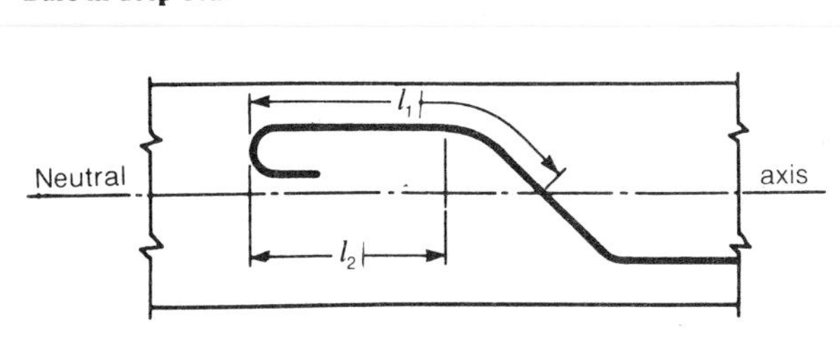

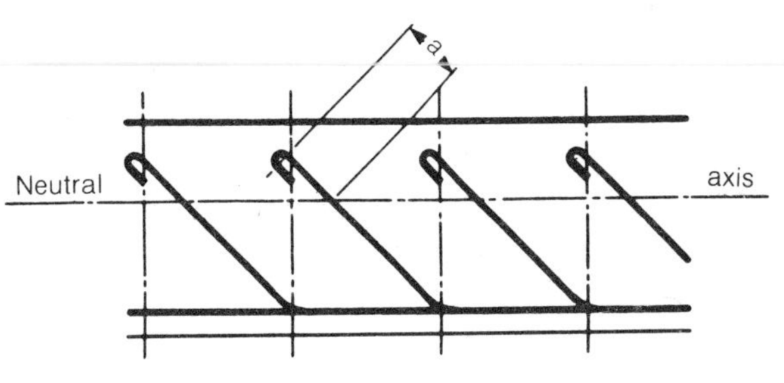

steel or 0.2% with deformed bars, with additional bars (mainly horizontal) in vicinity of supports.

Design shearing force. Must not exceed lesser of $blf'_c/10\gamma_m$ or $bhf'_c/10\gamma_m$, where f'_c is the compressive strength of the cylinders.

21.4.2 Kong-Robins-Sharp method

In ref. 43 Kong, Robins and Sharp propose the following for the ultimate shearing resistance V of a deep beam without web openings:

$$V = k_1[h - 0.35a_1]f_t b + k_2 \sum A a_2 \sin^2\theta/h$$

the notation being as given in *Table 148*. In this expression the first term represents the contribution of the concrete and the second that of the reinforcement, each bar being considered individually to obtain the summation shown. The values of coefficients k_1 and k_2 are empirical, and those suggested on *Table 148* take account of the necessary partial safety factors etc. When calculating the main reinforcement required, the authors recommend a lever-arm factor of $0.6h$ when $l \geqslant h$ and of $0.6l$ when $l \leqslant h$.

If an opening interrupts the diagonal passing from the inner face of the support to the nearer edge of the concentrated load, the modified expression for V is

$$V = k_1[\xi h - 0.35\alpha a_1]f_t b + k_2 \sum A a_2 \sin^2\theta/h$$

and when calculating $A_{s\,req}$ the lever-arm considered should be $0.75\xi h$ when $l \geqslant h$.

The application of the method is illustrated by the following example.

Example. Design the reinforcement for the deep beam shown in the diagram in *Table 148* which supports an ultimate load that (including self-weight) can be represented by the twin concentrated loads shown of 625 kN, using 25 grade concrete and mild-steel bars.

The concentrated loads exert a bending moment of $625 \times 10^3 \times 400 = 250 \times 10^6$ N mm on the beam. Thus the area of main reinforcement required is the greater of either

$$\frac{1.9M}{f_y l} = \frac{1.9 \times 250 \times 10^6}{250 \times 1650} = 1152\,\text{mm}^2$$

or

$$\frac{1.55M}{f_y \xi h} = \frac{1.55 \times 250 \times 10^6}{250 \times 800} = 1938\,\text{mm}^2$$

Provide four 25 mm bars ($A_s = 1963\,\text{mm}^2$).

Since $f_{cu} = 25\,\text{N/mm}^2$, take $f_t = 2.5\,\text{N/mm}^2$. Then, since $V = 625 \times 10^3$, the breadth of section required is given by

$$b \simeq \frac{0.55V}{k_1(\xi h - 0.35\alpha a_1)f_t} = \frac{0.55 \times 625 \times 10^3}{0.7(800 - 0.35 \times 300)2.5} = 283\,\text{mm}$$

Say $b = 300$ mm. Thus the shearing resistance provided by the concrete together with the main reinforcement only is

$$\begin{aligned} V_1 &= k_1(\xi h - 0.35\alpha a_1)f_t b + k_2 A_{sprov} d \sin^2\theta/h \\ &= 0.7\,(800 - 0.35 \times 300)\,2.5 \times 300 \\ &\quad + 100 \times 1963 \times 1425 \times 0.877/1500 \\ &= 528 \times 10^3\,\text{N} \end{aligned}$$

since $\tan\theta = 800/300$ and thus $\sin^2\theta = 0.877$.

Thus the balance of $625 \times 10^3 - 528 \times 10^3 = 97 \times 10^3$ must be provided by the web reinforcement. If horizontal links are provided at the depths shown in the diagram, $\sin^2\theta = 0.877$ for each link. Since

$$\begin{aligned} \sum A a_2 \sin^2\theta/h &= (200 + 350 + 750 + 900 + 1050 \\ &\quad + 1200 + 1350)A \times 0.877/1500 = 3.39A \end{aligned}$$

then

$$\begin{aligned} A &= (V - V_1)/(1.5k_2 \times 3.39) = 97 \times 10^3/(3.39 \times 100 \times 1.5) \\ &= 191\,\text{mm}^2 \end{aligned}$$

Ultimate shearing resistance provided by a single system of links

Limit-state
ULTIMATE VALUES **145**

Spacing of links (single system) (mm)	Factor	CP110 requirements: Mild steel $f_y = 250\ N/mm^2$ Bar size (mm) 6	8	10	12	CP110 requirements: High-yield steel $f_y = 425\ N/mm^2$ Bar size (mm) 6	8	10	12	BS8110 requirements: Mild steel $f_y = 250\ N/mm^2$ Bar size (mm) 6	8	10	12	BS8110 requirements: High-yield steel $f_y = 460\ N/mm^2$* Bar size (mm) 6	8	10	12	Minimum size of compression bar for given link spacing
50	K_u	246	437	683	984	418	743	1162	1673	246	437	683	984	452	804	1257	1810	6
	b_t	565	1005	1570	2261	942	1675	2617	3679	615	1093	1708	2460	1130	2010	3142	4525	
75	K_u	164	291	455	656	279	496	774	1115	164	291	455	656	301	536	838	1206	8
	b_t	376	670	1047	1507	628	1117	1745	2513	410	728	1139	1640	752	1340	2095	3015	
100	K_u	123	218	341	492	209	372	581	836	123	218	341	492	226	402	628	905	10
	b_t	282	502	785	1130	471	837	1308	1884	307	546	854	1230	565	1005	1570	2262	
125	K_u	98	175	273	393	167	297	465	669	98	175	273	393	181	321	502	724	12
	b_t	226	402	628	904	376	670	1047	1507	246	437	683	984	452	802	1255	1810	
150	K_u	82	146	227	328	139	248	387	578	82	146	227	328	150	268	419	603	16
	b_t	188	335	523	753	314	558	872	1256	205	364	569	820	375	670	1047	1507	
175	K_u	70	125	195	281	119	212	332	478	70	125	195	281	129	229	359	517	18
	b_t	161	287	448	646	269	478	748	1077	175	312	488	702	322	572	897	1292	
200	K_u	61	109	171	246	104	186	290	418	61	109	171	246	113	201	314	452	20
	b_t	141	251	392	565	235	418	654	942	153	273	427	615	282	502	785	1130	
225	K_u	55	97	152	218	93	165	258	371	54	97	152	218	100	178	279	402	20
	b_t	125	223	349	502	209	372	581	837	136	243	379	546	250	445	697	1005	
250	K_u	49	87	136	197	83	148	232	334	49	87	136	197	90	160	251	362	25
	b_t	113	201	314	452	188	335	523	754	123	218	341	492	225	400	627	905	
275	K_u	44	79	124	179	76	135	211	304	44	79	124	179	82	146	228	329	25
	b_t	102	182	285	411	171	304	476	685	111	198	310	447	205	365	570	822	
300	K_u	41	73	114	164	69	124	193	279	41	73	114	164	75	134	209	301	25
	b_t	94	167	261	377	157	279	436	628	102	182	284	410	187	335	522	752	
Shearing resistance when $s = 3/4d$		9220	16400	25620	36900	15680	27880	43560	62730	9220	16400	25620	36900	16970	30170	47150	67890	≯ 120

K_u ultimate shearing resistance provided by system in N per mm of effective depth
b_t maximum permissible width of section with nominal links unless $v < v_c/2$
*Permitted by BS8110 only.

Values of K_u provided by system in N per mm of effective depth

Bar arrangement	f_y (N/mm²) 250	425	460*	Bar arrangement	f_y (N/mm²) 250	425	460*	Bar arrangement	f_y (N/mm²) 250	425	460*
6@300	41	69	75	10@275	124	211	228	12@200 / 6@ 50	246	418	452
6@375	44	76	82	8@175	125	212	229	10@125	273	464	502
6@250	49	83	90	10@250	136	232	251	12@175	281	478	517
6@225	55	93	100	8@150	146	248	268	8@ 75	291	495	536
6@200	61	104	113	10@225	152	258	279				
6@175	70	119	129	12@300 / 6@ 75	164	279	301	12@150	328	577	603
8@300	73	124	134					10@100	341	581	628
8@275	79	135	146	10@200	171	290	314	12@125	393	669	724
6@150	82	139	150	8@125	175	297	321	8@ 50	437	743	804
8@250	87	148	160	12@275	179	304	329	10@ 75	455	774	838
8@225	97	165	178	10@175	195	332	359	12@100	492	836	905
6@125	98	167	181	12@250	197	334	362	12@ 75	656	1115	1206
8@200	109	186	201	12@225 / 8@100	218	371	402	10@ 50	683	1161	1257
10@300	114	193	209					12@ 75	984	1672	1206
6@100	123	209	226	10@150	227	387	419				

Note: maximum permissible width of section must be verified from table at top of page.
*Permitted by BS8110 only.

Chapter 22
Columns

22.1 SHORT COLUMNS UNDER AXIAL LOADING ONLY

Even when modular-ratio design is employed elsewhere in the structure, the carrying capacity of a short column loaded concentrically is almost always determined on the basis of conditions at failure, the compressive stress (or yield stress) in the reinforcement being considered independent of the compressive stress in the surrounding concrete. If modular-ratio principles are, however, employed the effective area of a column with separate links or ties is the area of the concrete plus α_e times the area of the longitudinal reinforcement. Thus for a short rectangular column the safe concentric load is given by

$$N_d = [A_c + (\alpha_e - 1)A_{sc}]f_{cc}$$

where N_d is the safe concentric load, A_c is the gross cross-sectional area of the member, A_{sc} is the area of the longitudinal reinforcement, and f_{cc} is the permissible stress in the concrete in direct compression. The value of α_e depends on the concrete, but often a value of 15 is assumed. The entire area of concrete is usually considered to be effective in supporting the load, but in some cases, as when the concrete cover is assumed to have spalled off in a fire in a building with a high fire risk, the safe direct load should be based on the area of the concrete in the core of the column only.

22.1.1 BS8110 and CP110 requirements

In contrast to earlier Codes where separate stresses were specified for concrete and steel in direct compression, in the expressions giving the ultimate resistance of axially loaded short columns provided in BS8110 and CP110 the values of f_y and f_{cu} are the same as those employed elsewhere, but suitable reduction factors are now embodied in the formulae themselves.

Both Codes differentiate between braced and unbraced columns. Braced columns are defined as those where the stability of the whole structure in the plane considered is provided by bracing or walls designed to resist all lateral forces. Where the type of structure precludes any possibility of the columns being subjected to significant moments, the ultimate axial loads are given by the following expressions:

BS8110: $N = 0.4f_{cu}A_c + 0.75f_yA_{sc}$

CP110: $N = 0.4f_{cu}A_c + 0.67f_yA_{sc}$

These expressions are derived from the strength of a section under pure axial load, reduced slightly to cater for an eccentricity to allow for constructional tolerances. Note that both here and in the corresponding formulae below the influence of the partial safety factors for materials is taken into account in the numerical factors provided, and suitable adjustments to these must be made if different partial safety factors are appropriate.

Where a column supports an approximately symmetrical arrangement of beams (i.e. the beams carry uniform imposed loads only and their spans differ by not more than 15%), the expressions for ultimate axial load are as follows:

BS8110: $N = 0.35f_{cu}A_c + 0.67f_yA_{sc}$

CP110: $N = 0.35f_{cu}A_c + 0.6f_yA_{sc}$

For square columns of various sizes and having a range of steel arrangements, values of N calculated from these formulae are listed in *Tables 149* and *150*. No deduction is made for the load-carrying capacity of the concrete displaced by the reinforcement. Comparison with calculations where this deduction is taken into account shows that, in the cases that the tables cover, the maximum difference in load-carrying capacity is only about 3%.

Unbraced short columns supporting a symmetrical arrangement of loading should be designed to withstand the given ultimate axial loading acting at a nominal eccentricity of $h/20$, although BS8110 also specifies that this eccentricity need not exceed a maximum of 20 mm. Assuming a ratio of x/h (or d_c/h) of unity (which may be slightly inaccurate in the case of very low values of ρ_1 when a rectangular stress-block is employed), it may be shown that the following expressions for N/bh correspond to this condition:

For a parabolic-rectangular stress-block:

$$\frac{N}{bh} = \left[k_1\left(\frac{d}{h} - k_2\right) + f_{yd1}\rho_1\left(\frac{d}{h} - \frac{1}{2}\right)\right] \bigg/ \left[\frac{d}{h} - \frac{9}{20}\right]$$

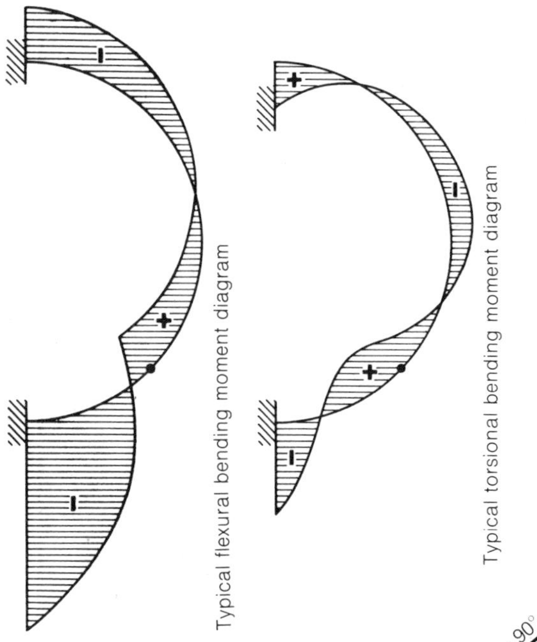
Typical flexural bending moment diagram
Typical torsional bending moment diagram

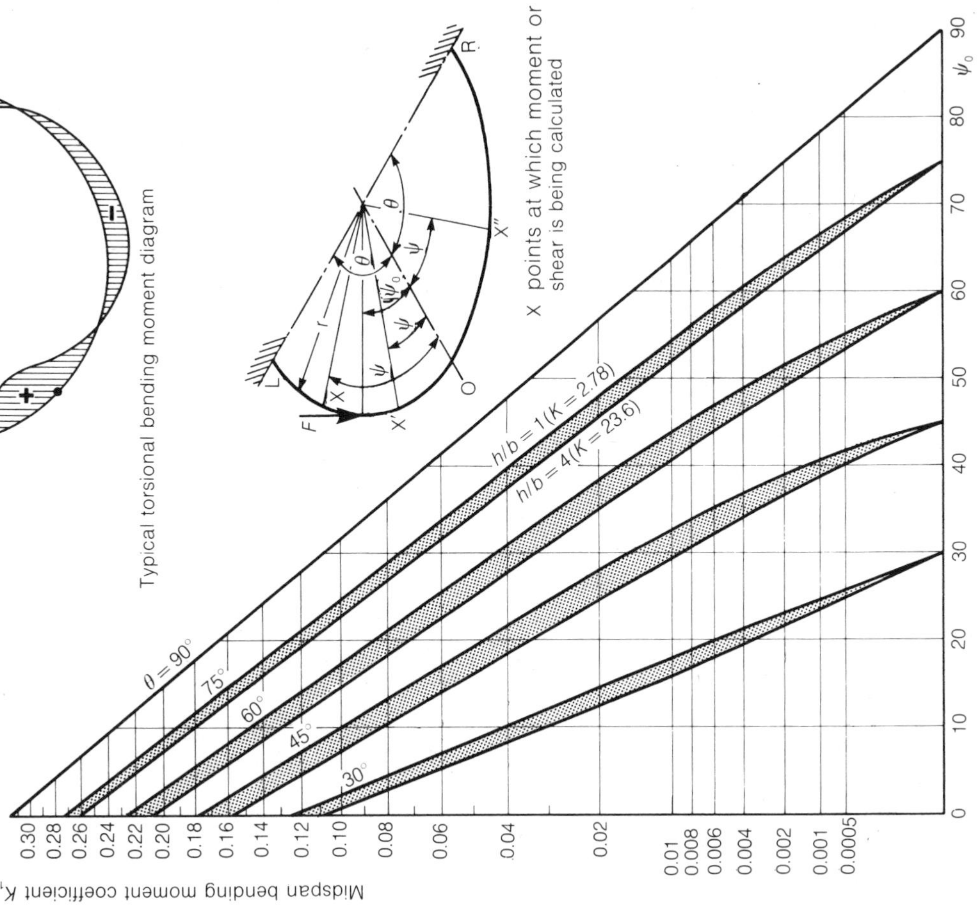
X points at which moment or shear is being calculated
L
R
O
F
X
X'
X''
h/b = 1 (K = 2.78)
h/b = 4 (K = 23.6)
θ = 90°
75°
60°
45°
30°
Midspan bending moment coefficient K1
ψ0

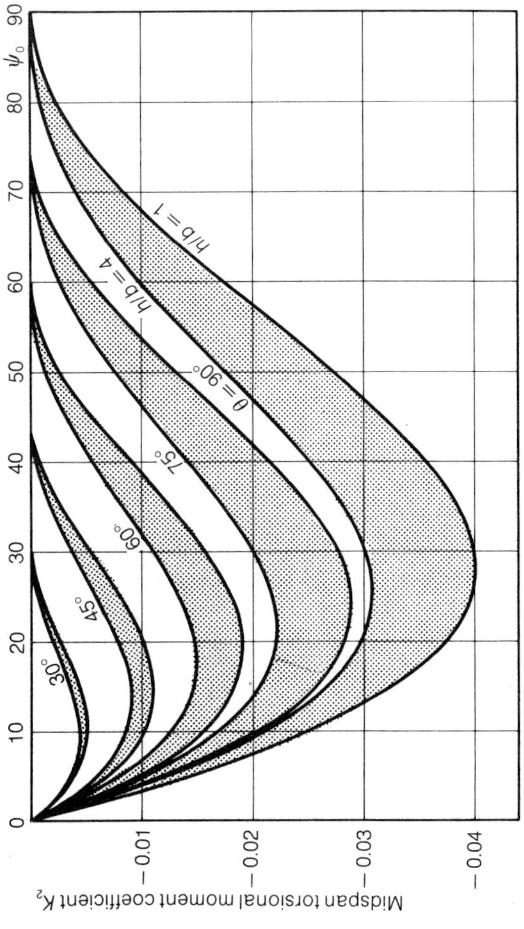
h/b = 1
h/b = 4
θ = 90°
75°
60°
45°
30°
Midspan torsional moment coefficient K2
ψ0

Between L and F (i.e. $\psi_0 \leq \psi \leq \theta$):

$$M = Fr[K_1 \cos\psi - K_2 \sin\psi + K_3 \sin\psi - \sin(\psi - \psi_0)]$$

$$T = Fr\{K_1 \sin\psi + K_2 \cos\psi + K_3(1 - \cos\psi) - [1 - \cos(\psi - \psi_0)]\}$$

$$V = F(1 - K_3)$$

Between F and O (i.e. $0 \leq \psi \leq \psi_0$):

$$M = Fr(K_1 \cos\psi - K_2 \sin\psi + K_3 \sin\psi)$$

$$T = Fr[K_1 \sin\psi + K_2 \cos\psi + K_3(1 - \cos\psi)]$$

$$V = -FK_3$$

Between O and R (i.e. $0 \leq \psi \leq \theta$)

$$M = Fr(K_1 \cos\psi + K_2 \sin\psi - K_3 \sin\psi)$$

$$T = Fr[-K_1 \sin\psi + K_2 \cos\psi + K_3(1 - \cos\psi)]$$

$$V = -FK_3$$

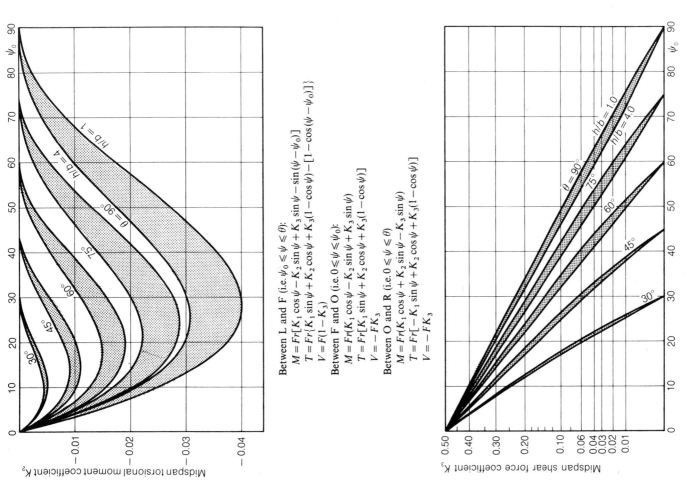

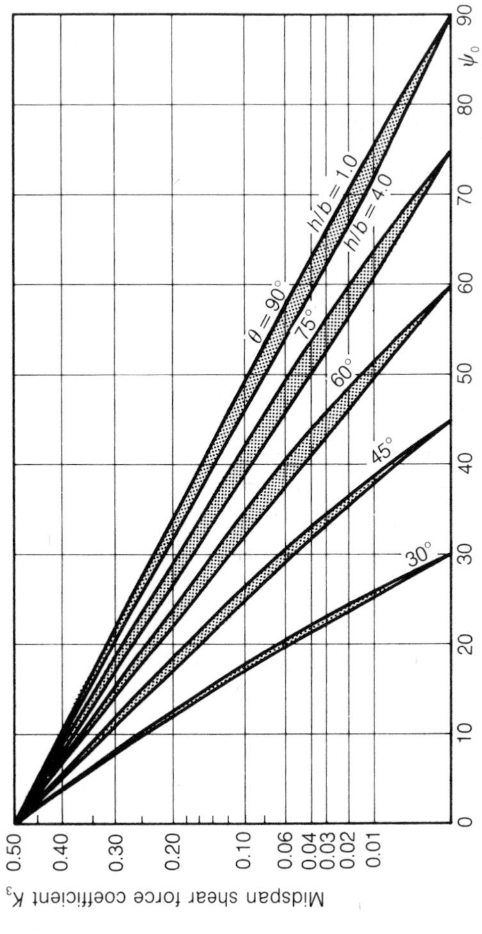
θ = 90°
h/b = 1.0
h/b = 4.0
75°
60°
45°
30°
Midspan shear force coefficient K3
ψ0

Bow girders—2: uniform loads

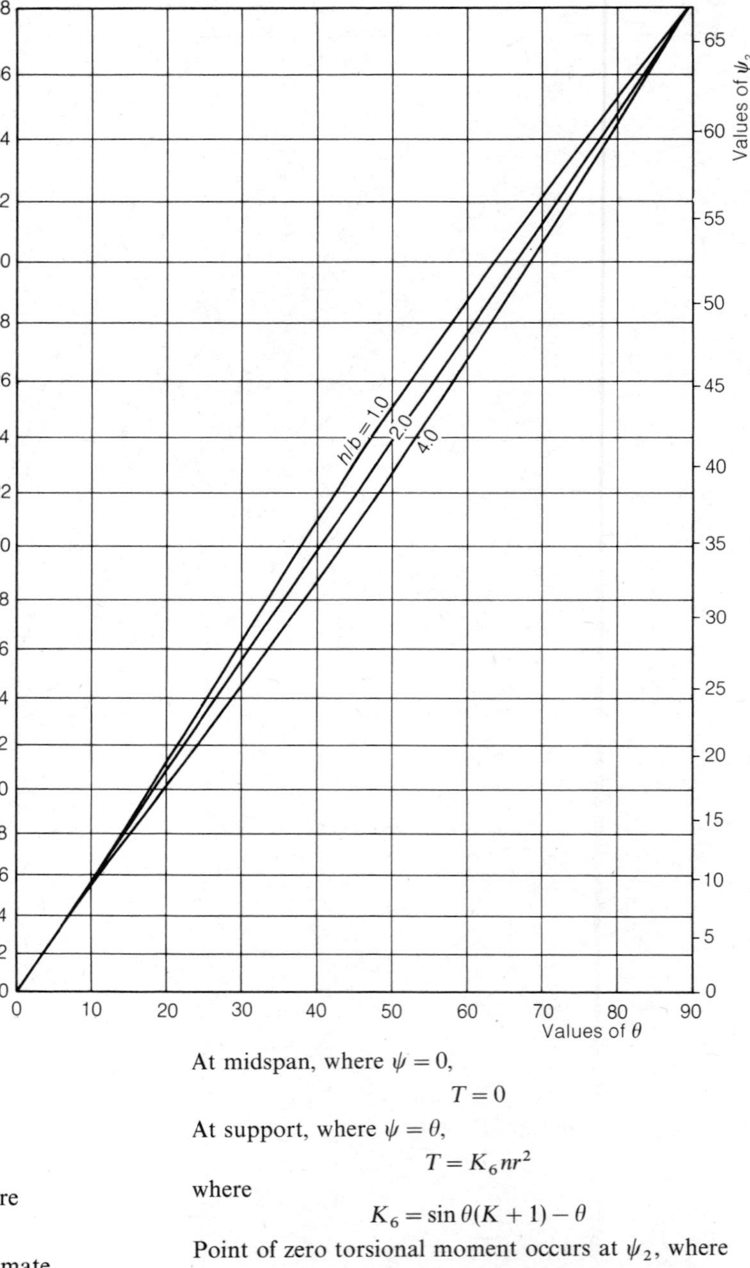

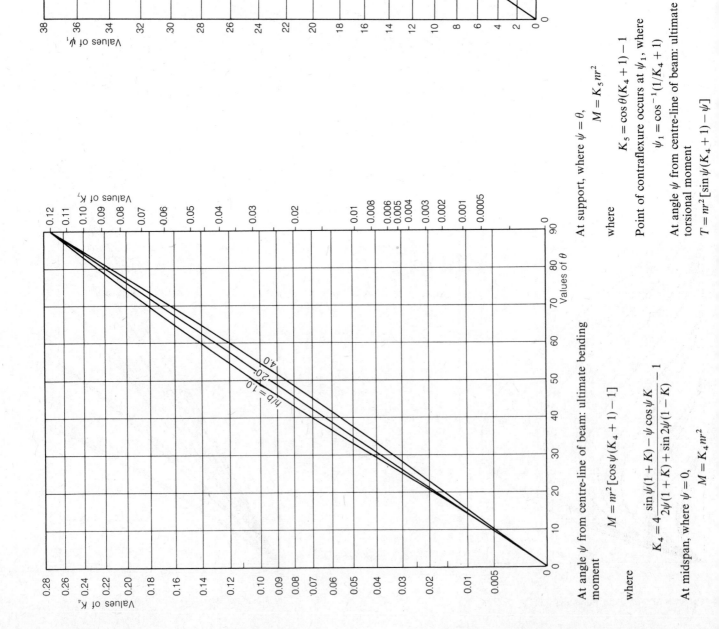

At angle ψ from centre-line of beam: ultimate bending moment

$$M = nr^2[\cos\psi(K_4 + 1) - 1]$$

where

$$K_4 = 4\frac{\sin\psi(1+K) - \psi\cos\psi K}{2\psi(1+K) + \sin 2\psi(1-K)} - 1$$

At midspan, where $\psi = 0$,

$$M = K_4 nr^2$$

At support, where $\psi = \theta$,

$$M = K_5 nr^2$$

where

$$K_5 = \cos\theta(K_4 + 1) - 1$$

Point of contraflexure occurs at ψ_1, where

$$\psi_1 = \cos^{-1}(1/K_4 + 1)$$

At angle ψ from centre-line of beam: ultimate torsional moment

$$T = nr^2[\sin\psi(K_4 + 1) - \psi]$$

At midspan, where $\psi = 0$,

$$T = 0$$

At support, where $\psi = \theta$,

$$T = K_6 nr^2$$

where

$$K_6 = \sin\theta(K + 1) - \theta$$

Point of zero torsional moment occurs at ψ_2, where

$$\sin\psi_2(K_4 + 1) = \psi_2$$

Maximum positive torsional moment occurs at point of zero bending moment, i.e. $\psi = \psi_1$: then

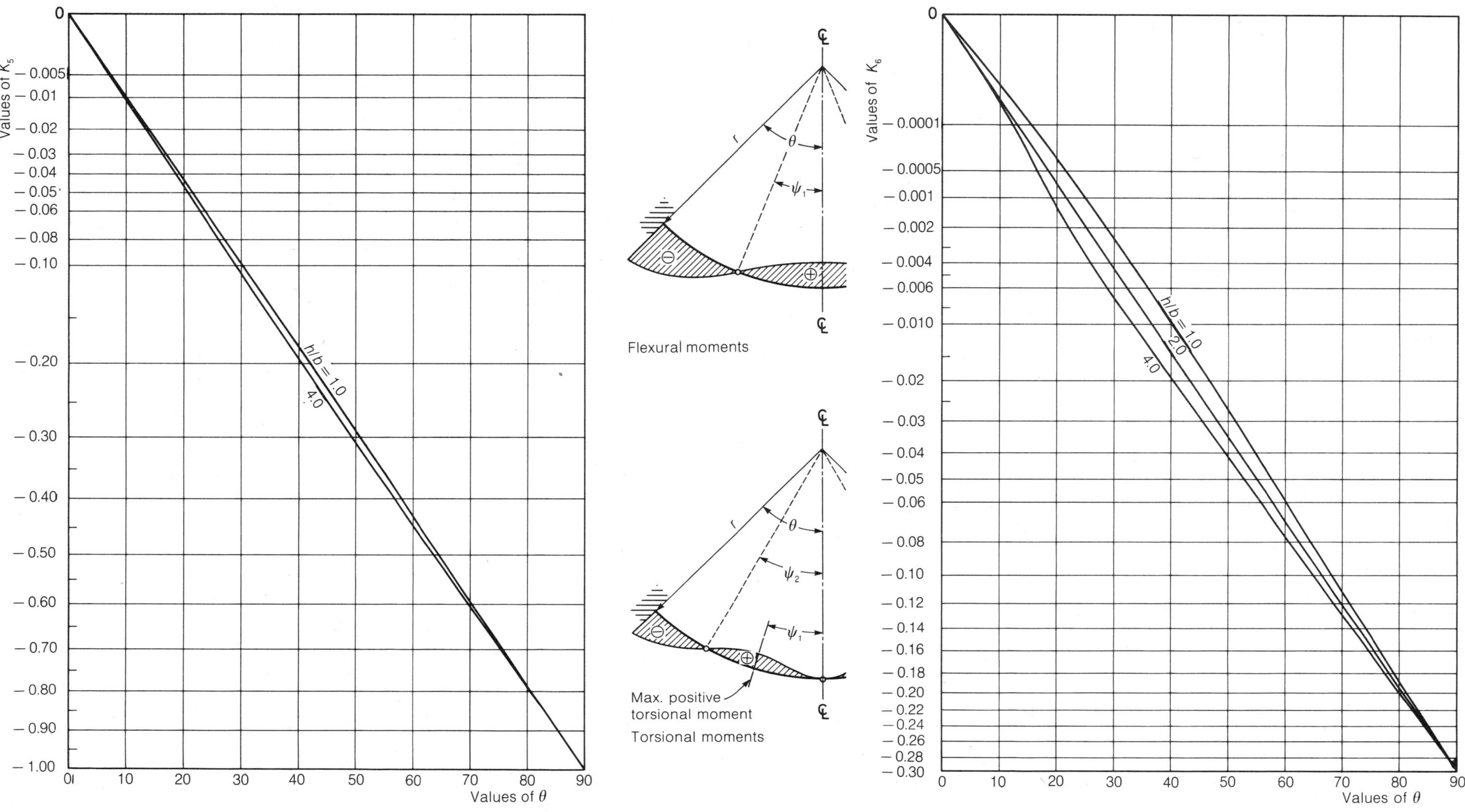
Values of K_5
$h/b = 1.0$
4.0
Values of θ
Flexural moments
Max. positive torsional moment
Torsional moments
Values of K_6
$h/b = 1.0$
2.0
4.0
Values of θ

For a rectangular stress-block according to BS8110:

$$\frac{N}{bh}=\left[0.402f_{cu}\left(\frac{d}{h}-\frac{9}{20}\right)+f_{yd1}\rho_1\left(\frac{d}{h}-\frac{1}{2}\right)\right]\bigg/\left[\frac{d}{h}-\frac{9}{20}\right]$$

For a rectangular stress-block according to CP110:

$$\frac{N}{bh}=\left[(0.4f_{cu}+f_{yd1}\rho_1)\left(\frac{d}{h}-\frac{1}{2}\right)\right]\bigg/\left[\frac{d}{h}-\frac{9}{20}\right]$$

For the simplified formulae given in CP110:

$$\frac{N}{bh}=\left[(0.4f_{cu}+0.72f_y\rho_1)\left(\frac{d}{h}-\frac{1}{2}\right)\right]\bigg/\left[\frac{d}{h}-\frac{9}{20}\right]$$

Although it is slightly more complex to apply, when working to CP110, it is normally preferable to utilize the expression corresponding to a parabolic-rectangular stress distribution since the ultimate load-carrying capacity of the section can be up to 18% higher than when the rectangular stress-block is assumed. With BS8110 requirements this difference is always less than 2%. The values given by the CP110 simplified expression are, of course, even lower owing to the assumption of a constant value of f_{yd1} of $0.72f_y$.

According to both Codes, the amount of longitudinal reinforcement should not exceed 6% of the total cross-sectional area of the section where columns are cast vertically and 8% where they are cast horizontally, the limit at laps being 10% in both cases. BS8110 stipulates a minimum amount of 0.4%. The corresponding minimum in CP110 is 1%; however, if for architectural or other reasons a larger column is provided than is necessary to support the ultimate load, a lower percentage of steel will suffice provided that $A_{sc}F_y \nless 0.15N$. The minimum ultimate axial loads for a given arrangement of steel resulting from this requirement are listed on *Table 150* and have been incorporated into the body of this table.

According to both Codes the links, which must be at least one-quarter of the size of the largest main bar or 6 mm, whichever is the greater, should be provided at a maximum spacing of twelve times the size of the smallest longitudinal bar, the link arrangement chosen being such that every corner and alternate bar or group of bars has a link passing around it with an included angle not exceeding 135°, and that all other bars must be within 150 mm of such restrained bars.

22.2 SHORT COLUMNS UNDER BENDING AND DIRECT FORCES: LIMIT-STATE METHOD

22.2.1 Uniaxial bending: BS8110 requirements

BS8110 permits column sections subjected to direct load and bending about one principal axis to be analysed according to the rigorous limit-state theory outlined in section 5.3, using either a parabolic-rectangular or a uniform rectangular stress-block.

Parabolic-rectangular stress-block. If the parabolic-rectangular concrete stress distribution is adopted the resulting equations for rectangular columns are

$$N=k_1xb+A'_{s1}f_{yd1}-A_{s2}f_{yd2}$$
$$M=k_1xb(\tfrac{1}{2}h-k_2x)+A'_{s1}f_{yd1}(\tfrac{1}{2}h-d')+A_{s2}f_{yd2}(d-\tfrac{1}{2}h)$$

where

$$k_1=0.445f_{cu}-0.008\,38(f_{cu})^{3/2}$$
$$k_2=\frac{1876-70.73(f_{cu})^{1/2}+f_{cu}}{3752-70.73(f_{cu})^{1/2}}$$
$$k_3=0.0566(f_{cu})^{1/2}$$

and f_{yd1} and f_{yd2} are the appropriate values of f_y for compression reinforcement A'_{s1} and tension reinforcement A_{s2} respectively, to be used for design purposes, and depend on the corresponding value of x/h (for example $f_{yd2}=0.87f_y$ when $x/d \leqslant 805/(1265+f_y)$. When $x>d$ (i.e. the reinforcement A_{s2} is in compression), the value of f_{yd2} should be taken as negative in the foregoing expressions for M and N. Values of k_1, k_2 and k_3 can be read from the scales on *Table 102*, and values of f_{yd1} and f_{yd2} can be calculated from the appropriate expressions on *Table 103* or read from the scales on *Table 104*.

The above expressions are those used to produce the charts provided in Part 3 of BS8110. Since the relationship between f_{cu} and k_1 and k_2 is complex, it has been found necessary to prepare sets of charts for each particular combination of f_{cu} and f_y. However, if the expressions are divided through by f_{cu} it is possible to produce single charts that cover the entire range of values of f_{cu}: such charts form *Tables 151* and *152*. These charts are actually calculated for a value of f_{cu} of 30 but analysis has shown that, when used for grades of concrete of from 20 to 50 any resulting errors are negligible. Furthermore, by expressing the amounts of reinforcement provided in terms of $\rho_1 f_y/f_{cu}$ it is possible to accommodate curves representing values of f_y of 250 and 460 N/mm^2 on the same chart. Intermediate values of f_y can then be considered by interpolating in the zones (shown shaded on the charts) between these bounding curves.

Uniform rectangular stress-block. If the equivalent rectangular stress-block is employed, the corresponding equations are

$$N=0.402f_{cu}xb+A'_{s1}f_{yd1}-A_{s2}f_{yd2}$$
$$M=0.201f_{cu}xb(h-0.9x)+A'_{s1}f_{yd1}(\tfrac{1}{2}h-d')+A_{s2}f_{yd2}(d-\tfrac{1}{2}h)$$

22.2.2 Uniaxial bending: CP110 requirements

CP110 permits column sections subjected to direct load with bending about one principal axis to be analysed either on the basis of the limit-state principles described in section 5.3, or by simplified formulae.

Parabolic-rectangular stress-block. The resulting expressions are identical to those given above (but calculations must take account of the differing stress–strain relationships specified for reinforcement in each Code). These expressions have been used to develop the charts provided in Part 2 of CP110. As before, by dividing throughout by f_{cu} it is possible to produce single charts that cover the entire range of values of f_{cu}. Such charts form *Tables 153* to *156*, where curves representing values of f_y of 250 and 425 N/mm^2 are shown on the same chart. Intermediate values of f_y can be considered by interpolating within the shaded zones between these bounding curves.

Design procedure

1. Calculate ultimate bending moment M acting on beam.
2. Calculate area of main reinforcement required from formula A.
3. Calculate ultimate shearing force V acting on beam.
4. Calculate suitable minimum breadth of beam (or check, if breadth is specified) from formula B.
5. Sketch elevation of beam and measure angle θ for main steel.
6. Calculate shearing resistance V_1 for beam with main reinforcement only from formula C: thus determine shearing resistance $(V - V_1)$ to be provided by web reinforcement.
7. From sketch of beam, measure values of θ and a_2 for each individual web bar.
8. Calculate area of web bars required from formula D.

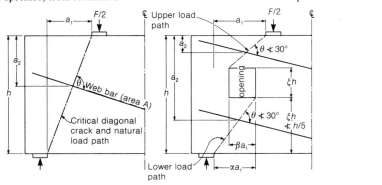

Design formula	Without openings in beam	With openings in beam
A	$A_{s\,req} \nless \dfrac{1.9M}{f_y l}$ or $\dfrac{1.9M}{f_y h}$	$A_{s\,req} \nless \dfrac{1.9M}{f_y l}$ or $\dfrac{1.55M}{f_y \xi h}$
B	$b \simeq \dfrac{0.65V}{k_1(h - 0.35a_1) f_t}$	$b \simeq \dfrac{0.55V}{k_1(\xi h - 0.35\alpha a_1) f_t}$
C	$V_1 = k_1(h - 0.35a_1) f_t b + k_2 A_{s\,prov} d \sin^2\theta/h$	$V_1 = k_1(\xi h - 0.35\alpha a_1) f_t b + k_2 A_{s\,prov} d \sin^2\theta/h$
D	$V - V_1 = k_2 \sum A a_2 \sin^2\theta/h$	$V - V_1 = 1.5k_2 \sum A a_2 \sin^2\theta/h$

Notes

1. The formulae are only known to be applicable if the following conditions apply: $l/h \ngtr 2$. Static loads only occur and these are applied to top of beam only. a_1/h is not greatly outside range of 0.23 to 0.70. Positive anchorage is provided to main reinforcement.
2. Restrictions to θ and ξh shown in diagrams only apply when opening intersects line of critical diagonal crack. If opening is reasonably clear of this line, the effect of the opening may be disregarded completely when considering shearing resistence.
3. For distributed loads, substitute statically equivalent twin concentrated loads (i.e. replace uniform load F by two concentrated loads of $F/2$ at distances of $l/4$ from supports.
4. The more nearly perpendicular a web bar is to the principal diagonal crack, the more effective it is in resisting shearing and limiting cracking: its effectiveness also increases with increasing depth a_2. However, inclined web reinforcement may be more expensive to bend and fix.
5. If openings are present, web reinforcement must pass both above and below them.

If cylinder splitting tensile strength is not known, estimate as follows:

cube strength f_{cu} (N/mm^2)	cylinder splitting tensile strength f_t(N/mm^2)
20	2.24
25	2.50
30	2.74
40	3.16
50	3.54

Notations

A	area of individual web bar
$A_{s\,req}, A_{s\,prov}$	minimum area of main steel required and actual area provided
a_1	clear distance from edge of load to face of support
αa_1	distance from inner edge of opening to face of support
βa_1	width of opening
a_2	depth at which web bar intersects critical diagonal crack
b	breadth of beam
d	effective depth to main steel
f_t	cylinder splitting tensile strength of concrete (see table on left below)
f_y	yield strength of reinforcement
h	overall depth of beam
k_1, k_2	empirical coefficients for concrete and reinforcement. Take k_1 as 0.7 for normal-weight concrete and 0.5 for light-weight concrete: take k_2 as 100 for plain round bars and 225 for deformed bars
l	span of beam between centres of supports
M	ultimate moment
V	ultimate shearing force
V_1	shearing force resisted by concrete and main reinforcement only
θ	angle between bar being considered and critical diagonal crack
ξ	distance of bottom of opening from beam soffit expressed as proportion of total depth of beam
ζ	depth of opening expressed as proportion of total depth of beam

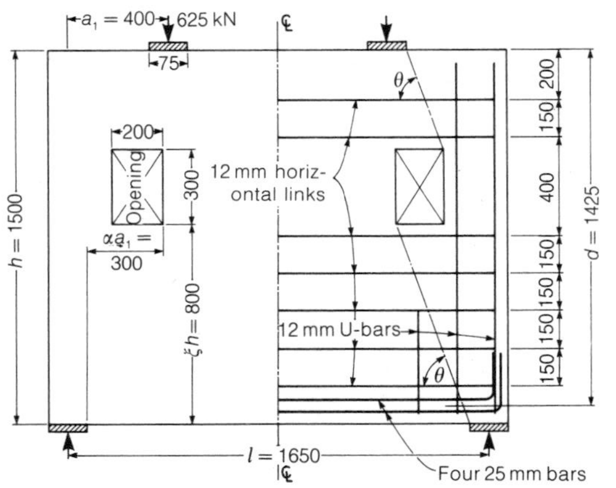

These charts have been extended to cover the situation where uniaxial bending is combined with direct tension and may thus be used to design sections subjected to such forces to meet ultimate limit-state requirements. However, when tension predominates, the limit-state of cracking becomes a controlling feature: brief notes of the design of sections in these circumstances are given in section 20.3.1. According to CP110, if the compressive force N is such that N/bhf_{cu} exceeds 0.2, it is unnecessary to check the section as regards cracking. For sections where the axial force (compression or tension) is small compared with the applied moment, the section should be considered as a beam when satisfying serviceability limit-state of cracking requirements.

Uniform rectangular stress-block. If the equivalent rectangular stress-block is employed, the corresponding equations are

$$N = \tfrac{2}{5} f_{cu} x b + A'_{s1} f_{yd1} - A_{s2} f_{yd2}$$
$$M = \tfrac{1}{5} f_{cu} x b(h - x) + A'_{s1} f_{yd1}(\tfrac{1}{2}h - d') + A_{s2} f_{yd2}(d - \tfrac{1}{2}h)$$

These expressions have been used to prepare the design charts provided in *Examples of the Design of Buildings* and in ref. 79.

CP110 simplified expressions. Sections may be analysed using the simplified expressions

$$N = \tfrac{2}{5} f_{cu} d_c b + 0.72 A'_{s1} f_y - A_{s2} f_{s2}$$
$$M = \tfrac{1}{5} f_{cu} d_c b(h - d_c) + 0.72 f_y A'_{s1}(\tfrac{1}{2}h - d') + A_{s2} f_{s2}(d - \tfrac{1}{2}h)$$

where $d_c \nless 2d'$ is the depth of concrete assumed to be in compression, and f_{s2} is the stress in the 'tension' reinforcement. The *Code Handbook* recommends that, when $2d' \leqslant d_c \leqslant h/2$, $f_{s2} = +0.87 f_y$; when $h/2 \leqslant d_c \leqslant d$, f_{s2} varies linearly from $+0.87 f_y$ to zero; when $d \leqslant d_c \leqslant h$, $f_{s2} = 0$; and when $d_c = h$, f_{s2} increases from zero to $-0.72 f_y$. Nominal reinforcement will suffice when

$$N = \tfrac{2}{5} f_{cu} b\left(h - \frac{2M}{N}\right)$$

provided that $M \leqslant [(h/2) - d']N$.

The foregoing expressions, which are obtained by considering a rectangular concrete stress-block having a uniform stress of $2f_{cu}/5$ and equating moments about the centre-line of section and direct forces, can be rearranged to give

$$\frac{N}{bhf_{cu}} = \frac{2}{5}\frac{d_c}{h} + 0.72\frac{f_y}{f_{cu}}\rho_c - \frac{f_{s2}}{f_{cu}}\rho_t$$

$$\frac{M}{bh^2 f_{cu}} = \frac{1}{5}\frac{d_c}{h}\left(1 - \frac{d_c}{h}\right) + 0.72\frac{f_y}{f_{cu}}\rho_c\left(\frac{1}{2} - \frac{d'}{h}\right) + \frac{f_{s2}}{f_{cu}}\rho_t\left(\frac{d}{h} - \frac{1}{2}\right)$$

Then if $\rho_t = \rho_c = \rho_1/2$, and for example when $d' = 0.1h$ and $d = 0.9h$,

$$\frac{N}{bhf_{cu}} = \frac{2}{5}\frac{d_c}{h} + \frac{f_y}{f_{cu}}\rho_1\left(0.36 - 0.5\frac{f_{s2}}{f_y}\right)$$

$$\frac{M}{bh^2 f_{cu}} = \frac{1}{5}\frac{d_c}{h}\left(1 - \frac{d_c}{h}\right) + \frac{f_y}{f_{cu}}\rho_1\left(0.144 + 0.2\frac{f_{s2}}{f_y}\right)$$

where f_{s2} is related directly to d_c as described above. Nominal reinforcement will suffice when

$$\frac{M}{bh^2 f_{cu}} = \frac{N}{bhf_{cu}}\left(\frac{1}{2} - \frac{5}{4}\frac{N}{bhf_{cu}}\right)$$

provided

$$\frac{M}{bh^2 f_{cu}} \leqslant \left(\frac{1}{2} - \frac{d'}{h}\right)\frac{N}{bhf_{cu}}$$

These expressions have been used to prepare the charts on *Tables 157* and *158*, which give values of $\rho_1 f_y/f_{cu}$ for given values of $M/bh^2 f_{cu}$ and N/bhf_{cu} when $d/h = 0.95$, 0.90, 0.85 or 0.80.

When $M \geqslant (d - h/2)N$, CP110 permits N to be neglected and the section designed instead for an increased moment of $M + (d - h/2)N$, the resulting area of tension steel needed being reduced by $\gamma_m N/f_y$. In effect this procedure implies the insertion of equal and opposite forces of value N along the line of the tension reinforcement. The upward force acts with N over lever arm $d - h/2$ to cause the additional moment, while the downward force on A_{s2} reduces the tension steel required. This technique is most useful where a reversal of moment cannot occur and it is uneconomical to have $A'_{s1} = A_{s2}$: see example 1 which follows. If the value adopted for x/d (and thus x/h) is the maximum that can be employed without reducing f_{yd2} below f_y/γ_m, the total amount of steel required when using this technique is never more, and often considerably less, than when equal steel is provided in both faces. However, when x/h exceeds 1/2, more compression steel than tension steel is necessary. This method is not explicitly mentioned in BS8110. Although not expressly forbidden, its failure to take account of strain compatibility is not approved.

When a reversal of moment cannot occur (e.g. where the moment in an exterior column is due to floor loading) and $M/N \simeq d - h/2$, it is always worth considering providing an unsymmetrical arrangement of reinforcement by substituting trial values of A'_{s1} and A_{s2} in the appropriate expressions above and examining the values of M and N thus obtained. If $M/N = d - h/2$, the line of action of N coincides with the position of the compression steel, of course, and virtually no tension steel is theoretically required. Charts have been produced for designing unsymmetrically reinforced rectangular sections to CP110: see ref. 85.

22.2.3 Biaxial bending: BS8110 requirements

For cases where a short column is subjected to a direct ultimate load N and ultimate bending moments M_x and M_y acting about the major and minor principal axes respectively, BS8110 provides expressions that convert the biaxial moments into a single equivalent increased moment acting about one axis only and thus enabling the methods and aids already described to be used to design the section. If M_x/h' exceeds M_y/b', the equivalent moment M'_x is given by $M_x + \beta M_y h'/b'$; otherwise the equivalent moment is $M_y + \beta M_x b'/x'$. In these expressions h' and b' represent the distances from the compressed face to the centre-line of the 'tension' steel (i.e. equivalent to the effective depth of a beam section) measured about the major and minor axes respectively, and $\beta = 1 - (7N/6bhf_{cu})$ (but not less than 0.3). When the expression for M'_x controls, the section must then be

Ultimate axial loads on short square columns: BS8110

COLUMNS NOT SUBJECTED TO SIGNIFICANT MOMENTS

Stresses (N/mm^2)	Size of square column (mm)	Diameter of main bars (4 no.) (mm) 16	20	25	32	40	Diameter of main bars (8 no.) (mm) 16	20	25	32	40
	300	1035	1112	1231	*1442*	*1748*	*1171*	*1324*	*1562*	Rcmt	exceeds
	350	1360	1437	1556	*1767*	*2073*	*1496*	*1649*	*1887*	*2310*	6%
$f_{cu} = 25$	400	1735	1812	1931	2142	*2448*	*1871*	*2024*	*2262*	*2685*	
	450	Rcmt	2237	2356	2567	2873	2296	2449	2687	3110	3721
$f_y = 250$	500	less	2712	2831	3042	3348	2771	2924	3162	3585	4196
	550	than	3237	3356	3567	3873	3296	3449	3687	4110	4721
	600	0.4%		*3931*	*4142*	*4448*	3871	4024	4262	4685	5296
	300	1212	1287	1403	*1610*	*1909*	*1345*	*1494*	*1727*	Rcmt	exceeds
	350	1602	1677	1793	*2000*	*2299*	*1735*	*1884*	*2117*	*2531*	6%
$f_{cu} = 30$	400	2052	2127	2243	2450	*2749*	*2185*	*2334*	*2567*	*2981*	
	450	Rcmt	2637	2753	2960	3259	2695	2844	3077	3491	4088
$f_y = 250$	500	less	3207	3323	3530	3829	3265	3414	3647	4061	4658
	550	than	3837	3953	4160	4459	3895	4044	4277	4691	5288
	600	0.4%		*4643*	*4850*	*5149*	4585	4734	4967	5381	5978
	300	1590	1637	1749	*1946*	*2231*	*1693*	*1835*	*2058*	Rcmt	exceeds
	350	2110	2157	2269	*2466*	*2751*	*2213*	*2355*	*2578*	*2973*	6%
$f_{cu} = 40$	400	2710	2757	2869	3066	*3351*	*2813*	*2955*	*3178*	*3573*	
	450	Rcmt	3437	3549	3746	4031	3493	3635	3858	4253	4823
$f_y = 250$	500	less	4197	4309	4506	4791	4253	4395	4618	5013	5583
	550	than	5037	5149	5346	5631	5093	5235	5458	5853	6423
	600	0.4%		*6069*	*6266*	*6551*	6013	6155	6378	6773	7343
For $f_y = 460\ N/mm^2$ add		126	197	309	506	791	253	395	618	1013	1583

BEAM LOADING APPROXIMATELY SYMMETRICAL

Stresses (N/mm^2)	Size of square column (mm)	Diameter of main bars (4 no.) (mm) 16	20	25	32	40	Diameter of main bars (8 no.) (mm) 16	20	25	32	40
	300	922	997	1116	*1326*	*1629*	*1056*	*1208*	*1445*	Rcmt	exceeds
	350	1206	1282	1400	*1610*	*1913*	*1341*	*1492*	*1729*	*2149*	6%
$f_{cu} = 25$	400	1534	1610	1728	1938	*2241*	*1669*	*1820*	*2057*	*2477*	
	450	Rcmt	1982	2100	2310	2613	2041	2192	2429	2849	3455
$f_y = 250$	500	less	2397	2516	2726	3029	2456	2608	2845	3265	3871
	550	than	2857	2975	3185	3488	2916	3067	3304	3724	4330
	600	0.4%		*3478*	*3688*	*3991*	3419	3570	3807	4227	4833
	300	1079	1155	1273	*1483*	*1786*	*1214*	*1365*	*1602*	Rcmt	exceeds
	350	1420	1496	1615	*1825*	*2128*	*1555*	*1707*	*1944*	*2363*	6%
$f_{cu} = 30$	400	1814	1890	2008	*2218*	*2521*	*1949*	*2100*	*2337*	*2757*	
	450	Rcmt	2336	2455	2665	2968	2395	2547	2784	3203	3810
$f_y = 250$	500	less	2835	2953	3163	3466	2894	3045	3282	3702	4308
	550	than	3386	3505	3715	4018	3445	3597	3834	4253	4860
	600	0.4%		*4108*	*4318*	*4621*	4049	4200	4437	4857	5463
	300	1394	1470	1588	*1798*	*2101*	*1529*	*1680*	*1917*	Rcmt	exceeds
	350	1849	1925	2043	*2253*	*2556*	*1984*	*2135*	*2372*	*2792*	6%
$f_{cu} = 40$	400	2374	2450	2568	2778	*3081*	*2509*	*2660*	*2897*	*3317*	
	450	Rcmt	3045	3163	3373	3676	3104	3255	3492	3912	4518
$f_y = 250$	500	less	3710	3828	4038	4341	3769	3920	4157	4577	5183
	550	than	4445	4563	4773	5076	4504	4655	4892	5312	5918
	600	0.4%		*5368*	*5578*	*5881*	5309	5460	5697	6117	6723
For $f_y = 460\ N/mm^2$ add		113	176	276	452	707	226	353	552	905	1414

Values of permissible load are in kN.
Values given in italics indicate less-practicable arrangements of bars (i.e. eight bars or large bars in small columns or four bars in large columns).
In calculating these values allowance has *not* been made for the area of concrete displaced by the reinforcement.

designed to resist axial load N with M'_x acting about the major axis; when M'_y dominates, design for N plus M'_y acting about the minor axis.

22.2.4 Biaxial bending: CP110 requirements

If a short column is subjected to a direct ultimate load N and biaxial ultimate bending moments M_x and M_y about the major and minor principal axes respectively, CP110 recommends that $\beta_x^{\alpha_n} + \beta_y^{\alpha_n} \leqslant 1$, where β is the ratio of the moment about an axis due to ultimate load to the maximum moment capacity about that axis assuming an ultimate axial load N, and

$$\alpha_n = \frac{5}{3}\frac{N}{N_{uz}} + \frac{2}{3}$$

where N_{uz} is the resistance of a given section to pure axial load and is given by

$$N_{uz} = \frac{9}{20} f_{cu} A_c + \frac{3}{4} f_y A_{sc}$$

Also $1 \ngtr \alpha_n \ngtr 2$. Values of N_{uz} for given values of f_{cu}, f_y and ρ can be read from the upper chart on *Table 159*, and the relationship between M_x/M_{ux}, M_y/M_{uy} and N/N_{uz} is illustrated by the lower chart. One possible design procedure employing these charts is illustrated in example 2 which follows.

To avoid this complex procedure, Beeby (ref. 70) has proposed the following approximate method:

1. Calculate

$$N_{uz} = N + 5\left(\frac{M_x}{2h - 3d'_h} + \frac{M_y}{2b - 3d'_b}\right)$$

where d'_h and d'_b are the depths to the 'compression' reinforcement in the directions of h and b respectively.
2. Calculate N_{uz}/N and hence determine α_n.
3. Calculate M_{ux} from the expression

$$M_{ux} = \sqrt[\alpha_n]{\left\{M_x^{\alpha_n} + \left[\frac{M_y(2h - 3d'_h)}{(2b - 3d'_b)}\right]^{\alpha_n}\right\}}$$

4. Finally, design the section to resist N combined with a uniaxial moment of M_{ux}.

Comparative calculations reported in ref. 70 indicate that the results obtained by using this procedure are unlikely to differ from those obtained by the exact method by more than 5% in practical cases. This discrepancy is well within the accuracy to which the column design charts provided in this *Handbook* and in Part 2 of CP110 can be read.

Example 1. Design a column section to resist an ultimate moment of 400 kN m and an axial load of 250 kN using grade 25 concrete and high-yield steel to BS8110 and CP110 requirements.

To BS8110 ($f_y = 460\,\text{N/mm}^2$). With 40 mm cover to the main bars, assume a section which has $h = 550$ mm and $b = 250$ mm. Assume $d/h = 0.9$ (i.e. $d' = 55$ mm). Now since

$$M/bh^2 f_{cu} = 400 \times 10^6/(250 \times 550^2 \times 25) = 0.212$$
$$N/bhf_{cu} = 250 \times 10^3/(250 \times 550 \times 25) = 0.073$$

from the right-hand chart forming *Table 151*, $\rho_1 f_y/f_{cu} = 0.52$, so that $\rho_1 = 0.52 \times 25/460 = 0.028$. Thus

$$A_{sc\,req} = 0.028 \times 250 \times 550 = 3850\,\text{mm}^2$$

Provide four 25 mm bars near each face.

Reference to chart 24 in Part 3 of BS8110 confirms that if

$$N/bh = 250 \times 10^3/(250 \times 550) = 1.8$$
$$M/bh^2 = 400 \times 10^6/(250 \times 550^2) = 5.3$$

$100\,A_{sc}/bh = 2.8$, so that

$$A_{sc} = 2.8 \times 250 \times 550/100 = 3850\,\text{mm}^2$$

To CP110 ($f_y = 425\,\text{N/mm}^2$). As before, assume a section which has $h = 550$ mm, $b = 250$ mm and $d/h = 0.9$. Again $M/bh^2 f_{cu} = 0.212$ and $N/bhf_{cu} = 0.073$. From the chart forming *Table 154*, $\rho_1 f_y/f_{cu} = 0.55$, so that $\rho_1 = 0.55 \times 25/425 = 0.032$. Thus

$$A_{sc\,req} = 0.032 \times 250 \times 550 = 4450\,\text{mm}^2$$

Provide two 32 mm bars plus two 20 mm bars near each face.

Reference to chart 24 in CP110: Part 2 confirms that, when $N/bh = 1.8$ and $M/bh^2 = 5.3$, $100\,A_{sc}/bh = 3.2$, so that

$$A_{sc} = 3.2 \times 250 \times 550/100 = 4450\,\text{mm}^2$$

Alternatively, neglect N and design for a total bending moment of $400 \times 10^6 + (550 - 53 - 275) \times 250 \times 10^3 = 455.5$ kN m. From the scales on *Table 102*, for $f_{cu} = 25\,\text{N/mm}^2$, $k_1 = 10.06\,\text{N/mm}^2$ and $k_2 = 0.4553$. Assume a maximum value of x/d corresponding to point C on the stress–strain design curve for reinforcement (*Table 103*), since this results in the most 'economical' arrangement. Thus when $f_y = 425\,\text{N/mm}^2$, $x/d = 0.476$. Now the resistance moment of the concrete alone $= k_1 bx(d - k_2 x) = 10.06 \times 250 \times 0.476 \times 497^2(1 - 0.4553 \times 0.476) = 231.7 \times 10^6$ N mm. Thus the resistance moment required from compression reinforcement $= 455.5 \times 10^6 - 231.7 \times 10^6 = 223.8 \times 10^6$ N mm, so that

$$A'_{s\,req} = \frac{M}{f_{yd1}(d - d')} = \frac{223.8 \times 10^6}{311.9(497 - 53)} = 1616\,\text{mm}^2$$

$$A_{s\,req} = \frac{k_1}{f_{yd2}} xb + A'_s \frac{f_{yd1}}{f_{yd2}}$$
$$= \frac{10.06 \times 0.476 \times 250 \times 497}{369.6} + \frac{1616 \times 311.9}{369.6} = 2974\,\text{mm}^2$$

The latter figure can now be reduced by $N/f_{yd2} = 250 \times 10^3/369.6 = 676$ mm, so that actual $A_s = 2298\,\text{mm}^2$. Thus in the present case the total area of reinforcement required using this method is only 3914 mm², showing a considerable saving over that needed when $A_{s1} = A_{s2}$.

Example 2. Design a section to resist a direct force of 1200 kN together with moments of 300 kN and 100 kN about the major and minor principal axes respectively, with $f_{cu} = 30\,\text{N/mm}^2$ and high-yield steel.

To BS8110 ($f_y = 460\,\text{N/mm}^2$). Try a section with $h = 600$ mm and $b = 300$ mm, and assume 40 mm cover to 40 mm main bars, so that $d'/h = 0.1$, $d'/b = 0.2$, $h' = 540$ mm and $b' = 240$ mm. Since $N/bhf_{cu} = 1200 \times 10^3/(300 \times 600 \times 30) =$

Ultimate axial loads on short square columns: CP110

COLUMNS NOT SUBJECTED TO SIGNIFICANT MOMENTS

Stresses (N/mm^2)	Size of square column (mm)	Diameter of main bars (4 no.)(mm) 16	20	25	32	40	Diameter of main bars (8 no.) (mm) 16	20	25	32	40
	300	855	930	1049	*1259*	*1562*	*989*	*1141*	*1378*		> 6%
$f_{cu} = 20$	350	1115	1190	1309	*1519*	*1822*	*1249*	*1401*	*1638*	*2058*	
	400	1340*	1490	1609	1819	2122	*1549*	*1701*	*1938*	*2358*	
	450		1830	1949	2159	2462	1889	2041	2278	2698	3304
$f_u = 250$	500		2094*	2329	2539	2842	2269	2421	2658	3078	3684
	550	Reinforcement		2749	2959	3262	2681*	2841	3078	3498	4104
	600	less than 1%		*3209*	*3419*	3722	< 1%	3301	3538	3958	4564
	300	1035	1110	1229	*1439*	*1742*	*1169*	*1321*	*1558*		> 6%
$f_{cu} = 25$	350	1340*	1435	1554	*1764*	*2067*	*1494*	*1646*	*1883*	*2303*	
	400		1810	1929	2139	*2442*	*1869*	*2021*	*2258*	*2678*	
	450		2094*	2354	2564	2867	2294	2446	2683	3103	3709
$f_y = 250$	500			2829	3039	3342	2681*	2921	3158	3578	4184
	550	Reinforcement		3272*	3564	3867		3446	3683	4103	4709
	600	less than 1%			*4139*	*4442*	< 1%	4021	4258	4678	5284
	300	1215	1290	1409	*1619*	*1922*	*1349*	*1501*	*1738*		> 6%
$f_{cu} = 30$	350	1340*	1680	1799	*2009*	*2312*	*1739*	*1891*	*2128*	*2548*	
	400		2094*	2249	2459	*2762*	*2189*	*2341*	*2578*	*2998*	
	450			2759	2969	3272	2681*	2851	3088	3508	4114
$f_y = 250$	500			3272*	3539	3842		3421	3658	4078	4684
	550	Reinforcement			4169	4472		4051	4288	4708	5314
	600	less than 1%			*4859*	*5162*	< 1%	4189*	4978	5398	6004
Maximum load on lightly loaded column		1340	2094	3272	5362	8378	2681	4189	6545	10723	16755
For $f_y = 425 N/mm^2$ add		94	148	230	377	589	189	295	460	754	1179
Maximum load on lightly loaded column		2279	3560	5563	9115	14242	4557	7121	11126	18230	28484

Values of permissible load are in kN.

BEAM LOADING APPROXIMATELY SYMMETRICAL

Stresses (N/mm^2)	Size of square column (mm)	Diameter of main bars (4 no.)(mm) 16	20	25	32	40	Diameter of main bars (8 no.) (mm) 16	20	25	32	40
	300	751	818	925	*1113*	*1384*	*871*	*1007*	*1219*		> 6%
$f_{cu} = 20$	350	978	1046	1152	*1340*	*1611*	*1099*	*1234*	*1447*	*1823*	
	400	1241	1308	1415	1603	*1874*	*1361*	*1497*	*1709*	*2085*	
	450	1340*	1606	1712	1900	2171	1659	1794	2007	2383	2925
$f_u = 250$	500		1938	2045	2233	2504	1991	2127	2339	2715	3258
	550	Reinforcement	2094*	2412	2600	2871	2359	2494	2707	3083	3625
	600	less than 1%			*3003*	*3274*	2681*	2897	3109	3485	4028
	300	908	976	1082	*1270*	*1541*	*1029*	*1164*	*1377*		> 6%
$f_{cu} = 25$	350	1193	1260	1366	*1554*	*1826*	*1313*	*1449*	*1661*	*2037*	
	400	1340*	1588	1695	1883	*2154*	*1641*	*1777*	*1989*	*2365*	
	450		1960	2066	2254	2526	2013	2149	2361	2737	3280
$f_y = 250$	500		2094*	2482	2670	2941	2429	2564	2777	3153	3695
	550	Reinforcement		2941	3129	3401	2681*	3024	3236	3612	4155
	600	less than 1%			*3633*	*3904*	< 1%	3527	3739	4115	4658
	300	1066	1133	1240	*1428*	*1699*	*1186*	*1322*	*1534*		> 6%
$f_{cu} = 30$	350	1340*	1475	1581	*1769*	*2040*	*1528*	*1663*	*1875*	*2251*	
	400		1868	1975	2163	*2434*	*1921*	*2057*	*2269*	*2645*	
	450		2094*	2421	2609	2880	2368	2503	2715	3091	3634
$f_y = 250$	500			2920	3108	3379	2681*	3002	3214	3590	4133
	550	Reinforcement		3272*	3659	3930		3553	3765	4141	4684
	600	less than 1%			*4263*	*4534*	< 1%	4157	4369	4745	5288
Maximum load on lightly loaded column		1340	2094	3272	5362	8378	2681	4189	6545	10723	16755
For $f_y = 425 N/mm^2$ add		84	132	206	337	528	169	264	412	676	1056
Maximum load on lightly loaded column		2279	3560	5563	9115	14242	4557	7121	11126	18230	28484

Values of permissible load are in kN.
Values given in italics indicate less practicable arrangements of bars (i.e. eight bars or large bars in small columns or four bars in large columns). In calculating these values allowance has *not* been made for the area of concrete displaced by the reinforcement.

*Asterisked values indicate maximum load that can be supported by a particular bar arrangement (irrespective of column size) when amount of longitudinal reinforcement is less than 1% and rules for lightly-loaded members apply (i.e. $N \leqslant f_y A_{sc}/0.15$).

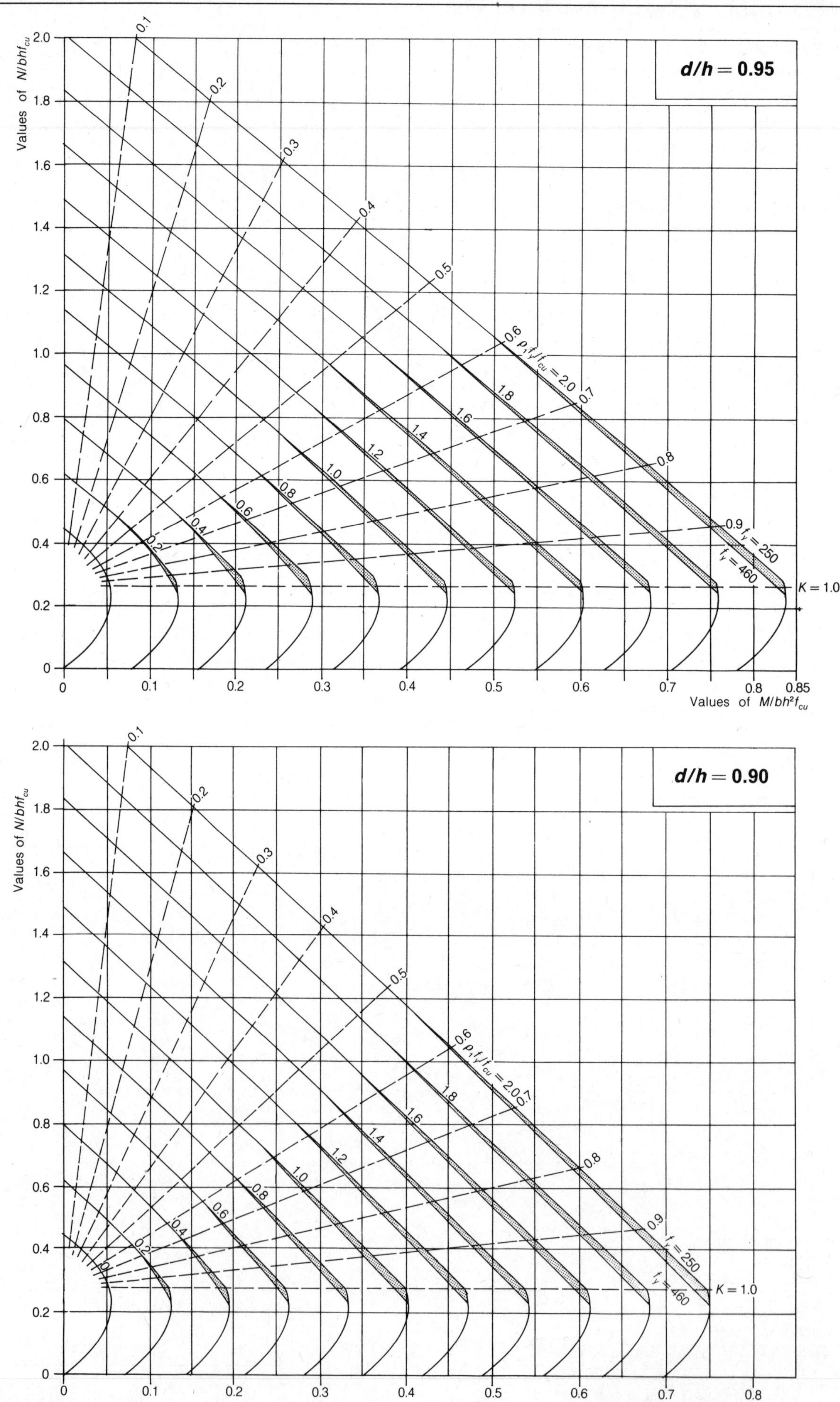
d/h = 0.95
Values of N/bhf_cu
Values of M/bh²f_cu
ρ₁f_y/f_cu = 2.0
1.8
1.6
1.4
1.2
1.0
0.8
0.6
0.4
0.2
0
0.1
0.2
0.3
0.4
0.5
0.6
0.7
0.8
0.9
K = 1.0
f_y = 250
f_y = 460
d/h = 0.90
Values of N/bhf_cu
Values of M/bh²f_cu
ρ₁f_y/f_cu = 2.0
K = 1.0
f_y = 250
f_y = 460

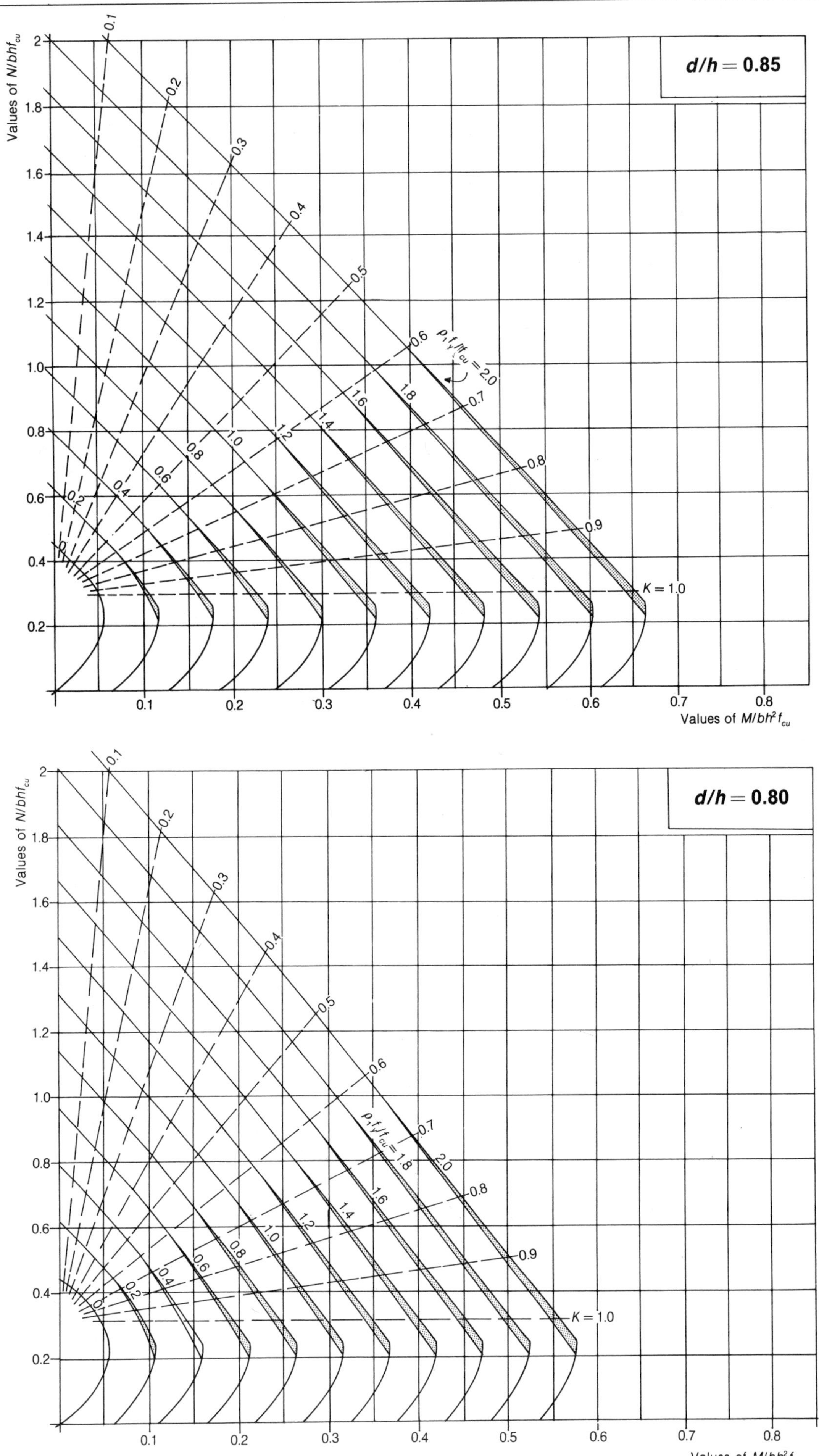
d/h = 0.85
d/h = 0.80
Values of N/bhf_cu
Values of M/bh²f_cu
ρ₁f_y/f_cu = 2.0
ρ₁f_y/f_cu = 1.8
K = 1.0

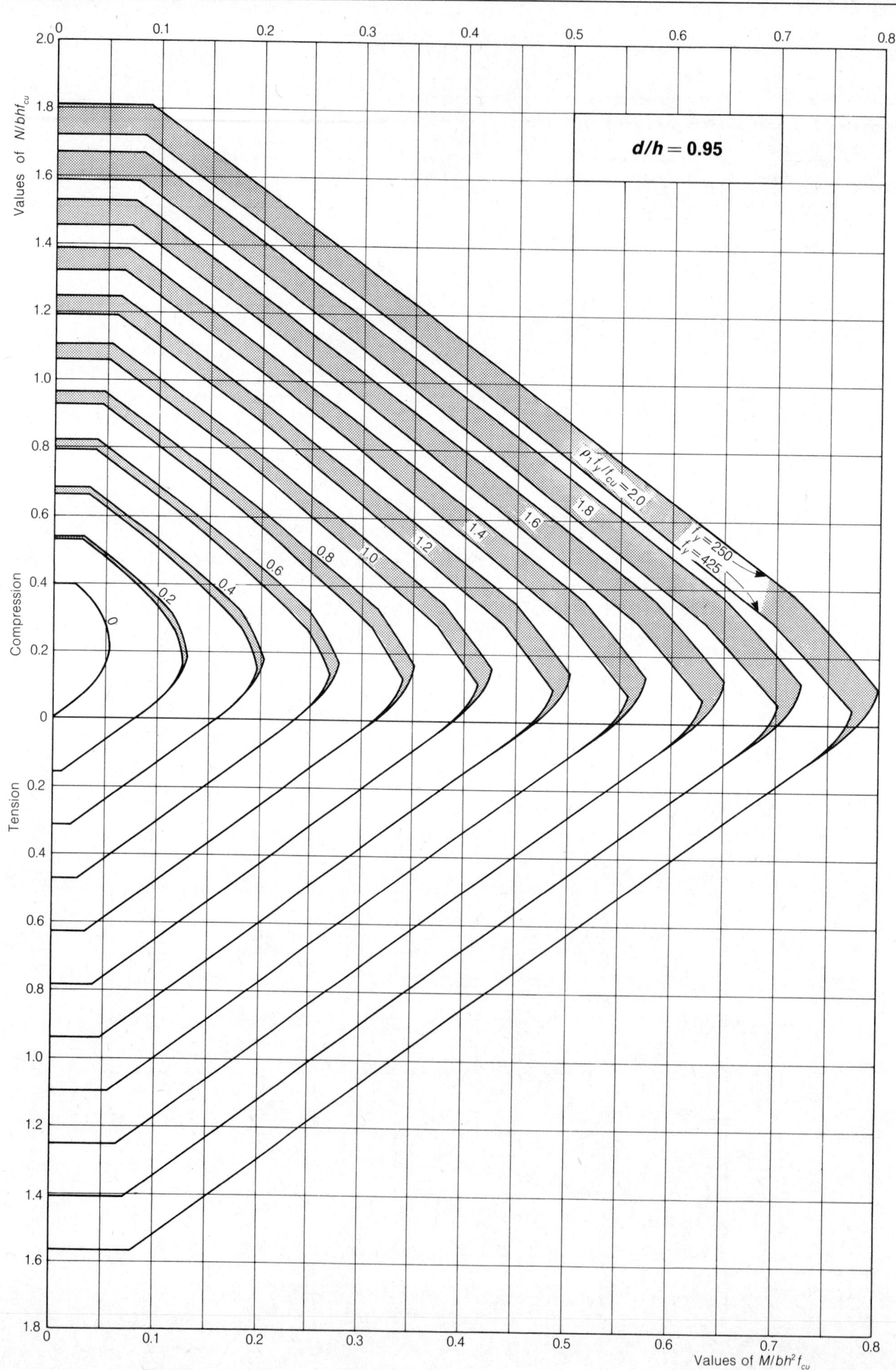
d/h = 0.95
Values of N/bhf_cu
Compression
Tension
Values of M/bh²f_cu
ρ₁f_y/f_cu = 2.0
1.8
1.6
1.4
1.2
1.0
0.8
0.6
0.4
0.2
0
f_y = 250
f_y = 425
0
0.1
0.2
0.3
0.4
0.5
0.6
0.7
0.8
2.0
1.8
1.6
1.4
1.2
1.0
0.8
0.6
0.4
0.2
0

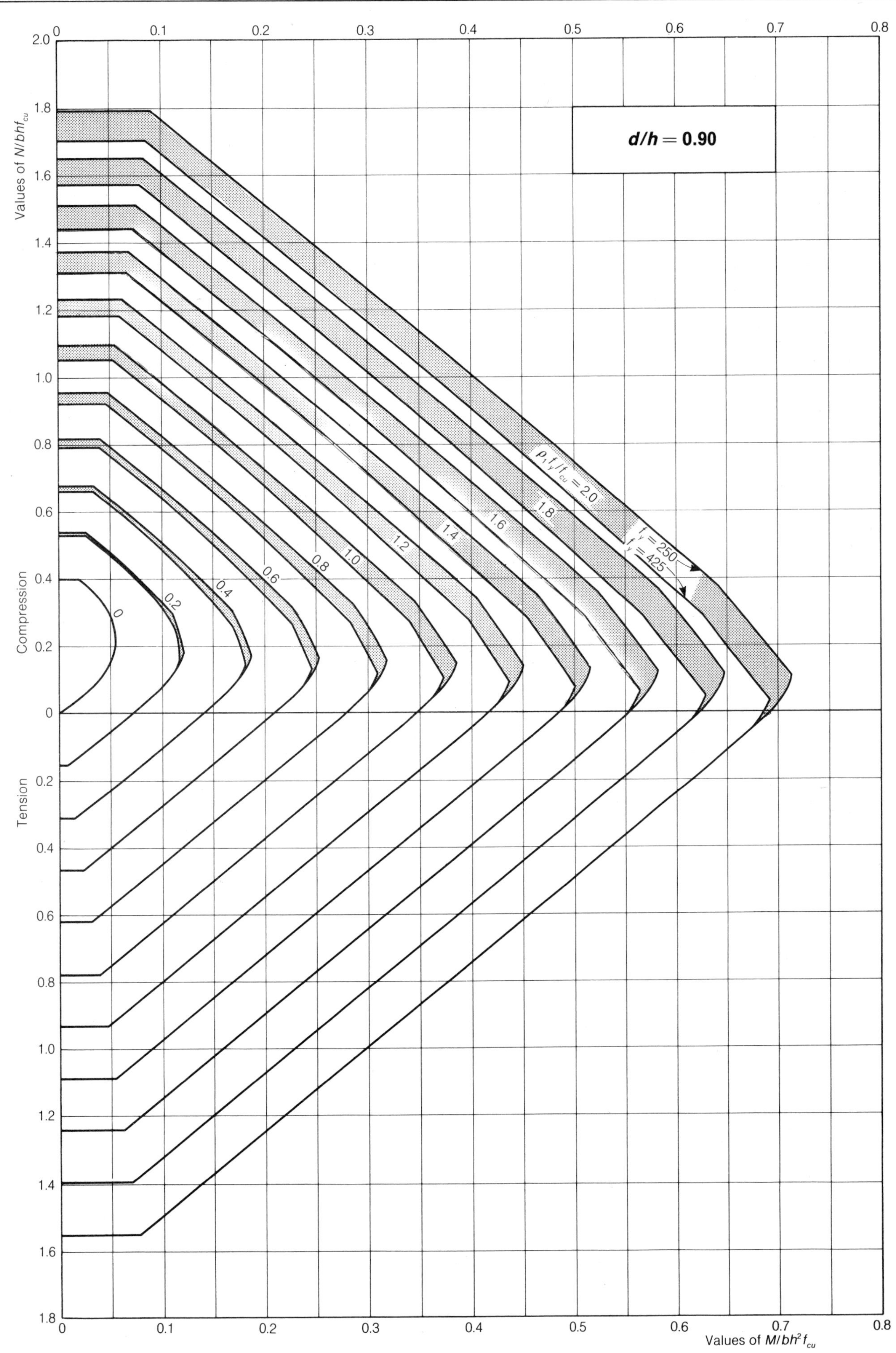

d/h = 0.90
Values of N/bhf_cu
Compression
Tension
Values of M/bh²f_cu
ρ₁f_y/f_cu = 2.0
1.8
1.6
1.4
1.2
1.0
0.8
0.6
0.4
0.2
0
f_y = 250
f_y = 425

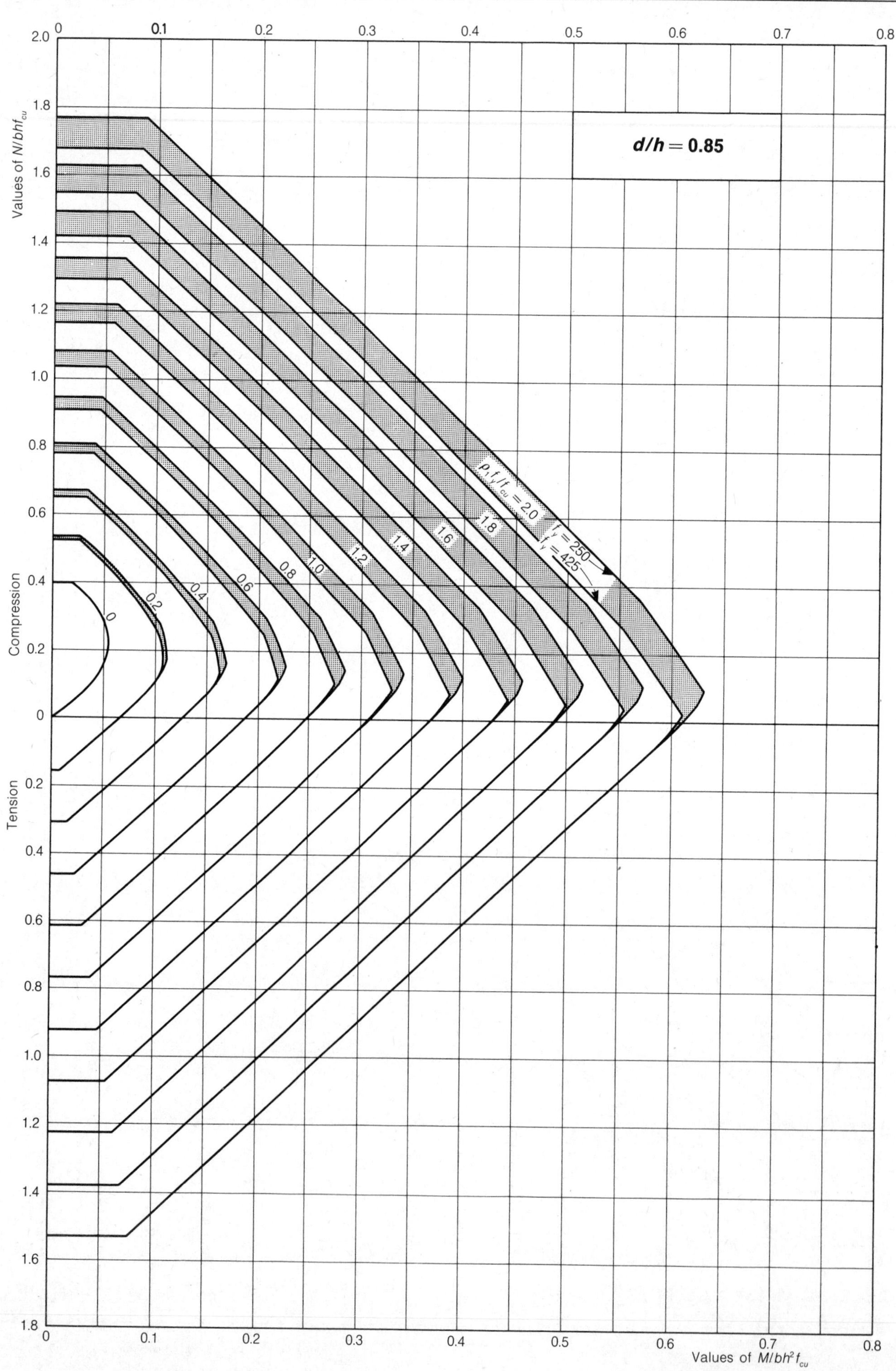
d/h = 0.85
Values of N/bhf_cu
Compression
Tension
Values of M/bh²f_cu
ρ₁f_y/f_cu = 2.0
1.8
1.6
1.4
1.2
1.0
0.8
0.6
0.4
0.2
0
f_y = 250
f_y = 425

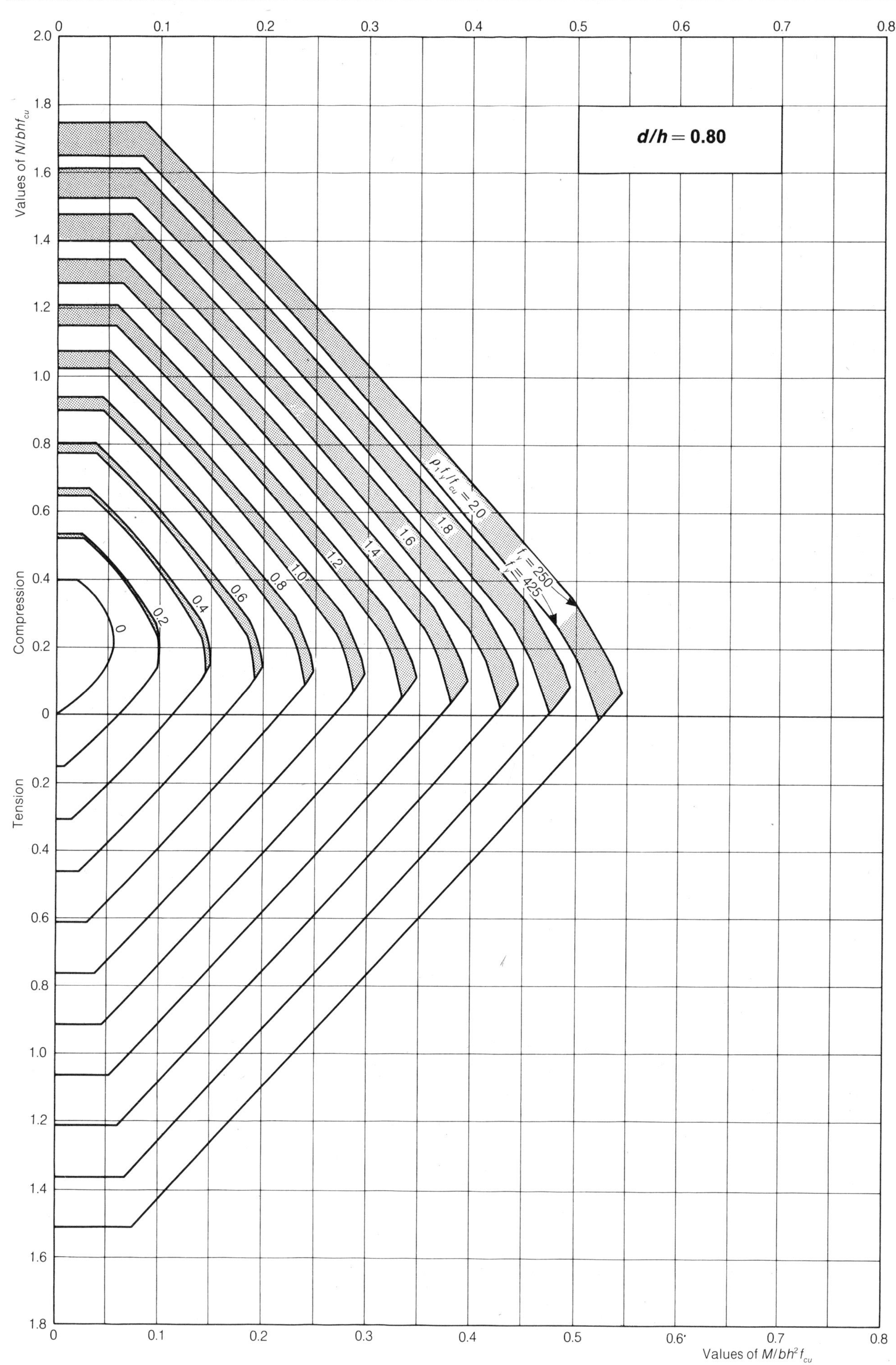
d/h = 0.80
Values of N/bhf_cu
Compression
Tension
Values of M/bh²f_cu
ρ₁f_y/f_cu = 2.0
1.8
1.6
1.4
1.2
1.0
0.8
0.6
0.4
0.2
0
f_y = 250
f_y = 425

0.222, $\beta = 1 - (7 \times 0.222/6) = 0.741$, and because M_x/h' $(= 300 \times 10^6/540 = 556 \times 10^3) > M_y/b'$ $(= 100 \times 10^6/240 = 417 \times 10^3)$, $M'_x = M_x + \beta M_y h'/b' = 300 \times 10^6 + 0.741 \times 100 \times 10^6 \times 540/240 = 467 \times 10^6$. Now with $M/bh^2f_{cu} = 467 \times 10^6/(300 \times 600^2 \times 30) = 0.144$, $N/bhf_{cu} = 0.222$ and $d'/h = 0.1$, from the right-hand chart forming *Table 152*, $\rho_1 f_{cu}/f_y = 0.26$, so that $\rho_1 = 0.26 \times 30/460 = 0.017$. Thus

$$A_{sc} = 0.017 \times 300 \times 600 = 3060\,\text{mm}^2$$

Provide four 32 mm bars, one near each corner of the section.

To CP110 ($f_y = 425\,\text{N/mm}^2$). Once again, try a section with $h = 600$ mm and $b = 300$ mm and assume 40 mm cover to 40 mm bars, so that $d'/h = 60/600 = 0.1$ and $d'/b = 60/300 = 0.2$. Then $M_x/bh^2f_{cu} = 300 \times 10^6/(300 \times 600^2 \times 30) = 0.0926$, $M_y/b^2hf_{cu} = 100 \times 10^6/(300^2 \times 600 \times 30) = 0.0617$ and $N/bhf_{cu} = 1.5 \times 10^6/(300 \times 600 \times 30) = 0.278$. Assume a ratio of M_y/M_{uy} of 0.6 say, so that $M_{uy}/b^2hf_{cu} = 0.0617/0.6 = 0.103$. Then, from *Table 156* with $M/bh^2f_{cu} = 0.103$ and $N/bhf_{cu} = 0.278$, read off $\rho_y f_y/f_{cu} = 0.26$: thus $\rho_y = 0.26 \times 30/425 = 0.0184$. From the upper chart on *Table 159*, if $f_{cu} = 30\,\text{N/mm}^2$, $f_y = 425\,\text{N/mm}^2$ and $\rho_1 = 0.184$, read off $N_{uz}/bh = 19$, so that $N/N_{uz} = 0.278 \times 30/19 = 0.44$. Now, from the lower chart, if $M_y/M_{uy} = 0.6$ and $N/N_{uz} = 0.44$, M_x/M_{ux} should be about 0.62, so that M_{ux}/bh^2f_{cu} should be about $0.0926/0.62 = 0.150$. From the chart forming *Table 154*, with $M/bh^2f_{cu} = 0.150$ and $N/bhf_{cu} = 0.278$, $\rho_x f_y/f_{cu} = 0.36$: thus $\rho_y = 0.36 \times 30/425 = 0.0254$.

Clearly, for a suitable section ρ_1 will lie somewhere between 0.0184 and 0.0254; try $\rho_1 = 0.022$ say. Now from *Table 156*, with $\rho_1 f_y/f_{cu} = 0.022 \times 425/30 = 0.31$ and $N/bhf_{cu} = 0.278$, $M_{uy}/b^2hf_{cu} = 0.12$ and thus $M_y/M_{uy} = 0.0617/0.12 = 0.529$. From *Table 154*, with $\rho_1 f_y/f_{cu} = 0.31$ and $N/bhf_{cu} = 0.278$, $M_{ux}/bh^2f_{cu} = 0.14$ and thus $M_x/M_{ux} = 0.0926/0.14 = 0.662$. From the upper chart on *Table 159* with $\rho_1 f_y = 425 \times 0.022 = 9.35$, $N_{uz}/bh = 20.5$ and thus $N/N_{uz} = 0.278 \times 30/20.5 = 0.406$. Thus $\alpha = (5/3)0.406 + (2/3) = 1.344$ and, since $0.662^{1.344} + 0.529^{1.344} = 1$, the section is satisfactory.

$$A_{screq} = 0.022 \times 300 \times 600 = 3960\,\text{mm}^2$$

Provide four 40 mm bars, one near each corner of the section.

This procedure is only valid if the bars are located at the corners of the section and thus contribute to the resistance of the section about axes. If not, the procedure must be modified accordingly. Details and an example are given in *Examples of the Design of Buildings*.

Using Beeby's method to design the foregoing section, $N_{uz} = 4.16 \times 10^6$ and thus $N/N_{uz} = 0.36$, so that $\alpha_n = 1.267$. The corresponding value of M_{ux} is thus 470×10^6 N mm. Now since $M_{ux}/bh^2f_{cu} = 0.145$ and $N/bhf_{cu} = 0.278$, $\rho_1 f_y/f_{cu} = 0.31$ and thus $\rho_1 = 0.022$ as obtained above.

One point that must be observed is that the ratios of M/M_u can be increased if the corresponding ratio of N/N_{uz} is higher. In other words, the limiting ratios of M/M_u correspond to the *minimum* ratio of N/N_{uz} and thus to the minimum value of N corresponding to the given values of M_x and M_y. This means that any condition in which relatively high bending moments act in conjunction with low axial load must be examined separately, if this is not the condition for which the section has been designed.

22.3 SHORT COLUMNS UNDER BENDING AND DIRECT FORCES: MODULAR-RATIO METHOD

The application of the modular-ratio method to sections subjected to bending and direct force is described more fully in section 5.14, and appropriate data are provided on *Tables 160–167*.

Table 160 covers the general case of any section subjected to direct thrust and uniaxial bending, while *Table 161* deals with rectangular columns having any reinforcement arrangement, modular ratio or value of d'/h. Where the reinforcement is disposed symmetrically in a symmetrical section and $\alpha_e = 15$, the design charts on *Tables 162* and *163* apply. The charts given on *Tables 164* and *165* apply to annular sections where $\alpha_e = 15$. *Table 166* gives information on uniaxial bending combined with direct tension, and biaxial bending and direct force is the subject of *Table 167*.

22.3.1 Uniaxial bending: general analysis

Example. The method outlined in *Table 160* for determining the stresses in a member having a non-rectangular cross-section is applied in the following example to the annular member shown at the foot of the table. The section is subject to combined bending and direct thrust.

Applied bending moment = 200 kN m. Applied direct force = 350 kN. Permissible stresses: $f_{st} = 140\,\text{N/mm}^2$; $f_{cr} = 7\,\text{N/mm}^2$, $\alpha_e = 15$. Eccentricity $e = 200 \times 10^3/350 = 571$ mm; $e/h = 571/1000 = 0.571$. Tensile and compressive stresses are likely to occur. Assume $x = 350$ mm (about $0.38d$).

The properties of the bars below the assumed neutral axis are considered in the accompanying table.

δA_s (mm^2)	a (mm)	$a - x$ (mm)	S (mm^3/10^3)	Sa (mm^4/10^6)	$\delta A_s a$ (mm^3/10^3)
628	500	150	94.2	47.1	314.2
628	653	303	190.4	124.3	410.3
628	783	433	272.1	213.0	492.0
628	870	520	326.7	284.3	546.6
314	900	550	172.8	155.5	282.7
2826			1056.2	824.2	2045.8

Depth to centre of tension $a_t = 824.2 \times 10^6/1056.2 \times 10^3 = 780$ mm.

The compressive area above the assumed neutral axis is divided into a series of horizontal strips, the properties of which are shown in the second table.

Depth to centre of compression $a_c = 4962.9 \times 10^6/36.5 \times 10^6 = 136$ mm. With $\alpha_e = 15$,

$$\bar{x} = \frac{(15 \times 2045.8 \times 10^3) + (40.65 \times 10^6)}{(15 \times 2826) + (220.5 \times 10^3)} = 271\,\text{mm}$$

The maximum stresses are given by

$$f_{cr} = \frac{350\,000 \times 350(571 + 780 - 271)}{(780 - 136)36.5 \times 10^6} = 5.62\,\text{N/mm}^2$$

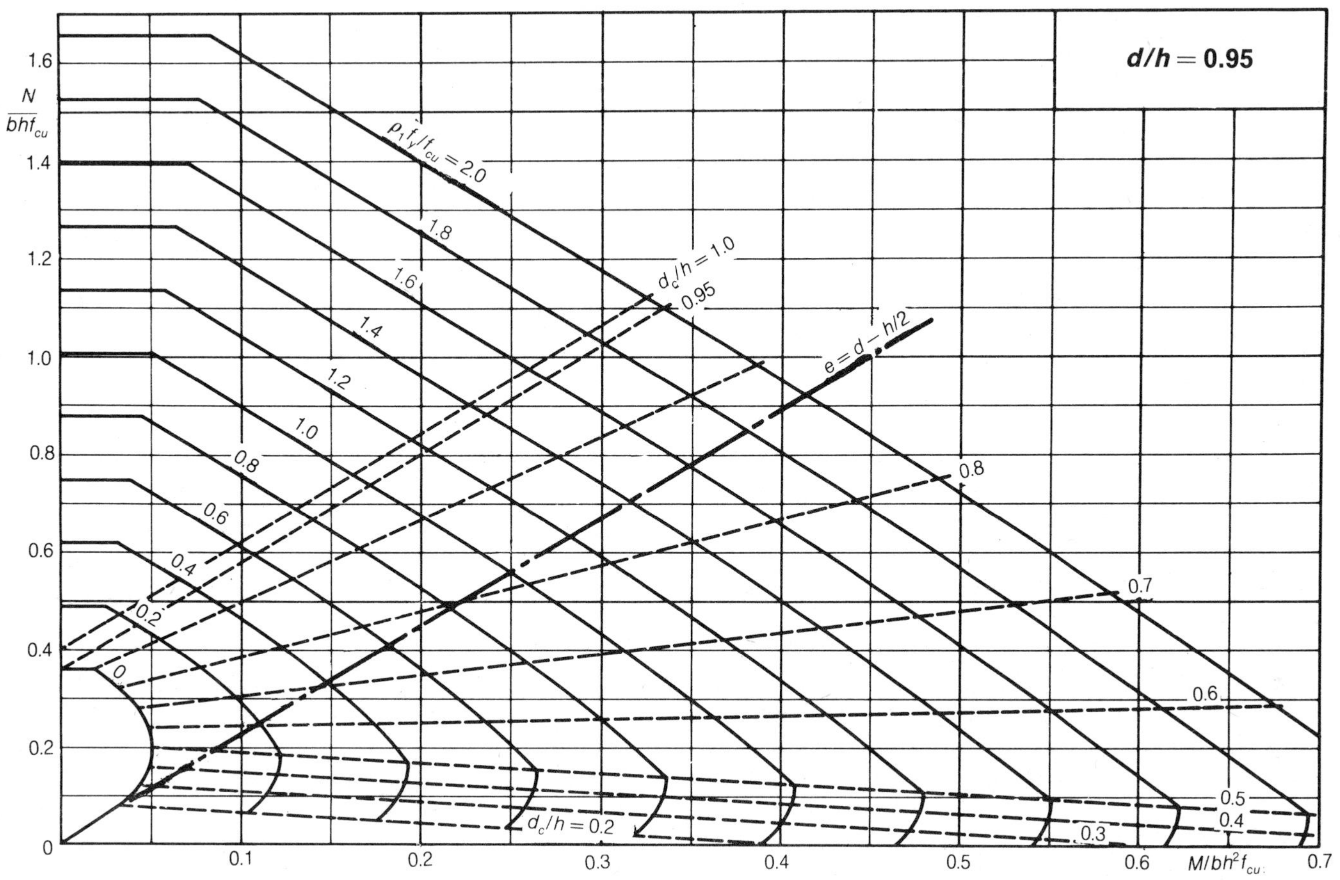

$d/h = 0.95$

N/bhf_{cu}: 0, 0.2, 0.4, 0.6, 0.8, 1.0, 1.2, 1.4, 1.6

M/bh^2f_{cu}: 0.1, 0.2, 0.3, 0.4, 0.5, 0.6, 0.7

$\rho_1 f_y/f_{cu} = 2.0$, 1.8, 1.6, 1.4, 1.2, 1.0, 0.8, 0.6, 0.4, 0.2, 0

$d_c/h = 1.0$, 0.95, 0.8, 0.7, 0.6, 0.5, 0.4, 0.3, $d_c/h = 0.2$

$e = d - h/2$

$d/h = 0.90$

N/bhf_{cu}: 0, 0.2, 0.4, 0.6, 0.8, 1.0, 1.2, 1.4, 1.6

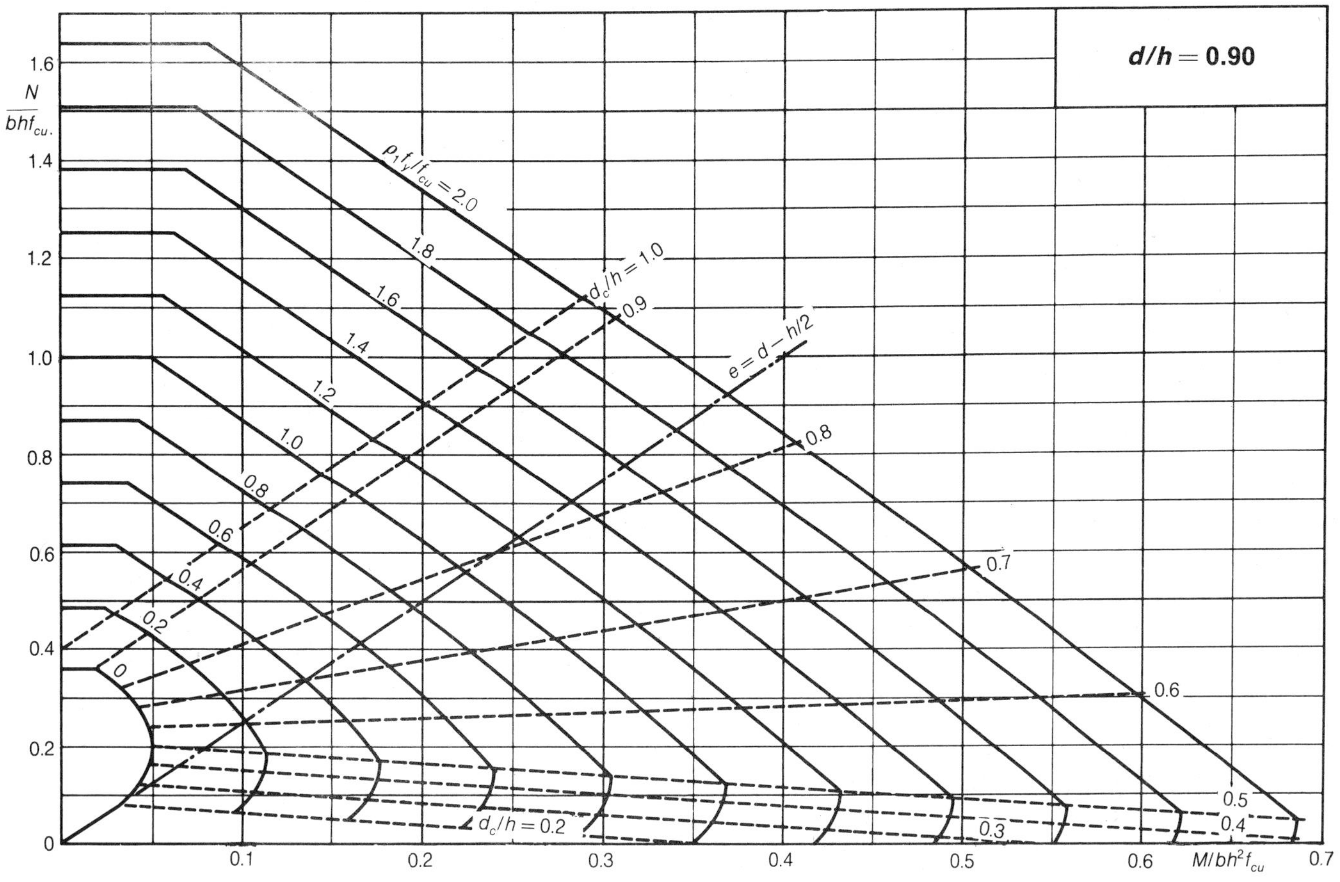

M/bh^2f_{cu}: 0.1, 0.2, 0.3, 0.4, 0.5, 0.6, 0.7

$\rho_1 f_y/f_{cu} = 2.0$, 1.8, 1.6, 1.4, 1.2, 1.0, 0.8, 0.6, 0.4, 0.2, 0

$d_c/h = 1.0$, 0.9, 0.8, 0.7, 0.6, 0.5, 0.4, 0.3, $d_c/h = 0.2$

$e = d - h/2$

Strip	b_s (mm)	h_s (mm)	$b_s h_s$ (mm²/10³)	$(\alpha_e-1)\delta A'_s$ (mm²/10³)	δA_{tr} (mm²/10³)	h_c (mm)	$x-h_c$ (mm)	$\delta A_{tr}(x-h_c)$ (mm²/10⁶)	$\delta A_{tr}h_c$ (mm²/10⁶)	$\delta A_{tr}h_c(x-h_c)$ (mm²/10⁶)
A	409	100	40.9	2.2	43.1	50	300	12.9	2.15	646.1
B	709	100	70.9	11.0	81.9	150	200	16.4	12.29	2458.3
C	554	100	55.4	8.8	64.2	250	100	6.4	16.04	1604.2
D	450	50	22.5	8.8	31.3	325	25	0.8	10.17	254.3
Σ					220.5			36.5	40.65	4926.9

$$f_{st} = \frac{(900-350)}{1056.2 \times 10^3}\left[\frac{(5.62 \times 36.5 \times 10^6)}{350} - 350\,000\right]$$

$$= 123.3\ \text{N/mm}^2$$

Check trial position of neutral axis:

$$\text{actual}\ x = 900 \bigg/ \left(1 + \frac{123.3}{15 \times 5.62}\right) = 365\ \text{mm}$$

compared with the assumed depth of 350 mm; thus a second trial is not necessary.

If such a trial were necessary, with say a greater depth than that assumed, the adjustment to the tabulations can readily be made by adding a further strip E, say 20 mm deep, to the compressive area and omitting from the reinforcement table any bars now included in the compression area. For the tension reinforcement, only the values of S and Sa are affected. In the compressive area the values of $x - h_c$ and consequently $\delta A_{tr}(x - h_c)$ and $\delta A_{tr}(x - h_c)h_c$ are affected. With these modifications the analysis then proceeds as shown for the first trial.

Note that if N_d is known to act at the centroid of the section, as would be the case of a chimney shaft,

$$e = \frac{M_d}{N_d} - \frac{1}{2}h + \bar{x}$$

22.3.2 Rectangular sections: uniaxial bending

Example. A rectangular member is 450 mm deep and 300 mm wide and is reinforced with two 25 mm bars in the top and three 25 mm bars in the bottom. The centres of the bars are 40 mm from the top and bottom faces respectively. Find the stresses produced in the section by the specified thrusts and bending moments, using *Table 161*. For all cases $h = 450$ mm; $b = 300$ mm; $d = 410$ mm; $d' = 40$ mm; $\alpha_e = 15$; $A_s = 1473\ \text{mm}^2$; $A'_s = 982\ \text{mm}^2$.

Case 1. $M_d = 25$ kN m; $N_d = 500$ kN acting at the centroid of the section.

Eccentricity $e = 25 \times 10^6/500 \times 10^3 = 50$ mm, which is less than $h/6$ (= 75 mm).

$$A_{tr} = (450 \times 300) + [14 \times (1473 + 982)] = 169\,300\ \text{mm}^2$$

$$J = \frac{1}{6} \times 450^2 \times 300 + \frac{14 \times 2455 \times 2}{450}(225 - 40)^2$$

$$= 15.4 \times 10^6\ \text{mm}^3$$

$$f_{cr} = \frac{500 \times 10^3}{169\,300} \pm \frac{25 \times 10^6}{15.4 \times 10^6}$$

$$= 4.58\ \text{N/mm}^2\ (\text{max.}) \qquad 1.32\ \text{N/mm}^2\ (\text{min.})$$

Case 2. $M_d = 25$ kN m; $N_d = 250$ kN acting at the centroid of the section.

Eccentricity $e = 25 \times 10^6/250 \times 10^3 = 100$ mm, which is greater than $h/6$ and less than $h/2$ (= 225 mm). A_{tr} and J are the same as in case 1.

$$f_{cr\,min} = \frac{250 \times 10^3}{169\,300} - \frac{25 \times 10^6}{15.4 \times 10^6} = 1.48 - 1.63 = -0.15\ \text{N/mm}^2$$

which is less than one-tenth of the allowable maximum compressive stress. Therefore the maximum compressive stress is $1.48 + 1.63 = 3.11\ \text{N/mm}^2$.

Case 3. $M_d = 40$ kN m; $N_d = 80$ kN with the line of action indefinite.

Eccentricity $e = 40 \times 10^6/80 \times 10^3 = 500$ mm, which is greater than $h/2$ and less than $3h/2$ (= 675 mm). With $\bar{x} = h/2$ approximately = 225 mm,

$$\beta_1 = \frac{500 - 225}{410} + 1 = 1.67$$

Assume that $x/d = 0.55$. Then $K_1 = 410 \times 300 \times 0.55 = 67\,700\ \text{mm}^2$. From *Table 161*, $\beta_2 = 0.224$ and $\beta_3 = 11.5$ approximately. Thus

$$f_{cr} = \frac{80 \times 10^3 \times 1.67}{(0.224 \times 300 \times 410) + 11.5 \times 982(1 - 40/410)}$$

$$= 3.54\ \text{N/mm}^2$$

and

$$f_{st} = \frac{3.54[(0.5 \times 67\,700) + (11.5 \times 982)] - 80 \times 10^3}{1473}$$

$$= 54.2\ \text{N/mm}^2$$

The value of x/d corresponding to these stresses is $1/[1 + (54.2/15 \times 3.54)] = 0.50$, compared with the assumed value of 0.55. Recalculate with an intermediate value of x/d of 0.51, for which $K_1 = 300 \times 410 \times 0.51 = 62\,730\ \text{mm}^2$. The accurate value of $\bar{x}$ is now

$$\bar{x} = \frac{(0.5 \times 410 \times 62\,730 \times 0.51) + (410 \times 15 \times 1473) + (14 \times 982 \times 40)}{62\,730 + (1473 \times 15) + (982 \times 14)}$$

$$= 164\ \text{mm}$$

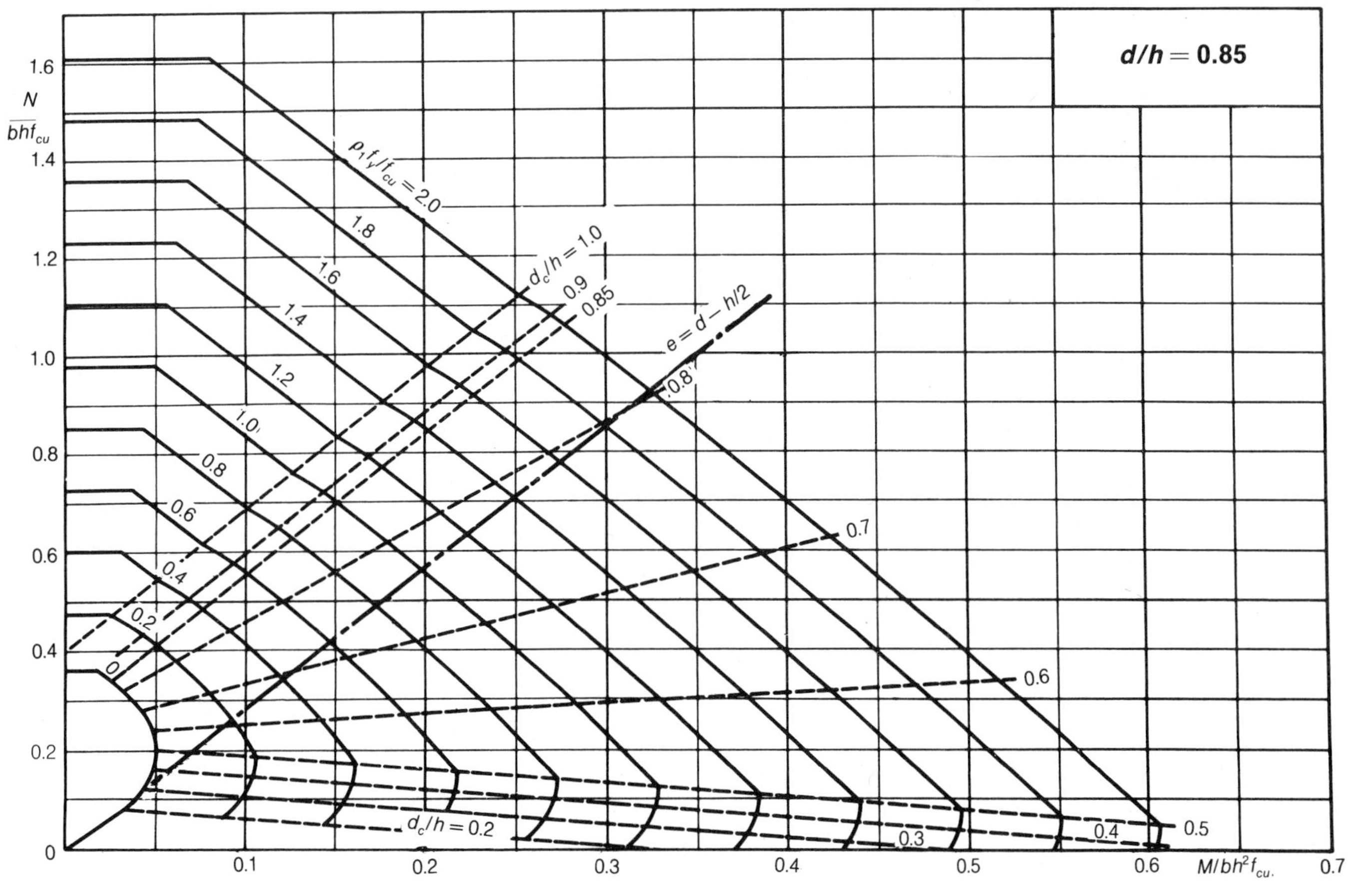

$d/h = 0.85$

N/bhf_{cu} — 0, 0.2, 0.4, 0.6, 0.8, 1.0, 1.2, 1.4, 1.6

M/bh^2f_{cu} — 0.1, 0.2, 0.3, 0.4, 0.5, 0.6, 0.7

$\rho_1 f_y/f_{cu} = 2.0$, 1.8, 1.6, 1.4, 1.2, 1.0, 0.8, 0.6, 0.4, 0.2, 0

$d_c/h = 1.0$, 0.9, 0.85, 0.8, 0.7, 0.6, 0.5, 0.4, 0.3, $d_c/h = 0.2$

$e = d - h/2$

$d/h = 0.80$

N/bhf_{cu} — 0, 0.2, 0.4, 0.6, 0.8, 1.0, 1.2, 1.4, 1.6

M/bh^2f_{cu} — 0.1, 0.2, 0.3, 0.4, 0.5, 0.6, 0.7

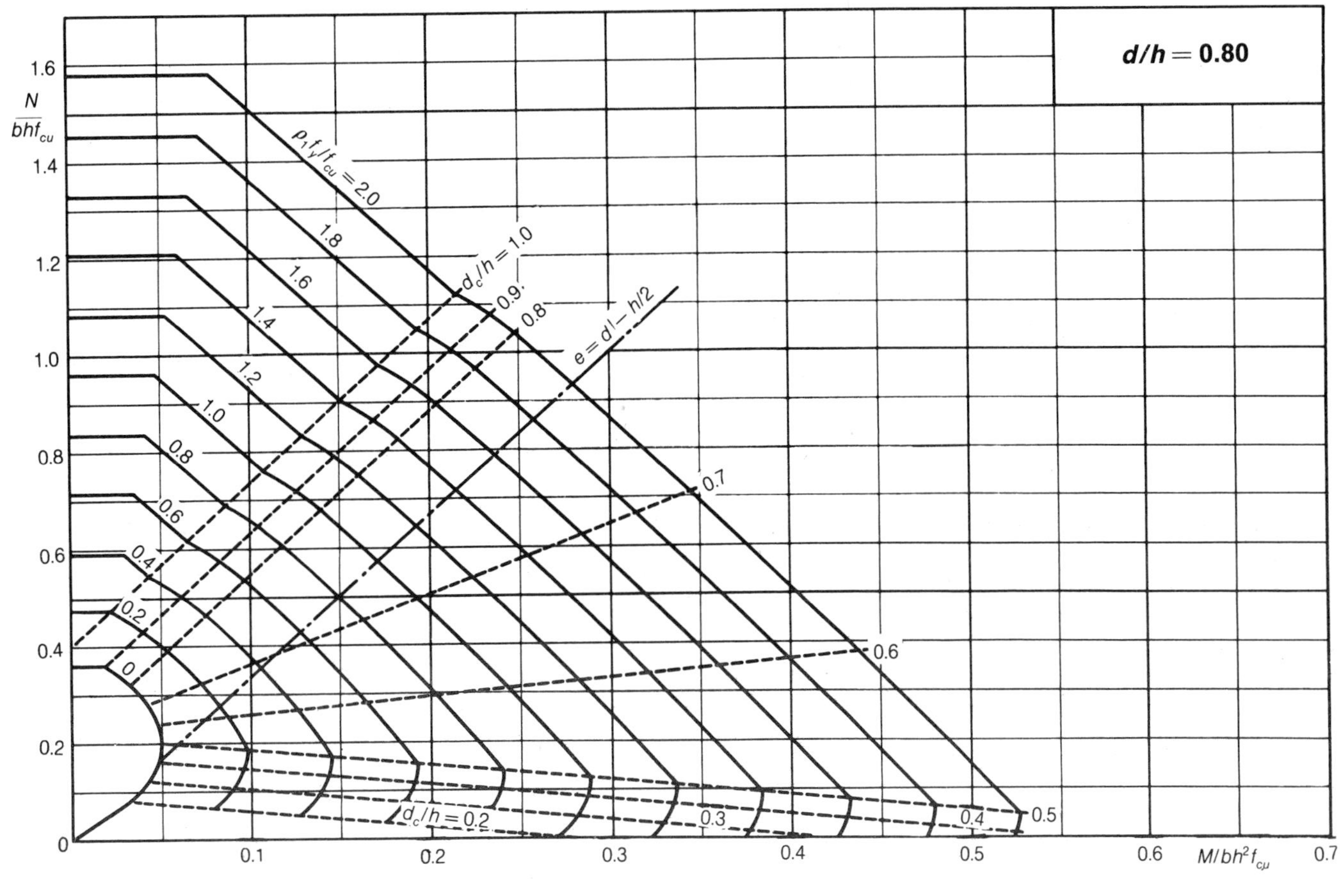

$\rho_1 f_y/f_{cu} = 2.0$, 1.8, 1.6, 1.4, 1.2, 1.0, 0.8, 0.6, 0.4, 0.2, 0

$d_c/h = 1.0$, 0.9, 0.8, 0.7, 0.6, 0.5, 0.4, 0.3, $d_c/h = 0.2$

$e = d - h/2$

(It is interesting to compare this value with the assumed approximate value of $h/2 = 225$ m.)

$$\beta_1 = \frac{450 - 164}{410} + 1 = 1.7 \qquad \beta_2 = 0.208 \qquad \beta_3 = 11.2$$

Now

$$f_{cr} = \frac{80 \times 10^3 \times 1.7}{(0.208 \times 300 \times 410) + (11.2 \times 982 \times 370/410)}$$

$$= 3.83\ \text{N/mm}^2$$

and

$$f_{st} = \frac{3.83[(0.5 \times 62\,730) + (11.2 \times 982)] - (80 \times 10^3)}{1473}$$

$$= 55.8\ \text{N/mm}^2$$

The corresponding value of x/d is now $1/[1 + (55.8/15 \times 3.83)] = 0.507$, which differs only marginally from the assumed value of 0.51.

Note that, if the line of action of N_d is known to be at the centroid of the section, there is no need to calculate $\bar{x}$, and $\beta_1 = 0.167$ as in the first trial.

22.3.3 Symmetrically reinforced rectangular columns

Equating axial forces and bending moments about the centre-line of a rectangular section subjected to direct force and bending, the following expressions are obtained.

When both tension and compression occur across the section:

$$\frac{N_d}{bhf_{cr}} = \frac{1}{2}\frac{x}{h} + \rho_c(\alpha_e - 1)\left(1 - \frac{d'}{h}\frac{h}{x}\right) - \rho_t\alpha_e\left(\frac{h}{x} - \frac{d'}{h}\frac{h}{x} - 1\right)$$

$$\frac{M_d}{bh^2f_{cr}} = \frac{1}{2}\frac{x}{h}\left(\frac{1}{2} - \frac{1}{3}\frac{x}{h}\right) + \rho_c(\alpha_e - 1)\left(1 - \frac{d'}{h}\frac{h}{x}\right)\left(\frac{1}{2} - \frac{d'}{h}\right)$$

$$+ \rho_t\alpha_e\left(\frac{h}{x} - \frac{d'}{h}\frac{h}{x} - 1\right)\left(\frac{1}{2} - \frac{d'}{h}\right)$$

Substituting, for example, $\rho_c = \rho_t = \rho_1/2$, $\alpha_e = 15$ and $d' = 0.1h$, these expressions simplify to

$$\frac{N_d}{bhf_{cr}} = \frac{1}{2}\frac{x}{h} + \rho_1\left(14.5 - 7.45\frac{h}{x}\right)$$

$$\frac{M_d}{bh^2f_{cr}} = \frac{1}{2}\frac{x}{h}\left(\frac{1}{2} - \frac{1}{3}\frac{x}{h}\right) + \rho_1\left(2.42\frac{h}{x} - 0.2\right)$$

and by substituting appropriate values of x/h and ρ_1, the related values of N_d/bhf_{cr} and M_d/bh^2f_{cr} can be obtained. Also, since the stresses are proportional to the distance from the neutral axis,

$$f_{st\,max} = \alpha_e f_{cr}(d - x)/x$$

When compression only occurs across section:

$$f_{cr\,max} = \frac{N_d}{A_{tr}} + \frac{M_d h}{2I_{tr}}$$

where, if $\rho_c = \rho_t = \rho_1/2$,

$$A_{tr} = bh[1 + \rho_1(\alpha_e - 1)]$$

$$I_{tr} = bh^3\left\{\frac{1}{12} + \left[\rho_1(\alpha_e - 1)\left(\frac{1}{2} - \frac{d'}{h}\right)\right]^2\right\}$$

Then if $\alpha_e = 15$ and $d' = 0.1h$, for example,

$$\frac{N_d}{bhf_{cr}} = (1 + 14\rho_1)\left[1 - \frac{M_d}{bh^2f_{cr}}\left(\frac{1}{4.48\rho_1 + 1/6}\right)\right]$$

This expression is valid where

$$\frac{N_d}{bhf_{cr}}\frac{4.48\rho_1 + 1/6}{(1 + 14\rho_1)} > \frac{M_d}{bh^2f_{cr}}$$

and by substituting appropriate values of ρ_1 and M_d/bh^2f_{cr}, the corresponding values of N_d/bhf_{cr} can be obtained.

Design charts derived in this way are provided on *Tables 162* and *163*.

22.3.4 Annular sections

Taylor and Turner (ref. 86) have shown that, if the individual reinforcing bars in an annular section are represented by an imaginary cylinder of steel providing the same cross-sectional area, the following expressions are obtained when the section is analysed using normal modular-ratio theory, and tension and compression occur across the section:

$$\frac{N}{rh_t f_{cr}} = 2(\sin\alpha - \alpha\cos\alpha - \rho_1\alpha_e\pi\cos\alpha)\Big/\left(1 + \frac{1}{2}\frac{h_t}{r} - \cos\alpha\right)$$

$$\frac{M}{r^2h_t f_{cr}} = (\alpha - \sin\alpha\cos\alpha + \rho_1\alpha_e\pi)\Big/\left(1 + \frac{1}{2}\frac{h_t}{r} - \cos\alpha\right)$$

where

$$\cos\alpha = \left(1 + \frac{1}{2}\frac{h}{r} - \alpha_e\frac{f_{cr}}{f_{st}}\right)\Big/\left(1 + \alpha_e\frac{f_{cr}}{f_{st}}\right)$$

By substituting appropriate values of α, α_e, h_t/r and ρ_1 in these expressions, the corresponding values of $N/rh_t f_{cr}$, $M/r^2h_t f_{cr}$ and f_{st}/f_{cr} calculated may be used to plot charts as shown on *Tables 164* and *165*. If a modular ratio of 15 is adopted, these charts may be used directly: for other values of α_e, the procedure described on *Table 165* should be followed.

If the section is loaded axially, $M/r^2h_t f_{cr} = 0$ and $N/rh_t f_{cr} = [1 + \rho_1(\alpha_e - 1)]2\pi$.

For other combinations of load and moment giving rise to compression across the entire section, the relationship between $N/rh_t f_{cr}$ and $M/r^2h_t f_{cr}$ is linear between the limiting values given by the above expressions and those for axial loading.

The following examples illustrate the use of *Tables 162–166.*

Example 1. Design a section to resist a bending moment of 100 kN m and a direct force of 500 kN if the maximum permissible stresses in the materials are $f_{cr} = 8.5\ \text{N/mm}^2$ and $f_{st} = 140\ \text{N/mm}^2$.

Assume initially that $d/h = 0.9$, and try a section with $b = 300$ mm and $h = 500$ mm. Then

$$M_d/bh^2f_{cr} = 100 \times 10^6/300 \times 500^2 \times 8.5 = 0.157$$
$$N_d/bhf_{cr} = 500 \times 10^3/300 \times 500 \times 8.5 = 0.392$$

Since $d/h = 0.9$, the upper chart on *Table 163* applies. Read

Values of ρ_1 for given values of f_y

$f_y =$ 250: 0, 0.02, 0.04, 0.06, 0.08

410: 0, 0.02, 0.04, 0.06, 0.08

425: 0, 0.02, 0.04, 0.06, 0.08

460: 0, 0.02, 0.04, 0.06, 0.08

Values of N_{uz}/bh (N/mm^2): 10, 20, 30, 40

$f_{cu} = 40$ N/mm^2, 35, 30, 25, 20

Values of $\rho_1 f_y$ (N/mm^2): 0, 10, 20, 30, 40

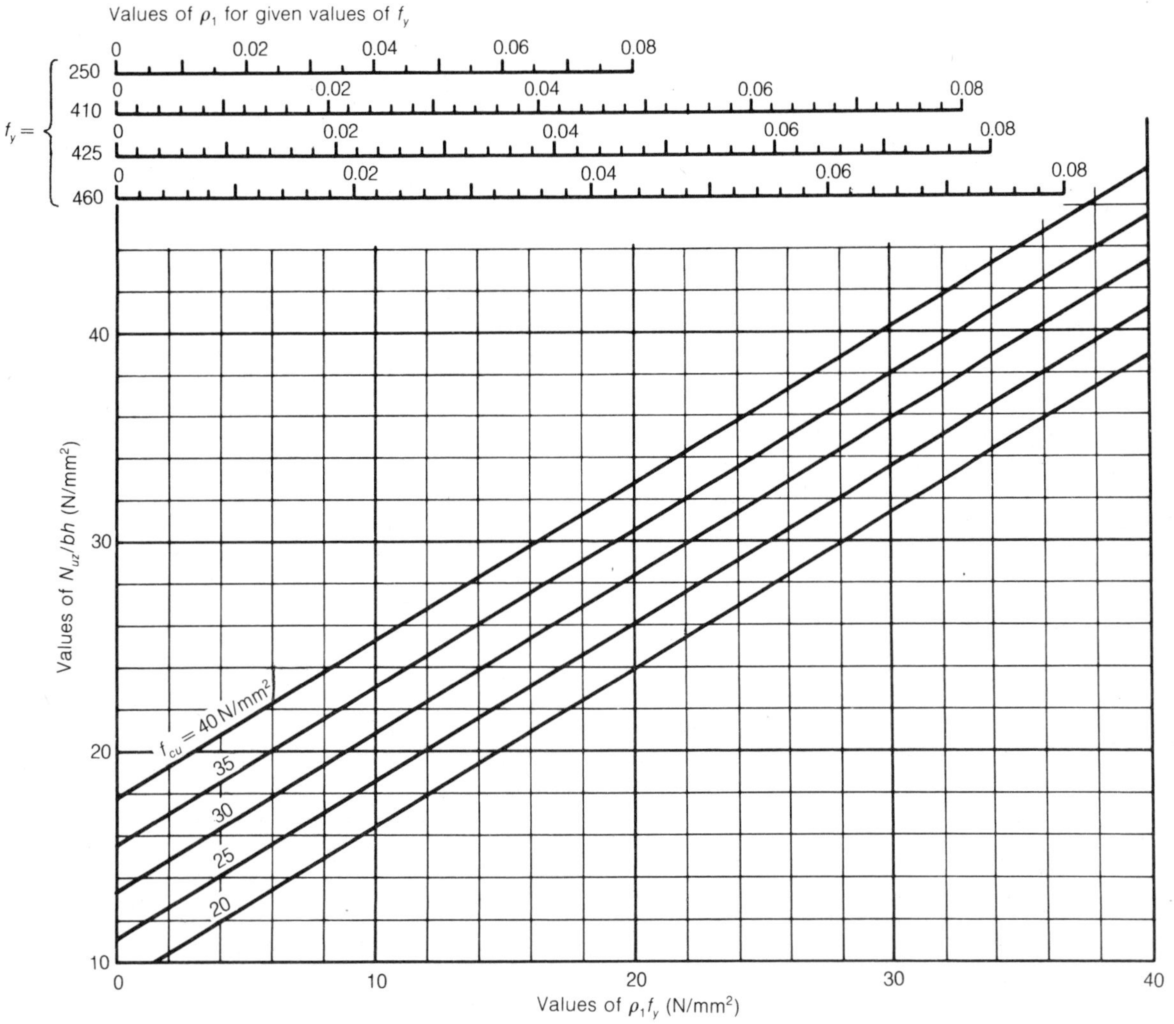

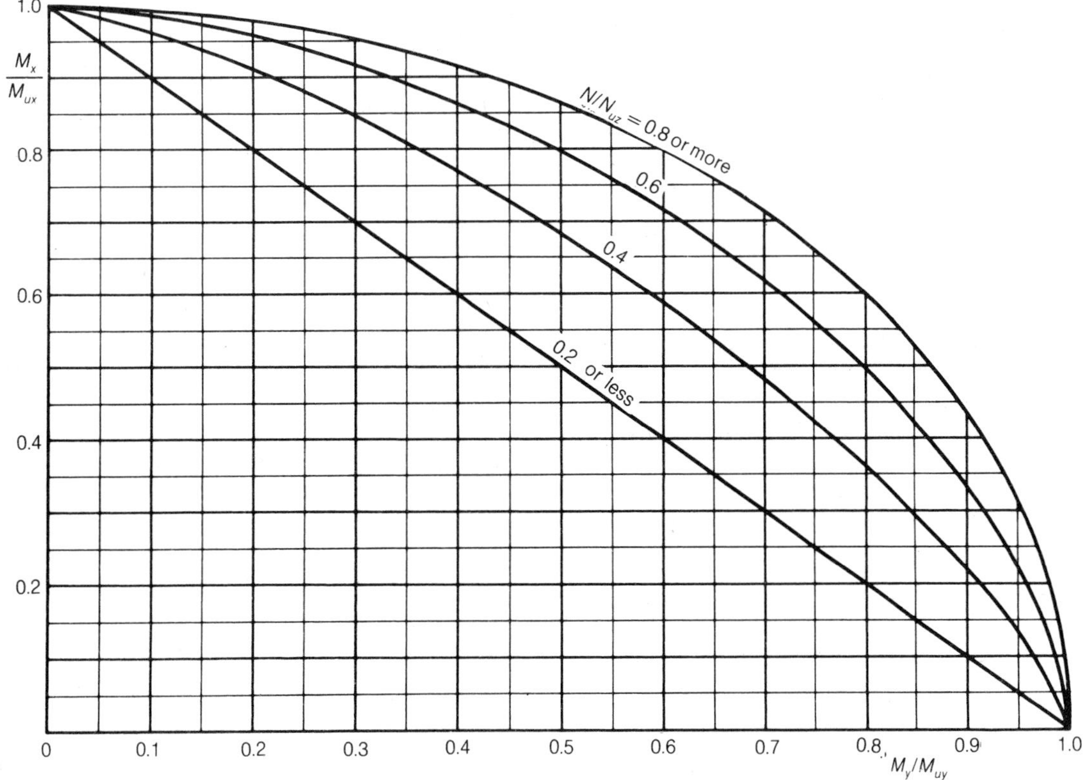

The method of using the charts on this page is described in section 22.2.4 and example 2 following that section.

$\rho_1 = 0.019$ and $x/h = 0.67$ corresponding to the given values of $M_d/bh^2 f_{cr}$ and N_d/bhf_{cr}. The total area of steel required is

$$A_{sc} = 0.019 \times 300 \times 500 = 2850\,\text{mm}^2$$

Provide five 20 mm bars near each face.

$$f_{st\,max} = \frac{15 \times 8.5(0.9 - 0.67)500}{0.67 \times 500} = 43.8\,\text{N/mm}^2$$

Example 2. Determine the maximum stresses in a trial section having $b = 300$ mm, $h = 500$ mm and reinforced with four 20 mm bars near each face (with 40 mm concrete cover) when subjected to a direct force of 500 kN and a moment of 25 kN m.

With 40 mm cover, $d' = 40 + 10 = 50$ mm, so that $d/h = 0.9$. Eccentricity $e = M_d/N_d = 25 \times 10^3/500 = 50$ mm and $e/h = 50/500 = 0.1$, while $\rho_1 = 8 \times 314/300 \times 500 = 0.017$. From the upper chart on *Table 163*, read off a value of N_d/bhf_{cr} of 0.82 corresponding to the given values of e/h and ρ_1. Then

$$f_{cr\,max} = \frac{500 \times 10^3}{0.82 \times 300 \times 500} = 4.07\,\text{N/mm}^2$$

The chart also indicates that compression only occurs over the entire section. Thus the maximum stress in the reinforcement is compressive and is less than $15 \times 4.07 = 61\,\text{N/mm}^2$. More accurately,

$$f_{sc\,max} = \alpha_e\left[f_{cr\,max} - \frac{M_d d'}{I_{tr}}\right]$$

$$= 15 f_{cr}\left[1 - \left\{(M_d/bh^2 f_{cr}) \middle/ \left[\frac{1}{12} + 14\rho_1\left(\frac{1}{2} - \frac{d'}{h}\right)^2\right]\right\}\frac{d'}{h}\right]$$

where $\alpha_e = 15$. Thus in the present case,

$$f_{sc\,max} = 15 \times 4.07[1 - (0.082 \times 0.1)/(\tfrac{1}{12} + 14 \times 0.017 \times 0.4^2)]$$
$$= 56.9\,\text{N/mm}^2$$

where the value of $M_d/bh^2 f_{cr} = 0.082$ is read from the chart at the intersection of the curves for the given values of e/h, ρ_1 and N_d/bhf_{cr}.

Example 3. Design a section to resist a bending moment of 100 kN m together with a direct thrust of 200 kN assuming maximum permissible stresses in the materials of 8.5 N/mm² and $f_{st} = 140\,\text{N/mm}^2$. (Compare with example 1.)

Assume that $d/h = 0.9$ and try a section with $b = 300$ mm and $h = 500$ mm as before. Now $e = M_d/N_d = 100 \times 10^6/200 \times 10^3 = 500$ mm and $e/h = 500/500 = 1$. From the upper chart on *Table 163* read off $\rho_1 = 0.015$ and $x/h = 0.41$ corresponding to

$$N_d/bhf_{cr} = 200 \times 10^3/300 \times 500 \times 8.5 = 0.157$$

$$M_d/bh^2 f_{cr} = 100 \times 10^6/300 \times 500^2 \times 8.5 = 0.157$$

Now

$$f_{st\,max} = \frac{\alpha_e f_{cr}(d-x)}{x} = \frac{15 \times 8.5(0.9 - 0.41)500}{0.41 \times 500}$$
$$= 152.4\,\text{N/mm}^2$$

which exceeds the permissible value. Since $\alpha_e f_{cr}/x = f_{st}/(d-x)$, the minimum ratio of x/h which will avoid f_{st} being exceeded is

$$\frac{\alpha_e f_{cr}}{\alpha_e f_{cr} + f_{st}}\left(\frac{d}{h}\right)$$

which in the present case is $(15 \times 8.5 \times 0.9)/(15 \times 8.5 + 140) = 0.43$. From the intersection of the curves for $M_d/bh^2 f_{cr} = 0.157$ and $x/h = 0.43$, read off $\rho_1 = 0.0155$. The total area of steel required $= 0.0155 \times 300 \times 500 = 2325\,\text{mm}^2$; provide four 20 mm bars near each face.

Example 4. A rectangular member is 400 mm deep and 250 mm wide and is reinforced with two 25 mm bars near the top face and three 25 mm bars near the bottom face. If $d = 348$ mm and $d' = 32$ mm, determine the stresses induced if $M_d = 10$ kN m and $N_d = 100$ kN (tension).

Table 166 applies. $A_{st} = 982\,\text{mm}^2$ and $A_{s2} = 1473\,\text{mm}^2$. $\bar{x} = 1473 \times 296/2455 = 178$ mm. $e = 10 \times 10^3/100 = 100$ mm, which is less than $d - d' - \bar{x} = 118$ mm. Then

$$f_{st1}(\text{in } A_{s1}) = \frac{100 \times 10^3(100 + 178)}{1473 \times 296} = 63.8\,\text{N/mm}^2$$

$$f_{st2}(\text{in } A_{s2}) = \frac{100 \times 10^3(296 - 100 - 178)}{982 \times 296} = 6.19\,\text{N/mm}^2$$

Example 5. Calculate the reinforcement required in a shaft having a mean radius of 1 m and a thickness of 100 mm when subjected to an axial load of 2 MN combined with a moment of 1.5 MN m. The maximum permissible stresses are $f_{cr} = 7\,\text{N/mm}^2$ and $f_{st} = 140\,\text{N/mm}^2$, and $\alpha_e = 15$.

From the upper chart on *Table 165*, with $h_t/r = 100/1000 = 0.1$, $M_d/r^2 h_t f_{cr} = 1.5 \times 10^9/(1000^2 \times 100 \times 7) = 2.14$

$$N_d/rh_t f_{cr} = 2 \times 10^6/(1000 \times 100 \times 7) = 2.86$$

$\rho_1 = 0.015$ and $f_{st}/f_{cr} = 5.8$. Thus

$$A_{sc\,req} = 0.015 \times \pi \times 1000 \times 100 \times 2 = 9425\,\text{mm}^2$$

Provide forty-eight 16 mm bars; these will be spaced at about 130 mm centres. The maximum stress in the reinforcement is $7 \times 5.8 = 41\,\text{N/mm}^2$.

22.4 SLENDER COLUMNS

If the ratio of the effective length of a column to its least radius of gyration exceeds about 50, the member is considered to be a 'long' or slender column and the safe load that it will support is less than that carried by a similar short column.

22.4.1 BS8110 design procedure

Provision for column slenderness is made in BS8110 and CP110 by a different procedure from that adopted in earlier Codes. According to BS8110, with braced columns of normal-weight concrete where the ratio of the effective height to the corresponding overall 'depth' of section about either principal axis exceeds 15, the same design methods as described in BS8110 for short columns subjected to axial load and uniaxial or biaxial bending are employed but the moment is increased to take account of any possible deflection of the column. For unbraced columns the corres-

Compressive stresses only

Equivalent area of strip: $\delta A_{tr} = b_s h_s + (\alpha_e - 1)\delta A'_s$

Equivalent area of transformed section: $A_{tr} = \sum \delta A_{tr}$

Depth to centroid of transformed section: $\bar{x} = \sum \delta A_{tr} h_c / A_{tr}$

Moment of inertia of transformed section about centroid:

$$I_{tr} = \sum \delta A_{tr}\left[\frac{(h_s)^2}{12} + (h_c - \bar{x})^2\right]$$

Compressive stresses:

$$f_{cr\,max} = \frac{N_d}{A_{tr}} + \frac{M_d \bar{x}}{I_{tr}} \qquad f_{cr\,min} = \frac{N_d}{A_{tr}} - \frac{M_d (h - \bar{x})}{I_{tr}}$$

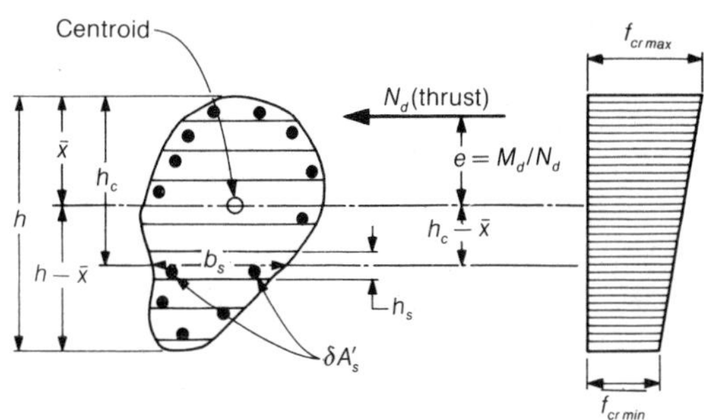

Combined compressive and tensile stresses

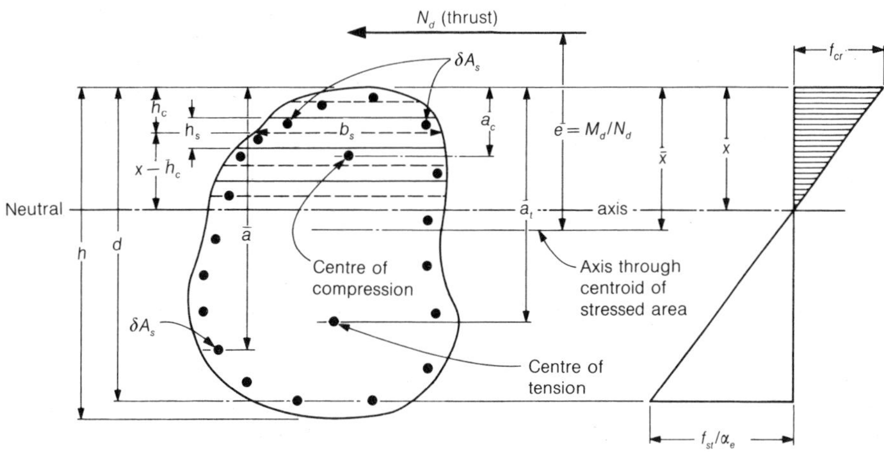

Assume a value of x.
Depth to centre of tension: $a_t = \sum Sa / \sum S$, where $S = (a - x)\delta A_s$
If all bars are of the same size: $a_t = \sum a(a - x) / \sum (a - x)$
Equivalent area of strip: $\delta A_{tr} = b_s h_s + (\alpha_e - 1)\delta A'_s$
Depth to centre of compression: $a_c = \sum (x - h_c) h_c \delta A_{tr} / \sum (x - h_c)\delta A_{tr}$
Position of centroid of stressed area:

$$\bar{x} = \frac{\alpha_e \sum \delta A_s a + \sum \delta A_{tr} h_c}{\alpha_e \sum \delta A_s + \sum \delta A_{tr}}$$

Maximum stresses:

$$f_{cr} = \frac{N_d x (e + a_t - \bar{x})}{(a_t - a_c)\sum (x - h_c)\delta A_{tr}}$$

$$f_{st} = \frac{(d - x)}{\sum S}\left[\frac{f_{cr}}{x}\sum (x - h_c)\delta A_{tr} - N_d\right]$$

Finally, check the assumed value of x by substituting these stresses in

$$\frac{x}{d} = \frac{1}{1 + f_{st}/(\alpha_e f_{cr})}$$

Example

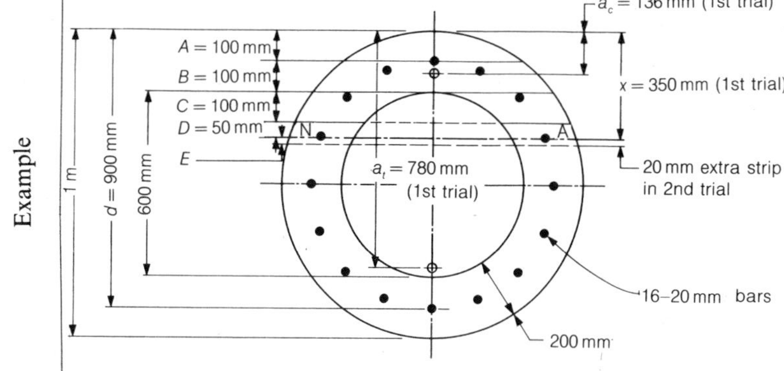

Thrust = 350 kN
Bending moment = 200 kN m

$$e = \frac{200 \times 10^3}{350} = 571\text{ mm}$$

ponding critical ratio is 10, as it is for lightweight concrete columns whether braced or not. For members of any cross-section and with any arrangement of reinforcement, BS8110 provides diagrams and tables indicating the additional moments that must be considered in braced and unbraced columns. However, when rectangular or circular sections are reinforced symmetrically the following simplified requirements apply.

For columns bending about a principal axis where the greater cross-sectional dimension is less than three times the lesser and for columns bending about the major axis where the ratio of l_e/h does not exceed 20, the total moment to be resisted at the point of maximum additional moment is

$$M_t = M_i + \beta Nh$$

where M_i is the initial moment due to normal ultimate load calculated by simple elastic analysis, and h is the overall depth of the cross-section in the plane of bending BS8110 states that with braced columns, M_i may be assumed to be equal to $0.4M_1 + 0.6M_2$ or $0.4M_2$, whichever is the greater, where M_1 and M_2 are the lesser and greater initial end moments acting on the column. The point of maximum additional moment is near the mid-height of the column, and at the ends only one-half of this additional moment need be considered. Thus the maximum uniaxial moment that need be taken into consideration when designing a slender column is either $M_i + \beta Nh$, $M_1 + \beta Nh/2$ or M_2, but in no case may this be less than Ne_{min}, where e_{min} is the lesser of $h/20$ or 20 mm.

For unbraced columns the additional moment must be assumed to act at the ends of the column, and so the total moment M_t to be resisted is $M_i + \beta Nh$, where M_i is the greater of the two end moments acting on the column.

When normal-weight concrete is used the slenderness factor β is given by

$$\beta = \frac{1}{2000}\left(\frac{l_e}{b'}\right)^2$$

where l_e is the effective height of the column in the plane being considered and b' is the smaller column dimension. If lightweight concrete is used, β should be multiplied by 5/3. Values of β corresponding to different l_e/h ratios can be read from the scales at the top of *Table 168*.

For columns bent about their major axis, where either the length of the shorter side is less than one-third that of the longer or the ratio of l_e/h exceeds 20, BS8110 recommends that the section is designed to resist biaxial bending but with an initial moment of zero about the minor axis.

In cases where the initial moments about both principal axes are significant, the section must be designed to resist biaxial bending. Additional moments are calculated about each axis separately but now taking b' as h, the depth of the section about the axis currently being considered. Each additional moment is combined with its appropriate initial moment to obtain the total moment acting about each principal axis, and these are then incorporated into a single equivalent uniaxial moment as described earlier for short columns subjected to biaxial bending.

The additional moment βNh evaluated above can be reduced by multiplication by a factor K of $(N_{uz} - N)/(N_{uz} - N_{bal}) \leqslant 1$, where N is the ultimate axial load for which the section is being designed, N_{uz} is the resistance of the trial section designed initially to resist N and M_t under pure axial load only, and N_{bal} is the axial load at which, for the section being considered, a maximum compressive strain of 0.0035 in the concrete and a tensile strain of 0.002 in the outermost layer of tension reinforcement are attained simultaneously. In this latter condition, which occurs when $x = 7d/11$, the corresponding tensile stress in the tension steel equals the compressive stress in the compression reinforcement provided that $d'/h \not> 0.214$. Thus if equal amounts of reinforcement with similar concrete cover are provided near both faces of a section, the resistance of the section to axial force when this condition occurs is that of the concrete alone, and the actual *proportion* of reinforcement provided does not influence the calculation of N_{bal} although the *position* of this reinforcement does. With a parabolic-rectangular stress-block,

$$\frac{N_{bal}}{bh} = k_1 x = \tfrac{4}{9} f_{cu}\left[1 - \frac{(f_{cu})^{1/2}}{53.05}\right]$$

$$= \frac{28}{99} f_{cu}\left[1 - \frac{(f_{cu})^{1/2}}{53.05}\right]\left(1 - \frac{d'}{h}\right)$$

For simplicity, BS8110 permits N_{bal} to be taken as $f_{cu}bd/4$ and N_{uz} is given by $0.45 f_{cu}A_c + 0.87 f_y A_{sc}$. Having evaluated N_{bal}, N_{uz} and N (or N_{bal}/bh, N_{uz}/bh and N/bh) for a particular trial section, N_{bal}/N and N_{uz}/N can be calculated and the appropriate value of K read from the lower chart on *Table 168*. The additional moment may now be modified, the total moment M_t calculated and the section redesigned to resist N and the increased value of M thus obtained. N_{bal} and N_{uz} are recalculated and a further value of K and thus M_t determined, the procedure being repeated until changes in K become negligible and a satiafactory section is obtained. If individual column design charts derived from rigorous limit-state analysis are used, such as those provided in Part 3 of BS8110 and *Examples of the Design of Buildings*, lines representing K can be included on the actual charts as described in section 5.15.1. This has also been done on the charts forming *Tables 151 and 152*.

In practice the cyclic trial-and-adjustment design procedure is actually less cumbersome than at first appears since, provided the dimensions of the concrete section remain satisfactory and the additional moment can be resisted by adjusting ρ_1 only, the value of N_{bal} remains unchanged throughout and it is merely necessary to alter N_{uz}, K, M_i and ρ_1 in turn. However, the lower chart on *Table 168* clearly shows that with low ratios, slight increases of N_{uz}/N markedly increase K. Thus to minimize 'recycling' it is advisable to reduce the value of K obtained from this chart by 20 to 30% if the ratio of N_{uz}/N is below 2 say, during the first cycle. This design procedure is illustrated in some detail in the example to follow.

In general the clear distance between the end restraints of a column should never be greater than 60 times the least lateral dimension, while the clear height of an unbraced unrestrained column must also not exceed $100\ b^2/h$ where b and h are the smaller and larger dimensions of the column.

If the average value of l_e/h for all columns at a particular level exceeds 20, the bases or other members connected to

Eccentricity about centroid of stressed area:

$$e = \frac{\text{bending moment}}{\text{thrust}} = \frac{M_d}{N_d}$$

Method applies to any modular ratio α_e, any proportions of A_s and A'_s and any ratio of d'/d

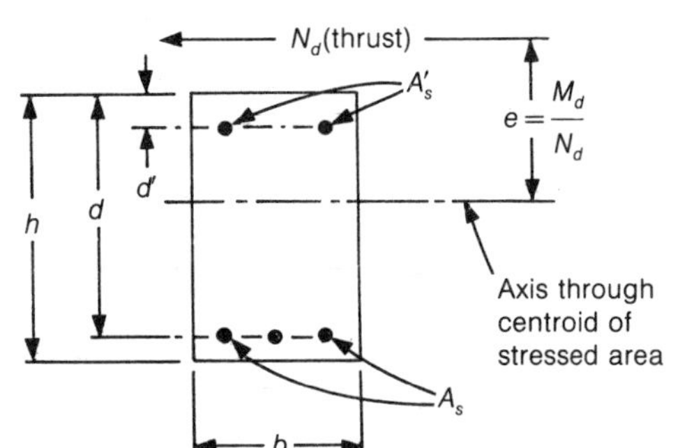

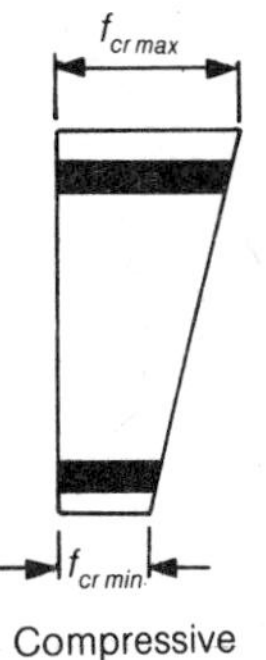

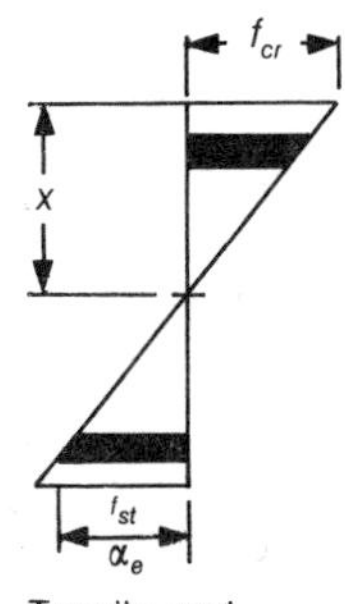

$e < h/6$

Approximate modulus of section $J = \frac{1}{6}bh^2 + \frac{2(\alpha_e - 1)A_{sc}}{h}(\frac{1}{2}h - d')^2$ $\quad A_{tr} = bd + (\alpha_e - 1)A_{sc}$

Stresses: $f_{cr\,max} = \frac{N_d}{A_{tr}} + \frac{M_d}{J}$ $\quad f_{cr\,min} = \frac{N_d}{A_{tr}} - \frac{M_d}{J}$ $\quad A_{sc} = A_s + A'_s$

$h/6 < e < h/2$

Compute $f_{cr\,min}$ by method for $e < h/6$; if positive, method applies.
If negative (or greater than permissible tensile stress in concrete), adopt method for $e > h/2$.

$e > h/2$

Assume value of x; evaluate x/d and $K_1 = bx$.
Determine depth to centroid of stressed area

$$\bar{x} = \frac{(1/2)K_1 x + \alpha_e A_s d + (\alpha_e - 1)A'_s d'}{K_1 + \alpha_e A_s + (\alpha_e - 1)A'_s} \quad (= h/2 \text{ approximately})$$

Calculate $\beta_1 = \frac{e - \bar{x}}{d} + 1$

Evaluate $\beta_2 = \frac{x}{2d}\left(1 - \frac{x}{3d}\right)$ and $\beta_3 = (\alpha_e - 1)\left(1 - \frac{d'}{x}\right)$ or obtain from table below.

Neutral-axis depth factor x/d			0.20	0.25	0.30	0.35	0.40	0.45	0.50	0.55	0.60	0.65	0.70	0.75
β_2 factor			0.093	0.114	0.135	0.155	0.173	0.191	0.208	0.224	0.240	0.254	0.268	0.281
Ratio of maximum stresses f_{st}/f_{cr} and factor β_3	$\alpha_e = 15$	Ratio of stresses	60	45	35	28	22.5	18.3	15	13.7	10	8	6.5	5
		d'/d 0.20	—	2.8	4.6	6.0	7.0	7.7	8.4	9.0	9.4	9.7	9.9	10.1
		0.15	3.5	5.6	7.0	8.0	8.8	9.4	9.8	10.2	10.5	10.7	11.0	11.2
		0.10	7.0	8.4	9.4	10.1	10.5	10.9	11.2	11.5	11.6	11.8	12.0	12.2
		0.05	10.5	11.2	11.6	12.0	12.3	12.4	12.6	12.7	12.9	12.9	13.0	13.0
	$\alpha_e = 12.5$	Ratio of stresses	50	37.5	29	23	18.8	15.2	12.5	10.2	8.3	6.8	5.4	4.2
		d'/d 0.20	—	2.3	3.8	4.9	5.7	6.3	6.9	7.4	7.7	8.0	8.1	8.3
		0.15	2.9	4.6	5.7	6.6	7.2	7.7	8.0	8.4	8.7	8.8	9.0	9.2
		0.10	5.7	6.9	7.7	8.3	8.6	9.0	9.2	9.5	9.6	9.8	9.9	10.0
		0.05	7.8	9.2	9.5	9.9	10.1	10.2	10.4	10.4	10.6	10.6	10.7	10.7
	$\alpha_e = 10$	Ratio of stresses	40	30	23.3	18.5	15	12.2	10	8.2	6.7	5.4	4.3	3.3
		d'/d 0.20	—	1.8	3.0	3.9	4.5	5.0	5.4	5.8	6.1	6.3	6.4	6.5
		0.15	2.3	3.6	4.5	5.1	5.6	6.1	6.3	6.6	6.8	6.9	7.1	7.2
		0.10	4.5	5.4	6.1	6.5	6.8	7.0	7.2	7.4	7.5	7.7	7.7	7.8
		0.05	6.8	7.2	7.5	7.7	7.9	8.0	8.1	8.2	8.3	8.3	8.4	8.4
	$\alpha_e = 8$	Ratio of stresses	32	24	18.6	14.8	12	9.8	8	6.5	5.4	4.3	3.4	2.6
		d'/d 0.20	—	1.4	2.3	3.0	3.5	3.9	4.2	4.5	4.7	4.9	5.0	5.1
		0.15	1.8	2.8	3.5	4.0	4.4	4.7	4.9	5.1	5.3	5.4	5.5	5.6
		0.10	3.5	4.2	4.7	5.1	5.3	5.5	5.6	5.8	5.8	6.0	6.0	6.1
		0.05	5.3	5.6	5.8	6.0	6.2	6.2	6.3	6.4	6.5	6.5	6.5	6.5

To determine stresses substitute evaluated factors in

$$f_{cr} = \frac{N_d \beta_1}{\beta_2 bd + \beta_3 A'_s(1 - d'/d)} \qquad f_{st} = [f_{cr}(\tfrac{1}{2}K_1 + \beta_3 A'_s) - N_d]/A_s$$

Check assumed value of x from $x = d/(1 + f_{st}/\alpha_e f_{cr})$ and recalculate with revised value of x/d if discrepancy exceeds 5%.

$e > 3h/2$

Calculate f_{cr} and f_{st} due to moment only and determine x for these stresses.

Evaluate $f_c = \frac{N_d}{bx + \alpha_e A_s + (\alpha_e - 1)A'_s}$. Then $f_{cr\,max} = f_{cr} + f_c$ and $f_{st\,max} = f_{st} - \alpha_e f_c$.

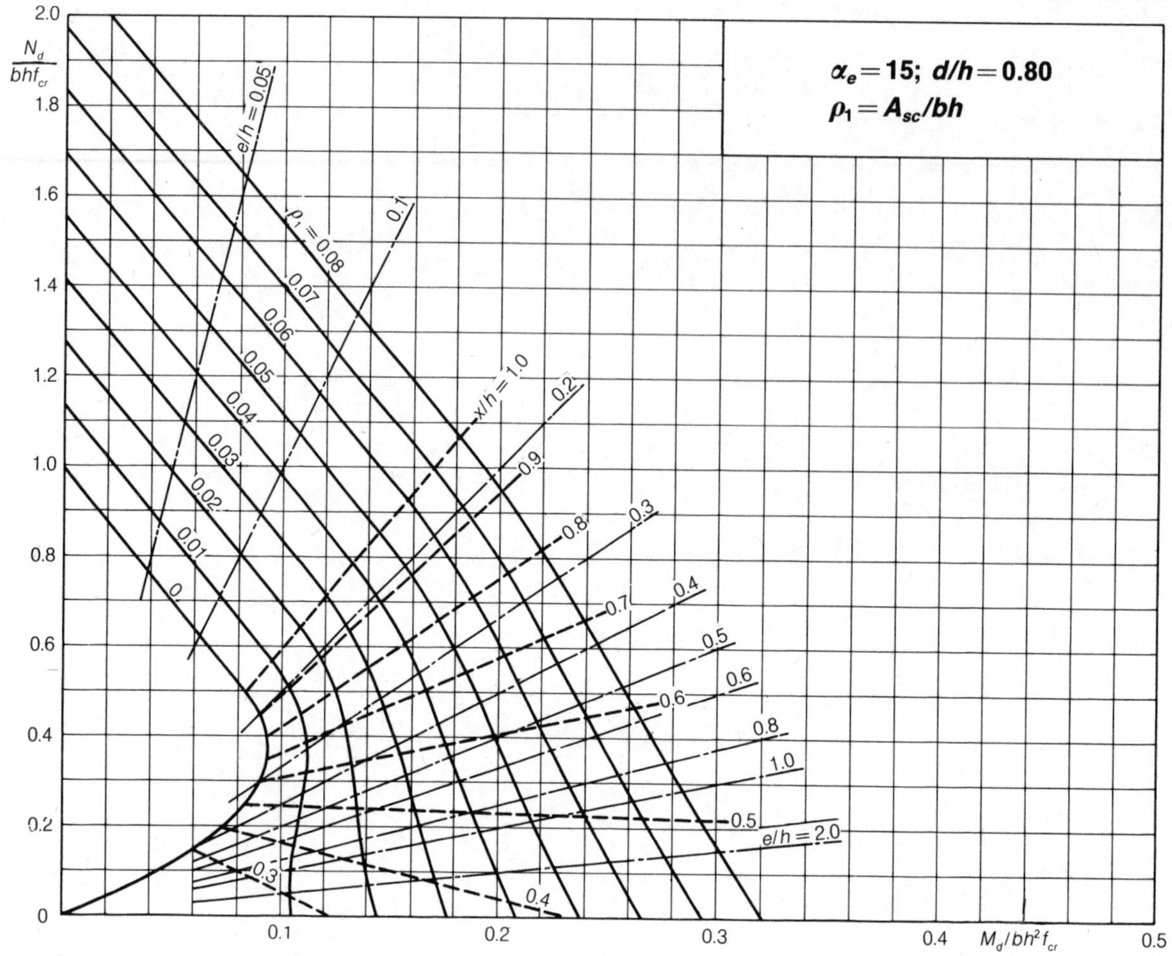

$\alpha_e = 15$; $d/h = 0.80$
$\rho_1 = A_{sc}/bh$

$\dfrac{N_d}{bhf_{cr}}$; $M_d/bh^2 f_{cr}$

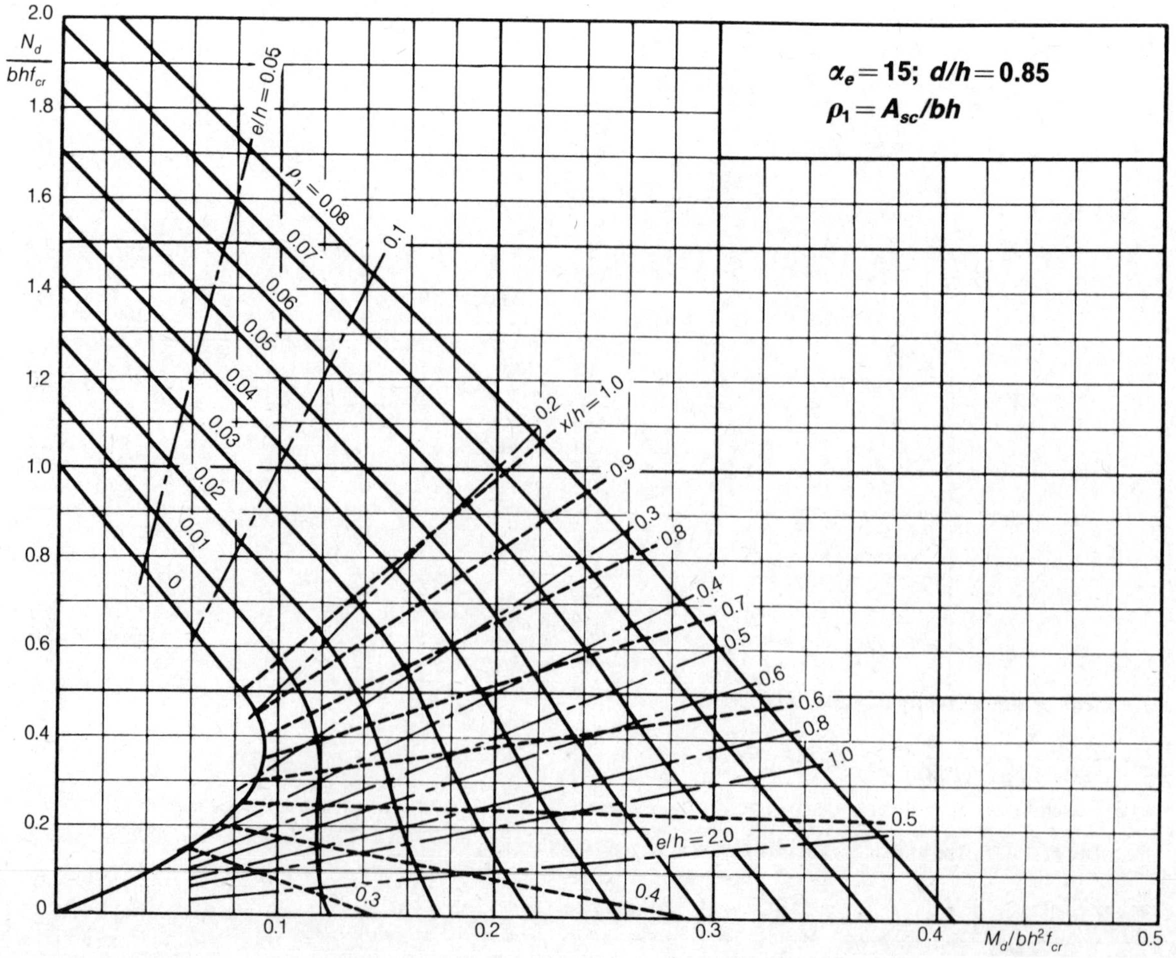

$\alpha_e = 15$; $d/h = 0.85$
$\rho_1 = A_{sc}/bh$

$\dfrac{N_d}{bhf_{cr}}$; $M_d/bh^2 f_{cr}$

$\alpha_e = 15$; $d/h = 0.90$
$\rho_1 = A_{sc}/bh$
$\frac{N_d}{bhf_{cr}}$
M_d/bh^2f_{cr}
$e/h = 0.05$
$\rho_1 = 0.08$
0.07
0.06
0.05
0.04
0.03
0.02
0.01
0
0.1
0.2
$x/h = 1.0$
0.3
0.9
0.8
0.4
0.5
0.7
0.6
0.8
0.6
1.0
0.5
$e/h = 2.0$
0.4
0.3
2.0
1.8
1.6
1.4
1.2
1.0
0.8
0.6
0.4
0.2
0
0.1
0.2
0.3
0.4
0.5

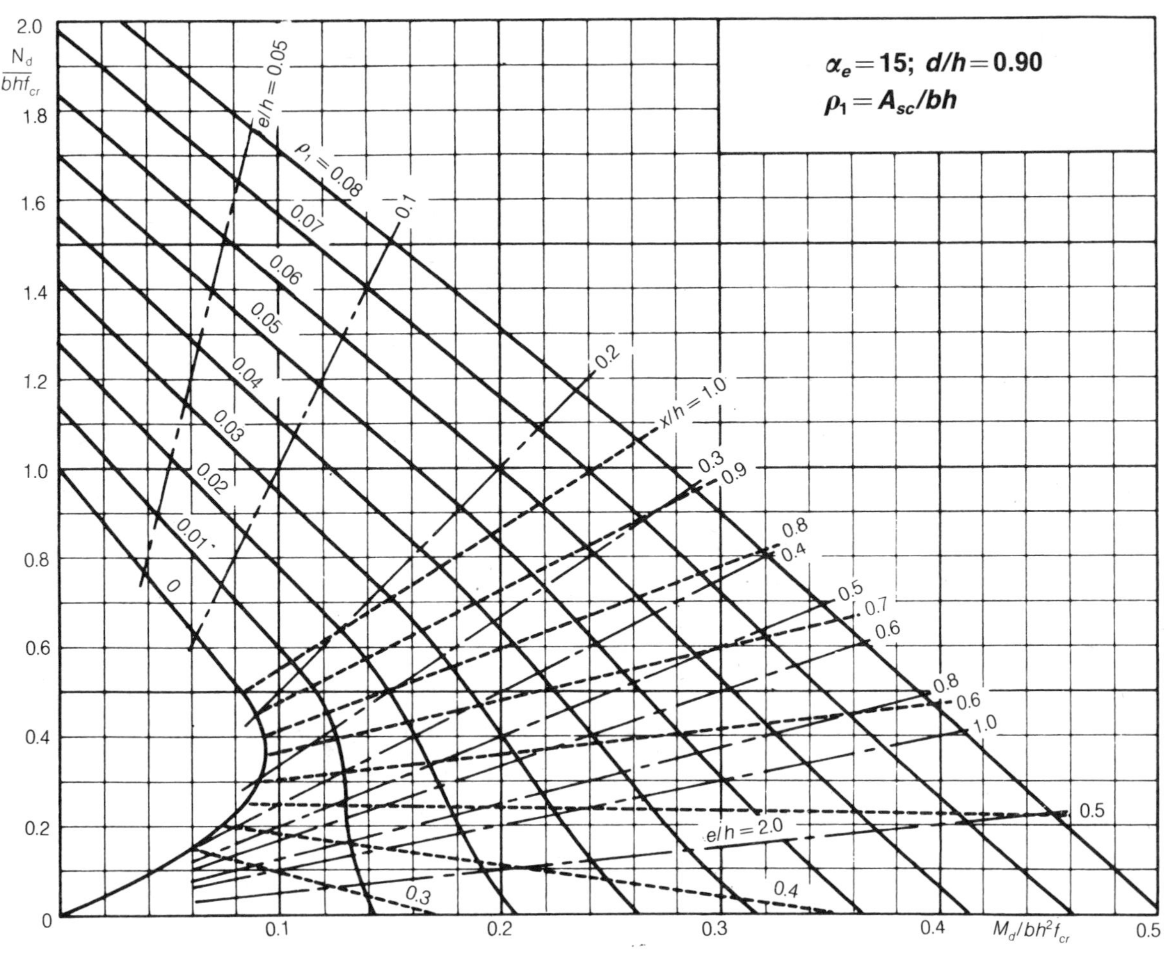

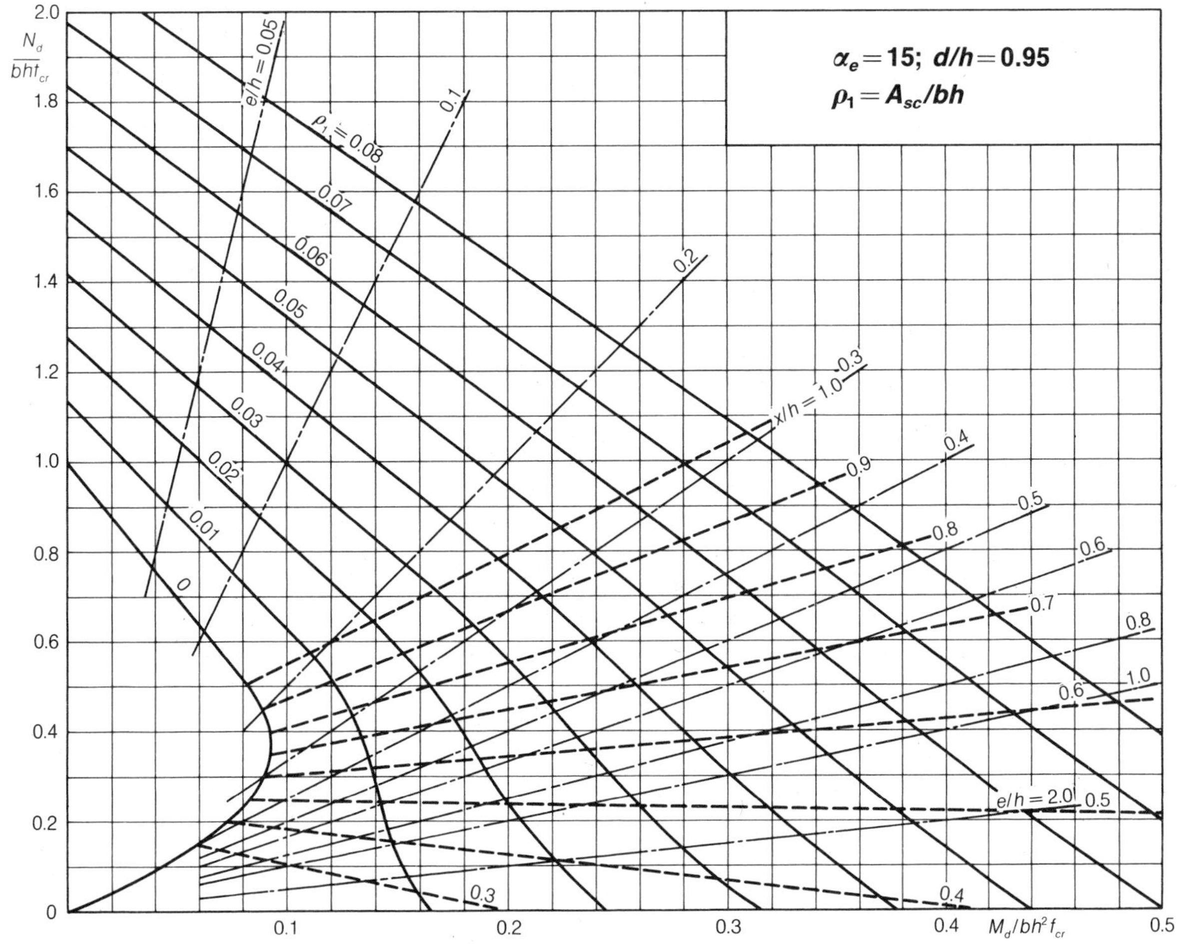

$\alpha_e = 15$; $d/h = 0.95$
$\rho_1 = A_{sc}/bh$
$\frac{N_d}{bhf_{cr}}$
M_d/bh^2f_{cr}
$e/h = 0.05$
$\rho_1 = 0.08$
0.07
0.06
0.05
0.04
0.03
0.02
0.01
0
0.1
0.2
$x/h = 1.0$
0.3
0.9
0.4
0.5
0.8
0.6
0.7
0.8
1.0
0.6
$e/h = 2.0$
0.5
0.4
0.3
2.0
1.8
1.6
1.4
1.2
1.0
0.8
0.6
0.4
0.2
0
0.1
0.2
0.3
0.4
0.5

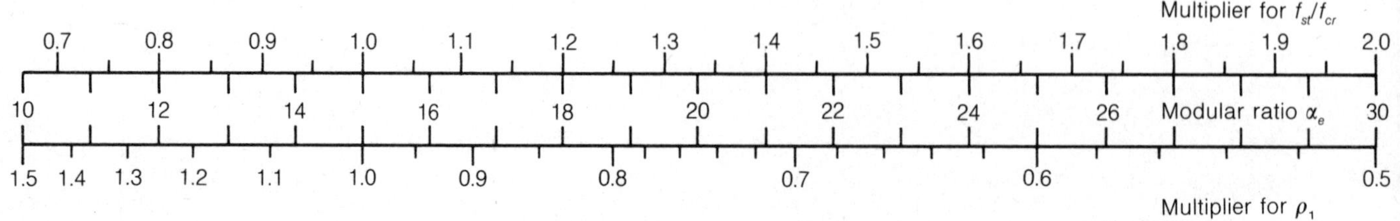

For values of modular ratio other than 15 multiply values of f_{st}/f_{cr} and ρ_1 read from charts below and in *Table 165* by multipliers obtained from scales above corresponding to modular ratio concerned.

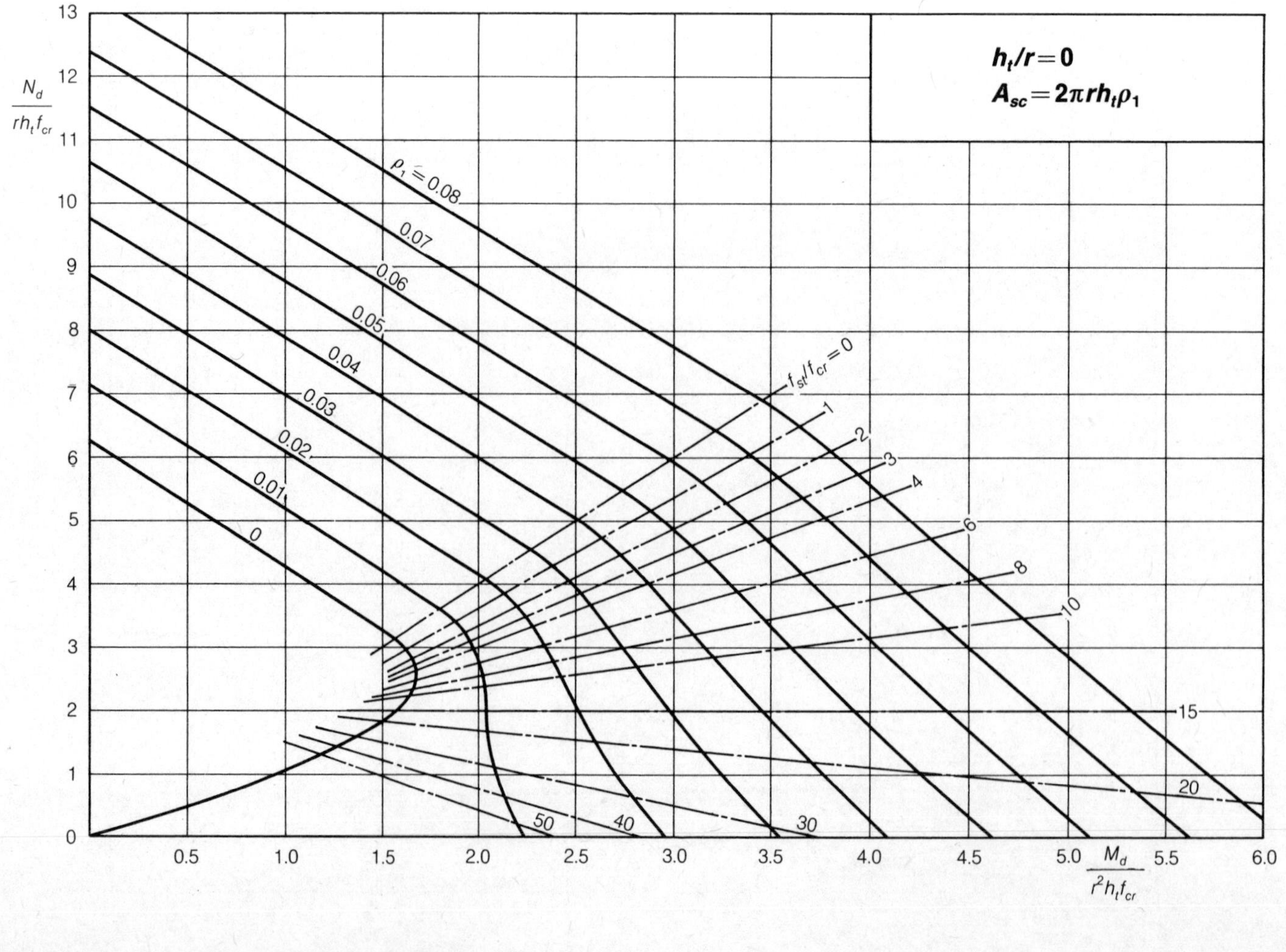

$h_t/r = 0$

$A_{sc} = 2\pi r h_t \rho_1$

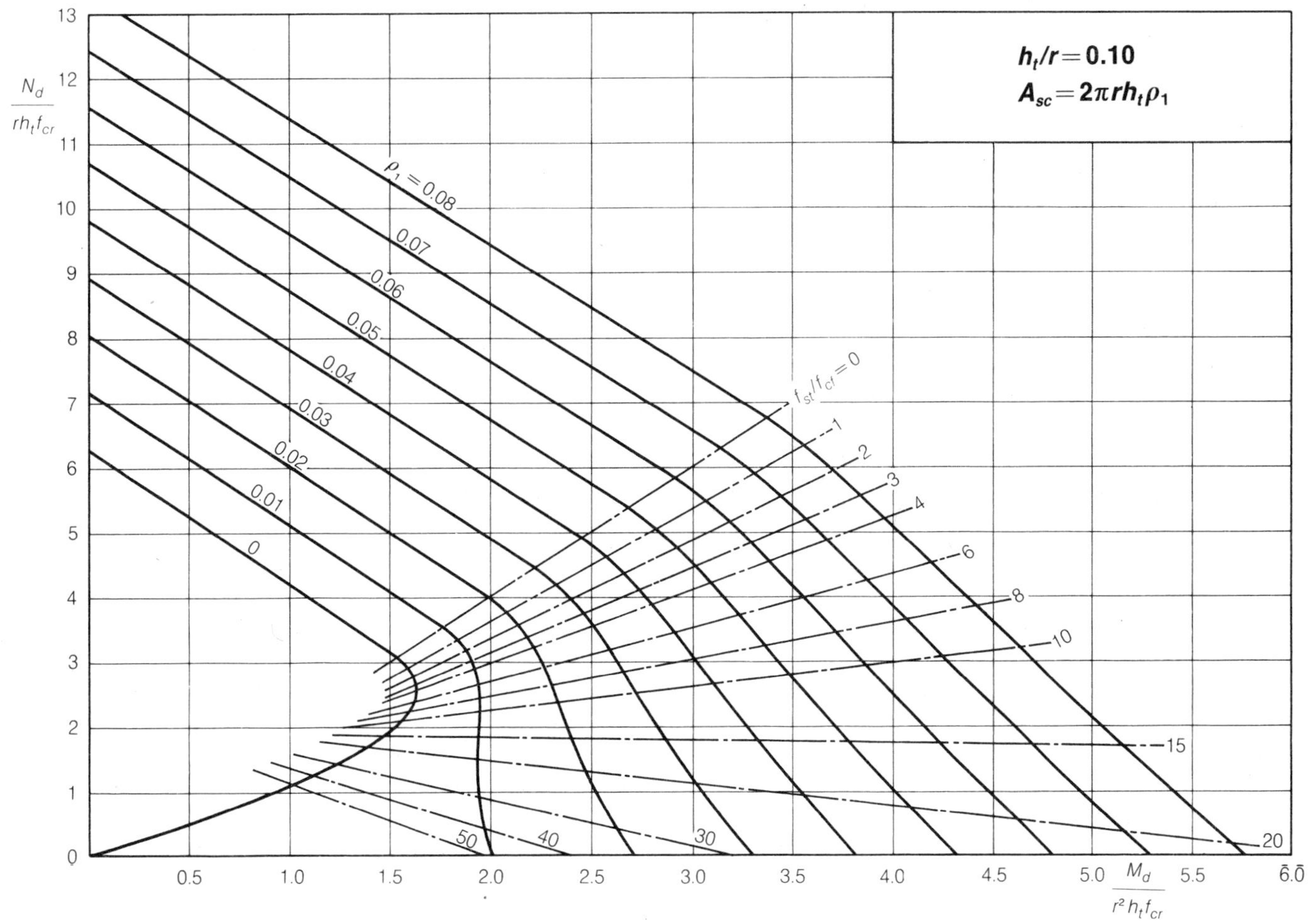

$h_t/r = 0.10$

$A_{sc} = 2\pi r h_t \rho_1$

$\frac{N_d}{r h_t f_{cr}}$; $\frac{M_d}{r^2 h_t f_{cr}}$; $\rho_1 = 0.08, 0.07, 0.06, 0.05, 0.04, 0.03, 0.02, 0.01, 0$; $f_{st}/f_{cr} = 0, 1, 2, 3, 4, 6, 8, 10, 15, 20, 30, 40, 50$

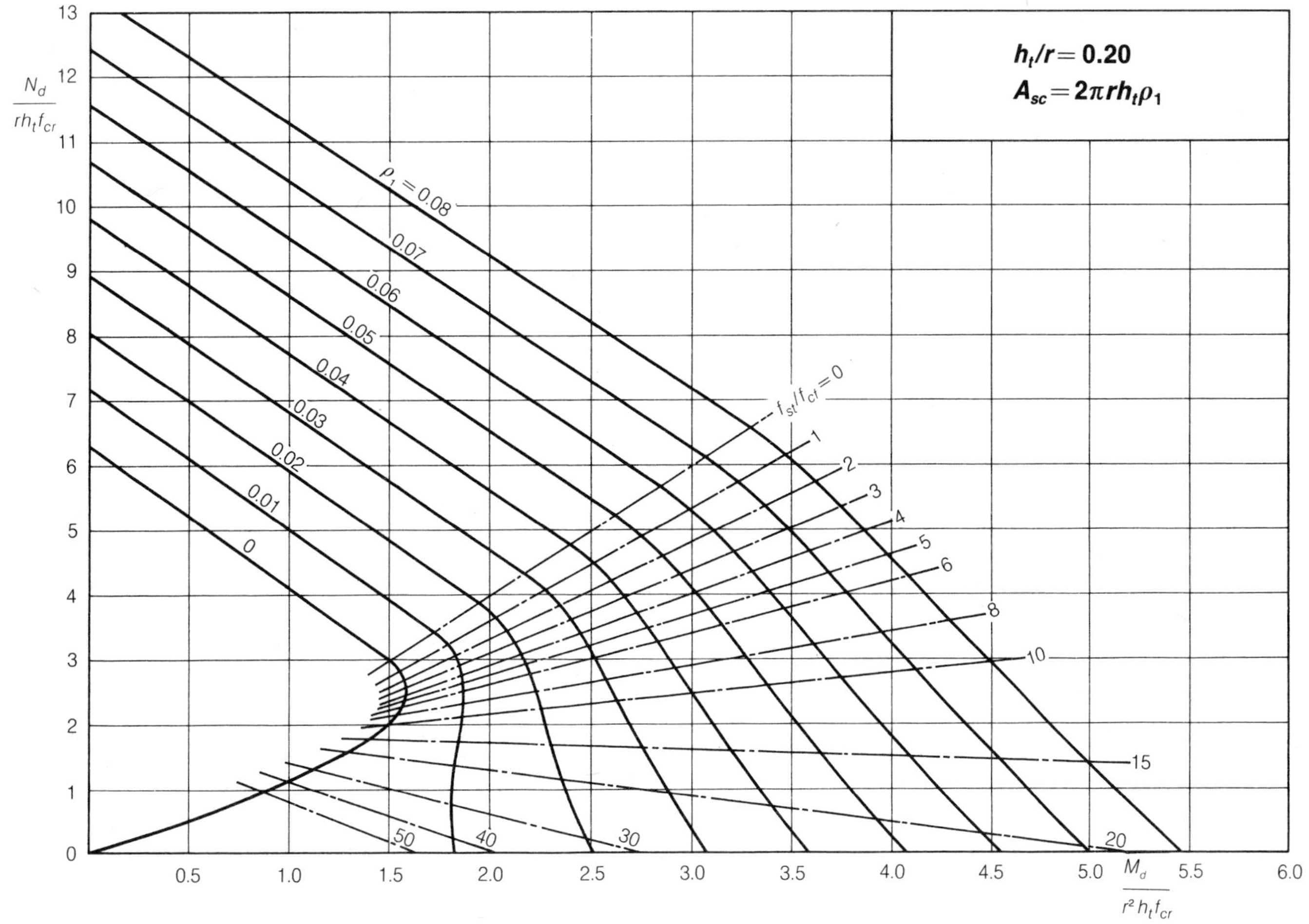

$h_t/r = 0.20$

$A_{sc} = 2\pi r h_t \rho_1$

$\frac{N_d}{r h_t f_{cr}}$; $\frac{M_d}{r^2 h_t f_{cr}}$; $\rho_1 = 0.08, 0.07, 0.06, 0.05, 0.04, 0.03, 0.02, 0.01, 0$; $f_{st}/f_{cr} = 0, 1, 2, 3, 4, 5, 6, 8, 10, 15, 20, 30, 40, 50$

the far ends of the slender columns must be designed to resist the total moments as described above.

22.4.2 CP110 requirements

The requirements of CP110 relating to slender columns are basically similar to those already described for BS8110 with certain exceptions. The critical ratios, above which the column is considered slender, are 12 and 10 for normal-weight and lightweight concretes respectively. For members of any cross-section and with any arrangement of reinforcement, CP110 provides diagrams indicating the additional moments that must be considered in braced and unbraced columns. However, when rectangular sections are reinforced symmetrically, the following simplified requirements apply.

For columns bending about the major axis where the overall depth of the cross-section is less than three times the breadth and for columns bending about the minor axis, the total moment to be resisted is

$$M_t = M_i + \alpha N h$$

where M_i is the maximum moment due to normal ultimate load calculated by simple elastic analysis and must not be taken as less than $Nh/20$, and h is the overall depth of the cross-section in the plane of bending. When normal-weight concrete is used the slenderness factor α is given by

$$\alpha = \frac{l_e}{1750}\left(\frac{l_e}{a}\right)^2\left(1 - 0.0035\frac{l_e}{a}\right)$$

where l_e is the greater of the two effective heights of the column (i.e. parallel to and at right angles to the plane of bending). Alternative methods of determining l_e are described in CP110 and details of these are given in *Table 169*. If lightweight concrete is employed α should be multiplied by 1.46. For columns bending about the minor axis, a is the overall depth in the plane of bending. For braced columns without transverse load, M_i may be reduced to $(2M_1/5) + (3M_2/5)$, where M_1 and M_2 are the lesser and greater initial end moments due to ultimate load, provided that $M_i \nless 2M_2/5$ and $M_t \nless M_2$. For columns bending about the major axis, a is the width at right angles to the plane of bending. Alternatively, CP110 permits such sections to be designed to resist biaxial bending with no initial moment about the minor axis. Ref. 36 suggests that this alternative approach may lead to significant economies and, owing to difficulties in arranging reinforcement effectively in sections less than 200 mm wide, the *Code Handbook* recommends its use for such narrow sections. It is important to note the foregoing definitions for a and h: a is *always* the lesser of the two cross-sectional dimensions, while h is *always* measured at right angles to the plane of bending (i.e. for columns bending about the minor axis, $a = h$).

If a slender section is to be designed to resist biaxial bending, the initial moment in each individual direction must be increased. Thus now

$$M_{tx} = M_{ix} + \alpha_x N h$$
$$M_{ty} = M_{iy} + \alpha_y N b$$

where

$$\alpha_x = \frac{1}{1750}\left(\frac{l_{ex}}{h}\right)^2\left(1 - 0.0035\frac{l_{ex}}{h}\right)$$

$$\alpha_y = \frac{1}{1750}\left(\frac{l_{ey}}{b}\right)^2\left(1 - 0.0035\frac{l_{ey}}{b}\right)$$

and l_{ex} and l_{ey} are the effective lengths relative to the major and minor axes respectively.

Values of α corresponding to values of l_e/a, where $a = h$ or b as appropriate, can be read from the scales at the top of *Table 168*.

As with BS8110, the additional moment $\alpha N h$ may be reduced by multiplication by a factor K, calculated from the terms N, N_{uz} and N_{bal}. N_{bal} is determined as described in section 22.4.1, although the simplification of the true expression to $f_{cu}bd/4$ is not given. Values of N_{bal}/bh for various values of d'/h and f_{cu} can be read from the upper chart on *Table 168*.

N_{uz} is given by $(0.45f_{cu} + 0.75f_y\rho_1)bh$, and values of N_{uz}/bh corresponding to various values of f_{cu} and $\rho_1 f_y$ may be read from the upper chart of *Table 159*. If f_y corresponds to one of the three principal steel stresses specified in CP110, the appropriate proportion of reinforcement can be projected vertically downwards from the related scale at the top of the chart.

The suggested design procedure is now identical to that already described for designing slender columns to BS8110 requirements.

In general the clear distance between the end restraints of a column should never be greater than 60 times the least lateral dimension, while the clear height of an unbraced unrestrained column must not exceed $100b^2/h$, where b and h are the 'breadth' and 'depth' respectively, of the section in the plane under consideration.

If the average value of l_e/h for all columns at a particular level exceeds 20, the bases or other members connected to the far ends of the slender columns must be designed to resist the total moments obtained as described above.

Example. Design a column section to resist an ultimate moment of 120 kN m about the major principal axis, together with a direct force of 2000 kN, if $f_{cu} = 30\ \text{N/mm}^2$ (normal-weight concrete) and using high-yield steel. The effective length of the column is 5 m.

BS8110 requirements ($f_y = 460\ \text{N/mm}^2$). Try a section with $h = 500$ mm and $b = 250$ mm, so that $d' = 40 + 16 = 56$ mm say, and $d'/h = 56/500 = 0.112$. Now $l_e/b = 5000/250 = 20$, so that an additional moment must be taken into account owing to slenderness. From the appropriate scale at the top of *Table 168*, for $l_e/h = 20$, $\beta = 0.20$, so that

$$\beta N h = 0.20 \times 2000 \times 10^3 \times 500 = 200 \times 10^6$$
$$M_t = 120 \times 10^6 + 200 \times 10^6 = 320 \times 10^6$$

Now

$$M_t/bh^2 f_{cu} = 320 \times 10^6/(250 \times 500^2 \times 30) = 0.171$$
$$N/bhf_{cu} = 2 \times 10^6/(250 \times 500 \times 30) = 0.533$$

From interpolation between the appropriate charts on *Tables 151* and *152*, $\rho_1 f_y/f_{cu} = 0.615$ and thus $\rho_1 = 0.04$. Also, from these charts, $K = 0.6$.

As previously suggested, reduce this value by 20%, thus obtaining $K = 0.5$. Then revised values are

Tensile stresses only: $e \not> z_s - \bar{x}_s$ (concrete ineffective in tension)

Irregular groups of bars

Group A_{s1} = bars in tension due to action of moment only

$$\bar{x}_s = \frac{A_{s1} z_s}{A_{s1} + A_{s2}}$$

Average tensile stresses in reinforcement:

In group A_{s1}: $f_{st1} = \dfrac{N_d(e + \bar{x}_s)}{z_s A_{s1}}$

In group A_{s2}: $f_{st2} = \dfrac{N_d(z_s - e - \bar{x}_s)}{z_s A_{s2}}$

Maximum tensile stress (in outer bar or bars in group A_{s1}):

$$f_{st1\,max} = f_{st2} + \left(\frac{z_s + a_1}{z_s}\right)(f_{st1} - f_{st2})$$

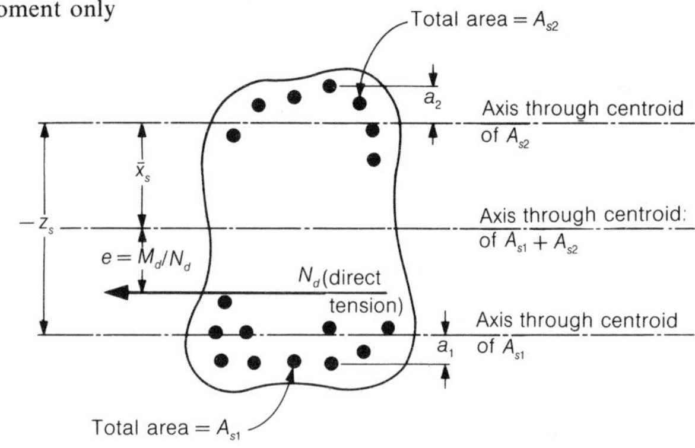

Regular groups of bars

If $A_{s1} \neq A_{s2}$, $\bar{x}_s = \dfrac{A_{s1} z_s}{A_{s1} + A_{s2}}$

Tensile stresses in reinforcement:

In group A_{s1}: $f_{st1} = \dfrac{N_d(e + \bar{x}_s)}{z_s A_{s1}}$

In group A_{s2}: $f_{st2} = \dfrac{N_d(z_s - e - \bar{x}_s)}{z_s A_{s2}}$

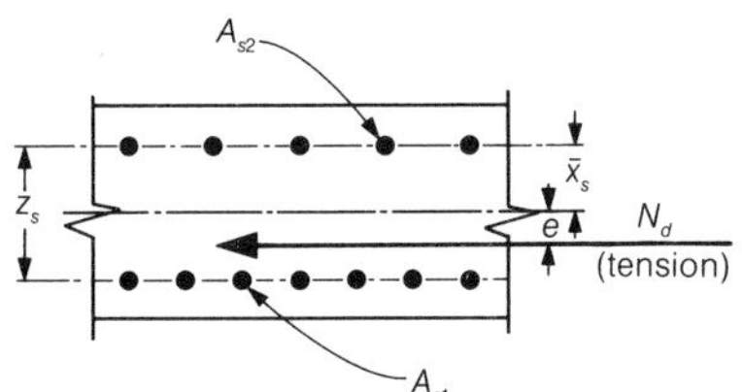

If $A_{s1} = A_{s2} = A_s$ at each face,

Tensile stresses:

In group A_{s1}: $f_{st1} = \dfrac{N_d[e + z_s/2]}{z_s A_s}$

In group A_{s2}: $f_{st2} = \dfrac{N_d[(z_s/2) - e]}{z_s A_s}$

Compressive and tensile stresses (concrete ineffective in tension)

Non-rectangular section

Assume depth to neutral axis x

Depth to centre of tension:

$$a_t = \frac{\sum Sa}{\sum S}$$

where $S = (a - x)\delta A_s$

If all bars are of same size:

$$a_t = \frac{\sum a(a - x)}{\sum (a - x)}$$

Equivalent area of strip:

$\delta A_{tr} = b_s h_s + (\alpha_e - 1)\delta A_s$

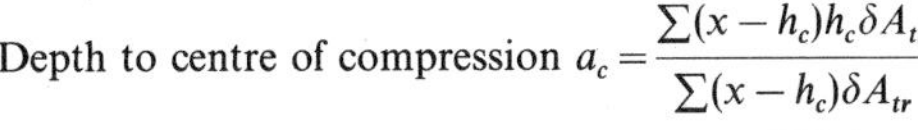

Depth to centre of compression $a_c = \dfrac{\sum (x - h_c) h_c \delta A_{tr}}{\sum (x - h_c)\delta A_{tr}}$

Position of centroid of stressed area: $\bar{x} = \dfrac{\alpha_e \sum \delta A_s a + \sum h_c \delta A_{tr}}{\alpha_e \sum \delta A_s + \sum \delta A_{tr}}$

Maximum stresses: $f_{cr} = \dfrac{N_d x(e - a_t + \bar{x})}{(a_t - a_c)\sum (x - h_c)\delta A_{tr}}$; $\quad f_{st} = \dfrac{(d - x)}{\sum S}\left[\dfrac{f_{cr}}{x}\sum (x - h_c)\delta A_{tr} + N_d\right]$

Finally check assumed value of x.

Rectangular section

$e > z_s - \bar{x}$

Assume value of x; evaluate x/d and $K_1 = bx$.

$$\bar{x} = \frac{(K_1 x/2) + \alpha_e A_s d + (\alpha_e - 1)A'_s d'}{K_1 + \alpha_e A_s + (\alpha_e - 1)A'_s} \left(= \tfrac{1}{2}h \text{ approx.}\right)$$

Calculate $\beta'_1 = \dfrac{e + \bar{x}}{d} - 1$; $\quad \beta_2 = \dfrac{1}{2}\dfrac{x}{d}\left(1 - \dfrac{1}{3}\dfrac{x}{d}\right)$

$$\beta_3 = (\alpha_e - 1)\left(1 - \frac{d'}{x}\right)$$

Determine stresses by substituting in

$$f_{cr} = \frac{N_d \beta'_1}{\beta_2 bd + \beta_3 A'_s(1 - d'/d)}$$

$f_{st} = [f_{cr}(\tfrac{1}{2}K_1 + \beta_3 A'_s) + N_d]/A_s$ Finally check assumed value of x.

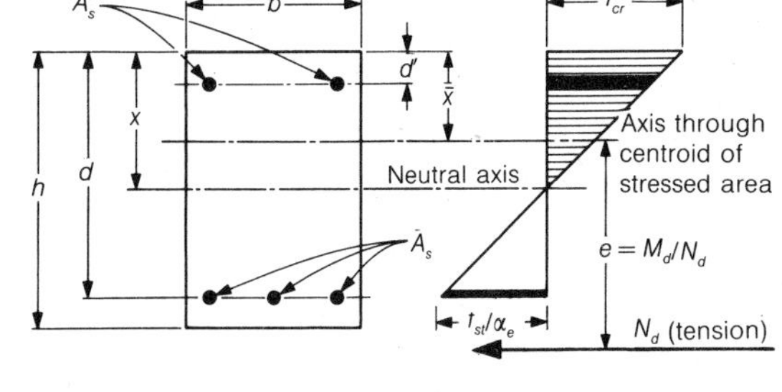

$e > \frac{3}{2}h$

Calculate f_{cr} and f_{st} due to moment only and determine x for these stresses.

Evaluate $f_c = \dfrac{N_d}{bx + \alpha_e A_s + (\alpha_e - 1)A'_s}$. Then $f_{cr\,max} = f_{cr} - f_c$ and $f_{st\,max} = f_{st} + \alpha_e f_c$

Approx. method for slabs

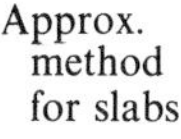

Evaluate $e = M_d/N_d$ and $e_s = e + \frac{1}{2}h - d$; then $A_{s\,req} = \dfrac{N_d}{f_{st}}\left(1 + \dfrac{e_s}{z}\right)$ or $f_{st} = \dfrac{N_d}{A_s}\left(1 + \dfrac{e_s}{z}\right)$

Rectangular member subjected to bending about two axes

Compressive stresses only developed

Section moduli:

J_{xo} about X-X, at edge A-B $= I_x/\bar{x}$

J_{xh} about X-X, at edge C-D $= I_x/(h - \bar{x})$

J_{yo} about Y-Y, at edge B-C $= I_y/\bar{y}$

J_{yb} about Y-Y, at edge A-D $= I_y/(b - \bar{y})$

M_{dy} bending moment in plane Y-Y

M_{dx} bending moment in plane X-X

A_{tr} transformed area $= bh + (\alpha_e - 1)A'_s$

Stresses: $f_{cc} = N_d/A_{tr}$ where $N_d =$ concentric thrust; if no thrust, $f_{cc} = 0$.

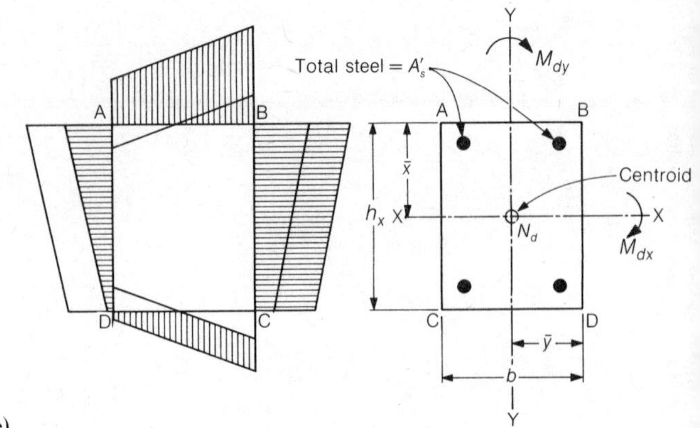

At A: $$f_{cr} = \left(f_{cc} + \frac{M_{dy}}{J_{xo}}\right) - \frac{M_{dx}}{J_{yb}}$$

At B: $$f_{cr} = \left(f_{cc} + \frac{M_{dy}}{J_{xo}}\right) + \frac{M_{dx}}{J_{yo}} \quad (= \text{maximum value})$$

At C: $$f_{cr} = \left(f_{cc} - \frac{M_{dy}}{J_{xh}}\right) + \frac{M_{dx}}{J_{yo}}$$

At D: $$f_{cr} = \left(f_{cc} - \frac{M_{dy}}{J_{xh}}\right) - \frac{M_{dx}}{J_{yb}} \quad (= \text{minimum value})$$

Tensile and compressive stresses

Notation as above, where applicable.

Also $$J_x = \tfrac{1}{6}xb^2 + \frac{(\alpha_e - 1)(A_s + A'_s)z_b^2}{2b}$$

Approximate stresses when $M_{dy} > M_{dx}$:

1. Calculate f_{st}, f_{cr} and x for M_{dy} combined with N_d or for M_{dy} alone if no thrust.
2. Calculate $M_{dx}/J_x = f_x$.
3. Resultant stresses are as follows:

   Compression in concrete at A: $f_{cA} = f_{cr} - f_x$

   Compression in concrete at B: $f_{cB} = f_{cr} + f_x$ (= maximum value)

   Tension in reinforcement at C: $f_{tC} = f_{st} - \alpha_e f_x$

   Tension in reinforcement at D: $f_{tD} = f_{st} + \alpha_e f_x$ (= maximum value)

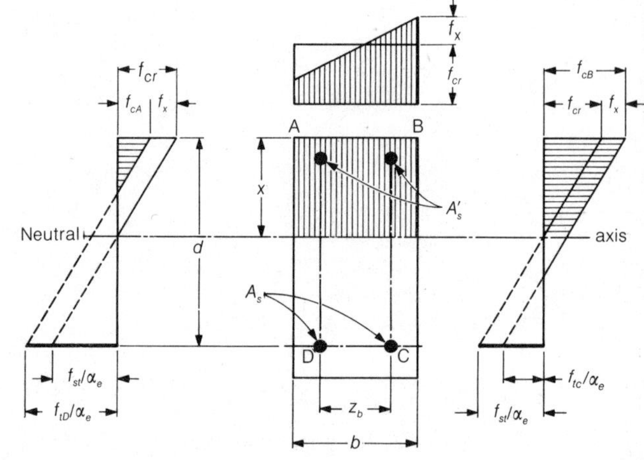

Principal stresses

f_{pt} principal tensile stress

f_{pc} principal compressive stress

θ inclination of principal plane N-N

f_{xt}, f_{yt} applied tensile (positive) stresses

f_{xc}, f_{yc} applied compressive (negative) stresses

v applied shearing stress

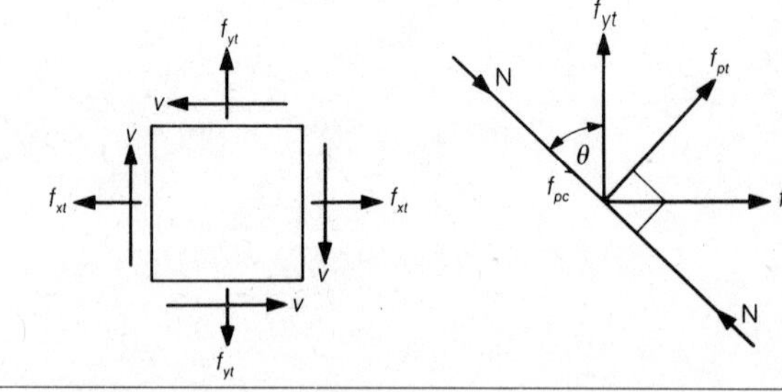

f_{xt} and f_{yt} tensile	$f_{pt} = -\tfrac{1}{2}(f_{xt} + f_{yt}) - \sqrt{\{[\tfrac{1}{2}(f_{xt} - f_{yt})]^2 + v^2\}}$ $f_{pc} = -\tfrac{1}{2}(f_{xt} + f_{yt}) + \sqrt{\{[\tfrac{1}{2}(f_{xt} - f_{yt})]^2 + v^2\}}$	$\tan 2\theta = 2v/(f_{xt} - f_{yt})$
f_{xt} tensile $f_{yt} = 0$	$f_{pt} = -\tfrac{1}{2}[\sqrt{(f_{xt}^2 + 4v^2)} + f_{xt}]$ $f_{pc} = \tfrac{1}{2}[\sqrt{(f_{xt}^2 + 4v^2)} - f_{xt}]$	$\tan 2\theta = 2v/f_{xt}$
f_{xc} compressive $f_{yt} = 0$	$f_{pt} = -\tfrac{1}{2}[\sqrt{(f_{xc}^2 + 4v^2)} - f_{xc}]$ $f_{pc} = \tfrac{1}{2}[\sqrt{(f_{xc}^2 + 4v^2)} + f_{xc}]$	$\tan 2\theta = -2v/f_{xc}$
v only	$f_{pt} = -v \quad f_{pc} = +v$	$\theta = 45°$

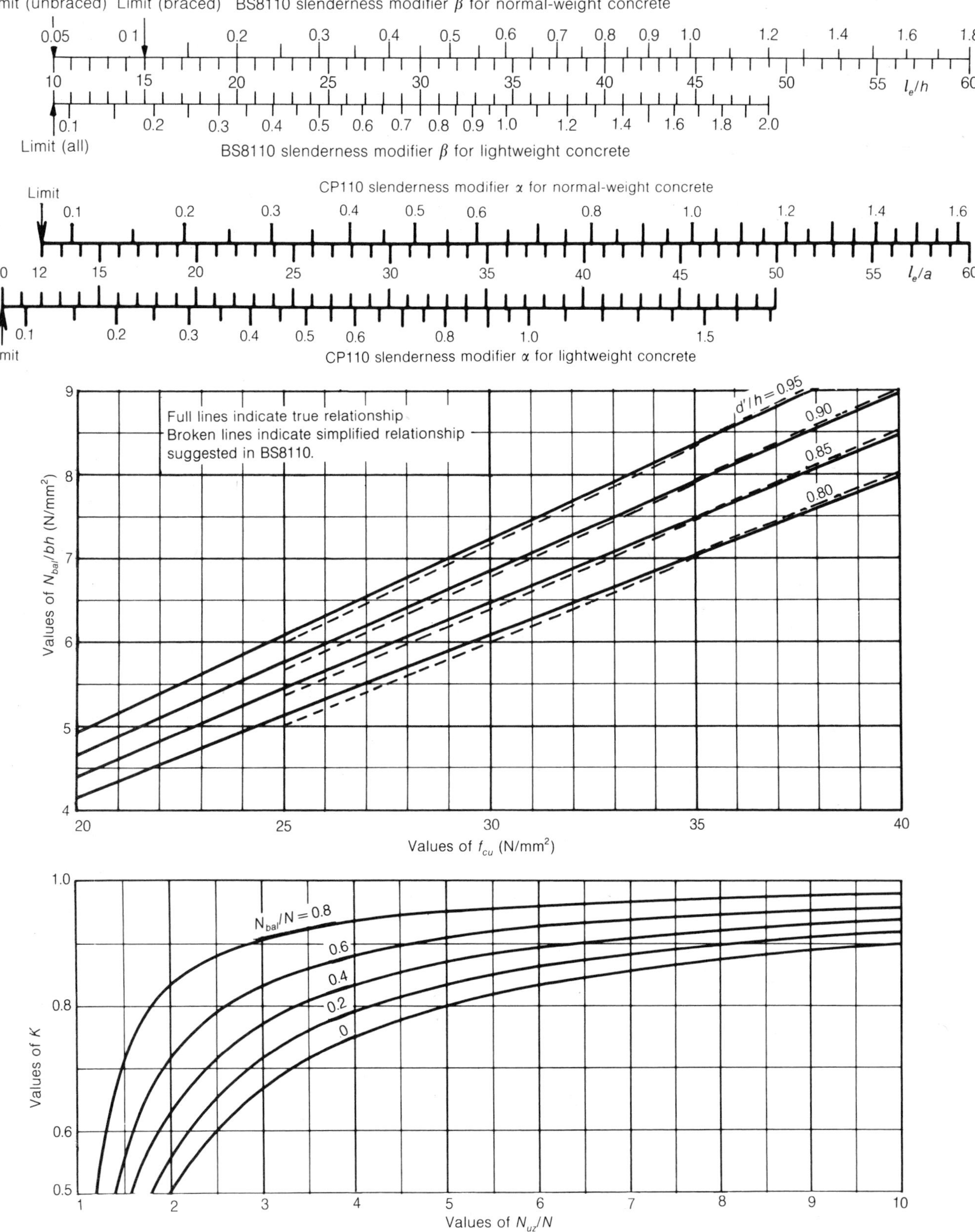

Outline of design procedure for slender columns

For BS8110

1. Determine β for appropriate ratio of l_e/b.
2. Calculate $M_t = M_i + \alpha Nh$, where M_i is the actual ultimate moment acting on section.
3. Design trial section to resist M_t and N and determine b, d, h and ρ_1.
4. Read N_{uz}/bh for trial section from upper chart in *Table 159*.
5. Read N_{bal}/bh for trial section from upper chart above.
6. Read K for trial section from lower chart above.
7. Recalculate $M_t = M_i + K\beta Nh$.
8. Repeat steps 3 to 7 until adjustment becomes negligible.

This procedure is illustrated in section 22.4.1.

For CP110

Follow identical procedure to that described above, having determined modifying factor α for appropriate ratio of l_e/a.

$$M_t = 120 \times 10^6 + 0.5 \times 200 \times 10^6 = 220 \times 10^6$$
$$M_t/bh^2f_{cu} = 220 \times 10^6/(250 \times 500^2 \times 30) = 0.117$$

Now with $N/bhf_{cu} = 0.533$ as before, interpolation between the relevant charts on *Tables 151* and *152* gives $\rho_1 = 0.028$ and $K = 0.5$. Thus

$$A_{sc} = 0.028 \times 250 \times 500 = 3500\,\text{mm}^2$$

Provide two 32 mm plus four 25 mm bars.

CP110 requirements ($f_y = 425\,\text{N/mm}^2$). Once again, try a section with $h = 500$ mm and $b = 250$ mm, so that $d' = 40 + 16 = 56$ mm and $d'/h = 0.112$. Now $l_e/b = 20$, so that an additional moment must again be taken into account owing to slenderness. From the appropriate scale at the top of *Table 168*, for $l_e/a = 20$, $\alpha = 0.21$, so that

$$\alpha Nh = 0.21 \times 2000 \times 10^3 \times 500 = 210 \times 10^6\,\text{N mm}$$
$$M_t = 120 \times 10^6 + 210 \times 10^6 = 330 \times 10^6$$

Now

$$M_t/bh^2f_{cu} = 330 \times 10^6/(250 \times 500^2 \times 30) = 0.176$$
$$N/bhf_{cu} = 2 \times 10^6/(250 \times 500 \times 30) = 0.533.$$

From interpolation between *Tables 154* and *155*, $\rho_1 f_y/f_{cu} = 0.75$ and thus $\rho_1 = 0.053$. For this trial section, with $f_{cu} = 30\,\text{N/mm}^2$ and $d'/h = 0.112$, $N_{bal}/bh = 6.75$ from the upper chart on *Table 168*. With $f_{cu} = 30\,\text{N/mm}^2$ and $\rho_1 f_y = 0.053 \times 425 = 22.53$, the upper chart on *Table 159* gives $N_{uz}/bh = 30.5$, so that $N_{bal}/N = 6.75/16 = 0.422$ and $N_{uz}/N = 30.5/16 = 1.91$. Entering the lower chart on *Table 168* with these ratios, read off $K = 0.62$.

As suggested earlier, reduce this value by 20% to obtain $K = 0.5$. Then the revised values are

$$M_t = 120 \times 10^6 + 0.5 \times 210 \times 10^6 = 225 \times 10^6\,\text{N mm}$$
$$M_t/bh^2f_{cu} = 225 \times 10^6/(250 \times 500^2 \times 30) = 0.120$$

Now with $N/bhf_{cu} = 0.533$ as before, from *Tables 154* and *155*, ρ_1 is 0.037. The ratio N_{bal}/N remains 6.75 as before but the upper chart on *Table 159* now gives $N_{uz} = 25.2$ with the revised value of ρ_1, so that N_{uz}/N becomes $25.2/16 = 1.58$. With these ratios, the lower chart on *Table 168* gives a value of K of 0.51, which is sufficiently close to the proposed value not to require further investigation.

Thus

$$A_{screq} = 0.037 \times 250 \times 500 = 4625\,\text{mm}^2$$

Provide six 32 mm bars.

22.4.3 Other methods

In earlier Codes of Practice the safe load on a slender column was often determined by evaluating the safe load on a similar short column and then multiplying the value thus obtained by a reduction factor β determined by the slenderness ratio. *Table 169* gives values of the reduction factor β which are based on the ratio of the effective length of the column to the least radius of gyration i, calculated from the following commonly accepted expressions: when $l_e/i \not> 50$, $\beta = 1$; and when $50 \leqslant l_e/i \leqslant 120$, $\beta = 1.5 - l_e/100i$. For columns with separate links the least radius of gyration should be calculated on the gross cross-sectional area of the section but, for members where helical binding is provided to increase the load-carrying capacity, the core section only should be considered, where the binding is assumed to assist in supporting the load on the member. In calculating the radius of gyration, the assistance of the reinforcement may be taken into account, assuming a modular ratio of 15. Radii of gyration of some common sections, taking account of the reinforcement, are given in *Tables 99* and *100*; similar data, but neglecting reinforcement, are provided in *Table 98*.

Effective column heights

BS8110 definitions

	Braced column			Unbraced column		
Type of fixity at end 2	Condition 1	Condition 2	Condition 3	Condition 1	Condition 2	Condition 3
Type of fixity at end 1						
End condition 1: Connected monolithically to beams at both sides > overall dimensions of column in plane considered	0.75	0.80	0.90	1.20	1.30	1.60
End condition 2: Connected monolithically to beams or slabs at both sides ≯ overall dimensions of column in plane considered	0.80	0.85	0.95	1.30	1.50	1.80
End condition 3: Connected to members not specifically designed to restraint rotation but which do provide some restraint	0.90	0.95	1.00	1.60	1.80	*
End condition 4: Unrestrained against both lateral movement and rotation	*	*	*	2.20	*	*

CP110 definitions

CP110 definitions	Effective height l_e
Braced: both ends properly restrained* in direction	$0.75l_0$
Braced: imperfectly restrained in direction at one or both ends	Between $0.75l_0$ and l_0 depending on efficiency of directional restraint
Partially braced or unbraced: properly restrained in direction at one end but imperfectly restrained in direction at the other	Between l_0 and $2l_0$ depending on efficiency of imperfect restraint

*The *Code Handbook* suggests proper restraint in direction may be reasonably assumed where the members not subject to compression framing into a junction supply twice the stiffness provided by the column (or more).

Alternatively, for framed structures, according to CP110, effective height of column may be calculated from following expressions.

Braced columns

l_e/l_0 is the lesser of

(i) $\left[\dfrac{14 + \alpha_{c1} + \alpha_{c2}}{20}\right]$; (ii) $\left(\dfrac{17 + \alpha_{c\,min}}{20}\right)$; or (iii) 1

Unbraced columns

l_e/l_0 is the lesser of

(i) $\left[\dfrac{10 + (3/2)(\alpha_{c1} + \alpha_{c2})}{10}\right]$ or (ii) $\left(\dfrac{20 + 3\alpha_{c\,min}}{10}\right)$

where

l_0 clear height between end restraints

α_{c1}, α_{c2} ratios of sum of column stiffnesses to sum of beam stiffnesses at each end of column under consideration

$\alpha_{c\,min}$ lesser of α_{c1} or α_{c2}

Stiffnesses should be determined by dividing the second moment of area of a member by its actual length, but only members framing into the column in the appropriate plane of bending may be taken into account. For column/base or beam/column junctions designed to resist nominal moments only, take a value of α_c of 10; for column/base junctions designed to resist full column moment, take a value of α_c of 1.

Reduction factors for 'long' columns

Based on least radius of gyration i (for general use)

Reduction factor β

Reduction factor β	1.0	0.9	0.8	0.7	0.6	0.5	0.4	0.3
Values of l_e/i	50 or less	60	70	80	90	100	110	120

If $l_e/i \not> 50$: $\beta = 1$. If $50 \leqslant l_e/i \leqslant 120$: $\beta = 1.5 - l_e/100i$.

Chapter 23
Walls

BS8110 and CP110 set out design requirements for both reinforced and plain concrete walls; the latter category also includes walls formed of interconnected precast concrete panels.

The design requirements for reinforced concrete walls, which are defined as vertical load-bearing members with a greatest lateral dimension exceeding four times the least lateral dimension and containing not less than 0.4% of vertical reinforcement, are similar to those for columns. The method of design of short or slender normal-weight or lightweight concrete walls subjected to axial load with or without bending corresponds to that previously described for the corresponding column section. It should be noted that the definitions of braced and unbraced walls differ slightly from those for columns, however, and in CP110 different upper slenderness limits are specified; details of these are given in *Table 170* for BS8110 and *Table 171* for CP110.

Plain concrete walls are dealt with in some detail in both Codes. By definition, such walls are really outside the scope of this book, but brief information regarding the principal differences between the Code requirements for plain and reinforced normal-weight and lightweight concrete walls are summarized in *Table 170*. For further guidance, reference should be made to the appropriate Code itself and also to the *Code Handbook*.

Walls to BS8110

Type		Reinforced concrete	Plain concrete
Defining requirements		$\rho_1 \not< 0.004$* $b/h \not< 4$. (If $b/h < 4$, section should be designed as column.)	In all other cases: some reinforcement may be needed to restrict cracking due to bending or shrinkage: for details see BS8110.
Braced wall	Stocky (i.e. short) wall	**Applicability:** for normal-weight concrete when $l_e/h \leqslant 15$; for lightweight concrete when $l_e/h \leqslant 10$. **Effective height:** determine as for columns (see *Table 169*). **Design formula:** Walls supporting an approximately symmetrical arrangement of slabs: $\frac{n_w}{h} = 0.35 f_{cu} + 0.67 \rho_1 f_y$. Walls subjected to axial load and transverse bending: Design as for columns (see *Tables 151* and *152*). Walls subjected to axial load with significant transverse and in-plane moments: adopt procedure described below.	**Applicability:** for normal-weight concrete when $l_e/h \leqslant 15$; for lightweight concrete when $l_e/h \leqslant 10$. **Effective height:** if lateral supports resist both lateral deflection and rotation: $l_e = (3/4) \times$ distance between lateral supports or $2 \times$ distance of lateral support from free edge. If lateral supports resist lateral deflection only: $l_e =$ distance between lateral supports or $(5/2) \times$ distance of lateral support from free edge. **Design formula:** $\frac{n_w}{h} = 0.3\left(1 - 2\frac{e_x}{h}\right) f_{cu}$
Braced wall	Slender wall	**Applicability:** for normal-weight concrete when $l_e/h > 15$; for lightweight concrete when $l_e/h > 10$. Maximum ratio of $l_e/h = 40$ when $\rho_1 \not> 0.01$ and 45 otherwise. **Effective height:** as defined for stocky braced walls above. **Design procedure:** section of wall supporting greatest axial load must be designed as slender column of unit width, as described in section 22.4.1, employing procedure for axial force combined with transverse and in-plane moments described below. If only single central layer of steel is to be provided, additional moment due to slenderness must be doubled.	**Applicability:** for normal-weight concrete when $l_e/h > 15$; for lightweight concrete when $l_e/h > 10$. Maximum ratio of $l_e/h = 30$. **Effective height:** as defined for stocky braced walls above. **Design formulae:** n_w/h is the lesser of the following: For normal-weight concrete only: $0.3\left[1 - 1.2\frac{e_x}{h} - 0.0008\left(\frac{l_e}{h}\right)^2\right] f_{cu}$ For lightweight concrete only: $0.3\left[1 - 1.2\frac{e_x}{h} - 0.0012\left(\frac{l_e}{h}\right)^2\right] f_{cu}$ For both types of concrete: $0.3\left[1 - 2\frac{e_x}{h}\right] f_{cu}$
Unbraced wall	Stocky (i.e. short) wall	**Applicability:** when $l_e/h \leqslant 0$. **Effective height:** as defined for stocky braced walls above. **Design procedure:** section of wall supporting greatest axial load must be designed to resist axial load + nominal moment corresponding to an eccentricity of $h/20$. Assuming a parabolic-rectangular stress-block. $\frac{n_w}{h} = \left[k_1\left(\frac{d}{h} - k_2\right) + \frac{f_y \rho_1}{1.15}\left(\frac{d}{h} - 0.5\right)\right] \Big/ \left(\frac{d}{h} - 0.45\right)$ where k_1 and k_2 may be read from *Table 102*.	**Applicability:** when $l_e/h \leqslant 10$. **Effective height:** $(3/2) \times$ actual height if floor or roof spans at right angles to wall at top of wall or $2 \times$ actual height otherwise. **Design formulae:** n_w/h is the lesser of the following: For normal-weight concrete only: $0.3\left[1 - 2\frac{e_{x2}}{h} - 0.0008\left(\frac{l_e}{h}\right)^2\right] f_{cu}$ For lightweight concrete only: $0.3\left[1 - 2\frac{e_{x2}}{h} - 0.0012\left(\frac{l_e}{h}\right)^2\right] f_{cu}$ For both types of concrete: $0.3\left[1 - 2\frac{e_{x1}}{h}\right] f_{cu}$
Unbraced wall	Slender wall	**Applicability:** when $l_e/h > 10$, maximum value of $l_e/h = 30$. **Effective height:** } as defined for **Design procedure:** } braced walls above.	**Applicability:** when $l_e/h > 10$. Maximum value of $l_e/h = 30$. **Effective height:** } as defined for short unbraced **Design formulae:** } walls above.

Notation

- b, h unit length and thickness of wall, respectively.
- d distance between compression face and centroid of less highly compressed reinforcement.
- $e_x (\not< h/20)$ resultant eccentricity of load at right angles to wall.
- $e_{x1}, e_{x2} (\not< h/20)$ resultant eccentricities at top and bottom of wall, respectively.
- n_w ultimate load (i.e. $1.4g_k + 1.6q_k$) per unit length of wall.
- ρ_1 A_s'/bh.

Procedure for considering axial force combined with transverse and in-plane moments

First determine forces on section, due to axial load plus moments resulting from horizontal forces, by an elastic analysis assuming that no tension occurs in concrete. Then calculate effects of transverse moments separately, and combine with axial force acting at point considered, obtained from previous calculation, using rigorous limit-state analysis.

Notes

Braced and unbraced walls: a braced wall is one where lateral stability of entire structure at right angles to plane of wall considered is provided by walls (or other means) designed to resist all lateral forces: otherwise, wall is unbraced. Stability in any direction of any multistorey building must not depend on unbraced walls alone.

Resultant eccentricity: loads transferred from floor or roof to wall are assumed to act at 1/3 of bearing width from face of support. Position of resultant eccentricity is then determined by simple statics.

Lateral support: see BS8110 for details of requirements for lateral support to resist deflection and rotation.

Chapter 24
Joints and intersections between members

The information given on *Tables 172* and *173* has been compiled from the published results of recent research undertaken by the Cement and Concrete Association (C & CA) and others. Brief notes on the recommended details are given below. In most cases the accompanying design formulae are derived from tests and the results obtained may not apply in less usual situations. In cases of uncertainty, the original references listed should be consulted.

Reference should also be made to the Concrete Society report on standard reinforced concrete details (ref. 96).

24.1 HALF JOINTS

The recommendations given in CP110 (clause 5.2.5.4), which result from the research described in ref. 94, are summarized on *Table 172*. The inclined links must intersect the line of action of F_v. If this cannot be ensured (e.g. if the inclined links may get displaced) or if horizontal forces may act, horizontal links must also be provided as shown.

24.2 CORBELS

Clause 5.2.7 of BS8110 and clause 5.2.4.1 and CP110 contain data for designing corbels. The information provided on *Table 172* is based on these recommendations plus information given in refs 82 and 83.

24.3 CONTINUOUS NIBS

The original recommendations in CP110 (clause 5.2.4.2) were modified in February 1976 owing to C & CA research (ref. 69). The revised Code proposals are summarized on *Table 172*, as are the requirements of BS8110 (clause 5.2.8). As a result of the C & CA investigations, the various methods of reinforcing such nibs illustrated in diagrams (a), (b) and (c) have been put forward. Method (a) is efficient but difficulties in incorporating the steel occur with shallow nibs if the vertical bends are to meet the minimum radii requirements in the Code. Method (b) is reasonably efficient and it is simple to anchor the reinforcement at the outer face of the nib. However, tests show that the capacity of the nib does not increase with an increase in the bar diameter, owing to splitting occurring along the line of the steel. It has been suggested (ref. 69) that method (c) combines the virtues of the two previous arrangements, while still being fairly simple to fix.

The C & CA design recommendations given on *Table 172* are based on the assumption of truss action (ref. 69), although BS8110 and CP110 suggest that such nibs should be designed as short cantilever slabs subjected to bending moments and shearing forces. Both methods generally lead to the need for similar amounts of reinforcement, however.

24.4 WALL-TO-WALL JUNCTIONS

24.4.1 Moment tending to close corner

Tests (ref. 95) have shown that when corners are subjected to moments tending to close them, the most likely cause of premature failure is due to bearing under the bend of the tension steel passing around the outside of the corner. Providing that the radius of this bend is gradual and that sufficient anchorage is provided for the lapping bars, no problems should arise. The Concrete Society recommends (ref. 96) the use of simple details such as (a) or (b) on *Table 173*.

24.4.2 Moment tending to open corner

With so-called 'opening' corners, the problems are somewhat greater and tests (ref. 95) have shown that many details fail at well below their calculated strength. The arrangement recommended by ref. 96 is that shown in (d) on *Table 173*. If at all possible, a concrete splay should be formed within the corner and the diagonal reinforcement A_{ss} located at a suitable distance from the surface of this. If this arrangement is impracticable, these diagonal bars should be included within the corner itself.

Detail (d) on *Table 173* is suitable for amounts of high-yield tension steel of up to 1%. If more tension reinforcement is provided, transverse links must be included as shown in (e). An alternative arrangement suggested in ref. 69 is that shown in (c). Special attention must be paid to bending and fixing the diagonal links, which must be designed to resist all the force in the main tension bars. Care must also be taken to provide adequate cover to these main bars where they pass round the inner corner.

Recent research by Noor (ref. 97) appears to indicate that

Walls to CP110 171

Type		Reinforced concrete	Plain concrete
Defining requirements		$\rho_1 \nless 0.004$*. $b/h \nless 4$. (If $b/h < 4$, section should be designed as column.) * If $\rho_1 < 0.01$, wall is considered as plain concrete for fire-resistance purposes.	In all other cases. If $b/h < 4$, values of λ_w must be multiplied by $\xi = \frac{1}{15}\left(\frac{b}{h} + 11\right) \nless 0.8.$ $e_x \nless 0.05h$ throughout.
Braced wall	Short wall	**Applicability:** for normal-weight concrete when $l_e/h \leqslant 12$; for lightweight concrete when $l_e/h \leqslant 10$. **Effective height:** determine as for columns (see *Table 169*). **Design formulae:** Walls loaded axially: $\frac{n_w}{h} = \frac{2}{5}f_{cu} + \frac{2}{3}\rho_1 f_y$ Walls supporting an approximately symmetrical arrangement of slabs: $\frac{n_w}{h} = \frac{7}{20}f_{cu} + \frac{3}{5}\rho_1 f_y$ Walls subjected to axial load and bending: design as for columns (see *Tables 153–158*).	**Applicability:** for normal-weight concrete when $l_e/h \leqslant 12$; for lightweight concrete when $l_e/h \leqslant 10$. **Effective height:** if lateral supports resist both lateral deflection and rotation: $l_e = (3/4) \times$ distance between lateral supports or $2 \times$ distance of lateral support from free edge. If lateral supports resist lateral deflection only: $l_e =$ distance between lateral supports or $(5/2) \times$ distance of lateral support from free edge. **Design formula:** $\frac{n_w}{h} = \left(1 - 2\frac{e_x}{h}\right)\lambda_w f_{cu}$
	Slender wall	**Applicability:** for normal-weight concrete when $l_e/h > 12$; for lightweight concrete when $l_e/h > 10$. Maximum ratio of $l_e/h = 40$ when $\rho_1 \ngtr 0.01$ and 45 otherwise. **Effective height:** determine as for columns (see *Table 169*). **Design procedure:** section of wall supporting greatest axial load must be designed as slender column of unit width, as described in section 22.4.2.	**Applicability:** for normal-weight concrete when $l_e/h > 12$; for lightweight concrete when $l_e/h > 10$. Maximum ratio of $l_e/h = 30$. **Effective height:** as defined for short braced walls above. **Design formulae:** n_w/h is the lesser of the following: For normal-weight concrete only: $\left[1 - 1.2\frac{e_x}{h} - 0.0008\left(\frac{l_e}{h}\right)^2\right]\lambda_w f_{cu}$ For lightweight concrete only: $\left[1 - 1.2\frac{e_x}{h} - 0.0012\left(\frac{l_e}{h}\right)^2\right]\lambda_w f_{cu}$ For both types of concrete: $\left[1 - 2\frac{e_x}{h}\right]\lambda_w f_{cu}$
Unbraced wall	Short wall	**Applicability:** as defined for short braced walls above. **Effective height:** determine as for columns (see *Table 169*). **Design procedure:** section of wall supporting greatest axial load must be designed to resist axial load + nominal moment corresponding to an eccentricity of $h/20$. Assuming a parabolic-rectangular stress-block. $\frac{n_w}{h} = \left[k_1\left(\frac{d}{h} - k_2\right) + f_{yd1}\rho_1\left(\frac{d}{h} - 0.5\right)\right] \Big/ \left(\frac{d}{h} - 0.45\right)$ where $f_{yd1} = 2000f_y/(2300 + f_y)$ and k_1 and k_2 may be read from *Table 102*.	**Applicability:** as defined for short braced walls above. **Effective height:** $(3/2) \times$ actual height if floor or roof spans at right angles to wall at top of wall or $2 \times$ actual height otherwise. **Design formulae:** n_w/h is the lesser of the following: For normal-weight concrete only: $\left[1 - 2\frac{e_{x2}}{h} - 0.0008\left(\frac{l_e}{h}\right)^2\right]\lambda_w f_{cu}$ For lightweight concrete only: $\left[1 - 2\frac{e_{x2}}{h} - 0.0012\left(\frac{l_e}{h}\right)^2\right]\lambda_w f_{cu}$ For both types of concrete: $\left[1 - 2\frac{e_{x1}}{h}\right]\lambda_w f_{cu}$
	Slender wall	**Applicability:** maximum value of $l_e/h = 30$. **Effective height:** } as defined for slender **Design procedure:** } braced walls above.	**Applicability:** as defined for slender braced walls above. **Effective height:** } as defined for short unbraced **Design formulae:** } walls above.

Notation

b, h unit length and thickness of wall, respectively.
d distance between compression face and centroid of less highly compressed reinforcement.
$e_x(\nless h/20)$ resultant eccentricity of load at right angles to wall.
$e_{x1}, e_{x2}(\nless h/20)$ resultant eccentricities at top and bottom of wall, respectively.
n_w ultimate load (i.e. $1.4g_k + 1.6q_k$) per unit length of wall.
ρ_1 A'_s/bh.
λ_w Stress-reduction coefficient. If $\psi =$ clear height between supports/length of wall, then:
For fully compacted concrete, grade 25 and above: $\lambda_w = (11 - 2\psi)/20$
For fully compacted concrete, grades 10 to 20: $\lambda_w = (17 - 2\psi)/40$
For no-fines concrete: $\lambda_w = (15 - 2\psi)/40$
If $1/2 > \psi > 3/2$, adopt these extreme values.
ξ multiplier for λ_w.

Notes

Braced and unbraced walls: a braced wall is one where lateral stability of entire structure at right angles to plane of wall considered is provided by walls (or other means) designed to resist all lateral forces: otherwise, wall is unbraced. Stability in any direction of any multistorey building must not depend on unbraced walls alone.

Resultant eccentricity: loads transferred from floor or roof to wall are assumed to act at 1/3 of bearing width from face of support. Position of resultant eccentricity is then determined by simple statics.

Lateral support: see CP110 for details of requirements for lateral support to resist deflection and rotation.

(b) is a valid alternative to (d) and, in fact, is more efficient when more than 0.35% of high-yield tension reinforcement is provided. If the empirical formulae devised by Noor are modified to include the appropriate partial safety factors for materials required by BS8110 and CP110, the following expressions are obtained. For (d),

$$A_s = \frac{10.2M_u - bd^2\sqrt{f_{cu}}}{350d(\sqrt{(f_{cu})} + 3.8\xi)}$$

where $f_{ys} = 425\ \text{N/mm}^2$ and $\xi = A_{ss}/A_s$. If no splay steel is provided (i.e. $\xi = 0$),

$$A_s = 0.0029\left(\frac{10.2M_u}{d\sqrt{f_{cu}}} - bd\right)$$

For (b),

$$A_s = \frac{16.3M_u - bd^2\sqrt{f_{cu}}}{730d(\sqrt{(f_{cu})} + 2.9\xi)}$$

Again, if $\xi = 0$, this expression simplifies to

$$A_s = 0.0014\left(\frac{16.3M_u}{d\sqrt{f_{cu}}} - bd\right)$$

24.5 JUNCTIONS BETWEEN BEAMS AND EXTERNAL COLUMNS

Research by Taylor (refs 95, 98) has shown that the forces in the joint are as shown in the sketch on *Table 173*. The inclined strut action across the corner due to the compressive thrusts in column and beam is accompanied by tensile forces acting at right angles. To ensure that, as a result, diagonal cracks do not form across the corner, a serviceability limit-state expression may be developed from the analysis set out in refs 69 and 98, as shown on the table.

To ensure that the joint has sufficient strength at the ultimate limit-state, an expression has also been developed to give the minimum amount of steel that is required to extend from the top of the beam into the column at the junction. In addition to meeting these requirements, it is recommended that the column sections above and below the joint should be designed to resist at least 50% and 70%, respectively, of the moment transferred from the beam into the column at the joint.

While research indicates that, unless carefully detailed as described, the actual strength of the joint between a beam and an external column may be as little as one-half of the calculated moment capacity, it seems that internal column/beam joints have considerable reserves of strength. Joints having a beam at one side of the column and a short cantilever on the other are more susceptible to a loss of strength, and it is desirable in such circumstances to design the junction between the column and the beam as an external joint, turning the steel from the beam down into the column as indicated on the diagrams, and then extending the cantilever reinforcement across the column to pass into the top of the beam.

The details shown are based on the recommendations given in ref. 96.

Nibs

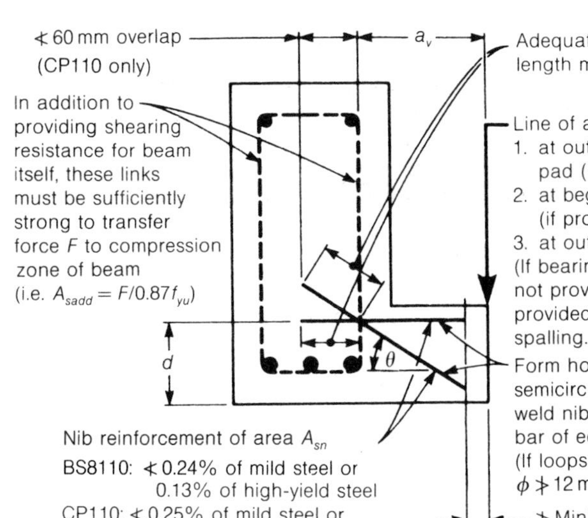

∢ 60 mm overlap (CP110 only)
a_v
Adequate anchorage-bond length must be provided
In addition to providing shearing resistance for beam itself, these links must be sufficiently strong to transfer force F to compression zone of beam (i.e. $A_{sadd} = F/0.87f_{yu}$)
Line of action of load F:
1. at outer edge of bearing pad (if provided); or
2. at beginning of chamfer (if provided); or
3. at outer edge of nib
(If bearing pad or chamfer is not provided, bars must be provided to prevent corner spalling.)
d
θ
Form horizontal or vertical semicircular loops here or weld nib steel to longitudinal bar of equal strength.
(If loops are vertical $\phi \not> 12$ mm.)
Nib reinforcement of area A_{sn}
BS8110: ∢ 0.24% of mild steel or 0.13% of high-yield steel
CP110: ∢ 0.25% of mild steel or 0.15% of high-yield steel
$\not>$ Minimum permissible cover

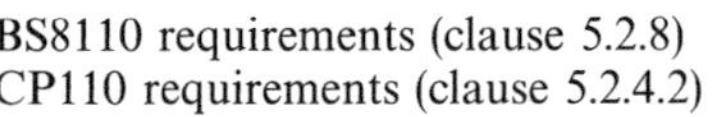

BS8110 requirements (clause 5.2.8)
CP110 requirements (clause 5.2.4.2)

1. Design A_{sn} to resist moment of $a_v F$
2. Check shearing resistance $2bd^2 v_c/a_v$ exceeds F (where v_c is allowable shearing resistance of concrete for steel proportion A_{sn}/bd, read from *Table 143*).

C & CA design recommendations

With horizontal nib steel: $A_{sn} = 1.15Fa_v/df_{yn}$

With inclined nib steel: $A_{sn} = 1.15F/f_{yn}\sin\theta$

where f_{yn} is yield stress in nib reinforcement

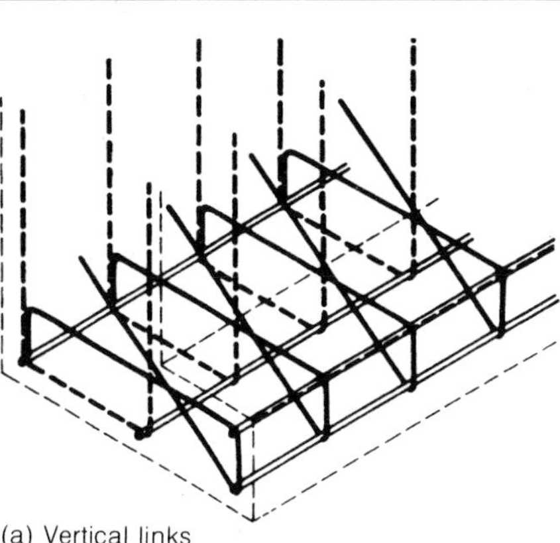

(a) Vertical links

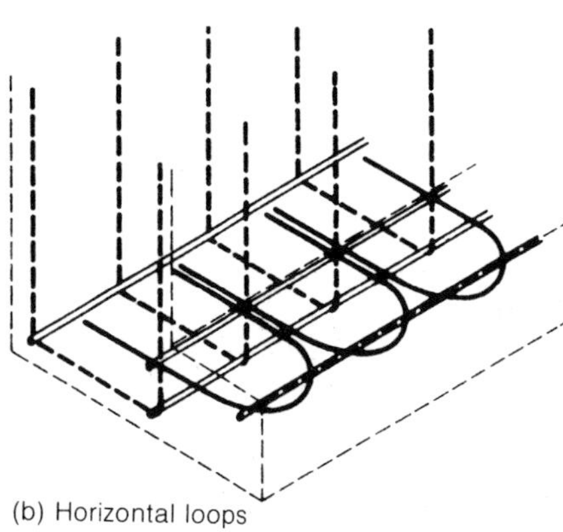

(b) Horizontal loops

Halving joints

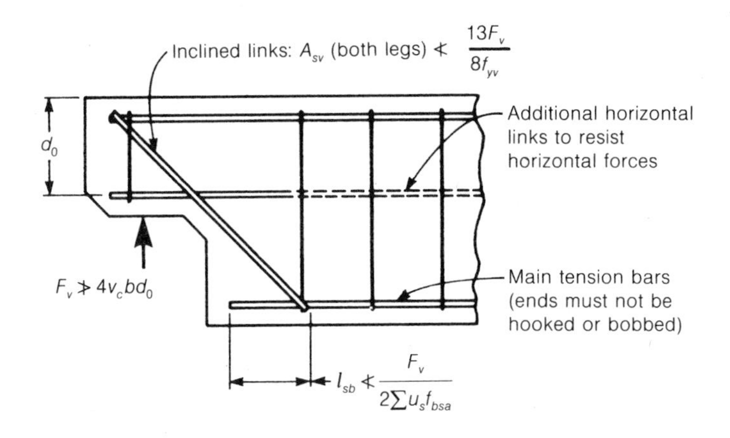

Inclined links: A_{sv} (both legs) ∢ $\dfrac{13F_v}{8f_{yv}}$
d_0
Additional horizontal links to resist horizontal forces
$F_v \not> 4v_c bd_0$
Main tension bars (ends must not be hooked or bobbed)
l_{sb} ∢ $\dfrac{F_v}{2\sum u_s f_{bsa}}$

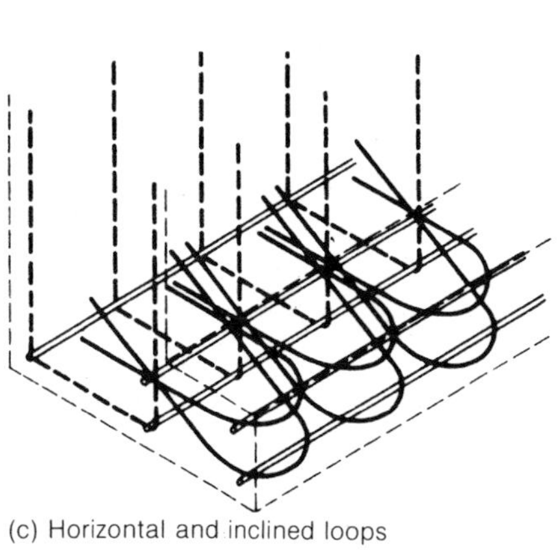

(c) Horizontal and inclined loops

Corbels

Design procedure

1. Determine depth d from considerations of shear
2. Then provide $A_s = a_v F_v/(d - \frac{1}{2}x) f_{yd2}$ where f_{yd2} is design stress in tension steel corresponding to x/d ratio obtained from *Table 104* and $x = \dfrac{5F_v}{\sin 2\theta b f_{cu}}$
3. Minimum allowable $A_s/bd = 0.004$: maximum $= 0.013$

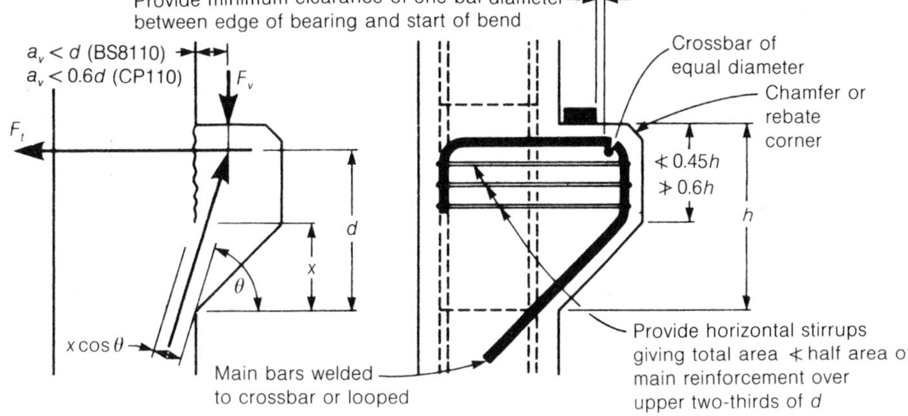

Provide minimum clearance of one bar diameter between edge of bearing and start of bend
$a_v < d$ (BS8110)
$a_v < 0.6d$ (CP110)
F_v
F_t
d
x
θ
$x\cos\theta$
Main bars welded to crossbar or looped
Crossbar of equal diameter
Chamfer or rebate corner
∢ 0.45h
$\not>$ 0.6h
h
Provide horizontal stirrups giving total area ∢ half area of main reinforcement over upper two-thirds of d

Chapter 25
Structures and foundations

25.1 STRUCTURAL STABILITY

To ensure structural stability and to provide a degree of resistance to the effects of excessive loading or accident, CP110 specifies that, when designing for ultimate wind loads, the horizontal force considered at any level should be not less than 0.015 times the total characteristic dead load above that level, and that this force should be distributed between the members providing resistance according to their stiffness and strength.

In addition, both BS8110 and CP110 specify that vertical and horizontal ties should be formed within the structural frame as indicated in the diagram on *Table 174* to resist the tensile forces T tabulated in the table. Each tie force depends on the appropriate coefficient F_t, which is related to the number of storeys n_o comprising the structure by the expression $F_t = 20 + 4n_o$ if $n_o \leqslant 10$; when $n_0 \geqslant 10$, $F_t = 60$. These forces are assumed to act independently of any other structural forces and thus the reinforcement already provided to meet other structural requirements may be considered to provide part or all of the amount required. For further information see section 6.1.1.

25.2 STAIRS

General notes on stairs are given in section 6.1.5. BS6399: Part 1 gives details of the characteristic imposed loads for which stairs in various buildings should be designed (see section 9.2.1). Cast *in situ* stairs designed as monolithic structures are generally designed to support the specified uniform load. However, stairs formed of individual treads (normally precast) cantilevering from a wall or central spine beam must be designed to resist the alternative concentrated load specified in BS6399. In designing such stairs, provision should also be made for *upward*-acting loads. It is not unknown for juvenile 'engineers' to demonstrate Archimedes' principles practically by inserting a lever between two treads and applying an upward test to destruction!

General requirements regarding stair dimensions etc. are contained in BS5395: 1977 'Stairs'.

25.2.1 Simple stairs

The following requirements regarding structural design are stated in BS8110 and CP110. They clearly only apply to relatively simple layouts (i.e. not to the specialized types considered separately below). The term 'stair' applies to either flight or landing, as appropriate.

Loading. Where stairs intersect at right angles, the loads on the common area may be divided equally between the stairs. Where stairs spanning in the direction of the flight are embedded at least 110 mm into the adjoining wall along at least part of the length, no load need be considered on the strip 150 mm wide adjoining the wall.

Effective width. This is normally equal to the actual width but, according to CP110 only, where the stair is built into the wall as described above, two-thirds of the embedded width but not more than 80 mm may be included in the effective width.

Effective span. If the stair is monolithic at the ends with supporting members spanning at right angles,

effective span = clear span plus one-half width of each supporting member

or plus 900 mm if the support thus considered is more than 1.8 m wide.

If the stair is freely supported,

effective span = distance between centre-lines of supports.

According to BS8110, the distance between the faces of supports plus the effective depth should be considered, if this is less.

BS8110 states that, if the stair flight occupies a distance of at least 60% of the effective span, the limiting span/effective-depth ratio may be increased by 15%.

25.2.2 Free-standing stairs

In ref. 125 Cusens and Kuang employ strain-energy principles to determine expressions relating the horizontal restraint force H and moment M_0 at the midpoint of a free-standing stair. By solving the two resulting equations simultaneously, the values of M_0 and H can then be substituted into general expressions to obtain the moments and forces at any point along the structure.

It is possible, by neglecting subsidiary terms, to simplify

Wall-to-wall intersections

(a)

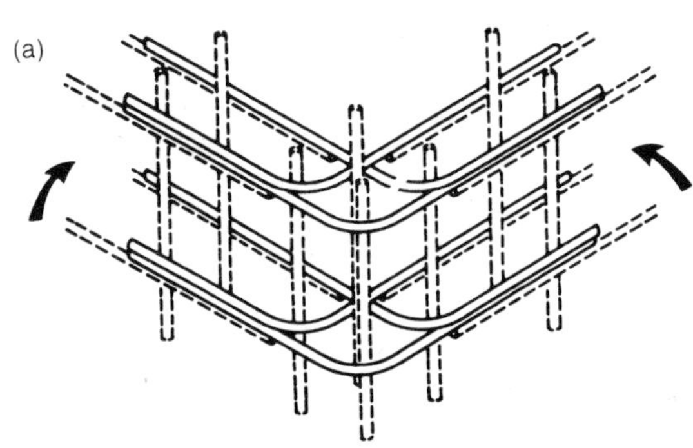

(This detail is only suitable where moments tend to close corner)

(b)

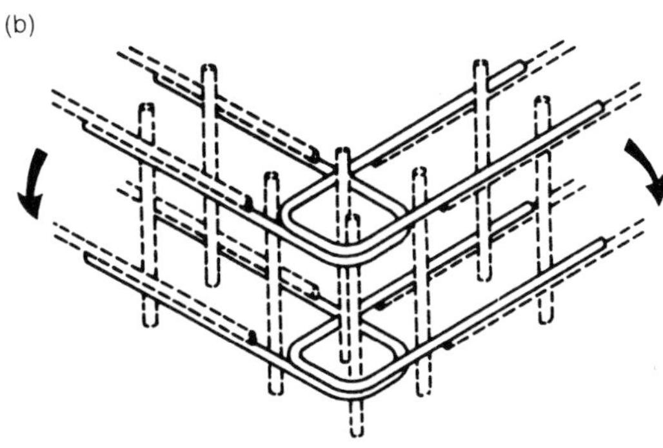

(c)

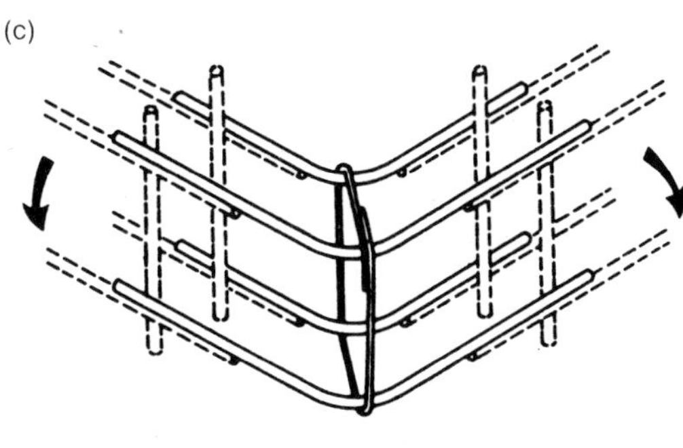

$$A_s = \frac{M_u}{0.87 f_y z} \qquad A_{sv} = \sqrt{(2)} f_y A_s / f_{yv}$$

(d)

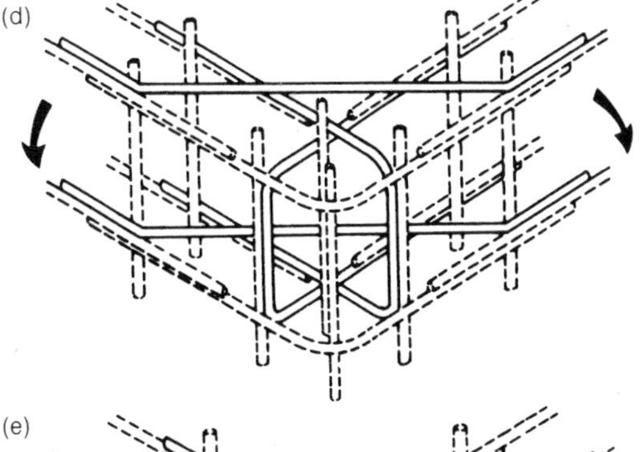

(e)

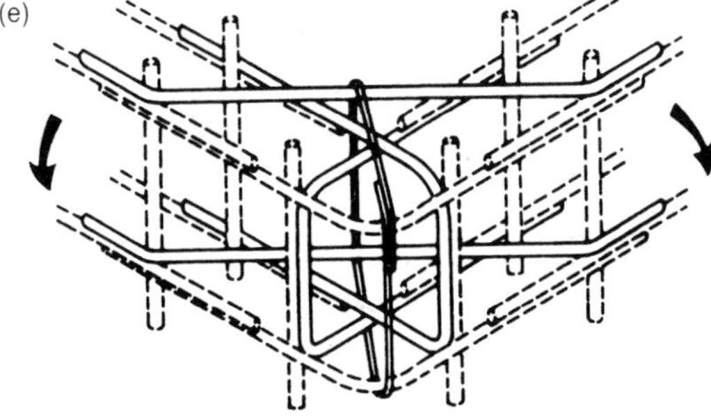

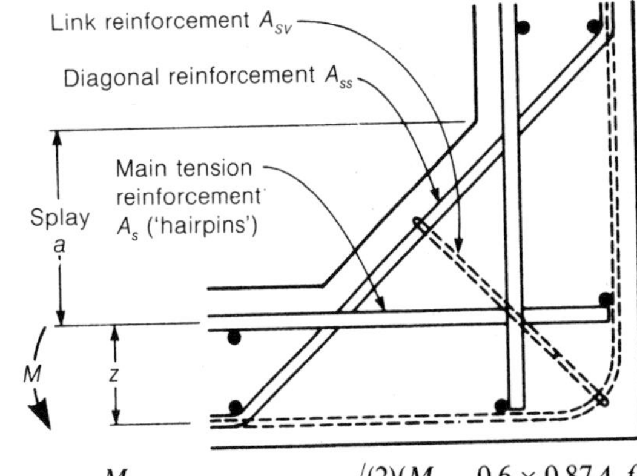

$$A_s = \frac{M_u}{0.87 f_y z} \qquad A_{ss} = \frac{\sqrt{(2)}(M_u - 0.6 \times 0.87 A_s f_y z)}{0.87 f_{ys}(a+z)}$$

If A_s (high-yield steel) $> bd/100$, $A_{sv} = 0.6 f_y A_s / f_{yv}$.

Also check radius of bend of hairpin $\nless 0.35\phi\left(\frac{5\phi + 2c}{\phi + 2c}\right)$

where c is cover in plane of bending.

Beam column intersections

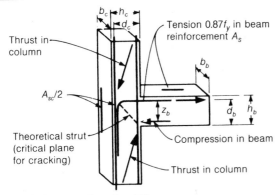

b_c h_c d_c
Tension $0.87f_y$ in beam reinforcement A_s
Thrust in column
b_b
$A_{sc}/2$
z_b d_b h_b
Theoretical strut (critical plane for cracking)
Compression in beam
Thrust in column

Limit-state of serviceability

$$\frac{5N_d}{b_c h_c}\left\{\sqrt{\left[1+\left(\frac{3M_d}{z_b N_d}\right)^2\right]}-1\right\} \ngtr f_{cu}$$

N_d thrust in column *above* beam and
M_d moment in beam, both *due to service loads*

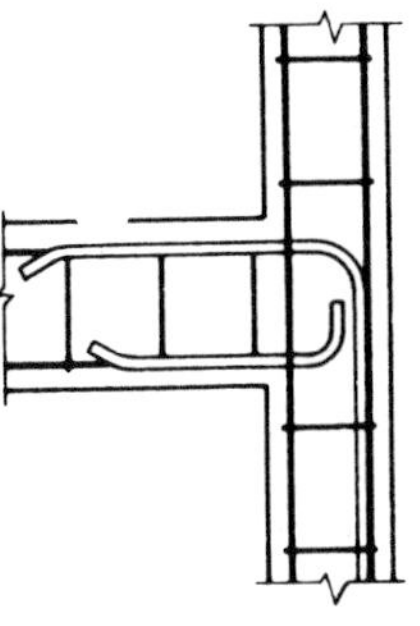

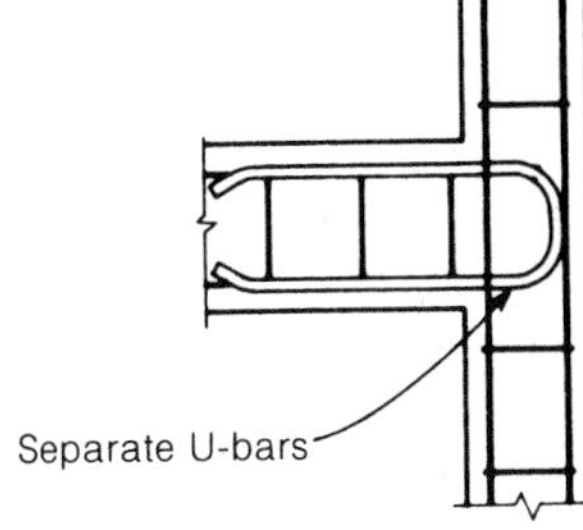

Ultimate limit-state

$$A_s \ngtr \left(3 + \frac{2d_c}{z_b}\right)\frac{\beta v_c b_c d_c}{0.87 f_y}$$

β ratio of ultimate resistance moment in beam at column face after redistribution to that before redistribution
v_c unit shearing resistance for column section corresponding to f_{cu} and $\rho = A_{sc}/2b_c d_c$ (read from *Table 143*)

Imposed load	M_v				M_h		T	
	At O	At B	At D	At A	At B in OB	Throughout AB	At B in BC	Throughout AB
Throughout	−35.87	−16.80	−1.16	−8.61	−73.67	−82.94	−7.35	−3.69
On flights only	−24.81	−9.22	+1.60	−10.67	−50.36	−56.68	−4.03	−2.55
On landing only	−31.32	−16.80	−3.14	−3.33	−64.86	−73.03	−7.35	−3.22

the basic equations produced by Cusens and Kuang. If this is done, the expressions given on *Table 175* are obtained, which yield H and M_0 directly. Comparisons between the values given by these simplified expressions and those presented by Cusens and Kuang made using a programmable calculator show that the resulting variations are negligible for values in the range encountered in concrete design.

The expressions given on *Table 175* assume a ratio of G/E of 0.4 as recommended in CP110 (the BS8110 recommendation of $G/E = 0.42$ leads to insignificant differences) and take C to be one-half of the St Venant value for plain concrete. As assumed by Cusens and Kuang, to determine the second moment of area of the landing only one-half of the actual width is considered.

A series of design charts for free-standing stairs has been generated by computer analysis: see ref. 128.

Example. Design a free-standing stair with the following dimensions to support total ultimate loads (including self-weight, finishes etc.) of 16.9 kN per metre on the flight and 15.0 kN per metre on the landing: $a = 2.7$ m; $b = 1.4$ m; $b_1 = 1.8$ m, $h_f = 100$ mm; $h_l = 175$ mm and $\phi = 30°$. The supports are fixed.

From the expressions given on *Table 175*, $H = 81.86$ kN per metre and thus $M_0 = 35.87$ kN m per metre. If Cusens and Kuang's exact expressions are employed to analyse this structure, $H = 81.89$ kN per metre and $M_0 = 35.67$ kN m per metre. There is thus an error of about 0.5% by using the approximate expression for M_0 and about one-tenth of this in H.

If these values are substituted into the remaining expressions on *Table 175*, the corresponding values of M_v, M_h and T throughout the structure can be found. Typical values for various combinations of load are shown in the accompanying table. Note that theoretically M_v reduces suddenly at B from −41.95 kN m per metre in OB (when both flights and landing carry imposed load) to −3.68 kN m per metre in BC, owing to the intersection with flight AB. Since the members forming the actual structures are of finite width, Cusens and Kuang recommend redistributing the moments across the width of the flight/landing intersections to give a value of M_v at B of $(-41.95 - 3.68)/2 = -22.82$ kN m per metre.

25.2.3 Sawtooth stairs

Cusens (ref. 126) has shown that, if axial shortening is neglected and the strain energy due to bending only is considered, the midspan moments for so-called sawtooth or slabless stairs are given by the general expression

$$M_s = \frac{nl^2(k_{11} + k_0 k_{12})}{j^2(k_{13} + k_0 k_{14})}$$

where k_0 = stiffness of tread/stiffness of riser and j is the number of treads.

If j is odd:

$$k_{11} = \tfrac{1}{16}j^2 + \tfrac{1}{48}j(j-1)(j-2)$$
$$k_{12} = \tfrac{1}{16}(j-1)^2 + \tfrac{1}{48}(j-1)(j-2)(j-3)$$
$$k_{13} = \tfrac{1}{2}j$$
$$k_{14} = \tfrac{1}{2}(j-1)$$

If j is even:

$$k_{11} = \tfrac{1}{48}j(j-1)(j-2)$$
$$k_{12} = \tfrac{1}{48}(j-1)(j-2)(j-3)$$
$$k_{13} = \tfrac{1}{2}(j-1)$$
$$k_{14} = \tfrac{1}{2}(j-2)$$

The chart on *Table 176* gives the *support-moment* coefficients for various ratios of k_0 and numbers of treads. Having found the support moment, the maximum midspan bending moment can be determined by using the appropriate expression on the table and subtracting the support moment.

Typical bending-moment and shearing-force diagrams for a stair are also shown on *Table 176*, together with suggested arrangements of reinforcement. Because of the stair profile, concentrations of stress occur in the re-entrant corners, and the actual stresses to be resisted will be larger than those calculated from the moments. To resist such stresses, Cusens recommends providing twice the reinforcement theoretically required unless suitable fillets or haunches are incorporated at these junctions. If this can be done, the actual steel provided need only be about 10% more than that theoretically necessary. The method of reinforcing the stair shown in diagram (a) is very suitable but is generally only practicable if haunches are provided. Otherwise the arrangement shown in diagram (b) should be adopted. A further possibility is to arrange the bars shown in diagram (a) on *Table 173* for wall-to-wall corners.

Stability: BS8110 and CP110 requirements

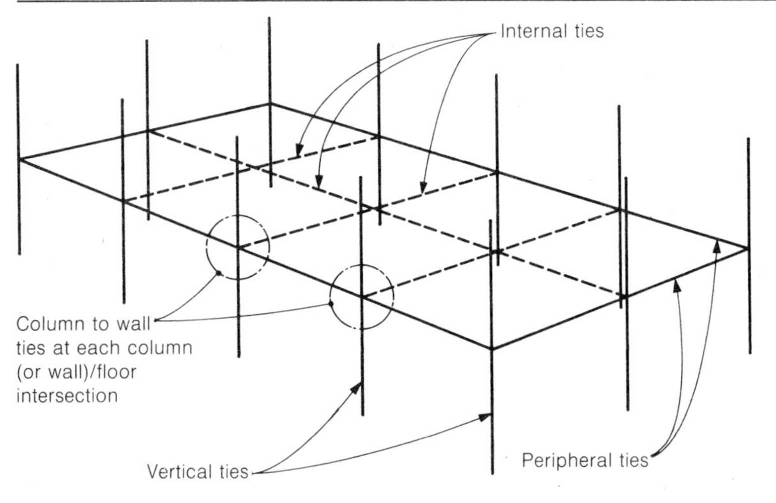

Notation

F_t tie-force coefficient (dimensionless)
n_o number of storeys (dimensionless)
l either greatest distance between centres of vertical load-bearing members; or 5 × clear storey height (below beams if provided); whichever is the *lesser* (metres)
l_0 floor to ceiling height (metres)
g_k average characteristic dead load (kN/m²)
q_k average characteristic imposed load (kN/m²)
T ultimate tensile force for which each tie is to be designed

Type of tie		Reinforcement required: Amount	Reinforcement required: Disposition etc.
Vertical (only required for buildings exceeding four storeys high)		Minima provided to comply with requirements for reinforced concrete walls and columns will suffice. *CP110 only*: For plain concrete walls where $\rho < 0.2\%$ and for precast structures see provisions in Clause 5.1.2.4.	
Horizontal (required in buildings of any height)	Peripheral	To resist $T = F_t$ kN	At each floor and roof level. In peripheral wall or within 1200 mm of edge of building.
	Internal	If $(g_k + q_k)l \leqslant 37.5$ kN/m, to resist $T = F_t$ kN/m width If $(g_k + q_k)l \geqslant 37.5$ kN/m, to resist $T = 0.0267(g_k + q_k)lF_t$ kN/m width	At each floor level. Either spread evenly through slab or grouped at beams, walls etc. In walls (within 500 mm of top or bottom of floor slab), floor slab or beams.
	External column and wall	To resist the greater of either (i) if $l_0 \leqslant 5$ m, $T = 0.4l_0F_t$ kN; if $l_0 \geqslant 5$ m, $T = 2F_t$ kN; (values for walls are per metre of horizontal length) or (ii) $0.03 \times$ total ultimate vertical load for which member has been designed, at floor level considered.	At each floor level, to anchor column or wall to floor structure. Reinforcement required may be partly or wholly provided by extending that used for peripheral or internal ties. Corner columns should be tied in both directions to resist forces T specified.

Number of storeys n_o	1	2	3	4	5	6	7	8	9	10 or more
Tie-force coefficient F_t	24	28	32	36	40	44	48	52	56	60

Tie details

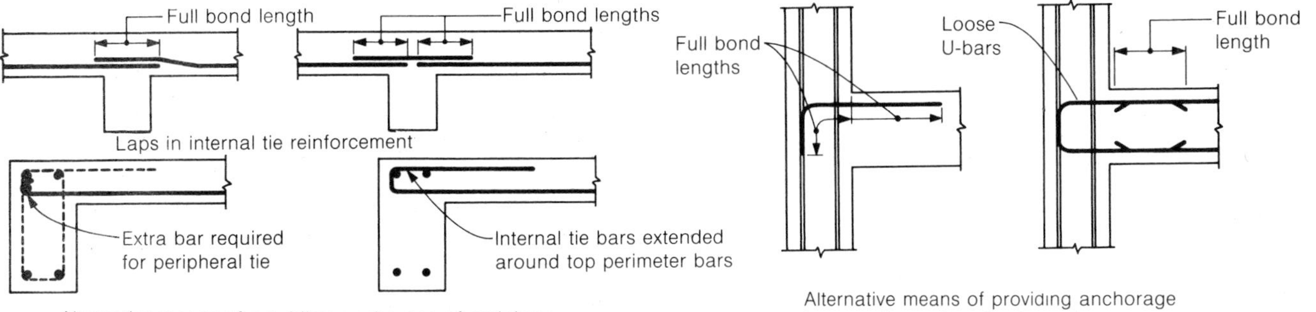

Alternative means of providing anchorage of periphery

Alternative means of providing anchorage between internal and column ties

Example. A slabless stair has seven treads, each 300 mm wide with risers 180 mm high, the thickness of both being 100 mm. It is to carry an imposed load of $3\,kN/m^2$ and is 1 metre wide. Design the stair.

The self-weight of the treads and risers (assuming no finishes are required) is given by

$$\frac{(0.3 \times 0.1) + (0.18 \times 0.1)}{0.3} \times 24 = 3.84\,kN/m^2$$

Thus total ultimate load = [(3.84 × 1.4) + (3.0 × 1.6)] 1.0 = 10.18 kN/m. Since $l_t = 300$ mm, $l_r = 180$ mm and $h_t = h_r = 100$ mm, $k = 180/300 = 0.6$. From the chart on *Table 176*, the support-moment coefficient = − 0.088. Thus

$$\text{support moment} = -0.088 \times 10.18 \times 2.1^2 = -3.95\,kN\,m$$

If $j = 7$,

$$\text{free bending moment} = \tfrac{1}{8} \times 10.18 \times 2.1^2\left(\frac{7^2+1}{7^2}\right) = 5.73\,kN\,m$$

Therefore maximum bending moment at midspan = 5.73 − 3.95 = 1.78 kN m.

25.2.4 Helical stairs

By using strain-energy principles it is possible to formulate, for symmetrically loaded helical stairs with fixed supports, the following two equations in M_0 and H:

$$M_0[K_1(k_5 + \tfrac{1}{2}\sin 2\theta) + k_5k_7] + HR_2[-K_1k_4 \tan\phi + k_4k_7 \tan\phi + k_5 \sin\phi \cos\phi(1-K_2)] + nR_1^2[K_1(k_5 + \tfrac{1}{2}\sin 2\theta - \sin\theta) + k_5k_7 + k_6k_7R_2/R_1] = 0$$

$$M_0[-K_1k_4 + k_4k_7 + (k_7 - K_2)k_5] + HR_2[\tfrac{1}{2}K_1 \tan\phi(\tfrac{1}{3}\theta^3 - \tfrac{1}{2}\theta^2 \sin 2\theta - 2k_4) + \tfrac{1}{2}k_7 \tan\phi(\tfrac{1}{3}\theta^3 + \tfrac{1}{2}\theta^2 \sin 2\theta + 2k_4) + 2k_4 \tan\phi(k_7 - K_2) + k_5 \cos^2\phi(\tan\phi + K_2 \cot\phi)] + nR_1^2[K_1(k_6 - k_4) + k_4k_7 + k_7(\theta^2 \sin\theta + 2k_6)R_2/R_1 + (k_7 - K_2)(k_5 + k_6R_2/R_1)] = 0$$

where

$$k_4 = \tfrac{1}{4}\theta \cos 2\theta - \tfrac{1}{8}\sin 2\theta$$
$$k_5 = \tfrac{1}{2}\theta - \tfrac{1}{4}\sin 2\theta$$
$$k_6 = \theta \cos\theta - \sin\theta$$
$$k_7 = \cos^2\phi + K_2 \sin^2\phi$$

$K_1 = GC/EI_1$, $K_2 = GC/EI_2$ and $\theta = \beta/2$.

These simultaneous equations may be solved on a programmable calculator or larger machine to give coefficients k_1 and k_2 representing M_0 and H respectively. If the values of M_0 and H are then resubstituted into the equations given on *Table 176*, the bending and torsional moments, shearing forces and thrust at any point along the stair may be calculated rapidly. Since the critical quantity controlling helical stair design is normally the vertical moment M_{vs} at the supports, a further coefficient k_3 can be derived to give this moment.

In ref. 127, Santathadaporn and Cusens present 36 design charts for helical stairs, covering ranges of β of 60° to 720°, ϕ of 20° to 50°, b/h of 0.5 to 16 and R_1/R_2 of 1.0 to 1.1, based on a ratio of G/E of 3/7. The four design charts provided on *Table 177* have been recalculated for a ratio of G/E of 0.4 as recommended in CP110 and by taking C to be one-half of the St Venant value for plain concrete. These charts cover ranges of β of 30° to 360° and ϕ of 20° to 40°, with values of b/h of 5 and 10 and R_1/R_2 of 1.0 and 1.1, these being the ranges most frequently met in helical stair design. Interpolation between the various curves and charts on *Table 177* will be sufficiently accurate for preliminary design purposes.

Example. Design a helicoidal stair having an angle of inclination ϕ of 25° to the horizontal plane to support a uniform imposed load of $3\,kN/m^2$. The stair is to have a width of 1.2 m and the minimum thickness of the slab is 120 mm, the radius to the inside of the stair R_i being 900 mm. The angle β turned through by the stair is 240°.

For radius of the centre-line of the load R_1 is

$$R_1 = \frac{2(R_0^3 - R_i^3)}{3(R_0^2 - R_i^2)} = \frac{2(2.1^3 - 0.9^3)}{3(2.1^2 - 0.9^2)} \simeq 1.58\,m$$

Then since the radius of the centre-line of the stair R_2 is $0.9 + (1/2)1.2 = 1.5$ m, $R_1/R_2 \simeq 1.05$ and $b/h = 1200/120 = 10$. Thus from the charts on *Table 177*, interpolating as necessary, $k_1 = -0.12$, $k_2 = +1.52$ and $k_3 = -0.32$. Assuming that the mean thickness in plan of the stair (including treads and finishes) is 220 mm, the self-weight of the stair is $0.22 \times 24 = 5.3\,kN/m^2$ and thus the total ultimate load = (3 × 1.6) + (5.3 × 1.4) = $12.22\,kN/m^2$. Thus

$$M_0 = -0.12 \times 12.22 \times 1.5^2 \times 1.2 = -3.96\,kN\,m$$
$$H = 1.52 \times 12.22 \times 1.5 \times 1.2 = 33.4\,kN$$

Also

$$M_{vs} = -0.32 \times 12.22 \times 1.5^2 \times 1.2 = -10.56\,kN\,m$$

The slab should now be checked to ensure that the thickness provided is sufficient to resist this final moment. Then, assuming this is so, the foregoing values of M_0 and H can be substituted into the equations for M_v, M_n, T, F, V_n and V_h given on *Table 176* to obtain the moments and forces along the stair, in order to detail the reinforcement. For example, when $\theta = 60°$, $M_v = 1.11$ kN m, $M_n = -48.17$ kN m, $T = 0.05$ kN m, $N = -36.5$ kN, $V_n = 9.68$ kN and $V_h = 16.7$ kN.

Typical distributions of moments and forces along the stair are shown on *Table 176*.

25.3 NON-PLANAR ROOFS

25.3.1 Prismatic structures

To design a simple prismatic roof or similar structure comprising a number of planar slabs for service loads and stresses, the resultant loads Q acting perpendicularly to each slab and the unbalanced thrusts N acting in the plane of each slab are determined first, taking into account the thrust of one slab on another. The slabs are then designed to resist the transverse bending moments due to loads Q assuming continuity and combination with the thrusts N. The longitudinal forces F due to the slabs bending in their own plane

Stairs 1: general information

Free-standing (or scissor) stair (landing unsupported)

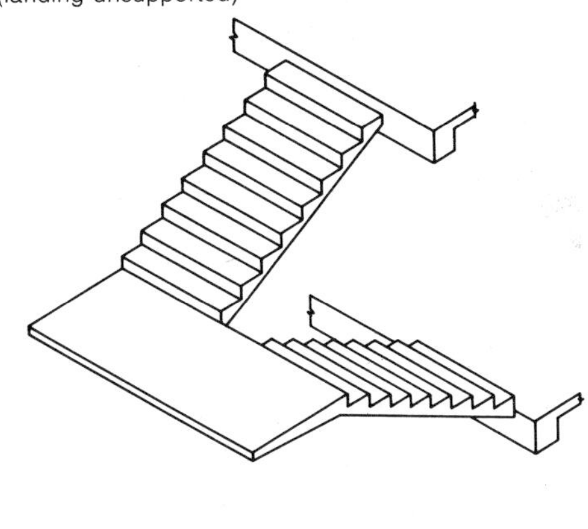

Individual precast treads cantilevered from spine beam

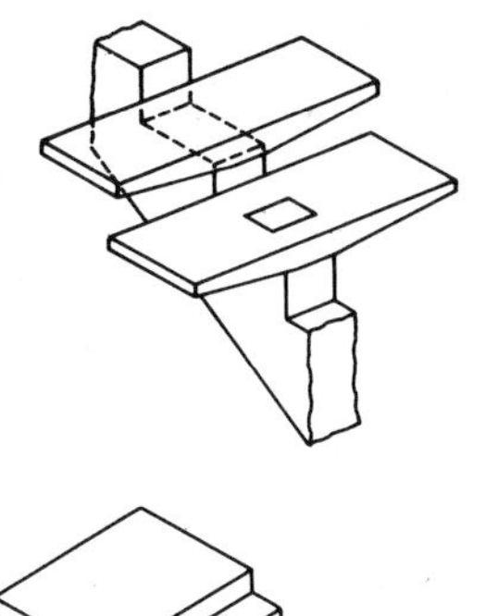

Helical stair

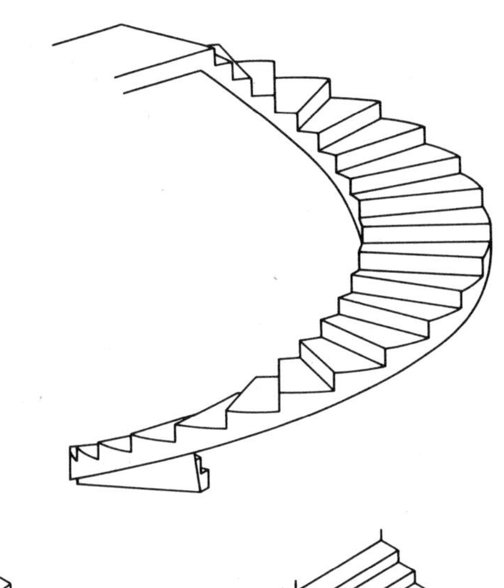

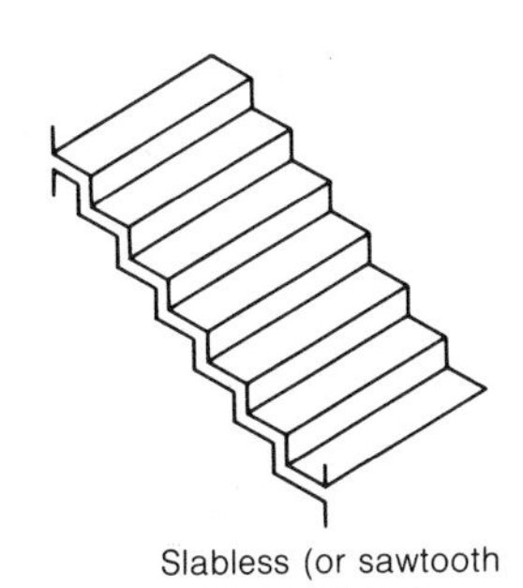

Slabless (or sawtooth or 'dog-leg') stair

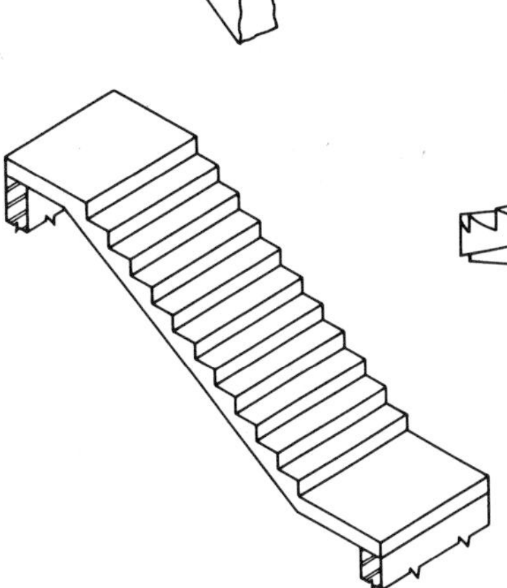

Simple straight stair

Landing arrangement for simple stair

General information

Optimum dimensions for stairs (BS5395) (mm)

Usage	Going	Rise	Min. width
Public	300	150	1000
Semi-public	275	165	1000
Private	250	175	800

General optimum dimensions:
2 × rise + going = 600 mm

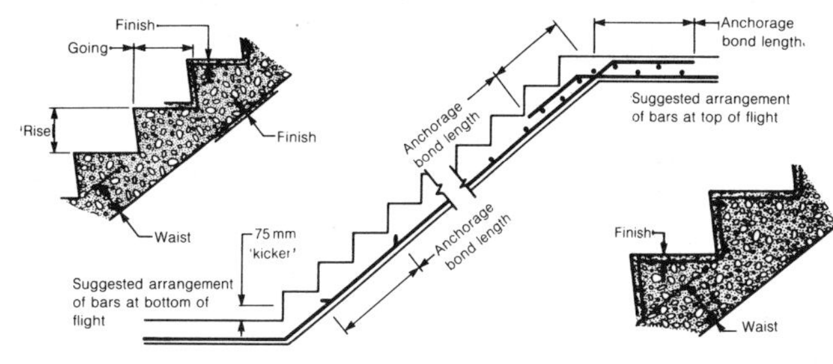

Free-standing stairs

If flights are freely supported at A and A′:

$$H = \left[n_l(b_1 + b)\left(1 + \frac{1}{2}\frac{b}{a}\sec\phi\right) + n_f a\cos\phi \right] \Big/ 2\tan\phi$$

If flights are fully fixed at A and A′:

$$H \simeq \left[n_l(b_1 + b)\left(4 + 3\frac{b}{a}\sec\phi\right) + 3n_f a\cos\phi \right] \Big/ \left\{ 2\tan\phi \; 4 + 3(b_1/a)^2 \Big/ \left[\frac{0.72}{1 + (h_f/b)^2} + \frac{1}{K} \right] \right\}$$

$$M_0 \simeq [Hb_1 \tan\phi - \tfrac{1}{4}n_l(b_1^2 - b^2)] \Big/ \left[\frac{1.44K}{1 + (h_f/b)^2} + 2 \right]$$

where $K = \left(\dfrac{h_f}{h_l}\right)^3 \left(\dfrac{b_1}{a}\right) \sec^2\phi$

Then for OB, at any point distance y from O:

$$M_v = -M_0 - \tfrac{1}{2}n_l y^2 \qquad M_h = -H_y \qquad T = -\tfrac{1}{2}n_l b y$$

For BC, at any point distance y from O:

$$M_v = -\tfrac{1}{2}n_l[\tfrac{1}{2}(b_1 + b) - y]^2 \qquad M_h = 0$$
$$T = -\tfrac{1}{2}n_l b[\tfrac{1}{2}(b_1 + b) - y]$$

For AB, at any point distance x from B:

$$M_v = Hx\sin\phi - \tfrac{1}{2}n_l(b_1 + b)(x\cos\phi + \tfrac{1}{2}b) - \tfrac{1}{2}n_f x^2\cos^2\phi$$
$$M_h = -\tfrac{1}{2}Hb_1\cos\phi - [M_0 + \tfrac{1}{8}n_l(b_1^2 - b^2)]\sin\phi$$
$$T = -\tfrac{1}{2}Hb_1\sin\phi + [M_0 + \tfrac{1}{8}n_l(b_1^2 - b^2)]\cos\phi$$

Additional notation

- a length of flight
- b width of flight and landing
- b_1 distance between centre-lines of flights
- H, M_0 horizontal restraint force and restraint moment at cut, respectively
- h_f, h_l slab depth of flight and of landing, respectively
- M_h, M_v, T horizontal and vertical bending moments and torsional moment at any point, respectively
- n_f, n_l ultimate load per unit length on flight and on landing, respectively
- x, y distances measured along flight and along Y-axis respectively
- ϕ slope of flight measured from horizontal

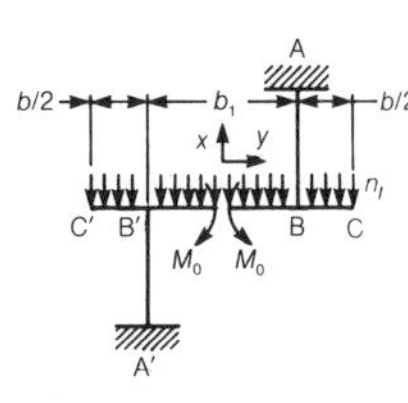

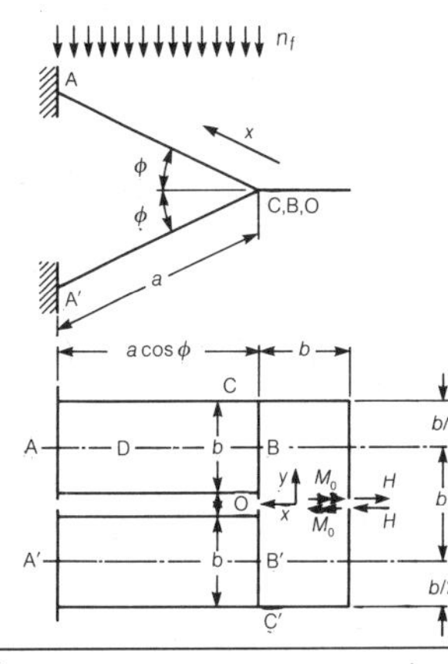

under the loads N are, for any two adjacent slabs AB and BC, calculated from formula (2) in *Table 178*, in which M_{AB} and M_{BC} are found from formula (1) if the structure is freely supported at the end of L. For each pair of slabs AB–BC, BC–CD etc. there is an equation like (2) containing three unknown forces F. If there are n pairs, there are $(n-1)$ equations and $(n+1)$ unknowns. The conditions at the outer edges a and z of the end slabs determine the forces F at these edges; for example, if the edges are unsupported, $F_a = F_z = 0$. The simultaneous equations are solved for the remaining unknown forces F_A, F_B, F_C etc. The longitudinal stress at any junction B is calculated from the formula (in *Table 178*) for f_B. Variation of the longitudinal stress from one function to the next is rectilinear. If f_B is negative, the stress is tensile and should be resisted by reinforcement. Shearing stresses are generally small.

25.3.2 Domes

A dome is designed for the total vertical load only, that is, for the weights of the slab and any covering on the slab, the weight of any ceiling or other distributed load suspended from the slab, and the imposed load. The intensity w of total service load = the equivalent load per unit area of surface of the dome. Horizontal service loads due to the wind and the effects of shrinking and changes in temperature are allowed for by assuming an ample imposed load, or by inserting more reinforcement than that required for the vertical load alone, or by designing for stresses well below the permissible values, or by combining any or all of these methods.

Segmental domes. Referring to the diagram and formulae in *Table 178*, the circumferential force acting in a horizontal plane in a unit strip S is T, and the corresponding force (the meridional thrust) acting tangentially to the surface of the dome is N. At the plane where θ is 51°48′, that is, at the plane of rupture, $T = 0$. Above this plane T is compressive and reaches a maximum value of $0.5wr$ at the crown of the dome ($\theta = 0$). Below this plane T is tensile, and equals $0.167wr$ when $\theta = 60°$ and $wr = 90°$. The meridional thrust N is $0.5wr$ at the crown, $0.618wr$ at the plane of rupture, $0.667wr$ when $\theta = 60°$, and wr when $\theta = 90°$; i.e. N increases from the crown towards the support and has its greatest value at the support.

For a concentrated load F on the crown of the dome, T is tensile; and T and the corresponding meridional compressive thrust N are given by the appropriate formulae in *Table 178*, the basis of which is that the load is concentrated on so small an area at the crown that it is equivalent to a point load. The theoretical stress at the crown is therefore infinite, but the practical impossibility of obtaining a point load invalidates the application of the formulae when $\theta = 0$ or very nearly so. For domes of varying thickness, see ref. 87.

Shallow segmental domes. Approximate analysis only is sufficient in the case of a shallow dome; appropriate formulae are given in *Table 178*.

Conical domes. In a conical dome, the circumferential forces are compressive throughout and at any horizontal plane x from the apex are given by the expression for T in *Table 178*, the corresponding force in the direction of the slope being N. The horizontal outward force per unit length of circumference at the bottom of the slope is T_r, and this force must be resisted by the supports or by a ring beam at the bottom of the slope.

25.3.3 Segmental shells

General notes on the design of cylindrical shell roofs and the use of *Table 179* are given in section 6.1.9.

Membrane action. Consideration of membrane action only gives the following membrane forces per unit width of slab due to the uniform loads shown on *Table 178*: to obtain stresses, divide by the thickness of shell h. Negative values of V indicate tension in the direction corresponding to an increase in x and a decrease in θ_x: positive values of F indicate tension. Reinforcement should be provided approximately in line with and to resist the principal tensile force. If the shell is supported along any edges the forces will be modified accordingly.

At any point:

Tangential force:

$$F_y = -(g + q\cos\theta_x)r\cos\theta_x$$

Longitudinal force:

$$F_x = -(1-x)\frac{x}{r}[g\cos\theta_x + 1.5q(\cos^2\theta_x - \sin^2\theta_x)]$$

Shearing force:

$$V_{xy} = (g + 1.5q\cos\theta_x)(2x - l)\sin\theta_x$$

Principal forces (due to membrane forces only):

$$F_p = \tfrac{1}{2}(F_x + F_y) \pm \sqrt{[\tfrac{1}{4}(F_x - F_y)^2 + V_{xy}^2]}$$

$$\tan 2\phi = \frac{2V_{xy}}{F_x - F_y}$$

At A (*at midpoint at edge:* $\theta_x = \theta$; $x = l/2$):

$$F_{yA} = -(g + q\cos\theta)r\cos\theta$$
$$F_{xA} = -\tfrac{1}{4}l^2[g\cos\theta + 1.5q(\cos^2\theta - \sin^2\theta)]/r$$
$$V_{xyA} = 0$$

At B (*midpoint at crown:* $\theta_x = 0$; $x = l/2$):

$$F_{yB} = -(g + q)r$$
$$F_{xB} = \tfrac{1}{4}l^2(g + 1.5q)/r$$
$$V_{xyB} = 0$$

At C (*at support at edge:* $\theta_x = \theta$; $x = 0$):

$$F_{yC} = -(g + q\cos\theta)r\cos\theta$$
$$V_{xyC} = -(g + 1.5q\cos\theta)l\sin\theta$$
$$F_{xC} = 0$$

At D (*at support at crown:* $\theta_x = 0$; $x = 0$):

$$F_{yD} = -(g + q)r$$
$$F_{xD} = 0$$
$$V_{xyD} = 0$$

Stairs 2: sawtooth and helical stairs

Sawtooth stairs

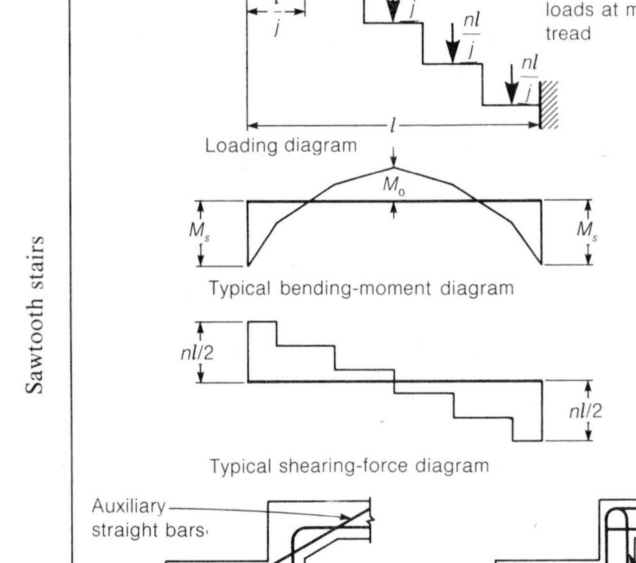

Possible arrangements of reinforcement

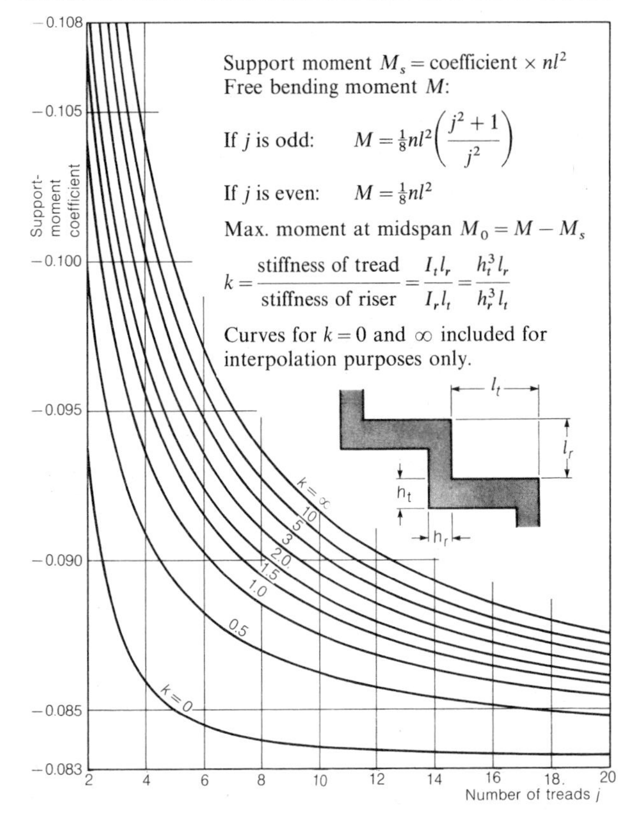

Helical stairs

At any point along stair

Lateral moment: $M_n = M_0 \sin\theta \sin\phi - HR_2\theta \tan\phi \cos\theta \sin\phi - HR_2 \sin\theta \cos\phi + nR_1 \sin\phi(R_1 \sin\theta - R_2\theta)$

Torsional moment: $T = (M_0 \sin\theta - HR_2\theta\cos\theta\tan\phi + nR_1^2 \sin\theta - nR_1R_2\theta)\cos\phi + HR_2 \sin\theta \sin\phi$

Vertical moment: $M_v = M_0 \cos\theta + HR_2\theta \tan\phi \sin\theta - nR_1^2(1 - \cos\theta)$

Thrust: $N = -H \sin\theta \cos\phi - nR_1\theta \sin\phi$

Lateral shearing force across stair: $V_n = nR_1\theta \cos\phi - H \sin\theta \sin\phi$

Radial horizontal shearing force: $V_h = H \cos\theta$

where

Redundant moment acting tangentially at midspan: $M_0 = k_1 nR_2^2$

Horizontal redundant force at midspan: $H = k_2 nR_2$

Vertical moment at supports: $M_{vs} = k_3 nR_2^2$

Additional notation

- I_1, I_2 second moment of area of stair section about horizontal axis and axis normal to slope, respectively
- n total loading per unit length projected along centre-line of load
- R_1 radius of centre-line of loading $= (2/3)(R_0^3 - R_i^3)/(R_0^2 - R_i^2)$
- R_2 radius of centre-line of steps $= (1/2)(R_i + R_0)$, where R_i and R_0 are the internal and external radii of the stair, respectively
- θ angle subtended in plan between point considered and midpoint of stair
- β total angle subtended by helix in plan
- ϕ slope of tangent to helix centre-line measured from horizontal

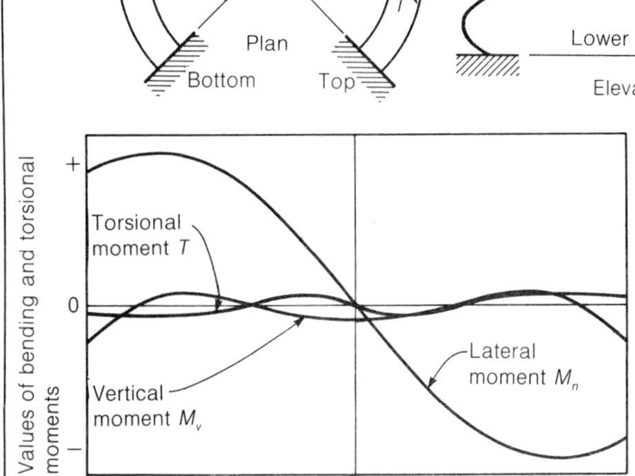

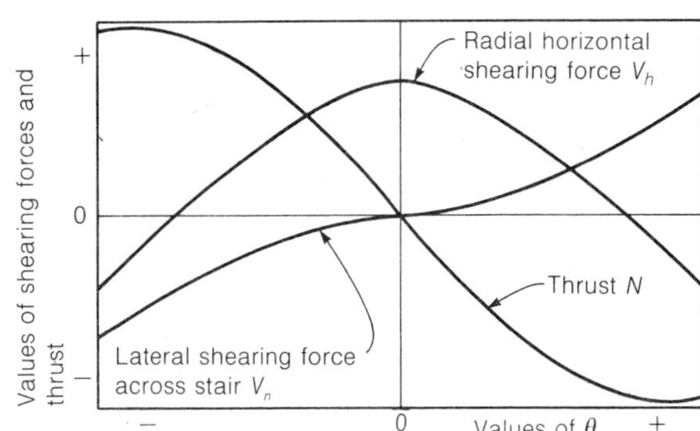

Stairs 3: design coefficients for helical stairs

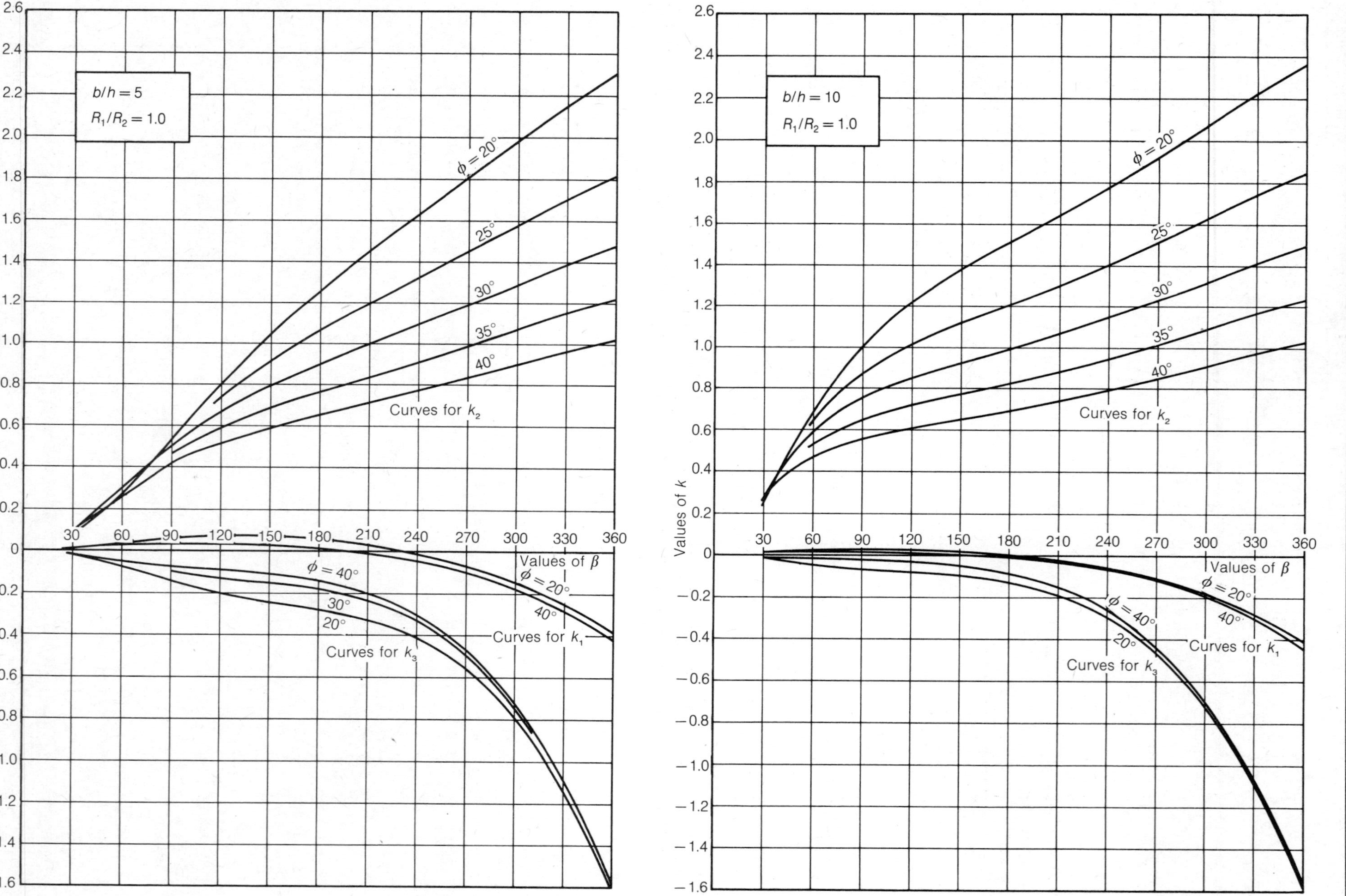

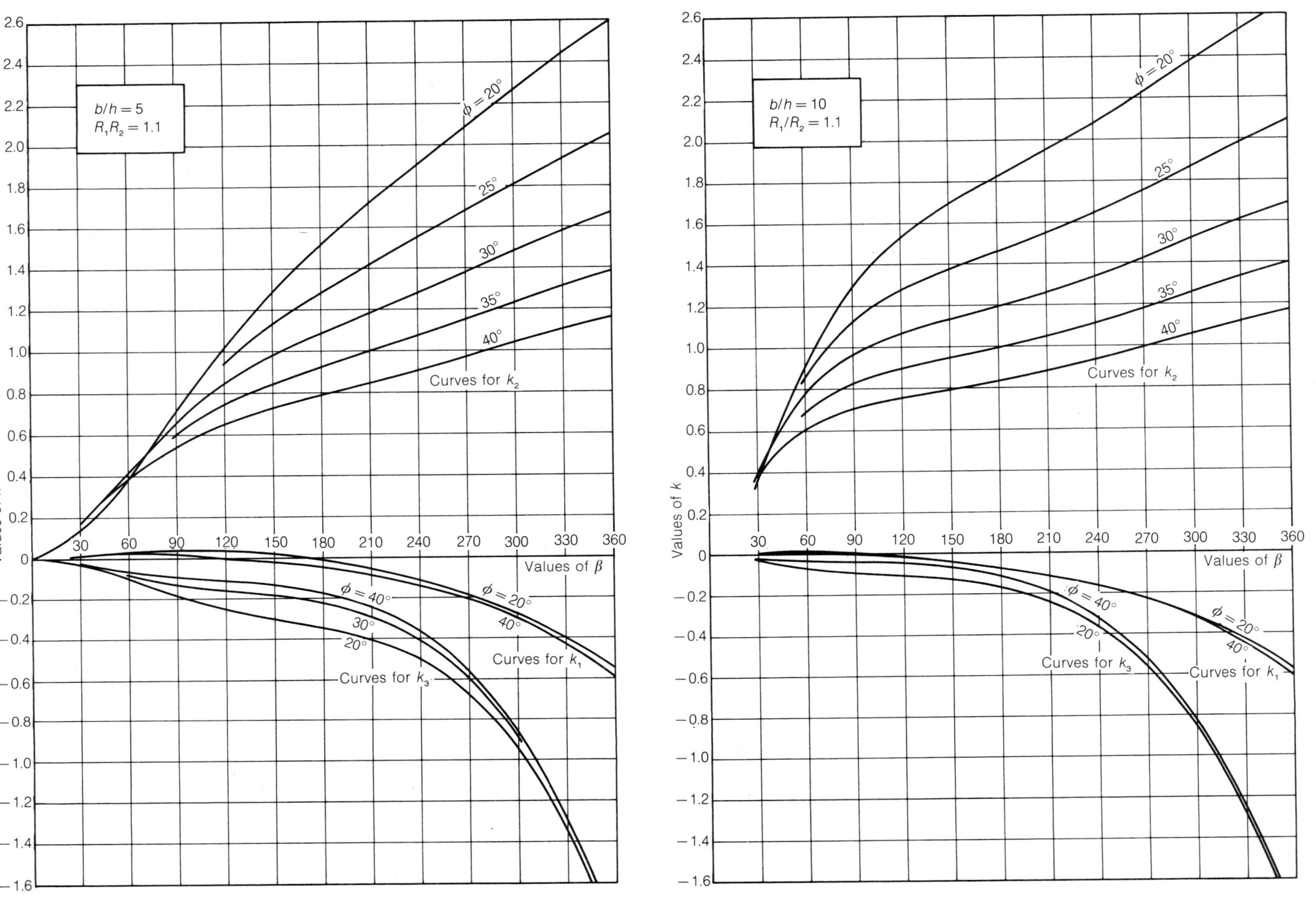
b/h = 5
R1R2 = 1.1
φ = 20°
25°
30°
35°
40°
Curves for k2
Values of k
Values of β
φ = 40°
30°
20°
Curves for k3
φ = 20°
40°
Curves for k1
b/h = 10
R1/R2 = 1.1
φ = 20°
25°
30°
35°
40°
Curves for k2
Values of k
Values of β
φ = 40°
20°
Curves for k3
φ = 20°
40°
Curves for k1

Beam action. If the ratio of the length of a cylindrical shell l to its radius r is at least 2.5, the longitudinal forces may be approximated with reasonable accuracy by calculating the moment of inertia I_{xx} and the vertical distance from the neutral axis to the crown $\bar{y}$ from the simplified approximate expressions

$$\bar{y} \simeq R - \frac{\sin\alpha}{\alpha}(R - \tfrac{2}{3}h)$$

$$I_{xx} \simeq R^2 h(R - \tfrac{3}{2}h)\left(\alpha + \sin\alpha\cos\alpha - 2\frac{\sin^2\alpha}{\alpha}\right)$$

Then if n is the total uniform load per unit area acting on the shell (i.e. including self-weight etc.), the maximum bending moment in a freely supported shell is given by

$$M = 2\theta rn \times \tfrac{1}{8}l^2 = \tfrac{1}{4}\theta rnl^2$$

Now, from the well-known relationship

$$\frac{M}{I_{xx}} = \frac{f}{y}$$

the horizontal forces F_x (top) and F_x (bottom) at midspan at the crown and springing of a shell of thickness h are given by the expressions

$$F_x(\text{top}) = \frac{M\bar{y}h}{I_{xx}}$$

$$F_x(\text{bottom}) = \frac{M[r(1-\cos\theta) - \bar{y}]h}{I_{xx}}$$

At the supports the total shearing force in the shell is

$$V = \tfrac{1}{2} \times 2\theta rnl = \theta rnl$$

The shearing stress v at any point is then given by the expression

$$v = \frac{VA\bar{x}}{2hI_{xx}}$$

where $A\bar{x}$ is the first moment of area about the neutral axis of the area of cross-section of shell, above the point at which the shearing stress is being determined.

The principal shortcoming of this approximate analysis is that it does not indicate in any simple manner the size of the transverse moments which occur in the shell. However, a tabular method has been devised by which these moments can be evaluated indirectly from the lateral components of the shearing stresses: for details see ref. 88.

25.3.4 Hyperbolic-paraboloidal shells

This surface, the simplest type of double-curved shell, is generated by the intersection of two separate sets of inclined straight lines (parallel to axes XX and YY respectively, as shown in the diagrams on *Table 178*). Vertical sections through the shell at angles to XX or YY are parabolic in shape and horizontal sections through the surface form hyperbolas; hence the name hyperbolic paraboloid.

Individual units such as those shown in diagrams (a) and (b) in *Table 178* can be used separately, being supported on columns or buttresses located at either the higher or the lower corners. Alternatively, groups of units can be combined to achieve roofs having attractive and unusual shapes: one example is shown in diagram (c). Some idea of the more unlikely forms that can be achieved may be obtained from ref. 89.

If the shell is shallow and the loading uniform, the shell acts as a membrane transferring uniform tensile and compressive forces of $F/2c$ (where F is the total load on the unit and c is the rise) parallel to the directions of principal curvature back to the edges of the shell. These forces are transmitted back to the supports along beams at the shell edges. The principal problems which arise when designing hyperbolic-paraboloidal shells involve the interaction between the shell and the supporting edge members, the design of the buttresses or ties needed to resist the horizontal component of the forces acting at the supports, and the fact that excessive deflections at unsupported shell edges lead to stresses that differ considerably from those determined by simplified theories.

Stability increases with sharpness of curvature of the shell, which also minimizes the forces and reactions within the shell, but to avoid the need for top forms the maximum slope must not exceed about 45°: this corresponds to a ratio of c/a or c/b in the diagrams on *Table 178* of $1/\sqrt{2}$. To ensure stability if a single unit is to be used, the ratio of c/a or c/b must be at least 1/5.

Useful introductions to the theory and design of hyperbolic-paraboloidal shells are given in refs 55 and 90.

25.4 BEARINGS, HINGES AND JOINTS

25.4.1 Hinges and bearings

A hinge is an element that can transmit a thrust and a shearing force, but permits rotation without restraint. If it is essential that hinge action is fully realized, this can be effected by providing a steel hinge, or by forming a hinge monolithic with the member as shown at (a) in *Table 181*; this so-called Mesnager hinge is sometimes provided in a frame of a large bunker to isolate the container from the substructure or to provide a hinge at the base of the columns of a hinged frame bridge. The hinge-bars *a* resist the entire horizontal shearing force; the so-called 'throat' of concrete at D must be sufficient to transfer all the compressive force from the upper to the lower part of the member. The hinge bars should be bound together by links *d*; the main vertical bars *e* should terminate on each side of the slot B and C. It may be advantageous during construction to provide bars extending across the slots, and to cut these bars on completion of the frame. The slots should be filled with bituminous material, lead, or a similar separating layer.

The foregoing form of hinge is now largely superseded by the Freyssinet hinge shown at (b). Here the large compressive stresses across the throat provide high shearing resistance and the inclusion of bars crossing the throat may, in fact, adversely affect the hinge. Tests have shown that, owing to biaxial or triaxial restraint, such hinges can withstand compressive stresses of many times the concrete cube strength without failure occurring. Bursting tension on each side of the throat normally controls the design of this type of hinge.

Prismatic structure (hipped plate construction)

N_{AB} etc. thrust in plane of slab AB etc. due to component of load and weight and of thrust in slab BC etc.

$M_{AB} = \frac{1}{8} N_{AB} L^2$; $M_{BC} = \frac{1}{8} N_{BC} L^2$, etc. (1)

Longitudinal stresses (tensile if negative) at junction B:

$$f_B = \frac{2}{h_{AB} l_{AB}} \left(\frac{3M_{AB}}{l_{AB}} - F_A - 2F_B \right)$$

$$= \frac{2}{h_{BC} l_{BC}} \left(2F_B + F_C - \frac{3M_{BC}}{l_{BC}} \right)$$

(similarly for junction C etc.)

Formulae for stabilizing forces, slabs AB and BC:

$$\frac{F_A}{h_{AB} l_{AB}} + 2F_B \left(\frac{1}{h_{AB} l_{AB}} + \frac{1}{h_{BC} l_{BC}} \right) + \frac{F_C}{h_{BC} l_{BC}} = 3 \left(\frac{M_{AB}}{h_{AB} l_{AB}^2} + \frac{M_{BC}}{h_{BC} l_{BC}^2} \right) \quad (2)$$

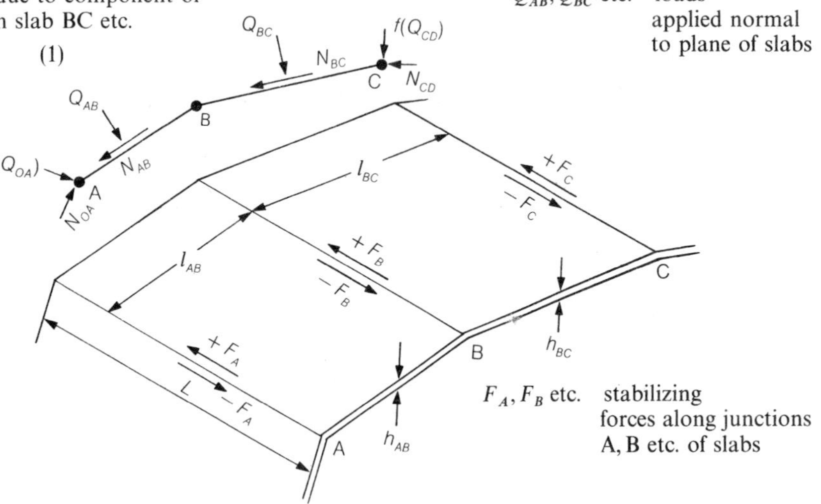

Q_{AB}, Q_{BC} etc. loads applied normal to plane of slabs

F_A, F_B etc. stabilizing forces along junctions A, B etc. of slabs

Dome

Segmental dome

T circumferential force (in horizontal plane) in unit strip at S.

N meridional thrust (acting tangentially) in unit strip at S.

Uniform load w per unit area of surface of dome:

$$T = wr \left[\frac{1 - \cos\theta - \cos^2\theta}{1 + \cos\theta} \right]; \quad N = -\frac{wr}{1 + \cos\theta}$$

At crown: $T = N = \frac{1}{2} wr$ (compression)

Load F concentrated at crown:

$$T = \frac{F}{2\pi r} \operatorname{cosec}^2\theta; \quad N = -\frac{F}{2\pi r \sin^2\theta}$$

(Formulae not applicable to small values of θ.)

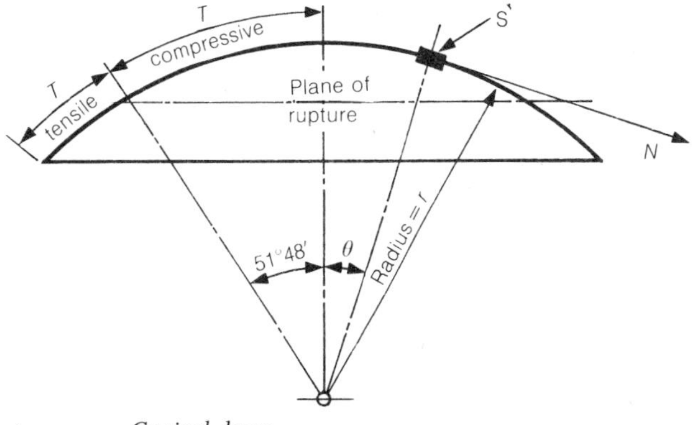

Shallow segmental dome (approx. method)

$$r = \frac{d^2}{8a} + \frac{1}{2} a$$

Total load on supports $= R = 2\pi raw$.

At springing: $N = -\frac{2Rr}{\pi d^2}$

Tensile force in ring beam at springing: $T_r = \frac{R(r-a)}{\pi d}$

w
a
d
N

Conical dome

In horizontal plane at x:

$T = -wx \tan^2\theta$ (i.e. compression) and $N = -\frac{wx}{2\cos^2\theta}$

At bottom:

$T_r = -wh \frac{\tan\theta}{2\cos\theta}$ per unit length of circumference

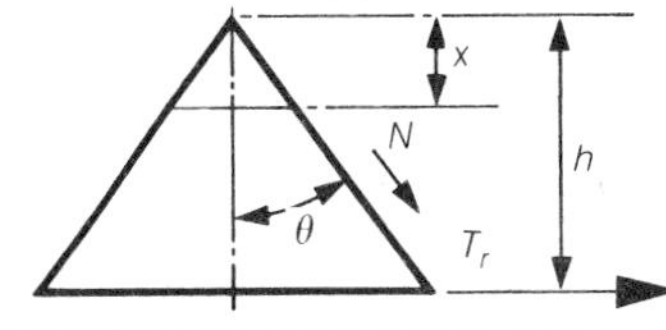

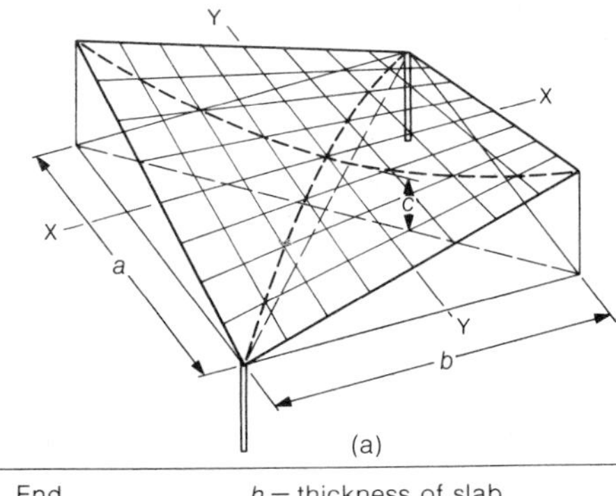

(a)

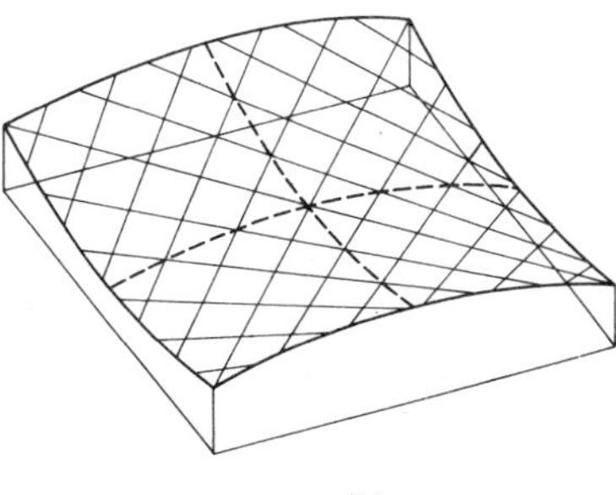

(b)

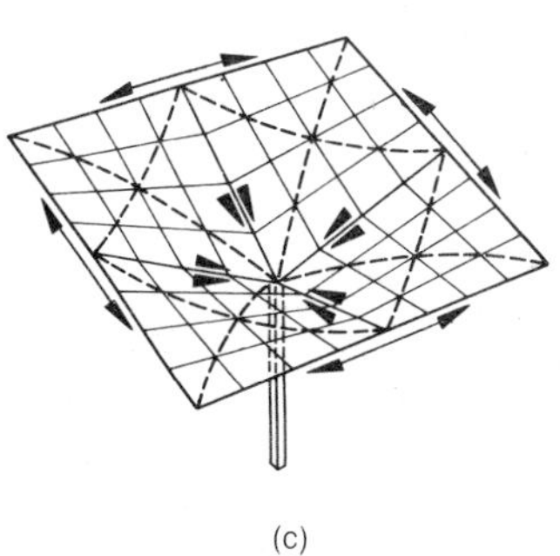

(c)

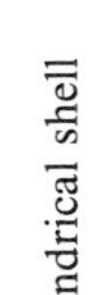

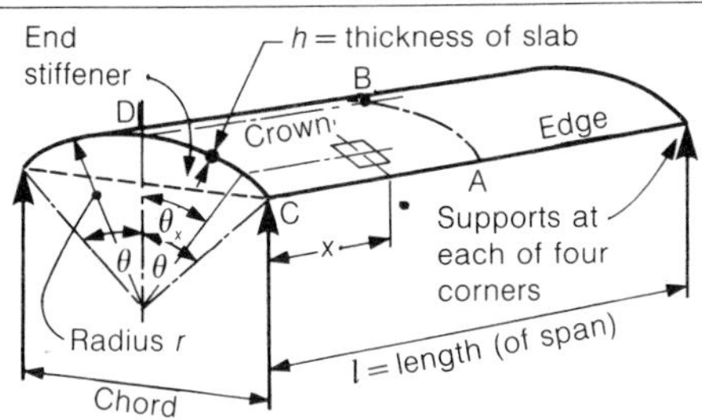

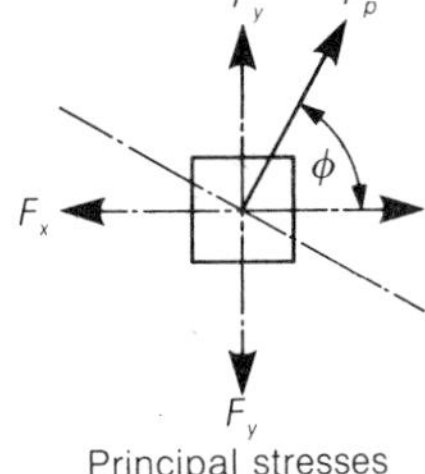

Principal stresses

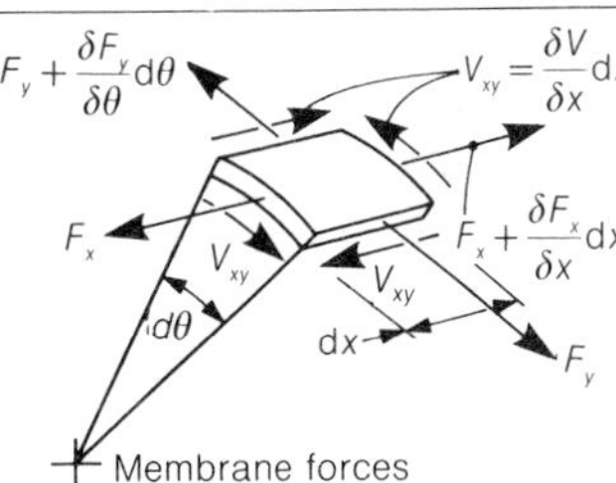

Membrane forces acting on element of slab

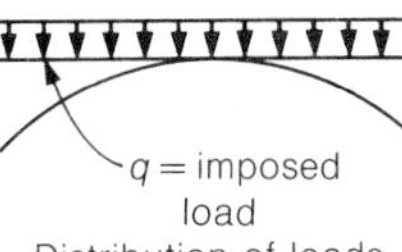

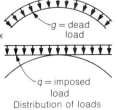

Distribution of loads

Shell roofs: empirical design method

Principal forces and moments required for design

	Feather-edged shell	Shell with valley beams	Shell with edge beams
Assumptions made	No valley beam No horizontal displacement or rotation at shell edge	Half-shell acts with half valley beam No horizontal displacement or rotation of valley beam	Edge beam does not deflect vertically but has no horizontal restraint except its own stiffness
Minimum value[(1)] of y	$\frac{l}{30}\left(1+\frac{l}{60}\right)$	$\frac{l}{30}\left(1+\frac{l}{60}\right)$	$\frac{l}{45}\left(1+\frac{l}{60}\right)$
Load per unit length supported by half-shell	$F_s = wr\psi + \frac{1}{2}W_b$	$F_s = 1.19\,Wy_s/y$	Read from graph on opposite page
Load per unit length supported by half-beam	—	$F_b = W - F_s$	$F_b = wr\psi - F_s$
Total tension in shell valley at midpsan	$N_{ls} = K_1 F_s l^2/y_s$ where $K_1 = 1.7$ when $K\psi \ngtr 1.75$ $K_1 = \frac{9.35}{9-2K\psi}$ when $K\psi > 1.75$[(2)]	$N_{ls} = \frac{K_2 Wl^2}{y}\left(\frac{y_s}{y} - 0.48\right)$ where $K_2 = 1.78$ when $K\psi \ngtr 1.75$ $K_2 = \frac{9.8}{9-2K\psi}$ when $K\psi > 1.75$[(2)]	$N_{ls} = \frac{K_3 F_s l^2}{y_s}$ where $K_3 = 0.17$ when $K\psi \ngtr 1.5$ $K_3 = \frac{1.02}{9-2K\psi}$ when $K\psi > 1.5$[(2)]
Total tension in beam at midspan	—	$N_{lb} = \frac{K_2 Wl^2}{y}\left(1.33 - \frac{y_s}{y}\right)$	$N_{lb} = \frac{22K_3 F_s l^2}{3y_s}$
Total shear in half-shell	$\sum V = 9.25\,Fl/\psi$	$\sum V = 8.45\,Fl/\psi$	$\sum V = 8.60\,Fl/\psi$
Maximum positive transverse bending moment[(3)]	$M_{dt} = \frac{6\times 10^{-5}F^2 l}{y_s}$	$M_{dt} = \frac{4.4\times 10^{-5}F^2 l}{y}$	$M_{dt} = \frac{5.2\times 10^{-5}F^2 l}{y_s}$
Transverse tension in shell	$N_t = 11.8\,wr\sqrt[4]{(l/a)}$	$N_t = 10.2\,wr\sqrt[4]{(l/a)}$	$N_t = 10.8\,wr$

Notes

1. If value of y adopted is less than that given by appropriate expression, max. longitudinal compressive stress and/or deflection at crown may be excessive and empirical method is inapplicable.

2. In such cases (i.e. 'short' shells) transverse bending moments M_{dt} given by formulae are less reliable and longitudinal moments may be significant, so caution should be adopted.

3. The distribution of transverse moments is as shown in sketch below, maximum value occurring at springing, where shell is thickened to at least 150 mm. Negative moment at crown is about 2/3 to 3/4 of max. positive moment, and steel provided top and bottom throughout shell to resist max. positive moment will suffice.

Springing — Crown

Typical distribution of M_{dt}

4. Beams should be designed as follows:

Valley beams: to resist load F_b plus direct tension (N_{lb} at midspan) plus horizontal shear between shell and valley beam varying from $4/lN_{lb}$ at support to zero at midspan

Edge beams: as continuous beam over internal columns to resist loads as valley beam.

Distributions of principal tension and shearing force in half-shell	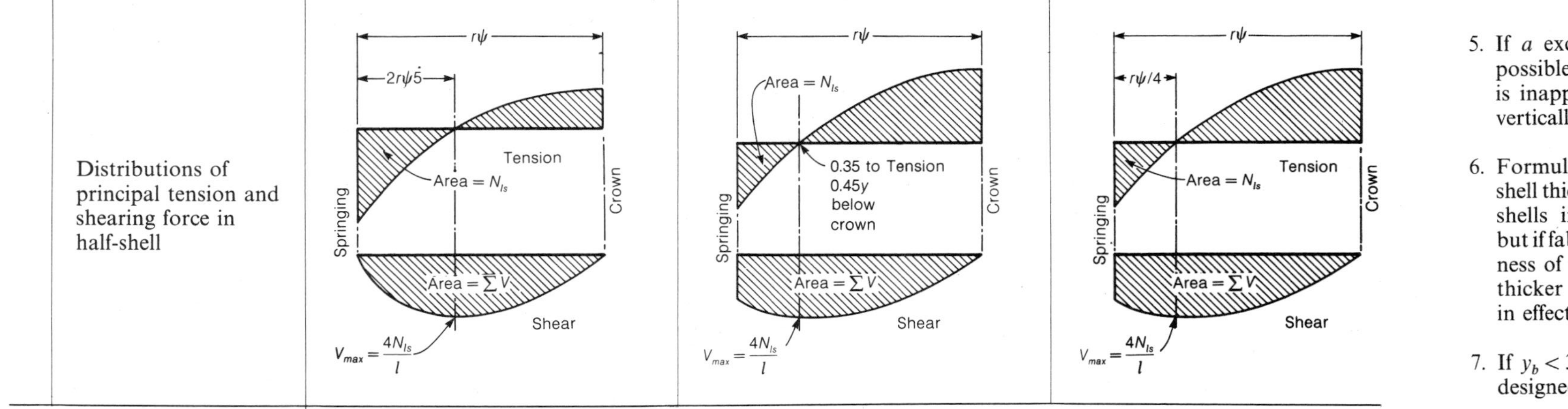
Reinforcement required[4]	Total tensile reinforcement required in half-shell $= N_{ls}/f_{st}$. Total shearing reinforcement required at 45° across corner $= \sum V/1.41 f_{stv}$. (The point at which this steel may be curtailed can be estimated by means of the shearing-force diagrams above.) Fabric reinforcement required to resist transverse moments $= M_{dt}/z f_{st}$ (top and bottom)[6].

5. If a exceeds 15 m, buckling is possible and empirical method is inapplicable unless shell has vertically supported edge beams.

6. Formulae give values of M_{dt} for shell thickness of 65 mm. Thicker shells induce higher moments but if fabric is designed for thickness of 65 mm it will suffice for thicker shell, owing to increase in effective depth.

7. If $y_b < 300$ mm, shell should be designed as feather-edged.

Notation

- a chord width of shell[5] (m)
- F_b load per unit length carried by beam (kg/m)
- F_s load per unit length carried by half-shell (kg/m)
- f_{st} permissible stress in tension reinforcement
- f_{stv} permissible stress in shearing reinforcement
- K shell parameter: $K = 0.925 \times \sqrt[4]{(r^3/l^2 t)}$
- l span of shell (m)
- M_{dt} transverse bending moment in shell (positive for tension on underside) (N m per metre)
- N_{lb} longitudinal tension in beam at midspan (N)
- N_{ls} longitudinal tension in shell valley at midspan (N)
- N_t transverse tension in shell (N)
- r radius of shell (m)
- t thickness of shell (m)
- V shear force per unit length (N/m)
- $\sum V$ sum of all shear forces in half-shell at stiffening beam (N)
- W total load per unit length of half-shell and valley beam, including all imposed loads and thickenings (kg/m)
- W_b load per unit length along valley additional to shell and valley beam load (kg/m)
- w load per unit area of shell, including self-weight, finishes and imposed load (kg/m²)
- y total depth from soffit of valley beam to crown of shell (m)
- y_s depth of shell from springing to crown (m)
- y_b depth of downstand of valley beam[7] (m)
- z lever-arm (within shell thickness)
- ψ angle subtended by half-shell (i.e. angle between radius and vertical at springing)

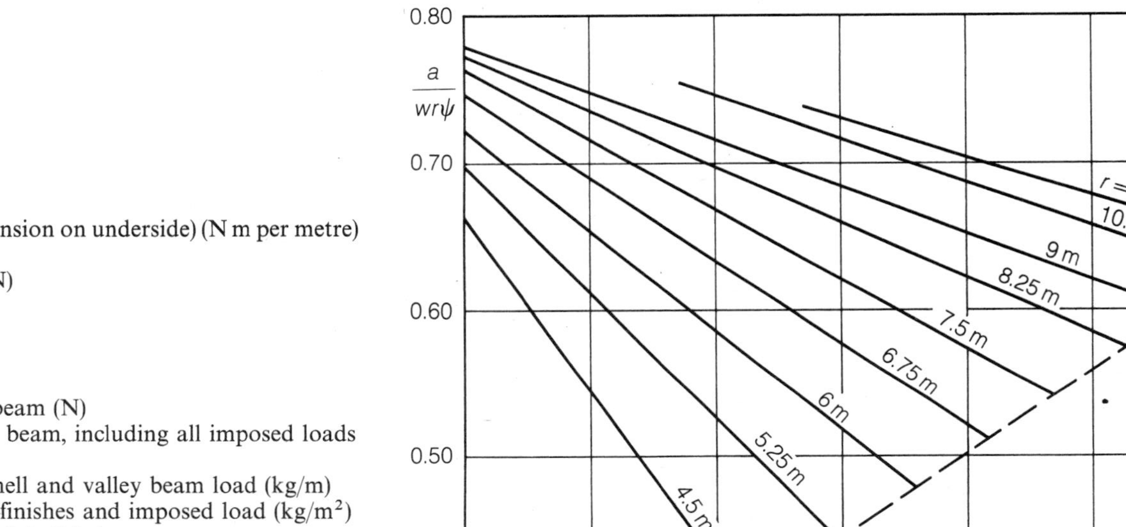

Other types of hinges and bearings are illustrated in *Table 181*:

(c) a hinge formed by the convex end of a concrete member bearing in a concave recess in the foundations
(d) a hinge suitable for the bearing of a girder where rotation, but not sliding, is required
(e) a bearing for a girder where sliding is required
(f) a mechanical hinge suitable for the base of a large portal frame or the abutment of a large hinged arch rib
(g) a transverse expansion joint in the deck of a bridge, which is suitable if the joint is in the slab or is formed between two transverse beams
(h) a rocker bearing suitable for girder bridges of spans of over 15 m or 50 ft; for shorter spans a sliding bearing as at (e) is sufficient
(j) a hinge suitable for the crown of a three-hinged arch when a mechanical hinge is not justified
(k) a bearing suitable for the support of a freely suspended span on a cantilever in an articulated bridge

To accommodate movements of 5 to 125 mm or about 1/4 to 5 in with or without rotation, elastomeric pad bearings may be used. By reinforcing the rubber pad with one or more steel plates, resistance to specified combinations of direct and shearing force can be provided. Such bearings are relatively cheap, easy to install and require no maintenance.

The introduction of sliding bearings of polytetrafluoroethylene (PTFE) has meant that mechanical bearings have become much less commonly used recently. PTFE is a fluorocarbon polymer having the least coefficients of static and dynamic friction of any known solid. In its pure form its compressive strength is low, but fillers may be incorporated to improve this and other detrimental properties without affecting the valuable low-friction attributes. Detailed information on these types of bearing can be obtained from ref. 91.

Permissible bearing pressures on plain and reinforced concrete under bearing plates are given in *Table 191*.

25.4.2 Expansion and contraction joints

The joints shown in *Table 182* are suitable for various structures.

Diagrams (a) to (d) illustrate the types of joint recommended in BS5337. The spacing of the expansion and contraction joints should be calculated as explained in section 20.3.1 to avoid the formation of cracks due to shrinkage and thermal movements. All the details shown in these diagrams are equally applicable to wall or floor construction. However, the waterbar should be positioned centrally within the wall section and on the underside of a floor slab, if it is supported on a smooth level layer of blinding concrete. Surface-type waterbars will not ensure that seepage does not occur unless rigidly supported from behind. If used in vertical situations, they must therefore be located on the internal face of a tank or reservoir (but on the external face of a basement where the intention is to keep ground-water out). Plain butt-joints as shown are preferable, unless it is necessary to transfer shear across the joint, in which case a joggle may be required. However, unless great care is taken during construction, a joggle is a potential point of weakness.

The joints shown in diagrams (e) and (f) are alternative designs for the junction between the floor and wall of a cylindrical tank which minimize or eliminate the restraint moment at this point. The jointing material beneath the wall must combine high resistance to direct loading (to ensure that it is not squeezed out by the weight of the wall above) with a low coefficient of friction (to permit the wall to slide sideways freely). Detail (e) utilizes rubber pads, while (f) relies on the action of a membrane of PTFE or some similar material. Because of the difficulties described, it may be better to employ monolithic construction if this is possible, and to design the wall to resist the resulting restraint moments induced.

The design and arrangement of joints to ensure watertight construction is discussed in detail in ref. 92.

Diagram (g) shows a vertical joint in the stem of a cantilever retaining wall; the spacing depends on the height of the wall but should not exceed 20 m or 60 ft. For low walls with thin stems a simple butt-joint is generally sufficient, but unequal deflection or tilting of one part of the wall relative to the next shows at the joint; a keyed joint as at (a) is therefore preferable for walls more than 1 m or 4 ft high and reduces the risk of percolation of moisture through the joint. The double chamfer improves the appearance. Where it is necessary to provide for an amount of expansion exceeding the probable amount of shrinkage, a space, say 12 mm or 1/2 in wide, should be left between the faces of the concrete and filled with resilient material.

In slabs laid on the ground (and not forming part of a foundation raft), construction joints should be permanent joints in predetermined positions, such as at the end of a day's work, at a restricted section, at a change of thickness, or at other positions where cracks are likely to occur. Diagrams (j) show such a joint that makes a definite break in the slab; this type of joint should be provided at intervals of about 5 m or 15 ft in the bottoms of reservoirs or in floors laid directly on the ground. The pad under the joint prevents one panel settling relatively to the other when laid on soft ground, but on firm ground the pad may not be necessary. When the floor is subject to abrasion, as in factories where wheeled containers travel across the joint, the edges should be protected by steel angles as indicated. If the ground is waterlogged, the alternative joint shown can be adopted.

In the case of cantilevered retaining walls it is not always necessary to extend the joint from the walls into the base slab, but a longitudinal joint parallel to the wall should be provided in the base slab to separate the base of the wall from the remainder of the floor when the area of the floor is considerable.

If permanent joints are provided in buildings it is necessary to carry the joint through the floors, roof slab (as at (k)) and walls (as at (l)). The joints in the walls should be made at the columns, in which case a double column as at (h) is provided; the space is filled with a joint filler. The copper strip or other type of waterbar must be notched where the links occur, the ends of the notched pieces being bent horizontally or cut off. At joints through suspended floors and flat roofs it is common for a double beam to be provided. A joint filler and waterbar are required in a joint in a roof. A joint in a floor should be sealed to prevent rubbish accumulating therein.

Bridges: types

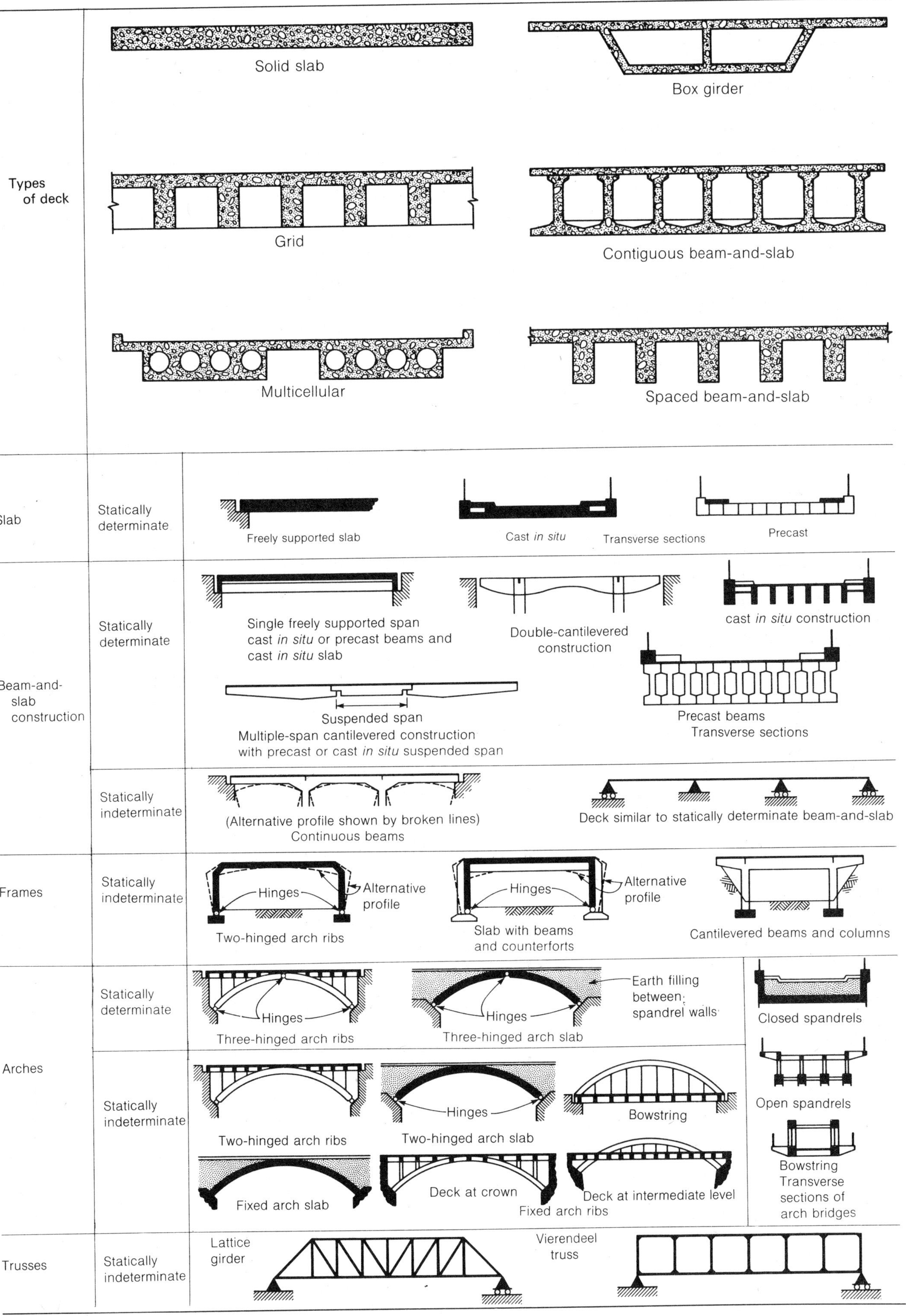
Types of deck
Solid slab
Box girder
Grid
Contiguous beam-and-slab
Multicellular
Spaced beam-and-slab
Slab
Statically determinate
Freely supported slab
Cast in situ
Transverse sections
Precast
Beam-and-slab construction
Statically determinate
Single freely supported span cast in situ or precast beams and cast in situ slab
Double-cantilevered construction
cast in situ construction
Suspended span
Multiple-span cantilevered construction with precast or cast in situ suspended span
Precast beams
Transverse sections
Statically indeterminate
(Alternative profile shown by broken lines)
Continuous beams
Deck similar to statically determinate beam-and-slab
Frames
Statically indeterminate
Hinges
Alternative profile
Two-hinged arch ribs
Hinges
Alternative profile
Slab with beams and counterforts
Cantilevered beams and columns
Arches
Statically determinate
Hinges
Three-hinged arch ribs
Hinges
Earth filling between spandrel walls
Three-hinged arch slab
Closed spandrels
Open spandrels
Statically indeterminate
Two-hinged arch ribs
Hinges
Two-hinged arch slab
Bowstring
Fixed arch slab
Deck at crown
Deck at intermediate level
Fixed arch ribs
Bowstring
Transverse sections of arch bridges
Trusses
Statically indeterminate
Lattice girder
Vierendeel truss

25.5 ROADS

As shown on *Table 183*, the overall thickness of the slab and the amount of reinforcement required depend on the total number of so-called 'standard axles' that will be carried during the lifetime of the road. A standard axle, which represents a load of 80 kN or 18 000 lb, is the most damaging class of axle permitted in the UK for normal vehicles conforming to the Construction and Use Regulations (see section 9.2.2). Tests by the AASHO have shown that the damage caused by an axle is approximately proportional to the fourth power of the applied axle load. Hence private cars do not contribute significantly to the damage, and design is based on the number of commercial vehicles (defined as goods or public-service vehicles having an unladen weight of more than 15 kN (3375 lb). If the road is likely to carry wheel distributions and loadings that differ greatly from normal the advice of the Engineering Intelligence Division of the Department of Transport should be obtained.

The procedure for determining the number of equivalent standard axles is described in Technical Memorandum H6/78 issued by the DTp. For various reasons, including the observation that, as the flow of commercial vehicles increases, an increasing proportion of them move into the faster traffic lanes, the simple method of evaluation described in ref. 59 has now been superseded. It is first necessary to determine the cumulative traffic of commercial vehicles during the life of the road by means of the nomogram shown. To obtain the number of standard axles, this value must now be multiplied by the appropriate factor from the table below. (The nomogram has been modified slightly from that which appears in ref. 102, and is reproduced by permission of the Director of the Transport and Road Research Laboratory, Crowthorne, Berks.) Note that TRRL report LR910 ('Commercial traffic: its estimated damaging effect 1945–2005'), which appeared in December 1979, suggests that the value of 2.75 for more than 2000 vehicles should be increased to 2.9. It also indicates the possibility that damage may be related to the fifth or even sixth power of the applied load, rather than the fourth power as stated earlier.

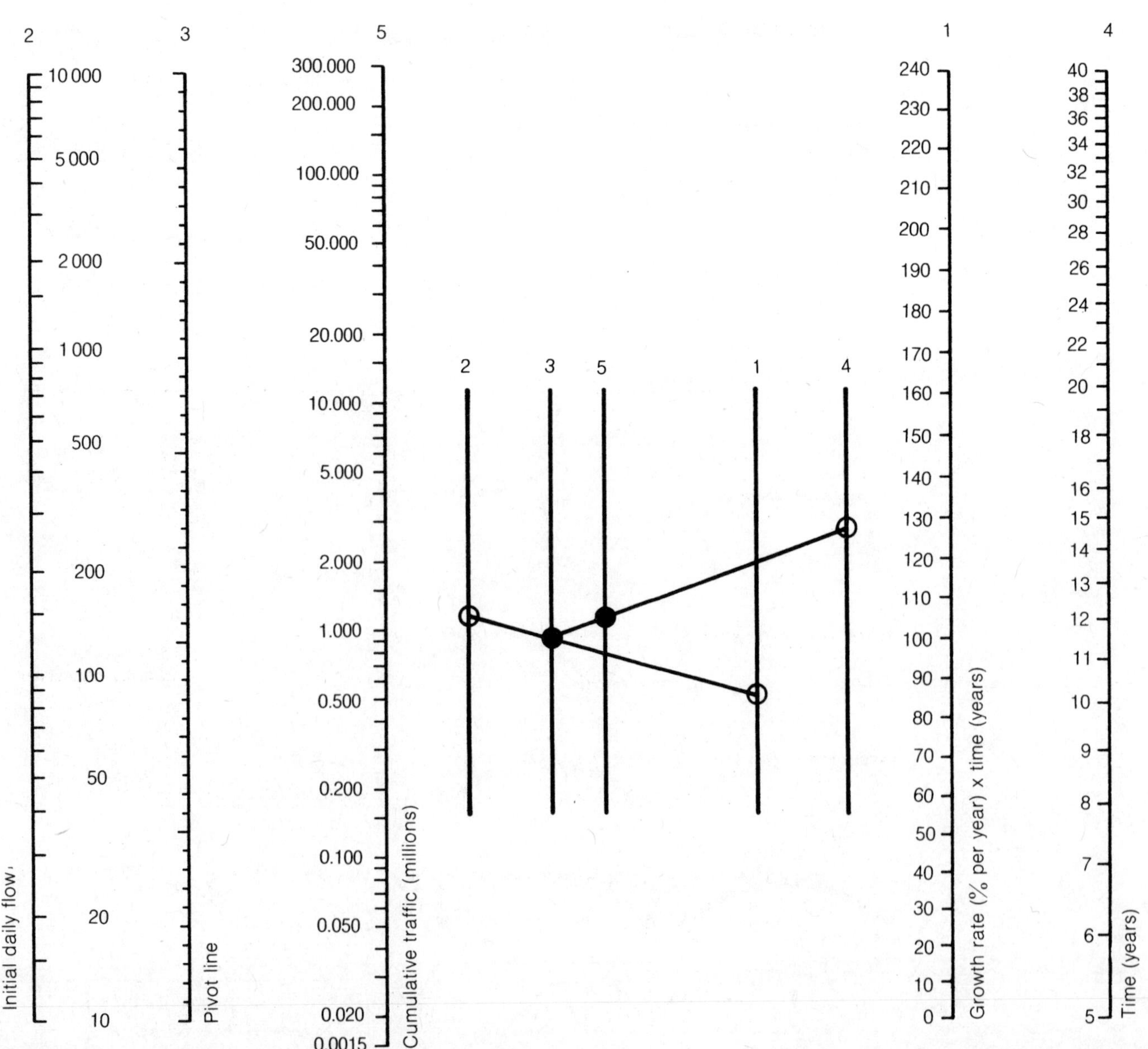

Hinges and bearings

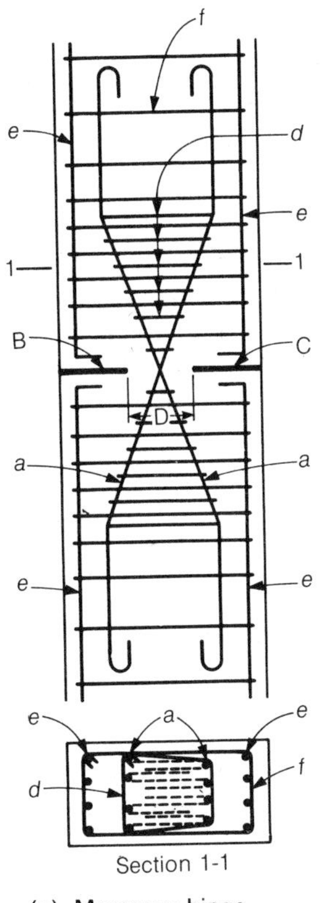

(a) Mesnager hinge

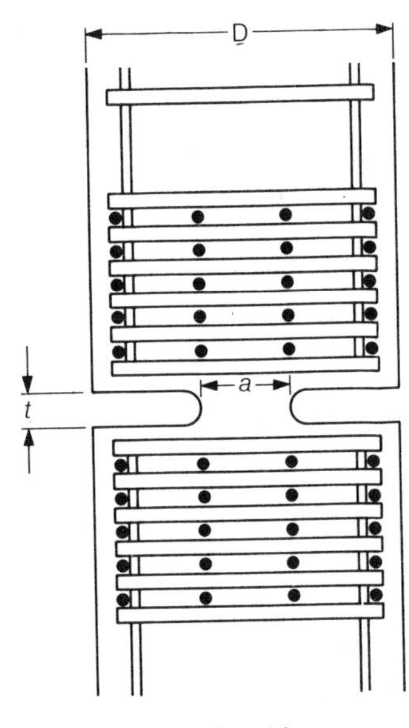

(b) Freyssinet hinge

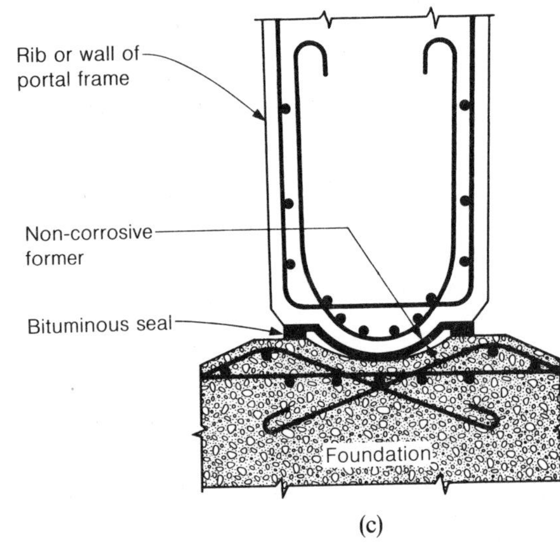

(c)

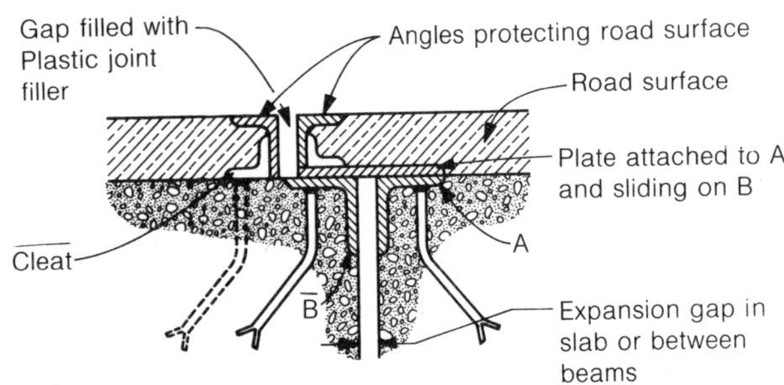

(g) Joint in deck of bridge

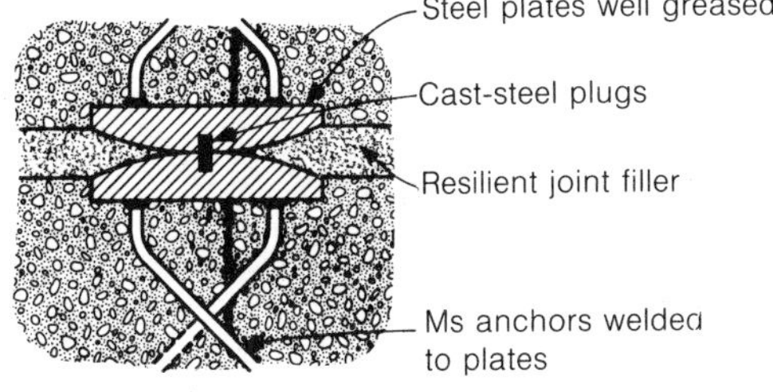

(d) Fixed-end bearing (hinge)

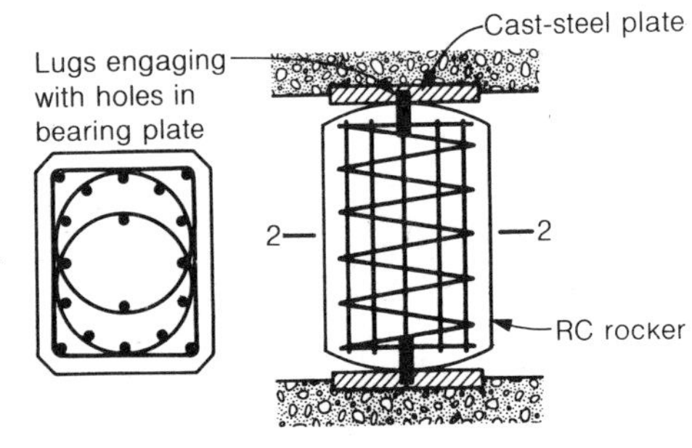

(h) Rocker bearing

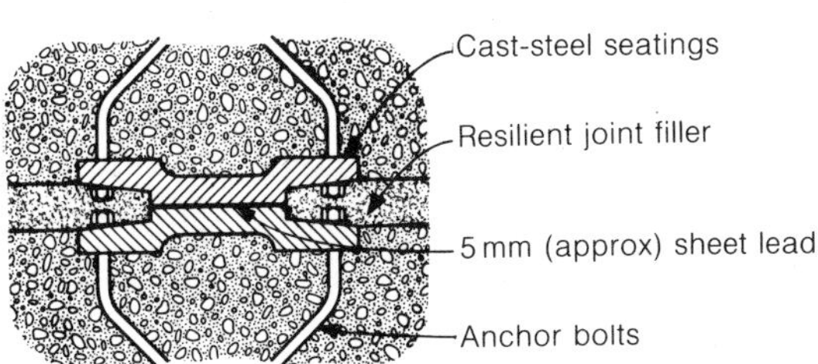

(e) Free-end bearing (hinge)

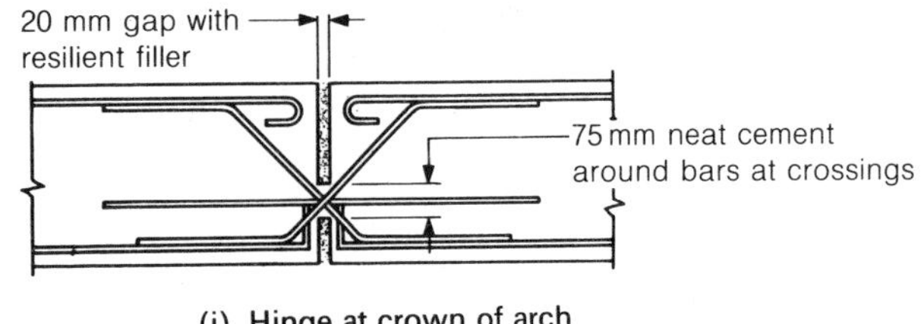

(j) Hinge at crown of arch

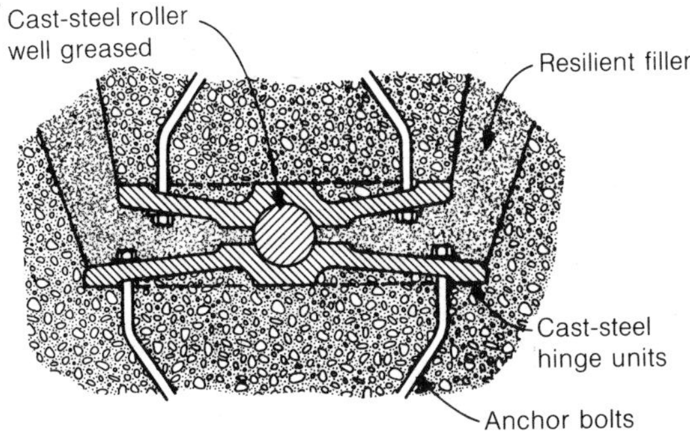

(f) Mechanical hinge

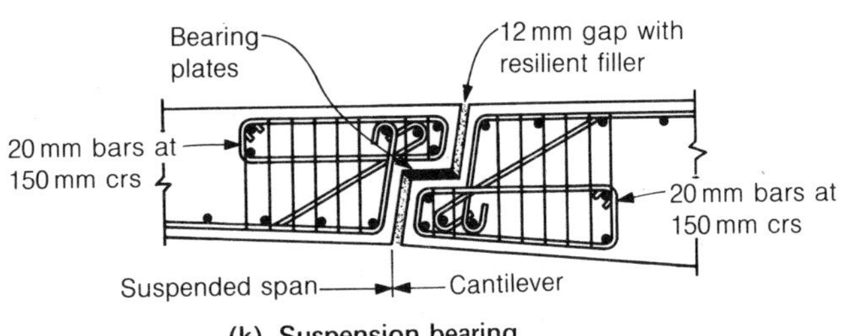

(k) Suspension bearing

Number of commercial vehicles per day in each direction at time of construction for which road is designed	Equivalent number of standard axles per commercial vehicle
Exceeding 2000	2.75
Between 1000 and 2000	2.25
Between 250 and 1000	1.25
All other roads	0.75

25.6 CYLINDRICAL TANKS AND WATER TOWERS

25.6.1 Walls of cylindrical tanks

Data for the analysis of walls of cylindrical tanks are given in *Table 184*. According to Reissner (translated by Carpenter, ref. 93) the bending moment M_A at the base of a wall of constant thickness h_A is given by the expression

$$M_A = \frac{K(K-1)}{24}\left(\frac{h_A d}{h^2}\right)^2 D_l h^3 = K_1 D_l h^3$$

where

$$K = \sqrt{\left(\frac{h^2}{h_A d}\right)}\sqrt[4]{[12(1-v^2)]}$$

Assuming Poisson's ratio v is zero (or v^2 is negligible compared with unity),

$$K = \sqrt{\left(\frac{h^2}{h_A d}\right)}\sqrt[4]{12}$$

Now the height $K_2 h$ above the base of the tank at which the maximum circumferential tension N_{max} occurs is given by the expression

$$\cosh KK_2 + \sinh KK_2 - \cos KK_2 - (2K-1)\sin KK_2 = 0$$

Then

$$N_{max} = \tfrac{1}{2}K_3 D_l hd$$

where

$$K_3 = (1-K_2) - \frac{\cos KK_2 + \left(\frac{K-1}{K}\right)\sin KK_2}{\cosh KK_2 + \sinh KK_2}$$

Values of K_1, K_2 and K_3, calculated on the assumption that $v = 0$, may be read from the scales on *Table 184*. If the true value of v is 0.2, the resulting coefficients K_1, K_2 and K_3 seldom differ by more than 2% from those given by the scales.

The following example illustrates the use of this material.

Example. Determine the service bending moments and direct tensile forces in the wall of a cylindrical water tower 6 m in diameter and 10 m deep with a wall thickness of 250 mm at the bottom.

Thus $d = 6$ m; $h = 10$ m; $h_A = 250$ mm; $D = 1000$ g/m^3; $h^2/dh_A = 10^2/(6 \times 0.25) = 66.7$. From *Table 184*, $K_1 = 0.002\,02$; $K_2 = 0.185$; and $K_3 = 0.884$.

Bending moment (vertical) at A $= 0.002\,02 \times 9.81 \times 10^3 = 19.8$ kN m per metre of circumference. Position of point of maximum circumferential tension $= 0.185 \times 10 = 1.85$ m above the bottom. Maximum circumferential tension is given by

$$N_{max} = 0.5 \times 9.81 \times 10 \times 6 \times 0.884$$
$$= 260 \text{ kN per metre height}$$

Note If the bottom is suspended, and monolithic with the wall, deformation of the bottom slab may produce vertical bending moments in the wall which must be combined with those due to restraint at the base of the wall. Similarly, the bending moments and shearing forces due to this restraint affect the resultant moments and tensions in the bottom.

25.6.2 Bottoms and roofs of elevated cylindrical tanks

Data for the design of the bottoms of elevated cylindrical tanks under service loads are given in the accompanying diagrams and in *Table 184*.

Bottoms with beams. At (a) each beam spans between opposite columns and carries one-quarter of the load of the bottom of the tank. The remaining half of the load, the weight of the wall and the load from the roof are transferred to the columns through the wall. In the arrangement shown at (b), each length of beam between columns carries the load on the shaded area, and the remainder of the load on the floor of the

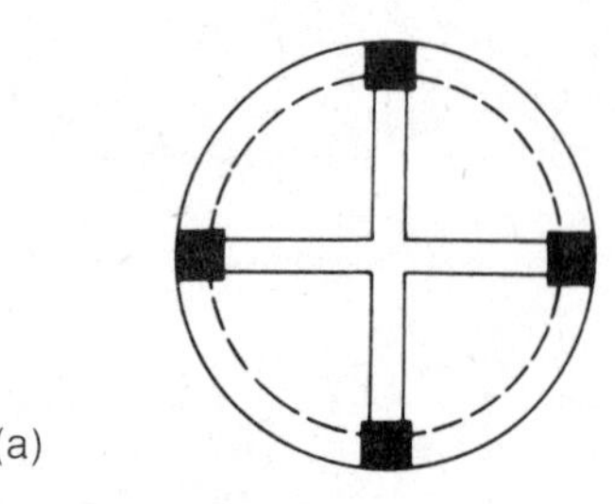
(a)

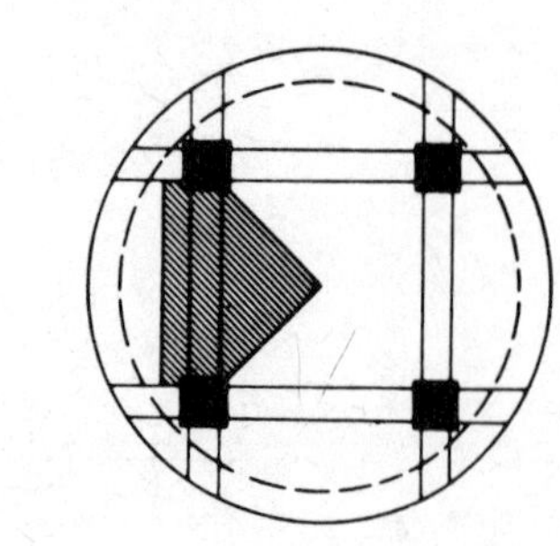
(b)

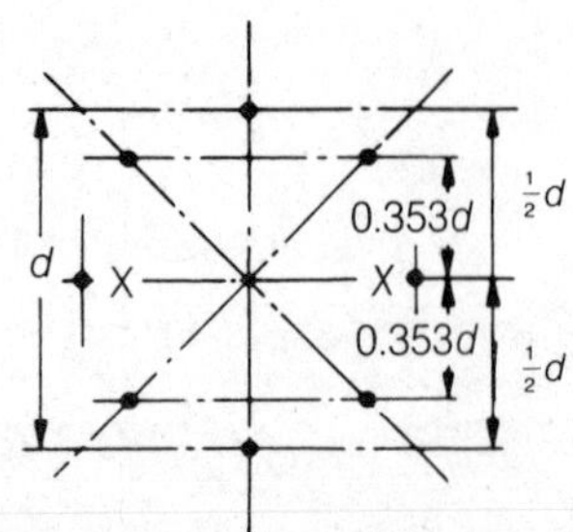

(c)

Expansion and contraction joints

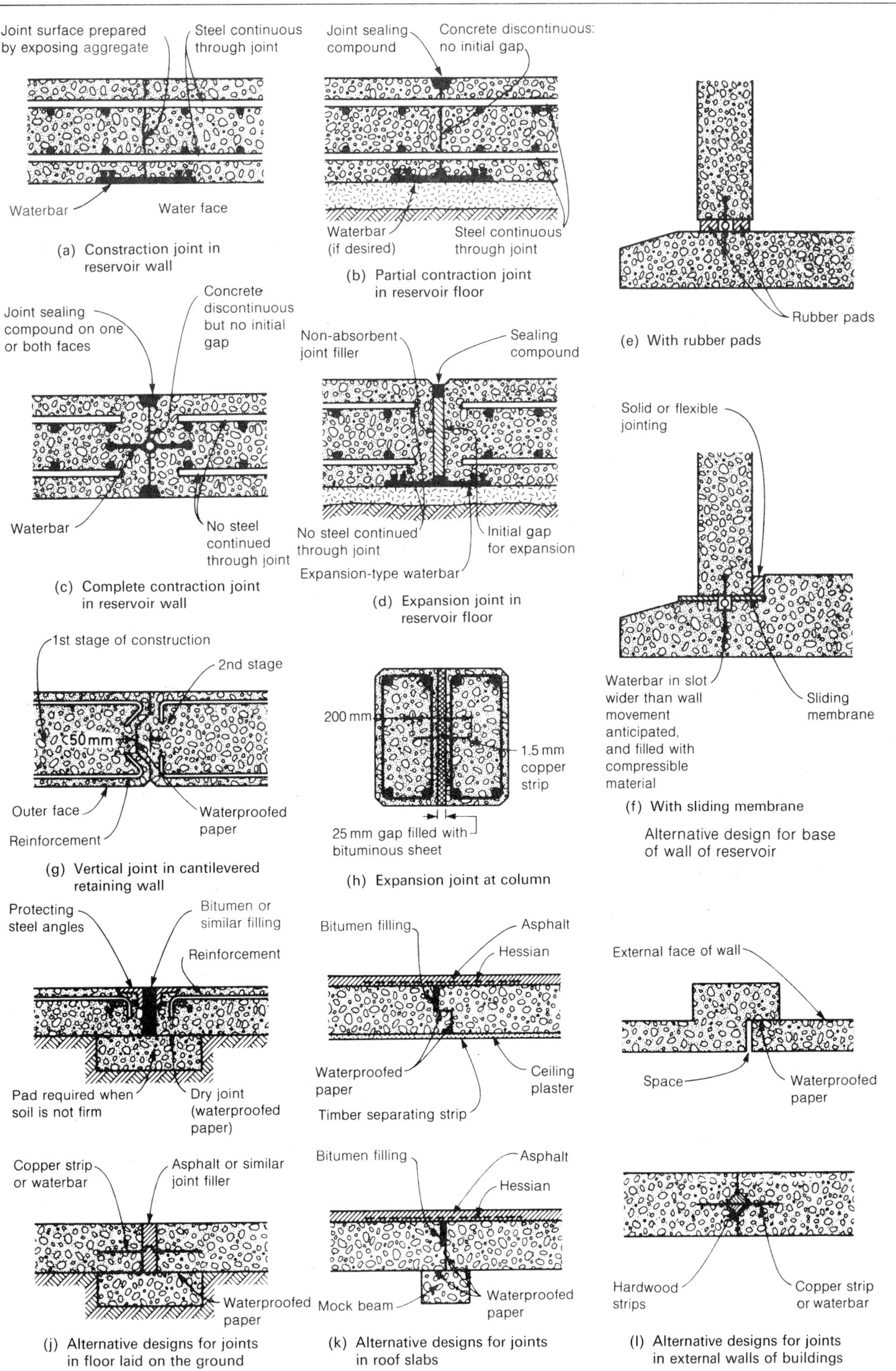

(a) Constraction joint in reservoir wall

(b) Partial contraction joint in reservoir floor

(e) With rubber pads

(c) Complete contraction joint in reservoir wall

(d) Expansion joint in reservoir floor

(f) With sliding membrane

Alternative design for base of wall of reservoir

(g) Vertical joint in cantilevered retaining wall

(h) Expansion joint at column

(j) Alternative designs for joints in floor laid on the ground

(k) Alternative designs for joints in roof slabs

(l) Alternative designs for joints in external walls of buildings tank, the weight of the walls and the load from the roof are equally divided between the eight cantilevered lengths of the beams. An alternative to this design is for the columns to be placed almost under the wall, in which case the cantilevers are unnecessary but secondary beams may be required.

Domed bottoms. For a tank of large diameter a domed bottom and roof of either of the types shown in *Table 184* are more economical, and although the formwork is much more costly the saving in concrete and reinforcement compared with beam-and-slab construction may be considerable. The ring beams A and C in the case of a simple domed bottom or roof resist the horizontal component of the thrust from the domes, and the thicknesses of the domes are determined by the magnitude of this thrust. The maximum compressive stress in the roof dome under service loads should be low, say 20% of the ordinary safe service stress, in order to allow an ample margin for local increases due to incidental concentrated loads and for irregular distribution of the imposed load. For the bottom dome, where the uniform distribution of the load is more assured, a higher service stress can be used, and about 0.5 to 1% of reinforcement should be provided in each direction. The service shearing stress around the periphery of the dome should also be calculated and sufficient thickness of concrete provided to resist the shearing forces. Expressions for the thrust and vertical shearing force around the edge of the dome and the resultant circumferential tension in the ring beams are given in *Table 184*. Domes can also be analysed by the method described in *Table 178*.

The bottom comprising a central dome and an outer conical part (called an Intze tank) illustrated at the foot of *Table 184* is economical for the largest tanks. The outward thrust from the top of the conical part is resisted by the ring beam B, and the difference between the inward thrust from the bottom of the conical part and the outward thrust from the domed part is resisted by the ring beam A. Expressions for the forces are given in *Table 184*. The proportions of the conical and domed parts can be arranged so that the resultant horizontal thrust on A is zero. Suitable proportions for bottoms of this type are given in *Table 184*, and the volume for a tank of diameter d_0 with these proportions is $0.604d_0^3$. The wall of the cylindrical part of the tank should be designed as described previously, account being taken of the vertical bending at the base of the wall and the effect of this bending on the conical part. The floor of a tank must be designed to resist, in addition to the forces and bending moments already described, any direct tension due to the vertical bending of the wall.

Example. Determine the principal forces due to service loads in the bottom of a cylindrical tank of the Intze type if $d_0 = 10$ m; $d = 8$ m; $\phi = 48°$; $\theta = 40°$; $F_1 = 2500$ kN; $F_2 = 2800$ kN; and $F_3 = 1300$ kN.

$\mathrm{Cosec}\,\theta = 1/\sin\theta = 1.55; \cot\theta = 1.192; \cot\phi = 0.900.$

From *Table 184*, the vertical shearing force per metre of periphery of dome is given by

$$V_1 = 2500/(8\pi) = 100\,\text{kN}$$

The thrust per metre of periphery of dome is

$$N_1 = 100 \times 1.55 = 155\,\text{kN}$$

The values of V_1 and N_1 determine the thickness of the dome at the springing.

Outward horizontal thrust from dome per metre of periphery of ring beam A:

$$H_1 = 100 \times 1.192 = 119.2\,\text{kN}$$

Shearing force per metre of inner periphery of conical portion:

$$V_2 = (2800 + 1300)/8\pi = 163\,\text{kN}$$

Inward thrust per metre of periphery of ring beam A from conical part:

$$H_2 = 163 \times 0.900 = 146.8\,\text{kN}$$

Resultant circumferential compression force in ring-beam A:

$$= 0.5 \times 8(119.2 - 146.8) = 110.4\,\text{kN}$$

(If H_1 exceeds H_2, the circumferential force is tensile; the ideal case occurs when H_1 and H_2 are equal, and thus produce zero force in B: see below.)

Shearing force per metre of outer periphery of conical part:

$$V_3 = 1300/10\pi = 41.4\,\text{kN}$$

Outward thrust per metre of periphery of ring beam B at top of conical part:

$$H_3 = 41.4 \times 0.900 = 37.2\,\text{kN}$$

Circumferential tension per metre of periphery of beam B at top of conical section:

$$= 0.5 \times 10 \times 37.2 = 186.2\,\text{kN}$$

The vertical wall must be reinforced for circumferential tension due to the horizontal pressure from the contained liquid: this tension is $0.5 \times 9.81 d_0 h_1$ kN per metre of height. The conical part must be reinforced to resist a circumferential tension, and the reinforcement can either be distributed throughout the height of the conical portion or be concentrated in the ring beams at the top and bottom.

In large-diameter Intze tanks the width of the ring beam A may be considerable, and if this is so the weight of water immediately above the beam should not be considered as contributing to the forces on the dome and conical part. With a wide beam, F_1 is the weight of the contents over the net area of the dome, and d is the internal diameter of the ring beam; F_2 is the weight of the contents over the net area of the conical part, and d for use with F_2 is the external diameter of the ring beam. If this adjustment is made for a ring beam of reasonable width in the foregoing example, H_1 would more nearly balance H_2.

25.6.3 Columns supporting elevated tanks

The thrust and tension produced in columns due to wind forces on a tank supported by the column can be calculated for a group of four columns are follows. If the total moment due to wind is M_w and the columns are a distance d apart,

Concrete roads

Stresses in road slabs

Q wheel load (N or lb)
h thickness of concrete slab (mm or in)
f maximum tensile and compressive stress (N/mm^2 or lb/in^2)
r radius of contact area of wheel on slab (mm or in)
r_1 equivalent radius of contact area (mm or in):
if $r < 1.724h$, $r_1 = \sqrt{(1.6r^2 + h^2)} - 0.675h$
if $r \geqslant 1.724h$, $r_1 = r$
E_c elastic modulus for concrete (N/mm^2 or lb/in^2)
r_2 radius of relative stiffness $= \sqrt[4]{[E_c h^3/12(1-v^2)k]}$ (mm or in)
v Poisson's ratio for concrete
r_3 coefficient (approx. equal to $5r_2$) (mm or in)
K dimensionless coefficient ($\ngtr 0.4$)
k modulus of reaction of ground (equal to the reciprocal of the deformation in inches when soil is loaded to 1 lb/in^2

Notes:
The formulae are applicable to both metric and imperial units provided the values used throughout are consistent.

Type of soil	Typical values of k N, mm units	in, lb units
Soft and plastic soils	13.57×10^{-3}	50
Firm soil	54.29×10^{-3}	200
Compact gravel and rock	135.7×10^{-3}	500

Maximum stresses

At corner: $f = \dfrac{3Q}{h^2}\left[1 - \left(\dfrac{r\sqrt{2}}{r_2}\right)^{0.6}\right]$

At an edge: $f = \dfrac{0.53(1+0.54v)Q}{h^2}\left[\log\left(\dfrac{E_c h^3}{k r_1^4}\right) - 0.71\right]$

Remote from edge or corner:

$$f = \frac{Q(1+v)}{h^2}\left[0.275\log\left(\frac{E_c h^3}{k r_1^4}\right) - 15K\left(\frac{r_2}{r_3}\right)^2\right]$$

Concrete road slabs per ref.59 (third edition)

				Total number of standard axles $\times 10^{-6}$	0.01	0.10	1.0	5	10	25	50	75	100
Concrete slab	Reinforced	Minimum thickness (mm)	Subgrade CBR	$\ngtr 2\%$	150	160	190	225	245	265	295	305	315
				$> 2\% \ngtr 15\%$	125	135	165	200	220	240	270	280	290
				$> 15\%$	100	110	140	175	195	215	245	255	265
		Maximum joint spacing (m)	Limestone aggregate		19.8	19.8	19.8	25.2	33.0	33.0	42.0	42.0	42.0
			Other aggregates		16.5	16.5	16.5	21.0	27.5	27.5	35.0	35.0	35.0
	Non-reinforced	Maximum joint spacing (m)	Subgrade CBR	$\ngtr 2\%$	175	185	195	225	245	265	295	305	315
				$> 2\% \ngtr 15\%$	150	160	170	200	220	240	270	280	290
				$> 15\%$	125	135	145	175	195	215	245	255	265
		Minimum thickness (mm)	Other than limestone aggregate: expansion joints $\ngtr$ 60 m apart if $h \nless$ 200 mm ($\ngtr$ 40 m otherwise); contraction joints at 5 m intervals. Limestone aggregate: increase these distances by 20%										
Reinforcement	Weight (kg/m^2)				1.8	2.0	2.5	3.3	3.7	4.3	4.9	5.3	5.55
	Equivalent BS long. mesh ref. no				261	261	261	341	434	434	555	555	555

Dowel bars in joints	Reinforced concrete slabs				Non-reinforced slabs	
	Expansion joints		Contraction joints		Warping joints	
Thickness of concrete slab (mm)	Diameter (mm)	Length (mm)	Diameter (mm)	Length (mm)	Diameter (mm)	Length (mm)
$\nless 150 \ngtr 180$	20	550	12	400	12	1400
$\nless 190 \ngtr 230$	25	650	20	500	12	1400
$\nless 240$	32	750	25	600	12	1400

Expansion joint in reinforced slab

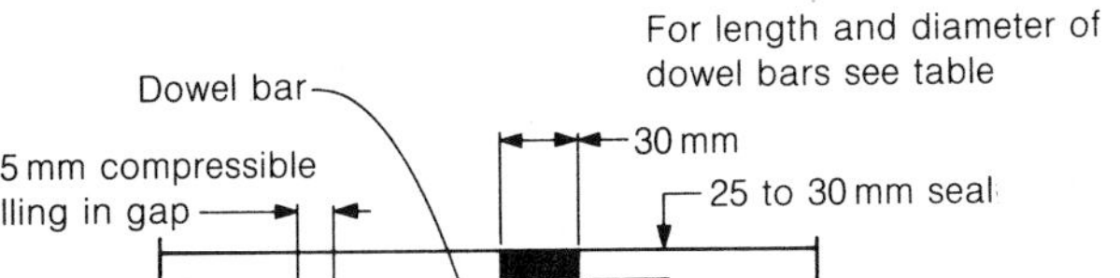

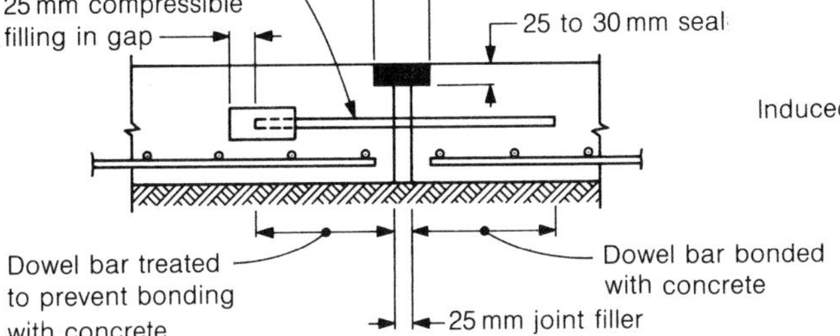

Warping joint in non-reinforced slab

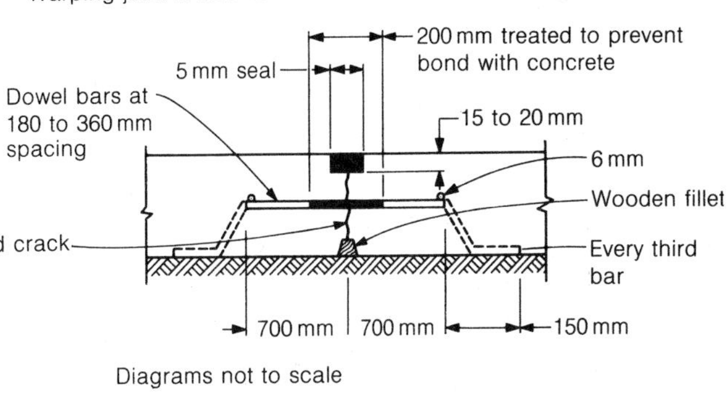

Diagrams not to scale

when the wind blows normal to the dimension d, the thrust on each column on the leeward side and the tension in each column on the windward side is $M_w/2d$. When the wind blows normal to a diagonal of the group, the thrust on the leeward corner column and the tension in the windward corner column $= M_w/d\sqrt{2}$.

For any other number of columns, the force on any column can be calculated from the equivalent moment of inertia of the group. For example, consider a wind moment of M_w due to the wind blowing normal to the X-X axis of the group of eight columns shown at diagram (c) in section 25.6.2.

The moment of inertia of the group about X-X $= [2 \times (d/2)^2] + [4 \times (0.353d)^2] = 1.0d^2$. The thrust on the extreme leeward column $= M_w \times 0.5d/1.0d^2 = M_w/2d$.

The forces on each of the other columns can be determined similarly, by substituting the appropriate lever-arm for $d/2$ in each case.

25.7 RECTANGULAR CONTAINERS

Example. A single rectangular container, the internal dimensions of which are 4 m by 4.8 m, is subject to a uniform horizontal pressure of 5 kN/m^2 at a certain depth. Determine the resulting maximum service moments and direct tensions at this depth, assuming that the walls span horizontally.

Assume that the walls are 150 mm thick; the effective spans are then 4.15 m and 4.95 m; hence $l_1/l_2 = 4.95/4.15 = 1.2$ (approx.); from *Table 185*, $k = 9.7$ (approx.) Then

Bending moment at corners
$= M_1 = ql_1^2/k = 5 \times 10^3 \times 4.15^2/9.7 =$ 8 880 N m per m
Free bending moment on l_1
$= (1/8) \times 5 \times 10^3 \times 4.15^2$ = 10 760 N m per m
deduct Bending moment at corner = 8 880 N m per m
Positive bending moment at
midspan of l_1 = 1 880 N m per m
Free bending moment on l_2
$= (1/8) \times 5 \times 10^3 \times 4.95^2$ = 15 310 N m per m
deduct Bending moment at corner = 8 880 N m per m
Positive bending moment at
midspan of l_2 = 6 430 N m per m

Direct tension in short side
$= ql_1/2 = 0.5 \times 5 \times 10^3 \times 4 = 10\,000$ N/m
Direct tension in long side
$= ql_2/2 = 0.5 \times 5 \times 10^3 \times 4.8 = 12\,000$ N/m

These service bending moments and direct tensions are combined as described in *Table 167*.

25.8 RETAINING WALLS

The chart on *Table 187* enables preliminary base dimensions to be established for simple cantilevered walls retaining non-cohesive or purely cohesive materials, and is a modified version of one first published by R. C. Hairsine (ref. 63). The resulting values, which are based on an analysis considering an idealized line structure (i.e. neglecting the thickness of wall and base) generally err slightly on the side of safety, and may then be checked by investigating the stability regarding overturning, sliding and overloading of the actual structure.

Stability and bearing pressure may be investigated for all types of soil by means of the chart but, as regards sliding, the chart is only valid for non-cohesive soils. If the soil considered is purely cohesive (i.e. $\theta \simeq 0°$), the ratio β does not enter the calculations when considering sliding; the appropriate design expression is

$$\alpha = \frac{\gamma_\mu k_2 D h_1}{2C_w}$$

where γ_μ is the factor of safety against sliding, k_2 is the coefficient of lateral pressure, D is the unit weight of the retained material, h_1 is the effective height of the wall, C_w is the cohesion between the clay and the wall and α is the proportion of the base breadth to the effective height of the wall. When α has been determined from the above equation, the curve for $\alpha/\sqrt{k_2}$ on the chart (ignoring β) can be used to check the values of ξ and $\tan\mu/\gamma_\mu\sqrt{k_2}$.

In the case of a cohesive soil with appreciable internal friction (i.e. $\theta \gg 0°$), the appropriate expression for safety against sliding is

$$\frac{\alpha}{\sqrt{k_2}} = \frac{\gamma_\mu\sqrt{k_2}}{2[(C_w/Dh_1) + \tan\mu(1-\beta)]}$$

where μ is the angle of friction between the base and the formation. This expression cannot be represented directly on the chart and must be evaluated separately. If several trial values of β are substituted into this equation, together with the appropriate constants, the resulting curve for $\alpha/\sqrt{k_2}$ can be sketched on to the chart and used to select appropriate values of α and β which meet the requirements regarding sliding, bearing and overturning.

For the idealized wall, if γ_{st} is the safety factor against overturning,

$$\gamma_{st} = 3(1-\beta^2)\alpha^2/k_2$$

If the bearing pressure at the heel of the base is zero, the proportion α is given by the expression

$$\alpha = \sqrt{\left[\frac{k_2}{(1+3\beta)(1-\beta)}\right]}$$

Then the ratio ξ of the maximum pressure under the toe of the base f_{max} to the vertical pressure Dh_1 is given by

$$\xi = \frac{k_2}{\alpha^2} + (1-3\beta)(1-\beta)$$

If uplift is allowed at the heel of the base,

$$\xi = \frac{4(1-\beta)^2\alpha^2}{3(1-\beta^2)\alpha^2 - k_2}$$

If μ is the angle of friction between base and formation,

$$\tan\mu = \frac{\gamma_\mu k_2}{2(1-\beta)\alpha}$$

Curves representing these five relationships are plotted on the chart. The design procedure is first to decide suitable

Forces and bending moments on walls

Direct tension in wall due to internal pressure

N (force per unit distance) $= \frac{1}{2}q_{lp}d = \frac{1}{2}D_l h_1 d$

$$A_{s\,req} = \frac{N}{f_{st}} = \frac{q_{lp}d}{2f_{st}} = \frac{D_l h_1 d}{2f_{st}} \text{ (area per unit height: elastic-strain analysis)}$$

$$\text{Minimum thickness of wall} = \frac{D_l h_1 d}{2}\left[\frac{1}{f_{ct}} - \frac{\alpha_e - 1}{f_{st}}\right] \text{ (elastic-strain analysis)}$$

(For information on the design of slabs forming walls of liquid-containing structures in direct tension in accordance with BS5337 see *Table 133.*)

Direct compression in wall of empty submerged or underground tank

$$f_{cc} = \frac{q_{ep}d}{2[h + (\alpha_e - 1)A_s]} \text{ (stress) (elastic-strain analysis)}$$

Bending moment due to restraint at base of wall

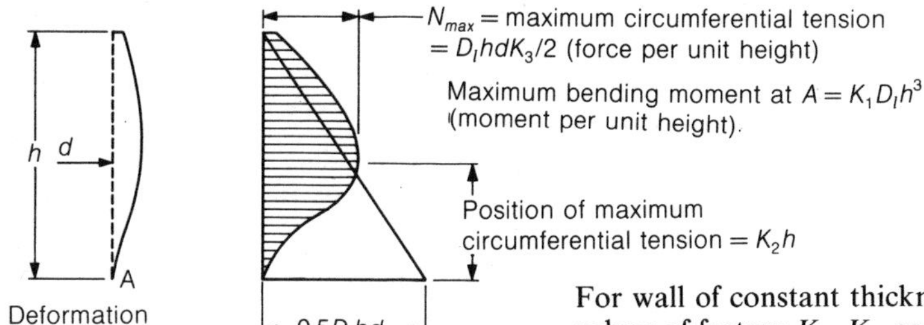

For wall of constant thickness values of factors K_1, K_2 and K_3 may be read from the scale below

Notation

- d diameter of tank
- D_l weight of contained liquid per unit volume
- q_{lp} internal pressure per unit area at depth h_1
- q_{ep} external pressure per unit area at depth h_1
- h depth of tank and maximum depth of contained liquid
- h_1 depth of liquid above level considered
- A_s area of circumferential reinforcement per unit height
- f_{st} permissible tensile stress in reinforcement
- f_{ct} permissible tensile stress in concrete
- h_A thickness of wall at A

If contents are dry granular materials, Substitute $D_l k_2$ for D_l, where

$$k_2 = \frac{1 - \sin\theta}{1 + \sin\theta}$$

and θ is the angle of internal friction (see *Table 17*).

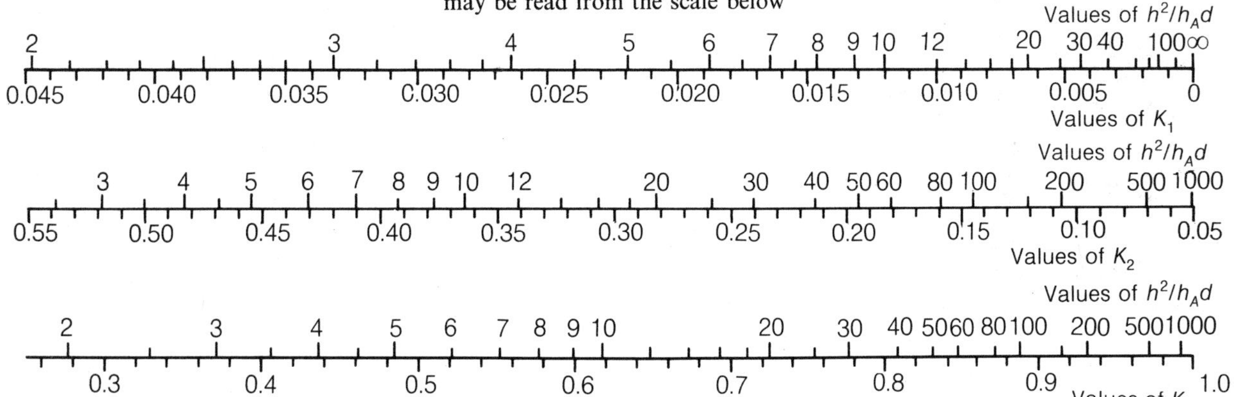

Domed bottoms

C

A

$\cos\theta = 1 - \frac{h_0}{r}$

d

θ

A

h_0

r = radius

V_1

F_1: weight of contents above dome including weight of dome

Shearing force $V_1 = F_1/\pi d$ (force per unit length of perimeter)

Circumferential tension in beam at $A = H_1 d/2 = 0.16F_1 \cot\theta$

$H_1 = V_1 \cot\theta$

N_1 = thrust at perimeter of dome $= V_1 \operatorname{cosec}\theta$ per unit length of perimeter

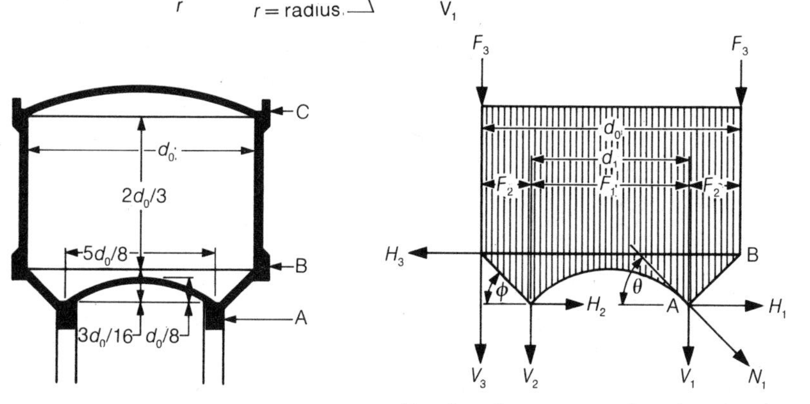

Reactions from cone Reactions from dome

Values of V_1, N_1 and H_1 as for simple dome above

$$V_2 = \frac{F_2 + F_3}{\pi d}$$

$$H_2 = V_2 \cot\phi$$

$$V_3 = \frac{F_3}{\pi d_0}$$

$$H_3 = V_3 \cot\phi$$

per unit length of appropriate periphery

(Ideal case occurs when $H_1 = H_2$)

Circumferential tension in beam at $A = \frac{1}{2}d(H_1 - H_2)$

- F_1 weight of contents above dome including weight of dome
- F_2 weight of contents above cone including weight of cone
- F_3 weight of wall etc. and all loads on roof including weight of roof etc.

values of γ_μ and γ_{st}. Appropriate values of D, k_2 and μ may be read from *Table 17* and a suitable limiting bearing pressure f_{max} obtained from *Table 191*. With these values, next calculate $\xi = f_{max}/Dh_1$ and $\tan\mu/\gamma_\mu\sqrt{k_2}$ and, from the graph, read off the corresponding minimum values of β and $\alpha/\sqrt{k_2}$ while checking that the safety factor against overturning is sufficient, and noting whether uplift occurs. It is normally unnecessary to insist that uplift does not occur (except with a gravity wall) but this restriction may be advisable where the occurrence of ground-water beneath the base heel would soften the formation and diminish the allowable bearing pressure.

25.8.1 Surcharge

If the surcharge is small in comparison with the total forces acting on the wall, it is simple and safe to convert the surcharge load to an extra height of retained material and, by adding this to h_1, to undertake the calculations with an equivalent total height h_e. However, if the surcharge is considerable, the best procedure is to calculate the resulting horizontal thrust F_s and overturning moment due to the surcharge as indicated on *Table 20*, and to add this to the thrust and moment due to the retained material alone to obtain a total thrust F and moment M. Then, if f_v is the vertical pressure at base level, by using the expressions $k_{est} = 6M/f_v h_h^2$ and $k_{e\mu} = 2F/f_v h_1$, the equivalent coefficients of lateral pressure for overturning k_{est} and sliding $k_{e\mu}$ can be substituted for k_2 in the expressions

$$\alpha/\sqrt{k_2} \qquad \text{and} \qquad \tan\mu/\gamma_\mu\sqrt{k_2}$$

respectively, and the foregoing design procedure followed.

25.8.2 Mass concrete walls

The stability of a mass concrete wall may be checked with the chart by assuming the idealized line structure to be retaining a material with a density of concrete. The equivalent coefficient of lateral pressure k_e is then given by the expressions $k_e = k_2 D/22.6$ and $\xi = f_{max}/22.6h_1$. The design chart is now used as previously described with this value of ξ, k_e substituted for k_2 and taking $\beta = 0$.

Example of sheet-pile wall. Prepare a preliminary design using service loads and stresses for a simple cantilevered sheet-pile wall 4 m high; angle of internal friction of earth = 35°. No surcharge. $h = 4$ m; $\theta = 35°$; $D = 16\,\text{kN/m}^3$.

Hence $k_1' = 1.4$ and $k_2' = 1.0$. Embedded length of pile = $1.0 \times 4 = 4$ m. Thus total length of pile = $4 + 4 = 8$ m. Span of sheet-pile for calculating bending moment = $l = 1.4 \times 4 = 5.6$ m. Total active pressure on back of wall on height $l = k_2 \times 16 \times 10^3 \times 5.6^2 \times 0.5$; from *Table 18*, $k_2 = 0.27$; therefore the total pressure = 67 700 N. The service bending moment = $67\,700 \times 0.33 \times 5.6 = 126\,400$ N m = 126.4 N m per mm width. With equal areas of reinforcement in tension and compression and with maximum service stresses of 140 N/mm² and 7 N/mm², using modular-ratio theory, $d = \sqrt{(126.4 \times 10^3/2.85)} = 211$ mm. With not less than 40 mm cover, the minimum thickness of pile required is approximately 300 mm, z is about 200 mm, and the reinforcement required in a pile 400 mm wide is

$$A_{sreq} \simeq 126\,400 \times 400/(140 \times 200) = 1806\,\text{mm}^2.$$

Provide a total of eight 25 mm bars (four bars near each face).

25.9 FOUNDATIONS

25.9.1 Separate bases

An introduction to separate bases is given in section 6.13.6. The following examples illustrated methods for these bases.

Example 1. Determine the variation of pressure beneath a reinforced concrete foundation 3 m long, 2.5 m wide and 600 mm thick and carrying a load of 1 MN placed with an eccentricity of 300 mm in the 3 m direction.

Weight of base = $3.0 \times 2.5 \times 0.6 \times 24\,\text{kN/m}^3 = 108$ kN.
Total load = $1000 + 108 = 1108$ kN.

Taking moments about the short side of the base:

$$M = (1000 \times 1.2) + (108 \times 1.5) = 1362\,\text{kN m}$$

Eccentricity = $(0.5 \times 3.0) - (1362/1108) = 0.27$ m. Since $l/6 = 3 \times 0.167 = 0.5$ m, $e < l/6$. Thus

$$k = 1 \pm \frac{6 \times 0.27}{3.0} = 1.54 \quad \text{or} \quad 0.46$$

$$\text{maximum ground pressure} = \frac{1.54 \times 1108}{3.0 \times 2.5} = 228\,\text{kN/m}^2$$

$$\text{minimum ground pressure} = \frac{0.46 \times 1108}{3.0 \times 2.5} = 68\,\text{kN/m}^2$$

Example 2. Design a base (using service loads and stresses) for a reinforced concrete column 400 mm square carrying a concentric service load of 600 kN; the ground pressure is not to exceed 150 N/m². Permissible service stresses are $f_{st} = 140\,\text{N/mm}^2$ and $f_{cr} = 7\,\text{N/mm}^2$. From the scales on the right-hand side of *Table 120*, if $f_{st}/f_{cr} = 140/7 = 20$, $x = 0.428$, $z = 0.857$ and $M_d/bd^2 f_{ct} = 0.183$.

Assume $F_{base} = 20$ kN. Then total load = $600 + 20 = 620$ kN. Now $l = \sqrt{(620/150)} = 2.03$ m; provide a base 2.1 m square.

$$f_{net} = 600/2.1^2 = 136\,\text{kN/m}^2$$
$$M_{xx} = \tfrac{1}{8} \times 136 \times 2.1(2.1 - 0.4)^2 = 103\,\text{kN m}$$

If $a_1 = 500$ mm, $d \nless \sqrt{[103 \times 10^3/(0.183 \times 7 \times 0.5)]} = 402$ mm; say $h = 500$ mm. If $c = 75$ mm, $d = 500 - 75 = 425$ mm, then

$$A_{sreq} = \frac{103 \times 10^3 \times 10^3}{0.857 \times 425 \times 140} = 2024\,\text{mm}^2$$

Provide ten 16 mm bars in each layer.

If the base is tapered from 500 mm at the column to 150 mm at the edge and if $a_2 = 0.4 + 2 \times (0.5 - 0.075) = 1.25$ m, then at the critical shear perimeter

$$d = \left[\frac{(h - h_1)(l - a_2)}{(l - a_1)}\right] + h_1 - c = \frac{350 \times 0.85}{1.6} + 150 - 75$$

$= 261$ mm approx.

Rectangular containers: moments in walls spanning horizontally

Form of container	Support-moment formulae	Bending moments $M = ql_1^2/k$. Bending-moment coefficients k — Ratio of l_2/l_1: 1/2	3/4	1	5/4	3/2	7/4	2	Reaction formulae (i.e. shearing force)
	$M_1 = \frac{q(l_1^3 + l_2^3)}{12(l_1 + l_2)}$	16.00	14.77	12	9.14	6.86	5.19	4.00	$R_{l1} = \frac{1}{2}ql_1$ $R_{l2} = \frac{1}{2}ql_2$
	$M_1 = \frac{q(l_1^3 + 3l_1^2 l_2 - l_2^3)}{12(l_1 + 2l_2)}$	10.11	10.61	12	15.02	22.59	60.63	—	$R_{l1} = \frac{1}{2}ql_1 + \frac{M_2 - M_1}{l_1}$
	$M_2 = \frac{q(l_1^3 + 2l_2^3)}{12(l_1 + 2l_2)}$	19.20	16.27	12	8.56	6.19	4.61	3.53	$R_{l2} = \frac{1}{2}ql_2$
	$M_1 = \frac{q(3l_1^3 + 6l_1^2 l_2 - l_2^3)}{12(3l_1 + 5l_2)}$	11.23	11.44	12	12.99	14.61	17.32	22.29	$R_{l1}(\text{end span}) = \frac{1}{2}ql_1 + \frac{M_2 - M_1}{l_1}$
	$M_2 = \frac{q(3l_1^3 + 5l_2^3)}{12(3l_1 + 5l_2)}$	18.21	15.85	12	8.70	6.34	4.73	3.63	$R_{l1}(\text{central span}) = \frac{1}{2}ql_1$ $R_{l2} = \frac{1}{2}ql_2$
	$M_1 = \frac{q(l_1 + l_2)(2l_1 - l_2)}{24}$	10.67	10.97	12	14.22	19.20	34.91	—	$R_{l1} = \frac{1}{2}ql_1 + \frac{M_2 - M_1}{l_1}$
	$M_2 = \frac{q(l_1^3 + l_2^3)}{12(l_1 + l_2)}$	16.00	14.77	12	9.14	6.86	5.19	4.00	$R_{l2} = \frac{1}{2}ql_2 + \frac{M_2 - M_3}{l_2}$
	$M_3 = \frac{q(l_1 + l_2)(2l_2 - l_1)}{24}$	—	27.43	12	7.11	4.80	3.49	2.67	
	$M_1 = \frac{q(6l_1^3 + 6l_1^2 l_2 - l_2^3)}{12(6l_1 + 5l_2)}$	11.49	11.61	12	12.73	13.94	15.89	19.20	$R_{l1}(\text{end span}) = \frac{1}{2}ql_1 + \frac{M_2 - M_1}{l_1}$
	$M_2 = \frac{q(6l_1^3 + 5l_2^3)}{12(6l_1 + 5l_2)}$	15.40	14.43	12	9.32	7.08	5.40	4.17	$R_{l1}(\text{central span}) = \frac{1}{2}ql_1$
	$M_3 = \frac{q(5l_2^3 + 9l_1 l_2^2 - 3l_1^3)}{12(6l_1 + 5l_2)}$	—	28.04	12	7.06	4.75	3.45	2.63	$R_{l2} = \frac{1}{2}ql_2 + \frac{M_2 - M_3}{l_2}$
	$M_1 = \frac{q(5l_1^3 + 6l_1^2 l_2 - l_2^3)}{60(l_1 + l_2)}$	11.43	11.57	12	12.80	14.12	16.27	20.00	$R_{l1}(\text{end span}) = \frac{1}{2}ql_1 + \frac{M_2 - M_1}{l_1}$
	$M_2 = \frac{q(l_1^3 + l_2^3)}{12(l_1 + l_2)}$	16.00	14.77	12	9.14	6.86	5.19	4.00	$R_{l1}(\text{central span}) = \frac{1}{2}ql_1$
	$M_3 = \frac{q(5l_2^3 + 6l_1 l_2^3 - l_1^3)}{60(l_1 + l_2)}$	80.00	23.41	12	7.44	5.11	3.74	2.86	$R_{l2}(\text{end span}) = \frac{1}{2}ql_2 + \frac{M_2 - M_3}{l_2}$ $R_{l2}(\text{central span}) = \frac{1}{2}ql_2$

Check for shearing resistance:

$$V_d = \frac{136}{4 \times 1.25}(2.1^2 - 1.25^2) = 76\,\text{kN/m approx.}$$

To resist shearing, the required $d = 76 \times 10^3/(0.86 \times 10^3 \times 0.7) = 126\,\text{mm}$, which is less than the value of $d = 261\,\text{mm}$ provided.

25.9.2 Combined bases (strip bases)

When more than one column or load is carried on a single base the centre of gravity of the several loads should, if possible, coincide with the centre of the area of the base, in which case the pressure under the base is uniformly distributed. The base should be symmetrically disposed about the line of the loads and may be rectangular in plan as in *Table 192*, trapezoidal as in *Table 192* or at (a) in the upper part of *Table 190*, or made up of a series of rectangles as at (b) in *Table 190*. In the last case each rectangle should be proportioned so that the load upon it acts at the centre of its area, and the area of each rectangle should be equal to the corresponding applied load divided by a safe bearing pressure, the value adopted for this pressure being the same for all rectangles.

If it is not practicable to proportion the bases as described the load will be eccentric, and thus the centre of pressure of the upward ground pressure will have the same eccentricity relative to the centre of the area of the base. If the base is so thick that it may be considered to act as a single rigid member, the ground pressure will vary according to the formulae for eccentric loads given in *Table 191*, and the pressure-distribution diagram is as at (c) in *Table 190*. If the base is comparatively thin this distribution may not be realized, and owing to the flexibility of the base the ground pressure may be greater immediately under the loads, giving a pressure distribution as at (d) in *Table 190*.

In the case of uniform distribution, or uniform variation of distribution, of pressure the longitudinal bending moment on the base at any section is the sum of anti-clockwise moments of each load to the left of the section minus the clockwise moment of the upward pressure between the section and the left-hand end of the base. This method of analysis gives larger values for longitudinal bending moments on the base than if a non-linear variation is assumed, and therefore the assumption of linear distribution, on which the formulae in *Table 192* (concentric load) and in the following example and in *Table 190* (eccentric load) are based, is safe.

Example. Find the service bending moment at the position of load F_2 on a strip base 15 m long and 1.5 m wide, supporting five unequal concentrated loads arranged eccentrically as shown in the diagram. The loads are $F_1 = 500\,\text{kN}$, $F_2 = 450\,\text{kN}$, $F_3 = 400\,\text{kN}$, $F_4 = 350\,\text{kN}$ and $F_5 = 300\,\text{kN}$; the distances are $z_1 = 14\,\text{m}$, $z_2 = 11\,\text{m}$, $z_3 = 8\,\text{m}$, $z_4 = 5\,\text{m}$ and $z_5 = 1.5\,\text{m}$.

The method is as follows. First obtain e from

$$e = \sum Fz/\sum F - \tfrac{1}{2}l \ngtr \tfrac{1}{6}l$$

Calculate f_{min} and f_{max} from the formulae in *Table 192*. Then

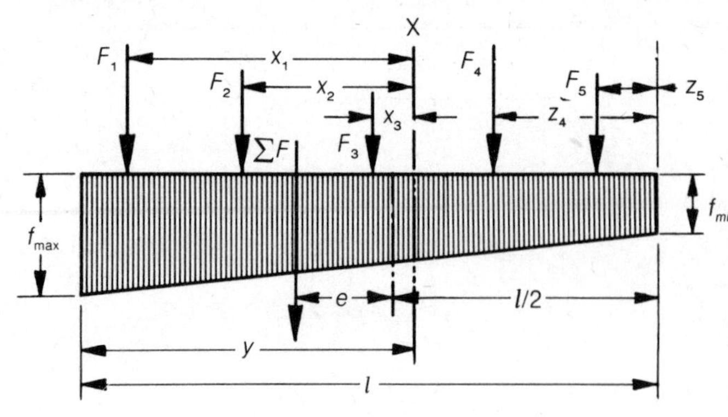

find

$$f_x = f_{min} + (f_{max} - f_{min})(l - y)/l$$
$$M_{xx} = F_x - \tfrac{1}{6}y^2(2f_{max} + f_x)b$$

So, to begin, $\sum F = 2000\,\text{kN}$ and

$$\sum Fz = (500 \times 14) + (450 \times 11) + (400 \times 8) + (350 \times 5) + (300 \times 1.5) = 17\,350$$

Therefore

$$e = 17\,350/2000 - (1/2)15 = 1.175\,\text{m}$$

which is less than $l/6 = 2.5\,\text{m}$. Thus

$$k = 1 \pm \frac{6 \times 1.175}{15} = 1.47 \quad \text{or} \quad 0.53$$

The pressures are:

$$f_{max} = \frac{1.47 \times 2000}{15 \times 1.5} = 130.7\,\text{kN/m}^2$$

$$f_{min} = \frac{0.53 \times 2000}{15 \times 1.5} = 47.1\,\text{kN/m}^2$$

At the load F_2, $y = 15 - 11 = 4\,\text{m}$. Therefore

$$f_x = \frac{(15 - 4)}{15}(130.7 - 47.1) + 47.1 = 108.4\,\text{kN/m}^2$$

Also $x_1 = 3$ and $x_2 = 0$. Therefore $F_x = F_1x_1 + F_2x_2 = 3 \times 500 = 1500\,\text{kN m}$. Finally,

$$M_{xx} = 1500 - \tfrac{1}{6} \times 4^2(2 \times 130.7 + 108.4)1.5 = 1500 - 1479 = +21\,\text{kN m}$$

Shearing forces. The shearing forces on combined bases, rectangular or trapezoidal in plan and carrying two loads, are calculated as for a double-cantilevered beam. For a strip base, the shearing force can be calculated by using the basic principle that the shearing force at any section is the algebraic sum of the vertical forces on one side of the section.

Longitudinal bending moments. The longitudinal positive bending moment on a base carrying two loads can be determined graphically from the two negative bending moments under the loads F_1 and F_2 and the 'free' positive bending moment M_x.

Minimum depth of foundation. The theoretical minimum depth at which a foundation should be placed can be determined from the formulae in *Table 191*, which can be

Pyramidal hoppe bottoms

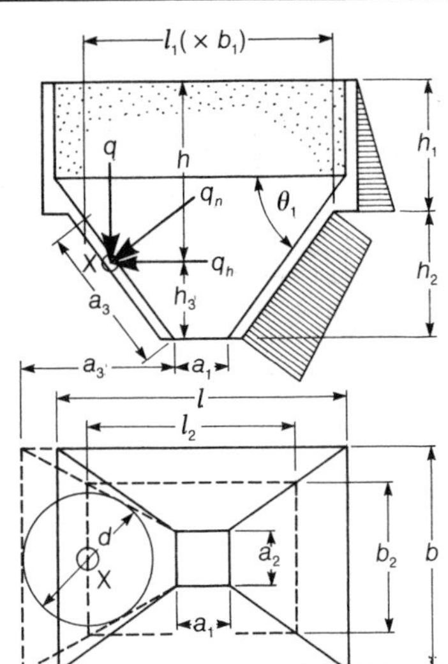

D weight of contents per unit volume

g_s weight of sloping slab per unit area

G_x total weight of hopper bottom below level of X

G total weight of hopper bottom of depth h_2

$$F_x = D\{\tfrac{1}{3}h_3[a_1a_2 + b_2l_2 + \sqrt{(a_1a_2b_2l_2)}] + b_2l_2h\} + G_x$$

$$F = D\{\tfrac{1}{3}h_2[a_1a_2 + b_1l_1 + \sqrt{(a_1a_2b_1l_1)}] + b_1l_1h_1\} + G$$

$$q = Dh; \quad q_h = k_2Dh; \quad q_n = q_h\sin^2\theta_1 + q\cos^2\theta_1 + g_s\cos\theta_1$$

Horizontal effects at midspan and corners of hopper bottom:

Bending moment $= \pm(1/32)q_nd^2$ per unit length of sloping slab

Direct tension $= (1/2)q_nl_2\sin\theta_1$ per unit length of sloping slab

Effects along slope:

Bending moment at centre and top of sloping slab $= \pm(1/32)q_nd^2$

Direct tension (in direction of slope) $= \dfrac{F_x}{2\sin\theta_1(l_2+b_2)}$ at centre

$= \dfrac{F}{2\sin\theta_1(l_1+b_1)}$ at top

Vertical hanging-up force $= \dfrac{F}{2(l_1+b_1)}$ at top

(per unit width of sloping slab)

Rectangular box culverts

Bending moments (per unit length of culvert)

$M_A = M_B \qquad M_C = M_D$

Pressures and uniform loads are per unit area of walls or slab.

Loads F and G are total loads per unit length of culvert. h and l are measured between centres of walls or slabs.

q_1 = pressure transferred to soil.

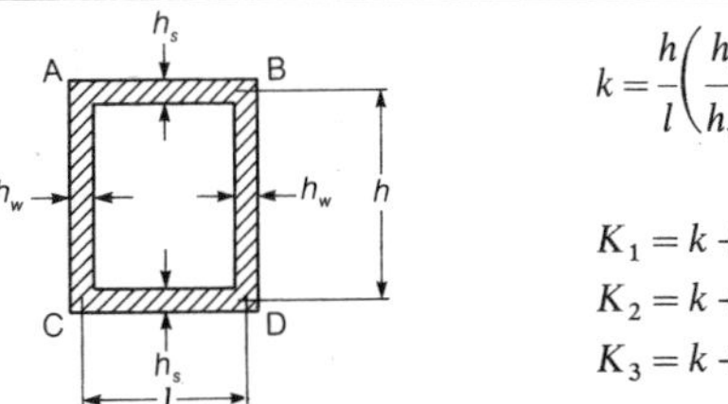

$$k = \frac{h}{l}\left(\frac{h_s}{h_w}\right)^3$$

$K_1 = k+1 \qquad K_4 = 4k+9$

$K_2 = k+2 \qquad K_5 = 2k+3$

$K_3 = k+3 \qquad K_6 = k+6$

$K_7 = 2k+7 \qquad K_8 = 3k+8$

Loading	Condition of supporting ground (limiting cases): Highly compressible		Non-compressible	
Concentrated load on roof	F; $q_1 = \dfrac{F}{l+h_w}$	$M_A = -\dfrac{FlK_4}{24K_1K_3}$; $M_C = \dfrac{K_6}{K_4}M_A$	F	$M_A = -\dfrac{Fl}{4K_2}$; $M_C = -\dfrac{M_A}{2}$
Uniform load on roof	q; $q_1 = q$	$\left.\begin{matrix}M_A\\M_C\end{matrix}\right\} = -\dfrac{ql^2}{12K_1}$	q	$M_A = -\dfrac{ql^2}{6K_2}$; $M_C = -\dfrac{M_A}{2}$
Weight of walls	G G; $q_1 = \dfrac{2G}{1+h_w}$	$M_A = +\dfrac{q_1l^2k}{12K_1K_3}$; $M_C = -\dfrac{K_5}{k}M_A$	G G	$M_A = M_C = 0$
Earth pressure on walls	q_{ep}	$M_A = -\dfrac{q_{ep}h^2kK_7}{60K_1K_3}$; $M_C = \dfrac{K_8}{K_7}M_A$	q_{ep}	$M_A = -\dfrac{q_{ep}h^2k}{30K_2}$; $M_C = \dfrac{K_8}{2k}M_A$
Earth (surcharge) pressure on walls	q_{ep}	$\left.\begin{matrix}M_A\\M_C\end{matrix}\right\} = -\dfrac{q_{ep}h^2k}{12K_1}$	q_{ep}	$M_A = -\dfrac{q_{ep}h^2k}{12K_2}$; $M_C = \dfrac{K_3}{k}M_A$
Hydrostatic (internal) pressure	q_{ip}; $q_1 = q_{ip}$	$M_A = +\dfrac{q_{ip}h^2kK_7}{60K_1K_3}$; $M_c = \dfrac{K_8}{K_7}M_A$	q_{ip}	$M_A = +\dfrac{q_{ip}h^2k}{30K_2}$; $M_C = \dfrac{K_8}{2k}M_A$
Excess hydrostatic (internal) pressure	q_{ip}; q_{ip}; $q_1 = q_{ip}$	$M_A = +\dfrac{q_{ip}(h^2kK_3 + l^2K_5)}{12K_1K_3}$; $M_C = +\dfrac{q_{ip}k(h^2K_3 - l^2)}{12K_1K_3}$	q_{ip}; q_{ip}	$M_A = +\dfrac{q_{ip}(h^2k + 2l^2)}{12K_2}$; $M_C = +\dfrac{q_{ip}(h^2K_3 - l^2)}{12K_2}$

transposed to give

$$h = f_{max} k_2^2 / D$$

or

$$h = \left[f_{max} - \frac{2C}{\sqrt{k_2}} \left(\frac{1}{k_2} + 1 \right) \right] \frac{k_2^2}{D}$$

25.9.3 Balanced bases

Referring to the diagrams in the upper right-hand corner of *Table 190*, a column is supported on the overhanging end C of the beam BC at (a) which is supported on a base at A and subjected to a counterbalance at B. The reaction at A, which depends on the relative values of BC and BA, can be provided by an ordinary reinforced concrete or plain concrete base designed for a concentric load. The counterbalance can mostly be provided by the load from another column as at (b), in which case the dead load on this column at B should be sufficient to counterbalance the dead and imposed loads on the column at C, and vice versa, with a sufficient margin of safety. It is often possible to arrange the column B immediately over A_1. Formulae giving the values of the reactions at A and A_1 are given in *Table 192*, but the probable variation in loads F_1 and F_2 (see diagram in *Table 192*) must be considered for bases of this type. If F_1 can vary from F_{1max} to F_{1min} and F_2 from F_{2max} to F_{2min}, the reaction R will vary from

$$R_{max} = eF_{1max}/l \quad \text{to} \quad R_{min} = eF_{1min}/l$$

Therefore R_1 and R_2 may have the following values:

$$R_{1max} = F_{1max} + F_{base1} + R_{max} + F_{beam}/2$$

$$R_{1min} = F_{1min} + F_{base1} + R_{min} + F_{beam}/2$$

$$R_{2max} = F_{2max} + F_{base2} - R_{min} + F_{beam}/2$$

$$R_{2min} = F_{2min} + F_{base2} - R_{max} + F_{beam}/2$$

Base 1 must therefore be designed for a maximum load of R_{1max} and base 2 for R_{2max}; but R_{2min} must always be positive and also sufficiently large to ensure a sufficient margin of safety in the counterbalance provided by base 2.

From the reactions the shearing forces and bending moments on the beam can be calculated.

If no column loads can be conveniently brought into service to counterbalance the column at C an anchorage must be provided at B by other means, such as the construction of a plain concrete counterweight as at (c) or the provision of tension piles.

If the column to be supported is a corner column loading the foundation eccentrically in two directions, one parallel to each building line, it is sometimes possible to introduce a diagonal balancing beam which is anchored by the adjacent internal column D as at (d). In other cases, however, the two wall beams meeting at the column can be designed as balancing beams to overcome the double eccentricity. The bending moment due to the cantilever action in the beam EC is equal to $F_E e_1$, where F_E is the column load, and the upward force on column C is $F_E e_1/(l_1 - e_1)$. Similarly the bending moment in beam EF is $F_E e_2$ and the upward force on column F is $F_E e_2/(l_2 - e_2)$.

25.9.4 Rafts

The load on and the spacing of the columns determine the shearing forces and bending moments which in turn determine the thickness of the raft. If this thickness does not exceed 300 mm a solid slab as at (a) in the lower part of *Table 190* is generally the most convenient form. If a slab at ground level is required, it is nearly always necessary to thicken the slab at the edge, as at (b), to ensure that the edge of the raft is deep enough below the ground to avoid weathering of the gound under the raft. If a greater thickness is required, beam-and-slab construction designed as an inverted floor, as at (c), is more economical. In cases where the total depth required exceeds 1 m (or 3 ft) or where a level top surface is required, cellular construction as at (d), consisting of a top and bottom slab with intermediate ribs, is adopted.

When the columns on a raft are not equally loaded or are not symmetrically arranged, the raft should be designed so that the centroid coincides with the centre of gravity of the loads. As this distributes the pressure on the ground uniformly, the area of the raft is equal to the total load (including the weight of the raft) divided by the safe bearing pressure. If this coincidence of centres of gravity is impracticable owing to the extent of the raft being limited on one or more sides, the plan of the raft should be made so that the eccentricity e_w of the total loading F_{tot} is a minimum, and this may produce a raft which is not rectangular in plan, as in the example illustrated at (f).

Maximum pressure on the ground (which should not exceed the safe bearing resistance and occurs at a_1) is given by

$$= \frac{F_{tot}}{A_{raft}} + \frac{F_{tot} e_w \alpha_1}{I_{raft}}$$

where A_{raft} is the total area of the raft and I_{raft} is the moment of inertia about the axis N-N which passes through the centroid of the raft and is normal to the line joining the centroid and the centre of gravity of the loads. The minimum ground pressure (at a_2) is given by

$$\frac{F_{tot}}{A_{raft}} - \frac{F_{tot} e_w a_2}{I_{raft}}$$

The intensity of ground pressure along the line N-N = F_{tot}/A_{raft}.

When the three pressures have been determined, the pressure at any other point or the mean pressure over any area can be assessed. Having arranged a rational system of beams or ribs dividing the slab into suitable panels, as suggested by the broken lines at (f), the panels of slabs and the beams can be designed for the bending moments and shearing forces due to the net upward pressures to which they are subjected.

25.10 IMPACT-DRIVEN PILES

25.10.1 Pile loading

In calculations for the loads on piles, any formulae can only give comparative values that must be combined with the results of tests and experience when assessing the safe load

Retaining walls

Types of retaining walls

Simple cantilevered walls

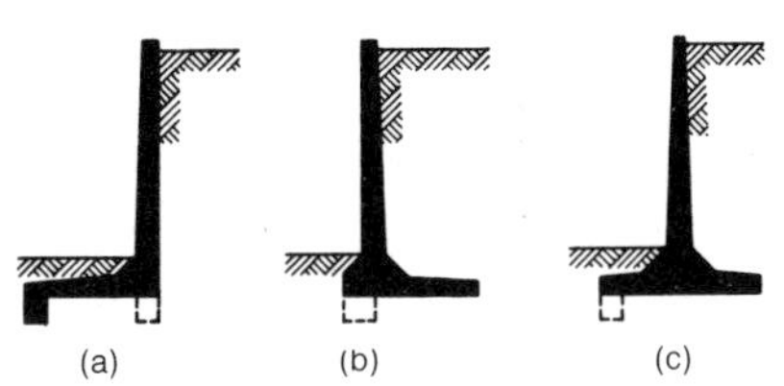

Walls with counterforts

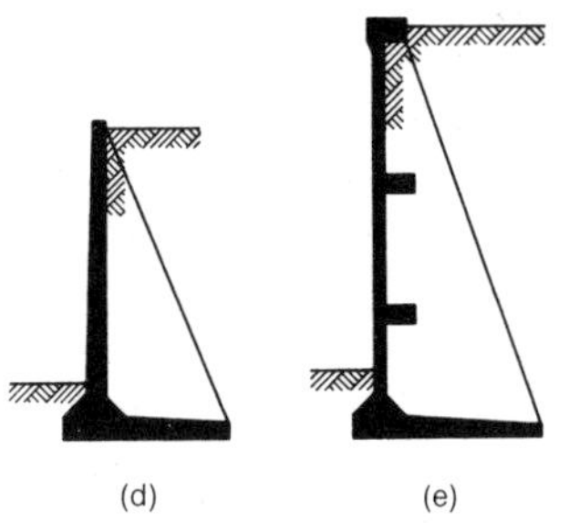

Sheet-pile wall

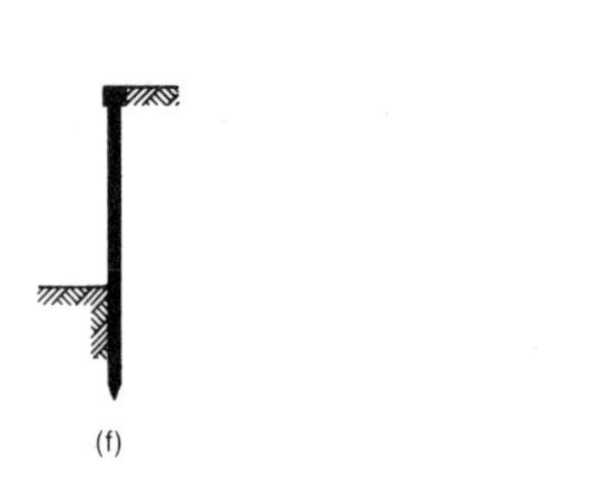

Cantilevered retaining walls

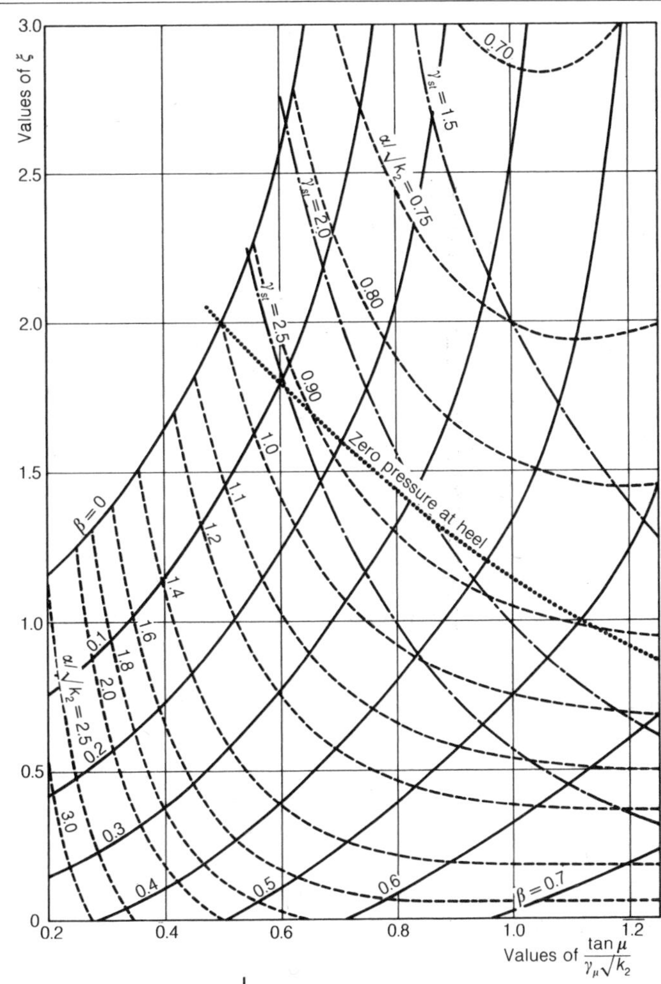

Values of controlling proportions α and β (based on idealized wall of zero thickness shown in sketch below) for given values of $\xi(=f_{max}/Dh)$ and $\tan\mu/(\gamma_\mu\sqrt{k_2})$ may be read from diagram above. For a more detailed explanation of the use of this chart, see section 2.5.8.

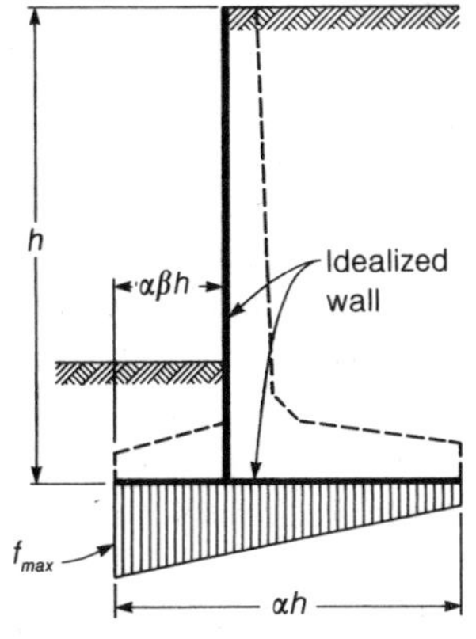

Pressures** and loads per unit length of wall

- F_v resultant of all vertical loads including weights of stem and base of wall, weight of earth on base, and surcharge on ground behind wall
- F_h^{**} resultant of all active horizontal pressures on height h
- $F_h'^{**}$ resultant of all active horizontal pressures acting on stem of wall above A-A

Bending moment at A-A $= F_h' z$
(also check bending moment at bottom of splay)

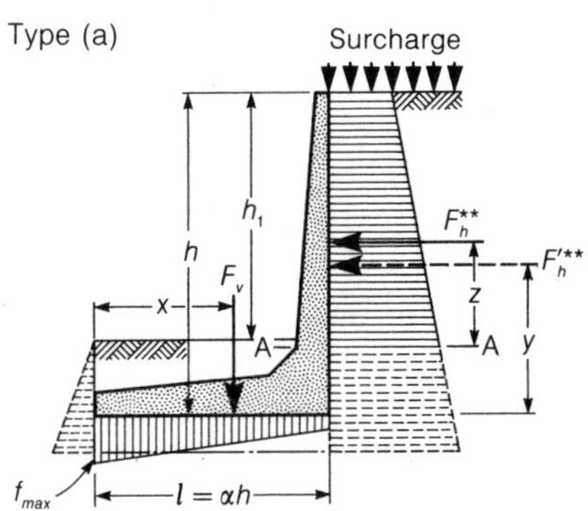

Type (b)

For stability: $F_v x \nless \gamma_{st} F_h y$

Resistance to sliding:
- Frictional resistance only: $\mu F_v \leqslant F_h \gamma_\mu$ (for granular soils only)
- Passive resistance only: passive resistance of ground in front of wall $\leqslant \gamma_p F_h$

Minimum factors of safety:
- against instability: $\gamma_{st} \nless 3/2$
- against sliding (friction): $\gamma_\mu \nless 3/2$
- against sliding (passive resistance): $\gamma_p \nless 2$.

Ground pressure: e = eccentricity of F_v and F_h combined

$$= \frac{F_h y}{F_v} + \tfrac{1}{2}l - x \ngtr \tfrac{1}{6}l$$

$$\text{Maximum ground pressure} = f_{max} = \xi D h = \frac{F_v}{l}\left(1 + \frac{6e}{l}\right)$$

$\ngtr$ safe bearing capacity

**See *Tables 17–20* for calculation of earth pressures on walls.

Simple cantilevered steel-pile walls without ties

Probable variation of pressure

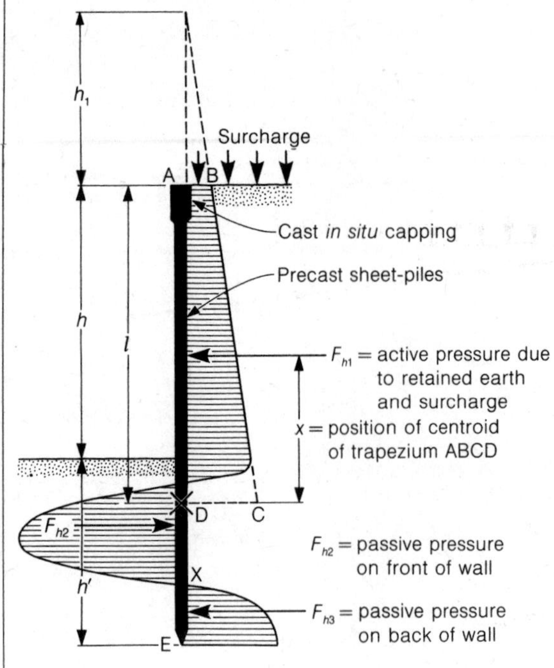

q_{epp} increase of passive resistance per unit depth
q_{epa} increase of active pressure per unit depth

For preliminary design:
maximum bending moment on sheet-pile $= F_{h1}x$
$F_{h1} = \frac{1}{2}q_{epa}l(2h_1 + l)$

Note: formulae applicable only if type and condition of soil is the same in front of and behind wall.

Approximate distribution of pressure for checking a design

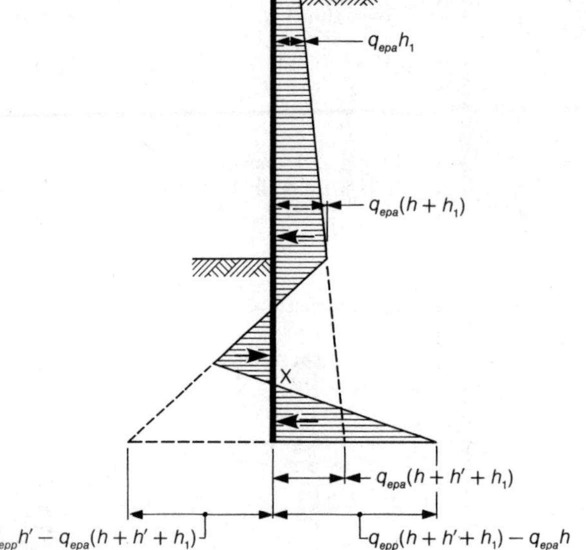

Formulae for checking a design:

Substitute known values of q_{epa}, h, h' and h_1 in

$$q_{epa}(h + h' + h_1)^3 - q_{epp}(h')^3 + \frac{[q_{epp}(h')^2 - q_{epa}(h + h' + h_1)^2]^2}{(q_{epp} - q_{epa})(h + 2h' + h_1)} = 0$$

to obtain an expression in the form

$$k_1 - k_2 q_{epp} + \frac{k_3(q_{epp} - k_4)^2}{q_{epp} - k_5} = 0$$

in which k_1, k_2, k_3, k_4 and k_5 are numerical values.

Calculate
$a = (k_3 - k_2)$
$b = (k_1 + k_2k_5 - 2k_3k_4)$
$c = (k_4^2k_3 - k_1k_5)$
and substitute in

$$q_{epp} = \frac{1}{2a}[\sqrt{(b^2 - 4ac)} - b]$$

Finally compare calculated value of q_{epp} with probable value, allowing for safety factor.

Steel-pile retaining walls

Angle of internal friction of ground	Condition at A: Free		Hinged		Fixed	
	k'_1	k'_2	k'_1	k'_2	k'_1	k'_2
20°	2.0	2.0	1.23	1.23	1.11	1.11
30°	1.5	1.3	1.08	0.88	1.07	0.87
35°	1.4	1.0	1.07	0.67	1.06	0.66
45°	1.3	0.8	1.06	0.56	1.05	0.55

Free = simple cantilevered wall. Hinged = tie at top of wall
Fixed = tie below top of wall.

Span of sheet-piles for calculation of bending moment* $= l = k'_1h$

Minimum embedded length of sheeting $= h' = k'_2h$

Tabulated values assume pressures triangularly distributed and are applicable to preliminary designs. For final designs actual conditions should be considered.

Bending-moment reduction factors (do not apply to simple cantilevered walls). Factors are due to pressure redistribution and not to reduction of pressure	Angle of internal friction of ground		5° or less	15°	20°	30°	35°	45° or more
	thickness of wall / span	0.02	1.00	0.80	0.70	0.56	0.48	0.36
		0.10	1.00	0.88	0.80	0.69	0.62	0.50
		0.20	1.00	0.92	0.86	0.78	0.72	0.60
		0.30	1.00	0.93	0.90	0.83	0.78	0.69
		0.40	1.00	0.96	0.91	0.87	0.83	0.76

189

Sheet-pile retaining walls with ties

Walls with ties at or near top

Sheet-pile wall with tie at top

For stability

$\gamma_{st} F_{h4} x \not< F_{h5} y$

γ_{st} = factor of safety (= say 1.5)

To prevent spewing in front of wall:

$$h' \not> \frac{k_2^2 f_w}{D}$$

f_w intensity of vertical pressure in ground at level of E due to weight of earth and surcharge

D weight of soil (unit vol.)

k_2 pressure factor*

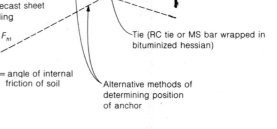

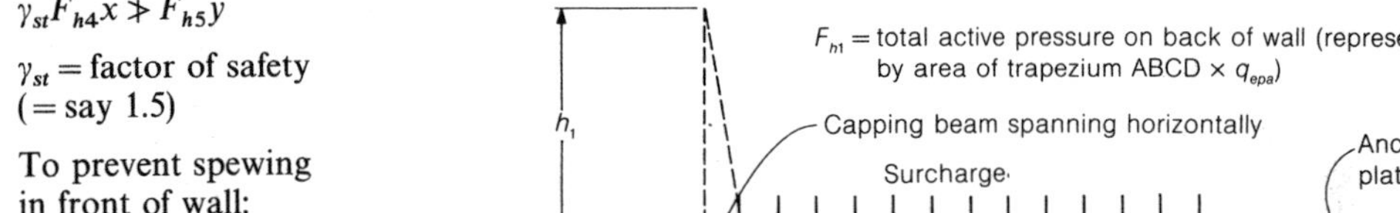

Note

Formulae apply only to preliminary designs and only if type and condition of soil is the same in front of and behind the wall.

Sheet-pile wall with tie at top

Sheet-pile wall with tie below top

$N = F_{h4} + F_{h6} - \frac{2}{3} F_{h5}$ but $\not< \frac{1}{2} F_{h4} + F_{h6}$

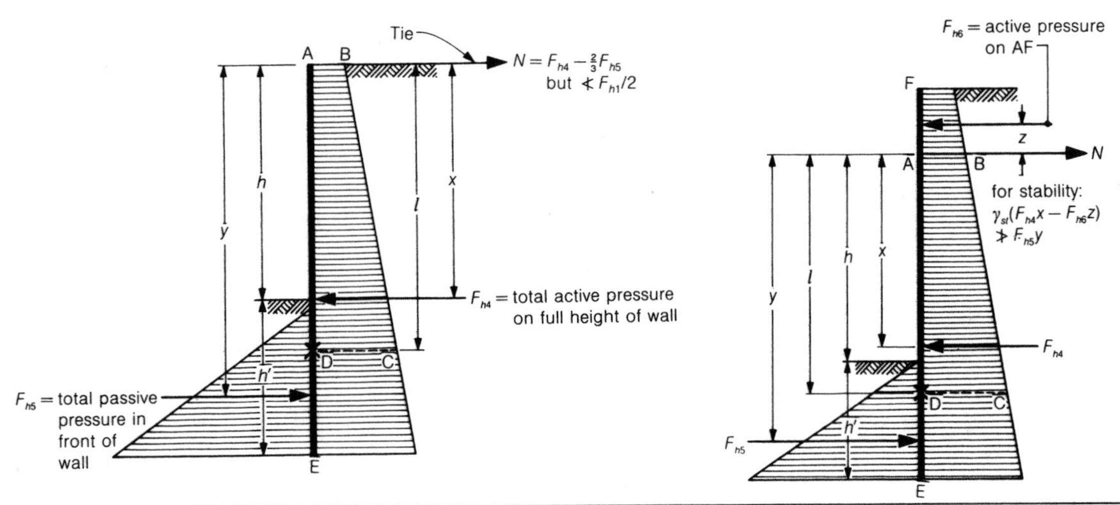

Walls with anchor-piles

Forces in anchor-piles

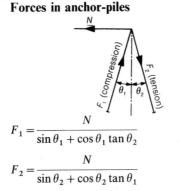

$$F_1 = \frac{N}{\sin\theta_1 + \cos\theta_1 \tan\theta_2}$$

$$F_2 = \frac{N}{\sin\theta_2 + \cos\theta_2 \tan\theta_1}$$

Sheet-pile wall with relieving platform

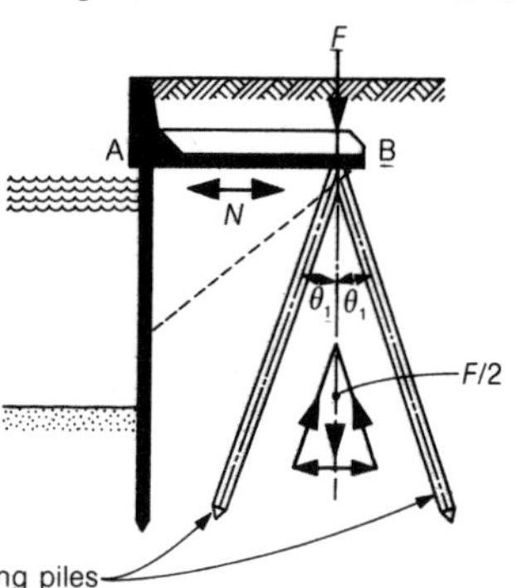

Forces in piles $= F_1 + \frac{1}{2} F \sec\theta_1$ (compression)

or $F_2 - \frac{1}{2} F \sec\theta_1$ (tension)

*See *Table 18* for values of k_2.

on a pile. The validity of dynamic formulae such as those due to Hiley and Faber is discussed in section 6.14.1. In their original form the Hiley and Faber formulae appear in imperial units: in *Table 193* these formulae have been modified by the incorporation of factors α_1, α_2 and α_3 to make them applicable to both SI and imperial systems of measurement.

Example. Estimate the safe service load on a 350 mm square pile 12 m long, driven into gravel by a 20 kN single-acting steam hammer falling 1 m with a final penetration of 4 blows per 10 mm; the weight of the helmet, dolly and stationary part of the hammer is 5 kN. The dolly is in good condition at the end of the driving.

Using the modified Hiley formula given in *Table 193*: self-weight of pile $= 12 \times 0.35^2 \times 23.6 = 35$ kN approx; $P = 35 + 5 = 40$ kN. $P/w = 40/20 = 2$. Effective drop $= H_1 = 0.9 \times 1000 = 900$ mm. For $P/w = 2$, $e = 0.37$. For medium driving, $c = 0.29$ for $l = 12$ m. Then the settlement load is

$$= \frac{20 \times 900 \times 0.37 \times 0.4}{1 + (25.4 \times 0.29 \times 0.4)} + 20 + 40 = 675 + 60 = 735\,\text{kN}$$

For this load the driving pressure is $735/0.35^2 = 6000\,\text{kN/mm}^2$, which is sufficiently close to the assumed value of $6900\,\text{kN/m}^2$. Thus the safe working load is, say, $(1/2) \times 735 - 35 = 333$ kN.

25.10.2 Piled jetties: design examples

Example 1: vertical piles only. See diagram (a) accompanying. Consider a single row of piles; therefore $n = 1$ for each line and $\sum n = 4$. Since the group is symmetrical, $X = (1/2) \times 9.0 = 4.5$ m. From *Table 195*:

$$M = (800 \times 0.75) - (100 \times 4.8) = +120\,\text{kN m}$$

The calculation of the load on the piles can be made as shown in the accompanying table.

The shearing force on each pile $= 100/4 = 25$ kN and the bending moment on each pile is $(1/2)25 \times 4.8 = 60$ kN m. The maximum load on any pile is 212 kN; say 250 kN including the self-weight of the pile.

Example 2: vertical and inclined piles. See diagram (b) accompanying. For each pile, A is assumed to be the same.

Pile no	x (m)	x^2 (m²)	k_w $\left(\frac{1}{\sum n}\right)$	k_m $\left(\frac{x}{nI}\right)$	Axial load $(k_w F_v + k_m M)$	
N_1	−4.5	20.25	+0.25	$-\frac{4.5}{45} = -0.100$	$(0.25 \times 800) - (0.100 \times 120)$	= 188 kN
N_2	−1.5	2.25	+0.25	$-\frac{1.5}{45} = -0.033$	$200 - (0.033 \times 120)$	= 196 kN
N_3	+1.5	2.25	+0.25	+0.033	200 + 4	= 204 kN
N_4	+4.5	20.25	+0.25	+0.100	200 + 12	= 212 kN

$I = \sum nx^2 = 45.00\,\text{m}^4$

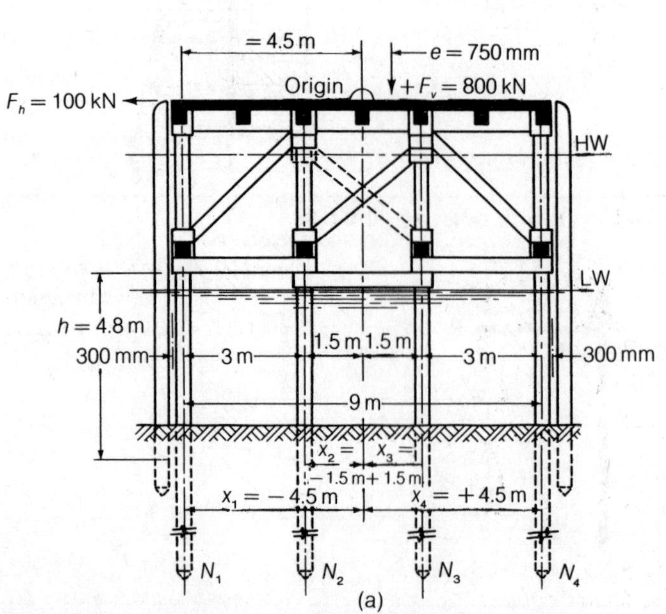

(a)

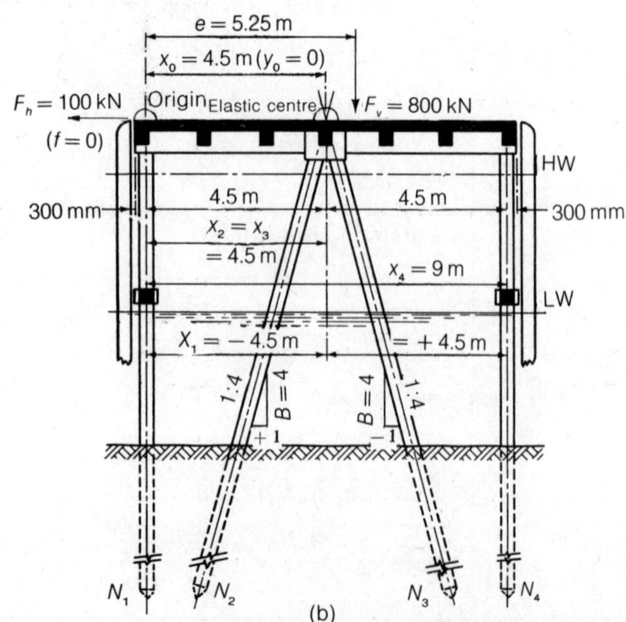

(b)

Foundations: types of combined bases

Combined foundation for line of loads

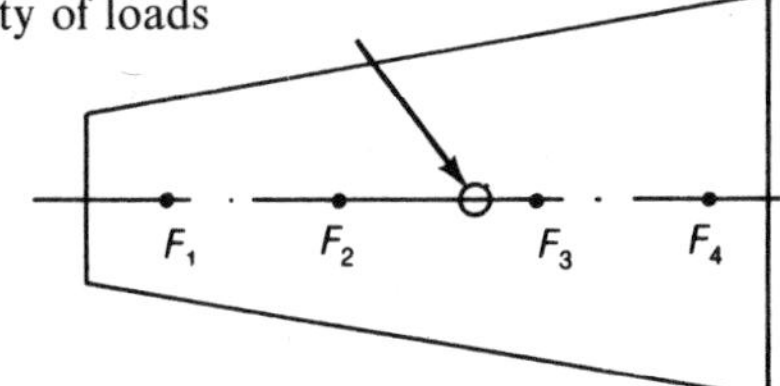

(a) ***Trapezoidal***

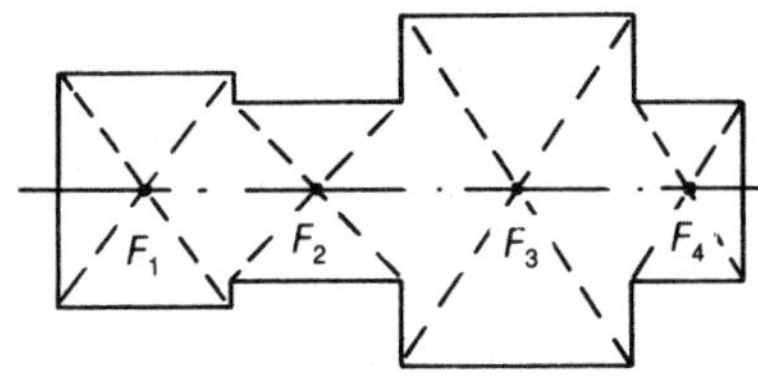

(b) ***Rectangular***

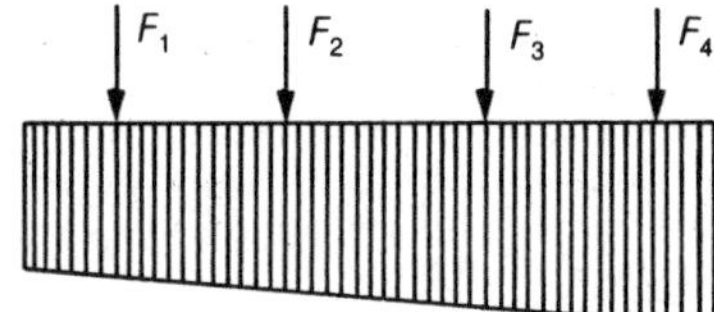

(c) ***Uniform variation of pressure***
(when CG and centroid not concident)

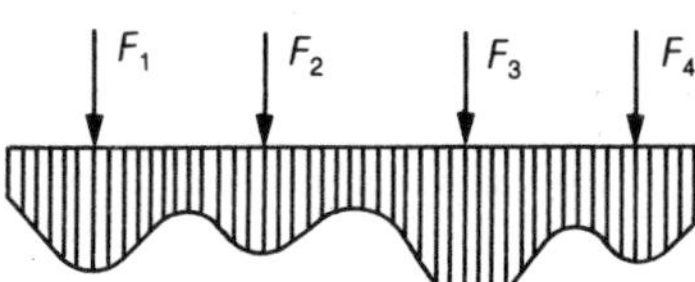

(d) ***Non-uniform variation of pressure***

Balanced foundations

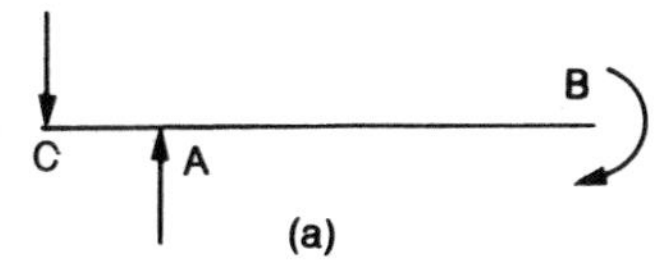

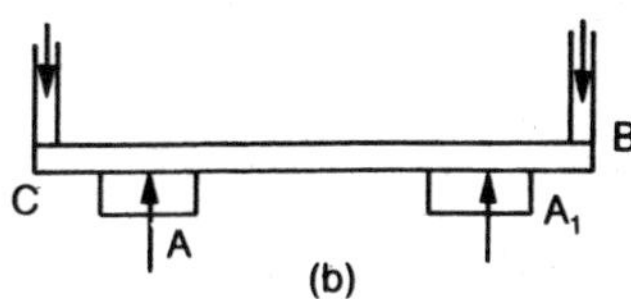

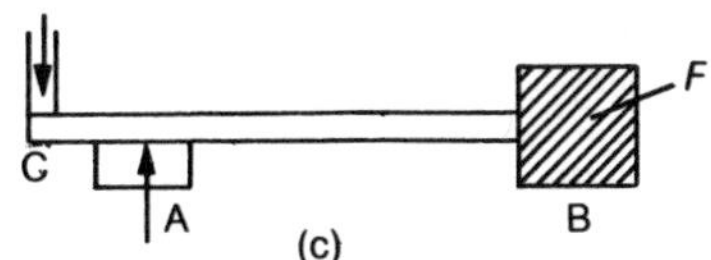

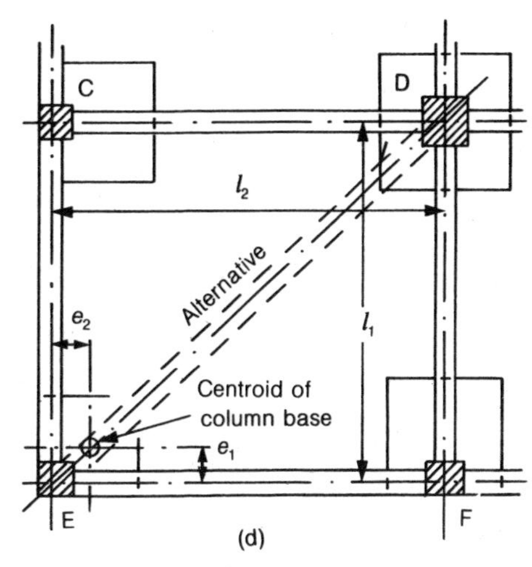

Rafts

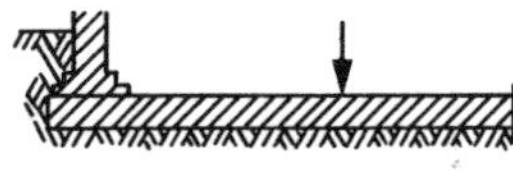

(a) ***Solid raft***

(b) ***Solid raft with thickening at edge***

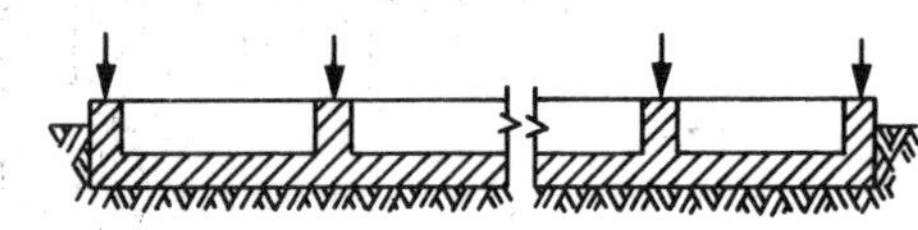

(c) ***Beam-and-slab raft***

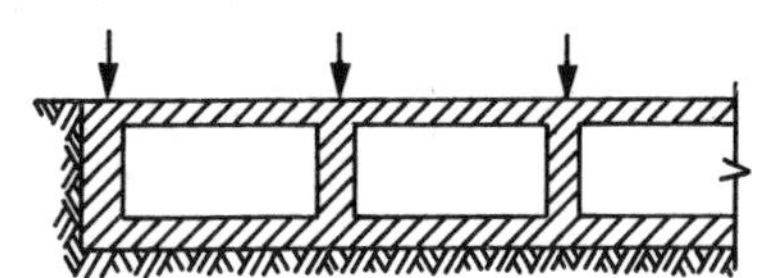

(d) ***Cellular raft***

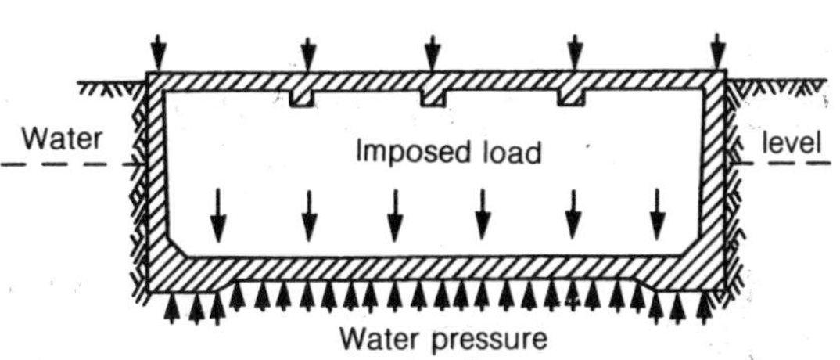

(e) ***Basement in wet ground***

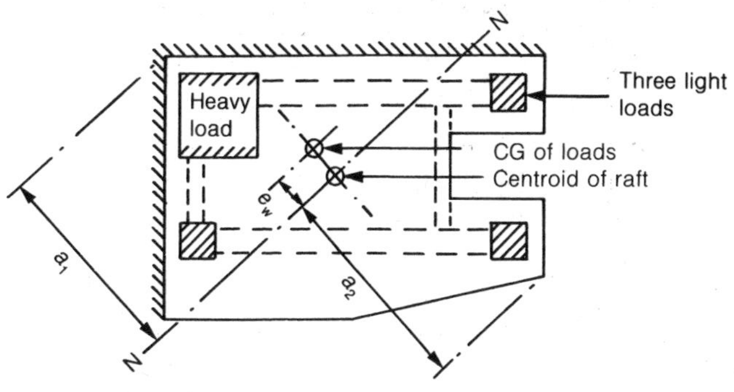

(f) ***Plan of eccentrically loaded raft***

Foundations: allowable pressure and separate bases

Safe bearing pressures on ground

Type of ground	Bearing pressure kN/m²	tons/ft²
Clay: soft	<75	<0.75
firm	75–150	0.75–1.5
stiff	150–300	1.5–3
very stiff, hard	300–600	3–6
Sand, uniform: loose	<100	<1
medium dense	100–300	1–3
compact	>300	>3
Gravel, sand and gravel: loose	<200	<2
medium dense	200–600	2–6
compact	>600	>6

Type of ground	Bearing pressure kN/m²	tons/ft²
Chalk: hard sound	600	6
Limestone: soft	600	6
Shale, mudstone: soft	600–1000	6–10
hard	2000	20
Sandstone: soft	2000	20
Schist, slate	3000	30
Sandstone, limestone: hard	4000	40
Rock: igneous and gneissic: sound	10000	100

Maximum ground pressure to prevent spewing, at depth h: In granular (cohesionless) soil: $f_{max} = Dh/k_2^2$

In cohesive soil: $f_{max} = \dfrac{Dh}{k_2^2} + \dfrac{2C}{\sqrt{k_2}}\left(\dfrac{1}{k_2} + 1\right)$

(both) but not greater than safe pressure as tabulated

For values of k_2 and C, see *Tables 17* and *18*.

Safe bearing pressures on constructional materials

Constructional material: Description	28-day cube strength N/mm²	lb/in²	Max. bearing pressure under uniform load MN/m²	lb/in²
Plain concrete 1:4:8	8.6	1 250	1.7	250
1:3:6	11.5	1 650	2.4	350
1:2::4	21.0	3 000	5.3	760
1:1½:3	25.5	3 750	6.5	950
1:1:2	30.0	4 500	7.6	1140
Masonry or brickwork (unreinforced) with 1:3 cement mortar	20.5	3 000	1.65	240
	27.5	4 000	2.05	300
	34.5	5 000	2.50	360
	52.0	7 500	3.50	510
	69.0	10 000	4.55	660
	96.5 or more	14 000 or more	5.85	850

Max. bearing pressure under eccentric load = 1.25 × that under uniform load
Max. bearing pressure under concentrated load = 1.5 × that under uniform load

Plain concrete: If slenderness ratio $k \leqslant 6$ use tabulated values of max. bearing pressure directly. If $6 \leqslant k \leqslant 27$, multiply tabulated value by $\alpha = 1.165 - 0.275k + 0.66e(6-k)$ where e = eccentricity of vertical loading as proportion of thickness. (Expression valid only when $\alpha \nless 0.2$.) For members having a cross-sectional area A of less than 0.3 m or 500 in², the max. bearing pressure calculated must be multiplied by the reduction factor $(9 + 10A)/12$ (metric units) or $(1500 + A)/2000$ (imperial units).

Masonry or brickwork: If slenderness ratio $k \leqslant 15$, use tabulated values of max. bearing pressure directly. If $15 \leqslant k \leqslant 24$, multiply tabulated value by $(45-k)/30$.

Distribution of pressure

Concentric load

$e = 0$

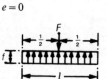

Eccentric load

$e \not> l/6$: $k = 1 \pm \dfrac{6e}{l}$

Eccentric load

$e > l/6$: $k = \dfrac{4l}{3(l-2e)}$

$f = kF/bl$

where

- l length of foundation
- b width of foundation
- F total load on foundation (including weight of base)
- F_{base} weight of base

Independent bases

Concentric load

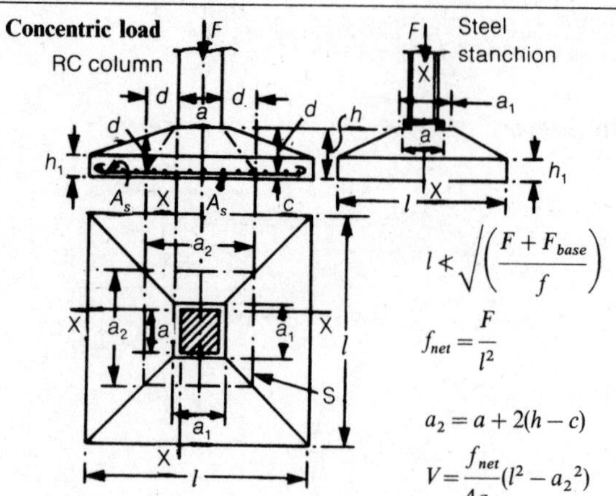

$$l \nless \sqrt{\left(\frac{F + F_{base}}{f}\right)}$$

$$f_{net} = \frac{F}{l^2}$$

$$a_2 = a + 2(h - c)$$

$$V = \frac{f_{net}}{4a_2}(l^2 - a_2^2)$$

per unit width

For RC column: $M_{XX} = \frac{1}{2} f_{net} l (l-a)^2$

For steel stanchion: $M_{XX} = \frac{1}{8} f_{net} l^2 (l-a)$

Eccentric load

$$e = \frac{F_v e_w + F_h h + M}{F_v + F_{base}}$$

Note signs of e_w, M and F_h

$$f_1 = f_{max} - f_{base}$$

$$f_2 = f_{min} - f_{base}$$

$$a_2 = \tfrac{1}{2}(l-a) + e_w$$

$$M_{YY} = \frac{F}{8b}(b-a)^2$$

$$M_{XX} = \frac{a_2^2 b}{2}\left[f_2 + \frac{a_2}{3l}(f_1 - f_2)\right]$$

$$\left.\begin{matrix} f_{max} \\ f_{min} \end{matrix}\right\rangle = \frac{F + F_{base}}{bl}\left(1 \pm \frac{6e}{l}\right) \left\langle \begin{matrix} \not> f_{lim} \\ \nless 0 \end{matrix}\right.$$

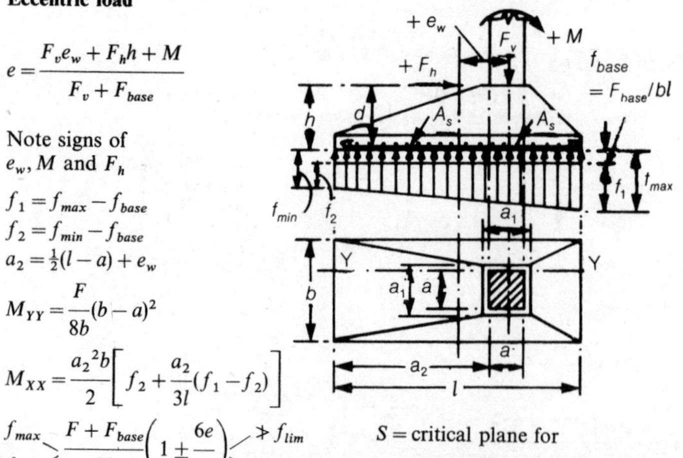

S = critical plane for shearing resistance (CP110)

Foundations: combined bases

Concentric load

Rectangular base

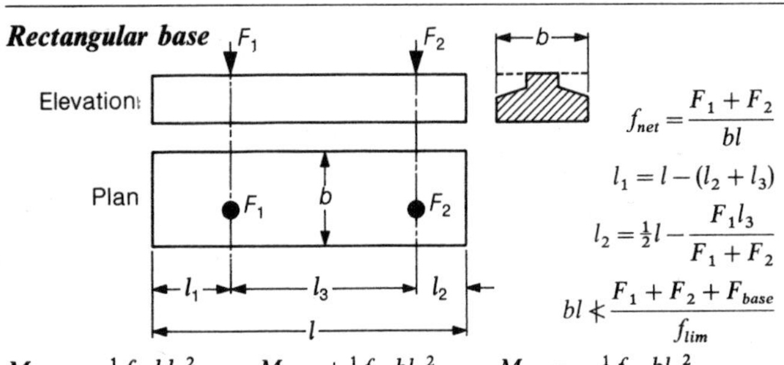

$$f_{net} = \frac{F_1 + F_2}{bl}$$

$$l_1 = l - (l_2 + l_3)$$

$$l_2 = \tfrac{1}{2}l - \frac{F_1 l_3}{F_1 + F_2}$$

$$bl \not< \frac{F_1 + F_2 + F_{base}}{f_{lim}}$$

$M_{11} = -\tfrac{1}{2} f_{net} b l_1^2$ $\quad M_x = +\tfrac{1}{8} f_{net} b l_3^2$ $\quad M_{22} = -\tfrac{1}{2} f_{net} b l_2^2$

Transverse bending moment (at each load) $= -\tfrac{1}{8} bF_1$ (or F_2)

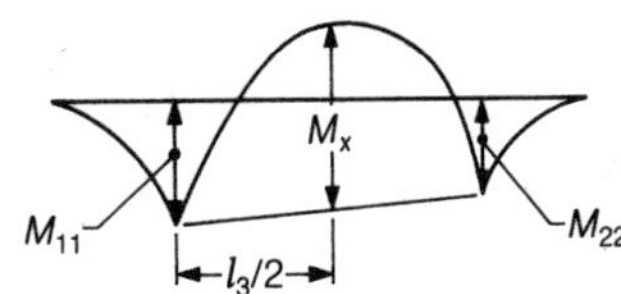

Trapezoidal base

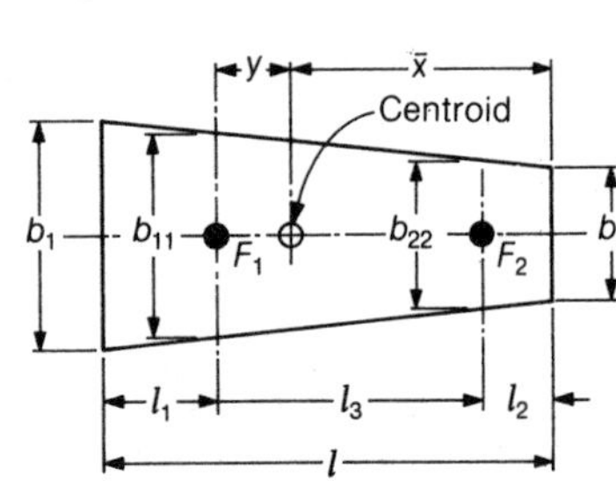

$$\bar{x} = \frac{l}{3}\left[\frac{2b_1 + b_2}{b_1 + b_2}\right]$$

$$y = \frac{F_2 l_3}{F_1 + F_2}$$

$$l_1 = l - (y + \bar{x})$$

$$l_2 = l - (l_3 + l_1)$$

$$f_{net} = \frac{2(F_1 + F_2)}{l(b_1 + b_2)}$$

$$b_{11} = b_2 + (b_1 - b_2)\frac{l - l_1}{l}$$

$$b_{22} = b_2 + (b_1 - b_2)\frac{l_2}{l}$$

$$\tfrac{1}{2}l(b_1 + b_2) \not< \frac{F_1 + F_2 + F_{base}}{f_{lim}}$$

Longitudinal bending moments (total)
(diagram similar to rectangular base concentrically loaded)

$M_{11} = -\tfrac{1}{6} l_1^2 (2b_1 + b_{11}) f_{net}$ $\quad M_{22} = -\tfrac{1}{6} l_2^2 (2b_2 + b_{22}) f_{net}$

$M_x = +\tfrac{1}{16} l_3^2 (b_{11} + b_{22}) f_{net}$ (approx.)

Transverse bending moments $= -\tfrac{1}{8} F_1 b_{11}$ at F_1: $-\tfrac{1}{8} F_2 b_{22}$ at F_2

General case for any number of loads

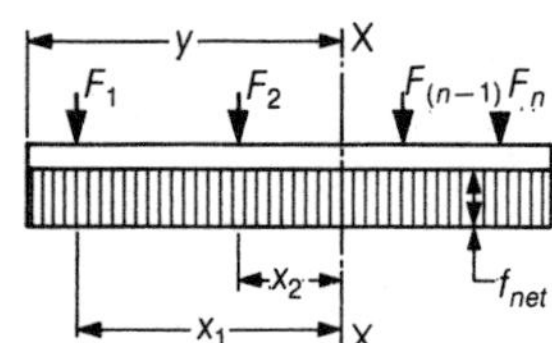

Bending moment at X-X:
$= \Sigma Fx - \tfrac{1}{2} b y^2 f_{net}$

Wall footings

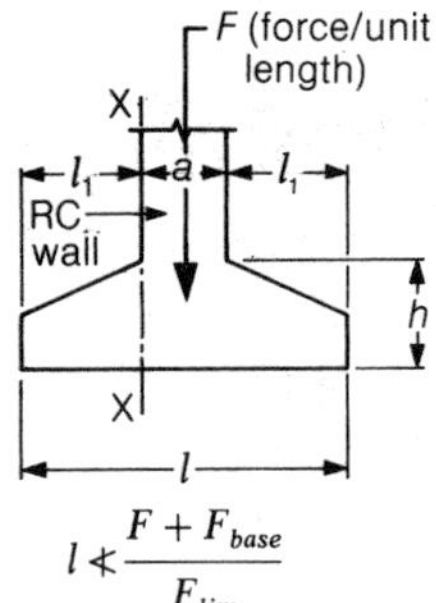

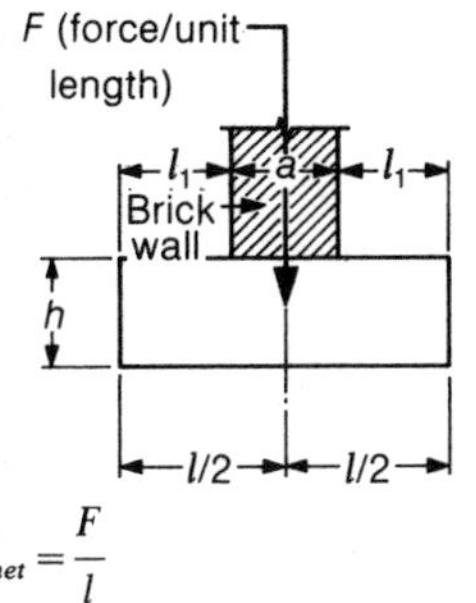

$$l \not< \frac{F + F_{base}}{F_{lim}} \qquad f_{net} = \frac{F}{l}$$

$M_x = \tfrac{1}{2} f_{net} l_1^2$ per unit length $\qquad M_x = \tfrac{1}{4} f_{net} l_1 l$ per unit length

Notes Notation additional to diagrams

$F, F_v =$ vertical imposed load: $F_h =$ horizontal imposed load
$f_{lim} =$ safe bearing pressure on ground
$f_{base} =$ bearing pressure induced by weight of base
$f_{net} =$ actual net upward pressure due to imposed loads only

Eccentric load (note sign and direction of F_v, F_h, M, e etc)

Rectangular base

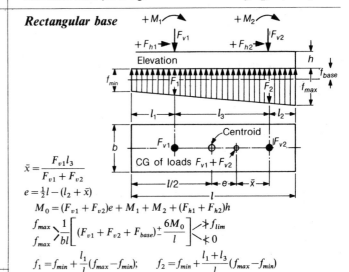

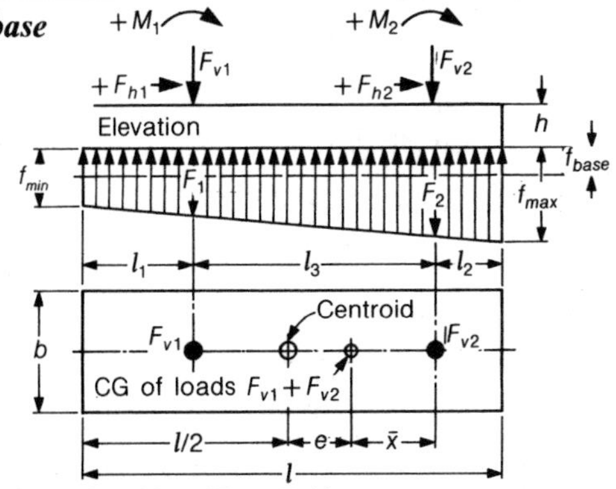

$$\bar{x} = \frac{F_{v1} l_3}{F_{v1} + F_{v2}}$$

$$e = \tfrac{1}{2}l - (l_2 + \bar{x})$$

$$M_0 = (F_{v1} + F_{v2})e + M_1 + M_2 + (F_{h1} + F_{h2})h$$

$$\begin{matrix} f_{max} \\ f_{max} \end{matrix} \frac{1}{bl}\left[(F_{v1} + F_{v2} + F_{base}) \pm \frac{6M_0}{l}\right] \begin{matrix} \not> f_{lim} \\ \not< 0 \end{matrix}$$

$$f_1 = f_{min} + \frac{l_1}{l}(f_{max} - f_{min}); \qquad f_2 = f_{min} + \frac{l_1 + l_3}{l}(f_{max} - f_{min})$$

Longitudinal bending moments (total)
(diagram similar to rectangular base loaded concentrically)

$M_{11} = -\tfrac{1}{6} b l_1^2 (2f_{min} + f_1 - 3f_{base})$

$M_x = +\tfrac{1}{16} b l_3^2 (f_1 + f_2)$ (approx.)

$M_{22} = -\tfrac{1}{6} b l_2^2 (2f_{max} + f_2 - 3f_{base})$

Transverse bending moments (at each load) $= -\tfrac{1}{8} bF_{e1}$ (or F_{v2})

Balanced bases

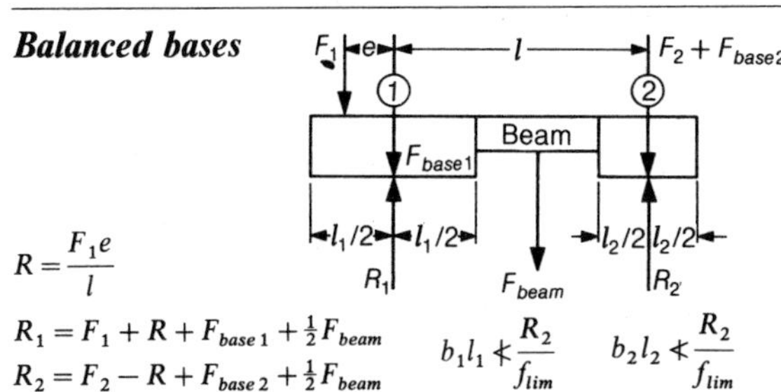

$$R = \frac{F_1 e}{l}$$

$R_1 = F_1 + R + F_{base\,1} + \tfrac{1}{2}F_{beam}$ $\qquad b_1 l_1 \not< \dfrac{R_2}{f_{lim}}$ $\qquad b_2 l_2 \not< \dfrac{R_2}{f_{lim}}$

$R_2 = F_2 - R + F_{base\,2} + \tfrac{1}{2}F_{beam}$

Longitudinal bending moment varies from $F_1 e$ at centre-line of ① to zero at centre-line of ②

Tied bases

$$b_1 l_1 \not< \frac{F_{v1} + F_{base\,1}}{f_{lim}}$$

$$b_2 l_2 \not< \frac{F_{v2} + F_{base\,2}}{f_{lim}}$$

$$M_{11} = M_1 + F_{h1}h$$

$$M_{22} = -(M_2 + F_{h2}h)$$

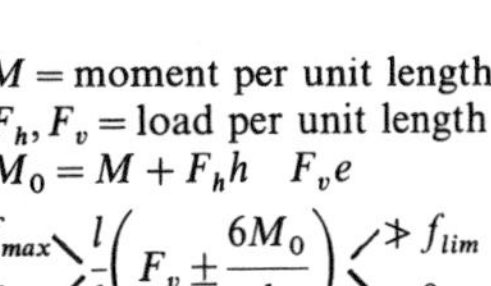

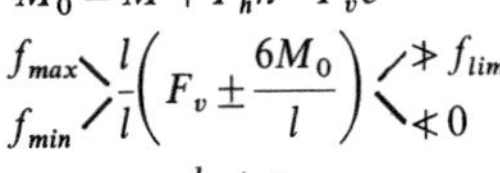

Shearing force on beam $= \dfrac{M_{11} - M_{22}}{l}$

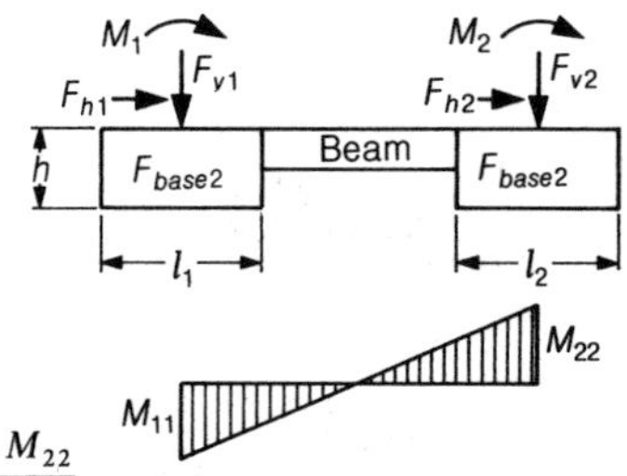

Wall footing

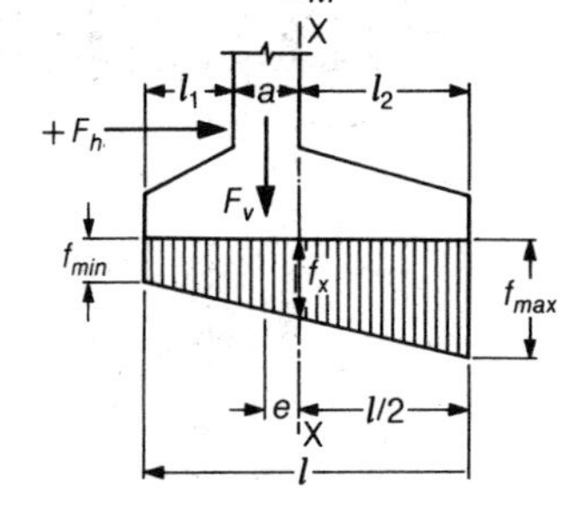

$M =$ moment per unit length
$F_h, F_v =$ load per unit length
$M_0 = M + F_h h \quad F_v e$

$$\begin{matrix} f_{max} \\ f_{min} \end{matrix} \frac{1}{l}\left(F_v \pm \frac{6M_0}{l}\right) \begin{matrix} \not> f_{lim} \\ \not< 0 \end{matrix}$$

$$f_x = f_{min} + \frac{l_1 + a}{l}(f_{max} - f_{min})$$

$M_x = \tfrac{1}{6} l_2^2 (f_x + 2f_{max} - 3f_{base})$
per unit length

Shearing force at X $= \tfrac{1}{2} l_2 (f_x + f_{max} - 2f_{base})$ per unit length

Units: Loads: Newtons or pounds
Dimensions: metres or feet
Moments: N-m or lb-ft
Pressures: N/m² or lb/ft²

All piles are driven to the same depth, so if A/l for piles N_1 and N_4 is unity, A/l for N_2 and $N_3 = 4/\sqrt{(1+4^2)} = 0.97$. Since the group is symmetrical, $\sum_2 = 0$, $\sum_3$ is not required, $\sum_4 = 0$, $k = \sum_1 \sum_5$, $x_0 = 9/2 = 4.5$ m, and $y_0 = 0$. Then

$$M = 800(5.25 - 4.5) + 0 = 600\ \text{kN m}.$$

The calculation is then as shown in the accompanying table.

Therefore $k = 3.826 \times 0.114 = 0.436$. The axial loads on the piles are:

$$N_1 = 1[(0.261 \times 800) + 0 - (0.111 \times 600)]$$
$$= 208.8 - 66.7 = 142.1\ \text{kN}$$

$$N_2 = 0.941[208.8 + (2.19 \times 100) + 0] = 402.6\ \text{kN}$$

$$N_3 = 0.941(208.8 - 219 + 0) = -9.6\ \text{kN (tension)}$$

or $+20$ kN including the self-weight of the pile.

$$N_4 = 208.8 + 66.7 = 275.5\ \text{kN}$$

Thus the maximum load on any pile is 402.6 kN; say 430 kN including the self-weight of the pile.

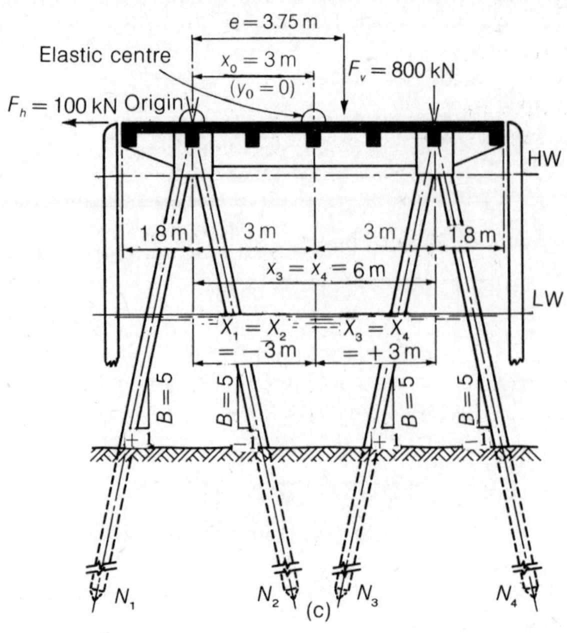

Pile no.	$\sum_1$	$\sum_5$	x (m)	X (m)	$\sum_6 = I$	k_p	k_w	k_h	k_M
N_1							$+\frac{0.114}{0.436}$		$-\frac{4.5}{40.5}$
	+1	0	0	−4.5	+20.25	+1	= +0.261	0	= −0.111
N_2	$+\frac{0.97 \times 4^2}{1+4^2}$	$+\frac{0.97}{1+4^2}$				$+\frac{0.97 \times 4}{\sqrt{(1+4^2)}}$		$+\frac{3.826}{4 \times 0.436}$	
	= +0.913	= +0.057	+4.5	0	0	= +0.941	+0.261	= +2.19	0
N_3	+0.913	= +0.057	+4.5	0	0	+0.941	+0.261	= −2.19	0
N_4	+1	0	+9	+4.5	+20.25	+1	+0.261	0	+0.111
Totals	+3.826	+0.114	—	—	+40.5	—	—	—	—

Example 3: inclined piles only. See diagram (c) accompanying. Tan $\theta = 0.2$. For each pile l and A are the same, and thus unity may be substituted for A/l. For piles N_1 and N_3, $B = +5$, and for N_2 and N_4, $B = -5$. Since the group is

Pile no.	$\sum_1$	$\sum_5$	x (m)	X (m)	$\sum_6 = I$	k_p	k_w	k_h	X/I
N_1	$\frac{5^2}{1+5^2}$	$\frac{1}{1+5^2}$			$0.9615(-3)^2$	$\frac{5}{\sqrt{(1+5^2)}}$	$\frac{0.1538}{0.5917}$	$+\frac{3.846}{5 \times 0.5917}$	$-\frac{3}{34.62}$
	= +0.9615	= +0.0385	0	−3.0	= +8.65	= +0.9806	= +0.26	= +1.3	= −0.0867
N_2								$-\frac{3.846}{5 \times 0.5917}$	
	+0.9615	+0.0385	0	−3.0	+8.65	+0.9806	+0.26	= −1.3	−0.0867
N_3									$+\frac{3}{34.62}$
	+0.9615	+0.0385	+6.0	+3.0	+8.65	+0.9806	+0.26	+1.3	= +0.0867
N_4	+0.9615	+0.0385	+6.0	+3.0	+8.65	+0.9806	+0.26	−1.3	+0.0867
Totals	+3.846	+0.1538	—	—	+34.62	—	—	—	—

Foundations: precast concrete piles

Hiley formula (modified)

Settlement load (tons or kN) $W_M = \dfrac{wH_1en}{1+\alpha_1 cn} + w + P$

where

- w weight of hammer (kN or tons)
- H_1 effective drop of hammer (mm or in)

$$\frac{\text{effective drop}}{\text{actual drop}} = \begin{cases} 1.0 \text{ for freely falling drop hammer} \\ 0.9 \text{ for single-acting steam hammer} \\ 0.8 \text{ for winch-operated drop hammer} \end{cases}$$

- l length of pile (m or ft)
- P weight of helmet, dolly and stationary parts of hammer plus weight of pile (kN or tons)
- n number of blows for final unit length of penetration (per mm or per inch)
- c temporary elastic compression factor

Read from table below or calculate from

$\alpha_1 c = \frac{1}{2}\alpha_3(c_1 + c_2 + c_3)$

where

c_1 (for pile) $= 0.044pl$ where l is in metres or $0.0134pl$ where l is in feet

c_2 (for helmet and dolly) $= 0.56p$ for helmet and packing or $0.11p$ without helmet

c_3 (for ground) $= 0.22p$ for gravel, $0.44p$ for clay, or $1.1p$ for peat

$\alpha_1 = \alpha_3 = 1$ when all values are in imperial units

$\alpha_1 = 25.4$ and $\alpha_3 = 64.8$ when all values are in SI units

p = driving pressure (tons/in^2 or kN/mm^2) $= W_M$/area of pile

Working load (including weight of pile) $= kW_M$ where $k = 1/3$ to $2/3$, the greater factor applying to hard-driving conditions

Efficiency of blow e	P/w	0.5	1.0	1.5	2.0	2.5	3	4	5	6	7
	With helmet and wooden dolly	0.69	0.53	0.44	0.37	0.33	0.30	0.25	0.21	0.19	0.17
	Pile-head and cap in poor condition	0.67	0.50	0.40	0.33	0.28	0.25	0.20	0.16	0.14	0.12

Compression factor c	Length of pile	p N/mm^2	p tons/in^2	6 m / 20 ft	9 m / 30 ft	12 m / 40 ft	15 m / 50 ft	18 m / 60 ft
	Easy driving	3.4	0.22	0.13	0.16	0.17	0.19	0.20
	Medium driving	6.9	0.45	0.24	0.27	0.29	0.33	0.36
	Hard driving	10.3	0.67	0.33	0.37	0.42	0.46	0.51
	Very hard driving	13.8	0.89	0.40	0.46	0.52	0.58	0.64

Tabulated values of c are minima and assume dolly and packing in good condition and compact ground

Faber formula for piles driven into clay

- H free fall of hammer (mm or in)
- d diameter or size of pile (mm or in)
- A_s area of sides of pile embedded in ground (m^2 or ft^2)
- F factor of safety (1.5 to 2.5)

$\alpha_2 = 1$ when all values are in given imperial units

$\alpha_2 = 107.3$ when all values are in given SI units

Safe load (kN or tons) $= \dfrac{wn(H - 0.143d)}{F(1 + 0{\cdot}08Hn)} + \dfrac{\alpha_2 A_s}{20}$

Points of lifting to produce min. BMs

Single-point lifting

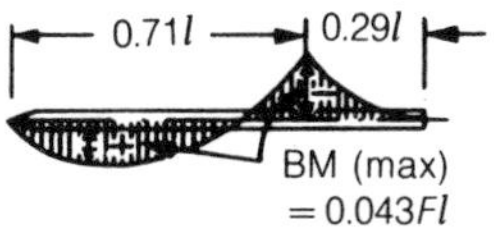

Two-point lifting

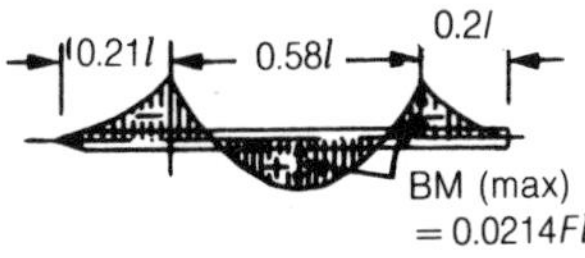

l length of pile
F total weight of pile

Short piles: Toggle holes near head (for guiding) can generally be used for lifting without producing excessive bending moments

Typical details of individual piles and shapes of shoes

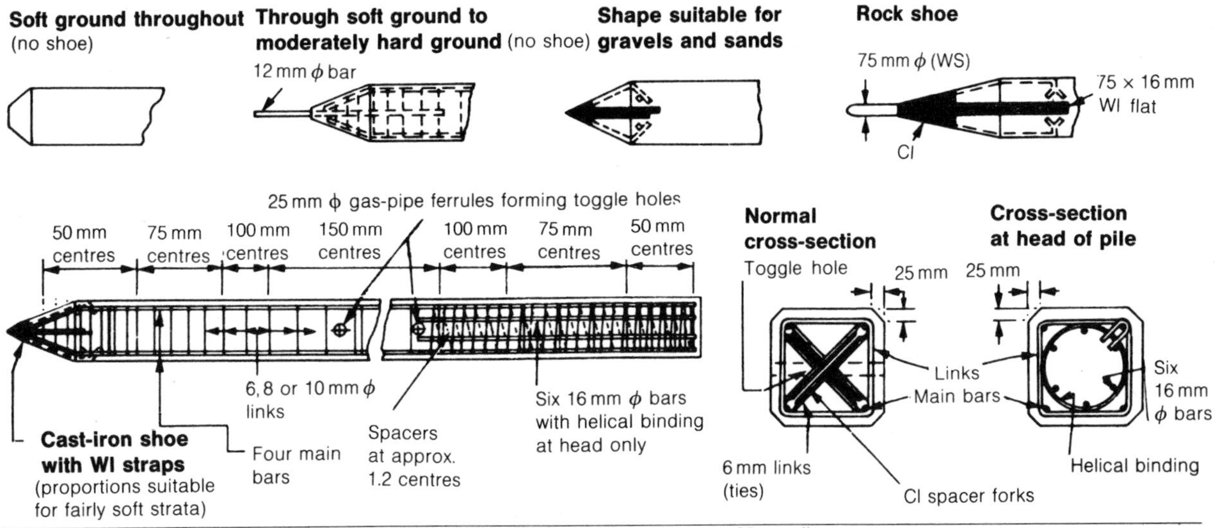

Shoes and interlocks for sheet piling

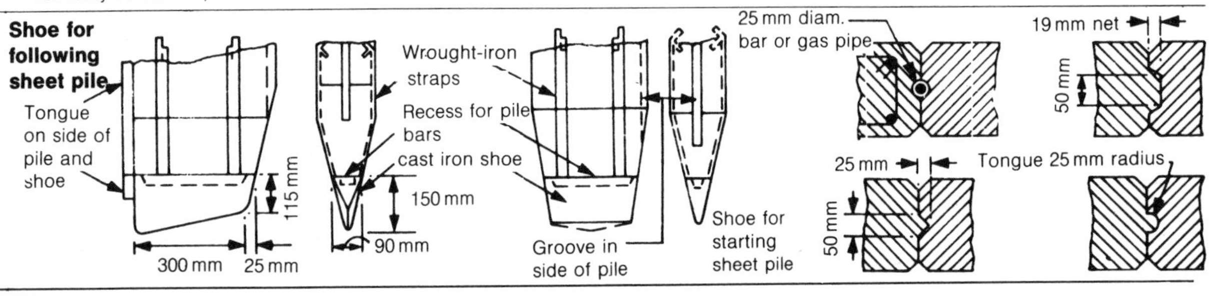

symmetrical, $\sum_2 = 0$, $\sum_3$ is not required, $\sum_4 = 0$, $J = \sum_1 \sum_5$, $x_0 = 3.0$ m, and $y_0 = 0$. $M = 800(3.75 - 3.0) + 0 = 600$ kN m. The calculation is then as shown in the accompanying table.

Therefore $k = 3.846 \times 0.1538 = 0.5917$. The axial loads on the piles are:

$$N_1 = 0.9806[(0.26 \times 800) + (1.3 \times 100) - (0.0867 \times 600)]$$
$$= 0.9806(208 + 130 - 52) = 280.4\,\text{kN}$$
$$N_2 = 0.9806(208 - 130 - 52) = 25.5\,\text{kN}$$
$$N_3 = 0.9806(208 + 130 + 52) = 382.4\,\text{kN}$$
$$N_4 = 0.9806(208 - 130 + 52) = 127.5\,\text{kN}$$

The maximum load on any pile is 382.4 kN; say 410 kN including the self-weight of the pile.

Notes on design examples. Design (a) comprises vertical piles only, design (b) vertical and inclined piles, and design (c) inclined piles only. In each case the group is symmetrical and is subjected to the same imposed loads. Designs (b) and (c) are special cases of symmetrical groups for which $\sum_4 = 0$ and therefore $y_0 = 0$; this condition applies only if the inclined piles are in symmetrical pairs, both piles in a pair meeting at the same pile-cap.

The design in (c) requires the smallest pile, but there is little difference between the designs in (b) and (c). Although the maximum load on any pile is least in the design in (a), the bending moment on the pile requires a pile of greater cross-sectional area to provide the necessary resistance to combined thrust and bending. The superiority of design (c) is greater if the horizontal force F_h is greater: if F_h were 200 kN (instead of 100 kN) the maximum loads (excluding the weight of the pile) would be 236 kN (and a large bending moment of 120 kN m) in design (a), 609 kN in design (b), and 510 kN in design (c). Design (b) is the most suitable when F_h is small; if F_h were 10 kN, the maximum loads would be 255 kN (and a correspondingly small bending moment of 6 kN m) in design (a), 217 kN in design (b), and 268 kN in design (c). Design (a) is most suitable when there is no horizontal load.

The foregoing calculations are similar whether imperial or metric units are employed.

Foundations: pile-cap design

Forces in idealized truss system

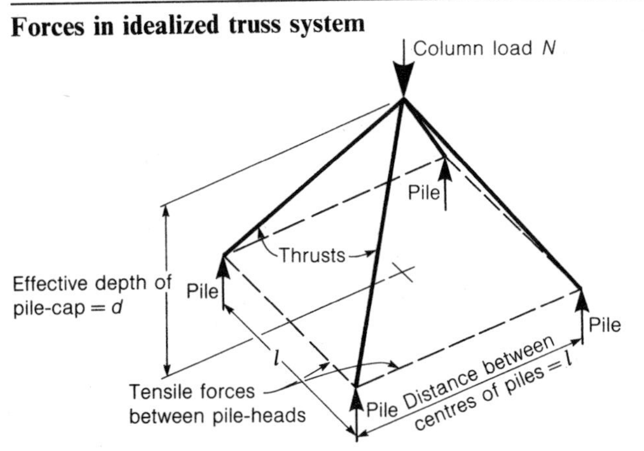

Design of reinforcement

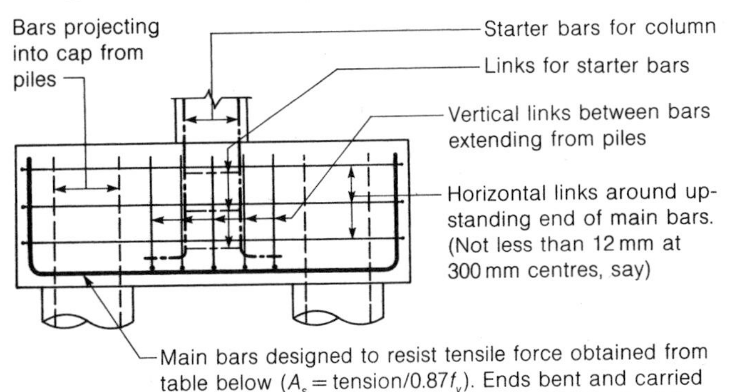

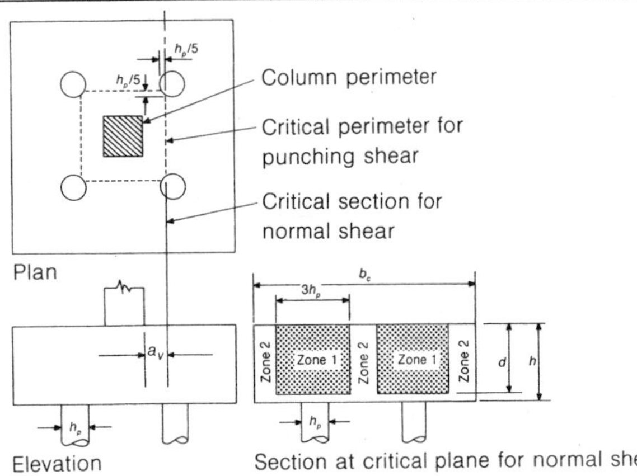

Shearing resistance to BS8110

Allowable shearing resistance $= (3nh_p v_{c1} \times 1.5d/a_v) + (b_C - 3nh_p) \times v_{c2} d$, where v_{c1} and v_{c2} are allowable shearing stresses in zones 1 and 2 respectively, read from *Table 142*, and n is number of zones 1. If no longitudinal bars are provided in zone 2, take $v_{c2} = 0$. If centre of any pile is further from column than critical plane, the force in that pile contributes to shear.

Punching shear

Check punching shear around column perimeter as described on *Table 64*. If pile spacing exceeds $3h_p$ also check punching shear on critical perimeter shown on diagram.

Recommended thickness of pile cap

(Cap thickness must also be sufficient to meet anchorage-bond length requirements of starter bars and normal and punching shear requirements.)

If $h_p \not> 550$ mm: $h = 2h_p + 100$; If $h_p > 550$ mm: $h = \frac{1}{3}(8h_p - 600)$

Number of piles	Dimensions of pile cap	Tensile force to be resisted by reinforcement: Neglecting of column	Tensile force to be resisted by reinforcement: Taking size of column into consideration
2	$l = \alpha h_p$; a; $h_p + 300$; $(\alpha+1)h_p + 300$	$\dfrac{Nl}{4d}$	$\dfrac{N}{12ld}(3l^2 - a^2)$
3	$h_p + 300$; Y; $l = \alpha h_p$; a; b; X—X; $(\frac{2}{7}\alpha + \frac{1}{2})h_p + 150$; $h_p + 250$; $(\frac{6}{7}\alpha + 1)h_p + 300$; $l = \alpha h_p$; $(\alpha+1)h_p + 300$	$\dfrac{Nl}{9d}$	Parallel to X-X: $\dfrac{N}{36ld}(4l^2 + b^2 - 3a^2)$ Parallel to Y-Y: $\dfrac{N}{18ld}(2l^2 - b^2)$
4	Y; X; a; b; X; $l = \alpha h_p$; Y; $(\alpha+1)h_p + 300$	$\dfrac{Nl}{8d}$	Parallel to X-X: $\dfrac{N}{24ld}(3l^2 - a^2)$ Parallel to Y-Y: $\dfrac{N}{24ld}(3l^2 - b^2)$
5	Y; X; a; b; X; $l = \sqrt{(2)}\alpha h_p$; Y; $[\sqrt{(2)}\alpha + 1]h_p + 300$	$\dfrac{Nl}{10d}$	Parallel to X-X: $\dfrac{N}{30ld}(3l^2 - a^2)$ Parallel to Y-Y: $\dfrac{N}{30ld}(3l^2 - b^2)$

Notation h_p diameter of pile; a, b dimensions of column; α spacing factor of piles (normally between 2 and 3 depending on ground conditions)

Groups containing vertical piles only

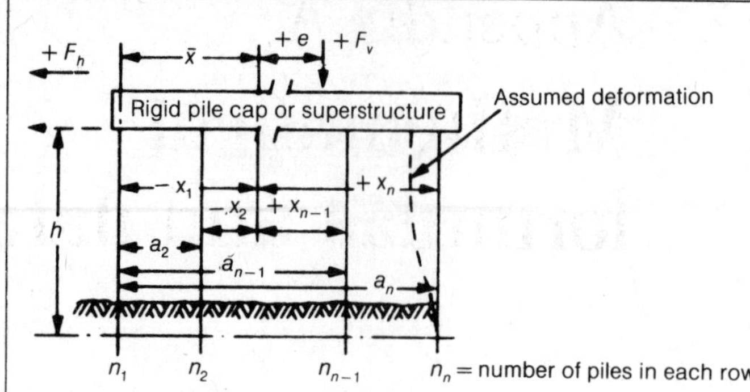

$\bar{x} = \Sigma an/\Sigma n$ (for symmetrical group $\bar{x} = a_n/2$)

$I = \Sigma nx^2$

Axial load on any pile:

$N_x = k_w F_v + k_m M$ plus weight of pile

$M = F_v e - F_h h$

$k_w = 1/\Sigma n; \quad k_m = x/I$

Shearing force on any pile $= V = F_h/\Sigma n$

Bending moment on any pile $= Vh/2$

Groups containing inclined piles with or without vertical piles

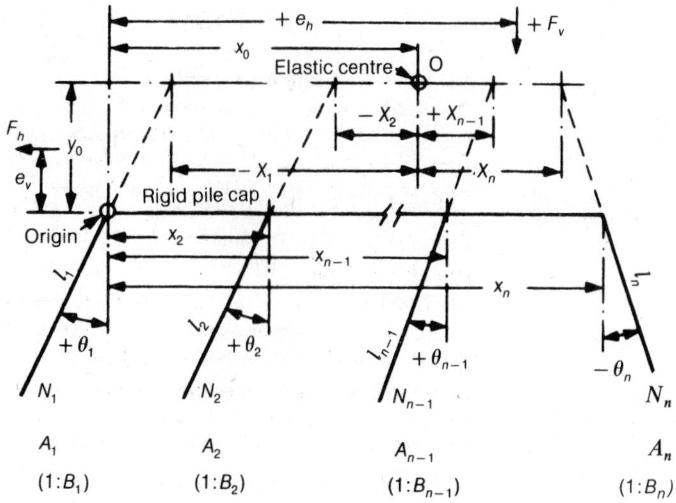

Axial load on any pile:

$N_x = k_p(k_w F_v + k_h F_h + k_m M)$

$M = F_v(e_h - x_0) + F_h(y_0 - e_v)$

Co-ordinates of elastic centre:

$x_0 = (\Sigma_3\Sigma_5 - \Sigma_2\Sigma_4)/k$

$y_0 = (\Sigma_2\Sigma_3 - \Sigma_1\Sigma_4)/k$

$k = \Sigma_1\Sigma_5 - \Sigma_2^2$

$J = A/l$

N_n pile reference and load

A_n cross-sectional area

$(1:B_n)$ slope of pile $= \tan\theta$

E is assumed to be constant

Summations	Piles inclined towards right	Vertical piles	Piles inclined towards left
$\Sigma_1 = \Sigma J\cos^2\theta$	$+\Sigma_R \frac{A}{l}\frac{B^2}{1+B^2}$	$+\Sigma_V \frac{A}{l}$	$+\Sigma_L \frac{A}{l}\frac{B^2}{1+B^2}$
$\Sigma_2 = \Sigma J\cos\theta\sin\theta$	$+\Sigma_R \frac{A}{l}\frac{B}{1+B^2}$	Nil	$-\Sigma_L \frac{A}{l}\frac{B}{1+B^2}$
$\Sigma_3 = \Sigma xJ\cos^2\theta$	$+\Sigma_R \frac{A}{l}\frac{B^2}{1+B^2}x$	$+\Sigma_V \frac{A}{l}x$	$+\Sigma_L \frac{A}{l}\frac{B^2}{1+B^2}x$
$\Sigma_4 = \Sigma xJ\cos\theta\sin\theta$	$+\Sigma_R \frac{A}{l}\frac{B}{1+B^2}x$	Nil	$-\Sigma_L \frac{A}{l}\frac{B}{1+B^2}x$
$\Sigma_5 = \Sigma J\sin^2\theta$	$+\Sigma_R \frac{A}{l}\frac{1}{1+B^2}$	Nil	$+\Sigma_L \frac{A}{l}\frac{1}{1+B^2}$
$\Sigma_6 = \Sigma X^2 J\cos^2\theta$	$+\Sigma_R \frac{A}{l}\frac{B^2}{1+B^2}X^2$	$+\Sigma_V \frac{A}{l}X^2$	$+\Sigma_L \frac{A}{l}\frac{B^2}{1+B^2}X^2$
$X = x - x_0 + y_0\tan\theta$	$x - x_0 + \frac{y_0}{B}$	$x - x_0$	$x - x_0 - \frac{y_0}{B}$
Coefficients in formula for N_x			
$k_p = J_x\cos\theta_x = \frac{A_x}{l_x}\frac{B}{\sqrt{(1+B^2)}}$	$+\frac{A}{l}\frac{B}{\sqrt{(1+B^2)}}$	$+\frac{A}{l}$	$+\frac{A}{l}\frac{B}{\sqrt{(1+B^2)}}$
$k_w = (\Sigma_5 - \tan\theta\,\Sigma_2)/k$	$+\left(\Sigma_5 - \frac{\Sigma_2}{B}\right)\Big/k$	$+\frac{\Sigma_5}{k}$	$+\left(\Sigma_5 + \frac{\Sigma_2}{B}\right)\Big/k$
$k_h = (\tan\theta\,\Sigma_1 - \Sigma_2)/k$	$+\left(\frac{\Sigma_1}{B} - \Sigma_2\right)\Big/k$	$-\frac{\Sigma_2}{k}$	$-\left(\frac{\Sigma_1}{B} + \Sigma_2\right)\Big/k$
$k_m = X/I = X/\Sigma_6$	$+\frac{X}{\Sigma_6}$	$+\frac{X}{\Sigma_6}$	$+\frac{X}{\Sigma_6}$

Note on symmetrical groups $\quad \Sigma_2 = 0; \quad k = \Sigma_1\Sigma_5; \quad x_0 = \frac{1}{2}x_n; \quad \Sigma_3$ is not required

Appendix A

Mathematical formulae and data

MATHEMATICAL AND TRIGONOMETRICAL FUNCTIONS

Trigonometrical formulae

$$\sin^2\theta + \cos^2\theta = 1$$
$$\sec^2\theta - \tan^2\theta = 1$$
$$\operatorname{cosec}^2\theta - \cot^2\theta = 1$$

$$\sin(\theta+\phi) = \sin\theta\cos\phi + \cos\theta\sin\phi$$
$$\sin(\theta-\phi) = \sin\theta\cos\phi - \cos\theta\sin\phi$$
$$\cos(\theta+\phi) = \cos\theta\cos\phi - \sin\theta\sin\phi$$
$$\cos(\theta-\phi) = \cos\theta\cos\phi + \sin\theta\sin\phi$$
$$\tan(\theta+\phi) = \frac{\tan\theta + \tan\phi}{1-\tan\theta\tan\phi}$$
$$\tan(\theta-\phi) = \frac{\tan\theta - \tan\phi}{1+\tan\theta\tan\phi}$$

$$\sin\theta + \sin\phi = 2\sin\tfrac{1}{2}(\theta+\phi)\cos\tfrac{1}{2}(\theta-\phi)$$
$$\sin\theta - \sin\phi = 2\cos\tfrac{1}{2}(\theta+\phi)\sin\tfrac{1}{2}(\theta-\phi)$$
$$\cos\theta + \cos\phi = 2\cos\tfrac{1}{2}(\theta+\phi)\cos\tfrac{1}{2}(\theta-\phi)$$
$$\cos\theta - \cos\phi = -2\sin\tfrac{1}{2}(\theta+\phi)\sin\tfrac{1}{2}(\theta-\phi)$$
$$\sin\theta\sin\phi = \tfrac{1}{2}[\cos(\theta-\phi) - \cos(\theta+\phi)]$$
$$\sin\theta\cos\phi = \tfrac{1}{2}[\sin(\theta+\phi) + \sin(\theta-\phi)]$$
$$\cos\theta\cos\phi = \tfrac{1}{2}[\cos(\theta+\phi) + \cos(\theta-\phi)]$$

OTHER DATA

Factors

$\pi = 355/113$ (approx.) $= 22/7$ (approx.) $= 3.141\,592\,654$ (approx.)
One radian $= 180°/\pi = 57.3°$ (approx.) $= 57.295\,779\,5$ (approx.)
Length of arc subtended by an angle of one radian = radius of arc

One degree Fahrenheit = 5/9 degree centigrade or Celsius
Temperature of t°F $= (t-32)/1.8$°C
Temperature of t°C $= (1.8t+32)$°F

Base of Napierian logarithms, e = 193/71 (approx.) = 2721/1001 (approx.) = 2.718 281 828 (approx.)
To convert common into Napierian logarithms, multiply by 76/33 (approx.) = 3919/1702 (approx.) = 2.302 585 093 (approx.).

Nominal value of $g = 9.806\,65\,\text{kg/s}^2 = 32.174\,\text{ft/s}^2$

Inscribed circle

Diameter of inscribed circle of a triangle:

$$D = 2b\sqrt{\left[a^2 - \left(\frac{a^2+b^2-c^2}{2b}\right)^2\right]}\Big/(a+b+c)$$

For isosceles triangle, $a = c$:

$$D = \frac{b\sqrt{(4a^2-b^2)}}{2a+b}$$

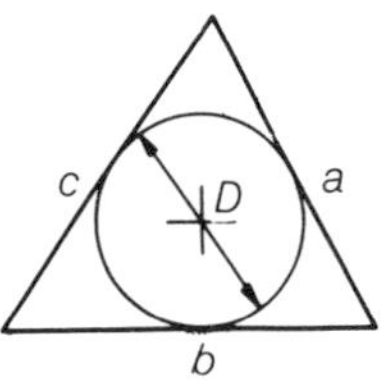

Solution of triangles

Applicable to any triangle ABC in which $AB = c$, $BC = a$, $AC = b$:

$$\frac{\sin A}{a} = \frac{\sin B}{b} = \frac{\sin C}{c}$$

$$\text{area} = \frac{bc\sin A}{2} = \frac{ac\sin B}{2} = \frac{ab\sin C}{2}$$

$$= \sqrt{[s(s-a)(s-b)(s-c)]} \quad \text{where} \quad s = (a+b+c)/2.$$

$$\sin\frac{A}{2} = \sqrt{\left[\frac{(s-b)(s-c)}{bc}\right]}$$

$$\cos A = \frac{b^2+c^2-a^2}{2bc}$$

Roots of quadratics

$$ax^2 + bx + c = 0$$

$$x = \frac{-b \pm \sqrt{(b^2 - 4ac)}}{2a} = -\frac{b}{2a}\left[1 \mp \sqrt{\left(1 - \frac{4ac}{b^2}\right)}\right]$$

Applications

1. Roof slopes, $s = \sqrt{(1 + H^2)}$:

   S 1.0 H

   (a) Limiting slope for inclined roof loading = 20°:

   $$H = \cot 20° = 2.7475$$

   Therefore limiting slope = 1:2.75.

   (b) Limiting slope for inclined roofs = 10°:

   $$H = \cot 10° = 5.6713$$

   Therefore limiting slope = 1:5.67.

2. Earth pressures:

$$k_2 = \frac{1 - \sin\theta}{1 + \sin\theta} = \tan^2\left(45° - \frac{\theta}{2}\right)$$

$$\frac{1}{k_2} = \frac{1 + \sin\theta}{1 - \sin\theta} = \tan^2\left(45° + \frac{\theta}{2}\right)$$

3. Hopper bottom slopes:
   Specified minimum slope in valley = ϕ.

$$Y/X = R$$

$$X = H \cot\phi/\sqrt{(1 + R^2)}$$

$$\tan\theta_x = \tan\phi\sqrt{(1 + R^2)}$$

$$\tan\theta_y = \tan\phi\sqrt{(1 + R^2)}/R$$

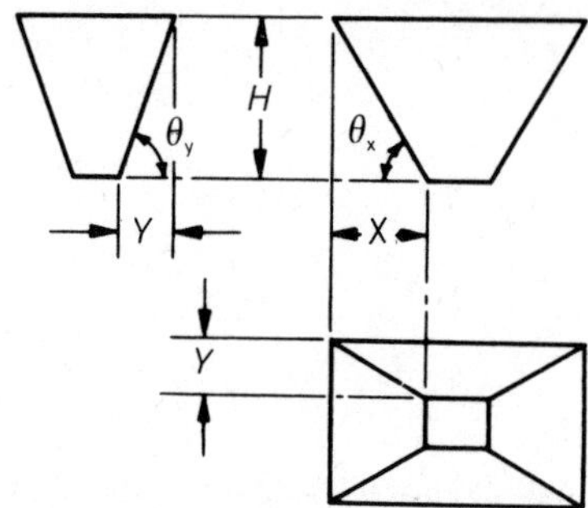

Appendix B
Metric/imperial length conversions

The metric and imperial equivalents of a range of lengths are given. The imperial equivalent of any metric length up to 16 m can be obtained by adding the equivalent for metres and tenths of metres from the upper part of this section, to that for hundredths and thousandths of metres (i.e. centimetres and millimetres) from the lower part. The maximum error of the resulting conversion cannot exceed 1/32 inch.

m	0.0	0.1	0.2	0.3	0.4	0.5	0.6	0.7	0.8	0.9
0	—	0′-3 15/16″	0′-7 7/8″	0′-11 13/16″	1′-3 3/4″	1′-7 11/16″	1′-11 5/8″	2′-3 9/16″	2′-7 1/2″	2′-11 7/16″
1	3′-3 3/8″	3′-7 5/16″	3′-11 1/4″	4′-3 3/16″	4′-7 1/8″	4′-11 1/16″	5′-3″	5′-6 15/16″	5′-10 7/8″	6′-2 13/16″
2	6′-6 3/4″	6′-10 11/16″	7′-2 5/8″	7′-6 9/16″	7′-10 1/2″	8′-2 7/16″	8′-6 3/8″	8′-10 5/16″	9′-2 1/4″	9′-6 3/16″
3	9′-10 1/8″	10′-2 1/16″	10′-5 31/32″	10′-9 29/32″	11′-1 27/32″	11′-5 25/32″	11′-9 23/32″	12′-1 21/32″	12′-5 19/32″	12′-9 17/32″
4	3′-1 15/32″	13′-5 13/32″	13′-9 11/32″	14′-1 9/32″	14′-5 7/32″	14′-9 5/32″	15′-1 3/32″	15′-5 1/32″	15′-8 31/32″	16′-0 29/32″
5	16′-4 27/32″	16′-8 25/32″	17′-0 23/32″	17′-4 21/32″	17′-8 19/32″	18′-0 17/32″	18′-4 15/32″	18′-8 13/32″	19′-0 11/32″	19′-4 9/32″
6	19′-8 7/32″	20′-0 5/32″	20′-4 3/32″	20′-8 1/32″	20′-11 31/32″	21′-3 29/32″	21′-7 27/32″	21′-11 25/32″	22′-3 23/32″	22′-7 21/32″
7	22′-11 19/32″	23′-3 17/32″	23′-7 15/32″	23′-11 13/32″	24′-3 11/32″	24′-7 9/32″	24′-11 7/32″	25′-3 5/32″	25′-7 3/32″	25′-11 1/32″
8	26′-2 31/32″	26′-6 29/32″	26′-10 27/32″	27′-2 25/32″	27′-6 23/32″	27′-10 21/32″	28′-2 19/32″	28′-6 17/32″	28′-10 15/32″	29′-2 13/32″
9	29′-6 11/32″	29′-10 9/32″	30′-2 7/32″	30′-6 5/32″	30′-10 3/32″	31′-2 1/32″	31′-5 15/16″	31′-9 7/8″	32′-1 13/16″	32′-5 3/4″
10	32′-9 11/16″	33′-1 5/8″	33′-5 9/16″	33′-9 1/2″	34′-1 7/16	34′-5 3/8″	34′-9 5/16″	35′-1 1/4″	35′-5 3/16″	35′-9 1/8″
11	36′-1 1/16″	36′-5″	36′-8 15/16″	37′-0 7/8″	37′-4 13/16″	37′-8 3/4″	38′-0 11/16″	38′-4 5/8″	38′-8 9/16″	39′-0 1/2″
12	39′-4 7/16″	39′-8 3/8″	40′-0 5/16″	40′-4 1/4″	40′-8 3/16″	41′-0 1/8″	41′-4 1/16″	41′-8″	41′-11 15/16″	42′-3 7/8″
13	42′-7 13/16″	42′-11 3/4″	43′-3 11/16″	43′-7 5/8″	43′-11 9/16″	44′-3 1/2″	44′-7 7/16″	44′-11 3/8″	45′-3 5/16″	45′-7 1/4″
14	45′-11 3/16″	46′-3 1/8″	46′-7 1/16″	46′-11″	47′-2 15/16″	47′-6 7/8″	47′-10 13/16″	48′-2 3/4″	48′-6 11/16″	48′-10 5/8″
15	49′-2 9/16″	49′-6 1/2″	49′-10 7/16″	50′-2 3/8″	50′-6 5/16″	50′-10 1/4″	51′-2 3/16′	51′-6 1/8″	51′-10 1/16″	52′-1 31/32″

m	0.000	0.001	0.002	0.003	0.004	0.005	0.006	0.007	0.008	0.009
0.00	—	1/32″	3/32″	1/8″	5/32″	3/16″	1/4″	9/32″	5/16″	11/32″
0.01	13/32″	7/16″	15/32″	1/2″	9/16″	19/32″	5/8″	21/32″	23/32″	3/4″
0.02	25/32″	13/16″	7/8″	29/32″	15/16″	31/32″	1 1/32″	1 1/16″	1 3/32″	1 5/32
0.03	1 3/16″	1 7/32″	1 1/4″	1 5/16″	1 11/32″	1 3/8″	1 13/32″	1 15/32″	1 1/2″	1 17/32″
0.04	1 9/16″	1 5/8″	1 21/32″	1 11/16″	1 23/32″	1 25/32″	1 13/16″	1 27/32″	1 7/8″	1 15/16″
0.05	1 31/32″	2″	2 1/16″	2 3/32″	2 1/8″	2 5/32″	2 7/32″	2 1/4″	2 9/32″	2 5/16″
0.06	2 3/8″	2 13/32″	2 7/16″	2 15/32″	2 17/32″	2 9/16″	2 19/32″	2 5/8″	2 11/16″	2 23/32″
0.07	2 3/4″	2 25/32″	2 27/32″	2 7/8″	2 29/32″	2 15/16″	3″	3 1/32″	3 1/16″	3 1/8″
0.08	3 5/32″	3 3/16″	3 7/32″	3 9/32″	3 5/16″	3 11/32″	3 3/8″	3 7/16″	3 15/32″	3 1/2″
0.09	3 17/32″	3 19/32″	3 5/8″	3 21/32″	3 11/16″	3 3/4″	3 25/32″	3 13/16″	3 27/32″	3 29/32″

ft	0″	1″	2″	3″	4″	5″	6″	7″	8″	9″	10″	11″
0	—	0.025	0.051	0.076	0.102	0.127	0.152	0.178	0.203	0.229	0.254	0.279
1	0.305	0.330	0.356	0.381	0.406	0.432	0.457	0.483	0.508	0.533	0.559	0.584
2	0.610	0.635	0.660	0.686	0.711	0.737	0.762	0.787	0.813	0.838	0.864	0.889
3	0.914	0.940	0.965	0.991	1.016	1.041	1.067	1.092	1.118	1.143	1.168	1.194
4	1.219	1.245	1.270	1.295	1.321	1.346	1.372	1.397	1.422	1.448	1.473	1.499
5	1.524	1.549	1.575	1.600	1.626	1.651	1.676	1.702	1.727	1.753	1.778	1.803
6	1.829	1.854	1.880	1.905	1.930	1.956	1.981	2.007	2.032	2.057	2.083	2.108
7	2.134	2.159	2.184	2.210	2.235	2.261	2.286	2.311	2.337	2.362	2.388	2.413
8	2.438	2.464	2.489	2.515	2.540	2.565	2.591	2.616	2.642	2.667	2.692	2.718
9	2.743	2.769	2.794	2.819	2.845	2.870	2.896	2.921	2.946	2.972	2.997	3.023
10	3.048	3.073	3.099	3.124	3.150	3.175	3.200	3.226	3.251	3.277	3.302	3.327
11	3.353	3.378	3.404	3.429	3.454	3.480	3.505	3.531	3.556	3.581	3.607	3.632
12	3.658	3.683	3.708	3.734	3.759	3.785	3.810	3.835	3.861	3.886	3.912	3.937
13	3.962	3.988	4.013	4.039	4.064	4.089	4.115	4.140	4.166	4.191	4.216	4.242
14	4.267	4.293	4.318	4.343	4.369	4.394	4.420	4.445	4.470	4.496	4.521	4.547
15	4.572	4.597	4.623	4.648	4.674	4.699	4.724	4.750	4.775	4.801	4.826	4.851
16	4.877	4.902	4.928	4.953	4.978	5.004	5.029	5.055	5.080	5.105	5.131	5.156
17	5.182	5.207	5.232	5.258	5.283	5.309	5.334	5.359	5.385	5.410	5.436	5.461
18	5.486	5.512	5.537	5.562	5.588	5.613	5.639	5.664	5.690	5.715	5.740	5.766
19	5.791	5.817	5.842	5.867	5.893	5.918	5.944	5.969	5.994	6.020	6.045	6.071
20	6.096	6.121	6.147	6.172	6.198	6.223	6.248	6.274	6.299	6.325	6.350	6.375
30	9.144	9.169	9.195	9.220	9.246	9.271	9.296	9.322	9.347	9.373	9.398	9.423
40	12.192	12.217	12.243	12.268	12.294	12.319	12.344	12.370	12.395	12.421	12.446	12.471
50	15.240	15.265	15.291	15.316	15.342	15.367	15.392	15.418	15.443	15.469	15.494	15.519

Fractions of an inch								
	$\frac{1}{32}$″ 0.79 mm	$\frac{5}{32}$″ 3.97 mm	$\frac{9}{32}$″ 7.14 mm	$\frac{13}{32}$″ 10.32 mm	$\frac{17}{32}$″ 13.49 mm	$\frac{21}{32}$″ 16.67 mm	$\frac{25}{32}$″ 19.84 mm	$\frac{29}{32}$″ 23.02 mm
	$\frac{1}{16}$″ 1.59 mm	$\frac{3}{16}$″ 4.76 mm	$\frac{5}{16}$″ 7.94 mm	$\frac{7}{16}$″ 11.11 mm	$\frac{9}{16}$″ 14.29 mm	$\frac{11}{16}$″ 17.46 mm	$\frac{13}{16}$″ 20.64 mm	$\frac{15}{16}$″ 23.81 mm
	$\frac{3}{32}$″ 2.38 mm	$\frac{7}{32}$″ 5.56 mm	$\frac{11}{32}$″ 8.73 mm	$\frac{15}{32}$″ 11.91 mm	$\frac{19}{32}$″ 15.08 mm	$\frac{23}{32}$″ 18.26 mm	$\frac{27}{32}$″ 21.43 mm	$\frac{31}{32}$″ 24.61 mm
	$\frac{1}{8}$″ 3.18 mm	$\frac{1}{4}$″ 6.35 mm	$\frac{3}{8}$″ 9.53 mm	$\frac{1}{2}$″ 12.70 mm	$\frac{5}{8}$″ 15.88 mm	$\frac{3}{4}$″ 19.05 mm	$\frac{7}{8}$″ 22.23 mm	

Appendix C

Metric/imperial equivalents for common units

Basic conversion factors

The following equivalents of SI units are given in imperial and, where applicable, metric technical units.

1 mm	= 0.039 37 in	1 in	= 25.4 mm	$1\ m^2$	$= 1.196\ yd^2$	$1\ yd^2$	$= 0.8361\ m^2$
1 m	= 3.281 ft	1 ft	= 0.3048 in	1 hectare	= 2.471 acres	1 acre	= 0.4047 hectares
	= 1.094 yd	1 yd	= 0.9144 m	$1 mm^3$	$= 0.000\,061\,02\ in^3$	$1\ in^3$	$= 16\,390\ mm^3$
1 km	= 0.6214 mile	1 mile	= 1.609 km	$1\ m^3$	$= 35.31\ ft^3$	$1\ ft^3$	$= 0.028\,32\ m^3$
$1\ mm^2$	$= 0.001\,55\ in^2$	$1\ in^2$	$= 645.2\ mm^2$		$= 1.308\ yd^3$	$1\ yd^3$	$= 0.7646\ m^3$
$1\ m^2$	$= 10.76\ ft^2$	$1\ ft^2$	$= 0.0929\ m^2$	$1\ mm^4$ (M of I)	$= 0.000\,002\,403\ in^4$	$1\ in^4$	$= 416\,200\ mm^4$

Force

1 N	= 0.2248 lbf	= 0.1020 kgf
4.448 N	= 1 lbf	= 0.4536 kgf
9.807 N	= 2.205 lbf	= 1 kgf

1 kN	= 0.1004 tonf	= 102.0 kgf	= 0.1020 tonne f
9.964 kN	= 1 tonf	= 1016 kgf	= 1.016 tonne f
9.807 kN	= 0.9842 tonf	= 1000 kgf	= 1 tonne f

Force per unit length

1 N/m	= 0.068 52 lbf/ft	= 0.1020 kgf/m
14.59 N/m	= 1 lbf/ft	= 1.488 kgf/m
9.807 N/m	= 0.672 lbf/ft	= 1 kgf/m

1 kN/m	= 0.0306 tonf/ft	= 0.1020 tonne f/m
32.69 kN/m	= 1 tonf/ft	= 3.333 tonne f/m
9.807 kN/m	= 0.3000 tonf/ft	= 1 tonne f/m

Force per unit area

$1\ N/mm^2$	$= 145.0\ lbf/in^2$	$= 10.20\ kgf/cm^2$
$0.006\,895\ N/mm^2$	$= 1\ lbf/in^2$	$= 0.0703\ kgf/cm^2$
$0.098\,07\ N/mm^2$	$= 14.22\ lbf/in^2$	$= 1\ kgf/cm^2$

$1\ N/mm^2$	$= 0.064\,75\ tonf/in^2$	$= 10.20\ kgf/cm^2$
$15.44\ N/mm^2$	$= 1\ tonf/in^2$	$= 157.5\ kgf/cm^2$
$0.098\,07\ N/mm^2$	$= 0.006\,350\ tonf/in^2$	$= 1\ kgf/cm^2$

$1\ N/m^2$	$= 0.020\,89\ lbf/ft^2$	$= 0.102\ kgf/m^2$
$47.88\ N/m^2$	$= 1\ lbf/ft^2$	$= 4.882\ kgf/m^2$
$9.807\ N/m^2$	$= 0.2048\ lbf/ft^2$	$= 1\ kgf/m^2$

$1\ N/mm^2$	$= 9.324\ tonf/ft^2$	$= 10.20\ kgf/cm^2$
$0.1073\ N/mm^2$	$= 1\ tonf/ft^2$	$= 1.094\ kgf/cm^2$
$0.098\,07\ N/mm^2$	$= 0.9144\ tonf/ft^2$	$= 1\ kgf/cm^2$

Force per unit volume

$1\ N/m^3$	$= 0.006\,366\ lbf/ft^3$	$= 0.102\ kgf/m^3$
$157.1\ N/m^3$	$= 1\ lbf/ft^3$	$= 16.02\ kgf/m^3$
$9.807\ N/m^3$	$= 0.0624\ lbf/ft^3$	$= 1\ kgf/m^3$

$1\ kN/m^3$	$= 0.002\,842\ tonf/ft^3$	$= 0.1020\ tonne\ f/m^3$
$351.9\ kN/m^3$	$= 1\ tonf/ft^3$	$= 35.88\ tonne\ f/m^3$
$9.807\ kN/m^3$	$= 0.027\,87\ tonf/ft^3$	$= 1\ tonne\ f/m^3$

$1\ kN/m^3$	$= 0.003\,684\ lbf/in^3$	$= 0.1020\ tonne\ f/m^3$
$271.4\ kN/m^3$	$= 1\ lbf/in^3$	$= 27.68\ tonne\ f/m^3$
$9.807\ kN/m^3$	$= 0.036\,13\ lbf/in^3$	$= 1\ tonne\ f/m^3$

Moment

1 N m	= 8.851 lbf in	= 0.7376 lbf ft	= 0.1020 kgf m
0.1130 N m	= 1 lbf in	= 0.083 33 lbf ft	= 0.011 52 kgf m
1.356 N m	= 12 lbf in	= 1 lbf ft	= 0.1383 kgf m
9.807 N m	= 86.80 lbf in	= 7.233 lbf ft	= 1 kgf m

Fluid capacity

1 litre = 0.22 imperial gallons = 0.2642 USA gallons
4.546 litres = 1 imperial gallon = 1.201 USA gallons
3.785 litres = 0.8327 imperial gallons = 1 USA gallon

Useful data

$1000\ kg/m^3 = 62.4\ lb/ft^3$ (density of water)
$23.6\ kN/m^3 = 2400\ kg/m^3 = 150\ lb/ft^3$ (nominal weight of reinforced concrete)
$14\ kN/mm^2$ (approx.) $= 140 \times 10^3\ kg/cm^2$ (approx.) $= 2 \times 10^6\ lb/in^2$ (nominal elastic modulus of concrete)
10×10^{-6} per °C $= 5.5 \times 10^{-6}$ per °F (nominal coefficient of linear expansion of concrete)

References and further reading

1. Institution of Structural Engineers (1951) Earth-retaining structures. Civil Engineering Code of Practice no. 2, London, p. 224

2. German Federal Republic Standards Institution (1964) DIN1055: Part 6. Design loads for buildings: loads in silo bins. Berlin, p. 6

3. Paterson, W. S. (1970) A selective bibliography on the design of hoppers and silos. CIRIA bibliography 1, p. 23

4. Walker, D. M. (1966) An approximate theory for pressures and arching in hoppers. *Chemical Engineering Science* **21**, pp. 975–99

5. Jenike, A. W. (1961) Gravity flow of bulk solids. Bulletin 108, University of Utah Engineering Experimental Station

6. Coates, R. C., Coutie, M. G. and Kong, F. K. (1972) *Structural Analysis*. Sunbury-on-Thames, Nelson, p. 496

7. Cross, H. and Morgan, N. D. (1932) *Continuous Frames of Reinforced Concrete*. New York, Wiley, p. 343

8. Cassie, W. F. (1954) *Structural Analysis*. London, Longmans Green, second edition, pp. 130–74

9. Blaszkowiak, S. and Kaczkowski, Z. (1966) *Iterative Methods in Structural Analysis*. London, Pergamon, p. 590

10. Rygol, J. (1968) *Structural Analysis by Direct Moment Distribution*. London, Crosby Lockwood, p. 407

11. Steedman, J. C. (1962) Charts for the determination of moment-distribution factors. *Concrete and Construction Engineering* **57**(9), pp. 348–53 and **57**(10), pp. 395–6

12. Marcus, H. (1932) *Die Theorie elastischer Gewebe und ihre Anwendung auf die Berechnung biegsamer Platten*. Berlin, Julius Springer

13. Bares, R. (1969) *Tables for the Analysis of Plates and Beams based on Elastic Theory*. Berlin, Bauverlag

14. Timoshenko, S. P. and Woinowsky-Krieger, S. (1959) *Theory of Plates and Shells*. New York, McGraw-Hill, second edition, p. 580

15. Roark, R. J. and Young, W. C. (1965) *Formulas for Stress and Strain*. New York, McGraw-Hill, fifth edition, p. 624

16. Wang, P.-C. (1966) *Numerical and Matrix Methods in Structural Mechanics*. New York, Wiley, p. 426

17. Johansen, K. W. (1962) *Yield-Line Theory*. London, Cement and Concrete Association, p. 181
This is an English translation of the original 1943 text on which yield-line theory is founded, but is generally less useful to the practising designer than the remaining references in this section.

18. Johansen, K. W. (1972) *Yield-Line Formulae for Slabs*. London, Cement and Concrete Association, p. 106
Gives design formulae for virtually every 'standard' slab shape and loading. Essential for practical design purposes.

19. Wood, R. H. (1961) *Plastic and Elastic Design of Slabs and Plates*. London, Thames and Hudson, p. 344
Relates collapse and elastic methods of slab analysis, but mainly from the viewpoint of research rather than practical design.

20. Jones, L. L. (1962) *Ultimate Load Analysis of Reinforced and Prestressed Concrete Structures*. London, Chatto and Windus, p. 248
About one-half of this easily readable book deals with the yield-line method, describing in detail the analysis of a number of 'standard' slabs.

21. Jones, L. L. and Wood, R. H.(1967) *Yield-Line Analysis of Slabs*. London, Thames and Hudson, Chatto and Windus, p. 405
The best English-language book dealing with yield-line theory, by the leading UK experts. Essential for designers using the method frequently and requiring more than 'standard' solutions.

22. Hillerborg, A. (1975) *Strip method of design*. London, Viewpoint, p. 225
The English translation of the basic text on the strip method (both simple and advanced) by its originator. Deals with theory and gives appropriate design formulae for many problems.

23. Pannell, F. N. (1966) Yield-line analysis. *Concrete and Constructional Engineering*. Series of six articles. Basic application of virtual-work methods in slab design. June pp. 209–16
Describes at greater length the empirical method introduced in this *Handbook*.
Economical distribution of reinforcement in rectangular slabs. July, pp. 229–33
Establishes expressions giving ratios of span to support and main to secondary reinforcement which minimize steel required while meeting serviceability requirements.
Edge conditions in flat plates. August, pp. 290–4
Discusses circumstances where it is advisable not to adopt yield mechanism in which cracks are assumed to run to a free edge and vice versa.
General principle of superposition in the design of rigid-plastic plates. September, pp. 323–6.
Deals with the application of Johansen's superposition theory, mentioned briefly in this *Handbook*.
Design of rectangular plates with banded orthotropic reinforcement. October, pp. 371–6
Two chief disadvantages in providing uniform isotropic or orthotropic steel over a complex slab are that it is uneconomical and that the calculation needed to investigate all possible modes of collapse is considerable. This article describes the division of such slabs into several individual systems, each of which is locally self-sufficient.
Non-rectangular slabs with orthotropic reinforcement. November, pp. 383–90
Explains in detail the application of the affinity theorems introduced in this *Handbook*.

24. Armer, G. S. T. (1968) The strip method: a new approach to the design of slabs. *Concrete* **2**(9), pp. 358–63
A useful, easily understood introduction to simple and advanced strip theory.

25. Fernando, J. S. and Kemp, K. O. (1978) A generalized strip deflexion method of reinforced concrete slab design. *Proceedings of the Institution of Civil Engineers, Part 2, Research and Theory* **65**, March, pp. 163–74

26. Anchor, R. D., Hill, A. W. and Hughes, B. P (1979) *Handbook on BS5337: 1976* ('The structural use of concrete for retaining aqueous liquids'). London, Viewpoint, p. 60

27. Naylor, N. (1950) Sidesway in symmetrical building frames. *The Structural Engineer* **28**(4), pp. 99–102

28. Fintel, M. (ed.) (1975) *Handbook of Structural Concrete.* New York, Van Nostrand Reinhold, p. 802

29. American Concrete Institute (1979) Building code requirements for reinforced concrete. ACI Standard 318–79. pp. 102, 132

30. Institution of Structural Engineers (1976) Report of working party on high alumina cement concrete. *The Structural Engineer* **54**(9), pp. 352–61

31. Kinnear, R. G. et al. (1965) *The Pressure of Concrete on Formwork.* CIRIA Report 1, April, p. 44

32. CEB-FIP (1978) Model code for concrete structures. Comite Euro-International du Beton (CEB), p. 471

33. The Concrete Society/Institution of Structural Engineers (1968) *The Detailing of Reinforced Concrete.* London, The Concrete Society, p. 31

34. Regan, P. E. and Yu, C. W. (1973) *Limit State Design of Structural Concrete.* London, Chatto and Windus, p. 325

35. Beeby, A. W. and Taylor, H. P. J. (1978) The use of simplified methods in CP110 – is rigour necessary? *The Structural Engineer* **56A**(8), pp. 209–15

36. Allen, A. H. (1974) *Reinforced Concrete Design to CP110 – Simply Explained.* London, Cement and Concrete Association, p. 227

37. Beeby, A. W. (1979) The prediction of crack widths in hardened concrete. *The Structural Engineer* **57A**(1), pp. 9–17

38. Baker, A. L. L. (1970) *Limit-State Design of Reinforced Concrete.* London, Cement and Concrete Association, pp. 157–65

39. Institution of Structural Engineers (1969) *The Shear Strength of Reinforced Concrete Beams.* London, p. 170

40. Schulz, M. and Chedraui, M. (1957) Tables for circularly curved horizontal beams with symmetrical uniform loads. *Journal of the American Concrete Institute* **28**(11), pp. 1033–40

41. Spyropoulos, P. J. (1963) Circularly curved beams transversely loaded. *Journal of the American Concrete Institute* **60**(10), pp. 1457–69

42. Leonhardt, F. and Walther, R. (1966) *Deep Beams.* Bulletin 178, Berlin, Deutcher Ausschuss fur Stahlbeton

43. Kong, F. K., Robins, P. J. and Sharp, G. R. (1975) The design of reinforced concrete deep beams in current practice. *The Structural Engineer* **53**(4), pp. 173–80

44 Ove Arup and Partners (1977) *The Design of Deep Beams in Reinforced Concrete.* CIRIA Guide 2, London, p. 131

45. Bennett, J. D. (1965) Circular members subjected to bending and thrust. *Concrete and Constructional Engineering* **60**(12), pp. 444–51

46. Bennett, J. D. (1958) Design of eccentrically-loaded columns by the load-factor method. Part 3: Unsymmetrical cold-worked reinforcement. *Concrete and Constructional Engineering* **53**(3), pp. 119–28. Part 4: Unsymmetrical mild steel reinforcement. *Concrete and Constructional Engineering* **53**(5), pp. 201–11

47. Bennett, J. D. (1957) Design of eccentrically-loaded columns by the load-factor method. Part 1: Symmetrical cold-worked reinforcement. *Concrete and Constructional Engineering* **52**(11), pp. 361–71. Part 2: Symmetrical mild steel reinforcement. *Concrete and Constructional Engineering* **52**(12), pp. 411–16

48. Scott, W. L., Glanville, Sir W. and Thomas, F. G. (1965) *Explanatory Handbook on the British Standard Code of Practice for Reinforced Concrete, CP114: 1957.* 2nd edn, London, Cement and Concrete Association, p. 172

49. Pannell, F. N. (1966) *Design Charts for Members Subjected to Biaxial Bending and Direct Thrust.* London, Concrete Publications, p. 52

50. Gibson, J. E. (1968) *The Design of Shell Roofs.* London, Spon, 3rd edn, p. 300

51. Chronowicz, A. (1959) *The Design of Shells.* London, Crosby Lockwood, p. 202

52. Tottenham, H. A. (1954) A simplified method of design for cylindrical shell roofs. *The Structural Engineer* **32**(6), pp. 161–80

53. Bennett, J. D. (1958) *Some Recent Developments in the Design of Reinforced Concrete Shell Roofs.* London, Reinforced Concrete Association, November, p. 24

54. Bennett, J. D. (1962) Empirical design of symmetrical cylindrical shells. Proceedings of the colloquium on simplified calculation methods, Brussels; September 1961. Amsterdam, North-Holland, pp. 314–32

55. Bennett, J. D. (1961) *The Structural Possibilities of Hyperbolic Paraboloids.* London, Reinforced Concrete Association, February, p. 25

56. Hambly, E. C. (1976) *Bridge Deck Behaviour.* London, Chapman and Hall, p. 272

57. Cusens, A. R. and Pama, R. P. (1974) *Bridge Deck Analysis.* London, Wiley-Interscience, p. 278

58. Best, B. C. (1974) *Methods of Analysis for Slab-type Structures.* London, Constructional Industry Research and Information Association, November, Technical Note 62, p. 18

59. Department of the Environment (1970) A guide to the structural design of pavements for new roads. Road Note 29, 3rd edn

60. Department of Transport (1978) Transport and Road Research Laboratory with the Cement and Concrete Association. *A Guide to Concrete Road Construction.* London, HMSO, 3rd edn, p. 82

61. Anchor, R. D., Hill, A. W. and Hughes, B. P. (1977) Papers presented at a colloquium on BS 5337 held at the IStructE on 14 April 1977. *The Structural Engineer* **55**(3), pp. 115–31. Discussion. *The Structural Engineer* **56A** (9), pp. 254–62

62. Pinfold, G. M. (1975) *Reinforced Concrete Chimneys and Towers.* London, Cement and Concrete Association, p. 233

63. Hairsine, R. C. (1972) A design chart for determining the optimum base proportions of free standing retaining walls. *Proceedings of the Institution of Civil Engineers* **51** (February), pp. 295–318

64. Irish, K. and Walker, W. P. (1969) *Foundations for reciprocating machines.* London, Cement and Concrete Association, p. 103

65. Barkan, D. D. (1962) *Dynamics of Bases and Foundations.* New York, McGraw-Hill, p. 434

Tomlinson, M. J. (1977) *Pile Design and Construction Practice.* London, Cement and Concrete Association, p. 413

67. Yan, H. T. (1954) Bloom base allowance in the design of pile caps. *Civil Engineering and Public Works Review* **49**(575), pp. 493–5; and (576), pp. 622–3.

68. Whittle, R. T. and Beattie, D. (1972) Standard pile caps. *Concrete* **6**(1), pp. 34–6; and **6**(2), pp. 29–31

69. Taylor, H. P. J. and Clarke, J. L. (1976) Some detailing pro-

blems in concrete frame structures. *The Structural Engineer* **54**(1), pp. 19–32

70. Beeby, A. W. (1978) *The Design of Sections for Flexure and Axial Load According to CP110*. London, Cement and Concrete Association, publication 44.002, p. 31

71. Beeby, A. W. (1978) *The Analysis of Beams in Plane Frames According to CP110*. London, Cement and Concrete Association, publication 44.001, p. 34

72. Fidler, C. (1883) Continuous girder bridges. *Proceedings of the Institution of Civil Engineers* **74**, p. 196

73. Ostenfeld, A. (1905) Graphische behandlung der kontinuierlichen träger... *Zeitung der Architecture und Ing. Ver.* **51**, p. 47

74. Salmon, E. H. (1931) *Materials and Structures* volume 1. London, Longmans Green, p. 638

75. Kong, F. K. and Evans, R. H. (1980) *Reinforced and Prestressed Concrete*. Walton-on-Thames, Nelson. 2nd edn, p. 412

76. Teychenne, D. C., Parrott, L. J. and Pomeroy, C. D. (1978) *The Estimation of the Elastic Modulus of Concrete for the Design of Structures*. Watford, Building Research Establishment Report CP23/78

77. British Standards Institution (1969) Draft code of practice for the structural use of concrete. p. 241

78. Institution of Structural Engineers/The Concrete Society (1978) *Design and Detailing of Concrete Structures for Fire Resistance*. London

79. Steedman, J. C. (1974) *Charts for Limit-State Design to CP110: Uniform Rectangular Stress-Block*. London, Cement and Concrete Association, publication 12.065, p. 20

80. Steedman, J. C. *Charts for the Design of Water-Containing Structures to BS5337* (unpublished)

81. Threlfall, A. J. (1978) *Design Charts for Water Retaining Structures to BS5337*. London, Cement and Concrete Association, publication 12.078, p. 66

82. Somerville, G. and Taylor, H. P. J. (1972) The influence of reinforcement detailing on the strength of concrete structures. *The Structural Engineer* **50**(1), pp. 7–19; and **50**(8), pp. 309–21

83. Somerville, G. (1972) *The Behaviour and Design of Reinforced Concrete Corbels*. London, Cement and Concrete Association, publication 42.472, p. 12

84. Regan, P. E. (1974) Design for punching shear. *The Structural Engineer*. **52**(6), pp. 197–207

85. Steedman, J. C. (1975) *Design Charts for Unsymmetrically-Reinforced Columns*. London, Cement and Concrete Association, publication 12.069, p. 60

86. Taylor, C. P. and Turner, L. (1960) *Reinforced Concrete Chimneys*. London, Concrete Publications, 2nd edn, pp. 40–53.

87. Terrington, J. S. and Turner, F. H. (1964) *Design of Non-planar Roofs*. London, Concrete Publications, p. 108

88. Krishna, J. and Jain, O. P. (1954) The beam strength of the reinforced concrete cylindrical shells. *Civil Engineering and Public Works Review* **49**, (578), pp. 838–40; and **49** (579), pp. 953–56

89. Faber, C. (1963) *Candela: the Shell Builder*. London, The Architectural Press, p. 240

90. Portland Cement Association (USA) (1960) *Elementary Analysis of Hyperbolic Paraboloid Shells*. PCA Structural and Railways Bureau, ST 85, p. 20

91. Lee, D. J. (1971) *The Theory and Practice of Bearings and Expansion Joints for Bridges*. London, Cement and Concrete Association, p. 65

92. Deacon, R. C. (1978) *Watertight Concrete Construction*. London, Cement and Concrete Association, publication 46.504, 2nd edn, p. 29

93. Carpenter, H. (1927) Restraint in circular tanks. *Concrete and Constructional Engineering* **22**(4), and **24**(6)

94. Reynolds, G. C. (1969) *The Strength of Half-joints in Reinforced Concrete Beams*. London, Cement and Concrete Association, publication 42.415

95. Balint, P. S. and Taylor, H. P. J. (1972) *Reinforcement Detailing of Frame Corner Joints with Particular reference to Opening Corners*. London, Cement and Concrete Association, publication 42.462, p. 16

96. The Concrete Society (1973) *Standard Reinforced Concrete Details* p. 28

97. Noor, F. A. (1977) Ultimate strength and cracking of wall corners. *Concrete* **11**(7), pp. 31–5

98. Taylor, H. P. J. (1974) *The Behaviour of In Situ Concrete Beam-Column Joints*. London, Cement and Concrete Association, publication 42.492

99. CIRIA (1974) *A Comparison of Quay Wall Design Methods*. Technical Note 54, p. 125

100. Cranston, W. B. (1972) *Analysis and Design of Reinforced Concrete Columns*. London, Cement and Concrete Association, publication 41.020, p. 28

101. CIRIA (1978) *Guide to the Design of Waterproof Basements*. CIRIA Guide 5, p. 38

102. Thrower, F. N., and Castledine, L. W. E. (1978) *The Design of New Road Pavements and of Overlays: Estimation of Commercial Traffic Flow*. Crowthorne, TRRL Laboratory Report 844, p. 14

103. Jenkins, W. M. (1969) *Matrix and Digital Computer Methods in Structural Analysis*. London, McGraw-Hill, p. 209

104. Zienkiewicz, O. C. (1977) *The Finite Element Method*. London, McGraw-Hill (UK), third edn, p. 787

105. Zienkiewicz, O. C., Brotton, D. M. and Morgan, L. (1976) A finite element primer for structural engineering. *The Structural Engineer* **54**(10), pp. 387–97

106. Rowe, R. E. (1958) *The Electronic Digital Computer, a New Tool for Structural Engineers*. London, Cement and Concrete Association, publication TRA/297, p. 16

107. Morice, P. B. (1969) The new look in structural analysis—a historical survey. *Concrete* **3** (10), pp. 415–17

108. HMSO (1970) *Communication from Designer to Site – Computers in Structural Engineering*. Report by a working group of the sub-committee on the application of computers in structural engineering. London, p. 72

109. The Concrete Society (1970) *Drawing and Detailing by Automated Procedures*. Papers presented at a symposium held at Birmingham University on 13 April

110. The Concrete Society (1970) *Automated Calculation and Detailing Techniques for Reinforced Concrete*. Papers presented at a symposium held in Bristol on 11 and 12 December

111. Alcock, D. G. and Shearing, B. H. (1970) GENESYS – an attempt to rationalize the use of computers in structural engineering. *The Structural Engineer* **48**(4), pp. 143–52; and discussion, **48**(9) pp. 371–4

112. Craddock, A. (1978) GENESYS as applied to detailed design of reinforced concrete structures. *The Structural Engineer* **56A**(10), pp. 277–82

113. Croft, D. D. (1978) The GLADYS system computer for the design of reinforced concrete elements. *The Structural Engineer* **56A**(10), pp. 282–6

114. Beeby, A. W. (1978) Reinforced concrete design calculations using small computers – DECIDE. *The Structural Engineer* **56A**(10), pp. 287–9

115. Bensasson, S. (1978) A state-of-the-art review of computer programs for the detailed design of reinforced concrete. *The Structural Engineer* **56A**(10), pp. 275–7

116. Bensasson, S. (1978) *Computer Programs for Continuous Beams – CP110*. Design Office Consortium Evaluation Report 2, Cambridge, p. 64

117. Institution of Structural Engineers (1967) *Standardization of Input Information for Computer Programs in Structural Engineering*. London, p. 161

118. Mills, P. and Brotton, D. M. (1979) Computer-aided detailing of reinforced concrete structures. *The Structural Engineer* **57A**(1), pp. 19–23

119. Jones, L. L. (1975) LUCID – an aid to structural detailing. *The Structural Engineer* **53**(1), pp. 13–22; and discussion, **53**(11), pp. 487–94

120. Wright, E. W. (1976) *Structural Design by Computer*. London, Van Nostrand Reinhold, p. 411

121. Gibson, J. E. (1975) *Computers in Structural Engineering*. London, Applied Science Publishers, p. 290

122. Alcock, D. G. (1977) *Illustrating BASIC*. Cambridge, Cambridge University Press, p. 134

123. Lewis, R and Blakeley, B. H. (1974) *Elements of BASIC*. Manchester, National Computing Centre Publications, 2nd edn, p. 103

124. Chandor, A. (1977) *The Penguin Dictionary of Computers*. Harmondsworth, Penguin, 2nd edn, p. 440

125. Cusens, A. R. and Kuang, Jing-Gwo (1965) A simplified method of analysing free-standings stairs. *Concrete and Constructional Engineering* **60**(5), pp. 167–172 and 194

126. Cusens, A. R. (1966) Analysis of slabless stairs. *Concrete and Constructional Engineering* **61**(10), pp. 359–64

127. Santathadaporn, Sakda, and Cusens, A. R. (1966) Charts for the design of helical stairs. *Concrete and Constructional Engineering* **61**(2), pp. 46–54

128. Khim Chye Gary Ong (1977) *Design Charts for Straight Free-Standing Stairs*. Thesis for University of Dundee, 29 charts

129. Newmark, M. N. (1942) Numerical procedure for computing deflections, moments and buckling loads. *Proceedings of the American Society of Civil Engineers* May

130. Taylor, R., Hayes, B. and Mohamedbhai, G. T. G. (1969) Coefficients for the design of slabs by the yield-line theory. *Concrete* **3**(5), pp. 171–2

131. Salvadori and Levy (1967) *Structural Design in Architecture*. Englewood Cliffs, Prentice-Hall, p. 457

132. Sargious M. (1975) *Pavements and Surfacings for Highways and Airports*. London, Applied Science Publishers, p. 619

133. Howard, R. A. (1985) Computers create more paper – graphics can reduce it. *The Structural Engineer* **63A**(1), pp. 13–15

134. Port, S. and Myers, A. P. (1985) Computer graphics and reinforced concrete detailing. *The Structural Engineer* **63A**(1), pp. 15–17

135. Parsons, T. J. (1985) GIPSYS – a CAD system developed by a user. *The Structural Engineer* **63A**(1), pp. 17–20

136. Whittle, R. (1985) Computer graphics related to an in-house drafting system. *The Structural Engineer* **63A**(1), pp. 20–21

137. Ross, C. T. F. (1982) *Computational Methods in Structural and Continuum Mechanics*. Chichester, Ellis Horwood, p. 177
Provides 14 program listings written in CBM PET BASIC for structural analysis, ranging from beams and pin-jointed plane trusses to grillage analysis and two-dimensional field problems. Extended versions of these programs are available on disk or microcassette tape for various microcomputers, and details can be obtained from the publishers.

138. Mosley, W. H. and Spencer, W. J. (1984) *Microcomputer Applications in Structural Engineering*. London, Macmillan Press, p. 258
Includes BASIC listings for various complete and part programs covering steel and reinforced concrete design as well as structural analysis. The programs are also available on disk for the Apple II microcomputer.

139. Brown, D. K. (1984) *An Introduction to the Finite Element Method using BASIC Programs*. London, Surrey University Press (Blackie), p. 188
Listings of four programs written in BASIC for the CBM PET 4000, ranging from pin-jointed frame analysis to finite-element analysis of the bending of thin plates.

140. Jenkins, W. M., Coulthard, J. M. and De Jesus, G. C. (1983) *BASIC Computing for Civil Engineers*. Wokingham, Van Nostrand Reinhold, p. 173
Includes numerous short BASIC programs ranging from numerical methods to structural analysis, steel and concrete design, surveying, hydraulics and geotechniques.

141. Milligan, G. W. E. and Houlsby, G. T. (1984) *BASIC Soil Mechanics*. London, Butterworth, p. 132
Incorporates listings for 24 BASIC programs dealing with a range of geotechnical problems. This is one of an expanding series of books providing short BASIC programs for different engineering applications.

142. Cope, R. J., Sawko, F. and Tickell, R. G. (1982) *Computer Methods for Civil Engineers*. Maidenhead, McGraw-Hill, p. 361
Incorporates many part and complete FORTRAN programs for different aspects of civil engineering including structural analysis and design, soil mechanics, hydraulics, management, and highway and traffic engineering.

143. Bowles, J. E. (1977) *Foundation Analysis and Design*. New York, McGraw-Hill, 2nd edn, p. 750
Includes as an appendix eleven FORTRAN listings of selected programs from the calculation of vertical or horizontal stresses using the Boussinesq equation to three-dimensional pile analysis.

144. Bowles, J. E. *Analytical and Computer Methods in Foundation Engineering*. New York, McGraw-Hill, p. 519
Embodies many FORTRAN listings for different aspects of foundation analysis and design.

145. Alcock, D. (1982) *Illustrating FORTRAN (The Portable Variety)*. Cambridge, Cambridge University Press, p. 134
An excellent companion to ref. 122.

146. Heilborn, J. (ed.) (1981) *Science and Engineering Programs, Apple II Edition*. Berkeley, Osborne/McGraw-Hill, p. 225
Provides program listings for various disciplines. The structural analysis programs determine the geometric properties of any arbitrary section (e.g. box girders etc.) and analyse continuous-beam systems that may include non-prismatic members.

147. Read, R. E. H., Adams, F. C. and Cooke, G. M. E. (1962) *Guidelines for the Construction of Fire Resisting Structural Elements*. Building Research Establishment Report, HMSO

148. Department of Transport (1973) *The design of highway bridge parapets*, DTp memo BE5, 3rd revision. London, HMSO

Index